LET'S GO

P9-BZM-150

■ THE RESOURCE FOR THE INDEPENDENT TRAVELER

"The guides are aimed not only at young budget travelers but at the indepedent traveler; a sort of streetwise cookbook for traveling alone."

—*The New York Times*

"Unbeatable; good sight-seeing advice; up-to-date info on restaurants, hotels, and inns; a commitment to money-saving travel; and a wry style that brightens nearly every page."

—*The Washington Post*

"Lighthearted and sophisticated, informative and fun to read. [Let's Go] helps the novice traveler navigate like a knowledgeable old hand."

—*Atlanta Journal-Constitution*

"A world-wise traveling companion—always ready with friendly advice and helpful hints, all sprinkled with a bit of wit."

—*The Philadelphia Inquirer*

■ THE BEST TRAVEL BARGAINS IN YOUR PRICE RANGE

"All the dirt, dirt cheap."

—*People*

"Anything you need to know about budget traveling is detailed in this book."

—*The Chicago Sun-Times*

"Let's Go follows the creed that you don't have to toss your life's savings to the wind to travel—unless you want to."

—*The Salt Lake Tribune*

■ REAL ADVICE FOR REAL EXPERIENCES

"The writers seem to have experienced every rooster-packed bus and lunar-surfaced mattress about which they write."

—*The New York Times*

"A guide should tell you what to expect from a destination. Here Let's Go shines."

—*The Chicago Tribune*

LET'S GO PUBLICATIONS

TRAVEL GUIDES

Alaska & the Pacific Northwest 2003
Australia 2003
Austria & Switzerland 2003
Britain & Ireland 2003
California 2003
Central America 8th edition
Chile 1st edition **NEW TITLE**
China 4th edition
Costa Rica 1st edition **NEW TITLE**
Eastern Europe 2003
Egypt 2nd edition
Europe 2003
France 2003
Germany 2003
Greece 2003
Hawaii 2003 **NEW TITLE**
India & Nepal 7th edition
Ireland 2003
Israel 4th edition
Italy 2003
Mexico 19th edition
Middle East 4th edition
New Zealand 6th edition
Peru, Ecuador & Bolivia 3rd edition
South Africa 5th edition
Southeast Asia 8th edition
Southwest USA 2003
Spain & Portugal 2003
Thailand 1st edition **NEW TITLE**
Turkey 5th edition
USA 2003
Western Europe 2003

CITY GUIDES

Amsterdam 2003
Barcelona 2003
Boston 2003
London 2003
New York City 2003
Paris 2003
Rome 2003
San Francisco 2003
Washington, D.C. 2003

MAP GUIDES

Amsterdam
Berlin
Boston
Chicago
Dublin
Florence
Hong Kong
London
Los Angeles
Madrid
New Orleans
New York City
Paris
Prague
Rome
San Francisco
Seattle
Sydney
Venice
Washington, D.C.

LET'S GO

SOUTH AFRICA
WITH COVERAGE OF
SOUTHERN AFRICA

KYLE D. HAWKINS EDITOR
TESS MULLEN ASSOCIATE EDITOR
SARAH LEVINE-GRONNINGSATER ASSOCIATE EDITOR

RESEARCHER-WRITERS
KELZIE E. BEEBE
LEILA CHIRAYATH
JOSHUA GARDNER
YUSUF RANDERA-REES
OWEN ROBINSON
RICK SLETTENHAAR
BRYDEN SWEENEY-TAYLOR

YAW D.K. OSSEO-ASARE MAP EDITOR
D. CODY DYDEK MANAGING EDITOR
ABHISHEK GUPTA TYPESETTER

ST. MARTIN'S PRESS ❧ NEW YORK

HELPING LET'S GO If you want to share your discoveries, suggestions, or corrections, please drop us a line. We read every piece of correspondence, whether a postcard, a 10-page email, or a coconut. Please note that mail received after May 2003 may be too late for the 2004 book, but will be kept for future editions. **Address mail to:**

> **Let's Go: South Africa**
> **67 Mount Auburn Street**
> **Cambridge, MA 02138**
> **USA**

Visit Let's Go at **http://www.letsgo.com,** or send email to:

> **feedback@letsgo.com**
> **Subject: "Let's Go: South Africa"**

In addition to the invaluable travel advice our readers share with us, many are kind enough to offer their services as researchers or editors. Unfortunately, our charter enables us to employ only currently enrolled Harvard students.

Maps by David Lindroth copyright © 2003 by St. Martin's Press.

Distributed outside the USA and Canada by Macmillan.

ISBN: 0-312-30592-3

10 9 8 7 6 5 4 3

Let's Go: South Africa is written by Let's Go Publications, 67 Mount Auburn Street, Cambridge, MA 02138, USA.

HOW TO USE THIS BOOK

Congratulations on your purchase of a brand new *Let's Go: South Africa!* What follows are some handling tips. (1) Bathe your *Let's Go* once weekly, paying particular attention to its claws and teeth. (2) Play with your *Let's Go* every day. Though at first the book may tend to "play rough," occasionally causing major flesh wounds, it will eventually settle down. (3) If your *Let's Go* begins foaming at the mouth or making gurgling noises, don't worry: this is a growth phase. (4) Shower your *Let's Go* with love; the book will give it back in return and then some.

ORGANIZATION OF THIS BOOK

WAAR BEGIN EK? **(WHERE DO I BEGIN?).** The first chapter, **Discover Southern Africa,** provides an overview of travel in the region, including **Suggested Itineraries** that give you an idea of what you absolutely *must* see. The **Essentials** section outlines the information you will need to prepare for your trip. If you read the next chapter, **History and Culture,** you won't sound like a dumb tourist on the road.

HOOFGEREG **(MAIN COURSE).** We begin in **Cape Town** and travel around the South African provinces before moving on to the two kingdoms surrounded by South Africa, and then west to east across the other African countries covered. The **black tabs** in the margins will help you navigate between chapters quickly.

NAGEREG **(DESSERT).** The appendix contains useful **conversions,** a **phrasebook,** and a **glossary** of words that are used in Southern African English. *Dis al!*

A FEW NOTES ABOUT LET'S GO FORMAT

PRICE RANGES AND RANKINGS. Our researchers list establishments in order of value from best to worst. Our absolute favorites are denoted by the Let's Go thumbs-up (🖒). Since the best value does not always mean the cheapest price, we have incorporated a system of price ranges into the guide. The price bracket is based on a scale from ❶ to ❺, with each icon corresponding to a specific price range. There is a table at the beginning of each country chapter that lists how prices fall within each bracket.

PHONE CODES AND TELEPHONE NUMBERS. The phone code for each region, city, or town appears opposite the name of that region, city, or town, and is denoted by the ☎ icon. Phone numbers in text are also preceded by the ☎ icon.

GRAYBOXES AND IKONBOXES. Grayboxes provide cultural insight or crude humor. **Whiteboxes,** on the other hand, provide important information such as warnings (⚠), helpful hints and further resources (🔍), and border crossings (🛂).

COUNTRY ESSENTIALS. The first few pages of each country chapter contain information about money, transportation, and many other tips. **"Life and Times"** gives some of the history and background of each country, while **"Today"** fills you in on some of the hot issues in the country today.

A NOTE TO OUR READERS
The information for this book was gathered by *Let's Go* researchers from May through August of 2002. Each listing is based on one researcher's opinion, formed during his or her visit at a particular time. Those traveling at other times may have different experiences since prices, dates, hours, and conditions are always subject to change. You are urged to check the facts presented in this book beforehand to avoid inconvenience and surprises.

WHO WE ARE

A NEW LET'S GO

With a sleeker look and innovative new content, we have revamped the entire series to reflect more than ever the needs and interests of the independent traveler. Here are just some of the improvements you will notice when traveling with the new *Let's Go*.

MORE PRICE OPTIONS

Still the best resource for budget travelers, *Let's Go* recognizes that everyone needs the occasional indulgence. Our "Big Splurges" indicate establishments that are actually worth those extra pennies (pulas, pesos, or pounds), and price-level symbols (❶ ❷ ❸ ❹ ❺) allow you to quickly determine whether an accommodation or restaurant will break the bank. We may have diversified, but we'll never lose our budget focus—"Hidden Deals" reveal the best-kept travel secrets.

BEYOND THE TOURIST EXPERIENCE

Our Alternatives to Tourism chapter offers ideas on immersing yourself in a new community through study, work, or volunteering.

AN INSIDER'S PERSPECTIVE

As always, every item is written and researched by our on-site writers. This year we have highlighted more viewpoints to help you gain an even more thorough understanding of the places you are visiting.

IN RECENT NEWS. *Let's Go* correspondents around the globe report back on current regional issues that may affect you as a traveler.

CONTRIBUTING WRITERS. Respected scholars and former *Let's Go* writers discuss topics on society and culture, going into greater depth than the usual guidebook summary.

THE LOCAL STORY. From the Parisian monk toting a cell phone to the Russian *babushka* confronting capitalism, *Let's Go* shares its revealing conversations with local personalities—a unique glimpse of what matters to real people.

FROM THE ROAD. Always helpful and sometimes downright hilarious, our researchers share useful insights on the typical (and atypical) travel experience.

SLIMMER SIZE

Don't be fooled by our new, smaller size. *Let's Go* is still packed with invaluable travel advice, but now it's easier to carry with a more compact design.

FORTY-THREE YEARS OF WISDOM

For over four decades *Let's Go* has provided the most up-to-date information on the hippest cafes, the most pristine beaches, and the best routes from border to border. It all started in 1960 when a few well-traveled students at Harvard University handed out a 20-page mimeographed pamphlet of their tips on budget travel to passengers on student charter flights to Europe. From humble beginnings, *Let's Go* has grown to cover six continents and *Let's Go: Europe* still reigns as the world's best-selling travel guide. This year we've beefed up our coverage of Latin America with *Let's Go: Costa Rica* and *Let's Go: Chile;* on the other side of the globe, we've added *Let's Go: Thailand* and *Let's Go: Hawaii.* Our new guides bring the total number of titles to 61, each infused with the spirit of adventure that travelers around the world have come to count on.

CONTENTS

IX

x

RESEARCHER-WRITERS

Kelzie E. Beebe   *Namibia*

This Boston marathon runner, soccer player, and outdoors guru took a break from the physics lab to trek across Namibia and expand our coverage by almost 50%. Whether she was having her pack stolen or declining marriage proposals, nothing came between Kelzie and her love of travel and Africa. While she may be the most hard-core researcher this company has seen, she shows how Namibia is a perfect vacation spot for outdoors enthusiasts of all skill levels.

Leila Chirayath   *Mozambique and Malawi*

Leila took a break from the jungles of Senegal to master the tamer realms of Mozambique and Malawi. A top-rate scholar writing a thesis on African development, Leila never tires of traveling in the developing world or studying Portuguese. She's been *everywhere*, including a six-month stint volunteering in Uganda. Although she packed lightly, she was never without her sense of humor while riding for 72 hours in the backs of trucks or taking a side jaunt into Rwanda.

Joshua Gardner   *Eastern South Africa and Swaziland*

After researching Romania for *Eastern Europe 2002*, Josh fulfilled a long-standing ambition by going to Africa. Whether sailing on the Olifants River, eating crocodile in Warmbaths, clubbing in Nelspruit, or getting naked at the largest spa in Swaziland, Josh loved every minute and didn't want to leave. A humble man, he still attributes much of his outstanding copy to Efrat for being the best receptionist ever and to those who helped him in Africa.

Yusuf Randera-Rees   *The South Coast and Garden Route*

Our native Jo'burger, Yusuf hit the road like opponents in his rugby matches. He tackled clubs, hostels, and restaurants like a hooker (just some rugby terminology) with his straightforward, no-nonsense writing style. A South African expert who has been everywhere a dozen times, he never seemed to lose his smile or good nature, even when falling off ostriches in Oudtshoorn or overcoming his fear of heights at the Bloukrans bungee.

Owen Robinson   *Botswana, Zambia and Zimbabwe*

Owen researched for *Central America 2000* and edited *South Africa 2002* before returning to the road in Botswana. Ever the Afrophile, he has studied at the University of Zimbabwe in Harare and has worked actively in the country's non-profit sector. Owen has been to almost 40 countries, but he says that all the coolest ones are in Southern Africa. He would know, after all; he's been a budget traveler in eight different Southern African countries.

Rick Slettenhaar *Gauteng and Western Cape*

After traveling all over his native Europe, this 6 ft. 8 in. Dutchman tried out the citylife of Jo'burg, Pretoria, and Cape Town. A veteran hiker and master of many languages, Rick combined his street smarts with his adventurous spirit to tame South Africa's biggest metropolis. When he wasn't touring with locals, he was fine-tuning our copy into the most precise it's ever been. Now that he's out of Africa, you can find this fun-loving giant crossing Spain on foot.

Bryden Sweeney-Taylor *Central South Africa and Lesotho*

This veteran of *Southwest USA 2002* and *Hawaii 2003* put his extensive outdoor and hiking skills to work in the wilds of Lesotho and South Africa. The result was top-notch coverage of some of the region's most pristine and underappreciated areas. Bryden possesses an incessant devotion to detailed research and a childish love of adventure—he still claims that he wants to be a cowboy when he grows up— both of which made his work among *Let's Go's* finest.

CONTRIBUTING WRITERS

Bekezela Ncube served as a Researcher-Writer for *Let's Go: South Africa 2002*. A native of Zimbabwe, Beke has lived in South Africa for the past five months, where she spent a semester studying at the University of Cape Town.

Emilou MacLean is working in Cape Town, South Africa with Medecins Sans Frontieres on the Access to Essential Medicines Campaign. She was an Associate Editor for *Let's Go: South Africa 2002*.

Mamongae Mahlare worked for Bain & Company in South Africa. This fall, she will be part of the incoming Harvard MBA class.

ACKNOWLEDGMENTS

LET'S GO

SAF Team thanks: Douglas and Greer Hawkins for editorial and language assistance. Murray Gott and Russell Davidson of the Oak Lodge in Cape Town for their research assistance. SAF 2002 and Cody for advice.

Kyle thanks: Sarah, Tess, D.K., and Cody for their hard work. Paul, Ben, and Seton for lost time on the basketball court. Scuzz and Jason for apartment-hunting in my absence. Louise for being there and helping me have fun all summer. Mom and Dad for getting me out of South Africa and back again so many times, and for their advice. Ouma and all my South African family for their endless love and support. My work is dedicated in memory of my South African hero, Edward Bands.

Tess thanks: Kyle for keeping me on track. Sarah for being a cool person. Harriett for letting me ask endless questions. Owen for laughter and unbelievable stories. Mark for getting me interested in Africa. Becca for being an great roommate and friend. Ben for making sure I had fun and for making me incredibly happy. Mom for being my best friend. Dad & Tiffany for love and support.

Sarah thanks: Kyle and Tess for the book. Eli for doors. Karoun for Target. Ben W. for optimism. Liz for Cape Cod. Jen/Ben G. for Cape Codders. Scrobs for Paris. Stefan for "coffee." Irene for Newport. The BG/Sara for emails. Taylor for the McFlurries. Noah for dysfunction/good times. Doulo for more than I ever deserve. Eno for novels, pictures, dreams. The Seneca. My family, the original LG enterprise.

DK thanks: The SAF bookteam for realizing the complexity of the African landscape, M&P for loving the world, C for existing, and Seeds for their flavor, jalapeno-style.

Editor
Kyle D. Hawkins
Associate Editors
Tess Mullen, Sarah Levine-Gronningsater
Managing Editor
D. Cody Dydek
Map Editor
Yaw D.K. Osseo-Asare

Publishing Director
Matthew Gibson
Editor-in-Chief
Brian R. Walsh
Production Manager
C. Winslow Clayton
Cartography Manager
Julie Stephens
Design Manager
Amy Cain
Editorial Managers
Christopher Blazejewski,
Abigail Burger, D. Cody Dydek,
Harriett Green, Angela Mi Young Hur,
Marla Kaplan, Celeste Ng
Financial Manager
Noah Askin
Marketing & Publicity Managers
Michelle Bowman, Adam M. Grant
New Media Managers
Jesse Tov, Kevin Yip
Online Manager
Amélie Cherlin
Personnel Managers
Alex Leichtman, Owen Robinson
Production Associates
Caleb Epps, David Muehlke
Network Administrators
Steven Aponte, Eduardo Montoya
Design Associate
Juice Fong
Financial Assistant
Suzanne Siu
Office Coordinators
Alex Ewing, Adam Kline,
Efrat Kussell

Director of Advertising Sales
Erik Patton
Senior Advertising Associates
Patrick Donovan, Barbara Eghan,
Fernanda Winthrop
Advertising Artwork Editor
Leif Holtzman
Cover Photo Research
Laura Wyss
President
Bradley J. Olson
General Manager
Robert B. Rombauer
Assistant General Manager
Anne E. Chisholm

DISCOVER SOUTHERN AFRICA

If you've got this book in one hand and a plane ticket to South Africa in the other, everyone you meet should be envious. You are in for some adventures that are difficult to describe. They will be mind-numbing, breath-taking, head-scratching, foot-stomping, Zulu-speaking, eye-opening, and, if you aren't careful, run-on-sentence-producing. No matter how many hyperbolic, hyphenated adjectives we try to use, none will adequately prepare you for standing in Kruger National Park watching lions on the morning hunt, bungee jumping over Victoria Falls, SCUBA diving in Lake Malawi, safari-ing in the Kalahari Desert, clubbing in Cape Town, basking on the beautiful beaches of the Indian Ocean, exploring Soweto, or skydiving over the African *veld* in Namibia. There is very little you *cannot* do in Southern Africa; it's got something for everyone.

South Africa itself may be thought of as an outdoor adventure paradise, but lions, rhinos and leopards (oh my!) aren't the only highlights of this cultural kaleidoscope. Culturally, this is the land the spawned Nelson Mandela, Charlize Theron, Dave Matthews, J.R.R. Tolkien, and plenty of others in between. The nation is perhaps most noticeable for its diversity, with eleven national languages and citizens of African, European, and Asian ancestry. Above all, South Africa offers the opportunity to experience life in a country that is still struggling to come to grips with a troubled past while finding its footing for a stable future.

Whatever you do, don't be fooled into thinking that South*ern* Africa ends in South Africa's Northern Province. Adventurous travelers will find that the other nations in the region possess their own thrills and lifestyles independent of South Africa. **Swaziland** is a nation of incredible natural beauty, elaborate tradition, and cultural vibrancy. **Lesotho,** a small kingdom that was able to maintain its independence from South Africa because of a ring of sheer mountains, has wonderful opportunities to trek through high passes on ponyback and pick up some great Basotho craftwork.

Namibia is an oft-overlooked but haunting landscape that includes desolate desert, ghost towns, and shipwrecks, as well as big game, rock paintings, and a world of watersports. **Botswana's** policy of ecotourism has kept the wilderness almost as wild as it can get. While opportunities can be both rich *and* expensive, plenty of adventure outfitters are game for budget business. Although political conditions in **Zimbabwe** have deteriorated in recent years, the spectacular Victoria Falls, which make Niagara look like a leaky faucet, still continue to thunder as they have for hundreds of thousands of years, and the Great Zimbabwe ruins are one of the most surreal archaeological sites on the continent.

Mozambique, while a more difficult country to travel through or across, offers pristine beaches with thriving local economies based around the sea, as well as the magnificent Mozambique Island, a UNESCO World Heritage site, in the north. Finally, **Malawi's** appeal is centered around its gorgeous inland sea, dotted with sailboats and filled with exotic species of fish; its high plateaus and mountain ranges give the hiker another reason to tour the country.

DISCOVER

CLOSEST ANIMAL ENCOUNTER: Savor *mopane* worms and ginger beetles in **Thohoyandou** (p. 342).

EXPAND YOUR CONSCIOUSNESS: If you're hunting for hippie hang-outs or a little eco-friendly fun, open your mind and alter your reality at **Rustler's Valley** (p. 389), where you can learn about permaculture. Explore the best **ecotourism** has to offer without exploiting the environment in **Swakopmund** (p. 494). Commune with fellow dreadheads in **Knysna** (p. 161) and **Port St. Johns** (p. 217), or mingle with tens of thousands of all cultures at the **Grahamstown Arts Festival** (p. 206). Spend a night with a rural Zulu family in **Eshowe** (p. 267).

WEIRD WANDERING: For some atypical traveling, try getting around Lesotho on the back of a **Basotho pony** (p. 432). If that doesn't thrill you, **sand boarding** in Swakopmund, Namibia (p. 498) is a sure shock at 80km per hr. Or, **bodysurf** down the Zambezi rapids in Victoria Falls (p. 590).

COOLEST UNTOURISTED DESTINATIONS: To see a 16th-century trading center in all its faded glory, make the long journey to **Ilha de Moçambique** (p. 631), on the Indian Ocean. If this isn't remote enough for you, drive your safari vehicle into the heart of the desert at **Central Kalahari Game Reserve** (p. 541).

WHEN TO GO

As a general rule, tourism in Southern Africa peaks during summer holidays for schools and universities in Dec.-Jan. During this time, as well as during the other school holidays in Apr., June, and Sept., national parks are heavily booked, and prices on coasts and in major tourist areas can go up significantly. See **Appendix,** p. 649, for a list of average monthly temperatures in Southern Africa; see country-specific **Essentials** for a list of national holidays.

SOUTH AFRICA, LESOTHO, AND SWAZILAND. Most of the **Western Cape** has a Mediterranean climate: warm, mild summers (usually around 26°C or 79°F), and wet, chilly winters (around 5°C or 41°F). March and May are the best months to visit, as the weather is very mild and the winds drop. Don't let this advice lull you into a false sense of security, however: the gods can be crazy, and the Western Cape in particular is known for its unpredictable weather. Spontaneous downpours and sporadic winds can occur anytime throughout the year. Beware the *berg* (mountain) wind, too: a hot, muggy wind, it begins at the Cape and can blow all the way to the east coast. **KwaZulu-Natal** feels tropical, with warm temperatures year-round. Summers can be hot and very humid; the best time to visit is during the light, sunny winters (with highs around 22°C or 72°F). In **Gauteng** and the **Northwest Province,** summer days tend to be warm and windless (with highs around 26°C or 79°F), and they may end with sudden deluges of rain. While winter days are clear and crisp, nights can drop below freezing, and it is common to see frost in the early morning. **Mpumalanga** is rainy in summer and hot throughout, especially in the *lowveld* and Kruger National Park. Mild and dry winters can be very cold at night, especially on the escarpment. The **Eastern Cape** tends to be very blustery. In the summer, parts of the **Northern Cape** experience scorching temperatures of around 40-45°C (104-113°F). Wildflowers are at their best in the **Namaqualand** and the **West Coast** during August and September.

BOTSWANA. The summers (Sept. to Nov.) are sweltering by day and pleasant at night, until the rains (Dec.-Apr.) take over and cool things down a bit; winter (May-Aug.) sets in soon after the rains subside. You can see game in Botswana's parks whenever you go, although many lodges close during the rainy season. Animals

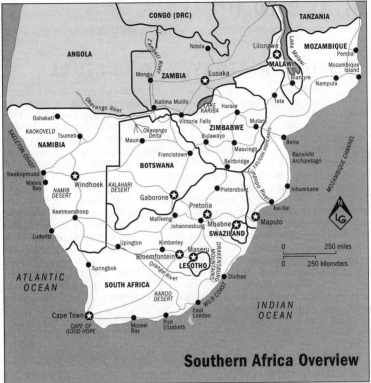

Southern Africa Overview

are best seen during the dry season, when they congregate at watering holes and grasses are lower.

NAMIBIA. Summer (Dec.-Feb.) in Namibia's interior is miserably hot. On the west coast, summers are blissful and packed, as all of Namibia flocks to the water for relief from the heat. However, the dry winters (May-Sept.) are prime angling season, and the best time to visit national parks; the temperature is comfortable and thirsty game come to strategically-placed waterholes to drink. Plus, travelers during these months avoid dangers and delays from flooded rural roads, particularly risky if one does not have a 4WD.

ZIMBABWE AND MALAWI. These countries' winters (May-Oct.) are generally very mild and dry, while the summers (Nov.-Mar.) are wet and hot. The Zambezi Valley, Midlands area, and the shores of Lake Malawi are warmer and drier than higher areas of the region.

MOZAMBIQUE. Temperatures here peak from October to March, although temperature variations between seasons are much less drastic than in other parts of the region. Parts of Mozambique get dumped on between December and March, especially in recent years as the swollen Zambezi and Limpopo rivers attest. As Mozambique is a very long country spanning a long stretch of the continent, the differences between Maputo and northern Mozambique are great: Maputo's climate is more temperate, while the north experiences tropical weather.

THINGS TO DO

For more specific regional attractions, see the **Highlights of the Region** section at the beginning of each chapter.

POLITICS, HISTORY, AND CULTURE

For social science buffs, the time is ripe in South Africa for exploring the history and legacy of apartheid. Only 10 years after Nelson Mandela's release from **Robben Island** (p. 101), the former prison has been transformed into a museum. **Cape Town** (p. 76) is a fantastic base from which to explore the history of South Africa's "coloured" and Muslim populations, especially at the **District Six Museum** (p. 99) and in the **Bo-Kaap** (p. 100). The **Eastern Cape**'s small towns offer insight into Boer life in the stifling **Karoo** (see p. 195), while its capital, **Port Elizabeth** (p. 184), boasts two of the best township tours in the country.

Trips further inland reveal the story of South Africa's development. Stop in at **Kimberley** (p. 405) to see the biggest diamond mine in the world. The history of **Johannesburg** (p. 291) is intertwined with the story of gold in South Africa. Gaze upon long-standing monuments to Afrikaner culture in **Pretoria** (p. 310), and visit the sites of the bloodiest battles in South African history in **KwaZulu-Natal** (p. 222).

In **Windhoek, Alte Feste** (p. 461) narrates the history of **Namibia** from colonization to independence, and **Katatura** (p. 469) is one of the more visitor-friendly townships. The ghost mining town **Kolmanskop** (p. 517), near Lüderitz, captures the spirit of the diamond rush in preserved buildings now half-buried in sand. Botswana's **Tsodilo Hills** (p. 557), although difficult to reach, contain some of the most unique and best-preserved examples of San rock art in the world. Finally, **Ilha de Moçambique** (p. 631), a UN World Heritage Site in the far northeast of the country, contains centuries-old churches and forts that were constructed by Portuguese spice traders in the very first days of European-African contact.

ADVENTURE SPORTS

The public transportation system in Southern Africa might consist mostly of jolting buses and minicabs, but there are other more exciting ways of moving around. **Cape Town** (p. 76) offers ways of getting down—abseiling, mountain biking, sandboarding, and skydiving—as well as getting up (kloofing) and across (paragliding). Nearby, the **Overberg Coast** (p. 140) is the best site for whale watching and—strictly for the masochistic—shark cage diving. Strenuous hikes and the highest bungee jump in the world will lure you to the **Garden Route** (p. 151). **Jeffreys Bay** (p. 193) and **Durban** (p. 222) have crests and tubes which are perfect for surfing. **Kruger Park** (p. 365) is world famous for its wildlife, including crocs, hippos, and big game. From here, cross the border into Zimbabwe for some whitewater rafting and bungee jumping at **Victoria Falls** (p. 586). **Swakopmund** (p. 494), on **Namibia's** coast, offers everything from desert safaris to skydiving to sand boarding. Botswana's **Okavango Delta** (p. 549) offers a unique way to see the animals: in a *mokoro*, a dugout canoe somewhat similar to a Venetian gondola. **Lake Malawi** (p. 646) has some of the area's most unique snorkeling and scuba diving, and invites sailing, kayaking, and top-notch sport fishing.

GREAT TREKKING

If it weren't for the stunning, rugged mountainscapes of South Africa, *The Hobbit* and *Lord of the Rings* might never have been written. Legend has it that it was during hikes in the **Drakensberg** (p. 238), the country's largest mountain range, that

J.R.R. Tolkien conceived his fantastic tales. The Drakensberg is, far and away, the best place to hike in South Africa, although there are also spectacular trails through the **Blyde River Canyon** (p. 378), **Winelands** (p. 119), and **Breede River Valley** (p. 130). **Tsitsikamma National Park's** famous **Otter Trail** (p. 171) is world-class, but books solid up to a year ahead of time. In **Lesotho**, you can trade in your weary legs for a pony at the famous **Malealea Lodge** (p. 433). Finally, a trip to South Africa would not be complete without a hike up **Table Mountain** (p. 104), from where you can savor the panoramic view of the peninsula. If your limbs are still crying out for more, fly home via **Namibia's Fish River Canyon Park** (p. 519), the largest canyon in the Southern Hemisphere with the most challenging hiking trail in all of Africa.

THE WILD SIDE

Southern Africa has a plethora of national parks and nature reserves. Some of them cater to tourists content to watch the animals from the safety of their cars, while others indulge those who are just itching to be out there amongst the baboons. Most South African parks have sound infrastructures with knowledgeable rangers who run day and night safaris; especially spectacular are the world-renowned **Kruger National Park** (p. 365), **Pilanesberg National Park** (p. 400), and **Hluhluwe-Umfolozi Game Reserve** (p. 285), all of which boast the Big Five—lion, buffalo, elephant, leopard, and rhino. The Western and Northern Cape are the only two provinces where you're better off sticking to wine—you'll admire the gorgeous scenery of the **Richtersveld** and **Kalahari Gemsbok National Parks,** but you're not likely to spot as much game. Visit Botswana's **Chobe National Park** (p. 558)—especially during the zebra migration season—or the **Okavango Delta** (p. 549), where you can explore the bird-filled waterways by *mokoro* boat and camp in the wild at the nearby **Moremi Game Reserve** (p. 551). Rivalling the Serengeti and Kruger, **Etosha National Park** (p. 484) in **Namibia** was once the bottom of a lake, and is now an eerie salt pan that attracts some of the finest game in Africa to its southern edges. **Malawi's** big game is a bit more scarce, but can be appreciated at **Liwonde National Park** (p. 648).

LIFE'S A BEACH

Southern Africa, with its thousands of miles of metamorphosing shore, does away with the idea of no-name-brand surf 'n' sand. Each of the beaches and coastlines has a distinct personality, allowing the discerning sun-worshipper to pick and choose. In **Cape Town** (p. 76), where the Indian Ocean meets the Atlantic, you can have your waters warm or iced. On the Atlantic side, at the base of spectacular mountains, chill out (literally) at chic, cosmopolitan **Clifton** and **Camps Bay** (p. 105), or secluded **Llandudno** and **Sandy Bay** (p. 105), where you'll spot some jaw-dropping drawer-dropping. The **Garden Route** (p. 151) offers a mixed bag of wild, sprawling strand and hip, yellow-polka-dot-bikini beaches. Waterbabies shouldn't miss **Jeffreys Bay** (p. 193), the surfing capital of the South Africa. A little farther east, the **Wild Coast** (p. 211) is exactly that—an untamed paradise of pointy dunes and undulating ocean. Small, touristy beaches flare into the blistering tropical bliss of **Durban** (p. 222). Islands and beaches near **Lüderitz** (p. 514), in **Namibia,** are cold and windswept, but provide the ideal habitat for seals and penguins, and the perfect atmosphere for viewing the less fortunate ships to sail into (literally) the Skeleton Coast. A bit further north, **Walvis Bay** (p. 502), an otherwise unremarkable port town, is known to bird-watchers worldwide as one of Southern Africa's premier birding sites. On the east coast, Mozambique's **Bazaruto Archipelago** (p. 623) basks in idyllic (if pricey) perfection, while budgeteers find their niche in the fishing villages near **Inhambane** (p. 621). In the African interior, **Lake Malawi** (p. 646) might not be a sea in the true sense of the word, but still offers enough beaches, watersports, and waves to give the Indian and Atlantic a run for their money.

SUGGESTED ITINERARIES

BEST OF SOUTH AFRICA (FOUR WEEK TOUR)

BEST OF SOUTH AFRICA (4 WEEKS)
Start with a week in **Cape Town** (p. 76), at the tip of Africa: hike up **Table Mountain** (p. 104), then cruise down on the cable car, marveling at the sprawling city below; take a spectacular scenic drive around the peninsula; take a boat to **Robben Island** (p. 101) for the 3hr. tour; by night, party to the decadent beat of the dance and jazz clubs. Next, go wine-tasting in **Stellenbosch** (p. 121), and let a frisky horse whisk you through valleys and vineyards. Now hug the coast, admiring the Cape Dutch architecture along the **Garden Route** (p. 151). Catch the famous steam train, **Outeniqua Choo-Tjoe** (p. 162), from George to Knysna, stopping at **Wilderness** (p. 160). In **Knysna** (p. 161), bike out to view the giant Knysna heads before moving on to party with the young, tanned, and beautiful at **Plettenberg Bay** (p. 166). Tackle the rugged terrain in the **Tsitsikamma National Park** (p. 171), suntan and surf on famous **Jeffreys Bay** (p. 193), then on to **Port Elizabeth** (p. 184), where fortune might pitch you the thrill of a night-cricket match and *boerewors* roll at St. George's Park. Drive through the Karoo desert to check out the spooky **Owl House** (p. 200) near Graaff-Reinet, then head to **Grahamstown** (p. 202)—with some good planning and some luck, you may be able to catch one of their world-famous festivals. Continue inland to visit a *sangoma* in **Lesotho** (p. 421), and try your hand at some of the country's amazing pony trekking. From here, explore the sheer

Drakensberg Range (p. 238) before bouncing back to the **Wild Coast** (p. 211) and **Durban** (p. 222) for some tropical beaches, colonial architecture, and spicy Indian cuisine. Continue up the coast toward **St. Lucia** and **Cape Vidal** (p. 277), exploring one of the most unique wetland ecosystems on earth. Now into **Swaziland** (p. 436), another tiny country that demonstrates both the good and the bad of a traditional monarchy. Slip out the northern side of the country and into **Kruger National Park** (p. 365) for a few days of the "big five," and walk around **Blyde River Canyon** (p. 378) on your way to **Johannesburg** (p. 291) for a few hair-raising final days. Take the **Soweto township tour** (p. 304) and—for an unusual watering hole—visit a *shebeen*. Relax under the jacarandas and royal palms of **Pretoria** (p. 310) before bidding *adieu* to this wonderful country.

THE CARELESS AND THE CARLESS: AN ITINERARY FOR DAREDEVILS (3 WEEKS) Fly into **Johannesburg** (p. 291). Flush out the jetlag with some traditional *maheu* beer in a Soweto *shebeen* and shake it on down to the *soukous* or *kwaito* rhythms of Hillbrow's dance clubs. Hop on a bus to **Durban** (p. 222) via the **Northern Drakensberg** (p. 240). Scour the mountains by foot, or with one of the world's only 4WD VW beetles. Try to get to Durban in time for the world's most grueling race, the **Comrade's Marathon,** and the famous horse race, the **Durban July** (1st Sa). Then horse around on your own by jet-skiing, paragliding, and scuba diving in the warm Indian waves. Go game-viewing on foot in the KwaZulu-Natal nature parks. Catch your breath on the bus trip to Cape Town, but only after stopping off at Port Shepstone to take a daytrip to the **Oribi Gorge** (p. 258) to abseil and go whitewater rafting. If you're not dizzy yet, ask the bus to stop at: **Port Edward** (p. 263), for deep-sea fishing; **Jeffreys Bay** (p. 193), for surfing; the **Tsitsikamma** (p. 171), for the 5-day Otter Trail; and **Plettenberg Bay** (p. 166), for hard-core partying. Ditch the bus from Knysna to George to ride the **Outeniqua Choo-Tjoe** (p. 162). Take a daytrip to **Oudtshoorn** (p.

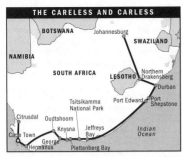

THE CARELESS AND CARLESS

DESERT TRAVERSES: NAMIBIA

135) for ostrich-riding, and some claustro-phobic hyperventilation in the Cango Caves; then have a whale of a time whale-watching in **Hermanus** (p. 140). Keep up the pace in **Cape Town** (p. 76) with hiking, *kloofing*, shark diving, sandboarding, and mountain biking. A daytrip to **Citrusdal** (p. 180) will send you skydiving. If you're still on your feet by this point, a good bout of clubbing in Cape Town is guaranteed to knock you out for good.

DESERT TRAVERSES: NAMIBIA (4 WEEKS)

Start in **Windhoek** (p. 461) for 4 days to shake off your jetlag and soak up your new surroundings. Walk among the wild, visiting **Daan Viljoen Park** (p. 470) as a daytrip. Back from the baboons, head north to **Waterberg Plateau National Park** (p. 475), and then whirl through Tsumeb on your way to **Etosha National Park** (p. 484). Spend a night at each of its 3 rest camps, while rhino, leopards, and lions come out of the dark for a sip and dip at camp water-holes. Make **Khorixas** (p. 488) your next base for at least 3 days while you visit **Vingerklip, Petrified Forest,** and **Twyfel-fontein** for some geo-oddities and ancient artistry. Head south for a hike into the **Brandberg** (p. 489) in search of the myste-rious White Lady, and then hit some highs en route to Bushman's Paradise at **Spitzko-ppe** (p. 493). Next, kick it at the coast in **Swakopmund** (p. 494): test your hand at angling or your guts with 80km per hour sandboarding down desert dunes. Check out 100,000 sweet and smelly seals at the **Cape Cross Seal Reserve** on the **Skeleton Coast** (p. 494). In **Walvis Bay** (p. 502), picnic with palm trees at Dune 7 or laze by the lagoon, unless paragliding and dune

biking are more your thing (you daredevil, you!). What's a day or two in the oldest desert in the world? Hike the **Sossusvlei and Sesriem Canyon** (p. 510) in the ancient Namib Desert, and leave the rest of the world in the dust. Say goodbye to **Namib-Naukluft Park** to tromp around on the **Giant's Playground** (p. 512), an unearthly pile of massive boulders in **Keet-manshoop**. Swing by **Lüderitz** (p. 514) for some motion in the ocean and grab some rock lobster before visiting a nearby ghost town. Challenge yourself one last time at **Fish River Canyon** (p. 519), rivaled only by the Grand Canyon and home to one of Africa's most challenging hiking trails, the **Fish River Hiking Trail.** Head back to Wind-hoek for a final farewell.

SAFARI HEAVEN: BOTSWANA (4 WEEKS)

Get you bearings in **Gaborone** (p. 527) for a few days, checking out the museums and shops. Rest for a night in the gold rush town of **Francistown** (p. 534) on your way to the **Tuli Block** (p. 539), where you the game is plentiful and the digs are cheap. Next, stock up in **Nata** (p. 546) and prepare to be stunned by the salty solitude of the desolate **Makgadikgadi Pan** (p. 543). Spend a night in the pans at **Planet Baobab** before heading to **Kasane** (p.

DISCOVER

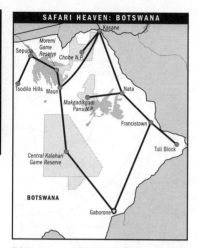

SAFARI HEAVEN: BOTSWANA

561), gateway to **Chobe National Park,** for beasts by day and booze cruises by night. After a few nights in Kasane, make your way to **Maun** (p. 552), where you can meet other travelers for a wild week in the **Okavango Delta** and **Moremi Game Reserve** (p. 551). Snake down the Delta in a boat pushed by pole, look out for lions and leopards, hunt for rock paintings, and dodge hungry, hungry hippos. From there, it's also a short stretch to the **Tsodilo Hills** (p. 557), site of over 3000 rock paintings, including the "Dancing..." well, you'll find out. See the ancient dunes of the **Central Kalahari Game Reserve** (p. 541). You can spend a week looking for lions and reflecting on the harsh wilderness of part of the largest desert expanse in the world. Before you get too existential, get your butt back to **Gaborone** for a few good-byes and cheap souvenirs. Have a happy safari!

PUTTING IT ALL TOGETHER: SOUTHERN AFRICA EPIC (12 WEEKS AND UP) This "dream itinerary," though both long and exhausting, would undoubtedly be one of the great experiences of your life; give it some thought, especially if you're the world traveler type. Start things off in cosmopolitan **Cape Town** (p. 76), reveling in the museums, history, nightlife, and amazing natural scenery that this world-class city has to offer. Take a few days to meander through the wine country around **Stellen-**

bosch (p. 121), getting loopy on fine merlots and chardonnays, before moving on to the **Garden Route** (p. 151) with its adventure sports, seaside villages, mouth-watering seafood, and laid-back atmosphere. Pass through **Grahamstown** (p. 195), catching a few museums and perhaps a festival, and then cross into **Lesotho** (p. 421), where pony trekking and an introduction into Basotho culture and spirituality await. Tramp through the national parks of the dramatic **Drakensberg Range** (p. 238) on the way back to the coast and **Durban** (p. 222), where Indian culture and superb beaches offer at least a few days of exploration and relaxation. Continue up the coast, stopping for a few days at **St. Lucia** and exploring nearby **Cape Vidal** (p. 277), and then head for the markets, cultural sights, and nature preserves of tiny **Swaziland** (p. 436), a country that deserves at least a week of exploration time. You can't come this close without spending at least a few days on safari in South Africa's **Kruger National Park** (p. 365); after successfully evading marauding bands of elephant and lion, cross yet another border to **Maputo, Mozambique** (p. 612). Spend a few days pounding the pavement of this fascinating capital, taking in the sights of the center and perhaps the smells of the fish market, and then hit the road once more, moving up the Mozambican coast to the beaches of **Inhambane** (p. 621). Save room in your budget for the idyllic (if exclusive) attraction of the **Bazaruto Archipelago** (p. 623), and return (slightly more tanned) to the road, to **Blantyre, Malawi** (p. 640), within easy reach of some excellent hiking in the airy heights of southern Malawi. Trade your hiking boots for flippers on the shores of **Lake Malawi** (p. 646), coming face to face with fish that prove that God does indeed have a sense of humor. Once you have your land legs back, take a flight across Zimbabwe to **Victoria Falls** (p. 586), one of the greatest wonders of the natural world. Bungee, paraglide, or raft to your heart's content, or merely soak in the spray from this world wonder. When you've seen enough of the thundering cascade (if you ever do), head for Botswana's **Chobe National Park** (p. 558) and prepare to see more elephants in one place than you ever knew existed in the entire world. If you thought this place was spectacular, just wait until you start your

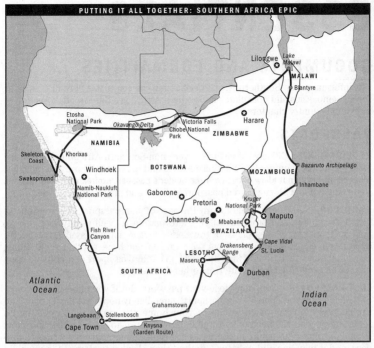

safari in the **Okavango Delta** (p. 549); spend a solid week in this, one of the most amazing natural areas on earth. After a long, bouncy trip across the Kalahari, pull into Namibia's **Etosha National Park** (p. 484) to marvel at the animals congregated at the salt pans. Stop at **Khorixas** (p. 488) and spend some time meandering around the weird rock formations, prehistoric paintings, and mountains that surround this outpost. Then on to **Swakopmund** (p. 494) and the **Skeleton Coast** (p. 499), where seal colonies, harsh but beautiful scenery,

and myriad adventure sports guarantee at least a few days of enjoyment. Continue south, through the shifting sand dunes of **Namib-Naukluft National Park** (p. 506), to the yawning expanses of **Fish River Canyon** (p. 519), which beckons hikers or just gazers. Cruise down the home stretch of the South African Atlantic Coast, spending a few days near **Langebaan** (p. 176) to wind down and see the wildflowers, before returning, triumphant, to the familiar haunts of **Cape Town.** Phew. We're out of breath just *thinking* about this.

ESSENTIALS

DOCUMENTS AND FORMALITIES

For information on Southern African **embassies and consulates** abroad as well as foreign embassies and consulates in Southern Africa, see the **Essentials** section of individual country chapters.

PASSPORTS

REQUIREMENTS. Citizens of virtually every non-Southern African country need valid passports to enter all of Southern Africa, and to reenter their own countries. **Most countries do not allow entrance if the holder's passport expires within six months.** Returning home with an expired passport is illegal and may result in a fine.

PHOTOCOPIES. Be sure to photocopy the page of your passport with your photo, passport number, and other identifying information, as well as any visas, travel insurance policies, plane tickets, or traveler's check serial numbers. Carry one set of copies in a safe place, apart from the originals, and leave another set at home. Consulates also recommend that you carry an expired passport or an official copy of your birth certificate separate from other documents.

LOST PASSPORTS. Fool, don't lose your passport! But if you choose not to take our advice, and you do lose your passport, immediately notify the local police and the nearest embassy or consulate of your home government. To expedite its replacement, you will need to know all information previously recorded and show ID and proof of citizenship. In some cases, a replacement may take weeks to process, and it may be valid only for a limited time. Any visas stamped in your old passport will be irretrievably lost, so you an no longer impress people in bars with all the places you've been. In an emergency, ask for immediate temporary traveling papers that will permit you to reenter your home country. Your passport is a public document belonging to your nation's government. You may have to surrender it to a foreign government official, but if you don't get it back in a reasonable amount of time, inform the nearest mission of your home country.

NEW PASSPORTS. File any new passport or renewal applications well in advance of your departure date. Most passport offices offer rush services for a steep fee, which may not even reach you in time. Citizens living abroad who need a passport or renewal should contact the nearest consular service of their home country.

Australia: Info ☎ 131 232; passports.australia@dfat.gov.au; www.dfat.gov.au/passports. Apply for a passport at a post office, passport office (in Adelaide, Brisbane, Canberra, Darwin, Hobart, Melbourne, Newcastle, Perth, or Sydney), or overseas diplomatic mission. Passports AUS$136 (32-page) or AUS$204 (64-page); valid for 10 years. Children AUS$68/$102; valid for five years. New passports are delivered 10 working days after they are ordered.

Canada: Canadian Passport Office, Department of Foreign Affairs and International Trade, Ottawa, ON K1A 0G3 (☎ 819 994 3500 or 800 567 6868; www.dfait-maeci.gc.ca/passport). Applications available at post offices, passport offices, and Canadian missions. Passports CDN$60; valid for 5 years (non-renewable).

Ireland: Pick up an application at a *Garda* station or post office, or request one from a passport office. Apply by mail to the Department of Foreign Affairs, Passport Office, Molesworth St., Dublin 2 (☎ 01 671 1633; fax 671 1092; www.irlgov.ie/iveagh), or the

Passport Office, Irish Life Building, 1A South Mall, Cork (☎021 27 25 25). Standard (32-page) passports €57; large (48-page) passports €69. Valid for 10 years. Under 18 or over 65 €12; valid for 3 years.

New Zealand: Send applications to the Passport Office, Department of International Affairs, P.O. Box 10526, Wellington, New Zealand (☎0800 22 50 50 or 04 474 81 00; fax 04 474 80 10; passports@dia.govt.nz; www.passports.govt.nz). Standard processing time is 10 working days. Passports NZ$71; valid for 10 years. Children under 16 NZ$36; valid for five years. 3-day "urgent service" available for an additional NZ$80.

South Africa: Department of Home Affairs, Private Bag X114, Pretoria, 0001. Passports are issued only in Pretoria, but all applications must still be submitted or forwarded to the nearest South African consulate. Processing time is 3 months or more. Standard (32-page) passports R735; "Jumbo" (48-page) passports R900; valid for 10 years. Under 16 around R435; valid for five years. For more information call 012 314 8911.

United Kingdom: Info ☎0870 521 0410; www.open.gov.uk/ukpass/ukpass.htm. Get an application from a passport office, main post office, travel agent, or online (for UK residents only) at www.ukpa.gov.uk/forms/f_app_pack.htm. Then apply by mail to or in person at a passport office. Passports UK£30 (UK£40 for 48-page passport); valid for 10 years. Under 15 UK£16; valid for 5 years. The process takes 4 weeks; faster service of 1 week or less (by personal visit to the offices listed above) costs at least 2x as much.

United States: Info ☎202 647 4000 (Department of State); www.travel.state.gov/passport_services.html. Apply at any federal or state courthouse, authorized post office, or US Passport Agency (in most major cities); see the "US Government, State Department" section of the telephone book or a post office for addresses. Processing takes 3-4 weeks. New passports US$60; valid for 10 years. Under 16 US$40; valid for 5 years. Passports may be renewed by mail or in person for US$40. Add US$35 for 3-day expedited service.

VISAS AND WORK PERMITS

VISAS. Visa requirements vary from the minimal and free (South Africa) to the ponderous and expensive (Mozambique). US citizens can take advantage of the **Center for International Business and Travel** (**CIBT;** ☎800 929 2428; www.cibt.com), which secures visas for travel to almost all countries for a variable service charge.

Be sure to double-check on entrance requirements (they can change without warning) at the nearest embassy or consulate for up-to-date information before departure. US citizens can also consult www.pueblo.gsa.gov/cic_text/travel/foreign/foreignentryreqs.html.

VISA REQS		AUS	CAN	IRE	NZ	SA	UK	US
	BOTSWANA	N	N	N	N	N	N	N
	LESOTHO	N	N	N	N	N	N	N
	MALAWI	N	N	N	N	N	N	N
	MOZAMBIQUE	Y	Y	Y	Y	Y	Y	Y
	NAMIBIA	N	N	N	N	N	N	N
	SOUTH AFRICA	N	N	N	N	N	N	N
	SWAZILAND	N	N	N	N	N	N	N
	ZAMBIA	N	N	N	N	N	N	Y
	ZIMBABWE	N	N	N	N	Y	N	Y

WORK PERMITS. Admission as a visitor does not include the right to work, which is authorized only by a special business visa and/or work permit. Entering most Southern African countries to study also requires a special permit. For more information, see **Alternatives to Tourism,** p. 45.

IDENTIFICATION

When you travel, carry two or more forms of identification on your person, including at least one photo ID; a passport combined with a driver's license or birth certificate is usually adequate. Many establishments, especially banks, may require several IDs in order to cash traveler's checks. Never carry all your forms of ID together; split them up in case of theft or loss.

STUDENT AND TEACHER IDENTIFICATION. The **International Student Identity Card (ISIC),** the most widely accepted form of student ID, provides discounts on sights, accommodations, food, and transport. The ISIC is preferable to an institution-specific card (such as a university ID) because it is more likely to be recognized (and honored) abroad. All cardholders have access to a 24hr. emergency helpline for medical, legal, and financial emergencies, and holders of US-issued cards are also eligible for insurance benefits (see **Insurance,** p. 24). Most student travel agencies worldwide issue ISICs. The card is valid from September of one year to December of the following year and costs AUS$15, CDN$15, or US$22. Applicants must be degree-seeking students of a secondary or post-secondary school and must be of at least 12 years of age. Because of the proliferation of fake ISICs, some services (particularly airlines) require additional proof of student identity, such as a school ID or a letter attesting to your student status, signed by your registrar and stamped with your school seal. The **International Teacher Identity Card (ITIC)** offers the same insurance coverage as well as similar but limited discounts. The fee is AUS$13, UK£5, or US$22. One of the most useful organizations (and web sites) is the **International Student Travel Confederation (ISTC),** Herengracht 479, 1017 BS Amsterdam, Netherlands (☎31 20 421 28 00; fax 421 28 10; istcinfo@istc.org; www.istc.org).

ISICONNECT SERVICE. If you are an ISIC card carrier and want to avoid buying individual calling cards or wish to consolidate all your means of communication during your trip, you can activate your ISIC's ISIConnect service, a powerful new integrated communications service (powered by eKit.com). With ISIConnect, one toll-free access number (☎0800 992 921 in South Africa) gives you access to several different methods of keeping in touch via the phone and Internet, including: a reduced-rate international calling plan that treats your ISIC card as a universal **calling card;** a **voicemail** box accessible from pay phones anywhere in the world or for free over the Internet; **faxmail** service for sending and receiving faxes via email, fax machines, or pay phones; various **email** capabilities, including a service that reads your email to you over the phone; an online **"travel safe"** for storing (and faxing) important documents and numbers; and a 24hr. emergency **help line** (via phone or email at ISIConnect@ekit.com) offering assistance and medical and legal referrals. To activate your ISIConnect account, visit the service's comprehensive web site (www.isiconnect.ekit.com) or call the customer service number of your home country (which is also your home country's access number): in Australia 800 114 478; in Canada 877 635 3575; in Ireland 800 555 180 or 800 577 980; in New Zealand 0800 114 478; in the UK 0800 376 2366 or 0800 169 8646; in the US 800 706 1333; and in South Africa 0800 992 921 or 0800 997 285. Note that ISIConnect does not yet function in Southern African countries outside of South Africa.

CUSTOMS

Upon entering Southern Africa, you must declare certain items from abroad and pay a duty on the value of those articles that exceed the allowance established by customs service. Keeping receipts for purchases made abroad will help establish values when you return. Make a list, including serial numbers, of carried valuables from home; if you register this list with customs before your departure and have an official stamp it, you will avoid import duty charges and ensure an easy passage upon your return. Upon returning home, you must declare all articles acquired abroad and pay a **duty** on the value of articles that exceed the allowance established by your country's customs service. Goods and gifts purchased at **duty-free** shops abroad are not exempt from duty or sales tax at your point of return; you must declare these items as well. For more specific information on customs requirements, contact the customs information center in your country.

MONEY

CURRENCY AND EXCHANGE

Obtaining Southern African currencies is typically not a problem; with the exceptions of South Africa and Botswana, however, **it is very difficult and expensive to change local currencies back into foreign currencies.** Many a traveler to Southern Africa has exchanged too much money at the beginning of a trip, only to find himself stuck at the end with a wad of worthless local cash. It is therefore very important to plan cash expenses carefully with the aim of having just enough local cash to complete a trip, and no more.

In much of Southern Africa, hard **US dollars** or **British pounds** will be exchangeable virtually anywhere, and can fetch astronomically good rates. *Let's Go* recommends that travelers exchange cash at *bureaux de change* whenever possible, as opposed to banks (which have lower rates) or informally. **Thomas Cook/Rennie's** is found in most Southern African countries, and tends to have very competitive rates. Finally, in **Mozambique** and **Zambia,** where routine purchases sometimes run into the millions of kwacha or meticais, beware of a popular scam that adds an extra "zero" to the end of a credit card slip or purchase price, in the hopes that the traveler won't notice the tenfold increase in such a large number.

For a currency conversion chart, see p. 50.

TRAVELER'S CHECKS

Traveler's checks are much safer than cash, but also have their disadvantages. First, traveler's checks often (but not always) fetch lower rates than cash at banks and *bureaux de change*. Second, travelers may have a difficult time finding places to exchange checks outside of capital cities and major international tourist destinations. Finally, some countries, such as Mozambique, levy a prohibitively hefty fee on all check exchanges. Most of the disadvantages mentioned here do not apply to the country of South Africa, where traveler's checks are a much more convenient means of payment.

While traveling, keep check receipts and records separate from the checks themselves. Also leave a list of check numbers with someone at home. Never countersign checks until you're ready to cash them, and always bring your passport with you to cash them. Always carry emergency cash.

American Express: These are by far the most widely accepted in Southern Africa. Checks available with commission at select banks and all AmEx offices. US residents can also purchase checks by phone (☎888 887 8986) or online (www.aexp.com). Checks available in US, Australian, British, Canadian, Japanese, and Euro currencies. *Cheques for Two* can be signed by either of 2 people traveling together. For purchase locations or more information contact AmEx's service centers: In the US and Canada ☎800 221 7282; in the UK ☎0800 521 313; in Australia ☎800 25 19 02; in New Zealand ☎0800 441 068; elsewhere US collect ☎801 964 6665.

Visa: Checks available (generally with commission) at banks worldwide. For the location of the nearest office, call Visa's service centers: In the US ☎800 227 6811; in the UK

☎0800 89 50 78; elsewhere UK collect ☎44 020 7937 8091. Checks available in US, British, Canadian, Japanese, and Euro currencies.

Travelex/Thomas Cook: In the US and Canada call ☎800 287 7362; in the UK call ☎0800 62 21 01; elsewhere call UK collect ☎44 1733 31 89 50.

CREDIT CARDS

Where they are accepted, credit cards often offer superior exchange rates—up to 5% better than the retail rate used by banks and other currency exchange establishments. Credit cards may also offer services such as insurance or emergency help, and are sometimes required to reserve hotel rooms or rental cars. **MasterCard** and **Visa** are the most welcomed; **American Express** cards are often accepted in South Africa, but are less useful in other countries. Safari operators and adventure activity operators throughout the region will typically accept a variety of credit cards. Credit cards are also useful for **cash advances,** which allow you to withdraw currency from associated banks and ATMs throughout Southern Africa instantly. Note that credit card advances are a more costly way of withdrawing cash than ATMs or traveler's checks. In an emergency, however, the transaction fee may be worth the cost. To be eligible for an advance, you need a **Personal Identification Number (PIN)** from your credit card company (see **Cash (ATM) Cards,** below).

CREDIT CARD COMPANIES

Visa (US ☎800 336 8472) and **MasterCard** (US ☎800 307 7309) are issued in cooperation with banks and other organizations. **American Express** (US ☎800 843 2273) may have a varying annual fee, depending on the card. AmEx cardholders may cash personal checks at AmEx offices abroad, access an emergency medical and legal assistance hotline (24hr.; in North America call ☎800 554 2639, elsewhere call US collect ☎202 554 2639), and enjoy American Express Travel Service benefits (including plane, hotel, and car rental reservation changes; baggage loss and flight insurance; mailgram and international cable services; and held mail).

CASH (ATM) CARDS

Cash cards—popularly called ATM cards—are becoming increasingly common in Southern Africa. Depending on the system that your home bank uses, you can most likely access your personal bank account from abroad. The two major international money networks accepted in Southern Africa are **Cirrus** (US ☎800 424 7787) and **PLUS** (US ☎800 843 7587). To locate ATMs around the world, call the above numbers, or consult www.visa.com/pd/atm or www.mastercard.com/atm.

GETTING MONEY FROM HOME

If you run out of money while traveling, the easiest and cheapest solution is to have someone back home make a deposit to your credit card or cash (ATM) card. Failing that, consider one of the following options.

WIRING MONEY

It is possible to arrange a **bank money transfer,** which means asking a bank back home to wire money to a bank in Southern Africa. This is the cheapest way to transfer cash, but it's also the slowest, usually taking several days or more. Money transfer services like **Western Union** are faster and more convenient than bank transfers—but also much pricier. Visit www.westernunion.com, or call in the US 800-325-6000, in Canada 800 235 0000, in the UK 0800 83 38 33, in Australia 800 501 500, in New Zealand 800 27 0000, or in South Africa ☎860 100 031. Money transfer services are also available at **American Express** and **Thomas Cook** offices.

US STATE DEPARTMENT (US CITIZENS ONLY)

In dire emergencies only, the US State Department will forward money within hours to the nearest consular office, which will then disburse it according to instructions for a US$15 fee. If you wish to use this service, you must contact the Overseas Citizens Service division of the US State Department (☎202-647-5225; nights, Sundays, and holidays ☎202-647-4000).

COSTS

If you stay in hostels and prepare simple meals for yourself, expect to spend anywhere from US$10 per person per day in Zambia, to US$50 per person per day in Botswana. Starting prices for budget accommodations run anywhere from US$2 per night in rural villages, to US$10 per night in Cape Town or Durban. A basic meal costs at least US$3. A simple but comfortable daily budget, allowing for occasional restaurant meals and splurges, might be around US$40/day in South Africa, US$60/day in Botswana, and US$30-35 per day elsewhere in the region.

TIPPING, BARGAINING, AND BARTERING

Tipping is, in most places, more of a voluntary recognition of good service than an expected part of the bill. Taxi drivers, waitstaff, hairdressers, and tour leaders are generally tipped between 10% and 15% for satisfactory service; porters generally receive US$0.30 for service; and gas station attendants are usually not tipped unless they perform an extra service, such as checking your car's fluids.

Bargaining is generally expected in the informal sector (stalls, markets, informal guide services, etc.), and often (but not always) inappropriate in the formal sector. However, hotel and hostel owners can be persuaded to knock down their prices in the low season. In Zimbabwe, backpackers have been known to smooth-talk their way into international resorts at hostel prices, due to the lack of tourists lately.

Bartering remains a popular form of exchange for artwork, crafts, and guide services, especially outside of South Africa. Travelers who bring Western apparel for exchange tend to have great success, especially if the apparel features brand-name or sports logos. Baseball caps are an appealing trade, as are watches, brand-name blue jeans, and basketball jerseys, particularly those of any NBA All-Star. American cigarettes are worth much more than their cash value. Finally, athletic sneakers (particularly Nike, Reebok, or Adidas) can often be traded for multiple pieces of high-quality artwork, as such items are extremely hard to come by locally.

SAFETY AND SECURITY

Safety is a major concern for most travelers to Southern Africa, and rightly so. As Africans feel the pinch of falling wages, rising inflation, and mounting unemployment, many turn to economic crimes such as pickpocketing, scam jobs, and robbery. Western tourists are prominent targets for this kind of activity. Many a traveler has returned from the region with a few items missing and some rattled nerves, but relatively few experience any physical harm. For the most part, staying safe involves a careful mixture of awareness, conservatism, and street smarts, as well as an ability to let go of valuables without argument if confronted by a robber.

Instability in Zimbabwe, Northern Namibia, South African townships, and elsewhere adds another dimension to the mix of concerns: political violence. Travelers should maintain a low political profile and a low level of political involvement at all times. Avoid carrying political leaflets or buttons, wearing shirts with political logos, attending political speeches and rallies, or criticizing a country's president, ruling party, police, or armed forces in public. Finally, get up-to-date local

THE ART OF THE DEAL Bargaining in most of Southern Africa is a given: no price is set in stone, and vendors and drivers will automatically quote you a price that is several times too high; it's up to you to get them down to a reasonable rate. Successful merchants enjoy the haggling (just remember that the shopkeepers do this for a living and have the benefit of experience). With the following tips and some finesse, you might be able to impress even the most hardened hawkers:

1. Bargaining needn't be a fierce struggle laced with barbs. Quite the opposite: good-natured wrangling with a cheerful smiling face may prove your biggest weapon.

2. Use your poker face. The less your face betrays your interest in the item the better. If you touch an item to inspect it, the vendor will be sure to "encourage" you to name a price or make a purchase. Coming back again and again to admire a trinket is a good way of ensuring that you pay a ridiculously high price. Never get too enthusiastic about the object in question; point out flaws in workmanship and design. Be cool.

3. Never underestimate the power of peer pressure. Bargaining with more than one person at a time always leads to higher prices. Alternately, try having a friend discourage you from your purchase—if you seem to be reluctant, the merchant will want to drop the price to interest you again.

4. Start low. Never feel guilty offering what seems to be a ridiculously low price. Your starting price should be no more than one-third to one-half the asking price.

advice on all potentially questionable areas on your itinerary. Consult your country's embassy, the police, and other travelers to gain a better idea of the level of risk in any particular area, and do enough homework beforehand to understand the basic significance of any new developments.

PERSONAL SAFETY

EXPLORING
To avoid unwanted attention, try to blend in as much as possible. Even in countries where almost everyone happens to be of a different race, a non-black traveler can be treated very differently depending on how well he or she "fits in" with local customs and etiquette—perceptions are not based merely on skin color. Respecting local customs (in many cases, dressing more conservatively) may placate would-be hecklers. Refrain from giving money and candy to children as it encourages begging. Instead, consider donating money to local charities or international development organizations such as OXFAM International (www.oxfam.org).

When walking at night, stick to busy, well-lit streets and avoid dark alleyways. Do not attempt to cross through parks, parking lots, or other large, deserted areas. Look for children playing, women walking, and other signs of an active community. If you feel uncomfortable, leave as quickly and directly as you can, but don't allow fear of the unknown to turn you into a hermit. Rural areas are generally safer than cities, but it is still not advisable to walk alone at night. Deserted beaches are particularly dangerous and even couples should not walk here at night, as gang rape unfortunately is not uncommon. If you are driving, try to reach your destination in the daylight hours. Be sure that someone at home knows your itinerary and never admit it if you're traveling alone.

SELF DEFENSE
A good self-defense course can give you ways to react to unwanted advances. **Impact, Prepare,** and **Model Mugging** can refer you to local self-defense courses in the US (☎ 800 345 5425). Visit the web site at www.impactsafety.org for a list of nearby chapters. Workshops (2-3hr.) start at US$50; full courses run US$350-500.

DRIVING

If you are using a **car,** learn local driving signals and wear a seatbelt. Children under 40 lbs. should ride only in a specially-designed carseat, available for a small fee from most car rental agencies. Study route maps before you hit the road, and if you plan on spending a lot of time on the road, you may want to bring spare parts. If your car breaks down, wait for the police to assist you. For long drives in desolate areas, invest in a cellular phone and a roadside assistance program. Be sure to park your vehicle in a garage or well traveled area, and use a steering wheel locking device in larger cities. **Sleeping in your car** is one of the most dangerous (and often illegal) ways to get your rest.

For info on the perils of **hitchhiking,** see p. 38.

TRAVEL ADVISORIES. The following government offices provide travel information and advisories by telephone, by fax, or via the web:

Australian Department of Foreign Affairs and Trade: ☎ 1300 555135; faxback service 02 6261 1299; www.dfat.gov.au.

Canadian Department of Foreign Affairs and International Trade (DFAIT): In Canada and the US call 800 267 6788, elsewhere call ☎ 613 944 6788; www.dfait-maeci.gc.ca. Call for their free booklet, *Bon Voyage...But.*

New Zealand Ministry of Foreign Affairs: ☎ 04 494 8500; fax 494 8506; www.mft.govt.nz/trav.html.

United Kingdom Foreign and Commonwealth Office: ☎ 020 7008 0232; fax 7008 0155; www.fco.gov.uk.

US Department of State: ☎ 202 647 5225; faxback service 647 3000; http://travel.state.gov. For *A Safe Trip Abroad,* call 202 512 1800.

TRANSPORTATION

If you are using a **car,** wear a seatbelt (it's the law). The quality of many Southern African roads is quite poor, especially outside of South Africa. Mozambican roads are especially problematic due to extensive flooding in recent years; Malawian roads are also notorious. The road conditions will often necessitate driving more slowly and cautiously than you would at home, and some areas may be impassable (or dangerous) without a **four-wheel-drive vehicle;** ask at a tourist center or car rental agency. **Drive carefully.** Study route maps before you hit the road, and be prepared to brake for roaming animals—in rental car vs. elephant matchups, the elephant almost always wins. Children under 40 lbs. (18kg) should ride only in a specially-designed carseat, available for a small fee from most car rental agencies. If you plan on spending a lot of time on the road, you may want to bring spare parts (especially spare wheels, in case of flat or shredded tires). For long drives in desolate areas, invest in a cellular phone and a roadside assistance program. Extra petrol and water tanks are musts for desert drives in Botswana and Namibia. Park your vehicle in a well-traveled area whenever possible, and *always* use a steering wheel locking device in larger cities. Try not to leave valuable possessions, such as radios or luggage, in your vehicle while you are away. If your tape deck or radio is removable, hide it in the trunk or take it with you.

Be particularly careful on **buses** and **minibus taxis;** see p. 38 for more information.

Thieves thrive on **trains;** professionals wait for tourists to fall asleep and then carry off everything they can. When traveling in pairs, sleep in alternating shifts; when alone, use good judgment in selecting a train compartment: never stay in an empty one, and use a lock to secure your pack to the luggage rack. Keep important documents and other valuables on your person and try to sleep on top bunks with your luggage stored above you (if not in bed with you).

FINANCIAL SECURITY

PROTECTING YOUR VALUABLES
With unemployment rising throughout the region, many are forced to turn to theft as a means of sustenance. Townships and major cities (Johannesburg foremost among them) are the highest risk areas, although travelers should never let their guard down wherever they are. There are a few steps you can take to minimize the financial risk associated with traveling. First, bring as little with you as possible. Leave expensive watches, jewelry, and electronic equipment at home; you'd probably break them or lose them anyway, and nothing is more certain to make you stick out than a proliferation of expensive gadgets. Second, buy a few padlocks to secure your belongings either in your pack—which you should never leave unattended—or in a locker. Third, avoid carrying large amounts of cash, if there are other practical financial options available such as traveler's checks or ATM/credit cards. Keep all financial assets in a money belt—not a "fanny pack"—along with your passport and ID cards. Fourth, keep at least one small cash reserve separate from your primary stash. This should entail about US$50 (US$ is best) sewn into or stored in the depths of your pack, along with your traveler's check numbers and important photocopies. Fifth, carry a fake wallet filled with a small amount of money and perhaps some old IDs to surrender in case of mugging.

CON ARTISTS, PICKPOCKETS, AND CORRUPTION
Con artists often work in groups, and children are among the most effective. Be aware of certain classics: sob stories that require money, rolls of bills "found" on the street, mustard spilled (or saliva spit) onto your shoulder distracting you for enough time to snatch your bag. If approached, keep a solid grip on your belongings, and act to cut off the conversation quickly and firmly.

In city crowds, especially on public transportation, **pickpockets** are highly skilled. In many situations in Africa, it is often difficult to avoid being jam-packed in with a bunch of strangers; in such cases, it might be a good idea to inconspicuously slip one hand in your own pocket and keep your fingertips on your wallet. If carrying a backpack or daypack in a crowd or queue, try to secure the zippers with a small padlock or tie, and/or carry the pack in front of you where you can see it.

Corruption-related crime is down across Southern Africa, but still occurs. Travelers have reported being stopped at police checkpoints and relieved of large sums of cash for a fictitious "infraction," such as missing a paper in the vehicle's registration. Border officials in some areas have also been known to levy surprise "exit fees" on travelers. There is frustratingly little that can be done to either prevent or remedy such instances, other than hiding as much cash as possible and claiming to be broke. Some countries, such as Botswana and South Africa, are aggressively pursuing national anti-corruption initiatives; in these cases, complaints to the police or embassy usually receive a powerful response.

DRUGS AND ALCOHOL
Most of Southern Africa does not legally differentiate between "hard" drugs and more mainstream ones such as marijuana. It is highly likely you will come across marijuana (also called *dagga* and *mbanje*) at some point. Cannabis crops flourish throughout the region, are sold at laughably low prices, and are extremely popular among many locals in both urban and rural settings. Travelers insist that discretion is crucial to avoiding trouble; be careful of your surroundings and know exactly what you're getting. *Never, ever* carry any illicit drug across a national border. Stay away from **mandrax;** this methadone-based drug is very addictive and very dangerous, and is even mixed with *dagga* on occasion.

HEALTH

Common sense is the simplest prescription for good health while you travel. Drink lots of fluids to prevent dehydration and constipation, and wear sturdy, broken-in shoes and clean socks.

The majority of travelers' illnesses are passed through food and water. This is mostly a concern in the game parks and rural areas, although major cities are not risk-free. Travelers are generally safe from life-threatening diseases provided they take some minor precautions. The major diseases to worry about are **HIV** (see p. 23), **malaria** (see p. 21), **tuberculosis** (see p. 23), and **schistosomiasis,** also called **bilharzia** (see p. 22). Medical facilities outside of South Africa are generally more limited than those within the country; Southern African travelers in need of imminent surgery or other treatment may want to invest in a flight to Johannesburg or Cape Town for the procedure. Consult country introductions for more information.

BEFORE YOU GO

In your **passport,** write the names of any people you wish to be contacted in case of a medical emergency, and also list any **allergies** or medical conditions of which you want doctors to be aware. Allergy sufferers might want to obtain a full supply of any necessary medication before the trip. Matching a prescription to a foreign equivalent is not always easy, safe, or possible. Carry up-to-date, legible prescriptions or a statement from your doctor stating the medication's trade name, manufacturer, chemical name, and dosage. While traveling, keep all medication with you in your carry-on luggage. For tips on packing a basic **first-aid kit,** see 18.

IMMUNIZATIONS

No vaccinations are required to enter Southern African countries unless you are traveling from countries that have incidences of yellow fever, such as certain African and South American countries. These visitors must have the yellow fever vaccination at least 10 days in advance of their visit, or the certificate won't be valid. The certificate is valid for 10 years from the time you get the shot. For a list of the countries that apply, consult the Centers for Disease Control (see below). The CDC also strongly recommends malaria pills for travelers to high risk areas (particularly game parks). Travelers over two years old should be sure that the following vaccines are up to date: MMR (for measles, mumps, and rubella); DTaP or Td (for diptheria, tetanus, and pertussis); IPV (for polio); HbCV (for haemophilus influenza B); and HBV (for hepatitis B). rabies shots, typhoid vaccine, Hepatitis A vaccine and/or immune globulin (IG) is recommended for travelers to Southern Africa. For recommendations on immunizations and prophylaxis, consult the CDC (see below) in the US or the equivalent in your home country.

USEFUL ORGANIZATIONS AND PUBLICATIONS

The US **Centers for Disease Control and Prevention** (☎877 394 8747 toll-free; fax 888 232 3299; www.cdc.gov/travel) maintains an international travelers' hotline and an informative web site. The CDC's comprehensive booklet *Health Information for International Travel*, an annual rundown of disease, immunization, and general health advice, is free online or US$25 via the Public Health Foundation (☎877 252 1200). Consult the appropriate government agency of your home country for consular information sheets on health, entry requirements, and other issues for various countries (see the listings in the box on **Travel Advisories,** p. 17). For quick information on health and other travel warnings, call the **Overseas Citizens Services** (☎202 647 5225; after-hours 202 647 4000), or contact a passport agency, embassy, or consulate abroad. US citizens can send a self-addressed, stamped envelope to the Overseas Citizens Services, Bureau of Consular Affairs, #4811, US Department of State, Washington, D.C. 20520. For information on medical evacuation services and travel insurance firms, see the US government's web site at http://travel.state.gov/medical.html or the **British Foreign and Commonwealth Office** (www.fco.gov.uk).

For detailed information on travel health, including a country-by-country overview of diseases, try the **International Travel Health Guide**, by Stuart Rose, MD (US$20; www.travmed.com). For general health info, contact the **American Red Cross** (☎ 800 564 1234; www.redcross.org).

MEDICAL ASSISTANCE ON THE ROAD

Standards at some government-run hospitals throughout Southern Africa have declined drastically in recent years—travelers are strongly recommended to go straight to a private hospital or medical center, even in non-emergency cases. Doctors and hospitals may need payment up front (some require the full amount up front), and US medical insurance is not always valid overseas (see **Insurance**, p. 24). Pharmacies in small towns may not have as wide a selection of medicines, and the staff may not speak fluent English. Countries with foreign currency shortages, particularly **Zimbabwe**, may have corresponding shortages of pharmaceuticals, both in hospitals and pharmacies. It is wise to bring a more than adequate supply of any prescription medicine to the region, as it may not be available locally.

If you are concerned about obtaining medical assistance while traveling, you may wish to employ special support services. The *MedPass* from **GlobalCare, Inc.**, 2001 Westside Pkwy., #120, Alpharetta, GA 30004, USA (☎ 800 860 1111; fax 770 677 0455; www.globalems.com), provides 24hr. international medical assistance, support, and medical evacuation resources. The **International Association for Medical Assistance to Travelers** (US ☎ 716 754 4883, Canada ☎ 416 652 0137, New Zealand ☎ 03 352 20 53; www.sentex.net/~iamat) has free membership, lists English-speaking doctors worldwide, and offers detailed info on immunization requirements and sanitation. If your regular **insurance** policy does not cover travel abroad, you may wish to purchase additional coverage (see p. 24).

Those with medical conditions (such as diabetes, allergies to antibiotics, epilepsy, heart conditions) may want to obtain a **Medic Alert** membership (first year US$35, annually thereafter US$20), which includes a stainless steel ID tag, among other benefits, like a 24hr. collect-call number. Contact the Medic Alert Foundation, 2323 Colorado Ave, Turlock, CA 95382, USA (☎ 888 633 4298; outside US ☎ 209 668 3333; www.medicalert.org).

ONCE IN SOUTHERN AFRICA

ENVIRONMENTAL HAZARDS

Heat exhaustion and dehydration: Heat exhaustion, characterized by dehydration and salt deficiency, can lead to fatigue, headaches, and wooziness. Avoid it by drinking plenty of fluids, eating salty foods (e.g. crackers), and avoiding dehydrating beverages. Wear a hat, sunglasses, and a lightweight longsleeve shirt in hot sun, and take time to acclimatize to the Southern African heat before seriously exerting yourself. Bring plenty of water (at least 5L per person per day) on hikes. Continuous heat stress can eventually lead to **heatstroke**, characterized by rising body temperature, severe headache, and cessation of sweating. Victims must be taken to a doctor immediately.

Sunburn: The sun is extremely powerful throughout Southern Africa, so bring strong sunscreen with you and apply it liberally and regularly. Wear good sunglasses to protect your eyes from ultraviolet rays. If you get sunburned, drink more fluids than usual and apply Calamine or an aloe-based lotion.

Hypothermia and frostbite: Travelers from countries where it is warm between May and September may be surprised to find chilly temperatures throughout Southern Africa during that time of year. In winter, the weather can shift rapidly. A rapid drop in body temperature is the clearest sign of overexposure to cold. Victims may also shiver, feel exhausted, have poor coordination or slurred speech, hallucinate, or suffer amnesia. *Do not let hypothermia victims fall asleep,* or their body temperature will continue to drop. To avoid hypothermia, keep dry, wear layers, and stay out of the wind. In wet weather, wool and synthetics retain heat whereas cotton and other fabrics make you colder. Drink warm beverages, and slowly warm the area with steady body contact.

High altitude: Allow your body a couple of days to adjust to less oxygen before exerting yourself. Note that alcohol is more potent and UV rays are stronger at high elevations.

INSECT-BORNE DISEASES

Many diseases in South Africa are transmitted by insects, especially **mosquitoes** (as well as fleas, ticks, and lice). Beware of insects in wet or forested areas, particularly while hiking and camping. Mosquitoes are most active from dusk to dawn. Use **insect repellents,** such as DEET, and soak or spray your gear with permethrin (licensed in the US for use on clothing). Wear long pants and long sleeves (tropicweight cottons can keep you comfortable in the heat), and buy a mosquito net. Wear shoes and socks, and tuck long pants into socks. Consider natural repellents that make you smelly to insects, like vitamin B-12 or garlic pills. To stop the itch after being bitten, try Calamine lotion or topical cortisones (like Cortaid), or take a bath with a half-cup of baking soda or oatmeal. **Ticks**—responsible for Lyme and other diseases—can be particularly dangerous in rural and forested regions. Pause periodically while walking to brush off ticks using a fine-toothed comb on your neck and scalp. Do not try to remove ticks by burning them or coating them with nail polish remover or petroleum jelly. Do not swim in fresh water—doing so might result in a "parasitic infection."

Malaria: Transmitted by *Anopheles* mosquitoes that bite at night. The malaria season starts in November, peaks between February and April, and tends to die down from May to October, although especially wet areas may be malarial year-round. Incubation periods vary from 6-8 days to months. Early symptoms include fever, chills, aches, and fatigue, followed by high fever and sweating, sometimes with vomiting and diarrhea. Left untreated, malaria can cause anemia, kidney failure, coma, and death. It is an especially serious threat to pregnant women. The risk is greatest in rural areas and game parks. Use mosquito repellent, particularly in the evenings, and take oral prophylactics, like **mefloquine** (sold under the name Lariam) or **doxycycline** (ask your doctor for a prescription). Be aware that these drugs can have very serious side effects, including slowed heart rate and nightmares. They are also not 100% guaranteed to prevent malaria symptoms. If you are planning to visit a malarial risk area, that anti-malarial medication before, during and after your trip. If you experience fever or flu-like symptoms up to a year after your visit, see your doctor. Consult a travel health professional or the CDC for a detailed map of malaria risk areas in Africa.

Dengue fever: An "urban viral infection" transmitted by *Aedes* mosquitoes, which bite during the day rather than at night. Dengue has flu-like symptoms and is often indicated by a rash 3-4 days after the onset of fever. Symptoms for the first 2-4 days include chills, high fever, headaches, swollen lymph nodes, muscle aches, and in some instances, a pink rash on the face. If you think you've contracted Dengue, see a doctor, drink plenty of liquids, and take fever medication such as acetaminophen (Tylenol). **Never take aspirin to treat Dengue.**

Other insect-borne diseases: Tick-bite fever usually affects people who have been tramping or camping in tall grass during the summer. Symptoms of the illness include headaches, fever, or hot and cold sweats.

ESSENTIALS

FOOD- AND WATER-BORNE DISEASES

Food and water in South Africa and Botswana are generally safe to consume "as is," but travelers in other countries may want to avoid uncooked fruits and vegetables, tap water, and ice. To purify water, bring it to a rolling boil for at least 10 minutes or treat it with **iodine** drops or tablets. Boiling is the most reliable treatment—some parasites such as *giardia* have exteriors that are iodine-resistant. In extremely rural areas, watch out for food from markets or street vendors that may have been washed in dirty water or fried in rancid cooking oil. Also stay away from unpasteurized dairy products. Always wash your hands before eating, or bring a quick-drying purifying liquid hand cleaner. Your bowels will thank you.

Traveler's diarrhea: Results from a temporary (and fairly common) reaction to the bacteria in new food ingredients. Try quick-energy, non-sugary foods with protein and carbohydrates to keep your strength up. Over-the-counter anti-diarrheals (e.g. Imodium) may counteract the problems, but can complicate serious infections. The most dangerous side effect of diarrhea is dehydration; drink 8oz. water with a ½ tsp. of sugar or honey and a pinch of salt, drink caffeine-free soft drinks, or munch on salted crackers. If you develop a fever or your symptoms don't go away after 4-5 days, consult a doctor.

Dysentery: Results from a serious intestinal infection caused by certain bacteria. The most common type is bacillary dysentery, also called shigellosis. Symptoms include bloody diarrhea (sometimes mixed with mucus), fever, and abdominal pain and tenderness. Seek medical help immediately. Bacillary dysentery generally only lasts a week, but it is highly contagious. Amoebic dysentery, which develops more slowly, is a more serious disease and may cause long-term damage if left untreated. A stool test can determine which kind you have. In an emergency, the drugs norfloxacin or ciprofloxacin (commonly known as Cipro) can be used. If you are traveling in high-risk regions (especially rural areas) consider obtaining a prescription before you leave home.

Cholera: An intestinal disease caused by a bacteria found in contaminated food. Travelers to South Africa and Lesotho are generally not at risk, but fatal outbreaks have occurred in other countries. Symptoms include diarrhea, dehydration, vomiting, and muscle cramps. See a doctor immediately; if left untreated, it may be deadly. Antibiotics are available, but the most important treatment is rehydration. Consult a doctor.

Hepatitis A: A viral infection of the liver acquired primarily through contaminated water, ice, shellfish, or unpeeled fruits and vegetables, and also from sexual contact. Symptoms include fatigue, fever, loss of appetite, nausea, dark urine, jaundice, vomiting, aches and pains, and light stools. Risk is highest in rural areas and the countryside, but is also present in urban areas. Ask your doctor about the vaccine (Havrix or Vaqta) or an injection of immune globulin (IG; formerly called gamma globulin).

Parasites: Microbes, tapeworms, etc. that hide in unsafe water and food. **Giardiasis,** for example, is acquired by drinking untreated water from streams or lakes. Symptoms include swollen glands or lymph nodes, fever, rashes or itchiness, digestive problems, eye problems, and anemia. Boil water, wear shoes, avoid bugs, and eat only cooked food.

Schistosomiasis (bilharzia): A parasitic disease found in and around South Africa, caused when flatworm larvae penetrate unbroken skin. Symptoms include an itchy localized rash, followed in 4-6 weeks by fever, fatigue, painful urination, diarrhea, loss of appetite, night sweats, and a hive-like rash on the body. The "most acute" infections may not have symptoms. Avoid swimming in stagnant water, especially in rural areas. If exposed to untreated water, rub the area vigorously with a towel and apply rubbing alcohol. Schistosomiasis can be treated with prescription drugs.

Typhoid fever: Caused by the salmonella bacteria; common in villages and rural areas. While mostly transmitted through contaminated food and water, it may also be acquired by direct contact with another person. Early symptoms include fever, headaches, fatigue, loss of appetite, constipation, and sometimes a rash on the abdomen or chest. Antibiotics can treat typhoid, but a vaccination (70-90% effective) is recommended.

OTHER INFECTIOUS DISEASES

Tuberculosis (TB): TB is more common in Africa than anywhere else in the world, and is considered to be one of the region's most pressing health problems after HIV/AIDS. TB most commonly affects the lungs, but may also affect the nervous and other systems. Symptoms include fever, weakness, weight loss, and coughing up blood. TB is contracted by breathing air contaminated by a TB-infected person. Travelers are most at risk if they share confined, poorly ventilated spaces with infected people, such as in rural hospitals, homeless shelters, or the home of an infected individual. Although a vaccine does exist, it is not very reliable and most physicians do not recommend it unless travelers will be in a particularly high-risk situation.

Rabies: Transmitted through the saliva of infected animals; fatal if untreated. Avoid contact with animals. By the time symptoms appear (thirst and muscle spasms), the disease is in its terminal stage. If you are bitten, wash the wound thoroughly, seek immediate medical care, and try to have the animal located. A rabies vaccine, which consists of 3 shots given over 21 days, is only semi-effective.

Hepatitis B: A viral infection of the liver transmitted via bodily fluids or needle sharing. Symptoms may not appear until years after infection. Symptoms include abdominal discomfort, nausea, vomiting, anorexia, and often progress to jaundice. Severity and symptoms vary. Vaccinations are recommended for health-care workers, sexually active travelers, and anyone planning to seek medical treatment abroad. The 3-shot vaccination series must begin 6 months before traveling.

Hepatitis C: Like Hep B, but the mode of transmission differs. IV drug users, those with occupational exposure to blood, hemodialysis patients, and recipients of blood transfusions are at the highest risk, but the disease can also be spread through sexual contact and sharing items like razors and toothbrushes that may have traces of blood on them.

AIDS, HIV, STDS

Acquired Immune Deficiency Syndrome (AIDS) is a tremendous problem in Africa. Always practice safe sex, and *never* share needles. Don't even consider becoming involved with a prostitute, as infection rates among them have reached nearly 100% in some areas. Finally, medical workers in all Southern African countries are required to unpackage fresh needles in front of their patients. If a doctor or nurse attempts to give an injection or take a blood sample with a needle that was opened out of your sight, you have the right to ask for a fresh needle.

For detailed information on **AIDS** in Africa, call the **US Centers for Disease Control's** 24hr. hotline at 800 342 2437, or contact the **Joint United Nations Programme on HIV/AIDS (UNAIDS),** 20 av. Appia 20, CH-1211 Geneva 27, Switzerland (☎41 22 791 36 66; fax 22 791 41 87).

Sexually transmitted diseases (STDs) such as gonorrhea, chlamydia, genital warts, syphilis, and herpes are easier to catch than HIV and can be almost as dangerous. **Hepatitis** B and C are also serious STDs (see **Other Infectious Diseases,** above). Though condoms may protect you from some STDs, oral or even tactile contact can lead to transmission. Warning signs for STDs include: swelling, sores, bumps, or blisters on sex organs, rectum, or mouth; burning and pain during urination and bowel movements; itching around sex organs; swelling or redness in the throat, flu-like symptoms. If these symptoms develop, see a doctor immediately.

WOMEN'S HEALTH

Women traveling in unsanitary conditions, especially in the more remote areas of Southern Africa, are vulnerable to **urinary tract** and **bladder infections,** common and severely uncomfortable bacterial infections that cause a burning sensation and painful and frequent urination. To avoid these infections, drink plenty of Vitamin-C-rich juice and clean water, and urinate frequently, especially right after inter-

AIDS infection rates in sub-Saharan Africa continue to rise. It is estimated that 40 million people in the world have AIDS—70% of whom are African. Today, 20% of adults in South Africa have AIDS. In some cities, the number is above 50%. In Botswana, 38.5% of adults now have the disease. Among commercial sex workers, the rate approaches 100% in some places. Many leaders are asking that developing countries have their debt forgiven to be able to fund prevention and treatment. The work force is dying off rapidly and life expectancy is plummeting, but drugs are too expensive. In 1999, it was noted that 80% of deaths are workers aged 20 to 50 years old. Recent statistics speculate that by 2010, life expectancy in South Africa will have dropped to 36, in Namibia and Zimbabwe to 33, and in Botswana to 42. By 2005, there will be 5 million AIDS orphans in South Africa. The latest treatments available in the industrialized world cost up to $15,000 a year. In Africa, even $4 a treatment is too much for countries that spend no more than $10 a year per citizen for all health care, but time is running out. In South Africa alone, there are an estimated 1700 new HIV infections every day. For more information, updated regularly, consult www.unaids.org.

course. Untreated, these infections can lead to kidney infections, sterility, and even death. If symptoms persist, see a doctor. **Vaginal yeast infections** may flare up in hot and humid climates. Wearing loosely fitting trousers or a skirt and cotton underwear will help, as will over-the-counter remedies like Monostat or Gynelotrimin. Bring supplies from home if you are prone to infection, as they may be difficult to find on the road. Since **tampons, pads,** and reliable **contraceptive devices** are also sometimes hard to find when traveling, bring supplies with you.

INSURANCE

Travel insurance generally covers four basic areas: medical/health problems, property loss, trip cancellation/interruption, and emergency evacuation. Although your regular insurance policies may well extend to travel-related accidents, you may consider purchasing travel insurance if the cost of potential trip cancellation/ interruption or emergency medical evacuation is greater than you can absorb. Prices for travel insurance purchased separately generally run about US$50 per week for full coverage, while trip cancellation/interruption may be purchased separately at a rate of about US$5.50 per US$100 of coverage. **Medical insurance** (especially university policies) often covers costs incurred abroad; check with your provider. **US Medicare** does not cover foreign travel. **Canadians** are protected by their home province's health insurance plan for up to 90 days after leaving the country; check with the provincial Ministry of Health or Health Plan Headquarters for details. **Homeowners' insurance** (or your family's coverage) often covers theft during travel and loss of travel documents (passport, plane ticket, railpass, etc.) up to US$500.

ISIC and **ITIC** (see p. 12) provide basic insurance benefits, including US$100 per day of in-hospital sickness for up to 60 days, US$3000 of accident-related medical reimbursement, and US$25,000 for emergency medical transport. Cardholders have access to a toll-free 24hr. helpline (run by the insurance provider **TravelGuard**) for medical, legal, and financial emergencies overseas (US and Canada ☎877 370 4742, elsewhere call US collect ☎715 345 0505). **American Express** (US ☎800 528 4800) grants most cardholders automatic car rental insurance (collision and theft, but not liability) and ground travel accident coverage of US$100,000 on flight purchases made with the card.

INSURANCE PROVIDERS. STA (see p. 30) offers a range of plans that can supplement your basic coverage. Other private insurance providers in the US and Canada include: **Access America** (☎800 284 8300); **Berkely Group/Carefree Travel Insurance** (☎800 323 3149; www.berkely.com); **Globalcare Travel Insurance** (☎800 821 2488; www.globalcare-cocco.com); and **Travel Assistance International** (☎800 821 2828; www.europ-assistance.com). Providers in the **UK** include **Columbus Direct** (☎020 7375 0011). In **Australia,** try **AFTA** (☎02 9375 4955).

ESSENTIALS

PACKING

Pack lightly: Lay out only what you absolutely need, then take half the clothes and twice the money. The less you have, the less you have to lose (or store, or carry on your back). Any extra space will be useful for any souvenirs or items you might pick up along the way.

Clothing: If you will be in Southern Africa between May and September, bring a warm jacket or a wool sweater. Always bring a rain jacket (Gore-Tex is both waterproof and breathable), sturdy shoes or hiking boots, and thick socks. A double pair of socks—light absorbent cotton inside and thick wool outside—will cushion feet, keep them dry, and help prevent blisters. Talcum powder in your shoes and on your feet can prevent sores, and moleskin is great for blisters. Also bring a comfortable pair of waterproof sandals for grubby hostel showers and for when the temperature skyrockets. Pack khakis or light cotton trousers instead of jeans. You may also want to add one nicer outfit and pair of shoes. If you plan to visit any religious or cultural sites, remember that you'll need something besides tank tops and shorts to be respectful.

Electric current: In Southern Africa, electricity is 220 volts AC, enough to fry any 110V North American appliance. Most outlets are made for round prongs, so even if your machine has a built-in converter, you'll also need an **adapter** to change the plug shape.

TOILETRIES. Toothbrushes, towels, cold-water soap, talcum powder (to keep feet dry), deodorant, razors, tampons, and condoms may be difficult to find, so bring extras along. Also bring extra pairs of contact lens and solution for your entire trip. Bring your glasses and a copy of your prescription in case you need emergency replacements. If you use heat disinfection, either switch temporarily to a chemical disinfection system (check first to make sure it's safe with your brand of lenses), or buy a converter to 220/240V.

First-aid kit: For a basic first-aid kit, pack: bandages, pain reliever, antibiotic cream, a thermometer, a Swiss Army knife, tweezers, moleskin, decongestant, motion-sickness remedy, diarrhea or upset-stomach medication (Pepto Bismol or Imodium), an antihistamine, sunscreen, insect repellent, burn ointment, and a syringe for emergencies (get an explanatory letter from your doctor).

Film: Film development is often expensive or unavailable in Southern Africa, so consider bringing along enough film for your entire trip and developing it at home. Less serious photographers may want to bring a disposable camera or two rather than an expensive permanent one. Despite disclaimers, airport security X-rays can fog film, so ask security to hand-inspect it. Always pack film in your carry-on luggage.

OTHER USEFUL ITEMS. For safety purposes, you should bring a **money belt** and small **padlock**. Basic **outdoors equipment** (plastic water bottle, compass, waterproof matches, pocketknife, sunglasses, sunscreen, hat) is also useful. **Other things** you're liable to forget: an umbrella; sealable **plastic bags** (for damp clothes, soap, food, and other spillables); an **alarm clock;** a flashlight; and a small **calculator.**

IMPORTANT DOCUMENTS. Don't forget your passport, traveler's checks, ATM and/or credit cards, and adequate ID (see p. 12). Also check that you have a hosteling membership card, a driver's license (see p. 12), and travel insurance forms.

ESSENTIALS

ACCOMMODATIONS

Accommodations in Southern Africa run the gamut from hip, cosmopolitan hostels, to Victorian guest houses with English breakfast, to concrete-block rooms with corrugated metal roofs, to traditional *rondavel*-style thatched huts. In South Africa, excellent hostels compete with one another to offer the most perks, including swimming pools, free tours, free coffee and tea, and free pick-up from airports and train stations. In Botswana, many accommodations cater to a posher crowd; sleek, tastefully decorated rooms with cable TV are easy to locate, but cheaper digs are often harder to come by. Throughout the rest of the region, the variety and quality of accommodations cover an extremely wide range. More touristed areas tend to have a wider range of options, including reasonably priced hostels, hotels, and *rondavels*. Camping is also a popular option in game areas and mountains. Those looking to go well "off the beaten path," however, will have to be more flexible in their accommodation options. Some rural lodgings do double as brothels, while others lack amenities such as electricity and running water.

Throughout Southern Africa, **rural homestays** provide a fascinating and culturally sensitive way to experience African life on a day-to-day basis. Local African families open their homes to visitors, who share in daily chores such as cooking, fetching water, and tending fields. This unique option helps contribute to the local economy, educates visitors in the realities and misperceptions of African life, and provides opportunities to develop personal friendships.

Especially within South Africa, many accommodations can be found well ahead of time and even reserved on the Internet. **Doorway** (www.doorway.co.za) is a general travel site with extensive accommodation listings; you can search by province, town, or category (self-catering, camping, etc.). **AA Travel Guides** has listings of accommodations for all countries in Southern Africa at their web site (www.aatravel.co.za). AA is the South African equivalent of the American Automobile Association (AAA); AAA members should enjoy reciprocity with the AA, provided they bring their membership cards. **Afriscape** has extensive listings on its database, and you can search by categories (www.afriscape.co.za).

The Internet Guide to Hostelling (www.hostels.com/za.html) provides a directory of hostels around the world—including many in South Africa and a few in other African countries—in addition to oodles of information about hostelling and backpacking worldwide. Another resource is **Hostelling International South Africa** which has many listings of hostels in South Africa; you can either check their web site or contact them directly to get the pamphlet *Backpacker Hostels in South Africa*. For their various services and lower rates at member hostels, hostelling associations, especially **Hostelling International (HI),** can definitely be worth joining. HI has quite a few member hostels in South Africa, but almost none in other Southern African countries. Refer to their web site (www.iyhf.org) for information on how to join. Applications are also available at HI hostels. Finally, refer to the **Hostels Association of South Africa,** 3rd fl. 73 St. George's St. Mall, P.O. Box 4402, Cape Town 8000 (☎021 424 2511; fax 424 4119; info@hisa.org.za; www.hisa.org.za).

Several travel guides and reservation services specialize in B&Bs and guest houses. The most extensive resource is probably Bed 'n Breakfast (Pty) Ltd., P.O. Box 91309, Auckland Park, South Africa 2006 (☎11 482 2206; fax 726 6915; www.bnb.co.za). They have B&B listings for just about every major town and city in the country. Information and listings of all types of accommodations are available from the Portfolio Collection, P.O. Box 132, Newlands, 7725, Cape Town (☎21 686 5400; fax 686 5310; www.portfoliocollection.co.za). They can mail you a wide range of brochures. Another good resource is the Guest House Association of Southern Africa, 27 Tennant Road, Kenilworth, Cape Town, 7800 (☎0860 1023 69; fax 27 21 797 3115 ; www.gha.org.za).

TRAVEL CENTRE

11 Hof st,Gardens,Cape Town,South Africa
e-mail:ashanti@iafrica.com

Tel:+27 21 424 4016   Fax:+27 21 423 8790

EXPEDITIONS   ACCOMMODATION

TRUCK SAFARIS   ADVENTURE

DAILY TOURS   BUS TICKETS

CAR HIRE

Specialists in Southern African travel for backpackers.
For loads of info & options visit us @

www.ashanti.co.za

Your African experience starts here

Many **colleges and universities** open their residence halls to travelers when school is not in session; some do so even during term-time. Getting a room may take a couple of phone calls and require advanced planning, but rates tend to be low, and many offer free local calls.

CAMPING AND THE OUTDOORS

WILDERNESS SAFETY: GROUND RULES

1. Stay warm, stay dry, and stay hydrated. If any of these becomes a problem, stop immediately and remedy it; don't wait for the situation to become more serious.

2. Always hike with a companion, and always make someone aware of your itinerary and when you expect to be back.

3. Keep up to date on weather forecasts, flood risks, and other conditions.

4. NEVER sleep in proximity to your food. Lock it in your safari vehicle, place it in a stuff sack and hang it high in a tree far from your tent, or, at the very least, seal it as completely as possible and hide it in undergrowth far from your tent.

5. If a lion, rhino, or other animal enters your camp, stay put. Do not try to leave your tent or get to your vehicle. Once the animal has finished off your food supply, it will likely lose interest and wander on, leaving you hungrier but still in one piece.

If you're spending any time at all in Southern Africa, you'll inevitably find yourself adventuring in some of the region's many national parks, wilderness hiking areas, or game reserves. If you're tenting or caravanning through Southern Africa, just keep two points in mind: first, always try to camp in designated campsites, not along roadsides or in the bush. Even if local residents aren't upset by your actions, local elephants and lions may feel differently. Second, consider shelling out the extra money for a hostel bed in major cities, especially in South Africa.

Although outdoors stores exist in abundance in South and Southern Africa, they often have a narrower selection, higher prices, and fewer established brand names than their counterparts in North America and Europe. Though some last-minute purchases can wait until the day before a safari, hiking trip, or camping excursion, it's a better idea to outfit yourself before arriving in Africa.

An excellent general resource for travelers planning on camping or spending time in the outdoors is the **Great Outdoor Recreation Pages** (www.gorp.com).

GETTING TO SOUTHERN AFRICA

BY PLANE

When it comes to airfare, a little effort can save you a bundle. If your plans are flexible enough to deal with the restrictions, courier fares are often the cheapest. Tickets bought from consolidators and standby seating are also good deals, but last-minute specials, airfare wars, and charter flights often beat these fares.

Timing: Airfares to Southern Africa peak between June and August, and the Christmas/New Year period (from the beginning of Dec. until mid-Jan.) is also an expensive period. Return-date flexibility is usually not an option for the budget traveler; traveling with an "open return" ticket can be pricier than fixing a return date when buying the ticket and paying later to change it.

Round-the-World (RTW): If Southern Africa is only 1 stop on a more extensive globe-hop, consider a RTW ticket. Tickets usually include at least 3 stops and are valid for about a year; prices range US$1200-5000. Try **Northwest Airlines/KLM** (US ☎800 447 4747; www.nwa.com) or **Star Alliance,** a consortium of 13 airlines including United Airlines (US ☎800 241 6522; www.star-alliance.com).

Gateway Cities: It will frequently be cheapest to fly to Johannesburg or Cape Town, and then take a regional flight to your starting point. A traveler flying from London to Maputo, for example, will pay US$700-1100 by flying London to Johannesburg to Maputo. Flying direct from Europe to Maputo, on the other hand, can cost upwards of US$2500. **South African Airways** (www.saa.co.za) offers excellent rates.

Fares: Round-trip fares to South Africa from the US range from US$1100-1600 (during the off-season) and from US$1600-2200 (during peak season). From Europe, they range from US$800-1200. These prices don't include any discounts or special deals, and they can go up if you wait too long to book. To other Southern African capitals, expect to pay an extra US$250-1000 if flying direct from Europe; consider an add-on from Johannesburg for US$100-300 instead.

 AIRCRAFT SAFETY. Although South African Airways boasts an excellent safety record, other airlines in Southern Africa may not always meet safety standards. The *Official Airline Guide* (www.oag.com) and many travel agencies can tell you the type and age of aircraft on a particular route. The **International Airline Passengers Association** (US ☎800 821 4272, UK ☎020 8681 6555) provides region-specific safety information. The **Federal Aviation Administration** (www.faa.gov) reviews the airline authorities for countries whose airlines enter the US. **US State Department** travel advisories (☎202 647 5225; travel.state.gov/travel_warnings.html) sometimes involve foreign carriers, especially when terrorist bombings or hijackings may be a threat.

BUDGET AND STUDENT TRAVEL AGENCIES

While knowledgeable agents specializing in flights to Southern Africa can make your life easy and help you save, they may not spend the time to find you the lowest possible fare—they get paid on commission. Students and under-27ers holding **ISIC and IYTC cards** (see p. 3), respectively, qualify for big discounts from student travel agencies. Most flights from budget agencies are on major airlines, but in peak season some may sell seats on less reliable chartered aircraft.

CTS Travel, 44 Goodge St., **London** W1T 2AD, UK (☎0207 636 0031; fax 0207 637 5328; ctsinfo@ctstravel.co.uk).

STA Travel, 7890 S. Hardy Dr., Ste. 110, Tempe AZ 85284, USA (24hr. reservations and info ☎800 781 4040; www.sta-travel.com). A student and youth travel organization with over 150 offices worldwide (check their web site for a listing of all their offices), including US offices in Boston, Chicago, L.A., New York, San Francisco, Seattle, and Washington, D.C. Ticket booking, travel insurance, railpasses, and more. In the UK, walk-in office 11 Goodge St., **London** W1T 2PF or call 0207 436 7779. In New Zealand, Shop 2B, 182 Queen St., **Auckland** (☎09 309 0458). In Australia, 366 Lygon St., **Carlton** Vic 3053 (☎03 9349 4344).

Travel CUTS (Canadian Universities Travel Services Limited), 187 College St., **Toronto,** ON M5T 1P7 (☎416 979 2406; fax 979 8167; www.travelcuts.com). 60 offices across Canada. Also in the UK, 295-A Regent St., **London** W1R 7YA (☎0207 255 1944).

COMMERCIAL AIRLINES

The commercial airlines' lowest regular offer is the **APEX** (Advance Purchase Excursion) fare, which provides confirmed reservations and allows "open-jaw" tickets. Generally, reservations must be made seven to 21 days ahead of departure,

20,160 minutes floating (in the sun).
5 minutes to book online (Boston to Fiji).

Save money & time on student and faculty
travel at StudentUniverse.com

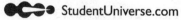 StudentUniverse.com   **Real Travel Deals**

FLIGHT PLANNING ON THE INTERNET.
Many airline sites offer special last-minute deals on the Web. Other sites do the legwork and compile the deals for you—try www.bestfares.com, www.flights.com, www.hotdeals.com, www.lowestfare.com, www.onetravel.com, and www.travelzoo.com. ■ StudentUniverse (www.studentuniverse.com), STA (www.sta-travel.com), and Orbitz.com provide quotes on student tickets, while Expedia (www.expedia.com) and Travelocity (www.travelocity.com) offer full travel services. Priceline (www.priceline.com) allows you to specify a price, and obligates you to buy any ticket that meets or beats it; be prepared for antisocial hours and odd routes. Skyauction (www.skyauction.com) allows you to bid on both last-minute and advance-purchase tickets. An indispensable resource on the Internet is the *Air Traveler's Handbook* (www.cs.cmu.edu/afs/cs/user/mkant/Public/Travel/airfare.html), a comprehensive listing of links to everything you need to know before you board a plane.

with seven- to 14-day minimum-stay and up to 90-day maximum-day restrictions. These fares carry hefty cancellation and change penalties (fees rise in summer). Book peak-season APEX fares early; by May you will have a hard time getting your desired departure date. Use **Microsoft Expedia** (expedia.msn.com) or **Travelocity** (www.travelocity.com) to get an idea of the lowest published fares, then use the resources outlined here to try and beat those fares. Low-season fares should be appreciably cheaper than the **high-season** (mid-June to Sept.) ones.

Although APEX fares are probably not the cheapest possible fares, they will give you a sense of the average commercial price, from which to measure other bargains. Specials advertised in newspapers may be cheaper but have more restrictions and fewer available seats. Carriers to Southern Africa include (phone numbers are US unless otherwise indicated):

Air France (☎ 800-237-2747; www.airfrance.com) flies from Paris (CDG) to Johannesburg (JNB) and Cape Town (CPT).

Air Zimbabwe (in Zimbabwe ☎ 04 575 111; www.airzimbabwe.com) flies from London Gatwick (LGW) and Frankfurt (FRA) direct to Harare (HRE) and Victoria Falls (VFA), and from HRE to 18 African destinations. Also flies to Brussels. Johannesburg is only destination within the Republic of South Africa.

British Airways (☎ 800-247-9297; www.britishairways.com) flies to JNB, CPT, HRE, VFA, Gaborone (GBE), WDH, Lusaka (LUN), and Lilongwe (LLW) via LGW.

El Al (☎ 800-223-6700; www.elal.com) flies to JNB via Tel Aviv (TLV).

KLM (☎ 800-374-7747; www.klm.com) flies to JNB and CPT via Amsterdam (AMS).

LAM Mozambique Airlines (in Portugal ☎ 351 21 321 9962; www.lam.co.mz) flies direct from Maputo (MPM) to Lisbon (LIS).

Qantas (☎ 800-227-4500; www.qantas.com) flies to JNB and CPT from Sydney (SYD).

Sabena (☎ 800-955-2000; www.sabena.com) flies to JNB via Brussels (BRU).

South African Airways (SAA) (☎ 800-722-9675; http://www.saa.co.za). The only airline to fly direct from six continents to Southern Africa, eliminating that pesky European layover. Direct flights from New York (JFK), Ft. Lauderdale (FLD), and São Paulo (GRU), as well as a number of European, Asian, and Australian cities.

SwissAir (☎ 800-221-4750; www.swissair.com) flies to JNB, CPT, and HRE via Zurich.

TAP Air Portugal (☎ 800-221-7370; www.tap-airportugal.pt) flies via LIS to JNB and MPM.

Virgin Atlantic (☎ 800-862-8621; www.virgin-atlantic.com) flies to JNB and CPT via LHR.

12 minutes to defrost (medium heat).
5 minutes to book online (LA to Rome).

Save money & time on student and faculty
travel at StudentUniverse.com

 StudentUniverse.com   **Real Travel Deals**

OTHER CHEAP ALTERNATIVES

AIR COURIER FLIGHTS

Those who travel light should consider courier flights. Couriers help transport cargo on international flights by guaranteeing delivery of the baggage claim slips from the company to a representative overseas. Couriers usually must travel with carry-ons only and must deal with complex restrictions on their flight. Most flights are round-trip only and have a limit of a single ticket per issue. These flights also generally operate only out of major gateway cities in North America (e.g. New York, Los Angeles, San Francisco, and Miami in the US; and Montreal, Toronto, or Vancouver in Canada), and rarely fly to Southern African countries other than South Africa. Round-trip courier fares from the US to South Africa run $750-1000 to Cape Town and Johannesburg. Groups such as the Air Courier Association (☎800-282-1202; www.aircourier.org) and the International Association of Air Travel Couriers, 220 South Dixie Hwy., P.O. Box 1349, Lake Worth, FL, USA 33460 (☎561-582-8320; iaatc@courier.org; www.courier.org) provide lists of courier opportunities for an annual fee.

TICKET CONSOLIDATORS

Ticket consolidators, or **"bucket shops,"** buy unsold tickets in bulk from commercial airlines and sell them at discounted rates. The best place to look is in the Sunday travel section of any major newspaper (such as *The New York Times*), where many bucket shops place tiny ads. Call quickly, as availability is typically extremely limited. Not all bucket shops are reliable establishments, so insist on a receipt that gives full details of restrictions, refunds, and tickets, and pay by credit card so you can stop payment if you never receive your tickets. For more information, see the information outlined below or check the web site **Consolidators FAQ** (www.travel-library.com/air-travel/consolidators.html).

TRAVELING FROM THE US AND CANADA. Travel Avenue (☎800-333-3335; www.travelavenue.com) searches for best available published fares and then uses several consolidators to attempt to beat that fare. Other consolidators worth trying are **Interworld** (☎305-443-4929); **Pennsylvania Travel** (☎800-331-0947); **Rebel** (☎800-227-3235; travel@rebeltours.com; www.rebeltours.com); and **Cheap Tickets** (☎800-377-1000; www.cheaptickets.com). Yet more consolidators on the web include the **Internet Travel Network** (www.itn.com); **SurplusTravel.com** (www.surplutravel.com); and **TravelHUB** (www.travelhub.com). Keep in mind that these are just suggestions to get you started in your research; *Let's Go* does not endorse any of these agencies. As always, be cautious, and research companies before you hand over your credit card number.

TRAVELING FROM THE UK, AUSTRALIA, AND NEW ZEALAND. In London, the **Air Travel Advisory Bureau** (☎020 7636 5000; www.atab.co.uk) can provide names of consolidators and discount flight specialists. From Australia and New Zealand, look for consolidator ads in the travel section of the *Sydney Morning Herald*.

BY BOAT

Interested in getting from a European port to Cape Town via the Atlantic Ocean? **SAFMarine,** a shipping company, offers travelers a spot on one of their ships for as little as US$10 per day. You need permission from the captain, but the trip from Europe to Cape Town takes less than 10 days. You can get off the ship at its stops along the way only if you have a valid visa. Ships do not have regular schedules or insurance; you travel at your own risk. Still, if you've got the time, it can be an

exciting (and very cheap) way of reaching South Africa from Europe. Write to SAFMarine at 22 Riebeeck St., Cape Town 8001. Alternatively, visit their web site: www.anr.safmarine.co.za/gauss and click on the "Passenger Travel" tab.

GETTING AROUND

BY BUS AND MINIBUS TAXI

A complex network of bus and minibus connections links the entire region. As a general rule, it is almost always possible to travel from town A to town B by bus; exactly how to do it is the hard part. Add in the frequent breakdowns and inexplicable national holidays, and bus travel can become quite an adventure.

The Southern African bus network can be broken down into three levels. On top are the **executive and tourist buses,** such as **Baz Bus, TransLux, Intercape,** and **Greyhound.** Mostly within South Africa, these operate between major cities with few stops, and offer such amenities as air conditioning, reclining seats, videos, toilets, and coffee and tea service. They are also, of course, the most expensive, and advance reservations are a very good idea. A second tier of bus services consists of the typical **"African buses,"** frequented by most working-class Africans. In South Africa, the major carrier is called **City to City;** in other countries, hundreds of small carriers operate individual routes. These buses typically leave from stations several miles from the center of town, and cost 25-50% the price of executive buses. Stifling heat, frequent stops, cramped seats, and breakdowns are typical. The third tier consists of long-distance **minibus taxis,** small vans that leave when full and tend to travel routes that the buses don't go. Vans designed for 12 people will carry up to 20, making moving one's arms a complicated procedure. Overnight minibuses, in particular, can be very dangerous. The trade-off, however, is that minibuses are cheap, leave frequently, go everywhere, and get there (too) fast.

While minibuses in most parts of Southern Africa are practical and frequent ways to get from one point to another, safety concerns in some areas should make you think twice before boarding. The reputations of minibus taxis in Johannesburg and Cape Town are particularly suspect; robberies are not uncommon, and news of "wars" (anything from scuffles to outright shooting) between competing drivers makes many travelers stick to other options. Reckless driving and speeding among South African long-distance minibus drivers has been a major problem in the past, but new, well-enforced legislation that mandates speed limits and license requirements has made this concern more infrequent. Always follow two rules: 1) talk to locals you trust to learn about minibus safety in your area, and 2) *never* board a minibus unless you are positive that this minibus will get you there. And don't even *consider* riding a minibus after dark.

BY TRAIN

Buses are generally faster, cheaper, and more convenient than trains in Southern Africa, but there are still some cases in which the train provides a worthwhile alternative. In **South Africa,** the rail system, **Spoornet,** has a well-developed network connecting all major cities. Although slower and more expensive than the bus, Spoornet offers comfy compartments in first and second class, reasonably priced dining cars that serve good meals, and the opportunity to experience a long-distance African train journey with relative ease. In **Namibia, Botswana,** and **Zimbabwe,** the train system is typically slower, less frequent, and as expensive as the bus. For overnight journeys, however, the train might be a better option, simply because

FIVE RULES OF MINIBUS ETIQUETTE

1. Don't produce large bank notes. Apart from being just plain inconsiderate, it makes you a robbery target.

2. If you sit near the driver, you should expect to collect money, calculate and give back change, and hang onto piles of cash and change until the driver can grab them.

3. Call out your stop at least 30 seconds before it arrives. "Here" and "over there" are not good enough; say things like "corner of Mandela" or "at the stop sign."

4. Don't sit in the farthest corner of the minibus if your stop is early on, unless you enjoy climbing over six irritated strangers.

5. When you get into a minibus that is not yet full, seat yourself so that others can get past you (i.e., not in the aisle).

FIVE RULES OF MINIBUS SANITY

1. Don't be rude or curt to the driver. He is the only person who can guide you to your stop, especially if you don't know the area.

2. Don't expect any privacy. If you are asked probing questions about your past, your life, or your past life, be prepared with a good lie; a few choice one-liners to deflect marriage proposals can't hurt, either.

3. Forget you've ever heard of a thing called deodorant—many of your fellow passengers still haven't.

4. Don't be offended if you're asked to hold someone's baby or toddler on your lap.

5. Always follow the five rules of minibus etiquette!

compartments offer a better opportunity to stretch out and get a good night's rest than a bus seat does. **Mozambique** has a deteriorated railway system that is almost completely useless for the traveler; tiny **Swaziland** and **Lesotho** have no tracks at all. For more information, see the **Transportation** sections of individual countries.

BY THUMB

 Let's Go strongly does not recommend hitching as a safe means of transportation, and none of the information printed here is intended to do so.

Given the infrequency (or nonexistence) of public transportation to certain popular destinations, travelers often need to find other ways to get where they're going. Hostels frequently have message boards where those seeking rides and those looking to share the cost of gas can meet up. Standing on the side of the highway or road with your hand out is much more dangerous than making a new friend at your hostel. Safety issues are always imperative, even when you're traveling with another person. If you hitch, you might be exposed to assault and sexual harassment (not to mention unsafe driving). Moreover, as a non-Southern African traveler in Southern Africa, you immediately stand out as foreign, and many people equate being foreign with being rich. **If you're a woman traveling alone, don't hitch.** It's just too dangerous. Avoid getting in the back of a two-door car (or any car that you can't get out of again in a hurry), and never let go of your backpack.

This said, it is also important to note that, in many parts of Southern Africa, hitchhiking has become an institutionalized part of the public transportation system, much like minibus taxis or buses. There is a well-known, if unwritten, set of "fares" between towns that is roughly the same price as the buses, and many Africans rely on hitchhiking to make shopping trips into the city or to visit relatives. In many towns, orderly queues form at certain well-known spots, and locals will file into vehicles as they arrive. In addition, long-distance truckers making journeys between Southern and Eastern Africa often supplement their incomes by informally taking on passengers in their cabs at set daily rates; many travelers have ridden all the way from the Cape to Nairobi on such arrangements. This semi-institutionalized hitchhiking is a much different matter than randomly sticking one's hand out on a roadside; the trick, however, lies in knowing exactly how these networks operate and exactly how to travel in them. If you can get a local to accompany you and show you the ropes, this might be a viable option; if all you're going on is a guess, however, stick to the buses.

BY CAR

Many of the more remote areas of Southern Africa are inaccessible without a car; public transportation options to these regions are nonexistent. Because very few travelers arrive in Southern Africa with a car (they're not so easy to squeeze into the suitcase), renting and purchasing are popular options.

RENTING

Renting a car in Southern Africa is cheap enough so that, split between three or four people who plan on doing a lot of traveling, it might actually wind up rivaling the cost of the bus or train. A 4WD is necessary for parts of Southern Africa, especially in game reserves, rural areas and national parks. Quality counts, so don't just go for the lowest price—cheaper cars tend to be less reliable and harder to handle on difficult terrain. Less expensive 4WD vehicles in particular tend to be more top-heavy, and are more dangerous when navigating particularly bumpy roads. In order to enter Swaziland, Botswana. Namibia, or Lesotho, renters need a letter of authority from their rental company.

RENTAL AGENCIES

The big worldwide agencies, including **Hertz, Avis,** and **Budget,** all have offices across Southern Africa; these are usually more expensive than local agencies, but their many locations make it easier to pick up and drop off vehicles at different points. You can generally make reservations before you leave by calling major international offices in your home country. However, occasionally the price and availability information they give doesn't jive with what the local offices in your country will tell you. Try checking with both numbers to make sure you get the best price and accurate information. Local desk numbers are included in town listings; for home-country numbers, call your toll-free directory.

South Africa also has a number of national chains, and most Southern African cities have independent operators who often have the best prices. If you're taking your own safari, certain companies specialize in off-road rentals, offering vehicles that include long-distance gas tanks, water tanks, repair kits, and full camping equipment. Though these companies tend to be more expensive than other options, you'll drive away with a full professional outfitting. Check in the **Transportation** section of the region you intend to visit for local rental agencies.

While it is legal for anyone over 18 to rent a car in South Africa, its hard to rent one if you're under 21. Some agencies require renters to be 25, and most charge those aged 21-24 an additional insurance fee. Policies and prices vary from agency to agency. Small local operations occasionally rent to people under 21, but be sure to ask about the insurance coverage and deductible, and always check the fine print. The best rental agencies in Southern Africa are in South Africa in Johannesburg (see p. 298), for access to Mozambique, Lesotho, Swaziland, Zimbabwe, and Botswana; Cape Town (see p. 85), for access to the western portion of South Africa; and Upington (see p. 411), for access to Botswana and Namibia.

COSTS & INSURANCE

Rental car prices start at around R203 a day from national companies, R130 from local agencies. Expect to pay more for larger cars and for 4 wheel drive. Cars with automatic transmission can cost up to R900 a day more than standard manuals (stick shift), and in some places, automatic transmission is hard to even find in the first place. It is difficult, no matter where you are, to find an automatic 4 wheel drive.

Many rental packages offer unlimited kilometers, while others offer three thousand kilometer per day with a surcharge of approximately R1.50 per kilometer after that. Return the car with a full tank of petroleum to avoid high fuel charges at the end. Be sure to ask whether the price includes insurance against theft and/or collision. Remember that if you are driving a conventional vehicle on an unpaved road in a rental car, you are almost never covered by insurance; ask about this before leaving the rental agency. Beware that cars rented on an American Express or Visa/Mastercard Gold or Platinum credit cards in Southern Africa might not carry the automatic insurance that they would in some other countries; check with your credit card company. Insurance plans almost always come with an excess (or deductible) of around R10,000 for conventional vehicles. This means you pay for all damages up to that sum, unless they are the fault of another vehicle. The excess you will be quoted applies to collisions with other vehicles; collisions with non-vehicles, such as trees, will cost you even more. The excess can often be reduced or waived entirely if you pay an additional charge, approximately around R200 per day.

BUYING A CAR

Buying a car instead of renting one might appeal to people who are planning to be in Africa for an extended period of time and wish to cover large distances. Reliable used vehicles cost around US$5000, but you can get most of your money back by reselling it when you leave, assuming you take care of it.

It is probably best to buy a car in Johannesburg, Cape Town, or the capital city of another country, where there are the greatest conglomeration of used car dealers and private sellers. Buying from a dealer is generally less expensive and more reliable, but it never hurts to check newspaper ads for deals. Many hostel notice-boards also often have notices from people trying to sell used cars. To avoid scams, it is best to buy a car through a contact you can trust.

In South Africa, cars being sold are required to have roadworthy certificates. Do not buy a vehicle without a roadworthy certificate, even though it might be cheaper. Also do not assume that simply because a car has a certificate, it is roadworthy—you should take it to a testing station and have it checked out—there is quite a good bit of corruption and private owners just might have bribed officials for certificates. To have your car checked and given the certificate of approval will run approximately R110. Once you have the roadworthy certificate, it is necessary to take the car to a vehicle registration center with the certificate, the registration book (that you will have received from the previous owner), your driver's license, and passport. A new registration document will cost under R250. In other Southern African countries, the roadworthy certificates may not be legally required, but it is still an excellent idea to get the car checked out before leaving town.

If you are unsure about the reliability of the car that you wish to buy, the Automobile Association of South Africa (☎011 315 2296; fax 315 1884) will check out the car for you for a fee (depending on the type of vehicle, members up to R543, non-members up to R503).

ON THE ROAD

Southern Africans drive on the **left side of the road,** and a "give way to the right" rule means that in unmarked intersections, a driver must yield to vehicles entering the intersection from his or her right. Many cars pass on the inside so be careful when changing lanes. **Buckle up,** or risk a fine. The speed limit is 80kph on rural roads and 120kph on most main roads. The limit in towns varies.

CAR ASSISTANCE

In South Africa, the **Automobile Association (AA),** Paxton House, Allandale Rd., Midrand 1685 (☎ 011 799 1000; toll-free breakdown line 0800 01 01 01; fax 799 1089; www.aasa.co.zm) is the national motor club. Nonmembers may, for a fee, use AA services in times of need. However, they expect that you will join afterwards.

DRIVING PERMITS AND CAR INSURANCE

INTERNATIONAL DRIVING PERMIT (IDP). International visitors who intend to drive in Southern Africa are encouraged to get an IDP, mainly for insurance purposes. However any driver's license is legal as long as it's in English and has a photograph on it. Your IDP, valid for one year, must be issued in your own country before you depart. You must be 18 years old to receive the IDP. A valid driver's license from your home country must always accompany the IDP. An application for an IDP usually needs to include one or two photos, a current local license, an additional form of identification, and a fee. To apply, contact the national or local branch of your home country's Automobile Association.

CAR INSURANCE. Most credit cards cover standard insurance. If you rent, lease, or borrow a car, you will need a **green card,** or **International Insurance Certificate,** to certify that you have liability insurance and that it applies abroad. Green cards can be obtained at car rental agencies, car dealers (for those leasing cars), some travel agents, and some border crossings. Rental agencies may require you to purchase theft insurance in countries that they consider to have a high risk of auto theft.

SPECIFIC CONCERNS

WOMEN TRAVELERS

Women exploring on their own face some real safety concerns, but it's easy to be adventurous without facing undue risks. The prevailing attitudes concerning women and society in Southern Africa have their effects on female travelers as well, particularly those traveling alone or without a male companion. Whistles, catcalls, and even half-joking marriage proposals are difficult to avoid, and female travelers should become comfortable with a few effective phrases to shut down unsolicited advances quickly and decisively. The concept of "personal space" is less defined in Southern Africa than in other places, but physical contact (hands on shoulders, attempted embraces, etc.) is inappropriate even in the context of the culture, and shouldn't be tolerated. If you feel intimidated, older women (and, sometimes, older men) can be sources of support.

For more information, pick up one of the following: *A Journey of One's Own: Uncommon Advice for the Independent Woman Traveler*, by Thalia Zepatos (Eighth Mountain Press; US$17; *Adventures in Good Company: The Complete Guide to Women's Tours and Outdoor Trips,* by Thalia Zepatos (Eighth Mountain Press; US$17); *Active Women Vacation Guide,* by Evelyn Kaye (Blue Panda Publications; US$18); *Travelers' Tales: Gutsy Women, Travel Tips and Wisdom for the Road,* by Marybeth Bond (Traveler's Tales; US$8).

Women's Safety These are some safety suggestions for female travelers, but many of these tips will apply to **male travelers** as well. It is wise to remember that male travelers and groups of travelers can also be easily susceptible to dangers on the road.

1) Try to stay in hostels that offer single rooms that lock from the inside.

2) Stick to centrally located accommodations that will allow you to avoid late-night treks home or rides on public transportation.

3) If you are planning to drink, make sure to keep tabs on your beverage and make sure that it comes from a closed container.

4) Always carry extra money for a phone call, bus or taxi. Hitching is never a good idea, even for groups. See **Getting There By Thumb**, p. 58.

5) When using public transportation, try to get a seat on the aisle so that no one can box you in, and choose seats that are well-lit at night.

6) Avoid looking like a tourist. Dress conservatively and try to blend in. You can't hide the fact that you're a foreigner, but you can look culturally savvy.

7) Always walk like you know where you're going, even if you really don't. Exude confidence. If you need to take out a map or your trusty ■ *Let's Go*, don't be conspicuous and don't stand on street corners looking lost. Make sure you know where you are going before exiting the car, hotel or restaurant.

8) Wear a conspicuous wedding band, carry photos of "your family," and mention that your strong, virile husband is waiting for you back at the hotel in order to avoid unwelcome advances.

9) Respond to verbal harassment by not answering. Feigned deafness, sitting motionless and staring straight ahead at nothing in particular will do a world of good in most cases. If harassment persists, a firm, loud, very public "Go Away!" is in order. Do not be afraid to use your voice or call attention to yourself.

10) Do not hesitate to seek out a police or a passerby if you are being harassed. It is helpful to approach older women; they often cast their own moral safety net.

11) Memorize the national emergency number of the country in which you are traveling, if it has one.

12) Carry a whistle on your keychain and mace in your bag. Some travelers also like to carry a knife in their pocket. (Make sure that whatever you take with you from home is legal to carry on the airplane. You might need to buy some of these safety tools once you arrive in Southern Africa.)

13) Consider taking a self-defense course before you go. These courses will prepare you for a potential attack, raise your confidence, and help you to read your surroundings. See **Self Defense**, p. 9.

14) Lastly, this may be a cliché, but we'll say it anyway: **trust your instincts.** Always make sure you know what is going on around you and get out of any situation that makes you feel uncomfortable.

OLDER TRAVELERS

Senior citizens, especially in South Africa, are eligible for a wide range of discounts on transportation (especially buses), museums, movies, theaters, and concerts. If you don't see a senior citizen price listed, ask, and you may be delightfully surprised. For **more information**, check out *No Problem! Worldwise Tips for Mature Adventurers*, by Janice Kenyon (Orca Book Publishers; US$16); or *A Senior's Guide to Healthy Travel*, by Donald L. Sullivan. (Career Press; US$13).

Travel agencies for seniors are growing in popularity. These offer trips to Southern Africa:

ElderTreks, 597 Markham St., Toronto, ON, M6G 2L7, Canada (☎416 588 5000; www.eldertreks.com). Expects to offer trips to South Africa in 2003.

Elderhostel, 11 Avenue de Lafayette, Boston, MA 021111 (☎877 426 8056; www.elderhostel.org). 17 days in South Africa with airfare $3775-3970.

BISEXUAL, GAY, AND LESBIAN TRAVELERS

The 1996 South African Constitution broke new ground when it specified that discrimination against homosexuals is illegal. Although the bisexual, gay, and lesbian scene in the country is decidedly low profile and not without controversy, the atmosphere in **South Africa** is more accepting of gays than almost anywhere else in the region. Within the country, levels of acceptance vary: Zulu, Afrikaner, and Indian communities, for example, are all fairly conservative and anti-homosexual; Cape Town, on the other hand, does have an active gay social life.

See the **Essentials** sections of individual country chapters for information, or visit the "World Legal Survey" on the **ILGA** web site (see below).

For **more information** about gay travel, try one of the following resources: *Spartacus International Gay Guide* (Bruno Gmunder Verlag; US$33); *Damron's Accommodations* and *The Women's Traveller* (Damron Travel Guides; 800 462 6654; www.damron.com; US$16-23); *Ferrari Guides' Gay Travel A to Z, Ferrari Guides' Men's Travel in Your Pocket, Ferrari Guides' Women's Travel in Your Pocket, Ferrari Guides' Inn Places* (Ferrari Guides; US$14-16); and *The Gay Vacation Guide: The Best Trips and How to Plan Them,* by Mark Chesnut (Citadel Press; US$15).

TRAVELERS WITH DISABILITIES

Wheelchair access is not common in Southern Africa. In South Africa and Botswana, almost all National Parks have special accommodations for disabled travelers. Still, it is a good idea to contact the National Parks Board for specific details on a particular park's facilities before you go. In other countries, accessibility is much more limited: as a general rule, parks that see a steady stream of Western tourism will be equipped to accommodate people with disabilities, while less developed or well-known parks will not be. All major airlines flying to Southern Africa can help disabled passengers, if arrangements are made in advance (see **Transportation By Plane,** p. 29). Sun Air reserves the right to approve the "carriage" of disabled passengers, so be sure to obtain approval when making a reservation. Renting **automatic cars with hand controls** can be arranged through Avis (reserve at least 72hr. in advance). Budget also has cars with hand controls in limited numbers; make plans in advance (see **Renting,** p. 39).

USEFUL ORGANIZATIONS

Mobility International USA (MIUSA), P.O. Box 10767, Eugene, OR 97440 (☎541-343-1284; info@miusa.org; www.miusa.org). Provides information about international exchange and internship opportunities for travelers with disabilities.

Society for the Advancement of Travel for the Handicapped (SATH). 347 5th Avenue, Suite 610, New York, NY 10016 (☎212-447-7284; sathtravel@aol.com, www.sath.org). An advocacy group that publishes free online travel information and the travel magazine *OPEN WORLD* (US$18, free for members). Annual Membership US$45; Students US$30.

TOUR AGENCIES

Wilderness Wheels Africa, 117 St. Georges Rd. Observatory, 2198, Johannesburg (☎011 648 5737; fax 648 6769). Arranges adventure safaris for paraplegics and other disabled travelers and their families in South Africa.

Flying Wheels Travel Service, 143 W. Bridge St., Owatonna, MN 55060 (☎ 800-535-6790; fax 507-451-1685, www.flyingwheelstravel.com). Arranges trips for groups and individuals in wheelchairs or with other limited mobility. Custom Itineraries to South Africa have included Cape Town, Stellenbosch, Cape of Good Hope, Johannesburg, Kruger National Park, Zambezi River, and Sun City.

MINORITY TRAVELERS

Since black people make up 87% of the population in South Africa and 95-99% in other countries, it is Caucasian, Indian, and Asian travelers who will find themselves in the minority. African-Americans will have widely varying experiences based on their skin tone. Lighter African-Americans will most likely be categorized by locals as "coloured," but may be treated with dubious suspicion. Dark-skinned African-Americans will find themselves assumed to be black Africans at first; this means that they may not feel as though they fit in anywhere. Signs proclaiming "Right of Admission Reserved" do not necessarily mean that an establishment enforces racist policies; most likely, proprietors intend to refuse peddlers. **Interracial couples** traveling together in Southern Africa may encounter hostility from whites and blacks alike: both groups often take a chilly view of interracial relationships, albeit for differing reasons.

Let's Go asks its writers to exclude establishments that discriminate. If you encounter discriminatory treatment, you should state your disapproval firmly but calmly—do not push the matter. Make it clear to the owners that another hostel or restaurant will be receiving your patronage. Please contact *Let's Go* if the establishment is listed in the guide, so that we can investigate the matter next year.

DIETARY CONCERNS

Vegetarians in Southern Africa will be able to fill their bellies nicely, despite the popularity of carnivore-oriented specialties such as *braais* (barbecue), *boerewors* (sausage) and *biltong* (jerky). For more info about dietary concerns, pick up a copy of *The Vegetarian Traveler: Where to Stay if You're Vegetarian,* by Jed and Susan Civic (Larson Publications; US$16), or contact the **North American Vegetarian Society,** P.O. Box 72, Dolgeville, NY 13329 (☎ 518-56-7970; www.navs-online.org). Travelers concerned with keeping kosher will have a much easier time in the more urbanized parts of South Africa, where there are substantial Jewish communities, than in other parts of the region, where Jewish citizens may number no more than a few hundred nationwide. Jewish travelers should contact synagogues in larger cities for information on kosher restaurants. **Jewish Travel Guide 2002,** by Michael Zaidner, lists synagogues, kosher restaurants, and Jewish institutions in over 80 countries (Vallentine-Mitchtell Publishers, US$17).

ALTERNATIVES TO TOURISM

Traveling from place to place around the world will be a memorable experience, but if you are looking for a more rewarding and complete way to see the world, you may want to consider Alternatives to Tourism. Working, volunteering, or studying for an extended period of time can be a better way to understand life in Southern Africa. This chapter outlines some of the different ways to get to know a new place, whether you want to pay your way through, or just get the personal satisfaction that comes from studying and volunteering. In most cases, you will feel that you partook in a more meaningful and educational experience—something that the average budget traveler often misses out on.

Because of its astonishingly high HIV and AIDS statistics (about one-third of the Zimbabwean population is infected), Southern Africa has become a common destination for those looking to do humanitarian work. An abundance of volunteer organizations provide an opportunity to assist in AIDS awareness education.

 VISA INFORMATION
Visa requirements vary throughout Southern Africa. Visitors from the US, UK, Canada, Australia, the EU, and Japan do not need visas for visits less than 90 days when going to Botswana or South Africa. Visitors from some EU countries need a visa to go to Namibia. Visitors from the US, Australia, Japan and many EU countries need visas to visit Zimbabwe (you can get these on arrival). All travelers need visas to visit Mozambique. In general, visas can be obtained through countries' embassies or consulates. If the country you are visiting does not have an embassy in your country, you may be able to get a visa at British High Commissions. In general, to obtain a visa you need to fill out the country's visa application forms and have a valid passport, two passport-type photos, and a copy of your return ticket. Sometimes you also need a copy of your itinerary. If you need a working visa, you need to obtain a letter from your employer. Fees generally run between US$30-54. Many countries have additional requirements; check with your country's consulate or embassy for more specific information.

STUDYING ABROAD

A quick survey of available study abroad opportunities reveals a bewildering variety of possibilities in Southern Africa. A good starting place on the web is **www.studyabroad.com,** and several excellent books are listed below. As you're perusing these options, remember that the fall semester runs from July to November (actually during the South African spring), and the spring semester goes from February to June. The field of programs in South Africa may seem immense (and it is), but the choices generally fit into one of two categories: direct enrollment in a South African university or action-based learning.

DIRECT ENROLLMENT IN A SOUTHERN AFRICAN UNIVERSITY
The majority of study abroad programs in Southern Africa act as arbiters, assisting in arrangements between international undergraduates and Southern African uni-

versities. For a fee, the program provides a comfortable interface for adventurous students, including any of a wide variety of services: enrollment in classes, location of housing, processing of visas, airline bookings, excursions, medical assistance, etc. "Why do I need a middleman?" you say. Aside from making your months prior to departure much less stressful, you will be thrilled once you arrive in Southern Africa to have an organization backing you up if things go wrong—let's just call it a security blanket of sorts. Here are a few options:

InterStudy, 63 Edward St., Medford, MA 02155 (☎800-663-1999; fax 391-7463; www.interstudy.org). This small non-profit offers fall, spring, and year-long programs in Durban, Pietermaritzburg, Cape Town, Johannesburg, and 5 other cities. Semester US$7760-9260; full-year US$13,160-16,010. Scholarships available.

American Universities International Program (AUIP), PMB 221, 305 West Magnolia St., Fort Collins, CO 80521 (☎970-495-0869; fax 484-6997; www.auip.com). Offers a 1-month field study out of Pretoria which ventures through South Africa, Swaziland, and Mozambique. US$3500, not including airfare.

American Institute for Foreign Study, River Plaza, 9 West Broad Street, Stamford, CT 06902 (☎800-727-2437; www.aifs.com). Organizes a semester program for college study at the University of Stellenbosch, outside of Cape Town. Semester US$8695; full-year US$15,890. Scholarships available.

Association of Commonwealth Universities (ACU), John Foster House, 36 Gordon Sq., London WC1H OPF (☎44 020 7380 6700; www.acu.ac.uk). Publishes information about Commonwealth universities in Botswana, Malawi, Mozambique, Namibia, South Africa, Swaziland, and South Africa.

Council on International Educational Exchange (CIEE), 633 Third Ave., 20th Floor, New York, NY 10017 (☎800-407-8839; www.ciee.org). Program at the University of Cape Town during fall, spring, and full year. If you call, request the program advisor for Africa. Semester US$9300; full-year US$16,800. Scholarships available.

Study Abroad Links, 1958 University Avenue, Berkeley, CA 94704 (☎510-649-8753; fax 644-8273; www.studyabroadlinks.com). Online search engine and directory for study abroad and educational travel. Includes links to programs in Botswana, Namibia, Zimbabwe and South Africa.

LANGUAGE SCHOOLS

Unlike American universities, language schools are frequently independently run international or local organizations or divisions of foreign universities that rarely offer college credit. Language schools are a good alternative to university study if you desire a deeper focus on the language or a slightly less rigorous course load. These programs are also good for younger high school students that might not feel comfortable with older students in a university program. The **Worldwide Classroom** program (www.worldwide.edu/ci/south_africa) is a particularly useful listing of language schools in South Africa that welcome international students; check their web site if you're looking for some specific locations. Otherwise, Cape Town hosts the **Language Teaching Center** (www.languageteachingcenter.co.za), which offers accommodations, sightseeing tours, and a variety of courses focusing on major world languages plus English, Afrikaans, Xhosa, and Zulu. They can accommodate students of all ages and abilities.

ACTION-BASED LEARNING PROGRAMS

Several programs in Southern Africa are affiliated much less closely with their host university and are more geared toward learning by doing; students often head out into the bush and do hands-on research. Both of the following programs combine this free-spirited philosophy with a serious academic agenda (including GPA requirements and an application process to get into the program):

School of International Training (SIT), Kipling Rd., Box 676, Brattleboro, VT 05302 (☎800-257-7751; fax 802-258-3296; www.sit.edu). Semester-long programs in Cape Town ("Multiculturalism and Social Change") and Durban ("Reconciliation and Development") explore modern themes in South African culture; a program in Botswana focuses on "Ecology and Conservation." See web site for descriptions. US$12,500-13,100. Scholarships available.

International Association for the Exchange of Students for Technical Experience (IAESTE), 10400 Little Patuxent Pkwy., Suite 250, Columbia, MD 21044-3519 (☎410-997-2200; www.aipt.org). 8 weeks to 1 year in South Africa for college students who have completed 2 years of technical study. US$25 application fee.

Lexia International, 25 South Main Street, Hanover, NH 03755 (☎800-775-3942; fax 603-643-9899; www.lexiaintl.org). The "Lexia in Cape Town" program includes independent research, language training, and field research opportunities during the summer (US$4850), fall and spring semesters (US$10,450), and academic year (US$19,850).

ALTERNATIVES TO TOURISM

WORKING

There are two main schools of thought. Some travelers want long-term jobs that allow them to get to know another part of the world in depth (e.g. teaching English, working in the tourist industry). Other travelers seek out short-term jobs to finance their travel. They usually seek employment in the service sector or in agriculture, working for a few weeks at a time to finance the next leg of their journey. This section discusses both short-term and long-term opportunities for working in Southern Africa. Make sure you understand your chosen country's **visa requirements** for working abroad. See the box on p. 45 for more information.

Before seeking work, keep in mind that any job you take is a job that a local could have. Many areas of Southern Africa face unemployment figures of over 50%. In order to keep jobs open for locals, you may want to consider volunteer work instead of paid employment.

LONG-TERM WORK

If you're planning on spending a substantial amount of time (more than three months) working in Southern Africa, search for a job well in advance. International placement agencies are often the easiest way to find employment abroad, especially for teaching English. **Internships,** usually for college students, are a good way to segue into working abroad, although they are often unpaid or poorly paid (many say the experience, however, is well worth it). Be wary of advertisements or companies that claim the ability to get you a job abroad for a fee—oftentimes the same listings are available online or in newspapers. It's best, if going through an organization, to use one that's somewhat reputable. Some good ones include:

TEACHING ENGLISH

Teaching jobs abroad are rarely well paid, although some elite private American schools can pay somewhat competitive salaries. Volunteering as a teacher in lieu of getting paid is also a popular option, and even in those cases, teachers often get some sort of a daily stipend to help with living expenses. Keep in mind that Southern African countries all have very low costs of living; one can live comfortably even on a relatively small teacher's stipend. In almost all cases, you must have at least a bachelor's degree to be a full-fledged teacher, although oftentimes college undergraduates can get summer positions teaching or tutoring.

Many schools require teachers to have a **Teaching English as a Foreign Language (TEFL)** certificate. This does not necessarily exclude you from finding a teaching job, but certified teachers often find higher-paying jobs. Native English speakers working in private schools are most often hired for English-immersion classrooms where no English is spoken. Those volunteering or teaching in public, poorer schools are more likely to be working in both English and the local native language. Placement agencies or university fellowship programs are the best resources for finding teaching jobs in Southern Africa. The alternative is to make contacts directly with schools or just to try your luck once you get there. If you are going to try the latter, the best time of the year is several weeks before the start of the school year. If you're looking for a good organization, try the **Fulbright English Teaching Assistantship,** U.S. Student Programs Division, Institute of International Education, 809 United Nations Plaza, New York, NY 10017-3580, (☎212-984-5330; www.iie.org). This competitive program sends college graduates to teach in various parts of Southern Africa.

SHORT-TERM WORK

Traveling for long periods of time can get expensive; therefore, many travelers try their hand at odd jobs for a few weeks at a time to make some extra cash to carry them through another month or two of touring around. Another popular option is to work several hours a day at a hostel in exchange for free or discounted room and/or board. Most often, these short-term jobs are found by word of mouth, or simply by talking to the owner of a hostel or restaurant. Many places, especially due to the high turnover in the tourism industry, are always eager for help, even if only temporary. *Let's Go* tries to list temporary jobs like these whenever possible; check the practical information sections in larger cities. Your best bet, though, is to check with the accommodations and restaurants you visit.

VOLUNTEERING

Volunteering can be one of the most fulfilling experiences you can have in life, especially if you combine it with the wonder of travel in a foreign land. Many volunteer services charge you a fee to participate in the program and to do work. These fees can be surprisingly hefty (although they frequently cover airfare and most, if not all, living expenses). Try to do research on a program before committing—talk to people who have previously participated and find out exactly what you're getting into, as living and working conditions can vary greatly. Different programs are geared toward different ages and levels of experience, so make sure that you are not taking on too much or too little. The more informed you are and the more realistic expectations you have, the more enjoyable the program will be.

Most people choose to go through a parent organization that takes care of logistical details, and frequently provides a group environment and support system. There are two main types of organizations—religious (often Catholic), and nonsectarian—although there are rarely restrictions on participation for either.

Child Family Health International, 953 Mission St., Suite 220, San Francisco, CA 94103 (☎415-957-9000; fax 501-423-6852; www.cfhi.org). Sends pre-med undergraduate and medical students to work with physicians in South Africa for 1 month, although the focus is more on working with the community and learning about health care rather than actually providing medical assistance. Must be at least 21 years old. US$1550, not including airfare.

Earthwatch, 3 Clocktower Pl. Suite 100, Box 75, Maynard, MA 01754 (☎800-776-0188 or 978-461-0081; www.earthwatch.org). Arranges 1- to 3-week programs in Namibia and South Africa to promote conservation of natural resources and help scientists with field work research. Fees vary based on program location and duration; costs average $2300 plus airfare.

Habitat for Humanity International, 121 Habitat St., Americus, GA 31709 (☎229-924-6935 ext. 2555; www.habitat.org). Volunteers build houses in Botswana, Malawi, Mozambique, South Africa, and Zimbabwe. From 2 weeks to 3 years. Short-term program costs range from US$1200-4000.

Peace Corps, 1111 20th St. NW, Washington, D.C. 20526 (☎800-424-8580; www.peacecorps.gov). Opportunities in a variety of fields in South Africa, Lesotho, Namibia, Malawi, and Mozambique. Volunteers must be US citizens, age 18 and over, and willing to make a 2-year commitment. A bachelor's degree is usually required.

Service Civil International Voluntary Service (SCI-IVS), SCI USA, 3213 W. Wheeler St., Seattle, WA 98199 (☎/fax 206-350-6585; www.sci-ivs.org). Arranges placement in work camps in Botswana, Lesotho, Swaziland, and South Africa for those 21+. Registration fee US$125.

Volunteers for Peace, 1034 Tiffany Rd., Belmont, VT 05730 (☎802-259-2759; www.vfp.org). Arranges placement in work camps in Botswana, Malawi, Mozambique, Namibia, South Africa, and Zimbabwe. US$20 membership required for registration (includes annual *International Workcamp Directory*). Programs average US$200-500 for 2-3 weeks (see web site).

FOR FURTHER READING ON ALTERNATIVES TO TOURISM

Alternatives to the Peace Corps: A directory of third world and U.S. volunteer opportunities, by Joan Powell. Food First Books, 2000 (US$10).

How to Live Your Dream of Volunteering Overseas, by Collins, DeZerega, and Heckscher. Penguin Books, 2002 (US$17).

International Directory of Voluntary Work, by Whetter and Pybus. Peterson's Guides and Vacation Work, 2000 (US$16).

International Jobs, by Kocher and Segal. Perseus Books, 1999 (US$18).

Work Abroad: The Complete Guide to Finding a Job Overseas, by Hubbs, Griffith, and Nolting. Transitions Abroad Publishing, 2000 ($16).

Work Your Way Around the World, by Susan Griffith. Worldview Publishing Services, 2001 (US$18).

Visions in Action, 2710 Ontario Rd. NW, Washington, DC 20009 (☎202-625-7402; fax 588-9344; www.visionsinaction.org). Volunteers spend 6-12 months in Johannesburg addressing social justice and democratization or 1 year in Zimbabwe working in development journalism. Must raise US$3800-5200 to cover expenses: airfare, visa, training (including Zulu or Shona language instruction), homestays, etc.

Sports Coaches' Outreach (SCORE), Sports Science Institute of South Africa, Boundary Rd., Newlands 7700, South Africa (☎021-689-6968; score@iafrica.com). Summer program for self-funding volunteers to coach sports in deprived communities and initiate community sporting activities. Most candidates have experience in physical education, but all interested parties should apply. Fee for one 6-month term is US$1200.

International Veterinary Students Association (IVSA) (www.ivsa.org), provides opportunities to work with animals in South Africa. Some veterinary experience and skills required. Check out the web site for more information.

SOUTH AFRICA

CURRENCY

USD $1 = R10.62	R10 = USD $0.94
AUD $1 = R5.76	R10 = AUD $1.75
CAD $1 = R6.78	R10 = CAD $1.47
EUR €1 = R10.37	R10 = EUR €0.96
GBP £1 = R16.26	R10 = GBP £0.62
BWP P1 = R1.69	R1 = BWP P0.59
MWK MK10 = R1.43	R1 = MWK MK7.03
MZM Mt10,000 = R4.54	R1 = MZM Mt2,202
NAD $1 = R1.00	R1 = NAD $1.00
ZWD Z$10 = R1.94	R1 = ZWD Z$5.15

PRICE RANGES. Price ranges, marked by the numbered icons below, are now included in food and accommodation descriptions. They are based on the lowest cost for one person, excluding special deals or prices. In the case of campgrounds, we include the cost of a car. The table below is a guide to how prices and icons match up.

SYMBOL	❶	❷	❸	❹	❺
ACCOMM.	R1-100	R101-200	R201-300	R301-400	R401+
FOOD	R1-25	R26-50	R51-100	R101-200	R201+

Over the course of around 2 million years, the southern part of Africa has seen both the origins of human life and the greatest kaleidoscope of human culture in the world. On the political end, South Africa has seen numerous (although only one "official") civil wars, created the second-most controversial form of government—apartheid—of the 20th century, and remained the last major white-ruled country in Africa. All this has happened in an area featuring the driest deserts, lushest forests, and tallest skyscrapers surrounded by two beautiful oceans. Whether you're into old battlefields, the Big Five (South African for the lion, leopard, elephant, buffalo, and rhinoceros), desert, jungle, sandy beaches, or native culture, you'll find it all somewhere between Cape Town in the west and Mpumalanga in the east.

LIFE AND TIMES

LAND

Most of South Africa is on a high-lying, central plateau, called the *Highveld*, bordered on the north by the Kalahari Basin. To the south, the plateau is ringed by a series of low mountain ranges called the Great Escarpment, which rises to a highest elevation of 3350m (11,000 ft.) in the Drakensberg Range running through Lesotho and KwaZulu-Natal. Fertile, narrow coastal plains extend from the escarpment to the sea. The Indian Ocean, to the east, is warmed by the tropical

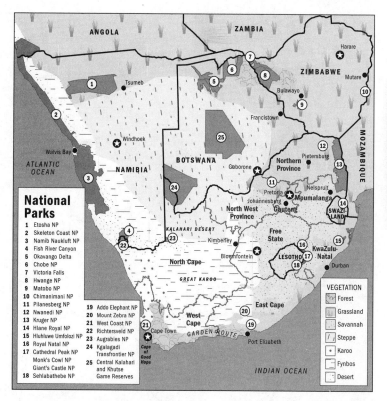

National Parks

1 Etosha NP
2 Skeleton Coast NP
3 Namib Naukluft NP
4 Fish River Canyon
5 Okavango Delta
6 Chobe NP
7 Victoria Falls
8 Hwange NP
9 Matobo NP
10 Chimanimani NP
11 Pilanesberg NP
12 Nwanedi NP
13 Kruger NP
14 Hlane Royal NP
15 Hluhluwe Umfolozi NP
16 Royal Natal NP
17 Cathedral Peak NP
   Monk's Cowl NP
   Giant's Castle NP
18 Sehlabathebe NP
19 Addo Elephant NP
20 Mount Zebra NP
21 West Coast NP
22 Richtersveld NP
23 Augrabies NP
24 Kgalagadi Transfrontier NP
25 Central Kalahari and Khutse Game Reserves

VEGETATION

Forest
Grassland
Savannah
Steppe
Karoo
Fynbos
Desert

Mozambique Current while on the west, the Atlantic Ocean is cooled by the icy Benguela Current coming up from the Antarctic. The two oceans, the prevailing winds and the topography of South Africa combine to create forest and subtropical savanna on the east coast and desert or semi-desert on the west coast. In general, South Africa has a temperate subtropical climate, and much of the land is semi-arid. Annual rainfall decreases from east to west, with only 6% of the land receiving more than 1m (40 in.) annually. The Mediterranean-like region around Cape Town is somewhat distinct, receiving its rain in the winter and dry, hot weather in the summer. The most important river in South Africa is the Orange, which flows west 2250km (1400 mi.) from the Drakensberg Range to the Atlantic.

FLORA AND FAUNA

Whereas South Africa has diverse and distinctive flora, the country is most famous for its magnificently large and colorful fauna. Much of this exciting wildlife can be found within the plethora of national parks and nature reserves. Some of these protected areas cater to tourists content to watch the animals and plants from the safety of their cars, while others indulge those who are just itching to be out there amongst the baboons. The world-renowned **Kruger National Park** (p. 365), **Pilanesberg National Park** (p. 400), and **Hluhluwe-Umfolozi Game Reserve** (p. 285) all boast the Big Five of the land mammals. The Western and Northern Cape are the only two

SOUTH AFRICA

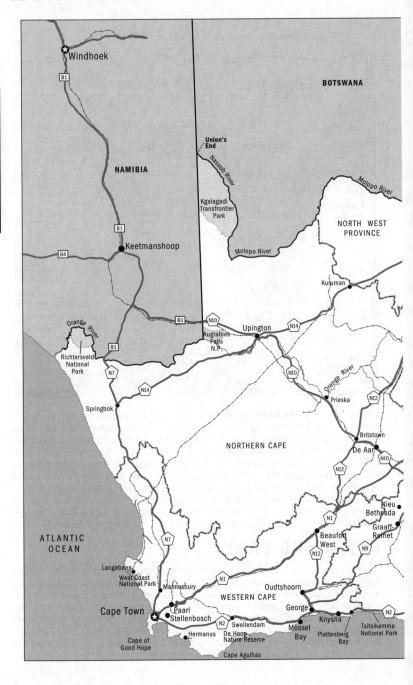

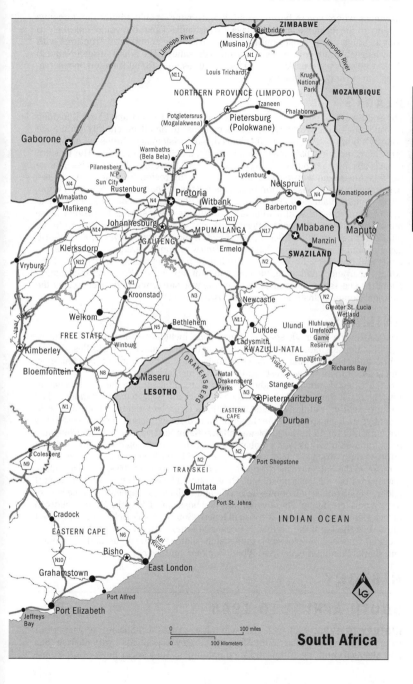

South Africa

provinces where you're better off sticking to wine—you'll admire the gorgeous scenery of the **Richtersveld** and **Kgalagadi Transfrontier Parks,** but you're not likely to spot as much game. Most South African parks have sound infrastructures with knowledgeable rangers who run day and night safaris. The South African National Parks web site (www.parks-sa.co.za) is a great resource for information on reservations and conservation efforts.

PLANTS

The southwestern part of the Western Cape is home to the Cape Floral Kingdom, the only one of the world's six plant "kingdoms" to find itself entirely within one country's borders. A variety of fine-leaved, narrow-stemmed shrubs called *fynbos* grow here, including 6252 species that are found only in South Africa. The Western Cape is also home to many of the country's 20,000 flowering plants species. Plantations of Australian wattle trees, introduced to the region for timber supply, are beginning to pose conservation problems for the *fynbos*. On the Northern Cape, the dry, sandy plains and granite mountains of the Namaqualand produce a splendid array of colorful wildflowers and succulents every spring. To protect these unique desert flora, **Namaqua National Park** was created in 1999 and is open to the public during August and September. Most of the country, however, is semi-arid savanna and temperate woodland. The *Highveld* prairies are covered with grasslands and few trees. Forests are rare, found in pockets along the valleys of the Great Escarpment and along the east and southern coasts. For more information about the vegetation of South Africa, see the web site (www.parks-sa.co.za) or the National Botanical Institute web site (www.nbi.ac.za).

ANIMALS

South Africa has over 200 species of mammals, including elephants, rhinoceroses, hippopotamuses, baboons, lions, leopards, antelopes, mongooses, gazelles, jackals, zebras and cheetahs. Many of these animals can only be found in protected areas and some of them are seriously endangered. The black rhinoceros is currently the most threatened animal in Southern Africa. Hunted for sport in the past two centuries, the black rhinoceros's horn was coveted for its use as a dagger handle and as an ingredient in traditional medicines. Efforts to protect and breed this animal in recent years have stemmed the threat of immediate extinction, and the best herds are currently found in the **Hluhlewe-Umfolozi Game Reserve** (see p. 278). Cheetahs, lions, mountain zebras, and elephants have also been targeted with preservation efforts. South Africa also has over 800 species of birds, including the ostrich, which is raised in the Cape Province for its feathers. There are over 100 species of snakes, one quarter of which are poisonous. Hikers should be especially careful of the puff adder, whose bite is poisonous. Lethargic and well camouflaged, the snake is easy to step on accidentally. These venomous bad boys have triangular heads, yellow to brown skins, and usually grow to 1m in length. South Africa's rich natural life is not limited to the land; the country's oceans abound with edible fish (snoek, cod, kingklip, mussels, rock lobster), game catch (tunny, red steenbras, and yellowtail), and sharks (hammerhead, Great White, Zambezi, and tiger).

HISTORY

SOUTH AFRICA TO 1948

HISTORY TO 1795. Archaeologists will tell you that for thousands of years prior to the European arrival in South Africa, the area was populated with **Khoisan** (**San** and **KhoiKhoi**) hunting and pastoral communities. They spent most of their time

basking in the sun and complaining about minibus taxis in downtown Johannesburg (some things never change). Eventually, about 2000 years ago, that got boring, and so they migrated south to the Cape of Good Hope. Their earliest
competitors were the **Bantu**-speaking **Sotho, Swazi, Xhosa,** and **Zulu,** who spoke a
click language that would forever confuse future European residents.

They remained unknown to Europe until 1487, when **Bartolomeu "Bart" Dias,** a
Portuguese explorer searching for a sea route to India, arrived at the Cape, which
he called the Cape of Storms. The Portuguese rulers, ecstatic that Dias had
rounded the African continent, changed the name to the more cheerful **Cape of
Good Hope** in order to attract tourists and *Let's Go* researcher-writers. In 1652, **Jan
van Riebeeck** of the **Dutch East India Company (VOC)** founded a small post at Table
Bay. The Company began assigning land to independent Dutch settlers, with the
understanding that settlers would grow wheat for the Company's use. To work the
land, the settlers imported slaves from Ceylon (Sri Lanka), the Dutch East Indies
(Malaysia and Indonesia), Madagascar, and Mozambique. It was the descendants
of these slaves as well as the progeny of mixed marriages who, over two centuries
later, were categorized as **"coloureds"** by the apartheid government. Settlers also
started producing wine in the fertile grape fields around Stellenbosch, thus providing a drinkable alternative to warm African beer.

Once they heard about the vineyards, poor Europeans looking for a change of
pace and booze flocked to South Africa. Settlers initially came from such countries as Holland, France, Germany, and Belgium. Germans outnumbered those
from Holland, so it seemed logical to make Dutch the primary language—silly
Europeans. **Afrikaans,** which originated as a colonial dialect of Dutch, developed
as the *lingua franca* of the region. The settlers, mingling first in dwelling and language and then in blood, came to be called **Afrikaners,** or **Boers** (not to be confused
with "boars" or "bores," both of which are equally abundant in South Africa). At
the turn of the 18th century, the Afrikaners grew discontent with the control the
VOC tried to exercise over them. Crying "*Ons is nou gatvol!*" ("We've had it up to
here!"), they moved inland, becoming *trekboers.*

The result was widespread contact between natives and white settlers, and by
"contact," we mean the settlers told the natives to move inland or else. By 1730, no
Khoi remained within 250 miles of Table Bay. Towards the end of the 18th century,
the Cape's remaining Boers began to stage more rebellions against the VOC; at the
same time, the *trekboers* provoked skirmishes with the Xhosa by organizing frequent military expeditions against the indigenous people.

THE BRITISH ARRIVE (1795-1819). In 1795, Britain invaded Cape Town to keep
the territory away from Holland's ally, France. The British imposed their language
and law on the Dutch settlers. They also granted emancipation to all slaves (1834)
and began extensive missionary work.

However, they faced two dilemmas: how best to cope with conflict between the
settlers and the Xhosa, and how exactly to pronounce "Xhosa." To strengthen the
Eastern frontier border, the British leaders sent some of their people to farm
(these Britons became known as the **1820 Settlers**), resulting in the establishment
of small towns such as Port Elizabeth and Grahamstown. During this period, British forces, trying to increase the boundaries of their rule, engaged the Xhosa in six
Frontier Wars. They finally subjugated the Xhosa towards the end of the 19th century and imprisoned several chiefs (including **Chief Hintsa,** whom they eventually
executed) on **Robben Island,** which later housed Nelson Mandela for 27 years.

The arrival of the British sparked Zulu and Boer unification movements. In the
19th century, the **Zulu** kingdom under **Shaka** (see **Shaka Zulu,** p. 268) concentrated
its forces and migrated inland, conquering other African communities in a series
of brutal struggles over space, trade, and survival. Around the same time, the

Boers strengthened their own identity in opposition to the assimilation programs of the British. In 1834, hundreds of farmers, crying *"Genoeg met die verdoemde Britte—weg is ons!"* ("Enough of the damned Brits, let's hit the road!") packed their wagons and embarked on the **Great Trek.** The exodus took them from the Cape to the north and east. Over a period of 20 years, many Boers—known now as **Voortrekkers**—traveled into Natal/Zululand (now **KwaZulu-Natal**) where they came into violent conflict with the Zulu and the British. They moved back over the Drakensberg Range into areas that they later proclaimed republics: the Orange Free State, now the **Free State;** and the Transvaal, portions of which are now **Gauteng.**

FIGHTING EVERYWHERE. From 1838-1880, South African history goes like this: Boers fight Zulus, Boers declare independence, Boers in Orange Free State fight Basutoland (now **Lesotho**), British seize Basotho territory, British fight Zulus, Zulus crushed. Major battles include the **Battle of Blood River** in 1838, when the Boers collided with the Zulus in Natal; and the **Battle of Isandlwana** in 1879, the Zulus' only major victory against British forces.

A labor shortage persisted during this period, even though many Africans became tenants on white-owned farms. To remedy this, whites shipped 6000 Indian indentured servants to Natal between 1860 and 1866. An Indian population slowly grew, enveloped between blacks and whites in the enforced racial hierarchy. Toward the end of the 1860s, the advent of capitalism demanded both land and labor, and indigenous Africans were seen as a source for both. The discovery of **diamonds** and **gold** in the Boer republics—in 1871 and 1886 respectively—fueled the British desire to control the country's resources. They seized the diamond fields and invaded the Transvaal, Zululand, and Pediland. Zulu, Ndebele, and Venda resistance collapsed, and, by the turn of the century, no autonomous African societies remained in South Africa.

DIAMONDS (1867-1898). It was the discovery of diamonds and gold that propelled South Africa's economy into the world market. Investment came from—and profits were reaped by—Britain, Europe, and North America. The main consequences in South Africa itself were major fluctuations in the population distribution and an ever-widening cleavage in wealth between the British imperialists and the predominantly black mine workers.

The craze began in April 1867 when a solitary diamond was found near **Hopetown** in the Cape Colony. By 1871, 20,000 whites had flocked to the diamond fields, using local natives as a source of cheap labor. In 1889, **De Beers Consolidated Mines,** owned by **Cecil John Rhodes,** became South Africa's sole diamond producer and started plotting irritating television commercials (see **Cecil John Rhodes,** p. 411).

In 1886, Frederick and Henry William Strueben discovered a rich deposit of gold in the **Witwatersrand,** a ridge of land 30 miles south of Pretoria. As with the diamond mines, the discovery of gold increased the demand for unskilled black labor; this, in turn, aggravated the proletarianization of the race. By 1899, 97,000 of the 109,000 people working in the gold industry were black. Owners also imported thousands of Chinese laborers.

THE ANGLO-BOER WAR (1899-1902). The Anglo-Boer War was not the first conflict between the British and the Boers, but it was the most brutal and consequential, marked by atrocities on both sides. Scuffles over rights to gold-rich land ignited the war after Cecil Rhodes, then prime minister of the Cape Colony, started secretly devising a plan in 1895 to oust President Paul Kruger and permanently secure Transvaal for the British Empire. However, the Boers were informed of his intentions, intensifying the tension. War broke out in 1899.

Over the course of the 2½-year war, 500,000 British troops fought against 87,000 Boers. Boer commandos took up guerrilla tactics, which the British countered by burning farms and setting up **concentration camps,** in which they confined Boer women and children. The results were horrific. Nearly 25,000 Boers died of disease and malnutrition in these camps; 14,000 blacks died in separate camps. The Boers, badly defeated, worked out a settlement with the British in 1902 with the **Peace of Vereeniging,** under which the Boers agreed to cede their republics and accept British supremacy. British High Commissioner Alfred Milner moved his government to Johannesburg and set about ensuring that the former Boer republics would be wholly absorbed into the British empire. Despite his efforts, British settlers only trickled into the Transvaal, and government-sponsored anglicization incited a more vigorous Afrikaner nationalism. Milner's plan failed because Afrikaners still made up a majority of the white population.

JOIN THE PARTY (1903-1909). In 1903, Boer leaders **Louis Botha** and **Jan Smuts** established the **Het Volk (The People) Party,** which canvassed sturdy support over the next two years. In 1907 the two republics—the Transvaal and the Orange Free State—were restored to Afrikaner control. Meanwhile, black farmers were being gradually pushed off their land through a series of taxes and restrictions, provoking an unsuccessful rebellion led by **Chief Bambatha** of the Zondi, which resulted in the massacre of tens of thousands of natives.

Such rebellions intensified whites' desire for political unity in order to facilitate control of the black population. In 1908, a national convention in Durban drafted a **constitution** for South Africa which established a unitary state with parliamentary sovereignty. This meant that even though the **Union of South Africa** was comprised of the initial four colonies (which at this point became "provinces"), only the national government had supreme legislature. The constitution ensured over-representation of rural voters, which benefited Afrikaner nationalism. It also recognized both English and Dutch (and later Afrikaans) as national languages. Aware of the fact that the entire arrangement gave whites a monopoly on political power, a group of blacks formed the **South African Native National Congress (SANNC)** in 1912, which evolved into the **African National Congress (ANC).** "Coloured" South Africans established the **African People's Organization,** and Indians led by **Mahatma Gandhi** resisted discriminatory laws with nonviolent methods.

FACTIONS ORGANIZE THEMSELVES (1910-1948). Despite the creation of the **Union of South Africa** in 1910, the first half of the 20th century was marked by an increasing division among various socio-economic and ethnic groups. One such divide fell between the more technologically advanced British South Africans and the poorer Afrikaner farmers and mine workers. Another came between whites who held political power and indigenous Africans who were subject to their authority.

To represent their divergent interests, Afrikaners formed political parties. Afrikaner nationalism manifested itself initially in the **National Party (NP)** under **J.B. Hertzog,** who had split from the **South Africa Party (SAP)** in 1914. A society of Afrikaners called the **Broederbond** (League of Brothers) was also becoming active in political affairs around this time. The **Great Depression** forced the merger of the NP and SAP into a new party in 1934. Following that, a different group of Afrikaner nationalists under **D.F. Malan** formed still *another* party: the **Purified National Party,** closely allied with the Broederbond and a pseudo-party: the **Federation of Afrikaans Cultural Associations (FAK).** Just when we thought they couldn't possibly have more political groups, along came an even more radical, extra-parliamentary group, the **Ossewa Brandwag (Ox-Wagon Sentinel).**

The split between the Afrikaner nationalists and the SAP revolved around increasing racial tensions between white and black workers. The British South Africans passed both the **1913 Land Act,** which made it illegal for blacks to pur-

SOUTH AFRICA

chase or lease land anywhere outside of blocked-off reserves, and the **1923 Urban Areas Act,** which called for segregation in urban areas and specified that blacks could only live in towns if they were needed there by whites. But from the 1920s onward, the SAP leaders were not nearly as committed to such policies as the Afrikaner nationalists. Hertzog, one such nationalist, stressed these differences when he created the National Party which won the 1924 election. As prime minister, Hertzog passed further discriminatory measures and denounced the SAP on the grounds that it was turning a blind eye to the *swart gevaar* (black threat).

In 1933, fearing a lack of new parties, the SAP formed a coalition government with the NP to try to avert economic depression: the two parties merged to form the **United Party (UP).** The coalition was short-lived; in 1939, Hertzog and others defected in protest over the party's decision to support Britain in **World War II.**

THE APARTHEID ERA

EARLY YEARS. In the 1948 elections, Prime Minister Smuts and the UP were ousted by D.F. Malan's National Party, bringing in the first all-Afrikaner government. The NP won a narrow victory on a platform of **apartheid** (literally meaning "apartness"), advocating total racial segregation. Drawing upon Dutch religious tenets and pseudo-scientific beliefs about racial difference, apartheid was based on the idea that the only way that each race could maintain its unique "cultural destiny" was by separation. Behind this misleading front, the National Party hid their real motive: total subjugation of the native population. The NP controlled South Africa for the next half-century, increasing its own political power and turning its platform of apartheid into a political, social, and economic reality.

EARLY APARTHEID LAWS

Prohibition of Mixed Marriages Act (1949). The first major apartheid legislation, it did exactly what its name indicates.

Immorality Act (1950). Prohibited all sexual relations between whites and blacks.

Population Registration Act (1950). Defined "race" and mandated the use of identity cards that would indicate a person's official race.

Group Areas Act (1950). Declared segregation in residential areas, resulting in the forceful evictions of numerous blacks from their homes.

Abolition of Passes Act (1952). Required all blacks to always carry a 96-page booklet outlining their rights of movement and criminal and employment records.

Separate Amenities Act (1953). Prohibited people of different races from sharing schools, hospitals, cinemas, shops, and toilets.

Job Reservation Act (1954). Designed to prevent whites from hiring lower-paid Africans to hold "traditional white" jobs. Resulted in the removal of thousands of Africans from their jobs.

While the 1950s was marked by segregation laws similar to those seen in the US South during the same time, apartheid policy shifted in the 1960s. Under **Hendrik Verwoerd** and **B.J. Vorster,** the emphasis of apartheid legislation changed to the complete removal of blacks from South African citizenship. Since discriminatory legislation seemed to National Party leaders only to cause more conflict in South Africa, they sped up the process by which the black reserves would eventually be transformed into self-governing, independent **homelands.** Publicly, nationalist leaders called this oppressive system **separate development,** but privately they hoped that establishing independent black states would increase white prosperity and, more importantly, draw attention and opposition away from their government.

They also counted on such separation to dilute the full force of the black community, since they decided to divide blacks into eight distinct ethnic groups.

Blacks, making up three-quarters of the population, were squeezed into 13% of the total land available in South Africa. Moreover, even though some homelands, like the **Transkei,** had considerable resources, most were woefully impoverished and undeveloped. The 87% of South African land allocated to whites, on the other hand, was the most valuable and arable—yet, it still required cultivation, and the government found blacks expedient for this reason. Any black person who did not perform "useful service" in South Africa's labor market was expected to go to the homelands which, instead of becoming autonomous, self-sufficient nations, soured into barren economic backwaters due to the heavy emigration of black males. The few homelands that did become independent in the South African government's eyes—Transkei in 1976, **Bophutswana** in 1977, **Venda** in 1979, and **Ciskei** in 1981—were not recognized by any foreign nations. Most of their labor force went to work for whites in South African cities.

APARTHEID RESISTANCE MOVEMENTS. The transition from apartheid to "separate development" was largely a response to increasing international and domestic opposition, which made discriminatory legislation (on the grounds of white supremacy alone) more difficult to bear. Not all South African whites supported apartheid. Some members of the **Dutch Reformed Church** voiced criticisms, while students from the University of Cape Town and the University of the Witwatersrand organized protests. A women's organization called the **Black Sash** participated in silent protests and provided legal advice to victimized blacks.

Soon after the National Party came to power, black resistance movements also became more organized and effective. The **African National Congress (ANC),** founded in 1912 to pursue African enfranchisement, organized a passive resistance movement along with the South African Indian Congress in the early 1950s. The ANC's leaders were **Walter Sisulu, Oliver Tambo,** and **Nelson Mandela.** The two groups, along with white opposition groups like the Congress of Democrats, also adopted a **Freedom Charter** in 1955 which called for basic human rights, equality before the law, freedom of speech, and social reforms.

Another group, the **Pan-Africanist Congress (PAC),** broke away from the ANC in 1959 because of the ANC's cooperation with white groups. In 1960, PAC leaders organized nationwide campaigns against the pass laws. In Sharpeville, the protests met with violent opposition from police forces, who opened fire on the crowd, killing 67 and wounding 186. Sharpeville and related demonstrations frightened the government into outlawing the ANC and the PAC, forcing their operations underground. The **Sharpeville massacre,** as it came to be known, also caused these resistance groups to reconsider their strategies. In the 1960s, the ANC, the PAC, and the African Resistance Movement decided that violence must be met with violence. They conducted over 200 bombings of various government buildings. In 1963, Mandela and Sisulu were charged with treason and were sentenced to life imprisonment on **Robben Island** off the coast of Cape Town. Other leaders were either arrested or exiled, but the ANC and PAC continued to organize armed resistance movements from outside the country.

Some of the most effective resistance came from outside these underground movements. The apartheid era generated a number of outspoken authors and playwrights of all races, whose writings contributed to a rising domestic and international awareness of the evils of apartheid (see **Literature,** p. 65). The 1970s also saw rapid growth of the economy and the development of black trade unions, which pressed for higher wages and better working conditions. Many young blacks were inspired by what became known as the **Black Consciousness Movement,** led by 22-year-old **Steve Biko.** In June 1976, in the township of **Soweto** on the outskirts of

SOUTH AFRICA

Johannesburg, students organized a massive protest against the use of Afrikaans as the official language of instruction in a **Bantu education** system. When police shot and killed a 13-year-old demonstrator in the **Soweto Uprising,** a wave of protests and interracial violence broke across the country. The subsequent police crackdown caused many young blacks to leave the country, many of whom joined the militant wings of the ANC and the PAC in exile.

APARTHEID IN CRISIS. Although the government reacted to internal protest with more repressive measures, the conflict of the 1970s clearly made the apartheid system difficult to maintain. In addition, international opposition to apartheid led to South Africa's growing isolation in the world, especially since the government in 1961 had declared South Africa a **republic,** and thus independent from the British Commonwealth. Although the economy grew rapidly in the 1960s and 70s, South Africa faced a "brain drain" as many highly skilled whites left the country. In 1974 and 1975, the restoration of power to blacks in **Angola** and **Mozambique,** former colonies of Portugal, exposed by contrast the oppression of blacks in South Africa. The new black Marxist governments in these countries were sympathetic to the ANC and the PAC (which held to certain communist tenets). In the civil wars that followed the demise of white government in Mozambique and Angola, the South African government gave resources and military support to the anti-Marxist forces. Surprisingly, South Africa could not even claim Cold War allies in this fight—the US refused to intervene, even though the Marxist regiments were backed by Cuba and the Soviet Union. This was a shock to the National Party, who had repeatedly tried to woo international support through active anti-communism.

Other factors served to make many within the National Party question the efficacy of apartheid. In 1977, the UN imposed an **embargo** on the sale of arms to South Africa. The progress of **civil rights** in the US made many American leaders vocally critical of the South African government, and foreign governments refused to recognize the government-enforced homelands as independent nations. In 1978, Prime Minister Vorster's inability to stop internal unrest led to the premiership of **P.W. Botha.** Botha advocated a **"total strategy"** which would respond to the "onslaught" upon South Africa. In 1983, he introduced a **new constitution** that would give some measure of political representation to "coloureds" and Indians. Blacks, however, were still given no voice in the new government.

Botha did attempt to reform some of the old segregation laws in the late 80s: he repealed the Immorality Act and the pass laws, and desegregated many public buildings. These amendments, however, remained tokens, designed to fend off international criticism. Domestic and international outrage reached an all-time high in the 1980s. The ANC, operating in exile, had joined 575 organizations to form, in 1983, the **United Democratic Front (UDF).** School and bus boycotts occurred throughout South Africa. Violence rose, even among the various black political parties. Tension ran especially high between ANC supporters and Zulu **Inkatha Freedom Party** members, led by **Chief Mangosuthu Buthelezi.**

Foreign relations turned sour when **Margaret Thatcher** and **Ronald Reagan** began to experience public pressure to impose sanctions on South Africa. Foreign businesses decreased their investments in South Africa, and **Chase-Manhattan Bank** caused a financial crisis by refusing to roll over its short-term loans. In 1986, the US Congress, over President Reagan's veto, passed a **Comprehensive Anti-Apartheid Act,** terminating air links, much importation, and new investments and loans.

In 1986, Botha declared a **state of emergency** in South Africa and resorted to extremely repressive and authoritarian measures to "restore order" to the Republic, which he felt was threatened by black opposition. This meant, among other things, detaining as many as 30,000 people without trial, demolishing black squatter camps, and completely censoring the media. It was clear, however, that Botha was not even satisfying his own electorate. Many previously supportive whites began to realize that, in the face of such widespread domestic and international opposition, the present system was no longer viable. Ironically, Botha's actions didn't appease the radical right-wing either; his decision to repeal pass laws only strengthened the neo-Nazi paramilitary group **Afrikaner-Weerstandsbeweging** (Afrikaner Resistance Movement), or **AWB,** and its leader, **Eugene Terre Blanche.**

THE END OF APARTHEID (1989-1994). In 1989, **F.W. De Klerk** replaced an aging, ailing Botha as president. De Klerk was considered an extremely conservative member of the National Party, but he was 21 years younger than Botha and realized that the system had to be changed drastically. In 1990, he shocked the world by announcing that he would release Mandela and other political leaders from prison, lift bans on the ANC, the PAC, and the UDF, and initiate negotiations towards a new constitution. Between 1990 and 1991, De Klerk effectively eroded the concrete blocks of apartheid one by one by repealing all the major discriminatory laws, including the Separate Amenities Act, the Group Areas Act, and the Population Registration Act. The government also began to introduce integrated education by reducing color barriers in schools. De Klerk did all this despite strong opposition from his own party and constituency.

The negotiation process for a new constitution formally began in December of 1991 with the **Convention for a Democratic South Africa (CODESA).** Mandela, having succeeded **Oliver Tambo** as president of the ANC, spearheaded talks for the party. However, CODESA was beset with problems from the start. For one thing, there was little agreement among blacks themselves as to the future of the nation. The PAC still did not want an alliance with the ANC and did not attend CODESA. Ongoing violence in Natal and the Transvaal between the Zulu supporters of the **Inkatha Freedom Party (IFP)** and the Xhosa members of the ANC stalled talks. The military wing of the National Party, anxious about its imminent loss of power, even made secret payments to Inkatha leader **Chief Mangosuthu Buthelezi** in return for organized Inkatha attacks on the ANC. The bargaining in CODESA led to compromises which, although supported by Mandela and De Klerk, threatened to alienate the leaders from their parties. De Klerk's whites did not want to forgo their privileges; Mandela's blacks did not want to concede any more power to the whites. Nevertheless, in the **1992 whites-only referendum,** the negotiation process won a thumbs up. In the same year, however, the ANC was forced to withdraw from CODESA negotiations after Inkatha members in police vehicles murdered 42 men, women, and children in what became known as the **Boipatong Massacre.** The ANC then organized nationwide **strikes** which effectively brought the economy to a halt.

By September 1992, Mandela and De Klerk were able to resume formal negotiations, and they made plans for a nationwide election in 1994. An interim constitution was adopted when the ANC and National Party met halfway between the former's wish for majority rule and the latter's wish to protect white interest. The groups agreed on universal adult suffrage, a bill to maintain human rights, and the elimination of the homeland governments. But there were still problems to be resolved. The **Conservative Party** (a right-wing group that had split from the National Party) formed an alliance with the extreme paramilitary **AWB** and also joined with the **IFP** in a **Freedom Alliance** to boycott the negotiations and the upcoming elections. The Freedom Alliance sought to maintain the autonomy of homelands and to create a separate homeland, a *volkstaat,* for Afrikaners.

Most of the various opposition groups finally decided to cooperate with the ANC and the National Party. In 1993, Mandela and De Klerk were jointly awarded the **Nobel Peace Prize** for their struggles. In April 1994, the **first all-race election** was held in South Africa. The ANC won 63% of the vote, the National Party 20%, and the IFP 10%. Nelson Mandela, as head of the ANC, was inaugurated as president on May 10 in a ceremony attended by 45 heads of state and the UN Secretary General.

SOUTH AFRICA

TODAY

THE NEW SOUTH AFRICA. The tasks that Mandela faced in 1994 were innumerable. He was committed to eradicating the widespread repercussions of the apartheid system, and in particular the inequality between blacks and whites. But he also had to maintain a growing economy that could provide jobs for everyone. During the build up to the 1994 elections, Mandela proposed a **Reconstruction and Development Program (RDP)** to reform health, housing, and education systems, and promote economic growth. The ANC, having won the elections, agreed to form a coalition with other parties called the **Government of National Unity.** This was an interim government created to write the **new constitution** before the next elections in 1999. In the meantime, they allocated 4.2 billion rand to the RDP and promised, among other things, to build 80,000 houses in 1994-95, a figure which they said would grow to 300,000 by the turn of the century. Mandela also passed the **Restitution of Land Rights Act,** which would return lands taken from blacks under apartheid. The process of writing up the **new constitution** took almost two years; it is perhaps the most ambitious constitution in the world, granting its citizens rights to housing, food, health care, education, and social security, and outlawing discrimination based on more than 15 categories. In 1996, the interim government finally approved its new constitution and, since then, South Africa's international standing has risen greatly. Mandela, in particular, was crucial to this process, helping to eliminate international sanctions and arms embargoes while facilitating trade agreements with the world's economic powers.

CONFRONTING APARTHEID CRIMES. The **Truth and Reconciliation Commission (TRC),** headed by Nobel Peace Prize laureate **Archbishop Desmond Tutu,** began the task of investigating the crimes of the apartheid era. The commission heard thousands of accounts by perpetrators, victims and their families. Through a very complex process, the commission sought to grant full amnesty to those who were able to prove that their crimes were politically motivated, and who publicly apologized to the victim or the victim's family. Some believe it is the best possible way of satisfying both apartheid victims and perpetrators; others feel that it is literally letting people get away with murder. Only 849 of the 7000 people who have applied to the TRC for amnesty have been pardoned. The murderers of activist **Chris Hani** and Black Consciousness leader **Steve Biko** were denied absolution for their crimes. On the other hand, **Jeffrey Benzien,** an apartheid assassin, was granted amnesty; he is now immune to prosecution in criminal and civil court. In July 1999, **Eugene De Kock,** the notorious colonel of a counterterrorism unit during apartheid, admitted to crimes filling 4000 pages—by far the longest application the TRC has seen. Former president **P.W. Botha,** on the other hand, refused to confront the committee, in spite of being accused of participating in the murders of eight anti-apartheid activists. The commission's web site, **www.truth.org.za,** provides the TRC's reports and public records, and explains its mission.

1999 ELECTIONS. South Africa's **second democratic general elections,** held on June 2, 1999, passed peacefully. The African National Congress won 266 seats; the Democratic Party 38; the Inkatha Freedom Party 34; the New National Party, formerly the National Party, 28; the United Democratic Movement 14; and the African Christian Democratic Party 6. **Thabo Mbeki** took over from Nelson Mandela as South Africa's president, and **Jacob Zuma** is deputy president.

Mandela and his government brought running water to three million and basic housing to half a million. Yet Mandela was unable to significantly mitigate four major national crises: **unemployment** (50% of the working-age population is reputedly unemployed), **education, crime,** and the growing **AIDS rate** (which some fear could wipe out a third of the population). **Affirmative action** has occurred at breakneck speed, but the government has not focused on how to train individuals. While instances of political crime have decreased, civilian crime remains astronomical. It is estimated that one in three South African women loses her virginity to a rapist. Even more troubling is that only one in six murderers is convicted. Little will change until the government commits to creating adequate security and investigatory infrastructures. Mbeki is more radical than Mandela, and his policies reflect his interest in expanding affirmative action even further. He has forcibly removed whites from jobs at all levels of society and replaced them by unskilled blacks. He fell victim to international ridicule when he denied that HIV causes AIDS, one of his nation's greatest problems. He also has done little to reduce unemployment and crime. In fact, Mbeki has blamed many of South Africa's problems on international conspiracies, perhaps correctly identifying many foreign governments' apparent inability to distinguish between South Africa and Zimbabwe.

South Africa has become a very different country since 1994, but it still has a long way to go in order to achieve a truly democratic and economically stable society. Those goals will remain distant until the government is able to adequately address government reform and its myriad social problems.

PEOPLE

DEMOGRAPHICS

POPULATION AND DEMOGRAPHY. South Africa's population is about 44 million, including an estimated two million illegal immigrants. Approximately 75% of the people are black, 13% are white, 9% are "coloured," and 3% are Asian (mostly Indian). Blacks may be roughly divided into nine different groups, although within these groups there are a number of smaller divisions. The two largest, by far, are the **Zulu** (22%) and the **Xhosa** (18%). The ethnic and political rivalry between these two major groups has had a defining impact on African politics. The Xhosas now make up the most powerful political party (ANC), and the Zulus retain a traditional kingdom in KwaZulu-Natal and make up the third most powerful political party, the Inkatha Freedom Party (IFP). The remaining African groups are (from largest to smallest): **Pedi, Sotho, Tswana, Tsonga, Swazi, Ndebele,** and **Venda.**

Afrikaners, descendants of 17th-century Dutch settlers, French Huguenots, and German Protestants, make up 60% of the white population. The Afrikaners formed the core of the National Party (now the New National Party) in South Africa, the seat of white power in government for most of the second half of the 20th century. The remaining whites are mostly English-speaking descendant from the **British** who began arriving in the Cape region in the early 19th century.

The mixed-race descendants of Africans, Indians and other Asians and Europeans are traditionally called **"coloureds."** The ancestry of coloureds goes back to the 17th century when slaves from Malaysia and Indonesia and women from the Far East were brought to South Africa. There was considerable interracial marriage prior to 1948. Coloureds usually speak Afrikaans and some English. There is also a small population of **Indians,** largely descendants of 19th-century immigrants and indentured laborers, and an even smaller Chinese population.

LANGUAGE

Because of its extraordinary diversity, South Africa has a whopping 11 official languages. Unfortunately, **you must be proficient in all of them** in order to successfully travel around South Africa (just kidding—English alone will be fine). In addition to **English** and **Afrikaans** (which has Dutch and German origins), there are nine black languages that correspond to the nine different ethnic groupings. There are about 90 different dialects of these languages and many other cultural variations. These languages were strictly oral until Europeans created a written form for them in the 1800s.

The majority of South Africans can communicate in many different languages, and more than 57% speak and understand English. Zulu is still the most widely spoken first language, used by 67% of the population. Afrikaans, spoken predominantly by whites and "coloureds," is a first language to 15% of the nation; Xhosa is a first language to 11.6%, and English to 9%. For a brief introduction to some important words and phrases in the major South African languages, see the **Glossary** and **Phrasebook** in the **Appendix** (p. 649).

CULTURE

FOOD AND DRINK

The many cultures that have contributed to South Africa's history have also contributed to its cuisine. At an early stage, Cape cooking was profoundly influenced by the Far Eastern slaves who were brought to the area by the Dutch. These slaves infused traditional Dutch dishes with spices, leading to the creation of such dishes as **sosaties**—kebabs in a spicy marinade—and **bobotie**—minced lamb or beef with a topping of baked egg, milk and toasted almonds. **Curries,** also a product of the Malay influence, are usually served with spicy, flavorful sauces, chutney (onions and fruits cooked with spices and vinegar) and *atchars* (pickles). Cape dwellers today are proud of their deliciously fresh seafood.

Traditional black **"chow"** (food in South African slang) relies heavily on beans, grain, and corn. **Putu,** a staple of the Zulu diet, is made by cooking cornmeal (known as "mealie meal") into a stiff, dry porridge and is eaten with **amasi,** a sour milk. The Afrikaners have developed their own version called **pap** which they serve with sweet tomato and onion relish known as **sous.** Cooked green maize and roasted mealie (corn) on the cob are favorite snacks, especially in cities. Homemade brews from cornmeal, sorghum seeds, or millet are common beverages.

The Great Trek resulted in some unique ways to preserve food as the Afrikaners made the long trip across arid territories. The best-known and perhaps best-tasting is **biltong**—salted, spiced and air-dried beef. Beef or lamb ribs were pickled in brine to make **soutribbetjies,** and scones were dried to make **beskuit** (called **rusks** in English) to be dunked in tea or coffee. **Bredie,** a stew of vegetables and meat, was cooked over campfires in three-legged, round-bellied iron pots. **Potjiekos,** or pot food, consists of layers of pork, beef, lamb, and different vegetables simmered over a low fire to blend the flavors and make the meat melt-in-the-mouth tender.

South African barbecues, or **braaivleis** (more commonly known as *braai*), also derive from the Great Trek. The staple is lamb chops, and **boerewors,** a juicy sausage with coarsely-chopped beef, pork, herbs and spices. **Vetkoeks** (fat cakes), made from yeast dough deep-fried in oil and eaten with savory mince or **Bovril** (South African-style Vegemite), are a dinner favorite.

Traditional Afrikaner sweets include **melktert** (milk tart), **soetkoekies,** cookies from the Cape area, and **koeksusters,** small plaited portions of dough, deep-fried and then dipped in a syrupy sauce which they soak up to become very sweet and moist. These have been adopted into black culture and are called **itwist.**

Specialties of Durban's Indian population include: **samosa,** a three-sided, deep-fried triangle with spicy meat and vegetable fillings; **biryani,** a blend of meat and spices marinated overnight in yogurt, and **roti,** a flat bread.

South Africa is home to a thriving **wine** industry, initiated in 1655 when the first governor of the Cape, Jan van Riebeeck, planted a vineyard and produced the first

Cape wine. Cape vineyards now offer 21,000 wines from which to choose (see **Winelands,** p. 119). Revelers may come across local and home-brewed specialties such as **"cane,"** a spirit distilled from sugar cane and frequently mixed with Coca-Cola. **Beer** brands in South Africa include Lion, Castle, Hansa, and Ohlssons, and are consumed with gusto at *braai* and sporting events. **Maheu** is a thick and sour homemade beer with a sorghum base.

IT'S CASTLE TIME? Lion and Castle Lager, the two most popular brewskies in South Africa, are both made by South African Breweries, which bought the US-based Miller Brewing Company in June 2002. With the acquisition, South African Breweries became the second largest brewery in the world (moving up from fourth) and acquired a foothold in the US market. American travelers should keep in mind that the next time you enjoy a Miller Lite, your money is going ultimately to the same people who make Lion and Castle.

CUSTOMS AND ETIQUETTE

South Africans are generally very outgoing. Many will engage you in conversation, often enthusiastically referring to the popular topic of national sports. White South Africans have continental manners. Initiating conversations with a firm handshake is key. Make eye contact and don't put your hands in your pockets while talking to someone. When you arrive at the airport, you might be greeted by porters with cupped hands. These men are not begging; rather they are indicating that they will be grateful for any tip you may give them.

AMONG AFRICANS. Always receive gifts and reach for things with two hands. Ladies don't always go first; African men usually enter the door before women do. Greetings are usually more involved than a simple "hello"—you should also ask how someone and their family are doing.

ZULUS. If you plan to visit a Zulu village or homestead, wait to enter until people notice you and invite you in. Do not stand when a Zulu chief or high ranking official walks towards you; your head should always be below his. Accept offers of food or drink (refusing them is insulting). Don't be surprised if children are shy when you approach them. People who are younger than you will not make eye contact and will not speak until you address them.

TABOOS. Do not point; it's rude, and it looks like you are trying to challenge someone. Indicate where objects are with an open hand instead. Making a "V" with your middle and index figures with your palm facing your body is very insulting.

THE ARTS

Like most aspects of the nation's culture, South Africa's arts scene is a conglomerate of English, Afrikaner, and African influences. One might hear native music blended with *NSYNC in the same marketplace. Art museums generally display both European and native works alongside one another. Indeed, South Africa's nickname—the "Rainbow Nation"—is perhaps best reflected in its arts.

LITERATURE. The first South African literature in English appeared following the arrival of the 1820 British settlers. **Olive Schreiner's** *The Story of an African Farm* (1883), considered to be the first truly South African novel, provides a realistic account of the stark landscape of a Karoo farm and reflects on European identity in Africa, and on the taming and possessing of the land.

The first novel by a black South African is *Mhudi* (1930), a romantic epic of Tswana life by **Sol Plaatje,** first general secretary of the ANC. It was only after

World War II that short stories, novels and autobiographies by black and "coloured" writers began to convey the realities of life in the townships and to initiate a literature of resistance. **Steve Biko** described the horrors of apartheid in his book *I Write What I Like.* Apartheid resulted in the exile, banning, or imprisonment of these writers and others. In the late 70s, **Staffrider** magazine published—largely for black audiences—radical black writing which can be sampled in *Ten Years of Staffrider* (1988). The best-known black women writers are **Miriam Tlali,** for her *Muriel at Metropolitan* (1975), and **Bessie Head,** who wrote about her place of exile in Botswana in stories such as those in *The Collector of Treasures* (1977), and about her own struggle with identity and madness in the novel *A Question of Power* (1974).

In the post-war period, writers such as **Alan Paton,** internationally acclaimed for his *Cry, The Beloved Country* (1948), and Nobel Prize winner **Nadine Gordimer** began writing novels which revealed black suffering produced by racial injustice, and the guilt and inertia of white liberal consciousness. **Rian Malan** explores his guilt as an Afrikaner in his famous non-fiction work, *My Traitor's Heart* (1991). Of more recent writing, **Nelson Mandela's** autobiography *Long Walk to Freedom* (1994) has been a best-seller. Even more recently, writers have turned to the Truth and Reconciliation Commission for subject matter: **Antjie Krog** has written an autobiographical work, *Country of My Skull* (1998), which deals with her problematic status as Afrikaner, and her role in the TRC hearings.

MUSIC. Far from crushing musical activity, the apartheid government's oppressive laws seem to have forced people to turn to music even more as a way to express their pain, frustration and cultural isolation. While artists at home were compelled to disguise their words by analogy (as in "Weeping," by **Bright Blue**), expatriate artists introduced the beat and strain of South Africa to an international audience.

Probably the most significant 20th-century musicians are the jazz pioneers of the 40s and 50s. The earliest traces of jazz can be found in *marabi* music, often played on organs or accordions, which began in the townships in the 1920s. This evolved into the *kwela* (urban jive) of the 40s and 50s. The **Jazz Epistles** brought together a mix of jazz, classical, and traditional South African music, and were the first black band to produce an album. They were extremely politically conscious, as were many other artists, such as **Miriam Makeba,** and were often banned in South Africa. **Abdullah Ibrahim's** "Cape Town Fringe" (1976) became an anthem for international protest in the wake of the Soweto uprising (see **Apartheid Resistance Movements,** p. 59). With the unraveling of apartheid in 1990, many exiled musicians returned to South Africa to experiment in new directions. **Hugh Masekela** surprised and inspired young fans with his 1995 album *Johannesburg,* which showcases hip-hop, rap, pop, and jazz. But politically conscious musicians were not only black: **Johnny Clegg** is known as the "white Zulu" to his fans because of his close contact with the Zulu people and his use of Zulu musical traditions. Clegg insisted on playing in South Africa with his multiracial band, **Juluka,** to present a racially mixed group to a segregated people. Clegg, whose initial songs were anthems composed for political prisoners, was arrested more than a dozen times by the apartheid government.

The South African music scene got its biggest international boost in the late 80s with the release of **Paul Simon's** *Graceland* album which included the vocals of the Zulu band **Ladysmith Black Mambazo.** Ladysmith is the most well-known exponent of *isicathamiya* songs, an a capella style from communities of Zulu migrant workers. The most popular female musicians include **Brenda Fassie** and **Yvonne Chaka Chaka,** both of whom began producing multi-platinum albums in the 80s and 90s. The country's best-known rap group is **Prophets of Da City,** while the unquestioned king of reggae is **Lucky Dube.** Probably the most popular form of music in recent years is **kwaito,** a staple of urban disco clubs that combines elements of hip-hop, rap, disco, and *mpaqanga.* Its best known artists are **Arthur, Abashante,** and **Boomshaka.** Other popular music forms include the Central African-inspired *soukous* and **kwasa kwasa,** which feature heavy beats juxtaposed with acoustic guitar.

FILM. South African films (both by and about South Africans) can give the traveler a quick, entertaining introduction to the history of the country, if one doesn't mind a little historical distortion now and then. The first films made about South Africa, including D.W. Griffith's **The Zulu's Heart** (1908) and the 1936 film adaptation of H. Rider Haggard's novel **King Solomon's Mines,** were noticeably one-sided, imperial, and often racist. It was not until the 1950s that films began to portray the harsh effects of township life, urban migration, and racial oppression. Sidney Poitier starred in a 1952 film adaptation of Paton's *Cry, the Beloved Country* that powerfully emphasized these themes. In the 1980s, at the height of violence and oppression, a series of films took critical views of the country. Richard Attenborough's 1987 **Cry Freedom** (starring Denzel Washington and Keven Kline) focused on the story of **Steve Biko,** the charismatic leader of the Black Consciousness movement murdered by security police in 1977. The 1989 film **A Dry White Season,** based on Andre Brink's international best-seller, was one of the first films about the apartheid-era made by a black person, **Euzhan Palcy. Shaka Zulu** (1987), tells the story of the famous chieftain (see **Shaka Zulu,** p. 268), and has been linked to Zulu nationalism and received support from Zulu Chief Mangosuthu Buthelezi.

Of course, not all films about South Africa deal with struggle. For anyone interested in safaris, **The Gods Must Be Crazy** (1980), a hilarious and touching story about a tribesman who finds a Coke bottle in the desert and sets out to throw it off the edge of the world, is a must-see.

VISUAL ART. The first artists in South Africa lived about 30,000 years ago, when the San people painted and engraved images on rock walls, stone or terra cotta. (Most of this rock art was discovered in caves in the Northwest Province, near the Vaal River.) Many of the earlier paintings depict tranquil scenes; after the European invasion, scenes of blood and terror are documented instead. The earliest European painters, however, were more interested in topographical issues. Mostly landscape artists, they produced works chiefly for patrons in their native Holland. **Charles Davidson Bell** and **Pieter Wenning** produced realist-romantic depictions of a conquered South Africa. While South African artists did not follow the avant garde trends of European art, some artists, such as **Strat Caldecott, Jan Hendrik Pierneef,** and **Irma Stern** ushered in modernist styles in the early 20th century. It was not until the 60s and 70s that artists expressed a genuine interest in the social realities of the country. In a movement called the **New Humanism,** artists like **Cecil Skotnes** emphasized an emotional response to the realities of South Africa.

Although black artists had little access to formal training in the apartheid era, they nonetheless produced a wide body of work known as **township art.** The first well-known black artists were **Gerard Sekoto** and **G.M. Pemba,** who depicted life in the townships in the first half of the 20th century. Whereas urban blacks have had less opportunity for serious artistic expression, blacks in rural areas who maintain their traditional cultures have contributed a wide array of crafts, murals, and applied arts to South African art. **Zulu beadwork** and **baskets,** for instance, which have been a part of traditional cultures since before colonization, have recently made their way into exhibits and collections throughout the country. **Ndebele** and **Basotho villages,** on the other hand, are magnificent works of art in their own right, the walls of the houses decorated with colorful geometric designs. The truest South African art may lie in artifacts and objects more than in paintings.

SPORTS AND RECREATION

Sport is probably the most popular cultural activity and form of entertainment in the nation. However, during the apartheid era, South Africa was banned from most international sporting events in the world's attempt to put pressure on the government to change. Since South Africa's re-admission in the early 1990s into global sports competitions, the nation has fielded teams in almost all international competitions, including, most recently, the **Soccer World Cup** in June 2002.

RUGBY. Sometimes labeled the "national religion" of South Africa, rugby fervor reached its apex in 1995. That year, the South African **Springboks** hosted, and won, the third **Rugby World Cup,** defeating New Zealand decisively in the championship match. The sport merits some explanation. Rugby looks like a combination of soccer and American football. Players try to score "tries" (touchdowns in US football) by advancing the ball into the end zone; they do so through a series of rushes and lateral passes. There is no forward passing in rugby. "Tries" count for five points and grant the possibility of a two-point conversion. Anyone can punt the ball away at any time. Under rugby rules, you can make contact only with the man carrying the ball; there is no blocking like in American football. And they don't wear any pads in rugby. Not even down there.

There is no rugby season *per se*, at least not in the same sense that there is a baseball season in America. Most games happen as part of tournaments throughout the year. Things kick off around February and end later in the year. Big tournaments include the Suer 12, the Currie Cup, and the World Cup. When in Jo'burg, the Springboks play in Ellis Park. If you're interested in watching rugby while in South Africa, check out the Springbok web site at **www.sarugby.net.** The web page also includes links (in the lower left corner) to amateur rugby leagues.

FOOTBALL (SOCCER). Despite the high-profile nature and competitiveness of South African rugby, football (soccer) is the most popular sport in the country. Although South Africans of all races have competed in the world's football leagues, football is traditionally the major sport of the black population. Anti-apartheid

---

ONE COUNTRY, ONE EMBLEM? Visitors to South
Africa who don't catch sight of the popular Springbok sports team logo simply don't have their eyes open. What may not be so clearly visible is the bitter contest over the meaning of this symbol. Because rugby had long been dominated by Afrikaners, the emblem itself became associated with apartheid. In the mid-1990s, prominent black sports officials began a serious campaign to remove the springbok as the emblem of South African sports teams. It was expected, in 1995, that the springbok would be replaced by the protea, South Africa's national flower. But at the outset of the 1995 Rugby World Cup final (which South Africa won), President Mandela walked out onto the field wearing a Springbok jersey and cap to greet captain Francois Pienaar. The mostly white audience shouted "Nelson! Nelson!" as he walked on and off the field. Shortly afterward, the National Sports Council reconsidered its decision and let the Springboks keep their stirring symbol. The Mbeki government, however, has recently reversed that decision. To the dismay of millions of Springbok fans world wide, the logo is now being phased out and replaced by the protea.

---

groups like the ANC and Steve Biko's Black Consciousness Movement often used football games as an opportunity to voice their concerns to the collected masses of blacks in townships. After the 1990 release of Mandela and other political prisoners, the ANC held rallies in Soweto's First National Bank Stadium, also known as Soccer City, in front of nearly 90,000 people.

CRICKET. Cricket remains an enormously popular spectator sport in South Africa, despite allegations that it is a tad boring. For many years, it was considered an elite and "imperial" game, played in British social clubs and schools. There are now two brands of the sport: one features five-day games, and the other features one-day games. Cricket fields are circular; there is no such thing as a "foul ball" like in baseball. Two sets of wickets stand in the middle of the field. The batsman stands at one wicket; the "bowler" (like a baseball pitcher) at the other. The bowler hurls a hard ball towards the batsman's wicket, only he must do so without bending his throwing arm. There are four ways to get a batter out: hit his wicket on a pitch, catch a ball he has hit, tag him while he is running, or knock down a wicket while he is on the run. The batsman scores every time he moves between the two wickets. A "home run"—hitting the ball out of the park—counts as a six runs.

What makes cricket matches last forever? The batsman only runs if he feels like it. We are not making this up. In five-day cricket, the batsman can sit there all day long blocking bowls. As a result of this, it is very difficult to get batsmen out. Typical five-day cricket scores run into the hundreds. It's not uncommon for a score to be 200-190. One-day cricket is much faster because each team only receives a limited number of "overs" (an over is a group of six bowls). Teams stack their best batsmen at the top of the lineup, and there is a lot more running.

To check on cricket games in South Africa, visit **www.cricket.org/ link_to_database/national/rsa.** The 2003 World Cup will take place in South Africa. Check the web site, or just flip on the TV when you get there.

HOLIDAYS AND FESTIVALS

The evolution of some South Africans holidays manifests how South Africa has changed over the past decade. December 16th—once called the Day of the Vow to celebrate the Boers' pact with God that lead to their victory in the Battle of Blood River—is now Reconciliation Day. Most businesses are closed on holidays. If a public holiday falls on a Sunday, it will be celebrated the following Monday.

Mar. 21: Human Rights Day (anniversary of Sharpeville massacre; see p. 59)

Apr. 17: Family Day

Apr. 27: Constitution Day

May 1: Workers Day

June 16: Youth Day (anniversary of Soweto uprising; see p. 59)

Aug. 9: National Women's Day

Sept. 24: Heritage Day

Dec. 16: Day of Reconciliation

Dec. 26: Day of Good Will

SOUTH AFRICA'S FESTIVALS (2003)

DATE	NAME & LOCATION	DESCRIPTION
New Year's Day	Coon Carnival, Cape Town	This New Year's parade hosted by Cape Town's coloureds has music, street-partying and rollicking good times
March	Mampoer Festival, Zeerust	This festival degenerates into drunken fun as people celebrate *mampoer,* a locally produced brandy.
Early Autumn	Klein Karoo Nasionale Kunstefees, Oudtshoorn	Tens of thousands of people come to this festival every year to celebrate arts and culture done in the Afrikaans language. There is a diverse array of cultural performances, as well as shopping and lots of beer.

DATE	NAME & LOCATION	DESCRIPTION
July	National Arts Festival, Grahamstown	Art, opera, film, student works and more are presented at this popular festival. There are also plays in many different South African languages.
October	Food and Wine Festival, Stellenbosch	Here you can try the region's famous wines.
Third week of October	Jacaranda Festival, Pretoria	Held while the Jacaranda trees are in full bloom, this festival has food, entertainment, and a flea market.

ADDITIONAL RESOURCES

GENERAL HISTORY

■ *Illustrated History of South Africa* (1994), published by Reader's Digest. One of the most popular (and colorful) history textbooks, it contains a good overview of South African history with numerous pictures.

Grounds of Contest (1990), by Malvern Van Wyck Smith. A useful survey of South African English literature; it is a vital piece in the establishment of the South African literary canon.

Twentieth-Century South Africa (1994), by William Beinart. Perhaps a bit too academic in tone for many readers, but interesting nevertheless. A useful 250-page outline of all the major events of the last 100 years.

FICTION AND NON-FICTION

The works listed below make good reading for most contemporary audiences. For additional suggestions related to South Africa's literary history, see **Literature,** p. 65.

■ *Cry, the Beloved Country* (1948), by Alan Paton. One of the most significant novels in South African history.

■ *The Power of One* (1989), by Bryce Courtenay. An excellent novel narrated by an English boy who grows up during the beginning of the apartheid era.

■ *Disgrace* (1999) by J.M. Coetzee. Winner the Booker Prize and widely regarded as Coetzee's finest. Good insight into Cape Town life.

Fools (1983), by Njabulo Ndebele. Stories of growing up in Soweto.

My Son's Story (1991), by Nadine Gordimer. Gordimer, who won a Nobel Prize in Literature, produced a number of books on life in South Africa. *My Son's Story*, at under 300 pages, is a somewhat confusing but shorter novel.

To Every Birth (1981), by Mongane Wally Serote. Describes in narrative form the infamous 1976 Soweto uprising.

FILM

Shaka Zulu (1987), dir. William Faure. Available as a miniseries and a more condensed movie, *Shaka Zulu* tells the story of the "most savage warrior of all time." In the US, the miniseries appears on TBS periodically.

Cry, the Beloved Country (1995), dir. Darrell Roodt. Based on Paton's classic novel (see above), this version stars James Earl Jones and Richard Harris.

Mandela (1987), dir. Philip Saville. A made-for-TV (and relatively low-quality) movie about the life of Nelson Mandela.

Cry Freedom (1987), dir. Richard Attenborough. The plot grows out of the assassination of activist Steve Biko. Features Kevin Kline and Denzel Washington.

The Power of One (1992), dir. John Avildsen. A vastly inferior retelling of Bryce Courtenay's classic novel. The film has some merits, but fans of the book will be gravely disappointed by the cheesy Hollywood-induced story variations.

ESSENTIALS

DOCUMENTS AND FORMALITIES

For information on visas, please see p. 11.

EMBASSIES AND CONSULATES ABROAD

Australia: Corner of Rhodes Place and State Circle, Yarralumla, Canberra (☎02 6273 2424; fax 02 6273 3543; info@rsa.emb.gov.au; www.rsa.emb.gov.au).

Botswana: Plot 5131 Kopanyo House, 3rd fl., Nelson Mandela Dr., Gaborone (☎267 30 48 00; fax 30 55 01/2).

Canada: 15 Sussex Dr., Ottawa, Ontario (☎613 744 0330; fax 613 711 1639; Consulate-General, Suite 2615, 1 Pl. Ville Marie, Montréal, Quebec (☎514 878 9217; fax 878 4751; sacongen@total.net; www.docuweb.ca/SouthAfrica).

Ireland: Alexandra House, 2nd fl., Earlsfort Ctr., Earlsfort Terr., Dublin (☎661 5553; fax 661 5590).

Malawi: Impco Building, Lilongwe (☎265 730 888).

Namibia: RSA House, Windhoek (☎61 205 7111; fax 61 22 4140 or 61 23 6093), at the corner of Jan Jonker and Nelson Mandela Ave.

UK: South Africa House, Trafalgar Sq., London (☎020 7451 7290/9; fax 020 7925 0367; general@southafricahouse.com; www.southafricahouse.com).

US: 3051 Massachusetts Ave. NW, Washington DC (☎202 232 4400; fax 202 265 1607; www.southafrica.net); 333 E. 38th St., 9th fl., New York City, NY (☎212 213 4880; fax 213 0102; sacg@southafrica-newyork.net; www.southafrica-newyork.net).

Zimbabwe: 7 Elcombe Ave., Belgravia, Harare (☎04 753 147-9/150-3; fax 04 908 or 04 753 187).

EMBASSIES AND CONSULATES IN SOUTH AFRICA

All the following embassies and consulates are in Pretoria unless otherwise noted.

Australia: 292 Orient St., Arcadia (☎12 342 3740; fax 12 342 8442); BP Ctr., 14th fl., Thibault Sq., Cape Town (☎21 419 5425/9; fax 21 419 7345; australia@new.co.za; www.australia.co.za).

Botswana: 24 Amos St., Colbyn (☎12 342 4760/1/2/3/4; fax 342 1845). 122 De Korte St., Braamfontein, Johannesburg (☎11 403 37480).

Canada: 1103 Arcadia St., Hatfield (☎12 422 3000; fax 12 422 3052; pret@dfait-maeci.gc.ca).

Ireland: Delheim Suite, Tulbach Park, 1234 Church St., Colbyn (☎12 342 5062; fax 12 342 4752).

Israel: Dashing Ctr., 339 Hilda St., Hatfield (☎12 421 2222/3/4; fax 12 342 1442).

Lesotho: 391 Anderson St., Menlo Park (☎12 467648; fax 12 467649).

Malawi: Embassy, PO Box 11172, Brooklyn (☎12 477 853).

Mozambique: 199 Beckett St. (☎12 343 7840; fax 12 343 6714).

Namibia: 702 Church St., Arcadia (☎12 344 5992; fax 12 344 5998).

The Netherlands: 825 Arcadia St. (☎12 344 3910; fax 12 343 9950; eapret@dutchembassy.co.za; www.dutchembassy.co.za).

New Zealand: Hatfield Gardens, Block C, 2nd fl., 1110 Arcadia St., Hatfield (☎12 342 8656/7/8; fax 12 342 8640).

Swaziland: 715 Government Ave. (☎12 344 1910; fax 12 343 0455), at Blackwood.

UK: 256 Glyn St., Hatfield (☎ 12483 1400; fax 483 1400; bhc@icon.co.za); 91 Parliament St., Cape Town (☎ 21 461 7220; fax 21 461 0017; britain@icon.co.za).

US: 877 Pretorius St., Arcadia (☎ 342 1048; fax 342 2244; SNewman@pd.state.gov; www.usembassy.state.gov/pretoria).

Zimbabwe: 798 Merton Ave., Arcadia (☎ 12 342 5125; fax 12 342 5126).

CURRENCY AND EXCHANGE

South Africa's currency unit is the **rand (R).** **ATM machines** and credit cards are more commonly accepted in South Africa than in other parts of Southern Africa and using an ATM or credit card will often get you better exchange rates. The most common **credit cards** are MasterCard (MC), Visa (V), and Diner's Club (DC). If you stay in hostels and prepare your own food, expect to spend anywhere from US$15 to $25 per person per day. Accommodations start at about US$8 per night for a dorm bed, while a basic sit-down meal costs US$5. Prices and living costs tend to be highest in the cities, especially in Cape Town, and considerably lower in towns and less developed areas. Personal checks are only very rarely accepted, and you should not expect to be able to pay for anything directly with traveler's checks.

HEALTH AND SAFETY

Emergency: (☎ 10 111). Free connection to police, ambulance, fire department. **Ambulance** ☎ 10 177.

South African Airways Travel Clinic: (☎ 0800 000 2609; www.travelclinic.co.za). Free travel advice on vaccinations, diagnosis, treatment, and care and the best source for info on malarial areas in Southern Africa.

Travelphone: (☎ 083 901 1011). 24hr. information service for tourists.

KEEPING IN TOUCH

TELEPHONES. A **calling card** is probably your cheapest bet for placing international calls. Calls are billed collect or to your account. **MCI WorldPhone** also provides access to **MCI's Traveler's Assist,** which gives legal and medical advice, exchange rate information, and translation services. Other phone companies provide similar services. **To obtain a calling card** from your national telecommunications service before leaving home, contact the appropriate company below:

Australia: Telstra **Australia Direct** (☎ 13 22 00).

Canada: Bell Canada **Direct** (☎ 800 565 4708).

Ireland: Telecom Éireann **Ireland Direct** (☎ 800 25 02 50).

New Zealand: Telecom New Zealand (☎ 0800 00 00 00).

South Africa: Telkom South Africa (☎ 09 03).

UK: British Telecom **BT Direct** (☎ 800 34 51 44).

US: AT&T (☎ 800-222-0300), **MCI** (☎ 800-950-5555), **Sprint** (☎ 800-877-4646).

When **dialing from outside South Africa,** omit the 0 at the beginning of the area code, but use it when dialing within the country. Public phones are coin- or card-operated. You can buy phone cards at post offices and airports. Wherever possible, use a calling card for international phone calls, as the long-distance rates for national phone services are often exorbitant. (Most coin phones are broken, as well.) You can usually make direct international calls from pay phones, but if you aren't using a calling card you may need to drop coins as quickly as words. **Prepaid phone cards** can be used in card-operated phones for direct international calls, but they are still less cost-efficient, and can only be purchased in denominations of up to R50—small amounts which are quickly devoured by Telkom South Africa's outrageous international rates. Look for pay phones in public areas, especially train stations, since private pay phones are often more expensive. Although incredibly convenient, in-room hotel calls invariably include an arbitrary and sky-high surcharge.

The expensive alternative to dialing direct or using a calling card is having an international operator place a **collect call (reverse charges)**. An English-speaking operator from your home country can be reached by dialing a service provider listed above, who typically place collect calls even if you don't have their card.

 PLACING INTERNATIONAL CALLS. To call Southern Africa from home or to place an international call from Southern Africa, dial:

1. The **international dialing prefix.** To dial out of **Australia,** dial 0011; **Canada** or the **US,** 011; the **Republic of Ireland, Zimbabwe, Lesotho, Swaziland, Botswana, New Zealand,** or the **UK,** 00; **Namibia** or **South Africa,** 09.

2. The **country code** of the country you want to call. To call **Australia,** dial 61; **Botswana,** 267; **Canada** or the **US,** 1; the **Republic of Ireland,** 353; **Lesotho,** 266; **Namibia,** 264; **New Zealand,** 64; **South Africa,** 27; **Swaziland,** 268; the **UK,** 44; **Zimbabwe,** 263.

3. The **city** or **area code.** *Let's Go* lists the phone codes for cities and towns opposite the city or town name, alongside the following icon: ☎. If the first digit is a zero (e.g., 020 for London), omit it when calling from abroad (e.g., dial 011 44 20 from Canada to reach London).

4. The **local number.**

For **directory assistance** within South Africa, **call 1023.** For general information, **call 10 118.** The simplest way to call within the country is to use a coin-operated phone. You can also buy prepaid phone cards. Every time you make a call, the phone charges the fee to your card until it has been exhausted. Always keep a spare phone card handy. Cards are generally sold at post offices, gas stations, and Telkom offices. Phone rates tend to be highest in the morning, lower in the evening, and lowest on Sunday and late at night. To call within other Southern African countries, see those **Essentials** sections.

MAIL. Airmail averages 4-8 days to the US and Europe and 1-2 weeks to Canada, Australia, and New Zealand, although times are less predictable when sending mail from smaller towns. (Mark "airmail" or "par avion" to avoid slow surface mail, which takes one to three months to cross the Atlantic and two to four to cross the Pacific.) Aerogrammes take less time, but don't try to sneak anything in your aerogramme besides your words; most post offices will charge exorbitant fees or simply refuse to send aerogrammes with enclosures.

It is usually safer and quicker, though more expensive, to send mail express or registered. Bring your passport (or other photo ID) for pick-up. **Federal Express** (US and Canada ☎800 247 4747; Australia ☎132 610; New Zealand ☎0800 733 339; UK ☎0800 123 800; www.fedex.com) can get a letter from New York to Johannesburg in three days for a whopping US$65 ($68 with pick-up); London to Johannesburg GBP30. By US Express Mail, a letter from New York would arrive within two business days (although they can make no guarantees) and costs about US$20.

Go to www.southafrica.co.za/postal.html for postal codes within South Africa.

INTERNET. Internet access is widespread in South Africa, even in the smaller towns. Impromptu email stations can be found in tourist offices, hostels, and occasionally people's homes, but cybercafes are the hip place to head in the bigger cities. These places are listed in the Orientation and Practical Information sections of cities and towns wherever Internet services are available. If in doubt, ask at the visitor center or tourism office. **Cybercafe Guide** (www.cyberiacafe.net/cyberia/guide/ccafe.htm) has a few listings in South Africa.

Though in some cases it is possible to forge a remote link with your home server, in most cases this is slower (and more expensive) than taking advantage of free **web-based email accounts,** including Hotmail (www.hotmail.com), RocketMail (www.rocketmail.com), and Yahoo! Mail (www.yahoo.com).

Travelers with laptops can use a modem to call an Internet service provider. Long-distance phone cards intended for such calls can defray high phone charges. Check with your long-distance phone provider to see if they offer this option.

TIME DIFFERENCE. South Africa is two hours ahead of GMT, one hour ahead of Central European Winter Time, and seven hours ahead of US Eastern Standard Winter Time. South Africa does not observe daylight savings time.

FROM WHERE I STAND
Life After Apartheid

Decades of resistance against apartheid came to an abrupt end with the release of Nelson Mandela, affectionately known as Madiba. February 1990, though inevitable, was still a surprise to the country. Although there had been rumors of his imminent release, these were, at the time, as unbelievable as the concept of apartheid itself.

Following Mandela's release, a multiparty Congress for Democratic South Africa (CODESA) was constituted. Its main aim was to prepare for and develop the constitution that would govern a democratic South Africa. The new Interim Constitution became effective April 27,1994 and the final constitution was completed two years later. The interdependence of transformation, reconciliation and reconstruction necessitated the constitution of The Truth and Reconciliation Commission (TRC) in 1995, which was mandated to deal with the violence and human right abuses that took place during apartheid. It was a tough process for many to embrace especially the victims. Most believed that justice was not being served, but they participated in the quest for the truth hoping it would help them move beyond their pain and suffering.

The run up to the April 1994 election was a particularly trying and exciting time. The groups that had been unified so strongly against apartheid were being rocked by political violence and resistant action from the right-wing political parties. At the same time the atmosphere was electric, pregnant with promise and hope of a 'better future for all'. Few days will ever be as memorable as April 27, 1994, the day of the first democratic elections, now commemorated as Freedom Day. The lines outside most voting stations stretched for miles, with people queuing for days in the scorching sun for that one minute when they would exercise their democratic rights and cast their votes for the very first time in history.

Many promises were made in the run up to the 1994 elections. For the majority of citizens, freedom promised—among other things—proper housing, clean water, electricity, food, quality education and health services. It also meant that one could go to any beach, any public place and drink from any tap. Freedom meant deliverance from whatever thorn bush was one's individual reality. Since becoming democratic, the government has made steady progress in addressing apartheid's legacy of inequality and poverty. Millions of people now have access to services that they were previously denied. Macroeconomic stability has been achieved, the country's standing in the international community and in particular as a voice for Africa's development has been acknowledged, and two successful democratic elections have been held. Slowly, South Africans are uniting to eradicate the legacies of the past.

A lot of work remains. It is impossible to describe the damage that apartheid has inflicted and the concentrated effort it will take to deliver on election promises. South Africans are realizing that the government alone will not be able to deliver them to the Promised Land. They recognize the importance of embracing the process, being proactive, persistent, patient and tolerant. This is unlike any other previous struggle they have faced; the enemy is not singular nor tangible or definable. Success requires strong leadership from all sectors of society. Recently, the country celebrated the 25th anniversary of the June 16 Soweto riots, the day youth took to the streets in open defiance of the apartheid government. Today youths are asking what they can do to participate constructively in this new struggle.

As South Africa seeks to deal with its domestic challenges, it remains involved in issues relating to the development of Africa, Southern Africa, and the world, recognizing that no country can solve its own problems and achieve lasting prosperity in isolation. The government has shown commitment to Africa's recovery through its efforts around the development of the New Partnership for Africa's Development (NEPAD) and the mobilization of support within the G8.

South Africa remains committed to building a united nation fighting for change. The unbreakable spirit of its people and their unshakable optimism provides the confidence that their dedicated efforts will deliver on the promises of democracy and freedom.

Mamongae Mahlare, a native of South Africa, worked for the international consulting firm Bain & Co. in South Africa.

WESTERN CAPE

The undulating landscape of the Western Cape bursts with enticing activities. The breathtaking accumulation of beautiful beaches, majestic mountains, ragged rock formations, and wildflowers that explode into color every spring creates a full spectrum of delights for the annual tourist hordes. This is one spot where you might want to eschew game-watching for people-watching. A stampede of party-goers lets loose in Cape Town, adventure activities quench every animalistic yearning for adrenaline, and the stellar winelands encourage visitors to drink up. This is not to say that the Western Cape lacks its own natural wonders: the annual migration of Southern Right whales, the hopping year-round marine life, the adorable assemblies of jackass penguins, and the roaming ostriches of the Karoo provide a counterpoint to the wealth of human hedonism. The region's flora creates a particular hue for the Western Cape, with verdant mountains gracefully jutting above the beaches of powdery sand and chilly waters.

The Western and Northern Cape are the only two provinces in South Africa without a black majority, in part because the Cape was repeatedly colonized by Europeans from the 17th to the 19th century. The Dutch first arrived in 1652, quickly followed by French, German, and Belgian settlers, and then by the British in 1795. Today, Afrikaners and English-speaking whites still live throughout the region. The majority of the people, however, are "coloureds"—a term which itself hides incredible variations—wvmho comprise 55% of the population. Xhosas make up the majority of the black population.

The diversity of the province attracts tourists as eclectic as the locals. Surfers and nature lovers, rock climbers and wine buffs, club-hoppers and backpackers all come to the Western Cape to indulge in the region's riches. Due to the area's remarkable budget tourism infrastructure, travelers on a tight budget will enjoy extravagant luxuries and unending hospitality for a pittance.

HIGHLIGHTS OF THE WESTERN CAPE

CAPE TOWN. Just about anything here is a true highlight, from the gripping history of Mandela's imprisonment at **Robben Island** (see p. 101) to the magnificent trails that ascend **Table Mountain** (see p. 108).

CAPE OF GOOD HOPE NATURE RESERVE. On the way to the awesome reserve (see p. 118), swim with the endearing jackass penguins of **Boulder's Beach** (see p. 116) before fighting off baboons at the picture-perfect **Cape Point** (see p. 108).

WINELANDS. While here, sample the vintages that put South African vineyards on the map (see p. 119) while admiring the green-gabled Cape Dutch architecture.

GARDEN ROUTE. Along the scenic gem (see p. 151), dive with sharks, go bungee jumping, or ride on Africa's oldest steam train, the **Outeniqua Choo-Tjoe** (p. 156).

CEDERBERG WILDERNESS AREA. Whitewater-raft down the Olifants River (see p. 180), and catch a glimpse of *fynbos* flora, the region's pride.

CAPE TOWN ☎ 021

Cape Town is known as the "Mother City," and like all mothers, she will leave a permanent mark upon your psyche. With any luck, therapy will not be required. Her landscape is both stunning and isolating—the presence of the titanic Table Mountain and the myriad beaches conspire to separate the metropolis from the rest of South Africa and the world at large. South Africa's most diverse city, Cape Town proves dizzying and dazzling in its limitless range of possibilities.

Still, beneath its glamorous veneer, Cape Town offers numerous insights into the pulse of the New South Africa. The vibrant scene around Long St., Kloof St., and Loop St. equals any hotspot elsewhere in the nation. The residue of apartheid is still apparent in the townships that push against the edges of the city and in nearby wealthy wine estates. These distinct realms produce a kaleidoscopic effect; the very nature of Cape Town shifts and evolves throughout different areas of the city. Cape Town embodies a range of experiences that are challenging, exhilarating, and, ultimately, irresistible.

HIGHLIGHTS OF CAPE TOWN

TABLE MOUNTAIN. This giant (p. 108) serves as backbone and backdrop for the city. Climbing or riding up and down the sides of the behemoth is always breathtaking.

DISTRICT SIX. This area (p. 99), along with the **Bo-Kaap** (p. 100) and the **Cape Flats** (p. 102) are musts for anyone interested in South Africa's past and present.

THE V&A WATERFRONT. Here, you'll fine packs of tourists (p. 101), but the worthwhile sights there **Robben Island** (p. 101) and the **Two Oceans Aquarium** (p. 101).

CAMPS BAY. Worship the sun and toast its farewell with sundowners (p. 105).

CAPE POINT. Wave to the bontebok and baboons (p. 108) and swim with the penguins at **Boulder's Beach** (p. 116).

◪ INTERCITY TRANSPORTATION

FLIGHTS

Airport: Cape Town International Airport (☎934 0407), 22km from the city center, is tiny and more pleasant than Johannesburg's airport. Captour **tourist information desks** in both the domestic and international terminals provide maps, brochures, and suggestions for accommodations. Reserve accommodations ahead of time—most hostels and B&Bs offer discounted or free airport pick-up. **The Backpackers Bus** will drive you to your accommodation from anywhere in the city. (☎082 809 9185; after hours ☎462 5888; bpackbus@mweb.co.za. Reserve in advance. 8am-6pm, R70; 6pm-8am, R90.) **Taxis** go into the city for R140, but the price can be bargained down.

Airlines: All airfares listed are for 14-day advance purchase and include VAT.

British Airways/Comair (☎683 4203) to **Durban** (2hr., 2-4 per day 6:45am-5:30pm, R1899) and **Johannesburg** (1hr., 7-13 per day 6:45am-7:05pm, R1899).

National Airlines (☎934 0350; fax 934 3373; www.nac.co.za/nationalairlines/natairmain.html) to **Springbok** (1½hr., M-F 8am, R2964).

Nationwide Air (☎936 2050; www.nationwideair.co.za) to **Johannesburg** (2hr., 3-4 per day 7am-5:45pm, R810).

South African Airways/Express/Airlink (☎936 1111; www.saa.co.za) to: **Durban** (2hr., 5-7 daily 6:30am-7pm, R1259); **East London** (1½hr., 2-3 per day 6am-6:15pm, R1234); **George** (1hr., 2-5 per day 6:30am-4:30pm, R1006); **Johannesburg** (2hr., 18-28 per day 6am-9:05pm, R1348); **Kimberley** (2hr.; M-F 6:40am and 4pm, Su 3pm; R2193); **Port Elizabeth** (1hr., 3-6 per day 6:10am-5:15pm, R732); **Upington** (1½hr., Su-F 3:15pm, R1280).

TRAINS

Station: Along Adderley St. from Hans Strijdom down to Strand, next to Golden Acre Mall. Bustling hub with a huge outside market and several travel offices. Sheltered inside is South Africa's first steam locomotive. Be aware of your valuables, as the station, particularly after dusk, attracts a rag-tag crew of petty thieves and pickpockets.

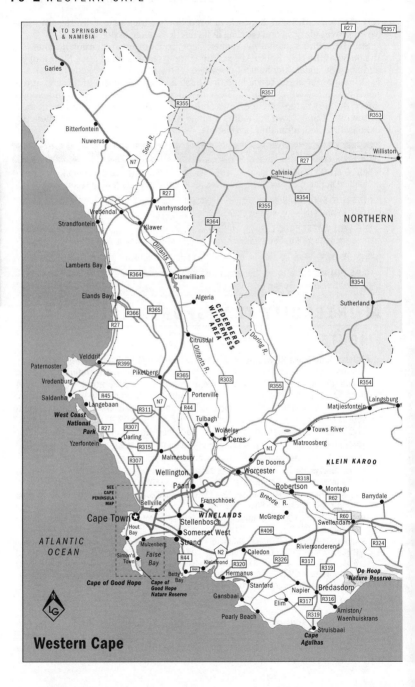

WESTERN CAPE

TO SPRINGBOK & NAMIBIA

Garies

Bitterfontein
Nuwerus

Vredendal
Strandfontein
Klawer

Lamberts Bay

Elands Bay

Velddrif
Paternoster
Vredenburg
Saldanha
Langebaan

West Coast National Park

Yzerfontein

Darling

Malmesbury

Wellington
Paarl

Bellville

Cape Town

Hout Bay

ATLANTIC OCEAN

Simon's Town

False Bay

Muizenberg

Cape of Good Hope

Betty's Bay

Cape of Good Hope Nature Reserve

Sout R.

Olifants R.

Vanrhynsdorp

Clanwilliam

Algeria

CEDERBERG WILDERNESS AREA

Citrusdal

Olifants R.

Piketberg

Porterville

Tulbagh
Wolseley
Ceres

Stellenbosch
Somerset West
Strand

WINELANDS

Franschhoek

Kleinmond
Hermanus
Stanford
Gansbaai

Pearly Beach

Calvinia

Doring R.

NORTHERN

Williston

Sutherland

Matjiesfontein
Laingsburg

Touws River
Matroosberg

KLEIN KAROO

De Doorns
Worcester

Robertson
Montagu
Barrydale

McGregor

Swellendam

Breede R.

Caledon
Riviersonderend

De Hoop Nature Reserve

Napier
Bredasdorp

Elim
Arniston/Waenhuiskrans

Struisbaai

Cape Agulhas

N7
R27
R27
R357
R355
R357
R353
R354
R355
R27
R364
R364
R365
R366
R27
R399
R45
R311
R27
R307
R307
R315
R44
R303
R355
R354
N7
N1
R318
R62
R60
R324
R406
N2
R44
R320
R326
R317
R319
R317
R316
R319

SEE CAPE PENINSULA MAP

N
LG

Western Cape

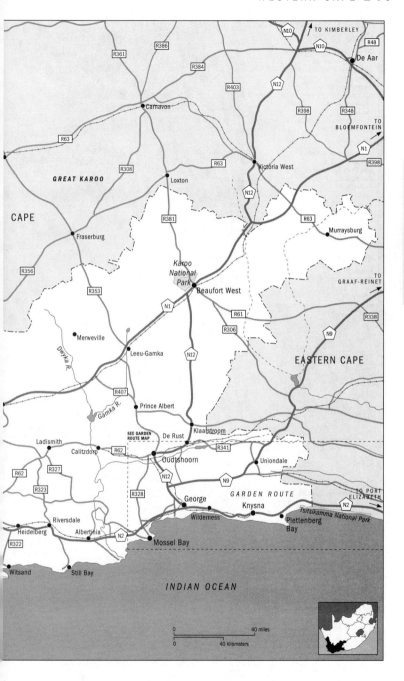

WESTERN CAPE

TO KIMBERLEY
N10
N10
R48
De Aar
R361
R386
R384
R403
N12
R398
R348
TO BLOEMFONTEIN
Carnavon
N1
R63
R308
R63
Victoria West
R398
GREAT KAROO
Loxton
N12
R63
CAPE
R381
Murraysburg
Fraserburg
Karoo National Park
R356
TO GRAAF-REINET
R353
Beaufort West
N1
R61
R338
Merweville
R306
N9
Leeu-Gamka
N12
EASTERN CAPE
Dwyka R.
R407
Gamka R.
Prince Albert
Klaarstroom
SEE GARDEN ROUTE MAP
De Rust
Ladismith
R341
Calitzdorp
R62
Oudtshoorn
Uniondale
R62
R327
N12
N9
R323
R328
GARDEN ROUTE
TO PORT ELIZABETH
George
N2
Riversdale
Wilderness
Knysna
Tsitsikamma National Park
Heidelberg
Albertinia
N2
Plettenberg Bay
R322
Mossel Bay
Witsand
Still Bay

INDIAN OCEAN

0   40 miles
0   40 kilometers

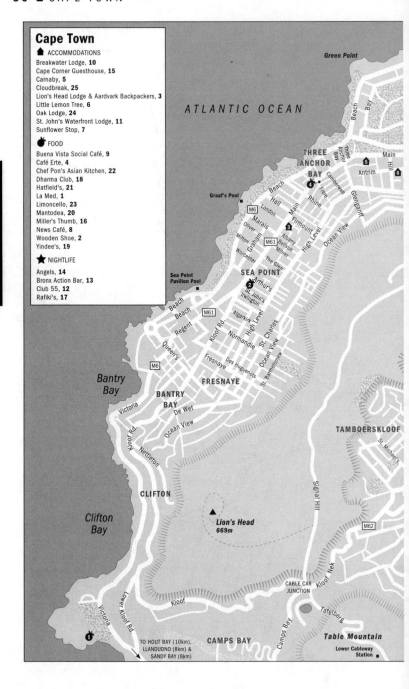

Cape Town

🏠 ACCOMMODATIONS

Breakwater Lodge, **10**
Cape Corner Guesthouse, **15**
Carnaby, **5**
Cloudbreak, **25**
Lion's Head Lodge & Aardvark Backpackers, **3**
Little Lemon Tree, **6**
Oak Lodge, **24**
St. John's Waterfront Lodge, **11**
Sunflower Stop, **7**

🍴 FOOD

Buena Vista Social Café, **9**
Café Erte, **4**
Chef Pon's Asian Kitchen, **22**
Dharma Club, **18**
Hatfield's, **21**
La Med, **1**
Limoncello, **23**
Mantodea, **20**
Miller's Thumb, **16**
News Café, **8**
Wooden Shoe, **2**
Yindee's, **19**

⭐ NIGHTLIFE

Angels, **14**
Bronx Action Bar, **13**
Club 55, **12**
Rafiki's, **17**

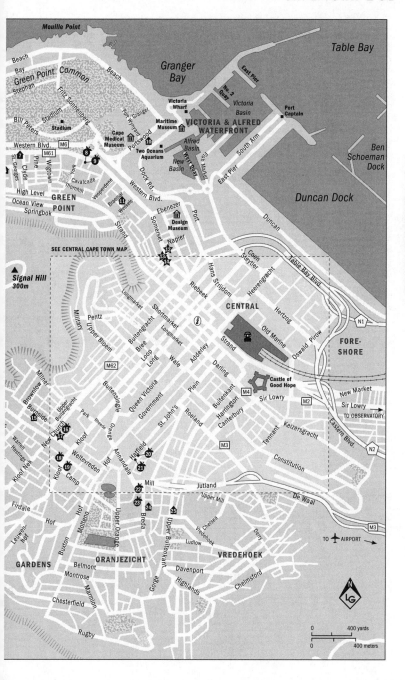

WESTERN CAPE

Table Bay

Mouille Point

Beach
Bay
Green Point Common
Stephan
Fritz Sonnenberg

Granger Bay

East Pier

Bill Peters
Stadium
Stadium
Western Blvd.
M6
M61
Wigtown
Pine
Clyde
St. Georges
Cavalcade
Thornhill
High Level
Ocean View
Springbok

No. 2 Quay

Victoria Wharf

Victoria Basin

Port Captain

Cape Medical Museum
Portswood
10
Two Oceans Aquarium

Maritime Museum
VICTORIA & ALFRED WATERFRONT

Alfred Basin

New Basin

Ben Schoeman Dock

South Arm

East Pier

Duncan Dock

Tort Wynyard
Granger
Dock Rd.
Western Blvd.
Strand
Braemar
Wessels
Vesperdene

GREEN POINT

Ebenezer

Design Museum
Somerset
Napier

Port

Duncan

SEE CENTRAL CAPE TOWN MAP

12
13
14

▲ Signal Hill 300m

Table Bay Blvd.

Coen Steytler
Hans Strijdom
Heerengracht
Hertzog

Riebeek

CENTRAL

N1

FORE-SHORE

Military
Pentz
Upper Bloem

Longmarket
Shortmarket
Buitengracht
Bree
Loop
Long
Longmarket
Wale
Adderley
Strand
Darling
Old Marine
Oswald Pirow

M62

Brownlow
Burnside
15
Upper Buitengracht
New Church
16
17
18
19
Kloof
Camp
Weltevreden
Warren
Hastings
Kloof Nek

Park
Rheede
Orange
Queen Victoria
Government
St. John's
Plein
Roeland
Buitenkant
Harrington
Canterbury
Sir Lowry

Castle of Good Hope
M4

New Market

Sir Lowry
TO OBSERVATORY

M2

N2

Eastern Blvd.

Keizersgracht
Tennant
Constitution

M3

Firdale
Leeuwen
hof
Hof

Buxton
Molteno
Upper Orange
Annandale
Hatfield
20
21
Mill
22
23
24
Breda
25
Jutland
Upper Mill
De Waal

Chelsea
Vredehoek
Chelmsford

M3

TO ✈ AIRPORT →

GARDENS
Belmont
Montrose
Marmion
Chesterfield
Rugby

ORANJEZICHT
Davenport
Highlands
Ludlow

VREDEHOEK

Upper Buitenkant
Gorge

N

0   400 yards
0   400 meters

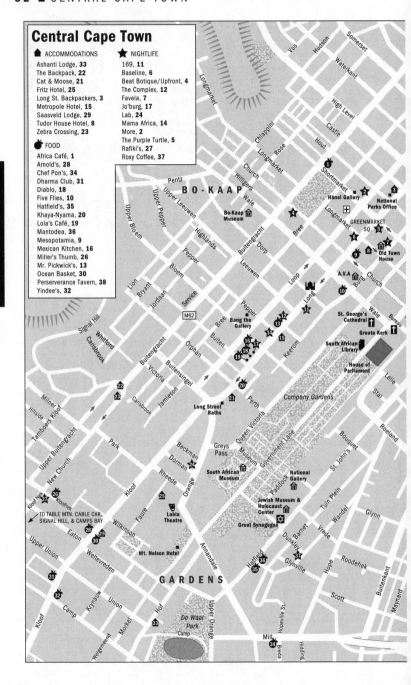

Central Cape Town

🏠 ACCOMMODATIONS

Ashanti Lodge, **33**
The Backpack, **22**
Cat & Moose, **21**
Fritz Hotel, **25**
Long St. Backpackers, **3**
Metropole Hotel, **15**
Saasveld Lodge, **29**
Tudor House Hotel, **8**
Zebra Crossing, **23**

🍎 FOOD

Africa Café, **1**
Arnold's, **28**
Chef Pon's, **34**
Dharma Club, **31**
Diablo, **18**
Five Flies, **10**
Hatfield's, **35**
Khaya-Nyama, **20**
Lola's Café, **19**
Mantodea, **36**
Mesopotamia, **9**
Mexican Kitchen, **16**
Miller's Thumb, **26**
Mr. Pickwick's, **13**
Ocean Basket, **30**
Perserverance Tavern, **38**
Yindee's, **32**

⭐ NIGHTLIFE

169, **11**
Baseline, **6**
Beat Botique/Upfront, **4**
The Complex, **12**
Favela, **7**
Jo'burg, **17**
Lab, **24**
Mama Africa, **14**
More, **2**
The Purple Turtle, **5**
Rafiki's, **27**
Roxy Coffee, **37**

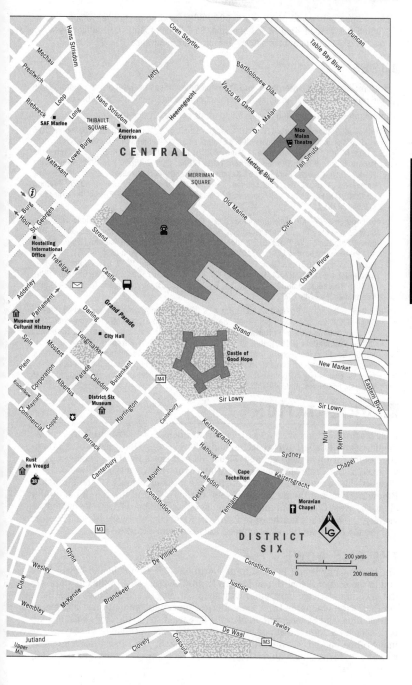

WESTERN CAPE

Lines: Spoornet (☎449 3871 or 086 000 8888; www.spoornet.co.za). Office open M-Tu and Th-F 7:30am-4pm, W 7:30am-3pm, Sa 7:30-10:45am. 40% student discounts on 2nd-class round-trip tickets in low season. Book in advance.

BUSES

Station: Greyhound, Intercape, and **Translux** have offices and departure points beside the train station along Adderley St., across from the intersection with Riebeeck St.

Companies: Prices are all one-way; round-trip is generally twice the fare.

Greyhound, 1 Adderley St. (☎418 4310; www.greyhound.co.za). Office open daily 8am-8pm. 10% student discount, 20% for seniors off-peak times, under 12 half-price. To: **Durban** (22¼hr., daily 11am, R390) via **Bloemfontein** (12¾hr., R305), **Harrismith** (18hr., R365), and **Pietermaritzburg** (21hr., R390); **Durban southern route** (26hr., daily 7:45pm, R390) via **Swellendam** (2¼hr., R80), **George** (7¼hr., R125), **Knysna** (8hr., R150), **Port Elizabeth** (12½hr., R205), **Grahamstown** (14hr., R220), **East London** (17hr., R230), and **Umtata** (19¾hr., R325); **Pretoria northern route** (20½hr., daily 8pm, R285) via **Kimberley** (12¾hr., R260) and **Johannesburg** (19½hr., R285).

Intercape (☎386 4400; www.intercape.co.za). Open daily 6am-6pm. Reservations desk open daily 8am-5pm. 24hr. phone reservations. 15% student discount, 10% senior discount. To: **Durban** (22hr.; Su, M, W, F; R375) via **Bloemfontein** (13hr., R270), **Harrismith** (16¾hr., R350), and **Pietermaritzburg** (21½hr., R370); **George** (6½hr., R125); **Knysna** (8hr., R135); **Port Elizabeth** (11½hr., R190), via George and Knysna; **Pretoria** (20½hr.; M, W, F, Su 8pm; R270) via **Johannesburg** (19hr., R270); **Upington** (11hr.; Su, M, W, F 6:15pm; R220) via **Citrusdal** (3hr., R125); **Windhoek, Namibia** (19½hr.; Su, Tu, Th, F; R380), via **Springbok** (8hr., R240), and **Keetmanshoop** (14hr., R320).

Baz Bus, 8 Rosedene Rd. (☎439 2323; fax 439 2343; info@bazbus.com; www.bazbus.com), in Sea Point. Office open daily 8am-8pm. The door-to-door, hop-on, hop-off route runs from Cape Town to: **Johannesburg/Pretoria** (R1500, round-trip R2500 via Swaziland), via **Hermanus** (R90); **Swellendam** (R160), through the Garden Route to **Port Elizabeth** (R655, round-trip R930); **East London** (R850); **Umtata** (R995); **Durban** (R1275, round-trip R1700), continuing north either through **St. Lucia** (R1525) and **Mbabane, Swaziland** (R1650). There are also direct fares to towns along the Garden Route and the south coast to Durban, with prices comparable to the main line buses. AmEx/DC/MC/V.

◪ ORIENTATION

Table Mountain, which overlooks the city from a height of 1000m, provides a spine-tingling view of Cape Town's beaches and suburbs (see p. 108), and acts as a reference point for those who get lost. **Signal Hill** and **Lion's Head** are smaller bumps annexed to the Table Mountain range. The **N2** runs between Cape Town and Port Elizabeth along the Garden Route; the **N1** runs to Johannesburg via the Karoo and Bloemfontein; and the **N7** goes between Cape Town and the Namibian border along the West Coast, continuing to Windhoek as Namibia's **B1.** In the immediate vicinity, the **N1** heads northeast to Paarl, the **R102** cuts eastward to Stellenbosch, and the **M4** heads south to Muizenberg, Kalk Bay, and Simon's Town.

THE CITY BOWL

The bustling city center lies just to the north of Table Mountain and Devil's Peak and to the east of Signal Hill and Lion's Head. The real pulse of the city throbs in the accommodations, bars, and funky shops of **Long, Kloof,** and **Loop St.** A more cerebral vibe emanates from the galleries, museums, and cultural intrigue of **Church, Bree,** and **Buitengracht St.** near the **Bo-Kaap** district (the city's Muslim quarter). **Adderley St.** and the **Strand** host the more commercial zone of the city, where many office buildings and travel centers are located. The closest residential city suburbs—which along with the city center are collectively referred to as the **City**

Bowl—are **Gardens, Oranjezicht, Vredehoek,** and **Tamberskloof.** These areas are a pleasant walk from the center of town through **Company Gardens** (the city's botanical gardens) along **Government Lane.**

THE V&A WATERFRONT

The **Victoria and Alfred (V&A) Waterfront,** north of the city center, is a popular destination for tourists and locals alike. From here it is easy to see the infamous **Robben Island,** where political prisoners were detained in the apartheid era (see p. 101). The Waterfront shops remain open late nights and on Sundays when all other shopping venues are laid to rest, and decent bands play in the outdoor amphitheater on sunny afternoons. There are also nightclubs, and a big warehouse that hosts exhibitions. Some locals call this area "tourism central," particularly because of the view and the big mall. This is not the place to wander if you're looking for lots of authentic local culture. Don't walk here—especially at night; take the shuttle bus from Adderley St. or the tourist office (daily; departing every 10-15min. 6am-11:30pm; R1.90).

THE ATLANTIC SEABOARD

Just a short distance west of the Waterfront, and partially separated from the rest of the city by Signal Hill and Lion's Head, are the residential suburbs that border the Atlantic: **Mouille Point, Green Point, Three Anchor Bay, Sea Point, Bantry Bay,** and the luxurious **Clifton.** You can get to most of these spots via Kloofnek Rd., which passes between the hills from downtown to the beaches. Above Clifton, the scenic **Victoria Rd.** winds along the shore to popular **Camps Bay,** with its white sand and turquoise water. Some of Cape Town's most beautiful beaches and houses are here. Green Point's huge Sunday morning market is just next to the sports stadium, while Sea Point's *forte* is its restaurants.

OBSERVATORY AND THE SOUTHERN SUBURBS

The southern suburbs of **Observatory, Mowbray, Rosebank, Rondebosch** (home of the University of Cape Town), and **Constantia** were formerly white residential areas but have become less so. Shops, pubs, and theaters line the main roads and stay open fairly late. The **University of Cape Town's** stately, vine-covered campus is above the main road on the slopes of **Table Mountain.** These suburbs, which end just before **Muizenberg** on the False Bay coast, are easily accessible by train. However, if you want to be close to the action, this is not the place to stay.

▐ LOCAL TRANSPORTATION

Cape Town's public transportation isn't well suited for sightseeing and is best avoided at night. Luckily, many of the main attractions are within walking distance of the city center. **Metro Trans Info** offers information on the Cape Peninsula's buses, trains, and taxis. (☎ 0800 656 463. Open 24hr.) In general, the most available forms of transit during the day are Rikki's Taxis or minibuses (see p. 86), while metered cabs are the smartest way to travel after dark.

TRAINS

Metrorail (☎ 403 9080 or 0800 656 463) conveniently serves the southern suburbs all the way to Simon's Town. These routes are fairly safe during peak hours, offer stunning ocean views, and often have a dining car. Purchasing a first-class ticket (R4.50-11.50) reduces the risk of being pickpocketed. Remember to **hold on to your ticket;** you'll need it to get off the train at your destination. Trains run from 5:30am to 6 or 7pm. Be cautious while traveling: the route to the Winelands is known to be risky. Travelers strongly recommend against waiting in the Muildersvlei station alone. Avoid the route from Paarl to Wellington at all costs. Overall, it is best to travel when the trains are busy and to avoid traveling after dark.

BUSES

Golden Arrow city buses run infrequently between 8:00am and 6:30pm, but have inexpensive, convenient routes from the city center to places such as Kirstenbosch, Sea Point, Camps Bay, Table Mountain, and Hout Bay with stops along the way. Buses, however, are slow and don't follow a direct route. On Sundays, there are few, if any, buses on most routes. The main **Grand Parade terminal** is on Castle Street, just behind the Golden Acre Shopping Mall and reasonably close to the train station; there is an information booth with current timetables. (☎0800 656 463; www.gabs.co.za. Tickets under R5; book of 10, R43. Prices are slightly more expensive between 4-6:30pm.) Special **waterfront buses** (R1.90) leave every 10 minutes. 6am-11:30pm from Adderley Street in front of the train station and from the tourist office.

MINIBUS TAXIS

Plentiful and popular, this mode of transport fills an otherwise empty niche. It is also a fundamental cultural experience for those who want to understand how most Capetonians live. Minibus taxis generally run until about 6pm (and those running later should be avoided for safety reasons). Minibuses will almost always wait until they are absolutely full before departing; prepare for a cramped wait if you board an emptier minibus. Most fares are under R4, and the routes go through townships and along the major roads in Cape Town and the Cape Peninsula. Travel throughout the city and to the beaches and southern suburbs is generally safe, while **travel to the townships should be avoided unless you are accompanied by a local.** Most depart from the main train station, either from the mammoth minibus terminals upstairs from Track 17 or from the main taxi areas downstairs. If you aren't sure which route to take, ask a security guard. Other minibuses head from Strand St., which runs alongside the train station to the beaches. Minibuses to and from the Waterfront leave from Adderley St. and in front of the Dock St. tourist information center, respectively, and cost R1.50. For those wishing to go from the Gardens into the city, minibuses run regularly along Kloof St. Minibuses also run frequently along Main Rd. through Sea Point and Green Point into the city.

TAXIS

There are several reliable taxi companies in Cape Town, though they tend to cost a bundle and you'll have to call in advance. Try **Unicab** (☎448 1720), **Marine Taxi** (☎434 0434), or **Sea Point Taxi** (☎434 4444). Cabs in Cape Town have numbers (next to the "TAXI" sign); take note of them in case you forget luggage or run into other problems. **Rikki's Intercity Transport** is a popular service that delivers travelers to destinations throughout the city for a pittance in small, open-back vans. (☎423 4888. R8-15 for most destination around Cape Town, R70 to the airport, R60 to Hout Bay, R50 to Kirstenbosch. M-F 7am-7pm, Sa 8am-2pm.) An inexpensive alternative at night is the 24hr. **Boogie Bus** (☎082 495 5698), which has fixed rates. Within the city, prices run about half the cost of a taxi, depending on the number of travelers. You must book before 9pm for late-night trips, and one hour to one day in advance for day trips. *On Addersley St. there are taxis whose drivers run 24hr. shifts. Avoid these if you can; they present safety concerns.*

CARS

RENTAL. Major car rental agencies have desks in the airport terminals. It's generally necessary to reserve cars—especially automatics—at least one week in advance during the high season. Minimum fees for a manual with limited kilometers and limited insurance are about R100 per day, R200 for automatics. A standard economy car runs R230-300. To rent a car, you must be over 21 years of age and have had a license for at least three years; those under 23 must pay an additional daily fee (R15-20). Full coverage insurance is a wise investment. For more on driving and renting a car in South Africa, see **Getting Around: By Car,** p. 39. ▧**Around About Cars Car Hire** (☎ 021 419 2727, 419 2729, or 082 419 2727; info@aroundaboutcars.com; www.aroundaboutcars.com) is a car rental company especially for backpackers. Unlimited kilometers, no age restrictions, free delivery, and drop-off. From R169 per day (R20 extra for A/C), R209 with complete coverage. **Comet Car Rental** has good rates and reliable service. (☎ 386 2411; fax 386 2430; www.cometcar.co.za. Open M-F 8am-5pm, Sa 8am-1pm.) **Africa Travel Center** (see p. 88) rents cars and provides travel advice. **Detour Traveller's Shop,** 234 Long Street, offers great rates for automatics. (☎/fax 424 1115; detourafrica@xsinet.co.za. Open M-F 8:30am-6pm, Sa 8:30am-1pm.) In addition, **Avis,** 123 Strand Street (☎ 424 1177) and **Budget** (120 Strand Street) provide alternatives.

PARKING. For those with a set of wheels, parking in town is bleak during the daytime—prepare to cruise. If hell freezes over and you happen to find a space on the streets, the cost is R2 per 30min. (M-F 8am-6pm, Sa 8am-1pm; all other times parking is free). You'll usually need an **ADO card,** available at convenience and grocery stores and the post office. Beyond that, full-day parking is available at the Grand Parade on Darling St. (R4 per hr.), at all malls, and at other small lots throughout the city. Though unofficial parking lot attendants will often look after your car for a small tip (R1-R2), security is suspect—always remove your radio if possible, lock the doors, leave nothing that could appear valuable on the seats, and arm as many anti-theft devices as possible. Many streets, especially in busy areas, have unofficial "parking attendants" as well. For a small fee, they offer to "watch" your car; drivers who decline this service will often find a mysterious dent or cracked window upon their return. Some people get around this by telling these attendants that they'll pay them when they get back.

BICYCLES, SCOOTERS, AND MOTORBIKES

Cape Town is bicycle-crazy. In March, the **Cape Argus cycle race** fills the town with 40,000 lunatics in lycra, and scads of two-wheel enthusiasts can be seen around town throughout the year. Be warned though: this is one hilly place. The road up to Signal Hill, in particular, is dangerously steep, with many turns and cars. **Downhill Adventures,** Shop 10, Overbeek Building, at the corner of Kloof, Orange, and Long St., rents bikes for R60-100 per day and will arrange mountain biking trips to various areas around Cape Town. (☎ 422 0388. Open M-F 8:30am-5pm, Sa 9am-1pm. AmEx/MC/V.) **African Buzz Scooter Sales and Rentals,** 202 Long St., rents scooters, with helmets and insurance; a driver's license and R1500 deposit are required. (☎ 423 0052. R160 per day with unlimited mileage, R120 in low season; book in advance.) For more horsepower, **Le Cap Motorcycle Hire,** 43 New Church St., is another good spot. They'll organize guided tours, and the owner, Jürgen, will fix your motor if problems arise. Check out the web site for the various prices. (☎ 423 0823; fax 423 5566; www.lecap.co.za. Wide assortment of bikes and long-term deals. Daily rates as low as R290 per day plus R1 per km.)

🔁 PRACTICAL INFORMATION

TOURIST AND FINANCIAL SERVICES

Tourist Offices: Cape Town Tourism Gateway or **Captour** (☎426 4260, answered 24hr.; fax 426 4266; capetown@tourismdirect.co.za; www.cape-town.org), ground floor of the Pinnacle Building, at the corner of Burg and Castle St. Offers a range of maps and information, they also arrange accommodations for 10% commission. Their advice is thorough, but they only give info about services that pay their membership fees, so ask about specifics at hostels themselves. They sell maps of the city center (R2) and have an Internet cafe (R10 for 15min., 10% student discount). Open M-F 8am-6pm, Sa 8:30am-2pm, Su and public holidays 9am-1pm. Several tourist bureaus are scattered around the city; look for signs with the green "i." **National Parks Board** (☎422 2810; fax 424 6211; www.parks-sa.co.za), at the corner of Castle and Burg St. Very helpful for planning visits to any national park. Books accommodations. Open M-F 9am-4:45pm.

Travel Agencies: Cape Town provides all forms of travel assistance and advice. Most hostels also offer information that emphasizes saving money—sometimes at the expense of quality. Before paying, check out details regarding liability, insurance, etc.

Africa Travel Center, 74 New Church St. (☎423 5555; fax 423 0065; backpack@backpackers.co.za; www.backpackers.co.za), at the Backpack Hostel. A class act; the zany ladies who run this agency offer almost unlimited information on tour bookings and budget travel. Great car rental rates. Open daily 8am-8:30pm. MC/V. AmEx for car rental only.

Hostelling International South Africa (HISA), 73 St. George's House, 3rd fl. (☎424 2511; fax 424 4119; info@hisa.org.za; www.hisa.org.za). Extremely amicable staff. Book reservations at HI hostels throughout South Africa. Buy HI memberships (R45). HI members also receive discounts on several tours and services when booking through them. Open M-F 9am-4:30pm.

One World Traveler's Space, 309 Long St. (☎/fax 423 0777; oneworld@mweb.co.za). Chill with helpful, no-pressure staff. Buys and sells used travel guides; sells road maps, magazines, CDs, novelty postcards. Arranges overland tours. Open M-F 9am-5pm, Sa 9am-1pm.

STA Travel, 31 Riebeeck St. (☎418 6570; fax 418 6470; info@cpt.statravel.co.za). Specializes in student and youth travel. One of the best bets for plane tickets out of Southern Africa. Offers good advice on tours. Open M-F 9am-5pm, Sa 9am-noon. AmEx/MC/V.

Overseas Visitors Club, 230 Long St. (☎424 6800; fax 423 4870; hross@ovc.co.za; www.ovc.co.za). Sells cheap tickets to major points around Africa as well as overseas and also serves as a hostel and booking center for coach tours. Open M-F 8:30am-5pm, Sa 9am-noon.

Banks: Surrounding Greenmarket Sq., St. George's House, and the commercial juggernaut that is the Waterfront. Many with **ATMs.**

Currency Exchange: Rennies/Thomas Cook Foreign Exchange (☎418 1206). Other branches on Riebeeck St. and at the V&A Waterfront. All branches open M-F 8:30am-5pm, Sa 9am-noon.

American Express: (☎421 5586), in Thibault Sq. Open M-F 9am-5pm, Sa 9am-noon. Or (☎419 3917), in V&A Waterfront Mall, to the right of the info center when your back is to Dock Rd. Open M-F 9am-7pm, Sa-Su 9am-5pm.

Western Union: 2 Long St. (☎418 2003). Open M-F 8:30am-5pm, Sa 9am-12:30pm.

LOCAL SERVICES

Luggage storage: At the main train station, near Platform 24. M 8am-6:45pm; Tu, Th, Sa, Su 8am-2:45pm; W 8am-3:45pm; F 6am-5:45pm.

Bookstores: Exclusive Books (☎419 0905), at the V&A Wharf Mall on the Waterfront. Open M-F 9am-10:30pm, Sa 9am-11pm. **The Traveler's Bookshop** (☎425 6880), also in the mall, offers guidebooks and foreign newspapers. Open daily 9am-10pm, travel bookshop 9am-9pm. Long St. has many good **used bookstores.**

Library: The **South African Library** (see **Sights,** p. 98) has nearly everything written about South Africa or anything written by a South African writer. Non-circulating. Open M-F 9am-5pm.

Gay and Lesbian Services: Gay esCape, 105 High Level Road, Green Point (☎439 3829; fax 439 3861; gayesc@cis.co.za; www.gayescape.co.za), is a terrific resource for gay and lesbian travelers, with information on accommodations, travel, entertainment, and nightlife. **GayNet Cape Town** (☎422 1925; www.gaynetcapetown.co.za), is a gay Internet travel guide. Office open M-F 8am-4pm. **Triangle Project** (☎448 3812; fax 448 4089; triangle@icon.co.za) provides counseling and a helpline for gays, lesbians, and bisexuals.

Laundromats: Most listed accommodations offer laundry machines or service. Otherwise, laundromats and dry cleaners abound. Full service R20-30 per 5kg.

EMERGENCY SERVICES

Emergency: Police (☎10 111); **ambulance** (☎10 177).

Hotlines: Rape Crisis Center (☎447 9762, after hours 083 222 5158); **AIDS Helpline** (☎0800 012 322); **Emergency Info or General Advice** (☎408 1022).

Police: Main office is downtown in Caledon Square, on Buitenkant Street between Albertus and Barrack Streets. The **Tourist Assistance Police Unit** (☎418 2853), in Tulbagh Square, responds to complaints from foreigners and tourists. Follow signs on Hansstrijdom Street, across from the train station; at night take a taxi, lest you be mugged a second time.

Pharmacy: Litekem Pharmacy, 24 Darling St. (☎461 8040). Also runs a health care clinic with a doctor and dentist. Open M-Sa 7am-11pm, Su 9am-11pm; clinic open M-F 8am-5:30pm, Sa 9am-1pm. **Glengariff Pharmacy** (☎434 8622), on Main Rd. on the edge of Sea Point and Three Anchor Bay, at the corner of Glengariff. Open M-Sa 8am-11pm, Su 9am-11pm. Many pharmacies along Main Rd. in Sea Point.

Hospital: Cape Town Medi-Clinic, 21 Hof St. (☎464 5764), has 24hr. walk-in service for all medical woes. **City Park Hospital,** 181 Longmarket St. (☎480 6111, emergency 0801 222 222 or 480 6272). On Loop St. between Longmarket and Shortmarket St., 2 blocks from Wale St. toward the water. The city center's main hospital. **Groote Schuur Hospital** (☎404 9111), at the intersection of De Waal (M3) and Eastern Blvd. (N2), closer to Rondebosch or Observatory. The world's first successful heart transplant took place here in 1967, a fact that every Capetonian seems to know.

COMMUNICATIONS

Internet Access: In the last two years, Cape Town has become one of the most wired (and wireless) cities in the world. You should have no trouble finding cybercafes every few blocks in the downtown area. Terminals abound in Sea Point and Long St., and most hostels listed in this guide have Internet access. Prices will vary across town, but speed should be decent. The **South African Library** (see p. 98) also offers cheap, though glacially slow, connections (R10 per 30min.).

Post Office: There are several post offices in the City Bowl. The **GPO,** with *Poste Restante,* is on the corner of Parliament and Darling St., on the second floor of the Game department store. Open M-F 8am-4:30pm, Sa 8am-noon.

Postal Code: 8001.

ACCOMMODATIONS AND CAMPING

> **PRICE RANGES.** Price ranges, marked by the numbered icons below, are now included in food and accommodation descriptions. They are based on the lowest cost for one person, excluding special deals. In the case of campgrounds, we include the cost of a car. The table below is a guide to how prices and icons match up.

SYMBOL	❶	❷	❸	❹	❺
ACCOMM.	R1-100	R101-200	R201-300	R301-400	R401+
FOOD	R1-25	R26-50	R51-100	R101-200	R201+

The fierce competition among Cape Town's hostels (a.k.a "backpackers"), hotels, B&Bs, and other lodgings has created a traveler's paradise in which high expectations are met for a handful of rand. Within the City Bowl, you can't throw a stone without hitting one of dozens of lodgings. Walk-ins are no problem, but the carless can ease their pains by calling ahead to arrange pick-up at the airport or train station. The rates listed in this section apply to both the low and high seasons, but bargaining works wonders in the winter. For longer-term stays, many of the hostels offer discounted rates, and apartments can be procured from the classified ads of *Cape Argus* or *Cape Ads*.

Long St., in the **City Center,** is the most central, although noise from the strip of bars and clubs and often lower maintenance standards detract from the ease of being front and center. Still, the nightlife and lower cost of hostels makes staying downtown an appealing option. **Gardens,** so named for its vague proximity to the Company's Gardens, is a mecca of high-quality hostels. The **Atlantic Coast,** including Sea Point and Green Point, though a little seedy around the edges, is closest to the finer beaches and crammed with late-night cafes, clubs, and convenience stores. Mini-cabs into town are easily accessible. Staying in artsy **Observatory,** a common spot for students and other long-termers, is fun but can make getting into town, especially at night, a bit of a challenge. The **University of Cape Town** has furnished rooms and flats available from December to February, but it's far from the center of things. Prices depend on duration of stay and room, but a standard B&B is R78 per person. Contact the Vacation Accommodation Office (☎ 650 3002; shovac@protem.uct.ac.za; www.uct.ac.za), in Rondebosch.

Unless stated otherwise, the listed accommodations have a common room with TV, bar, and a guest phone that accepts incoming calls. The hostels include a self-catering kitchen, Internet access, laundry facilities, and communal bathrooms, unless noted to the contrary. Many hostels add a 5% service charge for credit card.

CITY CENTER

HOSTELS

■ **The Backpack,** 74 New Church St. (☎ 423 5555; fax 423 0065; backpack@backpackers.co.za; www.backpackers.co.za). A super clean, colorful, and friendly hostel run with gusto by a dedicated and fun team of women. Within walking distance of the restaurants and nightlife of Long St., but far enough that the loud bass music won't keep you up at night. Numerous in and outdoor lounge areas, pool, and a buzzing cafe/bar (open daily 8am-midnight). Weekly *braais* (R40), tons of security precautions, and a gorgeous view of Table Mountain. Africa Travel Center is in the hostel office. Private, electronic safe R20 for up to 1 week. Reception 7:30am-8:30pm. Check-out 10am. Reserve by email; ask for discounts Apr.-June. Dorms R65-80; singles R180; doubles R250, with bath R300, additional people (beyond 2) R65 each. MC/V. ❶

■ **Zebra Crossing,** 82 New Church St. (☎/fax 422 1265; zebracross@intekom.co.za). Clean and attractively relaxed. Surrounding a tree-filled patio and swank lounges, ZC declares itself (in a whisper) to be the most serene backpackers in town. Bar open in the evenings. Reception 8am-8pm. Dorms R50; singles R100; doubles R150. ❶

Cat & Moose, 305 Long St. (☎/fax 423 7638; catandmoose@hotmail.com). Old building (circa 1791) just next to the Long St. Baths. Common rooms and courtyard with a tiny plunge pool are the real highlights. Best bet for those longing to be on Long St. Crowded 4- to 10-bed dorms have Oriental rugs over worn wooden floors. Video room. Nice bar/lounge. Free pick-up anywhere in the city before 10pm. Reception 8am-10pm. Check-out 10am. Low season room discounts for longer stays, but not for dorms. Dorms R55; doubles from R120. ❶

Long St. Backpackers, 209 Long St. (☎423 0615; fax 423 1842; longstbp @mweb.co.za; www.nis.za/~longstbp). Where Pepper St. meets Long St. A happening place with a lingering crowd. The discreet door leads to a stairway into a split-level courtyard. 2- to 4-bed dorms have numerous bathrooms (with dingy bathtubs). Bar is always lively; courtyard rooms hear it all. Free *potjie* on Su. Lockers. Check-in 24hr. Check-out noon. Dorms R60; singles R90; doubles R150, with bath R160. ❶

HOTELS AND B&BS

Tudor House Hotel, 153 Longmarket St. (☎424 1335; fax 423 1198; tudorhotel@iafrica.com). In Greenmarket Sq. Victorian hotel decorated with images of London. Some of the large rooms open onto balconies. Huge private bathrooms. Wheelchair accessible. Breakfast included. Reception 24hr. Singles in summer R295, in winter R265; doubles R495/R350; 4-person family rooms R185/R145 per person. AmEx/DC/MC/V. ❸

Metropole Hotel, 38 Long St. (☎423 6363; fax 426 5312; metrop@icon.co.za; www.chamonix.co.za/metropole). Classy place in the heart of town with lush red and pink hallways and an old-school lift. Rooms attractively decorated, with TV, bath, and A/C. Safe indoor parking. Wheelchair-accessible. Reception 24hr. Singles R175; doubles R255; 4-person family rooms R310. AmEx/MC/V. ❷

GARDENS AND NEARBY

HOSTELS

■ **Oak Lodge,** 21 Breda St. (☎465 6182; fax 465 6308; oaklodge@intekom.co.za; www.oaklodge.co.za). Off Orange St. Part lodge, part legend: the OL began as a commune; its charismatic staff ensure it remains a friendly meeting place attracting ex-lodgers, friends, and wanderers. Refined rooms feel like pleasant home. Masks and murals adorn the premises. Bar and chill smoking room. If you ever say the word "tequila," you have to buy everyone at the bar (including yourself) a shot of tequila. Free W *braais* and *potjiekos*. Reception 8am-midnight. Reserve 48hr. ahead Nov.-Apr. Spacious 6- to 10-bed dorms R55-60; doubles and triples R150-160; doubles in separate apartments R90 per person. Winter discounts. Save 10% on 7or more days if paid up front. ❶

■ **Ashanti Lodge (HI),** 11 Hof St. (☎424 4016; fax 423 8790; ashanti@iafrica.com; www.ashanti.co.za). A backpacker's palace, this cavernous hostel offers 134 beds. With an outdoor pool and a terrace overlooking Table Mountain, staying here doesn't feel like roughing it. Attracts large groups. Spacious cafe and bar open 7:30am-midnight. Lockers. Luggage storage R1 per item per day. Reception M-Sa 24hr., Su 7:30am-midnight. Book ahead. 6-bed dorms R70 per person; doubles with sinks R200; doubles with bath in quieter separate building R240. Camping R50. 10% HI discounts. 7th night free if you pay in advance. MC/V (5%). ❶

Cloudbreak (HI), 219 Upper Buitenkant St. (☎461 6892; fax 461 1458; cloudbrk@gem.co.za). Worn-in home to surfer dudes and chill lone travelers. Friendly staff won't take groups larger than 15 to avoid a cliquey atmosphere. Cave bar hosts many a friendly chess game and many a friendlier drunk. *Braai* once or twice a week (R25). Free covered parking. Reception 8:30am-10pm. Crowded 6-bed dorms R60; singles R130; doubles R160. 10% HI and ISIC discount. ❷

HOTELS AND B&BS

▨ **Fritz Hotel,** 1 Faure St. (☎480 9000; fax 480 9090; reception@fritzhotel.co.za; www.fritzhotel.co.za). Off Wilkinson, which is off Kloof St. Stylish and sumptuous. Stunning Art Deco rooms full of amenities like claw-footed tubs and private fax machines; it's that kind of place. Breakfast included. Singles in summer R450-600, in winter R300-350; doubles R500-650/R350-400. AmEx/MC/V. ❺

Saasveld Lodge, 73 Kloof St. (☎424 6169; fax 424 5397; saasveld@icon.co.za). Spartan white rooms with TV, fan, and phone. Several have mountain views. Breakfast included. Reception 24hr. Long-term discounts. Singles R250; doubles R350; self-catering family rooms R420. AmEx/DC/MC/V. ❸

Cape Corner Guest House, 25 Burnside Rd., Tamboerskloof (☎422 1363; capecnr@iafrica.com; www.capecorner.com). Off Buitengracht St. 4 rooms in a 105-year-old Victorian house. Each room includes private bathrooms, TV, minibar, and fireplace. Breakfast included. Singles in summer R350, in winter R275; doubles R450/R350. ❹

ATLANTIC COAST

HOSTELS

Sea Point is full of hostels, hotels, and B&Bs. A stroll through the area will reveal numerous places to stay. Rather than list them all, we've listed our favorites. If the ones below aren't to your liking, or if they're full, other options do exist.

▨ **Carnaby,** 219 Main Rd., Three Anchor Bay (☎439 7410; fax 439 1222; carnaby@netactive.co.za). 87 beds in a converted hotel with eclectic design. Pool, outdoor and indoor bar, charming staff, and cool crowd. Great Su fish *braai*, occasionally with live jazz. Singles and doubles have radio and bath. Internet R15 per 30min. Free airport pick-up for stay of 3 or more nights. Breakfast R7-11. Laundry R30 per load. Book ahead in high season. Reception 24hr. 6-bed dorms R55; 3- to 4-bed dorms with shower/bath R60; singles R135; doubles R145-195. AmEx/MC/V. ❷

The Sunflower Stop, 179 Main Rd., Green Point (☎434 6535; fax 434 6501; www.sunflowerstop.co.za; devine@sunflowerstop.co.za). Very clean hostel with a friendly staff and mellow-yellow-everywhere decor. Small and snazzy outside pool and bar. 4- to 12-bed dorms, some with triple bunks. Free airport pick-up 8am-7pm. Cheap breakfast in summer. Reception 8am-7pm. Check-out 11am. Dorms in summer R70, in winter R55; twins or doubles from R160/R150. ❶

Lion's Head Lodge/Aardvark Backpackers, 319 Main Rd., Sea Point (☎434 4163; fax 439 3813; lionhead@mweb.co.za). Slightly crowded 6- to 12-bed dorms with baths and kitchenettes. Hotel has 12 self-catering flats and 38 B&B rooms, with TVs, phones, and private bathrooms. Backpackers often stay in hotel doubles at backpacker prices. Dorms have large lockers and a phone for incoming calls only. Pool, pub, upscale restaurant, beer garden, and Internet cafe. Good choice for families. Internet R15 for 30min. Reception 24hr. Dorms R60; hotel doubles R240; hotel triples in summer R330, in winter R250; family room R350/R250. MC/V. ❶

St. John's Waterfront Lodge, 6 Braemar Rd., Green Point (☎439 1404; fax 439 1424; fredgeof@mweb.co.za; www.nis.za/stjohns). From Main Rd., turn up Wessels St., then right onto Braemar. Standard rooms. 2 houses, 2 pools, grassy grounds, balconies, and decks appeal to those seeking a backyard beach atmosphere. Laundry R12. Internet R20 per hr. Free travel advice. Book in advance. Discounts for longer stays. 8-bed dorms R60; singles R150; doubles R180. ❷

HOTELS AND B&BS

Breakwater Lodge, Portswood Rd., V&A Waterfront (☎406 1911; fax 406 1436; brkwater@fortesking-hotels.co.za). Formerly a prison and still institutional, but highly secure. Small, immaculate rooms with TV, phone, tea, and coffee. Self-catering kitchen on every floor. Parking. Internet. 2 restaurants and a pub. Breakfast R48. Reception 24hr. Check-in from 2pm. Check-out 10am. Singles R230, with bath R390; doubles R275/R450; 4-bed family unit R550. ❸

Little Lemon Tree, 9 Antrim Rd., Green Point (☎439 1990 or 082 338 2888; fax 434 4209; little-lemon@iafrica.com; www.little-lemon.com). Gorgeous with bright, floral paintings, private phone lines, and minibars in room. Tropical breakfast garden with a lovely pool. Airport pick-up R130. Breakfast included. Laundry facilities. Singles in summer R300-350, in winter R200-250; doubles R350/R250, with balcony R400/R300. All prices R100 less in low season. ❹

Cape Town Lodge, 101 Buitengracht St. (☎422 0030; fax 422 0090; www.capetownlodge.co.za; info@capetownlodge.co.za). 3 floors and 114 nice hotel rooms in the center of CT. Rooms include A/C, TV, minibar, fridge, VCR, electronic safe, and private baths. Breakfast R35-55. Reservations recommended. Reception 24hr. Singles R545; twins R545; doubles R625; family rooms R715; suites R825. AmEx/DC/MC/V. ❺

OBSERVATORY

HOSTELS

The Green Elephant (HI), 57 Milton Rd. (☎0800 222 722 or 448 6359; fax 448 0510; greenele@iafrica.com; www.hostels.co.za), uphill from Lower Main Rd., on the left. Fun place with worn aesthetic. Climbers gather before ascending the Cape's sundry summits. Climbing wall, pool, "honesty bar," *braais*. Jacuzzi available occasionally. Free airport pick-up. Reception 7am-10pm. Dorms R65; singles R160; doubles R195. 5% HI and ISIC discount. AmEx/MC/V. ❷

The Lodge, 36 Milton Rd. (☎/fax 448 6536; thelodge@mweb.co.za). Near The Green Elephant. For long-term visitors; min. 1-week stay. 5 houses on the same block with spacious rooms, Oriental rugs, and wandering pets. Pool. Reception 8am-10pm. Reservations required. 3- to 4-bed dorms R65; doubles R75 per person. For stays of at least a month: dorms R50; double R55 per person. Ask for discounts during winter. ❶

HOTELS AND B&BS

Koornhoop Manor House (☎/fax 448 0595; koornhoop@yahoo.com). On the corner of Wrensch and Nuttall Rd.; Wrensch is the 3rd to last street before Lower Main intersects Main; Nuttall is downhill. Sunny, airy garden in back, large rooms with bath, and grand breakfast buffet all provide tranquil and cheap luxury. Great for families (especially the 3-bedroom self-catering suite, R550). Parking available. Breakfast included. Reception 24hr. Singles R265; doubles R360. ❸

Observatory Guest House, 47-49 William St. (☎/fax 448 2014; obsguesthouse.cape@new.co.za). Call for directions. Smartly decorated rooms, most with bath and TV; heavy on African motifs. Jacuzzi and steam room (R50 per hr.), meditation garden (with meditating ducks), pool, and free parking. Breakfast R15. Reception 24hr. Singles R150; doubles R170. AmEx/MC/V. ❷

◘ FOOD

Cape Town keeps its devotees happy with an excellent food at low prices. While the range of culinary offerings proves pleasing to any palate, one institution dominates outside the confines of Cape Town restaurants: the unabashedly carnivorous, artery-clogging culture of the *braai*. Locals revel in the smoky bliss of sky-high flames and charred *boerewors* (sausages). Evening *braais* capture the gregarious flavor of Cape Town; a visit to the city is incomplete without the experience. Only a few restaurants serve **"Cape cuisine,"** a blend of Dutch, Malay, and other influences, which includes spicy Indonesian curries, *bredies* (stews), and *bobotie* (Malay minced beef and lamb). For more information, see **Food**, p. 64.

Strips of snazzy restaurants—from pizzerias to champagne bars—line Long St. in the City Center and Kloof St. in the Gardens. Main Rd. in Sea Point, Green Point, and Three Anchor Bay offer almost as many restaurants as accommodations. Main Rd. also hosts a handful of kosher restaurants. The elegant **Heritage Square**, at Bree and Shortmarket St., is home to numerous chic restaurants, shops, and bars, and its courtyards bustle gracefully on weekend nights. For a list and description of interesting upmarket restaurants—most of which offer a good value—pick up **The Food Map** available at Captour (see **Tourist Offices**, p. 88).

For **groceries,** supermarkets and convenience stores are scattered throughout the city. In the City Center, there is a 7-Eleven at the corner of Long and Kloof, a ShopRite in the Golden Acre Mall next to the train station, and another ShopRite farther up Kloof for those in Gardens. In Observatory, there is a Kwik-Spar on Station Rd., just off Lower Main Rd. In Sea Point, there is a Pick 'n Pay on Main Rd. Many street vendors also sell fresh and inexpensive produce.

For those feeling lazy after a day of jumping off mountains or uneasy about venturing out, **Mr. Delivery** can bring dishes from area restaurants to your door. (☎423 4177; www.mrdelivery.com. R20 minimum, R7.50-10 surcharge.)

BETTER LATE THAN NEVER? You may notice that many restaurants and clubs throughout South Africa advertise themselves as open until "late." You probably looked at your wristwatch and noticed that it doesn't have the number "late" anywhere on it. When is this magical "late" time? For restaurants, it's defined by whenever the last person leaves, usually between 10:30pm and 12:30am, depending on the day of the week and time of the year. For clubs, "late" can mean anything from 1am until the sun comes up, which technically would be "early."

CITY CENTER

▨ **Mesopotamia** (☎424 4664). Corner of Long and Church St. One of Long St.'s secrets, this restaurant was voted one of the 100 best restaurants in South Africa in 2000. A tapestry-draped, cushion-covered, candle-lit enclave of Kurdish delight. Excellent, reasonably priced traditional food. Try the set menu (R85) to get all the best. Great *baklava* (R19.50). Also a wide variety of vegetarian dishes. Belly dancing F-Sa (R10); book ahead. Free waterpipe afterwards. Open M-Sa 6-late. AmEx/MC/V. ❸

▨ **Diablo,** 224 Long St. (☎426 5484). The devil has more fun, and his food tastes better too. Tapas bar with lengthy delectable menu (R12-20). Good place to fill *el estómago* with *albóndigas* (meatballs in sherry sauce, R17) or *mejillones ajillo* (mussels in garlic butter sauce, R18). Open M-Sa 9am-midnight, Su 5pm-midnight. ❶

▨ **Mr. Pickwick's,** 158 Long St. (☎424 2696). Popular spot serving foot-long sandwiches (R24-33). Mr. Spottletoe (grilled chicken, roasted peppers, feta, and *tapenade*, R32) and Edwin Drood (mozzarella, tomato, and basil on a baguette, R24-33) are excellent.

Half sandwiches available. Legendary milkshakes R10. Delicious chunks of cheesecake R15.50. Open Su-Tu 8:30am-2am, W-Th 8:30am-3am, F-Sa 8:30am-4am. ❷

Khaya-Nyama, 267 Long St. (☎/fax 424 2917; khaya-nyama@mail.com; www.khaya-nyama.com). "House of Meat" in English, this intimate meatery prepares game while showing videos of roaming mammals and serving vodka through a springbok's ass. Mozambican shark R78. Nigerian gemsbok goulash R75. Arranges game tours and hunting trips (R500, including breakfast and lunch). Book meals and tours in advance. Open daily 5pm-midnight. ❸

Lola's Cafe, 228 Long St. (☎423 0885). On the corner of Long St. and Buiten St. Battles yuppie-ism with a retro jive. Though wall-papered in gravy packaging, Lola's serves strictly vegetarian fare, including curries, pastas, and sandwiches. Perfect for a late breakfast (R15-24, until to 4pm). Sit and sip outdoors on a lazy afternoon. Open M-Sa 8am-midnight, Su 8:30am-midnight. ❶

The Africa Cafe, 108 Shortmarket St. (☎422 0221). Amazing set menu: 14-16 all-you-can-eat samples of different African cuisine (salads, main dishes, and desserts), with many vegetarian options (R105 per person). Reservations required. Open M-Sa 6:30pm-late. AmEX/DC/MC/V. ❹

The Five Flies, 14-16 Keerom St. (☎424 4442; fax 423 1048; fiveflies@iafrica.com). Across from the Supreme Court. Save this one for a treat. A candlelit elegant space with cobbled atria, shiny checkered floor, and live music. Afro/Euro menu includes rosette of sole fillet with shrimp *thermidore*, Saldanha Bay mussels, and white chocolate parfait cup with Irish whiskey truffle. Pay by the number of courses: 2 courses, R85; 3, R105; 4, R120. Open M-F noon-3pm and 7-10:30pm, Sa-Su 7-10:30pm. ❹

Mama Africa, 178 Long St. (☎424 8634). At Long and Pepper St. Decent African wild game food, noteworthy decor, and excellent marimba bands play late into the evening. Starters around R20. Mixed grill R120. *Malva* (caramelized cake with ice cream) R20. If you don't eat *malva* at some point, you should be deported! Wheelchair-accessible. African band 8pm-late. Cover R10. Open M-Sa 7pm-late for dinner. Book ahead (as much as a week beforehand during weekends and summer). MC/V. ❹

The Famous Butcher's Grill, 101 Buitengracht St. (☎422 0880; fbgrill@iafrica.com). Wear the one nice shirt you brought and treat yourself to a great ostrich steak (personally picked from "the butcher's block") and some of the finest wines in town. Prices vary from R60 to R70. Steakhouse of the year 2000. Secure parking. M-F noon-late, Sa-Su 7pm-late. Make reservations on weekends. AmEx/DC/MC/V. ❸

Mexican Kitchen, 13 Bloem St. (☎423 1541). Just off Long St. Funky spot with all-you-can-eat buffet (lunch R35; dinner R49.50, Su-M R39.50) emphasizing quantity over quality. Everything is homemade with love. Open M-Th 10am-11pm, F 10am-11:30pm, Sa 11am-11:30pm, Su noon-11pm. Bar open past your bedtime. ❷

GARDENS

▨ **Mantodea,** 30 Wandel St. (☎461 5750; fax 461 5751; mantodea@wol.co.za). Across the road from Hatfields. "The kind of restaurant you've been *preying* for." Delicious, uncomplicated cuisine of creative combinations. Menu changes monthly but always includes great vegetarian dishes. Starters R20-30. Entrees R20-40. It doesn't get much better than this. M-Sa noon-3pm, Tu-Sa 6pm-late. AmEx/DC/MC/V. ❷

▨ **Yindee's,** 22 Camp St. (☎422 1012; fax 422 1014). Just off Kloof St. Swanky Thai place with romantic candlelit courtyard and classy interior. Spring rolls (R16.50). *Rama song kai* (spicy chicken dish with egg noodles) R43. Open M-F 12:30-2:30pm and 6:30-11pm, Sa 6:30-11pm. Long wait; book ahead. AmEx/DC/MC/V. ❷

▨ **Chef Pon's Asian Kitchen,** 12 Mill St. (☎465 5846). Chef Pon is Asia's culinary saint, and his restaurant is approaching religious popularity among locals. An unassuming eatery that concocts some of the best Thai and Asian fare around. Highlights include delicious aromatic crispy duck (R47) and sweet and sour calamari (R43). Open M-Sa 5:30pm-late. ❷

Hatfields, 129-131 Hatfield St. (☎465 7387; www.hatfieldsrestaurant.co.za). Off Annandale St. Quiet Italian restaurant in business for 17 years. Off the tourist trail and around corner from Roxy Coffee (see p. 111). Continental steaks, seafood, and big plates of good pasta in family-style setting (R26-33). Open M-F 12:30-3pm and 6pm-midnight, Sa 6pm-midnight. AmEx/DC/MC/V. ❷

Miller's Thumb, 10b Kloofnek Rd., Tamboerskloof (☎424 3838). At the intersection with New Church St. Lively, with delectable dishes. Grilled calamari that melt in your mouth R46. Line fish prepared in Cajun, Moroccan, or Malay styles R54. Open M and Sa-Su 6:30-10:30pm, Tu-F 12:30-2:30pm and 6:30-10:30pm. Book ahead. ❸

The Dharma Club, 68 Kloof St. (☎422 0909; thedharmaclub@thedharmaclub.com). This comfortably hip cocktail bar/restaurant serves *presque* gourmet African and Mediterranean fusion cuisine amid oak decor under a skylight. More dharma than a menu can summarize. Soy-glazed Norwegian salmon R69. Pan-fried chicken breast R55. Open daily 6pm-1am, food served 7-11pm. MC/V. ❸

Limoncello Ristorante, 8 Breda St. (☎461 5100 or 082 218 752; wapa@intekom.co.za). Just down the street from the Oak Lodge (see p. 91). A trendy, fresh, and young Southern Italian restaurant. Try the Calzoncino di Carne (R44) or any other great pasta or pizza around that price. Open M-F noon-3pm and 6-11pm, Sa 6-11pm. Reservations vital for dinner. ❷

The Perseverance Tavern, 83 Buitenkant St. (☎461 2440). This almost 200-year-old tavern has regularly served the likes of Cecil John Rhodes; today it caters to a decidedly more working-class, hard-drinking set. Daily specials: M burgers R15 (accompanied by fine live blues), Tu *espatados* R45, F all-you-can-eat ribs R44, Sa chicken and chips R14.50. Happy Hour M-F 5-6pm (beers R5). Pub lunches R15. Open daily 11am-late, kitchen open daily noon-3pm and 6-10:30pm. ❷

Charley's Bakery, 20 Roeland St. (☎461 5181; biesst@new.co.za). "Mucking afrazing food." A German baker makes delicious sandwiches, pies, and quiches. Try the sausage roll (R7.50) only with ketchup! Open M-F 7:30am-5pm. MC/V/DC. ❶

Arnold's, 60 Kloof St. (☎424 4344; fax 424 8941). A fine food and wine deli and cafe. Go check it out yourself. The game combo is among the best deals in town (R65). Also try the *Ice und Heiss* (R21) for dessert. Happy hour daily 4:30-6:30pm (all alcohol including wine half-price). Open daily 11am-11pm. AmEx/DC/MC/V. ❸

Ocean Basket, 75 Kloof St. (☎422 0323; fax 422 0322; feedback@oceanbasket.co.za; www.oceanbasket.co.za). Though in fact a chain of restaurants, this particular location is probably the best Ocean Basket in South Africa. Voted best seafood restaurant in Cape Town 2002. Offers exclusively Mediterranean seafood with some excellent seasonal specials at reasonable prices. Open M-Th noon-10pm, F-Sa noon-4pm, Su noon-9:30pm. Reservations only for lunch. AmEx/DC/MC/V. ❷

ATLANTIC COAST

La Med (☎438 5600), on Victoria Rd. next to Glen Country Club, halfway between Clifton and Camps Bay. Popular and pretentious venue for sundowners and burgers (R35). Hopping on Su afternoons and nights (see **Cafes, Pubs, and Bars,** p. 111). Cover F and Su on sunny days. Open May-Aug. M-F 3pm-late, Sa-Su noon-late. Sept.-Apr. daily noon-late. Kitchen closes M-F 9pm, Sa-Su 10pm. AmEx/DC/MC/V. ❷

The Wooden Shoe (☎439 4435), corner of Main Rd. and St. John's Rd., Sea Point. Vegetarians might want to skip this one. Meat-lovers, welcome to Nirvana! Since 1961, The

Wooden Shoe has served some of the best steaks in town (R50-60) in a small, cozy bar-like venue. Your steaks are prepared right behind the bar. To satisfy a big appetite, try the 750g steak, if you can. Open W-M 6pm-late. MC/V. ❸

Cafe Erte, 265A Main Rd., Sea Point (☎ 434 6624). Awkward but delightful cross between Hindu shrine and fluorescent bar serves as lively after-hours playground and lounge for a predominantly gay and lesbian crowd (see **Gay Nightlife,** p. 114). Vegetarian menu (meals R17-27). Internet R20 per hr. Open daily 10am to the wee hours; kitchen closes M-Th 3:30am, F-Su 4:30am. ❶

Avron's Place, 307 Main Rd., Sea Point (☎ 439 7610). Serves a wide variety of kosher dishes amid photos of New York City. Flagship Broadway Beef Ribs enjoy a rep as the best in town (R79). Burger R26. Sushi R36. Open Su-Th 11:30am-11pm, F 11:30am-4:30pm, Sa opens one hour after sundown. AmEx/DC/MC/V. ❸

News Cafe, 81 Main Rd., Greenpoint. (☎ 434 6196). In Exhibition building, corner of Ashstead and Somerset Rd., right next to the roundabout on the M6. The best place around for breakfast (R20-30 until noon) and pastries (R10-17). Also a popular bar where locals meet up before hitting the club scene. Open Su-Th 7:30am-11pm, F-Sa 7:30am-midnight. AmEx/DC/MC/V. ❶

Buena Vista Social Cafe, 81 Main Rd., Greenpoint (☎ 433 0611; fax 433 0610; buenavista@sadomain.co.za). Right above the News Cafe. A great Cuban refuge. Cafe, bar, tapas restaurant, and a lot of Latin/Cuban/Brazilian music. Tapas R20. Mojito R18-20. Open M-F noon-1am, Sa-Su 5pm-1am. MC/V. ❶

OBSERVATORY

Obz Cafe, 115 Lower Main Rd. (☎ 448 5555). Attracts jet-setters and students for sandwiches and salads (R30-60). Ask about the daily specials; they're excellent. Involved in local art events. Open daily 8am-1am, kitchen closes at midnight. AmEx/MC/V. ❸

Pancho's, 127 Lower Main Rd. (☎ 447 4854). Pure Tex-Mex absurdity: enormous sombreros, papier mâché cactuses, and a claim to being open 366 days a year. *Chimichangas* and veggie or beef fajitas R38. Fine sangria (only during summer) R5 per glass, R25 per jug. Fruit margaritas R14 per glass, R50 per jug. Offers a "Mexican portion": smaller portion for a lower price. Open daily 6pm-late. ❷

Cafe Ganesh, 388 Trill Rd. (☎ 448 3435). Just off Lower Main Rd. A mysterious mixture of Indian and South African cuisines. You'll have to experience it for yourself. Specials R30-40. Open Tu-Su 6pm-late. ❷

◷ SIGHTS

While the brilliance of the landscape surrounding Cape Town is unavoidable and undeniable, many overlook the thriving art scene found in the city's museums and galleries. Poignant memories of the injustices of the Apartheid Era lie beneath the veneer of neighborhoods such as Bo-Kaap and the Cape Flats, and many of Cape Town's art and cultural institutions deal with themes that are highly charged and of visceral importance to Capetonians. Often, museum guides and staff have first-hand experience with the issues and narratives being exhibited and will offer personal opinions and interpretations. Cape Town's unique and vibrant sights function as educational tools, but also as expressions, coping mechanisms, memorials, meeting places, and experiments.

Many of the city's sights are within walking distance of the city center and accessible by public transportation during the daytime. The Western Cape **Arts & Crafts Map** (available at Captour and various galleries) provides a comprehensive list of Cape Town's private galleries, larger museums, and main craft markets.

WESTERN CAPE

COMPANY'S GARDENS AND SURROUNDINGS

Adderley St. and its immediate surroundings serve as the soul of the City Bowl, with an appropriately hectic crush of activity that crowds the streets and sidewalks. The **Company's Garden,** which begins where Adderley St. turns into Government Ave., serves as a lush urban oasis. This expanse of exotic trees and colorful roses is the oldest garden in South Africa; it was originally established in 1652 as a vegetable garden by Jan van Riebeeck so that passing ships could restock with fresh produce. Its namesake neighborhood, **Gardens,** stretches from the southwest corner of the garden up to the base of Table Mountain.

SOUTH AFRICAN NATIONAL GALLERY. With contemporary African paintings and sculptures, the progressive gallery displays excellent apartheid-inspired art. Highlights include the disturbing *Butcher Boys* and *Botha's Baby* as well as works by Peter Schutz and Lucas Seage. The Gallery hosts frequent exhibitions on indigenous art, art collectives, and contemporary themes. *(Near the south end of the Company's Gardens.* ☎ *467 4660; fax 481 3993; sang@gem.co.za; www.museums.org.za/sang. Wheelchair accessible. Open Tu-Su 10am-5pm. R5; children, students, and seniors free.)*

SOUTH AFRICAN MUSEUM AND PLANETARIUM. Housed in a stately Victorian mansion, the most interesting aspect of this ethnographic museum is not the displays, but the controversy it has engendered. Many feel that the exhibits on Southern African hunter-gatherers and herders depict indigenous people as indistinct from the animals on display. A number of posted articles and disclaimers examine the controversy. The museum's Planetarium is popular with the young and old; inhabitants of the northern hemisphere shouldn't miss the night sky shows. *(25 Queen Victoria St., at the southwestern tip of Company's Garden.* ☎ *481 3800; fax 481 3993. Open daily 10am-5pm. R8, free W; students and children free. Planetarium open M-F 11am-3pm, Sa-Su 11am-4pm. 3 shows daily Sa-Su, 1 show daily M-F. Schedules at entrance. Daytime shows R10, children R5; evening shows, adults R12.)*

SOUTH AFRICAN CULTURAL HISTORY MUSEUM. The museum's collections are shown in a number of buildings around Cape Town, most of which are within walking distance of each other. The main building, housed in what originally served as a slave lodging for the Dutch East India Company, exhibits artifacts that illustrate and illuminate various cultures. While a large section of the museum is dedicated to an eclectic and somewhat random collection of materials from a range of times and places, including ancient Rome, Tibet, and Japan, the more interesting part of the museum displays artifacts of Cape history and narrates tales of (mostly white) Cape history. Some intriguing items include an original Afrikaans text (in Arabic script), a slave registry, a large collection of English-influenced Victoriana (stamps, clothing, dishes, and other domestic accessories), and a Mercedes Benz-sponsored collection of fancy items owned by the Dutch East India company. *(The Slave Lodge is near the northern end of the Company's Gardens, at the end of Adderley St., on the corner of Wale St.* ☎ *461 8280. Open daily 9:30am-4:30pm. A map to the other sites, including the Bo-Kaap Museum, Groot Constantia, Maritime Museum, Bertram House, and Koopmans-De Wet House, is available at the Lodge. R7, students R3, children R2.)*

HOUSES OF PARLIAMENT. This building complex holds South Africa's legislative branch. Public observations of Parliament are usually possible from August to December. *(Accessible from Parliament Ave.* ☎ *403 2911. 1hr. tours during Parliamentary recess M-F every hour on the hour 9am-noon. Book ahead. Free; passport required.)*

SOUTH AFRICAN LIBRARY. Founded in 1818 as one of the world's first free libraries, the collection has nearly all works written on South Africa or by South Africans. *(On the right at the beginning of the gardens.* ☎ *424 6320. Open M-F 9am-5pm.)*

MOUNT NELSON HOTEL. This pink, century-old accommodation often serves as the temporary residence for super-famous folk visiting town, placing it in an orbit far removed from budget-traveler-land. Nevertheless, you too can live the good life and eat tiny sandwiches at the ■**Sunday High Tea.** *(76 Orange St., just outside the southern end of Company's Garden. Recognizable by the horrid colonial-style uniforms worn by the porters; Rhodes' influence dies hard. Call ☎ 423 1000 for times and prices for tea, as it changes seasonally but hovers around R75. Don "smart casual" clothes.)*

JEWISH MUSEUM, GREAT SYNAGOGUE AND HOLOCAUST CENTER. Newly renovated, and super-hi-tech, the **Jewish Museum** provides amazing visual displays that describe South Africa's 150-year-old Jewry's "memory, reality and dream." Highlights include a walk-in reconstructed Lithuanian *shtetl*, discussion of Jews, Mandela and the struggle for freedom, and displays on enterprising Jewish South Africans like fashion guru Max Rose, "The Ostrich Feather King of South Africa."

The adjacent **Holocaust Center** is state-of-the-art. Serving as a memorial to victims of Nazism, its permanent exhibit focuses on South African Jewry and its ancestry, and makes mention of homosexuality, race, apartheid, and the relationship between Nazism and the National Party. The informative and moving display centers on the personal, and contains many well-chosen anecdotes and many chilling photographs, including a collection of ID photos submitted to Nazis by Jews just prior to their deportation to Auschwitz. **Cafe Riteve** is this Judaica complex's good kosher restaurant. *(88 Hatfield St. Jewish Museum: ☎ 465 1546; fax 465 0284; www.sajewishmuseum.co.za. Open Su-Th 10am-5pm, F 10am-2pm. R30, students/seniors R20, children R10. Holocaust Center: ☎ 462 5553; fax 462 5554; ctholocaust@mweb.co.za; www.museums.org.za/ctholocaust. Open Su-Th 10am-5pm, F 10am-1pm. Free, but donations appreciated. Cafe open Su-Th 8am-late, F 8am-3pm, Sa sundown-late. Parking near entrance at Cape Town High School field.)*

ST. GEORGE'S CATHEDRAL. During the apartheid era, Archbishop Desmond Tutu delivered numerous sermons decrying apartheid's evils within this Victorian Gothic building. In addition to the fine examples of stained-glass windows, interesting items include Leon Underwood's *The African Madonna* statue and the AIDS quilt by the north door. *(Open M-F 6:30am-5:30pm, Sa-Su 6:30am-1pm. Free.)*

CENTRAL BUSINESS DISTRICT (CBD)

■ **DISTRICT SIX MUSEUM.** This museum is a memorial to the residents of District Six, who were forcibly removed from their homes in 1966, under the National Party's Group Areas Act (see **The Scar of District Six,** above). The museum poignantly conveys the heartache and destruction these removals caused and covers other cases of forced removals throughout the world. On the floor is a personalized street map of the old District where former residents have written in their old addresses, and on the walls hang street signs recovered from the bulldozed site (ironically, the foreman who bulldozed District Six kept all the signs, and was reluctant to hand them over to the museum for fear of prosecution). The museum is staffed by ex-District Sixers, a number of whom have written about it and are eager to talk. Ask for a free self-guided tour map of District Six at the museum. *(25a Buitenkant St., in an old Methodist church on the corner of Albertus St. ☎ 461 4735; fax 461 8745. Open M-Sa 9am-4pm. Great pamphlet on life in District Six. R2. Free; donation appreciated.)*

■ **LONG STREET BATHS.** Built in 1906, the baths are good for a quick splash or a prolonged soak. There is a huge pool as well as Turkish baths and a sauna. *(☎ 400 3302. Open M-Sa 7am-7pm. Massages R35; Turkish bath R45; discounted combinations available. Ladies-only Turkish bath on M, Th, Sa. R7, monthly card R90.)*

WESTERN CAPE

THE SCAR OF DISTRICT SIX

East of the city center and at the foot of Table Mountain lies an unsightly vacant lot currently referred to as **Zonnebloem.** Only three decades ago it was a lively and diverse cultural mecca known as District Six, where middle-class residents of all races and religions happily coexisted, a slap in the face to the National Party's insistence that different races could not live in close contact. The pressurized melting pot inspired strong cultural and political ideals, jazz, and poetry.

In 1966, the National Party declared District Six a white-only district as defined by the **Group Areas Act of 1958.** Between 1966 and 1980, bulldozers razed the homes of over 60,000 residents, forcing them into townships (some of which the government perversely named after streets in District Six) and leaving only the churches and mosques that still stand. The memory of this martyred district is at once nostalgic and haunting for Cape Town citizens. With the exception of the hideous Cape Technikon, no one has yet dared build on this ground, which possesses something of a sacred aura. Restitution is underway, and a court operating out of the District Six Museum recently began adjudicating property claims by former residents in hope of bringing them back. The government plans to build low-cost housing to facilitate this process, though the settlement of claims will take years. The ability to replicate the vitality of the now ghost-like land seems dubious. For more on District Six, pick up *"Buckingham Palace," District Six* by Richard Rive or *The Spirit of District Six* by Cloete Breytenbach.

BO-KAAP. Also known as the **Malay Quarter,** this collection of suburbs north of Buitengracht St., is home to CT's Muslim population. Of the current population, an estimated 99% are descendants of slaves. Bo-Kaap is CT's oldest residential area, a distinction shown by its cobblestone streets and lively Dutch and Georgian architecture. During apartheid, the National Party decided not to destroy religious institutions, allowing the area to retain its Muslim character. Unfortunately, the Bo-Kaap has a crime problem; don't carry valuables. ■**Bo-Kaap Guided Tours** offers tours by the area's residents. *(☎ 422 1554 or 082 423 6932. Tours daily in morning and afternoon. Book one day in advance. R55.)* The **Bo-Kaap Museum** details the rich local history. *(71 Wale St. ☎ 424 3846. Open M-Sa 9:30am-4:30pm. R5, children R2.)*

CASTLE OF GOOD HOPE. This pentagonal military base is South Africa's oldest building and a tourist favorite. Currently the regional headquarters of the South African Army, the fortifications were once used by the ruling regimes to defend the Cape from invaders. Inside is a military museum, which celebrates the eras in which camouflage was considered too gauche for officers and gentlemen. See William Fehr's gigantic collection of landscape paintings detailing the development of South Africa between the 17th and 19th centuries. *(Between Darling and Strand St. east of Adderley St. ☎ 496 1249. Open daily 9am-4pm. R15, students and children R7; half-price on Su. William Fehr Collection open M-Sa 9am-4pm; second, on-street Buitenkant St. entrance for just the collection. Free. Once inside the gates, free tours of the castle are held M-Sa at 11am, noon, and 2pm. Key ceremony M-F at 10am. Changing of the Guard M-F at noon.)*

GRAND PARADE AND CITY HALL. Years ago, British troops used to flash a bit of pomp and circumstance here with uniformed demonstrations. After they left, the residents of District Six used the space as a market. Though peddlers still hawk their wares, the Grand Parade has more recently served as a venue for celebrations and demonstrations of political protest. *(East of Adderley St., down Darling.)* The turn-of-the-century City Hall presides over the Parade, its clock tower a half-sized Big Ben replica. Mandela delivered his famous Freedom Speech from the balcony of City Hall to a jubilant crowd of 250,000 in 1990 after being released from 27 years in captivity. *(☎ 462 1250. Performances Th and Su 8pm.)*

RUST EN VREUGD HISTORIC HOUSE AND GARDEN. Numerous portraits celebrate Cape Town's infancy, with a substantial collection of paintings from landscapist John Thomas Baines. The elegant house was originally an 18th-century home for a Dutch East India official and the attractive garden outside tries to approximate its 18th and 19th century antecedents. *(78 Buitenkant St. Entrance to the side, through the gardens.* ☎ *465 3628; fax 461 9620; jvanwyk@iziko.org.za. Open M-Sa 8:30am-4:30pm. Donation requested.)*

OLD TOWN HOUSE. A former city hall, the house holds the spectacular Michaelis Collection of paintings, as well as prints of historical Cape Town which reveal hedonistic revelry that would put the modern city to shame. Upstairs, works by Van Dyck, Frans Hals, and Rembrandt focus on rather dry portraits. Special exhibitions frequently complement the collection. The soothing courtyard inside the museum has a restaurant guarded by stone lions that salivate water. *(In Greenmarket Sq., at the corner of Longmarket and Burg St.* ☎ *424 6367; fax 461 9592. Open M-Sa 10am-5pm, Su 10am-4pm. Donations appreciated.)*

SOUTH AFRICAN SENDIGGESTIG (MISSIONARY MEETING-HOUSE) MUSEUM. A church erected by missionaries for slaves in 1804, the restored building provides a documentary of slavery in the Cape. Young men might also be interested to find out just how fun it was to stay at a YMCA at the turn of the century. *(40 Long St.* ☎ *423 6755. Open M-F 9am-4pm. Free.)*

V&A WATERFRONT AND GREEN POINT

The Victoria and Albert Waterfront is a popular and crowded destination that perspires commercialism from every pore. The original Alfred Basin dates back to 1860 and had to be expanded when shipping volume increased. The private Victoria & Alfred Waterfront Company opened the current, tourist-oriented area in 1988 on a landfill ironically made from the rubble of District Six. Unlike similar wharfs around the world, the docks remain active not only with throngs of tourists, but also with fishing boats. The expensive shops and restaurants are open late, every cranny is wheelchair accessible, and there's usually a decent band playing for free in the outside amphitheater on sunny afternoons. *(Take the Waterfront shuttle from in front of the Adderley St. train station; R1.90. The shuttle also operates daily between the Waterfront, the Cape Town Airport, and the Table Mountain cableway.* ☎ *418 2369; information center* ☎ *408 7600; fax 425 2165; info@waterfront.co.za; www.waterfront.co.za. Open in summer daily 9am-6pm; in winter M-F 9:30am-5pm, Sa-Su 9am-6pm. Info kiosks in the Victoria Wharf mall open daily 9am-9pm; info office that makes bookings open daily 9am-6pm.)*

TWO OCEANS AQUARIUM. The unique aquarium exhibits teach tourists how to sleep with the fishes. This aquarium is definitely worth a visit, as the meeting of the Indian and Atlantic Oceans has provided it with specimens that exist nowhere else in the world. The touch pool and ragged-tooth sharks prove particularly appealing for children, while exhausted parents tend to identify with the lethargic seals. For a more intimate view, certified **divers** can join the sharks without the hindrance of a cage. *(At Dock Rd., just before the main Waterfront complex.* ☎ *418 3823; infoline* ☎ *418 4644; fax 418 3952; www.aquarium.co.za. Open daily 9:30am-6pm. R45; students and seniors, R3; ages 4-17, R20; under 4, free. Shark diving daily 10am, noon, 2pm. R275, with gear rental R350. Must be certified with dive card or certificate. Book one or two days in advance. AmEx/DC/MC/V.)*

ROBBEN ISLAND. Catamarans leave Jetty One for a 3½hr. tour of this former political prison for black activists during apartheid. The main part of the tour is led by former prisoners who take visitors to Nelson Mandela's prison cell and to the lime quarry where the Nobel Laureate suffered damage to his vision from the bright limestone. The tour also details political resistance among the prisoners—including the clever means by which Mandela wrote *Long Walk to Freedom*. Some of the former prisoners are poignantly candid, and encourage and answer questions about their experiences before and during their incarceration, their feelings about the museum and how (in)accurate its portrayal of the prison is, as well as their feelings about their current work as tour guides and about the new South Africa in general. There is also a penguin look-out and a children's center with storytelling, including classics like Mandela's *Little Red Riding Hood Loses Her Civil Rights*, every hour on the hour from 10am to 3pm. The ride itself proves singularly thrilling, as sheets of water glance off the boat, temporarily concealing the amazing view of Table Mountain. *(From the back of the Visitors Center, walk towards the red clock-tower and follow the signs. ☎419 1300; fax 419 1057; info@robben-island.org.za or bookings@robben-island.org.za; www.robben-island.org.za. Tours daily 9am-3pm on the hour; in winter 9am-2pm. Summer R100, winter R50; ages 4-14 R50/R30. Book tickets well in advance. Tours might be cancelled due to weather. Note that the replacement boat, used when the Robben Island Cruisers are being serviced, can be slower and increase tour time by 1hr. Also be aware that many local boat companies offer trips to "Robben Island" but do not in fact visit the prison; be sure to ask. Mountain biking, and penguin tours also available.)*

CAPE MEDICAL MUSEUM. Housed in the former residence of the medical superintendent of the old City Hospital, this thorough collection of early 20th-century medical paraphernalia is worth a gander. The small yet thorough museum contains intriguing reconstructions of an apothecary, a dentist's surgery, a ward bed, and a frightening operating theater. Displays on the history of South African doctors, medicine during the Anglo-Boer War, and indigenous medicine are informative. *(Portswood Rd. in Green Point, across from the Breakwater Lodge and indicated on a street sign. ☎/fax 418 5663. Open Tu-F 9am-4pm.)*

TELKOM EXPLORATORIUM. The museum offers exhibits and over 50 hands-on displays, primarily on energy and telecommunications, with the enthusiasm of a mad scientist. While the triumphal, Clockwork Orange-esque atmosphere isn't anything to write home about, the free Internet access inside provides means by which do so. *(On Dock Rd., a bit beyond the main Waterfront complex, in the building behind and to the right of the Visitors Center. ☎419 5957; www.exploratorium.co.za. Open Tu-Su 9am-6pm; last entry 5:30pm. R12, students and children R7.)*

CAPE FLATS

To truly experience Cape Town, visitors should not miss the Cape Flats, to the east of Cape Town along the N2. A visit to these surrounding townships is essential for anyone interested in the uncensored history of South Africa and the painful reality of how over two-thirds of its citizens currently live. The drive from Cape Town to the airport is often the only glimpse visitors to Cape Town get of these barren townships, which were established under apartheid as "mens-only dormitories" to provide lily-white Cape Town with a cheap labor force. Blacks who could not find work, and thus had no legal place to live, were forced to set up squatter camps with tin shacks and plastic tarps for roofs. **Crossroads** is one such shantytown that still exists, despite attempts by the National Party to eradicate it. This township was the site of the much-publicized 1993 murder of white American Fulbright Scholar Amy Biehl by a black mob. Today, plans are in the works for her family and those of the accused to fund a nearby community center. **Langa** (the oldest township and birthplace of the Pan-African Congress), **Guguletu, Khayelitsha,** and predominantly "coloured" **Mitchell's Plain** are among the other townships, most of whose names were derived from streets of District Six.

TOURS. Since the labyrinthine townships are almost impossible to navigate and certain parts can be dangerous, it is necessary to go with a guide. There are many outstanding operators who provide a critical examination of life in the townships. The tours do an excellent job of humanizing the townships by introducing visitors to the residents (at schools, workshops, and *shebeen* taverns).

Township Crawling (www.townshipcrawling.com) is a quarterly magazine that presents socially responsible cultural and historical information about the Cape Town townships and tours. It is affiliated with **Thuthuka Tours** (☎ 082 979 5831; fax 689 9705), run by township residents. Half-Day Township Tours visit visitors to men's hostels, a traditional healer, a *shebeen*, and a craft market (M-F 9am-1pm or 1-5pm, R180). Thuthuka also offers an Evening Jazz Tour (F-Su, R180), a Gospel Tour (semi-formal dress required, 9am-1pm Su, lunch included; R180), and a Xhosa Folklore Tour (half-day, 1-5pm Sa).

Samuel at **Day Trippers** is a wonderfully personable guide to District Six and the townships. (☎ 082 970 0564, or contact him through The Backpack; see **Accommodations**, p. 94. R195 for a morning tour, additional R130 for tour of Robben Island.) **Grassroute Tours** provides an expertly detailed examination of District Six, Bo-Kaap, and the townships, and also does evening tours through jazz clubs. (☎ 797 0949 or 082 951 1016; grasrout@iafrica.com; www.grassroutetours.co.za. R160, children under 12 R80.) **One World Traveller's Space,** 309 Long St., arranges alternative township visits, in which visitors join a township resident on a *kombi* ride to their neighborhood before proceeding on an informal walking tour; see **Practical Information,** p. 88. (☎/fax 423 0777. R90.) **Green Turtle** tours offer a four-hour walking tour through Imizamo Yethu, near Hout Bay. (☎ 082 558 2963 or 462 3702; gturtle@mweb.co.za; www.greenturtletours.co.za. R230.)

SOUTHERN SUBURBS

■ **KIRSTENBOSCH NATIONAL BOTANICAL GARDENS.** Lying serenely on the eastern slopes of Table Mountain (see p. 106), the Gardens contain over 4500 species of some of the rarest and most beautiful flora in Southern Africa. Capetonians flock to this utopia for its picturesque picnicking conditions. The restaurant and cafe on the premises are also popular venues for champagne breakfasts. Undulating hills, winding paths, serene ponds, presumptuous peacocks, and lush gardens cover the 528ha of this estate. Two of the best paths lead you to the Fragrance Garden. Particularly recommended is the path for blind visitors, as it contains plants of the aromatic and tactile variety. The information center offers decent advice and maps on trails both up Table Mountain via Skeleton Gorge (see p. 107) and in the Gardens themselves. Sunday night concerts (jazz, folk, blues, carols, et. al.) are a delightfully popular event. *(10min. drive from the city center; take the M3/Rhodes Dr. to the M63. Golden Arrow runs two buses from the Grand Parade; call ☎ 0800 656 463 for times. Rikki's Taxi ☎ 423 4888. R40. ☎ 762 9120 or 761 4916; info ☎ 799 8783. Open daily Apr.-Aug. 8am-6pm; Sept.-Mar. 8am-7pm. R15, students and children R5. Free trail maps available. Guided tours every Tu and Sa at 11am are free; other times R10 per person. Guided walks can be arranged for groups. Contact the information office for wheelchair bookings. Sunday sunset concerts Dec.-Mar. 5:30-6:30pm. R25 admission after 3pm, children R10.)*

■ **GROOT CONSTANTIA.** The beautiful estate of this vineyard (the oldest in South Africa) was purchased in 1685 by Simon Van der Stel, governor of the Cape, and namesake of the other heavy hitter in the South African wine world, Stellenbosch. He transformed this scenic piece of farmland into several vineyards less than 20 years later. The impressive Cape Dutch Manor House where Van der Stel lived contains beautiful antique Cape furniture. An ornate mural of male cherubs adorns the front door. The lone female among this group was created when an apprentice mistakenly chiseled off a key anatomical part of one unfortunate male. The estate's wine tour is quite informative and includes a film and generous tasting. There is also a museum crammed with furniture and bric-a-brac, but some revisionist historian forgot to mention the slaves who did most of the work. The estate is government owned, and taxpayers groaned when the government wrote off R10 million in old loans. (☎ 794 5128. *Open daily 9am-5pm. Tours every hour on the hour 10am-4pm. Tastings R9. Tours R20, including tasting.*)

UNIVERSITY OF CAPE TOWN. The most prestigious university in South Africa, UCT is in the suburb of Rondebosch, at the foot of Devil's Peak. The campus is worth a visit for its attractive red-brick, ivy-clad buildings, the impressive Jamieson Hall with the Peak as backdrop, and the view over the Cape Flats. The upper part of campus is quite a hike from the main road in Rondebosch, so take one of the frequent shuttles. (*Follow signs from M3/Rhodes Dr. Minibuses run from Adderley St.*)

ELSEWHERE

⬛ TABLE MOUNTAIN CABLE CAR. Those looking for all the Table Mountain views without all the work pop into the cable car that glides up the mountain in five minutes. One rotation made along the route gives passengers both a full 360-degree view of the surroundings and extreme vertigo. The queues can stretch to unbelievable lengths, so expect a wait (up to 2hr. during peak season). It doesn't run in poor weather or high wind; definitely call ahead. Cable cars leave daily at regular and frequent intervals. (☎ 424 8181 or 424 0015; *www.tablemountain.co.za. Opening times and rates vary by season; check the web site for more information. The first car goes up at 8am or 8:30am, depending on season. The last car goes up at 5pm, 6pm, 7pm, or 9pm, depending on season. Rates range from R68-95, R35-50 for children.*)

RATANGA JUNCTION AMUSEMENT PARK. This theme park is the first of its kind in Africa. Head-rattling roller coasters, gargantuan water rides, and ample entertainment pavilions make for good, clean, wholesome fun. Within the park is the newly opened Docksides entertainment complex, with sprawling dance floors, drink specials, and ladies nights with strippers. (*Drive down the N1 toward Paarl and get off at the Sable Rd. exit; follow the signs. Open W-Su 10am-5pm. Closed in winter. R69, children under 1.3m R59; non-riders R29. Parking R2.50 per hr.*)

NEWLANDS. In this suburb, accessible via the M3 or the Metrorail, **South African Breweries** produces the flavors that monopolize national bars. (*3 Main Rd.* ☎ 658 7395. *Tours and tastings available by appointment M-F 10am and 2pm. Free.*) **Norwich Park Newlands** has been the site of many an international rugby showdown. (*On Boundary Rd.* ☎ 689 4921.) The **South African Rugby Museum,** on the premises, details the team's rich history. Those averse to spilled blood tend to opt for the adjacent **Newlands Cricket Ground;** mentioning the name of Hansie Cronje might induce a tear or a fistfight. (☎ 683 4934.) To arrange tours of the stadiums or the museum, contact Gateway to Newlands. (☎/fax 686 2150 or 082 461 8651; *gateway@dockside.co.za.*)

🏛 GALLERIES

A number of galleries line Church St., while more cutting-edge work is shown along Bree St. and Buitengracht St. and in some new spaces around Buitenkant St. Check web sites for updated information on exhibits.

Bang the Gallery!, 21 Pepper St. (☎/fax 422 1477; alexh@bangthegallery.co.za; www.bangthegallery.co.za). Large space exhibiting a number of artists of varying media. Regularly includes works by Alex Hamilton, Shany van den Berg, Solomon Siko, Karen Jay, and Craig Foster. Open M-F 10am-5pm, Sa 10am-2pm.

Hänel Gallery, 84 Shortmarket St. (☎431 1406; fax 423 5277; ehaenel@compuserve.com; www.hanelgallery.com). Exhibits monthly solo shows of South African and sometimes German artists. Open Tu-F 11am-5pm, Sa 10am-2pm.

Johans Borman Fine Art Gallery (☎423 6075; fax 426 4475). In the In-Fin-Art building on Upper Buitengracht St. at the corner of Buitensingle. Shows a large selection of Old Master paintings and glass work as well as a few contemporary mixed media pieces. Open M-F 10am-6pm, Sa 9am-2pm.

◙ BEACHES

SEA POINT AND GREEN POINT. The beach along Sea Point has a number of rock pools popular for bathing, despite their proximity to the city. Because of dangerous rocks and riptides (not to mention the oft-frigid Atlantic), most of the ocean here is not for swimming; the park and promenade along the shore, however, are great for a stroll amid panting joggers, amorous couples, and playful children.

Toward the end of Beach Rd. in Sea Point is the **Sea Point Pavilion Pool,** an Olympic-sized saltwater pool with high diving boards and several dipping pools. The main pool is much warmer than the ocean, making it a better place to sunbathe and swim. *(Open Nov. to mid-Apr. daily 7am-7pm. Lockers available. R6.)* **Graff's Pool** is a temperate rock pool marked by an inconspicuous sign near the intersection of Beach Rd. and Marais St., and while it is technically open to women, the sight of a bunch of male nudists enjoying the sea breeze tends to deter them. Graff's Pool is sometimes a congregating point for gay sun-bathers. *(Open 24hr. Free.)*

CLIFTON. For some hard-core beach activity, the luxurious suburb of Clifton has four interlinked beaches, all with quite different personalities. While the glacial water deters swimmers (except for quick dips or kamikaze sunbathers with overheated brains), volleyball, frisbee, and sunbathing pass the time adequately. **First Beach** is full of bronze surfers and surfettes; **Second Beach** with teeny-boppers; **Third Beach** with thirtysomethings; and **Fourth Beach** packs in the throngs and is the most-family oriented. Second Beach also sometimes serves as a favored meeting point for gay sunbathers. Third and Fourth have snack vendors and umbrella/chair rentals. Fire-throwers visit on some weeknights.

CAMPS BAY. Camps Bay has become a surfing and scuba diving venue, but it is also a good place for chilling beside (and, if masochistic, in) the turquoise waters. Just along Victoria Rd. after Clifton, Camps Bay stretches along an expanse of virginal sand where beach volleyball players thrive. The mountain peaks of the **Twelve Apostles** in the background make it one of the most breathtaking settings around Cape Town. Capetonians spend their summer days lolling on the beach before heading across the road to the numerous trendy restaurants to cool off with a cold beer. During Christmas and Easter holidays, Camps Bay is a hotspot, especially for watching the sunset. Surfing it not permitted on Camps Bay; go to Glen Beach if you want to ride some waves. *(Minibus taxis run along Victoria Rd., which becomes Beach Rd., from here to the rest of the Atlantic Coast, and to the center of town; R3. Beach chairs and shades can cost up to R50, especially if you ooze foreigner vibes; keep those vibes in tow.)*

LLANDUDNO. Llandudno Beach hides discreetly behind two granite boulders. Because of its remote location, a twisty 15km drive from Cape Town along the M6, the beach remains relatively peaceful (though parking is difficult on weekends), creating chilly but outstanding surfing conditions and uninterrupted tanning. Those who don't have tan lines should meander a bit farther down the M6 before dropping their drawers at **Sandy Bay,** the "unofficial" nudist beach. This isolated stretch of sand, accessible via a 15-minute walk from Llandudno, serves a mixed nudist scene on weekends; during the week, however, it's primarily a venue at which men, many gay, hang out.

HOUT BAY. Hout Bay's natural beauty and bountiful schools of fish manage to preclude its lapse into industrial unsightliness. The grey harbor, crowded with boats, remains the center of Hout Bay; while it may not be the V&A Waterfront, there is something to be said for a fishing port that retains a genuine, unpackaged quality. The **Sentinel** mountain peak towers 800m over the harbor, which offers little except for fish 'n chips stands, a couple of shabby museums, and some cute kitsch shops. The area near the drive to **Chapman's Peak** is sprouting new restaurants and bars and can be quite lively. Spectacular cruises run from the harbor to **Duiker Island,** also known as Seal Island, for the huge influx of the adorable creatures in the summer. Playful seals fly in and out of the water around the ships, while the island itself seems like a huge department store where every pup is lost and every cow runs around trying to identify her child by bark and smell. The island is only accessible by boat, as sharks number among the many island visitors. **Circe Launches** is the least expensive, with speedy 30-minute trips to Duiker Island or longer cruises that also circle around to Chapman's Peak. (☎ 790 1040. Duiker Island cruises daily 9:30 and 10:15am. R25, children R10.) **Drumbeat Charters** runs more frequently to Seal Island, Chapman's Peak, Sandy Beach, and a shipwreck site. *(☎ 438 9208 or 790 4859. Daily 9:15, 10, 11:30am, 1:30, 3:30pm; more times depending on season and demand. R40, children R18.)*

🔋 HIKING

Despite its proximity to the city and its domestic name, **Table Mountain,** with over 550 walks, can rock the world of most hikers and tourists. The easiest route is still quite a challenge for the average person, while the more difficult routes can be downright thrilling for seasoned hikers. Many tourists hike up and take the cable car down to spare their knees; one-way tickets can be purchased at the top. Even if you think you'll hike both ways, we urge you to bring enough money for a one-way ticket down. Trust us. Overlooking the Rhodes Memorial, neighboring **Devil's Peak** was named because of various local legends that accuse good ol' Satan of a smoking addiction so severe that he regularly obscures the mountaintop in a cloud of exhale. Shirley Brossy's *Walking Guide to Table Mountain* (R45) includes good tips on the entire range. To reach the trailheads, call Rikki's Taxi (☎ 423 4888, R10), catch the Kloof Nek bus at the Grand Parade station, or take the summer tourist shuttle from the Waterfront. *(Take Kloof Nek Rd. almost to the top, and turn left at the well-marked turn-off. The city bus runs at 7, 8am, 2, and 3pm.)*

🔋 **PLATTEKLIP GORGE.** This medium-difficulty hike is the most popular route to the summit of Table Mountain. From the lower cable station, it zigzags up a steep gorge, finally depositing its hikers at the upper cable station. For those who are reasonably fit, the gorge will take roughly one and a half hours to climb. The trail begins with a 30min. stint straight up, then a short hike along the Contour Path to the beginning of the gorge; a sign on the left designates the path, which is fairly straightforward. After absorbing the incredible view of the city from the top, turn right and walk along the mountain (follow the painted yellow footprints) until you reach the mobs of tourists at the upper cable station. Abseiling is available, if hanging off cliffs with the ocean looming behind sounds enticing (for more information, see **Adventure Outfitters,** p. 108). To check out False Bay instead of going straight to the cable car, follow the Maclear's Beacon trail.

THE PIPE TRACK. Although this route doesn't go to the top of Table Mountain, the staggering views of the Atlantic and Camps Bay make it one of the most popular hikes. *(The flat footpath runs for 4.5km (1½hr.) along the Twelve Apostles, the mountain crags overlooking the sea. The path begins at Kloof Nek, just west of the Tafelberg Rd. turn-off.)*

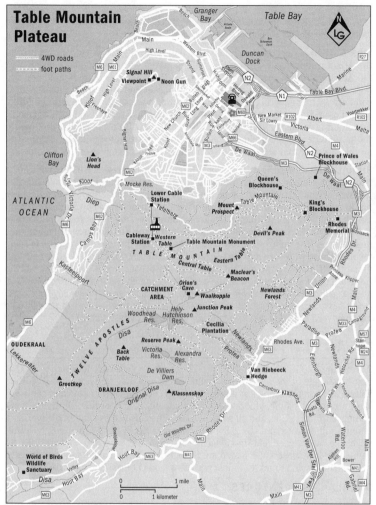

Table Mountain Plateau

- ----- 4WD roads
- ----- foot paths

SKELETON GORGE AND MACLEAR'S BEACON. With its origin at the Kirstenbosch Botanical Gardens, Skeleton Gorge is a difficult but popular hike that offers excellent conditions for summer scrambles. The generally shady path has dams and rivers for quick splashes of refreshment. Clearly marked signs lead the way initially, but at several points the trail is hard to follow. Some of the boulders demand elementary rock climbing, and at certain points you will ascend mountain streams. After some ladders, it's necessary to navigate slippery rocks until the main path reappears. At the top, proceed up the sand path for a few meters for a spectacular view of a hidden mountain lake. Retrace your steps to the signpost. *(To go to the very top of Table Mountain, follow the sign for Maclear's Beacon all the way to the upper cable station. Fit hikers can generally make the trek from Kirstenbosch to Maclear's Beacon in 3hr., plus another hr. to get to the Cableway. Alterna-*

tively, follow signs for Kasteelsport, which leads to a descent path called Nursery Ravine that returns to Kirstenbosch. This loop takes about 4hr. from the beginning of Skeleton Gorge. Exercise caution—descents down the path of ascent can prove treacherous.)

LION'S HEAD. This steep peak lies adjacent to the city center, separating it from the Atlantic suburbs and rewarding willing hikers with spectacular sunsets over the Atlantic. For an easy but vigorous hike, the summit is quite doable day and night in under an hour, even with a picnic basket and a bottle of wine. There is some tricky maneuvering up narrow trails, but it is possible even with children. Near the top, hikers have the option of scrambling up a set of fixed vertical chains, or detouring on flatter ground. The 360-degree view from the peak is well worth the minimal exertion, and sunsets over the city are unforgettable. During full moons, it seems that half of Cape Town ascends the summit to enjoy the show.

SIGNAL HILL. Formerly called "Lion's Rump," this low rise is well-known for the **Noon Gun,** a cannon fired from the hill every day at noon (except Sundays). The gun was originally placed to signal the time to ships in Table Bay; its practical use has long since expired, but the tradition lives on. During hikes up Signal Hill, wanderers might notice the unique, shimmery **Silver Tree,** a species found only in the Table Mountain area, but recently transplanted to the Kirstenbosch Botanical Gardens as well. The view of the bay and the coast from the top of Signal Hill is spectacular. Those with sore legs (or pressed for time) can call Rikki's Taxi, which will make the trip during the day. At night a car or private taxi is necessary, but the drive offers a knock-out view of the city lights from above. *(From the city, follow Kloof Nek Rd. up to the top until the well-marked junction for the cable car and Camps Bay/Clifton; take a right for the turn-off to Signal Hill. From the Lion's Head trailhead, walkers can continue up the tarred road and along the ridge for about 45min. to reach the hilltop.)*

▨ ADVENTURES

Adrenaline junkies thrive in this city. There are endless daredevil activities that take advantage of the nearby mountains, rivers, oceans—and hospitals. **Adventure Village,** 229 Long St., serves as a great one-stop shop for fearlessness and madness. They arrange abseiling, kloofing, bungee jumping, sand boarding, skydiving, paragliding, surfing, sailing, and all sorts of tours. They also advise and book overlanders and sell gear. (☎/fax 424 1580; after hours ☎082 859 0427; thrills@adventure-village.co.za; www.adventure-village.co.za. Open M-F 8am-7pm, Sa 8am-1pm, Su 9am-noon; low season M-F 8am-6pm, Sa 8am-1pm.) Backpackers lodges can also book activities and tours. For most activities, book at least one day in advance.

OVERLAND ADVENTURES

MOUNTAIN BIKING. Day Trippers offers mountain biking along the Constantiaberg Mountains in many of their tours to Cape Point and the Winelands. *(☎/fax 531 3274; trippers@iafrica.com; www.daytrippers.co.za. R235 for Constantiaberg trip on Su.)* **Downhill Adventures,** at the intersection of Long, Kloof, and Orange St., offers a rigorous three-hour Double Descent down Table Mountain for R250 (M, W, F, Su), which starts off at the upper Cable Station and continues down the mountain at high speeds. Halfway down, the group takes a break at a crystal clear rock pool, where bikers can swim and jump off a 14m cliff to get their hearts pounding even faster. The trip ends with a final descent down Devil's Peak, where the views of the city are astounding. Downhill Adventures also cycles to Cape Point on a more scenic trip (W, F, Sa) and swerves to the Winelands for R295. Bike rental also available. *(☎422 0388. Open M-F 8:30am-5pm, Sa 9am-noon.)*

ABSEILING. Abseiling, also known as rapelling, involves a scintillating descent down a mountain or cliff face in which you trust your life to the security of gravity, ropes, and harnesses. Giddy up. **Abseil Africa,** based in Adventure Village, offers two fantastically scenic options. The most popular is Table Mountain (see p. 106), which at 112m is the world's highest natural commercial abseil. The first 65m go straight down the mountain side, while the final stretch entails a "free-fall," during which the abseiler gently slides down the rope with ample time to enjoy the view of Camps Bay (R250). This abseil is excellent for even the most terrified first-timers. *(☎ 424 4760; abseil@iafrica.com; www.abseilafrica.co.za. Call ahead to find out if they're running on Table Mountain on a given day.)*

SANDBOARDING. Downhill Adventures (see p. 87) runs a full-day **sandboarding** expedition to the biggest sand dunes around the Cape for R395. Sandboarding— inspired by surfing and snowboarding—is easy to learn and great fun on a clement day, though be sure to bring sunscreen and shades and book ahead.

MOTOR BIKING. Bike 2 Oceans rents BMWs (R480 per day including 200km, insurance, helmets, and maps) and arranges raging biking tours through South Africa, Namibia, Lesotho, Swaziland, and Zimbabwe. (☎ 082 491 9124; bike2oceans@ intekom.co.za; www.bike2oceans.com.) **Adventure Village** arranges a **quad-biking** tour through bush and sand dunes (R350 for 2 hr., bikes are automatic and no license or previous experience is required).

AQUA ADVENTURES

SURFING. *Endless Summer* devotees might tell you Jeffreys Bay (see p. 175) is the place for real surfers, but Capetonians know better. The Cape Peninsula is a fantastic place for both beginner surfers and professionals to savor the overlap of the Indian and Atlantic Oceans. The most popular surfing spots in the area are **Kommetjie, Long Beach,** and **Big Bay** on the Atlantic coast. **Muizenberg** (see p. 115) is a good place for neophytes to practice the basics. The waves on the False Bay side of the Cape tend to be a little less intimidating, and the water is certainly warmer, but the surf is better along the Atlantic side of the peninsula. The biggest swells are in the winter. For up-to-date information on surfing conditions, call ☎ 788 5965. The **Surf Center,** at the corner of Castle and Burg St., rents boards and wetsuits. *(☎ 423 7853; surf@surf.co.za; www.surf.co.za. Open M-F 9am-5pm.)* **Downhill Adventures** (see p. 87) offers a day-long surfing academy (Tu, Th, Sa, Su; R450 including lunch; additional day R315). They also have a surf lodge in Kommetjie one minute away from Long Beach (R120 per night). Downhill Adventures can take experienced surfers to the best breaks, and Chris Ross at the Overseas Visitors Club can also point you in the right direction. For **windsurfing** lessons or rentals, contact **South African Windsurfari** (☎ 082 449 9819). **Sea kayaking** is also good around the Cape. **Adventure Village** (see p. 108) rents gear for R120 per two hours.

SCUBA DIVING. Scuba diving is possible with **Table Bay Diving** (☎ 419 8822; fax 418 5821; R1500 for a 4-day course, shore dive R80, boat dive R135); some of the best Cape Peninsula diving is located in False Bay in winter. The **Two Oceans Aquarium** (see p. 101) arranges cageless dives with ragged-tooth sharks and other sea predators.

POWER BOATING. Ocean Rafters (a.k.a **Atlantic Adventures**) offer exhilarating high speed rides on 10-seater, 200-hp/V8 engine power boats. The windier the day, the bumpier the ride, the wetter your pants. (R200 for 1hr. tour to Robben Island or Hout Bay. ☎ 425 3785 or 072 265 6600; info@atlanticadventures.co.za; www.atlanticadventures.co.za or www.oceanrafters.co.za.)

WESTERN CAPE

WESTERN CAPE

EXTREME ADVENTURES

KLOOFING. *Kloof* means "cliff." Kloofing is an unbeatable summer activity that involves climbing up cliffs and waterfalls, jumping off, and swimming in the water that is (hopefully) there to catch you (see **If Everybody Jumped Off a Cliff...**, p. 215). This activity takes advantage of natural obstacle courses and requires equipment and know-how, so be sure to go with a tour company that can provide an experienced guide. **Day Trippers** (see **Daytrips**, p. 114) runs their Suicide Gorge (5-18m or higher) trips twice a week (Tu and F, Nov.-Apr.), in which most of the day is spent winding along a river (R325, including lunch and a cold beer if you survive). **Abseil Africa** at Adventure Village (see p. 108) catapults *kloofers* into Kamikaze Kanyon, a draining yet exhilarating full-day journey that involves both abseiling down a waterfall and kloofing (R450; including breakfast, lunch, and light dinner).

PARAGLIDING AND SKYDIVING. Adventure Village (see p. 108) books **tandem paraglides,** the most graceful of local adventure activities. The stunning flight from Lion's Head, Signal Hill, Gordon's Bay, or Hermanus is breathtaking (R750; book at least a couple of days ahead). Paragliding lessons are also available. They also book **tandem skydives** for those anxious to experience a 30- to 40-second free-fall from 9500 ft. (R1000, bookings essential, video of your jump R350).

▣ ENTERTAINMENT

For complete listings, check out the *Cape Review*.

MOVIES

Labia Theatre, 68 Orange St. in the Gardens, is a venue for art films, so don't be misled by the name. Stop by to pick up a weekly schedule of mainstream and alternative films. (☎424 5927 or 918 8950 for credit card bookings; www.labia.co.za. R18, under 12 and HI members R15; main evening show R20, children R18; seniors R10, except for main evening show.) The other artsy filmhouse is affiliated with UCT's **Baxter** (☎685 7880), on Main Rd. in Rondebosch. The **Independent Armchair Theatre** (☎447 1514) on Lower Main Rd. in Observatory screens a variety of genres and also has Monday night Manga accompanied by DJs (9pm); comedy nights, film classics, and live music (R10). The **NuMetro Cinema** (☎419 9700) and **Ster-Kinekor Cinema Nouveau** (☎425 8222), both at the V&A Waterfront, show the latest features (R20-26, check *Cape Times* and *Cape Argus* for showtimes). Theaters at the **Cavendish Square Mall** in Claremont require a car. The **IMAX Cinema,** in the BMW Pavilion on Dock Rd., plays nausea-inducers on the largest screen in the Southern Hemisphere. Bookings are advisable at all cinemas, especially on weekends.

THEATER

▨**Comedy Warehouse,** 55 Somerset Rd., in Greenpoint (☎425 2175), is Cape Town's funniest venue; you'll laugh your bum off. They pride themselves on good humor and mixed drinks. Tuesdays feature open mike at 8:30pm (R10). Friday and Saturday are strictly stand-up from 9pm on (R30). Sundays offer improv (R30) in the vein of *Whose Line Is It Anyway?* UCT's **Baxter Theatre Center** (☎685 7880; fax 689 1880; bxtms@protem.uct.ac.za; www.uct.ac.za/org/baxter), on Main Rd. in Rondebosch, has a main theater, a concert hall, and a studio. It hosts shows that originate in Johannesburg, as well as comedy, drama, musicals, dance, and symphony concerts. The **Nico Theatre Center,** at the Foreshore between D.F. Malan and Jan Smuts St., hosts the **Cape Town Philharmonic,** in addition to frequent musicals, ballet, and operas. (☎421 7695; fax 421 5448; www.artscape.co.za. Open M-F 9am-5pm, Sa 9am-12:30pm. Student tickets available 30min. before the show, R40.) To witness some rising local talent, check out the **Little Theater & Arena Theater** (☎480

7129; fax 424 2355; cbylvest@hiddingh.uct.ac.za), downtown between Orange St. and Government Ave. UCT's drama students put on experimental theater here (R20, students R15). Also see the **Independent Armchair Theater** (see **Movies,** above). **On Broadway,** 21 Somerset Rd. (☎418 8338; www.onbroadway.co.za), offers popular gay theater, with performances mixing in cabaret and drag shows.

⌐⌐ MARKETS AND SHOPPING

All manner of goods, from African curios to utter crap, are on sale at the countless organized and informal markets scattered throughout the city. Bargaining is expected at the outdoor markets, but is much less common at a formal store. The **outdoor markets** around Cape Town, mostly open Monday through Saturday until 4:30pm, offer more bang for the haggling buck; the most sane markets run from Greenmarket Sq. and St. George's Mall, while the greatest variety awaits at the Grand Parade and Adderley St. Sunday's outdoor market next to **Green Point Stadium** is gigantic, and it is easy to feel lost among the maze of giant masks and giraffe-topped salad servers. (☎447 2257. Open Su 8am-5pm.) The **Pan African Market,** 76 Long St. in the building across from the Purple Turtle, has many shops offering African crafts and hair braiding, and some of the vendors give excellent drum lessons on Saturday mornings. (☎424 2957. Open M-F 9am-5pm, Sa 9am-3pm.) There is also an African craft market in **Kayelitsha,** in the Cape Flats (M and Th 10am-2pm). Call ☎853 2803 for information on taking a tour through the market. There are a number of crafts markets at the waterfront. Captour provides a map of the city's numerous craft markets and training centers.

▐ NIGHTLIFE

Cape Town rocks to varied beats, from understated, cooler-than-thou venues to wild drum-and-*didgeridoo* circles to trance parties that usher in the dawn. While the ephemeral scene frequently (and frustratingly) shifts in some of the here-today, gone-tomorrow pubs and clubs, those who want to find a place to party won't go home disappointed. The local music scene is also thriving, with outstanding indie, marimba, and jazz bands burning it up. Check the *Cape Review* or the Friday section of the *Mail & Guardian.* Online, visit www.clubbersguide.thunda.com for up-to-date information on clubs and parties in Cape Town.

Unfortunately, nightlife is still racially divided, and not too much of it is specifically African, with the predominantly white City Bowl remaining the center of the action. **Long and Loop St.** are the veins of Cape Town's nightlife, where thousands of people wander to the cacophonous soundtrack of myriad clubs. The large security presence on weekends make clubs feel quite safe. Observatory also serves up a central but slightly more sedate scene. Elsewhere in the city, nightlife tends to be quite dispersed, making it difficult to move between venues without the assistance of a cab or the Boogie Bus (see **Getting Around,** p. 86).

Cape Town is renowned for its welcoming **gay nightlife scene.** Captour publishes a free, annually revised **Pink Map,** available at the tourist office, detailing Cape Town's gay-friendly establishments.

CAFES, PUBS, AND BARS

▨ **La Med** (☎424 863). Overlooking the Atlantic between Clifton and Camps Bay; look for signs. Especially popular and very crowded on Su afternoons and nights, La Med's setting is jaw-dropping, with Lion's Head paragliders landing on the field below the terrace and Cape Town's best sunsets. Once inside, cliquey, well-heeled groups get down to swinging jams and cover bands. Frequent live music. R15 cover on F and Sa includes R5 drink voucher. Open daily 10am-late.

Roxy Coffee, 14 Wandel St. (☎461 8507). In Dunkley Sq. Intimate, funky coffee bar with mirrored tiles on the floor, candles on tables, and a cozy fireplace in the corner. Interesting selection of specialty coffees (R16) and desserts. Mediocre sandwiches and cakes. Open May-Aug. M-F 3pm-late, Sa-Su noon-late; Sept.-Apr. daily noon-late.

Jo'burg, 218 Long St. (☎422 0142). Hip hip and away. A chic crowd mingles under an upside-down rotating Jo'burg skyline. Naked Bart Simpson, inspiring photography, funky blue bar stools. Always loud, always busy. Heaving on weekends. Open M-F 5pm-4am, Sa noon-4am, Su 7pm-4am.

Rafiki's, 13b Kloofnek Rd. (☎426 4731). A languid lick of paradise. This large yet cozy, candle-lit space features live music, art shows, beanbags, and relaxed balconies with hammocks. Classy. Open M-Sa 4pm-late, Su 6pm-late.

Cafe Vacca Matta, 1A Seeff House, Foreshore (☎419 5550; fax 421 8866; www.vacca-matta.com). Near the Waterfront. An almost exact replica of the dance bar in the film *Coyote Ugly*. Women dancing on the bar, professional dancers, and a crowd going wild to loud music. Check the web site for theme parties. Open until very late W-Su nights.

The Shack, 45 De Villiers St., Zonnebloem (☎461 5892). Hangout for Cape Technikon students, who sprawl across all of the indoor and outdoor crannies of this titanic complex. Sweet music, billiards, delicious food. Only drawback is location; Zonnebloem is often considered an unsafe area. **206** (☎465 2106), inside, is a mini-funk club. No cover. Both open M-Th 4pm-late, F 1pm-really late, Sa-Su 6pm-late.

Cool Runnings (☎448 7656), corner of Lower Main Rd. and Station Rd., in Observatory. A hopping Jamaican-themed bar, mon. Wild specialties include The Pangalactic and Sex in the Bush. Huge terrace with sand. Lots of Thai and Caribbean options for Da Nibbles. Occasional live music. Open daily 10am-2am.

Touch of Madness, 12 Nuttal Rd., Observatory (☎448 2266; www.cafeatom.co.za). Turn onto Station St. from Lower Main Rd. and take the first right; it's the purple Victorian building on your right. Popular, posh cigar and whiskey lounge/bar for scenesters. Jazzy atmosphere is an extremely friendly hangout for gay and straight alike. Open daily 7pm-real late. AmEx/MC/V.

Buena Vista Social Cafe, 81 Main Rd., Greenpoint (☎433 0611; fax 433 0610; buenavista@sadomain.co.za). Right above the News Cafe (see p. 97). A great Cuban refuge. Cafe, bar, tapas restaurant, and a lot of Latin/Cuban/Brazilian music. Tapas R20. Mojito R18-20. Open M-F noon-1am, Sa-Su 5pm-1am. MC/V. ❶

DANCE CLUBS

Beat Boutique, 79 Church St. (www.sleaze.co.za/beat). On Longmarket St. Cape Town's *creme de la creme* when it comes to nightlife. This is currently one of the hottest places in the city. 2 dance floors and frequent special nights (see web site). F funky house, Sa progressive house. **Upfront,** attached, continues until sunrise on an enormous deck with amazing views. Cover R30. Open F-Sa 10pm-very late.

The Fez, 38 Hout St. and **Fez on the Beach,** The Drive in Camps Bay (☎082 681 4330 or 423 1456). One in the heart of downtown, the other on a deck overlooking Camps Bay. Moroccan *casbahs* host a variety of Cape Town's young and restless. Nomads come from afar for provisions (R18 on up). Fez is open M-Sa 9pm-late; Fez on the Beach is open in summer from the early afternoon until the sun rises. Popular during the week, especially funk Th when other venues are quiet. Dress code. Closed for renovations July 2002, but scheduled to reopen Sept. 2002. Cover R20.

Lab, 50 Orange St., Gardens (☎423 2112; fax 423 2177; info@lab-bar.co.za; www.lab-bar.co.za). Just beyond the very end of Long St. The "London Academy of Bartending" offers 112 spectacular cocktails of about R25 each and a great dance scene. W members only, Th gay night. No cover. Su, W, Th 6pm-2am, F-Sa 6pm-4am.

The Complex, 156 Long St. (☎424 1248). A combination of the Groove Bar, Legacy, and a record shop named Rugged Vinyl. Home to Cape Town's Drum 'n Bass, Deep Funky house, rave beat, and trance lovers. F "Expression night." Open daily 9pm-6am.

Organafix, 32 Glynn St., Gardens (☎083 490 2103; debbie@cafeerte.com; www.kwik-kut.com). Next to Drum Cafe. Intense venue sends the willing through the looking glass. Multimedia dance parties place premium on psychedelic images, astral projections, and a haze of (illegal) smoke. Pillows, couches, and munchies make it feel more like a private party than a club. Mostly trance. Will soon include a vegetarian restaurant and offer movie nights. Open W-Th 5pm-very late, F-Sa 3pm-very, very late. F pajama night.

The Lounge, 194 Long St. (☎424 7636). Colorful rooms and an enormous balcony. Cool relaxing furnishings for lounging. Full of local film-industry types. Chilling is at a premium, especially on the balcony. Superb drum 'n bass and breakbeats scene on W nights. F hip-hop. Cover R10. Open M, W-Sa 8pm-late.

169, 169 Long St. (☎426 1107). R&B/hip-hop nightclub. Includes a dance floor, lounge area with courtyard, and an enormous balcony. Bouncers more intimidating than Ray Lewis. Cover R30, dress code smart casual. Open W, F-Sa 10pm-5am.

More, 74 Loop St. (☎422 0544). Get ready to dance your feet off your legs to the house and funky beat. Thank goodness More has plenty of sofas for catching one's breath. Cover R30. F "party night." Open F-Sa 10:30pm-late.

Baseline, 74 Shortmarket St. (☎083 364 2505). Not to be confused with Johannesburg's Baseline. This new nightclub overlooking Long St. plays loud R&B, hip-hop, and groovy house. Cover R30. Open W, F-Sa 10pm-very late.

Favela, 34 Burg St. (☎083 430 1203). A small and very trendy club. Get a taste of funky house on W, R&B on F, and house on Sa. Prepare to be very trendy. Cover R20-40. Open W, F-Sa 10:30pm-late.

Stones, 166A Long St. (☎424 0418). Though only one of the 9 branches of Stones in Cape Town, its location makes this billiards bar the ideal place to relax before hitting the dance floor. A long bar, loud music (from hard rock to dance), and video screens get you in the mood while you show off your skills on one of the 19 pool tables. R2 per game. Open noon-late.

LIVE MUSIC

▨ **Mama Africa,** 178 Long St. (☎424 8634). On the corner of Long and Pepper St. Renowned venue for marimba music, with bands from all over Africa giving diners a beat to eat to. Decent bar with interior courtyard around the corner and upstairs. Bands play 8pm-midnight or so. Cover R10, even if you're eating. Open M-Sa 7pm-close.

▨ **The Drum Cafe,** 32 Glynn St. (☎461 1305; www.drumcafe.co.za). Off Buitenkant St., near Zonnebloem St. Take a taxi or drive. Drumming sessions can be either fantastic or abysmal, depending on who decides to rent and play/abuse a drum. Those who participate always have a blast. M group workshop (traditional West African). W facilitated circle (different African styles), Th freestyle jam, F surprise night, and Sa Tranz-Central. Frequent screenings, performances, alternapop and trance DJs. Cover R20, R10 after 11pm, drum hire R20. Open M-Sa 9pm until everyone's hands are sore.

Club Galaxy, 67 College Rd. (☎637 9132; clubgalaxy@iafrica.com). In Rylands. Popular jazz venue in the Cape Flats. Inviting for fusion (electric guitars and African drum beats) and hip-hop enthusiasts. Cover R20. Sa afternoons live jazz and a guaranteed full dance floor. Open Th-F 9pm-4am, Sa 3pm-4am.

The Jam, 43 De Villiers St., Zonnebloem (☎083 341 5627). Drive or take a taxi. This dimly lit loft next to The Shack is Cape Town's best indie music venue. A strange mix of indie and cheese. Live bands jam on weekends. W CD release parties, Th absurd banana parties. Cover R10-30. Open W-Sa from 9pm, bands go on at varied times.

Dizzy Jazz Cafe, 41 The Drive, in Camps Bay (☎438 2686). Popular, unpretentious spot for hot summer nights. Excellent live music daily from 9:30pm, off-season 6 nights a week (call for schedules). The view of the Atlantic from the veranda is incredible. Cover R20. Open daily 11am until everyone's dizzy.

The Purple Turtle (☎423 6194), at the corner of Long St. and Shortmarket St.; it's the big purple building with the powerful music. A loud, gothic feel. Serves the market vendors during the day. DJs, live heavy metal, and alternative. Happy Hour M-F 4-6pm, Sa 4-5pm. Open daily 10am-very late.

GAY NIGHTLIFE

Cape Town is so welcoming and integrated that the need for a distinct gay nightlife is minimized; almost all bars and clubs are gay-friendly. Additionally, the few self-proclaimed gay spots are some of the best establishments on the city's nightlife canvas (hence their popularity with the straight set). GayNet Cape Town's **Easter Dance** annually reasserts who rules the nightlife roost. Most of the gay clubs congregate around **Somerset Rd.** and **Waterkant St.,** close to Fat Boy's, the center of all things overwhelmingly hetero. The **South African Gay and Lesbian Film Festival** hits Cape Town in mid-February (www.oia.co.za). See **Gay and Lesbian Services,** p. 89, for more information. Also look out for the free *Pink Map* and *Cape Gay Guide.*

🖫 **55,** 22 Somerset Rd. (☎425 1849 or 083 479 9532). Bistro/bar/theater/club, 55 is *always* open. Two floors of dance floors and chill areas. Because it's been the most spirited and electrified club in Cape Town for a while, expect a significant straight crowd too on weekends. F-Sa club nights feature uplifting trance and progressive house.

Bronx Action Bar (☎419 9216), at Somerset and Napier Rd. On weekends, many sweaty boys (and some girls) pack this joint to the gills, dropping all pretenses to hop onto the bars and shake it. Weekdays are much more chill. Still bumping when everything else in town seems dead. No cover. Open daily 8pm-"past your bedtime."

Angels, 32 Somerset Rd. (☎419 8547). At Napier Rd. Trippy interior—lots of hanging, shiny objects and flashing traffic lights. The debaucherous **Detour** upstairs is darker, more intense, and laser-ridden. Wild, bass-heavy music with sweet house beats. Cover F R20, Sa R40; half-price before midnight. Open F-Sa 10pm-breakfast.

Cafe Erte, 265A Main Rd., Sea Point (☎434 6624). Fluorescent bar serves as lively after-hours playground and lounge of predominantly gay and lesbian crowd. Vegetarian menu (see **Food,** p. 97). Internet R20 per hr. Open daily 10am to the wee hours; kitchen closes M-Th 3:30am, F-Su 4:30am.

🖣 DAYTRIPS

There are several budget tour companies geared toward tourists and backpackers. Any of the backpackers accommodations can book tours or activities in the region, as can travel agencies (see p. 88). For daytrips around Cape Town, most backpackers use one of three companies. 🖫**Ferdinand's Tours and Adventures** (☎465 8550 or 083 462 0425; fax 465 8551; www.ferdinandstours.co.za; ferdinand@telko-msa.net) offers remarkably wild trips to the **Winelands** (R265). Ferdinand, whose tours take place in a raging mini-van with blaring tunes and room for dancing, has become a legend for his partying stamina, and it is unheard of for anyone to return from his Winelands trip in a state of sobriety or dissatisfaction. He also arranges a brewery tour, Hermanus, Cape Point, paragliding, and kloofing excursions and hiking trips in the Cederberg Wilderness Area (see p. 180), and can arrange tailor-made tours to suit your group's tastes and budgets. Book ahead. **The Baz Bus** (☎021 439 2323; info@bazbus.com; www.bazbus.com) also offers a fun Cape Peninsula tour (Tu-Su, R265, 10% discount for VIP and HI card holders). They'll use bus, bike, and boat to show you all the peninsula's highlights. **Day Trippers** (☎/fax 531 3274; trippers@iafrica.com; www.daytrippers.co.za) offers thoughtful trips for nature lovers. They have a Winelands tour (R235), and a biking and hiking tour to Cape Point and Boulder's Beach that is fun when the weather cooperates (R265). They also go to Hermanus from July to November to do whale-watching and biking (R350). Call for availability and book ahead, especially in summer.

NEAR CAPE TOWN

MUIZENBERG AND KALK BAY   ☎021

The train to Muizenberg from Cape Town (R8) takes 45min. By car, take the M4 all the way in. Peninsula Tourism, 52 Beach Rd., provides info and books accommodations. ☎788 6176. Open M-F 9am-5:30pm, Sa 9am-12:30pm.

Muizenberg is an ever-popular beach town just 25km south of Cape Town. Surfers, especially those mastering their technique, congregate here for consistent long waves, water that is not too deep, and mild temperatures. It's also a perfect beach for bathing, with safe swimming and a wide expanse of sand beside town shops and streets. The 19th-century bathing boxes at the end of the beach, immortalized in photos and postcards, can be rented, but only for an entire season.

There are also a few decent museums for those who are drying off. The acclaimed **Natale Labia Museum,** 192 Main Rd., on the right just after the beach turn-off when coming from Cape Town, is not the sex shop the name might imply. It exhibits the satellite collection of the South African National Gallery in a sumptuous abode that evokes the family's Venetian roots. (☎788 4106. Open Tu-Su 10am-5pm. R3, free on Su.) Just south of the Labia along Main Rd. is the **Rhodes Cottage,** where stately Cecil kicked the bucket in 1902. The house is surprisingly modest for a man who wanted to rule Africa, but the knick-knacks and memorabilia recall his massive ambitions. (☎788 1816. Open M-Sa 9:30am-4:30pm, Su 10:30am-1pm. Free, donations appreciated.) Just north of the Labia is the **South African Police Museum,** which houses a history of cop knick-knacks. Set in an old courthouse, the museum also narrates the tales of various South African psychopathic sex maniacs and serial killers through displays of stuffed toys. (Open M-F 8am-3:30pm, Sa 9am-1pm, Su 2-5pm. Free.) A bit farther down the road, the **Lindbergh Arts Foundation,** 18 Beach Rd., displays and sells the works of contemporary local artists. (☎788 2795. Open M-F 9am-4:30pm, Sa 10am-1pm. R5. No children.) Within walking distance of the town, the **Silver Mine Nature Reserve** offers some excellent day hikes and caving opportunities. (☎789 2455. R5 per person, R10 per vehicle.)

For accommodations, try ▧**Blue Oceans Backpackers ❶,** 3 Church Rd., in Muizenberg (☎788 9780 or 083 715 9410; fax 788 9785; info@blueoceans.co.za; www.blueoceans.co.za), behind ShopRite, close to Main Rd., 250m from the beach. In a freshly renovated 130-year-old building, this young hostel with its young owners is an oasis for surfers. Dorms are nice but individual rooms are better. (One-on-one surfing lessons from experienced surfer R300, including equipment. Make-your-own-surfboard workshop offered. Internet R20 for 30min. Reception 24hr. Dorms R60; singles R80; doubles R80 per person.) **Muizenberg Backpackers ❶** (☎788 1900; wipeout@iafrica.com), at the corner of Main and Camps Rd., about a block from the beach, is best for those who are in town to surf and have little concern for maintenance. The well-worn rooms remain comfortable. Surfboards, cocktails, coffee, cats, free bikes, and live music (Sa) accentuate the laid-back atmosphere of this backpackers, which is above the raucous **Wipeout Pub.** Reception 9am-2am. Dorms R59-65; doubles R120. Seventh night free.

Amberley Travellers Lodge ❷, 15 Amberley Rd., in Muizenberg, is close to the train station. From Main Rd., take the street next to the radio station. Spacious rooms with balconies and well-maintained facilities, for the quieter crowd. (☎788 7032 or 082 686 1869; fax 788 6881; amberley@worldonline.co.za; www.amberley-lodge.com. Internet R0.50 per min. Reception 9am-6pm. Check-out 11am. Singles R110; doubles R130; triples and quads R60 per person. For stays longer than 7 nights: singles R90; doubles R110; triples and quads R50 per person.)

The popular ■**Brass Bell Restaurant ❸**, a local institution, is in Kalk Bay at the waterfront, next to the train station. It's a triplex consisting of a pub, a casual eatery, and an upscale seafood restaurant. The pub hangs over the ocean, and is pretty wild, with bands playing on the outside deck and occasional rowdy party animals skinny-dipping in the tidal pools next door. The main restaurant serves noteworthy food: Seafarer's Pot includes a great calamari (R42-55), while many other seafood delights, such as a half-dozen oysters, are about R30. (☎788 5455. Pub open daily 11am-late; restaurant open daily noon-3:30pm and 6-11pm; closes 1hr. earlier during winter.) **The Acoustic Cafe ❶**, right next to Muizenberg Backpackers, serves simple meals in huge portions for small prices, such as rumpsteak with chips for R25. (☎788 1900. Open daily 7am-11pm. AmEx/DC/MC/V.) **Gaylords ❷**, 65 Main Rd., Muizenberg serves some of the best Indian curry around. Prices are all around R35. Try the traditional or seafood curry, and don't skip the desserts. (☎788 5470. Open W-Su 12:30pm-2:30pm, W-M 6:30pm-10pm. DC/MC/V.) **Cape to Cuba ❸**, 165 Main Rd. (☎788 1566; fax 788 3695) brings Cuba to your doorstep. Light up a big cigar and wear your Che t-shirt as you enjoy the excellent seafood. Main courses go for R45-65.

SIMON'S TOWN AND BOULDER'S BEACH

Simon's Town serves as a showcase for South Africa's naval and marine history, having acted as an important government center for 300 years. Named after Simon van der Stel, governor of the Cape from 1679 to 1699 and namesake of Stellenbosch (see p. 121), the port was originally a winter anchorage for the Dutch East India Company. Despite the interest generated by its museums and huge ships, the town is overshadowed by a flock of rotund black and white birds on the outskirts of town (see **Outdoors,** p. 116).

◪ PRACTICAL INFORMATION. The **train** from Cape Town (1hr., every hr. during the day, R10) along the suburban route offers incredible views on its way to central Simon's Town. Or, get to Boulder's Beach with **Rikki's Taxis** (☎786 2136; R120). A **tourist office** (☎786 3046) shares quarters with the Simon's Town Museum, while the **Peninsula Tourism Simon's Town Office**, 11 St. George's St., arranges accommodations and posts a list of options outside its office. (☎786 2436. Open M-F 9am-5:30pm, Sa 9:30am-1pm, Su 10am-1pm.)

▐◪ ACCOMMODATIONS AND FOOD. TopSail House ❷, 176 St. George's St., is a lovely converted convent that caters to budget travelers. The confessional is a kitchen, and the vestry, a toilet. (☎786 5537 or 082 677 7277. Dorms R70; doubles R160, with bath R180; "the chapel"—now a virtual honeymoon suite—R200.) **Boulder's Beach Guesthouse ❸**, 4 Boulder's Pl., is definitely for upscale penguin-lovers looking to splurge. (☎786 1758; boulders@iafrica.com; www.bouldersbeach.co.za. Breakfast included. Twins and doubles R245. AmEx/MC/V.)

◪ ▟ SIGHTS AND OUTDOORS. The true highlight awaits just south of Simon's Town at **Boulder's Beach,** where the amazing colony of endangered **African penguins**

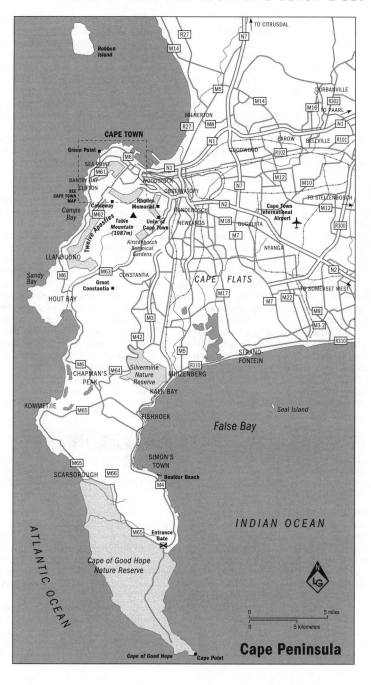

SEE CAPE TOWN MAP

TO CITRUSDAL

Robben Island

CAPE TOWN

Green Point
SEA POINT
BANTRY BAY
CLIFTON
Camps Bay
Cableway
Rhodes Memorial
Table Mountain (1087m)
Kirstenbosch Botanical Gardens

WOODSTOCK
OBSERVATORY
RONDEBOSCH
Univ. of Cape Town
NEWLANDS

MILNERTON

GOODWOOD
PAROW BELLVILLE
DURBANVILLE
TO PAARL

Cape Town International Airport
GUGULETA
TO STELLENBOSCH

NYANGA

TWELVE APOSTLES

LLANDUDNO
Sandy Bay
HOUT BAY

CONSTANTIA
Groot Constantia

CAPE FLATS

TO SOMERSET WEST

STRAND
FONTEIN

CHAPMAN'S PEAK
Silvermine Nature Reserve
MUIZENBERG
KALK BAY

KOMMETJIE
FISHHOEK

Seal Island

False Bay

SIMON'S TOWN
Boulder Beach

SCARBOROUGH

INDIAN OCEAN

ATLANTIC OCEAN

Entrance Gate

Cape of Good Hope Nature Reserve

0   5 miles
0   5 kilometers

Cape of Good Hope   Cape Point

Cape Peninsula

has made a home. The Boulder's Beach colony is one of only two mainland colonies in the world. The impossibly passive penguins, also known as jackass penguins because of their donkey-like crooning, spend their languid days observing the bizarre behavior of jackass tourists and busloads of schoolchildren who swim uneasily beside them. The penguins meander between areas depending on their mood: Gate 5 is the see and be seen area, complete with observation deck; Gate 4 is the tanning parlor, where lazy penguins rest on the rocks; Gate 3 is the pick-up area, featuring the romantic overtures of the wild; Gate 2 is mixed, with the penguins and swimming visitors intermingling; and Gate 1 is a wealthy residential suburb. Because of vandals mistreating the birds, there is now a guard who watches over them; the birds also fight back, and they'll bite those who come too close. The beach itself is lovely, with huge boulders forming little coves where people can swim safely and enjoy the sun. Gate 1 is wheelchair accessible. (☎786 2329. Open 8am-5pm. R10, ages 8-18 and seniors R5, under 8 free.)

Simon's Town Museum, on Court Rd., was built as the residence of the Cape governor in 1777. In previous incarnations, this venue has been used as a hospital, police station, and post office. The museum details both the history of the residence and of Simon's Town. (☎786 3046. Open M-F 9am-4pm, Sa 10am-4pm, Su 11am-4pm. R5; students, children, and seniors R1.) Next door, the **South African Naval Museum** has a bunch of gizmos and naval hardware to provide a quick fix for lovers of boats, explosions, and exploding boats. (☎787 4635. Open daily 10am-4pm. Free.) Farther down Main Rd. at the intersection with St. George's St., the **Warrior Toy Museum** offers a collection of dinky toys that chronicles the cultural history of the century. (☎786 1395. Open daily 10am-4pm. R3.) Downhill from the Toy Museum, the **Islam Cultural Museum,** on King George Way, explores the lives of the first Muslims to live in the Cape. The home in which the museum resides is the first dwelling reclaimed by "coloureds" in Simon's Town. (☎786 2302. Open Tu-F 11am-4pm, on weekends by appointment. R3; students and seniors R1, children R1.) In the heart of Simon's Town, amidst a collection of craft-sellers and small cafes, lies a statue to the curiously famous naval dog, **Just Nuisance,** who reportedly aided drunken sailors in finding their way. **Scratch Patch Mineral World,** just north of town toward Fishhoek, is a semi-precious gemstone factory where visitors sift through a patch of gems and fill pre-paid baggies. (☎786 2020. Open M-F 8am-4:45pm, Sa-Su 9am-5:30pm. Bags from R7.)

CAPE OF GOOD HOPE NATURE RESERVE

The Cape of Good Hope Nature Reserve exports its visitors away from Cape Town and into natural Africa. A wonderland where the Atlantic Ocean and False Bay meet, the reserve mixes jaw-dropping views, invigorating hikes, open bike trails, and some wild wildlife.

CAPE POINT. Cape Point lies at the tip of the Cape Peninsula, and for that reason, many people mistake it for the southernmost tip of Africa. In fact, that honor belongs to **Cape Agulhas** (see p. 150), which lies farther east along the coast. Still, standing on the rocky promontories of Cape Point and looking out at the ocean makes this feel like the bottom of the world. Another common misconception is that Cape Point divides the Atlantic and Indian Oceans. This is also untrue, though for all intents and purposes the False Bay seaboard is considered by South Africans to be part of the Indian and not the Atlantic.

The parking area itself is something of a trip, with ferocious baboons generally fighting with each other or with tourists for scraps of food. The view from atop the **cast-iron lighthouse** boggles the imagination with an unworldly panorama of Cape Town and the surrounding mountain. The lighthouse itself, however, has a troubled history; at 249m, it was often shrouded in mist, rendering it invisible to most drunken, wayfaring sailors even on clear days. This shortcoming produced ship-wrecked catastrophes and forced the construction of a second lighthouse in 1919 that still functions as the most powerful light on the African coast.

A hearty uphill 15-20 min. walk will take visitors from the baboon-infested parking lot to the original lighthouse. Alternatively, a **funicular railway** makes the ascent much easier for those of more leisurely persuasions.

CAPE OF GOOD HOPE. While marked only by an unassuming sign proclaiming it the southwesternmost point in Africa, the Cape of Good Hope still exudes a historical vibrancy. "X" marks the spot where Bartolomeu Dias rounded the coast in 1487 in his attempt to find a shipping route to the East. One decade later, Vasco da Gama used the beacon erected by Dias to find his own way around the coast before continuing to India. Just up the road, the agitated waves of **Neptune's Dairy** stir the waters of the Atlantic into a thick foam. *(Visit either by traversing a steep, rocky hiking trail from Cape Point, about a 1½hr. hike, or by driving or biking. Follow the road signs.)*

DIAS CROSS. In the center of the park, close to the information cabin, looms the Dias Cross, dedicated to the erstwhile mariner. The site itself is fairly non-descript, although it still functions as a navigational beacon to guide ships.

OLIFANTSBOS. In the northwestern section of the park, about 10km from the entrance, Olifantsbos is crowded with wildlife and shipwreck debris. Baboons often roam here. From Olifants Bay, the **Tucker Shipwreck Trail** provides a pleasant, 90min. hike for the morbid; two wrecks are still visible. *(Turn right at the entrance gate and drive to the end of the road. Turn left at the T-junction and follow the road to the end.)*

ELSEWHERE IN THE PARK. The area along the eastern coast of the peninsula offers numerous beaches and rock pools that make for delightful—and often pleasantly warm—swimming and surfing, especially around the **Venus Pools** and the **Black Rocks** area. Wild ostriches peck around these parts, as do Cape baboons, who join fishermen in capitalizing on the fruits of the sea. Also along the east coast, **Buffels Bay** serves as a recreation area with a beach and tidal pool. *(During the summer months, there's an extra charge to use these amenities.)*

THE WINELANDS

Because many travelers make the pilgrimage to the Winelands on the trail of ine-briated bliss, the non-alcohol-related profiles of these culturally rich destinations go overlooked. But of those who stop and look around, even the most adamant teetotalers will be hard-pressed to deny the appeal of the region. Gorgeous land-scapes, world-class museums, unique collections of wildlife, and one of the best student towns in all of South Africa only begin to detail the bountiful attractions. There are also, of course, some pretty good wines.

🎇 WINNING WINERIES

Winelands tours typically cover several of the best wineries in Stellenbosch, Fran-schhoek, and Paarl, but if you decide to explore on your own, here are a few to try out. The Wine Route Office in each town can give you more information.

STELLENBOSCH

🎇 **Rust en Vrede** (☎881 3881; fax 881 3000; info@rustenvrede.com; www.rusten-vrede.com). From Stellenbosch, take the R44 south and turn left at the sign. When Nelson Mandela and F.W. de Klerk won the Nobel Peace Prize, they sipped this wine at the ceremony. Free tastings. Open M-F 9am-5pm, Sa 9am-3pm.

WESTERN CAPE

■ **Simonsig** (☎ 888 4900; fax 888 4909; wine@simonsig.co.za; www.simonsig.co.za). From Stellenbosch, take the R44 north for about 7km, then take a left onto the M23. It's the first winery on the right. Famous for its award-winning "Cap Classique" (a.k.a. champagne, but we didn't tell you that!). Tours M-F 10am, 5pm; Sa 10am. Open M-F 8:30am-5pm, Sa 8:30am-4pm.

Muratie (☎ 882 2330; fax 882 2790; muratie@kingsley.co.za; www.muratie.co.za). Right off the R44 north of Stellenbosch. Thought to be the oldest vineyard in the area and the oldest South African cultivator of the Pinot Noir, Muratie is a charming estate and its tastings are in an 18th-century building strewn with cobwebs, paintings, and caricature drawings. Offers a selection of reds as well as port, and a fortified white dessert wine. Open M-F 9am-5pm, Sa 10am-4pm, Su 11am-3pm. R1 per taste, R10 per glass.

Blaauwklippen (☎ 880 0133; fax 880 0136). On the R44 between Stellenbosch and Somerset West. This vineyard sits on a beautiful estate with colorful vines clothing the lower slopes of the mountain in the backdrop. Altitude variations allow Blaauwklippen to produce radically different styles of wine on one farm. Horse-drawn carriage rides are also offered (Oct.-Apr. M-F 10am-noon and 2-4pm, Sa 10am-noon; min. 8 people; R5). Free cellar tours, by reservation, M-Th 11am and 3pm, F-Sa 11am. Open M-F 9am-4:45pm, Sa 9am-12:45pm. R10 for 5 tastes and a Blaauwklippen glass.

Morgenhof (☎ 889 5510; fax 889 5266; info@morgenhof.com; www.morgenhof.com). Dating from 1692, and set in a picturesque valley, Morgenhof cultivates high caliber wines. Open Nov.-Apr. M-Th 9am-5:30pm, F 9am-5pm, Sa-Su 10am-5pm; May-Oct. M-F 9am-4:30pm, Sa-Su 10am-3pm. R10 for 5 tastes.

Spier Wine Estates (☎ 809 1100; fax 809 1144; www.winecorp.co.za). From Stellenbosch, turn south on Strand St. and take the R44 south to the R310; continue south on the R310 and look for signs, or for the adjacent Spier train station. A huge, 300-year-old estate and wine farm close to Stellenbosch, Spier is the oldest running South African wine cellar. All buildings on the premises are national monuments, including the 1884 Manor House, which is adorned with brilliant paintings of a fictive antiquity. That said, the whole place reeks of what Stellenbosch could become if overtouristed; it's like a wine estate Disneyland. Open daily 9am-5pm. Tastings every hr. (R12). Open 9am-5pm. The Spier **Equestrian Center** offers horseback riding (R100 per hr.) and 1hr. carriage rides (R100, on request). For kids and cat-lovers, the Spier **Cheetah Park** allows visitors an opportunity to pet these extremely affable—and domesticated—cats. Cheetah park open daily 10am-5pm. R40, children R20. Feeding at 1pm. The Spier Summer Festival includes a wide variety of musical theater productions.

PAARL

■ **De Zoete Inval** (☎ 863 2375; fax 863 2817; dezoetinval@wine.co.za; www.dezoeteinval.co.za), off the R45 on the way to Franschhoek. Friendly, family-run winery, remarkable for its free tasting of 20-year-old Cabernet Sauvignon. Open M-Sa 9am-5pm.

KWV (☎ 807 3008), near the eastern end of Main St. An internationally famous vineyard and the world's largest. KWV's huge Cathedral Cellar, complete with barrel roof, is home to the five largest wine vats under one roof in the world. Ironically, while it's perhaps the best known of South African wine labels abroad, it isn't sold domestically. Over 100 natural wines as well as brandy, sherry, and ports. English-language tours M-Sa 10, 10:30, 11am, 2:15 and 3pm. R20 including wine and fortified wine tastings. Tasting of fortified wines only M-Sa noon-2pm and 3:30-4:30pm (R10). Sales M-Sa 9:45am-4:30pm.

Fairview (☎ 863 2450; fairback@iafrica.com). From Main St., go past the N1 onto the R101 and take the 2nd right. It's a perpetual wine and cheese party. Go to see the tower of goats; stay for the wine. R10 for a wine and cheese tasting, free after 4:30pm. Open M-F 8am-5pm, Sa 8am-1pm.

FRANSCHHOEK

⬛ Franschhoek Vineyards (☎876 2086; fax 876 3440; fhoekvin@mweb.co.za; www.fran-schhoekwines.co.za), off the R45 right before town. This wine cooperative samples and sells bottles from wineries throughout the area. Large store, coffee shop, restaurant, and audiovisual presentations. Wheelchair accessible. Open M-F 9:30am-5pm, Sa 9:30am-3pm, Su 11am-2pm.

La Motte (☎876 3119; fax 876 3446; cellar@la-motte.co.za; www.la-motte.co.za), off the R45 on the way into town coming from Stellenbosch. An ultra-civilized vineyard set in a plush floral valley. Known for their Millennium blend: much to the chagrin of other winers, La Motte copyrighted the "Millennium" wine name back in the 1980s. La Motte also hosts a classical concert series. Open M-F 9am-4:30pm, Sa 9am-noon.

Moreson (☎876 3055 or 876 3112; fax 876 2348; sales@moreson.co.za; www.more-son.co.za). Take Main Rd. (R45) north from Franschhoek. It's on your left after about 5km. A small wine estate that specializes in whites. Also includes a good restaurant. Tastings daily 11am-5pm.

STELLENBOSCH ☎021

Stellenbosch is a delectable vintage of a South African city, with a sublime mixture of world-class wines, student energy, and cultural complexity in a setting that remains intimate. Affectionately referred to as *Die Eikestad* (Oak Town), the city's tree-lined streets and well-preserved Cape Dutch architecture ooze pleasurable grandeur. Nearby, breathtaking wineries are set against brilliant panoramas and majestic peaks. The students of the University of Stellenbosch counter this serenity by sweating enthusiasm and vitality into the restless night air. After Cape Town, Stellenbosch is the oldest town in South Africa. In 1679, Cape Governor Simon van der Stel began encouraging Cape farmers to grow fruits and vegetables to supply ships headed to the East Indies. The settlers planted grapes, and the combination of rich soil, hot sun, and cool, brisk night air created exceptional ripening and cultivating conditions. The Stellenbosch Wine Route—the first in South Africa—became official in 1971, and today 29 cellars are open for visits and wine-tastings to carry on the region's legacy.

▐ TRANSPORTATION

Trains: ☎418 2443. To **Cape Town** (1hr.; M-Sa every hr. from Platform 1; 3rd class R5, 1st class R15).

 TRACK RECORDS. While most authorities on the matter report a relatively good safety record, the train can be a bit risky in these areas, no matter what class fare you buy. *Let's Go* recommends that you not carry a lot of gear or valuables with you, as there have been some reports of muggings in both the first- and third-class sections. Consider carrying a false wallet and stashing only the necessary amount of cash somewhere hidden on your person. Furthermore, do **not** travel by train after dark or on the weekends. The route between Paarl and Wellington is considered risky at any time of day or night.

Car Rental: ABAT Auto Rental (☎448 2150), rents small cars for R150 per day, R120 per day for 1 month or more, including 90% insurance and unlimited mileage. For full insurance, add R50 per day.

Minibus Taxis: Minicabs are the cheapest option within Stellenbosch and to Cape Town, the airport, Franschhoek, and Paarl. Services are run by **Eric** (☎082 344 3507), **Nelia** (☎083 772 7875), and **Antoinette** (☎082 478 9889).

Bicycle: The town is suited to two-wheelers. There are several biking trails along the Wine Route; ask at the tourist office. **Easy Rider** (☎886 4651; stumble@iafrica.com; see **Tours,** below) rents bikes and recommends good routes. Open daily 8am-5pm. R10 per hr., R50 per day. **Piet se Fiets** (☎887 3042), at the corner of Dorp St. and Piet Retief St. Open M-F 8am-5:30pm, Sa 8am-1pm. R10 per hr., R50 per day; license, ID, or R200 deposit required.

ORIENTATION AND PRACTICAL INFORMATION

Stellenbosch, a 30-minute, 48km drive east of Cape Town, is in the Jonkershoek river valley. Take the N2 to Exit 33; go north on the R310 until you hit Stellenbosch. The **Eerste (First) River** borders town on its south side. The **train station** is on the westernmost side, and the **Braak** (town square) is a few minutes' walk east from the station, just beyond the tourist office. **Dorp St.,** which runs alongside the river, is a busy main street and a national monument, thanks to its row of historic buildings. **Bird St.** and **Plein St.** are more central and more alive. **Merriman St.,** which is mostly a strip of gas stations and convenience stores, marks the northern end of the main part of town.

TOURIST, FINANCIAL, AND LOCAL SERVICES

Tourist Office: 36 Market St. (☎883 3584; fax 883 8017; eikestad@iafrica.com; www.istellenbosch.org.za). Just west of the *Braak*. From the train station, cross over to the brick walkway, head down Dorp St., and turn left onto Market St. (also referred to as Mark St.). Thorough information on wine tours, hiking, and biking routes. Pick up *Stellenbosch and its Wine Route.* Open Sept.-May M-F 8am-6pm, Sa 9am-5pm, Su 9:30am-4:30pm; June-Aug. M-F 9am-5pm, Sa-Su 9:30am-4:30pm.

Tours: Stellenbosch on Foot (☎883 3584) meets at the tourist office to roam the city. Oct.-Apr. M-F 10am and 3pm, 6pm twilight tour by arrangement; May-Sept. 11am and 3pm. R40 per person. **Easy Rider Tours** (☎886 4651; stumble@iafrica.com), based at the Stumble Inn (see below). Informative and entertaining day adventures to the Winelands. Specialist tour covers 5 different wineries, lunch, cheese tastings, cellar tours. (R195, R175 if you spend two nights at the Stumble Inn.)

Banks: Standard, Trust, United, and **First National** are open M-F 9am-5:30pm, Sa 8:30am-12:30pm. **ATMs** are all over the place.

Laundromat: Merri Go Round, 34 Merriman St. (☎887 9980), next to The Workshop (see **Food,** below). R20 per drop-off (drop-off and collect services run daily 8am-7:30pm). Open M-F 8am-5pm.

Bookstore: Ex Libris (☎886 6871), on Andringa St. just past Plein St., has a fairly large selection. Open M-F 9am-5pm, Sa 8:30am-12:30pm.

EMERGENCY AND COMMUNICATIONS

Pharmacy: Joernings Eikestad Pharmacy, 30 Bird St. (☎887 0019), at the corner of Plein St., across from the *Braak*. Open M-F 8:30am-7pm, Sa 8:15am-12:45pm, Su 10:30am-12:30pm.

Medical Services: Hospital (☎887 0310), at the corner of Rokewood and Saffraan. **Medi-Clinic** (☎883 8571) inside. No appointment necessary. 24hr. care.

Internet Access: ■Java i.net Cafe, 2 Ryneveld St. (☎ 887 6261), near intersection of Dorp and Ryneveld St. R10 per 30min., students R5. Open daily 9am-11pm. **Cyber-**

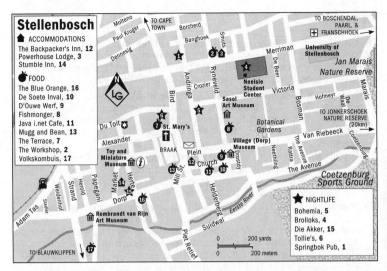

Stellenbosch

♠ ACCOMMODATIONS
The Backpacker's Inn, 12
Powerhouse Lodge, 3
Stumble Inn, 14

● FOOD
The Blue Orange, 16
De Soete Inval, 10
D'Ouwe Werf, 9
Fishmonger, 8
Java i.net Cafe, 11
Mugg and Bean, 13
The Terrace, 7
The Workshop, 2
Volkskombuis, 17

★ NIGHTLIFE
Bohemia, 5
Brolloks, 4
Die Akker, 15
Tollie's, 6
Springbok Pub, 1

WESTERN CAPE

sonic, 36 Market St. (☎886 3020; info@winelands.co.za), in the tourist office. R10 per 30min. Open daily 9am-7pm, but may also close with the tourist office.

Post Office: (☎883 2263), at the corner of Bird and Plein St. *Poste Restante.* Open M-Tu and Th-F 8:30am-4:30pm, W 9am-12:30pm, Sa 8am-noon. **Postal code:** 7600.

ACCOMMODATIONS

Stellenbosch respects and loves its budget travelers, offering them a high-quality array of cheap accommodations. The lack of similar choices in the rest of the Winelands makes Stellenbosch an ideal base for exploration of the region.

Stumble Inn Backpackers Lodge, 12 Market St. (☎/fax 887 4049; stumble@iafrica.com; www.jump.to/stumble). Personable, chill, funky backpackers with good music and fun hosts. Vibrant courtyard, pool, kitchen, and TV. Reasonably spacious dorms and firm beds. Discounts for 2-night stays from **Easy Rider Tours** (see **Tours,** above). Reception 7am-11pm, later by arrangement. Free Baz Bus pick-up from Somerset West. 10% ISIC discount. Dorms R60; doubles R160; triples R195. Camping R30. MC/V 5%. ❶

The Backpackers Inn (☎887 2020; fax 887 2010; bacpac1@global.co.za), in a passage-way off Church St. near Bird St. (on left at yellow jewellers sign), De Wet Center, first fl. Resembles a college dorm, with spartan, spacious rooms, a fully stocked communal kitchen, pool table, TV lounge, and students looking for alcohol. Laundry R20 per load. Reception 8am-11pm. HI discounts 10%. 6- to 8-bed dorms R60; doubles R160. ❶

Powerhouse Lodge, 34 Merriman St. (☎887 9980; phlodge@mweb.co.za; www.wine-lands.co.za/powerhouse). This converted powerhouse offers more elegant and upscale lodging, though they'll cut some deals for budget travelers. Huge rooms with bath, TV, coffee, phone, and fridge open onto pleasant decks. Breakfast in The Workshop included. 24hr. reception. Backpacker rooms are small but lovely. R150-220 per person; most doubles R400-500, R125 per extra person. AmEx/MC/V. ❷

University of Stellenbosch (☎808 9111; lcill@adm.sun.ac.za). Guest flats available throughout the year and holiday accommodations Dec. 15-Jan. 5. Rooms and suites have kitchens and attached baths. Singles start at R97; doubles R173. ❷

🔃 FOOD

The combination of a huge, hungry student population and loads of budget travelers has led Stellenbosch's restauranteurs to put their money where your mouth is. Expect superb food in big quantities for low, low prices. Many venues have daily specials in hopes of inspiring the shallow-of-pocket to drop by.

🔳 **The Workshop,** 34 Merriman St. (☎887 9985). Delectable and generous meals of intercontinental ilk in a hip, attractively furnished setting. Best burgers in town (R24) and remarkable vegetarian platter (aubergine, a mushroom tower, and *spanakopita;* R42). Elaborate cocktails (such as "smurf juice" and "sandy shag") for R15-24. Wheelchair accessible. Open M-Sa 10:30am-11pm. AmEx/MC/V. ❷

🔳 **Java i.net Cafe** (☎887 6261) corner of Church St. and Andringa St. Garnishes food with multimedia amusement. Terrace cafe with Internet cafe in back. Breakfasts (R15-30) are perfect hangover cures, and a good way to begin a day. Light meals for R30-R50. Open daily 9am-11pm. AmEx/DC/MC/V. ❷

🔳 **Volkskombuis** (☎887 2121; fax 883 3413), the only building at the Wagonweg on your right. Great Afrikaans-Cape Malay traditional cuisine and good regional wines in an intimate atmosphere (former slave quarters). Ostrich fillet R69, Cape Country Sampler R65. Stay away from the lamb's brain. Make reservations at least a day in advance; this place gets busy. Open M-Sa 6:30-9:30pm and M-Su noon-3pm. AmEx/DC/MC/V. ❸

The Blue Orange, 77-79 Dorp St. (☎887 2052; fax 886 5826; b-orange@iafrica.com). A farm and coffee shop with a glorious, plush garden terrace and even lovelier breakfasts. Health Breakfast R27.50, farm breakfast R30.50. 10% take-away discount. Open daily 9am-6pm. ❷

The Terrace, 50 Alexander St. (☎887 1942). Wide menu, wonderful staff, live music almost every night, and a mixed clientele of locals, tourists, and students. "Small" pizzas (R10-13) are enormous, and there's a substantial pub lunch menu, served all day, (most items under R20). Live music every night. Open daily 10am-2am. Kitchen closes at 10pm. AmEx/MC/V. ❶

D'Ouwe Werf, 30 Church St. (☎887 4608). Tree-canopied terrace and bubbling fountain ooze elegance and sophistication. Claims to be the oldest tavern in South Africa. About as traditional as Afrikaner food gets. Chicken pie (R44). Huge portions of *bobotie* (R44) and brilliant desserts (R9-15). Country platter combines some of their best: 2 dishes R58; 3 dishes R62; 4 dishes R69. Open daily 7am-9pm. ❷

De Soete Inval, 5 Ryneveld St. (☎886 4842; pancake@adept.co.za). Slightly overboard on the muzak, but fortunately, also overboard on the size and lusciousness of their Dutch-style pancakes. Savory toppings range from strawberries to beef goulash (R13-39). Book in advance for Dutch-Indonesian *rijsttafel* on Thursday and Friday nights (R50 for 4 courses). Open M-F 9am-10pm, Sa 9:30am-2pm, Su 9:30am-3pm. ❷

Fishmonger, 28 Ryneveld St. (☎887 7835). Serves some serious seafood beneath fishing nets spread across the ceiling. Entrees R40-60; salads R15-32; delectable prawn R8.50-21 each. Linefish pan R58.50, sushi at various prices. Open M-Sa noon-10:30pm, Su noon-9pm. AmEx/DC/MC/V. ❷

The Simonsberg Cheese Shop, 9 Stoffel Smit St. (☎809 1017). In a little yellow building on same road off the R44 as Bergkelder (see p. 125), making it a great complement to the wine tastings. The shop offers free tastings of a couple of their wares; weekly specials pull many excellent varieties under R10. Open M-F 9am-5pm, Sa 9am-1pm. ❶

Mugg & Bean (☎883 2972, fax 883 2761), corner of Mill St. and Church St. A coffee shop/restaurant that gained popularity for its R7 bottomless coffee or hot chocolate. Also food in big portions: huge gourmet sandwiches R22-37 (try the "AB FAB BLT"; R24). Breakfast R19-34, giant muffins R14. Open M-Sa 8am-10pm, Su 9am-10pm. AmEx/DC/MC/V. ❶

MUSEUMS

Most of Stellenbosch's major sights are easily walkable within a small downtown radius. Enjoying the wildlife and wineries on the outskirts of town, however, requires a bike or car (see **Practical Information,** p. 122). The bike trip is ambitious but feasible—bring enough water.

▨ VILLAGE (DORP) MUSEUM. This excellent examination of the city's residential history and domestic taste focuses on the trend toward opulence in Stellenbosch's homes. The museum features six restored houses dating from 1709 to 1929, and one house in the process of restoration. Everything is preserved as it was, including the rather sad sight of a dead cat on a bed in Schreuderhuis. *(18 Ryneveld St. Entrance on Ryneveld between Plein and Church St. ☎ 887 2902; fax 883 2232. Open M-Sa 9am-5pm, Su 2-5pm. R15, students and seniors R5, children R2.)*

SASOL ART MUSEUM. The University of Stellenbosch's terrific collection of sculptures, landscapes, and portraits provides a full survey of South African art over the last 200 years. The collections of Maggie Laubser's post-impressionist and expressionist works, as well as the series of lithographs from Oskar Kokoschka, are both worth a visit. Archaeology and anthropology exhibits detail the cultures and rituals of the Xhosa, Mfengu, and Thembu. *(52 Ryneveld St., between Victoria and Van Riebeeck St. ☎ 808 3691; www.sun.ac.za/usmuseum. Open Tu-F 9am-4pm, Sa 9am-5pm, Su 2-5pm. R2; students, seniors, and children free.)*

BERGKELDER. See a film about the history of wine making, take a cellar tour, and do some tasting. More interesting for its examination of the process of making wine than for the actual wine. Also contains the wine-making tool collection of the former Stellenryck Wijn Museum, including larger-than-life wine barrels. *(Head up the R44/Adam Tas St. across the train tracks; Bergkelder is on the left. ☎ 809 8492. Open M-F 9am-5pm, Sa 9am-1pm. Tours start at the visitors' center by the parking lot. 10am and 3pm in English and Afrikaans; 10:30am in English and German. Includes tasting. R12.)*

REMBRANDT VAN RIJN ART MUSEUM. This museum houses a small collection of South African artists, almost all 20th century. Sculptures of Anton van Wouw and the Gauguin-esque paintings of Irma Stern mix with more contemporary pieces, such as Willie Bester's *Crossroads*, a mixed media collage depicting the townships. *(31 Dorp St., close to Market St. Accessible through the entry courtyard on Aan-de-Wagen St. ☎ 809 8492. Open M-F 9am-12:45pm and 2-5pm, Sa 10am-1pm and 2-5pm. Free.)*

TOY AND MINIATURE MUSEUM. Herein lie delights for those stuck in childhood. Collections of baby dolls, the world's smallest kitchen crammed into a matchbox, a replica of the village museum, and the whole damn world packed into a single room. It *is* a small world, after all. *(Market St., behind the tourist office. ☎ 886 7888. Open M-Sa 9:30am-5pm, Su 2-5pm; May-Aug. closed Su. R5, children R1.)*

▨ OUTDOORS

The **Jonkershoek Nature Reserve** offers manifold trails for hikers, bikers, and drivers to indulge in the gorgeous scenery. There are also honey badgers and cobras, but the chances of seeing them are low; it's more the idea that one *could* see them. A 10km driving trail takes visitors through the highlights. (Take the R44 south, then the M12 east. ☎ 866 1560. Open daily 8am-6pm. R18, R9 for children under 12.) **Wiesenhof Wildpark** is a day picnic resort with swimming pools, roller skating, and a reserve with cheetahs, baboons and zebras. Since all the animals are wild, one can only see them from an enclosed car; for those who can take a tour prior to the 11am feedings, the animals often come right up to the cars. (Take the R44 north about 13.5km from Stellenbosch and look for the small signs. ☎875 5181; wiesenhof@intekom.co.za. Open daily Sept.-July 9:30am-6pm. R18, children under 12 R12.) **Butterfly World,** on the R44 north of Stellenbosch, just before the Paarl turnoff, houses approximately 21 species that flutter from plant to plant, less than an arm's length from the visitors in a way that is both dazzling and kind of creepy. (☎875 5628. Open daily 9am-5pm. R20, seniors R15, children R10.)

ENTERTAINMENT AND NIGHTLIFE

Stellenbosch loves its culture, and there are a number of festivals throughout the year to prove it. The **Stellenbosch Festival of Music and the Arts** is held every year from late September to late October. It features classical and local African music, art exhibits, crafts, street festivals, and children's programs. The concurrent **Spier Festival of Music, Theatre, and Opera** is an arts extravaganza. (For info and schedule, call ☎423 3351 or 883 3584. Discounts for students, seniors, and children.) The **Oude Libertas Amphitheatre,** near the intersection of Strand and Dorp St., also features a summer season of performances. For schedules and tickets, call Computicket (☎430 8000; www.computicket.com; open daily 9am-8pm).

Despite this confluence of classy pursuits, Stellenbosch lets its hair down, too. This bustling university town likes to party...a lot. The nightlife is robust, particularly in the area surrounding the Drostdy Center shopping area on Bird St., where everything is open late and debauched twentysomethings wander until dawn.

Bohemia (☎882 8375; www.bohemia.co.za), at the corner of Adrinda St. and Victoria St. Low-lit, chilled-out student bar complete with Egyptian hubbly bubbly (R25). A variety of live music 3-5 nights a week (check the web site). Open daily 10am-2am.

Springbok Pub (☎887 0547; fax 886 8816; stellbok@netactive.co.za), corner of Andringa St. and Merriman Ave. This student bar includes a dance floor, a pool-bar, and a cafe (named "The Rhodesian Arms") all in one complex. Expect a student crowd at all times, and prepare to go wild. R10 cover charge. Open M-Sa 11am-4am, Su 5pm-4am. Dance floor opens at 9pm, closed on Su. Pool bar opens at 5pm (6pm during winter).

Die Akker, 90 Dorp St. (☎883 3512, fax 883 9521). Traditional pub (one of the three oldest pubs in SA) always full of raucous students. Pub lunches between 11:30am-3:30pm. Pub of the year 1986. Popular on W. Open 10am-2am.

Brolloks (☎883 2410), in Neelsie Student Center, off Merriman Ave., past The Workshop; take a right after the bridge. Cave replica where Stellenbosch students sweat out scholastic anxieties. Waterfall doubles as a dip pool, but it's difficult to discern who's drenched from dancing to the unrelenting house and who jumped in. 10 pool tables. W, F, Sa guaranteed pumpin'. Occasional cover R10. Open daily 10am-late.

Tollie's, Shop 19, Drostdy Center (☎886 5497). On Bird St. Loud, jolly atmosphere spills out of this wood-laden interior filled with giant beer vats. To hell with wine! Tollie's has its own suds made fresh on the premises (0.5L draft R5, bottle R4). Live music 3 nights a week. No cover. Open M-Sa 10am-2am.

PAARL   ☎021

Paarl may not be as postcard perfect as the other two towns of the Winelands triumvirate, Stellenbosch and Franschhoek, but it more than makes up for this with the vineyards that surround it and a spate of interesting museums. Paarl was officially named in 1657 by the Dutch explorer Abraham Gabbema. After the expedition camped in the valley, the explorers awoke to more than just a hangover; the remnants of night-time rain glistened on the huge granite rocks, inspiring Gabbema to call the region "Peerlbergh," or Pearl Mountain. The aptness of the title is still visible on days when moisture brings out the shine in the rocks. Don't miss the Paarl's *raison d'être,* its Wine Route (see **Winning Wineries,** p. 119). Paarl

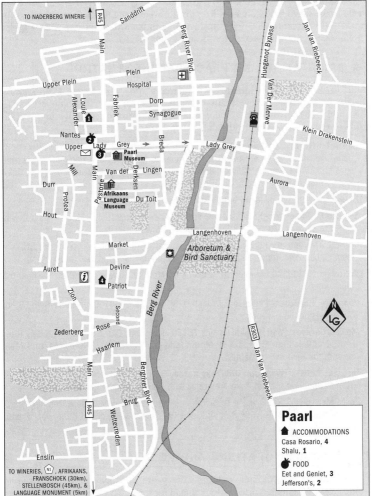

Paarl

🏠 ACCOMMODATIONS
Casa Rosario, **4**
Shalu, **1**

🍎 FOOD
Eet and Geniet, **3**
Jefferson's, **2**

holds the historical bookends of modern South Africa. The Society of True Afrikaners was founded here in 1875, spawning a movement of linguistic nationalism
that would later have political ramifications. Nelson Mandela served the final
years of his sentence in Paarl's Victor Verster Prison before his release sounded
apartheid's knell. This history takes front stage in Paarl's sightseeing, while the
views and booze at its area wineries proffer a slightly more hedonistic draw.

▣ TRANSPORTATION

Paarl lies along the N1 northeast of Cape Town and is not easy to navigate by foot.
Minibus taxis can take you to the center of town and out leaving from ShopRite on
Main St.; don't take them after dark. The **train station** is on Station Rd., just off the

east end of Main St., with trains to and from Cape Town (every 1-2hr., R15). **Paarl Radio Taxis** (☎872 5671) charges R6 per km. **Wine Route Rent-A-Car,** 23 Nantes St. (☎872 8513; wrrental@iafrica.com), rents cars from R79 per day. **Village Cycles** (☎872 8906) rents bikes and suggests short wine routes.

ORIENTATION AND PRACTICAL INFORMATION

Paarl's charms are more spread out than many other wine towns. **Main St.** runs for about 15km (the longest main street in South Africa) with a quick break in the middle at **Lady Grey St.,** the commercial center of town. Shops and restaurants dot Main St. only periodically, except around Lady Grey St.

Tourist Office: Paarl Tourism, 216 Main St. (☎872 3829; fax 872 9376; paarl@cis.co.za), at Auret St., stocks brochures to get a head start on finding key wine cellars, and has restaurant menus and accommodations listings starting at R100. Open M-F 9am-5pm, Sa 9am-1pm, Su 10am-1pm.

Banks: There are several major **banks** and **ATMs** downtown.

Bookstore: Paper Weight Bookstore, 45 Lady Grey St. (☎872 0596), near the intersection with Main St. Open M-F 8:30am-5pm, Sa 8am-1pm.

Market: The **flea market,** in Jan Philips Sq., next to the Nedbank on Nantes St., is a local place to eat, trade, and shop for clothes, pottery, and the like. Sa 8am-1pm.

Police (☎10 111), up Market St., which is off Main St. toward Lady Grey St., near the tourist office.

Pharmacy: Roodeberg Pharmacy, 171 Main St. (☎871 1034). Open M-Sa 8am-10pm, Su 9am-1pm and 6-10pm.

Medical Services: Paarl Hospital (☎872 7510), down Lady Grey St. and left on Berg River Blvd. On the left after Hospital St. **Medi-Clinic** (☎871 1330), on Berlyn St. off Optenhorst at the west end of Main St.

Internet Access: Webdome Internet Kafee, 318 Main Rd. (☎872 3018). R10 per 30min. Open M-Sa 10am-9pm; free drink with every hr. on the Internet.

Post Office (☎872 5337), at the corner of Main and Lady Grey St., behind the huge bank of **phones.** Open M-Tu, Th-F 8am-4:30pm, W 8:30am-4:30pm, Sa 8am-noon. **Postal code:** 7646.

ACCOMMODATIONS AND FOOD

The only hostel in town shut its doors a few years back, leaving only B&Bs in its wake, most of them high-priced. Book ahead for the summer, when Paarl is sometimes bustling with tourists getting their fix of South African wine, or try Stellenbosch for more budget options.

Shalu, 15 Louie St. (☎872 1215; fax 863 3629). From the tourist office, walk down Main St. past Lady Grey St., and then make a left on Ottawa St. The 2-story house is 1 block down, on the corner. Sleek interior and colorful rooms; upstairs rooms open onto veranda. Breakfast included. 24hr. reception, but call ahead if arriving after 7pm. Singles R140; doubles R240. ❷

Casa Rosario, 1 Patriot St. (☎872 2899; fax 872 1119). From the tourist office, walk one block from town center; it's on the left. Relaxing, with garden and pool. The 2 rooms (both with TV and kitchenette, one with A/C) sleep up to 4. Reception 7am-10pm. No children. Book ahead Nov.-Mar. R110-130 per person. ❷

Jefferson's Family Restaurant, 6 Commercial St. (☎872 6037). Pricey for those not movin' on up, but huge meals like surf 'n turf will satisfy small armies (R41). Entrees R30-50. No families (just kidding). Open daily 9am-11pm. DC/MC/V. ❷

Eet & Geniet, 317 Main St. (☎872 2608), across from the post office. A local favorite for take-away, with lunch of the day a steal at R12. Burgers, *boerewors,* salads, and light meals all under R17. Open M-F 6:30am-9pm, Sa 7am-2pm. ❶

👁 🎵 SIGHTS AND ENTERTAINMENT

Lording over the mountains, and rather inaccessible without a bike (steep trails!) or car, **the Afrikaans Language Monument** commemorates the town's significance as the cradle of the language movement. The majestic view of the valley from the monument is worth the trek. Enormous jutting obelisks (representing the "tongues" of the world) place Afrikaans as the biggest and most important language. Asking at the info center if they have the brochure in English won't endear you to the staff. (Head to the N1 end of Main St. and turn right at the mill, following the signs up the path. ☎863 2800. Open daily 8:30am-5pm. R5, children R2.) Back in town, the **Afrikaans Language Museum,** 11 Pastorie Ave. has interesting exhibits on the Afrikaans language and introduces you to some of the individuals who fought for its recognition. Not surprisingly, the descriptions are in Afrikaans, so non-speakers might want to pick up a brochure in English from the desk for an extra R2 or ask to borrow the accompanying English book during their visit. (☎872 3441. Open M-F 8am-5pm. R2, children R1.) The **Paarl Museum,** 303 Main St., offers an excellent examination of the history of Paarl's inhabitants. From the installation on the Khoikhoi, to the studies on slave abuse, to a critical examination of the apartheid era and its aftermath in the Western Cape, the museum proves surprisingly thorough. (☎872 2651. Open M-F 10am-5pm. R5, students and children free. Donations suggested.) The **Paarl Bird Sanctuary,** housing over 140 species of birds, is next to the Berg River; the entrance is off of Drommedaris Rd., across the railway line. (☎872 4972. Open daily 8am-7:30pm, during winter 8am-6pm. Free.)

FRANSCHHOEK   ☎021

Also known as "the Valley of the Huguenots," Franschhoek is a sleepy little village sitting in a fertile valley where the French first made wine in South Africa over 300 years ago. Today, Franschhoek provides other delectables to accompany the wine, including delightful cheeses, decadent chocolates, and detailed shops dedicated to wine accessories.

🔋 📶 ORIENTATION AND PRACTICAL INFORMATION. The little **Main Rd.,** which turns into **Huguenot Rd.,** runs the length of the village and is lined with all the small-town basics. There are no buses or trains, but **minibus taxis** run from Paarl (R5), departing from Daniel Hugo Rd. If you're driving or biking, take Exit 47 off the **N1** and turn off via Simondium to Franschhoek. The **R43** goes from Stellenbosch to Franschhoek. **Franschhoek Vallé Tourisme,** 68 Huguenot Rd., has a helpful staff and brochures on wine estates, accommodations, hiking trails, crafts, and horseback riding. (☎876 3603; fax 876 2768; info@franschhoek.co.za; www.franschhoek.co.za. Open M-Tu and Th-F 8:30am-4:30pm, W 9am-4:30pm, Sa 8am-noon.) **Post office,** 21 Huguenot Rd. (☎876 2342). **Postal code:** 7690.

👔 🏠 ACCOMMODATIONS AND FOOD. There are no hostels, though **Reeden Lodge ❷,** off Cabriere St., a 10-15min. walk from town, is gorgeous and affordable. The beautiful grounds include a pool and four cottages with self-catering facilities. (☎/fax 876 3174. Singles R200; doubles R340; 4-person cottages R680.)

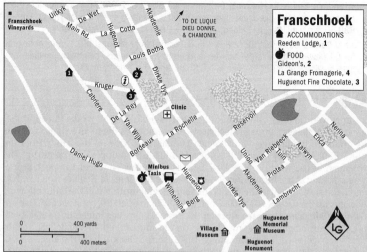

Franschhoek

🏠 ACCOMMODATIONS
Reeden Lodge, **1**

🍴 FOOD
Gideon's, **2**
La Grange Fromagerie, **4**
Huguenot Fine Chocolate, **3**

Franschhoek has many excellent eateries. **Gideon's ❷**, 29a Huguenot Rd., whips up delectable flapjacks. Souffle pancakes come with healthy lunch fillings (R26-36) or chock full of sugar (R15-27), all washed down with homemade ginger beer for R6.50. All food is kosher. (☎876 2227; fax 876 2563; pancakes@iafrica.com. Open M-Th 9am-5pm, F 9am-4pm, Su 9am-6pm.) **La Grange Fromagerie ❷**, 13 Daniel Hugo St., offers amazing cheese platters for R42. (☎876 2155. Open M-Sa 9am-5pm, Su 10am-5pm.) **Huguenot Fine Chocolates ❶** (☎876 4096), at Kruger St. and Huguenot Rd., sells (and offers daily free tastings) of delicious hand-made chocolates. Belgian chocolate R16.50 per 100g. (☎876 4096. Open M-F 8am-5:30pm, Sa-Su 9:30am-5pm.) The **Franschhoek Delicatessen ❶**, 38a Huguenot Rd., offers quiches (from R4), *tramezzinis* (R14-18), and other goodies. (☎876 3054. Open M-F 8:30am-2pm, Sa-Su 8:30m-2pm.)

🎥 🎵 **SIGHTS AND ENTERTAINMENT.** The spectacular **Franschhoek Wine Route** consists of 21 wine farms. The farms tend to be smaller and the route more compact than those of Stellenbosch or Paarl. Pick up the *Guide to the Valley of the Huguenots* at the tourist office for directions. The **Huguenot Memorial Museum**, which opened in 1967, is just next to the **Huguenot Monument** (which looks like a cricket wicket), and has information on the French Protestants who settled the valley. (Open M-Sa 9am-5pm, Su 2pm-5pm. Museum R5, children R1; monument R5, children R1.) For Huguenot enthusiasts who just can't get enough, there is also the **Franschhoek Village Museum,** 2 Huguenot Rd. (☎876 3408. Open W-Su 10am-3pm. R4.) Franschhoek celebrates cheese annually and hosts the **National Cheese Festival** in late April. They also celebrate their French roots during the Bastille Festival during the week before July 14th.

BREEDE RIVER VALLEY

The wind whips through the towns of the Breede River Valley and up into the snow-capped mountains that overlook the orchards, vineyards, and wheatlands carpeting the fertile valley floor, the largest fruit- and wine-producing region in the Western Cape. Many of its 15 quiet towns offer various "fruit route" tours in the surrounding area. Ceres is especially known for its lush grounds, and its name decorates juice boxes throughout South Africa. The mountains behind Montagu are *the* place to picnic and do some rock climbing. Many of the Afrikaner towns in the region have small house-museums where early settler homes are recreated; the Afrikaner struggle to preserve culture and language can be felt.

The valley is northeast of the Winelands on the western periphery of Little Karoo. The region stretches from Gouda and MacGregor in the southwest to Montagu in the east, with the Twanga-Karoo National Park providing the northern boundary. The tourist office for the region, **Breede River Valley Tourism** (☎ 023 347 6411; fax 347 1115; manager@breederivervalley.co.za; www.breederivervalley.co.za) is in Worcester. For a trip on the Breede River, **River Rafters** (☎ 712 5094; fax 712 5241; rafters@mweb.co.za) runs day-long rafting trips for R210 and three-day, two-night weekend trips for R595, including meals and accommodations.

TULBAGH   ☎ 023

The secluded valley of Tulbagh is another example of the Western Cape's natural beauty. The real draw to Tulbagh, though, is its fine Cape Dutch architecture. Picturesque Church St. is lined with galleries, cafes and B&B's in buildings that were restored to their original state after a 1969 earthquake shook them to the ground.

⌨ TRANSPORTATION. Tulbagh lies 130km to the northeast of Cape Town. By car from Cape Town, take the **N1** to the **R43** and follow it while it becomes the **R46** before the turn off to Tulbagh. Alternatively, you can take the slower but more scenic **R301**. From Worcester, take the R43, and from Ceres the R46. The road into town intersects **Van der Stel St.**, the town's main street. The famed **Church St.** is one block down the hill, running parallel to Van der Stel St. **Minibus taxis** leave from the Van der Stel St. hill south of town towards Ceres or come through town and stop at the Shell station. (To **Ceres,** R10; to **Cape Town,** R20).

⑦ PRACTICAL INFORMATION. The **tourist office,** 4 Church St., on the end opposite the entrance to town, has heaps of information on accommodations as well as the plethora of wine estates in the vicinity. (☎ 230 1348; tulbaghinfo@lando.co.za; www.tulbagh.com. Open M-F 9am-5pm, Sa 10am-4pm, Su 11am-4pm.) Van der Stel St. offers many necessities, including multiple **banks** with **ATMs, a grocery,** the **post office,** and a **pharmacy** (☎ 230 0150; open M-F 8:30am-1pm and 2-5:30pm, Sa 8:30am-12:30pm). **Postal code:** 6820.

⌂ ACCOMMODATIONS. Tulbagh and the surrounding area are awash with mid- to high-price B&Bs, with little in the way of cheap accommodations, especially for those without a car. **⬛Tulbagh Country House ❷,** 28 Church St., is across the road from Paddagang. Small but luxurious B&B with enormous well-decorated rooms and excellent facilities. Their breakfast is the best you'll ever have. You may want to return here for your honeymoon. (☎ 230 1171. R190 per person, May-Aug. R160 per person. AmEx/DC/MC/V.) **De Oude Herberg (The Old Inn) ❸,** 6 Church St., is one of the nice guest houses in the area, complete with a veranda for tea-sipping. Run by a personable couple, and smack dab in the middle of town. The house, restored after the quake, is a national monument and a perfect example of Tulbagh's hyper-pristine state. Its four large rooms are adamantly adorned with chintzes and doilies—the toilet paper comes ribbon-wrapped. (☎/fax 230 0260. Breakfast included. Singles R250; doubles R400. MC/V.) **Klipriver Park Holiday Resort ❶,** on Van der Stel St., is the cheapest place to stay, with campsites and basic chalets. (☎ 230 0506. Campsites R18-45; chalets R40-80 per person.) Away from Church St., the well-worn **Witzenberg Country Inn Guest House ❷,** 13 Piet Retief St. (Piet Retief runs uphill parallel to Van der Stel St.), offers clean pink rooms with double or twin beds and bath or shower. (☎ 230 0159; fax 230 0311; witzberg@mweb.co.za. Singles R165; doubles R290.)

WESTERN CAPE

🔘 **FOOD.** Though miniscule, Tulbagh capitalizes on its real estate with restaurants set in and serving up Cape Dutch ambience. 🔲 **Paddagang** ❷ is a culinary enclave, not to mention a sight in its own right. Set in an 1820s building on Church St., with a rose garden on the front lawn, and a hanging garden out back with bougainvillea and grapevines. Paddagang's entrees, such as Cape curried fish, run for R30-50. Wine cellar offers tastings daily from 9am to 4pm for R5. (☎230 0242; fax 230 0433. Open M-Tu, Th, Sa 8am-5pm; W, F 6pm-late; Su 8am-4pm.) **De Oude Herberg** ❷ (see **Accommodations,** above) does Cape cuisine on a candle-lit veranda at admirable prices. Entrees range between R20-45, with a tasty *bobotie* dish for R39. (☎230 0087. Open Tu-Su 8:30am-10pm.) **"Forty's"** ❷, 40 Church St., serves homemade pizzas, steaks, and pastas (R30-50) and drinks at the bar. The area behind the bar is still "earthquake damaged" with enormous cracks. (☎230 0567. Open Tu-Sa 6pm-late; kitchen closes 9:30pm.)

🔘🄰 **SIGHTS AND OUTDOORS.** In case you haven't caught on, a walk down Church St. should be the primary objective of every traveler to Tulbagh. The **Oude Kerk Museum** is a collection of several Cape Dutch houses preserved to mirror the Tulbagh life of old. The place to begin your visit is at the beginning of Church St. in the *Oude Kerk* ("Old Church," which, built in 1743, is the oldest in South Africa). Don't miss out on the graveyard, where you can see the tombs of assassinated locals and tombstones damaged by the earthquake. The main building has some displays on the history of Tulbagh, as well as a few paintings, a geological exhibit (read: how an earthquake destroyed our town), and some informative plaques on the town's 1969 restoration. The museum continues along Church St. at numbers 4 and 22—some of the houses that look like part of the museum are actually the homes of real people, so check before barging into someone's living room. (☎230 1041. Open Oct.-Apr. M-F 9am-5pm, Sa 9am-4pm, Su 11am-4pm; May-Sept. M-F 9am-5pm, Sa 10am-4pm. R5, children R2.) **De Oude Drostdy,** 4km out of town down Van der Stel St., was once the seat of governance in the region, but now contains a collection of Cape furniture and other household articles. More importantly, it is a good first stop on a **wine tour** of Tulbagh, as it offers free tastings. (☎230 0203. Open M-Sa 10am-1pm and 2-5pm, Su 2:30-5pm. Wine tasting M-F 8am-noon and 1-5pm, Sa 9am-12:30pm. Cellar tours M-F 11am and 3pm, Sa 11am. Free.) For a full listing of wine cellars and an accompanying map, check with the tourist office. **Silwerfontein Farm Cottage** offers a two-day **hike** on its premises through a pine forest, multiple *kloofs*, and to the Ontongs Cave. **Camping** ❶ is available, though the first night is in a converted double-decker bus. Bring your own water, food, and camping equipment. (R80 per person.) **Bikes** can be rented from Silwerfontein. (☎232 0531. Day visitors R15.)

CERES ☎023

Ask any South African what they know about Ceres (named after the Roman goddess of fertility), and they will inevitably say "fruit juice." As the most fertile area in the Breede River Valley, Ceres is the country's primary fruit juice producer. The town is also dubbed "the Switzerland of South Africa" for the wintertime snow-capped mountains that surround it, and eager South Africans come here sporadically during the winter in the hope of catching a rare snowfall.

Free tours of the **Ceres Fruit Growers Factory,** 3 Bon Cretien Rd. (☎316 9400), leave on Tuesdays and Thursdays at 10am. Go north through town on Voortrekker St., over the railway, and then right onto Bonchreten. Call to view the fruit juice factory by appointment. From November to January, you can picnic and pick cherries at the **Klondyke Cherry Farm.** (☎312 2085. Open daily 8am-4pm. R5.) The several hiking trails in the area include the **Disa** and the **Matroosberg;** maps are available at the tourist office. The trail to the **Toll House** (a national monument complete with tea garden) is an 8km walk that merges with the spectacular Mitchell's Pass (3hr.).

The trails leave from the Pine Forest Holiday Resort (☎316 1878), where permits are available. There are also several mountain biking routes, such as the sheep-riddled **Suurpootjie** or the 30km **Warm Bokkeveld** through various farms.

Ceres is along the **R46** (which leads to Citrusdal in the north and Tulbagh in the south), and the **R43** (running south to Worcester and Cape Town), which leads over the breathtaking Mitchell's Pass—look for the spectacular rock formations. **Minibus taxis** leave from the market on Voortrekker St. to go to Cape Town and back. The **tourist office** is in the **library** at the corner of Owen St. and Voortrekker St. and offers information about local activities ranging from 4x4 safaris to San homestay programs. (☎/fax 316 1287; info@ceres.org.za; www.ceres.org.za. Open M-Sa 7pm-10:30pm, Tu-Sa noon-2pm.) **The Village Guest House ❷**, 64 Vos St., off Voortrekker St., has modern rooms with televisions, fans, private bathrooms, and craft touches. There is a pool around back. (☎316 2035. Breakfast included. Singles R170; doubles R250.) The **restaurant ❷**, filled with works of local artists, serves good homestyle cooking, including calamari stews and steaks (R30-60). Even if you don't stay at the colonial **Belmont Hotel ❸** (☎312 1150), at the end of Porter St. off Voortrekker St., sample the food. Sunday lunch is quite popular (R72). **Oom Ben se Vat ❸** is their a la carte restaurant, and its pizzeria, **Pizza Nostra ❸**, has great Italian food. (Both open M-Tu, Th 9am-5pm, W 1-5pm, F 9am-4pm, Sa 9am-noon.)

MONTAGU ☎023

Montagu hides behind a mountain face, but is well known for what it can offer the ambitious rock climber: more of that mountain face. The village was founded in 1851, and eventually named after the Colonial Secretary of State, John Montagu. The traveler in need of some physical coddling and spiritual rejuvenation will appreciate the hot springs here, known as the Healing Waters. The radioactive springs were discovered when a pioneer's wagon got stuck in the rocks of a river bed. When the pioneer was trying to free it from the rocks, his hand became mangled in the wheels of the cart, and he and his crew were forced to pitch camp in the area for the night. Some of the crew traced the origin of the strangely cool river water to the springs, where the injured pioneer nursed his hand back to health in a matter of days. The Healing Waters, as the springs became known, have since attracted many a traveler in need of some physical and spiritual nourishment.

🖾🗗 ORIENTATION AND PRACTICAL INFORMATION. From the **N2**, the **R60** heads towards Robertson and Montagu, the latter being accessed via its own private road that passes through an arch blown into the mountain by the English. The town itself is tiny and easily navigable on foot. Entrance into Montagu from either direction leads to **Long St.** The main drag, **Bath St.,** is one block over. The helpful **tourist office,** 24 Bath St., is at the west end of town. (☎/fax 614 2471; montour@lando.co.za; www.lando.co.za/montagu. Open M-F 8:45am-4:45pm, Sa 9am-5pm, Su 9:30am-12:30pm.) The newly renovated **hospital** (☎614 1130) is on Hospital St., off of Church St., perpendicular to Bath St. Bath St. also has several **banks** with **ATMs**, a 24hr. **Engen station**, a **grocery store, pharmacies,** and the **post office. Internet** access is available at the red-painted **Printmor** (☎614 1838), on Bath St. at the corner of Mark St. **Postal code:** 6720.

🗗 ACCOMMODATIONS AND CAMPING. If you book your B&B accommodations through the tourist office, you will likely get a discount. Backpackers tend to congregate at the attractive **🖾De Bos Guest Farm ❶,** just after the bridge at the end of Bath St. (the end without the springs). The expansive and peaceful farm has a pool and is close to some walking trails. The 20-bed backpackers' barn has no bunks; the bungalows have self-catering facilities and rooms with baths. (☎614 2532 or 082 921 8959. Bedding R5. 24hr. Reception. Dorms R35; singles R100; doubles R130, R50 per extra person; bungalow doubles R140, R50 per extra person; camping R25. Book in advance weekends and holidays. Weekend 2-night min. stay.) An attractive B&B option is the **Aasvoelkrans ❸**, a unique curvy and classy home designed by the proprietor's daughter while she was studying at architecture school. Rooms are in separate cottages and are thoughtfully garnished with mini bottles of sherry, bouquets of lavender, and homemade biscuits. All three rooms are ensuite with verandas looking onto a garden filled with birds, horses, and a picturesque pool. Hardy, tasty breakfasts served in the most elegant of crockeries. (☎/fax 614 1228, plombard@lando.co.za. R300 per person, R270 if arranged through tourist office. Discounts available out of season. Book ahead.) **Montagu Springs ❹** (☎614 1050, fax 614 2235; www.montagusprings.co.za) is a pricier but excellent option. Three kilometers east of town down Bath St., take a left onto Uitvlucht St. Close to the springs with an attached bird sanctuary, this child-friendly chalet park is perhaps the better option for families. Most chalets accommodate four people, but some are larger. A pool, tennis courts, and playground are attached. (☎230 0567. "Villas" weekdays R420, weekends R590; "Golden Terraces" R340/R490; large Plettenbergs R280/R420; small Plettenbergs R240/R390.) The more basic **Montagu Caravan Park ❶** is just over the low bridge at the end of Bath St., just beyond De Bos. Less than scenic, the park is clean and green, and has a pool as well as small cabins outfitted with fridge and stove. (☎/fax 614 3034. Caravan sites R25 per person for up to 4 people and R15 for 4 or more; for Dec. and Apr. holidays R60 per person for less than 4; electricity R5. Camping R20 per person for up to 4 people; R15 per person for 4 or more. Cabin singles R50; doubles R140; quads R320, in season R400.)

⬛ FOOD. Jessica's ❷, 47 Bath St., named after the proprietors' dog and featuring dog-based art and images, is a quiet and quaint venue. Delicious homemade dishes include game (R40-70) and vegetarian options like butternut gnocchi on a bed of spinach gratinated with blue cheese sauce for R35. (☎614 1805. Open daily 6-10pm.) **Romano's Restaurant ❶**, 22 Church St., is a small family restaurant with clogs and pictures of happy sods smacked on the walls. Serving Dutch-Italian cuisine, they make pizzas (R18-30). (☎614 2398. Open M 6-10pm, Tu-Sa noon-2pm and 6-10pm.) **Preston's ❷**, 17 Bath St., has unhurried service but big portions of a standard mix of fish, steaks, and token vegetarian meals for R30-50. (☎614 3013. Open daily 10:30am-2:30pm and 5:30pm-late.) There's also a **take-away stand ❶** serving toasted sandwiches at the entrance to the springs, and a *braai* there every night—bring your own meat. (M-F R10, Sa-Su R15.)

⬛ SIGHTS. There are a number of decent wineries in Montagu, all of which hold free tastings and sell super-cheap bottles that make a great accompaniment at the springs or along the hiking trails. **Bloupunt Wines,** 12 Long St., cultivates excellent chardonnays and merlots. (☎/fax 614 2385. Open M-F 9am-12:30pm and 2-5pm, Sa 9:30am-12:30pm and 2-4pm.) On Bath St., **Montagu Co-op Wine Cellar,** next to the town golf course at the northeast end of Bath St., offers 30-min. tours of its stately estate. (☎614 1125. Open M-F 8am-12:30pm and 1:30-5pm, Sa 9am-noon.) **Joubert House** (☎614 1774), the oldest dwelling in Montagu, and the **Montagu Museum** (☎614 1950) are both basic museums, filled with knick-knacks, period furniture, and trinkets like old Dutch moustache cups. The delicious-smelling garden behind the museum sprouts herbal remedies. (Both on Long St. parallel to Bath St. Both open M-F 9am-5pm, Sa-Su 10am-noon. R3, children R1.) Montagu houses a number of painting and craft galleries and shops. Many line Bath St., and the tourist office provides a map and descriptions of the daily **"Arts and Crafts Route."**

◪ OUTDOORS. The **"hot" springs** may be a little disappointing to those over 10 years of age. The water is lukewarm rather than hot and the basin is rather crowded. They are open to day visitors at the Avalon Springs Hotel, 3km east of town. Both hot and cold springs spout from the comical animal statues that gape above the pools. There is a *braai*, cocktail bar, mini-golf, and several restaurants. (☎614 1150. Springs open daily 8am-11pm. Free for hotel guests. M-F R20, Sa-Su R22.50, children under 12 R12.50/15. Parking R5/10.) There are several **hiking trails** in Montagu, ranging from the leisurely to the ambitious. **Lover's Walk,** painstakingly restored after a 1981 flood washed it away, is a 2.2km-long footpath through some beautiful mountain scenery. Joggers have been known to frequent this relatively flat trail, though there are some rocky and wet parts that require tricky maneuvering. The path starts at Barry St., passes the entrance of Ou Meul and ends up at the hot springs at the Avalon Springs Resort. **Cogman's Kloof Trail** is just over 12km long, leveling off after the first two agonizingly steep kilometers; the view of Montagu from the top is stunning. **Bloupunt Hiking Trail** will take you twice as high (1000m), but it takes six to nine hours to hike all 15.5km. The vista at the summit lays nearly all of the towns in the Breede River Valley at your feet. Get a tourist office map for the latter two hikes which start at **Ou Meul.** (Open daily 6am-5:30pm. R5, children R2.50.) At the entrance, you can also arrange overnight **accommodations** (☎614 2471) on both routes in two six-bed stone cabins (R40 per person, children R20) or your own tents (R20 per person). Those in search of a less-demanding ascent of the mountains can be tugged along a 3hr. **tractor tour** to the summit of the Langeberg Mountains. Wear something warm. (☎614 2471. Book well in advance—these tours are worth all the hype. Rides W 10am, Sa 10am and 2pm. Lunch included. R40, under 13 R20.) **Rock climbing** is popular in Montagu; Ian Smuts of **Montagu Rock Adventures** (☎082 896 9914) leads abseiling, climbing, and hiking expeditions in the evenings and on weekends. **Dusty Sprockett Trails,** 78 Bath St., provides a slew of guided mountain bike adventures, ranging from 10 to 43km excursions. (☎/fax 614 1932; brunings@lando.co.za. R10-40 depending on length of route.)

NEAR MONTAGU

If you're around Montagu or on your way to Oudtshoorn, check out ◪**Ronnie's Sex Shop** (☎028 572 1153), on the R62 between Barrydal and Ladismith. This legendary bar, best described as being in the middle of nowhere, owes its popularity to the three-letter word added to its name. The bar, in fact, bears no resemblance to a real sex shop. The name is a joke designed to attract curious passers by. The joke worked, and the bar is now very successful. In case you drink a little too much, Ronnie offers a three-bed dorm for R60 per person. Ask for directions to the hot springs nearby. (Open Tu-Sa 10am-late.)

OUDTSHOORN   ☎044

Oudtshoorn farms out entertainment and mirth in the form of big, big birds that languish in the arid *Klein Karoo* (Little Karoo). An ostentatious ostrich industry has pecked its way into the hearts (and bellies, for those who can stomach it) of residents and visitors over the past century, making possible an array of gratuitous, silly wildlife activities that revolve around the landlocked bird. For those who want to get really landlocked, there are also the claustrophobic Cango Caves. Oudtshoorn is the only inland city that attracts the Garden Route crowd, and consequently it has a much more touristy feel than other Karoo towns.

WESTERN CAPE

BIG BIRD. Ostriches aren't your typical birds. First of all, they're bigger than any other bird today. Full-grown adults weigh about 120kg. They're also the only bird species with two toes on each foot. Although the birds aren't naturally very aggressive, they can be pretty treacherous for people who annoy them. An ostrich's defense system involves a forceful kick followed by dragging the sharp talon-like front toe downward across the offender's body; several people die each year from inadvertently stumbling upon a momma bird's eggs.

▣ TRANSPORTATION

Trains: To get to the **train station** (☎203 2203), go about 4km down Langenhoven St., and then turn left onto Station St. Station open M-F 8am-2pm, Su 4-6pm. To **Cape Town** (15hr., Su, 5:40pm) and **Port Elizabeth** (8½hr., M and F, 9:14am).

Buses: Make bookings at **Harvey World Travel** (☎272 3158; fax 272 3161; elsa.marais@harveyworld.co.za), on Church St. **Translux** goes to: **Cape Town** (6-7hr., daily, R150); **Johannesburg** (14hr., daily, R280); **Port Elizabeth** (7hr., daily, R160). **Backpackers Paradise** does pick-ups from **George** off the **Baz Bus**. Round-trip R30 if you stay there, otherwise round-trip R60.

Minibus Taxis: The station is behind the Spar on High St. They go to **Cape Town** (6hr., daily, R90) and **George** (1hr., 5 times per day, R14). Arrange Cape Town trips the night before; departures are early mornings.

▣ ℹ ORIENTATION AND PRACTICAL INFORMATION

Baron Van Reede St. is the main street and also the road to the Cango Caves and two of the ostrich farms. **Voortrekker St.** intersects Baron Van Reede St., and is the main road to Calitzdorp (and eventually Cape Town). On the other side of Voortrekker, Baron Van Reede St. becomes **Langenhoven St.,** which leads out of town toward George and the Garden Route. The **Central Business District** (CBD) is centered around **High St.,** which is parallel to and one block away from Baron Van Reede St. **Church St.** is the main cross street in the CBD.

Tourist Office (☎279 2532; otb@mweb.co.za; www.oudtshoorn.com), on Baron Van Reede St. near the corner of Voortrekker St. Open M-F 8am-5pm, Sa 9am-1pm.

Bank: First National Bank (☎272 2108), on High St. at the corner of Church St. Foreign exchange. Open M-F 8:30am-4pm, Sa 8:30-11am.

Police Station: (☎203 9000), in a fortress on Baron Van Reede St. between Church and St. John St. Open 24hr.

Pharmacy: Queen's Pharmacy (☎272 0400, emergency 082 453 6701), in Queens Mill Center on Voortrekker St. Open M-F 8:30am-5:30pm, Sa 8:30am-1pm and 6-8pm, Su 10am-noon and 6-8pm.

Medical Services: Hospital (☎272 8921), at the end of Church St. away from the CBD. **Cango Medi-Clinic** (☎272 0111), at the back of the hospital. Both open 24hr.

Internet Access: At **Backpacker's Paradise** (see **Accommodations,** p. 137).

Post Office: (☎279 1777), on Church St. between High and Baron Van Reede St. Open M-F 8:30am-4:30pm, Sa 8am-noon.

Postal code: 6625; Private box: 6620

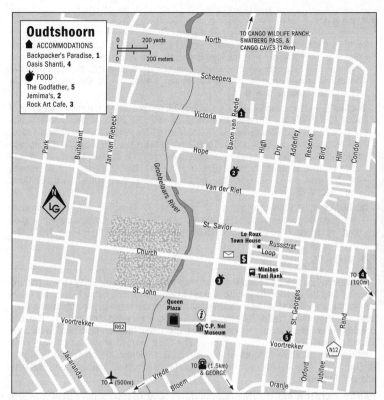

Oudtshoorn

♠ ACCOMMODATIONS
Backpacker's Paradise, 1
Oasis Shanti, 4

🍴 FOOD
The Godfather, 5
Jemima's, 2
Rock Art Cafe, 3

WESTERN CAPE

⚑ ACCOMMODATIONS

Both of the following accommodations in Oudtshoorn boast a swimming pool, kitchen, spacious TV lounge and pick-ups in George. Be sure to call ahead for availability during the high-season.

▨ **Backpackers Paradise,** 148 Baron van Reede St. (☎272 3436; fax 272 0877; jubilee@pixie.co.za). A well-organized and extremely comfortable backpackers that will keep you happily busy for as long as your heart desires. Bar and pool table. Television with DSTV. Also the primary organizer of mountain bike trips in the area. Provides discounts for all attractions. Convenient internet access. Ostrich egg breakfast R20 (veg. option also available). Ostrich *braai* for dinner every night R40. Per item laundry charge. Reception 7:30am–1pm. Check-out 10am. Dorms R55; doubles R60-80 per person. Camping R30. AmEx/MC/V and traveler's checks accepted. Fourth night is free. ❶

Oasis Shanti, 3 Church St. (☎/fax 279 1163; oasis@mailbox.co.za). A neat and fairly well-organized backpackers with a nice and relaxing pool. Offers a number of discounts for all the major attractions. Breakfast R12-17. Nightly ostrich *braai* R35. Laundry R10 per machine; R15 wash, dry, fold per load. Key deposit R50. Reception 7:30am-10pm. Check-out 10am. Dorms run from anywhere between R50-60, doubles R110-160. ❶

FOOD

Rock Art Café, 42 Baron van Reede St. (☎279 1927; 279 1928; rockart@wol.co.za). Closer to the Flintstones than the Hard Rock Cafe, with springbok skins on the floor and imitation San cave drawings on the walls. Spuds R23. Burgers R22-27. Often have live bands/performers, call for info. Smart casual. Wheelchair accessible. Open M-Sa 11am-2am, Su 6pm-2am. ●

Jemima's, 94 Baron van Reede St. (☎272 0808; jemima_za@yahoo.com). Voted one of *Wine Magazine*'s top 100 restaurants in South Africa for 2002. Jemima's never falters in providing impeccable service, a charming ambience, and above all delicious food. The restaurant is run by two sisters who change the menu often so that the produce from their family farm—used as ingredients in the meals—is as fresh as possible. Wheelchair accessible. Lunch: starters R18, entrees R27-42. Dinner: starters R18-34, entrees R42-52, steaks R38-58. Open Tu-Sa 11am-3pm and 6:30-10pm; Su 6:30-10pm. AmEx/MC/V. ●

The Godfather, 61 Voortrekker St. (☎272 5404; fax 272 4585; eat_with_us@yahoo.com; www.godfatheronroute62.com). A friendly Italian/South African restaurant with a good range of venison (R50-62). Pizzas R19-40. Take-away. Open M-Sa 6-11pm. MC/V. ●

SIGHTS

Oudtshoorn has beasts of burden emerging from every nook and cranny, turning the city and its surroundings into a giant petting zoo. The ostrich industry takes center stage as that was the creature that brought the town prosperity in the early 20th century, when "ostrich fashion" was in vogue (see **Big Bird,** p. 136). The arid conditions are ideal for the world's largest species of bird, and the ostrich farming industry itself is still running strong. The four ostrich show farms vary only slightly; they all allow visitors to ride and feed ostriches and provide insight into the industry. With vouchers from either of the two hostels, backpackers can usually get discounts.

CANGO OSTRICH FARM. This farm is the closest to the Cango Caves. Cango's most unique feature is Linda, their pride and joy, an ostrich who gives visitors a "kiss" in exchange for a kernel of corn held lightly between their lips—just don't think about how many other people she's kissed or where else that beak has been. *(About 14km from Oudtshoorn on Caves Rd. ☎272 4623; www.cangoostrich.co.za. Open 8:30am-4:30pm. 1hr. tour R32, children under 18 R12; group discounts available.)*

OUDSTHOORN OSTRICH SHOW FARM. Oudtshoorn offers slightly shorter tours that are also slightly less expensive, as well as ostrich jockey races, ostrich rides, and a look at the egg-incubation process. *(About 10km from Oudtshoorn on Caves Rd. ☎/ fax 279 1861 or 083 685 3565; oosf@freemail.absa.co.za; www.ostrichfarm.co.za. Open daily 8am-5pm. 45min. tour every 30min. R25, kids up to 18 R10.)*

SAFARI OSTRICH FARM. This farm features an "ostrich palace," a mansion built by one of the barons who got rich during the turn-of-the-century feather boom. *(Follow Voortrekker, then take the first left, which is toward Mossel Bay. The farm is on the left. ☎272 7311; fax 275 5896; karroovf@mweb.co.za; www.safariostrich.co.za. Open daily 8am-4:30pm. 1hr. tour R30, kids under 18 R10.)*

HIGHGATE OSTRICH SHOW FARM. Highgate is the oldest, biggest, and most authentic of Oudtshoorn's ostrich farms, as it is still a working farm today (the others are primarily just for show). Tours here are slightly longer and more detailed than at the other farms, and almost everyone gets a chance to ride a bird. *(To get to*

Highgate, head out of town toward Mossel Bay, past the Safari Ostrich Farm, and turn right at the sign. ☎272 7115; hoopershighgate@pixie.co.za; www.highgate.co.za. Open daily 7:30am-5pm. 1¼hr. tour R30, kids R12.)

C.P. NEL MUSEUM. The museum tells the story of the ostrich through the ages, exhibits range from deformed ostrich chicks preserved in formaldehyde to the feather-plumed hats that caused the rise and fall of the bird business. The museum also recounts the social history of Oudtshoorn and features a restored synagogue. *(3 Baron van Reede St. ☎/fax 272 7306; cpn.museum@pixie.co.za. Open M-F 8am-5pm, Sa 9am-5pm. R10, kids under 13 R3. Guided tours on request.)*

▨CANGO WILDLIFE RANCH. This ranch houses all kinds of wild and wonderful creatures. Placing some of the world's most endangered creatures in a haven in the middle of Oudtshoorn seems like an absurd idea, but has proved to be an inspired one, creating a fantastic spectacle. Visitors over 1.6 meters tall and older than 16 can't miss the cheetahs, who are so tame and friendly they are quite happy to be petted (R30). Whether or not you'd want to get into a cage with the completely wild jaguars, lions, or white Bengal tigers is another question altogether. *(About 3km from town down Baron van Reede St. ☎272 5593; fax 272 4167; cango@co.za. Open daily 8am-5pm. Tours last 45min. and run every 10-15min., low season every 30min.). R33; kids under 16 R20.)*

WILGEWANDEL CAMEL RIDES. If you've ever had the urge to ride a camel, here is your chance. The attached restaurant has cheap food; sandwiches cost R5-10. *(2km from the caves on Caves Rd. ☎272 0878. Open daily 10am-5pm. 10min. ride R12.)*

ANGORA RABBIT FARM. A visit here will leave you feeling soft and cuddly. A short tour, including petting, educates visitors about the rabbit farming industry. *(Across the road from the Cango Ostrich Farm. ☎272 6967. Open daily 9am-5pm. 30min. tour R10, children R6.)*

CANGO CAVES. Another sight drawing visitors to Oudtshoorn is Cango Caves, discovered in 1780 by a fearless soul who used only candlelight to find his way through the stalagmites and stalactites that had grown up and down over hundreds of thousands of years. Now, however, far less taxing tours commence hourly and half hourly; the standard tour involves a leisurely, hour-long stroll through the first three chambers while a guide points out interesting facts. The Adventure Tour, on the other hand, is a non-stop act of gymnastic prowess, as patrons must crawl, shimmy and roll through a maze of tight fits. Claustrophobes beware. *(30km from Oudtshoorn on Laves Rd. ☎272 7410; fax 272 8001; reservations@cangocaves.co.za; www.cangocaves.co.za. Open daily 8:30am-4:30pm. Standard tours start at 9am and run on the hour; Adventure Tours start at 9:30am and run every 30min. Standard tour R35, kids under 16 R22. Adventure Tour R50/R35.)*

OTHER ADVENTURES. Joyrides is a bike rental outfitter based Oasis Shanti. They will transport you and a rented bike up to the top of the Swartberg Pass. Then let gravity do its thing as you admire the view, descending the mighty inclines. Not just a fun time, it's also a good way to get to the Cango Caves and ostrich farms. *(3 Church St. ☎279 1163. R70 and R100 deposit for guests, R200 deposit for non-guests.)* On the way back, the truly fit can take a detour to the **Rus en Vrede** waterfall, a spectacular 90m cascade with ample picnic space at the bottom. The less athletic can also reach the falls by car; follow the signs from the road toward the Caves. *(☎272 7142. Open daily 9am-5:30pm; in winter 8:30am-5pm. R10 per car.)* **Backpackers Paradise** offers private spelunking expeditions that involve a cave crawl in overalls with lanterns. *(☎272 0725. 2½hr. trip R65.)*

WESTERN CAPE

🎵 🎭 ENTERTAINMENT AND NIGHTLIFE

Every year, Oudtshoorn puts on its party hats for one week in late March or early April to celebrate the **Klein Karoo National Arts Festival** (info ☎ 272 7771; kknk@mweb.co.za). The streets fill with shows, plays, concerts, temporary galleries, food and craft markets, and wine tastings. Most of the action is concentrated in the heart of town, close to the C.P. Nel Museum, and nearly all of the events are conducted in Afrikaans. This festival is so extravagant that it drains most of Oudtshoorn's partying energies for the rest of the year; though there are a couple of nightlife options, Oudtshoorn's two clubs open only on Wednesday, Friday, and Saturday nights. **Alcatraz** is an underground joint on High St., opposite the post office, underneath the pet shop. The dance floor fills with alternative, rave, colored lights, and lots of smoke. (☎ 082 492 2742. Cover R10. Open W and F-Sa 9pm-late.) **Wiljo's** doesn't get busy until 11pm, and when it does the crowd is a little more subdued. Aside from the occasional dancing, this place feels like a typical South African pub with smart casual dress required. (☎ 272 5642. R7.)

THE OVERBERG COAST

An area where the wildlife and plant life is like nowhere else in the world, this southernmost region of the African continent lies east of the Hottentots Holland Mountains and just south of the picturesque Langebergs. The name *Overberg* stems from a Dutch term meaning "over the mountains," first used by settlers contemplating what lay on the other side of the majestic peaks of Africa; the answer proved to be miles of rolling fertile land and a rugged coastline of unparalleled beauty.

The coastal area of the Overberg—known as the Whale Coast for the abundance of massive sea mammals found cavorting just offshore each year—extends east from Betty's Bay and Hangklip to the mouth of the Breede River. There is a scenic coastal road (the R44) that passes through each little fishing village between Cape Point and Cape Agulhas, the southernmost tip of Africa, where the frigid Atlantic Ocean and tropical Indian Ocean meet. While the road offers breathtaking views of mountains and oceans, it is a slalom of a drive. The Overberg is also home to Hermanus, the self-proclaimed "whale capital of the world," which is teeming with tourists who make the pilgrimage, binoculars in hand, to catch some lobtailing. Those who want to avoid the mobs head for the rugged coastline of De Hoop Nature Reserve, which offers moon-like serenity in its isolated sand dunes and some brilliant "undiscovered" vantage points for whale-watching.

The **Cape Overberg Tourism Association** (☎ 028 212 1511; fax 214 1427; cota@capeoverberg.co.za; www.capeoverberg.co.za) is in Caledon, an unassuming town with little to offer despite its title as the regional capital. The Overberg region is accessible from the Cape Peninsula via the stunning Sir Lowry's Pass along the N2, or by following the R44 along the coast.

HERMANUS   ☎ 028

Before you even have time to ask why locals call Hermanus "the whale capital of the world," you just might see a Southern Right Whale make one of its frequent seasonal appearances off the coast. The city has grown up around these huge sea mammals (and the accompanying tourist trade), as well as its glimmering beaches and beautiful nature reserve, which hosts a vast array of coastal *fynbos*. The Hermanus Whale Festival in late September and early October is a popular annual event celebrating the return of the whales. While Hermanus quiets down quite a bit off season, the past year or two has seen Hermanus' ever-burgeoning tourist industry recognize the allure of the budget traveler, making it a prime destination for those based in Cape Town or on their way to the Garden Route.

▐ TRANSPORTATION

Municipal legislation forbids any buses from entering Hermanus, but pick-ups from nearby Botriver can be arranged.

Buses: Baz Bus (☎021 439 2323) stops in Botriver, and Hermanus' hostels provide shuttles from there. To **Cape Town** (1½hr., daily 7:30pm, R90) and **Port Elizabeth** (11½hr., daily around 9:45am, R605). Reserve at the tourist office.

▌ PRACTICAL INFORMATION

Tourist Office: Hermanus Tourism Bureau, Mitchell St. (☎312 2629; fax 313 0305; infoburo@hermanus.co.za; www.hermanus.co.za/info), in the old station building parallel to Main Rd. and visible across an empty lot from Main Rd. near the center of town. Endless brochures and a lodging guide. Open M-Sa 9am-5pm, holidays 9am-noon. **Hermanus Accommodation Center,** 9 Myrtle Ln. (☎/fax 313 0004; hermanus@adept.co.za; www.adept.co.za/hermanus), at Church St., arranges self-catering flat rentals from R110 per person. Open M-F 9am-5pm, Sa 9am-noon.

Banks: Banks with **ATMs** in the town center. All open M-F 9am-3:30pm, Sa 9am-11am.

Bookstores: A number of secondhand shops cluster on Main Rd. near the Harbor. **Hemingway's Bookshop,** 12 Harbour Rd. (☎312 2739), is one of the best. Open M-F 9:30am-5pm, Sa 9:30am-4pm, Su 10am-3pm. You can swap books or buy used ones at **Jenny's Book Exchange,** 6 Victoria Sq. (☎312 1658), off Main Rd. Open M-F 9am-4:30pm, Sa 9am-1:30pm.

Laundry: Hermanus Dry Cleaners & Laundromat, 8 Mitchell St. (☎312 1487). 5kg for R22. Open M-F 8am-5pm, Sa 8am-noon.

Bike Rental: Hermanus Cycles, 125 Main Rd. (☎313 2052), just off Main St. towards Cape Town. R60 per day. Open M-F 8:30am-5pm, Sa 8:30am-noon.

Emergency: Police ☎312 2626; **fire** ☎312 2400; **ambulance** ☎312 3219.

Pharmacy: 145 Main Rd. (☎312 4039). Open M-F 8am-6:30pm, Sa 8am-1pm and 6:30-7:30pm, Su 10am-noon and 6:30-7:30pm.

Internet Access: Hermanus Computers, 69 Main Rd., Ste. 191 (☎313 0249; cell 082 661 8046; fax 313

IN RECENT NEWS

RURAL CIRCUMCISION: CULTURAL TRADITION OR HUMAN RIGHTS ABUSE

"Ndiyindoda!"— I am a man! This is the cry of the young Xhosa man as his foreskin is cut and he enters manhood. The problem with this age-old custom is that now, boys are dying.

A burning controversy is raging in South Africa over the existence of traditional initiation schools that are intricate to Xhosa culture. In his book "A Long Walk to Freedom," Nelson Mandela writes that an uncircumcised Xhosa man is a paradox because he is still looked up as a boy. Recently, however, the virtues of circumcision were again called into question. Some schools are run by incompetent healers whose inadequate care subsequent to circumcision led to a fair number of boys' wounds becoming infected, often fatally so. Evidence of severe physical abuse was also found.

Debate rages over not whether these schools should exist, but over how to regulate them. The government wants to grant power to the provinces to oversee the custom, but traditional leaders are unhappy, demanding that the government empower them to regulate the practice. It is, they say, a tradition that has existed in African culture for hundreds of years, and its dangers lie not in the act itself, but with the men who carry it out.

—Yusuf Randera-Rees

0278; icafe@hermanuscomputers.com; www.hermanuscomputers.com), offers fast Internet for R10 per 20min.

Post Office: ☎312 2319, on Main Rd. near the town center. Also issues abalone (*perlemoen*) fishing permits. **Postal code:** 7200.

ACCOMMODATIONS

The town's hostels are vying for business, offering cheap bike rental, daytrips, and other enticements to would-be guests; meanwhile, nearly every house in town has slapped up a B&B sign. Both the tourist office and accommodation center (see **Practical Information,** above) can find lodging. In whale season, it's essential to call ahead at least a day or two. During the low season (May-Aug.), prices bend like Play-doh, often dropping to 50% of those listed, so put on your haggling hat.

■ **Hermanus Backpackers,** 28 Flower St. (☎312 4293; fax 313 2727; moobag@mweb.co.za), off Main Rd. A busy backpackers with pool area, great bar and lounges for hanging out. Spacious dorms, good facilities, free breakfast, shuttles to beach and Baz Bus, and 5min. from cliff paths for whale-watching. Arranges free township tours, package excursions for the active, cheap meals, haircuts, and massages. Lockers. Families welcome. 6-7 bed dorms R45-50; doubles R130-140. ❶

■ **Moby's Backpackers,** 9 Mitchell St. (☎313 2361; fax 312 3519; moby@hermanus.co.za). Two blocks from the tourist office. Hostel ambience in ex-hotel facilities. All rooms include private bath. Breakfast included. Shuttle service. Pool, bar, restaurant. Key deposit R20. 4-6 bed dorms R60. Singles R125; doubles R170; triples R210; family suite R280. ❷

Zoete Inval, 23 Main Rd. (☎/fax 312 1242; zoetein@hermanus.co.za). B&B with small backpackers lodge out back. 6- and 8-bed dorms (one of which is females-only), as well as the backpacker double, are crowded and basic, but have a small kitchen and nice courtyard. The guesthouse's rooms (most with bath) are decorated with international themes. Parking. Internet access R15 per 20min. Breakfast R15-30. Laundry R30. Key deposit R50. Reception 8am-9pm. VIP discount R5-10. Dorms R60; guest house R120 per person, with bath R150. MC/V. ❷

Kenjockity Guest House, 15 Church St. (☎/fax 312 1772; kenjock@hermanus.co.za), Off Main Rd. The first guest house in Hermanus is also perhaps its friendliest. Large B&B with clean rooms. Breakfast included. R125 per person, with bath R165. MC/V. ❷

Hermanus Esplanade, 63 Marine Dr. (☎312 3610; fax 313 1125; info@hermanus-esplanade.com; www.hermanusesplanade.com). Large, two-level, self-catering flats and cottages good for groups and privacy, though rooms are drab and musty. Still, many cottages have dining areas, TV lounges, and balconies. Wheelchair accessible. More costly sea-facing rooms have awesome views. Reception M-Th 7:30am-8:30pm, F 7:30am-9pm, Sa 8am-8:30pm, Su 9am-8:30pm. Families welcome. Sea-facing doubles R260-340; mountain-facing doubles R180-235; 2-bedroom quads R320-410/250-315; 3-bedroom 6-person suites R365-475/R310-390. AmEx/DC/MC/V. ❸

FOOD

The obvious choice in this seaside town is seafood—so fresh that undercooked meals may still be flopping around on your plate. In high season, book ahead.

■ **Bientang's Cave** (☎312 3454), right on the water in the Old Harbor, off Marine Dr., down steep stairs under the sign. Most popular restaurant in Hermanus. Its prime location (in a cave) puts you nose-to-snout with the whales while tempting your tongue with loads of seafood. Also has a fine selection of white wines. Starters R10-48. Heaping basket of calamari and chips R48.50. Open Su-Th 10am-4pm, Sa 10am-4pm and 6:30-9:30pm;

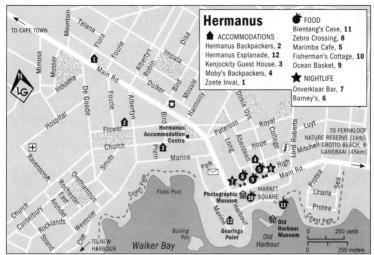

Hermanus

🐋 FOOD
Bientang's Cave, 11
Zebra Crossing, 8
Marimba Cafe, 5
Fisherman's Cottage, 10
Ocean Basket, 9

🏠 ACCOMMODATIONS
Hermanus Backpackers, 2
Hermanus Esplanade, 12
Kenjockity Guest House, 3
Moby's Backpackers, 4
Zoete Inval, 1

⭐ NIGHTLIFE
Onverklaar Bar, 7
Barney's, 6

WESTERN CAPE

in high season, open nightly for dinner. Closes sporadically, so book in advance, especially on weekends. MC/V. ❷

Zebra Crossing (☎312 3906), at Main and Long St. A coffee bar in the mornings and late evenings, a restaurant otherwise, hip all the time. Serves Cape cuisine (*bobotie* R19), breakfast (R13-27), and a staggeringly large seafood platter (R130, serves 2). Huge burgers around R20-35. Open M 9am-4pm, Tu-Sa 9am-2am, Su 10am-2am. Kitchen closes at 4pm. ❷

Marimba Cafe, Royal Ln. (☎312 2148), in a small shopping center facing 108 Main St., in front of a street chess board. An intimate, candlelit, pan-African restaurant at night. Good vegetarian items, such as spicy refried beans (R32). Tasty meatier grub, like *feijoada*—beans, chorizo, chicken, peppers, and onions (R45). Portions are copious and starters might be excessive. Open daily 7pm-late; in winter 6:30pm-late. Book ahead in season. ❷

The Rock, site 24a New Harbor (☎312 2920). From the center of town, drive along the seafront towards the New Harbor, enter the Harbor gates, and take the second left. Large glass windows afford a view that commands all of Walker Bay. Fresher than fresh seafood (R40-50), dimly lit and comfortable. Open daily 9am-10pm. ❷

Fisherman's Cottage (☎312 3642), at Lemm's corner, by the intersection of Harbor and Main Rd. You can enter by a marked path on Main St. across from Zebra Crossing. Unique seafood dishes in its small dwelling, excellent Thai seafood curry (R95), and fresh oysters (R20-45). Open daily 11am-late. Closed M-Tu during winter. ❷

The Ocean Basket, 139 Main Rd. (☎312 1313). Good, cheap option for fine seafood on a budget. Daily oyster menu. Garlic mussels (R22) and kingklip (R45) are both sizable and well prepared. Enormous seafood platter (R120 for 2). Non-smoking. Open M-Th 11:30am-9pm, F-Sa-Su 11:0am-10pm, Su 11:30am-8pm. AmEx/MC/V. ❷

👁 🏔 SIGHTS AND OUTDOORS

A WHALE OF A TIME. In town, the best vantage points from which to watch the **whales** are along the 12km cliff path from New Harbor to Grotto Beach: **Gearing's Point, Sievers Point,** and **Die Gang** are all popular grounds for blowhole spotting. "How popular?" you might ask. Well, last year, on the first day of the Whale Festi-

THE SOUTHERN RIGHT WHALE Southern Right Whales were originally given their names by whalers who deemed them the "right" whales to kill because of their oil and bone content and the fact that they float when dead. They are quite dark, with an occasional spot of white or gray on the back, and have a pair of blowholes, which explains the V-shaped blow experts use to identify them from afar. Their massive, oval-shaped heads are covered in callosities, wart-like bumps that come in different shapes and sizes so unique that scientists use them to identify specific whales in a group. Adult whales range between 14 and 18m long, and South African waters are estimated to hold about one thousand. Between 40 to 70 of these whales are thought to be in Walker Bay. Many oohs and aahs can be heard from shore when the whales start performing some of their most frequently photographed pet tricks:

Breaching: When whales lift their entire bodies out of the water in a graceful leap. Usually occurs 3-5 times in succession, may be done for communication purposes or just for excitement.

Lobtailing: When whales slap their tales on the surface of the water. Scientists believe this is for communication purposes, especially for sounding out warnings to sharks or rival whales. Pity the mother whale who has to deal with such a tantrum.

Spyhopping: When whales push themselves up vertically out of the water to get a 360° view of their surroundings.

Blowing: The act of expelling air from the lungs through the blowhole, resulting in a loud spout of water vapor. Spout shapes characterize different types of whales.

Grunting: A loud effusion, often heard at night, that carries as far as 2km.

val, a mama whale gave birth 50 yards off Gearing's Point, to an applauding crowd of thousands. Whales have also popped up within 5m of the rocks at Bientang's Cave (see **Food,** above).

Other popular lookouts peer from the cliff paths that line the hills above the ocean along Walker Bay. They are difficult to miss; if one walks toward the ocean from town, they run from the Old to New Harbors, with a bar for celebration at each end. Early morning types can sight scores of dassies (a sort of fat, hairy, man-rodent) that inhabit the cliff paths, a part of this complete breakfast experience. If paths and cliffs seem too removed from the action, up-close whale viewing is possible via boat. **Boat Based Whale Cruises** (☎315 1406) organizes trips, as do local backpackers.

For updates on whale sightings, Hermanus has the world's only **whale crier,** who walks through town daily from 10am to 4pm in whale-watching season, starting at the Old Harbor, and walking through town to the tourist office on Mitchell St. He blows his horn to keep everyone abreast of the latest whale sightings in the bay and will answer the questions of every eager tourist. The **Whale Route Hotline** also offers updates (☎083 910 1028; www.mtn.co.za/whaleroute).

FLORAL SIGHTS. A drive up Rotary Way grants a closer look at the indigenous *fynbos* vegetation and a stunning view of the town from above. (*Off Main St. 1km out of town toward Cape Town. Look for white entrance gates.*) The **Fernkloof Nature Reserve,** just above town, has an impressive floral display of coastal *fynbos* and other plant species, especially the different species of the protea flower. The reserve is one of only six floral "kingdoms" in the world. Over 50km of **hiking** paths traverse the reserve, and the panoramic views of Walker Bay and the town from above are exceptional. **Guided tours** can be arranged with the tourist office. (☎312 1122. Open at all times. Backpackers in town give lifts. Free.) There are more enjoyable views and a variety of *fynbos* at **Hoy's Koppie,** also the burial place of Sir William and Gertrude Mildred Hoy. Sir William, former general manager of the South African Railways, is the reason that there is no railway line through town—he didn't want to spoil the town's natural beauty.

MUSEUMS. The **Old Harbor Museum** contains exhibits on the whaling history of Hermanus and (part of) an impressive whale skeleton. (☎312 1475. Open M-Sa 9am-1pm and 2-5pm, Su and holidays noon-4pm. R2, children R1.) Back in Market Sq., in a small house across the yard beyond the parking lot, the dinky **Photographic Museum** briefly chronicles the development of Hermanus and looks at some of Jaws' jaws. (☎313 0418. Open M-Sa 9am-noon and 1-5pm, Su noon-4pm. R2, children R1. Free with ticket from Old Harbor Museum.)

THE BEACH. When it comes to soft sand, **Grotto Beach** is the candidate for bountiful offerings in Hermanus, stretching east to the mouth of the Klein River Lagoon. Surfers may want to head for **Kammabaai** (also known as Nancy's Beach or Lover's Cove) and **Voelklip** (on the way out of town toward Stanford). **Fick's Pool,** on Westcliff Rd., is a tidal pool popular for swimming, and **Langbaai** is ideal for windier days. There are also some great dive sites in Walker Bay.

CRUISING. Hermanus Adventure can transform civilized folk into pirates in just a few hours. They run *braai* cruises between Hermanus and Stanford (3-4hr., R125), breakfast cruises (2hr., R75), wine route trips (R55, picnic included), and bus tours (1½hr., R30) for landlubbers, and can arrange crayfish netting (summer only, R150), and fishing trips (3hr., R75). (☎313 2905 or 083 645 3333. 135 Main Rd. Office open daily 7am-6pm.)

♫ ☕ ENTERTAINMENT AND NIGHTLIFE

The **Whale Festival** (☎313 0928) runs for 11 days from the last week of September into early October, saturating the town with visitors who celebrate the mating and calving of whales. Over 30 performances, all celebrating the aforementioned procreation, run the gamut from cabaret, art exhibitions, and flea markets, to drinking while engaging in ocean voyeurism. In addition to other festivals that dot the months, the **Food and Wine Fair** (☎312 1113) takes place concurrently, whetting the palate for three days with cooking demonstrations and ample boozing. For those who need cultural gratification, the **Village Theatres cinema** (☎313 0551), in Village Sq. off Marine Dr., shows two films per week. The tourist office provides information about local **vineyards.**

For a town of its size, the nightlife is pretty fab. A number of pubs toast the tardy hours, adamantly refusing to close before it's "late." Most of these are in a conveniently compact and safe area at the intersection of Main Rd. by the harbor.

▨ **Onverklaar Bar,** 121 Main Rd. (☎312 1679), at Long St. above Zebra Crossing. The O-bar is the closest thing to a dance club in Hermanus. Those who aren't moved by the deep house can sink into the cushy couches next to the fireplace or play some pool. DJs nightly in summer, F-Sa in low season. Cover R10-20. Open nightly 8pm-2am.

Gecko, an annex of The Rock (see **Food,** above). Overlooking the Bay, these indoor and outdoor tables are Hermanus' prime location for sundowners. Open daily 11am-2am.

Fisherman's Cottage (☎312 3642), at Lemm's Corner by the Old Harbor, proudly wears the honor of being the smallest Southern Hemisphere bar. This tiny, tiny bar pays homage to grizzled old fishermen who resemble Poseidon and still manages to pound out the hipster pulse of Hermanus. Live bands (mostly cover bands) cut it up on weekends. No cover. Open daily 11am-late, closed M-Tu during winter.

Barney's Tavern, 12 High St. (☎313 0611), a Mediterranean-themed sports pub that blares out alternative music. Open M-Sa 4pm-4am, Su 7pm-4am.

NEAR HERMANUS: GANSBAAI AND PEARLY BEACH 028

Gansbaai, originally "Gangstat" or "goose fountain" after the geese who pioneered this coastal town, is now the unassuming white shark capital of the world. South Africa was the first country to protect the endangered shark species, and Dyer and Geyser islands, near Gansbaai, are nature reserves between which sharks hang out. Serving as a launching pad for a variety of shark sighting adventures, Gansbaai has been attracting an increasing number of visitors.

Backpackers and the Hermanus and Gansbaai tourist offices arrange tours and trips. **White Shark Adventures** offers cage diving where pairs of viewers descend into the ocean in cages and play with the surrounding sharks. (☎384 1380; fax 384 1381; sharkdiv@itec.co.za.) A divers' license is necessary for some trips.

For those who prefer to stay dry, Gansbaai offers a number of hiking options. The commanding 3½km **Duiwelsgat (Devil's Bottom) Hiking Trail** (1½hr.) hugs the coast of Walker Bay, presenting a succession of majestic views of the harbor. The trail also offers choice and relatively secluded vantage points for staring down blowholes. Check out the gushers from above **De Kelders**, the only freshwater cave on the African coast, about 3km down the trail. The relatively easy trail starts at the campsite, close to the Old Harbor. Although it is poorly marked by sporadic green footprints on the rocks, you can't go too far astray if you stay close to the coast. The self-proclaimed "coast of contrasts" also offers entertainment for the more sedate along the empty and soft stretches of sand at **Pearly Beach**, 20km out of town.

Gansbaai is about 40km east of Hermanus on the **R43**. The **tourist office,** just off Main Rd., piles on the info and books accommodations. (☎384 1439; gansbaai-info@telkomsa.net. Open M-F 9am-4pm, Sa 10am-noon.) There are no hostels in town, and the proliferation of B&B rooms start at R150 per person. As many tours and activities can be arranged in Hermanus, and include transportation, it is probably a better idea to stay there.

CALEDON ☎028

Bread. Flowers. Beer. Mineral water that won a prize at the Chicago World Fair of 1893. Not just any grocery list, all these items are part of Caledon's claims to fame. Other than that, the capital of the Overberg Coast has just enough diversion to make it a good pit stop on the way somewhere else, or a truly ingenious hideaway.

The **mineral baths** just outside of town are now housed in a ritzy spa resort, but the pleasure of a short, albeit pricey, dip is open to all. The pools are filled by water that is unfiltered and unheated, yet remarkably warm. Don't stay in for more than 15 min., and the curious color of the water should explain why. (On the grounds of The Caledon Casino, Hotel and Spa, on Nerina St.; take a right on Plein St., at the top of the hill from town, and follow it for about 5min. until you see signs. A somewhat precarious 30min. walk. ☎214 1271. Open daily 6am-8pm. R25, children R15.)

Just above town is the 56ha **Caledon Wild Flower Garden and Reserve,** a small and under-appreciated paean to all things *fynbos*. Follow the reserve's 10km Meiring **hiking trail,** which leads to Window Rock, for Cederberg-on-a-budget highlights (3-5hr.; bring your own water). The annual **Wildflower Show** (☎212 1511), during the second weekend of September, displays all of the different species in the area. It is touted as the largest flower show in all of South Africa, and its protea (the national flower) entrants often do well in the Chelsea Flower Show in London. The **Caledon House Museum,** 11 Constitution St., is a reconstructed late Victorian home that also contains a collection of 1950s works by Cape Town artist Peter Clark. (☎212 1511. Open M-F 8am-1pm and 2-5pm, Sa 9am-1pm.)

Plein St. is the main road that leads into town from Hermanus in the south and the **N2** to the north. All three **intercity buses** stop in Caledon at the Alexandra Hotel.

The **tourist office,** 22 Plein St., offers info on walking tours, a local artists gallery, a bakery shop, and other useful information. (☎212 1511; fax 214 1427. Open M-F 8am-1pm and 2-5pm, Sa 9am-1pm.)

SWELLENDAM   ☎028

Midway between Cape Town and the Garden Route, and set in a plush green patch of the Langerberg Mountains, Swellendam attracts adventure-seeking backpackers, new age proselytizers, and serene nature-loving vacationers alike. One of South Africa's oldest towns, Swellendam offers reasonably-priced outdoor adventure activities, swarms with trails for hiking, mountain biking, horseback riding and canoeing, and hosts a large museum plus coffee shops galore. Swellendam can also serve as a base for exploring the De Hoop Nature Reserve and Cape Agulhas.

⊏ TRANSPORTATION

Swellendam lies at the northeastern edge of the Overberg, 220km from Cape Town and from the mouth of the Garden Route along the **N2.**

Buses: All mainliners depart from the **Swellengrebel Hotel** on Voortrek St. **Intercape** (☎514 2135) has two daily buses to **Cape Town** (3hr., R65) and **Port Elizabeth** (7½hr., R120), via **Mossel Bay** (2½hr., R65) and **Knysna** (4hr., R90). **Greyhound** (☎021 418 4312) also has two daily buses to **Cape Town** (3hr., R75) and two to **East London** (11hr., R185), via the Garden Route towns and **Port Elizabeth** (7½hr., R135). The **Baz Bus** stops at Swellendam Backpackers.

⁊ PRACTICAL INFORMATION

Tourist Office: 36 Voortrek St. (☎/fax 514 2770; infoswd@sdm.dorea.co.za; www.swellendam.org.za.), has several brochures on B&Bs in the area. They also offer samples of the delicious local Youngberry Liqueur. Open M-F 9am-1pm and 2-5pm, Sa 9am-noon.) Information on outdoor and adventure activities as well as tours to nearby nature reserves is offered by the enthusiastic staff of **Swellendam Backpackers.**

Internet Access: Bramble Bush Coffee Shop (See **Food,** p. 148) R0.70 per min. Also, **The Grande Bazaar** (☎514 1942), a restaurant/cafe/gallery that also books accommodations. R0.50 per min. Open M-T 9am-5pm, W-Su 9am-10pm.

Post Office: On Voortrek St. between Rhenius and Fairbairn St. **Postal Code:** 6740.

⌀ ACCOMMODATIONS AND CAMPING

▧ **Swellendam Backpackers,** 5 Lichtenstein St. (☎514 2648; fax 514 1249; backpack@dorea.co.za). Spaciously cushioned between the peaceful slopes of the Langeberg Mountains near the town center. With the route to Cape Town at your back, go across the river, left on Berg St., and left on Lichtenstein St. A bodacious outdoorsy staff offers accommodations and tons of information for grubsters. There's a swimming pond out back, a little river, a blazing campfire on summer nights, and five little "Wendy House" wood cabins in back with double beds. Bikes R30 half day, R50 full day. Dinner R15-35. Internet access R15 per 30min. Reception 24hr. 4- to 8-bed dorms R45; singles R85-95; doubles R130; Wendy Houses R130; camping R30. ❶

Herberg Roosje van de Kaap, 5 Drostdy Street (☎/fax 514 3001; roosje@dorea.co.za), parallel and south of Voortrek Street, is a classy B&B and restaurant set in an 18th-century building. Some of the rooms are small, but the atmosphere is charming, and the hosts are welcoming. Singles R215; doubles R160 per person; garden singles R250; garden doubles R180 per person. R20 surcharge per person if paying by credit card. AmEx/MC/V. ❸

Swellendam Caravan Park (☎514 2705; fax 514 2695; swellendam@xsinet.co.za). 20 cottages and 100 caravan spots (SIC). Call for prices. ❶

🔋 FOOD

▨ **Mattsen's Steakhouse,** 44 Voortrek St. (☎514 2715), is next to the tourist office. Locals claim that they have the best steaks in the country (R45-60). Open Su-F noon-3pm and 6:30pm-late, Sa 6:30pm-late. AmEx/DC/MC/V. ❸

Bramble Bush Coffee Shop (☎514 3565; ndk9@worldonline.co.za), at the corner of Voortrek St. and Andrew Whyte St., is one of Swellendam's most pleasant cafes. Its large outdoor terrace is plant-lined, while its cozy interior serves as a gallery for local art. Big Breakfast R30. Internet access. Open M-F 9am-5pm, Sa-Su 9am-3pm. ❷

Zanddrift (☎514 1789), Swellengrebel St. next to the Drosty Museum, is renowned for all-you-can-eat homemade cooking. The menu is "take it or leave it"—dishes change each day and are recited to diners by the host-chef herself. Prices are reasonable if you plan to eat a lot. Soup R25, cold meat, cheese and fruit platter R45, hot platter R55. Vegetarian option available. Open F-W 9am-4pm. ❸

The Connection Restaurant, 132 Voortrek St. (☎514 1988), offers all-you-can-eat hot dinner platters for R65, with soup R70. Open Th-F and Su-Tu 11am-2:30pm and 6-10pm, Sa 6-10pm. ❸

The Goose and Bear Pub, 25 Voortrek St. (☎514 3101), is across from the Standard Bank. This is the pub for any time of day and has passable pub plates for pleasing prices. Steak with chips and salad R25, toasted sandwiches R7. Open M-Sa 11:30am-2am, Su 7pm-midnight. ❶

Herberg Roosje van de Kaap, 5 Drostdy St. (☎514 3001), is an upscale, tasteful place serving pizzas (R22-48) as well as more refined dishes. The restaurant is quite romantic, in a quiet B&B with candles everywhere. Sole (R34) and fillet *roosje* (R65-75; ostrich fillet R70) are both right on. Open Tu-Su 7pm-late. ❸

👁🔼 SIGHTS AND OUTDOORS

▨ **Faerie Sanctuary,** 37 Buitenkant St. (☎514 1786), off Murray St. A tranquil shrine to magic and childhood, from the infernal to the ethereal. This artist's home features loads of little elves and gnomes in its garden, creating a veritable journey through the looking glass. Open Tu-Su 9am-5pm. R5.

Drostdy Museum, 18 Swellengrebel St. (☎514 1138), is one of the larger museums in the region. Examine the history of Swellendam in three buildings, a carriage house, and a luscious rose garden. There's also an old jail for those who need to be disciplined and punished. Open M-F 9am-4:45pm, Sa-Su 10am-3:45pm. R10, children R1.

Swellendam Horse Trails (☎082 494 8279) zigzags its way up the slopes of the Langeberg Mountains, either on short excursions or full daytrips. Levels of difficulty vary. R85 per hr.; weekend trips available.

Bontebok National Park (☎343 1991), 6km from Swellendam on the N2 toward Mossel Bay, lies in the shadows of Langeberg's peaks. Wildlife in the park includes Bontebok antelope (the park's original *raison d'être* was to increase the population of this endangered species, which has since been fulfilled), the Cape Mountain Zebra, and birds of all feathers. Full-day hikes (including lunch) R550. The gravel trails are superb for **biking.** Open daily Oct.-Apr. 7am-7pm; May-Sept. 7am-6pm. Free.

 ADVENTURES

A number of outfits organize adventures and excursions into the natural surroundings. **Felix Unite** (☎ 021 683 6433), an adventure travel company in Cape Town, runs **whitewater rafting** and **cycling trips** along the Breede River near Swellendam.

SUIDPUNT

The feel of the Overberg Coast's Suidpunt region, an expanse that halts abruptly at the southernmost point of Africa, is that of uninterrupted desolation. The coastal quasi-peninsula rests between the Indian and Atlantic Oceans, conjoining the two at Cape Agulhas. Few venture out to these distant realms, leaving the region's beaches quieter and less cluttered than others in the province. Most come only to stand at the precipice of Africa, while others flock to the De Hoop Nature Reserve, gallivanting across its moonscape dunes in order to catch some glimpses of the Southern Right Whale, which makes spectacular annual appearances.

Most Suidpunt villages are small enough to spit across, lengthwise. Thus, amenities are few and transportation options scarce. The coastal drives are beautiful, though the often unpaved terrain can be hell on any car. Suidpunt is accessible from Swellendam and the **N2** via R316, R317, or R319. The **Suidpunt Tourism Bureau,** in Bredasdorp, at the intersection of the R316, 317, and 319, has brochures of what's going on in the region by season. They also attempt to help out with transportation and accommodations. (☎ 028 424 2584; fax 028 425 2731; suidpunt@brd.dorea.co.za; www.capeoverberg.co.za. Open M-F 8:30am-4:30pm, Sa 9am-1pm.)

BREDASDORP   ☎028

Bredasdorp is just that, a tiny *dorp* (village) at the intersection of the R316, 317, and 319. There is no public transport into town, but for those passing through on the drive to Arniston or Agulhas, it offers a museum with the taste for the macabre, and a nature walk. The **Bredasdorp Shipwreck Museum,** 6 Independent St. at the corner of Museum St., enlivens the city history by celebrating the ghosts of crashes past. The typical local history of the bed-and-chamber pot variety is made eerie by the fact that most objects on display floated ashore from wrecked liners. (Open M-F 9am-3:45pm. R5, children R2.) At the Shipwreck Museum, you can also ask for the key to the **Bottle Collection,** South Africa's largest such assembly, which sits in the Old Jail on Hoop between Van Riebeeck and All Saints St. The **Heuningberg Nature Reserve** (☎ 424 2584), at the southern end of town all the way down Van Riebeeck St., has some gorgeous trails that harbor nice destinations for a picnic.

ARNISTON/WAENHUISKRANS   ☎028

Arniston/Waenhuiskrans is a town so nice they named it twice. Lying at the end of the R316, 24km from Bredasdorp, the town's coast undulates with dunes and caves (the name *Waenhuiskrans* refers to a sizable sea cave—apparently roomy enough for a wagon to turn around in). The fishing village, Kassiesbaai, is a national monument in its own right, and the warm, blue waters are 100% Indian Ocean. Arniston makes for a good base from which to visit the southern coast.

⛏ ACCOMMODATIONS. The new ⬛**South of Africa Backpackers ❷,** off the R316 and on the same road as the missile testing site (see below), offers three-star hotel amenities at hostel prices. All 12 rooms offer TV and phone. The luxuries include: a swimming pool, billiards, free giant breakfast, gym, and sauna. Free pick-up is available from Bredasdorp. (☎ 445 9240; fax 445 9254; www.dieherberg.co.za. Singles R110; doubles R180; triples R225. DC/MC/V.)

WESTERN CAPE

⚠ OUTDOORS. While the **dunes** and **cave** in Arniston/Waenhuiskrans are worth-while as a daytrip, they are fairly tough to access without the benefit of a four wheel drive vehicle; it's not uncommon for two wheel drive vehicles to get stuck in the sand. It is better to park at the beach entrance and walk. Just inland, Arniston's **missile testing site** served as one of the focal areas in the development of missile capabilities for nuclear warheads prior to South Africa's abandonment of this operation in the mid-80s. The missile testing site is open to the public on two days every year—ask the Suidpunt tourist office in Bredasdorp. A different kind of danger lurks at the majestic **Waenhuiskrans Cave,** about 1km from the village. This enormous sea cavern, filled with bats as well as geological oddities from erosion by the sea, can be visited at low tide. Those who visit must exercise cau-tion, however, as getting stuck in the caves during high tide can be deadly. Hap-pily, the Suidpunt tourist office makes things easier and safer by providing daily tide schedules.

CAPE AGULHAS   ☎028

To many, it is known as 34°49'58" south, 20°00'12", but for the rest of us it is (with a drum roll), "The Southernmost Tip of Africa." A profound anticlimax marks this point, which would remain inconspicuous were it not for a sign identifying it as the merger of the Atlantic and Indian Oceans. Still, hard-core, glory-craving travelers will make the journey almost out of necessity, if only to say that they've "done it." L'Agulhas may lack character, but there's an undeniable thrill in gazing across the deep blue and imagining the not-so-far-off coastline of Antarctica. The road may not be too good and it is sometimes hard to turn around, so park your car early and walk the last bit.

The coastline on either side of Cape Agulhas is known as the "Graveyard of Ships;" over 250 have fallen victim to the treacherous winds and merciless waves along this stretch of rocky coast. The **L'Agulhas Lighthouse,** the second-oldest working lighthouse in the country, is still in use after a hundred and fifty years. It only takes a bit of heavy breathing to make it up the ladders to the top of the light-house tower, where a panoramic view of the meeting point of the two oceans awaits. The lighthouse also serves as L'Agulhas' surrogate tourist office and pro-vides local information. (☎435 6078. Open M-Sa 9am-4:45pm, Su 11am-3pm. R5, children R2.)

L'Agulhas lies at the southern tip of the **R319,** 38km from Bredasdorp. Although the town is very small, accommodations are available. The funky and bohemian **Southernmost ❷,** at the corner of Lighthouse Rd. and Van Breda St., or the first right down the hill from the lighthouse, has a hut-like Mediterranean-style B&B and hostel in the shadow of the lighthouse, and adds a pleasant dose of charm to the town. Outside, their olympic-size swimming pool is affectionately known as the ocean. No smoking or use of cell phones on the premises. During the winter, backpackers might be placed in the colder rooms. (☎435 6565; fax 435 6544; cowper@isat.co.za. Internet access. Backpackers R120-140; B&B singles R200; doubles R350.) **Lewende Hawe ❶,** 11 Krom St., is a decent option. From Main Rd. (approach-ing the lighthouse), take a right onto Duiker St., then the second right onto Krom St. Basic but clean small dorms in the back of a house. (☎435 7009 or 083 581 7211. R55-65, R5 surcharge for bedding.)

Nearby the **L'Agulhas Caravan Park ❶,** on Main Road, is clean and basic. (☎435 6015. Reception daily 8am-8pm. Sites R40-55, electricity included.) **Agulhas Sea-foods ❶,** on Main Road next to L'Agulhas Kafee, has delectable fish 'n chips for R10-15. (☎435 7207. Open M-Sa 9am-7pm, Su 9am-3pm; Apr. and Dec.-Jan. daily 8am-8pm.)

DE HOOP NATURE RESERVE   ☎028

The gargantuan sand dunes and picture-perfect coastline of De Hoop Nature Reserve make it one of the most satisfying destinations in the Western Cape, especially because so few have discovered its draw. The whale-watching here is considered the best in the Western Cape, and the lack of binocular-laden, *biltong*-munching tourists makes it that much more of a refreshing place to view some blowhole-spouting and lobtailing.

The wilderness in De Hoop is astounding; 36,000ha include a marine reserve (the entire coastal area), a wetland with several aquatic bird species, limestone hills 200m above sea level, the Potberg Mountain Range, and the impressive (up to 90m) sand dunes that line the coast. The flora, however, is even more remarkable, with over 1500 varieties of plants. Among the 86 species of mammals here are baboon, Cape Mountain zebra, bontebok, and the rarely seen leopard. The reserve is also home to 260 bird species, including the rare Cape vulture and the black oyster catcher. There are several drives and walks as well as more intense hiking trails, a mountain biking route (bring your own bike), tidal pools for swimming and snorkeling, and a game drive. The head office has a number of maps. Head to **Koppie Allen** in the middle of the coastal area for splendid whale-watching atop the dunes; the whales and their calves can often be spotted from here. Walk from the car park along the coastal trail in the reserve for 5km east or west. (50km east of Bredasdorp; 280km from Cape Town. From Swellendam or Cape Town, take the turn-off from the N2 between Swellendam and Bredasdorp. From Bredasdorp, take the Bredasdorp Malgas Rd. to the signposts. ☎028 542 1126; fax 542 1247; dehoopinfo@sdm.dorea.co.za. Open Sa-Th 7am-6pm, F 7am-7pm, last entry 1hr. prior to closing. R5. Bring your own supplies (or buy them in nearby Ouplaas). **Accommodations ❶** office open M-F 8am-4pm, Sa-Su 8-11am. 4-person self-catering cottages without bedding or kitchen utensils R100, R25 per extra person; fully equipped 4-person cottages R200, R50 per extra person; campsites R35, maximum 6 people. Book ahead.)

THE GARDEN ROUTE

The Garden Route navigates a stunning coastal tightrope between lush, swelling peaks and azure oceanic expanses. While the route originally centered around the tree-hugging hippie havens of Knysna and Plettenberg Bay, the undeniable appeal of a title conjuring a placid paradise convinced neighboring towns to get in on the action; the region dubbed the Garden Route now spreads from Storms River in the east to Mossel Bay in the west. The splendor of this gorgeous stretch entices a wealth of visitors seeking to capitalize on both the setting and the unbelievable amenities that have been built around it. Backpackers will enjoy a particularly regal life, as they are showered with offerings of food, drink, transport, delirium, and frenzy amidst the boundless activities. Despite this, the predominant and palpable tranquility produced by the spectacularly serene environment still leaves visitors at peace with the world.

MOSSEL BAY (MOSSELBAAI)   ☎044

When Bartolomeu Dias first set foot in Mossel Bay in 1488, he set in action a chain of events that would forever change the history of Africa. His landing marked the first encounter between Europeans and the area's KhoiKhoi inhabitants. When a KhoiKhoi was killed in an exchange with Dias's crew, Mossel Bay became the first page in South Africa's 500-year history of hostile race relations. The history buff will be interested in this village, but the thrill-seeker will also be satisfied, especially after encountering a Great White Shark face-to-face.

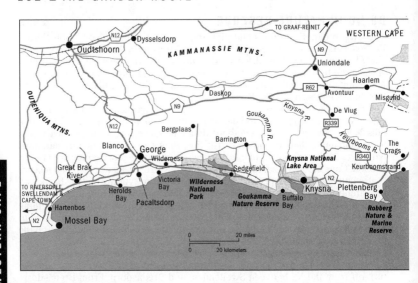

TRANSPORTATION

Buses: Baz Bus (☎ 021 439 2323, fax 691 2640) stops daily at local hostels on its way along the coast. Departs 2-2:30pm, 3:30-3:45pm. **Translux** (☎ 801 8202), **Intercape**, and **Greyhound** drop passengers off at the Shell Station in Voorbaai, about 10km from Mossel Bay. Most hostels will arrange pick-ups from the station. Buses run to: **Cape Town** (6hr., daily, R110-115); **Durban** (7hr., daily, R305-330); **George** (30min., daily, R60-80); **Pretoria,** (16hr., daily, R270). **Bay View Travel,** 12 Church St. (☎ 691 2644; fax 691 2640), has detailed schedules and tickets.

Minibus Taxis: On Marsh St., turn inland at the Milky Lane ice cream shop; the stand is on the left on an unmarked street. To: **Cape Town** (4hr., daily, R110); **George** (30min., many times daily, R12); **Port Elizabeth** (5hr., daily, R95).

ORIENTATION AND PRACTICAL INFORMATION

Mossel Bay has the only north-facing beach in South Africa. This means that when you face the water with **The Point** to your right and the western **Santos Beach** to your left, you're looking up toward Greece. All of Mossel Bay is situated between The Point and Santos, and the distance between them can be walked in 20min. Marsh St. is the main street and most services are either on this street or its side streets.

Tourist Office: Mossel Bay Tourism (☎ 691 2202; fax 690 3077; iti26050@mweb.co.za; www.sacape.co.za; www.gardenroute.net/mby), corner of Market and Church St. Open M-F 8am-6pm, Sa 9am-5pm; winter M-F 9am-5pm, Sa 9am-1pm.

Bank: Standard Bank, 85 Marsh St. (☎ 690 7136). Across from Edgars. Foreign exchange and **ATMs.** Open M-F 8:30am-3:30pm, Sa 8:30-11am.

Police: 2C George Rd. (☎ 690 3359; **emergency** ☎ 10 111).

Pharmacy: Fanie's Pharmacy, 93 Marsh St. (☎ 691 1505; fax 691 2687; after hours 082 744 9034). Open M-F 8:30am-8pm, Sa 8am-1pm and 6-8pm, Su (emergencies only) 10am-noon and 6-8pm.

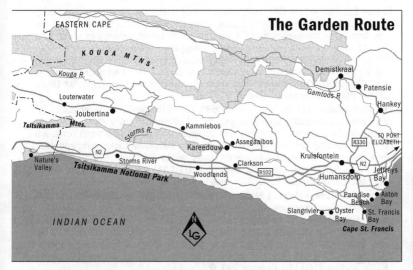

The Garden Route

EASTERN CAPE

KOUGA MTNS.

Kouga R.

Demistkraal

Patensie

Louterwater

Gamtoos R

Hankey

Joubertina

Tsitsikamma Mtns.

Storms R.

Kammiebos

Assegaaibos

Kareedouw

N2

Storms River

Clarkson

Kruisfontein

R330

TO PORT
ELIZABETH

Nature's
Valley

Tsitsikamma National Park

Woodlands

R102

N2

Humansdorp

Jeffreys
Bay

INDIAN OCEAN

Paradise
Beach

Aston
Bay

Slangrivier

Oyster
Bay

St. Francis
Bay

Cape St. Francis

WESTERN CAPE

Hospital: Bay View Hospital (☎ 691 3718), on Marsh St., 1km west of town on the corner of Ryktulbach St. in the big white building. On-the-spot payment required. **Ambulance** service (☎ 691 1911). Open 24hr.

Laundromat: 5 Marsh St. (☎/fax 690 3646). Self-service and drop-off. Washers R7; wash, dry, fold R8 per kg. Open M-F 8am-5pm, Sa 8am-1pm.

Internet Access: J+D Internet Cafe (☎ 691 2768; cgate@lantic.net; www.swd.co.za), in The Plaza, next to the post office on Marsh St. R9 per 15min., R16 per 30min., R28 per hr. R17 per hr. after 7pm. Open daily 9am-9pm. **Postnet,** 26 Bayside Center (☎ 690 7779; fax 690 5540; postnetm/bay@worldonline.co.za), offers Internet access (R10 per 15min.), faxing, and copying. Open M-F 8:15am-5pm, Sa 8:30am-12:45pm.

Post Office: (☎ 691 1308; fax 691 1771), corner of Marsh and Mitchell St. Open M-Tu and Th-F 8:30am-5pm, W 9am-5pm, Sa 8am-12:30pm.

Postal Code: 6500; deliveries 6506.

🏕 ACCOMMODATIONS AND CAMPING

Mossel Bay wins big points for its innovative accommodations. The offerings are solid, whether you sleep on a train, in a hut, or in the lap of contemporary luxury. Book ahead during South African holiday seasons.

🏠 **Khoi Village** (☎ 690 4940 or 083 346 53363), embedded in carved-out cliffs (where the Khoi once dwelled) at The Point. For those who pine for the nomadic life, these huts provide an unusual way to rough it. Need water? Fill an ostrich-egg jug. There's a toilet and 5 hot showers; the adventurous can opt to bathe in a rock pool and dry off by the fire. Breakfast included. Bookings essential. Reception 9am-late. R89 per person. ❶

Barnacle's, 112 High St. (☎/fax 690 4584; barnacles@mweb.co.za). Entrance around corner on Hill St. Sparkling backpackers with great facilities, brightly colored squeaky clean rooms, and gorgeous views of the sea from its balcony. Pool table and TV lounge. Breakfast R25. Laundry R10 per load. Internet: 1 terminal, only for use after 7pm; R10 per 15min., R15 per 30min., R25 per hr. Key deposit R20. Reception 8am-10pm. Check-out 10:30am. Dorms R60; doubles R150; flexi-room (sleeps 2-4) R70 per person; penthouse R180 (en suite). ❶

Santos Express (☎/fax 691 1995; santos.express@mweb.co.za; www.santosexpress.co.za). From the museum complex, facing the water, walk down the hill on the left, then follow the railroad tracks. Guests stay in preserved sleeper cars overlooking the sea. Unique, but a bit claustrophobic. Stunning views of the coastline may make up for the lack of comfort. Continental breakfast included except between Dec. 15 and Jan. 10. Kitchen and TV in dining car; restaurant in caboose. Laundry R8 per kg wash, dry, iron. Key deposit R20. 5-day min. stay in Dec. Reception 8am-10pm. Check-out 10am. Singles R90; R75 per person sharing. MC/V. ❶

The Park House, 121 High St. (☎/fax 691 1937; the_station@yeboxhosa.co.za; www.park-house.co.za). Spend the night in a 130-year-old stone mansion with an enchanted fairy garden. This lovely yard, complete with carp in the small pond, will make all who stay here relax. Recently divided into a separate backpackers and B&B. Free tennis rackets and balls for use on courts nearby. Bus pick-ups R15. Reception open daily 8am-10pm. Check-out 10am. Breakfast R15-25. Dinner R20-30. Dorms R60; backpacker doubles R160; B&B doubles R200. ❶

Mossel Bay Backpackers, 1 Marsh St. (☎/fax 691 3182; marquette@pixie.co.za; www.gardenrouteadventures.com). Comfortable, cozy backpackers. Close to The Point, an excellent location for surfers. On lazy days, the garden and swimming pool make excellent spots for lounging around. Free pick-ups but not drop-offs. Internet R10 per min. Blankets in dorms for R10 extra. Breakfast R15. Dinner R35. Lockers available, R20 deposit for a lock. Key deposit R20. Reception 7am-10pm. Dorms R60; singles R120; doubles R160-180. Camping R40. ❶

Old Post Office Tree Manor (☎691 3738; fax 691 3104; book@oldposttree.co.za; www.oldposttree.co.za), next door to Gannet Cafe. A stately hotel in one of Mossel Bay's oldest buildings. For couples eager for a romantic interlude, the special package offered in the Honeymoon Suite includes a jacuzzi and a bottle of sparkling wine (R750 per night). TV with MNET in all rooms. All meals served at Gannet. Internet approx. R1 per min. Reception 7am-11pm. Check-out 10am. Doubles from R330-480 per person sharing B&B. AmEx/MC/V. ❹

🔾🞖 FOOD AND NIGHTLIFE

Though pickings are a bit on the slim side, there are enough cheap venues to provide therapy for even the most traumatized of wallets. There are also a number of mid-range restaurants that offer classy cuisine. Book ahead in high season.

Santos Express Restaurant, next door to Santos Express (see **Accommodations**). Typical South African pub menu with a grand view of the waves. Converted train carriages stopped forever in their tracks along the Santos Beach create a unique atmosphere for a commonplace meal. Toasted sandwiches R6.50-9. Calamari R18.95. Schnitzel R35. Su buffet R35. Take-away. MC/V. ❷

The Gannet Cafe (☎691 1885; fax 691 3104; gannet@oldposttree.co.za), on Market St. next to the Museum Complex. One of the first and best seafood houses in Mossel Bay. Ask to sit in the lush outdoor garden or snuggle up by the fireplace inside. Pub lunch R25-31. Fish R52-169. Wheelchair accessible. Attached is the Blue Oyster cocktail bar, which has a pleasant view out over the water. Open M-F 7am-10:30pm, Sa-Su 8am-10:30pm. AmEx/MC/V. ❷

Khoi Village (☎690 4940), in the huts at The Point. Use a seashell to scoop away at an a la carte meal, including fish and meat prepared over an open fire. Rump steak R48. Lamb chops R39. Dinner served M-Sa 7pm-late. ❷

Tidal's (☎691 3777; fax 690 3430; lighthouseresortcc@intekom.co.za), above the water at the tip of The Point. A fairly downtrodden pub which is nevertheless popular in Mossel Bay. DJs on W and F nights; during school holidays W, F, Sa. Often have live bands—enquire ahead. A range of music. Pub open 9am-late. AmEx/MC/V.

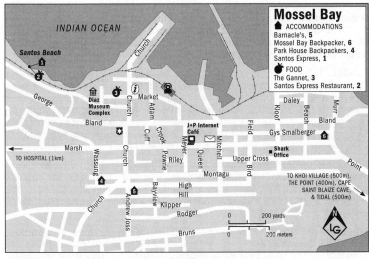

Mossel Bay
- ↑ ACCOMMODATIONS
  - Barnacle's, **5**
  - Mossel Bay Backpacker, **6**
  - Park House Backpackers, **4**
  - Santos Express, **1**
- ● FOOD
  - The Gannet, **3**
  - Santos Express Restaurant, **2**

INDIAN OCEAN

Santos Beach

George

Diaz Museum Complex

Bland

Market

Adam

J+P Internet Café

Daley

Gys Smalberger

Marsh

TO HOSPITAL (1km)

Wassung

Church

Cuff

Crook

Powrie

Meyer

Riley

Queen

Montagu

Mitchell

Upper Cross

Bird

Shark Office

TO KHOI VILLAGE (500m),
THE POINT (400m), CAPE
SAINT BLAIZE CAVE,
& TIDAL (500m)

High

Hill

Klipper

Rodger

Bruns

Bayview

Andrew Joss

Church

Field

Kloof

Beach

Murr

Bland

Point

0 ⸻ 200 yards
0 ⸻ 200 meters

☉ 🏃 SIGHTS AND ADVENTURES

DIAS MUSEUM COMPLEX. The **Maritime Museum** is a fascinating museum that displays artifacts from the Age of Exploration and Conquest, as well as the skewed, parched maps of the pre-Columbian world. The centerpiece is the life-size reproduction of Dias's original caravel. This replica ship sailed from Lisbon in 1987. (☎ *691 1067; fax 691 1915; diasmuseum@mweb.co.za; http://diasmuseum.com. M-F 8:15am-5pm, Sa-Su 9am-4pm. Tours on request but booking essential. R15, kids up to 18 R3.*) The shell collection in the **Shell Museum and Aquarium** is moderately impressive, but the aquarium amounts to little more than a few fish tanks. (*Same hours.* ☎ *691 1067 for whole complex. Aquarium free.*) The old granary seems to hold very little information, but the Cultural Museum just down the street does provide some insight into Khoi culture and the influence of the Anglo-Boer War on Mossel Bay. Outdoors, between the Shell and Maritime Museums, is the historic **Old Post Office Tree.** Early explorers left messages for each other in the trunk of this bushy tree, which is still used as a post office today. Behind the tree is the oft-mentioned spring that provided Dias's voyagers with fresh water. Yes, that puddle is the famous spring.

AROUND THE POINT. The history of the Khoisan is on display at The Point in the **Khoi Village.** This small open-air museum examines the ways of "the forgotten race of South Africa," which was devastated by Dias and those who followed in his footsteps. (☎ *690 4940. Open daily 9am-5pm. R2.*) **Cape Saint Blaize Cave,** a short hike up The Point's rocky promontories, has become a major archaeological site, due to the relics left behind by the Khoisan people who inhabited this natural shelter 80,000 years ago. This cave marks the beginning of the brilliant **St. Blaize Hiking Trail,** a rugged 13.5km march over some stunning coast and beneath a nearby lighthouse. The moderate 5hr. hike ends in Dana Bay.

SHARK-DIVING. Mossel Bay is one of the few spots where thrill-seekers without a diving license can stare down the bloody gullet of a hungry shark. ◪**Shark Africa Great White Shark Experience** might well be the most inviting cage-diving operator in South Africa, because divers don't need certification, and they offer a refund plan if the Great Whites don't appear. They don't lose much money, though, as 87% of their terrified passengers get a glimpse of the sea predators. (☎ 691 3796 or 082 455 2438; sharkafrica@mweb.co.za; www.sharkafrica.co.za. Cage dives R750, with 50% refunded if no sharks are seen; 2 people per cage. Boat deck viewing R450. Lunch included. No age restrictions. Book days ahead, if you dare.)

BUNGEE. If free falling is your thing, **Face Adrenalin** will throw you off the 65m Gouritz Bridge for an abrupt jump (the world's highest) or a solo or tandem swing between two neighboring bridges. This isn't just a sport for kids—seniors over 60 jump for free, and the record stands at 88. (The jump site is tough to reach without a car. Either head west on the N2 for 35km, or ask about transport at your accommodation. ☎ 697 7001; extremes@iafrica.com; www.faceadrenalin.com. Jumps daily 9am-5pm. R150; 2nd jump R100; solo swing R100-120; tandem swing R120. Min. age 14.)

BOTLIERSKOP GAME FARM. This game drive, 20min. from Mossel Bay, offers an up-close view of three of the Big Five. To get there by car, take the N2 toward George, turn onto the 401 at the Little Brak River, turn right at the end, and then take the next right. (☎ 696 6055 or 083 979 9949; botlier@mweb.co.za; www.botlierskop.co.za/botlierskop. R180.)

OTHER SIGHTS. Children may enjoy taking one of the cheap boat trips around **Seal Island. Romonza** (☎ 690 3101; romonza@mweb.co.za; www.mosselbay.co.za/romonza) and the **Seven Seas Pleasure Cruises** (☎ 691 3371; sevencs@mweb.co.za) offer similar trips and leave from the harbor below the tourist office. Estimates of the number of seals on the island range from 2000 to 4000. (1hr. Hourly 10am-5pm. R35, children R15. 2hr. sunset cruises R65. Whale-watching trips R240.)

GEORGE ☎ 044

As George claims to be the "Heart of the Garden Route," visitors might expect a town which has everything from the serenity and charm of nature to the gusto and zest of a vibrant culture. However, this kind of paradise is not what they will find. From its earliest days as a timber town, George has been very industrial and commercial, creating an atmosphere that remains to this day. George's industry does, however, have some redeeming aspects. First, blacks and "coloureds," who have few job opportunities elsewhere on the Garden Route, are able to find work in George, creating a diversity absent in the rest of the primarily lily-white region. Second, George's working-class personality gives it the feel of a "real" town, as opposed to the manicured perfection of the coastal vacation spots. Nature enthusiasts won't leave George completely empty-handed: hiking and mountain-biking opportunities await in the Outeniqua mountains that ring the town.

◨ TRANSPORTATION

Flights: George's airport is about 15km west of town, just off the N2. **South African Airways** (☎ 801 8430) flies to **Cape Town** (70min., 3 per day, R1000) and **Johannesburg** (2hr., 4 per day, R1275).

Trains: Outeniqua Choo-Tjoe (☎ 801 8288; see **Sights**, p. 159) chugs to **Knysna** (R60, under 15 R40) with a stop in **Wilderness.** Departs in summer M-Sa 9:30am and 2:15pm, in winter M, W and F 9:30am.

Car Rentals: Hertz (☎ 876 9999) and **Avis** (☎ 876 9314) are at the airport.

Buses: Bus lines stop at the lot off Cathedral St. (between York St. and Meade St.). Tickets sold at **South Cape Travel,** 111 York St. (☎ 874 6930). Open M-F 8:30am-5pm, Sa 9am-noon. **Translux, Intercape,** and **Greyhound** all offer service from George, though

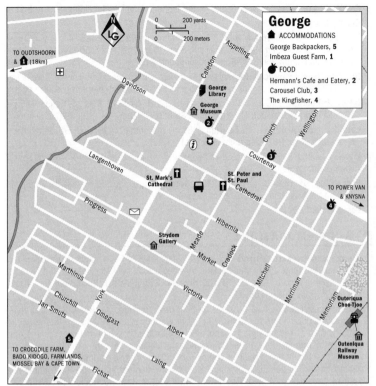

George

🏠 ACCOMMODATIONS
George Backpackers, 5
Imbeza Guest Farm, 1

🍴 FOOD
Hermann's Cafe and Eatery, 2
Carousel Club, 3
The Kingfisher, 4

only Translux serves all of the following destinations: **Bloemfontein** (9hr., daily, R220); **Cape Town** (6hr., daily, R120); **Durban** (19hr., daily, R305); **Johannesburg** (10hr., daily, R280); **Kimberley** (10hr., daily, R225); and **Port Elizabeth** (4½hr., daily, R110). **Baz Bus** (☎ 021 439 2323) stops daily at George Backpackers, and departs eastbound at 3pm and westbound at 2:45pm.

Minibus Taxis: The rank is in St. Mark's Sq., close to the church. To: **Cape Town** (5½hr., 3 per day, R90); **Mossel Bay** (45min., 4 per day, R12); **Port Elizabeth** (5hr., 2 per day, R83); and **Oudtshoorn** (45min., daily, R15).

Taxis: Zeelie Taxis (☎ 874 6707).

✈🛈 ORIENTATION AND PRACTICAL INFORMATION

Coming into town from the east, **Knysna Rd.** branches off from the N2 and proceeds into the CBD as **Courtenay St.** before finally heading out of town toward Oudt-shoorn as **Davidson St.** George's main drag, **York St.**, is perpendicular to Courtenay St. Most of the action occurs on these two streets and on cross streets that run parallel to Courtenay St. You can pick up a map (R1) at the tourist office.

Tourist Office: 124 York St. (☎ 801 9295; fax 873 5228; info@georgetourism.co.za; www.georgetourism.co.za). Open M-F 9am-5pm, Sa 9am-1pm.

Bank: First National Bank, 99 York St. (☎ 874 2434). *Bureau de change.* Open M-T, Th-F 8:30am-5pm, W 9-11am, Sa 8:30-11am.

Police: 37 Courtenay St. (☎873 2207). Behind large municipal building near York St.

Emergency: ☎ 10 177.

Pharmacy: Link's Pharmacy (☎873 5752, emergency 083 635 6882). Opposite Travel Bugs on York St. Open M-F 8:30am-1pm, Sa 8:30am-1pm and 5:30-8pm, Su and holidays 9:30am-noon and 5:30-8pm; prescriptions 24hr.

Hospital: George Provincial Hospital (☎874 5122). Quite a walk from York St. Turn left on Langenhoven St. (the continuation of Hibernia St.); it's about 2km down on the right.

Internet: Postnet, 118 York St. (☎874 4136; fax 874 4137). R10 per 5min.; R15 per 30min.; R25 per hr. Open M-F 8am-5pm, Sa 8:30am-1pm.

Laundry: (☎874 0311), on Courtenay St. at the corner of Mitchell St. Self-service. Washer R6, dryer R6. Open daily 7am-9pm.

Library: (☎801 9288), on Caledon St. behind the museum. Open M-Th 9am-7pm, F 10am-5pm, Sa 9am-12:30pm.

Post Office: 97 York St. (☎874 1212). Between Hibernia and Market St. Open M-F 8:30am-5pm, W 9am-5pm, Sa 8am-12pm.

Postal code: 6530.

■ ACCOMMODATIONS

George Backpackers, 29 York St. (☎874 7807; fax 874 6054; backpackers@worldonline.co.za). George's only backpackers provides a roof, basic facilities, and a TV room, but not much more. Bike hire (R100 deposit, R35 per day). Reception 7am-10pm. Dorms R50; doubles R180. ❶

Imbeza Guest Farm (☎886 0067). A 30min. drive from George. Head down Courtenay St. toward Oudtshoorn for 12km, turn left in Waboomskraal at the sign, turn left again after 3.6km at the hiking sign, and drive 2.4km past the pink house. Pick-ups from George by arrangement. In the Waboomskraal Valley, with a spectacular view of the Outeniqua Mountains. Excellent choice for families or travelers looking for someplace aesthetically and spiritually pleasing. Borders a wilderness area. Horseback riding R50 per hr. Breakfast included. Reception 24hr. Singles R130; doubles R190, with bath R240; 2 self-catering cottages (sleeping 4-6) R80 per person. ❷

■ FOOD AND NIGHTLIFE

Most restaurants in town are reasonably priced, and a couple provide exceptional value. During the week, nightlife consists of getting drunk and pretending that you're in another city. Nevertheless, for a few nights a week (W and F-Sa), everyone in town puts on their party pants, moving from Hermann's Cafe in the early evening to The Carousel later on.

The Kingfisher, 1 Courtenay St. (☎873 3127). Turn right on Courtenay St. at the museum; 1km down on the right. Creatively prepared fresh local seafood R36-42. Prawns R54-125. Take-away. Open daily noon-midnight. AmEx/MC/V. ❷

Hermann's Cafe and Eatery, 70 Courtenay St. (☎873 2052). Next to the museum. Located in the saloons of 2 retired trains, the novel setting is slightly tarnished by the tacky broken sign boards outside. Meat R44-54. Poultry R32-42. Smart casual. Open M-Sa 10:30am-late. AmEx/MC/V. ❷

Carousel Club, 38 Courtenay St. (☎ 873 4324). Across from Shell station. A cool venue worthy of club status in any city and definitely worth your partying energies. Nightly DJs play commercial music on the bottom floor and rave up above. Th is student night, with half-price on all local beers from 9pm-midnight. Cover for dance floor on W R10 and Sa R15. Beers R5. Open daily 6pm-5am.

SIGHTS

OUTENIQUA RAILWAY MUSEUM. On the outskirts of town, the cavernous former railway station holds an eerie collection of old trains, locomotives, and cars, making it feel like a transportation ghost town. The famous **Outeniqua Choo-Tjoe** leaves from this same spot. Most people come to George to see this, the last steam train in Africa that runs daily, evoking the grand bygone era of continental train travel. The scenery is magnificent (especially between George and Sedgefield), and many tourists take the round-trip ride to get a sense of the flow of the Garden Route. Be sure to sit on the right-hand side (to see the coast) and in the front (to avoid exhaust fumes). Book ahead in high season. Arrive early, allowing 30min. or so to look around the museum and then hop on, sit back, and be chugged away. *(2 Mission St. Turn right on Courtenay toward Knysna. ☎801 8274. Open M-Sa 7:30am-6pm. R5, under 15 R2. Tours available, but book in advance.)*

OUTENIQUA POWER VAN. This outfit offers panoramic views of the Outeniqua Mountains from the comfort of former railway inspection cars; it is the most leisurely way to explore the gorgeous passes that were chiseled into the peaks around George. The relaxed pace makes it a good option for families or older travelers. The "Power Excursion" goes up Outeniqua Mountain through the Montagu Pass in the power van. The more adventurous can take the power van up and cycle down. Consider bringing a helmet. *(Trips start at the Outeniqua Railway Museum on 2 Mission St. Turn right on Courtenay, toward Knysna, and right again over the bridge. ☎801 8239; fax 801 8246; opv@mweb.co.za. Bookings essential. Open daily 7:30am-5:30pm; winter 8:15am-4pm. Power van: 3hr. Two times per day in winter; every 2 hours from 7:30am in summer. R60, under 13 R45. Bike: R20 with your own, hire R60)*

GEORGE MUSEUM. This modest and somewhat historic museum has grown to include relics and knick-knacks from a number of eras, including everything from antique gramophones to giant saws. The back section of the building houses a history of the timber industry and the heyday lifestyles it created in George. Do not miss the whimsically detailed fairy paintings of **Ruby Reeves,** a hermit who supposedly lived with the "little people" who pepper her paintings. *(☎873 5343. Open M-F 9am-4:30pm. Free.)*

OUTDOORS AND ADVENTURES

Despite George's commercial focus, there are several sights and activities involving wildlife of varying degrees of ferocity. For those trying to get rid of a traveling companion, the **George Crocodile Park,** on York St. toward the N2, holds over 4000 of the hungry critters. *(☎873 4302. Wheelchair accessible. Open daily 9am-5pm. Feedings at 3pm, except in winter. R15, children R7.50. Cash only.)* **Bado Kidogo** ("in a little while") is a breeding farm for exotic birds. Visitors can stroll among the cages, enjoying the melodious cacophony created by over 2000 birds. *(Head out York St., turn up the R102 toward the airport, go right on the R404, and then left on the Geelhoutboom road. The bird farm is shortly after Farmlands. ☎/fax 870 7415. Wheelchair accessible. Open daily 9am-6pm; in winter 9am-5pm. R20, children R10. Cash only.)* While you're in the area, take the kids to the petting farm or go horseback riding at **Farmlands.** *(☎870 8013. Open daily May-Oct. 11am-4pm; Nov.-Apr. 10am-5pm. Book riding in advance. Guided horseback rides of all levels R60 per hr.; animal farm R7, children R5.)* Vigorous visitors can also join **Eco-Bound** for some thrilling descents down passes and dams on mountain bikes. Take the Power Van to the top of Montagu pass, then ride back down to George, 15km away. *(☎871 4455. In the same office as the Power Van, above. R90 including bike rental.)*

WILDERNESS   ☎ 044

Anyone who happens upon this peaceful one-street town surrounded by five rivers, a waterfall, two estuaries, expanses of indigenous forest, and the Indian Ocean thundering protectively in the background, will immediately see how aptly it is named. A local folktale gives an even more charming version of the town's naming: according to the story, a young suitor hoped to marry a woman whose love of the outdoors was so strong that she insisted on living in the wilderness; he solved the quandary by purchasing the land and renaming it "Wilderness." Regardless of the true story, the freshness and beauty of this place will please any who visit. With adventures to please the most daring, and many blissful spots for those who simply want to sit and take in nature, Wilderness caters to everyone, except perhaps the ever-partying city-lovers. Then again, even the most ardent city bum needs to get fresh air every now and then.

■ **∏** **ORIENTATION AND PRACTICAL INFORMATION.** Wilderness is a smooth, scenic 30km drive from George along the N2. The town itself has few roads, and most do not have clearly marked signs. Bare necessities can be found on George Rd., which leads directly to the N2. Most visitors choose to arrive on the regal **Outeniqua Choo-Tjoe** train (M-Sa 2 per day; in winter M, W, F once per day; R45) from George or Knysna. **Aarloo Taxis** runs to George (R45). **Greyhound** and **Translux** go to Cape Town (7hr., daily, R125) and Durban (16hr., daily, R295). The **tourist office,** on Leila's Rd., just off George Rd., sells maps (R2-5) and makes bookings. (☎/fax 877 0045; weta@wildernessinfo.co.za; www.wildernessinfo.co.za. Open daily 8am-6pm; low season M-F 8am-5pm, Sa 8am-1pm.) There are no banks or ATMs for foreign bank cards in town. In case of **emergency,** call ☎877 0011; for **medical emergencies,** ☎877 0177. The **post office** is at Wilderness Motors on Leila's Rd. (☎877 0541. Open M-F 8am-6pm, Sa 8am-noon.) **Postal code:** 6560.

∏ ◻ **ACCOMMODATIONS AND FOOD.** ▧ **Fairy Knowe Backpackers ❶** is a rustic, 19th-century farmhouse that embodies the Wilderness appeal and perfects the delicate balance between human dwellings and nature. The lawns go untamed, a pig roams free, and the feather mattresses and quilts are impossibly comfortable. It's about a 25min. walk to town (2km). The Outeniqua Choo-Tjoe will stop nearby, if you ask the conductor to stop there before your departure. (☎/fax 877 1285; fairybp@mweb.co.za. Breakfast R25. Reception 8am-9pm. Check-out 10am. 6-bed dorms R60; doubles R160. Camping R40.) If Fairy Knowe is the epitome of rustic charm, then ▧**The Beach House ❶** embodies beach living. Situated meters from the beach, which is accessible via a little walkway, the three doubles and one dorm provide superb accommodations. The lounge looks through big bay windows onto the sea. (☎877 0594; beachhouse@mweb.co.za. Internet R15 per 30min. Breakfast R25. Dinner R25. Laundry. Deposit R20. Reception 8am-9pm. Check-out 10am. Dorms R60; doubles R160.)

There are a few excellent restaurants in Wilderness. **Wilderness Grille ❷,** opposite the tourist office, has a typical pub menu, with most meals from R20-60 and grills for R49-53. Five set-course menus on Su are R45. (☎877 0808. Open daily 8:30am-10pm). **Kingfisher ❷,** 1 George Rd., has a menu mostly limited to seafood. (☎877 0288; k-fisher@mweb.co.za. Line fish R38-48. Fish 'n chips R24. Take-away. Open daily noon-midnight. AmEx/MC/V.)

∏ **OUTDOORS.** No one comes to an area called Wilderness to stay indoors. Worth a quick trip if you have a car, the so-called **Map of Africa** is a large section of land in the Outeniqua Mountains cut into an uncanny resemblance of the African continent by the Kaaiman's River. It is best seen from a viewpoint that can be reached by turning left at the end of George Rd. and following the road uphill until you see a sign marking the turn-off. Those without a car can rent a bike from Eden Adventures (see **Adventures**, below) and cycle the distance from town to the map along a trail which goes through the forest to the river. The local **beach** is great for swimming and surfing year-round, although due to strong riptides, folks shouldn't head into the water if the beach is otherwise vacant. The beach concludes at the **Touw River,** a lagoon that forms a bird-filled estuary amid majestic gorges and trees.

🄷 **HIKING. Wilderness National Park** was established 1987 to protect the stunning wetlands that border the Indian Ocean here. Amazing hikes of varying difficulty allow sightings of the rare Knysna Loerie and other birds. The park's four major trails all start at or near the park's Ebb and Flow reception area. The **Giant Kingfisher,** a 7km hike, follows the eastern bank of the Touw River to a waterfall. The **Pied Kingfisher,** a 10km circular route, passes Fairy Knowe, traces a section of coast, and visits the Wilderness rest camp before following the river back to the base. The **Half-Collared Kingfisher** follows the western bank of the Touw River for about 4km. Look for its trailhead near Ebb and Flow's water purification plant. Finally, the **Brown-Hooded Kingfisher** meanders among the Duiwe River and its tributaries, offering opportunities to play in small waterfalls and among rocks. Maps are available at Ebb and Flow, just off the N2. (☎877 1197; fax 877 0366. Open daily 8am-5pm; in season 8am-7pm. R10, children R5.)

🄷 **ADVENTURES.** The Wilderness lagoon is best explored by **canoe,** which can be rented at the Ebb and Flow office or Eden Adventures (see below). Three-day **canoeing trips** through the rivers of the park include a SATOUR guide, accommodations, drinking water, and cooking utensils, but no food (R150). **Eden Adventures,** close to Fairy Knowe on Freesia Ln. (just off Waterside Rd.), organizes magnificent activities in Wilderness highlighting the local history and environment. (☎877 0179 or 083 628 8547; fax 877 0267; tours@eden.co.za; www.eden.co.za. Kaaimans Canyon tour R220; wilderness canoeing and cycling tour R180; a 45m abseiling drop R220; full-day tour combining canoeing, cycling, abseiling and lunch R365; Kaaimans tour and abseiling R395. Canoe hire R25 per hr., R80 for the day. Bike hire R60 per day. New rock climbing and extreme kloofing tours are also available.) **Cloudbase Paragliding** is a paragliding school offering lessons, licensing, tours, accommodation, and tandem paraglides for the unlicensed. (☎/fax 877 1414; cloudbase-paragliding@mweb.co.za. Tandem R30 per 20min. Day course R500. Open daily 8:30am-6pm.)

NEAR WILDERNESS: VICTORIA BAY ☎044

The surging, swelling surf draws wave riders to this tiny outpost a couple kilometers west of Wilderness. The waves can ascend to peaks of 3m, providing the best breaks this side of J-Bay. **Land's End Guest House ❸,** at the very edge of the water, rents boards. (☎889 0123. R30 per half day, R50 per day. Bodyboards R25/R40. Rooms R250-500.) A beachfront **tourist office** operates the **campsite ❶** atop the cliffs that overlook the beach. (☎/fax 889 0081. Open daily 7:30am-4pm. Sites R119. Mar.-Nov. R59. Electricity available.) Next to the office, the **Victoria Bay Kiosk ❶** serves take-away breakfast for R16-25, sandwiches for R10-20, and pizzas for R12-30. (☎889 0168. Open daily 8am-6pm, depending on the weather.)

KNYSNA ☎044

If the Garden Route is making you feel culture-starved, Knysna (NIGH-zna) can save the day (and night) with a surprising number of art galleries, straw markets, restaurants, and live music venues. Knysna hosts an oyster festival every July, an arts festival in September, and, for the first time this April, a gay pride event called the Pink Loerie Festival. While Knysna has no beach (only a shallow lagoon), there are two stunning beaches not far away (at Noetzie and Buffalo Bay), and the surrounding area is famous for its forests and spectacular rocky heads. Those without a car may find these areas difficult to explore, but a lot can be done by bicycle, and most hostels organize inexpensive tours or provide free transportation. Anyone with a hippie streak will enjoy spending a day (or more) in Knysna proper.

▐ TRANSPORTATION

Trains: Outeniqua Choo-Tjoe (☎382 1361 or 382 7860; fax 382 3465), on Remembrance Ave., at the waterfront. From Main St., walk down Gray St. and turn right onto Waterfront Dr. Steam train to: **George** (2¾hr.); **Goukamma** (45min.); **Sedgefield** (1¼hr.); **Wilderness** (2hr.). Trains depart in summer M-Sa 9:15am and 2:15pm; in winter M, W and F 2:15pm; R60, children 3-15 R40.

Buses: Baz Bus (☎021 439 2323) serves all the backpackers in Knysna. **Intercape** and **Greyhound** conveniently stop in the middle of town at **Knysna Toyota,** on Main St. between Long and Queen St. **Translux** stops at the bus station opposite the waterfront. Make ticket bookings at **Knysna Reservations** (☎ 382 6960; fax 382 1609) for Translux, and at **Harvey Travel** (☎382 6960; fax 382 1609). Daily buses to: **Cape Town** (7hr., R145); **Johannesburg** (15hr., R345); **Port Elizabeth** (3½hr., R110).

Minibus Taxis: To get to the station from Main St., go down the stairs near the Nedbank, which is across the street from Cape to Cairo. Daily minibuses to: **George** (45min., R20); **Plettenberg Bay** (30min., R15); **Port Elizabeth** (3hr., R65). Long trips (i.e. to Cape Town) must be arranged with drivers the day before.

Taxis: Crown Cabs (☎382 1890 or 082 964 2714), **Benwill Shuttle** (☎082 728 5181), and **Knysna Shuttle** (☎082 965 5317).

Car Hire: Tempest, 14 Gray St. (☎382 0354). Also rents bikes for R45 per day, or R10 per hr.

Bike Rental: Available through most hostels at about R35 per day, R25 per half day.

▄✳ ▐ ORIENTATION AND PRACTICAL INFORMATION

Knysna's **Main St.** is about 1km inland from, and roughly parallel to, the waterfront. Most places of interest are down Main St. near the Woodmill Lane shopping complex or along the major cross streets between Main St. and the waterfront. Additional hotspots and craft stores congregate on the waterfront at the **Knysna Quays,** at the bottom of Grey St. near the railroad station. **Thesen's Island** (home of the **Oyster Company**) is at the end of Long St. A cluster of hostels perches above the center of town on and around Queen St.

Tourist Office: Tourism Bureau, 40 Main St. (☎382 5510; fax 3821646; knysna.tourism@pixie.co.za; www.knysna-info.co.za;). Past Grey St. Open M-F 8am-5pm, Sa 8:30am-1pm. During school holidays daily 8am-7pm, winter 8am-6pm. Check out the weekly "Action Ads" newspaper for info on everything happening in the area.

Banks: First National Bank (☎382 3034), corner of Main and Grey St., has ATMs and cashes traveler's checks. Open M-F 9am-3:30pm, Sa 8:30-11:30am.

Bookstore: Choices (☎ 382 1245), at the waterfront end of Woodmill Ln. Open M-F 9am-5pm, Sa 9am-1pm.

Laundromat: (☎382 7719), opposite Woodmill Ln. Shopping Center off Main St. R22 per 5kg wash, dry, fold. Open M-F 7am-7pm, Sa 7am-1:30pm.

Police: 11 Main St. (☎302 6600). Opposite the post office.

Pharmacy: Marine Pharmacy (☎382 5614; fax 382 5903; marinepharmacy@pixie.co.za), in the Jonker Building. on the corner of Grey and Main St., also has a **clinic** for travelers. Open M-F 8am-9pm, Sa 8am-1pm and 5-9pm, Su and holidays 9:30am-1pm and 5-9pm.

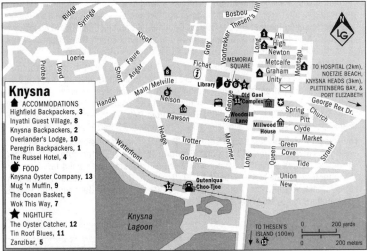

Knysna

♠ ACCOMMODATIONS
Highfield Backpackers, **3**
Inyathi Guest Village, **8**
Knysna Backpackers, **2**
Overlander's Lodge, **10**
Peregrin Backpackers, **1**
The Russel Hotel, **4**

🍴 FOOD
Knysna Oyster Company, **13**
Mug 'n Muffin, **9**
The Ocean Basket, **6**
Wok This Way, **7**

★ NIGHTLIFE
The Oyster Catcher, **12**
Tin Roof Blues, **11**
Zanzibar, **5**

WESTERN CAPE

Hospital: Knysna Private Hospital (☎ 384 1083), on Hunters Dr., about 2km toward Plettenberg Bay. Open 24hr. **Emergency** ☎ 10 177.

Internet Access: Cyber Perk (☎ 382 7547; loraine@cyberperk.co.za; www.cyberperk.co.za), in the Spar Center on Main St. Coffee and snacks available. 6 terminals. R10 per 30min. Open M-F 9am-6pm, Sa 10am-4pm.

Post Office: 6 Main St. (☎ 382 2945). M-Tu and Th-F 8:30am-5pm, W 9am-5pm, Sa 8am-1pm. **Postal code:** 6570.

▐ ACCOMMODATIONS

⧉ Overlander's Lodge, 11 Nelson St. (☎ 382 5920; overlanders@cyberperk.co.za; http://overlanders.co.za;). Fun, lively atmosphere with a log cabin feel bolstered by nightly bonfires and frequent outings to the beach. Forest canoe trip R140 for half day. Bike hire R50 full day, R30 half day. Scooters R150 per day. Internet R12 per 30min. Laundry R22 per 5kg. Key deposit R30. Reception 8:30am-6pm. Check-in 2pm. Check-out 11am. VIP member. Dorms R60 (only pillowcases provided); singles from R120; doubles from R155. ❶

Highfield Backpackers, 2 Graham St. (☎/fax 382 6266; highfield@hotmail.com). Comfortably worn, with roomy upstairs dorms featuring great views. Cool pool and bar area. Coin-operated Internet (R5 per 12min.). Continental breakfast included. Dinners R35. Key deposit R20. Reception 8am-10pm. Check-out 11am. Dorms R60-70; doubles R160-180, depending on season. ❶

Peregrin Backpackers, 16 High St. (☎/fax 382 3747; peregrin@cyberperk.co.za). Big ol' house high above town with spacious premises. Fairly standard rooms are less interesting than the trips offered here. These include shooting trips where guests can fire at targets under the supervision of a professional instructor. Bike hire R60 per day. Beach-buggy hire R180 per day. Internet R15 per 30min. Free continental breakfast. Dinner R30. Key deposit R50. Reception 7am-midnight. Dorms R60; singles R155; doubles from R155. ❶

Knysna Backpackers, 42 Queen St. (☎/fax 382 2554; knybpack@netactive.co.za). A recent makeover of this stately house (a national monument and Knysna's oldest hostel) left it with a sparkly finish, but it still has a lived-in feel to make it homey. Many of the windows offer scenic views of the town and ocean below, and it is ideal for the quieter backpacker. Internet R5 per 30min. Continental breakfast included. Laundry R15 per load. Key deposit R20 (dorms); R50 (doubles). Reception 8am-10pm. Check-in 8am. Check-out 10am. Dorms R70; twins R150; doubles R170. MC. ❶

Inyathi Guest Lodges, 52 Main St. (☎/fax 382 7768; inyathi-sa@mweb.co.za; www.inyathi-sa.com). An excellent upscale (but not exorbitant) alternative to the backpacker scene. Cool double cabins feature futons, stained-glass windows, and African curios. Ideally situated in the heart of Knysna but still surprisingly tranquil. All rooms have TV. Laundry R30 per load. Min. 3 nights from Dec. 15 to Jan 15. Reception daily 8am-8pm. Check-in 10am. Singles R185-245; doubles R235-295. MC/V. ❷

The Russel Hotel, (☎382 1052/58; fax 382 1083; russelhotel@mweb.co.za; www.russelhotel.co.za), corner of Long and Graham St. A new, 3-star hotel with cleanly designed fixtures and TV in every room. Interlinking rooms are a good family option. Laundry R22 per load. Key deposit R100. Reception 7am-11pm, out of season 7am-9pm. Check-in 2pm. Check-out 11am. R199-300 per person, depending on season. B&B option. AmEx/MC/V. ❷

🍴 FOOD

Knysna's hipster vibe extends to its notable network of independent cafes. Though many of these venues close around sunset, numerous pubs fill the cheap food void until late. The annual **Oyster Festival** happens in early July.

▨ Paquita's (☎384 0408; fax 384 0803), on George Rex Dr., The Heads. Stellar views on the water's edge. Pizzas are excellent and cheap (R30-45). The seafood (R40-80) is about as fresh as you can get, and the pasta (R25-35) is sure to please. Open daily 10am-10pm. AmEx/MC/V. ❷

Knysna Oyster Company (☎382 6941; fax 382 6943; knysnaoysterco@mweb.co.za; www.oyster.co.za), on the slightly grubby Thesen's Island. Popular spot to pop down a few salty aphrodisiacs, particularly since the restaurant is attached to an oyster farm that harvests 3.4-3.6 million oysters annually. Serves cultivated and coastal oysters. Taste R2.50-3.50, plate R20-45. Standard oyster farm tours explain how oysters are farmed and offer a tasting (tour R5, 15-20min.). The executive tour includes the standard tour education along with a glass of sparkling wine, a bottle of the house wine, and 6 oysters (tour R50; both tours run every hour on the hour from 10am-5pm daily). Open daily 10am-10pm; winter 10am-5pm. ❶

Wok This Way (☎382 1106), in Memorial Sq. on Main St., between Grey and Long St. Delicious and cheap Chinese food. Eat in or take-away. Typical Chinese dishes, mostly R18-40. Five-course set-menu dinner R45. Five-course set-menu lunch R32. Open M-Tu 5-9:30pm, W-Su 11am-3pm and 5-9:30pm. No reservations taken in season. MC/V. ❷

Mug 'n Muffin (☎ 382 5990), in Mulberry Gardens next to Spar. A simple but enjoyable coffee shop which serves good breakfasts and fantastic health shakes (R12.50). Juices R4.50-12. Breakfast R15-27.50. Overlander's backpackers get a 10% discount. ❶

The Ocean Basket (☎382 1010; fax 382 9988), in Memorial Sq. on Main St. Recommended by locals and savvy tourists for exquisite seafood. Starters R18-21. Entrees begin at R36. Open M-Sa 11:30am-10pm, Su 11:30am-3pm. AmEx/MC/V. ❷

🎵 🎭 ENTERTAINMENT AND NIGHTLIFE

Artists saturate Knysna, showcasing their talents during the **Nederburg Knysna Arts Experience** every year in September and October. The program features food, theater, live music, and a bevy of creators from the world over. (For information call the Festival Office; ☎382 0875.) More regular and less high-brow culture flashes frequently onto the screens of the old-style **Knysna Movie House,** 50 Main St. (☎382 7813; fax 382 7814. R18, R20 after 5:15pm.)

▨ **Tin Roof Blues** (☎382 0864; fax 382 1719; tinroof@cyberperk.co.za), on Main St. between Long St. and Saint George St. Best live music venue on Garden Route. Cavernous loft, with walls decorated with images of blues legends. The music vibe changes every night, with bands playing jazz, blues, rock, or reggae. Check what's on before you head down. Big screen TV shows sports on occasion. Beers R6.50-7. Shooters R6.50-7. No cover unless there's a big name band. Bands go on around 10:30pm F-Sa. Open daily noon-late; out of season 5pm-late.

Zanzibar Lounge (☎382 0386; zanzi@cyberperk.co.za; www.gosouth.co.za/zanzibar), on Main St. opposite Tin Roof Blues. A slightly fancier cigar lounge which makes the ideal place to chill before heading out for a big night at a dancing venue. Live music covers a wide range depending on who's booked (usually F and Sa). DJs spin regularly in summer. Cover only for some acts. Open daily noon-late; low season 5pm-late.

Al's Night Club (☎382 6305), at the waterfront end of Queen St. One room plays classic and indy rock, the other has techno/rave. Folks file in after midnight to bust a move. Cover R10, R10-25 for live bands. Open W-Sa 8pm-4am.

Oyster Catcher (☎/fax 382 9995), on the waterfront. Wash down an oyster with champagne as the sun sets over the Knysna Lagoon. Cocktails R20. Glass of champagne R9. Oysters R36-48 for 6. Usually live music on F and Su. Open daily 10am-midnight, low season 11am-7:30pm.

◉ SIGHTS

Knysna Fine Art, 8 Grey St., is a commercial gallery hosting mostly contemporary South African artists' work, as well as some international pieces. (☎382 5846; fax 382 6530. Wheelchair accessible. Open M-F 9am-5pm, Sa 9am-2pm. Pick-ups in Knysna can be arranged.) The **Millwood House Museum,** on Lower Queen St., is the town's historical museum. (☎382 5066. Open M-F 9:30am-4:30pm, Sa 9:30am-12:30pm. Tours on request. Free.) The **Old Gaol Complex,** at Queen and Main St., has a number of mini-museums: the **Angling Museum,** which delights seafaring, speargun toting gangstas; the **Maritime Museum,** featuring paintings and boat models; and the **Knysna Art Gallery,** showcasing landscapes by local artists. (☎382 5066; fax 382 1480. All museums in the Gaol Complex open M-F 9:30am-4:30pm, Sa 9:30am-1pm. Wheelchair accessible. Free.)

BREWERY. Every weekday, visitors can tour **Mitchell's Knysna Brewery** at 10:30am to see the entire brewing process and taste four local brands. All visitors take home a souvenir 90ml tasting glass and can buy natural brews. *(Just off Vigilance Dr. and accessible from George Rex Dr. ☎382 4685; fax 382 5818. Open M-F 8am-1pm and 2-5pm, Sa 9am-1pm. 15-20min. tours and tasting R15; tasting only R10. Call before heading over.)*

◮ ▦ OUTDOORS AND ADVENTURES

THE HEADS. The Knynsa area brims with fantastic coastal scenery, but nowhere rivals the **Knysna Heads,** two gigantic rock formations standing sentinel over the ocean inlet leading to Knysna. About 1km from downtown at the end of George Rex Dr., The Heads are best reached by car or bike. If you have a car, drive up The Heads, past millionaires' homes, to get to the **Bar View Lookout.** A wooden boardwalk lets visitors peer down at the storming surf and beach.

NOETZIE BEACH. This stretch of sand provides a less disturbing seaside alternative to The Heads; a series of residential stone castles overlooks the swimmable lagoon. This beach remains uncrowded and peaceful, although 4WD tracks marring the sand serve as an unhappy reminder that you're not alone. *(To get there, take the N2 toward Plettenberg Bay and turn right at the sign, following the dirt road for 5km.)*

SCUBA DIVING. The Heads offer some terrific diving opportunities, including the wreck dive in the channel. **Waterfront Divers,** at The Heads, runs diving tours (R60) and rents gear. *(☎ 384 0831. Open daily 8am-5pm. Gear R50 per 2hr.)*

ABSEILING. SEAL Adventures offers fabulous half-day abseiling trips amid stunning scenery. The journey starts with a canoe trip across the lagoon to the Featherbed Nature Reserve. There are three abseils to choose from: Beachcomber Caves (30m), Needlepoints (55m), or Thy Kingdom Come, the world's highest commercial abseil site (120m). No experience necessary. Bookings can be arranged through any backpackers, or by calling SEAL directly. *(☎ 381 0068; info@sealadventures.co.za; www.sealadventures.co.za. Trips daily 8:30am and 1:30pm, plus occasional night abseils. Combination quad bike and abseil R350. Booking essential.)* **Waterfront Divers** (see above) runs a 90m abseil (R180) at Kranhoek.

OTHER ADVENTURES. Waterfront Divers (see above) can arrange **river creeking** and **tubing** (R250), **canoeing** and **kayaking** (R150), **paintballing** (R40 per person and R0.50 per ball), **sunset cruises** including oysters and champagne (R150-200), **township tours** (R150), and **surfing** and **windsurfing** (R150). Book directly or through your hostel.

NEAR KNYSNA: BUFFALO BAY　　　　　　　　　　☎ 044

Only 25km from Knysna, the small seaside community of Buffalo Bay (Buffelsbaai) can hardly be called a town, but easily lives up to the title of "holiday retreat." **Wildside Backpackers ❶** has a near-perfect location right on the beach. Not surprisingly, it tends to be somewhat sandy inside, but a variety of beachy amenities make this the perfect beach bum vacation spot. *(☎ 383 0610. Dorms R50; doubles R130. R15 discount every 3rd night.)* Right next to the hostel, the **Goukamma Nature and Marine Reserve** presents a different sort of wild side. The Nature Reserve spans 2500ha, with the Marine Reserve stretching 14km along the coastline and 1.8km out to sea. Goukamma's coastal dune forest and *fynbos* vegetation support a variety of life, but it's Goukamma's bird life that causes the biggest stir. Among the 220 species of bird that have been recorded here are the rare African black oystercatcher and the endangered African penguin. A bushcamp, *rondavel,* and river lodge within the park are available for overnight accommodation but must be booked well in advance. *(☎ 383 0042. Open daily 8am-6pm. Bushcamp from R65 per person; rondavels from R55 per person; river lodge from R55 per person.)* To get to Buffalo Bay, take the Buffelsbaai exit off the N2, about 20km west of Knysna, or take the shuttle from Highfield Backpackers in Knysna.

PLETTENBERG BAY　　　　　　　　　　☎ 044

Plettenberg Bay basks in the glow of its radiant beaches, beautiful oceans, and hopping marine life. While the town has built a reputation as a playground for the wealthy, its residents also make it one of the most hospitable and welcoming places for budget travelers in South Africa. A 7km stretch of sandy heaven greets the deluge of visitors who come to capitalize on the city's goodwill. December sees the climax of this influx, when torrents of tourists pour in for the (in)famous New Year's Eve Party, considered by many to be the wildest in South Africa.

▐▀ TRANSPORTATION

Buses: Baz Bus (☎021 439 2323) services the town's hostels. **Translux** (☎382 1471), **Intercape,** and **Greyhound** stop at Shell Ultra City (☎533 0141; open daily 8am-8pm), at the corner of Marine Dr. and the N2. All go daily to: **Cape Town** (8hr., R145-185); **Durban** (18hr., R275-290); **George** (85min., R80-95); **Knysna** (30min., R30-80); **Port Elizabeth** (3hr., R80-95). Intercape and Translux run daily to **Pretoria** (19hr., R300) via **Johannesburg** (18hr., R300). Bookings for Intercape can be made at Tony's Info Center (☎533 5663; fax 533 6013), and bookings for Greyhound and Translux can be made at Harvey World Travel (☎533 0484).

Minibus Taxis: The rank is 2 blocks up Kloof St. from Main St. Minibuses to: **George** (1½hr., frequent, R32); **Knysna** (30min., frequent, R20); **Port Elizabeth** (2hr., twice daily, R95). Transfer in George or Port Elizabeth for more far-flung destinations.

Taxis: Big Foot Express (☎533 7777).

◼◼ ◼ ORIENTATION AND PRACTICAL INFORMATION

Downtown Plett is very small, its streets slanting down to the ocean. Most amenities can be found on **Main St.**, which runs parallel to the water, or along the cross streets above it.

Tourist Office: Plettenberg Tourist Office (☎533 4065; fax 5334066; info@plettenberg-bay.co.za; www.plettenbergbay.co.za), on Kloof St., 1 block uphill from Main St. 24hr. accommodations listings are posted outside. Open M-F 8:30am-5pm, Sa 9am-1pm; Dec.-Jan. M-F 8:30am-5pm, Sa-Su 9am-1pm.

Banks: Standard Bank (☎533 2010; fax 533 0388), 17 Main St. Open M-F 8:30am-3:30pm, Sa 8:30am-11am.

Bookstore: Village Bookshop (☎533 1450), on Main St. in Yellowwoods Ctr. between Crescent St. and Kloof St. Open M-F 8am-6pm, Sa 8am-1pm, Su 9am-1pm.

Library: (☎533 2053), on Anchor St. Open M-F 9:30am-5:15pm, Sa 9:30am-noon.

Laundry: Central Laundromat (☎/fax 533 4403). Wash, dry, fold R8 per kg; min. R25. Wash only R6 per kg; min. R20. Open M-F 8am-5pm.

Emergency: ☎10 111.

Police: 1 Main St. (☎533 2100). Uphill from the post office.

Pharmacy: Lookout Pharmacy, Lookout Center Main St. (☎/fax 533 1970). **Emergency:** ☎533 6222. Open daily 8am-6pm; Dec.-Jan. 8am-8pm.

Hospital: (☎533 0212; fax 533 0888; medsac@mweb.co.za). Follow Strand Street inland until it becomes Marine Drive, approximately 1kilometer out of town on the right. Open 24hr.

Internet Access: The Computer Shop and Internet Cafe (☎533 6007; tcs_plett@mweb.co.za), the Square, Main St. 9 terminals. Queues in season; quieter in evenings. R0.50 per min., minimum R5. Open M-F 8am-6pm, Sa 9am-2pm; Dec.-Jan. daily 9am-9pm. **Simunye Community Center** (☎533 2050), in Kwanokuthula township, has 10 terminals and charges a mere R10 per hour.

Post Office: (☎533 1260). Facing the water, follow Main St. uphill to the right past stores; the post office is on the left. Fax and *Poste Restante.* Open M-F 8am-5pm, Sa 8am-noon.

Postal code: 6600.

FROM THE ROAD

THE GOOD WITH THE BAD

If you're ever in Plett in December, you may have heard about the New Year's Eve party on Central. Some say it's the best in South Africa...all I know is that it's better than Cape T██

I was in Plett last New Year's, hoping that that night (unlike every other New Year's I had experienced) would be an unbelievable time. By 8pm, the beach was packed, and by 9pm, people were falling in love on the beach thanks to a man named Charles Glass and his product Castle Lager. A stage provided the entertainment, but not as many people were as interested in the music as they were in the increasingly good-looking people around them. Somehow I managed to find myself with a group of young black men around their fire. All of a sudden, one of them stood up and began singing "Nkosi Sikelele I'Afrika" (South Africa's national anthem). The song attracted attention from the groups of ████ white teenagers around us ████ azingly some began singing along. In a rush of excitement we rose to our feet and went into a huddle, white South Africans alongside black alongside coloured, singing a song that had once symbolized the antiapartheid movement but now symbolized the ██ unity of a nation that was once horribly divided. When the song ended we all became a bit embarrassed at our outburst of emotion and patriotism, and I ended up slinking sheepishly away to find my group of friends. While it lasted, though, it was a beautiful moment, one that made me hopeful for my country's future.

(Continued on next page)

⌐ ACCOMMODATIONS AND CAMPING

▨ **Stanley Island** (☎/fax 535 9442; cell 083 650 6346; bhbecke@global.co.za; backpacker_island@hotmail.com), 7km east along the N2. Just after the Keurbooms River Bridge, turn left onto the unmarked dirt road, bearing left again under the bridge; park on the mainland and honk repeatedly for the ferry. The carless can try calling from town; the owners are unlikely to make a special trip, but they're happy to pick travelers up on errand runs. While its location in the middle of the river isolates it from the rest of Plett, it is ideal as a quiet retreat, or, for those with cars, as a base from which to visit Plett and the Tsitsikamma. Easy access to watersports. Glider flights R250 per 30min. Internet R15 per 30min. Attached restaurant serves meals: lunch R25-30, breakfast R25, dinner R45-55. Laundry R20 per load. Reception 8am-10pm. Check-in 2pm; check-out 10am (both flexible). Dorms R60; doubles R190; upmarket rooms R250-500. AmEx/MC/V. ❶

▨ **Deios Guest House and Nothando Backpackers,** 3 and 5 Wilder St. (☎/fax 533 0220; www.deios.co.za). "Nothando," meaning "love" in Xhosa, permeates this cozily furnished, central lodging. This is the type of establishment that gives you that warm homely feeling without ever losing its backpacker vibe. Light-hearted bar is adorned with classic Gary Larson cartoons. Breakfast R25-30. Lunch R15-20. Dinner R40-45. Reception 8am-8pm. Check-in 11am. Check-out 10am (flexible). Nothando: Dorms R60; doubles R170-180. Guest House, including breakfast, R160 per person; Sept. to mid-Jan. R250 per person. ❶

Weldon Kaya (☎533 2437; fax 533 4364; info@weldonkaya.com; www.weldonkaya.com), 3.5km west of Plett, at the junction of the N2 and Piesang Valley Rd. A brilliant choice for that upmarket splurge you've been saving for. The unforgettable "Afro Village" is brilliantly constructed of recycled materials—old car windshields serve as windows in luxurious *rondavels*, while a former reservoir is now a pool. Wheelchair accessible. Laundry R20 per 6kg. 3 night min. in Dec.-Jan. Reception 8:30am-5pm. Check-in 2pm. Check-out 11am. R200 per person. Oct. 1-Apr. 30. R325 per person. ❸

Bosavern, 38 Cutty Sark Ave. (☎ 533 1312; fax 533 0758; info@bosavern.co.za, www.bosavern.co.za). A chic establishment with clean lines, big beds, and all the modern conveniences. Features a spectacular view of the Bay from the comfort of the pool. Some interesting suites good for families but prior arrangement must be made for kids under 16. R 89-100 for 3-course dinner. Internet R40 per 30min. Laundry R50 per load. Reception 8am-8pm. R270 per person sharing B&B; suites R350/R575 per person sharing B&B. MC/V. ❸

✦ FOOD

❧ **Blue Chili** (☎533 5104). Upstairs in the One Plett complex on Marine Drive. Vaguely trippy landscapes illuminated by the trademark blue chili create a psychedelic atmosphere. During daylight, the bay provides a glittering backdrop to the outdoor seating. Delicious, spicy Tex-Mex cuisine of burritos (R25-40), fiesta pans (R50-260), and steaks and grills (R30-65). 10% discount for *Let's Go* readers if you say, "Que pasa, amigo?" Open M-F 11am-11pm, Sa-Su 6pm-11pm. ❷

Weldon Kaya Restaurant (☎533 2437; fax 533 4364; info@weldonkaya.com; www.weldonkaya.com), in the lodge (see **Accommodations**, p. 168). Middle Eastern and African foods, served up on recycled LP records. Much like the lodge, the decor is eccentric and eclectic, with the awesome beer-bottle chandelier a favorite. Traditional dancing on Sa in season. Wheelchair accessible. In-season, African *meze* for R100 per kg. Entrees R39-52. Open daily 8:30am-1am. AmEx/MC/V. ❷

The Lookout Deck (☎533 1379). Turn down Hill St. from Main St. and follow signs to the tree-hidden entrance by Lookout Beach. Downstairs restaurant is quite expensive, but the typical seafood fare served upstairs on deck is reasonably priced. The great views from the outside deck are the real attraction. Breakfasts R17.50-42. Seafood R29.50-89.90. No reservations. Major hangout for youngsters in Dec.-Jan. Take-away. Wheelchair accessible. Open daily 9:30am-8:30pm. AmEx/MC/V. ❷

✦ NIGHTLIFE

During the winter months, the local nightlife (or lack thereof) can leave clubhoppers a bit dispirited. Cheer up by heading for **Flashbacks Lounge,** at the corner of Main St. and Crescent St. This local bar with pool tables, a small dance space, and a popular patio for chilling has the most action around. Flashbacks is particularly crowded on Wednesday, Friday and Saturday. (☎533 4714; www.flashbacks.co.za. Live music in Dec.-Jan. During the year DJ mostly plays commercial CDs. Occasional cover with live bands. Open M-Sa noon-2am, Dec.-Jan. open M-Sa noon-2am, Su 6pm-2am. Wheelchair accessible. Beers R7. Shooters R7.)

✦ SIGHTS

Plettenberg Bay was originally christened "Bahia Formosa" (beautiful bay) by early Portuguese explorers, and it's easy to see where they got the

(Continued from previous page)

As the night wore on and the initial happy drunkenness gave way to more belligerent emotions, attention was drawn to the group of poor young colored men and boys sitting along the fence near the edge of the beach watching the activities of the mostly white crowd. It is a well known fact that some of the desperately poor people from Plett's surrounding townships come down to the beach on New Year's Eve to try to pick up belongings that have been left behind or that people are not paying attention to. Sadly, a group of 18-year-old boys, determined to bolster their macho images, decided to take advantage of these poorer people. The boys left a pair of their shoes on the sand about 5 yards from them and then watched as a small man came over and picked them up. As soon as this happened they pounced and began punching and kicking the man. My friend and I intervened to stop the beating, but not before the man had received some harsh blows. The boys, far from showing remorse, refused to accept the futility or cruelty of their actions and maintained—despite our remonstrations—that the man deserved what he got.

This is the paradox of South Africa. At one moment you may think it is a symbol of hope for the rest of humanity, and at the next it is nothing more than a self-destructing pool of intolerance. In time the bigotry will fade, but you can never forget that this is not only a country of incredible beauty, but also of intricate social and political issues that are never far from the surface.

—*Yusuf Randera-Rees*

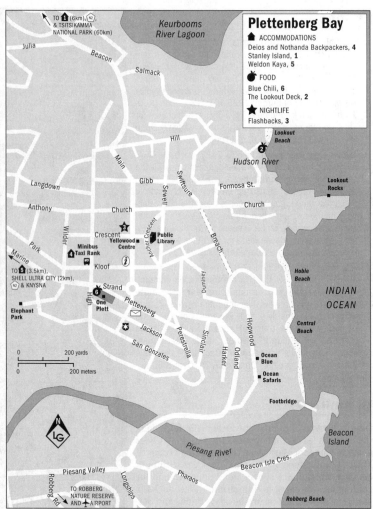

Plettenberg Bay

🏠 ACCOMMODATIONS
Deios and Nothanda Backpackers, **4**
Stanley Island, **1**
Weldon Kaya, **5**

🍎 FOOD
Blue Chili, **6**
The Lookout Deck, **2**

★ NIGHTLIFE
Flashbacks, **3**

name. The possibilities for capitalizing on Plett's gorgeous scenery seem limitless. The bay teems with sea creatures, including dolphins, seals, whales, and occasionally sharks. The diversity and concentration of marine species has attracted its share of scientific attention in recent years, leading to the establishment of the **MTN Center for Dolphin Studies,** in the same building as Ocean Safaris (see below), a non-profit marine mammal research institute whose goal is to "observe and conserve." **Ocean Blue,** in Milkwood Center on Hopwood St., has a permit to go within 50m of Southern Right Whales. (☎/fax 533 5083; cell 083 701 3583; info@oceanadventures.co.za; www.oceanadventures.co.za. R250 per person, R150 12 and under. *Let's Go* discount of R30. Open daily 7:30-5pm, summer 6am-8pm.) **Dolphin Safaris,** next door to Ocean Blue on Hopwood St., houses the Center for Dolphin Studies and has the same permit as Ocean Blue. (☎/fax 533 4963; cell 082

784 5729; info@oceansafaris.co.za; www.oceansafaris.co.za. "Close Encounter" tour R275, classic R250.) The nearby **Robberg Nature and Marine Reserve** features spectacular views of the Indian Ocean and its marine residents. Three circular trails of various length and intensity delve into the peninsula reserve, passing caves and a lighthouse, while a challenging 7km one-way hike around the peninsula begins at the reserve entrance. The Reserve is reachable by walking 5km down the beach from town; most hostels can also arrange rides. By car, head downhill on Strand St., turn right onto Piesang River Rd. at the small roundabout after the bridge, then turn left on Robberg Rd. and follow the signs. (Manager ☎ 533 2125; gate ☎ 533 3424. Open daily Dec.-Jan. 7am-8pm; rest of year daily 7am-5:30pm. R15, kids 6-18 R8.) About 9 kilometers west of Plett on the N2, the **Knysna Elephant Park** serves as a playground for seven young and adorable African elephants. (☎ 532 7732. Open daily 8:30am-4pm in winter; 8:30am-5pm in summer. R60, ages 3-12 R30. Sunset Safari R500/R250.)

Township tours explore both the depressing realities of apartheid, and the amazing resilience and optimism of its countless victims. **Ocean Blue** (see above) coordinates a trip to Qolweni Township, highlighted by events of gumbooting, dancing and singing. (Th evenings; 1hr.; R60, under 12 R30. Performances in the township theatre R70/R35.)

✦ ADVENTURES

By land, by sea, or even by air, Plett's variety of adventures can suit just about anyone's fancy. Mountain bikers can get their fix in the Hakerville Forest on the **Hakerville Mountain** trail (☎ 532 7777; half-day R61 without bike, R6 with bike). **The Bike Shop** rents bikes. (☎ 533 1111. Open M-F 8am-5pm, Sa 8am-1pm. R60 per half-day, R90 per day.) **Dolphin Adventures** offers half-day **sea kayaking** trips up to Robberg Reserve. (☎ 384 1536; martin@dolphinkayak.com; www.dolphinkayak.com. R170.) **Real Cape Adventures** (☎ 082 556 2520 or 082 920 3696; www.seakayak.co.za) offers a range of tours for R180 per day. **Valley Riding Center** offers horseback rides along trails and beaches. (☎ 082 767 7427; 2-hour tours R200.)

Abseil Africa runs a remarkable full-day abseiling expedition called "The Lost World." The trip navigates through a gorge and requires three abseils, two of which descend down waterfalls—one of which is a dizzying 90m high. A beautiful, shaded hike returns you to the top. The trip is open to beginners, but is best attempted only by veterans or novices undaunted by the prospect of eating algae. A 45m abseil in the Robberg Reserve is also offered. Sturdy walking shoes are required. (☎ 533 6188 or 082 850 3168. R150 for 3 abseils; "Lost World" trips R250 including lunch; 2 hours "Wild Side" trips R150. Book at least 1 day in advance.) **Glider flights** are also available and worth every minute. (☎ 072 170 7533; R250 per 30min. Bookings essential).

TSITSIKAMMA NATIONAL PARK ☎ 042

Though technically in the Eastern Cape, Tsitsikamma National Park proudly claims the title "the garden of the Garden Route," protecting an 80km stretch of rocky coastline backed by the looming Tsitsikamma Mountains. Including everything from sleepy seaside towns to untamed wilderness, Tsitsikamma is one of the last fragments of the pre-industrial Indian Ocean coast, when forests descended uninterrupted to the sea and the cape clawless otter and minute blue duiker existed in abundance. Although a network of well-kept trails have vaulted the park to international fame as one of the best hiking spots anywhere, even non-hikers can sample Tsitsikamma's beauty.

AT A GLANCE

AREA: 500 sq. km.

CLIMATE: Temperate, with wet, chilly winters (May-Jul.) and warm, drier summers (Nov.-Mar.)

HIGHLIGHTS: The 5-day Otter Trail, Monkeyland, and Bloukrans bungee jump.

GATEWAYS: Plettenberg Bay (p. 166), Storms River, Nature's Valley.

FEES & RESERVATIONS: Day permits R18, ages 2-16 R10. For Otter Trail bookings (required many months in advance), call ☎ 021 422 2810.

◆ ⚡ 2 ORIENTATION AND PRACTICAL INFORMATION

The central wilderness of gorgeous Tsitsikamma is flanked on the east and west by **Storms River** and **Nature's Valley,** respectively. Both villages are within the boundaries of the park and make convenient bases for daytrips elsewhere within its bounds. A quiet collection of summer holiday homes, **Nature's Valley** has a very nice beach and a few hiking trails worth exploring—the only downside is that almost no services can easily be found here. The village proper (at the end of the long, winding R102) consists of four streets running roughly parallel to the shore. Closest to the water is St. Michael's St. Moving inland, the streets are St. Andrew's St., St. George's St., and Forest St. **Storms River,** near the eastern edge of the park, is a better option for running errands or participating in organized activities. The entire "town," as it is, consists of one block along the main street (the N2). **Greyhound** runs daily from the Petrolport in Storms River to: Cape Town (10hr., daily, R165); Port Elizabeth (3hr, daily, R70); Durban (17hr., daily, R265). Baz Bus stops daily in Storms River before heading to Cape Town (12hr., 10:15am) and Port Elizabeth (3hr., 7pm). **Baz Bus** is also the only carrier to serve Nature's Valley, running daily to Cape Town (11hr., 11:15am) and Port Elizabeth (4hr., 6:15pm). For **tourist information**, head to **Storms River Adventures** (☎ 280 3561; fax 280 3563. Open daily 9am-5pm.) A conveniently located **ATM** is at the **Petrolport** in Storms River, just over the bridge and around the corner.

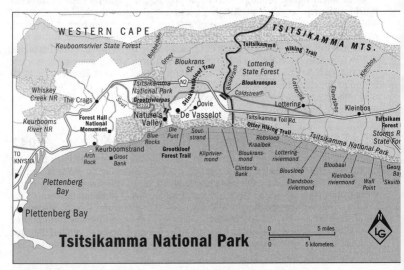

Tsitsikamma National Park

ACCOMMODATIONS AND CAMPING

NATURE'S VALLEY

Hiker's Haven, 411 St. Patrick's Rd. (☎ 531 6805; fax 531 6812; pat-bond@mweb.co.za). On the left end of St. George's St., facing the water. Ideal for hikers recovering from long treks. Dorm beds in one huge loft. Free sailboats and windsurfing boards. DSTV and pool. Breakfast R30. Laundry R10 per wash, R10 per dry. Reception 7:30am-10pm. Dorms R60; doubles R95; en suite R130 per person. MC/V. ❶

Tsitsikamma Village Inn (☎ 281 1711; fax 281 1669; info@village-inn.co.za; www.village-inn.co.za), drive off the N2 into Storms River Village and take a left at the first stop street. The inn is on the right. A large and elegant inn, with sprawling grounds and breathtaking views of the surrounding mountains. Rooms are big and come with TV, fan, phone etc. Great pool area for a bit of summer sun. Reception 24hr. Check-in and check-out 10am. B&B R380 per person. AmEx/MC/V. ❹

STORMS RIVER

Storms River Rainbow Lodge (☎/fax 281 1530; rainbowl@lantic.net), 65km outside Plettenberg Bay. Take the turn-off to Storm's River Village from the N2. Turn right at the first stop street, and the lodge will be on your left after about 800m. A fairly rudimentary establishment which offers standard and unspectacular budget accommodations. Minimum 3-day stay in season. Breakfast R25. Laundry R15 per load. Kids under 18 must be with parents. Reception 7am-11pm. Check-in 1pm. Check-out 10am. Dorms R65; family room R110 per person (en suite); self-catering chalets R125 per person. Camping R40. ❶

Tube 'n Axe (☎ 281 1757; tubenaze@breathe.com), on Darnell St. One of the most chill backpackers you'll ever find...and that's definitely saying something. The setting is idyllic, which masks the plethora of hair-raising activities offered here and at the nearby Storms River Adventures (see **Sights and Adventures,** below). Horse riding (2-2½hr., R90) and bike rental (R150 per hr., R250 per 2hr.). 15m tree abseil in garden. Breakfast R15-20. Dinner R30-35. Dorms R60; doubles R150. Camping R40. ❶

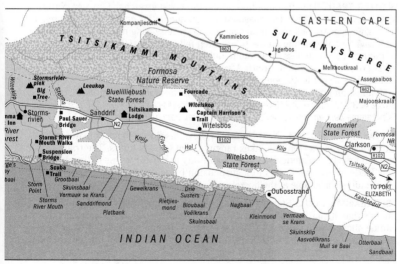

WESTERN CAPE

FOOD

NATURE'S VALLEY

Nature's Valley Restaurant, Pub, and Trading Store (☎531 6835; www.cyberperk.co.za/naturesvalley; beefy@cyberperk.co.za), from Port Elizabeth, take the Nature's Valley R102 turnoff just after the N2 tollgate. From Plett Bay, take the R102 P.E., Humansdorp turnoff just after passing the Crags. Serves hamburgers (R20-30), sandwiches (R17-20), and seafood and steak entrees (R30-40). May give special prices to backpackers who ask for them. Small stock of groceries for trips into the park. Shop open daily 8:30am-5pm; restaurant 10am-8:45pm. AmEx/MC/V. ❶

De Oude Martha, in Tsitsikamma Village Inn (see **Accommodations** p. 173). A pleasantly decorated Cape-style restaurant serving typical South African fare. A la carte buffet most nights (R90). Main Courses R30-100. Open 7:30am-11pm. AmEx/MC/V. ❸

STORMS RIVER

Rafter's Rest at Armagh Country Guesthouse (☎281 1512; fax 281 1510; armagh@mweb.co.za; www.the armagh.com). A special, eccentric setting, hidden amongst the cool foliage of a lush garden, makes you feel both content and hungry. Buffet R75-105. Light lunches R15-35. Soups, breads and fish courses also available. Open daily noon-2pm, 7-9pm. MC/V. ❸

◈ HIKING

Tsitsikamma's world-class hiking opportunities are no longer the well-kept secret that they used to be. The government's eco-friendly policy of limiting the daily number of hikers means that the wilderness here is pristine and that would-be trekkers must make plans long in advance. More spontaneous types can still enjoy the wilderness, however: day hikes abound in the area, and a lucky few may even be able to snag a last-minute spot on one of the famous trails.

◈ **OTTER TRAIL.** This five-day hike along the coast stretches between Nature's Valley and Storms River. The coastal trail is an undulating course that takes hikers through exquisite rock formations, around deep refreshing tidal pools, and past a waterfall that, depending on the tides, often falls right into the sea. Add glimpses of the rare cape clawless otter and minute blue duiker, and you've got one of the most spectacular trails in South Africa—and one of the most in-demand, with waiting lists a year long. Don't give up hope, however: lucky hikers may be able to grab a last-minute cancellation. *(To book, contact the National Parks Office in Pretoria.* ☎ *012 428 9111; fax 012 343 0905); reservations@parks-sa.co.za. Open M-F 7:30am-4pm. Tsitsikamma park emergency* ☎ *281 1607. Otter trail permits R400 per person.)*

DE VASSELOT SECTION. Near Nature's Valley, this side of the park features a network of interconnected day hikes ranging from two-six hours. The trails give a good (if brief) introduction to the park and vary in difficulty. One of the most popular leads up wooden stairs to a suspension bridge and a lookout point. More information is available at the hostels in Nature's Valley.

TSITSIKAMMA TRAIL. Starting in Nature's Valley, this five-day trek may be less famous than its larger sibling, the Otter Trail, but its obscurity also means that it can be hiked without a year's advance planning. Running parallel to Otter Trail a few kilometers inland, the trail explores the park's forests and mountains and rivals Otter in natural beauty. The first 3km of the trail make a spectacular day

hike: walkers climb from one rock pool to the next before reaching the culmina-
tion, a tall waterfall. Much of the trail involves scrambling over slippery rocks.

👁 🗺 SIGHTS AND ADVENTURES

🐒 **MONKEYLAND.** Though its name suggests a tacky theme park or fenced-in zoo,
Monkeyland is the first and only free-roaming primate sanctuary in the world. This
nature reserve protects thirteen species of monkey rescued from laboratories and
private owners. The monkeys meander freely through the enclosed forest. Very
informative one-hour guided walking tours are led by knowledgeable rangers and
leave visitors with a wealth of information about both the monkeys and the vegetation in which they live. *(Off the N2, just west of the Nature's Valley turn-off. ☎ 044 534
8906; fax 534 8907; monkeys@global.co.za; www.monkeyland.co.za. R66, children R33.
Open daily 8am-5pm; tours leave every half hour.)*

🐒 **STORMS RIVER ADVENTURES.** SRA runs fantastic adventure tours including
the Tsitsikamma Canopy Tour (3hr., R395); a guided car tour through the Storms
River Pass (2½hr., R55-65); blackwater tubing (5½hr., R295); a combination abseil,
tubing, mountain biking and hike (8hr., R495); abseiling (R120); mountain biking
(4hr., R175); Eco Wilderness Boat Cruises (R35, kids 2-16 R20); Tsitsikamma
Marine Tour (2½hr., R125, lunch R35) and scuba diving courses. *(Heading into Storms
River Village, take the second road to the left. The adventure company is on the right. 042 281
1836; fax 042 281 1609; adventure@gardenroute.co.za; www.stormsriver.com.)*

BLOUKRANS BUNGEE JUMP. The big draw in Bloukrans is sheer terror. **Face
Adrenalin's** 216m bungee jump off of the Bloukrans River Bridge on the N2 is
the biggest jump in the world, dwarfing the 110m jump over the Zambezi River
at Victoria Falls, Zimbabwe (see p. 586). The first plunge has you in free-fall for
five unbelievable seconds, followed by three seconds of stretching, before you
reverse directions and re-live the experience in several rebound bounces. Face
Adrenalin doesn't offer refunds for people who get to the edge and turn back,
but with the company's gleaming safety record and highly professional style,
fewer than 1% (of more than 14,000 jumpers in over 11 years) have chickened
out. The timid can check out the action from an observation point. There's no
public transport to the jump site, but most of the hotels in Plett and Nature's
Valley will help you find a lift. *(☎ 281 1458/0832313528; extremes@iafrica.com;
www.faceadrenalin.com. Office open 9am-5pm. 18+, 16+ with parental consent. Min.
weight 45kg. 1st jump R500; 2nd jump on the same day R300. Bridge walk R50, winch
ride R100. Jump videos R60.)*

THE WEST COAST

Few wayfarers venture north of Cape Town to explore the western coast, yet the
region holds hidden treasures for those willing to make the trek to see the flora,
fauna, and aqua. Densely populated with exotic species of *fynbos* (Afrikaans for
"fine bush," comprised mainly of proteas—the national flower—and heath) and a
whole host of animal species rarely seen in the rest of South Africa, the coast is
pristinely beautiful, especially in the springtime when wildflowers add a deep
blush to its complexion. Salty fishing villages produce seafood unrivaled in their
low prices, and at sunset many of the locals hold old-fashioned fish-*braais*. The
allure of the Western Cape, however, does not lie in its towns, unless one is deeply
interested in seeing Afrikaner culture face-to-face (including some of its more
insular attitudes). The real reason to go is for the area's natural wonders: flowers,
sea cliffs, rock art, animals, and sandstone formations. As archaeologists have dis-

covered, the ground here is rich with thousands of prehistoric fossils, including the distinguished "Eve's Footprint" (see **Footprints,** p. 177). The **West Coast National Park,** rubbing shoulders with the indigo-blue **Langebaan Lagoon,** is itself a compelling reason to visit. To do anything around here, it is essential to hire a car. The **West Coast Tourism Office** (☎ 022 433 2380; fax 433 2172) is in Moorreesburg.

LANGEBAAN   ☎022

A sprawl of holiday homes beside a turquoise lagoon, Langebaan is a two-season tourist destination. During the spring flower season, bird-watchers and nature lovers use Langebaan as a base to explore the **West Coast National Park.** As the weather ripens into summer, kitesurfers and windsurfers follow the tradewinds to the **Langebaan lagoon,** which offers world-class conditions for watersports.

■✦🛈 ORIENTATION AND PRACTICAL INFORMATION. By car, take the R27 north from Cape Town 100km and turn left at the highway sign; the center of town is 11km from this intersection. **Oostewal St.,** perpendicular to **Bree St.,** is the main road through town. Most businesses are on or around these roads. The lagoon is at the end of Bree St. Langebaan's **tourist office** is next to the National Park office at the end of Hoof St., just off Bree St. (☎ 772 1515; fax 722 1531; www.langebaan-info.com. Open M-F 9:30am-4:30pm, Sa 9:30am-noon.) The local **library** is at the corner of Bree St. and Oostewal St. (☎ 772 2115. Open M-Sa 9am-5pm.) **Langebaan Launderette** (☎ 772 1771; open M-F 8am-5pm, Sa 8:30am-noon) is on Oostewal St., opposite the **police station** (☎ 772 2111). The **ambulance service** (☎ 10 177) and medical facilities are on Oostewal St. just before Bree St. coming into town (☎ 772 2470; emergency after hours ☎ 083 286 1569; open M-F 8:30am-6pm, Sa 8:30am-1pm, Su 11am-noon). **Internet** is available at **Charly's,** in the Marra shopping center at the corner of Suffren St. and Bree St. (☎ 772 1208. R10 for 30min. Open daily 8:30am-late.) The **post office** with *Poste Restante* is on Bree St. (☎ 772 2710. Open M-F 8:30am-1pm and 2-4:30pm.) **Postal code:** 7357.

🛏 ACCOMMODATIONS AND CAMPING. The accommodations in Langebaan are mid-range, catering to South African holiday-makers. It is advisable to book ahead during holiday season. Low-season travelers can benefit from discounted rates at the accommodations that remain open. There are camping sites at **The Old Caravan Park** (☎ 772 2115) and on Suffrens St. off Bree St. The tourist office has a list of guest houses in the area. **Windstone Equestrian Center & Backpackers ❶** is 10km north of the Langebaan exit on the R27. Take a right onto the R45 to Hopefield, and then a right after 1km to Windstone Kennels. A car is needed to reach this out-of-the-way hostel, but it's worth the extra petrol. Peacocks roam, horses frolic, and tourists swim in a heated pool. Proprietors are friendly and can arrange horse rides. 4-bed dorms, and 1 family room with private bath around a central kitchen. (☎ 766 1645; fax 766 1038; winder@mweb.co.za; www.windstone.co.za. Dorms R60; family rooms R160. Camping R35. Group discounts available.) **Sea Winds ❶** is on the corner of Oostewal St. and the road to the country club, north of the center of town. Sloped cathedral ceilings, a modern living/dining room with hearth, and a covered front porch give this B&B a country-home feel, as does the 10min. walk to the lagoon. (☎/fax 772 1612. Doubles R90 per person.) **Dealmore Properties ❸,** on Bree St., is a real estate agency that can help you find accommodations such as flats (R300+ per night) or houses on the beach (R500+ per night). Book ahead, especially if you need bedding. (☎ 772 2291; cell 082 574 6993; fax 772 1155; dealmore@freemailabsa.co.za. M-Sa 9am-5pm, Su 9am-2pm.)

FOOTPRINTS An absolute paradise for archaeologists, the western coast of South Africa contains some of the richest fossil deposits in the world. Testifying to this fact is a paleontologist's 1997 discovery of what some scientists are calling **"Eve's Footprint,"** a 117,000-year-old pair of female footprints set in a calcified sand dune on the shores of Langebaan Lagoon. They are the oldest footprints of modern man ever discovered, and they lend considerable support to the theory that humankind originated in southwestern Africa. The prints consist of two marks made by a left and a right foot as well as a badly-eroded, unidentifiable third mark. It is nearly a miracle that the prints exist intact today, as they endured thousands of years unprotected while the sand dune aged and turned into rock. Exceptionally tame environmental circumstances prevented the footprints from being swept away by the wind or destroyed by the rising sea level. Scientists speculate that the "Langebaan Woman" (who may in fact have been a young male) walked over the dunes after a heavy rain, when the hard sand was wet enough to hold her prints. Dry sand then covered the prints and eventually turned to rock, preserving the marks inside. The South African National Parks Board has authorized the creation of the West Coast Fossil Park (☎021 424 3330). So, for now, the footprints reside in the South African Museum in Cape Town (see p. 98).

WESTERN CAPE

❏ FOOD. Die Strandloper ❸ is legendary among locals. This eccentric seafood restaurant offers 4hr., 10-course meals. Dining at covered picnic tables on the beach, patrons enjoy a view of the ocean while glutting themselves on mussels, crayfish (lobster), and angel fish (all-you-can-eat R95). Lunch is at noon, dinner at 6pm. Diners must arrive promptly to enjoy all the courses. BYOB, or purchase beers and ciders from the adjacent **Beach Bar** hut. Reservations essential. (From Oostewal St., turn onto the road to Club Mykonos. Die Strandloper is 2km down on the left. ☎772 2490.) **Spinnakers ❷**, on Bree St., is decorated with calm bleached wood, large Matisse prints, candles, and a view of the lagoon from corner seats. Enjoy exquisitely-prepared catch of the day (R40) and an eclectic selection of starters ranging from giant mushrooms with smoked salmon and blue cheese to fried camembert with chili jam (R25). (☎772 1278 Open daily 9am-11pm. AmEx/DC/MC/V.) **Pearly's on the Beach ❸**, is at the end of Bree St. to the left. A beach restaurant on a porch that overlooks the lagoon, Pearly's offers the only "nightlife" in Langebaan and serves English breakfast daily (R28). Hollandaise beefsteak costs R65-75. (☎772 2734. Open M-F 11am-late (in season 10am-late), Sa-Su 9am-late.)

⚏ ADVENTURES. For those interested in summer sports, the **Cape Sports Center** on Main St., off Bree St., is the best starting point. They rent **watersport** and **mountain biking equipment,** including windsurfs, kitesurfs, surfboards, kayaks, and mountain bikes (R35 per 2hr., R95 per day). They also offer **windsurfing lessons** (R195 per hr. with equipment), 3hr. guided tours around the lagoon in a kayak for R150, and will arrange accommodations and an **airport shuttle** (R300 per group each way) for those beach bums planning to stay a few days or more. (☎772 1114; cwcsa@iafrica.com. Open daily 9am-7pm. MC/V.) **Tropico** (☎082 556 5418), at the Club Mykonos marina, also offers day-long **pleasure cruises** for R50-60. Inquire about boat tours at the tourist office.

WEST COAST NATIONAL PARK ☎022

The 30,000ha of West Coast National Park's salt marshes, 20,000-year-old sand dunes and arid expanses surround an iridescent aquamarine lagoon spotted with islands that 250 bird species call home. Animals ranging from the Cape fur seal to the blue wildebeest also hang their hats within its confines. For an

FROM THE ROAD

POACHING AFRICA'S MOST PRECIOUS RESOURCES

Natural beauty governs all that is appealing about African continent. The word "Africa" conjures up images of lions on the prowl, herds of elephant at their watering hole, and of the rhinoceros suckling her young. The great thrill of Africa is that it is different. Nowhere else in the world can one be on safari in the morning and whale watching after lunch. Nowhere else in the world are there signs to "Beware of kudu", and that "Stopping and feeding of baboons is strictly prohibited". And nowhere else in the world is there such wide spread and soul-destroying poverty.

This is one of the great dilemmas facing South Africa. As a resource, tourism contributes 5-6% of South Africa's GDP, and a vital cog in this industry is wildlife and game-viewing. The Kruger National Park alone welcomes well over 1 million guests annually, generating turnover in the region of R200 million, not to mention the ripple effects it has on surrounding areas and the national economy. And yet South Africa's natural resources are being depleted through hunting and through the annexation of animals' natural environs by human beings. Just recently a man was arrested in the Limpopo Province for the poaching of rhino, and the government believes that linked syndicates are operating in 54 other reserves. One of the methods these syndicates use is to pay villagers on the Park perimeters to cut the fence so that animals escape and can then be shot as problem animals. The problem of

(Continued on next page)

overall view of the park, drive along the two roads that traverse this Y-shaped landmass (a map is distributed at the entrance). They cut through the *strandveld* (sand scrub), a plant community adapted to the harsh Western Cape climate. In the spring, the park is a necessary shrine to the flower pilgrimage path. To view the other ecosystems by car, take advantage of the dirt road excursions; head up a mountain to a sea cliff, or down to a bird hide in the salt marshes. As you explore, mind the 50km per hour speed limit and don't try to race the ostriches—the loser won't be you or the ostrich, but the unwitting turtles who regularly scuttle across the road.

⊞ PRACTICAL INFORMATION. The park's main entrance lies 90km north of Cape Town off the **R27** (a few minutes from the turn-off to Yzerfontein). The highway turn-off is well-marked, as is the second entrance from the southern end of Langebaan, 7km south of town. There's no public transportation service within the West Coast National Park, but a minibus taxi from Cape Town will get you there. The privately-owned Postberg section of the park, home to several antelope, is open during the flower season (Aug.-Sept.) from 9am-5pm; the rest of the park is open 24hr. all year. (☎ 772 2144; fax 772 2607. Admission R20, children R12; low season R12/R8. The **Geelbek Information Center** at the heel of the lagoon and 4km from the entrance, is the starting point for all park excursions. (☎ 772 2799. Open M-F 7:30am-4pm, Sa-Su 9:30am-4pm.) It offers a tea garden, self-catering beach cottages, and house boats. (☎ 772 2799. Open M-F &:30am-4pm, Sa-Su 9:30am-4pm. Tea garden open W-Su 10am-4pm. Cottages R280 for 4 people; houseboats R600 for 4 people. To book a houseboat, call ☎ 012 428 9111).

⊞ ADVENTURES. To get a truly wild experience, you'll need a sturdy pair of hiking boots and determination. From the Geelbek Information Center, one 16km trail passes through the *strandveld* and salt marshes to the Atlantic Ocean, while a 14km trail encircles the dunes. For the hardiest outbackers, the park offers the **Strandveld Educational Trail,** a two-day, three-night package that includes self-guided tours of both trails and overnight lodging. (☎/fax 772 2798; R60 per person plus R25 for bedding.) The park supports 28% of the total bird diversity of Southern Africa; ornithologists lead three-hour **cruises** to islands in the lagoon inhabited by rare species. While there is **scuba diving, windsurfing, water-skiing, boating, swimming, fishing,** and **sailing** in limited areas of the park, camping is not allowed.

PATERNOSTER ☎ 022

In Paternoster, commerce and nightlife are almost as frigid as the water—little interrupts the pleasing similitude of days and nights in this fishing village. All the better to sit on a veranda with an unopened book and become one with the rhythm of the waves. Not all boats fare well on the rocks of Paternoster Bay. One local tale claims that the town owes its name to an ancient shipwreck: the Paternoster, a Dutch merchant vessel, which crashed on the shoreline three centuries ago. The sodden wood of generations litters the bay's mammoth promontory, but the boats, a decrepit and paint-chipped lot, still strike out every morning to net crayfish and snoek (indigenous fish). Even the seagulls of the bay are cunning fishers: blue-grey mussel shells ceaselessly crunch beneath cars and feet, left after the gulls drop their plentiful quarry on the tar roads to crack the shells.

🔽 PRACTICAL INFORMATION. From Cape Town, take the **R27** 125km to the **R45**, which goes through Vredenburg and continues 15km directly into Paternoster. **St. Augustine Rd.** is Paternoster's main street. It passes the modest commercial center and leads directly to the bay. The **Oep ve Koep**, an antique shop at the beginning of St. Augustine Rd., acts as the unofficial **tourist office**. (☎ 752 2632 or 083701 6905. Open M-Sa 10am-4:30pm, Su 11am-4:30pm.) There are public **phones** in front of the **Paternoster Superette** on the way into town.

🔽🔽 ACCOMMODATIONS AND FOOD. The splurge-worthy 🔽**Blue Dolphin ❸**, on St. Augustine Rd., can be reached by taking a right at the tourist office and following the gravel road until it turns right onto a tar road; the B&B is at the end, right on the beach. This Cape Dutch home has a resident parrot and four bedrooms decorated with 19th-century antiques, as well as perks including TVs, heated towel rails, and teddy bears. Each room and two verandas offer spectacular views of the beach. A beach cottage (2 bedrooms and a loft with two single beds) is also available for two nights or more. (☎752 2001. Breakfast included. Reservations recommended. Singles R250; doubles and cottages R170 per person.) 🔽**Voorstrandt Restaurant ❸** is the only building on the beach side of Strandloop Way. It's right on the beach with right-on seafood. The stunning view alone makes it worth a visit. (☎752 2038. Enormous seafood platter R165. Crayfish R75-95. Fish of the day R45. Open daily 10am-10pm.) Inquire at the tourist office about lodging at the **Mosselbank B&B ❷**. It has three sunny rooms with pri-

(Continued from previous page)

deforestation is also an alarming one, with over 3 million rural households using wood as fuel to meet their energy requirements.

But what do you do when people are starving? How can you blame a rural villager for cutting a fence if it means their family does not go hungry? How can you blame people for chopping down trees when they are cold? The government cannot simply throw offenders in jail. This would be to deny the poverty that faces millions of Africans on a daily basis. No, another approach must be found to prevent rural people from assisting these syndicates and indeed from destroying their own surroundings.

The answer to this problem lies in getting local people invested in their environment so that they have a vested interest in the well-being of the animals and ecological system around them. Instead of telling people "You need to leave these animals alone because they bring money to the country", local people need to be given jobs in game reserves, given a share of the profits that these resources hold, so that the material benefits of nature are no longer an abstract concept for them. This is happening: For the past few years the South African National Parks have been creating links with communities on the perimeter of their parks in the hope of creating a new era of wildlife management in which the local community plays an essential role.

This is the only way that the balance between human survival and the survival of the Earth's great reserves of big game can be maintained.

—Yusuf Randera-Rees

vate entrances, and *braai* and self-catering kitchen facilities. The beach is only a 100 meter walk away. (☎752 2632 or 083 701 6905. Breakfast R30. Singles R170; doubles R120.)

■■ **SIGHTS AND ADVENTURES.** View the bay and surrounding mountains from the **Cape Columbine Nature Reserve.** Take St. Augustine Rd. 6km past downtown Paternoster, following the signs for Tietiesbaai. You can climb to the top of the lighthouse to view the bay and surrounding mountains. Camping (caravan or tent) is welcome, but make reservations at least three months in advance for December holidays. (☎752 2718. R65; low-season M-Th R45, F-Su R65. Admission R9, children R6.) For fishing trips, kayak tours, diving, hiking, bird watching, and other one hour to one week excursion concoctions, contact **West Coast Guided Trails** (☎082 926 2267; info@kayaktrails.com; www.kayaktrails.com) or **Sowandre** (☎083 480 4930; andre@ratrce.co.za; www.ratrace.co.za). Equipment, food, and accommodations provided. Prices range from R150 for a traditional fishing morning to R700 for a weekend of yacht-based kayaking and diving.

OLIFANTS RIVER VALLEY

The Olifants River Valley stretches 300km between the towns of **Citrusdal** and **Bitterfontein.** When Dutch pioneers topped the Piekenierskloof Pass in the 1660s, they christened the valley for its population of elephants (*olifant* is Afrikaans for "elephant"). The vista from the Pass is arresting, although roaming pachyderms have bowed out to be replaced by the agrarian efficiency of South Africa's third-largest citrus-producing region. Squat trees range across the hills, their fruits an orange and yellow confetti sprinkled over the landscape; in the winter, their tangy scent spritzes the air. The **Cederberg Mountain Range,** rising in jagged, erratic peaks of sandstone and hiding ancient Khoisan rock art in its caves, provides an austere contrast to the deep valley below.

CITRUSDAL   ☎022

These clusters of orange trees create a great base from which to explore the wilderness of the **Cederberg** (see p. 180) and the **Olifants Wine Route.** The nearby hot springs and bath resorts, the spring flowers along scenic driving routes, and free wine tastings at the local **Goue Vallei (Golden Valley) Vineyards** attract visitors throughout the year. For the brazen lot, the Citrusdal area also offers a range of **outdoor adventures** including hiking, mountain biking, fishing, parachuting and, of course, skinny-dipping in the warm, earthy waters.

🛈 **PRACTICAL INFORMATION.** To get into town, take the **N7** from Cape Town for 180km and turn off at the sign for Citrusdal; after 1km, turn left onto **Voortrekker St.,** which leads into the center of town. **Minibus taxis** run along the N7 from Cape Town to Springbok, but, as is the case with most of this region, a car is the best bet. There are no local car rental companies, so hire one before arriving in town. The **tourist office** is annexed to Uitspan Coffee Shop on Voortrekker St. (☎921 3210. Open M-F 8am-5pm, Sa 8am-1pm.) Voortrekker St. is home to most services, including an **ATM** (in front of the **Standard Bank**); **police station** (☎921 2011; next to the library and post office); **pharmacy** (☎921 2159; after hours ☎921 2272; fax 921 3440; open M-Th 8am-5:30pm, F 8am-6pm, Sa 8am-12:30pm); **Internet** (at the Cederberg Lodge; open with reception at the hotel; R1 per min.); and **post office,** with *Poste Restante.* (☎921 2250. Open M-F 8am-5pm, Sa 8am-noon.) **Postal code:** 7340.

⌐⌐ ACCOMMODATIONS AND FOOD. Since Citrusdal proper is not the area's main attraction, it's worth wandering outside of town for budget accommodations. An easy 17km from Citrusdal down a signposted road near the N7 (take a right after the turn-off to Craig Royston) are ◙**The Baths ❷,** a small spatype resort with mineral pools, whirlpools, and jacuzzis filled with natural 43-degree-celsius water. Day visitors may moisten and plunge in the magical hot and cold elixirs here for a mere R30 (half-price for children and M-F), but reserve in advance. (☎921 3609; fax 921 3988; baths@kingsley.co.za. Key deposit R50. Linens R10. Book well in advance. Campsites M-Th R30, F-Sa R40; children R15/R20. Double cottages R290, quads R380, sextets R460. Rooms with bunkbeds M-Th R120, F-Sa R150 per person. AmEx/MC/V.)

⌐ OLIFANTS RIVER VALLEY WINE ROUTE. Thanks to fertile soil, the Olifants River Valley is an ideal wine-producing region. Under apartheid, there was little domestic demand for red wines and no possibility of export. But with the lifting of sanctions, the wineries of the Olifants River Valley began experimenting with red wines, and discovered that the pebbled Karoo soil produces excellent bottles of that dark, sultry stuff. Olifants winemakers deservedly boast that their reds from the dominant cellars of Paarl and Stellenbosch are the most distinguished wines in national competitions and international sales. Eight wine cellars—six cooperatives and two privately owned—line more than 100km of the N7 from Citrusdal to Vredendahl. Each March, they collaborate on the Vineyard Feast, a three-day festival in Vredendahl, with live music, food stalls, and of course, copious wine-tasting. (Free tastings and cellar tours M-F 8am-1pm and 2-5pm, Sa 8am-noon.) All wineries are well marked along the N7; with a designated driver, a day of wine-tasting (free) and wine-purchasing (bottles of dry whites start at R10!) is a cheap way to get a flavor for the West Coast's inland towns. Call the Olifants River Wine Trust (☎027 213 3126) for information. Two of the best are in Vredendahl and Klawer. Vredendahl (☎027 213 1080) is the largest cooperative winery in the Southern Hemisphere, with 160 members and an input of 60,000 tons of grapes per year. From the N7 at Klawer take the R363 for 30km to Vredendahl. At the center of Vrehendal, turn right onto the R27. After a bridge, the winery is on the right side of the road. Klawer (☎027 246 1530; www.wine.co.za) is on the N7, 300km north of Cape Town. (Most stores and tastings are open M-F 8am-5pm and Sa 8:30am-12:30pm.)

If The Baths are booked, or if you want a more private splash, go next door to the new and still-developing **Elephant Leisure Resort ❸.** While the waters here are a few degrees cooler, the pool smaller, and the trees sparser, the immaculate and fully-equipped air-conditioned cabins feature TVs, phones, microwaves, and a lighted jacuzzi on each veranda. (☎921 2884; fax 921 2886; elephant@kingsley.co.za. 2-person chalet R225 per person, 4-person chalet R110 per person. Bed and breakfast service R275 per person, with dinner R350 per person.) For those who prefer to reside in town, the **Cederberg Lodge ❷,** 66 Voortrekker St., provides clean, spacious and air-conditioned hotel rooms, upholstered in garish pink, orange, and green. Squash, tennis, golf, and volleyball are offered on the grounds. (☎921 2221; fax 921 2704; cedarberglodge@kingsley.co.za; www.cedarberglodge.co.za. Breakfast R30-40. Singles R115-200; doubles R150-250.) Another option in town is the clean and green **Citrusdal Caravan Park ❸,** just past the bridge on the left-hand side of the road connecting Citrusdal to the N7. It has 66 camping and caravan sites. (☎/fax 921 3145. Reception 24hr. R70 for a lot and up to 4 people, R10 per extra person; R30 for individual campers.)

Just outside of town, immediately before the turn-off from the N7, is the █**Craig Royston ❶** travel stop, which has a tiny museum, a small theater, and a traditional farm shop with appetizing light meals. Taste wines from the entire region for R5, an appealing option for wine-lovers who do not have the time to undertake the 3hr. tour offered by Citrus Tours (see below). The gracious proprietor, committed to enhancing regional cultural activity beyond wine, will eagerly share tales about the 200-year-old Craig Royston farm and outpost. He might accompany you into the museum, a dusty room filled with an eclectic selection of farm historiana ranging from 19th-century enema jugs to wheelchairs. The food, served on the veranda at the other end of the building, is deliciously homemade; hand-churned butter and rum shortbread both sell for R5, and the Deli Platter is R25. (☎921 2963. Open daily 8am-6pm. Dinner theaters every 2nd F.)

◙▨ **SIGHTS AND ADVENTURES.** Venture around the Goue Vallei winery, Goede Hoop Citrus Co-op, or local orange groves with **Citrus Tours.** The winery tour ends with a free wine tasting. Watch the oranges as they bop along conveyor belts, plucked up by inspectors and photographed by computers that assess their quality. The attention given to each fruit is awesome, as is the synchronicity of humans and machines. (☎921 3210. Tours can be arranged M-F 9am-5pm. R10 per person per site. Reduced rates for large groups.) **Skydiving Citrusdal** (☎462 5666), on the road towards the springs, is a great outfit through which daredevils may test their courage. The town also holds an annual **Citrus Festival** in September, which includes a mountain bike rally called the "Crowning of the Festival Queen."

FREEDOM'S REALITY

The Achievements and Failures of Today's South Africa

The struggle, as the South African anti-apartheid movement is known, is now a memory. For almost five decades of apartheid rule, and centuries of colonial rule that preceded it, people risked death and imprisonment as they challenged oppression in a variety of ways, struggling for non-racialism, pan-Africanism, African rule, or "genuine" democracy. What emerged from years of protest was arguably the most liberal constitution in the world, a one-person one-vote electoral system, an unprecedented attempt at reconciliation, in the hope that the future would diverge from the past.

In the "New South Africa" the president is an African leader of a majority-African population. Seven out of nine provinces are controlled by the African National Congress, once an illegal underground organization. South Africa is now a regional leader and is no longer ostracized by the international community for its racial discrimination.

Even a decade after the end of legalized segregation, the transition between old and new has not eased all of apartheid's burdens. After voting in their first election in 1994, most people returned home to long-neglected homelands. The country that produced the world's first heart transplant still had corrupt hospitals, under-resourced rural clinics, and an escalating HIV/AIDS problem. Their country had the world's highest rape and murder rates, with a police force trained to stop protests (and sometimes torture or kill protesters) but inadequately funded to stop crime. A new constitution declared a universal right to education, but schools continued to "train and teach people in accordance with their opportunities in life, according to the sphere in which they live." The new government was faced with fifteen departments of education, and governmental expenditures on white students were four times greater than those spent on African students.

Some positive advances took place. The government adopted a multilingual national anthem. Public holidays—such as Human Rights Day and Youth Day—memorialized the Sharpeville massacre and the Soweto uprising, respectively. A Truth and Reconciliation Commission began the process of reconstruction. Still, genuine progress in land reform, education equalization, health care, and crime reduction is elusive.

The ANC government's first attempt at broad reform, the Reconstruction and Development Program (RDP), lasted barely two years. More promise than reality, the RDP was based on public works projects, massive housing construction, land redistribution, and an ambitious welfare system. Its successor, Growth, Employment and Redistribution (GEAR), prioritized economic growth over public sector reforms. GEAR presumed that land redistribution, health and education advances, and housing construction would arise from more rapid economic liberalization. The result has been a declining GDP growth rate coupled with an increasing inequality and a virtual abandonment of radical equalization or redistributive reforms.

Houses constructed after 1994 are easily identifiable because there are so few. Township residents create or resurrect additional corrugated iron shacks more often than formal housing structures. Vigilante justice is now the accepted (and effective) method of crime reduction. HIV/AIDS is overwhelming public health facilities, yet few resources are devoted to alleviating the growing crisis. To many, the ANC's priorities of regional political leadership and integration into the international economic community have subsumed the dreams of post-apartheid transformation and development.

Yet dreams live on. Committed activism is challenging today's government to realize its promises. In one of the most improbable transitions of the twentieth century, the Old South Africa became the New South Africa without all-out war and with a conscious process of reconciliation. But to exist beyond its constitutional promises, the New South Africa must face the challenges of HIV/AIDS, land distribution, housing, and education. It must use the tools it has—especially a radical constitution, and a population that will not accept inequity lying down—to shape its future.

Emilou MacLean is working in Cape Town, South Africa with Medecins Sans Frontieres on the Access to Essential Medicines Campaign. She was the Assistant Editor for Let's Go South Africa 2002.

EASTERN CAPE

The Eastern Cape combines everything South Africa has to offer—wild, secluded beaches with superb surf, accessible game parks, haunting deserts, and cities sizzling with nightlife. The region's rich political history has given birth to some of South Africa's most poignant heritage. When Europeans clashed with the indigenous African population, the Eastern Cape became a war zone between Afrikaners arriving from Cape Town and Xhosas. When British settlers in 1820 found themselves caught between the warring parties, they confined themselves to the relative safety of Grahamstown and Port Elizabeth. Under apartheid, the Eastern Cape was a stronghold of the opposition struggle, the blacks of its region being shuffled into the Ciskei and Transkei "homelands." Steve Biko's Black Consciousness Movement originated here, and the man himself is buried just outside of King William's Town. Nelson Mandelola was born in the province and has now retired to his ancestral village near Umtata.

Eastern Cape remains one of South Africa's poorest provinces, with unemployment in some areas topping 80%. With astounding sights and a rich history, tourism is one of the province's most promising prospects. Between the Wild Coast's heavenly beaches and Grahamstown's worldwide arts extravaganza, from Schotia Game Reserve's roaming wildlife to the Karoo's romantic deserts, Eastern Cape is an unforgettable part of any visit to South Africa.

HIGHLIGHTS OF THE EASTERN CAPE

The July **Grahamstown festival** (see p. 195), the 2nd largest arts festival in the world, draws an energetic troop of actors, musicians, dancers, artists, and revelers.

Figments of the imagination come to life at the **Owl House** (see p. 200), a surreal niche of eerie creativity.

In **Addo Elephant Park** (see p. 192), diminutive but industrious dung beetles compete for attention with their hard-to-miss neighbors.

Ease into the surfing scene at **Jeffreys Bay** (Jeffreys Bay, p. 193), and fight your way to the top of the crests and swells.

PORT ELIZABETH   ☎ 041

Founded in 1799 by English settlers displaced during the Afrikaner-Zulu wars, P.E. is also home to the oldest township in South Africa. Known as **Red Location** for the color of its rusted metal roofs, the township was first inhabited in 1902 by black residents accused of spreading the plague. During apartheid, P.E. became the site of political atrocities when police beat **Steve Biko** and **Siphiwe Mtunkula** in the building at 44 Strand St.

P.E. today stands as a reminder of the successes of the country's black population. The residents of **Walmer township** were among the proud few to resist relocation and remain in what were previously white suburban areas; the **boycotts** organized here by Steve Biko were powerful symbols of black resistance during the apartheid era. Post-apartheid, P.E. became the first major South African city to elect a black mayor. Tourists are glad to learn that the city's crime rate has remained remarkably low by South African standards.

At the edge of Algoa Bay, Port Elizabeth is today South Africa's second largest city by area and fifth largest in population (over 1.2 million). With 40km of shore-

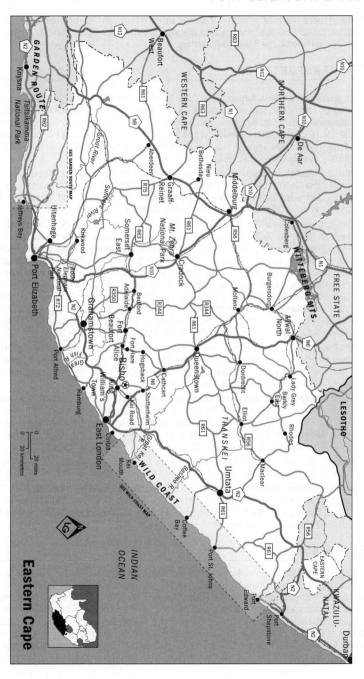

EASTERN CAPE

Eastern Cape

line and more hours of sunshine than any other coastal city in the country, it's no surprise that P.E. is the "watersport capital of South Africa." P.E. also has the best nightlife between Cape Town and Durban.

⌐ TRANSPORTATION

Flights: Port Elizabeth Airport (☎507 7319 or 581 2984), 4km northwest of Central District. From Beach Rd., turn inland on La Roche Rd. just before McDonald's. La Roche becomes Alister Miller Rd.; the airport is on the left, 2km from the water. Taxis from city center R15. **South Africa Airways** (☎507 1111) flies to: **Johannesburg** (1¼hr.,7 times daily, R120); **Cape Town** (1¼hr., 4 times daily, R850); **Durban** (1¼hr, 4 times daily, R850); **East London** (1½hr. daily, R1130).

Trains: The **station** (☎507 2647), is on Strand St., parallel to Govan Mbeki Ave., 1 block closer to the water. Daily service to **Johannesburg** (19hr.; 2:30pm; second class R225, first class R325) via **Addo** (R20/R50), **Cradock** (R70/95), and **Bloemfontein** (12hr., R140/R205). Change in Bloemfontein for **Cape Town** trains.

Buses: Greyhound (☎363 4555; fax 363 3559), **Intercape** (☎586 0055) and **Translux** (☎392 1333; fax 507 2366) all service Port Elizabeth. Call to reserve tickets. Though each line offers several pick-up spots, those listed here are the most central. **Greyhound** stops at 107 Govan Mbeki Ave. Open M-F 9am-4pm, Sa 9am-noon. **Intercape** stops on Fleming St. just behind Market Sq. **Translux** stops at the train station. Major routes for all include: **Cape Town** (12hr., 5 times per day, R190), with stops along the Garden Route; **Durban** (13hr., 5 times per day, R245-255) via **East London** (4hr., R90-100); **Johannesburg** (14hr., 3 times per day, R275-295). **Baz Bus** (☎021 439 2323) stops at all of P.E.'s hostels along its coastal route. **City to City** bus also runs to: **Cape Town** (daily, R130); **East London** (daily, R50); **Johannesburg** (daily, R170).

Minibus Taxis: A long-distance rank is opposite the train station. **Norwich Long Distance** (☎585 7253) runs to: **Cape Town** (10hr., twice daily, R200); **Graaff-Reinet** (3hr.; Tu, Th, F, and Su; R80); **Knysna** (2½hr., twice daily, R80). Call the day before to check departure times and to guarantee a seat.

Local Transportation: Algoa Bus Company (☎404 1200; fax 453 7437) runs a loop linking Rink St., Govan Mbeki Ave., Beachfront, and Greenacres Shopping Mall. Fares average R2.50. Buses depart from central station under Market Sq. Passengers enter from Market Sq. or Traduna Mall. Buses run from early morning until about 7pm. There are local **minibus taxis** along Strand St.

Taxis: Eagle Taxis (☎528 4439) and **Flexi Cabs** (☎585 8114, 082 297 2053 or 082 978 9750) both offer 24hr. service.

Car Hire: Economic Car Hire, 104 Heugh Rd., Walmer (☎5815826 or 082 800 4258; econhire@iafrica.com). **Imperial** (☎581 1268), **Avis** (☎581 7200), **Budget** (☎581 4242), **Tempest** (☎581 1256), **Hertz** (508 6600) and **Eurocar** (☎581 1547) all have offices at the airport open from the first to the last flight.

◼✈ ORIENTATION

P.E. is divided into two major areas: **Beachfront** and **Central.** The Beachfront district extends along the beach up to the western border of the Central Business District. **King's Beach,** in Humewood, is the closest beach to Central, a prime tourist area featuring excellent hostels and pubs. Central is divided into Lower and Upper. Between Lower and Upper Central, the **Donkin Reserve,** marked by a **lighthouse,** is the site of the main tourist office and a useful landmark for orientation. **Lower Central** is home to the Central Business District, train and bus stations, and the industrial harbor. Main **Govan Mbeki Ave.** runs parallel to the water, known at

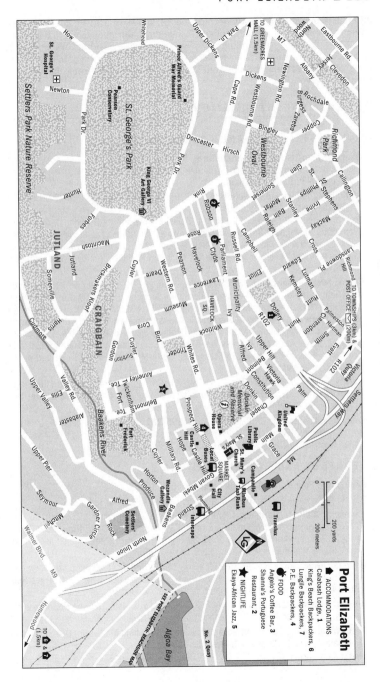

EASTERN CAPE

Port Elizabeth

ACCOMMODATIONS
Calabash Lodge, 1
King's Beach Backpackers, 6
Lungile Backpackers, 7
P.E. Backpackers, 4

FOOD
Angelo's Coffee Bar, 3
Shanna's Portuguese
Restaurant, 2

NIGHTLIFE
Ekaya-African Jazz, 5

different points as Baakens, Humewood, Beach, and Marine St. A number of cross-streets run inland from Govan Mbeki Ave. and make the steep climb to **Upper Central,** a racially integrated community of small businesses and historic buildings. **Rink St.** is Upper Central's main stretch of road. Host to a stretch of trendy restaurants and bars, **Parliament St.** diagonally intersects Rink St. before running to the Donkin Reserve.

🔟 PRACTICAL INFORMATION

TOURIST, FINANCIAL, AND LOCAL SERVICES

Tourist Office: Tourism Port Elizabeth (☎585 8884; fax 585 2564; information@tourismpe.co.za; www.ibhayi.com), in the lighthouse on Donkin Reserve. Open M-F 8am-4:30pm, Sa-Su 9:30am-3:30pm.

Tours: Bay Tourism and Tours (☎585 5427, 083 231 9242, or 083 369 4722; fax 584 0016; gary@baytours.co.za; www.baytours.co.za), in the Old Children's Museum, at the corner of Beach Rd. and Brooks Hill Dr. Satellite office on the Beachfront. Open daily 9am-5pm. **Springfield Safari and Tours** is popular for those looking to get off of the tourist track. Tailor-made tours can include hunting at private game farms, camping, and visits to see Mountain Zebras, Karoo, or Addo Elephants. Run by a registered specialist game guide.

Banks: First National Bank, 68 Govan Mbeki Ave. (☎506 6111; fax 586 1955). Open M-F 9am-3:30pm, Sa 8:30-11am. Other major branches, with **ATMs,** at 10 Rink St. (☎585 7781) and Walmer Park Shopping Mall (☎368 6132). **Rennies Foreign Exchange** (☎368 5890) has branches in the Walmer Park Mall and the Greenacres Mall. 1.5% commission, R30 min. charge. Both branches open M-F 9am-4:15pm, Sa 9am-12:15pm. **American Express** has a branch at the Boardwalk Casino (☎583 2025; fax 583 3470; emergency 082 591 9321). Open M-F 8am-10pm, Sa-Su and public holidays 10am-2pm.

Library: (☎585 8133; fax 585 1279), in Market Sq. at the end of Govan Mbeki Ave. Temporary membership available for a minimum of one month. Open M 1-6pm, Tu-F 9am-6pm, Sa 8:30am-1pm.

Laundromat: Automat, 6A Parliment St. (☎585 7870). Dry cleaning and drop-off services. Self-service washers R7; dryers R2 per 10 min. Wash, dry, and fold R18 per 5kg. Open M-F 7:30am-7pm, Sa 7:30am-6pm, Su 7:30am-5pm.

EMERGENCY AND COMMUNICATIONS

Emergency: Police ☎10 111; **ambulance** ☎10 177.

Police: In Flamingo Sq. on Govan Mbeki Ave. (☎394 6316; fax 394 6385).

Pharmacy: Rink St. Pharmacy, 4 Rink St. (☎585 5167, emergency 368 6570); fax 582 3773; rspharm@icom.za). Open M-F 8am-5:30pm, Sa 8am-1pm. **Humewood Pharmacy,** 19 Humewood Rd. (☎/fax 585 3294). In Humeway Center. Open M-Th 8am-7:30pm, F 8am-6pm, Sa 8am-3pm, Su 9:15am-1:30pm.

Hospital: Greenacres Hospital (☎/fax 363 0250; lindaab@netcare.co.za; www.netcare.co.za), at the corner of Rochelle Rd. and Cape Rd. in Greenacre. **St. Georges Hospital,** 40 Park Dr. (☎392 6000; mandystevens@afrox.boc.com). In Central.

Internet Access: Funtasia (☎363 4681), in Greenacres Mall, up Cape Rd. Accessible by bus. R12.50 per 30min. 8 terminals. Open M-Sa 9am-midnight, Su 9am-11pm.

Post Office: (☎585 8311), on Govan Mbeki Ave., 3km from Market Sq. Open M-Tu and Th-F 8am-4:30pm, W 8:30am-4:40pm, Sa 8am-noon.

Postal code: 6001.

ACCOMMODATIONS AND CAMPING

Though popular for their easy access to Beachfront, most of the hotels and B&Bs crowding Humewood and Summerstrand are quite expensive. Fortunately, two hostels stand within several blocks of the beach and within stumbling distance of the Brookes Pavilion, P.E.'s nightlife nucleus.

Lungile Backpackers, 12 La Roche Dr. (☎582 2042 or 082 825 6181; fax 582 2083; lungile@netactive.co.za). In Humewood, 2 blocks from Beach Rd. and McDonald's. A fantastically lively, clean and innovative backpackers with an inviting pool, active social life and some of the nicest doubles you can find for the price. The owners will happily arrange any activities the P.E. has to offer. Free continental breakfast. Dinner R20-30. Laundry R12 per load. Key deposit R20. Internet R0.50 per min. Dorms R50-55; singles R80; doubles and twins R110-150. Camping R35. Traveler's checks accepted. ❶

Port Elizabeth Backpackers, 7 Prospect Hill (☎586 0697; fax 585 2032; pebak-pak@global.co.za; www.pebakpak.info). Halfway up the hill. From the corner of Govan Mbeki Ave. and Whites Rd., climb the stairs of Prospect Hill. By car, drive up Whites Rd., turn left onto Belmont Terr., and follow signs downhill. With its prime location in Upper Central, this 100-year-old house is a good place to settle if you can be away from the beach. TV lounge with MNET. Free boogie boards and sandboards. Bookings for buses. Breakfast R20. Dinner R25-35. Laundry R20 per load. Key deposit R30. Internet R1 per min. Luggage storage. 24hr. reception. Dorms R55-60; singles R90; doubles R150. ❶

The Caboose (☎584 0638; fax 584 0637; www.caboose.co.za), up the road from Brookes Pavilion. A lovely and large log cabin geared towards families. Big TV lounge and social area. More expensive sports-themed rooms with TV available. Key deposit R30. Reception 7am-11pm. Singles R118; doubles 163; triples R182. ❷

Carslogic Bed and Breakfast, 11 Seventh Ave., Sommertrand (☎583 5251; fax 583 1802; clephane@netactive.co.za; www.carslogic.co.za). A pleasant option for those seeking to remove themselves from children, noise, and the rigors of the city. Sparkling pool, well-lit rooms and all modern conveniences. Breakfast included. Laundry R5 per item. Reception 24hr. Check-in 1pm. Check-out 11am. 4-star rating. Doubles R380-600. AmEx/MC/V. ❷

Calabash Lodge, 8 Dollery St. (☎ 585 6162; fax 585 0985; calabash@iafrica.com; www.axxess.web.za/calabash). Take Russell Rd. uphill from Govan Mbeki Ave. about 2km, turn right onto Irvine St., then right again on Campbell St. After 2 blocks, turn left onto Dollery St.; Calabash is at the bottom of the crescent on the right. Charming rooms provide a happy medium between noisy dorms and staid lodges. Free bus and airport pick-ups. Breakfast included. All rooms with bath. Laundry R25 for 5kg. Reception 24hr. Check-in and check-out 11am. Rooms R150 per person. ❷

King's Beach Backpackers, 41 Windemere Rd. (☎585 8113; fax 585 1693; www.backpackafrica.co.za), in Humewood. A relaxed environment in a homey setting. The self-catering kitchen is plastered with the graffiti of wise former visitors. Breakfast included. Key deposit R20. Internet R7 per 15min; R35 per 1½hr. Reception 6:30am-10pm. Dorms R55; doubles R130. Camping R35. ❶

FOOD

Typical fast-food chains line the beachfront; Brookes Pavilion offers a better beachside alternative. Parliament St., in Upper Central, is lined with restaurants and coffee shops serving up international cuisine, South African style.

Angelo's Coffee Bar, 10 Parliament St. (☎585 2929). Locally acclaimed food served in a cosmopolitan, *très chic* atmosphere. Surprisingly cheap, despite the pretense. Cakes

R7.90-9.90. Croissants R9.80-12.80. Pasta under R20. Open M-Sa 8am-11pm, Su 8:30am-11pm. No reservations. AmEx/MC/V. ❶

Shanna's Portuguese Restaurant, 19 Robson St. (☎082 443 7842 or 082 296 2892). Off Rink St. An authentic Portuguese restaurant. Starters R8-15. Entrees R35-60. Reservations essential. Open M-F 11am-late, Sa 6pm-late. MC/V. ❷

Zorba's Grill & Tavern (☎586 3804), in Dolphin Leap Center above 7-11. An understated and stylish restaurant with traditional Greek music and an authentically Greek ambiance. Smart casual. Take-away. Light meals R20-35. Grill R26-51. Mediterranean specials R42-89. Open M-Sa noon-3pm, 6-11pm; Su noon-3pm. AmEx/MC/V. ❷

The Mediterranean (☎582 3981; fax 582 3982), in Dolphins Leap Center opposite Zorba's. The relaxing blue hues that decorate this restaurant work in tandem with the ocean views to create a thoroughly mellow vibe. Nice view of the sea with a big outside deck. Specializes in seafood. Take away. Smart casual. Seafood R32-R125. Full sushi bar (R14-70). Open daily noon-3pm and 6pm-close. AmEx/MC/V. ❸

♫ 🎭 ENTERTAINMENT AND NIGHTLIFE

Humewood beachfront and the area around Parliament St. are P.E.'s nightlife hotspots. At night, the only transport between the two is a taxi (R20-25). Many start the night in one of the restaurants or bars near Parliament, before heading down to Brookes Pavilion (on Beach Rd. next to the Oceanarium) for more live music and dancing.

◪ **Tapas al Sol** (☎/fax 584 0660; www.tapas.co.za), upstairs in Brookes Pavilion. A typical Spanish pub, complete with loud beer-saturated twenty-somethings. Dancing and drinking spill out onto the open-air deck. Live music (usually alternative) offered Tu-Sa 9pm. Cover for big-name bands. "Hectic Wednesday" (beers R4, tequila R3). "Super Saturday" (8-10pm, drink two-for-one). 5L kegs R60. Most nights DJs spin anything from '70s to rave. Open daily 11am-2am.

Cagney's Action Cafe (☎082 881 1155), in the Kine Center on Rink St. Small '50s diner with pictures of Hollywood stars. Large dance crowds during the week. Karaoke nightly from 10pm on. DJs play a range of music nightly. F and Sa cover. Sa ladies free. Beers from R7. Shots from R5.50. 18+. Open M, Su 8pm-late, Tu-Sa 7pm-late.

Ekhaya-African Jazz, 2 Western Rd. (☎586 1156). Opposite Edward and grand hotels. A true African jazz joint with buck skins on floors, logs as chairs and Castle Lager in abundance. Delicacies include sheep head (R10) and tripe and offal (R8). Quarts R6.80, whiskey R6. Live jazz on Su night from 6pm. Open daily 10am-2pm.

Toby Joe's (☎584 0082), downstairs in Brookes Pavilion. A spacious pub/club with a young vibe. Popular with people from many backgrounds in P.E. Live bands on most Th and Su. Other nights DJs play everything from '60s to commercial dance. Calamari and chips R25. T-bone R30. No cover. W buy-one-get-one-free from 9-10pm and 11pm-midnight. Open W, F and Sa 11am-2am; Tu, Th and Su 11am-midnight.

👁 SIGHTS

TOWNSHIP TOURS. Separated from the city center, P.E's townships cannot be easily visited without an organized tour. The tours listed below offer an in-depth experience and historical perspective.

◪ **Molo Tours** (☎581 7085 or 082 970 4037; molotours@mweb.co.za). Offers the chance to spend a social evening in the township. Tours may include a meal in a local home, an in-depth history discussion, visits to a boys' initiation (for men only), community choir practices, jazz concerts, or a local *shebeen*. Pick-up at P.E. hostels. Tours daily

4:30pm; earlier tours can be arranged. 4hr., R150. Daytrips to local game parks R250.

Calabash Tours (☎585 6162; calabash@iafrica.com). Offers day and night options. The "Real City Tour" emphasizes the momentous changes of the last decade, focusing on P.E.'s unwritten history. Stops include a community-run school, the workshop of local artists, and explores the history and diversity of the townships. The evening option offers a more social focus, featuring *shebeen* dinners, live music, cheap drinks, and all-around fun. Real City Tour daily 3½-4hr., R180. *Shebeen* Tour nightly (meets at 4pm). R200.

Tanaqua Indigenous Tours (☎083 270 9924 or 083 995 6345; waldoadams@hotmail.com). Offers "complete city tour" (R150-180), stopping in the townships and colonial sectors. Township tours (R180-200) examines the township areas in-depth. A whale watch (R350), a full day Addo Elephant Park trip (R300), and an Addo-Schotia combination trips are available (9am-10pm, lunch and dinner, R950). Book ahead.

BAYWORLD MUSEUM COMPLEX. This complex houses the Port Elizabeth Museum, Oceanarium, and Snake Park. The **Museum** has dinosaur skeletons, musical instruments, photo exhibits, and mounted big game. The **Oceanarium** has dolphin and seal performances daily at 11am and 3pm and lets qualified divers swim with the sharks in their tanks every Wednesday. Booking essential. Africa's **Snake Park** not only provides thrills and chills, but anti-venom for use throughout South Africa. *(On the beachfront in Humewood. ☎584 0650; fax 584 0661; sandy@bayworld.co.za; www.bayworld.co.za. Museum open daily 9am-4:30pm. Oceanarium open daily 9am-12:45pm, 2-4:30pm. Snake park open daily 9am-1pm, 2-4:30pm. Combo ticket: R25, children under 14 R12, senior citizens R21. Oceanarium: R17/R9; senior citizens R14. P.E. Museum and snake park R10/R5, senior citizens R8.)*

NO. 7 CASTLE HILL. Built in 1827, No. 7 Castle Hill is one of the oldest surviving settler houses in P.E. Today, it is the

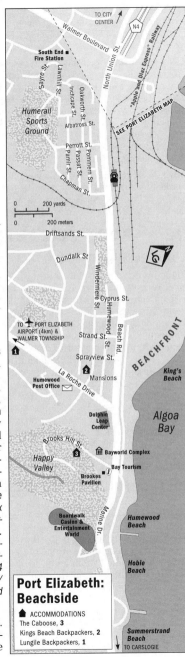

Port Elizabeth: Beachside

▲ ACCOMMODATIONS
The Caboose, **3**
Kings Beach Backpackers, **2**
Lungile Backpackers, **1**

EASTERN CAPE

city's historical museum, restored to its mid-19th century glory, complete with a working peach-peeler in the basement kitchen and an old doll house. (☎582 2818; fax 586 4962. Open M-F 8:30am-1pm, 2-4:30pm. R6, children under 12 R3. Tours provided on request; call ahead to arrange.)

ART GALLERIES. Wezandla Gallery and Coffee Shop is Port Elizabeth's funky artist epicenter, also a fun place to browse and have a snack. The brightly decorated gallery displays local crafts and paintings by regional artists. (27 Baakens St. ☎585 1186 or 082 893 7905; fax 585 1186; baer@global.co.za. Open M-F 9am-5pm, Sa 9am-1pm, will open on Su by request. Call ahead.) **King George VI Art Gallery** exhibits a large rotating collection of South African art. (1 Park Dr. At the corner of Rink and Western St. on the edge of St. George's Park. ☎586 1030; fax 586 3234; kgg@kgg.gov.za; www.kgg.gov.za. Open M-F 8:30am-5pm, Sa-Su 2-5pm. On the first Su of every month there are art displays in St. George's Park from 9am-2pm. Free.)

DONKIN HERITAGE TRAIL. A self-guided walking tour of the city, Donkin Trail is marked by a painted blue line on the pavement. The trail begins and ends in Market Sq. in Lower Central, and winds around St. George's Park. (R12. Detailed booklet with info about 47 sites along the trail is available at Donkin Reserve info center.)

NEAR PORT ELIZABETH

ADDO ELEPHANT PARK

A 45min. drive from P.E., Addo Elephant Park is one of the Eastern Cape's most reliable locations for spotting big game. Founded in 1931 to protect the 11 elephants not yet killed by hunters seeking ivory, the park's 320 elephants today make its 18,000ha home to the densest tusker population in the world. The elephants are easier to spot in the dry season as they flock to shrinking watering holes. Addo also supports several hundred kudu, red hartebeest, Cape buffalo, and black rhino, as well as the illustrious dung beetle. **Pembury Tours** (☎581 2581; fax 581 2332; shuttle@pemburytours.com) provides a guide, transport and lunch for a full-day excursion (R450 per person). It's also possible to drive through the park yourself. For groups, it's probably worth it to forgo the guide and hire a car. (From Port Elizabeth, head east on the N2 and follow the signs. Reception open daily 7am-7pm. Park open daily 6am-7pm. In winter 7am-5:30pm. Maps provided. The park religiously enforces two rules: no citrus fruit or pets in the park, and visitors must remain inside their vehicle; violating either rule will result in expulsion. R20, children under 16 R10. To book stays in Addo campsites call ☎042 233 0556/7 or 021 422 2810; fax 233 0199; reservations@parks-sa.co.za; www.parks-sa.co.za. Camping R85 for 2 people, R15 per extra person. Electricity included.)

SCHOTIA PRIVATE GAME RESERVE

Home to the only free-feeding lions in the Eastern Cape, Schotia attracts visitors hoping to catch a glimpse of the beast on the hunt. The reserve also has other free-range game, including zebra, warthog, jackal, and crocodile. As it is a private reserve, the only way to enjoy the acacia-covered hills of Schotia is to book through their main office or one of the private tour companies in P.E. The game drive, entitled the "Tooth and Claw Night Safari," begins at 4pm and continues until after nightfall (temperature plunges; dress for weather). Thanks to the stadium-caliber spotlights attached to each vehicle, visitors can take their own snapshots. A morning tour is also offered. At 8pm, the vehicles return to the open-air lapa for a safari meal. (East of Addo Elephant Park. Take the N2 east from Port Elizabeth and follow the signs. ☎042 235 1436; fax 235 1368; schotia@intekom.co.za; www.schotia.com. Booking essential. Open daily. Guided game drive R450, meal included. Game drive R250. Transfers from P.E. R100. AmEx/MC/V.)

JEFFREYS BAY   ☎042

Surf's up all year round in Jeffreys Bay. Hardy (sometimes foolhardy) surfers brave freezing water, winter storms, and even hungry sharks to ride the world famous "Super Tubes" wave here. In the early 1990s, J-Bay (as locals call it) was one of the fastest-growing towns in South Africa, but the "white gold" industry (calamari—not cocaine) proved less lucrative than had been hoped. As a result, the town has traded its driftnets for surfboards, turning this and nearby Cape St. Francis into a mega gnarly, tubular rush for all the surfer-dudes. But whether you surf or not, Jeffreys Bay is a chill place to spend a few days.

▐ TRANSPORTATION

Buses: Baz Bus (☎021 439 2323) is your best option to get to J-Bay. Buses depart daily to **Cape Town** (13hr., 8:30am) and **Port Elizabeth** (90min., 8:30pm). Main line buses including Intercape, Translux, and Greyhound come only as close as Humansdorp, 15km away. **Sunshine Express** (☎293 2221 or 082 956 2687; fax 293 1911) provides a shuttle service from town to **Port Elizabeth** (1hr., R70); other points served upon request. Buses run according to bookings. Door-to-door service.

Minibus Taxis: On Saint Francis St. between Goedehoop St. and Salamander St. Minibuses go to **Humansdorp** (1hr., R10) and to **Port Elizabeth** (1½hr., R22).

◢◣ ▐ ORIENTATION AND PRACTICAL INFORMATION

The main drag, **Da Gama Rd.**, stretches along the coast for about 10km, but most businesses and accommodation are near the main beach. Downtown is sandwiched between the cross streets of **Woltemade St.** (to the west) and **De Reyger St.** (to the east). **Super Tubes** beach is 5km from downtown. The intersection at Da Gama and **Groedehoop** is quite big, with a Spar and other shops clustered there.

Tourist Office: (☎293 2588; fax 293 2227; jbay-tourism@agnet.co.za; www.jeffreysbay-tourism.com). At the corner of Da Gama Rd. and Dromedaris, in same building as Shell Museum. Open M-F 8:30am-5pm, Sa and holidays 9am-noon.

Banks: Standard Bank (☎293 1646), at the corner of Jeffrey and Goedehoop St. Open M-F 8:30am-3:30pm, Sa 8:30-11am. **First National Bank,** 5 Goedehoop St. (☎293 1515). Open M-F 9am-3:30pm, Sa 8:30-11am.

Laundromat: Easy Wash (☎293 2724), beneath Le Grotto. Machine R8, dryer R10-30. Wash, dry, fold R8 per kg. Drop-off service. Open M-F 8am-5pm, Sa 8am-1pm.

Police: 6 Woltemade St. (☎293 1133). **Emergency:** ☎10 111.

Pharmacy: Jeffreys Bay Pharmacy (☎293 1606, emergency 083 656 0970), at the corner of Da Gama Rd. and Goedehoop St. Open M-F 8am-5pm, Sa 8am-1pm.

Hospital: The nearest hospital is in **Humansdorp** (☎295 1100).

Internet: The Network, 5 Drommedaris St. (☎293 3239; jbaycyber@lantic.co.za). Near the main beach. R30 per hr. Open M-F 9am-5pm, Sa 9am-3pm.

Post Office: 9 De Reyger St. (☎293 1200). Open M-Tu and Th-F 8:30am-6:30pm, W 9am-4:30pm, Sa 8am-noon. **Postal code:** 6330.

▐ ACCOMMODATIONS AND CAMPING

Wetsuits don't feature deep pockets, so the J-Bay accommodations scene is geared toward budget wave riders. Most places offer surfer services such as free boards and daily transport to Super Tubes. Many pick up from Humansdorp, and some will drive out to Port Elizabeth if arrangements are made in advance.

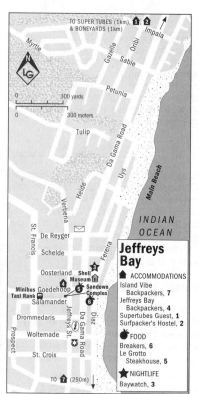

Jeffreys Bay

♠ ACCOMMODATIONS
Island Vibe
  Backpackers, 7
Jeffreys Bay
  Backpackers, 4
Supertubes Guest, 1
Surfpacker's Hostel, 2

🍴 FOOD
Breakers, 6
Le Grotto
  Steakhouse, 5

★ NIGHTLIFE
Baywatch, 3

Island Vibe, 10 Dageraad St. (☎293 1625; ivive@lantie.net; www.islandvibe-backpackers.com). From downtown, head down Da Gama Rd. (to the right facing the beach), turning left at its end onto Dageraad St. A bit of a hike from town, but it's worth it for the oceanside location. When it's too dark to surf, the action migrates to the bar; those not up for a party can chill in the garden and listen to whales doing some migrating of their own. Many activities can be arranged, including a surf school (2hr., R120), township tours, canoeing, and horseback riding. Dinners R20-30. Key deposit R20. Laundry R35 per load. Internet R1 per min. Bike hire R15 per day. Outriggers R50 per day. Surf boards and wetsuits R50 per day. 10% discount at Billabong Factory shop in town. Nightly happy hour 5:30-6:30pm. Dorms R50; doubles R140-160. Camping R35. ❶

Jeffreys Bay Backpackers (HI), 12 Jeffreys St. (☎293 1379; fax 296 1763; back-pac@netactive.co.za; www.hisa.org.za). The oldest backpackers in the area, with by far the most convenient location. A garden greets you on arrival and the "3rd night free" policy from Feb.-Nov. will encourage you to stay. Key deposit R20. Reception 8am-11pm. Dorms R80; singles R70; doubles R120. ❶

Supertubes Guest House, 6-12 Pepper St. (☎/fax 293 2957; cell 082 659 2855; supertubes@agnet.co.za). By the legendary waves. Posh guest house rooms come with TV, bath, self-catering kitchen, and great views. A great rags-to-riches story is that the adjacent house (previously a threadbare backpackers) has been converted into 4-star luxury suites equipped with heated towel racks, baths in every en suite bathroom and bar fridges. Check-in 2pm. Check-out 11am. Laundry R50 per 8kg. Dinner R60. Reception 24hr. Lodge R200; suites 350; singles in the suites R500. AmEx/MC/V. ❸

Surfpackers (☎293 2671; fax 293 3964; surfpackers@telkomsa.net; www.surfpack-ers.co.za), on Pepper St. across from Supertubes Guest House. Owners try to create a caring environment. Alcohol abuse is not allowed. Free surfboards for guests with experience and free wetsuits for everyone. All self-catering. Internet R0.50 per min. Free laundry. Reception 7am-10pm. Dorms R60; doubles R120. ❶

🔆 🍽 FOOD AND NIGHTLIFE

🍴 **Le Grotto Steakhouse** (☎293 2612 or 082 555 3936; fax 293 3355; legrotto@intekom.co.za), upstairs in Sandown Complex on Jeffreys St., between Goedehoop St. and Salamander St. A big uncomplicated restaurant known for very tasty meat. Black and white pictures of celebrities are all over the place. 1kg jumbo rump R65.50. Burgers R15.50-24.50. Grill R39.50-63.50. Take-away. Carvery on Sundays. Open M-Sa 11am-10pm, Su 11am-2pm. AmEx/MC/V. ❷

Boneyards (☎ 293 2306; pierre@boneyards.co.za; www.boneyards.co.za), at the far end of Da Gama Rd. near Wavecrest and Magna Tubes. This beachside bar and restaurant offers a more mellow party scene than some of the other more dance-oriented venues. The seafood is fresh, and live music, normally rock, plays 3 times a week. W evening is "backpacker's evening"— you can get a 3-course meal for R35. Su is African day with live reggae and drum circles. Open daily 8am-2am; low season 11am-2am. ❷

The Breakers, 22 Diaz Rd. (☎ 293 1975 or 082 782 2726) at Ferreira St. This relatively high-brow restaurant's most attractive feature is the fish tank that stretches all the way around the bar. Take away. Seafood R47-250. Cold starters and salads R8.50-33. Outside deck. Open M-Sa noon-3pm, 6-10pm; Su 6-10:30pm. ❹

Baywatch, 24 Diaz St. (☎ 293 1801) in Time Square Center. This beachfront club convincingly hawks itself as "*the* place to be" in J-Bay. Spend the early evening out on the deck enjoying a beautiful sunset view of the sea; after dark, head inside for a few drinks and to groove to anything from "boeremusiek" to rave to *kwaito*. Beers from R5.50. Shooters from R5. Live music often in Dec. Cover charge in Dec. Open daily 11am-2am.

📷 🎒 SIGHTS AND ADVENTURES

The one-room **Shell Museum,** by the tourist office, displays the future of beach-combing. (Open M-Sa 9am-4pm, Su 9am-1pm. Free.) For a personal approach to the townships surrounding J-Bay, **Goodman Alla** offers a walking tour of his neck of the woods. (3-4hr., R40. Book through Island Vibe Backpackers.) **Aloe Afrika** (☎ 296 2974 or 082 576 4259; aloe@agnet.co.za) runs a wild half-day rumble through a gorge that includes **abseiling, kloofing, swimming,** and **foefie sliding.** They also run **sandboarding** trips (both trips daily, 9am and 2pm, R150). Beachside **horseback** rides are also available (R150). The **Jeffrey's Bay Surf School** based at Island Vibe, (see **Accommodations** p. 193), provides lessons by the Eastern Province Development surf team coach, special thick beginner boards, wetsuits and rash vests (2hr., R120). They also offer custom-made, all-inclusive surf packages.

🏄 SURFING

Hundreds of die-hard wetsuits invade this town to try their luck with the waves. To join the gang, head down Da Gama Rd. about 2km to either **Magna Tubes** (a fast, intermediate wave), **Super Tubes** (a huge, long wave recommended only for experienced surfers), or the more rudimentary **Tubes.** On a good day (July is best), the waves connect, thrilling the sure-footed with an unbelievable five-minute ride. **Surfer's Point,** next to Tubes, and **Kitchen Windows,** a peak that breaks both ways near Main Beach, are best for the less experienced. The celebration of surf climaxes in July during the **Billabong Surf Classic** (www.billabongpro.com).

THE KAROO

Christened "the land of thirst," the Karoo is not your average tourist destination. Its unhappy history is plagued by the terrible dissolution of the indigenous Khoi, the ravaging Anglo-Boer wars, and the desperate retreat of the Xhosa from Shaka Zulu (see **History,** p. 54). The livelihood of its inhabitants now depends on arid plains, covered with rocky outcropping and grazing sheep. Although such a stark land may seem, at first glance, to hold little interest for travelers, visitors soon find that the Karoo's appeal lies in its isolation. The depths of the Valley of Desolation and the twisted world of Helen Martin's Owl House are striking and thought-provoking. The dedicated lifestyle of an agricultural community provides a contrast to the happy-go-lucky towns of the Garden Route.

GRAAFF-REINET ☎049

This site was the exact centerpoint of Gondwanaland, the former supercontinent of the Southern Hemisphere, which eventually split into South America, Africa, India, Australia, and Antarctica. Later, the Anglo-Boer war gave blacks and "coloureds" a long-awaited opportunity to rise against their Afrikaner masters. This collective trauma may be one of the reasons that Graaff-Reinet's residents have erected more monuments than any other South African city, earning the town the nickname "Jewel of the Karoo." In the 1980s, a wealthy local businessman started the Save Reinet Foundation, which offered interest-free loans to homeowners who agreed to restore the facades of their houses to their 19th-century look. If you ignore the satellite dishes atop many historical roofs, a stroll down the street can feel like a foray into the past.

▐ TRANSPORTATION

Intercape runs buses to: Pretoria (12hr., daily, R240) via Johannesburg (11hr., daily, R240); Plettenberg Bay (5½hr., daily, R170); Port Elizabeth (4hr., daily, R170); Durban (16hr., daily, R315) via Bloemfontein (5½hr., daily, R165). **Translux** runs to: Pretoria (Tu-Th, Sa-Su; R220-265) via Johannesburg (R220-265); Cape Town (daily, R195); East London (daily, R150). **City to City** goes to Cape Town (daily, R110) and Umtata (7hr., daily, R100). **Greyhound** runs to: Pretoria (daily, R260); Port Elizabeth (daily, R180); Durban (daily, R330) via Bloemfontein (R170). All pick-ups and drop-offs are at the **Engen Garage** on Church St. The **minibus taxi** rank is in Market Sq. Walk up Church St. until Caledon St., turn right, then right again. Minibuses go to Cape Town (7hr., 5 per week, R140) and Port Elizabeth (3½hr., 5 per week, R75).

✳❷ ORIENTATION AND PRACTICAL INFORMATION

The R75, known as the "Mohair Route," runs from the industrial city of Uitenhage through miles and miles of uninhabited land before finally reaching Graaff-Reinet. In town, it becomes **College Rd.**, which turns into **Church (Kerk) St.**, the main drag. On Church St. lie the Drostdy Hotel, the tourist office, the post office, and all the banks. Church St. ends at the big church. The cross street at the church is **Caledon St.**, which has a number of shops and places to eat. Turning left on Caledon and right onto Stockenstrom (parallel to Church St.), follow it out of town to the Karoo Nature Reserve. Following Caledon to the right leads to the **N9**, the road to Nieu Bethesda, Cradock, Middleburg, and eventually Johannesburg.

The **tourist office,** 38 Church St., has info on the area and books bus tickets. (☎/fax 892 4248; info@graafreinet.co.za; www.graaffreinet.co.za. Open M-F 8am-5pm, Sa 9am-noon.) Services include: **First National Bank,** 12 Church St. (☎892 2271; open M-F 9am-3:30pm, Sa 8:30-11am); **ABSA Bank,** 5 Church St. (☎892 4144; open M-F 8:30am-4:30pm, Sa 8am-11am); the **police station,** Middle St., down from Church St. (☎892 2283; open 24hr.); **Merino Pharmacy,** 52 Church St. (☎892 3366; emergency ☎083 305 9937; open M-F 8am-5pm, Sa 8am-1pm); **Midland Hospital,** go down Church St. until it becomes College Rd., then right onto Albertyn St. (☎892 2211; open 24hr.); **Internet** at Iets Anders, on Middle St. (☎892 2085; 1 terminal; R34 per hr.; open Tu-Su 8am-6pm); the **post office,** 28 Church St., opposite the museum (☎892 2221; open M-F 8:30am-4:30pm, Sa 8am-noon). **Postal code:** 6280.

▐ ACCOMMODATIONS

Because relatively few backpackers abandon the beaten coastal path to come to Graaff-Reinet, the hostel scene here isn't as developed as it is in other towns the

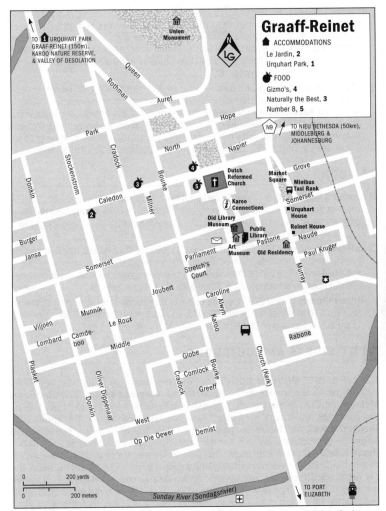

Graaff-Reinet

🏠 ACCOMMODATIONS

Le Jardin, **2**
Urquhart Park, **1**

🍎 FOOD

Gizmo's, **4**
Naturally the Best, **3**
Number 8, **5**

EASTERN CAPE

same size. Those who do visit often choose to stay in nearby Nieu Bethesda (see p. 199), which is even more isolated (albeit peacefully so).

Le Jardin Backpackin', 130 Caledon St. (☎082 644 4938; lejardinbackpackers@hotmail.com; www.abchool.com/backpackers). Entrance on Dorkin St. Not your typical South African backpackers, Le Jardin is run by an elderly and energetic couple who share their house with backpackers. Homey feel. Reception 24hr. Safe parking. All rooms R60 per person. ❶

Urquhart Park Graaff-Reinet (☎/fax 892 2136), on the parched road to the Valley of Desolation. Well-kept caravan park not too far from town. Check-out 10am. Reception 9am-9pm. *Rondavels* R80; upscale bungalows with 2 beds and bath R100. Two-bedroom chalets with kitchen R200-R250 for up to 4 people, R15 per extra person; 6-person caravan sites R50-R60. Some prices go up during school holidays. ❶

Cypress Cottages, 80 Dorkin St. (☎892 3965; cypress@yebo.co.za; www.cypresscottage.co.za). A fantastic option for families and couples, nestled in a gorgeous garden with a stunning mountain view. Partitioned into private units where guests are served breakfast at their own leisure. TV in rooms. Crystal-clear boarhole for swimming. Booking essential. Laundry. Reception 6am-10pm. Singles R250-300; doubles R400-500. Kids under 12 stay for half-price. ❸

Villa Reinet Guest Lodge, 83 Somerset St. (☎082 555 5563; villa_reinet@worldonline.co.za). A classy and more expensive option for the discerning traveler. The main house is a national monument, and the rooms are spacious and elegant, each with a different theme. Some rooms have TV and the main lodge is equipped with DVD and surround sound. Special home movie screenings are arranged (R75). Check-out 10am. Breakfast R32. Dinner R95. Laundry. Rooms R200-300 per person. MC/V. ❸

🛑 FOOD

🍴 **Number 8 Pub & Grill,** 8 Church St. (☎892 4464). A typical South African pub, ideal for any occasion. Family room, quiet dining room, and a lively hang-out area. Try the Karoo lamb chops (R36) or the *espetada* (R46). Vegetarian platter R35. Open daily 11am-11pm; bar open 11am-late. ❷

🍴 **Naturally the Best,** 104 Caledon St. (☎891 0937). Yes, indeed. Options include healthy, open-face sandwiches on homemade rye bread (R18-22), *tramezzini* (R21), and breakfasts (R16-24). If the snacks don't keep you here, the furry stock of mohair clothing certainly will. Open M-F 8:30am-5pm, Sa 8:30am-1pm. ❶

Gizmo's Pizzeria (☎892 3041), on the corner of Caledon and Queen St. Wood-oven pizzas served in a barn-styled interior. Vegetarian platter R30. Pizzas R18-50. Open daily 11am-10pm. Bar open 11am-late. Take-away. MC/V. ❷

👁 🎨 SIGHTS AND OUTDOORS

GRAAFF-REINET MUSEUM COMPLEX. Four museums, each housed in a 19th-century residence, make up the **Graaff-Reinet Museum Complex.** The **Old Library Museum,** on Church St., has an impressive collection of local prehistoric fossils, San paintings, and surreal Afrikaner formal wear from the turn of the century. The **Urquhart House,** on Market St., has a large collection of Victorian furniture and holds the genealogical records for the area. Behind it on Murray St., the **Reinet House** is best known for its huge vine, said to be one of the largest in the world. Planted in 1870, the vine remarkably still produces fruit. The fourth museum, the **Old Residency,** 1 Parsonage St., features an impressive collection of musical instruments and a good depiction of the Anglo-Boer War. *(All museums: ☎892 3801; graaffreinetmuseum@intelcom.co.za. Open M-F 8am-12:30pm and 2-5pm, Sa Old Residency and Urquhart House 9am-noon, Sa-Su Reinet House and Old Library 9am-4pm. Admission to all four museums R15, under 18 R8; any 3 R10/R6; any 1 R5-7/2.)*

HESTER RUPERT ART MUSEUM. Originally a church, this museum now has a collection of South African art that spans a wide range of 20th century artistic movements. *(Next door to the Old Library Museum on Church St. ☎892 2121. Open M-F 10am-noon and 3-5pm, Sa-Su 10am-noon. R5, children R3.)*

KAROO NATURE RESERVE. The reserve surrounding Graaff-Reinet isn't as regulated as most national parks, but it has better roads and free entrance. The most famous feature at the reserve is the **Valley of Desolation,** a rock formation of pillared columns often referred to as the quintessential Karoo landmark, showing the effects of erosion. Visitors drive to a high altitude and from there enjoy a great bird's-eye view of the columns and Graaff-Reinet. There is a short 1.5km hike leading to all the best lookout points (wear sturdy shoes). There is also a **game viewing area,** with wildebeest, zebra, kudu, springbok, and mountain redbuck. Though there are better game drives in the Eastern Cape, Karoo's free admission is rare, and the low underbrush makes game sighting easy. For longer hikes in the park, the **Eerstefontein Day Walk** starts at the Spandaukop gate off the Aberdeen Rd. Walkers then have the option of taking a 5km, 11km, or 14km hike, all of moderate difficulty. Those lacking a car but in good physical shape can rent a bike from Karoo Connection at R30 per half-day, R50 per full day. *(The Valley is 14km outside Graaff-Reinet. Take the road to Murraysburg and turn left 5km out of town. To get to the game viewing area, travel 8km outside of town along the road to Murraysburg. ☎892 3453. The Drie Koppe Hiking trail: R2; hut R15 per person, max. 10 people.)*

🔊 ADVENTURES

Karoo Connections acts much like a tourist center, with tons of info on Graaff-Reinet and the surrounding areas, tours to suit many different interests, **Internet access** (R45 per hr.), and **bicycle hire** (half/full day R30/R50). For those without transport, their tours are probably the best way to see the surrounding scenery. Cultural and historical tours include a **town walk** (2hr., R75), **Umasizakhe township walk** (2½hr., R95), **Anglo-Boer War tour** (2½hr., R95), and **Khoisan rock engravings** (2½hr., R95). Landscape and nature tours include the **Valley of Desolation** (2½hr., R90), **Karoo Nature Reserve** (2hr., R90), and **Mountain Zebra National Park** (half-day R330, full-day R495). Defying gravity and seeing the Karoo from the air is another option, whether it is in a **microlight** (30min., R450), or a **Cessna airplane** (45min., R650). A number of farm experiences are also available. *(7 Church St. ☎892 3978 or 082 339 8646; fax 891 1061; karooconnections@intekom.co.za.)*

NIEU BETHESDA ☎049

A small farming village with no more than 1000 inhabitants, a few streets, and one or two shops, Nieu Bethesda has achieved a high level of prominence. Its unlikely celebrity exists because of an artist named Helen Martins and the dazzling world she created. Reclusive and unrecognized during her lifetime, Martins used her home as a canvas on which to experiment with light and color (see **Owl House,** below). Ironically, her life, traumatic and secluded, has opened up this isolated farming village to the rest of the world.

■ ? ORIENTATION AND PRACTICAL INFORMATION

From Graaff-Reinet, follow the N9 toward Middleburg; turn left after 24km onto the extremely well-maintained gravel road. Those without a car can call the Owl House Backpackers (see **Accommodations**) for pick-up from Graaff-Reinet. Nieu Bethesda itself is small enough that most street names aren't really used or necessary. You can always orient yourself around **Martin St.,** the main road through town, or the **Owl House,** one block away. There are no banks or ATMs in Nieu Bethesda. The **post office** (☎841 1611; open M-F 8:30am-noon and 2-6pm) is next door to the **police** (☎841 1608; open M-F 8am-4pm, on-call 24hr.), one street away from Martin St. (in the opposite direction from Owl House). **Postal code:** 6286.

⌂ ◖ ACCOMMODATIONS AND FOOD

At the **Owl House Backpackers ❶** on Martin St., brilliant stars and a peaceful atmosphere more than compensate for the lack of backpacker nightlife (☎841 1642; fax 841 1657; owlhouse@global.co.za; http://welcome.to/owlhouse). Internet and laundry. Bicycle hire R20 per hr., R50 per day. Breakfast R20-28, lunch R24, dinner R15-35. Graaff-Reinet pick-ups R50. Dorms R50; doubles R120; cottages R150.) **The Village Inn ❶**, on the same street as the Owl House, serves breakfast (R15-25) and lunch (R16-25). It also rents cheap, self-catering cottages for R80-90 per person. (☎841 1605. Restaurant open Tu-Su 8am-10pm; in-season open daily.) The **Sneewitjie Restaurant ❷** is a delightfully cheerful community-run initiative to raise funds for the local school, where you can get traditional, no-nonsense South African food. (Take the road heading toward Cradock. Instead of turning off to Cradock, keep going straight. Sneewitjie is on your left. Meals of veggies and meat R30. Pudding R8. Vegetarian meals can be arranged. ☎841 1656. Open daily 6-9pm.)

🅖 SIGHTS

🦉THE OWL HOUSE. At once eerie and inspiring, disturbing and thought-provoking, the Owl House is one of South Africa's most surreal sights, one that should not be missed by tourists who find themselves anywhere near the Karoo. The house's preserved decor gives insight into the stifling family life that Helen Martins sought to escape through her art. After her parents' death in the 1940s, Helen's fascination with light, color, and the interplay of reflection and space led her to begin to transform the house that was her birthplace and home for many years. Inside, walls and windows are carpeted with a fine layer of ground-up colored glass that produces a sparkling effect. The house's mundane spaces have been filled with art: bottles of crushed glass replace food in the pantry and very little light penetrates the glass-encrusted windows. The backyard sculpture garden seems to have been Helen's true love. From commonplace materials, Helen and Koos Malgas—an itinerant sheepshearer who spent 12 years sculpting for Helen—put together an otherworldly fantasia in this crowded, chain-linked plot. Owls, camels, bejeweled hostesses, and scenes from Eastern religions all jumble together. In 1976, at the age of 78 and with failing health and eyesight, "Miss Helen" took her own life by swallowing caustic soda. Since then, at her own request, the house has been preserved as a museum. (*☎841 1603; owlhouse@ixinet.co.za; www.owlhouse.co.za. Open in summer daily 8am-6pm, in winter 9am-5pm. Tours on request. R10, students R6, 6-person family R30.*)

THE RUSTY LIZARD. Clive Lawrence looks at discarded pieces of agricultural machinery and sees birds, lizards, flowers, and cowboys. With a little bit of soldering and repositioning, the most mundane items—from exhaust pipes to bicycle chains—are reincarnated as magical creatures and sculptures. Ask for a guided tour of the collection, or let your self-guided imagination run wild. (*Near the church, 3 blocks from Martin St. away from the Owl House. ☎841 1666. Open daily 8am-6pm or whenever Clive is at home. Free, though donations are encouraged.*)

GANORA. The owners of this 4000ha farm just outside Nieu Bethesda were pleased one day to discover that signs of some of the land's ancient inhabitants still remained. They now lead excursions around Ganora to show off artifacts, fossils, Anglo-Boer War rock engravings, and San cave paintings. The fossil walk reveals several well-preserved specimens and mammal-like reptiles pre-dating dinosaurs. (*From Nieu Bethesda, head toward Cradock for 8km. ☎/fax 841 1302; ganora@owlhouse.info; http://ganora-tours. 1hr. excursions R30; 3-4hr. R65; full-day excursions including traditional meal R125. Horseback riding R40 per hr. Free walking trail through canyon town. Self-catering cottage sleeps up to 6, R95 per person. Camping in a San cave R30. Booking essential. Meals available. Breakfast R25, dinner R40-65.*)

IBIS ART CENTER. This center houses a contemporary collection of paintings and sculptures, many for sale, by local and national artists. Attached is a curio shop and accommodation booking office. (*On Martin St. ☎841 1623; ibis@intelcom.co.za; www.ibisartscentre.co.za. Open M-Sa 8:30am-4pm. Free.*)

CRADOCK   ☎ 048

In the vast desert of the Karoo, Cradock holds a near-silent vigil as a small residential outpost. In the dry plains, solitary windmills stand tall and wheel out their water slowly. In town, they stand small and silver in the souvenir shops (R20-40). Besides shopping for windmills, walking the streets, and admiring old houses, there isn't too much to do in Cradock. Olive Schreiner, author of *The Story of an African Farm*, would sympathize; she spent her adolescence here, but found the town stifling and couldn't wait to move on. Her house, now a museum, is the only real spot of interest in town, although its proximity to the magnificent **Mountain Zebra National Park** and the exhilarating whitewater rafting on the **Great Fish River** draw a few visitors to its dusty streets.

▐ TRANSPORTATION. The **train station** (☎801 8212) is across the river on Kerk St. (open M, W-F 4am-1pm; Tu, Sa-Su 4am-4pm). Trains run to Johannesburg (15hr.; Su-M, W-F 7pm; R100-165), via Bloemfontein (7hr., R55-130), and Port Elizabeth (2hr., R35-90). **Bus** tickets can be booked at **Strugwig Motors** on Voortrekker St., toward the Port Elizabeth highway. (☎881 2787. Open for bookings daily 9am-5pm.) Buses run to Cape Town (10hr., daily, R205) and East London (4½hr., daily, R130) via Queenstown (1½hr., R130). **City to City** runs to Cape Town (daily, R130). The **minibus taxi** rank is on Beerens St., just down from Stockenstroom St. Minibuses to **Port Elizabeth** (2½hr., 5am daily, R55-60) and **Queenstown** (1½hr., every morning, R43).

▌▐ ORIENTATION AND PRACTICAL INFORMATION. Most of Cradock's restaurants and hotels, as well as its **tourist office** lie along **Stockenstroom Street,** which runs parallel to the Great Fish River. The banks and post office are along **Adderley Street,** the next block inland. **Voortrekker Street** runs perpendicular to both and leads to the Port Elizabeth Hwy. The **Tourist office** is on Stockenstroom St. (☎881 2383; fax 881 1421; www.cradock.co.za. Open M-F 8:30am-12:30pm and 2-4:30pm.) Services include: **Standard Bank,** Frere St. (☎881 3029; open M-F 8:30am-12:45pm, 2-3:30pm; Sa 8:30am-11am); **police station** (☎881 7000), corner of Frere and Durban St., across from Standard Bank; **Waterson Pharmacy** (☎881 2872), on Adderley St. (Open M-F 8:30am-1pm and 2-5pm, Sa 8:30am-1pm); **Cradock Province Hospital,** two blocks farther from the center of town (☎881 2123; open 24hr.); and the **post office,** on Adderley St. (☎881 3040; open M-F 8:30am-4:30pm, Sa 8am-noon). **Postal code:** 5880.

▐ ACCOMMODATIONS AND CAMPING. Those with tents can camp at **Cradock Spa ❶,** 4km from town on Marlow Rd. (heading toward Graaff-Reinet). Although the spa features indoor and outdoor pools as well as a natural sulphur spring, it cannot be classified as the most luxurious accommodation. (☎881 2709. Camping R40 per site plus R11 per person; chalets in winter R124-208, in summer R168-251 low/high season.) In Cradock proper, the best budget option is at **106 Cawood St. ❶,** a charming white house on a quiet residential street. (☎/fax 881 3840. Table tennis. Darts. Safe parking. Breakfast R15-20. Lunch R20-30. Laundry. Reception 24hr. R80 per person.) The best-known accommodation in Cradock is undoubtedly **Die Tuishuise ❷,** 21 restored mid 19th-century houses decorated in the style of the artisans who once lived in them. The houses sleep between one and eight people and are ideal for groups seeking solace. (☎881 1322; tuishuise@eastcape.net. Meals available at Victoria Manor. Breakfast included. Reception 7am-11pm. Check-out 10am. R200 per person. AmEx/MC/V.) Of Cradock's many B&Bs, the best value is **Heritage House ❷,** 45 Bree St., around the corner from the Olive Schreiner House.

The lovely 180-year-old house is complemented by an enormous yard with gardens and a pool. (☎/fax 881 3210. Reception 7am-9:30pm. Breakfast included. Laundry. R140 per person.)

▣ FOOD. For tasty, inexpensive meals, locals head uphill to **Fiddler's Restaurant ❶**, 24 Voortrekker St., adjacent to the Total petrol station. The pizzas, starting at R16, come highly recommended. (☎881 1497. Take-away. Grills from R13-38. Open daily 7:30am-10pm. MC/V.) **Albert ❸**, in the Victoria Manor Hotel on Voortrekker St., serves tasty and filling three-course set menu dinners for R80. (☎881 1650. Reservations required. Smart casual.)

▣▨ SIGHTS AND OUTDOORS. The **Olive Schreiner Museum,** 9 Cross St., is the childhood home of the author of *The Story of an African Farm*, considered to be the first truly South African novel. From Stockenstroom St., turn right onto Cross St., walk about three blocks, and the museum is on the left. The museum displays a fascinating photographic biography of her life and the lives of other Anglo-Boer War writers. (☎881 5251. Open M-F 8:30am-12:45pm and 2-4:30pm; weekend hours by arrangement. Tours on request. Minimum R5 donation.) For more excitement, **Amanzi River Adventures,** 2 Naested St., takes adventurous travelers rafting on the Great Fish River and several other nearby rivers. Adrenaline-pumping trips run on class I-V rapids. (☎/fax 881 2976; aman@intekom.co.za.)

NEAR CRADOCK: MOUNTAIN ZEBRA NATIONAL PARK

The Mountain Zebra National Park was founded as a sanctuary for the Cape Mountain zebra, a rare species distinguished from more common zebra by its shorter mane and tendency to live in tightly-knit family groups. The species is only found in the mountainous areas of the Cape Province and is considered one of the rarest mammals in the world. The park is also home to a variety of antelope, Cape buffalo, and a few wild cats, including the lynx. Hiking is only allowed on the short trails near the rangers station where you won't see much wildlife, but the **game drives** are a treat if you have your own car. The best game drive is the **Rooiplatz Route** (2hr.). To get the most out of the experience, it's best to spend the night. (☎881 2427 or 012 346 6065; fax 881 3943. Open daily 6am-7pm; in winter 7am-6pm. R10, children R5. Campsites R40 for 2 people, R15 per extra person. Fully-equipped B&B chalets R290 for 2 people, R60-95 per extra person. Call to book.)

GRAHAMSTOWN ☎046

With lesser-known science and business festivals in April and September and its amazingly immense arts festival in July, Grahamstown always seems to be preparing to host some huge event. During the arts festival, people from all over the world bring spectacular creations and pile into Grahamstown to be immersed in the vibrant cultural explosion. While Grahamstown catches its breath during the other times of the year, it becomes a (relatively) normal university town, filled with lots of students, lots of studying, and peace and quiet.

In its early days, this cultural hotspot had a much less festive demeanor: it was once a site from which the Xhosa were pushed further and further north in the face of the land-hungry British. Founded in 1812 as a military outpost, Grahamstown began to grow in size and importance in the 1820s as settler families left their farms in search of more secure trades. Much of the city's history remains preserved in its old buildings, including the magnificent Cathedral of St. Michael and St. George (which has the tallest spire in South Africa).

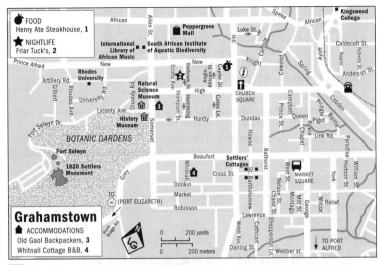

Grahamstown

♠ ACCOMMODATIONS
Old Gaol Backpackers, 3
Whitnall Cottage B&B, 4

⊨ TRANSPORTATION

Buses: Greyhound runs to **Cape Town** (14hr., daily, R235) via **Knysna** (6½hr., R110) and **Durban** (12hr., daily, R220) via **East London** (2hr., R110). **Intercape** runs to: **Cape Town** (daily, R225) via **Knysna** (R110); **Durban** (twice daily, R225) via **East London** (R105); **Port Elizabeth** (1½hr., R95, daily). **Translux** runs to: **Cape Town** (daily, R200) via **Kynsna** (R110); **Durban** (daily, R205); **Johannesburg** (10hr., daily, R250); **East London** (daily, R95); **Port Elizabeth** (daily, R70). All services offer a 15% student discount. **Baz Bus** stops at Old Gaol Backpackers.

Minibus taxis: Ranks are at Beaufort St. on the way to the township and on Raglan Rd. **Border Taxis** (☎622 2025) runs to: **King William's Town** (R35); **Port Alfred** (R20); **Port Elizabeth** (R40). **Uncedo Taxis** (☎622 2852) runs to: **East London** (R45); **Port Alfred** (R20); **Port Elizabeth** (R40).

Car Rental: Avis, in the Rhodes University Admin. Building (☎622 8233; fax 622 5090).

⊞ ORIENTATION

Somerset St. runs between Rhodes University and Grahamstown's business district. **Bathurst St.** is a wide shopping avenue that runs parallel to Somerset St. The area between these two streets is the center of downtown. Facing Rhodes University, the left-most street is **Beaufort St.**, home to the police station and a number of petrol stations. Next comes **High St.**, which is split by Church Sq. and filled with arts and crafts markets during the festival. Above High St. is **New St.**, the center of Grahamstown's restaurant scene.

⚐ PRACTICAL INFORMATION

Tourist Office: 63 High St. (☎622 3241; fax 622 3266; info@grahamstown.co.za; www.grahamstown.co.za). Up-to-date festival information and brochures on Grahamstown history. Pick up a free accommodations guide and map of the city center. Translux booking agent. **Internet** R15 per 30min. Open M-F 8:30am-5pm, Sa 8:30-noon.

Travel Agency: Sure Travel (☎ 622 2235; fax 622 3982), in Peppergrove Mall, on African St. Open M-F 8am-4:30pm, Sa 9-11:30am.

Banks: First National Bank, 102 High St. (☎ 622 7318). Open M-Tu, Th-F 8:30am-3:30pm; W 9am-3:30pm; Sa 8:30-11am. **Standard Bank,** Church Sq. (☎ 603 4700). Open M-F 9am-3:30pm, Sa 8:30-11am.

Bookstore: Checkers (☎ 622 6122), on High St. Open M-F 8am-5pm, Sa 9am-1pm.

Police: 16 Beaufort St. (☎ 603 9111, 603 9145, or 10 111). Open 24hr.

Pharmacy: Grahamstown Pharmacy, 117 High St. (☎ 622 7116). Open M-F 8am-6pm, Sa 8:30am-1pm, every 2nd Su 6-7pm. AmEx/MC/V.

Hospital: Settlers Hospital (☎ 622 2215), 15min. walk from town. Facing the front of the cathedral, turn left and walk down Hill St.; turn left at African St., right onto Milner St., and follow signs. Open 24hr.

Internet Access: Postnet, 123 High St., Shop 1a (☎ 636 2445). 2 terminals. R8 per 10min. Fax and postal services. Open M-F 8:30am-5:30pm, Sa 8:30am-1pm.

Post Office: 101 High St. (☎ 622 2340). Fax and *Poste Restante*. Open M-Tu, Th-F 8:30am-4:30pm, Sa 8am-noon.

Postal code: 6139.

⚓ ACCOMMODATIONS AND CAMPING

Though easy to find during most of the year, bargain backpackers and B&Bs are often booked months in advance during the festival. Standard hotels have no qualms about kicking their prices into the stratosphere, so it requires some creativity and patience to find a bed at a reasonable price.

Old Gaol Backpackers, 40 Somerset St. (☎ 636 1001). National monument status prevents owners from altering this converted 19th-century prison. Spotless rooms separated by thick stone walls retain their ancient, fortified feel and are accessible only through small steel doors. The harsh atmosphere won't appeal to every backpacker, and comfier budget accommodation can be arranged at Weth's Backpackers (see below). Breakfast R20; dinner R30. Laundry R20 per load. Reception open 8am-10pm. Dorms R45; doubles R110. ❶

Old Cock House, 10 Market St. (☎ 636 1287; cockhouse@imaginet.co.za). On the corner of Market and George St. Winner of the Automobile Association's best "Heritage Accommodation" award in 2002, the Cock House is a luxuriously comfortable guest house that lists Nelson Mandela as its most famous patron. TV and electric blankets in all rooms. Breakfast included. Laundry. Reception daily 7am-11pm. Singles R330; doubles R270. Both rates include breakfast. AmEx/MC/V. ❹

Whitnall's Cottage B&B, 2 Whitnall St. (☎ 622 8007). This is the cheapest centrally located B&B, but be advised if you are sensitive to living in a very religious environment: the house is adorned with a relatively large array of paraphenalia. Check-out 9am. Reception open 7am-8pm. Singles R100; doubles R200. ❶

◨ FOOD

Monkey Puzzle (☎ 622 5318), in Botanic Gardens, off the road to the Monument. Outdoor restaurant amidst lush foliage makes guests feel hidden. Student special of 6 beers and *shawerma* for R40 on Sunday nights. Steaks (including kudu and ostrich) R38-55. Kitchen open Tu, Th, Sa 6-10pm; F 12:30-10:30pm; Su 11am-10pm. Bar open Tu, Th, Sa 4pm-2am; F noon-2am; Su 11am-2am. ❷

The Mad Hatter, 118 High St. (☎622 9411). Blue, green, and orange add an appropriately curious color scheme to the Alice in Wonderland theme, turning the entire joint into a surreal tableau. Outdoor seating available. Vegetarian breakfast R23. Cottage salad R26. Wide sandwich selection R11-14. Open M-Th 7:30am-5:30pm, F 7:30am-late, Sa 8:30am-3pm. AmEx/MC/V. ❶

Calabash, 123 High St. (☎046 422 2324). A tribute to the African culture in the middle of Grahamstown's decidedly English colonial atmosphere. Traditional Xhosa Hotpots R45-47. Soups and salads R13-20. Calabash burgers R28. Reservations recommended. Open daily 7am-11:30pm. AmEx/MC/V. ❷

Henry Ate Steakhouse, 8 New St. (☎622 7261). One of the oldest and definitely the most regal restaurant in Grahamstown. Meat dishes satisfy every category of carnivore. Smart casual. Su lunch special: 3 courses R40. Starters R16-20. Open Tu-Sa 5pm-11pm, Su noon-3pm. AmEx/MC/V. ❷

◎ SIGHTS

ALBANY MUSEUM. The town's central museum is divided into three separate branches: Observatory, Natural Science, and Human History. The **Observatory Museum** is the restored Victorian home of Mr. Galpin, Grahamstown's late scientific jack-of-all-trades, and showcases the products of his academic schizophrenia. The first South African diamond was identified here, and upstairs is the only working *camera obscura* in the Southern Hemisphere. Built in 1882, it gives a 360° moving image of what's happening in and around Grahamstown. The quality of the pictures is astounding, but cannot match that of the sole tour guide, whose voice and knowledge alone are worth the price of admission. *(67 Bathurst St. ☎622 2312. Open Tu-F 9am-1pm and 2-5pm, Sa 9am-1pm. R8, students and children R5.)*

The **Natural Science Museum** features exhibits on birds, mammals, space, and the Earth, including a "Dinosaurs of the Eastern Cape" display showcasing the first dinosaur ever unearthed in South Africa. The **History Museum** has in-depth exhibits on the lives of the settlers of 1820, a genealogical office, and a gallery on contact and conflict, with relatively unbiased information on the Eastern Cape wars between the Xhosa and the British. Displays include some exquisite beadwork and traditional Xhosa attire. *(Museums are side-by-side on Somerset St. ☎622 2312. Both open Tu-F 9:30am-1pm and 2-5pm, Sa 9:30am-1pm. Each museum R8, students and children R5.)*

DAKAWA ART PROJECT. The organizers of the Dakawa project are dedicated to community revitalization. Having founded an artistic and entrepreneurial skills center for the education of local artists, the project seeks to support traditional artistic effort. Organizers assist in the sale of works at local fairs and markets and provide the entrepreneurial skills necessary for artists to support themselves and their art. Visitors are welcome to meet the artists and watch them at work, as they transform rough pieces into exquisite carvings, weavings, and paintings. *(From Somerset St., turn right onto African St. and follow to large intersection where African becomes Caldecott St. At the next intersection, bear left onto Currie St. Dakawa is on the right. ☎622 9733. Open M-F 8am-4:30pm, Sa-Su 8am-4:30pm.)*

SOUTH AFRICAN INSTITUTE FOR AQUATIC BIODIVERSITY. Something lurks beneath the surface of this Institute, where a basement laboratory houses the second-largest collection of preserved fish in the southern hemisphere. If you've got the time, spend it strolling amongst the 2km of fish-covered shelves and get blown away by the ferocity of the jaws of a Great White. Above-ground exhibits are devoted to the story of the coelacanth, a 200-million-year-old fish thought to be extinct until the 1930s. *(On Somerset St. near the University. ☎636 1002. Open M-F 8am-1pm and 2-5pm. Free. Tours can be arranged on request.)*

INTERNATIONAL LIBRARY OF AFRICAN MUSIC (ILAM). Part of the Rhodes University campus, the ILAM houses a large collection of instruments and recordings. Innovation abounds, with instruments created from everything and anything. Those with a special interest in African music can call to make an appointment for a demonstration. *(From Somerset St., turn left on Prince Alfred St.; look for signs to the right. Director ☎ 603 8557. Open M-F 8:30am-12:45pm and 2:15-4:35pm. Donations appreciated.)*

UMTHATHI TRAINING PROJECT. A non-profit organization aimed at enriching the lives of Grahamstown's underprivileged residents. The group offers a township tour and a meal. The tour includes visits to Xhosa homes and schools. *(Spoornet Station Building on Lower High St. ☎ 622 4450. Open M-F 8am-1pm, 2-5pm.)*

⚑ NIGHTLIFE

Pop Art Cafe, 16-18 New St (☎ 622 4729). This inventively decorated student "jol," a popular bar/club, has a backyard garden that provides it with a themed dance floor. Mixed crowds ensure a range of music, and a visiting DJ spins monthly. Beer R7, cocktails R10-20. Free. Cover during Festival R30, R20 before 10pm. Open M-Sa noon-late.

Rat and Parrot, 59a New St. (☎ 622 5002). This dark wood pub attracts straight-laced rugby and cricket-loving Rhodes students. The Rat (as it is affectionately called) is almost always crowded, filled with a young, cheerful vibe. Open daily 11am-2am.

Friar Tuck's Pub 'n Grill (☎ 622 4511) on Bertram St., off New St. The newest party venue in Grahamstown, blasting mostly commercial CDs to a mostly Rhodes student crowd. Open daily 11am-2am. Free.

⚑ GRAHAMSTOWN ART FESTIVAL

Once a year, Grahamstown explodes into the most vibrant city in Africa. For 11 days in July, thousands of arts patrons converge for the second largest arts festival in the world (only Scotland's Edinburgh festival is larger). Streets are packed with foreigners and South Africans from all walks of life. Universities and high school classrooms transform into backpackers, sports fields become campsites, and numerous private residences throw open their doors, all to make room for the influx of culture vultures descending upon Grahamstown.

FESTIVAL TIPS

Before arriving in Grahamstown, try to get your hands on a copy of the **Festival Booking Kit** (see below), published by the Grahamstown Foundation. Book far in advance for the larger productions put on in the **Monument Theatre.** Upon arrival in Grahamstown, it's best to purchase tickets for smaller performances ASAP. There are many precautions you can take in order to make yourself a happier *festino* (festival-goer). Be cautious with what you carry and display—such hectic streets are prime territory for pickpockets and petty thieves. Save plenty of time to bargain with craft vendors and frequent the festival's **fringe shows** (alternative productions by up-and-coming theater and music students). The bulky, official **festival program** (R30) can be purchased at the hill-top **Monument,** the festival's official base of operations. The **CUE,** the daily festival newspaper, provides additional news and tips. Dress in layers if you can— Grahamstown weather is highly temperamental, especially in July. Comfortable shoes and feet will make long hours of cultural absorption more enjoyable.

In its 28th year in 2002, the Grahamstown Festival showcased nearly 200 plays, cabarets, art exhibits, films, modern and classical music concerts, dance performances, and lectures. Hundreds of other activities and events form a supplement to the main schedule with Festival "Fringe," including over 1000 crafts vendors, two Jazz Festivals, and Wordfest—a celebration of the written word. For first-time *festinos*, the high-octane goings-on can be quite overwhelming, even with the help of exceptionally gracious locals and festival staff. The internationally available **Festival Booking Kit** lists the dates, times, and locations of the events composing the main festival. This kit can be ordered from the **National Arts Festival Grahamstown Foundation** (☎603 1164; fax 622 3082; naf@foundation.org.za; www.nafest.co.za).

█.█ FESTIVAL ACCOMMODATIONS AND FOOD. With almost 100,000 people squeezing into Grahamstown, it's a wonder that everyone finds a place to bed down for the night. Most hotels and B&Bs are booked well in advance of the festival, often at grossly inflated prices. But never fear: housing somehow appears for late-comers and stragglers alike. True daredevils might find it easiest to locate a spare stretch of floor (though such a method has obvious risks). Accommodation at the backpackers (see **Accommodations**, p. 204) is first come, first served, so it's worth an attempt the morning you arrive; if full, they usually try to help visitors sort out alternative places to stay. Most high schools offer campsites for less than R30. For those who prefer a roof over their head, **Rhodes University, Kingswood College** and **Victoria Girls High School**, on break during the festival, open up their dorms to *festinos* for around R100 per night. Reservations can be made on arrival or through the **Grahamstown Accommodation Guild** at 65 High St. (☎622 5777; fax 622 8949; booking@grahamstownaccomm.co.za; www.grahamstownaccom.co.za). The Guild will either be able to find you housing directly or refer you to one of numerous housing agencies for assistance. Festival food comes in all shapes, sizes, and varieties, from Belgian waffles to *boerewors*. There is always food available just behind the Cathedral in Church Sq. or on the Village Green, and a number of homes also become makeshift restaurants for the week.

EAST LONDON ☎043

The industrial capital of the Eastern Cape and the key transportation hub into the Ciskei and Transkei homelands, East London is rife with warehouses, manufacturing firms, and impersonal buildings. While downtown features the Steve Biko memorial monument and a surprisingly good museum and art gallery, most visitors head straight to the beach. Tales abound of shark visits to Nahoon Beach and Bonza Bay—East London's most popular stretches of shore—but surfers claim there's no danger. If you do spot a "shark warning" sign, you're better off visiting wildlife at Mpongo Park or just lying on the sand.

█ TRANSPORTATION

Flights: East London Airport (☎706 0211). From downtown, follow Fleet St. until it becomes the R72. Continue for about 5km after crossing the Buffalo River; the airport is on the right. For a shuttle from town to the airport, call ☎082 569 3599 at least a day in advance (starting at R50 from most locations). **South African Airways** (☎706 0203) flies to: **Cape Town** (2½hr., 3 per day, R1012); **Durban** (1¼hr., 2-3 per day, R1000); **Johannesburg** (1½hr., 4 per day, R1037).

Trains: Train station (☎086 000 8888; www.spoornet.co.za), on Station St. at the corner of Terminus St. It's called "Shosholoza Mail"—don't be confused. One train to **Johannesburg** (18hr.; noon; 2nd class R200, 1st class R295) via **Bloemfontein** (13hr.; 2nd class R125, 1st class R180). Open M-F 8am-5pm; Sa-Su 8am-noon. Trains run every day except W and Sa. Arrive 30min. prior to departure.

Buses: Start down Esplanade St. towards Eastern Beach, turn inland onto Moore St., then onto Windmill Rd; the bus complex is on the right. **Greyhound** office (☎743 9284) open M-Sa 7:30am-7:30pm, Su 10am-7:30pm. **Intercape** office (☎722 2254; fax 722 2235) open M-Sa 8am-5pm, Su 10am-noon and 2-4pm. **Translux** office (☎700 9099) open daily 7:30am-8:30pm. All lines run buses to: **Cape Town** (17hr., 3 per day, R230); **Durban** (10hr., 3 per day, R155); **Johannesburg** (13hr., 2 per day, R285); **Port Elizabeth** (4hr., 3 per day, R115). **Baz Bus** (☎021 439 2323) picks up backpackers from both Grahamstown hostels daily en route to **Durban** or **Port Elizabeth.**

Minibus Taxis: Long-distance minibuses wait at corner of North and Buffalo St. From Oxford St., turn left onto North St. To: **King William's Town** (30min., R20); **Port Elizabeth** (2½hr., R77); **Queenstown** (1¾hr., R37.50); **Umtata** (2½hr., R65).

Taxi: Hermon's Taxi (☎743 8076) or **Nyongo Taxis** (☎741 0481).

■✱🔢 ORIENTATION

Oxford St. runs through the central business district (CBD) and houses the tourist office, banks, and post office. Running parallel to Oxford St., **Station St.** is home to the train station. **Fleet St.** is perpendicular to Oxford St. and leads to the beachfront suburb of Quigney. Lined with most accommodations, food, and nightlife stops, **Esplanade St.** wraps around the waterfront from Orient Beach to Eastern Beach. From downtown, drive up Oxford St. to reach the Vincent Park Shopping Mall, on Devereux St., as well as the town's museums.

Tourist Office: 35 Argyle St. (24hr. hotline ☎722 6015; fax 743 5091; eltout@mweb.co.za; www.tourismbuffalocity.co.za). Turn off Oxford St. at City Hall and the statue of Steve Biko. Open M-F 8:15am-4:30pm, Sa 9am-noon.

Banks: ABSA, 85 Oxford St. (☎722 3128; fax 722 1283). *Bureau de change.* Open M-F 8:30am-3:30pm, Sa 8-11am. **Rennies,** 23 Chamberlain St. (☎726 0698). Doesn't charge commission to exchange traveler's checks. Open M-F 9am-4pm, Sa 9-11am.

Laundromat: Wishing Well Laundrette (☎722 2805), in Inverleith Center at the corner of Currie and Inverleith. Wash/dry R8 per kg. R9 per machine, R5 per dryer. Open M-F 7:45am-5:30pm, Sa 8:15am-5pm, Su 9am-4pm.

Police: 3 Fleet St. (☎722 5555). Walk down Oxford St., turning right toward Market Sq. onto Fleet St; the station is on the left.

Hospital: East London Private Hospital, 32 Albany St. (☎722 3128). Head up Oxford St. and turn left onto Albany St. The hospital is on the left.

Internet: Sugarshack Backpackers (see **Accommodations,** below). R1 per min.; R0.50 from 7pm-7am and on weekends. **East London Backpackers** (R36 per hr.).

Post Office: (☎743 3855), on Oxford St. between Terminus and Union St. Open M-Tu and Th-F 8:30am-4:30pm, W 9am-4:30pm, Sa 8am-noon. **Postal code:** 5211.

🏠 ACCOMMODATIONS AND CAMPING

Niki-nana Backpackers, 4 Hillview Rd. (☎/fax 722 8509; info@nikinana.co.za; www.nikinana.co.za). Follow Esplanade until it leads into Currie Rd. Take a left on Bonanza, then a right onto Hillview. Zebra-stripe decor makes Niki-nana impossible for motorists to miss. This small, lovingly furnished backpacker exudes a relaxed, African-themed vibe. Pool. Free airport bus and shuttle. Reception 24hr. Laundry R25 per load. 7th night free. Breakfast R20. Lunch R20. Dinner R35. Key deposit R20. Pool table. Internet R10-15 per hr. Dorms R55; doubles R140. ●

Sugarshack Backpackers (☎722 8240 or 083 320 5406; sugarsk@iafrica.com), at the far end of Esplanade St. after it becomes one-way. From Mire St., turn right onto John

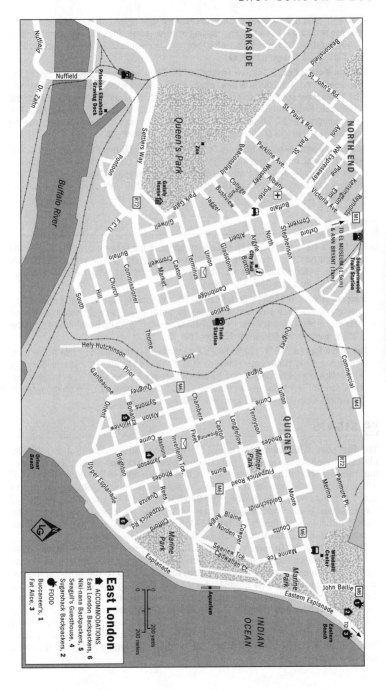

East London

⌂ ACCOMMODATIONS
East London Backpackers, 6
Niki-nana Backpackers, 5
Seagull's Guesthouse, 4
Sugarshack Backpackers, 2

◆ FOOD
Buccaneer's, 1
Fat Alice, 3

EASTERN CAPE

Bailie St. past the entrance to Buccaneer's, then right again onto Esplanade. Close to the ocean and the bus stop. Free surfing lessons, horse rides (R130), sandboarding (R60), bowling and more. Laundry R30 per load. Internet R0.50-1 per min. Dorms R50; doubles R120. Camping R40. ❶

Dolphin View Lodge, 6 Seaview Terrace (☎702 8600; after hours 082 904 9833). Off Esplanade from O'Hagan's. A new, classy and upmarket establishment removed from the backpacker scene. Plush couches and big comfy beds definitely make it worth the extra cash. Reception 8am-5pm. Check-out noon. Breakfast included; dinner R85. Per-item laundry charge. Singles R220; doubles R400. Prices exclude VAT. Self-catering apartment sleeping 8 people available at R5000 per month. ❸

Seagull's Guesthouse, 34 Bonanza St. (☎722 1049). Off Currie St., on the right. A reasonable option for all those with slightly deeper pockets. Clean, old-fashioned rooms all have TV. Laundry R15 per load. Key deposit R200. Reception 24hr. Check-out 10am. Singles R120, with breakfast R135; doubles R180/R205. Self-catering flat R280 per night. DC/MC/V. ❷

🍴 FOOD

▨ **Fat Alice's** (☎/fax 726 7541), in Nahoon opposite the caravan park. An eclectically decorated restaurant featuring international cuisine. Some nice vegetarian options available. Reservations preferred. Starters R17-23. Main dishes R29-52. Open Tu-Sa 7pm-10pm, Su 11am-3pm. MC/V. ❷

Buccaneer's (☎743 5171), on John Bailie St., overlooking Esplanade and next to Sugarshack. Good value pub food, especially for those staying at Sugarshack; a voucher gets you a free beer with every meal. Pool tables and TV. "Lite bites" R8-26, "For the hungry" R25-34. No one under 18 after 7pm. ❶

The Black Pan (☎743 3710), in King's Entertainment Center next to Virgin Active Gym. A new and funky family eatery ideal no matter how old you are. Art students' paintings and sculptures are on display and for sale. A special kids' room with a babysitter is provided. Lots of vegetarian dishes (R22.50-25.50). Steaks from R30. Reservations taken. Take-away. Open daily 7am-11pm. MC/V. ❶

👁 SIGHTS

The **East London Museum,** 319 Oxford St., houses exhibits of natural and African history, including the world's only dodo bird egg and anthropological displays highlighting the cultures of the Xhosa and Khoi-San. (☎743 0686. Open M-F 9:30am-5pm, Sa 2-5pm, Su 11am-4pm. R5, senior citizens R3, children under 18 R0.50, students with valid ID free.) The **Gately House,** 1 Park Gates Rd., a satellite of the museum, is also worth a visit. Built in 1878 by the city's first mayor, John Gately, it displays his family's original belongings. (☎722 2141. Open Tu-Th 10am-1pm and 2-5pm, F 10am-1pm, Sa-Su 3-5pm. Admission by donation.)

The **Ann Bryant Art Gallery,** 9 St. Mark's Rd., a well-preserved late-Victorian mansion, displays a collection of mostly 18th- and 19th-century European works, as well as an exhibition on Southern African art from 1920 to the present. Inquire about the resident ghost. (☎722 4044; fax 743 1729. Gallery open M-F 9am-5pm, Sa 9am-noon. Free, but donation requested.) If art and history aren't your bag, check out the **East London Aquarium,** on the Esplanade. Though small and of limited interest to adults, the aquarium's seal shows and fish feeding will delight the young—or the young at heart. (☎705 2637; fax 743 6801; fela@iafrica.com. Open daily 9am-5pm, seal shows 11:30am and 3:30pm, fish feeding 10:30am and 3pm. R8, ages 3-16 and senior citizens R6.)

NIGHTLIFE

East London's night scene is focused around a small but quality group of establishments which cater to most tastes. **The Hub,** on Bonza Bay Rd in Beacon Bay, is a prime spot. The stainless steel interior, 2m mirror ball, and sunken dance floor give it a classy air. "Fiesta nights" take place on Sa (drinks R5 all night). There is a guest DJ twice per month, and otherwise mostly pop and dance music. Cover W and F R20, before 10pm R10; Sa R30. Open W, F 9pm-2am, Sa 9pm-4am.)

The dance floor at **Buccaneer's** (see **Food,** above) hosts some of South Africa's biggest bands. (Cover W-Sa R5 after 7pm. Live bands R10.) For a quieter night, visit the **Ster-Kinekor Cinema** (☎ 086 0300 2222) at Vincent Park Mall.

THE WILD COAST

Between the Great Kei River in the south and the Umtamvuna River in the north lies an expanse of land graciously named "the Wild Coast." Perhaps it earned its name from its array of wildlife, intense indigenous forests, rolling grass hills, and subtropical thickets. Perhaps the name refers to the untamed feel of a land inhabited by countless species, each providing a flash of color, distinct melody, and another set of footprints for the eager hiker to discover. Or perhaps the name refers to the traditions and culture of the struggling population living within pastel, thatched-roof homesteads dotting the hills. Whatever the etymology, the area's beauty and cultural vibrance has not been cost-free. As one of the "homelands" created during apartheid, the Wild Coast—part of the Transkei—was starved of investment, left with little infrastructure and little organized tourism.

The region is almost entirely made up of Xhosa people, whose political activism and power has been rivaled only by

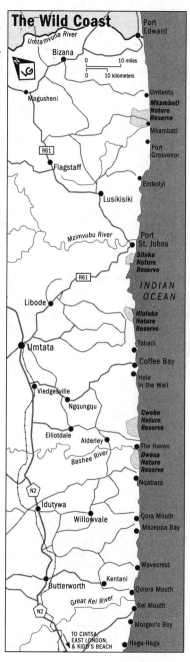

The Wild Coast

EASTERN CAPE

that of the neighboring Zulus, their long-time political foes and now uncomfortable bedfellows. An intertwined white bohemian class thrives on the area's isolation as well as on its *dagga* (marijuana)—it hasn't been nicknamed the "Ganja Coast" for nothing.

The most popular destinations—Port St. Johns, Coffee Bay, and Cintsa—have well-developed backpacker services, including shuttles to Umtata and East London. However, remote parts of the Wild Coast are highly rewarding to those who make the extra effort to reach them. The highlights of the area are the five secluded nature reserves (Dwesa, Cwebe, Hluleka, Silaka, and Mkambati), most of which can be reached along the multi-day hiking trails that stretch the length of the coast. Once you have eaten fresh oysters off the rocks after spending the night in an isolated coastal reserve, you may be ready to trade civilization for the Wild.

CINTSA ☎ 043

Close to the Wild Coast but not actually a part of it, Cintsa invites travelers in to the Transkei's relaxed way of life. Somewhat built-up, Cintsa has more of a holiday feel to it than the other stops further down the coast in the Transkei. Many of the holiday homes lie behind coastal bush, and the beaches are not overly populated, allowing a touch of refreshment after East London's concrete sprawl. Two exceptional backpackers allow you to enjoy the coastal town and its offerings with a pinch of adventure thrown into the mix.

■ ⁊ ORIENTATION AND PRACTICAL INFORMATION. To get to Cintsa from the N2, take Exit 26, about 25km northeast of East London, and follow the signs for East Coast Resorts. The **Cintsa River** and the salty estuary into which it flows divide the Cintsa area into two parts. The town center resides on the northern shore of the estuary and is called **Cintsa East;** south of the estuary is **Cintsa West.** About 16km from Exit 26, a turn-off for Cintsa West leads down to the two hostels of note. Four kilometers down the road, another turn-off leads to Cintsa East (12km). It takes about 10min. to walk from Cintsa West to Cintsa East along the beach, but nearly 30min. to drive there due to indirect roads.

If you are carless, call one of the hostels listed below; both provide free pick-up from East London almost daily. Alternatively, take the **Baz Bus** (☎ 021 439 2323), which stops at both of the hostels on its way to or from East London. There is **no tourist office** in town, but the owners of Buccaneer's (see **Accommodations,** above) are knowledgeable and helpful. There is an **ATM** next door to the Cintsa East Store and Bakery, a.k.a. Fred's Store (☎ 738 5202), in the Cintsa shopping center on Cintsa Dr. in Cintsa East just past the country club. Fred will give cash advances from credit cards for an extra 5%, and the store sells **groceries** and delicious fresh bread. Michaela's (see **Food,** below) accepts US, British, and Australian currency. The nearest **hospital** is in East London (see p. 208). There is **Internet access** at Buccaneer's and Moonshine (R40 per hr.). The **post office** is in the Cintsa East Store and Bakery (open daily 6:30am-6pm). **Postal code:** 5275.

▐ ▐ ACCOMMODATIONS AND FOOD. Follow the signs at the final Cintsa West turn-off to reach ▨ **Buccaneer's ❷,** well deserving of its reputation as one of the best backpackers in the country.The complex of dorms and private doubles offers a stunning view of wide golden beaches, inviting surf, and a line of hills stretching to the estuary's sandy southern banks. Rooms are clean, comfortable and often luxurious. A fully equipped bar (bringing Cintsa's nightlife to your doorstep) is accompanied by a swimming pool, *braai*, and a long table for delicious home-cooked meals (breakfast R10-25; sandwich bar from R10; dinner R25-45; Sa night 3 course-traditional Xhosa meal with wine R48). Buccaneer's offers a dizzying array of complimentary frills, including canoes, surfboards, bodyboards, a small climbing wall, volleyball court, cultural performances, sundowner trips, and even transport to a local *shebeen* (all activities also offer free wine). Buccaneer's also runs fundraising programs for a school nearby that guests can visit. **Cintsa Adventure Co.** (see **Outdoors,** below) is based here. (☎734 3012; fax 734 3749; cintsabp@iafrica.com; www.cintsa.com. Internet R25 per 30min. Reception 8am-10pm. Check-out 11am. Key deposit R50. Laundry R25 per load. Dorms R60; doubles R150-165. Camping R30. MC/V.)

Cintsa Moonshine Backpackers ❶, near the beach, is a castle painted with geckos and excited bushmen. It lacks the hyper-positive vibe and 180-degree view of Buccaneer's, but shares amenities with the nearby Cintsa West Resort; guests can plunge into the sparkling pool and use the squash tennis courts free of charge. Generally for a more quiet and mature crowd. Dorms are single-sex. (☎734 3590; fax 734 3990. Laundry R25 per load. Breakfast R25. Dinner R30. Dorms R50; singles R180; doubles R120. Camping R25.) Next to Cintsa Moonshine Backpackers in Cintsa West, the **Cintsa Bay Pub and Grub ❶** has a sun deck with ocean views and a shady pub area. Standard surf and turf menu includes breakfasts (R7-24), light lunches (R18-27), and burgers (R17). (☎734 3230 or 083 283 7024. Open Su-M 9:30-4pm, Tu-Sa 9:30am-9pm.) Next to Fred's store in Cintsa East is **Pig n' Pool ❷,** an uncomplicated pub and grill with pool tables and TVs. (☎738 5240. Open M 8am-6pm, Tu-Su 8am-9pm. Toasties R7.50-11.50; "specialities" R32.50-48.)

For a fancier feast, treat yourself to a meal at ▨**Michaela's ❸,** on Steenbras Dr. in Cintsa East. Enjoy the funicular ride or climb the 133 steps to the restaurant; its altitude, quality, and price are all loftier than most. The large outer deck provides a panoramic view of forest and ocean, which makes it the perfect spot for drinks or a romantic meal. (☎738 5139; info@michaelas.co.za; www.michaelas.co.za. Bookings essential. Open M, W-Sa 11am-2:30pm and 6-9:30pm, Su 12:30-2:30pm. Bar open daily until late. Sunday buffet R75. Fillet steak R69.)

◪ OUTDOORS. Cintsa Adventure Company (based at Buccaneer's; see **Accommodations and Food,** p. 212) offers a ton of activities. For the bodaciously far-out, the full-day surf school, including two meals and all equipment, is a great deal at R150, dude. For culture buffs, the Southern Kei day tour, with a visit to traditional Xhosa villages, a Xhosa historical site, and lunch on the Kobonaga River, is sure to please (R235). Other options are the full-day abseiling and ropes course, with training and climbing on-site at the Kwelega River (R125, lunch included), and a 4-day African heartland trip, with visits to the stunning 100m Magwa Fallas and mountain biking through the Mibikaba Nature Reserve (R1000, all meals included). The recently-opened **Inkwenkwezi Private Game Reserve** (☎734 3234; fax 734 3888; pgr@inkwenkwezi.co.za; www.inkwenkwezi.co.za) offers a taste of the Big Five from a coastal haven. The reserve's two rhinos have become relatively accustomed to humans and often hang out near the front entrance. A 3-4hr. 4x4 tour through Inkwenkwezi (Xhosa for "stars in the sky") will give you a glimpse of many of the park's residents (R125), while the same amount of time on horseback will provide a more intimate view (R100; no experience necessary). Three rides depart daily; book ahead. Private vehicles are not allowed in the park.

◪ SURFING. Any possible coastline adventure, including sunrise and sunset horseback rides on the beach, can be planned and arranged at the hostels. But you don't need guidance to surf—just dive in. The town's **surfing** haven lies directly in front of **Cintsa East,** where the beach break generates peaks with rights as well as lefts for all the goofy-footed board riders. Farther southwest in front of **Cintsa West,** the generic right-hand point break often has good rights on bigger swells. For the best waves in the area, head down to **Queensberry Bay,** a right-hand point break that can handle swells up to 4m. To get there, take the Gonubie exit from the N2 and follow the signs to East Coast Resorts.

EASTERN CAPE

COFFEE BAY   ☎ 047

Coffee Bay's main advantage (or disadvantage) is its feeling of being nowhere in particular—or at least very far from anywhere. Homesteads dotting the horizon from one hill to the next accentuate the vastness of the surrounding space. With a magical cast of local flavors at work, it can be very difficult to rationally explain how time seems to fly by here. Don't even try—just enjoy it.

TRANSPORTATION. Coffee Bay is one of the few destinations in the Transkei with a paved road from the N2. However, with the number of potholes, goats, sheep, cattle, horses, and pigs in the road, even paved driving is still an adventure. The turn-off for Coffee Bay is 21km from Umtata and another 80km from Coffee Bay itself. For those arriving in Umtata, the **Baz Bus, Greyhound,** or **Translux,** shuttles from all the backpackers can arrange to meet these buses at the Shell Ultra City and, for about R35, take you to their respective hostels. **Minibus taxis** head from Umtata to Mqanduli (R12), and from there to Coffee Bay (R18).

ORIENTATION AND PRACTICAL INFORMATION. The road from the N2 enters town down a steep hill, leading eventually across the Bomvu River. There are **no ATMs, banks,** or **currency exchange** options in Coffee Bay. The **police station** is 5km from town on the road to the N2. (Open 24hr.) The closest decent **hospital** is in Umtata (see p. 216). **Pay phones** are outside the **Bomvu River Grocery Store,** on the far side of the river next to the Coffee Shack. (Open M-F 7am-7pm, Sa-Su 8am-5pm.) The **post office** is in the Coffee Bay Shop next to the Ocean View Hotel. (☎ 575 2015. Open daily 7am-5pm.) **Postal code:** 5082.

ACCOMMODATIONS AND FOOD. With several quality backpackers in Coffee Bay, you can't go wrong. Offering visitors a "holistic alternative" is **Bomvu Backpackers ❶,** on the far side of the river. If you're into yoga and the Reiki healing method (a method of healing by transferring energy), then this is your place. The drum circle, surf shop, volleyball court, and horse rides definitely provide ample alternatives to the "alternative." There is also a restaurant that dishes up organic food. Around July every year they host a musical festival at their natural amphitheater on the banks of the river. (☎/fax 575 2073; bomvu@interkom.co.za; www.bomvubackpackers.co.za. Umtata pick-ups R35; call ahead. Reception daily 8am-5pm. Breakfast R10-20. Dinner R25-50. Laundry R10. Dorms R50; loft dorms R45; doubles R100-140. AmEx/MC/V.) **The Coffee Shack ❶,** across the road from the Bomvu, is known up and down the coast for its location and party atmosphere. Whether they've got you revelling in a traditional Xhosa headman's evening (every Friday night, R30 for dinner in traditional village, R20 of which goes to the community), testing the extent of your nerves with abseiling (R75), or riding waves for hours on Umdumbi Beach (full day including lessons R50), you will never, ever, be bored. (☎ 575 2048, 082 236 2251; coffeeshack@wildcoast.com. Internet R0.50 per min. Dinner R25. Dorms R50; doubles R120. Camping R25.)

Four Winds Lodge and Backpackers ❶, is a newly-opened backpacker a 5min. walk from the beach. The owners' curio shop—with shells and sticks undertaking a creative metamorphosis—might inspire artistic leanings. To get here, look for the zebra-striped walls and the "this is it" sign on the road from Umtata, or call and arrange a shuttle. (Breakfast R15-20. Dinner R25. Reception 24hr. Dorms R45; singles R75; doubles R150.) Virtually every night, local children perform traditional singing and dancing at Bomvu and Coffee Shack; be ready to give a few rand (or more). Blatantly, the most luxurious and expensive option in Coffee Bay is the **Ocean View Hotel ❹.** To get there, turn off the road into town at the low-level bridge and follow the signs for about 1km. The room furnishings are comfortable if not spectacular, which is more than compensated for by the stunning views, particularly in the sea-facing rooms. Large pool and trampoline. Mountain bike hire R20 for half-day. Free boogie board rental. Guided hikes to Hole in Wall R40. (☎/fax 575 2005/6; oceanview@coffeebay.co.za; www.oceanview.co.za. Reception 7am-10pm. Sea-facing rooms R325. Garden-facing rooms R250. AmEx/D/MC/V.)

IF EVERYBODY JUMPED OFF A CLIFF...

...you probably would, too. Cliff jumping (*kloofing*) is an increasingly popular pastime in South Africa. Although die-hards will find cliffs from which to throw themselves all over the country, the most commonly jumped cliffs are found between Cape Town and the Wild Coast. Jumps range from the height of a regular diving board to as high as your insanity will take you—some *kloofers* have been known to leap from heights of over 30m. When it comes to *kloofing*, peer pressure works in magical ways.

◨ ⚑ **SIGHTS AND OUTDOORS.** Coffee Bay has several local craft shops for the artistically inclined. Opposite the police station, 5km before Coffee Bay, is a brightly painted complex housing the **Masizame's Women Project,** a place for local artisans to display their work. (Open daily 6:30am-6pm.) Another interesting stop is **Mawawa's Crafts,** 250m from Coffee Shack on the way back out of town. The right-hand point in front of the Ocean View Hotel is a popular **surfing** break. The breakers at **Mdumbi,** a 2½hr. hike to the north, are the kindest in the area. In and around Coffee Bay, **hikes** abound in a choose-your-own-adventure deluge of opportunities. Take either a 6km hike south out to **Hole in the Wall** (p. 215), or hike to the mouths of the Mpuzi, Umtata, and Mdumbi Rivers. There are no formal trails; part of the beauty is finding the best route. Bring R5 and old shoes for the ferry across the Umtata River mouth.

NEAR COFFEE BAY: HOLE IN THE WALL   ☎ 047

About 6km south of Coffee Bay on rough roads, there is a hole carved into a cliff face out at sea. It provides exquisite scenery and a cliff-jump site with a difference. From a ledge on the side of the hole, those with nerves of steel—and a good swimming background—can hold their breath, wait for the right wave, and dive into the turbulent waters below. This is a "don't-try-it-alone" jump; make sure you are with someone who knows when and how to do the dive. The waves below can be very powerful. If you hiked and dove and don't have the energy to hike back, nearby **Hole in the Wall Backpackers ❶** provides cozy budget accommodations and organizes cultural tours, horse trail rides, free surfboards, and bodyboards. Shooters from the bar are R5. Take the Hole in the Wall turn-off on the Coffee Bay Rd and look for the hostel after about 32km. Free pick-ups from The Coffee Shack are available. (☎ 575 0009 or 083 317 8786; fax 575 0010. Breakfast R10-20. Dinner R30. Laundry R15 per load. Cultural tours R20. Trail tides R50 per hr. Reception 8am-8pm. Dorms R55; doubles R130. Camping R35. 4th night free. AmEx/DC/MC/V.)

UMTATA   ☎ 047

Umtata's derives its name from the river running through it. The river itself was named by the Amangcengana, who heaved their dead into the water with the cry, "*mThate Bawo!*" ("Take him, father!"). Today, Umtata is one of the less pleasant places to pass time. It is, however, the largest city in the Transkei and the only place near Coffee Bay or Port St. Johns with bank service, hospitals, and large shopping centers. It is also the only bus stop near PSJ or Coffee Bay.

EASTERN CAPE

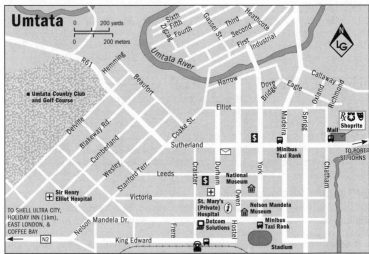

☰ TRANSPORTATION. **Translux, Intercape,** and **Greyhound** run daily to: **Cape Town** (17hr., R210-330); **Durban** (8hr., R150-170); **East London** (R95-115); **Port Elizabeth** (9hr., R175-195). Translux also runs to **Pretoria** and **Johannesburg** (daily, 12hr., R210-230). All buses, including the **Baz Bus,** stop at the Shell Ultra City petrol station. **Shuttles** from hostels in Port St. Johns and Coffee Bay meet travelers at the Ultra City daily. The **minibus taxi** ranks are beside the train station and at the corner of Sutherland and Madeira St. There is also a rank in the parking lot of the ShopRite Center along the road to Port St. Johns.

🛈 PRACTICAL INFORMATION. The **Eastern Cape Tourism Board,** 64 Owen St., has free maps of Umtata and the Wild Coast, as well as information for the entire Wild Coast up to the Kei River Mouth. (☎531 5290/2; fax 531 5291; ect-bwc@icon.co.za; www.ectourism.co.za. Open M-F 8am-4:30pm, Sa-Su 9am-3:30pm.) **Swift Travel,** in the City Center Building on York Rd., does bookings for all buses. (☎531 1641; fax 531 1646.) The mall on Sutherland houses several **ATMs,** a ShopRite **supermarket,** a **police station,** a **pharmacy,** and a **cinema,** on the R61 on the way out of town toward Port St. Johns. To change cash or traveler's checks, try **First National Bank** at the corner of York and Sutherland, or **Standard Bank** on Leeds between Craister and Durham. (Both open M-F 9am-3:30pm, Sa 8:30-11am.) Other services include: **Umtata General Hospital,** 1km south on the N2 between the Shell Ultra City and the airport turn-off sign (☎301 3000; open 24hr.); **St. Mary's Hospital,** 30 Durham St. (☎531 2911; fax 532 3125); **Dotcom Solutions,** 45 Nelson Mandela Dr. (☎532 2572), with 9 Internet terminals, printing, scanning and fax capabilities; **post office,** on the corner of Sutherland and Durham St. (Open M-F 8am-4:30pm, Sa 8am-noon.) **Postal code:** 5100.

🛏🍴 ACCOMMODATIONS AND FOOD. Spend the night at the **Holiday Inn ❹,** about 1km toward town from the Shell Ultra City. The safety is worth the extra rand, and the luxury includes a casino, swimming pool, and plush rooms with TVs and air conditioning. (☎537 0181; fax 537 0919. R403 per room; weekends R363.) **Barbara's Guest House ❸,** 55 Nelson Mandela Dr., is a cheaper and far more personal alternative to the Holiday Inn. The clean rooms all come with TV and bar.

(☎531 1751; fax 531 1754; barbp@cybertrade.co.za. 5 items washed daily free of charge. Breakfast and dinner buffets included. Reception 6am-10pm. Singles R280; doubles R200 per person.)

▣ **SIGHTS.** The new **Nelson Mandela Museum,** on the corner of Owen and Nelson Mandela Rd., is a proud and powerful tribute to Africa's favorite son. Audio-visual displays and informative wall hangings about his life and the history of the resistance struggle round off an impressive and interesting museum. Free tours can be arranged through reception. (☎532 5110 or 082 494 1740; mandelamuseum@intekom.co.za. Open M-F 9am-4pm, Sa 9am-12:30pm.) The **National Museum,** on the corner of Victoria and York St., has no doubt seen better days but does contain some interesting exhibits about the resistance movement, South African culture, and certain indigenous flora and fauna. (☎531 2427; fax 532 3006. Open M-Th 8am-4:30pm, F 8am-4pm. Free.)

THE WILD COAST HIKING TRAIL: FROM PORT ST. JOHNS TO COFFEE BAY

If the easy life—posh backpackers, the cushy Baz Bus, free *braai*—has been making you soft, try walking the full length of the Transkei coastline along the Wild Coast Hiking Trail, a 14-day project. Those too pampered for the full trek might opt for the section between Port St. Johns and Coffee Bay, a popular five-day journey. Much of the hiking takes place along the beach on some of the most stunning stretches of sand, dune, and sea in South Africa. The people of the communities of Pondo and Bomvana along the way are gracious and will help out in a pinch, but you should be fully equipped for the journey with backpacks, bedding, cooking gear, and food. Rest huts along the way have toilets and fresh water (which needs to be purified or boiled). The trail includes a number of estuary crossings; you are advised to work inland until you find a shallow ford. To start the trail from Port St. Johns, you *must* first get a permit at the **Nature Conservation Office** in Umtata. (☎531 2711. Rm. 33 of the municipal building. Open M-Th 8am-1pm and 2-4:30pm, F 8am-1pm and 2-4pm.) Permits for the five-day trail cost R30. Take your permit to the **Silaka Nature Reserve** at Second Beach between dawn and dusk to walk the trail.

EASTERN CAPE

PORT ST. JOHNS

☎047

With an abundance of *dagga* and more dreadlocks per capita than anywhere in South Africa, Port St. Johns seems like a hippie haven. Jungle spills down out of the mountains, right up to the edge of the road into town. This secluded part of the country is home to the Amapondo people (a division of the Xhosa). The area, however, is named for a ship that was wrecked near the mouth of the Umzimvubu River (meaning "place of the hippopotamus") in 1552.

▣ TRANSPORTATION

Minibus taxis: Pick one up opposite the main shopping center and Needles Hotel located at the entrance to town. Local minibuses also travel between First and Second Beach for R6.

Taxis: Depart from various taxi ranks depending on the time of day. Taxis come from **Durban** (5hr., R60) and **Umtata** (2hr., R20).

■■ 🛈 ORIENTATION AND PRACTICAL INFORMATION

Port St. Johns is the northernmost of the Wild Coast towns, on the **R61,** about 96km from the N2 at Umtata. From Port Edward to PSJ (about 210km along the R61), the last 18km (after Lusikisiki) is unpaved. PSJ is divided into two sections, conveniently called **First Beach** and **Second Beach.** The town center sits beside the Umzimvubu River at First Beach. A 5km tarred road marks the way to Second Beach; follow the signs for Amapondo or Second Beach Backpackers. Along a dirt road and across a bridge at the end of the tarred road on the left are accommodations; the road to the **Silaka Nature Reserve** is on the right.

Tourist office: In Town Entrance Square on the way into town. Maps free-R15. Open M-F 9am-4:30pm.

Bank: Meeg Bank, 6 Meeg Bank Center, Westgate St. Changes major currency and traveler's checks. Open M-F 9am-3:30pm, Sa 8:30am-11am.

Police: (☎564 1133), off the main road just before First Beach, past Jungle Monkey Backpackers on the left.

Clinic: (☎564 1255), at the end of the gravel road past the police station and museum. **Dr. O'Mahoney** (☎564 1225; after hours 564 1125), on Bridge St. parallel to the main road in town, is recommended for office visits. The closest **hospital** is in Umtata.

Internet: Lazy Lagoon (☎564 1105), in Lloyds Cottages on Second Beach, near Ikaya (see **Accommodations,** below). 7 terminals with Internet. Wireless network for people with laptops allows web-surfing on the beach. (Note: *Let's Go* does not recommend web-surfing on the beach; it makes you look like a loser.) R15 for 30min. M-Tu and Th-F 8:30am-4:30pm, W 9am-4:30pm, Sa 8am-noon. Open daily 8am-10pm.

Post office: (☎564 1111), on the road to First Beach, opposite Town Hall. Open M-F 8:30am-4:30pm, Sa 8am-noon.

Postal code: 5120.

🏠 ACCOMMODATIONS

Most accommodations in and around town offer weekly or even monthly rates (PSJ is the kind of place where people come for a few nights and end up staying a few months). Second Beach is more attractive and safer for swimming, although First Beach accommodations are closer to most services.

NEAR SECOND BEACH

📷 **Ikaya le Intlabati,** a.k.a. **The Beach House** (☎564 1266), attached to the Jakotz Clothing workshop across the bridge and to the left. A tranquil and clean tropical hostel. All rooms are private, perfect for the couple eager to escape from dorm life. Kitchen and bathrooms are shared, with the exception of 2 self-catering chalets (ideal for families). A short path leads to the sand. The safest parking in town is out back, thanks in no small part to the five German shepherds that call Ikaya home. Herb garden for guests' use. No prepared meals, but the small food and drink store saves a trip into town. Laundry R40 per 2kg. Reception open 8am-8pm. R60 per person. ❶

📷 **Amapondo Backpackers,** (☎564 1344, 083 315 3130; amapanda@wildcoast.co.za), up the hill above the road to Second Beach from First Beach. Activities include lunch in a Xhosa village, booze cruises, dolphin trips, and hikes. Call a day ahead for a shuttle from Umtata. 5th night's accommodation free. Breakfast R6-25. Dinner R25-50. Laundry R15 per load. Internet R30 for 30min. Reception 8am-late. Dorms R60; doubles R120; honeymoon tent R45. ❶

The Lodge (☎564 1171; thelodge@wildcoast.com; www.ruraltourism.org.za/portstjohns), next door to Ikaya. Caters to an older and more refined crowd than any of the backpackers, with a nicely tended garden and stunning views of Second Beach. Breakfast included. Dinner R30. Reception 8am-5pm. Singles R210; doubles R300. ❸

NEAR FIRST BEACH

THE LOCAL STORY

▨ **Mama Constance's Place** (book through Jungle Monkey, below), offers a rare opportunity to stay in an Amapondo community. Mama Constance, a Xhosa woman with a deep laugh and quick wit, lives in Mtumbane (halfway to Second Beach, a 30min. walk from PSJ) and cooks meals herself (dinner and breakfast, vegetarian meals available). She can sleep 6-8 people in close quarters. Bring a sleeping bag, candles, toilet paper, and, of course, enough to pay Mama. R80. ❶

Jungle Monkey (☎564 1517; guest 564 1516; junglemonkeybp@yahoo.co.uk), next door to The Island. Brightly colored murals at every turn and an arts and crafts section for guests to use at their leisure. Pool table and free surf lessons as well. Canoeing on the lagoon, guided hikes, and mountain bike rental (R25 for half-day). Breakfast R20. Dinner R25-35. Reception 24hr. Check-out 3:30pm. Dorms R45-60; doubles R120-140. ❶

The Island (☎564 1958 or 082 813 1611; the island@wildcoast.co.za), opposite the high school on First Beach. An anomaly in PSJ, with its satellite TV and DVD collection. Doubles as a restaurant. Breakfast R12-30. Dinner R35-40. Internet R25 for 30min. Laundry R30 per load. Reception 7am-10pm. Dorms R55; doubles R120; triples R180. Log cabin R190. Camping R35, with tent R30. Teepee R50. ❶

◪ FOOD

Hippo Restaurant and Take-aways (☎082 961 6635), across from Outspan Inn on the main road into PSJ from First Beach. A typical local South African take-away joint. Not visually stunning, but a good bargain. Generous helpings of chicken, rice, and beans R12. Open daily 6:30am-9pm. ❶

The Restaurant (☎564 1345; fax 564 1057), in the Outspan Inn on the road from First to Second Beach. As the name suggests, this place has a simple atmosphere. The owner/chef/bar lady is incredibly accommodating and will fix almost any dish if adequate warning is given. Menu changes daily. Starters R13. Entrees R38. Open daily 7-10am, 4:30-8:30pm. AmEx/D/MC/V. ❷

SO YOU THINK YOU'RE ON A BUDGET?

Thando Labase is a security guard at the Shell service station in Umtata

Q: What work do you do?
A: Sometimes I work in the shop checking receipts, sometimes I watch the cars.
Q: How many hours do you work a day?
A: 12 hours a day.
Q: What time do you work?
A: I work from 6 in the morning to 6 late (in the evening).
Q: How much money do you earn a month?
A: I earn R1500.
Q: How do you spend that money?
A: I give my mum R500, R350 goes to my school fees, I pay R120 for my room in my flat in the township and with the rest I buy some small groceries.
Q: I think that leaves you with just over R500 a month to spend. That's about R18 per day. What do you eat?
A: Every day I eat 3 boiled eggs, 3 bananas, and a small juice.
Q: How long you been living like this?
A: This is my third year now.

Lily Lodge (☎564 1229; lilys@cybertreat.co.za), off the road to Second Beach. From Second Beach, facing the water, climb wood steps on your left. Elegant, multi-course set menu with delicious seafood. Lovely views from the deck. Breakfast R25. Lunch and dinner R60. Open daily 7-9am, 1-2:30pm, and 6-9pm. Attached is the Lily Lodge, which has rooms for R210 per person, dinner and breakfast included. ❸

👁 SIGHTS

The **National Museum,** up the hill a block beyond the police station, is a Freemason lodge with "National Museum" stenciled over the front door. Old photos and stuffed fauna give one sort of impression; the Amapondo penis sheaths *(isidla)* give another. Two local musicians sometimes play the *maseguana* and the *ugumpu uhadi* here. (☎564 1265. Open M-Th 8am-4:30pm, F 8am-4pm. Free, but donations welcome.) For a taste of local culture, visit one of the many **sangomas** (traditional healers) in and around PSJ; ask a hostel owner to arrange a trip.

🎧 NIGHTLIFE

Bambooze Bush Bar (☎564 1084), across the bridge at Second Beach. Quiet spot near the beach. Nice pub with pool table and outdoor seating around a fireplace. Shooters R5. F and Sa R1 off all beers and R2 off other drinks. Open M-Sa sunset to sunrise.

Club Vuyani (☎083 963 3149), on the beach. In PSJ spirit, this club has no official hours. Some weekends it is open all day, with speakers on the beach, blasting foot-tapping, pelvis-rotating *quasa quasa* and *kwaito* beats for locals and adventurous travelers. Occasional pool and dart competitions.Open F-Sa 9pm-late.

🏕 OUTDOORS

Port St. Johns is a great base for exploring the Wild Coast. The **Isinuka Sulphur Springs** offer an afternoon of mud-splashing and all-natural facials. Summer is the best time of year to visit the springs. Minibus taxis head towards the springs (R4), while the Island and Amapondo (see **Accommodations,** p. 218) run free trips. By car, go 7km out of town on the Umtata road and look for the springs on your left. **The Gap and the Blowhole** is a violent confrontation between earth and sea, with the might of the ocean forced skywards through a small hole. From Second Beach, follow the path (on your left when facing the water) 30min. to the gravel road that leads through the Mtumbane township. From the road, the path down to The Gap involves a cable and ladder to help with the steep descent. **Eagle's Nest** offers a stunning view of the town and ocean; the hour-long path starts behind the Coastal Needles Hotel along the road into town. To reach a sparkling **waterfall** from Second Beach, follow the Bulolo River inland about 30min.

Just 2km from Second Beach (turn right across the small bridge and walk up the road, or ask someone to show you the shorter path along the coast), the small but beautiful **Silaka Nature Reserve** practically guarantees all visitors an up-close view of zebras and wildebeest. There are a variety of day hikes. (☎564 1177. Chalets available. R200 for up to 4 people.) The reserve is also the start of the five-day **PSJ-Coffee Bay hiking trail** along the coast (see p. 217). Most lodgings in town can give you maps and info. (Reserve admission R5. Open daily 6am-8pm.)

NEAR PORT ST. JOHNS: PERMACULTURE FARMS

Several permaculture farms a bit out of town are well worth a visit (or an extended stay) for the environmentally minded. Permaculture emphasizes sustainability and an understanding the conditions under which different crops grow naturally. To reach one of these farms, **Forest Glade,** head across the river toward Lusikisiki and turn right immediately after the bridge. The farm is about 1.5km up a dirt road on the left. Forest Glade is currently in the process of creating a two-sided farm: one side will be strictly vegetarian and the other will be "dual-catering." The farm generates its own solar energy and sells surplus organic crops. To contact Brother G or Juda, speak to The Island's owners. (See **Accommodations,** p. 218.)

EASTERN CAPE

KWAZULU-NATAL

KwaZulu-Natal was founded in 1994 when the former British province of Natal and the Zulu homelands merged. With mountains, plains, forests, and coastline, this region is a microcosm of South Africa. KwaZulu-Natal offers the spectacular game of Hluhluwe-Umfolozi without the Kruger-Park-like crowds. The Drakensberg range is heaven for hikers, and the St. Lucia estuary is one of the most important wetlands areas in the world. The Zulu culture, which thrives in cities as well as Zulu villages, is one of the most vibrant cultures in Africa. Filled with battlefields where British and Boer forces fought the Zulu, the region is also a historical cross-roads. Yet even though the province is culturally and historically one of South Africa's most important, it doesn't take itself too seriously. From the neon-lit towns of the South Coast to diverse Durban, relaxation rules still apply.

HIGHLIGHTS OF KWAZULU-NATAL

Play hide-and-seek with big game in **Hluhluwe-Umfolozi Game Reserve** (see p. 285).

Mangrove trees cluster in the **St. Lucia estuary** (see p. 277), where fishermen compete with snorkelers and ecotourists.

Escape from the crowds of Durban to peaceful **Pietermaritzburg** (see p. 250), a city dotted with Victorian architecture and fascinating museums.

DURBAN ☎ 031

Life here revolves around the water, whether it's the beachfront surf or the bustling harbor. There's the sense that the city is always busy. The bright lights of the Golden Mile keep a twinkling vigil over the white sands and night surfers well after the crowds have migrated from beach to nightclub. Meanwhile, the main harbor is constantly abuzz with imports and exports from around the globe. Durban's nearly four million inhabitants of European, Asian, and African descent lend the city a defining diversity. Magnificent mosques, bazaars, and Indian temples stand in striking contrast to the lingering remnants of British colonial architecture and colorful African markets. As does any big South African city, Durban has its share of concrete-slab high rises, overpopulated shantytowns, traffic congestion, and crime. With over 200 sunny days every year, the weather is almost tropical, and summer humidity can get oppressive. Even so, stretches of beautiful beaches and a relaxed, friendly atmosphere attract hordes of tourists, beach-deprived Jo'burgers, and wave-hungry surfers year-round. The city also offers numerous museums, and markets featuring everything from the latest electronics to traditional Zulu medicines. It is also an excellent base for exploring KwaZulu-Natal, with dozens of companies offering tours through Zululand, Swaziland, Lesotho, the Drakensberg, and the region's numerous game parks.

✈ INTERCITY TRANSPORT

FLIGHTS

Airport: Durban International Airport (☎451 6667) is about 15km south of the city along the N2. Taxis between the city and airport cost R90-120. Shuttles run from the corner Smith and Aliwal in town center. Hotels can arrange for pick-ups.

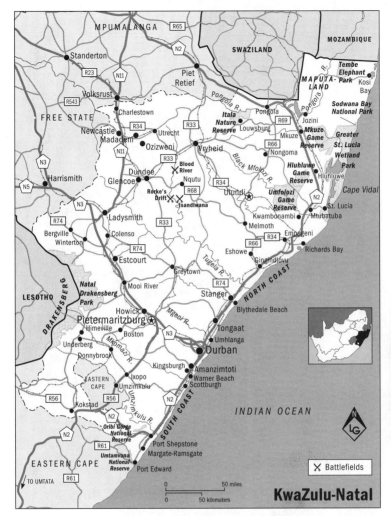

KwaZulu-Natal

X Battlefields

K W A Z U L U - N A T A L

British Airways/Comair (☎ 450 7000) flies to **Cape Town** (2 hours; M-F 3 flights daily 6:30am-6:15pm, Sa and Su 1 daily; R1100) and **Johannesburg** (1 hour, every hour 6:30am-10pm, R750).

Nationwide Air (☎ 450 2087) flies solely to **Johannesburg** (1 hour, 3-4 daily 7:15am-6:15pm, R1000).

South African Airways (☎ 250 1111) flies to: **Bloemfontein** (1¼ hours, 1-2 daily, R1000); **Cape Town** (2 hours, 6-7 flights daily 6:20am-7:40pm, R1500); **East London** (1¼ hours, 2-4 flights daily 6am-5:30pm, R850); **George** (2 hours, daily 12:05am, R1500); **Johannesburg** (1 hour, approximately every hour 6:30am-10pm, 6:30am, R1100); **Nelspruit** (1¼ hours, daily 10:35am, R1100); **Pietermaritzburg** (20 minutes; daily 7am, 3:30pm; R194); **Port Elizabeth** (1¼ hours, 3-4 daily 6:15am-5:15pm, R889); **Ulundi** (1¼ hours, M-F 7am and 3:30pm, R194).

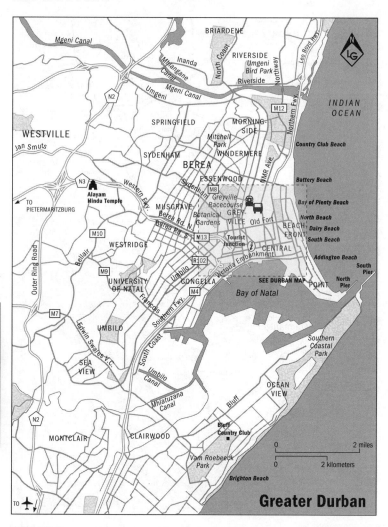

Greater Durban

TRAINS

Durban Station, on Umgeni Rd. east of Greyville Race Course, serves both suburban and mainline trains to Johannesburg and Cape Town. The information and booking offices are near the NMR Ave. entrance. **Metrorail Information Office** has schedules for all trains. (☎361 7609. Open M-Sa 6am-6:30pm.) Book mainline trains at Mainline Booking Office. (☎308 8118. Open M-F 7:30am-4pm, Sa 8am-noon.) *Trans Natal* runs to **Johannesburg** (13hr.; M, W-F, and Su 6:30pm; R215/145) via **Pietermaritzburg** (2hr., R45/30) and **Newcastle** (8hr., R130/85). *Trans Orange* runs to **Cape Town** (36hr., W 5:30pm R560/380) via **Pietermaritzburg** (2hr., R45/30) and **Bloemfontein** (16hr., R235/160). Call **Shosholoza Meyl** (☎361 7550) for *Trans Natal* and *Trans Orange* inquiries.

BUSES

Durban Bus Station, on NMR Ave. next to the train station, serves all long-distance buses except Baz Bus.

Translux (☎ 308 8111; fax 369 7963) runs to: **Cape Town** (25hr., daily, R380) via **Pietermaritzburg** (1hr., R45) and **Bloemfontein** (9¼hr., R150); **Pretoria** (9hr., 3 per day, R90-155) via Pietermaritzburg and **Johannesburg** (8hr., R90); **Port Elizabeth** (14hr., daily, R200-245) via **Grahamstown** (12hr., R205); **Umtata** (6hr., R140). Open daily 6:30am-10:30pm.

Greyhound (☎ 309 7830/8) runs to: **Cape Town** (22hr., daily, R390) via **Grahamstown** (11¾hr., R205), **Port Elizabeth** (14hr., R255), and **Knysna** (19hr.,R295); **Pretoria** (8hr., 5 per day, R170) via **Pietermaritzburg** (1¼hr., R80) and **Johannesburg** (7¼hr., R140). Open daily 6am-10:30pm.

Intercape (☎ 309 2144) goes to: **Cape Town** (R390); **Grahamstown** (R185); **Johannesburg** (R99); **Pietermaritzburg** (R70); **Umtata** (R115). Open daily 5:30am-10pm.

Eldo's Golden Wheels (☎ 309 2144; fax 301 2182). Buses to: **Johannesburg** (7hr.; 1-2 per day; R130, students 120) via **Pietermaritzburg** (1hr., R45). Open daily 7am-10:30pm.

Baz Bus has an office at Tourist Junction. Durban is a nighttime stopover point for buses coming north from Port Elizabeth and south from Johannesburg/Pretoria and Swaziland. Reservations can be made through hostels or by calling the main office in Cape Town (☎ 021 439 2323). Buses leave Durban at 7am for: **Johannesburg/Pretoria** (direct R210, with stopovers R595); **Port Elizabeth** (direct R295; with stopovers R635); **Manzini** (direct R425; with stopovers R395); **Cape Town** (direct R425; with stopovers R1275). Trips to **Cape Town** and other points south of Port Elizabeth require an overnight stay in Port Elizabeth.

MINIBUS TAXIS

Ranks are on Osborne St. and Umgeni Rd. opposite the train station, along Brook St. behind the Berea Rd. railway station, and on Alice St. in Berea. They are labeled with destinations and numbered (somewhat inaccurately) to help you find the general location of the right taxi. Taxi locations change frequently. If possible, avoid taking taxis late at night. If a night journey is unavoidable, go directly to the right taxi and wait in it. Crime is common in this neighborhood. Don't idle, especially if you have lots of luggage with you.

From Osborne St., taxis run to: Empangeni (2¼hr., R35-40, Rank 70): Johannesburg (6hr., R100-110, Rank 74); Newcastle (4hr., R60-70, Rank 66). From Brook St., taxis run to Port Shepstone (1½hr., R30, Rank 61a). Taxis run from the corner of Alice and Grey St. to Pietermaritzburg (1hr., R20).

⊞ ORIENTATION

Durban lies on a quasi-peninsula, framed by the Indian Ocean and the Bay of Natal. The beachfront lies on the eastern edge of the city, while the harbor is on the southern border. Parallel to the beachfront is **Marine Parade,** home to a number of restaurants and all of Durban's posh coastal hotels. Back a few blocks from the coast are **Point Rd.** and **Prince Alfred Rd.** (the latter runs the full north-south expanse of the city as either Prince Alfred, Stanger, or Cato Rd.). Most of Durban's major streets run east-west as to-the-beach or away-from-the-beach thoroughfares. **Victoria Embankment** runs along the northern edge of the harbor. Moving inland block by block are **Smith, West, Pine,** and **Commercial St.** (home of Tourist Junction). The area around Tourist Junction is a museum mecca. Nearby on Smith

KWAZULU-NATAL

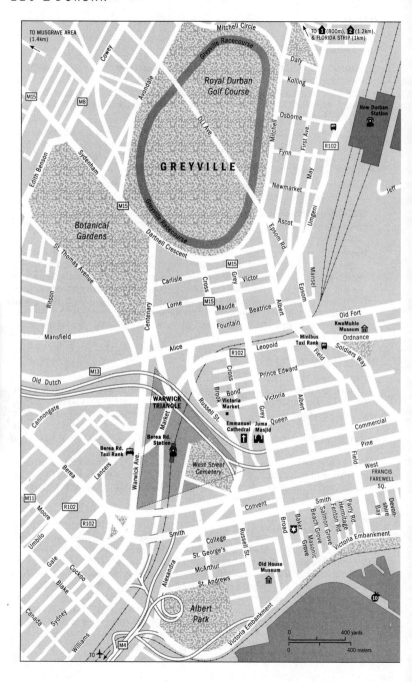

TO MUSGRAVE AREA
(1.4km)

Mitchell Circle

TO 1 (800m), 2 (1.2km),
& FLORIDA STRIP (1km)

Greyville Racecourse

Daly

Cowey

Avondale

Kolling

Royal Durban
Golf Course

Osborne

Mitchell

New Durban
Station

M15

M8

DL Ave.

Fynn

First Ave.

R102

Sydenham

GREYVILLE

Newmarket

Edith Benson

M15

Ascot

Epsom Rd.

Umgeni

Mansel

Botanical
Gardens

Greyville Racecourse

Dartnell Crescent

Old Fort

St. Thomas Avenue

Carlisle

Victor

KwaMuhle
Museum

Ritson

M15

Cross

Grey

Ordnance

Lorne

M15

Maude

Beatrice

Albert

Soldiers Way

Mansfield

Centenary

Fountain

Field

Leopold

Minibus
Taxi Rank

Alice

R102

Old Dutch

M13

Cross

Prince Edward

Brook

Victoria

Albert

Cannongate

WARWICK
TRIANGLE

Russell St.

Bond
Victoria
Market

Grey

Victoria

Queen

Commercial

Emmanuel
Cathedral

Juma
Masjid

Berea Rd.
Taxi Rank

Berea Rd.
Station

Pine

Market

Warwick Ave.

West Street
Cemetery

Field

West
FRANCIS
FAREWELL
SQ.

Berea

Lancers

M11

R102

Convent

Smith

Hermitage

Parry Rd.

Devon-
shire
Bay

Moore

R102

Fenton Rd.

Salmon Grove

Beach Grove

Masonic
Grove

Victoria Embankment

Umbilo

Smith

College

Russell St.

Baker

Broad

Gale

St. George's

Alexandra

McArthur

Old House
Museum

Cuckoo

St. Andrews

Blake

Albert
Park

10

Canada

Sydney

Victoria Embankment

Williams

M4

TO

0   400 yards

0   400 meters

KWAZULU-NATAL

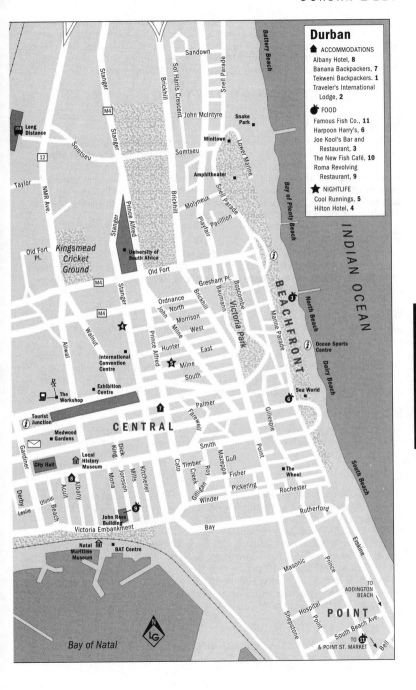

Durban

♠ ACCOMMODATIONS
Albany Hotel, **8**
Banana Backpackers, **7**
Tekweni Backpackers. **1**
Traveler's International
Lodge, **2**

🍎 FOOD
Famous Fish Co., **11**
Harpoon Harry's, **6**
Joe Kool's Bar and
Restaurant, **3**
The New Fish Café, **10**
Roma Revolving
Restaurant, **9**

★ NIGHTLIFE
Cool Runnings, **5**
Hilton Hotel, **4**

KWAZULU-NATAL

St. are most of Durban's business services. At the southern end of Commercial St. is Warwick Junction, the unofficial business hub of Durban where barter and tender is at its height in the network of surrounding markets. The other two major east-west routes, **Old Fort Rd.** and **Argyle St.**, serve as direct routes to the beach from the upscale hillside neighborhoods of **Berea** and **Morningside.**

⌐ LOCAL TRANSPORTATION

BY BUS

Durban Transport runs local buses throughout the city (☎ 309 5942 or 309 4126; M-F 9am-5pm). Timetables can be obtained from Tourist Junction. The **ticket office** is next door to the main bus terminal (open M-F 6am-5:30pm, Sa 7am-noon). Prices for **Durban Aquiline** are by zone (R0.50-2.50). **Mynah Shuttle Service** has faster service. (☎ 309 4126. R1.20-2.50 or 10 passes for R25.) The double-decker, open-roof **Durban Rickshaw bus** offers a hop-on, hop-off service throughout the city. (☎ 083 289 0509; fax 205 5713. R40 for a full-day pass.)

BY TRAIN

Metrorail Booking Office sells tickets to all local trains. (☎ 361 7794. Open 24hr.) Trains run to **Stanger, Cato Ridge,** and **Kelso** (R12/R7), as well as **Pinetown, Crossmoor, Umlazi, Wests,** and **KwaMashu** (R6.50/R3.50). Service is very frequent during the week, with about 20 trains per day.

BY MINIBUS TAXI

Minibus taxis can be caught almost anywhere in the city (R1.50). They tend to travel the exact public bus routes more frequently and for a cheaper price than the buses. Private minibuses also run along the major roads (R1 for any city destination) and post the major landmarks of their routes on their windshields. Minibus taxi ranks near Soldier's Way and along Leopold St. serve as bases for local buses and taxis, mostly to townships such as **KwaMashu, Umlazi,** and **Isipingo.**

BY TAXI

Numerous taxi services operate throughout the city, including **Mozzie's Taxis** (☎ 263 0467) and **Eagle Taxis** (☎ 337 8333 or 0800 330 336). Taxis cost R15-45 to get around the city.

BY CAR

The **Automobile Association** office in the Musgrave Center, Musgrove Rd., offers maps, accommodation reservations, special rates on car rentals, and roadside assistance. (Roadside assistance ☎ 0800 010 101; Emergency Medical Rescue 0800 033 007. Open M-F 8:30am-5pm, Sa 9am-3:30pm, Su 10am-2pm.)

Several **car rental** companies have offices in Durban: **Avis,** on the corner of Ulundi and Beachwalk Rd. behind the Royal Hotel (☎ 304 1741 or 0800 02 1111; fax 304 5517; open M-F 7:30am-5:30pm, Sa 8am-1pm, Su 9am-noon); **Budget,** 108 Ordinance Rd. (☎ 086 001 6622; www.budget.co.za; open M-F 8am-5:pm, Sa 8am-noon); **Tempest Car Hire,** on the corner of Victoria Embankment and Stanger Rd. (☎ 368 5231. Open M-F 8am-5pm, Sa 8am-noon).

BY BICYCLE

Fun Hire, on South Beach, rents bikes. (☎ 332 2579. Open daily 7:30am-6:30pm. Low-season times vary; call ahead. R15 per hr.; tandem R25 per hr.)

KWAZULU-NATAL

▼ PRACTICAL INFORMATION

TOURIST AND FINANCIAL SERVICES

Tourist Offices: Tourist Junction, 160 Pine St., in old railway station. Durban's tourism superstore. At the top of the marble stairs is **Tourist Information Office** (☎304 4934; www.durbanexperience.co.za; open M-F 8am-5pm, Sa 9am-2pm), with a branch of the **Natal Parks Board** (☎304 4934). The **Tourist Information Beach Office** (☎332 2595) in the Ocean Sports Center on Marine Parade just north of West St., has a similar arsenal of leaflets and maps. Open M-F 8am-5pm, Sa 8:30am-4:30pm, Su 9am-4pm. All can make tour and accommodation bookings. Both *What's On in Durban* and *Durban for All Seasons* are free and useful guides to Durban's events, entertainment, and restaurants, and are distributed at tourist offices and hotels. Both contain useful maps as well.

Embassies and Consulates: Australia, 24 Buro Crescent, Mayville (☎209 7351; fax 209 4081); **Canada,** P.O. Box 1454 (☎309 9695; fax 303 9694); **UK,** 22 Gardiner St. (☎305 3041); **US,** 31st fl. Old Mutual Building, 331 West St. (☎307 4737). Most open M-F 9am-4:30pm.

Banks: Main branches and **ATMs** line Smith St., east of City Hall.

American Express: 10th floor Nedbank Center, 1 Durban Club Place (☎301 5541). Open M-F 8:30am-4:30pm, Sa 9-11am.

LOCAL SERVICES

Luggage Storage: Ocean Sports Center (☎368 5842), on Marine Parade just north of West St. Lockers R5 per day. Long-term storage R100 per month, ages 17 and under R50 per month; R500 per year. Bring your own padlock. Open daily in summer 5am-7pm, winter 6:30am-5:30pm. Luggage storage also available in **Durban Station Cloakroom** (☎361 7462) for R5 per article per day. Open M, W-F 6am-6pm, Sa 6am-noon.

Library: Durban Library (☎311 2212), 1st fl. of City Hall. Tourists may check out up to 3 books for a refundable deposit of R50 and R6.50 per book. Open M-F 8:30am-5:00pm, Sa 8:30am-1pm.

Ticket Agencies: Computicket (☎083 915 8000) sells tickets to movies, performances, and Greyhound bus trips. Open M-F 9am-4:55pm, Sa 9am-2:55pm. **Ticketweb** is in Computicket's telephone service (☎086 140 0500; info@ticketweb.co.za; www.ticketweb.co.za).

Markets: Each weekend swarms of artisans and performers descend on **Point Waterfront Flea Market** (☎301 9400), at the harbor entrance near Famous Fish Co. **Victoria Street Market** (☎082 558 3614), in the heart of the Indian market district, is considerably cheaper than the posh shopping centers downtown. Open M-F 6am-6pm, Sa 6am-2pm, Su 10am-2pm. Next to the Victoria Market is the **Warwick Junction,** with everything from underwear to saris to witch doctor potions.

Laundromats: Throughout the city, particularly in shopping centers. R30-45 gets a load washed, dried, and ironed the same day. Self-serve wash R3-6, dry R10-15. Most open M-F 7am-5pm, Sa 7am-5pm, Su 8am-noon. Good choices include **Circle Laundry,** 3B Point Rd. (☎368 5804), and **Wishy Washy,** Shop 17 Broad St. (☎307 5110).

Public Toilets/Showers/Swimming Pools: Public toilets are near City Hall and in all the lifeguard stations, some of which have showers as well. Hot showers available in the **Ocean Sports Center** (☎368 5842), R5 per day. Open daily 5am-7pm; off-season 6am-6pm. There are public wading pools all along Marine Parade. **Rachel Finlayson Pool** (☎337 2721) is open M-Su 6am-5pm. R5.90, children R3.50, spectators R5.50.

Weather Conditions: ☎082 162; maritime ☎307 4135.

KWAZULU-NATAL

EMERGENCY AND COMMUNICATIONS

Emergency: Police ☎10 111; **ambulance** ☎10 177; **fire** ☎361 0000.

Police: ☎300 3333; general inquiries ☎306 4422; **Tourist Support Unit** ☎332 5923; **Beach patrol** ☎368 2207.

Crisis Lines: Citizens' Advice Bureau (☎304 5548 or 304 8386). Open M-F 8am-2pm. **Rape Crisis Line** (☎312 2323). **Wildlife Rehabilitation** (☎462 1127). **Child Line** (☎303 2222 or 0800 055 555). **Sea Rescue Services** (☎337 2200)

Pharmacies: Along all of the major streets of Durban. Most open M-F 9am-6pm, Sa 9am-2pm. For late-night assistance call ☎207 3946 or 305 6151.

Hospitals: Addington (☎327 2000), off Erskine Rd. south of South Beach. **Entabeni** (☎204 1300). **St. Augustine's** (☎268 5000).

Internet Access: The Internet Cafe, Shop 71, corner of Commercial Rd. and Aliwal St., 2nd floor of The Workshop (☎305 6998 or 304 0915), in city center, about a block from Tourist Junction. Also offers scanning, Word, Excel, and faxing. Open daily 8:30am-7pm. R15 per 30min.

Post Office: (☎333 3601), corner of West and Gardiner St. This old colonial-style building was the site of the convention that united the Cape Colony, the Transvaal, the Orange Free State, and Natal to form the Union of South Africa in 1910 and once served as Durban's town hall. Write home about it. Fax and *Poste Restante*. Open M-Tu and Th-F 8am-4:30pm, W 8:30am-4:30pm, Sa 8am-noon. Branches at Marine Parade and Point Rd. **Postal Code:** 4001.

ꞁꞁ ꞁꞁ ACCOMMODATIONS AND CAMPING

Downtown and near the beach, tucked between the skyscrapers of the expensive chain hotels, are some reasonably priced backpackers and hotels. Most backpackers are near grocery stores and have self-catering kitchens; most hotels have pubs and restaurants attached. Though downtown accommodations are convenient, the city can be noisy, polluted, and dangerous at night. Hostels in Greyville and Morningside—on the hill overlooking the city—are only a bus ride away, and the neighborhoods are quieter. These areas have all necessary amenities: clubs, restaurants, and supermarkets. Prices listed are for low and high season.

▨ **Tekweni Backpackers,** 169 9th Ave. (☎303 1433; fax 303 4369; guest 303 3339; tekwenihostel@global.co.za). Managers double as bartenders and social coordinators, often organizing weekend trips to local nightclubs. Communal atmosphere, with a spacious yard, bar and pool. Quiet neighborhood, with 2 grocery stores just steps away. Taxi service and twice weekly "bring 'n *braais*" barbecues. Self-catering kitchen. Dorms R60; doubles R120; snazzy suites with bath R180; camping R40. HI discount R5. ❶

▨ **Nomads Backpackers,** 70 Essenwood (☎202 9709 or 082 920 5882; www.zing.co.za/nomads). Next to Musgrave Mall. Prime location. A backpackers with a social and international outlook, Nomads strives to ensure a "vibe" in their dorms. Pool and lounge. Internet access (R0.50-1 per min.). Laundry R25. Breakfast. Dinner R25. Reception open 6:30am-midnight. Key deposit R20. Dorms R50; doubles R130. ❶

▨ **Hippo Hide Lodge and Backpackers,** 2 Jesmond Rd., Berea (☎207 4366; michelle@hippohide.co.za; www.hippohide.co.za). On a tiny road in the middle of a relatively quiet neighborhood, Hippo Hide is a genuine find. Immaculately clean rooms are complimented by a lush garden, pool, and intimate family atmosphere. Pool. Internet. Laundry. Library. Self-catering kitchen. Dorms R65; singles R90; doubles R160-200. ❶

▨ **Traveler's International Lodge,** 743 Currie Rd. (☎303 1064; travelers-lodge@saol.com; www.travelerslodge.webprovider.com). New owner Donovan Alexander promised to turn what is already an immaculately kept hostel into an amazing one. New features such as a drumming circle and aromatherapy compliment the existing bar, pool table, TV room, self-catering kitchen and prime location (Florida St. is just around the corner). The tourist info office can organize just about anything, and the owners will cook you breakfast for R15 and an evening meal for R30. Dorms R65; singles R110; doubles R150. ❷

Big J's Backpackers, 47 Essenwood (☎202 3023; bjbackpack@hotmail.com). Across from Nomads. Feel free to add to Big J's already trippy wall murals using the paints and brushes put at your disposal by the hostel. Previously run by an interior design student this old house is admittedly ramshackle, but may appeal to backpackers who enjoy randomly found beach cloth for decoration and plastic tire advertisements as their shower curtains. Well-stocked library. Pool. Bar. TV lounge. Laundry. Ping-pong. Dorms R50; doubles R100. Camping R30. ❷

Banana Backpackers, 61 Pine St. (☎368 4062; guest 379 571; fax 562 8673; aroutes@iafrica.com). 1st fl. of Ambassador House. Despite the hustle, bustle, and potential nighttime danger of the city center, hostel is spacious and stone's throw from everything you need, including the beach. Near Workshop and Tourist Junction. The breezy green courtyard area will help you forget about the urban howling outside and is a great spot to relax. Breakfast and dinner R15-20. Dorms R60; private room with bunkbed R80, R140 for 2; private room with double bed R135, R170 for 2, R210 for 3. ❶

The Albany Hotel, 225 Smith St. (☎304 4381; fax 307; www.albany.co.za; albany@iafrica.com). Next to Playhouse Complex opposite City Hall. Central location can be a bit noisy. Rooms have an antiseptic but comfortable feel—each with TV, bath, and A/C. Attached bar and restaurant feature a live band on Tu and Sa and karaoke on F. Breakfast included. Key deposit R100. Check-out 10am. Singles R211; doubles R297. ❸

The Bordello B&B, 47-49 Campbell Ave. (☎309 6019). The Bordello was named in honor of its history as a house of ill repute. Don't be fooled through, the Bordello is chic, sophisticated and morally suitable. Brass, crystal and clay touched evoke an earthy Moroccan feel, and the rooms are tastefully furnished. Fairly expensive, but worth the right kind of bang for your buck. Internet. TV. Attached bathroom. Bookings less than three days in advance require credit card payment of full amount. Single and doubles R200-350 per person. AmEx/Diners/MC/V. ❸

◨ FOOD

Most Durban restaurants serve common fare, and thousands of small take-out joints provide cheap snacks. The city is also home to hundreds of pushcarts and trailers that vend cheap eats. One local favorite is a filling and healthy "bunny chow"—a third of a loaf of bread with the middle torn out, filled with curry.

CENTRAL, BEACHFRONT, AND HARBOR AREAS

Joe Kool's (☎332 9697), on North Beach. "When at Joe's, do what Joe would do; be kool and have a party." This is the message on the menu at Joe Kool's, undeniably one of Durban's social hot spots. The size of the restaurant allows for a mixed crowd in every sense, with music supplied by DJs every evening. Su is busiest, and M night is "men's night," with half-price meals; all day Tu is for the ladies (half-price meals and free cocktail on arrival); and W is "boy-girl" couples night (half-price meals). Entrees R18.50-28. Burgers R24-33. All cocktails R14.50. Open M-Su 8am-10pm (kitchen); M-Su 8am-late. AmEx/DC/MC/V. ❶

Roma Revolving Restaurant (☎337 6707), 32nd fl. of John Ross House, off Victoria Embankment. One of the 40 revolving restaurants in the world. Spectacular views as night falls; if you eat for an hour, you get to see all of Durban from your seat. Roma has developed a reputation both for its game (crocodile R74, ostrich R69, blesbok R69)

THE LOCAL STORY

WHAT DID APARTHEID MEAN?

Joanna Moanakoena is a domestic Worker in Durban.

Q: What does your day consist of?

A: I wake up at 4:30 am every morning and at 4:45am I go for a run. By 7am I go upstairs, have a cup of tea and start my days work, washing the dishes, cleaning, doing laundry, cooking and driving.

Q: How long have you been working for your current family?

A: 9 years

Q: And how long have you been in this job?

A: I moved from my home in Rustenburg when I was 30 years old. I am now 50 years old.

Q: How far did you get in school?

A: I got to standard two (fourth grade).

Q: Why did you stop school?

A: My mom was also a domestic worker so she didn't have enough money. The older people at my home didn't believe in girls going to school. My mum worked in Johannesburg and once a month she used to buy about ten loaves of bread, butter it, dry it out and send it to us at home. It was very dry but we really liked it. She also sent sugar and tea. She would send it to us in Rustenburg where we lived with my grandmother.

Q: What did you do in between leaving school and starting work?

A: I just stayed at home in the rural areas. We had to fetch water from a river about 5 miles away and fetch fire wood. We carried it all on our heads. We ate pap and milk from the cow.

(Continued on next page)

and for its management staffers, who have run the restaurant for almost 30 years. Entrees R15-35. Kitchen open daily noon-2:30pm and 6-10:30pm. MC/V. ❷

Harpoon Harry's (☎ 337 5511), in Beach Hotel, at the intersection of Marine Parade and West St. Harpoon Harry's occupies a stand alongside **Pier 108,** its slightly cheaper and less sophisticated sister restaurant. Both serve a fairly varied and inexpensive array of seafood and steaks. Friendly staff. Live music Tu-Su 7-11pm, Sa noon-2pm. Jug of draught beer R30. Entrees R19-23. Grill R37-R49. Open M-Sa 9am-10:30pm, Su 9am-10pm. Bar open M-Sa 9am-11pm, Su 9am-10:30pm. AmEx/DC/MC/V. ❶

The New Fish Cafe, 31 Yacht Mole, Victoria Embankment (☎ 305 5062). A fairly up-market and pleasant seafood restaurant. An enjoyable location particularly during the day because of its view of the Point Yacht Club. Professional staff. Wheelchair accessible. Open daily noon-3pm, 6:30-10pm. AmEx/DC/MC/V. ❸

Famous Fish Co. (☎ 368 1060), King's Battery, Point Waterfront. Fairly difficult to get to with public transport except in the holiday season, when Mynah Bus runs here. Ideal if you have money to spend and an afternoon to chat away. Located in a battery used in WWII to protect Durban from naval assault, the Fish Company now freely allows ships to glide into dock at the nearby harbor. Beautiful views from upper and lower decks. Meat dishes R50-65. Combos R59-80. Reservations taken. Open M-Sa noon-4pm, 6-10:30pm; Su noon-4pm, 6-10pm. AmEx/DC/MC/V. ❸

FLORIDA STRIP

Florida Strip houses many fast food restaurants and bars, as well as some of the varied ethnic cuisine present everywhere in Durban.

Baanthai, 138 Florida Rd. (☎ 303 4270; www.sawebs.co.za/baanthai). Entrance on 8th Ave. Decorated in plush greens and reds. Specializes in Thai cuisine. Set menu R72 for three courses. Meals R25-R62. Open M-F noon-2:30pm and 7-10:30pm, Sa 4-10:30pm. ❸

Yorgo's Taverna, 200 Florida Rd, down the passageway. An upstairs location. Take the Mynah Bus to Mitchell Park or Musgrave Circle, both stop on Florida Rd. Stay long enough on a Sa evening and you're likely to see some plates broken Greek-style in this authentic Mediterranean restaurant. Try their speciality *meze* platter (R22.50) or lamb shank (R49). Friendly staff. Reservations taken. Entrees from R12.50. Open M-Sa noon-3pm and 6pm-2am. AmEx/Diners.MC/V. ❶

Vintage-Tandoori Restaurant, 20 Windermere Rd (☎ 309 1328). Excellent North Indian and Indo-Chinese food. Cozy atmosphere and friendly staff make Vintage a great dining option. Chefs trained in India are flown over to South Africa. Try the *Chicken Tawa* (R40). Entrees R19-54. 19 beer types from R7. Open daily noon-3pm, 6-10:30pm. ❷

BEREA

John Dory's, 36 Silverton Rd., Musgrave (☎202 6677; www.johndorys.co.za). Popular inland spot with an extensive array of seafood, including sushi. Ladies' "chooseday" every Tuesday—women get all meals for R35. Entrees R5-R46. Shellfish platter R294. Open M-Su noon-4pm, 5:30pm-10:30pm. AmEx/MC/V. ❷

Palki, 225 Musgrave Rd. (☎201 0019). 1st fl. of Tinsley House. Small, authentic Indian restaurant with everything from the chefs to the tables and decorations imported from India. Prides itself on its *dosa*. Sunday buffet R40-45. *Masala Dosa* R21. Open daily 11am-3pm and 6-10:30pm, AmEx/MC/V. ❶

Legends Cafe, Shop 221 Musgrave Mall (☎201 0733). Part of an exciting new project by KwaZulu-Natal Tourism, Legends seeks to provide "more than a meal." Equipped with fully stocked travel center and African crafts store, this is the ideal place for tourists to experience the best of everything this province has to offer. Buffet Tu-Sa evenings. Entrees R20-25. Late night menu R20-53. Open M-Su noon-3am. AmEx/MC/V. ❶

◉ �🏛 SIGHTS & MUSEUMS

▓**CITY HALL.** The beautiful architecture of Durban's City Hall resembles that of the city hall of Belfast. Inside, the **Durban Natural Science Museum** and **Durban Art Gallery** occupy the second and third floors, respectively. The perfect pre-safari stop, the **Durban Natural Science Museum** is packed full of stuffed creatures often larger than their spectators and interesting audio-visual displays. (☎311 2256. Open M-Sa 8:30am-4pm, Su 11am-4pm.) At the back is the **KwaZulu-wazi Activity Center,** which encourages visitors to truly experience some of Africa's natural phenomena by touching, hearing and smelling the exhibits. (☎311 2255. Open M-Su 10am-2pm. Free.)

JUMA MASJID. Right in the middle of the markets at the corner of Grey and Queen St. lies the largest mosque in the Southern Hemisphere. The marble interior is peaceful in the midst of the haggling just outside, and the silent, carpeted worship hall adds to the mosque's calm, simple elegance. Unfortunately, the mosque was threatened with reprisal bomb attacks after September 11th and is now closed except at prayer times. However, tours can be

(Continued from previous page)

Q: Did you have any children when you started working?

A: Yes, I had one son.

Q: Did your son live with you?

A: No, it was apartheid time so I didn't even think of him living with me. He stayed at home (in Rustenburg) with my mum. He's 23 years old now.

Q: Did you have any children subsequently?

A: Yes, I had two more sons. The middle one also lives at home. The youngest was allowed to live with me at the house of my current employers. We have a flat on the same premises. He is now 10 years old.

Q: What would you say democracy in South Africa has meant to you?

A: Things are 100 hundred percent better. My son can live with me now. He can go to school at a good school in the suburbs not like my other sons who had to go to silly schools at home (in Rustenburg). At home we also have electricity and running water which we never had before.

arranged if booked at least two days in advance. *(Entrance on Queen St. ☎306 4858. Open daily 6:30am-7pm. Women should wear ankle-length dresses or pants and long sleeves. Men should wear long pants. Shoes must be removed before entering. No photography or video cameras are permitted.)*

PARKS AND GARDENS. Durban has a number of well-tended public parks. **Medwood Gardens,** on West St. opposite City Hall, is a lovely oasis in the midst of the urban rush. **Durban Botanical Gardens,** on Sydenham Hill Rd. west of the Greyville Race Track, is one of the more relaxing spots in Durban with plants from all over the world. *(Gardens open Sept. 16-Apr. 15 7:30am-5:45pm; Apr. 16.-Sept. 15 7:30am-5:15pm. Free.)* **Mitchell Park,** off Florida Rd. in Morningside, is popular for picnicking and jogging. *(Open daily 8am-5pm.)*

KWAMUHLE MUSEUM. Although less entertaining that some of Durban's other museums, the Apartheid Museum, as it is known, is an invaluable stop for any visitor. The building was once the Department of Native Affairs, where every black South African in Natal was required to register. KwaMuhle, Zulu for "the beautiful place," was named for a white man who worked in the Department and fought against apartheid within the system's constraints. The museum now houses memorable video and photo exhibits tracing the history of racial laws in the city. A life-sized model of a tiny township shack speaks despite its voiceless, motionless inhabitants. *(130 Ordinance Rd. ☎311 2237. Open M-Sa 8:30am-4pm, Su 11am-4pm. Free.)*

NATAL MARITIME MUSEUM. Here, visitors have free run of the *SAS Durban* (a tugboat), the *SAS J.R. More* (a salvage tug), and the *SAS Ulundi* (a minesweeper). Get lost below decks, spin the ships' wheels, crawl through hatches, and climb down ladders that would be off-limits anywhere else. It's a *bona fide* museum, but it feels like a playground. *(On Victoria Embankment, next to BAT Center. ☎311 2231. Open M-Sa 8:30am-3:30pm, Su 11:30am-4pm. R3, ages 6-12 R1.50.)*

NATAL SHARKS BOARD. Not technically a museum, the Sharks Board is still the place to visit for deep and dangerous creatures. Audio-visual presentations entertain and educate. Those strong of stomach can even observe dissections. The display hall contains a large variety of lifelike sharks including the foreboding 892kg Great White. *(1a Herrwood Dr., Umhlanga Rocks. ☎566 0400; www.shark.co.za. Presentations Tu-Th 9am and 2pm and Su at 2pm, followed by shark dissections. Audio-visual displays every M-Th every hour from noon-3pm. R6.)*

♬ ENTERTAINMENT

TOURS

Walkabout Tours can be booked through any Tourist Information Office. The **Oriental Walkabout** emphasizes Durban's Indian influence, visiting Victoria St. Market, Emmanuel Cathedral, local mosques, and the Sari Emporium; the **Historical Walkabout** explores Durban's colonial history through architecture, visiting Durban's first railway station, St. Paul's Cathedral, Winston Churchill's Memorial Tablet, Francis Farewell Gardens, local statues, and the history museum. *(2¾hr., depart from the Tourist Junction M-F 9:40am, R25.)*

Tekweni Ecotours (☎303 1199; fax 303 4369; tekweni@global.co.za; www.tekweniecotours.co.za) is the best resource for local daytrips and winner of the Durban Mayoral Award for Excellence in Community Tourism. Organizers pride themselves on showing you the "real" KwaZulu-Natal, showing a less popularized and commercialized side of Durban. Day trips include: "Thekwini City Explorer," a cultural tour of Durban (R225); "Living Treasures of Durban," a visit to two reserves in one day (R325); and "Face to Face with the People," a tour of the valley of a thousand hills (R245, overnight option R435).

PERFORMING ARTS

Performances and performance spaces are relatively rare in Durban. The **BAT Center** (see p. 237) is a good place to start, but most major productions are put on at the **Playhouse Complex**, which houses five theaters, including a 1225-seat opera. (231 Smith St. ☎ 369 9444; info@playhousecompany.com; wwwplayhousecompany.com. Most shows begin Tu-Su 7:30-8pm. Tickets from R40. Occasional free shows during festivals.) Downstairs, **The Cellar** is a lively cabaret joint. (Box office open M-F 9am-5pm, Sa 9am-12:30pm. Cabaret Tu-Su at 7:30pm or 8pm. R110, including 3-course dinner.) *The Playhouse News*, available free from Tourist Junction and the Playhouse, has monthly schedules.

⬚ ADVENTURES

OVERLAND ADVENTURES

SAFARIS. Tekweni Ecotours also offers safaris through St. Lucia and Hluhluwe-Umfolozi Game Parks in search of all the big critters. (Tu dawn, R1485.) Their Drakensberg camping safari includes horse riding, river tubing (in season) and San rock art (Sa dawn, R1285). Each safari lasts three days. You can combine them with a walking tour (see **Tours,** above) for a seven-day adventure (R2895).

AQUATIC ADVENTURES

SURFING. Surf Zone, in the Ocean Sports complex on Marine Parade, rents surf and bodyboards, and lessons can be arranged from the best in the business. They also have an enormous selection of wetsuits and other beach gear. (☎ 368 5818. Open M 9am-5pm, Tu-F 8am-5pm, Su 8am-4pm. Rentals R25 per hr., R50 for 4hr., R70 per day.) **Fun Hire** rents surf and boogie boards and has lower rates for daily and weekly rentals. (☎ 332 2579. Open M-F 8:30am-6pm, Sa-Su 7am-7pm; low season Th-Su 8am-6pm. R5 per hr.) To learn to surf, visitors can attend **Surf Camp** at 85 Windermere flats, right on the beachfront. (☎ 082 530 3785 or 072 224 1136; nbsurf@hotmail.com; www.surfweb.co.za. R550 for 5-day course, including equipment.)

CRUISES. Harbor tours and pleasure cruises await those of a drier disposition. **Isle of Capri Pleasure Cruises,** at the end of Point "A" Shed, Small Craft Basin, New Water Front Point, offers 20km educational tours of the harbor. During public holidays, they offer deep-sea cruises that depart at 11:30am

THE LOCAL STORY

SO THAT'S TWO LION AND ONE LEOPARD EACH DAY BEFORE BED

I was on my way to the Victoria Street Market to do some research and out of the corner of my eye I see baby crocodiles. Dead ones. I look along the sidewalk and there are bones, skins and teeth of what must have been at least 20-30 different animals.

Q: What are the things you are selling here?

A: I have lion, crocodile, eagle, hyena, leopard and many others.

Q: Where do you catch these animals?

A: The crocodiles I go to the river and set my trap. I stay in a hotel over night and when I come in the morning the baby crocodiles are inside. Then I kill them one by one. I get the hyena and leopard from game reserves once they are too old. I paid R200 for an old leopard. I catch the eagles at some cliffs in Barberton. I shoot it with rubber bullets and it falls.

Q: What do you use these animal parts for?

A: I sell them to people for medicine.

Q: Can you give me some examples of what you use the different things for?

A: People can use the lining of the lion's stomach to rub on their eyes and then if they want to rob someone or to listen to what someone is saying those people won't be able to see them. It makes them invisible. If they eat some of the fat of the lion it will clear their chest. All of these animals do things like that.

and 2:30pm. They also offer shorter harbor cruises on a more regular basis. Call for details. (☎/fax 337 7751. Open daily 9am-4pm. 1¼hr. deep sea cruises R25, or 1hr. harbor cruises, children R17.)

DIVING AND DEEP SEA FISHING. Other aquatic adventures are a bit more cash for the splash. Deep-sea fishing trips are available on **Gratuity,** a 10m boat equipped for marlin, sailfish, and shark fishing. (☎564 5736 or 082 448 1781. Day and night cruises for up to 10. R500-1000. Fishing R2800-3000.) Slightly cheaper trips available on **Casea Charters,** whose 6m boat is equipped for just about anything except for marlin. All equipment is provided and you get to keep what you catch. (☎561 7381 or 083 690 2511. 2hr. for R200 per person, 3hr. for R250 per person, and 5hr. for R350 per person. Open from 8am in winter and 5am in summer.) The many famous reefs off the coast of Natal make the ocean around Durban great for diving. **NAUI Underwater World,** 251 Point Rd., sells and rents scuba gear and offers courses for divers of all skill levels. (☎337 5586 or 332 5820. Basic course R1500; advanced R1000; master course R1995-5000. Prices do not include equipment rental. Non-refundable deposit R500.)

Aliwal Shoal, 5km offshore from Scottburgh and 60km south of Durban, is a ragged tooth shark breeding ground that has been a shipping hazard for centuries. Several diving companies work out of Scottburgh's northern neighbor Umkomaas, taking trips out to the shoal to dive among shipwrecks, tiger sharks, and Great Whites. **Sea Fever** is one of the most popular companies. (☎039 973 1328. R220 including equipment; 2 dives R320; beginner's diving license course R1395 with crew pack, R1895 without.) **Metrorail** runs trains from Durban to Scottburgh on the beachfront opposite the Cutty Shark Hotel. (☎031 361 7609. Trains every hr. M-F 3:55am-6:33pm, Sa 3:55am-6:15pm.)

◪ **BEACHES NEAR DURBAN. Green Point's** right hand point break still attracts surfers 5km north of the city. Without shark nets, surfing these famous waves carries greater risk. It's a slightly hairy paddle out, but the peeling beauties are to die for. Take the R102 turn-off for Clansthal Beach on the way to Scottburgh, and follow the veering road to the right; drive all the way to the end and cut through the brush to the point. Without a car, it's a R10 ride from Durban to nearby Clansthal. In the other direction from Durban, **Warner Beach** is a relatively secluded area with great surf 40km towards Port Shepstone on the N2.

AIRBORNE ADVENTURES

For those who wish to see the ocean from above, **Blue Sky Paragliding** offers a low-altitude weekend course for beginners and a basic license course consisting of 25 solo flights. Motorized paraglider rides and lessons for licensed paragliders are also offered. (☎083 955 9120; tristam@blusky.co.za; www.blusky.co.za. Beginners R450-850; license course R3500 plus equipment rental; motorized rides R250.)

◨ CRAFTS

Craft vendors are stationed all over the streets of Durban; women from surrounding villages set up shop downtown and near the beach in Berea from 9am-5pm. **Victoria Street Market** offers a wide array of African crafts at fairly good prices. **The ◪African Art Center,** in Tourist Junction, is a wonderful initiative, selling the artwork of local artists trained by the Center, as well as that of professionals. Nothing from the pillow covers to the hand-crafted sculptures brings the center a profit. Prices range from a few rand to thousands. (☎/fax 304 7915; afriart@iafrica.com. Open M-F 8:30am-5pm, Sa 9am-1pm.) The **BAT Center,** off Victoria Embankment, has an enormous studio where you can see artists in their element. Much of the work created here is sold throughout South Africa and the world. (☎332 0451. Studio open Tu-F 8:00am-4:30pm, Sa 10am-3:30pm, Su 10am-2pm.)

▚ NIGHTLIFE

Durban may play third fiddle to Cape Town and Jo'burg in terms of size, but it can still get just as funky. Nightlife ranges from the gritty West St. beachfront and industrial areas around Umbilo Rd. to the glossy suburbs of Berea and Morningside. These diverse nightspots often attract segregated crowds.

LIVE MUSIC

▧ **Center for Jazz and Popular Music** (☎260 3385), at the University of Natal. Take South Ridge Road, turn right into Queen Elizabeth Ave. and take the first left into 75th Anniversary Avenue until you come to a traffic circle; the Center in on your left. The best option for jazz fans on a shoestring budget. Free jazz concerts always draw a crowd. Arrive at least 30min. before the show if you want a seat. Howard College holds concerts on Mondays. Darius Brubeck, son of jazz great Dave, runs the Center and often plays here with his band. Open W only. Music starts at 5:15pm. Entrance R5.

▧ **The BAT Center,** 45 Maritime Pl. (☎332 0451), off Victoria Embankment, Durban Harbor; next to Natal Maritime Museum. One of Durban's cultural hubs, the BAT Center is a maze of galleries, studios, boutiques, coffee shops, and performance halls with all sorts of visual and audio creativity. Drumming circle Tu 7pm. Poetry circle W 5pm. Chill on the deck, enjoy a beer and soak up the sight of the evening sun hitting the ocean. Cool. F and Su afternoon jazz. Call for schedule and ask for Richard Ellis.

Hilton Hotel, (☎336 8204), opposite the I.C.C. on Walnut St. A consummately classy venue hosting live jazz every Th evening from 8pm, "European DJs" every F, and *kwaito* music on Sa and Su. Attracts an upscale crowd. Ages 18 and over. Smart casual dress. Free on Th. R20 cover on other nights.

BARS

▧ **Beanbag Bohemia (BBB),** 18 Windermere Rd. (☎309 6019). Ground zero for Durban's "scene," the place to see and be seen—preferably smoking a foreign cigarette from behind a martini at a corner table. Regular art exhibits and a clientele that includes members of Durban's art community inspires a creative and sophisticated ambience. Downstairs bar is a great pre-club venue, particularly on W, F and Sa nights. Great hangover breakfasts R30-50. Main courses R37-65. Open M-Tu, Th, and Su 10am-midnight; W, F-Sa 10am-1am. AmEx/DC/MC/V.

Cool Runnings, 49 Milne St. (☎368 5604). A laid-back Caribbean tavern, refreshing from the moment you walk in. Murals of Bob Marley adorn the walls and shirts are optional. Well hidden amidst industrial buildings, this is the perfect place to kick back after a stressful day in the city. Drum circle Th 8pm. Bob Marley shooter R5. Live music F 9pm-late. Open daily noon-6am.

Monkey Bar (☎312 9436), at Florida and Lambert Rd. A loud sign greets you on arrival at Monkey Bar, a venue patently hip and young. "Beware of Flying Bottles" warns a sign on the bar, referring to the bartenders' constant flaring. On Th nights a DJ sets up his decks and spins as background to fire-blowing displays. Open M-Sa 11am-12:30am.

Roman Lounge, 200 Florida Rd. (☎312 9436). The gay pride flag fluttering outside is symbolic of this lounge's popularity with Durban's gay community. Lights are dimmed and decor is fairly modern, lending the bar a sophisticated feel. A charming balcony, fully stocked bar and comfortable couches makes this a relaxing place to while away the evening. Open daily 4pm-late.

CLUBS

330, 330 Point Rd. (☎377 7172). Think you're a club kid? Prove it with South Africa's rave bunnies at 330, once rated one of the top ten in the world. Hipsters guzzle energy drinks, bop with ecstasy, and blissfully pulse to the pretty blinking lights. Use the rest of the week to recover. Then do it all over again. Open Sa 10pm-whenever.

Tilt, 11 Walnut St. One of Durban's more racially mixed clubs, though still predominantly white. Definitely a dance venue although less frenzied than 330. Bump to the bass, then catch your breath in the cozy chill room. Especially jumping on F. Cover R25. Open F-Sa 9pm-8am.

Nite Fever, 121 Argyle St., Greyville (☎309 8422). Hard-to-miss location with a 10m tall neon-lit, bell-bottom-wearing man on the front of the building. Don your biggest hairdo and get down to Durban's favorite hits. Tu is Pig's Night; guys (cover R30) and girls (cover R25) get certain drinks free until 11pm.

THE DRAKENSBERG RANGE

Though the Drakensberg mountains may only be the home of dragons and goblins in the novels it inspired, such as J.R.R. Tolkien's *The Lord of the Rings*, it is still hard to explore the range without sensing a hint of the mystical. Stretching endlessly, both along the ground and toward the sky, the Drakensberg Range is a geological monument with a majesty that cannot be grasped in just a glance or a photograph. Towering over the rest of KwaZulu-Natal like huge guardians, these peaks seen to have a life of their own. A veritable paradise for outdoor enthusiasts, the 'Berg abounds with hikes, climbs, camping, 4x4 trails, pony treks, and an unspoiled remoteness that will leave an indelible mark in your memory.

The mighty Drakensberg define the eastern border of Lesotho with a kilometer-high wall of solid rock, an imposing border fence for the "Mountain Kingdom." The large Natal Drakensberg Park that traces this border has a plethora of amenities for nature-nervous cityslickers. However, the park's more developed access areas are merely islands of luxury in the midst of a wild hinterland, where camping in caves and multi-day wilderness treks offer a taste of true wilderness.

In the north, Royal Natal National Park's Amphitheatre, a 5km curve of sheer 1000m cliffs, tempts climbers and sight-seekers alike with some of the most spectacular scenery in the range. From here south, the horizon belongs to the peaks, crags, and occasional humps of the central Drakensberg, visible at a distance from the small towns along the way. Cathedral Peak offers a taste of the wild in its numerous valleys, accessible only by kilometers of rugged trail. Monk's Cowl is like a Drakensberg highlight film, with looming summits, rolling grasslands, and sparkling waterfalls. Giant's Castle is home to large populations of game and some of the best preserved rock art anywhere. The untamed southern 'Berg is accessible only by kilometers of dirt roads. Quieter access points such as Mkhomazi, Loteni, Vergelegen, Cobham, and Garden Castle cluster around Sani Pass, the only road that manages to breach the Lesotho border from KwaZulu-Natal. Though the Park ends at Garden Castle, the wilderness continues south into Lesotho.

TAKE HEED, GENTLE READER. Two practical items are common to most of the parks: an entrance fee, including a community and rescue levy (R15); and a prohibition on the use of firewood from the forests—be sure to bring a stove for cooking. For more information, see **Outdoors Essentials,** p. 22-24.

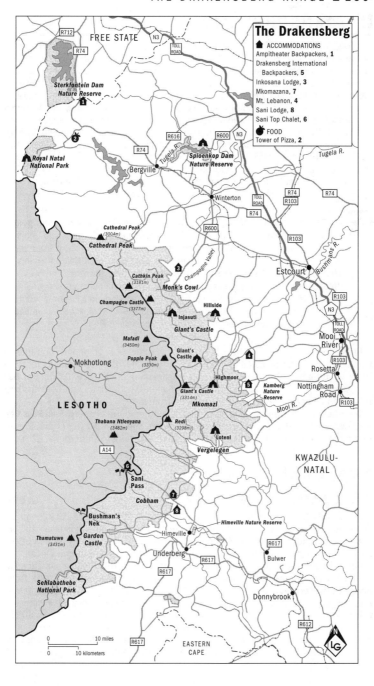

The Drakensberg

ACCOMMODATIONS
Ampitheater Backpackers, **1**
Drakensberg International
 Backpackers, **5**
Inkosana Lodge, **3**
Mkomazana, **7**
Mt. Lebanon, **4**
Sani Lodge, **8**
Sani Top Chalet, **6**

FOOD
Tower of Pizza, **2**

FREE STATE

Sterkfontein Dam
Nature Reserve

Royal Natal
National Park

Bergville

Spioenkop Dam
Nature Reserve

Tugela R.

Winterton

Cathedral Peak
(3004m)
Cathedral Peak

Cathkin Peak
(3181m)
Monk's Cowl

Champagne Castle
(3377m)

Champagne Valley

Estcourt

Bushman's R.

Hillside

Injasuti

Giant's Castle

Mafadi
(3450m)

Popple Peak
(3330m)

Mokhotlong

Giant's
Castle

Highmoor

Giant's Castle
(3314m)
Mkomazi

Kamberg
Nature Reserve

Mooi
River

Rosetta

Nottingham
Road

Mooi R.

LESOTHO

Thabana Ntlenyana
(3482m)

Redi
(3298m)

Loteni

Vergelegen

KWAZULU-
NATAL

A14

Sani
Pass

Cobham

Bushman's
Nek

Thamatuwe
(3431m)
Garden
Castle

Himeville

Himeville Nature Reserve

Underberg

Bulwer

Sehlabathebe
National Park

Donnybrook

0   10 miles
0   10 kilometers

EASTERN
CAPE

KWAZULU-NATAL

⌐ TRANSPORTATION

Several small towns off the **N3** serve as gateways to the 'Berg, providing transportation and necessities, but little else. There's a surprising dearth of good outdoor stores here, so plan on getting your camping equipment before you leave the big city. Getting to Drakensberg towns can be tricky, though not impossible; renting a car in one of the nearby cities, like Pietermaritzburg, Durban, or even Jo'burg, is probably the best option. **Bergville** is the closest town to Royal Natal, and **Winterton** is closest to Cathedral Peak and Monk's Cowl. These two towns are accessible via the **R74** off the N3 (from Durban or Johannesburg) or off the **N5** (from Bethlehem). It's possible to take a **minibus taxi** to Bergville from Estcourt (R15), Harrismith (R20), or Ladysmith (R15). From there, you can take another to Winterton (R8) or to the townships near the parks (around R10). **Baz Bus** (☎ 021 439 2323) from **Durban** (3hr.; Tu, F, and Su; R110) stops at First National Bank in Winterton, as does the bus from Johannesburg/Pretoria (6hr.; W, F, and Su; R110).

 BORDER CROSSING: TO LESOTHO The major Lesotho border post for KwaZulu-Natal is at the top of Sani Pass, accesible via Himeville and Underberg. The border can also be crossed on foot pretty much anywhere along the entire range; this is most often done between Bushman's Nek and Sehlabathebe National Park. The nearest sizeable Lesotho town to Sani Pass is **Mokhotlong,** which is still a good 50km away. Some tour operators can arrange trips to Mokhotlong and deeper into Lesotho via Sani Pass from Pietermaritzburg and Underberg. **Minibus taxis** also run from Underberg to Mokhotlong (around R50). See **Lesotho: Essentials,** p. 424, for more information.

Mooi River (see p. 247), right off of the N3, is the closest transportation hub to Giant's Castle. **Greyhound** (☎ 011 830 1400 or 031 309 7830) runs buses to Mooi River from **Durban** (2hr., daily, R85) and **Johannesburg** (7½hr., R160). The **Baz Bus** also stops in Mooi River at Wimpy's; Mt. Lebanon Backpackers and Drakensberg International Lodge (see p. 246) will pick up from here.

Underberg is the base of operations for the Southern Drakensberg. **Sani Pass Carriers** (☎/fax 033 701 1017) run between Underberg and Kokstad (R80), and Pietermaritzburg (R90). **Minibus taxis** run from Pietermaritzburg to Underberg (R25).

NORTHERN 'BERG

ROYAL NATAL NATIONAL PARK   ☎ 036

Royal Natal, the northernmost section of the Natal Drakensberg Park, contains some of the range's most breathtaking scenery. The 150-million-year-old, 1000m-high sheer basalt cliffs of the **Amphitheatre** stretch 5km along the heights of the park. Flowing down from the continental divide toward the Indian Ocean, the Thukela River thunders over a section of the Amphitheatre, plunging a distance of 284m. During the rainy season (Jan.-Mar.), this drop, known as **Tugela Falls,** becomes the second highest waterfall in the world at 976m. In the lowlands below, the river is dammed and, through several feats of engineering, provides water for thirsty Jo'burg. Hikers and climbers from across South Africa and around the world come to take in the mountain scenery and test their limits on a number of renowned routes. If you reach the top of the Amphitheatre, the next challenge is the great **Mont-Aux-Sources,** a magnificent peak at the continental divide.

⑦ PRACTICAL INFORMATION. Take the R74 about 29km from Bergville or 47km from Harrismith and head west at the "Northern Drakensberg" sign. From there, it is a 17km drive to the park entrance. Gates are open Oct.-Mar. daily 5am-7pm and Apr.-Sept. daily 6am-6pm. The entrance fee is R15 per person. Purchase topographical maps (R25) and the handy *Royal Natal Walks and Hikes Booklet* (R12) at the **Reception and Visitors Information Center,** 3km beyond the entrance station on the park road. (☎438 6412. Open M-F 8am-12:30pm and 2-4:30pm.)

⑥⑥ ACCOMMODATIONS AND FOOD. No trip to the Northern 'Berg would be complete without a night at the cozy **Amphitheatre Backpackers ❶.** Take the R74 to the top of Oliviershoek Pass (37km from Bergville, 39km for Harrismith), and then follow the signs. The Baz Bus also stops here. Located in an old sandstone house amidst a postcard setting that provides relatively easy access to both the foot and top of the Ampitheater, this is a perfect base from which to explore the 'Berg. The Ampitheatre Shuttle (R20, including park admission) runs from the lodge to the national park daily 8:30am. They run day tours to the top of the Amphitheater and Tugela falls (R145) as well as into Lesotho (R150) on almost a daily basis and can arrange a myriad of activities including Zulu weaving and village tours, biking and rafting. (☎438 6106 or 082 547 1171; www.amphibackpackers.co.za; amphibackpackers@worldonline.co.za. Breakfast R5-20. Lunch R18. Dinner R30. Dorms R45; doubles R130. Camping R30.) For camping in the park, try **Mahai Camp,** up the road from the reception area, or the smaller, more secluded **Rugged Glen Camp ❶.** Four kilometers from the park entrance in a northern valley of the park, campgrounds have toilets, hot showers, kitchen, and laundry. (☎438 6310. Camping R43, children R22.50.)

There are also several pricier accommodation options near Royal Natal. On the road to the park, **Tower of Pizza ❷** prepares home-baked pies in a wood oven and offers boldly colored rooms with original artwork. They also have **Internet access** at R20 for 30min. (☎/fax 438 6480. Open daily noon-9pm. Pizzas R20-40. Single Zulu huts or *rondavels,* doubles and 2-bedroom flats R190 per person. Breakfast only. Cash only.) One of the best restaurants in the region is **Caterpillar Catfish Cookhouse ❷,** on the R74 at the top of Oliviershoek Pass. Despite the name, trout is the specialty here and R50 will get you an amazing fish prepared any way you like. (☎438 6004. Open M-Sa 8am-10:30pm, Su 8am-10pm. Entrees R40-60.) For those staying in the park without the desire to cook for themselves, most of the hotels have restaurants. **Esibayeni Restaurant ❷** at Hlalanathi Resort is the best bet. (☎438 6004. Open M-Sa 8am-10:30pm, Su 8am-10pm. Entrees R40-60.)

⑪ OUTDOORS. Short walks in the park wind their way to the lush **Cascades** and **McKinley's Pool** (5km, 1hr.), **Tiger Falls** (7km, 2hr.), and **Gudu Falls** (9km, 3½hr.), all of which offer spectacular river views and good chances to swim or just soak your feet. The walk up the **Gorge** (5hr., 22.5km, moderate difficulty) follows the Thukela River toward the base of the Ampitheatre and is a Royal Natal classic. The trail climbs in and out of the magnificent path cut by the river through the rock, and if you climb high enough (during the wet season), you can watch the river plummet over the ridge, forming spectacular **Tugela Falls,** the second highest waterfall on the planet (after Venezuela's Angel Falls). There are nearly two dozen longer hikes, including the **Surprise Ridge** to **Cannibal Cave** (23km, 7hr.) and **Mont-Aux-Sources** (45km, 17hr.). Most are half- or full-day hikes, but the Mont-Aux-Sources is a rugged overnight trek. Camping is allowed on the mountain, but you must first confer with the ranger at the Visitors Center. Always sign in at the park register, and keep an eye on notoriously unpredictable weather conditions. The top of the

Amphitheatre can be reached without the struggle via a two-hour drive from the park entrance through the Free State (ask for directions at the Visitors Center), bringing you to the Sentinel car park and Witzieshoek Mountain Lodge. From here you can climb to Mont-Aux-Sources and back in six hours. While this is the shorter option, don't be fooled into thinking it's easy—the near-vertical climb, decorated with the occasional chain ladder, is exhausting. Hiring a local guide to lead the way is a great option for getting off the beaten track. Contact Royal Natal Community Guides (☎ 083 575 0762 or 083 340 2067) for more information. Acclaimed **horseback riding trips** leave from the Rugged Glen stables outside the park, on the way to the campground. (☎ 438 6422 or 082 422 8361. R30-40 per hr.) Fishing in the park requires a license (R50) from the Visitors Center; you are not allowed to catch anything but trout and must have your own equipment.

NEAREST TOWN: BERGVILLE ☎ 036

Bergville, the closest outpost to Royal Natal National Park, is a one-horse town, and the horse doesn't do much. **Tatham Rd.** and **West St.** are the main drags, and they intersect in the center of town. **Minibus taxis** leave from the rank on **Kingsway Rd.,** a block down West St. from South St., and head to: Estcourt (R15); Harrismith (R20); Hlangalani, the closest township to the park entrance (R10); Ladysmith (R15); Winterton (R8). Contact the Bergville Taxi Association (☎ 448 1170) for more information. The **Tourism Association,** on Tatham Rd. opposite the BP Station, has information on the entire Drakensberg range, particularly the central and northern 'Berg. (☎ 448 1557; www.drakensberg.org.za; info@drakensberg.org.za. Open M-F 9am-5pm, Sa 10am-noon.) Services include: **First National Bank,** on South St. opposite the Spar, with a 24hr. **ATM** (☎ 448 1037; M-F 9am-3:30pm, Sa 8:30-11am); **Bergville Library,** on Tatham Rd., next to the Tourism Association (☎ 448 1103; open M-Th 9am-1:30pm and 2-5pm, F 8am-1:30pm and 2-4pm); **emergency** services (☎ 10177); **police station,** on Sharratt St. on the south side of town (☎ 448 1095, open 24hr.); **Bergville Pharmacy,** 14 Tatham Rd. (open M-F 7am-4pm, Sa 7am-1pm); **Emmaus Lutheran Hospital,** on the way to Cathedral Peak (☎ 488 1570; open 24hr.). The **post office,** on Tatham Rd. next to the tourism association, offers copy, fax, and *Poste Restante.* (☎ 448 1570. Open M-Tu and Th-F 8:30am-4:30pm, W 9am-4:30pm, Sa 8am-noon.) **Postal code:** 3350.

If you're looking to bed down for the night, **Bergville Caravan Park ❶,** about 1km from town on South St. heading to Winterton, is the best budget option in town. There is no charge for pick-ups in Bergville or Winterton. (☎/fax 448 1273. Toilets, hot showers, kitchen, and laundry. Singles R50; doubles R80; 4-bed rooms R160. Camping and caravan R20 per person, R25 with electricity.) For a break from your typical meat and potatoes, head to **Bingelela,** 3km from town on the R74. The innovative cuisine is a great way to end a long day. (☎ 448 1336. Open daily noon-late.)

CENTRAL 'BERG

MONK'S COWL ☎ 036

This section of the Ukhahlamba Drakensberg Park suits the tastes of the jet set. The R600, which winds its way from Winterton to the very base of the central escarpment, passes through some of the most developed countryside in the region, with golf courses and luxury resorts at every turn. Yet, by merely facing west and climbing upwards, all the clamor and commotion of the crowds is left far below, blotted out by the sublime faces of Sterkhorn (2973m), Cathkin Peak (3148) and Champagne Castle (3377km).

🔢 **PRACTICAL INFORMATION.** The road into the park, the **R600,** is lined with country clubs, restaurants, and craft shops as well as limited services for travelers. About 19km from the park and 13km from Winterton in the Thokozisa complex (see p. 244) is the info-stocked **Central Drakensberg Tourism Association,** which makes reservations for accommodations, sights, and trips in the area. (☎488 1207; fax 488 1795; cdta@futurenet.co.za. Open daily 8:30am-5pm.) The entrance to the park also serves as the Visitors Center. (☎/fax 036 468 1103 or 036 468 1202. Entrance fee R15. Open Oct.-Mar. 5am-7pm; Apr.-Sept. 6am-6pm.) **Buffalo Thorn Community Guides** (☎082 216 9974) lead treks of all difficulties.

🔢 **ACCOMMODATIONS AND FOOD.** The best place to stay in the entire Central 'Berg is 🔲**Inkosana Lodge ❶,** 8km from the Monk's Cowl park entrance on the R600. This fantastic place is a simple but extraordinarily tasteful backpackers providing pristine camping, posh dorms, and spacious doubles. It's run by Ed, who knows everything there is to know about hiking in the Central 'Berg. He'll help organize **horseback safaris** (3hr., R120), **overnight hikes** with equipment (R200 per person), and **whitewater rafting** (R225). Free pick-up from Baz Bus/minibus taxi stop in Winterton. (☎/fax 468 1202; inkosana@futurenet.co.za; www.inkosana.nf.net. Laundry. Swimming pool. Breakfast R30. Dinner R50. Dorms R65; doubles R85 per person; family suite R110 per person. Camping R35.) Several of the resorts in the area, such as **The Nest** (☎468 1068) and **Dragon's Peak Park** (☎468 1031), have reasonable low-season prices and specials, so shop around if Inkosana happens to be full. If you're hungry, 🔲**Thokozisa Fusion Cafe ❷,** at the intersection of the R600 and the Bergville-Estcourt Rd., is an oasis of creativity, with tables set in a shady, tranquil garden where they serve innovative lunches and breakfast all day (R15-35) and a rustic dining room, which is home to unique dinners (R30-50). The cafe also doubles as a small deli. (☎488 1273. Open daily 8:30am-10pm.) Other dining options include the resorts and the **Monk's Cowl Country Club ❷.** (☎468 1300. Meals R30-50. Open daily 9am-late.)

🔢 **HIKING.** The trails that criss-cross this section of the park are excellent, providing visitors access to lush river valleys, grassy plateaus, and the peaks of the Drakensberg itself. Easy day-hikes to **Sterkspruit Falls** (2.5km) and **Nandi Falls** (5km) afford sensational views and some great swimming. More challenging treks such as **Hlatikulu Forest** (6km) and **The Sphinx** (4km) climb the hills and top out for some spectacular vistas. Real mountain goats can tackle the alpine heights of **Blind Man's Corner** (11km) or **Sterkhorn Peak** (2973m, 14km), or an overnight trip to the solitude of **Zulu Cave** (moderate), the impressive **Grey's Pass** (strenuous), or **Champagne Castle** (3377m, very strenuous). Like almost all the hikes in the 'Berg, these overnight sagas are both stunning and difficult; ensure your own safety and give back to the local economy by going up with a guide. (See **Buffalo Thorn Guides,** p. 243). The park doesn't have any huts, but camping is allowed away from the trails (R20 per night). Cave camping may be booked in advance at the Visitors Center, where you can also buy a topographical map (R25). Pitching a tent in the park's campground, which has toilets, hot showers, kitchen, and laundry, costs R41.

CATHEDRAL PEAK NATIONAL PARK ☎036

Sitting in the middle of the range, Cathedral Peak is fittingly named, not only because of its imposing might but also for its role as a focal point of the entire Drakensberg. From its summit looking south you can see the heights of Champagne Castle, Monk's Cowl and beyond. To the north, the striking profiles of the Amphitheatre and Devil's Tooth belie the fact that they are several days away by foot. The reserve itself is a quieter, more remote hiking option than either of its

KWAZULU-NATAL

neighbors, and those who head into the stunning hills for a daytrip or an overnight adventure are not likely to encounter another soul.

There is a R15 per person entrance fee for the park, payable at the park gates, which are supposedly open 24hr. You can tackle Cathedral Peak's trails on your own with a topographic map (R25) or with a guide, which can be arranged at the Visitors Center, on the road to the hotel. Some daytrip highlights include the unforgettable hike to Cathedral Peak itself (12hr., very strenuous, park for R20 at the hotel), a beautiful trek through Rainbow Gorge (5hr., moderate), and the Baboon Rock trail (5hr., moderate). Terrific overnight hikes include the Organ Pipes hike (which you can get a headstart on by driving up Mike's Pass; R30 per vehicle), Umlambonja Pass, and the Didima Gorge trail, which is adorned with lots and lots of Bushmen rock art (the Didima Gorge area is protected, so guides are required).

The ancient and somewhat pretentious **Cathedral Peak Hotel ❺** (☎488 1888) has a monopoly on park lodging (prices start at R400). The only cheap options are the **campsites** (R33) and **shelter huts** (R56 per person). Backcountry camping along the trails costs R20; if you plan to camp in one of the park's fifteen caves, call the **Visitors Center** a few days in advance for a reservation and permit. (☎036 488 1880; fax 488 1677. Open M-Sa 8am-12:30pm and 2-4:30pm, Su 8:30am-12:30pm and 2-3pm.) Good places to stock up on fresh supplies are **Hill-Billy's** farm stand, on the R600 next to Inkosana Lodge (open M-F 1-4:30pm, Sa 8:30am-1:30pm); and **Valley Bakery,** on R600 toward Thokozisa (open M-F 7am-5pm, Sa 7am-1pm).

NEAREST TOWN: WINTERTON   ☎036

Winterton is the closest town to both Champagne Castle and Cathedral Peak, but has little to offer visitors apart from the basic necessities. If Bergville is a one-horse town, then Winterton is a pony—an undernourished midget-pony. Leave it behind and head up into a beautiful national park.

Winterton lies on the R74, 23km from the Bergville and 44km from Estcourt. Springfield Rd. is the main drag in town. Minibus taxis pick up and drop off at the entrance to town, on the Bergville side. Taxis run to Bergville (R4), Estcourt (R1), and Ladysmith (R1). The **Baz Bus** (☎021 439 2323; www.bazbus.com; info@bazbus.com) stops at the First National Bank on Springfield Rd. (to Johannesburg on Tu, W, F, Su and Durban on W, F, Su 1:30pm). There is no real tourist information center in town, so head down the road to **Central Drakensberg Information** at Thokozisa. (☎488 1207; cdta@futurenet.co.za. Open daily 8:30am-5pm.) Services include: **First National Bank,** on the R74 (Springfield Rd.); 24hr. **ATM** (☎488 1045; open M-F 9:15am-1pm); **Winterton Library and Museum**, Church St. (☎488 1620; open M-F 8:30am-4pm); **police,** on President St. off the main road (☎488 1502; open 24hr.); **Winterton Pharmacy,** in the heart of downtown (☎488 1177; open M-F 8:30am-5pm, Sa 8:30am-noon); **Emmaus Lutheran Hospital,** on the way to Cathedral Peak (☎488 1570; open 24hr.); **Internet Access** at **Quantum Stationery,** across from the post office (☎488 1368; R36 per hr.; open M-F 8am-4:30pm, Sa 9am-noon). The **post office,** on the main road, has a fax and *Poste Restante.* (☎488 1014. Open M-Tu and Th-F 8:30am-4:30pm, W 9am-4:30pm, Sa 8am-noon.) **Postal code:** 3340.

The place to stay for cheap in the region is **Inkosana Lodge** in Champagne Valley (see above). They'll pick you up in Winterton (free) or Estcourt (R30). For those seeking a bit more privacy, there is an array of reasonably priced B&Bs and guest houses around town. One of the best is **The Swallow's Nest,** on the R74 just east of town, which offers a large cottage for four or more as well as individual rooms in the main house, all in a secluded garden setting. (☎488 1009. Full English breakfast. R140-150 per person.) Down the road, a bit closer to town, **The Purple House** and its neighbor, **Lilac Lodge,** both provide a funky alternative to your typical B&B. (☎488 1025. Self-catering rooms R100 per person; B&B singles R140; doubles

R270.) Apart from a few coffee shops and a chain pub, there isn't much by way of a restaurant in town. Your best bet for a substantial meal is down the road at Thokozisa Cafe (see above). **Spioenkop Nature Reserve** (☎488 1578), 14km northeast of Winterton on the road to Ladysmith (turn-off from the R74 1km north of town), has a variety of big game, including rhino and giraffe. **Fishing** in the dam is popular. The Spioenkop battlefield, important in the siege of Ladysmith during the Anglo-Boer War, shoulders the dam and can be approached from the Bergville-Ladysmith road. The reserve has a tented bush camp (R120 per person, minimum two), chalets (R84 per person), and powered campsites (R38). Book in advance. (Park gates open daily Oct.-Mar. 6am-7pm; Apr.-Sept. 6am-6pm. Park offices open M-F 8am-12:30pm and 2-4:30pm, Sa-Su 8am-noon and 2-4pm.)

SOUTHERN 'BERG

GIANT'S CASTLE NATURE RESERVE ☎036

Named for the fortress-like basalt rock formation that hovers over it, Giant's Castle Nature Reserve—the centerpiece of the 'Berg—is as much a sanctuary for visitors as it is for the eland, the largest of South African antelopes, that the park was established in 1904 to protect. Hikers and climbers tackle terrain carved by the elements. Rivulets seep from sandstone faces, springs bubble among spongy peat, and thousands of trickles of water coalesce to form **Bushman's River,** which flows its way to the unseen Indian Ocean. The Bushmen themselves must have found the grassy plateaus and deep valleys to their liking as well. The reserve contains superb tableaus featuring some of the best preserved rock art in all of Southern Africa. But the king of the pristine domain may be the lammergeyer, or bearded vulture, which soars on a 10 ft. wingspan above the mountains and rivers.

◪ PRACTICAL INFORMATION. To reach the reserve from Mooi River, take Giant's Castle Rd., an extension of Lawrence Rd., up the hill from downtown and follow the signs. The entrance gate is 64km from town. From Estcourt, take the Ntabamhlope Rd., which departs from the intersection of Conner and Lorne St., and follow the signs. All roads are paved. The **reception office,** 8km from the entrance gate, sells topographical hiking maps for R25 and walking guides for R4. (☎036 353 3718; bookings 033 845 1000. Open daily 8am-4:30pm.) The park's gates are open Oct.-Mar. from 5am-7pm and Apr.-Sept. from 6am-6pm. The entrance fee is R20, R10 for children. **Petrol** is available at the main gate. **Weather Info:** ☎082 231 1602.

◪ ACCOMMODATIONS AND CAMPING. Budget accommodations within Giant's Castle must be earned; hikes to **Meander Hut** (2hr.), **Bannerman Hut** (4hr.), **Centenary Hut** (6hr.) or **Giant's Hut** in the shadow of Giant's Castle (4hr.) lead to 4- and 8-person dwellings with toilet and cold water taps, but no cooking facilities or heat (R54 per person). There are no formal campsites in the central portion of Giant's Castle, but backcountry camping is possible for R20. Just take care to avoid the "intensive use zones" (marked on all topo maps), where camping is prohibited. Cushy, newly remodeled self-catering chalets at the **Giant's Castle camp,** booked in advance through **KZN Wildlife** (☎033 845 1000), cost R220 per adult, R115 per child (min. R330). Breakfast, lunch, and snacks are served at the coffee shop by the reception office. Open daily 8:30am-3:30pm.

The nearest accommodations are at **Mt. Lebanon Park ❶,** about 25km south on a sign-posted (and pot-holed) dirt road off the route to Kamberg. From Mooi River, take the Giant's Castle Rd. 38km to the T-junction and turn left. The road to Mt.

K W A Z U L U - N A T A L

Lebanon will be well posted on your right. They will also pick up from Mooi River. **Waterfalls** and **Bushman paintings** are within hiking distance. **Horseback riding** treks are available (R120 for a 3hr. trip; R500 per day for a multi-day trip) and can be the best way to get an up-close look at some of the far-away sights. (☎ 033 263 2214 or 082 399 9278; lebanonpark@freemail.absa.co.za. Breakfast R20. Lunch R30. Dinner R40. Laundry R7.50. Dorms R60; B&B R80, with dinner R120; doubles R120.) **Drakensberg International Backpackers Lodge ❶**, set on the Grace Valley Farm, is in a valley south of Giant's Castle, 42km from the park entrance on the road to Highmoor. From Mooi River, take the R103 south to the town of Rosetta. In the center of Rosetta, turn right, and head 31km on the road to Kamberg before turning off toward Highmoor; it's 4km down this road on your left. The lodge offers varied adventures: **horseback trips** (R120 for 2hr., R40 for each additional hr.) and "merry" **mushroom hunts**—nature walks that put the "fun" back in "fungi." (Meals R35. Internet R20 for 30min. Dorms from R60; doubles R70 per person. Camping R40 per person.) A hidden treasure is **Injisuthi ❶**, the northernmost section of the Giant's Castle reserve. The turn-off to this isolated, pristine valley is on the Bergville-Estcourt Rd., west of the town of Loskop and east of the R600. Park offices are 30km away. Known for its Bushman paintings and the highest peak in South Africa (**Mafadi**, at 3446m), Injisuthi has a campground and chalets. (☎ 036 431 7848. Camping R37 per person. Gates open Oct.-Mar. 5am-7pm, Apr.-Sept. 6am-6pm. Entrance fee R15. Reception office open daily 8am-12:30pm and 2-4:30pm.)

⚑ OUTDOORS. From the main camp and reception office, it's about 2km to the Main Caves and Site Museum, which feature magnificent Bushman rock art and interesting interpretative displays. The cave may only be entered on a guided tour (every hr. daily 9am-3pm, R15). For the carrion enthusiast, the park offers a day-trip out to the **lammergeyer hide,** where visitors can watch the rare bearded vulture, one of the world's largest birds, pick and peck. These trips are ridiculously popular, so book a year (yes, a year) in advance (☎ 036 353 3616; R100 per person, min. 3 people). Hiking is one of the best ways to appreciate the reserve, and there are a number of possibilities for all abilities. Champagne Pools (3km, 1hr.) and Grysbuck Bush (8km, 3½hr.) provide beautiful river views and great swimming. More involved treks include World's View (14km, 4½hr.), with incredible vistas of the whole escarpment from Giant's Castle to Champagne Castle; and Bannerman's Path-Langalibalele Path (15.6km, 5½hr.), which sets you directly beneath The Thumb (3055m). Those looking for an overnight challenge can tackle Giant's Castle (3314m) itself (26km), spending a night or two in Giant's Hut.

South of Giant's Castle , the Highmoor Nature Reserve boasts the highest access road in all of the Little 'Berg (the Drakensberg foothills). A hike from the entrance station takes you across a grassy plateau teeming with wildlife and provides some of the best views of the entire central escarpment, which unfolds before you stretching north. (☎ 033 263 7240. Entrance fee R15).

Entabeni Education Center, further down the road to Mt. Lebanon Park (☎ 033 263 2441; entabeni@futurenet.co.za), has a remarkable crane center that is home to a number of native African species, including the endangered blue crane, South Africa's national bird. Free tours of the facility are available daily.

Injisuthi offers some remarkable rock art and hiking on its own. Walks to view the spectacular Bushmen paintings at the renowned **Battle Cave** can be booked through the park office. (☎ 036 431 7848. R30 per person.) Treks through **Cataract Valley** (19km, 6hr.) and **Wonder Valley** (18km, 5hr.) both visit caves along the way and provide a real taste of solitude.

NEAREST TOWN: MOOI RIVER   ☎033

The nearest transportation hub for Giant's Castle is the hamlet of Mooi River, a commercial center for the region just off the N3. The town is 64km east of the Giant's Castle main entrance, 158km southeast of Harrismith, and 61km northwest of Pietermaritzberg. The downtown area straddles the railroad tracks with plenty of inexpensive markets on either side. **Greyhound** tickets are sold by **Mooi River Outfitters** next to Midlands Pharmacy. To **Durban** (2hr., R85) and **Jo'burg** (7hr., R160). (☎263 1467. Open M-F 8am-4pm, Sa 8am-11am. Booking fee R5.) Buses stop at Mooi River Motors, part of the service oasis Mooi One-Stop, 2km from town along the highway. The **Baz Bus** (☎021 439 2323; www.bazbus.com; info@bazbus.com) stops at Wimpy's, next to Mooi One-Stop and Mooi River Motors, and goes to: **Winterton** (Tu, F, Su); **Johannesburg** (Tu, F, Su); **Pietermaritzburg** (W, F, Su); **Durban** (W, F, Su). **N3 Motors**, on the R103 to Estcourt (☎263 1372), is an agent for **Budget Rent-A-Car**. **Mooi River Motors** (☎263 1197), next to the Mooi One-Stop, doubles as an office for **Imperial Car Rental**. One **minibus taxi** stand is beside the train tracks on Lawrence Rd. across from Mooi River Outfitters, near the Snack-n-Dash; the other is adjacent to the traffic roundabout in the center of town. Taxis run from both to: **Estcourt** (R10); **Hlatikulu** (R10); **Pietermaritzburg** (R20).

The countryside surrounding the Mooi River is chock-full of B&Bs catering to all price ranges. Your best bet in the town itself for a reasonable bed as well as a stellar meal is the **Argyle Arms Hotel ❶**, 65 Lawrence Rd. It features 13 rooms, a dining room and a bar just large enough to be able to place your order. (☎263 1106; argylearms@3i.co.za. R100 per person.) Services include: **First National Bank,** on the corner of Lawrence and Claughton, which has 24hr. **ATMs** (☎263 1041; open M-F 9am-12:45pm and 2-3:30pm, Sa 8:30-11am); **Mooi River Library,** Claughton Ter. (open Tu-F 9am-12:45pm and 1:30-4:30pm, Sa 9am-11am); **Moodley's Laundry,** 35 Market St. (☎263 1390); **emergency** services (☎10177); **police station** (☎263 1141; open 24hr.), south of town on Fife Rd.; **Midlands Pharmacy,** on Lawrence Rd. downtown (☎263 1471 or after hours ☎263 1487; open M-F 8:30am-1pm and 2-5pm, Sa 8:30am-1pm); **Internet** at **Statnet,** inside the Prince Kamboli Superstore on Lawrence Rd. (☎263 2699; open M-F 8am-5pm); **post office,** in the Prince Kamboli Superstore (☎263 1408; open M-F 8:30am-4:30pm, Sa 8:30am-noon). **Postal code:** 3300. The nearest **hospital** is in Pietermaritzburg (see p. 250).

SANI PASS   ☎033

At 2783m, Sani Pass is the highest border crossing in Africa and the most breathtaking way to enter Lesotho. Even if you're not bound for Lesotho, a trip up the pass is well worth your while. Hairpin turns, sheer drops, and slick roads ensure an adrenaline-filled experience as you climb toward the mountain kingdom. After climbing, you can have a drink at the highest pub in Africa while calming your nerves and enjoying the splendor of the excellent view.

▟▞ TRANSPORTATION AND PRACTICAL INFORMATION

The Sani Pass Rd. is 3km north of Himeville off the main road (which leads to Nottingham Rd.). From this junction, it is 23km of dirt trail to the South African border post. The road up the pass itself is steep, unpaved, and (beyond the South African border post) virtually impassable without a 4WD or a pack animal. A 2WD, however, suffices on the South African side; just take it slow and prepare for bumps.

Sani is in the heart of the Southern Drakensberg, the wildest and least developed section of the range. The rugged mountain scenery in the **Cobham Nature Reserve** on the South African side of the border is spectacular. (**Cobham Forest Sta-**

tion, at the end of D7 out of Himeville, has more information. Open daily 8am-5pm.) There are enough worthwhile hikes and tours to keep you occupied for days, as well as budget accommodations to keep you comfortable at night. **Thabana Ntlenyana,** the highest peak in Southern Africa (3482m), is only a day hike away from the pass. The **South Africa border post** (☎702 1169) is open daily 8am-4pm, and the **Lesotho border post,** 8km away, is open daily 7am-5pm. Lesotho charges a R6 toll for entry plus additional rand depending on how long you'll be in the country (R2 for five days). The roughest section of the road, the 8km between the border posts, is an invigorating hike (3hr.); you can park at the South African border post to walk up. For R180, tour operators in Underberg and Himeville run daytrips up the pass and back (see **Adventures,** p. 249). If you are planning to cross into Lesotho for a while, be aware that once you arrive in the mountain kingdom, it's a long way (about 50km) to the next town with gas, food, and accommodations. You can hire a local guide at the Sani Top Chalet for hikes into Lesotho.

■ ☐ ACCOMMODATIONS AND FOOD

The ▩**Sani Top Chalet ❶,** in Lesotho near the border crossing, is on the way to Mokhotlong (a 2hr., 52km drive), the next town of reasonable size and the only gas stop between Sani Pass and the rest of the country. The chalet hosts the **highest pub in Africa** (2874m), featuring scrumptious food and a friendly staff, and its backpackers' dorm has an incredible view from every window. However, this place gets absolutely freezing in winter (late Apr.-late Aug.), so come prepared. Dorms have a kitchen and hot showers. (In South Africa: ☎702 1158 or 082 715 1131; sanitop.info@futurenet.org.za; www.sanitop.co.za. Lunch R15-30. Dinner R45. Dorms R50; honeymoon *rondavels* R180 per person. Camping R30.)

There are two **backpackers** on the way to the pass on the South African side of the border (along the Sani Pass Rd.), each offering inexpensive beds and nearby hiking trails. **Mkomazana ❶,** 5km past Sani Pass Hotel on the road to Sani Pass, is a hidden treasure. The large compound, with a converted barn and several outbuildings housing its guests, provides the basics, including a kitchen, hot showers, a pay phone, and even a stocked bar. (☎702 0340 or 083 661 5044; sound.advice@pixie.co.za or wendy@mkomazana.co.za; www.mkomazana.co.za. Internet. Dorms R35-50; doubles R80-150. Camping R25.)

Sani Lodge ❶, 11km up Sani Pass Rd., offers basic accommodations as well as lots of information and a smorgasbord of activities to keep you busy. As an added bonus, the lodge's hostess offers aromatherapy massages to get your fatigued muscles back in order before you tackle the next trail (full-body massage 1¼hr., R120). You can also arrange for **San rock painting** tours (R120), horseback riding (R45 per hr., R190 per day), tours to Lesotho, or **homestays** with Zulu couples (R165 per person, including meals). There are free pick-ups from Underberg and Himeville. (☎702 0330; www.suchet.futurenet.co.za. Breakfast R20. Lunch R15-25. Dinner R35. Self-catering facilities. Laundry. Internet R20 per 30min. Dorms R50; singles R65; doubles R120; honeymoon *rondavels* R140. Camping R30.)

For **food,** a **supermarket** is in Underberg. The campervan across from the Lesotho border post is actually a disguised diner; meat, veggies, and *pap* run R8. **The Giant's Tea Cup Garden,** next to Sani Lodge, serves reasonably priced breakfast and lunch (R20-30). Otherwise, head for the hostels.

◪ HIKING

The view from the road up to the pass is a treat in itself, but drivers will more likely be concerned with keeping an eye on the precipitous drop rather than the iced waterfalls and millions of years' worth of basalt and sandstone rocks. A good guide, hired either on top at Sani Pass Chalet or through one of the South African tour companies in Underberg, will point out the sights along the way, including **Moshoeshoe's Finger** (named after the first Basotho leader), the **Giant's Steps,** and the **Twelve Apostles.** The 8km hike takes a leisurely three hours going up and about half that going down. Soaring above Sani Pass, **Thabana Ntlenyana** (3482km) is the highest point in Africa south of Kilimanjaro. The peak is only a day hike away from Sani Top and can be reached from the Sani Top Chalet via a 28km, 10hr. round-trip route. Your best bet is to hire a local guide through the Sani Top Chalet since the peaks are hard to differentiate, and maps are hard to get. Be aware: sudden blizzards in winter or lightning storms in summer can make the hike life-threatening.

The big hike around here is **Giant's Cup Trail,** which runs from the foot of Sani Pass to **Bushman's Nek** (60km, 5 days). The trail passes through mountain grasslands with views of the Drakensberg crest. Nights are spent in five farmhouses or huts (Pholela, Mzimkhulwana, Winterhoek, Swiman, and Bushman's Nek) with toilets and cold water facilities. Hikers can park at Mkomazana (see **Accommodations,** p. 223), 3km from the trailhead on Sani Pass Rd. Be sure to arrange a pick-up at Bushman's Nek with one of the hostels or Sani Pass Carriers. It is illegal to collect firewood, though there is occasionally some supplied at Pholela and Swiman. Read the KwaZulu-Natal Nature Conservation Service's *Giant's Cup Hiking Trail* booklet for more information. (☎845 1002, bookings ☎845 1000. R51 per night. Register with a hostel or park office before leaving.)

Mkomazana (see above) has its own hikes, including the stunning **Plateau View** (2hr.) and **Balancing Rocks and San Paintings** (5hr.). The moderate **Salt and Pepper Trail,** named for the sandstone pillars topping the ridge, involves some brief climbs and a 2km trek across an expansive grassland popular with baboons. From Sani Lodge (see above), you can take a short walk to the **Mkomazana Waterfall** (2hr.) or **Yellowwood Pool** (3hr.) for a refreshing dip. Longer hikes include **Gxalingenwa** (5hr.), with terrific river views, and **Ndlovini** (6hr.), a strenuous peak climb. National Park permits (R10, available at hostel) are required for most walks.

◪ OUTDOORS

Thaba Tours, based in Underberg, runs backpackers up the pass on a day tour (R180) and also offers more extensive forays into Lesotho (3 days, 2 nights from R1800). Their office on the Main Rd. acts as an accommodations booking center, as well. (☎701 2888 or 083 353 5958; thabatours@futurenet.co.za; www.futurenet.co.za/thabatours. Open daily 8:30am-4:30pm.) **Major Adventures,** next to the Underberg Inn, offers guided rock art tours (R80) and birding tours, as well as fascinating Basotho village tours in Lesotho via Sani Pass. Their office doubles as the local tourism information center. (☎701 1628 or 082 298 2135; info@majoradventures.com; www.majoradventures.com. Open daily 8:30am-5pm.) **Sani Top Chalet** has a day-tour package (R140, including lunch) that can be booked from **Southern Drakensberg Travel and Tips** (a.k.a. the Sani Top Chalet booking office) in Himeville. (☎702 1902. Open M-F 8am-4pm.) Finally, there are tours run out of Mkomazana Backpackers and Sani Lodge (see **Accommodations,** p. 223). **Light Flight** (☎701 1318 or 701 1091) gives you a bird's-eye view of the Drakensberg via microflights. Alternatively, soar from a local peak with **Wild Sky Paragliding.** (☎039 832 0224; wildsky@pixie.co.za. R150 for a tandem flight.)

NEAREST TOWNS: HIMEVILLE AND UNDERBERG ☎033

Himeville is the nearest town to Sani Pass, lying 34km from the top of the pass and 26km from the South African border post; Underberg is another 6km south along a paved road. Underberg is the metropolis of the Southern 'Berg, so you will find

KWAZULU-NATAL

yourself here if you are planning any excursion in the area. Extended layovers warrant a visit to the **Himeville Fort and Museum,** where the capable Mike Clark will fill you in on the area's history and culture. (☎702 1184. Open Tu-Su 9am-12:30pm.)

There isn't any regular, dependable transport between the hostels and the towns; your best bet is to hail a passing minibus taxi, or call the hostels to arrange transport on a delivery day. Once you're there, some travelers recommend mooching a ride off whoever's going into town on errands. **Sani Pass Carriers** (☎/fax 701 1017), on Old Main Rd., runs between Underberg and Pietermaritzburg (M-Sa, R90), Kokstad (on demand, 2 passenger minimum, R80).

Minibus taxis, stationed outside the Boxer store in Underberg, run to Pietermaritzburg (R25) and Bushman's Nek (R12). There is also a good chance of catching a minibus taxi into Lesotho. **Interstate** runs from Pietermaritzburg to Kokstad via Underberg (M-Sa 9:30am, R20). For tourist information, head to **Major Adventures** (see **Tours,** above) by the Underberg Inn (☎701 1628; open daily 8:30am-5pm) or **Southern Drakensberg Travel and Tips** in Himeville (☎702 1902; open M-F 8am-4pm). **First National Bank** has an **ATM** (☎701 1480; open M-F 9am-12:45pm and 2-3:30pm, Sa 8:30-11am). **White Cottage Books,** in the Clock Tower Mall, has a surprisingly good selection of books on Africa. (☎701 1589. Open M-F 9am-4:30pm, Sa 8:30am-2pm, Su 10am-4:30pm). **NUD Sports,** on the Main Rd. is the last place to stock up on backpacking supplies. (☎701 1096. Open M-F 8:30am-4:30pm, Sa 8:30am-noon.)

Other services include: **Drakensberg Dry Cleaning** (☎701 2474; open M-Th 8:30am-4:30pm, F 8:30am-4pm, Sa 8:30am-noon); **Sani Pharmacy,** down the street from **KwikSpar** (☎701 1034 or after hours 701 1955; open M-F 8am-5pm, Sa 8am-12:15pm); **emergency services** (☎101 777); **police,** on Arbuckle Rd. (☎702 1300; open 24hr.); **Riverview Country Hospital,** on the road to Pietermaritzburg (☎701 1339; emergency 701 1911; after hours 082 922 5911; open M-F 8am-4:30pm, Sa 8am-noon); **Internet** at **Cyberbuzz,** next to KwikSpar in Underberg (☎701 1317; open M-Th 9:30am-6pm, F 9:30am-6:30pm, Sa 10am-6:30pm, Su 10am-6pm; R15 per hr.). The **post office,** in the KwikSpar supermarket, has *Poste Restante.* (☎701 1118. Open M-F 8am-4:30pm, Sa 8am-noon.) **Postal code:** 3256 or 3257.

In the center of town, the **Underberg Inn ❶** has converted some space into "backpacker" rooms; that means there's no bedding. (☎701 1412. Dorms R70; singles R160; doubles R130 per person. Breakfast included.) The classic **Himeville Arms ❶** has done likewise and features a pool. (☎702 1305; himevillearms@futurenet.co.za. Dorms R70, R90 including breakfast; rooms R205 per person, including breakfast.) If you have to stay in town, your best bet is to pitch a tent at the **Himeville Nature Reserve ❶,** just east of downtown Himeville. They have showers and electricity, as well as wildebeest. (Open daily Apr.-Sept. 6am-6pm, Oct.-Mar. 5am-7pm. Camping R32 per person.) The hotels in both towns feature good if somewhat upscale restaurants. For a more down-home experience and a taste of the cultural life of local farmers, head to **Mike's Restaurant ❷,** on the road to Swartberg. The trout (R40) is excellent. (☎701 1565. Open M-Tu and Th-F 7:30am-2:30pm and 5-10pm, W 5-10pm, Su 7:30am-2:30pm.) You can try your culinary genius by stocking up on steaks, *boerewors,* and red peppers at the **KwikSpar** and then trying to make your own *braai.* (☎701 1554. Open daily 7am-7pm.)

PIETERMARITZBURG ☎033

Pietermaritzburg lies in a deep valley in the Natal midlands, one hour northwest of sprawling Durban. Also called *Umgungunhlovu* ("The Place of the Elephant"), the city was founded in 1838 by Voortrekkers moving north into Natal from the Cape. Over time the town has had a couple of different names. Though originally named "Pieter*mauritz*burg," after Pietermauritz Retief, the leader of the first trek into Natal, it was rechristened "Pieter*maritz*burg" in 1938 to honor Gert Maritz,

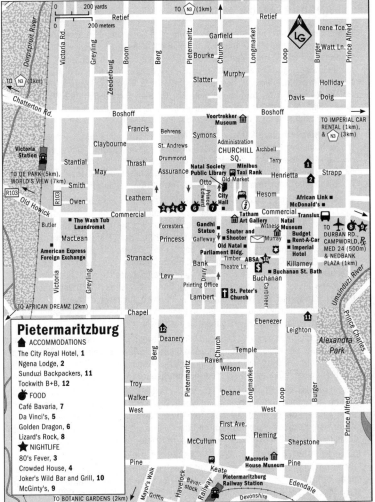

Pietermaritzburg

🏠 ACCOMMODATIONS

The City Royal Hotel, **1**
Ngena Lodge, **2**
Sunduzi Backpackers, **11**
Tockwith B+B, **12**

🍴 FOOD

Café Bavaria, **7**
Da Vinci's, **5**
Golden Dragon, **6**
Lizard's Rock, **8**

★ NIGHTLIFE

80's Fever, **3**
Crowded House, **4**
Joker's Wild Bar and Grill, **10**
McGinty's, **9**

KWAZULU-NATAL

the leader of the second trek into the region. Locals today refer to it as "Mauritzburg" or "PMB." Pietermaritzburg is renowned for its extensive links with figures such as Mahatma Gandhi and Nelson Mandela. Today, the city remains youthful and diverse, unspoiled by tourist hordes or an excess of modern architecture. Pietermaritzburg is one of the best preserved Victorian cities in the world. The sedate, regal structures (including the largest brick building in the southern hemisphere) that dot the downtown area stand in stark contrast to the harsh glass, steel, and concrete brutes built elsewhere. Though it is known as "The City in the Country," and agriculture is the backbone of the local economy, Pietermaritzburg has enough good museums and galleries—not to mention malls, restaurants, pubs, and clubs—to be one of South Africa's cultural destinations. It is a wonderful hybrid of big-city and small-town influences, with plenty of character, and is definitely worth a slot on any itinerary.

▛ TRANSPORTATION

Flights: Oribi Airport, 6km southeast of town. Take Commercial Rd. toward University of Natal, where it turns into Durban Rd. It eventually joins the N3. Follow to the N3, then take the turn-off left onto Market Rd, Exit 74. Continue past the shopping area on the left, following signs. The airport is on your left. A minibus taxi from rank #1 at the local bus stand behind Publicity House runs there for a few rand. **South African Airlink** (☎386 2923) flies to: **Durban** (20min., M-F 9:25am and 5:55pm, R270); **Johannesburg** (1¼hr.; M-F 6 flights daily 6:25am-7:30pm, Sa-Su 10:20am and 3:45pm; R1000-2000); **Ulundi** (40min., M-F 7:35am and 4:05pm, R270).

Trains: Pietermaritzburg Railway Station (☎897 2350), corner of Church and Pine St. Where Mahatma Gandhi found himself after he was unceremoniously ejected from a night train for asserting his right to a first class cabin on the route from Durban to Pretoria. The **Trans Natal** runs to **Johannesburg** (11hr.; daily; second class R125, first class R185) and the **Trans Oranje** goes to **Cape Town** (34hr., 1 per week, R360/R530).

Buses: The Baz Bus (☎021 439 2323; info@bazbus.com; www.bazbus.com), stops at Ngena Lodge. It heads for Durban on W, F, Su and Jo'burg on Tu, F, and Su. **Capital Coach** (☎342 3026), in Publicity House, is a booking agent for **Greyhound, Translux,** and **Intercape. Greyhound** goes to: **Cape Town** (20hr., daily, R358); **Durban** (1hr., 4 per day, R90); **Johannesburg** (6-8hr., 5 per day, R175). Pick-up at McDonald's on Burger St. **Translux** goes to: **Cape Town** (20hr., daily, R375); **Durban** (1hr., 3 per day, R30); **Johannesburg** (6-8hr., 3 per day, R155). Pick up at Garage across the street from McDonald's. **Intercape** goes to: **Cape Town** (daily, R375); **Durban** (2 per day, R60); **Johannesburg** (2 per day, R155). Pick-up at the Woodburn Shell Service Station on Durban Rd. Facing Publicity House in the city center, turn right on Commercial Rd. The Woodburn station is at the bottom of the hill. Buses leave from 5:15am-midnight.

Minibus taxis: There are stands at Churchill Sq. between Church and Longmarket St. and one on Keate St. between Pietermaritz and Church. Taxis to: **Durban** (1hr., R20); **Johannesburg** (5hr., R80); **Ladysmith** (1½hr., R40); **Newcastle** (3hr., R50); **Umtata** (5hr., R70). For more information, call the **Pietermaritzburg Taxi Association** (☎345 2504).

Local transportation: The best place to catch a **taxi** is along Longmarket St. between the minibus taxi stand and Commercial Rd. For R70 you can go anywhere in the city or suburbs. As there are different taxi ranks for different destinations, ask at the tourist office if you want to catch a minibus taxi, and they will assist you. You can also call **Capital Taxis** (☎390 1242; open 24hr.) to come pick you up.

Car rental: Budget, 224 Loop St. (☎342 8335; after hours 082 860 4750). Open M-F 8am-5pm, Sa 8am-noon. **Imperial,** 381 Boshoff St. (☎394 2728). Open M-F 7am-5pm, Sa 7:30am-12:30pm. Several companies have offices at the airport: **Imperial** (☎386 2077; open M-F 7am-5pm); **Avis** (☎386 6101, after hours 082 573 3024); and **Budget** (☎342 8433; after hours 083 381 3045; open M-F 8am-5pm, Sa 8am-noon). Expect to pay between R300-400 per day for a week-long economy car rental.

▟ ▜ ORIENTATION AND PRACTICAL INFORMATION

About 80km northwest of Durban and 225km southeast of Harrismith, Pietermaritzburg sits in a bowl-shaped depression surrounded by the sweeping farm country of the Natal midlands. The city center is a strict grid with numerous alleys doubling as shortcuts from thoroughfare to thoroughfare. Most places of interest are in the rectangle demarcated by **Boshoff, Berg, Chapel,** and **Loop St.** To the north is **Northdale,** an old Indian residential neighborhood that is one of the more dangerous areas of the city proper. To the west is the wealthy white suburb of Hilton, and to the south is the University of Natal, which rests in another plush residential area of the city. To the southwest is Edendale, a predominantly black section of town.

Tourist office: Pietermaritzburg Publicity Association, 177 Commercial Rd. (☎345 1348; fax 394 3535; info@pmbtourism.co.za; www.pmbtourism.co.za). In a Victorian building called Publicity House on the corner of Longmarket St. and Commercial Rd. Open M-F 8am-5pm, Sa 8am-1pm. The office also runs half-day walking tours (R50) and half-day and full-day driving tours of town (R175/250), as well as Midlands Meander tours (R250).

Tours: Hiking and recreation info and bookings for campsites and cottages in the KwaZulu-Natal Parks System may be found at **KZN Wildlife** in **Queen Elizabeth Park,** near Hilton (☎845 1999; www.kznwildlife.co.za). Open M-F 8:10am-4:15pm. Bookings for cottages must be made here or over the phone. Both **Africa Link,** 241 Commercial Rd (☎345 3175; afrilink@futurenet.co.za; www.africalink.co.za) and **Sibonene Tours** (☎390 2377) offer tours to the townships south of the city.

Banks: ABSA Bank, 194 Longmarket (☎845 6600; fax 394 4873). Open M-F 8:30am-3:30pm and Sa 8am-11am. Many **ATMS. Nedbank,** 239 Church St. (☎345 2371), is a local **AmEx** representative. **American Express Foreign Exchange,** 151 Victoria Rd. Open M-F 8:30am-4:30pm, Sa 8:30am-noon.

Bookstore: Shuter and Shooter, 230 Church St. (☎394 6830). Eager staff caters to literary needs. Open M and W-F 8:15am-4:55pm, Tu 8:30am-4:55pm, Sa 8am-12:55pm.

Library: Natal Society Public Library, 260 Church St. (☎345 2383). Open M-F 8:30am-5pm, Sa 8:30am-1pm.

Outdoor gear: Campworld, 10 Durban Rd. (345 5141). The place in PMB to stock up for the backcountry. Open M-F 8am-5pm, Sa 8:30am-12:30pm.

Laundromat: The Wash Tub Laundromat, 12 Commercial Rd. (☎345-7458). Open M–F 7am-6pm, Sa 7am-4pm, Su 8am-3pm.

Pool: Buchanan Street Bath. Open M-F 9:30am-5:30pm, Sa 8-10:30am. R5.50 per person.

Weather: ☎082 162.

Emergency: Police ☎10 111. **Ambulance** ☎10 177.

Police: 231 Loop St. (☎342 2211). Open 24hr.

Crisis line (rape): ☎394 4444.

Pharmacy: Scottsville Pharmacy, 64 Durban Rd. (☎386 1029). Open M-F 8:30am-9:30pm, Sa 8:30am-12:30pm and 3-9:30pm, Su 9am-2pm and 4-9:30pm.

Hospital: Med 24 (☎342 7023). On Payn St. off Commercial Rd. heading toward Durban. Open 24hr.

Internet access: The Hive, 50 Durban Rd. (☎342 8988). Take Commercial Rd. toward the University until its name changes to Durban in Nedbank Plaza. 8 terminals and an amiable owner. Open M-Th 9am-8pm, F and Sa 9am-9pm, Su 10am-4pm. R7 for 15min.

Post office: 220 Longmarket St. (☎345 5880). Fax and *Poste Restante*. Open M-Tu and Th-F 8:30am-4:30pm, W 9am-4:30pm, Sa 8am-noon.

Postal code: 3200.

▟ ACCOMMODATIONS

Pietermaritzburg is a more of a university town than a tourist destination and budget accommodations are quite hard to come by.

🏠 **Ngena Lodge,** 293 Burger St. (☎ 345 6237; ngena@sai.co.za). On Burger between Commercial and Boshoff; look for the world flags. Owner Sandi and her charming son offer the weary backpacker a warm smile and spotless surroundings. A safari theme accents the eating area and TV lounge. Laundry and self-catering kitchen. Dorms R60; singles and doubles R80 per person. ❶

African Dreamz, 30 Taunton Rd. (☎ 394 5141). Head west on Chapel out of city center, turn right at first stop light, driveway marked only by "30" on right side of road. Although just beyond the bustle of downtown, this B&B, with its gardens, tennis court, and pool, feels a world away from the city. Single R125, sharing R95 per person. ❷

Tockwith B&B, 208 Chapel St. (☎ 342 5802; megfrean@lantic.net). Between Loop and Burger. Victorian oasis near downtown. Spacious cottage as well as B&B in the English style. Pool, garden and airport shuttle. R100 per person; cottage R300 (sleeps 5). ❷

Sunduzi Backpackers, 140 Berg St. (☎ 394 0072; sunduzi@hotmail.com or sunduzi@futurenet.co.za). Backpackers at Sunduzi feel like part of the family, and they might as well be. Guests live alongside the owners, sharing the living room, kitchen, fireplace and dining room of this central PMB home. Restaurants, clubs, and pubs are a stone's throw away. Day tours of PMB R150, including lunch. Internet R30 per hr. Dorms R45; singles R50; doubles R55 per person. Camping R25. ❶

City Royal Hotel, 301 Burger St. (☎ 394 7072; frontoffice@cityroyalhotel.co.za; www.cityroyalhotel.co.za). Right next to Ngena Lodge. With an excellent location, in-house bar, and nice rooms with TVs, it's a great place for anyone willing to spend a little more for some privacy. Singles R230, with breakfast R250; doubles R260/280. ❸

🍴 FOOD

Golden Dragon Chinese Restaurant, 121 Commercial Rd. (☎ 345 7745). Basement spot in Karos Capital Towers. Interior decor attempts Eastern ambience amidst PMB's urban hubbub: wicker and lilies abound. With almost everything under R25, it's a great value. Open M-Sa 10:30am-3pm and 5:30-10pm, Su 11am-8pm. Cash only. ❶

The Lizard's Rock, 40 Durban Rd. (☎ 345 0615). Next to Nedbank Plaza out by the University. This funky joint puts a little bit of an eclectic twist on traditional South African fare (R20-50), and has some variety for vegetarians. Nice patio and lawn. ❶

Da Vinci Restaurant and Bar, 117 Commercial Rd. (☎ 345 6632). Near the corner of Commercial Rd. and Pietermaritz St. Popular spot with subdued, romantic feel. Candlelit tables, zebra-print curtains, and Da Vinci prints. Excellent choice for dinner. Pasta R25, seafood R35-40, pizza R20-30, pub lunches R10-20. DJ and dance-floor nightly. Open daily noon-2:30pm and 6-10:30pm. Bar open noon-4am; live band Su nights. ❷

Cafe Bavaria (☎ 345 1952), in the NBS building at corner of Commercial Rd. and Prince Edward St. Traditional diner with tiny booths perfect for sharing a milkshake. Very popular spot for breakfast and lunch. Curries and sandwiches R5-20. Burgers R10-20. Other entrees R20-40. Open M-F 7am-5pm, Sa 7am-1:30pm. ❶

🎵 🎬 ENTERTAINMENT AND NIGHTLIFE

Crowded House, 97 Commercial (☎ 345 5972). *The* place to see and be seen with local teens and 20-somethings. Biggest dance floor in town. Check out "Pig Night" on Tu when 3hr. of drinks is R25. Cover R5; drinks R6-8. Open Tu-Sa 8pm-4am.

80's Fever, 91 Commercial Rd. (☎ 342 9127). Combination sports bar, pool hall, and disco frequented by the college crowd, especially Th nights, when drinks are free for students between 8-9pm. Contrary to implication, even the most recent hits are played here. Cover R10; ladies free on Tu nights. Open Tu, Th-Sa 8pm-late.

McGinty's, 50 Durban Rd. (☎342 3365). The town's attempt at a "traditional Irish pub." Whether you're convinced of this depends on how many pints of Kilkenny you pound with other lads and lasses before the night expires. Beer R7-10. Fish and chips R26. Open M-Sa 11:30am-midnight, Su noon-10pm.

Joker's Wild Bar and Grill, 2 Club Ln. (☎342 8220). This entertainment complex attracts a diverse clientele, and with two bars, two restaurants, karaoke (Su night), and 10-pin bowling (adults R18, students R15), it has something for all. Curry of the day R18.50. Pizza R15-30. Veggie burger R15. Open daily 8am-late; bowling 9am-midnight.

SIGHTS AND ADVENTURES

NATAL NATIONAL BOTANICAL GARDENS. These are some of the most spectacular gardens in South Africa. A wide, tree-lined avenue near the entrance leads away from a bell called "The Lady Enchantress," weaving through beautiful landscaped lawns resplendent with flora from all over the world and just right for an afternoon siesta. *(On Mayors Walk, southwest of the city center. ☎344 3585. R5, children R2. Occasional guided walks R5-10.)*

TATHAM ART GALLERY. The gallery has a large collection of modern drawings, paintings, and sculpture from all over KwaZulu-Natal, some of which deal with apartheid and the 1991 floods, as well as a selection of earlier works from around the world. Community and youth art is also routinely displayed and sold. One of the more striking pieces is Willie Bester's *1913 Land Act*—a bench made of barbed wire, bullets, grenades, telephone wire, and miniature coffins. *(On Commercial Rd. at the intersection with Longmarket St. ☎342 1804. Open Tu-Su 10am-6pm. Free.)*

NATAL MUSEUM. This veritable Noah's ark holds thousands of natural curiosities, each one a bit more bizarre and exotic than the last. Look for the demonic aye-aye, a primate from Madagascar, and the king cheetah, with stripes instead of spots. And just when you think you couldn't be more stunned, wait until you see the huge live Madagascan Hissing Cockroaches (we're talking two inches here). Upstairs, the Hall of Traditional Cultures and Natal History, featuring homemade guns and a wide array of subversive posters and t-shirts, provides some insight into the struggle against apartheid. *(237 Loop St. ☎345 1404. Open M-F 9am-4:30pm, Sa 10am-4:30pm, Su 11am-3pm. R4, ages 4-17 R1, under 4 free.)*

VOORTREKKER MUSEUM. The museum comes in several parts. The **Main Building,** the old Longmarket Girls' School, houses the museum shop and rotating exhibits on the KwaZulu-Natal culture, with an emphasis on non-white contributions. The **Church of the Vow,** built in 1840 after the Battle of Blood River, houses exhibits of dolls, toys, pipes, and the personal articles of several famous Voortrekkers. The **annex** has tools, rifles, and a wagon from the Great Trek, as well as explanations of soap-making, coffee-making, and home remedies of the Voortrekkers. The Church will eventually be dedicated almost exclusively to Voortrekker religion and education. Finally, **Andries Pretorius House** was dismantled at its original site in the suburb of Edendale and rebuilt in its present location. This newest part of the Voortrekker museum is furnished much as it would have been after Pretorius built it in 1842. It houses handicrafts by Boer POWs in British prisons in India, Sri Lanka, and Bermuda, as well as old carriages and farming equipment. *(On the corner of Longmarket and Boshoff St. ☎394 6834. Open M-F 9am-4pm, Sa 9am-1pm. R3, students and seniors R1.50, children R1.)*

ADVENTURES. The ⚑**Pietermaritzburg Parachute Club,** gathers at the airport on weekends and public holidays to pre-party and jump. The clubhouse has pool, darts, and a ready supply of beer. Outside is camping and *braai*. A bunkhouse offers accommodation (R12) to those brave enough to attempt a jump the next day. (☎ 386 6346 or 082 859 7787; blueskies@futurenet.co.za. Tandem jumps R800; static-line diving courses R600. Qualified jumpers only R120.) **World's View** is an amazing overlook towering above Pietermaritzburg and the surrounding midlands as well as a whole series of hiking trails that can be reached by following Commercial Rd. (which becomes Old Howick Rd.) for 7km to World's View Rd.

THE SOUTH COAST

The South Coast (or Hibiscus Coast, as it is sometimes known) is a relaxed playground for travelers who have had enough of big cities and cold mountains. Cane fields, lush nature reserves, picturesque gorges, neon-lit towns, and rambling golf courses lie alongside some of the most spectacular beaches in the country. Warm weather graces this area year-round, though winter nights can be a bit chilly and occasionally rainy. Also known as the "slow coast," the South Coast exudes a stress-free vibe; if you can't afford to rent a convertible and cruise, hop on a bike and fill your lungs with the region's sweet seaside air. A word of caution, however: while the towns nearer to Durban can feel rather plastic, the waters are safer there than at the beaches farther south, which often lack shark nets.

PORT SHEPSTONE   ☎039

Port Shepstone, at the northern edge of the Hibiscus Coast, took off in 1879 when William Bazley, one of the world's first underwater demolition experts, was hired by a sugar farmer to blast away the rocks that barred the entrance to the harbor. Thousands of explosives later, the harbor opened the way for sugar and coffee farms to develop along the nearby river. After a limestone quarry opened, Port Shepstone became one of the region's major industrial centers. Even today, Port Shepstone remains the nerve center of the South Coast, with the largest hospitals, schools, banks, and industries. For the tourist, however, the town is most important as an information resource center and springboard for the Hibiscus Coast, including the nearby **Oribi Gorge Nature Reserve** (see p. 258).

▐▀ TRANSPORTATION

Buses: Margate Mini Coach (☎312 1406; minicoach@margate.co.za) stops at the Bedford Center off Aitken St., running to **Durban** (2hr.; 2 per day; round-trip R60, same-day return R85) and **Margate** (30min., 2 per day, same prices). **Translux, Greyhound** and **Intercape** run daily to: **Durban** (1½hr., R80); **East London** (12½hr., R245); **Port Elizabeth** (12hr., R245); **Umtata** (4¼hr., R145). Bookings for buses at **Sure Sheppie Travel,** Shop 4a Oribi Plaza (☎682 5301; fax 682 5409; janetg@sheppietravel@galileosa.co.za; www.suretravel.co.za), corner of Station and Sinclair Rd. Open M-F 8:30am-4:30pm, Sa 8:30-11:30am.

Minibus Taxis: The minibus taxi stand is at the top of the hill on Ryder St. off Escombe. Taxis run to: **Cape Town** (24hr., R400); **Durban** (2hr., R23); **Margate** (30min., R5); **Port Edward** (1hr., R10).

◼◢ ◳ ORIENTATION

Port Shepstone lies just below the Umzimkulu River, about 110km south of Durban along the **N2**, which runs along the southeastern edge of town. Just south of the bridge over the river, **Aiken St.** climbs uphill to the right, crossing **Connor, Shepstone,** and **Escombe St.** before ending at **Robinson St.** Parallel to and south of Aiken

St. are **Wooley, Reynolds, Bazley St.**, and **Ryder Rd.** Most services are around Oribi Plaza Pick 'n Pay at the corner of Station Rd. and Sinclair Rd., or off the R102.

Tourist Office: Hibiscus Coast Tourism (☎682 2455; fax 682 7337; www.thehibiscus-coast.co.za), in the Oribi Good Health Pharmacy. Useful source for information on accommodations, maps, and entertainment. Open M-F 9am-4pm, in high season also Sa 9am-noon.

Banks: First National Bank (☎682 2106) and **ABSA Bank** (☎682 0108; fax 682 4606), both on Aiken St. Open M-F 8:30am-3:30pm, Sa 8:30-11am.

Laundromat: Coastal Laundromat (☎682 4277), on Marine Dr. near the Oribi Plaza. R28 per 6kg load. Open M-F 7am-5:30pm, Sa 7am-1pm.

Emergency: ☎10 111.

Police Station: (☎682 1031; fax 688 1196), at the top of Wooley St. Open 24hr.

Pharmacy: Oribi Good Health Pharmacy (☎682 0847). Houses tourist information office. Open M-F 9am-5:30pm, Sa 9am-1pm. AmEx/MC/V. Several other pharmacies surround the 2 hospitals.

Hospital: Both the **Provincial Hospital** (☎682 1111) and the private **Hibiscus Hospital** (☎682 4882) are on Bazley St. as it heads uphill from the N2. Both open 24hr.

Internet Access: Comport Computers (☎682 2039), in Oribi Plaza. R10 per 15min. 5 ISDN terminals. Open M-F 9am-7pm, Sa 9am-6pm, Su 9am-2pm. **Postnet**, also in Oribi Plaza. R20 per 30min. 1 terminal. Open M-F 8am-4:30pm, 8:30am-noon.

Post Office: 17 Aiken St. (☎682 1015). Fax and *Poste Restante*. Open M-Tu and Th-F 8:30am-4:30pm, W 9am-4:30pm, Sa 8am-noon.

Postal Code: 4240.

▐ ◖ ACCOMMODATIONS AND FOOD

Port Shepstone is the center of services and amenities, and the small villages nearby host the best budget backpackers. Several snack shops and chain restaurants populate the shopping centers along the highway.

▨ **Mantis and Moon Backpackers Lodge**, 7/178 Station Rd. Umzumbe (☎684 6256; travelsa@saol.com). 15min. outside of town toward Durban on the R102. Take a right on Station Rd. in Umzumbe. Probably one of the only places in the world where, for as little as R60, you can enjoy the luxury of having a pod, jacuzzi, fire pit, and sun deck cocooned in lush vegetation. The three romantic doubles, in which electricity is replaced by candles and the mood is set by (optional) burning incense, make this an intriguing getaway spot for couples. Organizes the usual bevy of activities, such as diving and trips to Oribi Gorge. Baz Bus stop. Breakfast R16. Lunch and dinner menu R16-35. Laundry R25 per 5kg. Internet R35 per hr. Reception 24hr. Dorms R60; singles R100; doubles R150, with bath R180. Camping R45. ❶

▨ **The Spot**, 23 Ambleside Rd. (☎695 1318; fax 695 0439; spotbackpackers@netac-tive.co.za). Coming from Port Shepstone toward Durban, turn off the R102 6km north of town at the 2nd set of traffic lights; follow signs toward Umtentweni Beach. An idyllic setting near a perfectly unspoiled beach. Owners are friendly, helpful, and willing to organize the usual activities and transport into town. Warm water, shark nets, great waves, a small pub, cheap eats, pool table, and ping pong. Sheets and pillows, but no sleeping bags. Baz Bus stop. Breakfast R5-20. Dinner R20-25. Reception 7:30am-10:30pm. Check-out 10am. Reservations accepted. Dorms R55; doubles R130. ❶

Kapenta Bay Resort 11/12 Port Edward St. (☎682 5528). Turn off at the Oribi Plaza, left onto Sinclair and a right onto Princess Elizabeth. The hotel is on your left. Reasonably luxurious and home to a pool and game room. 2min. walk from the beach. Suites

KWAZULU-NATAL

house 4 people, with a TV lounge, dining area, and kitchenette. Attached bar and restaurant (breakfast R45; lunch and dinner buffet R55-60; open daily 6am-10:30pm). Check-in 2pm. Check-out 10am. Guests may use reception's Internet. Suites in high season R720, in low season R472; 4 people R910 high season, R880 low season. ❷

⊙ SIGHTS

BANANA EXPRESS. This narrow-gauge train meanders 122km, traveling for a short distance along the coast before turning inland through cane fields, forests, farms, and villages. Formerly Port Shepstone's most famous tourist attraction, the Banana Express has succumbed to the growing vegetation, leaving a lot of visible shrub and not much else. For those still interested, it offers either a 90min. trip to the historic town of Izotsha or a 6½hr. trip around the area . The longer trip stops at Paddock Station, where you can either stay for a *braai* or take a guided tour of the Oribi Gorge on a courtesy bus (see p. 258). The train then returns to Port Shepstone via the gorge. (☎682 4821. *Train to Izotsha: 2nd-class R40, first-class R50, under 3 R20/R25; return to Port Shepstone R120, children R6. Izotsha tour: round-trip R120, R60. Oribi Gorge bus tour R285.*)

PORT SHEPSTONE MARITIME MUSEUM. The Maritime Museum plots all the shipwrecks along the eastern coast and has an interesting display on the Harbor's history. The cast-iron lighthouse down the road behind the building was cast in Britain and shipped to Natal in the 1890s. Before its arrival, lanterns hung on scaffolding; occasionally, sheets were the only things used to guide ships into the harbor. *(2km south of Aiken St., down the N2 on the left. ☎688 2195. Open M-F 8:30am-4pm.)*

NEAR PORT SHEPSTONE: ORIBI GORGE NATURE RESERVE

About 22 kilometers inland from Port Shepstone along the N2, the **Oribi Gorge** forms a 330m-deep, 2km-wide, and 15km-long green gash in the middle of sugar cane, banana, and coffee fields. Cliffs and thick green forests lead to the winding **Umzimkulwana River** at the bottom. There are five **trails** (varying from 1-9km) along the floor and up the walls of the gorge, from which you can enjoy the scenery and spot monkeys, snakes, trees, and birds. The **park office** at the hutted camp offers a **visitor's guide** (R5), which describes the gorge's history, wildlife, and trails. (☎679 1644 or 083 284 9326. Office open M-F 8am-12:30pm and 2-4:30pm, Sa-Su 8:30am-3pm. Open daily sunup to sundown. R10)

The **Oribi Gorge Hotel** has the most breathtaking **viewpoints** that the gorge has to offer (R9; free for guests). All viewpoints are within walking distance of the hotel. The hotel also organizes the area's adventure activities, including abseiling, rafting, tubing, and air tours. The 110m **abseiling** course next to the waterfall is the highest commercial course in the world. (Beginners welcome. 1st run R156, 2nd run R78. Daily during peak seasons and roughly twice a week in the low season; inquire about specific times.) Or, you can choose to **whitewater raft** Class IV rapids or a more relaxing Class II course. (Full day R260, including lunch. Min. 4 people.) Rafting is a seasonal activity dependent on the water level. The hotel is currently in the process of constructing the world's highest gorge swing (85-100m). Contact the hotel for details; book in advance.

Campsites ❶ near the park entrance provide fully equipped budget accommodation, but prices vary greatly depending on the season. All accommodations have access to showers and toilets. There is a communal kitchen, and the larger huts are self-catering. Guests can access a separate dining room, lounge area, and swimming pool. (☎679 1644 or 083 284 9326. 2-bed huts R100-R160 per person, min.; 7-bed huts R385-R665; 10-person cottages R400-R600.) The more expensive option is the **Oribi Gorge Hotel** ❸, off the road to Oribi Flats, 10km before the park turn-off. Built in the 1800s, the hotel has simple, homey rooms and elegant wooden furnishings. Call ahead for a free pick-up from Port Shepstone. (☎687 0253 or 082 337 3746; oribigorge@worldonline.co.za. Breakfast included. Reception daily 7am-9pm. Singles R250; doubles R380; children R95, under 6 free.)

MARGATE AND RAMSGATE ☎039

Margate and Ramsgate, only 3km apart, are the most popular seaside resort towns on the KwaZulu-Natal coast. Although Margate's neon-saturated downtown consists mostly of fast-food restaurants, beachwear stores, and a couple of casinos, the beach is spotless and the local wildlife is not limited to surfer dudes. During the December holidays, vacationers eager to escape Jo'burg's bustle flood the streets and make for wild, Pamplona-style partying. If you are lucky—or savvy— enough to be in Margate in early June, catch the annual **Sardine Run** and experience a slightly more chilled-out town that is nevertheless still full of people. Hundreds of shoals of sardines en route to Mozambican waters come close to the shore, causing a feeding frenzy with cape gannets, seagulls, and fishermen alike scooping up passing fish. At about the same time, humpback whales breach and slap their tails as they pass by the coast on their way to calve off the shores of Mozambique. Occasional pods pass by in winter, but snorkelers, surfers, and sunbathers are more common. No matter what time of year, the weather is always beautiful, the swells inspiring, and excellent restaurants serve some of the most mouth-watering (if costly) meals in the province.

▐ TRANSPORTATION

Flights: Margate Airport, 4km west of Erasmus and National Rd. intersection; follow signs. **South African Airlink** (☎312 1017 or 317 3267; fax 312 1018; www.saairlink.co.za) flies to and from **Johannesburg** (1½hr., 1-2 per day, one-way R824-1063). Lower fares require 21-day advance booking. Office open M-F 8:30am-4:30pm and Sa 11am-1:30pm, Su 11am-6pm.

Buses: Margate Mini Coach (☎312 1406; margate-minicoach@margate.co.za; www.margate.co.za/minicoach.htm) runs buses to **Durban** (2hr.; 3 per day; R65 one-way, R85 round-trip). Pick-up and drop-off in southern Margate near Country Kitchen Restaurant on Marine Dr. Booking office in the Gird Mowat Bldg. farther north on Marine Dr. Open M-F 8:30am-4pm, Sa 8:30-11am. **Luxliner** (☎315 7306 or 0800 003 537; intercity@luxliner.co.za) connects Margate and **Pretoria** (11hr., 1-3 per week, R226) via **Johannesburg, Pietermaritzburg, Estcourt,** and towns along the South Coast. Book at tourist office. **Lucky Bus Company** (☎312 0150), in Emoyeni Ctr., runs buses to **Port Shepstone** (30min., 2 per day, R4.50) and **Port Edward** (4 per day, R4.50).

Minibus Taxis: Parked at Emoyeni Ctr. and along Marine Dr. To: **Durban** (R28.50); **Port Edward** (R5); **Port Shepstone** (R3.50). Local minibuses run from Emoyeni Ctr. and along Marine Dr. for about R3.

Taxis: Busy Bee Taxis (☎082 368 1007).

Car Rentals: Budget (☎317 3202), **Avis** (☎312 0094), and **Imperial** (☎312 1346) all have offices in the airport.

▐ ▐ ORIENTATION AND PRACTICAL INFORMATION

Margate is about 120km south of Durban along the **Old National Rd.** (also the R620). Another route to the town is the well-maintained but toll-ridden R61. Old National Rd. and **Marine Dr.,** the two main roads in town, branch off from each other at the

KWAZULU-NATAL

northern end of town and rejoin at the southern end. Marine Dr. runs about one block from the coast. Parallel to it, along the water, is the **Panorama Parade.** The **Emoyeni Center** is a shopping center near the intersection of National and **Erasmus Rd.** From the intersection, Erasmus runs east past **Uplands Rd.,** which branches off to the left and runs downhill to Marine Dr. West of the Erasmus and National Rd. intersection, along **Wartski Dr.,** is the **Hibiscus Mall;** signs lead west from here to the airport. Follow Marine Dr./Old National Rd. for 3km south after they join back together to the center of **Ramsgate,** a one-street (and one-horse) town.

Tourist Office: Hibiscus Coast Tourism (☎312 2322; fax 312 1886; margate@hibiscus-coast.co.za), on Panorama Parade at the southern end of the beach, near Wimpy's. Info on every town from Hiberdene to Port Edward. Open M-F 8:30am-4pm, Sa 9am-noon.

Banks: Standard Bank (☎312 1411), on Marine Dr. south of Uplands Rd. Open M-F 8:30am-3:30pm, Sa 8:30-11am. **First National Bank** (☎312 1415), also on Marine Dr. opposite Standard Bank. Open M-F 9am-3:30pm, Sa 8:30-11am. Both have **ATMs.**

Bookstore: Ramsgate Stationers (☎312 0303), in Hibiscus Mall. Family-run store with great staff and selection. Open M-F 8am-5:30pm, Sa 8am-1pm, Su 8am-12:30pm.

Laundromat: Uvongo, 225 Marine Dr. (☎312 2507 or 082 450 2645.) R25 per load. M-F 8:30am-5pm, Sa 7-10am.

Internet Access: Towers (fax 317 1187), corner of Old Main Rd. and Marine Dr. Eight terminals. R0.50 per minute. Open M-F 8am-5pm, Sa 9am-5pm, Su noon-5pm. **Postnet** (☎317 2273), in Checkers Center on Marine Dr. One terminal. R7.50 per 15min.

Emergency: Ambulance (☎315 5444, 312 1000, or 317 1122). **Fire** (☎314 4471).

Police: ☎312 2524 or 312 2523. At Erasmus and National Rd. Open 24hr.

Pharmacy: Medical Center Pharmacy (☎312 0370), opposite Casino Cinema on Marine Dr. north of Uplands Rd. Largest pharmacy in town and always the last to close. Open M-F 8am-6pm, Sa 8am-1pm, Su 9am-noon.

Hospital: Margate Private Hospital (☎317 3201; fax 317 3326; margatehospital@margatehospital.co.za), on Wartski Dr., a block up from Hibiscus Mall. Open 24hr.

Post Office: ☎312 0111. On the corner of Post Office Rd. and Marine Dr. Fax and *Poste Restante.* Open M-Tu, Th-F 8:30am-4:30pm, W 9am-4:30pm, Sa 8am-noon.

Postal code: 4275.

ACCOMMODATIONS AND CAMPING

Prices vary drastically by season, increasing during the peak months of April, July, October, December, and especially during Christmas and New Year's, when advance reservations are absolutely necessary.

Margate Backpackers, 14 Collis St. (☎/fax 312 2176). Off the R620 toward Uvongo and Shelly Beach, north of Margate in Manaba. The cheapest option in Margate with clean, uncomplicated rooms close to the beach. Owned by a man with 18 years of lifeguard experience on South African coastlines. A place for good times and great stories. Diving, dolphin/whale watching trips, and tours to Oribi organized. Breakfast R15. Dinner R25. Pool table, satellite TV and bar. Phone for free pick-up. Reception 24hr. Check-out 11am. Dorms R50; doubles R140-160. Camping R40. ❶

Kenilworth-on-Sea (☎312 0342; fax 312 0504; www.kenilworth@interkom.co.za), on Marine Dr. 300m south of the post office. Old-fashioned guest lodge with clean rooms, restaurant, pool and TV lounge. Decent view of the sea from the garden. Reception open 7am-8pm daily. Check-out 10am; check-in noon-onwards. Breakfast and dinner included. R185-215 high season, R138-158 low season. ❷

Ramsgate Holiday Cottages (☎314 4308), booking office next to the Bistro, south of Ramsgate. Variety of self-catering cottages scattered throughout the area. Two-person sea breeze cottages with gorgeous sea views R150; up to R300 during holidays. Large, multi-bedroom houses on beachfront R300; in December R600-850. ❷

The Sunlawns Hotel (☎/fax 312 1078), on Hibiscus Ave. Turn off Marine Drive onto Uplands Rd. and follow to Hibiscus Ave. An unsophisticated hotel with simple doubles and unimaginative decor. Traditional Scottish pub. Attached toilet/bath. Breakfast included. Bar, pool table, TV lounge. Doubles high season R160, low season R125; with dinner R185/R150. ❷

🍴 FOOD

Marine Dr. is lined with chain restaurants, snack shops, and fast-food outlets where you can pick up a delightfully greasy snack for under R20, but some of the best restaurants in the province are away from the beach during the high season. It's a good idea to make reservations for these jewels.

▨ **La Petite Normandie** (☎317 1818), on the R620, off Marine Dr. in northern Ramsgate, just past the Margate-Ramsgate border. Gourmet French restaurant. Stylish, sophisticated feel and enchanting meals. Decorated with hand-stenciled designs, lanterns, and antique chests. Great wine list. Most entrees, including magnificent duck and rabbit dishes, R28-60. Open daily noon-2pm and 7pm until things wind down. ❷

▨ **Trattoria La Terrazza** (☎316 6162; fax 316 8031; masniki@venturenet.co.za), at the end of Outlook Rd. off the R61 South-broom (south) exit, 10km from Margate. The kind of enchanting setting that makes you want to stretch out your dining experience for as long as possible. Recently voted on of the top 100 restaurants in South Africa. Open terrace looks out onto the Umkobi Lagoon. Delectable Italian dishes include *pepperoni ripieni* (R27) and *tagliata fiorentina* (R60). Mozambican crabs R82. Wines from R32. Reservations essential. Open Tu 6:30-10pm, W-Su 12:30-2pm, 6:30-10pm. MC/V. ❷

Larry's (☎317 2277), on the corner of W. O' Conner and Panorama Parade, opposite the tourist information office. Currently striving to make the Guiness Book of Records for the restaurant with the most patrons' names on its walls, Larry's is a wonderfully and unashamedly quirky family restaurant. Scores of pirate-shaped cushions hang from the ceiling, watching patrons tear into great meat and seafood dishes (R35-98). 6 shooters R35. No reservations. Open in summer daily 10am-late, in winter 10am-10pm. ❸

O Rentiro de Pescador (☎317 4544; ocean555@mweb.co.za), Continental Court, Marine Dr. A fairly uninspired attempt at creating a pocket of Portugal in Margate. Still, the Mozambican chicken (R45) is worth a visit. Starters R7-24. Shellfish R60-165. Open daily noon-3pm and 5:30-10pm. AmEx/MC/V. ❹

📷 SIGHTS

The **Margate Art Museum,** on Viking Rd., off the road to the airport, features paintings, sculptures, and ceramics by local and national artists. (☎312 2525. Open Tu-F 9am-1pm and 1:30-5pm, Sa 10am-4pm. Free.) **Zizamele Tours,** a community tourism project based at the Mud Hut Gallery on Marine Dr., offers tours to the nearby township of Gamalakhe. You get to meet a Zulu *inkosi* (leader) and *sangoma* (healer). Next, you are taken on a historical and informative tour of rural Umzumbe and treated to Iscathmlya music (Zulu *a capella*). You can spend the night sleeping in the Umzumbe valley. (☎317 4473; fax 317 4498; afritours@telkomsa.net. 3-4hr. tour R150; overnight stay, breakfast included, R110; min. 6 people.)

KWAZULU-NATAL

⚔ ADVENTURES

To enjoy the South Coast's lush scenery from solid ground, go for a customized **horseback-riding trip** (☎ 082 676 1899). If you prefer reptiles to mammals, the **Riverbend Crocodile Farm**, 8km south of Margate on the R61, is home to more than 200 Nile crocodiles, from newborns to 50-year-old, 5m leviathans. Riverbend breeds 3000 hatchlings every year; check out the mating shallows and the sand banks where eggs are laid. An art gallery and the Crocpot restaurant and tea garden are attached. (☎/fax 316 6204. Open M-F 8:30am-4:30pm; Sa 9am-4:30pm, low season 9am-1pm.; Su 9am-5pm. Public feedings Su 3pm. R20, students R15, children 2-6 R10. Wheelchair accessible. MC/V.)

Margate's ever-present sun, brilliant surf, and wide golden beaches continue to draw the crowds to its waterfront. Rideable waves peel right from the point and break along the beach. Surfers and swimmers enjoy the safety of shark nets year-round, except during sardine season in June and July. **Whale-watching** is especially popular during the winter. To get even closer, you can make use of several boats that run tours. Call Wayne Harrison at **Adventure Extreme** to take a memorable, environmentally conscious whale and dolphin cruise. (☎ 315 0894 or 082 960 7682; wayden@venturenet.co.za; www.kznwhale.co.za. R150, ages 6-16 R100.) **Manteray Beach Hire,** on the beach, rents beach equipment by the day. (☎ 083 459 3373. Surfboards R30, bodyboards R25, wetsuits R20. 1½hr. surfing lessons R120 including equipment. Open daily 8am-4pm.) **Deep-sea fishing** can be arranged at **Sensational.** (Call Denise at 083 226 5634 or 082 232 1370. R320, low season R290.)

For those with steel nerves, **African Dive Adventures** and **Kenilworth-on-Sea** (see **Accommodations,** p. 260) organize shark dives near the Protea Banks Reef, one of the best shark-diving spots in the world. Get up close and personal with Zambezi, Ragged Tooth, Hammerhead and Tiger sharks. (Shark-diving R130, plus equipment. Equipment R30 per item. Full diving courses R1300-3500.)

♞ NIGHTLIFE

The club scene in Margate is small, but people still come from afar to drink and dance the night away. **Backline Sports Bar,** off Marine Dr., is the biggest club in town. It has pool tables, big-screen TVs, a spacious dance floor, and occasional live bands and raves. (☎ 317 4358. Open daily 7pm-late; closed low season M and Th. Cover R10-20.) The pitch-black walls in **Birdcage,** off Marine Dr. in Ramsgate, give the impression of being in outer space—an illusion destroyed only by the pool table and the dancers rooted firmly to the floor. (☎ 314 9097. Open daily 5pm-2am.) Finally, **Casino Cinema** will keep you up-to-date with all the current box-office releases. (☎ 312 0741. Ticket office open daily 1:30-3pm, 4:30-8pm. Call for tickets if the office is closed. R16 for early shows, R18 for 8:15pm shows; children R10, seniors R8.)

KEEP YOUR EYE ON THE KRAAL If you trace back the genealogy of the electrified-cable fence in South Africa, you will find that its distant ancestor (and its contemporary in many parts) is the *kraal*. Kraal is an Afrikaans word that has been adopted into South African English to describe the circular enclosures erected by Zulu families to protect themselves and their cattle from the marauding of large carnivores and stealthy enemies. However, the word has come to stand for the entirety of a Zulu family dwelling, including the thatched *rondavels* within. Throughout Zululand, those who cannot scrape together enough rand for an electrified-cable or razor-wire fence still build their *kraals* the old-fashioned way.

KWAZULU-NATAL

PORT EDWARD   ☎ 039

There's a kind of magic in the air around Port Edward. You can feel it when you talk to the woman who runs the Vuna Valley Backpackers: she encourages children to listen for fairies living in the trees. Or you can sense it when you meet the man who owns the largest private collection of astronomical devices in South Africa and is not yet ready to conclude whether UFOs exist. This small, enchanting town stretches from the ocean back to the jungle-like forest along the banks of the Umtamvuna River. It is this river that marks the boundary between the Eastern Cape and KwaZulu-Natal, making Port Edward the last stop on the way south to the Wild Coast. The town is quiet, but there is plenty to see and do. Its attractions, however, are rather far apart for those on foot, and there is little public transportation. Still, any effort to make it here will be well rewarded with clean, calm beaches, the scenic Umtamvuna Nature Reserve, and unique, high-quality crafts.

▐ TRANSPORTATION

Buses: It's easiest to take a bus from Durban to the Wild Coast Sun Casino, and then a minibus taxi from the casino to the taxi stand near town. **Gass Buses** (☎253 1048) stop several times a day at the petrol station on the Owen Ellis side of the highway intersection. They run to **Durban** (R35) and **Lusikisiki** (R25), where connecting buses run to **Port St. Johns.** Schedules change frequently, so call ahead or ask at the petrol station.

Minibus Taxis: The taxi association (☎313 1416) has a stand at the Port Edward R61 intersection; it often pays to head to the Shelton taxi stand across the river (R2.50), where minibuses run to **Bizana** (R10), **Durban** (R25), and **Port Shepstone** (R10).

✦ ⁊ ORIENTATION AND PRACTICAL INFORMATION

Port Edward lies on both sides of the **R61,** about 160km southwest of Durban. From the highway intersection, the signs for Port Edward point down **Owen Ellis Rd.** toward the center of town and the beach. The road winds about 1km from the highway before **Ramsey Rd.** branches off to the right toward the **Strawberry Lane Center.** Owen Ellis Rd. veers left, passing the **Port Edward Mall** and the post office before terminating at the **Port Edward Holiday Resort** and the beach. On the opposite side of the highway, **Izingolweni Rd.** leads past **Old Pont Rd.** (the second left, about 3km from the highway) to the Beacon Hill entrance of the **Umtamvuna River Nature Reserve** about 8km away. The R61 itself continues southeast, crossing the Umtamvuna River into the Transkei about 4km from the intersection.

Tourist Office: (☎/fax 313 1211; portedward@thehibiscuscoast.co.za), on Owen Ellis between Ramsey Rd. and the Port Edward Mall. Open M-F 8:30am-4pm, Sa 9am-noon.

Banks: There are 3 banks in the Port Edward Mall. **ABSA** (☎ 313 2386) has the best hours but does not change traveler's checks. (Open M-F 8:30am-3:30pm, Sa 8-11am.) Change currency and traveler's checks at **First National Bank** (☎313 2355; open M-F 9:30am-2pm) or **Standard Bank** (☎313 2290; open M-F 9:30am-2pm). There is a 24hr. ABSA **ATM** in the shopping center at the highway intersection.

Library (☎313 2281; pelib@venturenet.co.za), next to the tourist office. Open M and W 8:30am-4pm, Tu and Th 9am-5pm, F 9am-4:45pm, Sa 9am-noon.

Supermarket: KwikSpar (☎313 2321), next to the Port Edward Mall. Open M-Sa 7:30am-7pm, Su 8am-5pm.

Laundry: Laundrette, in Strawberry Lane Ctr. Wash and dry R25 per load. Wash, dry, iron R40. Self-service 24hr. After hours, tokens can be bought at Marc One video shop. Open M-F 7:30am-4:30pm, Sa 7am-1pm.

KWAZULU-NATAL

Pharmacies: Port Edward Pharmacy (☎313 1263, emergency 082 335 4604; fax 313 2098), in the Port Edward Mall. Open M-F 8:30am-5pm, Sa 8:30am-1pm.

Police: ☎313 2266, emergency ☎10 111. off Owen Ellis Rd. just above the golf course. Open 24hr.

Medical Assistance: Dr. Dennis P. Van Zyl (☎313 2380), in the **Port Edward Medical Center** at the intersection of Owen Ellis and Ramsey Rd. Open M-F 8:30am-5:45pm, Sa 8:30am-12:45pm.

Internet Access: Career Development College (☎313 1367), near the post office. R10 per 15min. Printing and scanning also available. Open M-Sa 9am-7pm.

Post Office: ☎313 2222. On Owen Ellis Rd. across from the Port Edward Mall. Open M-Tu and Th-F 8:30am-4:30pm, W 9am-4:30pm, Sa 8am-noon.

Postal Code: 4295.

▐ ACCOMMODATIONS AND CAMPING

Backpacking chalets and hostels can be found on Old Pont and Izingolweni Rd. along the perimeter of the nature reserve. There are also hotels and guest houses near the beach off Owen Ellis Rd. Though a stay in town is convenient, the more remote places near the park are quieter, offer spectacular views, and are sometimes significantly less expensive. Hostel owners are usually happy to pick up guests who arrive in Port Edward without a car; call ahead to make arrangements.

AROUND PORT EDWARD

▨ **Kuboboyi Backpackers** (☎319 1371 or 072 222 7760; fax 319 1372; kuboboyi@hotmail.com), from Durban follow the N2 south, then take the R61. Take the second Leisure Bay turnoff on your left. At the first right you'll see the huge sign. Backpacker rates belie the sheer quality of what is surely one of South Africa's finest backpackers. Incredible food, heart-warming hospitality and spectacular 180° panoramic views make this an essential stop for any visitor to the Hibiscus Coast. Tons of activities can be arranged and a weekly Zulu cultural evening is planned. Port Shepstone pick-up R35. Lunch and dinner R35. Laundry R15 per load. Internet R30-40 per hr. HI discounts. Dorms R60; singles R100; doubles R150. Camping R35. ❶

The Flying Rhino Backpackers, 68 Effingham Parade (☎ 084 326 0376 or 313 0632). Take exit to Trafalgar off the R61, turn right onto Cunningham Pl., right at the T-Junction onto Effingham Parade. A fairly quiet hostel with a large, stunning garden-*cum*-campsite. The inviting *braai* area adds to the hospitable and calm atmosphere. Meals on request from R30. Shuttle from Port Shepstone R35. Dorms R60; doubles R140-160. Camping R40 per person. Group discounts can be arranged. ❶

Windsor Guest House, 180 Harrow Ave. (☎313 2389; umtam@venturenet.co.za; www.mrinfo.co.za). Entrance on Indaba Rd. Often used as an overflow accommodation for the Wild Coast Sun but nowhere near as luxurious or nice. Reasonable doubles with good views. Breakfast included. TV in room. Reception 7am-8:30pm. Check-out by 10:30am. Singles R250-300; R150-250 per person. AmEx/DC/MC/V. ❸

NEAR THE UMTAMVUNA VALLEY NATURE RESERVE

▨ **Vuna Valley Backpackers** (☎083 992 6999 or 313 1118; vunavalley@hotmail.com). On Mitchell Rd. at the end of Old Pont Rd., near the lower entrance to the nature reserve. Nestled in the Umtamvuna Valley on the border of the Transkei, the only sounds here are made by nature or you. The owner is lovely and encourages guests to join her in covering the walls of the hostel with brightly covered murals. Port Shepstone pick-up R35. Breakfast included. Dinner R30. Dorms R60; doubles R140. Camping R35. ❶

Clearwater Chalets (☎313 1130 or 083 549 6710; tabbott@venturenet.co.za). Follow signs for Clearwater Chalets at the end of District Rd. 595 off Izingolweni Rd., about 5km from highway. Simple, tidy chalets with spectacular views of the hills across the Umtamvuna Gorge, beside the nature reserve's hiking trails. Owners have a wealth of knowledge about indigenous flora. Free shuttle from Port Edward. Continental breakfast R25. Key deposit R150. Reception open daily 8am-6pm. Backpacker accommodations R50; doubles R100-150; 4- to 6-person chalets R200-300. ❶

The Space Center (☎313 2891). Off Izingolweni Rd. 4km from highway. Entertainment here is different from the usual hostel fare. The owner has assembled the largest collection of astronomical equipment in South Africa and is only too happy to discuss and explain his toys. His enthusiasm for the audio-visual spectacle also includes a huge TV screen and a laser-lit dance floor. Hiking trails and breathtaking views round out the eccentric and worthwhile package. Call for pick-up. Breakfast included. Singles R60. Also has *rondavels* and doubles. ❶

🍴 FOOD

The Webb (☎313 2593), in the Port Edward Mall. A simple restaurant with wild and eccentric ideas about pizza. Pizzas R10-39. Burgers R19-27. Fully stocked bar. Open daily 11am-10pm; low season M-Sa 11am-10pm. AmEx/DC/MC/V. ❶

Waterfront Restaurant (☎313 2301), attached to the Port Edward Holiday Resort. Specializes in seafood and overlooks the ocean. Seafood R35. Pub lunch R17-31. Takeaway cafe offers fish and chips (R14.50), curry and rice (R15), and sandwiches (R8-10). Open daily 8am-late; low season Su-M 8am-2pm, Tu-Sa 8am-late. ❷

Mother's Sports Bar and Grille (☎313 2169), on Owen Ellis Rd. past the Port Edward Mall, next to the Windwood Lodge. The closest thing you'll get to nightlife in Port Edward, with big screen TV, pool tables, and beers at R6 a bottle. Attached in Sleeper's Restaurant. Open daily 7am-2am. ❶

Sleeper's Restaurant (☎313 2373), on Owen Ellis Rd., attached to Mother's Sports Bar. Quiet, with reasonable deals for hungry travelers. W "Rib Mania" (full R30, half R23). F prawn specials, with 10 for R45. Open daily 7am-10am, noon-2pm, and 6-10pm. ❷

🎨 CRAFTS

POTTERY. There are several craft shops and pottery studios in and around Port Edward; see the work progress from inception to completion. At **Emithini,** you can browse through a dizzying collection of hand-painted and tie-dyed fabrics and clothing. Prices range from R30 to R650. *(On Old Pont Rd. ☎313 1241. Open daily 8am-4:30pm. Low season closed 2nd weekend of every month.)* **Zanner Pottery Studio** features slip-cast pottery, which is made from liquid clay ("slip") that is poured into a mold and baked, glazed, baked, glazed, and baked again. *(Closer to town on Old Pont Rd. ☎313 2382. Open daily 8am-5pm.)* Bright hand-painted mugs, plates, and teapots inhabit a well-tended garden. Also worth a visit is **Jo Arkell Pottery,** on Old Pont Rd., which has spunkier handmade work, including banana leaf stationery. *(☎313 1672. Open M-F 9am-12:30pm and 1:30-4:30pm.)*

CRAFTS. 🖼**Skhumba Crafts,** hidden amidst the greenery of Margate's surrounding forests, is a gem for artistic inspiration and master craftsmanship. The highlight of this fantastic little wooden complex, which includes a coffee shop and small stage for open-air performances, is a shop selling handmade leather shoes, belts and masks. The owner has been doing leather-work for the last 17 years, and it shows in the style and quality of his work. *(☎316 8212. Just off the R61 between Margate and Port Edward. Shoe prices R425-725.)* **Rob and Karen Bauchop** make internationally

KWAZULU-NATAL

acclaimed custom knives and swords in their workshop. Orders usually take about one month, but they have some pieces on display and are happy to show visitors what they do. The workshop is in Munster, about 7km north of Port Edward on R61. From the highway, head toward the coast 1km; the workshop is on the left just before the police station. *(☎/fax 319 2449; bauchopknives@hotmail.com.)*

👁 🧗 SIGHTS AND ADVENTURES

With a name like Port Edward, there's got to be a beach somewhere. You'll find the blue, peaceful waters of the Indian Ocean down Owen Ellis Rd. to Beach Rd. However, there is more to Port Edward than sand and waves. If you dare tear yourself away, head inland and discover the other side of this sleepy town.

AMADIBA ADVENTURES. An initiative entirely owned and operated by the community, Amadiba offers horse and hiking trails from Port Edward to the Umtentu River mouth in the Transkei. The European Union marveled at Amadiba's potential and brought significant financial support to expand the project along the full length of the Wild Coast, bringing over 60 jobs to the local people and attracting tourists without destruction. Fully operational trails run from Port Edward to Umtentu; 4-day trails take you there and back while 6-day trails allow some canoeing and more exploration in the nature reserve. Several pilot trails between Port St. Johns and Port Edward allow homestays with village families. Prices include all gear, food, accommodation, and activities. This is not only an opportunity to see some of the most spectacular scenery South Africa has to offer; it is a chance to contribute to the growth of a community and a country. It is tourism at its best. *(☎ 039 305 6455; fax 039 305 6456. R600-780 per person per day. Options are flexible.)*

THE SPACE CENTER. The owner of this one-of-a-kind museum/observatory/guest farm (see **Accommodations,** p. 265) gives a variety of tours as well as space exploration demonstrations. Reservations are essential. *(On Izingolweni Rd. past Old Pont. ☎ 313 2891. Audio-video slide shows 11am and 3pm daily in season; min. 10 people. Open daily 10am-5pm. R25, children R15.)*

UMTAMVUNA NATURE RESERVE. Stretching 25km along the northern shore of the Umtamvuna River, the reserve is famous for its rare trees, many of which are unique to the reserve. Cliffs capped by grasslands surround the gorge's lush forest, and baboons hang in the trees. Six trails, varying in length from 500m to 8km, snake along the floor and sides of the ravine, taking hikers through subtropical vegetation brimming with many colorful, sweetly singing, tree-clinging forms of wildlife. *The Umtamvuna Nature Reserve*, available at the tourist office and at the main entrance of the park (R10), describes the park's natural history. *(Two entrances: the main entrance 8km from the highway on Izingolweni Rd., and another at the end of Old Pont Rd. ☎ 313 2383. Trail maps available at entrances. No accommodations in the park, but caravaning and camping facilities are available. Open daily 7am-5pm. R10.)*

BEAVER CREEK COFFEE FARM. This caffeine haven supplies restaurants and grocery stores throughout the South Coast. A tour shows you the entire journey from seedling to tree to bean to miraculous brew (R10). Afterward, buy coffee liqueurs (R35 for 340ml) or java accessories in the shop. *(About 4.5km from the highway on Izingolweni Rd. ☎ 313 2347. Tours daily at 10am, noon, 2pm. Open M-Sa 9am-5pm, Su 9am-11am; high season also Su 9am-5pm.)*

NEAR PORT EDWARD: WILD COAST SUN CASINO   ☎039

About 5km south of Port Edward along the R161, the **Wild Coast Sun Casino** ❺ (☎ 305 9111) draws slot machine addicts from all over South Africa. With over 1000 slot machines, six restaurants, tennis and squash courts, table tennis, go-carts, miniature golf, bowling, beauty salons, boutiques, and all the alcohol you can funnel down your throat, fun here is abundant and expensive. Rooms in the impressive hotel begin at R662 per night (the cheapest double, although if you ask they sometimes have specials), so plan a daytrip and stay in Port Edward. If you do strike it rich and decide to stay in the hotel, keep your balcony door closed at night or else the cheeky monkeys may slip in and wreak havoc. The attached **Waterworld** (☎305 3024), at the mouth of the Umtamvuna River, has everything from waterskiing to booze cruises.

Also accessible from the casino is the intertidal **petrified forest.** Ask someone in town about the tide chart, and head down past the stable to the beach at low tide. Walk south along the coast (to the right when facing the water) for about 1km to come upon tree stumps and other fossilized impressions at the water's edge. To come here without paying the R10 entrance to the casino complex, drive through the entrance on the far right (for buses and staff) and tell the person in the booth that you're just there for the petrified forest. Across the highway from the casino is the **Mazamba Craft Village,** an enormous collection of imitation thatched huts filled with Xhosa crafts. (☎039 305 6083. Open M-Sa 8am-4:30pm, Su 8:30am-4:30pm.)

ZULULAND

Zululand, the ancestral home of the Zulu people, is a remarkable place both for its natural beauty and its rich history. The area's beauty can be seen in its dusty brown plains, gently rolling hills, river valleys, lush forests, waving grasslands, and staggering cliffs. The area's history, meanwhile, is proud, tragic, and bloody. During the *mfecane* ("the great crushing") in the early 19th century, the Zulu kingdom, led by legendary Shaka Zulu, swept into present-day Zululand from the north, annihilating or assimilating the peoples in its path. Shaka's empire expanded rapidly to become one of the largest in Southern Africa. Later clashes between the Zulus and Europeans involved great loss of life on both sides and eventually spelled the end of Zulu military might. These battles are commemorated today by monuments and cemeteries that dot the landscape like a web of unanswered questions.

To an outsider, it might seem like the only surviving trace of Zululand's former glory is in the myths and memories of its people. Today, many of the Zulu people live in poverty. Much of their society has recently been devastated by cholera, malaria, and HIV/AIDS, problems heightened by illiteracy and poor health care. But despite these problems, the Zulus are still a proud, strong, hopeful people. Opportunities for visitors to experience Zulu culture range from genuine and respectful to shallow and artificial. If you can distinguish the one from the other, you might be surprised by how much you can learn and experience.

ESHOWE ☎035

The small town of Eshowe is the center of the Zulu Nation. Those who step inland from the coastline are bound to encounter an African experience they never knew they were waiting for. Several twists and turns on a winding, scenic route hide Eshowe from view until, quite suddenly, you find yourself cooled by the breezes of the Indian Ocean and surrounded by modest dwellings and businesses. Founded by Zulu Prince Cetshwayo in 1860, Eshowe, loosely translated as "the wind sighing through the trees," was the site of a 10-week siege during the Anglo-Zulu War of 1879 and eventually became the capital of British Zululand. The birthplace and home of King Shaka (see above) is nearby. Eshowe may not be filled with raucous nightlife and exciting game drives, but it is brimming with stories and experiences.

SHAKA ZULU (1787-1828) Senzangakona, chief of the Zulus, and Nandi, the orphaned princess of the neighboring Elangeni group, met "accidentally" on a trail late one night. When an Elangeni messenger later reported that Nandi was pregnant, Senzangakona was extremely embarrassed, replying that her swollen belly must be the work of *iShaka*—an intestinal beetle. And so the babe got his name. After Shaka was born, an untraditional marriage between his parents failed, and he was sent back to the unwelcoming Elangeni with his mother. During the widespread famine of 1802, the adolescent Shaka and his mother were evicted from the clan and wandered homeless until they were accepted by the Mtetwa people. Here, Shaka grew and established a reputation for being a ferocious and creative warrior—inventor of the *iKlwa*, a short stabbing spear named for the sound it made when pulled from a victim's corpse. He eventually returned to the Zulus and forged an army that swept through Southern Africa like an avalanche, consuming or destroying every clan in its path. Though father of a new nation, Shaka could not even manage to govern himself when his mother died in 1827. Mad with grief, he executed close to 7000 Zulus and decreed that for one year no crops could be planted and no milk consumed. Pregnant women and their husbands were killed and milk cows slaughtered so that calves would experience the loss of a mother. Shaka was eventually assassinated by two of his half-brothers, but he remains the most dramatic symbol of a long, and violent Zulu heritage.

▐ TRANSPORTATION

The **Baz Bus** (☎ 021 439 2323) stops at Hotel George (6 buses per week) before heading west to Durban and east to Swaziland. The **minibus taxi rank** is behind the Chicken Licken near the roundabout on Main St. Minibuses to: Durban (2hr., R35); Empangeni (45min., R20); Gingindlovu (20min., R7); Johannesburg (7hr., R110); KwaDukuza/Stanger (45min., R25); Nkwalini (20min., R7); Ulundi (1hr., R30).

✳ ▐ ORIENTATION AND PRACTICAL INFORMATION

Eshowe lies about 150km north of Durban. Heading north from Durban on the N2, turn left onto the R66, which takes you into Eshowe. The main street through town is **Osborne St.**, which runs north-south parallel to the R66 on its west side. The two streets that connect Osborne St. to the R66 are **Kangela Rd.** on the northern side of town and **John Ross Hwy.** on the southern side of town. Kangela Rd. continues west past the hospital and then forms the northern boundary of the **Dlinza Forest.** John Ross Hwy. meets Osborne St. at a rotary, and **Main St.** leads west from that rotary past several hotels and toward **Fort Nongqayi.** Most of the town's shops and services are on Osborne St., or in the Eshowe Mall, at the corner of Osborne and Kangela St., just north of the center.

The **Eshowe Tourist Office** is on the corner of Osborne Rd. and Hutchinson St. (☎474 1141; open M-F 7:30am-4pm). Services include: **ABSA Bank** with **ATM,** on Osborne St. in the center of town (☎474 5601; open M-F 8:30am-3:30pm, Sa 8-11am); **Edwards Pharmacy,** on Osborne St. (☎474 1137; after hours 082 771 6644; open M-F 8am-5pm, Sa 8am-1pm); **Eshowe Hospital,** on Kangela Rd. west of the intersection with Osborne St. (☎474 2071; open 24hr. for emergencies); **Police, Traffic Control,** and **Fire Services** (☎474 2909 or 10 111 for police, 10 177 for ambulance) at 3 Hutchinson St. Surprisingly quick **Internet** access can be found at **Postnet,** in the Eshowe Mall at Osborne and Kangela Rd. (☎474 2222. Open M-F 8am-5pm, Sa 8am-1pm. 20min. R10; R1 per printed page.) The **post office** has *Poste Restante* and **telephones.** (☎474 4455. Open M-Tu and Th-F 8:30am-4:30pm, W 9am-4:30pm, Sa 8am-noon.) **Postal code:** 3815.

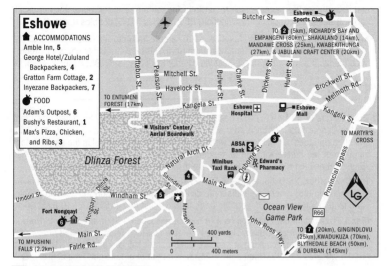

Eshowe

♠ ACCOMMODATIONS
Amble Inn, **5**
George Hotel/Zululand
  Backpackers, **4**
Gratton Farm Cottage, **2**
Inyezane Backpackers, **7**

● FOOD
Adam's Outpost, **6**
Bushy's Restaurant, **1**
Max's Pizza, Chicken,
  and Ribs, **3**

■ ACCOMMODATIONS

▨ **Inyezane Backpackers,** off the R66 between Eshowe and Gingindlovu (☎337 1326 or 082 704 4766; inyezane@ethniczulu.com; www.inyezane.lodge.tc). Inyezane is about 20km from Eshowe, so travelers without cars would probably be better off staying in Eshowe itself. For travelers with cars, however, Inyezane is worth the trip. To get there, take the R66 south from Eshowe, turn right onto the D134 dirt road just before Gingindlovu, and follow signs. A funky sort of place out in the middle of the cane fields, Inyezane offers all the usual things, like pleasant dorms, living room, and bar, with the added attractions of a steam room, wood-fired herbal bath, and mud baths. The artistically inclined can paint their own shirts, sarongs, and wall hangings, try their hand at pottery, or make paper out of zebra dung. A wide selection of tours, homestays, and cultural experiences are also available. Far from the lights and noise of the cities, Inyezane offers peace and quiet under a star-filled African sky. Laundry R30. Steam room and herbal bath R60 each; mud bath R35; fabric printing R60-240; pottery R150; paper making R80; tours and cultural experiences R60-250. Special rates on car rentals available. Dorms R50; singles R90; doubles R130, with A/C R150. Camping R35. ●

George Hotel/Zululand Backpackers, 38 Main St. (☎/fax 474 4919 or ☎082 492 6918; info@eshowe.com; www.eshowe.com). Zululand Backpackers is situated in the back of the George Hotel. It offers decent dorms with a communal kitchen and *braai* area, and guests have access to the George Hotel's bar, restaurant, and huge swimming pool. Freebies include 500mL of beer on your first night, one bundle of washing, and short tours of the town. The enthusiastic owners know Zululand well and can arrange cultural tours, including trips to traditional weddings, *sangoma* (traditional healer) initiation ceremonies, and other Zulu events (R195-250). Outdoor adventures include rock-sliding (see **Outdoors,** p. 270) and canoeing. Dorms R55; singles R85; doubles R150. Camping R30. Hotel singles R195; doubles R295; breakfast included. ●

Gratton Farm Cottage (☎/fax 474 1619 or ☎083 777 3815; dyardley@netactive.co.za). A relaxing B&B about 5km out of town on the R66 toward Melmoth, overlooking a rambling farm and nearby lake. Two rooms sleep up to 6 and feature TV, fan, heater, coffee maker, and views of surrounding cane fields. Communal lounge, dining area, and bar. The perfect place to settle in for some peace and quiet. Kitchen available. Breakfast R20. Dinner (2hr. notice) R50. Singles R195; doubles R300. ❷

Amble Inn, 116 Main St. (☎/fax 474 1300; ambleinn@corpdial.co.za). Close to the George Hotel, down Main St. and away from town, this pleasant lodge offers nice rooms and plenty of privacy. Breakfast included. Dinner R50. Singles R195; doubles R295. ❷

🍴 FOOD

▧ **The Quarters** (☎474 4919). The best food in town is at this warmly furnished restaurant at the George Hotel. Choose from a menu of hearty dishes like roast leg of lamb with mashed potatoes or chicken curry with rice. Thirsty? Have your meal in the bar next door and shoot the breeze with the bartender. Basic breakfast of cereal and fruit R14. Full English Breakfast R30. Dinner R25-40. Open 7-9am, noon-2pm, and 6:30-8pm. ❷

The Chatterbox, 26 Osborne Rd. (☎474 2738). Soak up the local atmosphere (maybe some gossip too) in a clean and simple diner atmosphere. Friendly interior and people, and large, tasty servings. Vegetarian options. Breakfast R17.50; lunch R10-R25. ❶

Max's Pizza, Chicken, and Ribs (☎474 5357), on Osborne St. in the center of town. If you are in the center of town, skip the mediocre fast-food joints and head straight for the good down-home cooking at Max's. Grilled quarter chicken and chips R14. Burgers R10-13. Pizzas R15-25. Open daily 7:45am-9pm. Eat in or take-out. Free delivery. ❶

Adams' Outpost (☎474 1787), at Fort Nongqayi. An elegant lunch spot in the shadow of the Fort, serving sandwiches, salads, meats, and seafood (entrees R20-40). Open M-F 9am-4pm, F 6-9pm, and Su 10am-3pm. ❷

Memory Lane Coffee Shop (☎474 5560), inside the Eshowe Mall, at Osborne St. and Kangela Rd. A quintessential "cafe shoppe," with understated decor and a large menu. Breakfast R15-25, served until 11am. Lunch R10-35. Open M-Sa 8am-5pm. ❶

Bushy's Restaurant at Eshowe Sports Club (☎474 2214), on Butcher St., off the R66 as it heads north (towards Melmoth/Empangeni). Serves seafood (R20-40), meaty pub lunches (R15), and indulgent grills (R34). Open daily noon-2pm and 6:30-9:30pm. ❷

👁 🗻 SIGHTS AND OUTDOORS

FORT NONGQAYI. An imposing stark-white structure, the fort was erected by the British in 1883 to house the Zululand Native Police and the Cape Mounted Rifles. Displays include traditional Zulu dress, a section of the fort's original floor, animal skulls, and memorabilia from the golden age of Anglo-Zulu conflict. The museum shop sells local crafts and history books. (*Follow Main St. past the George Hotel and police headquarters, turn right onto Windham Rd., and make a left onto Nongqayi Rd.* ☎474 1141. Open M-F 7:30am-4pm, Sa-Su 9am-4pm. R20 also includes entrance to Vukani Collection Museum. Donations appreciated.)

VUKANI COLLECTION MUSEUM. This small museum showcases beautiful examples of Zulu basketry, pottery, woodwork, beadwork, and tapestry. The pieces in the museum were originally part of a private collection owned by Rev. Kjell LoFroth, a Swedish missionary in Zululand. (*Located behind Fort Nongqayi, on Nongqayi Rd.* ☎474 1141. Open daily 9am-4pm.)

DLINZA FOREST RESERVE. This 250ha nature reserve in the middle of town is the spot for picnicking and bird-watching. Dlinza has more than 65 different species of birds, from the Purple-crested Lourie to the endangered Spotted Thrush. A 125m **aerial boardwalk** allows you to see the forest as the birds do and culminates in a 20m platform with a view of the Indian Ocean. For those who prefer to stay on the ground, the **Impunzi Trail** (20min.) and **Unkonka Trail** (30min.) begin at the Visitors Center and wind their way past more trees than you can shake a stick at. The lengthy **Prince Dabulamanzi Trail** begins at Dlinza and leads through indigenous forests to Entumeni Forest Reserve; inquire at the visitors' center for details. Early morning is said to be the best time for bird watching. Do not drink or swim in the streams, as there may be bilharzia in the water. *(Entrance to the forest is off Kangela Rd., northwest of the town center.* ☎ *474 4029. Gates open Sept.-Apr. 6am-6pm, May-Aug. 8am-5pm. R20 for entrance to the boardwalk, students R10.)*

OTHER OUTDOORS. A trail leads from Fort Nongqayi to the 5m-high **Mpushini Falls** (20min.); the attendant at the museum can point the way. If you have a little extra time on your hands, visit the small **Ocean View Game Park,** south of town on the John Ross Hwy., below the prison. Quiet in comparison to Kruger or Hluhluwe, Ocean View still delights with frisky herds of zebra, wildebeest, and gazelle. Farther out of town, approximately 17km from Eshowe on the Nkandla Rd., is **Entumeni Forest Reserve.** Established in 1970, Entumeni covers 750ha and consists mainly of a huge gorge covered in forests. The reserve is home to blue duiker, bushbuck, zebra, birds, and the rare Miller's Tiger moth, thought until recently to be extinct. Facilities consist of a clearing in the forest with two picnic tables. Two steep and strenuous hiking trails also begin at this clearing. *(Follow Kangela Rd. west for 13.2km, turn left and continue 3.5km to the forest entrance.* ☎ *476 6776. Gates open Sept.-Apr. 6am-6pm, May-Aug. 8am-5pm.)*

SPORTING EVENTS. The Eshowe Sports Club hosts weekly cricket, rugby, field hockey, and football matches between local teams. These games are a good place to meet locals and get away from tourists. Games are generally on the weekends; call ahead to find out what's up. *(On Butcher St., off the R66 north of town.* ☎ *474 2214.)*

CULTURAL TOURS

These tours are, far and away, the best reason to come to Eshowe and a fascinating way to gain a greater understanding of Zulu culture. **Umemluo** (girl's coming of age), **ukunqwambisa** (*sangoma* graduation), **uthomba** (boy's initiation), and **Zulu wedding** ceremonies are frequent events in this region. These ceremonies would happen with or without the presence of the tourists, thus eliminating some of the showcase feel of some other South African cultural experiences. Zulus go out of their way to make sure that visitors understand the nature of the ceremonies. **Overnight homestays** in the villages also offer a unique, first-hand opportunity to understand Zulu culture. Leaving from Martyr's Cross (see **Nkwalini Valley,** p. 274), visitors hike down into the valley below to their host family, where they spend the day, night and morning. On *sangoma* **visits,** visitors can sit with a local healer and ask questions about their tradition, herbal knowledge, bone-throwing techniques, and initiation process. The *sangoma* then tells the visitor's fortune and answers questions about health, love, money, and any other burning mysteries. Skittish visitors beware: your fortune may reveal an obstacle that can only be overcome with the killing of a chicken. Enthusiastic and somewhat informal tours of **KwaZulu-Natal battlefields** and sites in the **Nkwalini Valley** are given by Henry Bird, an amateur historian and SATOUR-registered guide. *(Cultural tours can be arranged through the George Hotel at 474 4919, or directly with Graham Chennells at 082 492 6918, Victor Mduduzi Mdluli at 072 152 0636, or Walter Cele at 082 665 9038. Ceremony visits R195-250. Overnight homestays R250. Henry Bird offers battlefield tours for R300 and Nkwalini Valley tours for R75; 474 2348, ahbird@netactive.co.za.)*

FESTIVALS. Several annual Zulu festivals take place around Eshowe. Not many tourists know about them, making them a good opportunity to interact with Zulu people in a natural way. The **Shembe Festival** takes place throughout October and draws pilgrims from far and wide for traditional religious celebrations. The **Reed Dance** occurs on the first Saturday in September. The festival of **First Fruits** is celebrated on February 23rd about 60km from Eshowe. Inquire at the George Hotel/ Zululand Backpackers for details.

NEAR ESHOWE

NKWALINI VALLEY

The Nkwalini Valley, the region immediately to the north of Eshowe, is a fertile patchwork quilt of sugar cane, citrus trees, and coffee plantations stretching almost 100 sq. km. The sights are relatively remote and inconspicuous and are best seen by car or on the local tours out of Eshowe.

If you follow Kangela Rd. east out of town, you should reach **Martyr's Cross.** The route is complex, so ask the tour office or locals for directions. The cross was placed here in 1877 in memory of Maqhamusela Khanyile, a Zulu who, after studying with missionaries, wanted to convert to Christianity. When he was ordered to denounce Christianity and pronounce allegiance to the Zulu nation before an enormous crowd, he refused and was executed; his body was left on top of the hill. According to local legend, that afternoon a thunderstorm engulfed the hill and his body disappeared, carried by God into the heavens during the storm. The site affords a 270-degree view of the valley below.

Mandawe Cross, a church built in the 1960s by Catholics to commemorate the efforts of local missionaries, is about 30min. by car from Eshowe. Follow the R66 about 10km north of town, turn right on the R230, and follow the exceptionally cratered road past several villages to the church. Be advised that this road is not recommended for travelers without a 4WD vehicle. The circular stone church, built in the shape of an inverted milking pail, is used every Sunday by the faithful who trek from surrounding villages. If it's open, the three-ladder climb to the top reveals a view of the Indian Ocean on a clear day.

About 14km north of Eshowe on the R66, **Shakaland** is built on and from the set of the acclaimed film *Shaka Zulu* and arranged as a traditional Zulu *umuzi* (homestead). It inspires controversy among locals and visitors alike: some describe it as a superficial, Disneyfied version of Zulu life, while others claim that it to be the closest most tourists will ever come to real Zulu culture. (☎460 0912; shakares@iafrica.com; www.shakaland.com. 3hr. tours at 11am and 12:30pm; R148 per person includes tour, lunch, and Zulu dance performance. Overnight visits begin at 4pm; R470 includes tour, drinks, dinner, accommodations, and breakfast; backpacker discounts available.)

KwaBekithunga is the home of the Fakude family and a cultural village that can be visited only by prior arrangement. To get there, follow the R66 north from Eshowe and turn right onto the R34 toward Empangeni. After 7km, turn right onto a dirt road and follow signs for KwaBekithunga/Stewart's Farm. Twelve Zulu families live and work on the premises, and Zulu cultural programs are available. Accommodation is available in Zulu beehive huts with toilets and showers; the camp has a thatched-roof bar and restaurant. (☎035 460 0644; fax 460 0867. Cultural programs R120, including a meal. Huts R75, with dinner and breakfast R150.)

The **Jabulani Craft Center** is 20km out of Eshowe towards Empangeni, on the R34. Their motto is, "We are in the people business, not the money business." If you are growing tired of the typical curio stand, this is the place to go wild with your shopping budget and contribute to a good cause. The center has workshops and housing specially equipped for disabled craftspeople. If you ask, you can get a tour around the workshop while they're working. Their beautiful creations—from animal-skin drums and spears to pottery, woodcarvings, and beadwork—are sold in a small thatched showroom next to the workshop. Proceeds from the sale of crafts provide assistance to the disabled of KwaZulu-Natal. Note that bargaining and haggling are not especially appropriate here. (☎/fax 928 144. Open daily 8am-5pm.)

KWADUKUZA (STANGER)   ☎ 032

KwaDukuza lies just off the N2 about 70km southwest of Eshowe. This little town, often known by its European title of Stanger, is the final resting place of the mighty King Shaka (see **Shaka Zulu**, p. 268), founder of the Zulu Nation. Toward the end of his life, Shaka relocated his capital to the warmth of the north coast, where he established a maze of huts later dubbed KwaDukuza, "the place of the lost person." On September 22, 1828, Shaka was stabbed to death by his half-brothers Dingane and Mhlangane as he sat watching the setting sun outside his cattle *kraal*. Dingane subsequently seized control of the kingdom and burned KwaDukuza to the ground. In 1873, the British built a town on this spot and named it after William Stanger, the surveyor-general of Natal. Now, after 126 years, the original name has been restored to pay tribute to its Zulu roots. KwaDukuza consists of a few crowded streets of shops and no-nonsense restaurants and is refreshingly free of shopping centers. The large Indian population supports a number of spice shops and Bollywood movie theaters. Tourists are notably absent, and the town is worth a quick visit just to see a regular African town going about its business. **King Shaka's grave,** next to the site of his murder, is on King Shaka St., the main road through town, near the intersection with Cato Rd. **The Dukuza Interpretive Center,** a museum right behind the simple tombstone, has small exhibits of traditional dress and weapons, and features a small theater showing three free films about Shaka and Zulu history. (☎552 7210. Open M-F 8am-4pm, Sa-Su 9am-4pm.)

BLYTHEDALE BEACH   ☎ 032

Blythedale Beach is across the N2 from KwaDukuza, about 70km southwest of Eshowe. A small, upscale, mainly white community, Blythedale consists of a row of lodges and holiday flats beside a pristine stretch of shark-netted beach. The R74 leads into town from the N2, becoming Umvoti St. in town. Umvoti St. turns sharply right at a rotary and leads along the coast. At the second rotary you come to, the public beach will be on your left. Blythedale has dolphins year-round and also witnesses the annual whale migration north toward Mozambique beginning in June or July. While there are no restaurants around Blythedale, several of the hotels and lodges offer meals for their clientele. The comfortable beach-side accommodations can provide a relaxing, secluded hiatus for the weary, especially after rigorous site-hopping and game-spotting. The **Bush and Beach Lodge ❶,** 71 Umvoti Dr., off the rotary where Umvoti St. turns to the right, has a cool pool surrounded by lush vegetation, a luxurious private bar, and a *braai* pit. Front rooms have an ocean view. (☎551 1496 or 083 404 1257. Light breakfast R15. Full English breakfast R25. Dorms R50, including bedding; doubles R90 per person; fully serviced 2-bedroom cottage for up to 8 people R300 per person, in low season R180 per person. MC/V.) **Channel Sands Holiday Cottages ❶,** right next door to Bush and Beach, provides 20 cottages of varying size and amenities, each sleeping up to six. Separated from the beach by no more than a hedge, visitors enjoy a beautiful view of the ocean. Tennis and swimming are available. (☎551 2266; csands@worldonline.co.za. 6-person cottage R300, low season R240. Prices for backpackers negotiable.) **Dolphin Coast MiniVillas ❷,** on Umvoti St. just past the second rotary, has single, double, triple, and quad cottages in varying degrees of luxury and a swimming pool, all just up a hill from the beach. Minivillas have en suite bath and kitchens. (☎551 1277. Call from KwaDukuza 9am-5pm for free pick-up. Book ahead in season. Singles and doubles R190-260; triples and quads R220-320.)

KWAZULU-NATAL

THE LOCAL STORY

GRAY MAGUIRE

Gray Maguire, age 22, is the manager of Isinkwe Backpackers in Monzi, near St. Lucia. He grew up in Jo'burg and Cape Town. Starting when he was 18, Gray spent two years as a guide for an overland tour company, leading groups of around 25 people on a truck through Africa for periods of around two weeks.

Q: What makes overland tours different from other tours?

A: My experience has been fairly limited, but I would say that there are three kinds of tours in Africa. The first is the normal day tour, which is a relatively impersonal experience but is usually slightly more professional than other tours. It's usually more money for something you could be getting cheaper. The second kind is an organized tour on a big bus, which is basically comprised of what would be a series of smaller day tours. Then there are overland tours, which are more for backpackers, for people who are interested in having a good time. They give backpackers a way to travel with a bit more security than usual. I mean, if you get stuck in some war zone on a tour, you could still be screwed, but at the end of the day, it's not your call to fix it.

Q: What was your best experience on a tour?

A: I guess my most impressive memory was when I first tracked down an elephant on foot while I was leading a group on a walking tour in the Okavango Delta. It charged from five meters away....I was the only person who got a photo.

EMPANGENI ☎ 035

The medium-sized town of Empangeni makes for a decent half-day stop on the way through Zululand. The Art and Cultural History Museum has some worthwhile exhibits on the area's past and present, and the tourist office has a number of cultural projects in the works, from a "Royal Zulu Hike" to a Zulu arts and crafts shop. Aside from this, Empangeni has little to offer aside from a big mall where you can stock up on supplies before getting back to the countryside.

■ ⁊ ORIENTATION AND PRACTICAL INFO.
Empangeni lies about 3km west of the N2 on the R34. The R34 runs approximately north-south through town and is also known as **Main Rd.** Heading north into town from the N2 on Main Rd., the center of town will be to your right, beginning around **Turnbull St.** and ending at **Biyela St.** Between Turnbull and Biyela is the main street through town, **Maxwell St.** Shops and services are here and on **Union St.**, which runs parallel to Maxwell one block to the south but does not intersect Main Rd. But the real motherload of shops and services is in the mall, **Sanlam Center**, on Maxwell St. between **Commercial Rd.** and **Smith St.**

Empangeni Museum (see **Sights**, below) books **Greyhound** buses to Durban (3¼ hr., 5:30pm, R90) and Pretoria/Johannesburg (9¼hr., 12:15pm, R180). The **minibus taxi** stand is on Maxwell St. near the intersection with Main Rd., across from the post office. Taxis go to: Durban (2hr., R40); Johannesburg (6hr., R100); KwaDukuza (1hr., R30); KwaMbonambi (30min., R15); Ulundi (1hr., R30). There is a **tourist office** at the back of Empangeni Museum. (☎792 1283. Open Tu-F 9am-4pm, Sa 9am-noon.) Services include: **First National Bank** with **ATM**, 8 Union St. (☎772 6763; open M-F 9am-3:30pm, Sa 8:30-11am); **Pick 'n Pay** supermarket, in Sanlam Center (☎772 3434; open M-F 8am-6pm, Sa 7:30am-3pm, Su 9am-2pm); **Edward's Pharmacy**, 10 Union St. (☎772 1611; open M-F 8am-5:30pm, Sa 8am-1pm); **hospital** (☎902 8500; open 24hr.); **Izindaba Internet Cafe**, 4 Paul Ave., off Main (☎772 1145; open M-F 8:30am-4:30pm; R36 per hr.); **telephones** at the intersection of Commercial Rd. and Union St. The **post office**, on Maxwell St., has *Poste Restante*. (☎772 1121. Open M-Tu and Th-F 8:30am-4:30pm, W 9am-4:30pm, Sa 8am-noon.) **Postal code:** 3880.

⌐ ⌐ ACCOMMODATIONS AND FOOD. Your best bet for budget accommodations in Empangeni is **Golf View Lodge ❷**, on Old Main Rd., which runs parallel to Main Rd. just south of town. To get there, follow

Main Rd. north from the N2 and, before you reach the center of Empangeni, turn left at the Spar supermarket onto Frank Bull Rd. and make an immediate right onto Old Main Rd. Golf View is a quiet, unpretentious lodge perched on a little hill overlooking the road. Rooms are clean and comfortable. (☎772 3949. Breakfast included. Singles R130; doubles with bathroom R250-280.) Restaurants in town include **Porky's ❷**, a homey "family diner" with pub-style decor, large helpings, and friendly staff. Pork shanks R50; pasta, burgers, and meat dishes R20-50. (☎792 3180 or 792 3185. Open daily noon until the last customer leaves. Smart casual dress for dinner.) A good spot for lunch is **Mocha Java Cafe ❶**, in Sanlam Center. Breakfast (R10-20) is served all day, along with pita sandwiches (R14.50) and other fare. (☎772 7570. Open M-F 8:30am-4:30pm, Sa 8:30am-1pm.)

◙ ♫ SIGHTS AND OUTDOORS. The only tourist attraction in town is the **Empangeni Art and Cultural History Museum**, on Turnbull St. The museum has permanent exhibitions on traditional Zulu culture and the early days of the sugar cane industry, as well as a sizeable collection of oil paintings and temporary exhibits of local art. Highlights include photographs of early sugar farms and displays of traditional Zulu clothing and crafts. (☎901 1618 or 901 1617. Open Tu-F 9am-4pm, Sa 9am-noon. R1, students R0.50.) **Enseleni Nature Reserve**, about 13km north of Empangeni on the N2, has picnic spots and a 7km hiking trail on which you may come face to face with the local animal life, mostly zebra and impala. There is also an Environmental Awareness Center with conservation-related information. (☎792 0034. Gates open daily 7am-6pm. Office and environmental awareness center open M-F 7am-4:30pm, Sa-Su 7am-1pm.)

RICHARD'S BAY ☎035

Richard's Bay is a haphazard mix of beach resort, fishing village, mall, and processing plant. The town center is dominated by large shopping malls, while the surrounding areas are home to the aluminum processing plants that make Richard's Bay one of the major industrial centers in the region. Unless you are an avid shopper or very enthusiastic about aluminum, you can afford to skip these parts of town and head straight for the waterfront, where you can grab lunch beside the pleasant harbor or catch some sun at the beach.

▐ TRANSPORTATION. Greyhound (☎011 249 8900 or 031 309 7830) runs to Durban (3¼ hr., 6:30pm, R90) and Pretoria/Johannesburg (9¼hr., 11:50am,

(Continued from previous page)

Q: What was your worst experience on a tour?

A: My second tour as a tour leader. I remember trying to drive 16 hours straight from Windhoek to the Delta after I had been up all night. We got lost and stuck and ran out of water, and the truck had no alternator. I hadn't eaten in five days. And in addition to that, there were...I guess the nicest way to put it is girl problems. It was a nightmare, start to finish.

Q: Where do you see yourself in 10 years?

A: I want to go to South America and run trips into the Amazon. Boat tours, walking trips, hopefully make some money. Then maybe I'll get to the States or Canada or Europe and start studying. Hopefully in 10 years I'll be a world-famous social anthropologist, and I can write big fat books and sell them for lots of money. Either that or some crappy politician.

Q: Where do you see South Africa in 10 years?

A: I see a lot of hope for the country....we certainly have our problems, but we are the only country in Africa with a first-world infrastructure. We are also the brains of Southern Africa—we produce the skills that Africa needs. Our people are becoming increasingly educated. If we stick to essential things, like education, AIDS prevention, and transportation, I believe we will come right.

R180). The **minibus taxi** stand is behind the Bay Plaza shopping center, across Bullion Blvd. from the Boardwalk Shopping Center. Taxis run to: Durban (2hr., R40); Empangeni (15min., R12); Gingindlovu (45min., R20); Johannesburg (6hr., R120); KwaDukuza/Stanger (1½hr., R40); Mtubatuba (45min., R16); Pietermaritzburg (3½hr., R70); Pongola (2hr., R65); Ulundi (1½hr., R35); Vryheid (1hr., R30).

■◼◼ ORIENTATION AND PRACTICAL INFORMATION. Richard's Bay lies about 15km east of the N2, where the R34 meets the ocean. Coming east into town from the N2, the R34 becomes **John Ross Pkwy.** Turn left from John Ross Pkwy. onto **North Central Arterial Rd.** and then left again onto **Bullion Blvd.** to reach the downtown area, dominated by the Boardwalk Shopping Center and the Bay Hospital. To reach the waterfront, continue straight on John Ross Pkwy. past the intersection with North Central Arterial, turn right onto **Bayview Blvd.**, bear right onto **Bridgetown Rd.**, cross the canal and take your first right, then turn left onto **Newark Rd.** and follow signs for **Tuzi Gazi Waterfront** and the **Small Craft Harbor.** To reach the **Alkanstrand,** the town's main beach, turn right onto Bayview Rd. from John Ross Hwy. and follow it as it curves to the left and dead-ends near the beach. The **airport** is north of town in a residential area called Birdswood.

Richard's Bay Tourism Association, in a small building at the Small Craft Harbor, next to the Quaywalk shopping and restaurant area, provides maps and information on tours, accommodations, and transportation. (☎ 788 0039; fax 788 0040. Open M-Th 8am-4pm, F 8am-3pm, Sa-Su 10am-2pm.) **The Boardwalk shopping area,** at the corner of Bullion Blvd. and Krugerrand St., offers every service imaginable, including: **Standard Bank** with **ATM** (☎ 789 7060; open M-F 9am-3:30pm, Sa 8:30-11am); **Internet access** at Postnet (☎ 789 9756; open M-F 8am-5:30pm, Sa 8am-noon; R40 per hr.); **Pick 'n Pay** grocery store (☎ 798 3267; open M-F 8am-6pm, Sa 8am-3pm, Su 9am-3pm); **Central Apteek** (☎ 789 3910; open M-W and F 8am-6pm, Th 8am-5:30pm, Sa 8am-1pm). Other services include the **Bay Hospital,** across Krugerrand St. from the Boardwalk Plaza (☎ 780 6111 or 789 1234; open 24hr.) and the **post office,** in the Checkers Center behind the Boardwalk (☎ 789 1215; open M-Tu and Th-F 8:30am-4:30pm, W 9am-4:30pm, Sa 8am-noon). **Postal code:** 3900.

◼◻ ACCOMMODATIONS AND FOOD. There are few budget accommodations available in Richard's Bay itself, though you can contact a few non-exorbitant B&Bs through the tourist office. Off the P106 (to Esikhawini) about 4km south of the R34 halfway between Empangeni and Richard's Bay, **Harbour Lights ❶** lies deep in the middle of a sugarcane field. It is the closest budget accommodation available, though sufficiently out of the way to make a stay in Empangeni or KwaMbonambi more tempting. Harbor Lights offers a wide variety of accommodations, from dormitories to Zulu beehive huts to luxury B&B flats. There is a self-catering kitchen, TV lounge, swimming pool, and petting zoo, and various tours and activities can be arranged. Free transport from Empangeni and Richard's Bay bus stations. Internet available. Visitors should make dinner reservations before noon—there are no restaurants within 10km. (☎/fax 796 6239 or ☎ 083 631 6410; zebra@harbourlights.co.za; www.harbourlights.co.za. Check-out 10am. Dorms and Zulu huts R50 per person; budget rooms R70 per person; self-catering singles R140; doubles R220; each additional person R60. Camping R60-80 per site.)

The Small Craft Harbor (Tuzi Gazi Waterfront) has some good, inexpensive restaurants, and there are numerous reasonable restaurants and fast-food joints in the Boardwalk Center. **Upper Deck Restaurant/Anchor's Cast Tavern ❷** is on Bridgetown Rd. at the Small Craft Harbor, past the turnoff for Tuzi Gazi Waterfront on the way to Naval Island. Sit at one of their outside tables overlooking the harbor and choose from a menu of seafaring and non-seafaring entrees including vegetarian lasagna (R26) and curries (R22.50). Most entrees are R20-40. (☎ 788 0219. Restaurant open T-Su 10am-late; tavern open daily 10am to late. MC/V.) **Ruben's Pizzeria ❷,** on the Tuzi Gazi waterfront, serves pizza, pasta, salads, and a range of lip-smacking dishes amidst cheery red and green decor. Entrees range from R20 to 40. (☎788 0135. Open M-Sa 11am-10pm.) Bars at the Tuzi Gazi Waterfront include the **Slipway** (☎788 0202; open daily 9:30am-late) and the **Green Iguana** (☎788 0939; open daily 10am-late).

🏃 **OUTDOORS. Alkantstrand,** the main public beach in town, features the second-highest vegetated sand dunes in the world. Shark netting protects swimmers and surfers. The **Bay Crocodile Sanctuary,** off John Ross Pkwy. at Medway Rd., has crocodile pools, a reptile park, and a petting zoo. (☎083 303 5543. Open daily 9am-4:30pm; crocodile feeding Su 11:30am; snake demos Sa 3pm; night tours by appointment. R12, children R6.)

MTUBATUBA   ☎035

Mtubatuba ("he who has pummeled one") was named after a local Zulu chief whose mother endured a very difficult delivery. Today, the small town houses workers from the surrounding paper mills, sugar cane fields, and refineries. Although Mtubatuba has little to offer in terms of sights and activities, its strategic location between St. Lucia and Hluhluwe-Umfolozi Park makes it a convenient place to stop while exploring the area. If you decide to spend time in Mtubatuba, inquire about "Songs of Zululand," a program occasionally run by the town that includes performances of Zulu song and dance by local schoolchildren.

Mtubatuba sits near the intersection of the N2 and the R618, about 30km west of St. Lucia. Turn off the N2 at the sign for St. Lucia, turn left onto the R618, and make a quick right onto **John Ross Highway** to reach the center of town. To find additional shops and services, make a left from John Ross Highway at the Power Spar onto **St. Lucia Rd.** The **minibus taxi** rank is just off John Ross Highway, near the intersection with St. Lucia Rd. There is no tourist office in Mtubatuba; your best bet for **information** is to enquire at local businesses or B&Bs. Services include: **Standard Bank,** with an **ATM,** 30 Jan Smuts Ave., off St. Lucia Rd. across the railway tracks (☎ 550 0047; open M-F 9am-3:30pm, Sa 8:30-11am); **Power Spar** supermarket, at the intersection of John Ross Highway and St. Lucia Rd. (open daily 7am-7pm.); and the **post office,** on St. Lucia Rd. across the railway tracks, with fax and *Poste Restante* services (☎ 550 0019; open M-Tu and Th-F 8:30am-4:30pm, W 9am-4:30pm, Sa 8am-noon.) **Postal code:** 3935. Somewhat surprisingly, a lovely B&B in Mtubatuba, **Mtuba B&B ❷,** 243 Celtis St. Turn right off of John Ross Highway just after the Power Spar, make your next left onto the road leading to the N2, make your next right, and turn left onto Celtis St. Double rooms are spacious and comfortable, and a pleasant deck overlooks the pool and garden. (☎550 0538; ida@bnbmtuba.co.za. Breakfast included; dinner available. R185 per person.)

ST. LUCIA   ☎035

St. Lucia has long served as the Afrikaner holiday-seeker's destination of choice. The town itself is a long strip of holiday flats, restaurants, and fishing charters, only five minutes by car from a golden stretch of beach. St. Lucia is the only South African town inside a nature reserve, and visitors may spot hippos and crocodiles on a casual night drive through the streets. When the trappings of tourism begin to wear on you, you can head out to the shores of Lake St. Lucia and the surrounding wetlands, which offer attractions that range from hiking and snorkeling to fishing and boat cruises. Though St. Lucia has become a bit more diverse over the years, several entrenched old South African attitudes remain, and occasionally whispered remarks and scornful looks (usually from white South African tourists, not locals) may require non-white visitors to bring a little extra emotional armor.

✈ 🔏 ORIENTATION AND PRACTICAL INFORMATION

St. Lucia lies at the eastern end of the R618, about 30km east of the N2. Coming into town on the R618, you will pass over a bridge and come to a small rotary. Turning right here will put you onto **McKenzie St.,** the main drag through town. At the end of town is a second rotary; turning left here will bring you to the KwaZulu-Natal Nature Conservation Services Office. **Katonkel Ave.** and **Dolfyn Ave.** intersect McKenzie St. in town. If you turn left instead of right at that first rotary as you come into town, you will reach the St. Lucia Crocodile Center; a right turn here leads to the beach, while continuing straight leads, in about 40km, to Cape Vidal.

There are **tourist offices** all over town—they provide various kinds of information but are mainly interested in booking tours and boat charters. One of the more helpful offices is **St. Lucia Safaris,** next to the Key West Cocktail Bar. (☎ 590 1047; bornfree@stlucia.co.za. Open M-F 8am-6pm, Sa 9am-1pm.) The **KwaZulu-Natal Nature Conservation Services Office** is the main office for booking park accommodations and boat tours up the estuary; it doubles as a curio shop. To get there, take a left at the rotary at the end of town, just past Bib's Backpackers. (☎ 590 1340 or 033 845 1000; fax 590 1343. Open daily 8am-12:30pm and 2-4:30pm.) There is no police station or hospital in town. Services include: **First National Bank** with **ATM,** in the Dolphin Shopping Center on McKenzie St. (☎ 590 1088; open M, W, F 9am-1pm, off-season closed W); **Spar Grocery Store** (open daily 7am-7pm); **St. Lucia Laundromat,** on McKenzie St. (open daily 7am-7pm); **Internet access** at Bib's International Backpackers (open daily 7am-10pm; R30 per hr.); and the **post office,** off Flamingo St. behind the Spar, with fax and *Poste Restante* (☎ 590 1022; open M-Tu and Th-F 8:30am-1pm and 2-4:30pm, W 9am-1pm and 2-4:30pm, Sa and the first and last day of the month 8am-noon). **Postal code:** 3936.

▐ ACCOMMODATIONS

Perhaps the most authentic way to experience the wetlands is by staying in one of the three **campsites** run by the Parks Board: Sugarloaf, Iphiva, or Eden Park. Sugarloaf has power outlets and a swimming pool, and all campsites have bathrooms and drinking water. (R48-53 per person, children under twelve enjoy half price.) Bookings can be made through the KwaZulu-Natal Nature Conservation Services office (see **Practical Information,** p. 243). For a small town, St. Lucia has an absurd number of accommodations, including B&Bs, self-catering holiday flats, and hostels.

▨ **Bib's International Backpackers** (☎ 590 1056; fax 590 1360; info@bibs.co.za; www.bibs.co.za), on McKenzie St. near the rotary at the end of town. Reception is just beyond the Jungle 2 Jungle Restaurant, in front of the backpackers. This popular hostel and Baz Bus stop has a happening outdoor bar and *braai* area, and the friendly owners offer free daily activities and rides to the beach. Clean, comfortable rooms without ceilings are partitioned in a tall, thatched building—the large open air-space over head allows sleep-talkers' most sordid secrets to travel with ease. Separate dorms and chalets are also available. The staff wash your dishes until 10pm and make your bed daily. Swimming pool (sometimes doubling as a crocodile den, though hopefully not while you're in it), TV lounge, and self-catering kitchen. Launch tours and **wetland tours** are available, as well as **nighttime game drives** in St. Lucia. Cape Vidal snorkeling R275; Hluhluwe game drives half-day R200, full-day R300; whale-watching R280; sea kayaking R175; deep sea fishing R350. Internet access. Laundry services. Pool table and table tennis. Dorms R55; doubles R130, self-catering with kitchen and bath R170; 3-bed chalets R130. ❶

▒**Isinkwe Wetlands Backpackers** (☎550 4433), at Monzi, 15km from St. Lucia on the road to Mtubatuba. Follow the R618 east from Mtubatuba toward St. Lucia. After about 20km, turn right onto the road to Monzi. This road will be the only paved road leading to the right off the R618 between Mtubatuba and St. Lucia. From this road, turn left into Monzi, a gated community and country club, and follow signs to Isinkwe. Although it's a bit of a drive from St. Lucia, Isinkwe offers enough attractions to make it worth the while of anyone able to get there. A beautiful lodge tucked away in the woods, Isinkwe is the ideal place to relax and watch the stars, far from the noise of town. Dorms are clean, bright and very comfortable. A large living room with pool table and communal kitchen is available, and the pool and outdoor patio command a good view of the surrounding countryside. The management can arrange all kinds of tours and activities. Dorms R60; doubles R160. Camping R45 per person.

Stokkiesdraai, 74 McKenzie St. (☎/fax 590 1216; st.lucia@mweb.co.za; www.stokkies-draai.com). Near the center of town, across from Spar supermarket. Stokkiesdraai, which means "playing truant," offers peace and privacy at backpacker prices and is one of the only establishments in town with a view of the estuary. Both dorms and holiday flats are available—the latter come with private kitchens and are fully serviced. *Braai* and swimming pool. Satellite TV and bathrooms in all flats and backpacker lounge. Many kinds of tours and activities can be arranged. Dorms R60; doubles R130. Prices for flats are negotiable but are in the same price range as dorm rooms.

▐ FOOD

St. Pizza (☎/fax 590 1048), on McKenzie St. in the center of town. This popular restaurant, pub, and take-out serves good, hearty food and has a nice outdoor area under a thatched roof. Their wood-fired pizza oven comes in handy when the town's power goes out, which generally happens several times a week. Despite their name, seafood is their speciality. Entrees R25-R40. Pizzas R20-R35. Open daily 9:45am-10pm. ❷

Quarterdeck Restaurant/Key West Pub (☎590 1116), on McKenzie St. in the center of town. The restaurant is a good place for seafood (R30-60), and the attached pub is the most happening spot in town, where tourists mix with locals in an atmosphere of happy intoxication. Interesting choice of mixed drinks includes the Mermaid's Orgasm and the Raging Bull (R22 each), beers (R6.50), and shooters (R6). Restaurant open daily 10am-2:30pm and 5-10pm; pub open daily noon-2am. ❶

Paradiso (☎590 1190), in the center of town. This quiet restaurant serves a good selection of Portuguese and Austrian specialties and understands that the secret to cooking good seafood is using only the freshest ingredients. Indoor and outdoor seating. Portuguese-style chicken R44. Grilled sole R59. Open Tu-Su 11am-late. ❸

Lagosta (☎590 2197), in the center of town next to Spar. The downstairs take-out counter does a brisk business, while the upstairs dining room serves seafood and Portuguese specialties in a more elegant setting. Grilled marinated calamari and grilled flat chicken each R39.50. Open daily 11am-2:30pm and 6-9pm.❷

Beach Bums, in the center of town next to Paradiso. This informal restaurant with outdoor picnic-style tables is the place to go for lunch. Cheese, tomato, mushroom, and onion crepe R18. Half roasted chicken with chips and salad R26. Delicious individual chicken and mushroom pies R5. Open daily 8am-5pm. ❶

◕ SIGHTS

For an in-depth look at Zulu culture, visit **Khula Village,** a Zulu community off the R618 between St. Lucia and Mtubatuba. Their interactive tours let you visit traditional *kraals, sangomas,* and artisans and experience Zulu storytelling, music,

FROM THE ROAD

SURFING IN ST. LUCIA

I arrived in St. Lucia on a Friday and stayed up drinking until 6am with my Australian friend Phil. It came out in the course of our conversation that I had never been surfing before, and Phil, horrified, determined to take me first thing the next morning.

We made it to the beach at 2pm, both feeling a little fragile. "These waves are crap," said Phil, surveying some of the biggest waves I had ever seen. It took us the better part of an hour to paddle out to past where the waves were breaking, mainly because the waves kept catching my board and pulling me under. By the time we had made it out beyond the break, I felt like I had a full day of activity under my belt already. "Are you in good shape?" asked Phil. "What do you think?" I gasped.

I tried to ride a few waves in, but wasn't able to stand up, and I kept going farther and farther out to keep from being pulled under. Phil came and told me that if I kept going, I would reach Australia. After a few hours, I went back to our car to get some water. I noticed a nearby sign that we hadn't seen on the way in: "Warning: unprotected beach with dangerous currents." It was erected in memory of someone who drowned there a few years back. I decided to stay on the beach after that, but I told Phil to catch one for me, and also that surfing is for crazy people.

—Joshua Gardner

and dancing. Tours depart from Siyabonga craft market in St. Lucia. For more information or bookings, contact Marrah Nene (☎083 525 0228) or Phillip Mkhwanazi (☎082 958 1237). The **St. Lucia Crocodile Center** (☎590 1386), 1km from town on the road to Cape Vidal, is part museum and part zoo. It features dioramas of all the park's ecosystems, exhibits on crocodile growth and development, a cycad garden, and an impressive snake park. One sinister exhibit displays the skull of a crocodile that drowned a woman in the park, complete with machete gashes inflicted by a guide who struggled to save her. Pens are filled with live specimens—Nile crocodiles, dwarf crocodiles, and long-snouted crocodiles are up close and personal. The Center also has an expansive curio shop and a relaxing tea garden serving snacks. (Open M-F 7:30am-4:30pm, Sa 8:30am-5pm, Su 9am-4pm. Croc feeding Sa at 3pm, and W in summer at 6:30pm; R30, children R15. Post-feeding Zulu dance show free, donations accepted. Croc demonstrations Su 11:30am; entrance to croc Center R15, children R10; weekends R20, children R15. "Snake talk" Sa 2pm; R20, children R15.)

The biggest local craft market, the **Siyabonga Craft Center** (☎590 1452), to the left of the bridge leading into town, is a thatched shelter for dozens of boisterous local craft vendors selling hand-woven baskets, wooden carvings, and beaded jewelry. (Open daily 7am-5pm.)

🥾 HIKING

Guided **wetlands walks** with armed rangers (full day, R35 per person) can be arranged through the KZN Nature Conservation Services Office in St. Lucia (see **Practical Information**). For the more adventurous, there are 5-day **wilderness trails** that can also be booked through the St. Lucia KZN office. Prices run around R1380 per person, including food and accommodation. There are several **hiking trails** that do not require a tour guide:

GwalaGwala Trail (1½km) starts at the end of McKenzie St. and loops through an incredibly dense forest just above the river.

iMvubu Trail (3hr., 10km) leaves from the Crocodile Center and takes you through mangroves, marsh, and swamp forest. 3 shorter hikes leave from the same trailhead, winding their way through the nearby hills and to the ocean.

Mziki Trail (3 days, R40 per night) leaves from Mission Rocks and includes respite in a modestly comfortable 8-bed trail hut.

Emoyeni Trail (5 days, R30 per night) also leaves from Mission Rocks. Hikers must bring their own tent.

Additional trails also begin at Mission Rocks, on the road to Cape Vidal. Book all overnight trails through the KZN office at Mission Rocks (☎590 9002). To get to Mission Rocks, you will need to enter the Greater St. Lucia Wetland Park (R20 per person, R35 per vehicle). Overnight hikers also pay a one-time community levy (R5 if camping, R10 if staying in a hutted accommodation).

🔼🔃 OUTDOORS AND ADVENTURES

BOAT CHARTERS. The town of St. Lucia lies between the Indian Ocean and the St. Lucia estuary, both of which provide opportunities to observe aquatic life. The best way to do some croc and hippo-spotting is to cruise the estuary on one of three available boats run by competing tour operators. **Born Free Cruises** provides the most comprehensive of these tours, an entertaining two-hour float down the estuary. (☎590 1174 or 083 283 1528. Trips daily 9am, noon, 3pm. R80, children under 10 R40.) Born Free also organizes **whale-watching trips** (R280) and **turtle-spotting tours** (Oct.-Mar.; R425). **Advantage/St. Lucia Tours and Charters** (☎590 1259, 590 1199 or 083 487 2762; fax 590 1053; advantage@zululink.co.za; www.wetlands.co.za/advantage) and **Fannas Spirit of St. Lucia** (☎590 1363) have similar tours and prices. Bib's Backpackers can also provide information and book tours.

FISHING. Fishing is one of St. Lucia's principal attractions. The **Bait and Tackle Shop** (☎/fax 590 1257), next to the Engen Station, and the **St. Lucia Fishing Den** (☎590 1450) both enthusiastically provide for the fisherman's every need. The two stores each contain a doomsday arsenal of rods, reels, bait, and beer. They also offer full-day deep-sea fishing charters for R300-R900. The Bait and Tackle Shop also rents equipment. (Bait and Tackle Shop open daily 7am-7pm. Fishing Den open daily 8am-6pm.) A fishing license (R25 for a month, R40 for a year), required for ages 13 and up, is available at the Nature Conservation Services Office (☎590 9002) or the post office.

KAYAKING AND WATER SPORTS. Chalupsky St. Lucia Kayak Safaris (☎550 5036 or 083 448 6466; wayne@chalupsky.com; www.chalupsky.com) runs half- or full-day kayak trips (full day R175) and half-day snorkeling (R250) excursions on Lake St. Lucia. They can be booked through Bib's Backpackers. At the **Ponta Lucia Beach Shop**, next to the Wimpy's on McKenzie St., you can rent boogieboards for R50 per day plus a R50 deposit. This well-stocked establishment also rents snorkeling gear for the same price. (☎590 1396. Open daily 8am-5pm.)

NEAR ST. LUCIA

CAPE VIDAL

Cape Vidal is a particularly choice stretch of beach about 40km north of St. Lucia. To get there, turn left at the rotary as you enter St. Lucia from the R618 and continue straight for 40km. Part of the beach is enclosed by an offshore reef, forming a bay that is ideal for **snorkeling** and **swimming**. The other, less protected areas of the beach are favored by body surfers, anglers, and water-skiers. For visitors who prefer to stay dry, the dune forests surrounding the beach offer good hiking and bird-watching opportunities. There is also a 1.5km **guided walking trail** that should be booked a day in advance (R20 per person). **Accommodation** options include campsites (R53 per person, minimum R212), fully equipped and serviced log cabins (R160 per person, minimum R480), and fully equipped fishing shacks (R70 per person, minimum R280). The upmarket Bhangazi bush lodge has a cook (you supply the food) and a field ranger to lead you on day walks (R210 per person, minimum R840). Children under 12 are about half price for all accommodations. (☎ 033 845 1000 or fax 033 845 1001 to book cabins, shacks, or the bush lodge. Book well in advance for holidays and long weekends.) To book campsites, call the **KZN Nature Conservation Office,** which is off the road just before the beach (☎ 035 590 9012; fax 035 590 9007; www.rhino.org.za). The KZN office has a **shop** that sells basic foodstuffs, but it's wise to bring your own food. (Office and shop open M-Sa 8am-12:30pm and 2-4pm, Su 8am-12:30pm and 2-3:30pm.) Cape Vidal is only part of the larger Greater St. Lucia Wetland Park. (Entrance R20 per person, R35 per vehicle. Gates open Apr.-Sept. 6am-6pm, Oct.-Mar. 5am-7pm.) The road between St. Lucia and Cape Vidal has a number of picnic sites, walking trails, and beaches. For more information on these attractions, contact the KZN office at Mission Rocks (☎ 035 590 9002). For travelers without cars, Bib's Backpackers and countless tour companies in St. Lucia run daytrips to Cape Vidal.

KWAMBONAMBI   ☎ 035

King Shaka (see **Shaka Zulu,** p. 268) spent the first 18 years of his life with the Mtetwa people in KwaMbonambi, and the spears that helped propel his empire across southeastern Africa were fashioned here. With a population of about 600 (including squatters), Kwambo, as it is locally known, is now a tiny hamlet in the heart of Zululand and a relaxing place from which to explore the immediate environs of Richard's Bay, the Hluhluwe-Umfolozi Game Reserve, and the Greater St. Lucia Wetland Park. In addition, there are a lot of good flora and fauna to be seen in the nearby Kwambo Conservancy, a private nature reserve maintained by the area's two big paper and pulp companies. The Conservatory is a bird-watcher's paradise and a testament to the growing environmental awareness in the region.

Kwambonambi lies about 30km north of Empangeni on the N2. From the N2 heading north from Durban, the KwaMbonambi turn-off is to the left. Take the turn-off and continue straight for about 1km, crossing the railroad tracks and passing the turn-off to the industrial area. The first street to the left is **Regia St.,** the main street in town. Past Regia St. are **Albizia St., Bredelia St.,** and then **Wedgewood Ave.** There is an **ATM** in the **Spar Supermarket** (open M-Sa 8am-5pm) on Regia St. Go to Mtubatuba to change currency. The KwaMbonambi **post office,** 23 Regia St., doesn't offer *Poste Restante.* (☎ 580 4269. Open M-Tu and Th-F 8:30am-4:30pm, W 9am-4:30pm, Sa 8am-noon.) **Postal code:** 3915.

The only accommodation available right in KwaMbonambi is **Cuckoo's Nest Backpackers ❶,** 28 Albizia St. Cuckoo's Nest is a quiet, relaxed place offering dorms and a variety of doubles, including a tree house. There's an outdoor bar, swimming pool, and a large backyard where the owners sometimes give "fire shows," in which they spin, throw, and catch various burning objects. They offer numerous tours and visits with Crocodile Kwambo, a local character who has crocodiles for pets and is a great resource for learning about conservation in KwaZulu-Natal. You can also arrange for free to attend a Zulu church on Sunday morning or make a trip to an isolated beach, about 30km out of Kwambo, for a good beach *braai.* (☎ 580 1001 or 580 1002; cuckoos@mweb.co.za. Continental breakfast included. Dinner free on the first night, R25 thereafter. Dorms R55; doubles R140; triples R180. Camping R35 per person.) There are a few mundane take-away shops, grocery stores, and tea rooms on Regia St. (Most open M-F 8am-5pm, Sa 8am-1pm.) If you're hungry, the **KwaMbonambi Country Club ❶,** has a very pleasant restaurant offering hearty meals (R15-25). To get there, follow Albizia St. past Cuckoo's Nest and make your next right onto Carissa St.—the entrance to the Club will be directly in front of you. Happy hour (daily 5:30-6:30pm) features half-price beers that are bound to make you less happy the next morning. (☎580 1321. Open Tu-Su 10am-late.) If **golf** is your thing, head over to Kwambonambi Country Club (see above) for a round or two. People staying at Cuckoo's Nest are entitled to member rates, which means you can play 18 holes for around R30. For the ambitious with a 4WD vehicle, the 50km dirt road across the N2 from the KwaMbonambi turn-off leads to the **Mapelane Nature Reserve,** which offers good beaches and fishing in a secluded location. Accommodations consist of campsites and 5-bed log cabins. (☎590 1407. Gates close Apr.-Sept. 6pm; Oct.-Mar. 7pm. Reservations must be made through the KwaZulu-Natal Nature Conservation Service: ☎033 845 1000 for cabins; 590 1407 for campsites. Cabins R140 per person, R420 minimum. Camping R45 per person, R90 minimum.)

HLUHLUWE   ☎035

The town of Hluhluwe ("shoo-SHLoo-wee") lies just off the N2 to the west of the Greater St. Lucia Wetland Park. Hluhluwe is little more than a supply base for the rural population and visitors to the parks in the surrounding area. The town's one paved street, **Main St.,** dead-ends on a dirt road. **Minibus taxis** run from the rank off Main St. to: **Durban** (2½hr., R60); **Empangeni** (1hr., R30) via KwaMbonambi (30min., R25); **Johannesburg** (6hr., R100); **Mtubatuba** (30min., R20); and **Pongola** (1½hr., R40). The best place to get information about game ranches and accommodations is the **Hluhluwe Tourist Information Office** next to the Engen Station. (☎562 0353 or 562 0966. Open M-F 8:30am-5pm, Sa 9am-1pm, Su 10am-noon.) Services include: **First National Bank,** on Main St., with **ATM** (☎562 0226; open M-F 9am-12:45pm and 2-3:30pm, Sa 8:30-11am); **Spar Market** (open M-F 8am-5:30pm, Sa 8am-2pm, Su 8am-1pm); **Hluhluwe Pharmacy,** on Main St. (☎562 0028; open M-F 8am-5pm, Sa 8am-1pm); and the **post office,** with *Poste Restante* (☎562 0018; open M-Tu and Th-F 8:30am-4:30pm, W 9am-4:30pm, Sa 8am-noon). **Postal code:** 3960.

⌂ ACCOMMODATIONS AND CAMPING. Most of the accommodations in the Hluhluwe area are out of the way; carless travelers should plan ahead to arrange transportation. **Isinkwe Bushlands Backpackers ❷** is near the Bushlands exit off the N2, 14km south of town. Those who make it this far are rewarded with a beautiful oasis in the *veld*. Deep inside 22ha of indigenous forest, this lodge has clean, cozy rooms, a Zulu beehive hut (where you will likely end up with one of the backpackers' dogs as a bedmate), and a rustic lounge/dining area with bar, patio, and swimming pool. Isinkwe has a rustic, welcoming feel and friendly hosts that go out of their way to make your stay pleasant. There is also a pool and a star-gazers deck to enjoy. Hearty meals are available. Guided game drives into Hluhluwe/Umfolozi Park also available (R350 per person, half-day R275; breakfast and *braai* lunch included). There are also daytrips including whale watching, kayaking, and snorkeling. (☎562 2258 or 562 2262; fax 562 2273; isinkwe@saol.com; www.africasfari.co.za/insinkwe. Internet R30 per hr. Dorms R60; rustic doubles R65 per person; double or quad cabins R75 per person. Camping R40 per person or R45 per person if you use their tents.)

Emdoneni Lodge and Game Farm ❷, before Isinkwe on the Bushlands exit off the N2, offers chalets, *rondavels*, and luxury chalets. Though more expensive than Isinkwe, Emdoneni has wandering impala, nyala, and reedbuck, as well as a cheetah and serval-cat farm where you can schmooze (inside the cages!) with some big cats as they munch on their dinner. (☎562 2256 or 562 2257; sunseekr@iafrica.com. Self-catering *rondavels* R180 per person or R315 including dinner, bed, and breakfast; chalets R140/ R275; luxury chalets R220/R355. Cheetah feeding time

M-Sa 4:30pm. R40, children R20.) **Ezulwini Game Lodge ②** is a remote lodge near False Bay, 13km out of Hluhluwe. Take a left at the end of Main St., towards False Bay, and watch for signs. Situated on a game reserve, Ezulwini is visited by giraffe, zebra, kudu, and nyala. The lodge is quiet, peaceful, reasonably priced, and offers a plethora of accommodation choices, from rooms and cottages to cozy tree houses and log cabins, complete with fridges, kitchenettes, and bathrooms. A swimming pool offers respite from hot, humid wetland days. Game drives available. (☎/fax 562 2100. Breakfast R35; dinner R70. Order meals two days in advance. Double rooms R120 per person; double cottages R165 per person; double tree house R120 per person; 6-person log cabin R130 per person.)

▢ FOOD. Many of the guest houses and game lodges serve expensive meals. Unless you're staying at Isinkwe, those on a shoe-string budget may have to settle for **Spar** self-catering or a **Wimpy's** burger. The posh, wood-paneled **Savannah Restaurant ②**, attached to Ilala Weavers (see **Sights**, below) is the luxury alternative. A few years ago the restaurant catered for the crew of the movie *I Dreamed of Africa*; you can dine from the same plates as Kim Basinger did. (☎ 562 0836 or 072 260 6171. Meals R30-60. Open daily 10am-10pm.)

◪ SIGHTS. Ilala Weavers, to the left at the end of Main St., past the turn-off to False Bay, is a craft shop that sells Zulu baskets, handcrafts, drums, and jewelry. There is also a small museum displaying crafts from the past hundred years or so. The gallery/store is supplied by the neighboring **Thembalethu Craft Village,** a lived-in Zulu *kraal* where craftspeople spend their days weaving baskets, carving, and bead-working—all of which you can watch on a guided tour. (☎ 562 0630 or 072 260 6171. Tours R10. Open M-F 8am-5pm, Sa-Su 9am-4pm.) **Dumazulu Traditional Village and Lodge** is down the Bushlands turn-off road, after Isinkwe and Emdoneni. Here you'll find a collection of huts and a restaurant built next door to a Zulu cultural village. Each hut style is representative of a different regional ethnic group. Zulu cultural shows include spectacular dancing, as well as demonstrations of spear-making, beadwork, and pottery. (☎ 562 2260 or 031 337 4222; fax 031 368 2322; glczulu@iafrica.com; www.glczulu.co.za. Tours R75. Book ahead.) A snake and crocodile park is also on the premises. (R25. Three reptile shows a day.)

▧ ADVENTURES. A left at the end of Main St. in town and a 15km drive lead to **False Bay Park,** on the western shore of Lake St. Lucia. False Bay is renowned for its fossilized coral reefs and exquisite scenery. Activities include game viewing, bird watching, fishing, and boating. In addition, there are three hiking trails in the park: the **Dugandlovu Trail** (16km) has a hut for overnight accommodation, the **Mpophomeni Trail** (10km) day hike, and the **Ingwe Trail** is a pleasant 6km walk. There is a swimming pool; unfortunately, there is no swimming in the lake, unless you want to swim alongside crocodiles and hippos, which, trust us, you don't. (☎ 035 562 0425. Gates open Oct.-Mar. 5am-8pm, Apr.-Sept. 6am-8pm. Office open daily 8am-12:30pm and 2-4pm. Admission R20, children R10. Campsites R41 per person, min. R82; quad huts R95 per person, min. R190.) The beautiful **Hluhluwe River Lodge** (☎ 562 0246), adjacent to False Bay Park, on the shore of Lake St. Lucia, offers boat trips, Hluhluwe game drives, morning guided canoe tours and Sand Forest drives which focus on the medicinal value of the local trees (all tours R150 per person, min. 4 people). **Isinkwe Backpackers** (see p. 249) offers a variety of tours and activities throughout the area. (Full-day Hluhluwe game drives R350 per person, half-day R275, breakfast and *braai* lunch included. Full-day Umfolozi or Mkuze drives R420 per person; whale watching R245; kayaking and snorkeling R275.)

NEAR HLUHLUWE

HLUHLUWE-UMFOLOZI GAME RESERVE

Hluhluwe and Umfolozi Game Reserves, founded April 30, 1895, were the first game reserves in Africa and only the second and third in the world. The two were linked by the Corridor Reserve in 1989, and the three combined cover an area of 96,000 hectares, shaped roughly like an hourglass. The park is the only area in KwaZulu-Natal where all of the Big Five congregate. There are also cheetah, crocodile, hippo, impala, waterbuck, nyala, warthog, kudu, giraffe, and thousands of bird species. Vegetation in the reserves is plentiful and varied, with palm trees, leafy thickets, and thorny acacia thriving within a few kilometers of each other. Standing at one of the many viewpoints and looking out across a mountainous landscape, visitors can decipher the roaming shapes of large game silhouetted against the horizon. Chances are you won't go too long without spotting some critters, due to the small size of the reserve and the abundance of animals. Aside from its animal life, the Reserve is also worth visiting for its tremendous natural beauty, complete with lovely hilltops, meandering streams, and dense forests. (Gates open Nov.-Feb. 5am-7pm, Mar.-Oct. 6am-6pm. Main camp offices open daily 8am-12:30pm and 2-4pm. Entrance R30, children R15, vehicles R35.)

Accommodations options include chalets, rest huts, tented camps, bush camps, and bush lodges. The main camp in the Hluhluwe section is the luxurious **Hilltop Camp ❷**; in the Umfolozi section, it's **Mpila Camp ❷**. Rates in the various camps range from R170 to R340 per person per night; most camps have exorbitant minimum charges, so day-tripping from a hostel outside the park may be a better option. (☎ 033 845 1000 or fax 033 845 1001 for reservations.)

To see some game, you can drive through the park or go as part of an organized game drive, though organized tours aren't cheap (see **Isinkwe Backpackers,** p. 249). A great way to experience the park is by walking on a wilderness trail with an astute guide. The **Umfolozi Wilderness Trail** is a four-night odyssey that costs R1725, including food. Two-night weekend trails are R975. These are the only legal ways to see the park without a motor vehicle. All bookings should be made through the **KwaZulu-Natal Nature Conservation Services office.** (☎ 033 845 1000; 845 1002 for general info. Book up to three months in advance.)

While it is illegal to exit your vehicle alone in most of the park, four self-guided trails begin at the major camps. While in the reserve, be sure to take advantage of the "hides," where you can quietly hold vigil over well-used watering holes and watch animals, hopefully oblivious to your presence, enjoy a drink. If you're getting car-sick and have a little extra rand to spend, short walks with armed guides are R60 per person. If, on the other hand, you can't get enough of driving around, three-hour **game drives** are available once during the day and once at night at Hilltop and Mpila camps for R90. **Boat cruises** are R60 per person. If you are lucky enough to visit Umfolozi while the Black Umfolozi River is flooding (best chances Oct.-Mar.), **river rafting** tours can also be arranged (half-day R150, full-day R225). Call ahead to enquire before making any river rafting plans.

GREATER ST. LUCIA WETLAND PARK WESTERN SHORES

The turn-off to the western shores of **Lake St. Lucia** is 20km north of Mtubatuba on the N2. After 12km, turn left and drive another 14km to reach **Fanies Island.** One of KwaZulu-Natal's most secluded camps, this spot is popular with anglers and birdwatchers. Despite its isolation, the island has a swimming pool, two kitchens, and an ablution block, as well as a "rustic conference center" for those tired of conventional boardrooms. The **Umkhiwane Trail** is a 5km hike through coastal forests and wetlands. A boat is available for rental. Don't try to swim in the lake; the water is home to hippos and crocodiles who would be happy to make you part of their holiday memories. (☎ 035 550 9035 for campsite reservations; 033 845 1000 for hutted camp reservations. Entry R20, children R10. Rustic 2-person huts R110 per person; 7-person chalets R130 per person, min. R520. Camping R38. Gates open Oct.-Mar. 5am-8pm, Apr.-Sept. 6am-8pm. Office open daily 8am-12:30pm and 2-4pm.)

Continuing straight at the turn-off to Fanies Island for another 4km leads to the **Charters Creek camp,** on the shoreline of Lake St. Lucia. This fisherman's heaven also has plentiful birdlife, beautiful hiking trails, and a swimming pool to keep non-anglers busy. The **Isikhova Trail** is a 7km hike through the coastal forest, while the **Umkumbe Trail** is 5km long and traverses a variety of ecosystems. A boat is available for rental, and there are daily guided boat tours at 10am, weather permitting. Don't swim in the lake. The office has a shop that sells some basic supplies, but bring your own food. (☎ 033 845 1000 M-Th; 550 9000 F-Su. Entry R20, children R10. 7-bed cottages R120 per person, min. R480; 2-bed chalets R145 per person; 2-bed huts R110 per person; 3-bed huts R110 per person, min. R220; 4-bed huts R110 per person, min. R220. Camping R38 per person, min. R76. Gates open Oct.-Mar. 5am-8pm, Apr.-Sept. 6am-8pm. Office open daily 8am-12:30pm and 2-4pm.)

The **Zamimpilo Community Market,** off the N2 about 20km south of Hluhluwe, is a community project there are small, basic shops for local handicraft and fruit vendors. The market has one of the largest selections of curios in KwaZulu-Natal, and money spent here goes to the local community. There is also a traditional Zulu village and a tea garden behind the shops. (☎ 083 519 2951. Open daily 6am-6pm.)

SODWANA BAY ☎ 035

The combination of warm waters, miles of shoreline, forested sand dunes, 4000-year-old coral reefs, and over 1200 species of fish have made Sodwana Bay a premier destination for scuba diving and fishing. There is not much out-of-water civilization, but below the surface, coral reefs teem with life and the vibrant colors of the fish rival the lights of any big city. Most travelers head to Sodwana for strictly aquatic purposes, though there are also some hiking options for those looking to stay dry. Anglers, divers, and the like favor the uncrowded off-season. During school holidays and the hot summer months, hordes of Afrikaner vacationers and fishermen migrate here and to Kosi Bay to drink like fish while catching a few as well. The beaches are packed with people and prices rise accordingly. Go from Sunday to Wednesday to appreciate the Bay's underwater offerings while remaining on good terms with your wallet at the same time.

▣ TRANSPORTATION

The **Baz Bus** (☎ 031 304 0556) has a drop-off in Hluhluwe. Most of the establishments in Sodwana Bay, including Coral Divers and Mseni Lodge, can arrange transportation the rest of the way. Be warned that all of the accommodations are several kilometers from the beach itself.

▣ ▣ ORIENTATION AND PRACTICAL INFORMATION

The only paved road to Sodwana Bay separates from the N2 at Hluhluwe and leads northeast, turning sharply right at the small town of Mbazwana. Driving into Sodwana Bay, visitors will pass through one set of park gates, then past the row of establishments that constitute the town, and then through a second set of park gates and into the reserve proper, where **Coral Divers** and **Mseni Lodge** are located.

Entrance to the park will set you back R20, and a R200 deposit is required for late entry. There is also a daily fee of R35 for staying in the park. The road to the **beach** turns off the main road between the two sets of park gates; look for the parking lot. The **Parks Board reception office** is at the second set of park gates. (☎ 571 0051. Open M-Th 8am-4:30pm, F-Sa 7am-4:30pm.) Some **tourist information** is available at Captain Lee Restaurant. (☎ 571 0231 or 082 6060 559. Office open M-F 8am-4pm.) Services include: **groceries** at Boxer Silver Sands general store, just outside the inner set of park gates (open daily 8am-5pm); **emergency** (☎ 082 821 4281); **police** in Mbazwana (☎ 571 0005); and **pay phones** outside the Parks Board Office.

▐▛ ACCOMMODATIONS AND CAMPING

Coral Divers (☎ 035 571 0050 or 571 0290; coraldivers@mweb.co.za; www.coraldivers.co.za), off the roundabout inside the inner set of park gates. This well-run diving charter with a laid-back vibe and a young, friendly staff of avid divers is probably the best value for any budget traveler in search of underwater adventures. Basic and clean, though the baths proudly proclaim that they are "Maintained by Wildlife." *Braai* pit, TV lounge, and swimming pool. Breakfast R28. Dinner R46; catering package of breakfast and dinner R60. Book ahead for all meals. Laundry services available. Reception 7am-9pm; open later in summer. Check-out 11am. Accommodations sleep 2; prices are per person. Lighted tents Su-W R45, Th-Sa R90; standard huts (with linen) R150; luxury huts with bath R180. ❷

Vis Agie Charters (☎/fax 571 0104 or 082 440 4141; www.vis-agie.com; visa1234@iafrica.com), on the main road between the two sets of park gates. A fishing charter service and lodge with a restaurant and bar that has the feel of a beach house. Accommodation is available in dormitories, 2-bedroom and 3-bedroom cabins, and aquarium-themed *rondavels*. Breakfast R45. Lunch R30. Dinner R60 (advance booking necessary). Lodge has full self-catering facilities, TV, laundry service, electricity, and free tea and coffee. Hire linen or bring your own. Reservations recommended. R120 per person self-catering; R155 bed and breakfast; R225 dinner, bed, and breakfast. ❷

Sodwana Bay Campsites (Parks Board ☎ 571 0051 or 571 0052), inside the inner set of park gates. Minimum stay 2 nights, in high season 4 nights. Campsites R33, upgraded sites with water and electricity at Gwala Gwala camp R45; 5- and 8-bed log cabins with kitchen, lounge, and full bath R130 per person. ❶

▐ FOOD

Mseni Lodge Restaurant (☎ 571 0284 or 082 567 7583), inside the second set of park gates. Not only does Mseni's serve some of the best food in town, but its location overlooking the bay makes it the ideal place to see the sunset. Skip the ground floor and head directly upstairs to fully appreciate the view. Full English breakfast (R45). Lunch menu (R15-38). Dinner menu (R28-45). *Prix fixe* lunch or dinner (R75). Open daily 7-11am, 12:30-3pm, and 7-10pm. Reservations recommended. ❷

Leatherbacks (☎ 571 0043; fax 571 0144), inside Sodwana Bay Lodge, on the main road between the two sets of park gates. Contrary to implication, there's no turtle soup on the menu, but you can find a pleasant array of seafood, chicken, pizza, and steak. A younger crowd plays pool and watches rugby downstairs at the bar, while the upper crust sips Jack and Coke a floor up in the main restaurant. A la carte menu including vegetarian dishes (R20-70). Open daily 7-10:30am, noon-5pm, and 7-10pm; downstairs bar open 4pm-late. ❷

Captain Lee Restaurant (☎/fax 571 0231), on the main road between the two sets of park gates. Vegetarians, be warned. The menu falls under two categories: "Things that

KWAZULU-NATAL

Swim or Float" and "Things that Moo or Crow." Although sparsely decorated, the restaurant's windows and patio (which face the Maputoland countryside) make for a pleasant sunset dining experience. Seafood dishes R35-130. Pizza R18-30. Steaks R40-55. Open daily 8am-10pm. ❸

⬛ AQUATIC ADVENTURES

SCUBA DIVING. Divers who know what they are doing and have the proper certifications can rent gear from **Sandton Scuba,** on the beach (☎463 2201 or 082 451 3529) or from **Coral Divers** (see **Accommodations and Camping,** above). Prices run about R40 per item. The less experienced can arrange dive packages with Coral Divers or with **Mseni Lodge** (☎571 0284 or 571 0257). A five-dive package runs between R520 and R600. A single 2-mile dive costs R140; 5-mile R155; 7-mile R170; 9-mile R180. The distances indicate how far out you go, not how far down (hopefully). Night dives are R200. For absolute beginners, packages are available for R650 that include training, equipment, and one dive. Coral Divers also offers packages that include several nights of accommodation, a number of dives, and advanced diving training courses.

ANGLING AND SNORKELING. North of Sodwana Bay, **Mabibi** has its own variety of aquatic species. From Mbazwana, a road with signs runs north to a turn-off leading to the Mabibi area. You must obtain an entrance permit from the Sodwana Bay Parks Office and arrive early, as only 20 vehicles per day are allowed inside. (Permit R120; expires after 1 year.)

⬛ OUTDOORS

Sodwana Bay has activities to keep the hydrophobic busy while their friends are frolicking with fish. Hikers may appreciate the closeness of the **Mngobozeleni Trail,** which starts at the Parks Board reception office, where you can purchase a booklet detailing the paths (R5). This mild 5km trail makes for a good afternoon activity, but don't expect to see much wildlife. The trees, marked for identification, are the most interesting part of the hike. If you're in the mood to see things that move, head west to the **Mkhuze Game Reserve.** Although the Parks Board pamphlet lists a number of big game species you can observe, make sure to bring your binoculars; Mkhuze is a bird-watching heaven. Drive there and enter the hides on foot for a day (gates open Oct.-Mar. daily 5am-7pm; Apr.-Sept. daily 6am-6pm) or call the Parks Board (☎573 9003) to book tented, hutted, or lodge accommodations for overnight trips. Bring your own food. **Horse Riding** can be arranged through Sandton Scuba (☎463 2201 or 082 451 3529) on the beach.

ULUNDI   ☎035

Out of Zululand's brown rolling hills and endless, stark savannah grasslands a spattering of humble homes emerges that slowly creeps up on the dusty, unremarkable town of Ulundi. According to Zulu tradition, when a new king came to power, it was customary for him to build a new capital. Ulundi was built after Cetshwayo became king in 1873. In 1879, Ulundi was the scene of the final, decisive battle of the Anglo-Zulu war and was torched by 5000 victorious British soldiers. The town was subsequently rebuilt and became the capital of the apartheid-era homeland of KwaZulu. Today, after the merging of KwaZulu with the originally whites-only province of Natal, Ulundi shares joint-capital status with Pietermaritzburg. This town may have little to offer fun-seekers, but its history provides a valuable commentary on the proud and troubled history of the Zulu people.

Ulundi lies 85km north of Eshowe on the R66. The **KwaZulu-Natal Legislative Building** (☎ 874 4166) stands opposite the R66 from the Ithala Center. The front entrance is off the road that branches to the left off the R66 about 500m north of Princess Magogo St. Parking lots filled with black Mercedes sporting cyan-shaded windows surround the conspicuously modern building. Outside the assembly room is a family tree of the Zulu kings, a set of vibrant tapestries depicting the history of the Zulu nation, and a statue commemorating the Battle of Isandlawana. Free tours can be arranged by phone. About 500m past the airport on King Cetshwayo St. is the **Ulundi Battlefield,** where the British overran the city in what became the last battle of the Anglo-Zulu War. Today, there is a modest memorial to the British and Zulu casualties and a small graveyard. About 4km farther down the road is the **Ondini Cultural Museum,** which stands at Ondini ("the high place"), the site of King Cetshwayo's ill-fated *kraal.* There is a guided trail through the remains of Ondini's former majesty, as well as several displays on the royal *kraal* and the Battle of Ulundi. There are also exhibits in the main museum of traditional Zulu, Xhosa, and Ndebele women's attire, as well as displays of traditional beadwork, children's toys, beer-making, and a replica of a traditional Zulu hut. (☎ 870 2050; fax 870 2054; amafahq@mweb.co.za. Open daily 9am-4pm. R10, children R5.)

For accommodations, **Ondini Cultural Museum ❶,** about 5km down King Cetshwayo St. past the airport, is the only wallet-friendly place to stay in Ulundi. Accommodations include double huts with private baths, double *rondavels* with communal baths, and a 10-bed Zulu beehive hut. Huts are set around an *isibaya* (*kraal*) in a secluded clearing near the museum and may be rather lonely for individuals. (☎ 870 2050; fax 870 2054; amafahq@mweb.co.za. *Rondavels* and beehive R85 per person, huts with private bath R120 per person.) The only true restaurant in town is at the **Holiday Inn Garden Court ❸,** on Princess Magogo St. just past Mkabayi St. The Holiday Inn offers single rooms for R454 and doubles for R558. (☎ 870 1012. Breakfast buffet R51; a la carte lunch R30-60; dinner buffet R72; children's menu R10-20.) Other options in Ulundi are pretty much limited to fast food and take-away joints on Mkabayi St. (Most open daily 9am-7pm.)

Minibus taxis run from the shopping center opposite the Holiday Inn on Princess Magogo near Princess Mkabayi St. to: Durban (3½hr., R60); Empangeni (1½hr., R30); Eshowe (1½hr., R30); Johannesburg (5hr., R90); and Vryheid (1½hr., R30). Services include: **Standard Bank,** in Ithala Center on Mkabayi St. (☎ 870 0714 or 870 0715; open M-F 9am-3:30pm, Sa 8:30-11am); **Spar** supermarket, on Mkabayi St. (open daily 8am-8pm); **Ondini Pharmacy,** on Mkabayi St. (☎ 870 1336 or 870 1062; open M-F 9am-6pm, Sa 9am-2pm); **Ekuphileni Medical Center,** in the Spar plaza on Mkabayi St. (☎ 072 141 2981; open M-F 8am-8pm, Sa 8am-1pm, Su 10am-1pm); **Nkonjeni Mission Hospital,** about 12km north of town on the R66 (☎ 873 0013; open 24hr.). The **post office,** at the back of Ithala Center on Mkabayi St., has **phones** and *Poste Restante.* (☎ 870 0905. Open M-Tu and Th-F 8:30am-4:30pm, W 9am-4:30pm, Sa 8am-noon.) **Postal code:** 3838.

PONGOLA   ☎ 034

With its lush surroundings and welcoming community, Pongola is a good base for exploring the remote areas of northern Zululand. The main trade center for sugar cane farmers and laborers in the area, Pongola is very close to Swaziland's border. None of the bus companies make it this far, making visits difficult for the carless.

■ ⁊ **ORIENTATION AND PRACTICAL INFORMATION.** The N2 from Durban becomes **Piet Retief St.** as it enters town from the east, passing **Lukas Meyer St.** on the right and the R66 to Ulundi on the left. After 1km is **Martins St.** to the right and then **Naude St.** to the right before the N2 continues on to Johannesburg. The center of town is along Piet Retief St. between Martins St. and Naude St. and continues one block north of Piet Retief to **Nieuwe Republiek St.** Within this square is a row of shops and services called **Sodwana Corridor.**

The **Pongola Taxi Association** (☎413 2491) has a taxi rank on the N2 at Naude St., near the Shell garage, with taxis running to: **Durban** (4hr., R1600); **Empangeni** (2hr., R1300); **Johannesburg** (4hr., R1600); **Newcastle** (2½hr., R1300); **Nongoma** (1½hr., R700); **Vryheid** (1½hr., R700). The **Pongola Info Lapa** is in the Pongola Arts & Crafts Center, across the N2 from Naude St., and offers a small collection of maps, brochures, and other information. (☎413 1144; fax 413 2100. Open M-F 8am-5pm, Sa-Su 9am-noon.) Services include: **ABSA Bank** with **ATM** and foreign exchange, on Nieuwe Republiek St. (open M-F 8:30am-3:30pm, Sa 8:30-11am); **Spar** supermarket, on Naude St. (open M-F 8:30am-5:30pm, Sa 8:30am-1:30pm, Su 9:30am-12:30pm); **police station,** at the intersection of Martins and Hans Strydom St., just northeast of the center (☎413 1201); the **Pongola Hospital,** 82 Hans Dons St., east of the center (☎413 1372; open 24hr.). **Pongola Apteek,** a pharmacy, is on Piet Retief St. (☎413 1331. Open M-F 8am-5pm, Sa 9am-1pm.) The **post office,** at Nieuwe Republiek and Martins St., has *Poste Restante.* (☎413 1530. Open M-Tu and Th-F 8:30am-4:30pm, W 9am-4:30pm, Sa 8am-noon.) **Postal code:** 3170.

⌂❑ ACCOMMODATIONS AND FOOD. The tourist office has info on many guest houses in the area that are accessible to travelers with wheels. **Casa Mia ❶,** five minutes from town by car, is a luxurious guest house set in a lovely sub-tropical garden with swimming pool. Rooms are extremely comfortable and beautifully decorated in African style. (Take the N2 about 5km toward Empangeni and turn right down the road marked "Suikermeule"; the guest house will be on your left in a few miles. ☎413 1713 or 083 228 1822; fax 413 2100; casamia@lantic.net. Doubles R165 plus VAT.) **Pongola Caravan Park ❶,** off the N2 on the eastern side of town near Lukas Meyer St., offers spacious, clean, and bright chalets. Attractions include a duck pond, playground, and swimming pool. (☎413 1789. Self-catering chalets R195 for 1, R175 per person sharing, children under 14 R75. Campsites R50 for 1, R90 for 2; R30 per extra person.) **Pongola Country Lodge ❸,** on Jan Millie St., is right in the center of town. The pink motel-style rooms surround a pool and newly replanted gardens. (☎413 1352. Singles with TV R240; doubles R360.) **Koppie Alleen Guest House ❸,** 2km from the N2 on R66, is an elegant B&B surrounded by stunning gardens and a swimming pool. Each room sports a TV lounge, a mini-bar, and fresh flowers daily. Rooms sleep up to four. (☎413 1281 or 083 228 2533. Breakfast included. R205 per person plus VAT.) **DJ's Fast Food ❷,** next to the Caltex Station across from the Arts & Crafts Center, offers steaks, fish, and breakfasts. Most entrees are R30-50. (☎422 198. Open daily 7am-10pm.)

NEAR PONGOLA: ITHALA GAME RESERVE

The Ithala Game Reserve covers nearly 30,000ha of mountainous *thornveld*, brimming with all of the Big Five except lions. The diverse topography (400-1450m) gives rise to a diversity of habitats, flora, and fauna, making any drive special. Spectacular routes cut through rugged terrain, approaching steep cliffs and escarpments. (Gates open Oct.-Mar. daily 5am-7pm; Apr.-Sept. 6am-6pm. Admission R30 per person, R30 per vehicle.)

The few **campsites ❷** in the reserve cost R22 and can be booked through the camp office. If you have some extra cash, consider splurging on the chalets at the spectacular and luxurious Ntshondwe. Self-catering accommodations at three rustic bush camps are also available. (Chalets R210 per person for self-catering or R280 per person with dinner and breakfast; bush camps R170 per person self-catering. Book chalets or huts with the KwaZulu-Natal Nature Conservation Services Reservations; ☎0331 845 1000; fax 845 1001. Last minute bookings can be made through the camp office; ☎034 907 5105. Call at least 24hr. in advance.)

KWAZULU-NATAL

GAUTENG

Although gold-rich Gauteng is South Africa's smallest province, it is also the most densely populated (with 8 million inhabitants) and heavily industrialized. In fact, Gauteng is single-handedly responsible for almost 25% of the economic output of the entire African continent. A century of development has transformed Gauteng's physical and economic landscape, resulting in the soaring skyscrapers, tangled freeways, and mega-shopping malls that dominate the province.

The history of the province is a tale of two cities: though barely 50km apart, Pretoria and Johannesburg developed under very different circumstances. As South Africa's old-guard administrative center, Pretoria served as humble capital to the poor but fiercely independent Zuid-Afrikaansche Republiek (ZAR), whose leaders fought for half a century to establish a national identity independent of British control. In 1884, the discovery of the richest gold-bearing reef in history, just southwest of Pretoria, changed the destiny of this backwater region forever. Within five years, Johannesburg, appropriately dubbed Egoli ("city of gold"), had become the largest and richest city on the continent.

From the township of Soweto, cradle to many liberation legends, the fight to abolish apartheid raged across present-day Gauteng to Pretoria's Union Buildings, where the city's successive ruling white governments tightened the screws of repression to their breaking point. Amid magnificent architecture and memorable museums, Pretoria and Johannesburg remain sites with powerfully recorded historical memories—some slowly fading and many more still fresh.

HIGHLIGHTS OF GAUTENG

Evidence of bravery in the face of apartheid hides behind the grim exterior of **Soweto,** South Africa's largest township (see p. 311).

Johannesburg's **Market Theatre** complex (see p. 310) is home to some of the best restaurants in the city, as well as museums, three cutting-edge theaters, and Kippie's Jazz Bar (see p. 308), one of the best jazz venues in all of Africa.

The **Voortrekker Monument** (see p. 320), the ultimate symbol of Afrikaner nationalism, stands unabashedly near the nation's capital.

JOHANNESBURG ☎ 011

Sixty kilometers southwest of Pretoria, "Jo'burg" presents quite the contrast to its older sibling. Born in 1886 during the greatest gold rush of all time, Jo'burg is today a city on the decline. Much of the downtown area has fallen into urban decay; millions of suburbanites never venture downtown anymore. Though some black citizens have moved into the middle and upper classes, countless others still live in abject poverty. Townships and squatter camps ringing the city clash with the lush, luxurious, and primarily white suburbs of Rosebank and Sandton. One glance at the barbed wire, alarms, dogs, and personal guards employed to protect these elite estates is an education in Jo'burg's crime problems. Sadly, the fears of the wealthy and the vague paranoia of visitors are not completely without grounding, as the city's crime and unemployment rates remain stratospheric.

Truth be told, most tourists do not stay in Jo'burg for very long. With rapid transport connections, many barely step outside Park Station, it's easy to come

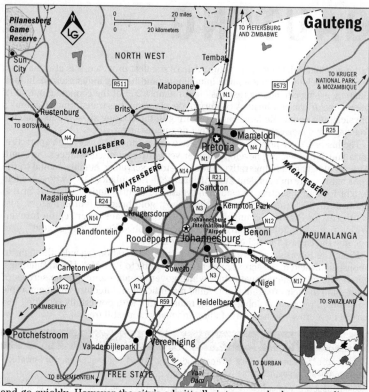

and go quickly. However the city's admittedly intense and edgy personality can also attract visitors. Johannesburg boasts a vibrant social scene with a dizzying array of clubs, pubs, and *shebeens*. Its intense personality has given rise to the hard-edged hip-hop and *kwaito* sounds of Hillbrow and the dazzling jazz of the Newtown district. The sounds and images of Newtown and Soweto are crucial to visitors who come to Johannesburg searching for a way to comprehend its difficult history.

⬛ INTERCITY TRANSPORTATION

FLIGHTS

Airport: Johannesburg International Airport (☎921 6262), is in Kempton Park, a 25min. drive east of downtown. Virtually all major carriers have international service to and from Jo'burg. **Magic Bus** service (☎914 4321) offers shuttle services to Johannesburg (R170-210 for the first member of a party; R30 for each additional party member up to seven). **Johannesburg Airport Shuttle** (☎394 6902) carries travelers from Terminal 3 to Grace Hotel in Rosebank, as well as to hotels in the Sandton area, and offers door-to-door special service (daily, every hr. 5:30am-11pm, R75). Many hostels offer **free airport pick-up** for guests; be sure to arrange a pick-up time prior to arrival, as late-night taxis into town cost upward of R160.

SAFETY IN JO'BURG: TEN COMMANDMENTS.

1. Johannesburg is a large and turbulent city. Take every precaution to ensure your safety, even in broad daylight in the busiest commercial districts.

2. Travelers are most vulnerable during arrival in or departure from the city; move purposefully and remain alert.

3. Don't wander the city until you've settled down and deposited your bags.

4. Seek and heed the advice of your hosts or trustworthy locals on security concerns. Do get second and third opinions, but never fully ignore a warning.

5. Avoid carrying large amounts of cash and other valuables into the Central Business District and Hillbrow.

6. Gain a pre-arrival familiarity with your area. Referring to a map in public is a dead giveaway to any ruffian plotting mischief.

7. When venturing into dangerous areas, stash cab fare and the number of a reliable taxi company on your person (inside your sock is an option).

8. Your caution must be color-blind; contrary to popular prejudice, criminals in Johannesburg come in a full spectrum of skin color.

9. If you are accosted, cooperate and follow instructions. Your life is more important than your camera.

10. **Beware of paranoia.** Dire warnings notwithstanding, Johannesburg is not that different from other big cities. Be savvy, but remember to enjoy yourself.

Airlines: The best source for internal flights is ■ **Kulula.com,** a South African airline that offers very cheap flights without standard amenities such as in-flight meals and business class. Their prices can't be beat for flights from Jo'burg to Cape Town or Durban and back. The prices listed below are round-trip, 21-day advance purchase.

British Airways/Comair (☎921 8600 or 0860 011 474) flies to: **Cape Town** (2¼hr., 6-13 flights daily 6:30am-7pm, R1230); **Durban** (1¼hr., 4-10 flights daily 6:45am-6pm, R638); **Port Elizabeth** (1¾hr., 2-4 flights daily 6:45am-6pm, R1116); **Victoria Falls** (1¾hr., daily 12:15pm, R2844); **Windhoek Int'l** (1hr., Tu-Su noon, R2506).

Nationwide Airlines (☎327 3000) flies to: **Cape Town** (2¼hr., 3-5 flights daily 7:10am-6pm, R1459); **Durban** (1hr., 4-5 flights daily 7:25am-6:15pm, R821); **George** (2hr.; M and Th-Sa 7:50am, Su 4pm; R1345); **Livingstone, Zambia** (1½hr.; M, W, Th, F, Sa 11:20am; R3200).

South African Airways/Express/Airlink (☎0860 359722) flies to: **Blantyre** (2¼hr.; Sa, W 10:15am; R2490); **Bloemfontein** (1¼hr., 3-7 flights daily 6:10am-6:35pm, R729); **Bulawayo** (1½hr., daily 10:30am, R1650); **Cape Town** (1¼hr., a zillion flights daily 6am-9:05pm, R1276); **Durban** (1½hr., 15-22 flights daily 6am-9:05pm, R706); **East London** (1½hr., 5-6 flights daily 6:15am-6:50pm, R820); **Gaborone** (1hr., 1-4 flights daily 6:30am-4:25pm, R1024); **George** (2hr., 2-4 flights daily 6am-4:25pm, R1208); **Harare** (1½hr., daily 10:40am and Su-W 7:05pm, R1970); **Kimberley** (1½hr., 1-4 flights daily 6am-5:45pm, R1026); **Lilongwe** (2¼hr., Th-M 10:20am, R2490); **Livingstone** (1¾hr.; Su, Tu, F 11:35am; R3160); **Manzini** (1hr., 4 flights daily 6:50am-4:15pm, R1037); **Maputo** (1hr., daily 2:10pm and F-Sa 9:30am, R1380); **Margate** (1½hr.; daily 11:50am, Su 4pm, F 6:30pm; R912); **Maseru** (1hr. 10min.; daily 6:45, 9:15am, 3:45pm; R1047); **Nelspruit** (50min., 3-6 flights daily 6:45am-4pm, R866); **Phalaborwa** (1hr.; M-Sa 10:40am and 4:10pm, M-F 6:40am; R969); **Pietermaritzburg** (1¼hr., 2-7 flights daily 6:30am-6:10pm, R821); **Pietersburg** (50min., 1-4 flights daily 7:20am-5pm, R866); **Plettenberg Bay** (2½hr.; Su-F 9:50am, Sa 7:30am and 1:20pm; R1414); **Port Elizabeth** (1¾hr., 4-7 flights daily 6:05am-5pm, R980); **Richards Bay** (1½hr, 1-4 flights daily 6am-4:30pm, R923); **Skukuza** (1¼hr.; daily 10:30am and 12:55pm, F 9:35am; R1721); **Sun City** (35min., Su-M and W-F 12:35pm, R502); **Umtata** (1½hr., 1-3 flights daily 6:20am-3:15pm, R1254); **Upington** (1½hr., daily 6:15am, R1368); **Victoria Falls** (1½hr., daily 9:10am and Th-Su 2pm, R3160); **Walvis Bay** (1½hr.; M-F 10:40am, Su 7:15am; R2277); **Windhoek Eros** (1hr.; M-F 6:15am and 4:25pm, Su 9:30am and 3pm; R1977); **Windhoek Int'l** (1hr.; Su-F 11am and 7:10pm, Sa 11am; R1977).

GAUTENG

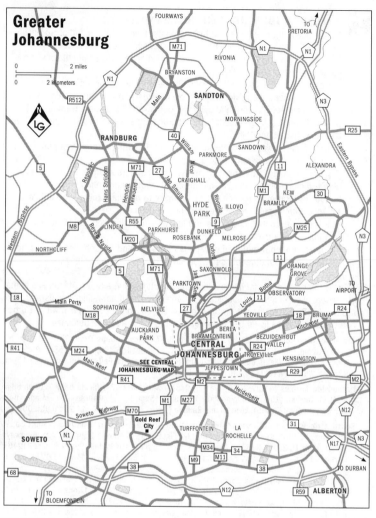

Greater Johannesburg

TRAINS

Trains: Trains arrive at and depart from **Park Station**, a bustling travel hub in central Johannesburg. Long-distance trains are generally en route to or from Pretoria. Be aware of your luggage and valuables at all times. **Luggage storage** available on the station's lower level (open M-Sa 6am-7pm, Su 7am-6pm; R2 per day per piece).

Lines: Spoornet runs the trains listed below. (☎773 2944, reservations ☎086 000 8888; www.spoornet.co.za). Open M-Tu and Th-F 7:30am-4pm, W 7:30am-3pm, Sa 7:30-10:45am. 40% student discounts available on 2nd-class round-trip tickets during low season. Book tickets in advance.

Algoa line to **Port Elizabeth** (19hr., daily 2:30pm, R215/R315) via **Bloemfontein.**

Amatola line to **East London** (20hr., daily 12:45pm, R200/R295) via **Bloemfontein.**

Diamond Express line to **Kimberley** (10hr., Su-F 7:35pm, R100/R150).

Komati line to **Maputo Post, Mozambique** (17½hr., daily 6:10pm, R110/R160).

Trans-Karoo line to **Cape Town** (28hr., daily 12:30pm, R290/R430) via **Kimberley** and **Worcester.**

Trans-Natal line to **Durban** (13½hr., daily 6:30pm, R145/R215) via **Pietermaritzburg.**

BUSES

Station: Greyhound, Intercape, and **Translux** all depart from Park Station. Ticket offices open 7am-9pm. AmEx/MC/DC/V.

Companies: Prices listed are all one-way; round-trip is generally twice the fare.

Greyhound (☎249 8900; www.greyhound.co.za). To: **Bloemfontein** (6½hr., 4 times daily, R150); **Bulawayo** (12¼hr., once daily, R270) via **Pietersburg** (4¼hr., twice daily, R130) and **Messina** (6¾hr., twice daily, R150); **Cape Town** (18hr., 3 times daily, R250-385); **Durban** (7hr., 7 times daily, R120-160) via **Pietermaritzburg** (6hr., 7 times daily, R120-180); **East London** (12½hr., once daily, R245); **Harare** (16½hr., once daily, R320) via Pietersburg, Messina, and **Masvingo** (13hr., R305); **Kimberley** (7½hr., twice daily, R160); **Nelspruit** (5½hr., 4 times daily, R125-150); **Port Elizabeth** (14hr., twice daily, R275-295) via **Grahamstown** (12hr., twice daily, R265); **Umtata** (11¼hr., once daily, R180).

Intercape (☎012 380 4400; www.intercape.co.za). To: **Bloemfontein** (6hr., once daily, R160); **Cape Town** (19hr., once daily, R250); **Durban** (7½hr.; 8am, 1:30pm, 10pm; R99-155) via **Pietermaritzburg** (6½hr., 2 or 3 times daily, R99-145); **Knysna** (17hr., R305); **Mossel Bay** (16½hr., once daily, R280); **Oudtshoorn** (15hr., twice daily, R260); **Upington** (10hr.; once daily; R250) via **Kuruman** (6hr., once daily, R175) and **Vryburg** (5hr., once daily, R150).

Baz Bus (☎021 439 2323; www.bazbus.co.za). To **Cape Town** (R685 direct; via **Swaziland** R1850; via the **Drakensberg** R1500) with door-to-door service. Perfect for "hoppers." Tickets available at most hostels.

MINIBUSES

Minibus Taxis: Long-distance minibus taxis depart from Park Station, along Wanderers and King George St., with a few ranks along De Villiers St. (For local minibus travel, see **By Minibus Taxi,** p. 299.) Ranks are a mugger's paradise, so show up with luggage only when you know exactly where you're headed. Locals advise catching minibuses at a known stop along their route (gas stations, road stalls) rather than from crowded taxi ranks. Ask hostel owners for known locations. Destinations include: **Durban** (R85); **Gaborone** (R87); **Kimberley** (R73); **Mafikeng/Mmabatho** (R47); **Maputo** (R107); **Mbabane** (R60); **Venda** (R70).

 Minibus taxis in Johannesburg are nicknamed "riding coffins" for a good reason: drivers often speed for long distances at night, causing an alarmingly high number of accidents in which many passengers are killed. As a result, *Let's Go* does not recommend minibus taxis for intercity or long-distance travel.

✈ ORIENTATION

While Johannesburg is indeed large, tourist areas of interest are fairly compact. With some orientation and some map savvy, Jo'burg can be quite easily navigated.

CENTRAL JOHANNESBURG

Central Jo'burg refers to the legion of skyscrapers and office buildings of the Central Business District, Braamfontein, and Joubert Park, as well as the high-rise residential apartments of Hillbrow and Berea. Northeast of the city rises the **Berea Telecommunications Tower,** a useful beacon for the disoriented traveler.

GAUTENG

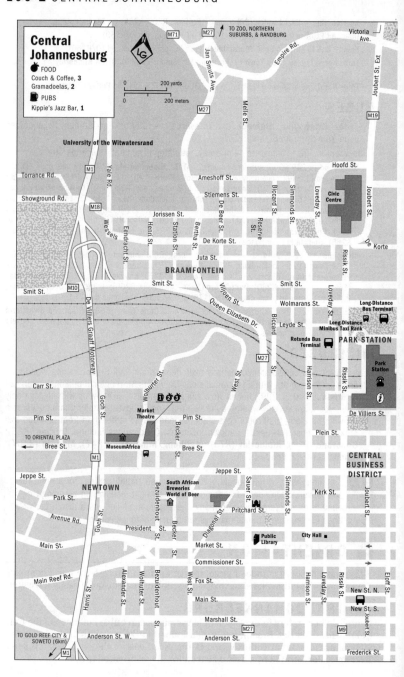

Central Johannesburg

🍎 FOOD
Couch & Coffee, **3**
Gramadoelas, **2**

🏠 PUBS
Kippie's Jazz Bar, **1**

TO ZOO, NORTHERN SUBURBS, & RANDBURG

M71 M27 M27 M19

Victoria Ave.

Empire Rd.

Jan Smuts Ave.

Mellie St.

Joubert St. Ext

0   200 yards
0   200 meters

University of the Witwatersrand

Torrance Rd.

Showground Rd.

Ameshoff St.

Hoofd St.

Civic Centre

Stiemens St.

Jorissen St.

Biccard St.

Simmonds St.

Loveday St.

Joubert St.

De Korte

M1

Yale Rd.

M18

Wessels

Eendracht St.

Henri St.

Station St.

Bertha St.

De Beer St.

Reserve St.

De Korte St.

Juta St.

Rissik St.

BRAAMFONTEIN

Smit St.

M10

Smit St.

Vliegen St.

Queen Elizabeth Dr.

Smit St.

Wolmarans St.

Leyde St.

Loveday St.

Biccard St.

Long-Distance Bus Terminal

Long-Distance Minibus Taxi Rank

Rotunda Bus Terminal

PARK STATION

De Villiers Graaff Motorway

Goch St.

Wolhuter St.

M27

West St.

Harrison St.

Rissik St.

Park Station

Carr St.

ⒺⒻⒼ

Market Theatre

Pim St.

Becker St.

De Villiers St.

Pim St.

Plein St.

Bree St.

🏛️ MuseumAfrica

Bree St.

CENTRAL BUSINESS DISTRICT

TO ORIENTAL PLAZA ←

Jeppe St.

NEWTOWN

Park St.

Avenue Rd.

Main St.

M1

Goch St.

Bezuidenhout St.

Becker St.

President St.

Diagonal St.

Jeppe St.

South African Breweries World of Beer

Sauer St.

Pritchard St.

Simmonds St.

Kerk St.

Joubert St.

Market St.

🏛️

📕 Public Library

City Hall ■

Commissioner St.

Main St.

Main Reef Rd.

Harris St.

Alexander St.

Wolhuter St.

Bezuidenhout St.

West St.

Fox St.

Main St.

Marshall St.

Harrison St.

Loveday St.

Rissik St.

Eloff St.

Joubert St.

New St. N.
New St. S.

TO GOLD REEF CITY & SOWETO (6km)

Anderson St. W.

Anderson St.

M27   M9

M1

Frederick St.

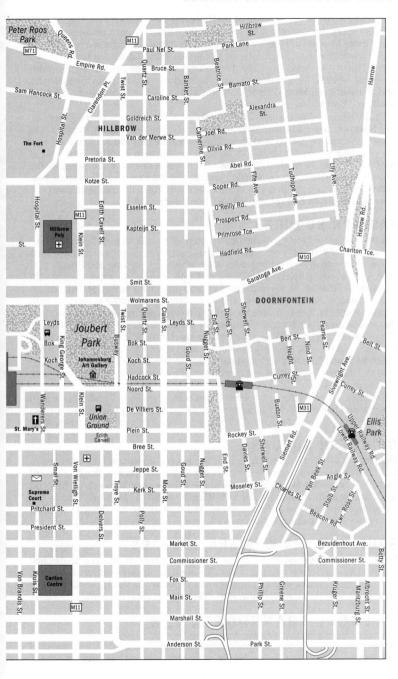

Peter Roos Park
Queens Rd.
M71
M11
Empire Rd.
Paul Nel St.
Park Lane
Hillbrow St.
Bruce St.
Quartz St.
Beatrice St.
Barnato St.
Harrow
Sam Hancock St.
Twist St.
Caroline St.
Banket St.
Clarendon Pl.
Alexandra St.
Goldreich St.
HILLBROW
Van der Merwe St.
Joel Rd.
Catherine St.
Olivia Rd.
The Fort
Pretoria St.
Abel Rd.
Lily Ave.
Kotze St.
Soper Rd.
Tudhope Ave.
Fife Ave.
Harrow Rd.
Hospital St.
Hospital St.
M11
Esselen St.
O'Reilly Rd.
Prospect Rd.
Charlton Tce.
Edith Cavell St.
Klein St.
Hillbrow Poly
Kapteijn St.
Primrose Tce.
St.
Hadfield Rd.
M10
Smit St.
Saratoga Ave.
Wolmarans St.
DOORNFONTEIN
Leyds
Twist St.
Quartz St.
Claim St.
Leyds St.
Davies St.
Sherwell St.
Beit St.
Pearse St.
Beit St.
Bok
Joubert Park
End St.
Nugget St.
Height
Nind St.
Sivewright Ave.
King George St.
Busway
Bok St.
Koch
Johannesburg Art Gallery
Koch St.
Goud St.
Currey St.
Currey St.
Hadcock St.
Klein St.
Noord St.
Buxton St.
Upper Railway Rd.
Ellis Park
Wanderers St.
Union Ground
De Villiers St.
M31
Lower Railway Rd.
St. Mary's St.
Edith Carvell
Plein St.
Rockey St.
Davies St.
Sherwell St.
Siemert Rd.
Van Beek St.
Angle St.
Bree St.
End St.
Stab St.
Lwr. Ross St.
Von Wielligh St.
Jeppe St.
Goud St.
Nugget St.
Moseley St.
Charles St.
Beacon Rd.
Smal St.
Troye St.
Kerk St.
Mool St.
Supreme Court
Pritchard St.
Delvers St.
Poly St.
President St.
Bezuidenhout Ave.
Betty St.
Market St.
Commissioner St.
Commissioner St.
Von Brandis St.
Kruis St.
Carlton Centre
Fox St.
Main St.
Phillip St.
Greene St.
Kruger St.
Albrecht St.
Maritzburg St.
Von Brandis St.
M11
Marshall St.
Anderson St.
Park St.

One block east of Park Station along **Wolmarans St.** is **Joubert Park,** home to the Johannesburg Art Gallery. **Hillbrow** stands immediately north of Joubert Park, while **Berea** lies east of Hillbrow. **Be cautious:** Hillbrow has garnered notoriety as the roughest, toughest neighborhood in Johannesburg. Looking toward the city center (using the station as a central reference), the **Central Business District (CBD)** lies south of the railway line cutting through the city. Streets form a rectangular grid: **Commissioner, Market, Jeppe,** and **Bree St.** run east-west; **Simmonds, Harrison, Rissik,** and **Eloff St.** run north-south.

On the western edge of the CBD, south of the railway lines and west of Sauer St., lies **Newtown,** home to the cultural precinct, the Market Theatre complex, the MuseumAfrica, and the Oriental Plaza. The **minibus taxi rank** and **bus stop** at the corner of Bree and Sauer St. primarily services the northern suburbs. Northwest of the CBD, beyond the rail line, **Braamfontein** is home to a number of businesses, the University of Witwatersrand's main campus, and the consulates and trade missions that have not yet fled into the northern suburbs. The area's primary east-west arteries are **De Korte St.** and, a block north, **Jorissen St.**

EASTERN SUBURBS

Yeoville, including Bellevue (immediately east of Yeoville across Cavendish St.) forms a buffer zone between the overflowing inner-city ghettos of Hillbrow and Berea and the middle-class residences of Observatory, Cyrildene, and Bruma. Yeoville centers around **Raleigh St.,** running east from Harrow St. at the junction with Kenmere St. Raleigh St. becomes the one-way eastbound **Rockey St.,** a seamless chain of shops, restaurants, pubs, and clubs. Westbound traffic is diverted onto parallel **Hunter St.** The two streams of traffic merge again at the intersection with **De Larey St.,** together becoming **Observatory St.** (the street's third name change). Yeoville's best accommodations are within a short walk of Raleigh/Rockey/Observatory St., and most hostels offer directions with this mega-street as their starting point. **Be aware:** the areas surrounding Rockey St. are becoming a target for muggers and thieves; use caution and carry minimal cash and valuables, especially on nighttime forays.

To the east, Observatory St. becomes **Marcia St.** as it enters the affluent suburb of **Cyrildene,** home to New Chinatown, before leading on to the massive Bruma Flea Market. Continuing eastward will bring you to the freeway and the **airport.**

NORTHERN SUBURBS

Melville, just north of Brixton and Braamfontein off **Barry Hertzog Ave.,** is the trendiest of the northern suburbs, especially around **3rd** and **7th Ave.** Running east of Melville is **Jan Smuts Ave.,** which leads to the affluent neighborhoods of Westcliff and Parktown. Johannesburg Zoo is further down Smuts Ave., followed by the suburbs of Rosebank, Hyde Park, and Dunkeld West. Home to Jo'burg's non-white *nouveau riche,* **Rosebank** is filled with chic shops, markets, clubs, and hotels.

SOUTHERN AND WESTERN SUBURBS

West of the city beyond Newtown lie the working-class residential areas once reserved for Johannesburg's Indian and "colored" populations—Brixton, Mayfair, and Amalgam. Farther south of these is mine country. As the M1 south freeway runs out of town, it passes the township of **Soweto** and gritty industrial factories.

▐ LOCAL TRANSPORTATION

Johannesburg's public transport infrastructure hinges on its formalized **municipal bus** network and the less formal but far more comprehensive **minibus taxi** routes.

Unfortunately, neither is very reliable after nightfall. Jo'burg's **metro-rail** system is useful primarily for reaching Pretoria. **Metered taxis** are expensive, but may be the only option after 7pm, when bus and minibus taxi services peter out.

BY BUS

 As of July 2002, the Jo'burg bus system was undergoing a major overhaul. The new system, to be named "Blue IQ," will feature substantially different routes from those of the previous regime. Travelers should visit **www.blueiq.co.za** for updates and more information.

Main bus terminal (☎403 4300), off Eloff St. at Ghandi Square, between the north and south arms of New St., 2 blocks east of the Carlton Center. Route maps are available at the on-site **info center,** but aren't entirely reliable. Most services stop at 6pm.

BY MINIBUS TAXI

Though many locals continue to express safety concerns, minibus taxis are still the most flexible and cost-effective means of local and long-distance transport (see **Getting Around by Minibus Taxi,** p. 28). Remain cautious and alert at the main ranks on **Bree St.** near the Market Theatre and at the **Union Ground** next to Joubert Park. Both have inordinately high crime rates, and hapless suitcase-laden travelers are the most common victims. Don't travel with bulky or valuable luggage. It's safest to direct route queries to the local minibus-association-run **Comutanet info kiosks** nearby. Inform your driver of your local destination prior to departure.

BY TAXI

Metered taxis can be found near or at the taxi ranks in the city center and at the corner of Raleigh and Kenmere St. in Yeoville. Elsewhere, the vicinity of shopping malls makes fertile ground for cab-hunting. Calling a taxi from an established firm lowers the risk of mugging or overcharge. **Maxi Taxis** (☎648 1212) and **Rose Taxi** (☎403 9625) both offer prompt, reliable service. While taxis have no specific quitting time, service is generally only reliable until 7:30pm. Expect to pay R4-5 per kilometer, and be sure to settle on a fare before hopping in, lest your driver be tempted to extend your route.

 HAND SIGNALS. To catch a taxi or minibus heading inbound toward the city center, **raise your index finger.** To travel within the area, **point your index finger downward,** as if to signal "here." A **thumb** will communicate its universal message, although *Let's Go* does not recommend hitching.

BY CAR

Renting a car is a cheap and convenient way of getting around this megalopolis. Ask hostel managers for special deals. Prices listed below are per day, assuming an average four-day rental. Weigh distance into your best-option equation.

Car Rental: Avis (☎086 102 1111). Special backpackers' deal for as low as R198; insurance included. **Budget** (☎086 101 6622). Cars from R70 plus R1.15 per km; airport tax and insurance included. **Sani** (☎083 659 2123). Special backpackers' deal for about R200 per day, including insurance. **Swan's** (☎975 0799). R99 per day plus R0.50 per km; first 125km free, although you'll rapidly use that up.

🛈 PRACTICAL INFORMATION

TOURIST AND FINANCIAL SERVICES

Tourist offices: South African Tourism Office (☎970 1669), at Terminal 2 in the airport international arrivals hall and at **Bojanala Place** (☎778 8000), 12 Rivonia Ave., Illovo. Open M-F 7am-9pm. **Gauteng Tourism Authority** (☎327 2000 or 340 9000), in Shop 401 at the Rosebank Mall. Offers the best maps and most comprehensive information packets on Johannesburg and surrounding areas.

Tours: A plethora of tour companies run trips in and around Jo'burg, as well as to attractions farther afield (Sun City, Kruger National Park, and various villages).

Bundu Bus (☎675 0767; sryan@bundusafaris.co.za). Offers safaris to **Kruger Park** (M, W, F only; 3 days R3600, 4 days R2100), **Swaziland** (R3500), and northern **KwaZulu-Natal,** with opportunities to stay with local village families (see **Tours,** p. 312).

African Prime Tours (☎794 5708), runs half-day tour of **Soweto** (R190), as well as full-day tours of **Lesedi Cultural Village** (R510) and the **Lion Park** (R320).

Other: Jabulani Tours (☎082 649 6368) offers overnight stays in and half-day tours of Soweto; free pick-up from anywhere in Jo'burg. **Springbok Atlas** (☎396 1053) has half-day Soweto trips for R255.

Travel agencies: STA Travel (☎447 5414), Rosebank Mall, first fl. Open M-F 9am-5pm, Sa 8:30am-12:30pm. **Harvey World Travel,** in Eastgate Mall (☎733 1110; open M-F 9am-5pm) and in Sandton City (☎616 1241; open M-F 9am-5pm, Sa 9am-1pm). The local **Thomas Cook** agency, Harvey offers comprehensive travel services. **Travelphone** (☎012 664 6404) is an info service offering flight schedules for all airlines, embassy numbers, exchange rates, and restaurant listings. Available daily 8am-5pm.

Banks: Jo'burg streets are lined with banks and **ATMs.**

American Express: Central office in Braamfontein (☎359 0111) and branch offices in Rosebank (☎880 8859), Sandton City (☎884 6161), and the Randburg Waterfront (☎789 3204). All offices open M-F 9am-4pm.

LOCAL SERVICES

Libraries: Johannesburg Central Library (☎836 3787), corner of Market and Fraser St., in CBD, 1 block east of Newtown. Open M-F 10am-5pm, Sa 9am-1pm.

Laundromat: Dizzy Lizzy Laundromat (☎726 8797), on the corner of 4th Ave. and 5th St., Melville. Wash R9, dry R10. Detergent and softener extra. Ironing R3-R11 per item. Drop-off service available.

EMERGENCY AND COMMUNICATIONS

Emergency: Police ☎10 111; **ambulance** ☎10 177 or 403 4227. **Netcare** (☎082 911) offers a private ambulance service that is faster but also more expensive.

Breakdown Services: AA Breakdowns (☎0800 010 101). Open 24hr. Members of the U.S.-based AAA have reciprocity with the South African AA.

Hotlines: National Gay and Lesbian Coalition (☎487 3810).

Medical services: Johannesburg General Hospital (☎488 4911), corner of York and Jubilee St. opposite Johannesburg College of Education, in Parktown. In non-emergency situations, many hostels can suggest private practitioners.

Internet access: Internet cafes line Raleigh St., near Yeoville center. **Milky Way Internet Cafe** (☎487 1340), 2nd fl. of Times Sq. on Raleigh St. in Yeoville. Slow connections, but a reasonable R5 per 30min. Open M-F 9am-8pm, Sa 9am-6pm, Su 4-8pm. **Sunset Boulevard** (☎083 517 4060), 78 4th Ave., Melville. Good connection for R18 per

30min. Open daily 10am-9pm, Tu 10am-6pm. Most **hostels** also offer Internet service at a going rate of R15 per 30min.

Post office: (☎336 1361). Corner of Von Brandis and Jeppe St., with *Poste Restante.* Open M-F 8:30am-3:30pm, Sa 8am-1pm.

Postal code: 2001.

ACCOMMODATIONS AND CAMPING

PRICE RANGES. Price ranges, marked by the numbered icons below, are now included in food and accommodation descriptions. They are based on the lowest cost for one person, excluding special deals or prices. In the case of campgrounds, we include the cost of a car. The table below is a guide to how prices and icons match up.

SYMBOL	❶	❷	❸	❹	❺
ACCOMM.	R1-100	R101-200	R201-300	R301-400	R401+
FOOD	R1-25	R26-50	R51-100	R101-200	R201+

In the blink of an eye, **Yeoville** transformed from a backpackers' mecca into a neighborhood plagued by crime. As a result, the nightlife and budget hostels that once thrived here have begun to migrate north, settling in the more palatable **northern suburbs.** Viable **camping** and **caravanning** options are limited to the periphery of the city. If you absolutely must camp under the starry Jo'burg sky, call ahead to one of the following hostels; many allow tents to be pitched in the backyard.

YEOVILLE AND OBSERVATORY

Eastgate Backpackers, 41 Hans Pirow Ave. (☎616 2741; egatebp@netactive.co.za), off Observatory/Marcia St. Located in a safe residential area, this attractive two-story building has comfortable rooms and dorms. Separate women-only accommodations available. Near Bruma Flea Market, Eastgate Mall, and New Chinatown. Play Julia Child in 2 open kitchens, or partake of prepared meals (R10-25). Management can arrange tours. Free pick-up from airport, bus station, or central Jo'burg. Internet R15 per 30min., 15min. minimum. Dorms R50; singles R120; doubles R140, with bath R170. ❶

Brown Sugar, 75 Observatory Ave. (☎648 7397; brownsugar2000@hotmail.com). About 2km from Yeoville's Rockey St. (Observatory Ave.). This popular hostel is in a villa that was built by a notorious gangster. It's on a hill and has a view of the city from rooftop balconies. Dorms consist of floor-level mattresses. Communal bathrooms are not in top condition (even by backpackers' undemanding standards), but guests will enjoy the jacuzzi and social atmosphere. Self-catered breakfast included. Meals R20. Internet R25 per 30min. Free pick-up from the airport or bus station. Dorms R60; singles R120; doubles R150, with bath R180. Ask about camping prices. ❶

NORTHERN AND EASTERN SUBURBS

🏆**Backpackers Ritz,** 1A North Rd. (☎325 7125; ritz@iafrica.com). Off Jan Smuts Ave. in Dunkeld West, at the end of a quiet cul-de-sac. Parts of this mansion survived the Boer War. The cavernous bar feels almost medieval. Unbeatable views, especially from gardens and rotunda dorm rooms. Communal kitchen and baths. Very friendly staff. Internet R20 per 30min. Tour booking services. Free pick-up from airport or anywhere around Jo'burg. Dorms R70; singles R125; doubles R180. AmEx/MC/V. ❶

GAUTENG

THE BIG SPLURGE

SOWETO BY NIGHT

Soweto can be a downright dangerous place to venture any time day or night, but the risks can be mitigated by hiring a professional guide. If you're willing to drop some cash on a really great night out, check out the "Soweto By Night" deal, offered by The Rock restaurant (see p. 304). For R400, you get a meal at a *Let's Go* favorite followed by a pub tour of Soweto's *shebeens*. Pick-up available. Call The Rock for reservations (recommended).

Rockeys of Fourways, 22 Campbell Rd., Craigavon (☎465 4219). Comfortable rooms and dorms, as well as one of the city's best camping options. Well-maintained facilities. Before hitting the sack, chill out at the great bar. Women-only dorms available. Easily accessible from the airport highway and close to the Fourways Mall and Monte Casino playground. Tours and daytrips arranged. Internet R10 per 15min. Free pick-up. Dorms R60; singles R110; doubles R160, with bath R200. AmEx/DC/MC/V. ❶

Airport Backpackers, 3 Mohawk St., Rhodesfield (☎394 0485 or 083 227 0971; airportbackpack@hotmail.com). 2km from airport in remote residential community; best for those with cars. Spacious and comfortable, with carpeted floors and understated decor. Internet R15 per 30min. Pleasant outdoor bar affords killer views of landings. Free airport pick-up and drop-off. Dorms R65; singles R120; twin (single room, two beds) R150; doubles R160. ❶

MELVILLE

Pension Idube, 11 Walton Ave. (☎482 4055; idube@mail.com). 5min. walk down 7th Ave. from heart of Melville, adjacent to Aukland Park. Take Melville bus #67 from center to Walton Ave. The proximity of this family-style guest house allows foot access to Melville's trendy nightlife and eateries. Spacious guest rooms and shiny hardwood floors. Cool backyard and pool provide a perfect place to recover from a raucous night. Light breakfast included. Singles R135 (R100 for extended stay), with bath R170; doubles R170/R240. Other discounts available for extended stays. Make reservations about a week in advance. ❷

The Melville Turret Guest House, 118 2nd Ave. (☎482 7197). Corner of 9th St., Braamfontein, and the CBD. Immaculate rooms with private bathrooms, TV, and under-floor heating. Breakfast included. Internet. Singles R250; doubles R380. Rooms with "outside bathroom" R170 per person. AmEx/DC/MC/V. ❷

❏ FOOD

Dining options in Johannesburg run the gamut from cheap take-away chains that dominate downtown to flashier fast-food joints in the northern suburbs and expensive gourmet establishments. For the best combination of quality and convenience, **Rosebank** and its shopping centers offer dozens of concentrated options. Over the past year or two, however, the trendy suburb **Melville** has become one of the most promising spots for great food and nightlife. Other worthwhile spots include: the **Bruma/Eastgate** area just east of Yeoville, with the newer of Johannesburg's two **Chinatowns; Oriental Plaza** in Newtown, with some of the best Indian cuisine in Jo'burg served from its stalls and shops; and the **Market Theatre Complex (MTC)** on Bree St. in the Newtown Cultural Precinct. Even with all of these options, **vegetarians** in Jo'burg may still be forced to make do with very few menu choices. Unless otherwise stated, restaurants accept major credit cards and are fully licensed to sell alcoholic beverages.

MELVILLE

🍴 **Cafe MezzaLuna,** shop 9A 7th St. (☎482 2477 or 482 2478). A little more expensive and classy than your usual backpackers' restaurant, but its fusion of Continental cuisine and great atmosphere make it worth your rands and appetite. The ostrich fillet (R51) is the most popular dish. Entrees R34-52. Make reservations on weekends. Open daily 7:30am-1am; kitchen closes at midnight. MC/V. ❷

Catz Pyjamas, 7 Main Rd. (☎726 8596). At 3rd St., upstairs. Patrons follow in the steps of such illustrious figures as Garfield and Hobbes as they climb the stairway to this large eatery and bar. Criss-crossing roof beams and lofty ceilings imply a warehouse motif, and unobtrusive felines regard diners from the walls. Wide selection of munchies and more substantial entrees offered. Many a late-night reveler will also grab a quick "breakfast" (R19.50-33.50) before heading home. Salads R25.50-27. Large pizzas R29.50-38. Sandwiches R20-30. Open 24hr. ❷

Full Stop Cafe, shop 4a 7th Ave., Melville (☎726 3801). Stop "where good food and people mix" for a great taste of African or Italian cuisine. The menu covers various vegetarian pastas and pizzas, and the prices stop at R55. Try the Alla Boscaiola pizza (R36.30). Make reservations on weekends. Open daily 8am-1am. ❷

CBD AND THE NEWTOWN CULTURAL PRECINCT

🍴 **Gramadoelas** (☎838 6960 or 082 880 5555). In MTC. Designed to recreate an African *valhalla* (Khoisan for "warriors' paradise"), Gramadoelas's pan-African cuisine has delighted such luminaries as Harry Belafonte, Catherine Deneuve, and Nelson Mandela. Mr. Mandela's personal favorite, *umgqosho* (braised beef shin with beans and maize; R33), is just one of many delectable offerings. Entrees run between R30-50. Reservations recommended. Open M 6-11pm; Tu-Sa noon-3pm, 6-11pm. ❷

Couch & Coffee, in MTC on Bree St., across from Gramadoelas. This new place was built on the site of the once-famous Yard of Ale and Kofifi, and it aims at the same local artsy and freethinking crowd of the MTC as its predecessors did. Besides being a coffee shop with comfortable couches, it offers a creative cuisine that varies from European to African. The Tramazinis (R15-20) will delight vegetarians and meat-eaters alike. ❶

NEW CHINATOWN

🍴 **Kitchenboy in Chinatown,** 18 Derrick Ave., Cyrildene (☎622 0483). The famous owner, Braam Kruger (restaurant critic, nude painter and hard-core hedonist) sets out as Kitchenboy on a crusade to "save the world from bad taste." Entrees in his Oriental-Afrikaner cuisine go for R60 to R80 but will easily serve two. He takes great pride in his "Harley-Davidson Fish" and his "Fish Pretending to Be a Bunch of Grapes" (both R75). The atmosphere is enriched by his many nude paintings and by the music of his vinyl recordings. Limousine pick-up service offered. Make reservations on weekends. Open Tu-Sa 7pm-late. ❸

Happy Man, 13c Derrick Ave., off Marcia Street in Cyrildene (☎615 7680). One of Jo'burg's best Chinese restaurants, it offers typical Chinese dishes of unusual quality. Service is quick, and large entrees go from R20 to R50. Take-out available. Open Th-Tu 10am-10pm. ❷

YEOVILLE

Time Square Cafe, 38 Raleigh St. (☎648 6906 or 487 1219). This is busiest of Time Square chain eateries; finding a seat can be impossible. Artsy crowd, colorful atmosphere, and an international menu. *Zivas-Yemen* (dough filled with cheese), a Pljeskavica-Yugoslav burger, and Mediterranean dishes R22.50-41. Open daily 9am-2am. ❷

Charros Curry (☎487 1068), in the Time Square Complex at the corner of Raleigh St. and Fortesque Rd. Dine among Yeoville's Pan-African intellectuals while enjoying spicy curries, *biryanis*, and *samosas*, all for less than R40. South Africa's oft-slighted vegetarians will find refuge here. Open M-Sa 11:30am-3pm and 5-10:30pm. ❷

ROSEBANK

▨ **Kranx** (☎880 3442), or "Cranks," on the Cradock Ave. side of Rosebank Mall. Exotically titled Thai and Vietnamese dishes (R39-69) will tantalize the imagination and delight the taste buds. Weekday Thai lunch specials R25. F and Sa night blues sessions. Make reservations. Open daily 11:30am-4pm and 6pm-1am; kitchen closes at 11:30pm. ❷

Shula's Bakery and Cafe, 173 Oxford Rd. (☎880 6969), in Rosebank. Kosher restaurant offers yummy pastries. You can't go wrong with chocolate cake or a meal of inventive pizzas, pastas, and salads (R34-45). No meat. Open Su-F 7am-7pm. ❷

SOWETO

▨ **Wandie's Place,** 618 Dube St. (☎982 2796). A Soweto legend in the shadow of Winnie Mandela's sprawling mansion, Wandie has surprised his guests with Sowetan cuisine since 1981. The premises were originally an extension of Wandie's own house and are still flanked by residential homes. The divine buffet of 40 dishes, including spicy oxtail stew, *potjie kos* (vegetable and beef stew), salads, and desserts, has been enjoyed by the likes of Quincy Jones and Evander Holyfield (R90). Open daily 9am-late. ❸

Palazzo di Stella, 616 Mutambo Street, Dlamini (☎083 756 7213). The *Palazzo's* stage pulses with some of Soweto's most cutting-edge jazz. African buffet arranged for large groups (R65). A la carte menu available. Live jazz F-Su, cover R20-60. Open daily 8am-10pm; 24hr. pizza take-away. ❸

Sakhumzi Restaurant, 6980 Vilakazi Street, Orlando West, Soweto (☎536 1267). Next to Archbishop Desmond Tutu's house and a stone's throw away from former president Nelson Mandela's house, this small-scaled restaurant offers hefty breakfasts and sumptuous lunches of Sowetan cuisine (*pap, samp, mhodu*, various vegetarian salads, etc.). All you can eat for R45. Call in advance. MC/V. ❷

RANDBURG WATERFRONT

▨ **The Rock** (☎789 7272), at the Randburg Waterfront. Generous portions of traditional African fare, including *mogodu* (tripe with *pap* and vegetables, R35) and a Soweto T-bone (R36.50). *Mamelodi* (600g ribs with chips, *pap*, and salad; R42.50). Benches overlooking the water allow patrons to soak up the sunshine and soulful African jazz. Relax until the moon rises, when The Rock becomes a pounding venue for *kwaito*, reggae and hip-hop. Su jazz, M South African music, Tu South African jazz, W African continental music. Open Su-Th 9am-11pm, F-Sa 9am-late. ❷

◎ SIGHTS

For most visitors, Jo'burg's pragmatic architecture, busy streets, and reputation as a mugging trap make it little more than a stopover point. But scattered among the grimy office buildings are several hidden gems, ranging from museums to unique

GAUTENG

buildings to historic sites. In the city center, a lively informal economy of traders hawks everything from vegetables to VCRs—some of them of undoubtedly dubious origin. Outside the city center, the **northern suburbs** are glimmering pockets of affluence, while nearby **Soweto** reveals Jo'burg's suffering—a visit to the township will give you real insight into Jo'burg's surreal socioeconomic extremes.

CENTRAL BUSINESS DISTRICT

Connection-bound passengers arriving via Jo'burg's central train and bus stations often hope to dash downtown for a speedy **stopover tour.** Any map of central Johannesburg will illustrate the expansive grid network that is the CBD. For those hankering for their bit of downtown Jo'burg, dress discreetly and secure all valuables before venturing out.

CBD STOPOVER TOUR. Exiting the train station onto the main concourse, head left toward **DeVilliers St.** Follow DeVilliers to the left, then take a left onto Eloff St. From Eloff, a right on Jeppe Street and seven city blocks will bring you the beginning of **Diagonal Street**, a unique slant angled through Jo'burg's otherwise predictable grid and home to the glass-faceted **De Beers** office tower (diamonds, diamonds, diamonds) and many traditional **medicine shops.** Head back toward the station by taking a left onto Commissioner, then left again onto Von Weilligh St. after 12 blocks (becoming Klein St.). **Johannesburg Art Gallery** is beyond Noord St., to the right of the Pretoria Taxi Station.

MARKET THEATRE COMPLEX. MTC is home to the Market Theatre Photogallery, the French Cultural Institute, the Foundation for the Creative Arts, studios, workshops, curio stores, and flower shops. *(On Bree St., north of Jeppe St. Photogallery. ☎ 832 1641, open Tu-Sa 10am-5pm. Free.)*

MUSEUMAFRICA. Aiming to trace South African history from the dawn of time to the present day, MuseumAfrica's exhibits on Afrikaner life fit into a larger, comprehensive display of the history of all South Africans. Don't miss the amazing exhibit on the 1956-61 treason trials. *(121 Bree St. ☎ 833 5624. Adjacent to the Market Theatre Complex (see above). Open Tu-Su 9am-5pm. R5; children, students, and seniors R2.)*

JOHANNESBURG ART GALLERY. Appreciation for and patronage of this classic gallery has recently been in decline, along with the museum's deteriorating exterior. The gallery houses a reputable collection of Dutch, British, and (white) South African artwork. Its curators have finally loosened up in the last few years, freeing up its walls to feature a wide range of African artwork. *(☎ 725 3130. Hoek St., at the southern end of Joubert Park.)*

BRAAMFONTEIN

Braamfontein remains the last stronghold of multinationals resisting flight to the suburbs. Towering office buildings rise above its streets.

UNIVERSITY OF WITWATERSRAND. "Wits," extending west from the corner of Jan Smuts and Jorissen St., is Braamfontein's main attraction. With nearly 20,000 students, it is the largest English-language university in the country and was a rare multiracial enclave during apartheid. It prides itself on its distinguished alums, including Nelson Mandela, who studied here for his post-graduate degree.

OTHER SIGHTS. Gertrude Posel Art Gallery, in the Senate House near the university, hosts a collection of African art. *(☎ 716 3632. Open Tu-F 10am-4:30pm.)* The **Johannesburg Planetarium** offers shows and displays aimed at demystifing the southern heavens. Check the bus schedules before making the trek. *(On Yale Rd. ☎ 717 1392.)*

GAUTENG

HILLBROW AND BEREA

If you're looking to get mugged, it's tough to find a better spot than Hillbrow. Beyond Joubert Park, the tightly packed high-rises of Central Jo'burg's northeastern quadrant tower above some of Africa's most vibrant and densely populated streets. Bustling to the varied beats of Congolese, West African, and Southern African music, these lively neighborhoods are home to much musical vitality and color. Unfortunately, they also suffer from high crime rates. Visitors are advised to venture here only in daylight and with reliable transportation. Be sure to study your map and gain a familiarity with the neighborhoods prior to arrival, and steer clear of areas beyond the main thoroughfares.

NORTHERN SUBURBS

RANDBURG WATERFRONT. Part shopping mall, part entertainment center, Randburg houses a cinema, glow-in-the-dark bowling alleys, miniature golf, laser tag, a carousel, and dining options that cater to every taste. *(Off Republic Dr. in Randburg. From Central Jo'burg, take M27 north for about 20km, exiting at Republic Dr. ☎ 789 5052.)*

JOHANNESBURG ZOO. Less a zoo than a large grassy park, this spot beckons late-afternoon naps. The polar bears win the prize for most-unlikely-to-be-spotted species. *(Follow the signs off of Jan Smuts in Parktown; turn onto Upper Park Dr. ☎ 646 2000. Open daily 8:30am-5:30pm. R15, children under 12 R10; parking R6.)* The **Museum of Military History** is on the eastern edge of the grounds. Tanks, fighter planes, submarines, and swords display South Africa's involvement in the battles that shaped its military past. *(☎ 646 5513. Open daily 9am-4:30pm. R5, seniors R3, children R2.)*

SOWETO

An acronym for SOuth WEstern TOwnship, Soweto's 38 suburbs are home to over 5.9 million residents packed into an almost 200 sq. km area. Born of the squatter camps and woeful housing erected by the government for laboring mine workers of the late 20th century, Soweto's poorer townships still resemble their corrugated iron origins. The 7000 people in Motsoaledi Informal Settlement Village share 250 communal toilets and seven taps of running water. Candles and kerosene lamps serve in place of electricity, while radios and TVs run on car batteries that can be recharged at the nearest filling station. However, Soweto also contains wealthier neighborhoods that come considerably closer to the northern suburbs in appearance. In fact, even some white people have settled here.

TOWNSHIP TOURS Since most South African townships are well out of sight of city centers and tourist areas, it's possible to travel through the entire country without ever seeing one. A huge proportion of South Africa's population, however, calls the townships home, and much of South Africa's grassroots culture and vitality thrives in them. After being sealed off from the rest of the world for so long, township residents welcome visitors with a special warmth: many of them are eager to share their world with interested outsiders and also to learn more from visitors about their own homes and countries. A few exceptional tours penetrate the townships, discussing how the legacy of apartheid lives on today, and allowing participants to gain a glimpse of everyday township life. If participating in a township tour, be conscious of whether the township tour benefits the community visited.

On June 16, 1976, students in Soweto organized a famous demonstration against the use of Afrikaans as the language of instruction in schools. When reactionary police shot and killed some of the protestors, a series of riots and demonstrations erupted nationwide (see the **Hector Peterson Museum**, p. 307). As news programs flashed headlines all over the world, Soweto became a tragic international symbol of the struggle against apartheid.

Though Soweto is considered the wealthiest township in South Africa, the majority of its residents still live in grinding poverty. In some parts of Soweto, crime is a major concern. In general, it is safe to walk on the streets by day in groups. Nevertheless, make sure you are familiar with the area before heading out and always remain careful. The best and safest way of discovering Soweto is, you guessed it, by hiring a guide or going on an official township tour.

TOURS. Since the mazelike townships are almost impossible to navigate independently and parts can be dangerous, it is necessary to go with a guide who knows the area. Many outstanding operators provide a critical examination of life in the townships, with historical background and a broader contextualization. The tour companies are particularly effective at humanizing the townships and their residents. Half-day tours allow a cursory view of the major sights; longer excursions often include visits to *shebeens* or homestays. (See **Practical Information,** p. 300.)

APARTHEID MUSEUM. This newly opened and very impressive museum deals with the history of South African apartheid. Many films and a continuously updated section on the present day make the various aspects of the institution much more vivid. Plan to spend at least three hours. (☎ *496 1822. Northern Parkway, next to Gold Reef City. Open Tu-Su 10am-5pm. R20; students, children and senior citizens R10.)*

REGINA MUNDI CATHOLIC CHURCH. One of the largest churches on the continent (standing room 6000), Regina Mundi contains one of only two black Madonnas in South Africa. During apartheid, political speeches were delivered from its pulpit by such luminaries as Nobel Peace Prize winner Desmond Tutu. The bullet holes scarring its ceilings stand as testament to the area's problems with violence.

FREEDOM SQUARE. On June 26, 1955, 3000 delegates from throughout South Africa gathered in this square to sign the ANC's freedom charter. **Avalon Cemetery,** nearby, is the resting place of many of Soweto's legendary activists. At its entrance stands a marble memorial with the inscription "Never, Never Again," dedicated to the children slain in the 1976 Soweto uprising. In 1992, a renowned anti-apartheid campaigner, Helen Joseph, became the first white person to be buried here, interred alongside her lifelong friend and fellow activist Lilian Ngoyi. Former South African Communist Party leader Joe Slovo's final resting place is marked with a marble hammer-and-sickle emblem.

HECTOR PETERSON MUSEUM. Named in honor of a 14-year-old victim of police gunfire, this makeshift museum recalls the horror of the Soweto uprising. Photographs—some taken on the fateful day in 1976—capture the initial terror and subsequent turmoil. Among these is the famous photograph of Hector being carried in the arms of an older boy while his sister weeps alongside. The story behind this photo alone makes the museum worth a visit. *(Down the street from Mandela Museum, at Vilakazi St. and Koma Rd. Open daily 9:30am-4:30pm. R5.)*

NELSON MANDELA MUSEUM. The humble bungalow in which Nelson Mandela lived before his arrest and trial in 1956 is now open to visitors. Not far from its front door are the swimming pool and landscaped grounds of Winnie Mandela's mansion (referred to by locals as "Beverly Hills"). *(At the corner of Vilakazi St. and the Klipspruit Valley road in Dube. Open 8am-6pm. Closes at 5pm during winter. Free.)*

THE JABULANI AREA. A tall tower honors philanthropist Sir Ernest Oppenheimer for his efforts to obtain housing for Soweto residents. From its vantage point you can see nearly all of Soweto, and the surrounding gardens and sculptures of the

Credo Mutwa Cultural Village. Farther along Koma Rd. is the **Five Roses Bowl,** the centerpiece of the Mofolo recreational park and erstwhile home of the world-famous **Soweto String Quartet.**

⚏ ENTERTAINMENT

PERFORMING ARTS AND CINEMAS

The three stages of the **Market Theatre Complex** (see p. 305) comprise the cutting edge of the local theatrical scene. **Windybrow Theater,** on Nugget St. between Joubert Park and Hillbrow, also hosts forward-looking productions. Show-goers should be aware of safety concerns after dark. On the university campus in Braamfontein, **Wits Theater** (☎ 716 3939) is the center for student productions. Most productions sell tickets through **Computicket** (☎ 340 8100). Check the *Star* newspaper for full listings. Rosebank's **Cinema Nouveau** (☎ 880 2866) does its best to provide Gauteng with art house fare; times and prices are published in daily papers.

SPECTATOR SPORTS

Much of the city's sporting action takes place in Doornfontein, east of the city center along Wolmarans St. **Ellis Park Rugby Stadium** (☎ 402 8644) and the **Standard Bank Arena** (☎ 402 3510) host a regular procession of rugby and track and field events. For top-notch action, **Soccer City** (☎ 494 3640), on Nasrec Rd. just off the Soweto highway, hosts hotly contested league games, featuring the local Orlando Pirates. **Wanderers Club Cricket Ground,** on Corlett Dr. just off Oxford Rd. in Illovo, and the **Cricket Stadium** (☎ 788 1008) often host world-class games. Motor sports enthusiasts head to the **Kyalami Race Track,** on Allandale Rd. in Midrand. Check out any daily paper for up-to-date happenings.

⚏ SHOPPING

Among the most popular of Jo'burg's weekend flea markets is the **Rosebank Flea Market,** held on Sunday afternoons in the car park of the Rosebank Mall, with its local handicrafts and trinkets (check out the paper made from recycled rhino dung). **Flea Market World,** an open-air bazaar offering bargains on crafts and clothing, is also well-liked. (Open daily 9am-5pm. R1.50.) The informal **Trading Market** occupies the entire city block between Cavendish and Bedford on Rockey St. in Yeoville and sells fresh produce and clothing. (Open daily 6am-10pm.) On Saturday mornings, the parking lot opposite the Market Theater and MuseumAfrica becomes one of Jo'burg's largest flea markets. Farther west along Bree St., the **Oriental Plaza,** a bazaar-like mall influenced by Jo'burg's Indian population, hosts over 300 traders. Several *muti* shops along Diagonal St. peddle herbal remedies, while the small cluster of Indian shops next door give a taste of old-time commerce.

⚏ NIGHTLIFE

CENTRAL JO'BURG

⚏ **Kippie's Jazz Bar** (☎ 838 1271; www.kippies.co.za), at the Market Theater Complex. One of South Africa's best-known jazz venues, this club is named for legendary musician Kippie Moeketsi. An ideal place to take in local jazz and the tunes of top contemporary foreign artists. Strangely, smoking is prohibited. M night poetry once a month. Live jazz Th-Sa and occasionally on Su. Cover around R30; call in advance. Open W-M 9am-3am.

YEOVILLE, HILLBROW, AND BEREA

Heed the warnings of an earned nickname; these neighborhoods are not referred to as "thieves' paradise" for nothing. Mugging and car theft are not uncommon. Exercise 24hr. caution and hit the streets in groups.

Tandoor, 26 Rockey St. (☎487 1569). Set atop a roof in Yeoville. Amidst burning fires and drumming sounds, this is the place to be for *kwaito*, reggae, and world beats. Enter through a dark tunnel and ascend into a mix of sheikh, rasta, and student clubbers enjoying live reggae (Sa 3-8pm) or traditional African bands (Su at sunset). Th is most hopping night. 3 pool tables. Cover R10-20. Open M-Tu 4pm-midnight, W-Su noon-late.

ROSEBANK

Cantina Tequila (☎447 5323). At the corner of Jan Smuts and Wells St., just 1km south of the Rosebank Complex. Margaritas galore. "Mambo Robot" replicates the Mexican tricolor flag. Fish bowl cocktails are a good deal and serve 4-5 people. Cocktails R25-30. Meals R65-95. Live bands F-Sa (mostly Latin and dance music). Open M-Sa noon-late.

MELVILLE

When Yeoville turned to the Dark Side, Melville became the guardian of Jo'burg's nightlife. This part of the town resembles London's Camben Town in all its splendors, with a sense of safety that is quite un-Jo'burg. Of course, always remain careful: if you found your way here, so might Jo'burg's less upstanding citizens.

The Bass Line, 7 7th St. (☎482 6915; www.thebassline.co.za). One of the top live music venues in the country. Giants of the local and international music scene showcase quickly evolving, distinctly South African sounds before a continuously full house. A magnet for black artists and professionals, the crowd is among the most cosmopolitan in the city. Drinks R8-14. Cover R30 most nights; up to R150 when big names perform. Book ahead for popular acts. Open Tu-Su 7pm-late.

Cool Runnings, 27A 4th Ave. (☎482 4786). When you enter the Jamaican microcosm of Cool Runnings, walk past the bar towards the back "outside deck." This is one of Jo'burg's best places to enjoy a cocktail (try the Feeling Irie for R20) or a Hubbly Bubbly waterpipe. Relaxation will follow. Tu African drumming. Open 11am-2am.

Xai-Xai, shop 7, 7th Ave. (☎482 6990). A chill Mozambican cocktail lounge where a mixed but young crowd meets up for inventive drinks (Short Island Ice Tea, Sour Jack Maputo) and a blend of Mozambican, Cuban, and Brazilian music. A social place to relax after eating and before dancing. Expect a full house and a welcoming crowd on weekends. Open noon-late.

Ratz, 9B 7th St. (☎726 2019). Bona fide Mexican restaurant and nighttime haunt for Jo'burg's 24+ party crowd. Guests perched on tree-stump stoolz eat chicken burritos. Concoctionz like Ratz Poison (R25; "one drink will do") intoxicate happy hour patronz (M-F 5-7pm, cocktails R15). Open daily 5pm-late.

Roxy's Rhythm Bar, 20 Main Rd. (☎726 6019). This newly renovated dance mega-complex encompasses 6 bars on multiple floors. Students groove on the roof garden. Music varies from hip-hop and breakbeat (Th) to alternative and pop and dance. Students with ID free on M. Tu metal night. W new bands. F, Sa the "best live bands in South Africa." Free drinks Th 8-10pm. Cover R10-25. Open M-Sa 6pm-late.

GAY NIGHTLIFE

The concentration of gay venues along **Braamfontein's** Henri and Juta Streets has been endearingly named "The Heartland." The magazines *Outright*, *Exit*, and *Woman on Woman*, available at newspaper kiosks, cover the GLBT scene

GAUTENG

throughout South Africa. Pick up a free copy of Gauteng Province's own *Rush* magazine at any GLBT bar or club in Jo'burg.

■ **Therapy,** 39A Juta St. (☎339 7791). Juta is a small street between the thoroughfares of De Korte St.and Smit St. Thumping rave is in session just once a week. 2 dance floors and several lounges. Don't miss the "Great and Secret Show"; hush, hush. Open Sa and public holidays 7pm-very late. F straight night (but gay-friendly) with the name "Guess."

PRETORIA   ☎012

Named after Andries Pretorius, leader of the Boer forces at the 1838 Battle of Blood River (see **Fighting, Fighting Everywhere,** p. 56), Pretoria has served as South Africa's administrative capital since 1910. A long-time bastion of Afrikaner nationalism, Pretoria is fraught with reminders of the white supremacy that dominated 20th-century South Africa. Monuments and statues commemorate the struggles of the Voortrekkers who settled here in the 19th century. The city is now host to a large educated middle class, a showcase of urban integration in South Africa.

Pretoria's attractions include 33 museums, a number of pleasant parks (Springbok, Burgers, and Jan Celliers), and a wealth of impressive architecture. In October, 80,000 jacaranda trees burst into bloom, painting tree-lined parks and otherwise drab avenues with splashes of purple. A lively international student contingent has brought other types of vivacity to old Pretoria, including a burgeoning nightlife and a wide range of cosmopolitan culinary options.

■ INTERCITY TRANSPORTATION

FLIGHTS

Pretoria's international flights are served by **Johannesburg International Airport** (see p. 292), roughly 50km southwest of Pretoria. From the airport, the **Pretoria Shuttle** (☎322 0904) drops passengers at the tourist office in Sammy Marks Square (every 2hr. M-F 7:15am-7:15pm, Sa 8:15am-8:15pm; R95). Shuttles also run from the center to the airport (every 2hr. M-F 7am-7pm, Sa 6:15am and 8am; then every 2hr. until 6pm). Specific pick-ups and drop-offs can be arranged at variable costs. A **taxi** from the airport into the city may cost upwards of R150; only a few hostels offer a pick-up service for a fee. From the tourist office, taxis can cover the short distance to most hotels and hostels.

TRAINS

The **Pretoria Railway Station** is near the corner of Paul Kruger and Scheiding St.

Spoornet (☎086 000 8888). Office open M-F 8am-4pm, Su 8-10am. Main rail lines include: Komati to **Komatipoort** (2nd-class R100, first-class R140) via **Nelspruit** (R80/ R110); Trans-Karoo to **Cape Town** (27hr., daily, R305/R450) via **Johannesburg** (1hr., R25) and **Kimberley** (11hr., R115/R170); Bosvelder to **Louis Trichardt** (15hr., daily, R90/R130) via **Pietersburg** (R90/R110). For **Bloemfontein,** take the **Diamond Express** from Johannesburg.

BUS AND MINIBUS TAXIS

Long-distance buses to and from Pretoria depart from the **Railway Station.** Buses heading south or west from the Johannesburg/Pretoria area originate here and proceed to their destinations via Johannesburg. **Minibus taxis** are scarce in Pretoria; those to be found are near the railway station and along Boom St. near the zoo.

Greyhound (☎323 1154; www.greyhound.co.za). Office open daily 6:30am-10pm. To: **Bloemfontein** (7½hr., daily, R150); **Bulawayo** (11hr., Su-F, R270) via **Pietersburg** (3hr., daily, R130) and **Messina** (5½hr., daily, R150); **Cape Town** (15hr., daily, R390); **Durban** (9hr., daily, R170) via **Pietermaritzburg** (8hr., daily, R170); **East London** (12½hr., daily, R285); **Harare** (16hr., Su-F, R320) via Pietersburg, Messina, and **Masvingo** (12hr., Su-F, R295); **Kimberley** (15hr., daily, R160); **Nelspruit** (6½hr., daily, R125); **Port Elizabeth** (17hr., daily, R295) via **Grahamstown** (15hr., daily, R265); **Umtata** (12½hr., daily, R200).

Intercape (☎660 0070 or 654 4114; open daily 6am-9pm; www.intercape.co.za) is the only travel option for most of the North West and Northern Cape provinces. To: **Bloemfontein** (7½hr., daily, R260); **Cape Town** (18hr., daily, R385); **Durban** (10¼hr., twice daily, R170) via **Pietermaritzburg** (8hr., daily, R145); **Plettenberg Bay** (20¼hr., daily, R310) via **Oudtshoorn** (17½hr., daily, R260), **Mossel Bay** (19¼hr., daily, R280), and **Knysna** (19¾hr., daily, R305); **Port Elizabeth** (16hr., daily, R260); **Upington** (13hr., Tu-Th, R250) via **Kuruman** (8hr., daily, R175); **Windhoek** (25hr.; Tu, Th, F, Su; R525).

Baz Bus (☎021 439 2323). Office open M-F 8am-9pm. Picks up and drops off at Pretoria hostels. Reservations may be made directly through hostels. Its "hop on, hop off" service is a great way of exploring South Africa. To: **Cape Town** via **Swaziland** (M, W, Sa; R1850) or via **Drakensberg** (M, F, Su; R1500); or "the loop" via **Johannesburg, Durban,** and **Swaziland** (clockwise or counterclockwise, 3 times per week, R800).

❖ ORIENTATION

As suburbia rapidly spills out from Jo'burg, the line separating Pretoria from its sprawling neighbor is becoming increasingly obscured. The Johannesburg airport is halfway between the two cities, only 50km from Pretoria, making the smaller city a convenient (and more welcoming) initial destination. Watch for the University of South Africa's looming concrete administration building, the unofficial boundary of Pretoria.

CENTRAL PRETORIA

Though Pretoria is a fairly large city, most of its acreage is taken up by the city's continuous residential expansion. The heart of the metropolis itself is a conveniently compact grid that centers on **Church Sq.** The main east-west thoroughfare is **Church St.**, which runs from the **National Botanical Gardens** in the east, through Church Sq. and the pedestrian mall and past **Arcadia**, into the far western suburbs. At 26km, it is the longest straight street in the Southern Hemisphere (what an honor). **Paul Kruger St.** is the most centrally located of the north-south streets. It's also the primary link between the local transportation hub at Church Sq. and the **Pretoria Railway Station** at the southern end of the street.

While museums and monuments are liberally distributed throughout the city center, the area around **Visagie St.** has a particularly high concentration. This area, encompassing the **Museum of Culture (African Window), City Hall, Burgers Park, Transvaal Museum,** and several other sights, is now a Museum Mall with paved walkways, ornate street lamps, and helpful directional arrows to the major attractions. West of the city center, Church St. runs through the **Heroes Acre** cemetery and the **Pretoria West Showgrounds** before entering Pretoria's large working-class suburbs of **Danville, Lotus Gardens,** and **Atteridgeville. Marabastad** and the **Asiatic Bazaar** stand a few blocks north of the cemetery, west of the **National Zoo.** A few blocks east of Church Sq., **Sammy Marks Sq.** is overshadowed by the **South African Reserve Bank,** the obsidian tower that is Pretoria's tallest building. Next to Sammy Marks Sq. stands the hulking multi-stage **State Theater**, adjacent to **J.G. Strijdom Sq.**, where one of apartheid's cold-blooded designers is commemorated in bronze.

GAUTENG

Mogul

R101

National Zoo
Aquarium

De Waal

Boom

Boom

R101

Boom

Du Toit

MARABASTAD

Asiatic Bazaar

Brown St.

Eleventh

Grand

Tenth

R101

Bloed

CENTRAL

Andries

Van der Walt

Prinsloo

Marlammen
Temple

Seventh

Stand

Struben

Bosman

Felrs

Paul Kruger

Malan Dr. E.

N4

Cowie

Proes

TO SUN CITY

Vermeulen

Palace of
Justice

Malan Dr. W.

Heroes' Acre

Kruger
House

Booth

Schubart

Grootkerk

Palace of Parliament

City Buses

Mintaal

Queen

Mosque

SAMMY MARKS
SQ.

Tourist
Police

R104

Church

Church

CHURCH
SQ.

Bank

Bureau

Central

State
Theatre

Prince's
Park

Kruger
Church

Parliament

Pretorius

Volkstem

Police
Museum

Claude Malan
Museum

Princes Park

Potgieter

Schoeman

M2

M2

M2

Skinner Ln.

Skinner

M1

Visagie

R101

R101

National Museum
of Culture

City
Hall

Minnaar

Transvaal
Museum

Burger Pk.

Minnaar

Prinsloo

Bosman

Paul Kruger

Andries

Burgers
Park

Artillery Row

Christina

Hoop

M11

Jacob Maré

Melrose
House

Read

Van der Walt

Intercity
Buses

M11

Scheiding

Loop

Tuflen

Rhodes

Dequar

N14

Skietpoort

Second Ave.

Koch

Clara

Berea
Park

Third

Second

First

Ben Schoeman

First St.

Second St.

Railway

Train
Station

Soetdoring

Ludo

Oasis

Klawer

Capa

Papawel

Fifth Ave.

Willow

Harmony

Correctional
Services
Museum

John Keevy

R28

John Keevy

Ben Schoeman Hwy.

TO JOHANNESBURG

R101

Voortrekker
Monument

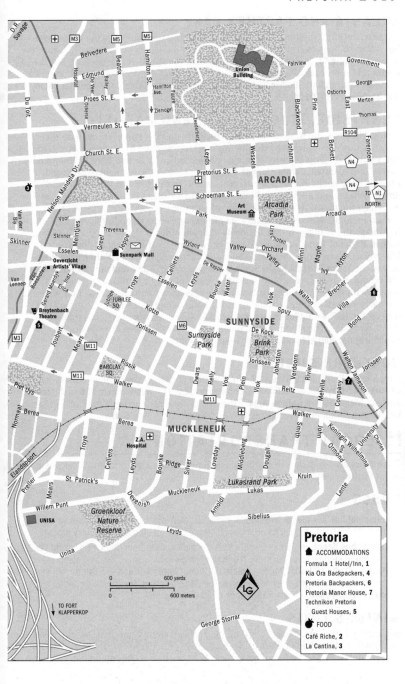

Pretoria

♠ ACCOMMODATIONS

Formula 1 Hotel/Inn, **1**
Kia Ora Backpackers, **4**
Pretoria Backpackers, **6**
Pretoria Manor House, **7**
Technikon Pretoria
  Guest Houses, **5**

🍅 FOOD

Café Riche, **2**
La Cantina, **3**

GAUTENG

ARCADIA AND FARTHER EAST

Home to the city's diplomatic community, Arcadia's centerpiece is the **Union Building,** a few kilometers from the city. East of the building, the area between Church St. and **Arcadia St.** is dotted with embassies and official residences, as are the neighborhoods north of Church St. as far east as **Bryntirion** and **Colby St.** Church St. continues through the **Colbyn Valley** nature area before reaching the **National Botanical Gardens** as the **R104.**

SUNNYSIDE, MUCKLENEUK, AND HATFIELD

Sunnyside, once the pride of Pretoria's nightlife and the height of culinary diversity, has now been nicknamed "Slummyside" in response to its recent economic and cultural decline. Almost all major restaurants, clubs, and bars have moved east or closed down. **Gerard Moerdyk St.** is perhaps the only remnant of Sunnyside's once-thriving social scene. The street features the **Breytenbach Theater, Oeverzicht Artists' Village,** and a few bars. Locals discourage visiting Sunnyside at night, and even daytime may now be unsafe for a solo tourist.

Farther south, **Muckleneuk** is an area of mixed residential and diplomatic neighborhoods and is home to the **University of South Africa's** main campus. The **South African National Parks Board** headquarters is close to the university on **Leyds St.** Directly to the east of Sunnyside stands the main campus of the **University of Pretoria** and the **Loftus Versfeld Rugby Stadium** on Jorissen St. Adjoining the campus' eastern boundary is the suburb of **Hatfield.** Students from Pretoria's four universities mingle with wealthy dot-com executives in this ultra-trendy neighborhood where the party continues long into the morning hours along **Burnett St.** The action centers on the **Hatfield Galleries** and **Hatfield Sq.** which boast an array of restaurants, clubs, and pubs. The street is even busier on weekends, when crowds flock to the flea market at **Hatfield Mall,** across from the square.

NORTHERN SUBURBS

Paul Kruger St. runs north past the **National Zoo** and the residential neighborhoods of **Parktown, Mayville,** and **Eloffsdal,** before reaching the **Wonderboom Nature Reserve** and the **Magaliesberg Natural Area.** These reserves mark the beginning of a green belt running west into the foothills of the Magaliesberg Mountains.

▐▄ LOCAL TRANSPORTATION

Comprehensive, regular bus services, combined with a local minibus taxi system, make Pretoria quite easy to navigate.

BUSES

Municipal bus service (☎ 308 0839). The most reliable and affordable means of transport. R3.20-6.90, depending on distance covered. R1.90 surcharge for bulky luggage.

Central bus depot, in Church Sq. Buses begin their circuits from Church Sq. along Vermeulen, Pretorius, and Church St. The **inquiry office** in Church Sq. issues a comprehensive timetable (R2.50). Routes radiate out from Church Sq. and are listed clockwise beginning with Colbyn. Service M-F 5am-7pm, Sa 5am-3pm. No service on public holidays. Repeat usage tickets R183; book of 20 coupons R52-107.

MINIBUS TAXIS

Minibus taxis are particularly convenient for travel along Church St. and between Sunnyside and Hatfield on Park St. Fares averages R3. In the city, minibuses heading up Church St. can be found on Van der Walt St., near J.G. Strijdom Sq.

TAXIS

Metered taxis congregate outside the tourist office at Sammy Marks Sq. and at the corner of Paul Kruger and Pretorius, just up from Church Sq. There are also large taxi ranks outside the Hatfield and Sunnypark malls. Among the more reputable companies are **Rixi Taxi** (☎325 8072 or 0800 325 807) and **CBD Mini Cab Taxi** (☎323 2241 or 323 2242). The standard fare is R5 per km.

⚄ PRACTICAL INFORMATION

TOURIST AND TRAVEL SERVICES

Tourist Office: Tourist Information, Church Sq. (☎337 4430). On the ground floor of the Nederlandsche Bank Building. Open M-F 8am-4:30pm, Sa 9am-noon. **Pretoria Airport Shuttle Office,** corner of Visagie and Van der Walt St. (☎322 0904). On the ground fl. of the Capital Protea Hotel. Open daily 6am-7pm.

Tours: Pretoria Backpackers Adventure Center, 425 Farenden St., Sunnyside (☎083 302 1976). Offers wide range of budget travel packages and advice on destinations throughout Southern Africa. Also handles bookings. Open daily 7am-midnight. **Kia Ora Backpackers,** 257 Jacob Mare St. (☎322 4803), offers similar services. **Travel the Planet,** Church Sq. (☎337 4415), on the ground fl. of the Nederlandsche Bank Building, is the touring division of the Tourist Information Office. Also offers **bike rental.**

Budget Travel: STA Travel, 1102 Hilda St. (☎342 5292; www.statravel.co.za), off Burnett St. in Hatfield. Open M-F 9am-5pm, Sa 9am-1pm.

Parks: National Parks Board, 643 Leyds St. (☎428 9111). Handles bookings for the country's parks. Open M-F 8am-5pm, Sa 8am-1pm.

Embassies and Consulates: See **Embassies and Consulates in South Africa,** p. 71.

Banks: Most banks cash traveler's checks and change currency, but commissions vary and can be painfully high. **AmEx** (☎320 2149), at Shop 4 (☎346 3580), in the Bank Forum Building. Open M-F 8:30am-5pm; phone lines staffed daily 7:30am-5pm.

LOCAL SERVICES

Bookstores: As in any major city, bookstores can be found scattered throughout Pretoria. **CNA** (☎320 4007), in the Tramshed complex on Schoeman St., offers a good selection of popular books, maps, and stationery. Open M-F 8:30am-5pm, Sa 8am-1pm. **Exclusive Books,** 89 Brooklyn Mall, Fehrsen St. (☎346 5864), offers a wide selection of literature.

Laundromats: Prevalent in the major shopping areas. Most offer self-service, drop-off service, and dry cleaning. **Schoeman Laundrette,** on Schoeman St. between Bosman and Paul Krugar St. Washing and drying (R13-17 per load). Dry cleaning. Open M-Su 6:30am-9:30pm. **Bosman St. Laundry and Dry Cleaners,** on Bosman St. between Schoeman and Pretorius St. R4 per wash, R4 per dry. Drop-off R9 per load. Open M-F 8am-8pm, Sa 8am-5pm, Su 8am-1pm.

EMERGENCY AND COMMUNICATIONS

Emergency: Police, ☎10 111; **ambulance,** ☎10 177.

Police: Pretoria Central Police (☎353 4000), at the corner of Pretorius and Bosmans St. Open 24hr. Travelers calling to report **lost passports or traveler's checks** should ask for Mrs. Erica Knox, Civilian Volunteer.

Hotline: Gay and Lesbian Organization of Pretoria (☎344 6501).

Hospitals: Pretoria Academic Hospital (☎354 1000), on Dr. Savage Rd. at the corner of Voortrekker St., and north of the Union Building. A provincial hospital with a 24hr. casualty unit. The **College Medical Center** (☎440 2622 or 440 2623), at the corner of Mears and Rissik St. in Sunnyside, is the closest hospital with 24hr. personnel.

Internet Access: Odyssey Internet Cafe, off the corner of Esselen and Jeppe St. in the Pavilion shopping arcade in Sunnyside (☎082 627 0179; open daily 8am-2am); and in the Hatfield Gallery in Hatfield (☎362 2467; open daily 9am-midnight). R5 per 15min. Printing R0.50 per page.

Post Office: Pretoria General Post Office (☎421 7000 or 0800 114 488), on the western side of Church Sq. For *Poste Restante,* go directly to the inquiries desk down the hall on the Church St. side of the building. Open M-Tu and Th-F 8:30am-4:30pm, W 9am-4:30pm, Sa 8am-noon.

Postal Code: 0001.

ACCOMMODATIONS AND CAMPING

Pretoria has no shortage of budget accommodations. With well-situated hotels and hostels, and a more heartily pronounced backpacker subculture, Pretoria is known to be a bit more welcoming to the travel-weary visitor than Jo'burg. Hostels in the city center are a stone's throw from museums and monuments, while those in Arcadia and Hatfield sit amid the stunning Union Buildings, surrounded by the restaurants and nightlife of eastern Pretoria.

CENTRAL PRETORIA

Kia Ora Backpackers, 257 Jacob Mare St. (☎322 4803; hostel@freemail.absa.co.za; members.freemail.absa.co.za/hostel). Central Pretoria's premier backpackers. Private rooms with hardwood floors, spacious dorms, and a large common kitchen. Women-only accommodations available. Take in a cold one and the daily soaps downstairs in the "Hole in the Wall" pub. Guests have access to a private resort on the Bronkhorstpruit Dam (R100 per night; R100 per transfer). Laundry R20. Internet access R15 per 30min. Baz Bus stop. Dorms R65; singles R110, with bath R140; doubles R160. AmEx/DC/MC/V. ❶

Formula 1 Hotel/Inn, 81-85 Pretorius St. (hotel ☎323 8331, inn ☎324 1304). Off Potgeiter St. 3-person rooms in these antiseptically clean hotels appeal only to those who think living in a cabinet would be too spacious. Flat rates regardless of occupancy. Open 24hr. Inn rooms R145. Hotel rooms with bath R185. ❷

SUNNYSIDE AND MUCKLENEUK

Pretoria Backpackers (HI), 425 Farenden St., Clydesdale (☎343 9754). Spacious dorms and stunning guest house rooms. Electric blanket on every bed. Women-only dorms available. Beauty salon offers intriguing "Dead Sea mud bath" treatments. Communal kitchen serves complimentary soup 6-7pm. *Braai* every Sa. Day trips and safaris organized. Free airport pick-up if booked in advance. Breakfast R20. Laundry R20. Internet R15 per 30min. Key deposit R100. Dorms R60-70; singles R120; doubles R75-80 per person. Camping R35. ❶

Technikon Pretoria Guest Houses (☎341 0890 or 341 0849; fax 341-2052), on the corner of Rissik and Joubert St. near Gerard Moerdyk St. Unexpected luxury on the UNISA campus. Spacious rooms in a comfortable on-campus apartment complex and the veritable Victorian mansion just down the road. Breakfast included. Dinner available upon request. Singles with balcony and bath R150, in Victorian home R190; with balcony, bath, lounge, and kitchenette R200. Doubles R250/R320/R340. ❷

Pretoria Manor House, 605 Jorrisen St. (☎344 3562; www.sararinow.com). At the corner of Hugh St. A 2-house B&B and recent recipient of the "Host of the Year" award. 14 rooms complete with TV, telephone, and winter heat. Guests relax in the shade of thatched huts after dips in the pool. Breakfast included. Lunch and dinner available upon request. Singles R285; doubles R390. AmEx/DC/MC/V. ❸

ARCADIA, HATFIELD, AND FARTHER EAST

⛺ **North South Backpackers Lodge,** 355 Glynn St. (☎362 0989; fax 362 0960; northsouth@mweb.co.za). Off Burnett St. A 5min. walk from Hatfield's myriad bars, restaurants, and discos. Lighthearted suburban hostel with attractive rooms, abundant diversions, and very friendly hosts. Fireplace provides the perfect place to congregate, especially after *braai* and pool parties. Common kitchen, TV room, and book exchange. Internet R20 per 30min. Laundry R20 per load. Key deposit R50. Check-out 10am. Dorms R70; singles R170; doubles R180. Camping R40. ❶

Simply the Best, 292 Talana Ave., Villiera (☎329 0801). One of Pretoria's largest fig trees spreads its enchanting umbrella over this hostel bar and brick-oven pizzeria; its mammoth roots are fed by the gurgling spring nearby. Communal kitchens. Internet R15 per 30min. Laundry R25 per load. Free pick-up from Pretoria. Knowledgeable management arranges day trips to Pretoria and environs. Spacious dorms R50; singles R90; doubles R140. Camping R35. ❶

Hatfield Backpackers, 1226 Park St. (☎362 5501; hatbackpackers@mweb.co.za). "Alternative" management make this novel new hostel a brow-lifting choice. Guests enjoy a common kitchen, and veritable Internet cafe (5 computers; R7.50 per 15min.) Downstairs at the pub, the special draught beer is a rare find. Laundry R10 per load. Dorms R60; flat-rate rooms R150, can accommodate up to 3. Camping R50. ❶

Pebble'n Palms, 124 Allcock St., Colbyn (☎433 739 or 082 577 7575; www.pebblenpalm.co.za). From Church St., turn left onto Amos St., left onto Glynn St., and left again onto Allcock. A real steal. This elegant thatched-roof mansion lies well away from Pretoria's urban heart. All rooms have TV, fridge, and attached bath. Breakfast. Singles R180; doubles R300. ❷

🍴 FOOD

CENTRAL PRETORIA

🍴 **Cafe Riche,** 2 Church Sq. (☎328 3173). Across from post office. 1920s elegance revisited. Waiters greet customers in white shirts and bow ties. Doubles as an unofficial tourist info center. Boer and Brit Breakfast (sausage, ham, eggs, and spicy Sheba sauce) R32.50. Apple and cheese omelette R26. Belgian and German beer. Live jazz (F 5pm-midnight, Su 11am-6pm). Open daily 6am-midnight. ❷

La Cantina, 395 Pretorius St. (☎322 4211). At the eastern edge of the city center near the corner of Pretorius and Du Toit St. With garlic wreaths strung about the counter and plastic bunches of globe grapes hung from the ceiling, *La Cantina* is the closest you can get to Italian flavor this side of the Kalahari. In business for over 25 years now, and it will likely last another 25 or more. Businessmen crowd tables at lunchtime, families and couples at dinner. All dishes made from scratch. Pizza (R23-33) or pasta (R21-31). Open M-Sa noon-2:30pm and 6-10pm. ❷

HATFIELD

🍴 **Tings 'n Times** (☎362 5538 or 362 5537), shop 16, tucked inside the ground floor of Hatfield Galleries, off Burnett St. Live reggae and rock bands entertain. Budding Rastafarians and yuppies collide. The newsletter-*cum*-menu bemoans the state of the world.

Bob Marley would have been proud to hang here. Stuffed pita sandwiches R15-30. Cover R5-R10 on band nights. Open M-Sa noon-2am, Su 6pm-2am. ❶

🏮**Eastwood's Tavern,** 391 Eastwood St. (☎344 0243). This Pretoria News Pub Winner 2001 is always happening. Young crowds converge for the best steak in town and great dance music from morning into the wee hours. Prices vary from R27-R99, and you get to pick your own piece of meat. Show up early to get a table; they only accept reservations for F lunch. Packed with fans during rugby games. Open daily 10:30am-late. ❸

The Seafood Platter, 526 Duncan St. (☎362 1144 or 082 374 4421). You probably won't regret a taste of the seafood South Africa prides itself on. The Seafood Platter for Two (R115) is a good way to start. Most one-person entrees cost R22-R90. Open Su-F 10:30am-3pm, daily 5:30-10pm. ❸

Mozzarella's, shop 34 Hatfield Sq., Burnett St. (☎362 6464). Traditional Italian cuisine the way only South Africans make it. Try the Panama pizza (R40) or the lamb shank (R46). Young and casual Pretorians quiet their appetites here. Open daily 11am-10:30pm. MC/V/DC/AmEx. ❷

Up the Creek, 494 Hilda St. (☎362 3712). A music venue and restaurant hidden in Hatfield Sq.'s far corner. Have a taste of the student menu and of Pretoria's best and worst music M at open mike night. Open daily noon-1:30am. MC/V/DC/AmEx. ❶

🎯 SIGHTS

As the seat of South Africa's government for well over a century, Pretoria and its environs are filled with relics documenting the nation's turbulent and emotionally charged past. Long regarded as the purest citadel of the Afrikaner nation, Pretoria is home to more than its fair share of monuments, statues, and grandiose constructions, erected granite and bronze edifices symbolizing supremacy and domination.

CENTRAL PRETORIA

Church Sq., in the very center of town and at the nexus of the local bus network, is an ideal starting point for a walking tour of the city. The old facades of the buildings around the square showcase gradual architectural changes. The century-old **Palace of Justice,** which forms part of the facade on the northern side of the square, houses the Gauteng division of the **South African Supreme Court.** Among those convicted here was Nelson Mandela, who would later occupy a government office just a few kilometers east. The **Ou Raadsaal (Old Government Building),** opposite the palace, dates back to 1887 and owes its architecture to French and German Baroque influences. The **General Post Office,** part of the western facade, features sculptures by Anton Van Wouw above its entrance. The **Paul Kruger statue** is the centerpiece of the park. Depicted as a rather dour-faced diplomat, Kruger is surrounded by bronze figures of Voortrekker sentries; the dark metal is mellowed by the wide grassy expanse, where Pretorians may be found enjoying an afternoon nap. The area encompassing **Burgers Park, Melrose House, City Hall,** the **National Museum of Culture,** and the **Transvaal Museum** has been renovated to allow for easy signpost navigation between these sights.

MELROSE HOUSE. This grandiose pseudo-Victorian mansion served as headquarters of the British forces during the Anglo-Boer War. After three long and violent years, the Treaty of Vereeniging was signed (perhaps over tea?) in the Melrose dining room, ending the Anglo-Boer War. The estate has been maintained as a national monument. Once bombed during a 1990 attack by the white supremacist Afrikaner Resistance Movement, Melrose and its reconstructed drawing room have since seen more peaceful days. *(275 Jacob Mare St., between Andries and Van der Walt St. ☎322 2805. Open Tu-Su 10am-5pm. R3.)*

BURGERS PARK. Pretoria's oldest public park, Burgers occupies a large square in the middle of downtown. Comprised of gardens and a central pavilion, the grounds once catered to the elite and their tea parties. The park provides a placid daytime respite from the city, but when night descends, visitors would do well to look elsewhere for tea parties or grassy knolls. *(Open daily 8am-6pm.)*

NATIONAL ZOO AND AQUARIUM. South Africa's largest zoo houses 97 mammal, 161 bird, and 106 reptile species, as well as representatives of the aquatic world. The komodo dragon exhibit is the centerpiece of recent renovations and expansion. The guide transforms the Reptile House into an adventure. For a pseudo-safari experience, golf carts may be rented for R60 per hour, 8am-3:30pm. *(Corner of Kruger and Boom St. ☎328 3265; zoologic@cis.co.za. Open daily Sept.-Apr. 8am-6pm; May-Aug. 8am-5:30pm. R20, children R14.)*

TRANSVAAL MUSEUM. A massive stone building, distinguished by the giant whale skeleton next to its entrance, the Transvaal houses an excellent repository of natural history, including an extensive display of South African geology and evidence of the origin of humanity in Southern Africa. A new exhibition offers a more interactive method of exploring. The museum is also home to "Mrs. Ples," one of the world's most intact humanoid skulls. *(On Paul Kruger St., between Visagie and Minnaar St. ☎322 7632. Open M-Sa 9am-5pm, Su 11am-5pm. R6, students and children R3.50.)*

CITY HALL. A large courtyard of fountains and flowerbeds fill the forecourt of this Greco-Roman inspired building. Statues of Andries and Marthinus Pretorius lord imperiously over the well-kept grounds. Have a glance at the frieze above the main columns for a particularly offensive example of apartheid public art. *(Directly across from the Transvaal Museum.)*

KRUGER HOUSE. Home of the former president and his wife from 1884 to 1900, this house contains many of the Krugers' possessions and letters. The simplicity of the home reflects Kruger's lifestyle; his very own train is parked out back. Includes a detailed exhibit on the Boer republics and their struggles. *(West of Church Sq., at the corner of Church and Potgieter St. ☎326 9172. Open daily M-F 8:30am-4:30pm, Sa-Su 9am-4:30pm. R10, students and children R5.)*

SCIENCE AND TECHNOLOGY MUSEUM. This section of a floor in an office building pays tribute to the history of science while repeating its mantra "U + Science = Fun" at every turn. A few minutes in the Physikon room helps prove this, with hands-on exhibits demonstrating all of those axioms and principles you never memorized. *(On Skinner St., at Andries St. ☎322 6404. Open M-F 8am-4pm. R5, students R4.)*

THE HIDDEN DEAL

BACKPACKING TOURS

Pretoria Backpackers (see p. 316) isn't just for lodging. They also offer some of the best value tours in the business. The friendly staff can arrange sightseeing trips according to your interests and needs. What's more, they can do so on short notice virtually anytime. Flexibility is the name of their game.

If you're looking for ideas, try their tours of Jo'burg and Soweto, a safe and (relatively) thorough way to see both areas. They'll include a stop at the much-heralded Apartheid Museum. Those who are really adventurous and into long car rides can try the Victoria Falls tour. That's right, they'll take you all the way up to Victoria Falls in Zimbabwe, although it does take some advance notice, and it's more than a couple of rand.

Tour prices depend completely on how much you want to do and see and how many people are in your group (2-person minimum). Still, this is an especially great deal for those who want to see the nation on the cheap courtesy of the experts.

OTHER SIGHTS. The Asiatic Bazaar lies west of the zoo along Boom St., in the swirling multiracial stew of **Marabastad.** Here, amid open-air butcheries, wholesale produce stalls, and minibus taxi ranks, is the **Miriammen Hindu Temple,** an ornate place of worship dedicated to a Hindu goddess. The temple rests at the corner of 7th and Sturben St. and is discernible by its white, green, and red tower. Visitors are welcome, but must remove their shoes.

ARCADIA

UNION BUILDINGS. These grand structures—the seat of South Africa's government—are perched atop Meintjeskop, a hill just west of the city center with a commanding view of Pretoria. Amid landscaped gardens, architect Herbert Baker's sandstone masterpiece originally housed the entire executive branch of the government. Today, the western wing contains the office of the president, which can be distinguished by its green-tinted, bulletproof windows. In 1994, Nelson Mandela was inaugurated in a ceremony on the balcony while South Africans and dignitaries, including 60 heads of state, looked on from the lawn below. Visitors can get no closer than the driveway, but the beautifully manicured gardens along the hillside and the views of Pretoria make the trip worthwhile.

PRETORIA ART MUSEUM. The museum, set at the edge of Arcadia Park, hosts a collection of works by South African artists such as Anton van Wouw and Jacob Pierneef. A small sculpture garden and etchings by Gauguin, Chagall, Dali, and Picasso round out the collection. Black artists' works are interspersed throughout the galleries. *(2 blocks south of the Union Building, at the corner of Wessels and Schoeman St. ☎ 344 1807. Open Tu and Th-Sa 10am-5pm, W 10am-8pm, Su noon-5pm. R3.)*

NATIONAL BOTANICAL GARDENS. The 77ha gardens host over 20,000 indigenous plants and often feature weekend concerts and flea markets. *(On Cussonia Dr. in Brummeria, east of Pretoria along Church St. ☎ 804 3200. Open daily 6am-6pm. R7.)*

AROUND PRETORIA

VOORTREKKER MONUMENT AND MUSEUM. The monument stands as the most potent symbol of the Afrikaners' belief in their destiny as the "white tribe of Africa," and pays tribute to the 20,000 Voortrekker pioneers who left the Cape Colony in 1834 and 1835. Designed by Gerard Moerdyk and constructed from 1938-49, this massive granite structure is regarded by many conservative Afrikaners as holy ground. Every Dec. 16 at noon light shines through the ceiling onto a symbolic grave to commemorate those fallen in the battle against the Zulus on that date. Gracing the inside wall is a marble frieze (one of the largest in the world) depicting the trekkers' 20-year history (including the killing of 4000 Zulu warriors, the construction of the Church of Vow, and the signing of the Sand River Convention in 1852), and their Great Trek to escape British rule. During the apartheid era, blacks were allowed to visit only at designated times. *(3km south of Pretoria along the R101. Buses run from Church Sq. terminus to Valhalla and Voortrekkerhoogte every 10min. during the week. Be warned: it's a steep climb from the bus stop to the monument. ☎ 326 6770. Open Th-Tu 8am-5pm, Sept.-Mar. until 6pm; W 8am-8pm. R18; students R10, children R6. Parking R6.)*

There is also a small **Voortrekker Museum,** highlighting the lifestyle and migratory routes of the Trekkers. *(On the hillside below the monument. Open daily 9am-4:30pm.)* Plans are to move the Voortrekker Museum into the basement of the monument. Surrounding the monument is the **Voortrekker Monument Nature Reserve,** home to small herds of antelope and zebra. A short distance west of the monument lies **Fort Schanskop,** one of four forts built to guard Pretoria during the Boer War.

PREMIER DIAMOND MINE. One of the world's richest diamond mines, Premier achieved worldwide recognition in 1905 with the discovery of the 3106-carat Cullinan diamond, the world's largest rough stone. The Cullinan diamond was later cut into several gems, including the 530-carat Great Star of Africa, the largest cut gem in the world, currently set in the British royal scepter. **Premier Diamond Tours,** based at the mines, offers surface tours that include video displays and replicas of famous stones. A walking tour includes an opportunity to prospect among piles of Kimberlite ore, although you can't take any finds with you. **Pretoria Backpackers Tours** (see p. 316) provides transport to the Premier Diamond Tour. *(Mine: 95 Oak Ave., 40km east of the city. To get there, take the R104, which begins as Vermeulen St. before merging into Church St. ☎734 0081. Tours M-Sa 9:30am and 1:30pm. R25; no children under 10. R250 with transport from Pretoria Backpackers. Book in advance.)*

SMUTS HOUSE MUSEUM. This humble house of wood and galvanized iron was moved 100km in 1909 to become the home of Jan Christian Smuts (1870-1950), general, international statesman, farmer, lawyer, scientist, author, and botanist. Give the man some credit; he had 26 university degrees. Filled with relics of Smuts' life, the house is an intimate portrait of the historical giant who wrote the preamble to the UN Charter and served twice as South Africa's Prime Minister. Mrs. Smuts claimed to have seen the ghost of an old man with whiskers in the Dark Room, and occasional tourist reports corroborate the sighting. *(16km south of Pretoria on the 4000ha Doornkloof farm. Take Louis Botha Ave.–the N1 or the M18–to the little town of Irene and follow the road signs to Doornkloof/Smuts House. ☎667 1176. Open M-F 9:30am-4:30pm, Sa-Su 9:30am-5pm. R5, students and children R3.)*

The expansive grounds of Doornkloof are perfect for a picnic and they host the **Irene Village Market** on the second and final Saturdays of each month. Arts, crafts, antiques, fruit, and bread are sold in the midst of live music and children's entertainment. *(Call 012 667 1659 for exact dates. 9am-2pm.)*

TSWAING CRATER. The crater is 1.4km wide and 200m deep, an awesome relic of a meteorite impact 200,000 years ago. Also known as Soutpan (which, like *Tswaing,* means "salt pan"), this eco-museum includes a small brine lake, the salt and soda deposits of which attract humans and wildlife alike. The long drive may deter all but the geologically inclined. There is also a comprehensive educational tour that includes a visit to a small **Ndebele village,** where indigenous life is preserved; call ahead to arrange for a guide. *(50km northwest of Pretoria along the M35. ☎790 2302. Open daily 7:30am-4pm. R7, with guide R12.)*

⤵ ENTERTAINMENT

Theater and film listings appear in the *Mail and Guardian* and *Pretoria News.*

CINEMAS. Pretoria's many movie theaters play mostly Hollywood blockbusters. The giant **Sterland Cineplex** (☎341 7569), at the corner of Beatrix and Schoeman St., offers the widest choice on its 14 screens. Other conveniently located theaters include the **Hatfield Nu Metro** (☎362 5899), on Burnett St., and the **Ster Kinekor Tramshed** (☎320 4300 or 320 4301), at the corner of Van der Walt and Schoeman St.

THEATERS. The **State Theatre** (☎322 1665), at the corner of Prinsloo and Church St., puts up impressive drama, dance, and music productions on its five stages; current information is posted on its doors and in the local daily papers (*Beeld, The Star,* or *The Pretoria News*). The **Teaterhuisie Community Theatre** (☎341 9411), directly behind the Pancake Palace on Gerard Moerdyk St., stages small, professional performances nightly at 7pm. The **Breytenbach Theater** (☎444 834), on Gerard Moerdyk St., is a smaller venue that features performances ranging from

GAUTENG

avant-garde student productions to elementary school pageants (R10-20). The adjacent **Moon Box** (☎341 1766) offers weekend cabaret.

FESTIVALS. The **Pretoria Show** (☎327 1487) takes place in the third week of August, kicking off the festival season, followed by **Oktoberfest** (☎803 4106), in late September. Pretoria's **Jacaranda Festival** (☎342 1660), in the third of week of October, celebrates the city's purple petals.

▣ MARKETS

Pretoria has several options available for mall-weary shoppers and avid bargain hunters. The **Hatfield Flea Market,** outside the mall on Burnett St., is widely regarded as Pretoria's best market, offering handicrafts, used books, artwork, and other bargain miscellany. (☎342 3769. Open Su and public holidays 9:30am-5:30pm.) **Sunnypark Flea Market,** at the corner of Esselen and Jeppe St., is another popular stop. (☎083 300 5200. Open Sa 8am-2pm, Su 11am-5pm.)

▣ NIGHTLIFE

While Pretoria often projects a staid, almost stodgy image (especially when contrasted with wild, on-the-edge Johannesburg), the city's large student population and increasing number of tourists have produced a nightlife boom. Hatfield is a popular, cosmopolitan area. The townships west of the city have a selection of taverns and *shebeens*, but consider them off limits unless accompanied by a local.

SUNNYSIDE

Zwakala, 150 Gerard Moerdyk St. Though the name of this jazz bar means "Come in," expect to find only local youngsters here. Beers R5.50. Open 3pm-late. Cash only.

HATFIELD

▣ **Tings 'n Times,** (☎362 5538), Hatfield Galleries, shop 16. Also a happening night spot, with live reggae and rock bands (see **Food,** p. 317).

Cool Runnings, 1071 Burnett St. (☎362 0100). The tropical patio, reminiscent of a Jamaican beachfront, is only the beginning of this labyrinth of rooms and patios that comprise Hatfield's busiest nighttime hangout. Music to suit a variety of tastes, from hip-hop to reggae; F night DJ. Cover R5 on dance nights. Open 10am-late.

McGinty's Irish Pub (☎362 7176), in the southeastern corner of Hatfield Sq. Good Irish Guinness in copious quantities at low cost (R15). By nightfall, it's standing room only; come prepared to battle for your bottle of stout. Open M-Sa 11am-2am.

News Cafe, (☎362 7190), corner of Hilda St. and Burnett, at Hatfield Sq. The first of South Africa's News Cafes, this bar draws a 23+ crowd each night. Enjoy the Ziva cocktail (R25) or any other drink (R8-25). Major newspapers available, of course. Open daily 7am-late. MC/V/DC/AmEx.

Up the Creek, 494 Hilda St., (☎362 3712). In the far corner of Hatfield Sq. A laid-back music venue. Try the pink gorgeous cocktail (R22.50). From noon-7pm all Bacardi drinks R7.50. Get R10 cocktails during "cocktail hour" daily 7:30-8:30pm. Cover R5.50. (See **Food,** p. 317.)

GAY NIGHTLIFE

Pretoria's selection of gay and lesbian clubs is continuing to grow, but it's likely that you'll run into the same people in several clubs in the same evening. Consult the latest issues of *Exit, Outright,* and *Gay Pages* for comprehensive listings of events, shows, and special attractions.

Stardust, The Embassy (☎321 9316), in the President Arcade on Pretorius St., between Andries and Van der Walt St. Ascend the escalator to an 18+ all-night house party. With several bars serving each floor, this mega-complex reigns as Pretoria's largest constellation of gay life. Mirrors, silver curtains, and black lights add to the midnight glitz. Su drag show. Cover R10-30. Open W and F-Su 8pm-late.

Gayteway, 95 Gerard Moerdyk St., Sunnyside (☎082 456 2585). A very happening gay/lesbian club. Tu stripshow, Th Karaoke, Sa Mister or Miss competitions. M happy hour 5-7pm. Always straight-friendly. Open literally *all* weekend from F noon until M 2am, and on weekdays noon-late.

NEAR PRETORIA

MAGALIESBERG ☎014

With its charming farmhouses and rolling pastures, the agricultural village of Magaliesberg (ma-HAL-ees-berg), provides a day trip from the megalopolis or a picturesque base from which to explore the nearby mountain range and adjacent Hartebeespoort Dam areas. The surrounding farmland is dotted with battle sites from the Anglo-Boer war and the Ndebele chief Mzilikazi's numerous bloody campaigns. Contemporary explorers will find it an extremely welcoming town with quaint accommodations and stunning scenery. The mountain range itself offers easy to medium trails; most lodges can arrange day or overnight hikes.

■◪ **ORIENTATION AND PRACTICAL INFORMATION.** Magaliesberg is 100km from Johannesburg on the R24. Drivers from Pretoria should follow the R560, turning left and driving for an hour on R24 (also known as **Rustenburg Rd.,** along which lie most of the village's businesses). Tourist information and reservation facilities are provided by the **Magaliesberg Information Office** (☎771 733), at shop 3 in the Magaliesberg Mall off Rustenburg Rd. There are **no banks** in the village and only one ATM, but most businesses accept major credit cards. Public transport to Magaliesberg from surrounding towns and cities is limited to **minibus taxis.** The **police station** is on Derby Koster Rd. (☎577 1315. 24hr.)

◪◩ **ACCOMMODATIONS AND FOOD.** Magaliesberg's relaxed atmosphere and proximity to Pretoria and Johannesburg have made it a premier getaway spot for city dwellers. Accommodation rates vary substantially, with the lowest prices between May and August. Near the De Wildt Wildlife and Cheetah Center, **Simply the Best ❶** offers a real taste of the African *bushveld* and countless adventures for the restless traveller. Visitors can relax and enjoy *braais* or engage in nearby adventures: hiking in the Magaliesberg mountains, exploring the 4x4 trails, abseiling, or partaking in watersports on the Hartebeesport Dam. (☎504 1679 or 072 262 3570. Free pick-up from Pretoria. Dorms R40; singles R70; doubles R120, with bath R130.) Twenty-five kilometers out of town off the R560, **Rustig Farmhouse ❶** is set at the base of the family's mountain. Hiking trails cover the mountain from top to bottom; trail huts wait along the way. Call well in advance for reservations, as the farmhouse accommodates 10 and is rented to one family at a time. (☎576 1241. Farmhouse R100 per person; trail huts R60 per person. Hiking R25 per day.)

◙ **SIGHTS.** Aspiring anthropologists should pay a visit to the ▨**Sterkfontein Cave,** where archaeologists unearthed the fossilized remains of "Mrs. Ples" *(Plesianthropus transvaalenis)*, a prehistoric female primate regarded by some to be the "missing link" between apes and humans. (☎011 956 6342. Tours every 30min. 9am-4pm. R12, ages 6-14 R5.) Alongside the **Rhino and Lion Nature Reserve** (☎011 957 0034), the stalagmite and stalactite formations of massive **Kromdraai Wondercave** include the "Praying Madonna." (☎011 957 0106. 1hr. guided tours, daily on the hour 8am-5pm; night tours available by appointment. R38, children R15.) Also within the conservancy is the **Old Kromdraai Gold Mine,** founded in 1881, reputed to be the earliest Witwatersrand mine. (☎011 957 0034. Open Tu-Su 8am-5pm. Guided tours every hr. R28, ages 3-12 R15.)

ACTIONS AND CONSEQUENCES
South African Politicians Deal with AIDS

Although apartheid was abolished in 1994, its effects still haunt South Africa. Among apartheid's legacies is the fast-spreading epidemic HIV/AIDS. Current statistics reveal an HIV/AIDS prevalence rate of 20%, and the epidemic may not have reached its peak. Blacks are the most highly affected subset of the Southern African population.

Many theories have been put forth to explain the extraordinary rapidity with which the HIV virus has spread in South Africa. One long-held myth of "Africa's hyper-sexuality" attributed the pandemic's unabated spread to promiscuity among Sub-Saharan Africa black population. However, the Durex Global Sex Survey belies this assumption with statistics that show that Americans have more sexual partners, and, on average, are sexually active at an earlier age (16.3 years) than Africans are (17.1 years).

It is more plausible that institutions established under apartheid are at the heart of HIV/AIDS' rapid rate of transmission. Whiteside and Sumter, the authors of "AIDS: The Challenge for South Africa," loosely define susceptibility to HIV/AIDS as the chance of infection, based on the number of sexual partners a person has as well as on the frequency of intercourse. Under apartheid, South Africa was a highly susceptible society.

For example, the migrant labor system under apartheid forced men to leave their families for long periods of time to work. Many workers, away from their regular sexual partners, engaged in intercourse with prostitutes. The excellent system of roads constructed during the apartheid era facilitated travel and, hence, communication of the disease. Migrant workers and the commercial sex workers they came into contact with eventually formed an extensive network of transmission. Returning home, the workers spread the virus to wives and girlfriends before returning to the city.

South Africa shows how high income can be a curse as well as a blessing. According to one theory concerning the relationship between income, social society and HIV/AIDS, a country with low social cohesion and high income is more susceptible to rapidly spread disease. South Africa fits the criteria for a rapidly spreading pandemic. The large rifts in civil society caused by apartheid and the inequitable economic system of South Africa made created a climate susceptible to the spread of HIV/AIDS.

There are cases where HIV/AIDS was even intentionally used to derail the anti-apartheid movement. It is reported that in the 1980's, government operatives assigned HIV-positive blacks in their employ to strategic sites, including two Hillbrow Hotels, to spread the virus among prostitutes.

While the apartheid government may have increased spread of HIV/AIDS in South Africa, today's ANC government has also been accused of harming anti-AIDS efforts. Controversial statements and legislation have received worldwide criticism. Local and international critics have questioned the commitment of Thabo Mbeki's government to the anti-AIDS campaign and the government has fought legal battles with civil groups (e.g. Treatment Action Campaign over the provision of nevirapine to pregnant mothers to prevent mother-to-child transmission) over government policy.

South Africans are taking matters into their own hands. The LoveLife campaign is a national advertising effort targeting teenagers and teaching responsibility. (Look out for their cryptic billboards along the highways.) Former President Nelson Mandela is a spokesperson for the anti-AIDS campaign and has criticized ANC reluctance to acknowledge HIV/AIDS as an urgent problem. Doctors have secretly defied government policy and prescribed antiretroviral drugs and nevirapine to patients despite government orders that such prescriptions be allowed only at certain pilot sites. Such efforts provide a source of hope that the goal "Towards an AIDS-free generation" is a feasible target.

Source: AIDS: The Challenge for South Africa. Sumter, C. and Whiteside A.

Bekezela Ncube was a Researcher-Writer for Let's Go: South Africa 2002. *A native of Zimbabwe, Bekezela has lived in South Africa for the past 5 months, where she spent a semester studying at the University of Cape Town.*

NORTHERN PROVINCE (LIMPOPO)

Sandwiched between the Gauteng Province and neighboring Botswana and Zimbabwe, the Northern Province is characterized by a variety of terrains and an eclectic mix of peoples. Despite being South Africa's poorest province, it is one of the country's most productive agricultural areas. Although it attracts fewer tourists than other areas, this province boasts both natural beauty and a rich history. Controversy over recently proposed legislation to change the province's name to Limpopo has shown that age-old tensions are still very real. All visitors should know that names in the Northern Province can change faster than Winnie Mandela's mood ring (see **What's in a Name?,** What's In a Name?, p. 328).

Perhaps one commonality among the people of the Northern Province is their love of the land. The dusty flat *bushveld* in the west rises into soft rolling mountains to the north, falling again into harsh dry bush punctuated with scattered baobab trees, while soft savannah grass blankets the lowveld in the far east. Farther south, the Letaba District swells with sub-tropical hills, valleys, and the rocky outcrops of the Klein Drakensberg. This attractive, varied landscape guarantees adventure for those willing to travel off the beaten track. Visitors to the province will bask in an unprecedented feeling of freedom while enjoying the many outdoor pursuits of the area, including isolated camping in the *bushveld*, vigorous hiking along the secluded trails of the Drakensberg, enticing climbs up the waterfalls of the Magoebaskloof Pass, and trekking with game in the salt pans.

HIGHLIGHTS OF THE NORTHERN PROVINCE

Explore the mighty **Drakensberg** and **Magoebaskloof Pass** (see p. 347) by foot, 4x4, or horse, then watch the stars from one of the unique accommodations near Tzaneen.

Visit the **Makapansgat Cave** (see p. 333), which holds many hominid fossils and is the site of Voortrekker Piet Potgietersrus' last stand against the Sotho people.

The **Ben Lavin Nature Reserve** in Louis Trichardt (see p. 337) features inexpensive accommodation smack in the middle of a 2500ha *bushveld* park complete with trails, safaris, and guided hikes.

WARMBATHS (BELA BELA)   ☎014

Warmbaths, the gateway to the Northern Province, lies only 36km from the border of Gauteng, the commercial and political center of South Africa. Nevertheless, this small town seems a universe away from the hustle of big cities. In fact, the only thing rushing in this town is its hot spring water, which gushes from the ground at a rate of 22,000L per hour. Though these springs have been here since the Iron Age, it was not until 1873 that they were officially "discovered." Travelers should not expect to find natural pools bubbling among rocks in the *bushveld*; instead, the source of the springs is encompassed by a thriving resort that abounds with

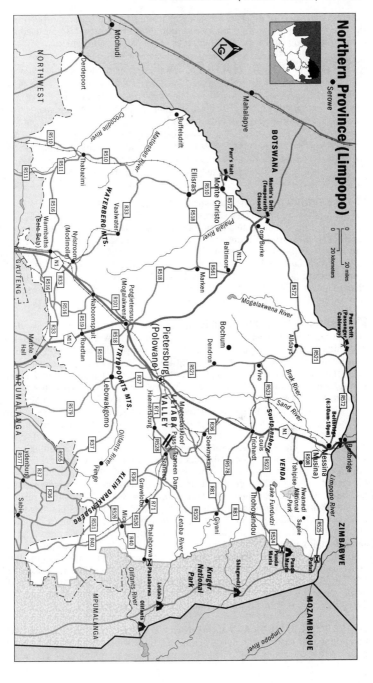

Northern Province (Limpopo)

different activities for all ages, including hydrotherapy and water sports. Though the spa is clearly the town's main attraction, Warmbaths can also be used as a comfortable stop on the way to other areas of the Northern Province.

WHAT'S IN A NAME? What's up with all the name changes in the Northern Province? Or should we say Limpopo? Is it Warmbaths or Bela Bela? Pietersburg or Polokwane? The government of the Northern Province has recently begun a major effort to replace Afrikaner names with their native-language antecedents. For many blacks, restoring original tribal names is a way of symbolically reclaiming the land and remembering Africa's pre-colonial history. To some whites, however, the rejection of Afrikaner names implies a rejection of the Afrikaners and their culture. Moreover, many people of both races argue that the money spent on changing names is much more urgently needed for the other problems confronting the Northern Province.

⌐ TRANSPORTATION. The **train station** is southeast of town, off Potgieter St., the road to Nylstroom, down a short dirt road. **Spoornet** (☎ 011 773 2944 or 011 773-2992/3994) runs to and from Johannesburg (3½hr.; departs daily 2:28am; second class R40, first class R55). **Greyhound** (☎ 011 830 1301) stops just outside of town and runs to Bulawayo (11hr.; Sa-Th 10am, F midnight; R215) via Pietersburg (2¼hr., R90), Louis Trichardt (3¾hr., R105), and Messina (4¾hr., R115); and to Johannesburg (2¼hr., daily 3:30am, R90) via Pretoria (1½hr., R90). For Harare, change buses in Messina. Book ahead at Overkruin Real Estate, on the second floor of the ABSA building on the corner of Marx St. and Sutter St.

◧◪ ORIENTATION AND PRACTICAL INFORMATION. Warmbaths lies about an hour north of Pretoria off the N1. The main street in Warmbaths is **Voortrekker St.**, which runs east-west past the Spa. **Sutter St.** runs parallel to Voortrekker to the south. **Pretoria St.** intersects the two. All three are host to major establishments. From the Warmbaths train station, walk out to the paved road, Potgieter, and turn left. A right on Pretoria will bring you to Voortrekker and the center of town.
  Warmbad Tourism, in the Waterfront Complex, 500m south of town on Marx St., can help you find local accommodations and activities, and provide maps of town for R15. (☎ 736 3694; fax 736 2890. Open M-F 8am-5pm, Sa 9am-2pm, Su 9am-noon.) **Overkruin Real Estate** (☎ 736 3766), which used to be Sibongile Charters and still handles their business, is on the second floor of the ABSA building in the shopping complex on the corner of Marx St. and Sutter St. They're useful for Greyhound tickets and other intercity transportation. **Standard Bank,** 42 Voortrekker St., provides the most comprehensive financial services, including **foreign exchange** and **ATM.** (☎ 736 2272. Open M-F 9am-3:30pm, Sa 8:30-11am.) Other services include: **Pick 'n Pay Supermarket,** in the same complex as the ABSA building (☎ 736 6050; open M-F 7am-7pm, Sa 7am-6pm, Su 7am-2pm); **Police station** (☎ 736 2402), 500m out of town on Van der Merwe St., off Potgieter St.; **Medlin Apteek,** in the same complex as the ABSA building. (☎ 736 2285; open M-F 8am-5:30pm, Sa 8am-1pm, Su 10am-noon.); **St. Vincent's Hospital,** 20 Quagga St., 500m west of the town center (☎ 736 2310.); **Internet access** at **ComTec,** 43a Voortrekker St. (☎ 736-2628; R10 per 30 min.; open M-F 8am-5pm, Sa 8am-noon); and the **post office** (☎ 763 3451), near the corner of Pretoria and Voortrekker St. (open M-Tu and Th-F 8:30am-4:30pm, W 9am-4:30pm, Sa 8am-noon). **Postal code:** 0480.

▐ ACCOMMODATIONS AND CAMPING. Warmbaths offers a variety of accommodations that cater to the needs of visitors, mainly city dwellers who come to relax on the weekends. The tourist office can arrange accommodations at a variety of establishments, from guest houses to secluded game lodges. If you prefer to make your own arrangements, good deals can be found at townhouses and holiday flats, which are reasonably priced but may raise their rates on the weekends. Call ahead if staying on a Friday or Saturday night. Many of these places offer a pick-up service from the bus and train stops in town. **Baden-Baden Spa Townhouses ❷**, 51 Luna Rd., is one block off Voortrekker St. With your back to the Aventura Spa entrance, turn left and head down Voortrekker to Grobler St., where you take a right. Luna Rd. is the first road on the right. Two-level self-catering villas have two or three bedrooms, three baths, a living room, a kitchen, balcony and backyard and sleep four to eight people. (☎736 2941 or 083 513 6472. Check-out 10am. M-F R110 per person, Sa-Su R150.) Spacious and cheerful self-catering rooms which sleep up to eight people are available at **Hoogland Spa ❸**, 45 Luna Rd. Follow directions to Baden-Baden and continue 100m along Luna Rd. (☎/fax 736 5928. Wheelchair accessible. Rooms low-season M-Th R220, F-Su R375; high-season M-Th R300, F-Su R400-475. Students and senior citizens 20% discount.) **Tobe's Inn ❶**, 46 Voortrekker, offers basic but pleasant rooms at a good price. (Breakfast R20. R100 per person.) Also on Voortrekker is the **Aventura Spa ❶** with powered caravan and tent sites. (☎736 2200. Check-in 3pm. Check-out 11am. Caravans and tents low-season R75, high-season R100; plus R30/R40 per person. MC/V.)

◖◗ FOOD. Greenfield's Cafe ❷, in the Waterfront Complex on Marx St., across the bridge from town heading south, has a good selection of breakfast platters (R13-25), burgers (R20-27) and grills (R40-50). A few vegetarian dishes are also available. (☎736 3272. Open daily 7am-10pm.) More centrally located is **The Keg ❷**, in the Elephant Springs Hotel, corner of Sutter and Marx St. Dinners are R20-50. (☎736-2101. Open M-Sa 7am-10pm, Su 8am-9pm.) After hours, music and pool tables are at **Rockies Bar and Restaurant,** in the Circle Center at the western end of Voortrekker St. (Open daily 9am-late.)

◪ OUTDOORS. The **mineral baths** at the Aventura Spa aren't just a sit-n-soak. The park has a water-ski cable, hydrotherapy, mini golf, and tons of other water activities. (☎736-2200. Springs open daily 9am-5pm; outdoor pool reopens 6-9pm. R40.) **Thaba Kwena Crocodile Farm** lies about 15km north of Warmbaths. Take the R101 toward Nylstroom and turn left on Groot Nylsoog St.; the farm is 4km down on the left. The largest crocodile farm in South Africa, Thaba Kwena is home to 18,000 of these magnificent beasts, most of whom will eventually show up in the form of wallets and sausages. Here you can view 250 adults and hundreds of babies basking in the sun and pretending they are not watching your every move. Excellent free tours are provided. (☎736 5059; fax 736 4774. Open daily 9am-4pm. R15.)

NYLSTROOM (MODIMOLLE) ☎014

Nylstroom, which means "source of the Nile," was founded in 1866 by a group of devoutly religious Voortrekkers who had fled the Cape in search of a British-free Christian holy land. Mistaking a fertile stream running north for the headwaters of the Nile, these so-called "Jerusalem Travelers" believed they had reached Egypt and set up camp. A nearby hill shaped like a pyramid (now known as Kranskop) convinced them further of their "discovery." The hill was actually a holy mountain for the indigenous people, who call it *Modimolle* or "place of the spirits." Today Nylstroom is a small town popular mainly for its proximity to the Waterberg mountains and for its annual grape festival in early January.

◧ TRANSPORTATION. To get to Voortreeker St. (which leads to Nylstroom's center) from the train station, stand in the station parking lot with the tracks behind you, follow the road that leads directly forward two blocks until it ends, turn left, and make your first right onto Rivier St., which will lead you eventually to Voortrekker. The **train** (☎011 773 2944 or 011 773 2992/ 3994) from Johannesburg arrives in Nylstroom at 11pm, so make plans for someone to meet you. Trains run daily from Nylstroom to Johannesburg (4hr., departs daily 1:58am, R60). **Greyhound** (☎011 830 1301) stops on Voortrekker St. and runs to Bulawayo (10¾hr.; Sa-Th 10:20am, F 12:20am; R215) via Pietersburg (2hr., R90), Louis Trichardt (3¼hr., R105), and Messina (4½hr., R115); Johannesburg (2½hr., daily 3:10am, R90) via Warmbaths (20min., R85) and Pretoria (1hr. 50min., R90).

ORIENTATION AND PRACTICAL INFORMATION. Nylstroom is about 1½ hours north of Pretoria on the R101. The R101 (which becomes Voortrekker St.) leads right into the heart of Nylstroom, where it intersects the town's main road, Potgieter St., which runs east-west. If driving from Warmbaths, make a right onto Potgieter St. from Voortrekker St. Almost everything you need is on Potgieter or its side-streets. Minimal **tourist information** is available at the **library,** on the corner of Kerk St. and Field St., which intersects Voortrekker at the First National Bank. (Open M-F 9am-5pm, Sa 9am-noon.) Other services include: **ABSA Bank,** on the corner of Pretoria and Potgieter (☎717 5321; open M-F 8:30am-3:30pm, Sa 8-11am); **Score Supermarket,** on the corner of Potgieter St. and Voortrekker St. (☎717 1113; open M-F 8am-6:30pm, Sa 8am-5pm, Su 8am-1pm); **Protea Pharmacy,** 88 Potgieter (☎717 5351 or 717 3752; open M-F 8am-6pm, Sa 8am-1pm and 5-6pm, Su 10am-noon and 5-6pm) and **Van Heerden Pharmacy,** 95 Potgeiter St. (☎717 2181; after hours 014 717 2836 or 083 409 9008), which alternate being open on Sa.; **medical clinic,** at the corner of Voortrekker and Kerk St. (☎717 1332/3; open M-F 8am-5pm, Sa 8am-1pm and 5:30-6:30pm, Su 10:30-11:30am and 5:30-6:30pm); **police** (☎718 1000), at the corner of Kerk St. and Hertzog St.; and the **post office,** on Potgieter St. between Pretorius and Landdros (open M-Tu and Th-F 8:30am-4:30pm, W 9am-4:30pm, Sa 8am-noon). **Postal code:** 0510.

ACCOMMODATIONS AND FOOD. One of Nylstroom's best B&Bs for comfort and hospitality is the **Pink Gables Guest House,** 3 De Beer St., a 15min. walk up Voortrekker toward Warmbaths. (☎717 5076. Breakfast included. Check-out 10am. Singles R150; doubles and triples R125 per person. MC/V.) Also very pleasant is the **Komma Weer Guest House,** 17 Rupert St. Follow Potgieter St. west past Voortrekker St., turn left onto Van Niekerk St., then right onto

IN RECENT NEWS

THE LITTLE GREEN RIBBON

Anyone traveling through the Northern Province and Mpumalanga will probably have noticed people wearing a small green ribbon attached to their clothing by a star or similar medallion. These people are not deputy police officers; they are members of a religion called the Zion Christian Church. The ZCC is based near Pietersburg and counts hundreds of thousands of South Africans, almost all of them black, as members. ZCC doctrine is said to draw upon the Old and New Testaments but also contain uniquely African elements. Adherants refrain from eating pork and using alcohol, tobacco, and other drugs, and have a reputation for honesty and civil behavior. Every Easter, thousands of the faithful descend upon the main church for prayer and celebration. The ZCC is growing rapidly and may soon be one of the largest and most influential faiths in South Africa.

Rupert St. (☎ 717 5539. Wheelchair accessible. Breakfast included. Dinner R35 by request. Check-out 10am. Singles R150; doubles R250.) There are a few take-away restaurants along Potgieter St., but for finer dining, **Pepe's Restaurant** (☎ 717 4114) offers an enticing menu of Italian pastas (up to R45) and intriguing grilles (up to R60). The *Fillet Mafioso* is a criminally succulent fillet steak with prawns. (Open Tu-Sa 11am-3pm and 6-10pm, Su 11:30am-3pm. Reservations recommended, especially weekends. DC/MC/V.) After hours, hit **Vic's Sports Bar**, on Potgieter St., for drinks, pool, and sports on the big-screen TV. (☎ 717-4941. Open M-F 10am-4am, Sa 10am-2am.)

◩ ⚑ SIGHTS AND OUTDOORS. The sights in town are few but historically noteworthy. Most noteworthy is the site of a **concentration camp,** at the corner of Potgieter and Van Riebeeck St., where Afrikaners were detained by British troops during the Anglo-Boer War. At present, the ground is the site of Eenheid Primary School, but the original gates (with tell-tale barbed wire) form the main entrance of the school. The camp was closed in 1902, after 544 women and children were killed and buried in the **cemetery** on Voortrekker Rd.

The **Waterberg** mountains extend from outside of Nylstroom to north of Potgietersrus. The **Nylsvley Nature Reserve** is an International Nature Sanctuary and one of the country's best spots for bird watching and small game viewing. (35km north of Nylstroom and clearly marked from the R101. ☎ 743 1074. Gates open daily 6am-6pm. R12.) For those itching to get into the bush, the **Sable Valley Hiking Trail** is a two-day, 22km route covering valleys, gorges, savanna, and mountain streams. The trail is 20km from Nylstroom off the R101. Look for the Serendipity sign. (☎ 743 1665 or 082 553 3266. Restricted to groups of 2-20 people over age 18. 4x4 trails and horseback riding available. Camping with electricity from R40-80 per adult; book at least one month in advance.) The **Lekkerbreek Hiking Trail** is a two-day, 12km circular route through the Waterberg. Make reservations at least one day before. An overnight hut stay is included. (☎ 715 2593. Take the R33 west from Nylstroom. Turn left after 5km and go 5km down, trail headquarters on the right. R30.)

In the same area is the **Kierpersol Hiking Trail,** a 20km trail through the Waterberg that can be done in one day (R30 per day). There are also cabins for R80 and a game drive for R30. (Take the R33 west towards Vaalwater. After 2km, turn right at the Kiepersol sign. ☎ 715 2295 or 082 689 0433.)

POTGIETERSRUS (MOGALAKWENA) ☎ 015

By 1854, the Voortrekkers had reached the location of modern day Potgietersrus, settling land along the way. Naturally, the land occupation conflicted with the interests of the Ndebele people, and hostilities arose, culminating in an attack on a hunting party led by Hermanus Potgieter, a Boer leader. Potgieter and many others were killed before the Boers retaliated. The Ndebele fled into the Makapansgat caves, where roughly 1500 people starved to death while the Boers maintained their offensive on the caves' entrances. Potgieter's nephew, Piet Potgieter, was killed in the offensive, and the town is now named in his honor. Despite its bloody origins, this small town of about 10,000 is a pleasant base for exploring the Waterberg Mountains flanking both sides of the town.

▣ TRANSPORTATION. The **train** from Johannesburg stops in Potgietersrus at 1am. There are **no taxis** in town. **Greyhound** stops on Voortrekker St., and runs to Bulawayo (9hr.; Sa-Th 11:20am, F 1:20am; R200) via Pietersburg (1hr., R85), Louis Trichardt (2hr. 20min., R85), and Messina (3 ½hr., R90); Johannesburg (3¾hr., daily 2:05am, R105) via Nylstroom (1hr., R85) and Pretoria (3hr., R105).

NORTHERN PROVINCE

▓ ▛ ORIENTATION AND PRACTICAL INFORMATION. Potgietersrus lies about 2 hours north of Pretoria on either the N1 or the R101. The **R101,** also known as the **N11,** becomes the main road, **Voortrekker St.,** in town. From the train station, turn right onto Van Riebeeck St. and continue until it intersects Voortrekker St. The **tourist info center,** 97 Voortrekker, is in front of the Arend Dieperink Museum between Kruger and Van Riebeeck St. (☎491 8458; open M-F 7:30am1pm and 2-4:30pm). Services include: **ABSA Bank,** 76 Voortrekker St., with **ATMs** and **exchange** (☎409 1500; open M-F 8:30am-3:30pm, Sa 8-11am); **police station,** 300m from Voortrekker St. on the corner of Retief and Rabe St. (☎409 1400; open 24hr.); **Potgietersrus Pharmacy,** on Voortrekker St. (☎491 3165; open M-F 8am-9pm, Sa 8am-1pm and 5-9pm, Su 9am-12:30pm and 5-9pm); **PotMed,** a private clinic, 106 Voortrekker (491-5019; open daily 10:30am-11am, 3pm-4pm, 7pm-8pm); **hospital,** at the corner of Geyser and Rabe St. (☎491 2236); **ambulance** (☎10 177); and the **post office,** on Ruiter near Retief St., with *Poste Restante* (☎491 4141; open M-Tu and Th-F 8:30am-4:30pm, W 9am-4:30pm, Sa 8am-noon). **Postal code:** 0060.

▛ ACCOMMODATIONS. Seba Cottage Guest House ❷, 139 Schoeman St. From the info center, walk down Voortrekker toward Pretoria and turn right onto Voor; walk through four intersections and turn left onto Schoeman at the fifth. Seba Cottage offers storybook country cottages with self-catering kitchens and baths. (☎491 2927. Wheelchair accessible. Breakfast R30. Singles R165; doubles R275.) You can also take advantage of the unusual and affordable facilities offered at the **Game Breeding Center.** A 10min. walk towards Pietersburg on Voortrekker, this four-room guest house has private baths, self-catering kitchens, and *braai.* The park entrance fee is included with the room. (☎491 4314. Wheelchair accessible. Check-out 10am. R90 per person.) **Jaagbaan B&B ❷** lies 12km south of town, just off the R101, which runs parallel to the N1. A white-washed farmhouse encircled by mountains and landscaped gardens, this friendly home is a tranquil getaway with lovely rooms amid beautiful scenery. (☎491 7833. Wheelchair accessible. Breakfast included; dinner R30 by request. Singles R150; doubles R200.)

About 10km north of town, **Thabaphaswa Recreational Park ❶** has 100km of hiking and mountain biking trails which run through the park's *bushveld* setting. It offers rustic simplicity with a permanent tent (R50 per person) and 4-5 person huts with a central stove. To get there head north on the R101, turn left at the sign for Percy Fyfe, left again at the sign for Thabaphaswa, and follow signs for the homestead. (☎491 4882. Book a month in advance. Huts R63 per person; R100 with bedding and utensils provided. Camping R34 per person; bring your own tent.)

About 17km beyond Thabaphaswa, 35km north of Potgietersrus, the **Percy Fyfe Nature Reserve** has tents and houses without electricity set against a picturesque mountainside. There are extensive hiking and mountain biking trails, a wide variety of birds, and a breeding site for endangered antelope and buffalo. (☎491 5678. Book in advance. Tents R30 per person; houses R100 per person.)

▟ FOOD. Cafe Italia ❷, 81 Voortrekker St., near Van Riebeeck St., offers a great pizza deal, with prices slashed for every two pizzas ordered. One large chicken mushroom costs R42.50. Two cheese pizzas cost R55 total. Vegetarian pizza and pasta (up to R16) also available. (☎491 3792. Open M-Th 8am-8:30pm, F-Sa 8am-9:30pm, Su 10am-2pm and 5-8pm.) **El Teas Coffee Shoppe ❶,** 112 Voortrekker, near Voor St., offers tea, scones, and light meals in an elegant setting. They just may live up to their claim to be "the nicest place in town to have morning coffee," with their sunny patio overlooking a rose garden. Scones and muffins (R10), sweet and savory pancakes (R6-22), and open sandwiches (R16-19) are offered. (☎491 6906. Open M-F 8am-6pm, Sa 8am-2pm, Su 11am-1pm.) A great bakery serving fresh rolls

(R0.50) and Chelsea buns (R1.50) is **Butterfield Bread ❶**, at the corner of Potgieter St. and Voortrekker St. (☎491 8788. Open daily 6am-7pm.) After hours, drinks and pool are at **Las Vegas,** 50 Ruiter St., which runs parallel to and north of Voortrekker. (Open M-Sa 10am-late.)

◙ ♫ SIGHTS AND OUTDOORS. The **Arend Dieperink Museum,** on Voortrekker St. between Kruger and Van Riebeeck St., has excellent exhibits on Sotho pottery and handicrafts, as well as a large collection of Voortrekker artifacts. (☎491-9600. Open M-F 8am-4pm. R3, children under 6 free.) The **Makapansgat Valley,** 19km from town, has preserved the most extended and comprehensive hominid fossil record in the world. The Makapan Cave is a rich site for Iron Age fossils as well as an important place in Voortrekker history. The clash between the Voortrekkers and the Ndebele people took place here, and the cave was declared a national monument in 1936. (Tours normally booked for groups of 10 or more. Book at least 1 week in advance at the Arend Dieperink Museum. R200 plus R15 per person, students R10. No children under 12.) The **Game Breeding Center,** within walking distance from the town center on Voortrekker St. toward Pietersburg, contains 1500ha of game farm with 35 species of mammals and birds. The center aims to breed endangered animals indigenous to Africa, Southeast Asia, and South America. Game drives go out in the morning and during the day for feeding, as well as by request in the evenings. Picnic and *braai* facilities available. (☎491 4314. R10. Game drives R25.)

PIETERSBURG (POLOKWANE) ☎015

Named in 1886 after the famous Voortrekker leader General Piet Jacobus Joubert, Pietersburg is the capital of the Northern Province and has developed into its administrative and economic center. Hurried businessmen are common in Pietersburg, and it is said that the town's population as much as doubles during the workday, as people come into town on errands from all over the Northern Province. But although hustle and bustle may reign supreme, Pietersburg has managed to retain some character, as well as a few worthwhile museums. The town boasts that it has the highest number of statues per capita in its public gardens. Travelers who are not impressed by that distinction can at least use Pietersburg as a base for exploring surrounding nature reserves, or as a stopping point on the way to Zimbabwe, the *lowveld,* or Kruger National Park.

◰ TRANSPORTATION

Flights: Pietersburg International (Gateway) Airport is about 2km. north of town on the N1. Follow signs for Pietersburg International/Military Base. **South African Airlink** (☎288 0164) flies to **Johannesburg** (55min.; 1-4 flights daily 8:30am-6:10pm; R1004).

Trains: The **train station,** on Hospitaal St., is 1km north of town center. **Spoornet** (☎022 996 202 or 011 773 2992/3994) runs to **Johannesburg** (6½hr.; 11:22pm; 2nd class R75, 1st class R110), via **Pretoria** (5hr., R65/R90); and **Messina** (7hr., 3am, R60/R90). Office open M-F 7am-9pm; reservations desk hours 7:30am-4pm.

Buses: North Link Tours (☎291 1867), in Library Gardens Ctr., books seats on North Link buses. The **Translux** ticket office (☎295 5548) is in the AZMO complex at 49 Gen. Joubert St. Tickets must be booked in advance. Schedules may change, so call ahead to confirm before making your travel plans. Buses leave from Hans van Rensburg St. between Grobler and Jorissen St.

Northlink Buses run to **Johannesburg** (4hr., daily 10pm, R100) via **Pretoria** (3½hr., R80); **Phalaborwa** (3hr., Th-Su 5pm, R75) via **Tzaneen** (1½hr., R45).

Greyhound runs to **Bulawayo** (10hr.; Sa-Th 12:20pm, F 2:30am; R195) via **Louis Trichardt** (1hr. 20min., R85) and **Messina** (2½hr., R85); **Harare** (10¾hr.; Su-F 3am, Sa 6pm; R220) via **Louis Trichardt** (1¼hr., R85), **Messina** (2½hr., R85), and **Masvingo** (8¼hr., R200); **Johannesburg**; (4hr., daily 1:30am and M-Sa 10:05am, R125) via **Nylstroom** (1¾hr., R90), **Warmbaths** (2hr., R90), and **Pretoria** (3½hr., R125).

Translux runs to **Bulawayo** (10¼hr., daily 1:15am, R165) via **Louis Trichardt** (1½hr., R45) and **Messina** (3hr., R70); **Harare** (12hr.; T, Th, F, Su 2:45am; R220) via **Louis Trichardt** (1½hr., R45), **Messina** (3hr., R70), and **Masvingo** (8¼hr., R140); **Johannesburg** (4hr.; daily 2:05am; M, W, F and Su 9:30am; W 10:30am; Su 1:30am; R115) via **Pretoria** (5¼hr., R115); and **Lusaka** (1¾1hr., T and F 1:45pm, R320) via **Louis Trichardt** (1½hr., R45), **Messina** (3hr., R70), **Masvingo** (8¼hr., R140), and **Harare** (12hr., R220).

Taxis: City Taxi (☎ 288 0142) to airport (R25) and train station (R15).

Car Rental: Avis (☎ 288 0171), **Budget** (☎ 288 0169), **Imperial** (☎ 288 0097), and **Tempest** (☎ 288 0219), all at Gateway Airport. A 4-door manual compact car averages R100-200 per day; insurance extra.

ORIENTATION

Pietersburg lies 273km north of Pretoria on the **N1.** The highway exit to Pietersburg turns into **Grobler St.,** a one-way road running east through the city center. South of Grobler, **Thabo Mbeki St.** runs west one-way, leading back to the N1. The rectangle enclosed by Grobler, Thabo Mbeki, **Market,** and **Dorp St.** (to the east) is the center of Pietersburg. The Library Gardens Center covers the block between Grobler St., **Jorissen St., Hans van Rensburg St.,** and **Schoeman St. Market St.** runs north towards the train station, Gateway Airport, and the N1 to Louis Trichardt.

PRACTICAL INFORMATION

Tourist Office: The Polokwane Municipality Marketing Dept., on Landdros Mare St. between Thabo Mbeki St. and Bodenstein St. (☎ 290 2010; www.pietersburg.org.za). Provides town info and arranges regional tours. The **Northern Province Tourism Board** (☎ 288-0099), in the airport, has maps and info about Pietersburg and the rest of the province.

Banks: Banks with **ATMs** crowd the city center. **Standard Bank** (☎ 295 9146), corner of Thabo Mbeki St. and Schoeman St. Open M-F 9am-3:30pm, Sa 8:30-11am. **ABSA Bank,** on Landdros Mare St. near Thabo Mbeki, has ATMs and foreign exchange. Open M-F 8:30am-3:30pm, Sa 8-11am.

Supermarket: Checkers Supermarket (☎ 295 2100), in Checkers Center complex on Hans van Rensburg near corner of Grobler St. Open M-Th 8am-6pm, F 8am-7pm, Sa 8am-5pm, Su 8am-2pm.

Emergency: ☎ 10 111; **ambulance:** ☎ 10 177.

Police: ☎ 290 6577 or 290 6578, on corner of Bodenstein and Schoeman St.

Pharmacy: Japie Visser Apteek, on Grobler and Mark St. (☎ 295 9171.) Open M-Sa 8am-9pm, Su 9am-1pm and 5-9pm.

Hospital/Medical Services: Redimed (☎ 295 4050 or 295 4052), 23a Thabo Mbeki St. near Hans van Rensburg St. Open 24hr.

Internet Access: Postnet (☎ 295 4290) in the Library Gardens Center. R10 per 20min. (Open M-F 7:30am-5pm, Sa 8am-1pm.)

NORTHERN PROVINCE

Pietersburg (Polokwane)

▲ ACCOMMODATIONS
Arnotha's Lodge, 7
Golden Pillow, 1
Jacaranda, 4

🍴 FOOD
Dolce Vita, 6
Houndog Cafe, 5
Monty's Pub and Grill, 8
Pebbles Cafe, The Manor, 2
The Restaurant, 3

Post Office: (☎291 3200), on Landdros Maré St. near Thabo Mbeki, opposite Civic Ctr. *Poste Restante.* (Open M-Tu and Th-F 8:30am-4:30pm, W 9am-4:30pm, Sa 8am-noon.)

Postal Code: 0699.

🏠 ACCOMMODATIONS

Guest houses and hotels in Pietersburg cater mostly to businesspeople, and those traveling cheap will have to stretch their budgets to stay in town. Rates are cheaper on the weekends, when corporate folks leave. Whenever you plan to visit, call ahead for reservations. There are simply not enough accommodations for everyone visiting Pietersburg, especially on weekdays, and those without reservations will likely find themselves out of luck.

Arnotha's Lodge, 42 Hans van Rensburg St. (☎291 3390; fax 291 3394). Face direction of traffic on Grobler, turn right down Rensburg and walk two blocks. Traveler's mecca for self-sufficient pilgrims. Spacious rooms have modern baths and kitchenettes. Breakfast R18, under 12 free. Check-out 10am. Singles R147; doubles R170. ❷

Jacaranda, 57 Voortrekker St. (☎295 5554; fax 295 5557), at Grobler. The establishment, in a quiet area not too far from the town center, consists of pretty bungalow-apartment style accommodations in a gated complex with secure parking. Jacaranda has rooms with TV, fridge, and shower. Laundry available. Breakfast M-F (R29). Checkout 10am. Singles R169; doubles R229. ❷

Golden Pillow, 57 Thabo Mbeki St. (☎295 2970). Between Hoog and Ost. Pleasant rooms with kitchenettes open onto outside walkways. Breakfast included. Recently renovated restaurant and pub. Singles M-Th R240, F-Su R180; doubles R320/260. ❷

◖◗ ☕ FOOD AND NIGHTLIFE

Pebbles Cafe/The Manor, 39 Grobler St. (☎295 6999). Near the corner of Compensatie St. In the former house of South African parliamentarian Tom Naude, Pebbles blends exemplary dining with fine home cooking. Wood floors, wicker chairs and a grate fire give the place a homey atmosphere. One can forgive the corny titles on the menu (the salads are dubbed "forest ferns"). Crepes, pitas, and sandwiches R15-30. Dinners R30-50. Open M-F 8am until late, Sa 8am-3pm, Su 9am-3pm. ❷

The Restaurant (☎291 1918). Corner of Dorp and Thabo Mbeki St. Gray walls with orange trim and white lights give the restaurant a hint of Halloween. The trace of the Gothic extends to ornate benches, kerosene lamps, handpainted tables, and rattan blinds. Offerings include Chinese *chow mein*, Indian lamb curry, South African grilles and vegetarian dishes. Open M and Sa 6pm-late, Tu-F 12:30pm-late. ❷

Houndog Cafe (☎291 1989). On Hans van Rensburg opposite the Checkers Center. This casual lunch spot is a local favorite, with high-quality burgers (R10-15), filled potatoes (R15-20), and crepes (R10-15). Open M-Th 7am-6pm, F-Sa 7am-9pm. ❶

Dolce Vita, 53 Hans van Rensburg (☎295 8483). Between Grobler and Thabo Mbeki Street. An upscale restaurant specializing in seafood, but with a wide variety of menu choices including poultry (R36-47) and steaks (R40-70). Low wood beams and wooden partitions lend an air of intimacy. Open M-F noon-4:30pm and 6pm-late, Sa 6pm-late. ❷❶

Monty's Pub and Grill, 46 Landdros Maré St. (☎295-8980), is the casual but happening place for Pietersburg nightlife. Down a few lagers at their hardwood bar or shoot pool with the young crowd. Pub food R20-25. Open M-Sa 11am-late. Happy hours W-Sa, Th karaoke.

⊙ SIGHTS

The **Pietersburg Museum,** in an historic Irish House on the corner of Thabo Mbeki St. and Landdros Maré St., displays the area's history from the Stone Age through the Voortrekker period to the industrialized Pietersburg of this century. (☎290 2182. Open M-F 8am-4pm, Sa 9am-noon, Su 3-5pm. Free.) The **Hugh Exton Photographic Museum** is part tribute to Hugh Exton, nationally renowned Pietersburg photographer, and part photo documentary of the town's first 50 years. It is housed in the civic park, in Pietersburg's first Dutch Reformed Church. (Open M-F 9am-3:30pm, Su 3-5pm. Free.) Sculptures and paintings fill the **Art Museum,** a modest gallery housing a variety of contemporary South African art. (Located at the back of the Library Gardens Center. ☎ 290 2177. Open M-F 9am-4:30pm, Sa 9am-noon. Free.) The **Bakone Malapa Open Air Museum** details the history and culture of the Northern Sotho (Bakone) who once lived on the land where the museum now stands. A Bakone tour guide leads visitors through a recreated ancient village and a replica of a modern-day family dwelling. (9 kilometers south of town on the Cheunespoort road, Kerk St. ☎295 2867. 30-40min. tours daily. Open daily 8:30am-12:30pm and 1:30-3:30pm. R3, children R1.50.)

⚄ OUTDOORS

The 9600ha **Pietersburg Game Reserve**, 5km south of the city down Dorp St., is home to more than 21 species of game, including zebra, giraffe, and white rhinos. Visitors can observe the wildlife while strolling the hiking trail, or from a car on the 20km road through the park. Make sure to grab a map from the entrance before you begin. (☎ 290 2331. R5, children R2. R5 per car. Open daily 7am-4:30pm.) The **Pietersburg Bird Sanctuary**, north of the city up Market St. (the R521 highway), is not as action-packed. Although the bird sanctuary has over 280 species, many birds are not visible during the day. It is best to go in the early morning. (☎ 290 2497. Open daily 7am-6pm. R5, children R2. R5 per car.)

LOUIS TRICHARDT   ☎ 015

North of Pietersburg, the dusty countryside becomes greener and more majestic as tall pine trees and larger indigenous bushes replace smaller *bushveld* shrubs. Louis Trichardt sits in this transitional area, shadowed by the Soutpansberg ("salt pan mountain") range to the north. Named after a Boer leader who led a group of early colonizers through the area to Mozambique, Louis Trichardt serves as a good springboard from which to explore the Soutpansberg and Venda territory.

⊏ TRANSPORTATION

Trains: The station is on the south side of town, on Burger St. near Pretorius. **Spoornet** (☎ 519 4202, 011 773 2992, or 773 3994) goes to **Johannesburg** (11hr.; daily 7:27pm; 2nd class R110, 1st class R130) via **Pretoria** (9hr., R85/R120); **Messina** (3½hr., daily 6:39am, R30/R40).

Buses: Book through the **Louis Trichardt Travel Agency** (☎ 516 5042), in the arcade on Burger St. between Trichardt and Devenish St. Open M-F 8am-1pm and 2-4pm, Sa 9-11am. Sa hours only valid after the 15th of the month.

Greyhound (☎ 011 830 1301) runs to: **Bulawayo** (6½hr.; M-Th and Su 1:40pm, F 3:50am; R170) via **Messina** (1¼hr., R85); **Harare** (10¾hr.; M-F and Su 4:20am, Sa 7:20pm; R210) via **Messina** (1¼hr., R85) and **Masvingo** (7hr., R115); **Johannesburg** (6¼hr., daily 11:30pm and M-Sa 8:15am, R135) via **Pietersburg** (1¼hr., R85), **Nylstroom** (1¾hr., R105), **Warmbaths** (3¾hr., R105), and **Pretoria** (5½hr., R135).

Translux (☎ 011 774 3333) picks up at the tourist office and runs to: **Bulawayo** (8¾hr., daily 2:45am, R165) via **Messina** (1½hr., R45); **Harare** (10½hr.; T, Th, F, Su 4:15am; R210) via **Messina** (1½hr., R45) and **Masvingo** (6¾hr., R125); **Lusaka** (21hr., T and F 3:15pm, R320) via **Messina** (1½hr., R45), **Masvingo** (7hr., R125), and **Harare** (10¾hr., R220).

Minibus taxis: The local rank is next to the OK Bazaar on Burger St. The long distance taxi rank is in Extension 4 just off the N1 highway at Rissik St. Minibuses go to: **Messina** (R25), **Pietersburg** (R25), **Thohoyandou** (R20), and **Tzaneen** (R30).

⊞ ⑦ ORIENTATION AND PRACTICAL INFORMATION

The town's main artery is **Trichardt St.**, which runs west from the **N1** at the second of the three stop signs. Everything you could possibly need can be found on Trichardt St., or within a block of Trichardt on **Krogh St.** or **Burger St.**

Tourist Office: Soutpansberg Tourism and Marketing Office (☎ 516 0040; info@tourismsoutpansberg.co.za.) At northern end of town facing the N1; look for the "i" sign on the awning next to Noise Boys shop. Accommodations, activities, maps, brochures, and hiking info. Open M-F 8am-5pm, Sa 8am-1pm.

NORTHERN PROVINCE

Bank: ABSA Bank (☎516 0161). Corner of Krogh St. and Trichardt St., with **ATMs.** Open M-F 8:30am-3:30pm, Sa 8-11am.

Laundromat: Easy Washy, corner of Kruger and Devenish St. in the ShopRite plaza. Open daily 8am-4:45pm. Wash R5, dry R5, plus R1 service fee per machine.

Pharmacy: Becks Pharmacy (☎516 4953). On Krogh St. across from the post office. Open M-F 8am-5pm, Sa 8am-1pm.

Police: ☎516 1587. Corner of Krogh and Devenish St.

Hospital: ☎516 0148. Corner of Hospitaal and Snyman St., north of the town center. **Songwozi Medical Center,** 89 Burger St. (☎ 516 3497). Open M-F 8am-6pm, Sa 8am-4pm, Su 10am-2pm.

Internet access: PCS Computers (☎083 300 9082). On Krogh between Joubert and Rissik, behind the Shell station. R20 per hr. Open M-F 8am-9pm.

Post office: ☎516 0111. On Krogh near Trichardt St. with *Poste Restante.* Open M-Tu and Th-F 8:30am-4:30pm, W 9am-4pm, Sa 8am-noon.

Postal Code: 0920.

ACCOMMODATIONS AND CAMPING

Lutombo B&B, 141 Anderson St. (☎516 0850; fax 516 1846). Follow Trichardt west, take a right on Anderson St. 2 blocks up from Krogh St. By far the town's highest-quality accommodation, Lutombo, meaning "blue vault of heaven," provides very comfortable rooms in a quiet suburban area with flourishing shady garden, pool and home atmosphere. Breakfast included. Dinner R40 by request. Singles R150; doubles R210. ❷

Inn On Louis Trichart (☎517 7088), on the N1 about 5km north of town. An upscale hotel in an historic building now run by Inns of Zimbabwe, the Inn On provides better-than-average rooms in an elegant setting with pool and tennis court. Breakfast and dinner included. Singles R250; doubles R450. Children under 2 free. ❸

Carousel Lodge (☎516 4482), 100m off Rissik St. on Klein St., on southern end of town. Follow Trichardt St. east, turn right on Grobler and left on Rissik. Alternatively, call for free pick-up. Offers standard hotel rooms with TV, kitchenette, and bath. Overnight safaris and horseback riding. Breakfast R30 by request. Limited wheelchair access. Check-out 9:30am. Singles R140; doubles R210; triples R240; quads R270. MC/V. ❷

Cloud's End Hotel (☎517 7021; fax 517 7187), 2km north of town to the left off the N1. Decent 3-star rooms, with good camping facilities, pool, tennis court, cricket field, and hikes in surrounding forests. Breakfast included. One wheelchair-accessible room. Check-out 11am. Singles R210, R275 with dinner; doubles R360/490; tents and caravans R35 for 2, R5 per additional person, R5 for electricity. MC/V. ❶

FOOD

Cafe d'Art (☎516 4068 or 516 5760), on Krogh St. near corner of Ruh St. Adjacent to an art gallery. The Cafe exudes muted trendiness, complete with blue theme, iron grille chairs, and modern wall paintings. Toasted sandwiches and burgers R8-23. Main entrees R28-47. Decent vegetarian selection. Open M-Sa 10am-9pm. ❷

Robot Coffee Shoppe (☎516 0171), on Krogh St. between Trichardt St. and Devenish St. Skip the fatty oxtail and go for homemade cakes in this reclusive cafe at the rear of Robot Hardware Store. Unique atmosphere for a power-tool-and-caffeine fix. Sandwiches R9. Light meals up to R16. Pancakes R9. Open M-F 8am-5pm, Sa 8am-1pm. ❶

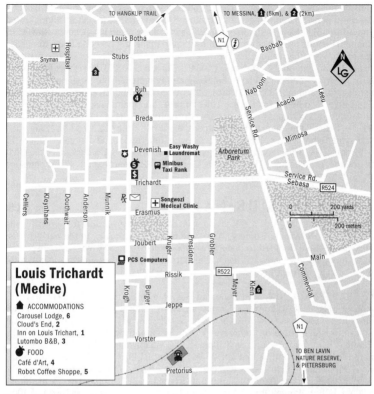

Louis Trichardt (Medire)

🏠 ACCOMMODATIONS
Carousel Lodge, 6
Cloud's End, 2
Inn on Louis Trichart, 1
Lutombo B&B, 3
🍴 FOOD
Café d'Art, 4
Robot Coffee Shoppe, 5

OUTDOORS

Louis Trichardt lies at the foothills of the Soutpansberg, a mountain range with two hidden salt pans and a number of nature reserves with trails. Most are to the west of Louis Trichardt off the R522. The Louis Trichardt tourist office has extensive information on reserves and hikes in this area. The **Arboretum Park** houses 145 species of indigenous trees as well as an old graveyard where several original Voortrekkers rest. (Corner of the N1 and Trichardt St.) **Hangklip Trail** is a two-day course through an evergreen forest, open grasslands, and plantations in the Soutpansberg. It is rated as "easy," so even novice hikers can gape at monkeys, woodpeckers, and other wildlife along the 21km trail. The trailhead and booking office are just out of town. (From town, follow Krogh north. It will quickly become Forestry Rd. and lead you to the picnic area and Hangklip office. Info ☎012 481 3615; reservations ☎013 764 1058; ecotour@mail.safcol.co.za.) A 2500ha *bushveld* park, the **Ben Lavin Nature Reserve** houses over 50 mammal species and 230 bird species. There are walking safaris and 18km of trails, including one overnight trail. Activities and accommodations should be booked at least one month in advance. (12km south of town; follow the N1 south 8km, turn left at sign. Park entrance 3.5km on the left. ☎516 4534 or 083 675 9231; benlavin@mweb.co.za. Day visits 6am-6pm, open 24hr. for overnight guests. R30, children under 16 R10. 1-day safari R120; 2-day R215. Half-day bike rental R20, full day R40. Caravan sites R35; hired tents R69; 2-5 person lodges with shower and kitchen R250 for 2 people, R65 per extra person; 2-person huts R190, R60 per extra person.) Featuring salt pan tours, San cave paintings, short hiking trails, and affordable lodgings, the **Bergpan salt pans and eco resort** lies 80km northwest of Louis Trichardt on the other side of the Soutpansberg. (Take the R522, Rissik St., west until Vivo, then follow the R521 north toward Alldays 6km out of Vivo and turn right. Resort 6km on the right. ☎/fax 593 0127 or ☎ 593 0042. Day visitors R25. Tours R10. Prices per person: 2-4 bedroom self-catering units R70-90; camping house R45, bedding R5; camping R25.) At **Medike,** the cliffs of the Sand River Gorge and the dry Sand River bed house over 200 species of birds and mammals, 250 kinds of trees, and numerous hiking trails which curve through the heart of the mountains. (36km west of Louis Trichardt in central Soutpansberg. Follow the R522 west for 29km, then turn right at the sign for Medike, just before the train tracks, and continue 6 km. ☎ 516 0481 or 082 893 2958; medike@mweb.co.za. Day visitors R20. Cottages R100 plus R20 per person or R80 plus R60 per person. Campsites R25; tent rental R50; discounts for those staying two days or more).

MESSINA (MUSINA) ☎ 015

For most of the past century, Messina was a quiet copper-mining town on the outskirts of South African society. When the mine closed down in the early 1990s, Messina seemed doomed to become a *spookiedorp* (ghost town). The discovery of diamonds a few years ago has saved it from that fate, but Messina is still little more than an outpost for transnational travelers following the N1 to Zimbabwe.

⌷ TRANSPORTATION. The Spoornet **Bosvelder** train (☎ 011 773 2944, 011 773 2992 or 011 773 3994) goes to **Johannesburg** (13hr.; daily 4:30pm; economy R75, 2nd class R125, 1st class R185). **Greyhound** (☎ 534 2220 or 011 830 1301) runs from the Limpopo River Lodge to **Bulawayo** (7½hr.; M-Th and Su 2:50pm, F 5am; R155); **Harare** (9½hr.; Su-F 5:30am, Sa 8:30pm; R185) via **Masvingo** (6hr., R105); **Johannesburg** (6hr. 45min.; daily 10pm and M-Sa 7:15am; R145) via **Louis Trichardt** (1½hr., R85), **Pietersburg** (3½hr., R85), and **Pretoria** (7hr., R135). **Translux** (☎ 534 2220 or 012 315 2230) also runs from the Limpopo River Lodge to **Bulawayo** (7¼hr., daily 4:20am, R185); **Harare** (9hr.; T, Th, F, Su 5:30am; R215) via **Masvingo** (5¼hr., R100); **Johannesburg** (7½hr.; daily 11:05pm; Su 10:15pm; M and Th 7:15am; Tu, Th, and Sa 6:15am; R140) via **Louis Trichardt** (1¼hr., R45) and **Pretoria** (6½hr., R140); **Lusaka** (18¼hr.) via **Masvingo** (5¼hr., R100) and **Harare** (9¼hr., R215). **City to City** also runs a bus from the Engen station, just south of the Limpopo River Lodge, to **Johannesburg** at half the price and half the reliability (9hr., between 7-10am daily, R80).

⌷ PRACTICAL INFORMATION. Messina's tiny heart stretches for 500m along the **N1,** also known as National Road, starting at the Limpopo River Lodge on the right and ending at the large **Spar** on the left as you are going north. The **train station** (☎ 534 7225) is on National Rd., just before Spar. The Zimbabwean **border post,** Beitbridge, is approximately 10km north of town along the N1. (Open daily 5:30am-10:30pm; R86 toll per vehicle. Don't be fooled by "officials" trying to sell you forms, and watch out for pickpockets.) For more info about public transport, border-crossing fees, and car rentals, visit **Manica Messina Travel Office,** in the Limpopo shopping complex on the N1 past the BP and opposite Spar. (☎ 534 2220; fax 534 2233. Open M-F 8am-1pm, 2-4:30pm.) Tourist info, including accommodations and local activities, can be found at **Messina Limpopo Valley Tourism Association,** (☎ 534 3500), on Limpopo Ave. off National Rd. Services include: **Spar supermarket** (☎ 534 0746; open M-F 8am-5pm, Sa 8am-1pm) on National Rd.; **ABSA** bank, on National Rd. next to the Limpopo River Lodge, with **ATM** and foreign exchange (open M-F 8:30am-3:30pm, Sa 8-11am); **police station** (☎ 10 111, or 534 2000), on

Limpopo St.; **hospital** (☎ 534 0446), on the N1 at the north end of town; **ambulance** (☎ 10 111 or 534 0061); **Messina Apteek** (☎ 534 0812 or 083 302 2132; open M-F 8am-7pm, Sa 8am-1pm); **Internet** at The Computer Shop, next to a needlework shop opposite Spar (☎ 534 1206; open M-F 8am-5pm; R15 per 30min.); and the **post office**, on the south end of town, off Irwin St., with *Poste Restante* (☎ 534 2308; open M-Tu and Th-F 8:30am-4:30pm, W 9am-4:30pm, Sa 8am-noon). **Postal code:** 0900.

⚐ ACCOMMODATIONS AND CAMPING. Limpopo River Lodge ❶, 6 National Rd., is an older hotel in the town center that can get noisy in the early morning. Reasonably clean but rather dull rooms have TV, A/C, and phones. (☎ 534 0204 or 534 0205. Reception 24hr. Check-out 10am. Singles R95, with bath R105; doubles R115/R140. MC/V.) Turn right onto the R508 (Irwin St.) to Tshipise to get to **The Guest House B&B ❸**, which has luxurious rooms with satellite TV and A/C. It's only a 5min. walk from town. (☎ 534 3517 or 082 780 0579. Breakfast included. Lunch R35. Dinner R85 by request. Free email. Fax and telephone facilities also available. Check-out 9am. Singles R280; doubles R380.) **Baobab Caravan Park ❷** is the first site as you enter town from the south. (☎ 534 3504. Check-out 9am. Partially wheelchair accessible. Singles R175; doubles R200; triples R260; quads R320. Campsites R40, plus R15 per person, up to 6 people. MC/V.)

❒ FOOD. Of Messina's eateries, the least mediocre is perhaps **Horseshoes Pub and Grill**, on National Rd. opposite the Limpopo River Lodge. Burgers (R15-25), pizzas (R20-30), and light meals (R25-35) are available. (☎ 534 0223. Open daily 7am-midnight). Farther down National Rd. around Limpopo St., a number of small take-out places do a brisk business in local foods and may even have a small sitting area. One such place is Oasis Banquet and Bakery (☎ 534 0556. Open daily 8am-10pm).

⚑ OUTDOORS. The 37,000ha **Messina Nature Reserve** encompasses part of the former Baobab Forest Reserve, which was established in 1926 to save the trees from paper factories. Since then, the baobabs within the reserve have been declared a national monument to ensure that the uniquely African trees will last as a protected symbol of the region. The reserve also contains birds, game-viewing roads, and an 8km hiking trail which costs R5. (☎ 534 3235 or 534 2307. Gates open M-F 7:30am-4pm. R7 per vehicle, R5 per person, under 16 R2.50. Tent sites R35; cabin R120 for up to 6 people.) The quirkiest baobab resides outside Messina: the **elephant tree,** a baobab with a swooping branch and sprawling roots, is said to resemble an elephant in mid-stride. (From the N1 turn onto the R508 to Tshipise and take a left at the elephant tree sign. Turn right where the road terminates at a T intersection. The first left takes you to the park where the "elephant" stands.) For an impressive **view of Zimbabwe** across the sprawling Limpopo river, follow the N1 to the Beitbridge border control. Just before the gate, turn left towards the service station and immediately right onto a dirt road. The road becomes paved again after 300m running along the three-tiered barbed wire fence that is the border, affording some great views of the Limpopo. Drive carefully around Beitbridge, as this area is a stopping point for trucks and can get quite congested.

VENDA

The Venda is a valley softly carpeted in green and laced with sacred rainforests and rumbling waterfalls. Here, the VhaVenda have been able to preserve their rich culture more faithfully than most other indigenous peoples in South Africa. Once a separate country and an apartheid homeland (see p. 38), Venda today is characterized by respect for the land, tradition, and people of all kinds.

The VhaVenda trace their ancestry to a group of Karanga-Rowzi people who migrated south across the Limpopo River 300 years ago. Under the leadership of Chief Dimbanyika, they eventually settled in the northern Soutpansberg foothills. During the 19th century, the VhaVenda thrived under Chief Thohoyandou and remained unconquered despite attempts by Boer, Swazi, Pedi, and Tsonga forces. It was not until 1898 that the VhaVenda succumbed to a Boer army of 4000 men. During the Apartheid Era, Venda became a homeland for the VhaVenda people, and in 1979 it was declared an independent republic separate from South Africa, with the hastily-constructed town of Thohoyandou serving as its capital. Today, most services for travelers are centralized in larger towns such as Louis Trichardt.

After South Africa's democratic elections in 1994, Venda rejoined South Africa and was incorporated into the Northern Province. Although it is no longer an officially segregated homeland, the area remains almost completely VhaVenda and is saturated with a strong sense of culture. Important legends are expressed through wood carvings and pottery, prized throughout Southern Africa for their high-quality workmanship. Strongly self-sufficient, the area has supported itself through mining, craftmaking, and bountiful harvests of fruits and nuts.

WHEN IN VENDA...

DO: Say **greetings and farewells**—they are not mere formalities in Venda culture, but are instead a way for strangers to acknowledge respect for each other. Travelers who want to feel welcome in Venda should be prepared to greet everyone with whom they make eye contact. When speaking, wear a big smile and draw out vowel sounds. To say hello (or goodbye), women should say "Aa!" while men should say "Ndaa!" For both men and women, "good morning" is "ndi matsheloni" and "good evening" is "ndi madekuana." The response to all three is "a uhudi." Extend **courtesies** to your hosts. To thank someone for their help, it is customary to give a gift of food. Don't be surprised if the VhaVenda suddenly bestow you with pawpaws, oranges, or other fruits in season. "Thank you" is "ndo liuhuwa," often followed by a handshake and handclasp.

DON'T: Kill or eat a python or a crocodile—they are both taboo creatures for the VhaVenda. Among older VhaVenda people, fish are also taboo because they keep the lakes and rivers from running dry; it's not wise to eat them.

THOHOYANDOU   ☎015

Though the town of Thohoyandou (toe-yahn-DOE) has little to offer visitors in search of landmarks and liveliness, its supplies and services, especially in the open market in the center of town, make it an adequate base camp for adventurous exploration. Before settling down, one may want to consider Louis Trichardt as a less confusing and subjectively more pleasant introduction to the region. If you've already set on Thohoyandou, it's best to book accommodations and tours, stock up on protein-rich *mopane* worms, and hop back into your vehicle. The outlying villages and mountain hiking opportunities deserve a full day's exploration.

⌐ TRANSPORTATION. Thohoyandou Travel and Tours, in the Venda Tusk Hotel, books Translux tickets. (☎962-5314. Open M-F 8am-6pm, Sa 8am-4pm, Su 8am-noon.) **Translux** runs to Johannesburg (daily 7:15am, R140) via Louis Trichart (R40). For Harare, change buses in Louis Trichart. **Minibuses** depart from a park just outside the shopping complex and run to destinations throughout Venda. From the Score shopping center, walk through the arcade marked "City Fashion Center." Ask a local to direct you to the minibus bound for your desired destination (R2-10). To get here by car, head east on **R523** out of Louis Trichardt for 50km;

the highway becomes Louis Trichardt St. and runs through the middle of Thohoyandou.

⚑ PRACTICAL INFORMATION. Some tourist info is available at **Ditike Travel and Tourism** (☎ 964 1921, ask for Irene), about 2km from town on the R524 toward Louis Trichart. Coming from Sibasa, go through Thohoyandou and turn right at the T-junction. **Tours** can be arranged here, at Bouganvilla Lodge, or directly with Mr. Dima (see **Sights**, p. 343). Thohoyandou's major services are arranged around a series of interconnected shopping plazas off the main road, currently even more confusing than usual because of construction. To get to the main shopping plaza, follow the main road away from Sibasa and turn left after the Caltex station. Turn left again at National Legal Aid Funerals, proceed past Checkout supermarket, and turn right after Hardware City. The main plaza, centered around a Score supermarket, will be on your right. Services include: **ABSA Bank** with **ATMs**, at the rear of the main plaza (☎ 962 5501; open M-F 8:30am-3:30pm, Sa 8-11am); **Alpha Omega Pharmacy,** in the main plaza (open M-F 8am-5pm, Sa 8am-1pm); **police** (☎ 962 5097); **ambulance** (☎ 962 4177); **Mveledzo Clinic,** on the main road (☎ 962-5662, open 24hr.); **Score grocery,** also in the main plaza (open M-F 7am-5pm, Sa 7am-4pm, Su 8am-noon); and the **post office,** in an orange brick building behind the main plaza (☎ 962 3275; open M-Tu and Th-F 8:30am-4:30pm, W 9am-4:30pm). **Postal code:** 0950.

⚏⚏ ACCOMMODATIONS AND FOOD. Bougainvilla Lodge ❷ is the more attractive of the town's two establishments. On the main road halfway between Sibasa and Thohoyandou before the entrance to Unit C, their rooms have fans, TV, and secure parking. (☎ 962 4064; fax 962 3576. Limited wheelchair access. Reservations recommended. Reception 24hr. Check-out 10am. Economy singles R195; doubles R230; triples R290. Credit cards accepted.) Less attractive but cheaper is **Acacia Park ❷,** on the 524 toward Punda Maria. Coming from Sibasa, proceed through Thohoyandou and turn left at the T-junction. Rather dingy chalets have two twin beds, bath, and kitchenette, and may be co-inhabited by six-legged friends. (☎ 962 3095; fax 962 2506. Wheelchair accessible. Check-out 10am. Chalets R125 per person; powered caravan sites and camping sites R45 plus R15 per person.)

Thohoyandou has its fair share of take-out joints and fast-food chains, but the open market centered around the shopping plaza parking lots is a more interesting—and healthy—option. Vendors sell a bounty of ready-to-eat snacks for pocket change. Feast on two handfuls of bananas (R2), a mug of boiled peanuts (R1), a bag of oranges (R2), or a small bucket of *mopane* **worms** (R5). The worms, called "*mopane* sausages" when cooked, are a great source of protein, and many Venda believe they are good for the heart. (Market open M-F 8am-4:30pm, Sa 8am-1pm.)

Many small food stores in the various shopping plazas sell the raw materials for traditional Venda cooking. Dairy products are available at **Hygenik** (open M-F 7am-4pm) and bread is available at the numerous bakeries (R2-4 per loaf). Those who can stomach antennae can sample some ginger beetles, which—true to their name—taste like a jolt of burning ginger. To prepare the little buggers, steam them with a bit of water, then pan-fry until golden brown and crunchy.

◙ SIGHTS. To really explore Venda, it is necessary to find a tour guide. At best, travelers who attempt to see Venda on their own will miss out on the legends and historical tales surrounding the sights. At worst, they won't find the sights at all. The man who used to give tours for the Venda government, **▨Mr. Mashudu Dima,** has gone private. He now gives informed tours of the Venda region and its people. Make sure to book a few days in advance, because his "perfect tours" are very popular. (☎ 964 1577 or 082 401 9756. Half-day tours from R300, full-day from R400.) Alternative but more expensive tours—good bets if Mr. Dima is booked—include

Four Corners Tours (☎083 339 7493; fax 015 962 0039) or **Great North Cultural Tours** (☎015 962 1500). Those short on time or money can take a half-day tour to must-see, less-accessible sights such as Lake Fundudzi and the Vhutanda Sacred Forest. **Lake Fundudzi** (meaning "to bow your head in homage"), is one of the largest lakes in South Africa and is a sacred site for the VhaVenda people (the ashes of the royal family of Chief Netshiava were scattered here). The lake is now protected by one of the chief's descendants, who only allows VhaVenda women and children to approach its shores. Lake Fundudzi bears an ethereal veil of mist. The **Sacred Forest** is a lush stretch of woods in the Thathe-Vondo forest. Visitors must keep to the main road, or face the wrath of the legendary Chief Nethathe, who changed into a white lion to protect the trees and flowers. Travelers can ask to visit local village artisans, who can only be found with the help of a guide, or to a local *sangoma* or traditional healer. *Sangomas* cure disease with traditional medicines and tell fortunes by a pattern of cattle bones thrown on the ground. During the summer, visitors should ask about the **Domba dance ceremony,** a rite of initiation for girls passing into womanhood still performed in a few villages. Even if you miss the ceremonies, you can still see the Domba dance: It danced all over Venda and mimics the movement of the python as many young girls circle a huge sacred drum.

⚑ OUTDOORS. Venda is an appealing mix of *bushveld* and indigenous forest with both dry places and areas with copious water. Unfortunately for the outdoors lover, many of the sites are sacred, and hiking by the general public is forbidden. One hike that is open to the public is the four-day **Mabudashango Trail** (☎963 1001 or 963 1211.) The 50km trail starts at the Thathe-Vondo tourist station and winds through the Soutpansberg forests past waterfalls and dams. **Phiphidi Waterfalls** is a worthwhile site that is simple to find without a guide. In late August or early September, these falls are the site of a sacred rain-making ceremony. The sister of the Venda chief comes to the flat rock at the top of the falls at sunrise and makes a rain offering to the ancestors. Travelers can do a bit of their own divining if they listen closely: an echoing noise from the falls means there is no rain to come, while a low rumbling noise means rain is on its way. There are rough-hewn picnic and *braai* facilities; get your firewood at the gate, for legend says that those who steal wood from the sacred forest will be destroyed by ancestral spirits. (Take the R523 from Thohoyandou past Sibasa 10km to the T intersection. Follow the sign left and well down the dirt road; watch for the "Phiphidi" sign. Minibuses also run from the Thohoyandou shopping complex to the falls. Open daily 8am-4:30pm. R2.)

NWANEDI NATIONAL PARK ☎015

82km north of Thohoyandou and Sibasa, the luscious evergreen environment gives way to dry *mopane veld* and thin acacia woods. Nwanedi (wah-NAY-dee) National Park is an 18,000ha chunk of this terrain, set against the rocky backdrop of the northern Soutpansberg and centered around two artificial lakes, Nwanedi Dam and Luphephe Dam. The area is peaceful, scenic, and provides the best accommodations in the Venda region. These range from camping and caravan sites to upscale chalets. There are a number of pleasant hikes in the park, the most popular of which is the beautiful and tongue-twisting **Tshihovhohovho Falls.** Visitors are likely to see buck dashing through the bush and may even glimpse a white rhino lolling in the shade. Other activities include **fishing, canoeing,** and eating delicious meaty dishes in the excellent restaurant (R25-50). This area is not very accessible by public transportation. Although minibuses run from Sibasa (R10), private cars are necessary to enjoy the park. From Thohoyandou, drive north on the main road through Sibasa, past the Sibasa ShopRite, until the road ends at a T-junction; turn right, away from Donald Fraser, and follow signs to Thengwe and past it. Beyond Thengwe, the tar road turns to dirt. Follow this road for 30km, past the sign for Nwanedi and through the village of Muswodi. The first sign, before you reach Muswodi, is for a reserve road only accessible by 4x4. Turn left at Muswodi and travel another 20km through Folovhodwe into Nwanedi. Park reception is the 2nd house on left, across from the park gates. (☎539 0723 or 539 0753. Gates open daily 6am-6pm. Reception daily 7am-7pm. Breakfast included. R5 per person, R7 per vehicle. Camping R35. *Rondavels* R120, chalets R125.)

THE MIGHTY (FUNNY-LOOKING) BAOBAB

You could mistake its massive bulbous trunk and gnarled limbs for the fossilized remains of an unfortunate mammal, but this object firmly planted in the soil and reaching its many twisted arms toward the sky is living flora known as the baobab tree. Often called the monkey-bread tree or the cream of tartar tree, the baobab *(Adansonia digitata)* is native to tropical Africa and one of the biggest tree species in the world, not because of its height (about 18m), but because of its width and breadth. It can grow up to 9m wide, and its branches often spread up to 9m beyond the trunk, which in itself is so vast that it is often hollowed out and used as a dwelling or water reservoir. The tree's roots can extend outward for many miles. One local legend says that the baobab's peculiar shape is the work of the devil, who plucked the tree from the earth, overturned it, and thrust its branches into the ground, leaving the roots to dangle in the air. Another story claims that spirits inhabit the tree's flowers and that anyone who picks the flowers will be cursed and eaten by lions. French author Antoine de St. Exupery used the baobab as a symbol of European colonialism in Africa. In addition to providing food for the imagination, the baobab has practical uses. Oval yellow-green fruit contain stones covered in a white pulp. The pulp, rich in vitamins, is eaten, as well as made into cold drinks, fuel, soap, and medicine. Extract from the bark is sometimes used as a substitute for anti-malarial quinine, and the wood is carved to make drinking vessels, canoes, and musical instruments.

SAGOLE

Three hundred years ago, the Venda hunter Sagole discovered some pools of water as hot as earth burnt by the sun, and moved his people from the hills to settle near these hot springs. Today, Sagole is a tiny village, miles from the nearest paved road, that offers visitors a glimpse of traditional rural life in South Africa. Along the dusty roads, children drive rickety donkey carts, men gather outside the town *drankwinkel* (liquor store), and women walk with enormous clay water jugs balanced on their heads. You can't get farther away from tourists than this. Since there are few amenities here and supplies at the restaurant and the supermarket are spartan at best, travelers should bring their own provisions.

To reach town, follow the same route as to Nwanedi (see p. 344) but instead of turning left at Muswodi toward the park, turn right toward **Sagole Spa;** the entrance to the resort (the only place to stay in the village) is about 15 kilometers down the road on the left. Drivers should beware of belligerent donkeys along the road. Outside the entrance to the Spa is the **post office** (open M-F 8:30am-4:30pm), a **bar,** a small **restaurant** (open daily 6am-7pm), and a **supermarket** (open M-Sa 7am-6pm), all lined up along the main road. Visitors can find accommodations inside the main gate to the Spa, where there are rather small *rondavels* with no power (R65, with bath R90). There are also spacious though spartan cottages that sleep up to six. Each cottage has its own hot spring pool. All this is a bargain for two or more people at R220 per night. Dorms are also available (R10; open daily 6am-6pm).

About 4km from the main road, just before Sagole and marked by a signpost off to the left as you come into the town, is the **Big Tree**. Upon first encounter one can only stare at it and think, "Man, that's a BIG ol' tree." After an estimated 3000 years of prodigious growth, this **baobab** is arguably the largest in Southern Africa (Tzaneen's mighty baobab looks like this tree's baby brother), with a 43m trunk and roots that extend for 5km.

LETABA DISTRICT

Most people who speed through the Letaba District on the way to Kruger National Park or Blyde River Canyon don't know what they are missing. Like most places of natural beauty, Letaba is better seen on foot for a few days than through a car window at 120km per hour. Those who make the commitment to explore will be rewarded with tangled stretches of indigenous forest amidst swaying grasslands and green hills, valleys with silver-sheeted dams, sheer mountain springs, and unexpected waterfalls spilling into pools far below. Letaba is called the "Garden of the Rain Queen," since it was the dwelling place of the Rain Queen Modjadji and is a rich agricultural area that grows most of South Africa's mangos, papayas, avocados, and tea leaves. The valley stretches from Haenertsburg through Tzaneen to Duivelskloof, hemmed in on the north by the forested Magoebaskloof Pass and on the south by the imposing rock faces of the Wolkberg Mountains (see p. 347).

The R71 leads east from Pietersburg to Haenertsburg. Here the road forks, and travelers can proceed to Tzaneen either on the mellow R528—which affords a few glimpses of the northern Drakensberg—or on the R71 down the beautiful (albeit steep and winding) Magoebaskloof Pass. The pass's namesake was Chief Makgoba, a Pedi chief who, along with a diverse band of breakaways, collaborated with Boers to raid neighboring lands. This fragile alliance was severed when Chief Makgoba refused to pay the government "hut tax." In response, the angered Boers turned on Makgoba and his followers, enlisting Swazi mercenaries to track the group through the treacherous terrain. The Swazis eventually located and killed Makgoba in the pass that now bears his name. A car is necessary to fully enjoy the valley, as outdoors destinations are often far from the town centers.

⚠ LETABA DISTRICT: OUTDOORS

The Greater Letaba District is South Africa's best kept secret (though not for long, as an international airport is under construction in Tzaneen). The district cradles peaceful hikes and waterfall pools that invite a dip, even in winter, and offers plenty of opportunities for overland antics in several ecological environments. To the south lies the mighty **Northern Drakensberg**, with rocky cliffs looming over the Letaba Valley. To the west is the **Magoebaskloof (ma-HO-ba-skloof) Pass,** a haven of hills and valleys blanketed in forests with an abundance of waterfalls and mountain streams. The owners of both **Satvik** and **Granny Dot's** (see **Accommodations,** p. 296) will lead area trips via 4X4. Daytrips will set you back R50-100 depending on the destination and duration. If you prefer to do it yourself, the tourist offices in Tzaneen and Haenertsburg can provide information. The **phone code** for all the numbers listed below is 015.

53km north of Tzaneen lies **Modjadji Cycad Reserve**, a beautiful mountainside of ancient ferns. There are pleasant picnic facilities and four walking trails through the forest. (Head north from Tzaneen on the R36 past the Big Baobab through Ga-Kapane and follow the sign to Ga-Modjaji, the village of the Rain Queen, 7km off the R36. Take a right off the tar road onto a bumpy dirt road, then take the left fork and head up the mountain for 5km. The reserve will be past the mountain village on the left. R2, plus R5 per car.) At the main park station of the **New Agatha Plantation** lies the head of the **Rooikat Hiking Trail.** This 11km circular forest route has picnic spots, river pools, and some steep gradients that reward the hiker with fantastic views of the Wolkberg and the Letaba Valley. Be sure to pick up a map; in some parts, the trail is hard to see. (Take the circular Agatha Rd. route south from the center of Tzaneen. About 1km after passing the turn-off to Granny Dot's on your right, the Plantation will be on your right. ☎307 4310.) South of Tzaneen off the R36, the **Wolkberg Wilderness Area** is a delightfully undeveloped stretch of forests and grasslands containing the Drakensberg's northernmost peaks. A 4WD vehicle is recommended for getting there. Access is by foot only, and self-reliance is imperative. (☎276 1303 or 276 4763. Camping permitted, but there are no facilities. No fires; bring gas stoves. Reservations required.) **Lekgalameetse Nature Reserve** has stunning scenery, swimming spots, and day and overnight trails. (44km south of Tzaneen. 4WD recommended. Take the R36 south toward Lydenburg, turn off at Ofcalco Rd. ☎303 0015.)

Magoebaskloof Pass boasts many sites, including the **Debegeni Waterfall**, a gorgeous gusher that puts the average trickling waterfall to shame. The surrounding area is tastefully developed and has wooden bridges and *braai*. In the summer, visitors can swim in any of the cool, natural pools along the breadth of the falls. Swimmers should think twice before stepping on the wet rocks, as a few unfortunate people have found them to be perilously slick. (To get there, take the R71 from Tzaneen about 14km toward Pietersburg and follow the signs for Debengeni Waterfall and SAFCOL hiking trails. Gate open daily 8am-5pm. R5.) Driving farther along the same gravel road past the waterfall (4WD highly recommended) will take you through the **Woodbush Forest,** the largest indigenous forest in the Northern Province. One or two kilometers from the falls is the **DeHoek Forest Station,** where the **Dokolewa** and **Grootbosch Trails** begin and end. These challenging three-day trails take hikers through the forest and afford magnificent views of the *lowveld*. Also in the area, up the same road, are the **Magoebaskloof Trails.** They include two-, three-, and five-day trails, plus day-hikes in the majestic Magoebaskloof range. (Book all hikes with SAFCOL, ☎276 4722. R50 per day.) Closer to Haenertsburg, the 11km **Louis Changuion Trail** affords breathtaking views and is not too difficult for inexperienced hikers. (Haenertsburg info center, ☎276 5047. Maps at tourist office.) **Filly's Way** offers one- and two-hour horseback rides through the Magoebaskloof area, traversing mountains and valleys for R70/R100. (☎276 6200. Tourist office 276 5047.) On the estate of Kings Walden Lodge, the **Kings Walden Garden** is a beautiful playground of reflecting pools and rosebushes with a stunning view of the Drakensberg's northern tip. Particularly striking is the stark white bluegum tree at the edge of the lawn, which owes its ivory pallor to a bolt of lightning. (Take Agatha Rd. south from the center of Tzaneen about 11 km. Take a left at the T junction and pass Granny Dot's on your right. Take a left at the sign that leads back to Tzaneen and KWG will be on your right. ☎ 307 3262. Open daily 9am-late. R5, children free.) Yet another "big" baobab, **Big Baobab** is a must-see for the pub and wine cellar built into its hollowed-out trunk. Sadly, the pub only turns on its taps for pre-booked functions. (40km north of Tzaneen. Head north on the R36, through Duivelskloof, and turn off at the "Sunland Baobab" sign. ☎309 9039, 082 413 8882, or 083 453 2228. Gates open daily 8am-6pm. R10.)

TZANEEN ☎015

With a population of 80,000 and a thriving business district, Tzaneen (zah-NEEN) is one of the largest commercial centers in the Northern Province. In spite of its productivity, Tzaneen (known as the "jewel of the north") manages to be a modern town without congestion or concrete sprawl; indeed, it offers all the services of nearby Pietersburg in an environment that will impress, not distress, the aesthetically inclined. Much of Tzaneen's charm lies in its refusal to conform to the grid-pattern of urban development; Instead of cutting right-angles, its streets wind and meander like mountain streams. With excellent accommodations and good supplies, Tzaneen is the perfect home base for exploring the Greater Letaba region.

[⌐ TRANSPORTATION. North Link** (☎ 307 2950 or 015 291 1867) runs daily buses to Johannesburg (6hr., M-Sa 8:30am, R135) and Phalaborwa (1½hr.; Th, F, Su 6:30pm; R35). **Minibus taxis** stop behind Tzaneng Mall and go to Phalaborwa (R30), Pretoria (R65), and Johannesburg (R70). To Pietersburg, make a connection in Boyne (R20). To rent a car, visit **Avis,** on Danie Joubert St. in the Delta Building. (☎ 307 1573. Open M-F 8am-5pm, Sa 8am-noon.)

▟▐ ORIENTATION AND PRACTICAL INFORMATION. Tzaneen lies 80km east of Pietersburg on the R71. Directions to the town center are clearly marked on all major routes. The main street through town is **Danie Joubert St.,** lined with shops, restaurants and most town services. On the northern end of Danie Joubert St. is a big four-way stop. Coming from the center of town, a right turn here leads to the **R71** east toward Phalaborwa; left is **R528** southwest toward George's Valley. The R528 connects with the R36, which, in turn, connects with the R71 heading west to Pietersburg. Going straight leads to **Voortrekker St.** running north to Tzaneen Dam.

The **tourist office** is at 25 Danie Joubert St. (☎ 307 1294; alfa@mweb.co.za. Open M-F 8am-5pm and Sa 9am-noon.) Services include: **Trappers Trading Company,** for camping equipment, in Tzaneng Mall (☎ 307 5668; open M-F 8am-5pm, Sa 8am-1pm; MC/V); **Standard Bank,** at the corner of Morgan and Lannie St., with **ATMs** (☎ 307 3785; open M-F 8:30am 3:30pm, Sa 8:30-11am); **Pick 'n Pay supermarket,** in the mall (open M-F 9am-6pm, Sa 8am-3pm, Su 9am-1pm); **police** (☎ 10 111 or 306-2129), on Danie Joubert St.; **Clicks Pharmacy,** in the mall (open M-F 8:30am-5:30pm, Sa 8:30am-1pm); **Van Velden Hospital,** on Claude Wheatley St. (☎ 307 4475; open 24hr.); **ProCom Internet Cafe,** 18 Peace St. (☎ 307 4836; open M-F 8am-7pm, Sa 9am-1pm; R15 per 30min.); the **post office,** with *Poste Restante,* on the corner of Morgan and Lannie St. (☎ 307 3616; open M-Tu and Th-F 8:30am-4:30pm, W 9am-4:30pm, Sa 8am-noon). **Postal code:** 0850.

▐ ACCOMMODATIONS AND CAMPING. **▨Satvik Village Backpackers ❶,** on George's Valley Rd. (R528), is an affordable haven of bungalows located right on the Tzaneen Dam that attracts a number of backpackers. Coming from Tzaneen, drive past the bright green Satvik farm stall on the left; the hostel is 50m farther down on the right. Highlights include nightly campfires, a pizza oven, swimming in the Dam, tropical vegetation, and, mmmm, *braai.* The thatch-roofed rooms are colorfully painted and quite cheerful, but lack electrical outlets and can be a bit chilly on winter nights. The showers are constructed of bamboo and huge palm leaves and create the perfect outdoor hygienic experience. Monkeys run rampant in these parts, so pack your belongings and hide your bananas. Common lounge and kitchen. Daytrips to mountain sites are available. Perfect for active nature-lovers. (☎/fax 307 3920; satvik@pixie.co.za. Laundry. Check-out 10am. Dorms R50; doubles R140; 2- to 4-person cottages with bath R250. Campsites R25 per person.) If backpacking isn't your style, head for **▨Granny Dot's Country Spot ❷,** which lives up to its slogan, "Home away from home—only better." To get to Granny's, follow Danie Joubert St. south until it turns into Peace St. Turn onto Agatha and continue south 11.5km to the T-junction. Turn left; the turn-off for the cottage is on the right at the bottom of the hill (look for the sign). A family homestead since 1944, Granny Dot's features comfortable rooms, great food, a lovely view of the Agatha forests, self-catering units, a pub, and a com-

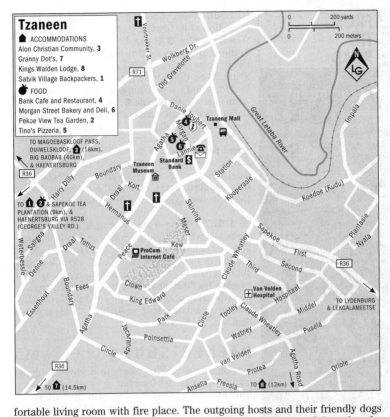

Tzaneen

🏠 ACCOMMODATIONS
Alon Christian Community, **3**
Granny Dot's, **7**
Kings Walden Lodge, **8**
Satvik Village Backpackers, **1**

🍴 FOOD
Bank Cafe and Restaurant, **4**
Morgan Street Bakery and Deli, **6**
Pekoe View Tea Garden, **2**
Tino's Pizzeria, **5**

fortable living room with fire place. The outgoing hosts and their friendly dogs will show you to a dam on the property where you can swim or fish, and to the Rooikat hiking trail, which is only a short walk away. (☎307 5149 or 083 702 3431; mwbisset@mweb.co.za. 4X4 drives into the Wolksberg (R60). Limited wheelchair access. Breakfast included; dinner by request. Singles R180; doubles from R280. Credit cards accepted.) More elegant than Granny Dot's but less homey, **Kings Walden Lodge ❸** is off of Agatha Rd. From town, take the R36 toward Lydenburg and follow signs onto Claude Wheatley St., which becomes Agatha Rd. This idyllic, old-fashioned getaway is surrounded by beautiful gardens and a stunning view of the northern Klein Drakensberg. (☎307 3262 or 083 380 3262. Guided hikes. Wheelchair accessible. Breakfast included. Check-out noon. Dinner R85 on request. R245 per person. Credit cards accepted.) **Alon Christian Community ❶** provides a unique alternative to the hostels and the mountain lodges. An amazing estate on a working farm run by a group of Christian missionaries just outside of Duiwelskloof, Alon is a beautiful example of a community. The rooms are nicely decorated, immaculately clean, and enjoy a sweeping view of the entire Tzaneen Valley, Magoebaskloof, and the Drakensberg Range. The community welcomes all visitors, regardless of spiritual affiliation, but be prepared to hear the gospel. There are no fixed rates, but donations are accepted in the form of money or labor. Contact Jonathan in advance at ☎083 444 9138 or email alona@tzaneen.co.za.

NORTHERN PROVINCE

FROM THE ROAD

LOST AND FOUND

When I was traveling in the Northern Province, I spent a few nights at a place called Satvik Backpackers in Tzaneen. I arrived there in the afternoon after a long, hot, frustrating day of research and immediately went for a long swim in the lake. When it began to get dark, I went to sit around the fire with the other backpackers and a fantastically thin old man named Joezi, who worked at the hostel. Three of the backpackers were from Holland and invited me to go hiking in the Wolkberg wilderness with them the next day.

We set out early in their car, following the directions they had gotten from the manager of the Magoebaskloof Hotel, a German named Horst. We must have taken a wrong turn somewhere, because we kept driving and driving and the road got worse and worse, and there was no sign of the forest station where the trails were supposed to begin. When the potholes in the road got so bad that the bottom of the car was striking the ground, we got out and walked beside the car to reduce the weight inside. When the road got worse than that, we left the car and struck out on foot.

We followed an old dirt road that led us uphill around steep precipices overlooking the valley below, and the terrain gradually changed from grassland to thick forest. After about three hours, we had run out of water and jelly sandwiches and were thinking about turning back. Just then, a Land Rover came hurtling down the dirt road and stopped beside us.

Inside was Horst and his wife, a rancher named John and his wife, and

(Continued on next page)

🍴 **FOOD.** Feast your eyes on the luscious green tea plantation while treating your taste buds at the **Pekoe View Tea Garden ❶** at Sapekoe Plantation, 9km from Tzaneen. Delicious sandwiches (R10), garden salads (R25), home baking (R6-10), and, of course, tea (R3-8) await you. (Take the R71 west toward Magoebaskloof Pass and Haenertsburg. ☎ 305-4321. Open daily 10am-5pm.) **Tino's Pizzeria ❶**, on Agatha St., has good Italian food, pizza, pasta, and cocktails. The garlic foccaccia bread (R15-35) is great. (☎ 307-1893. Open daily 12pm-10pm. Sunday brunch available.) **Morgan Street Bakery and Deli ❶**, on Morgan St., has good sandwiches (R5-10) and fresh bread (R3-5). (Open daily 6:30am-5:30pm.) After hours, shoot pool at **Bank Cafe and Restaurant,** next to the tourist office on Danie Joubert. (Open daily 7am-9pm.)

🔲 **SIGHTS. Tzaneen Museum,** on Agatha near Skirving St., showcases Tsonga, Sotho, and Afrikaner artifacts, including a sacred drum donated by Modjadji, the fourth Rain Queen. (☎ 307 2425. Open M-F 9am-4pm, Sa 9am-noon. Free, donations accepted.) The **Sapekoe Tea Plantation** offers the opportunity to learn everything about the production of tea in Letaba District on a plantation tour. (☎ 305 4321. Tours available Sept.-Mar., M-Sa 11am.)

HAENERTSBURG ☎ 015

Driving east from Pietersburg to Haenertsburg, the land rapidly changes from flat, dry *bushveld* to steep hills and valleys covered in lush green forests. Perched up in the hills, Haenertsburg looks like a little piece of Austria transplanted to Africa. A tiny village of just one main street, this is a lovely place to enjoy a quiet meal before or after enjoying the great outdoors of the Letaba District. Originally a gold rush town that sprung up in 1887, Haenertsburg is now a destination for the avid hiker, the urban escapee, and the nature lover.

🛈 **PRACTICAL INFORMATION.** Two hundred meters off the main highway up Rissik St. is the **Magoebaskloof Tourism Association,** at the Atholl Arms, which can arrange accommodations and activities. (☎ 276 5047. Open M-F 9am-5pm, Sa 9am-noon.) Services include: **police station** (☎ 276 4771 or 276 4772.), off Rissik on Rush St.; 24hr. **medical service** from Dr. Richard Gorbaszevicz (☎ 276-4710); and the **post office,** on Rush St. across from the police station (open M-Tu and Th-F 8:30am-1pm and 2-4:30pm, W 9am-1pm and 2-4:30pm, Sa 8am-noon). **Postal code:** 0730.

▛ ACCOMMODATIONS. It's worth stopping in Haenertsburg just to spend the night at the ▨**Bali Will Will Farm Guest House ❷.** From the R71, turn into Haenertsburg and left onto Rush St. At the T intersection turn left; the guest house is 5km down the dirt road. Situated on a beautiful working timber farm with a glorious view of the surrounding countryside, this highly recommended farmhouse features lovely rooms, great food, and charming hosts. (☎276 2212. Breakfast included; dinner by request. Singles R130; doubles R240. Self-catering cottage R200 for 2 people, each additional person R85.) The **Log Cabin ❷,** about 7km after Haenertsburg toward Tzaneen, marked by a sign on the left-hand side of the R71, is exactly what the name implies. (☎276 4242, 276 2104 or 083 269 3552. Breakfast R30. Check-out 10am. Singles R140; doubles R240.)

◨ ᒍ FOOD AND ENTERTAINMENT. Picasso's ❶, in a big cabin-style building right off the R71 in Haenertsburg, offers some of the finest pancakes in the province. They're warm and very satisfying, in both sweet and savory incarnations (R15-22). Sandwiches and salads are also served. (☎276-4724. Open daily 8:30am-4:30pm, and F-Sa 6:30-10pm.) The **Iron Crown Mountain Pub ❶,** on Rissik St. next to the BP station, offers a good variety of "pub food" (R12-35) and a place to shoot some pool. Every Friday night, the locals flock here for pizzas baked in a big stone oven out back. (☎276-4755. Open M noon-late, Tu-Th 11am-late, F-Su 10am-late.) In the last week of September and first week of October, Haenertsburg holds its annual **Spring Festival.** The azaleas, crab apple flowers, and cherry blossoms that splash the hillsides with glowing colors are the real attractions of this small country festival, which features craft stalls.

PHALABORWA ☎015

Phalaborwa (pa-la-BOR-ah), a pleasant little town at one of the gates of Kruger National Park, has become a popular base for exploring the Park, offering better accommodations at lower prices than those available in the Park itself. The town grew up around a phosphate and copper mine, now one of the largest opencast mines in the world. But forget those old images of mining towns with ramshackle log cabins and air blackened by smokestack grime. Phalaborwa is new, clean, and surprisingly attractive, thanks to the community-minded efforts of the mining companies, which are still by far the town's biggest employers. A tidy community of parks and shops traversed by wide roads, Phalaborwa today provides all the amenities of a friendly small town, all within a stone's throw of Kruger Park.

(Continued from previous page)

some farm hands sitting in the back. It turned out that we had wandered onto John's property and were over 16km from the forest station. We all piled into the back with the farm hands and went back to John's house for lunch. He showed us some prehistoric stone tools he had found that morning and then took us to explore some caves on the property. He said there was one cave he wanted to check out in particular, as he had been chased out of it by a leopard a few days before. When we got there, he sent his dogs in first, then Horst with a flashlight and pistol, and then the rest of us. We only found bats and porcupine quills.

At sundown, we drove up to the top of a mountain called the Iron Crown with a cooler of drinks and watched the sun go down in the valley below. The last rays of the sun illuminated dark green forests on the rolling hills that stretched into the distance as far as we could see and reflected brilliant flashes of light as it caught lakes and rivers. The baboons had come out to watch us and we could see rows of their dark shapes sitting on the ledges above our vantage point. Without speaking, we listened to the quiet noises around us for a long time before going home.

—Joshua Gardner

TRANSPORTATION. The **Phalaborwa/Kruger Park Airport** is off President Steyn St. on the northeast side of town. **South African Airways Airlink** (☎781 5823 or 781 5833) flies to **Johannesburg** (1hr.; M-F 3 flights per day, Sa-Su 2 per day; R858 one-way with advance notice, R2300 round trip). **North Link** (☎011 773 5857) buses stop in front of Impala Protea Inn on the corner of Palm Ave. and Essenhout St. and run to **Johannesburg** (4½hr., daily) and **Pietersburg** (3hr., daily). **Translux** 011 774 3333) also has service to Johannesburg. The **minibus taxi** rank is on the corner of Melor and Sealene St., behind ShopRite. Minibuses travel to **Hoedspruit** (R25), **Kruger Gate** (R10), and **Tzaneen** (R25).

ORIENTATION AND PRACTICAL INFORMATION. Phalaborwa is spread over a wide area, with residential streets and undeveloped land separating the central business district from outlying restaurants and accommodations, most of which lie east of town on **Koper Rd.** The main road is **Hendrick Van Eck Dr.,** which leads west to Tzaneen and east to the Phalaborwa gate of Kruger National Park. This gate is the most convenient for the Letaba and Balule rest camps, and is within reasonable distance of the Tambotie and Satara camps. The business district lies west of **Selati Rd.,** between **Tambotie St.** and **Sealene Rd.**

Outdoor Trading (☎083 227 8287), on Palm Ave. near the mall, has camping gear. (Open M-F 8am-5pm, Sa 8am-1pm.) Services include: **Phalaborwa Tourism** (☎781-6770), on Wildewy Ave; the **Tourist Information phone line** (☎780 6392; M-Th 7am-6pm and F 7am-4pm); **ABSA Bank,** with **ATMs,** on Wilger St. (open M-F 8:30am-3:30pm, Sa 8-11am); **emergency** ☎10 111; **CNA** (☎082 285 1436), a pharmacy in the Phalaborwa Mall (open M-F 8am-6pm, Sa-Su 9am-1pm); **Phalaborwa Hospital** (☎781 3511), on Grosvenor Crescent St.; **Net-O-Mania,** in Phalaborwa Mall, for Internet access (R24 per hr.; open M-F 8am-5pm, Sa 8am-1pm); **Pick 'n Pay,** a supermarket in Phalaborwa Mall (open M-F 8am-7pm, Sa 8am-6pm, Su 8am-1pm). The **Post Office** (☎781 1711), at Selati St. and Tambotie St. has *Poste Restante.* (Open M-Tu and Th-F 8:30am-4:30pm, W 9am-4:30pm, Sa 8am-noon.) **Postal code:**1390.

ACCOMMODATIONS. Elephant Walk Backpackers ❶, 30 Anna Scheepers St. (☎781 2758, 781 5860 or 082 495 0575) feels more like a comfortable apartment than a hostel. On Hendrick Van Eck St. going east toward Kruger, turn right at the Spar onto Koper Rd., right onto Essenhout St., and then left onto Anna Scheepers St. The owner of the hostel is the real gem. A virtual tourist board within one woman, she will tell you anything you want to know about Phalaborwa and book all types of trips into Kruger. She also has a B&B and two huge self-catering cottages at Phalaborwa Gate. (Free pick-up from town, secure parking, and fully equipped kitchen. Dorms R60; doubles R70, with breakfast R90. B&B singles R120; doubles R200. Cottages R90 per person, children R60, min. R270.) Colorful and bright, both in decor and personality, **Daan & Zena's B&B ❶,** 15 Birkenhead St., prides itself on being the friendliest place to stay in Phalaborwa. Going east on Hendrik Van Eck St. toward Kruger Park, turn left at the Spar onto President Kruger and then left onto Birkenhead. Signs off Hendrick Van Eck St. will lead you directly to the B&B. Zena paints all of the rooms herself with bright blues and pinks, and Daan paints the atmosphere with his local knowledge and enthusiasm. The rooms include TVs, and there is a swimming pool and courtesy bar. Daan can tell you about local township tours. (☎781 6049, 082 920 8808 or 082 920 0071; daan-zena@nix.co.za; twosummers.com/daanzena.htm. Communal lounge and kitchen and secure parking. Breakfast R20. Dinner R30. Laundry R15. Singles R80; doubles with private bath R200; 4-person cottages R100 per person.) **Matomani Lodge ❸,** on Essenhout at Selati St., is a peaceful, family-run place within walking distance of all the action in Phalaborwa. "Budget suites" contain two bedrooms, kitchen, bath, and dining area. Tours to Kruger can be arranged. (Breakfast R45. Dinner R50. Singles R215; doubles R290.)

🗋🗒 **FOOD AND NIGHTLIFE. Buffalo Pub and Grill ❶** (☎ 781 0829), at the corner of Lekkerbreek St. and Hendrick Van Eck St., is a friendly, informal place for good food and beer. Offerings include burgers (R10), steaks (R20-30), great chicken stir-fry (R15). It's lively on weekends and Wednesday nights. (Open daily 11am-late, kitchen closes 10pm.) **Sefapane Lodge ❷** (☎ 781 7041), on Koper Rd., is the best place in town for a fine sit-down meal. Main courses and grills cost R30-50; salads cost R12-20. (Open daily 6:30-9am and 6:30-9pm. **Catagoonz ❶** (☎ 781 3478), on Wildewy Rd. near the center of town, is the center of nightlife in Phalaborwa. Its large bar has a dance floor, pool tables, and live entertainment. (Open M-Sa 8pm-late.)

🗗🗒 **SIGHTS AND ADVENTURES.** Phalaborwa's lifeline, the open-cast **Phalaborwa Copper Mine,** is the largest artificially constructed hole in Africa and the second biggest copper mine in the world at 2km wide and 1km deep. You could put Big Ben inside the hole and it would look as big as a peanut in a coffee mug. (On Koper (Copper) Rd. near Kruger Park's Phalaborwa gate. ☎ 780 2911 or 780 2809. Book ahead for tours. Tours F 9am leave from the mine's main gate and stay above ground. Or ask the owners of Elephant Walk or Daan and Zena's to take you up to the lookout point for a great aerial view. Free.) Located in the first residential house in Phalaborwa, the **Foskor Museum** is a small, private museum, outlining the history of mining in the area, and makes a nice prelude to a copper mine visit. (16 Tambotie St. ☎ 789 2024. Open M-Th 1pm-4pm. Free, but call in advance.)

For one of the biggest thrills in South Africa, take off at sunrise on a **microlight flip** through the Kruger Park. You can skim just a few meters above the Olifants River, barely out of reach of snapping crocodiles and hippos. At R250 for 30 minutes or R500 for an hour, these flights are pricey, but the unique bird's-eye perspective on Kruger is worth the money, not to mention the fact that you'll fly over sections of the park that auto tourists never see. (☎ 082 956 1502. Minimum 2 people.) Alternately, take a **river safari** on the Olifants River, in search of fast-snapping crocodiles and thirsty elephants. **Olifants Safaris** offers popular evening cruises on a two-level boat with a full bar, ending in a night-time *braai* at their camp by the riverside. (☎ 781 0061 or 082 450 5230. Cruises R50 per person.) **Select-A-Safari** is more expensive but has an excellent reputation for professionalism and service. (☎ 781 3418 or 082 331 6937; select-a-safari@twosummers.com; www.twosummers.com/safari.htm. Cruises R150 per person.) **Jumbo River Safaris** also offers various safari options. (☎ 781 6168 or 083 580 5703. Cruises R50 per person, R350 minimum.) For those who prefer to stay on dry land, **Bataleur Street Stables** offers horesback riding around the area (☎ 082 802 2103).

MPUMALANGA

Spectacular scenery and roaming game lure travelers to Mpumalanga, a region of mountains, canyons, green forests, and sprawling *lowveld*. Mpumalanga means "sunrise," an appropriate name for an eastern province. A web of scenic drives and hiking trails traverses the province, appetizers to the region's premier attractions of Blyde River Canyon and Kruger National Park.

In the 19th century, this territory was a gold mine (literally) for fortune hunters. Vestiges of this era include abandoned mine shafts, prospector's trenches, and old oxcart roads. When quantities of gold were discovered elsewhere in 1876, gold mining in the *lowveld* was replaced by timber farming. A local timber merchant planted tracts of fast-growing eucalyptus (blue-gum) and pine trees, launching the successful tree plantations that today blanket the hills. However, most visitors don't come to Mpumalanga for its trees. Almost certainly the most popular destination is Kruger National Park, South Africa's oldest, largest, and most famous national park. Traversed by a network of paved roads and rest camps, Kruger offers the opportunity to see hundreds of animal species, including the famous Big Five, in their natural habitat. Although the majority of the park lies in the Northern Province, most visitors enter through the Mpumalanga gates.

West of Kruger, the *lowveld* escalates into the heady heights of the northern Drakensberg (peaking at about 2500m). Within this range is the fabulous Panorama Route, a natural amusement park of waterfalls, cliff-top vantage points, and outdoor pools. The awe-inspiring Blyde River Canyon—mother of all mountain cavities—lies at the northern edge of the route, its sheer cliffs and glimmering waters among South Africa's most stunning sights.

HIGHLIGHTS OF MPUMALANGA

An immense reserve dedicated to the conservation of South Africa's wildlife, **Kruger National Park** (see p. 365) is prime territory for spotting the Big Five.

Explore **Kaapsehoop** (see p. 359), enjoy the hospitality of local guest houses, and look out for wild horses roaming the village.

The **Blyde River Canyon Nature Reserve** (see p. 378) is spectacular from any vantage point, from the top of the Blydepoort Dam to the green depths of the canyon itself.

Hike through the forest surrounding **Sabie** (see p. 376) to one of the area's seven **waterfalls** for a swim or a picnic.

But apart from all the things to see in Mpumalanga, there is also lots to do. The province's extensive hiking trails range from the casual to the intense, while those with a taste for more excitement can choose from a range of outdoor adventures that include mountain biking, rafting, horseback riding, canyon-swinging, and hot-air ballooning. Mpumalanga is a worthy destination for nature lovers and outdoor enthusiasts, however they choose to experience the world around them.

NELSPRUIT ☎ 013

Nelspruit (NEL-sprate, pop. 24,000) is the capital of Mpumalanga and one of the fastest-growing cities in South Africa. The city was founded in 1905 in connection with the construction of a railway line between Pretoria and Maputo. But things only began taking off when South Africa's post-apartheid government drew up new provinces and made Nelspruit a provincial capital. Today, the city's bustling

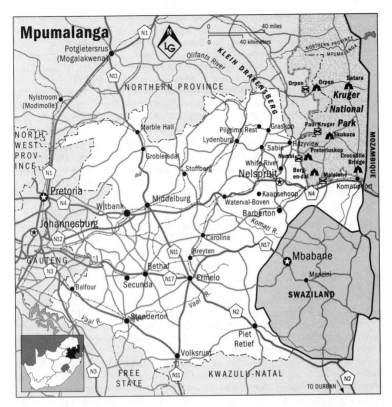

Central Business District stands in sharp contrast to the rural feel of most of the province and is one of the few places in Mpumalanga where you may even witness a traffic jam. Meanwhile, the steamy climate and palms are reminders that Mozambique and the Indian Ocean are just a few hours away. Most travelers use Nelspruit as a base supply camp, a place to buy some new duds, catch a movie, and log on to that dormant email account before heading back into nature. With good accommodations and restaurants, active nightlife, and a contingent of international backpackers, Nelspruit provides a welcome break from the slow pace of the province.

TRANSPORTATION

Flights: Nelspruit Airport (☎ 741 3192) is southwest of town off the Kaapsehoop Rd. **South African Airlink** (☎ 741 3557 or 741 3536) flies to **Durban** (1¼hr., daily, R1292 one-way) and **Johannesburg** (1hr., 5 times daily, R996 one-way).

Trains: Spoornet's **Komati Train** runs daily to **Johannesburg** (10hr.; daily 8:39pm; 2nd-class R90, first-class R130) and **Komatipoort** (3hr., daily 4:15am, R25/40), traveling in the dead of night—not the safest time. A connecting train travels from Komatipoort to **Maputo, Mozambique** (7hr.; 57,500Mt). Spoornet tickets should be purchased at least 1 day before departure from the **train station** (☎ 752 9257 or 752 9207), on the corner of Andrew St. and Henshall St. (Open M-F 7:30am-4pm.)

Buses: Greyhound, Translux, and **Mats Trans** buses stop in front of the Promenade Hotel. Greyhound tickets can be bought at the Greyhound office (☎753 2100) in the Promenade Hotel (open M-F 7am-9pm, Sa 7am-noon and 4-9pm, Su 3-9pm) and Translux tickets can be bought at Lowveld Promotions, which is moving to the Promenade Hotel (☎752 6108 or 752 5134). Greyhound runs to **Johannesburg** (5½hr.; M-Sa 7:30am, Su 4:15pm; R125). Translux also runs to **Johannesburg** (5½hr., daily 11:30am, R108). Mats Trans buses (☎753 6000) go to **Barberton** (40min., every hr. 1-4pm, R10). **City-bug** (☎741 4117) runs a shuttle to **Pretoria** (3½hr.; M-F 6 and 10am, Sa 6am, Su noon; R145) with a stop in **Johannesburg** (3hr., R145 or R160 to the airport). Book buses a few days in advance.

Minibus Taxis: Minibuses line up at the back of Nelspruit Plaza, on the corner of Henshall and Bester St., near the train station. Be careful after dark. To **Barberton** (R10); **Johannesburg** (R70); **Maputo, Mozambique** (R70); and **Sabie** (R15). There are also large inter-city buses that leave from a parking lot near the corner of Bester St. and Petroleum St., just east of the center.

Taxis: City Bug (☎741 4117 or 744 0128). One-way from city center to the airport R35.

Car Rental: National (☎752 4335) and **Tempest** (☎755 3481) are the cheaper alternatives to **Avis** (☎741 1087), **Budget** (☎741 3885), **Europcar** (☎741 3062), **Hertz** (☎741 2837), and **Imperial** (☎741 3210). All are at the airport.

■✳️🛈 ORIENTATION AND PRACTICAL INFORMATION

The N4 runs east-west through the center of Nelspruit, becoming **Louis Trichardt St.** in town, and extending west to Pretoria and east to Malelane and Komatipoort. The main north-south conduit is the R40, which runs south to Barberton and north to White River and Hazyview past the new **Riverside Mall**. It intersects with the N4/Louis Trichardt St. as **General Dan Pienaar St.** just west of the town's Central Business District (CBD). Shops, malls, and restaurants flank Louis Trichardt St. and **Paul Kruger St.,** while most banks are on **Brown St.,** one block north of Louis Trichardt St. A number of shops and services are also in the **Promenade Center,** on Louis Trichardt St. between Voortrekker St. and Henshall St. South of the town center is a suburban neighborhood with backpackers, pubs, restaurants, and strip malls, dominated by the **SonPark Center** on **Piet Retief St.** Paul Kruger St. becomes **Ferreira St.,** and putters south to this busy area. West of town off Louis Trichardt St. is **Kaapsehoop Rd.,** leading to the airport and Kaapsehoop.

Tourist office: Lowveld Tourism (☎755 1988; fax 755 1350; nelspruit@soft.co.za), in the foyer of the Civic Center, with maps. Heading east toward the CBD, turn right off the N4 at "Civic Center" onto Nell St. Open M-F 8am-4:30pm, Sa 9am-5pm, Su 10am-2pm.

Banks: First National Bank (☎754 2000) on Bester and Voortrekker St. Open M-F 9am-3:30pm, Sa 8-11am. **Standard Bank** on Brown St. Open M-F 8:30am-3:30pm, Sa 8:30-11am. **ATMs** at both banks, **SonPark Center,** and throughout the CBD.

Consulates: Mozambique (☎752 7396 or 753 2089), in the CVA building on Bester near De Waal St. To obtain a visa (R85), bring 2 ID photos (which you can get at any pharmacy) and fill out a form. Allow 24hr. for processing. Open M-F 8:30am-3pm, visa section open M-F 8:30-11am.

Bookstores: Exclusive Books (☎757 0352), on White River Rd. in the Riverside Mall, has a large selection. Open M-F 9am-9pm, Sa 9am-10pm, Su 9am-8pm.

Camping and Outdoor Gear: Trappers Trading Co. (☎757 1345), in the Riverside Value Mart, north of town off the R40, just before the Riverside Mall. Open M-F 8am-5pm, Sa 8am-3pm, Su 9am-1pm.

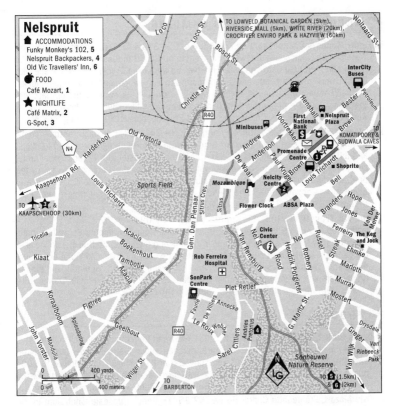

Nelspruit

▲ ACCOMMODATIONS
Funky Monkey's 102, **5**
Nelspruit Backpackers, **4**
Old Vic Travellers' Inn, **6**

● FOOD
Café Mozart, **1**

★ NIGHTLIFE
Café Matrix, **2**
G-Spot, **3**

Supermarket: ShopRite, on Louis Trichardt St. in the center of town. Open M-F 8am-6pm, Sa 8am-5pm, Su 9am-1pm. **Kwik Spar,** in SonPark Center. Open daily 7am-9pm.

Laundry: Village Laundrette (☎ 755 2844), in the Village Center on Marloth St. Open M-F 7:30am-5pm, Sa 8am-1pm.

Emergency: ☎ 10 177 or 753 2285.

Police: ☎ 10 111 or 759 1000, at the corner of Henshall and Bester St.

Pharmacy: Family Circle, 31 Promenade Center (☎ 752 4860, emergency ☎ 741 1769). Open M-F 8am-6:30pm, Sa 8am-2pm.

Hospital: Nelspruit Private Hospital (☎ 759 0500), off John Vorster St. on the south side of town. **Rob Ferreira Hospital** (☎ 741 3031), on Piet Retief near Gen. Dan Pienaar St.

Telephones: There is a bank of phones outside the post office (watch your wallets here). Public telephones throughout the city and at Riverside Mall allow international calls, with no less risk to your wallet.

Internet Access: Nexus Internet Cafe (☎ 741 2237 or 741 2303), in the back of the SonPark Center. R12 per 30min., R20 per hr. Open M-Th 8am-9pm, F-Sa 8am-10pm, Su 11am-5pm. **Rendez-Vous** (☎ 752 8504), in the Promenade Center. R20 per hr. Open M-F 8am-5pm, Sa 9am-2pm.

Post Office: On Voortrekker St. next to Promenade Center. *Poste Restante.* Open M-Tu and Th-F 8:30am-4:30pm, W 9am-4:30pm, Sa 8am-noon. **Postal Code:** 1200.

M P U M A L A N G A

⛰ ACCOMMODATIONS AND CAMPING

🏠 **Funky Monkeys Backpackers** (☎ 744 0534 or 083 310 4755). Corner of Van Wijk and Waterbok St., 3km south of town. Driving south on Gen. Dan Pienaar, turn left onto Piet Retief and then right onto Van Wijk. Free pick-up from town. A friendly, lively place with bright colors, funky artwork, and an outdoor patio with swimming pool and hammocks. A steady stream of charming, colorful people, including the owner, hang out late into the night around a pink table with hanging lamps. It's like college without the homework. Laundry available. Dorms R50; singles R65; doubles R120. Camping R25. ❶

🏠 **Nelspruit Backpackers,** 9 Andries Pretorius St. (☎ 741 2237; nelback@hotmail.com). Driving south on Gen. Dan Pienaar, turn left onto Piet Retief, right onto Sarel Cilliers, and left onto Andries Pretorius. A relaxed, comfortable hostel with TV room, pool table, swimming pool, and outdoors bar with vintage reggae posters. Catch some rays by the pool, wander into adjoining Nelspruit Nature Reserve, or book tours to Kruger Park and Blyde River Canyon through the friendly, knowledgeable owners. Laundry available. Dorms R50; doubles R120. Camping R35 per person. ❶

Old Vic Travellers' Inn, 12 Impala St. (☎ 744 0993 or 083 340 1508; oldvic@mweb.co.za). Off Van Wijk St., 500m downhill from 12A Impala St. Follow directions to Funky Monkeys, turn right onto Waterbok and then left onto Duiker; Old Vic is at the intersection of Duiker and Impala. If hostels are not your style, Old Vic offers peace, quiet, and privacy at reasonable prices. Also has swimming pool, car rental, and trips to Kruger Park and elsewhere. Breakfast included. Laundry R35 per bundle. Dorms R60; singles R90, with private bath R140; doubles R140/160. ❶

🍴 FOOD

Ocean Basket, 17 Ferreira St. (☎ 752 7193). Set apart from the crowded city center, this cantaloupe-colored seafood restaurant is perched above a street corner in the southeast suburban area of town. Calamari curry starter R10. Kingklip and rice R28. 200g prawn R35. Selection of Italian desserts, with *baklava* and black forest cake thrown in for cosmopolitan variety, R12. Open M-Sa 11am-9:30pm, Su 11am-8:30pm. ❷

Cafe Mozart, Promenade Center 56 (☎ 752 2637). Popular upscale lunch spot in the center of town. Large-tiled floors, Rococo flower sculptures, and classical music. Patrons could listen to an entire symphony while choosing from the 4-page list of drinks alone. Heavenly flavored coffees R8. Breakfast "quartets" R19-24. *Tramazinno* (toasted pita bread with mozzarella cheese and a meat topping) R15.50. Decadent Salzburg cheesecake R10. Open daily 8am-4:30pm. ❷

Hillside Tavern (☎ 755 5040), in the Village Center at the end of Marloth St. A cozy restaurant and pub serving mostly Continental food. Oxtail in red wine R56. Good steaks and seafood, excellent service. Open daily noon-2pm and 6pm-late, closed Sa lunch. ❸

👁 ⛰ SIGHTS AND OUTDOORS

Established in 1969, the 25ha **Lowveld National Botanical Gardens** straddle the Crocodile River, supporting over 600 tree species and 245 bird species. Highlights include waterfalls, a tropical rain forest, and the most comprehensive collection of African cycads in the country. The gardens are the perfect place to escape the urban sprawl. A trail through the indigenous rain forest meanders past twisting fig trees and a hippo pool, while a two-hour **Riverside Trail** runs alongside the Crocodile River. To get there, follow General Dan Pienaar out of town; the gardens lie 5km north on the R40, toward White River. (☎ 752 5531. Open Oct.-Apr. daily 8am-6pm, May- Sept. daily 8am-5:15pm. Cafe closes at 5pm. R7, children and "scholars" R3. Maps R3 at the entrance gate.)

Once used by the Swazi king as a refuge from hostile Zulus, the **Sudwala Caves'** fascinating limestone formations warrant the 6hr. Crystal Cave Tour offered on the first Saturday of every month. To get there, head north on the N4 for 25km, then straight down. (☎733 4152. 1hr. guided tours 8:30am-4:30pm. R30, children 5-15 R16. Crystal Tour R90 and must be booked well in advance.)

🔊 🎤 ENTERTAINMENT AND NIGHTLIFE

The **Keg and Jock,** on the corner of Van der Merwe and Ferreira St., is an appealing bar and restaurant south of the center. A spacious tiered layout, glossy wooden picnic tables, and wide green umbrellas make a great place to while away the evening with a beer. (☎755 4969. Beer R6-10. Open daily 11:30am-late.) If you are in the mood to dance, **Cafe Matrix,** in the NelCity Plaza at the corner of Louis Tri-chardt and Kruger St., is where Nelspruit's young ravers get down to a trance beat. (Open F-Sa 10pm-late.) **G-Spot,** on the Kaapsehoop Road before the airport turn-off, is a local bar with occasional live entertainment. (☎072 291 6070. Open M-Tu and Th 11am-10pm, W 11am-2pm, F-Sa 11am-late, Su 11am-8pm.) **Blue Moon** (☎744 9033), on Uitkyk Rd. off Ferreira St. south of town, is a popular concert venue.

NEAR NELSPRUIT: KAAPSEHOOP ☎013

Kaapsehoop is a tiny mountainside hamlet with storybook charm. The town itself is just a handful of brick and wood-plank buildings scattered on a hilltop of grass fields and jutting sandstone rocks. Wild horses roam the surrounding forest and often trot into town to graze in people's backyards. When the sun shines, Kaapse-hoop seems like the perfect setting for an old-fashioned romance; but when the mist rolls in, the town looks positively sinister, making it easy to see why its founders once dubbed the place Duiwel's Kantoor ("the devil's office"). Swept up in South Africa's late 19th century gold fever, Kaapsehoop began as a miners' camp in 1882. Prospectors who took refuge from the vicious tsetse flies in these mountains eventually changed the settlement's name to Kaapsche Hoop, or "pla-teau of hope." In the 120 years since this bygone era of gold diggers, oxcarts, and wattle huts, Kaapsehoop has marched to the unhurried beat of a different drum, transforming from mining town to agricultural and forestry village, though grow-ing very little in size. The population of wild horses still outnumbers the 120 human inhabitants. Kaapsehoop offers hiking and horseback riding and makes a good daytrip from Nelspruit (30km).

🏠🍴 ACCOMMODATIONS AND FOOD. Kaapsehoop Horse Trails, 12km down the Berlin dirt road past the Berlin Forestry Station, is a lovely farm with good views of the hills, pleasant cottages, and lots of horses. Coming from Nelspruit, turn right before town on the dirt road to the Berlin Forest Station and continue a few kilo-meters past the Forest Station. Visitors are welcome to take a ride through the for-est. (☎734 4995. Furnished luxury cottage R150 per person for 1-3, R580 total for 4-6; self-catering trail-house rooms R90 per person, catered R140. Camping R50.) Take the main road, Kruger St., through town and turn right onto Kantoor St. at the Koek 'n Pan Restaurant to reach **Silver Mist Guest House ❷,** a pleasant guest house currently undergoing renovations. Rooms have en suite bath and TV. (☎734 4429. Breakfast included. Singles R190; doubles R340.) **Koek 'n Pan Restaurant,** at the end of the main road, serves good sandwiches (around R15), salads, and light lunches. (☎082 601 5455. Open M-F 8:30am-5pm, Sa 8am-5pm.) **The Green Venus,** on the main road, is a charming rustic pub and restaurant serving brick-oven pizzas (R15-30) and cheaper sandwiches. (☎734 4332. Open Tu-Su 11am-late, kitchen open 11:30am-4pm and 6-10pm. Closed Su night.)

ᴷᴸ OUTDOORS. Kaapsehoop's wild horses are supposedly descendants of horses owned by the gold miners of old. Domesticated horses can be saddled at **Kaapsehoop Horse Trails,** on the main road not far from town. Take the Berlin turn-off and follow the dirt road for 12km, past the Berlin Forestry Station. The guided horse trails lead riders through indigenous forest, plantation, and grassland, and afford fantastic views of the cycad-filled escarpment. If you're there for the full moon, don't miss out on one of the **moonlight rides.** (☎734 4995. 1½hr. trail R100; 2½hr. R140; 4-6hr. day ride R170; moonlight rides R100 with dinner; weekend trail R375-500; 3-day wilderness trail R650.) In the same area is a network of **hiking trails,** the easiest of which is a 1.5km stroll from the old cemetery to a beautiful waterfall. In addition, there is a 1hr. **nature walk** from town that runs to the escarpment, culminating in a lookout point over the De Kaap Valley. Additional two- to five-day trails can be booked through the station. For more information, call 012 418 3615 or contact the Nelspruit **SAFCOL office** (☎752 3244). Birders can visit the **Blue Swallow Natural Heritage Site,** a 500ha reserve for the endangered blue swallow. Visits are by appointment only. For more info, contact Edward Thembi at 072 340 5588.

BARBERTON   ☎013

Hidden in the De Kaap Valley of the Makonjwa mountain range, Barberton is a gold mine of a village. A small, peaceful place with good views of the surrounding countryside, Barberton has as a sense of history but is not as self-consciously done up for tourists as other towns. Travelers with an appreciation for period architecture will enjoy seeing the preserved Victorian homes and elegant turn-of-the-century buildings scattered around town. Prospectors' trenches remain cut into the hillsides and old mine shafts are still around, including one that you can hike through. In addition to its natural beauty and historical monuments, Barberton also offers good values for food and accommodation, making the town a natural place for a few days of R&R.

▐ TRANSPORTATION

Buses: Mats Trans (☎753 6000) serves Barberton. The buses leave from the corner of Crown and General St., and head to: **Kaapmuiden** (1hr.; 5:30, 10am, 1, 7pm; R5) and **Nelspruit** (40min.; 5, 5:30, 6:30, and 7am; R5.50).

Minibus Taxis: There are two ranks: a local one on the corner of Halder and Adcock St. next to Tip Top Music, and a regional one on General St. at the entrance to Emjindini township, about 2km north of town. A taxi between ranks costs R2.50. All minibuses going out of town leave from the township rank. To get to **Kruger National Park,** take a taxi to **Kaapmuiden** (1hr., R8) and then another one to **Malelane gate.** Minibuses run direct to **Nelspruit** (40min., R10). To get to the **Oshoek border** into Swaziland (no minibuses go to the closer Bulembu post), take a taxi to **Badplaas** (1½hr., R15), then to **Lochiel,** and finally to the **Oshoek border** (5hr.). The tourist office has minibus taxi info.

▐✷▐ ORIENTATION AND PRACTICAL INFORMATION

Barberton lies 45km south of Nelspruit on the R40. Coming from Nelspruit, the turn-off from the R40 toward Barberton is **General St.,** which leads south past **Emjindini** township and into town. General St. intersects with the main road through town, **Crown St.,** which leads east and turns into **Sheba St.** Sheba St. curves northward and intersects with the R40. A right turn at this intersection leads to Swaziland, continuing straight leads to Kaapmuiden and the Kruger National Park.

WHO THE #$%! IS JOCK?

You see his name everywhere: Jock of the Bushveld, Jock of the Bushveld statue, Jock of the Bushveld monument. You wonder, who is this bloody Jock character, and what's his claim to fame? Jock is South Africa's most famous canine, a tough little Staffordshire terrier who traveled the 19th-century trade routes with his master, Percy Fitzpatrick. Fitzpatrick belonged to a group of adventurous men called "transport riders," who made a living selling supplies in the Transvaal mining towns. These riders drove oxcarts over the mountains and through the *lowveld* to the port at Delagoa Bay (now Maputo), where they stocked up on goods to bring west. While accompanying Fitzpatrick on these journeys, Jock kept himself busy protecting his master from the perils of the wilderness. Blissfully ignorant of the importance of size, the pup fought off baboons, lions, and crocodiles with his squat Staffie might. In the end, Jock fell victim to the cruelest of predators: a misfired bullet from a neighbor's rifle. But his legend lives on in Percy Fitzpatrick's book *Jock of the Bushveld*, an amalgamation of transport riders' stories fused into the biography of one dog. The book (which has been made into a film and is required reading in all South African schools) has made Jock into a canine legend, personifying the dogged but free spirit of the frontier days. Jock's trail can be traced from Lydenburg to Pilgrim's Rest, Sabie, Pretoriuskop in Kruger National Park, Barberton, and Maputo. A statue of the little hero can be seen at the town hall in Barberton, and his tombstone rests below a somber acacia tree in Kaapmuiden.

Tourist office: Barberton Tourist Information Bureau (☎712 2121; fax 712 5120; barinfo@corpdial.co.za or umjindi@mweb.co.za), in Market Square, on Crown St. This very helpful office provides accurate maps, facts, and advice about what to see and how to get around the area. Open M-F 8am-4:30pm, Sa 8:30am-noon. If it's closed, ask for info at **Origins** (☎712 5055), at 20 Sheba Rd. Open M-F 8am-5pm, Sa 9am-1pm.

Banks: Standard Bank (☎712 3126), with **ATM** on the corner of Crown and President St. Open M-F 9am-3:30pm, Sa 8:30-11am.

Supermarket: ShopRite, on the corner of Crown and Adcock St. Open M-F 8am-6pm, Sa 7:30am-3pm, Su 8am-1pm. **Friendly Supermarket,** inside the Eureka Center at General and Nourse St. Open M-Sa 8am-8pm, Su 8am-3pm.

Pharmacy: Eksteen Apteek (☎712 2181), on Crown St. in the center of town. Open M-F 8am-5:15pm, Sa 8am-1pm, alternate Sundays 11am-noon.

Hospital: Medi Clinic Hospital (☎712 4279), where Sheba St. meets the R40. 24hr.

Police: (☎712 5522), on the corner of General St. and De Villiers St.

Telephones: Banks of phones are outside the post office and on Crown St. in front of the tourist office.

Post Office: Inside the Eureka Center, at General St. and Nourse St. Open M-F 8:30am-2pm, Sa 8:30am-3pm.

Postal Code: 1300.

🏠 ACCOMMODATIONS

Hillside Lodge B&B, 62 Pilgrim St. (☎712 4466 or 082 490 1901; hillside-lodg@mweb.co.za). Perched on a hillside just above town, this B&B offers visitors peace and quiet. Watch the sunset from the veranda or relax in the swimming pool. Organized tours of Mpumalanga. Breakfast included. Singles R150-170; doubles R270-300. ❷

Old Coach Road Guest House (☎719 9755; oldcoach@global.co.za), 12km from town on the R38 toward Kaapmuiden. Set in a haven of mountaintops and acacia trees within a nature reserve, the guest house offers modern rooms with bright decor. Swimming pool, hiking trails, and sundowner bar. Dining room offers views as outstanding as its meals. Call ahead for pick-up at Barberton or Nelspruit. Breakfast included. R180 per person. Discount for children under 9 years. 30% discount with *Let's Go.* ❷

Fountain Baths, 48 Pilgrim St. (☎712 2707; fax 712 3361). Near the corner of Sheba St. and Crown St. With the overall ambiance of a 19th-century hotel, cottages are arranged around a courtyard swimming pool and have a kitchen, bath, and antique furniture. Rooms on the veranda with shared baths are just as comfortable, though they lack kitchens. Cottages R120 per person sharing; veranda rooms R100 per person. ❶

🞄🞄 FOOD AND NIGHTLIFE

🞖 **The Gold Mine** (☎712 4373), in the Eureka Center, next to Friendly Supermarket. A large, mellow restaurant with maroon benches, yellow lanterns, and very good food. Pub lunches R15-20. Crumbed sole R41.50. Vegetarian lasagna R29.50. Tipsy tart R10. Open Tu-F noon-3pm and 6-10pm, M and Sa 6-10pm. Reserve on weekends. ❷

De Hollandse Hoek (☎712 4376), in the Eureka Center at the corner of Nourse and President St. An open, informal sort of place specializing in the Dutch delicacies of *krokets* (fried oblong treats stuffed with chicken or beef and mushrooms; R12.50). Also serves salads, sandwiches, pancakes, and pizza. Main dishes R20-30. Tom will make his amazing version of *bami* (Indonesian noodles with beef, garlic, and vegetables) upon request. Open daily 8am-8pm. ❶

Coco Pan (☎712 2653), at the eastern end of Crown St., next to the Caltex station. Through the small door at the back of this shop is a spacious dining room whose walls are adorned with pictures of the town's founders and miners of yore. Breakfast R20. Double thick milkshakes R8. Fried trout R30. Open M-Sa 8am-9pm, Su 8am-8pm. ❶

John Henry's Pub (☎712 2653), on De Villiers St., or enter from Coco Pan. A large basement room with bar, dance floor, and gambling machines. Dance music on weekends, occasional live acts. Open M-Sa 4pm-late.

🞄🞄 SIGHTS AND ADVENTURES

HOUSE MUSEUMS. These two museums offer an intimate look into everyday life at the turn of the century. Things are so faithfully preserved that you feel like the owners have just stepped out and will be back any moment. At the corner of Bowness and Lee St., the **Belhaven House Museum** is a beautifully restored late Victorian- style house that re-creates the lifestyle of an upper-class family. The **Stopforth House Museum** was rebuilt with wood and iron and depicts the life of a middle-class family. *(On the corner of Bowness and President St. Guided tours for each House Museum every hr. M-F 10am-3pm. R10 for both.)*

PILGRIM STREET MONUMENTS. The grand **De Kaap Stock Exchange Building,** built in 1887, hosted the first gold exchange in South Africa. The 1887 **Globe Tavern,** one of over 200 pubs that existed in Barberton during the gold rush, is today a trendy turquoise and purple coffee shop. The **Lewis and Marks** building was the first two-story building in Barberton and is now an *a la carte* restaurant.

EUREKA CITY. Those who really want to sink their picks into the history of the area should head over to the ghost town ruins of **Eureka City,** a mountaintop gold-mining town that thrived between 1886 and 1925. Miners built this elevated town to escape the scourge of malaria and tsetse flies in the valley below, descending during the day to work in the still-rich **Sheba Mine.** *(Day-long tours to Eureka City leave*

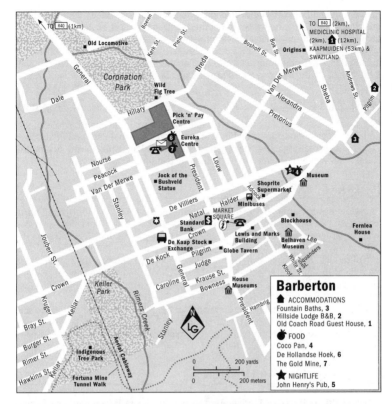

Barberton

▲ ACCOMMODATIONS
Fountain Baths, 3
Hillside Lodge B&B, 2
Old Coach Road Guest House, 1

🍴 FOOD
Coco Pan, 4
De Hollandse Hoek, 6
The Gold Mine, 7

★ NIGHTLIFE
John Henry's Pub, 5

daily at 9am from the municipal museum. For information and reservations, contact Origins, 20 Sheba Rd. ☎ 712 5055. 4-person minimum. R240 per person including lunch, entrance fees, and equipment; children under 12 half price.)

HIKING TRAILS. The **Fortuna Mine Walk** begins at Keller Park and leads 2km through the forest, passing through a 100-year-old ore-transport tunnel. The 600m tunnel is pitch-black and not for the faint of heart. Bring a flashlight to light your way. The **Pioneer Hiking Trail** is a difficult two-day, 18km trek through the forest, past creeks, a waterfall, and old mine tunnels. The trail begins 6km west of Barberton at the Ivy Store Base Camp on Moodie's Estates, and there are two huts for overnight stays. (☎ 082 268 4701 or 082 445 4467, or ask at the tourist office. R45 per person.) The **Queen Rose Hiking Trail** is a two-day, 20km hike of average difficulty. It begins near the Nelshoogte Forest Station east of Barberton and follows the Montrose and Queens Rivers through the mountains between Barberton and Badplaas. (☎ 013 712 2247, or ask at the tourist office.)

MALELANE ☎013

The Malelane gate is the closest entrance to Kruger Park from Nelspruit, Johannesburg, and Pretoria. As such, the tiny town of Malelane is a convenient place to stock up on food before entering the park, where prices of standard goods skyrocket. Off the N4 is a 24hr. Engen station and a few shops. If you are really dying

MPUMALANGA

to stay the night, **River Cottage ❸** is quite pleasant, if a bit pricey, and is a three-minute drive from the highway. To get there, turn onto Air St. at the Engen station, then right again after passing beneath the train tracks. Follow the signs to the cottages. (☎ 790 0825 or 082 921 5215; fax 790 1281. Singles R240; doubles R360 including breakfast.) Tourist information is available at **Daph's Leather Barn,** in the Spar Center right off the highway. (☎ 790 1013. Open M-F 8:30am-5pm, Sa 8:30am-1pm.)

HAZYVIEW ☎ 013

Hazyview consists of a few dusty strip malls and a wealth of superb accommodations within easy daytripping distance of the Kruger National Park and Blyde River Canyon. Its proximity to two park gates (Numbi and Paul Kruger) and its plentiful budget digs make Hazyview a great launching pad for a Kruger adventure.

▮ TRANSPORTATION

Hazyview lies about 50km north of Nelspruit on the R538 or R40. Driving north from Nelspruit/White River to Hazyview on the R40, a right turn at the T-junction leads to Kruger's **Numbi Gate** (see p. 367), 16km away, via the R538 and then the R569. A left at the T-junction leads to the main intersection in town, the intersection of the R40 and R536, with the Blue Haze shopping center on the corner. Turning right at this main intersection onto the R536 leads 45km to **Paul Kruger** gate and Skukuza camp. Straight ahead is the R40 to Bushbuckridge, with the **ShopRite Center** on the left and turn-offs in a few kilometers to Sabie and Graskop.

All major bus lines, including **Greyhound** (☎ 011 830 1301), have service to and from Nelspruit; take a minibus taxi from there or call Big 5 Backpackers or Kruger Park Backpackers to arrange pick-up. The **minibus taxi** rank is behind the Engen petrol station. Minibuses run to **Nelspruit** and **Sabie** (R12), and **Johannesburg** (R60).

▮ PRACTICAL INFORMATION

Tourist Office: Hazyview Tourism Association/Panorama Information and Central Reservations (☎ 737 7414 or 737 8191), in the ShopRite Center on the R40. Arranges transportation including **Europcar Rent-A-Car** service, accommodations, and activities. Open M-F 9am-5pm, Sa 9am-1pm.

Bank: ABSA Bank, first fl. of Blue Haze Mall. Open M-F 8:30am-3:30pm, Sa 8-11am.

Laundromat: Hazyview Laundrette (☎ 737 7808), in the Blue Haze Mall. Open M-F 7:30am-5pm, Sa 7:30am-1pm.

Supermarket: ShopRite, in the center of town, on the R40 near the intersection with the R536. Open M-F 8am-6pm, Sa 8am-5pm, Su 8am-1pm.

Police (☎ 737 7328), on the R40 between the ShopRite Center and the Blue Haze Mall.

Pharmacy: The Park Pharmacy (☎ 737 7775), in the Blue Haze Mall. Open M-F 8am-5:30pm, Sa 8am-1:30pm, Su 10am-1pm.

Clinic (☎ 737 7321), in the Blue Haze Mall. Consulting hours daily 8am-5pm.

Internet Access: Hazynet Internet Cafe (☎ 737 7811), in the ShopRite Center. R15 for 15 minutes. Open M-F 8am-5pm, Sa-Su 9am-1pm.

Post Office: On the R40 between the Blue Haze Mall and ShopRite Center. *Poste Restante.* Open M-Tu and Th-F 8:30am-4:30pm, W 9am-4:30pm, Sa 8am-noon.

Postal code: 1242.

🏠 ACCOMMODATIONS AND CAMPING

Big 5 Backpackers (☎ 737 7378 or 083 524 6615), 5km from town on the R40 toward Witrivier. Look for big pink "Backpackers" sign. Small hilltop retreat with down-to-earth vibe. Big 5 is the destination of choice for backpackers, offering a TV lounge, roomy kitchen, comfortable rooms, and *braai*. Allen, the owner, provides local information and organizes great trips into Kruger. Dorms R50; doubles R135 and R150. ❶

Umvubu Game Farm (☎ 737 6352), 1km from town on the R536 Sabie Rd. Comfortable 2-person cabins and 4-person tents with kitchen and bath overlook dam which attracts zebra, giraffe, and hippos. Popular with young families, Umvubu is the least expensive private game reserve in the area. Cabins R160 off-season and weekends, R230 in season. Tents R400/R520. Camping R70 up to 2 people, R15 per extra person. ❷

Perry's View (☎ 737 8374; www.perrysview.co.za), 3km from Hazyview on the R536 to Sabie. Two-level self-catering cottages have three bedrooms, vaulted ceilings, fully equipped kitchens, and private verandas. Breakfast R30. Dinner a la carte. Cabins R130 per person up to 3 people off-season, R150 in season; R100 per extra person. ❷

🍴 FOOD

The Ant & Elephant (☎ 737 8172), a few kilometers from town on the R536 to Sabie. An elegant restaurant with good service, large portions, and a pleasant outdoor seating area. Serves a wide selection of fish, meats, and vegetarian options. Entrees R30-60. Its popularity with the locals makes reservations a necessity. Open Tu-Su 6pm-late, kitchen closes at 9pm. ❷

Tembi (☎ 737 7729), about 500m north of town on the R40 toward Bushbuckridge. A charming little restaurant and B&B tucked into the forest. Serves good fish, grills, and veggie options. Entrees R40-60. Open M-Sa 6:30pm-9pm. ❸

T-Thyme, in the ShopRite Center, next to the tourist office. This sidewalk cafe and sandwich shop provides a great break from frantic grocery shopping. Sample tea (R6), coffee (R7), sandwiches (R10-14), or the best burgers in town (R15-20). Open M-F 8am-4pm, Sa 9am-1pm. ❶

📷 🎿 SIGHTS AND ADVENTURES

The **Shangana Cultural Village** is a traditional village which gives visitors a feel for Shangana culture and craftsmanship. Its meals are true events, filled with drums, dancing, and byala beer. *(Four kilometers from Hazyview on the R535 Graskop Rd. ☎ 737 7000. 1hr. tours daily 9, 10, 11am, 3, and 4pm; R55. Daily noon tour includes lunch, R115. 3hr. dinner tour Su and Th 5:30pm; R160. Call ahead).* **Quad Adventures** offers off-road quad biking trips through the Sabie River Valley. *(☎ 737 8266 or 072 263 0073. R260 for 1hr., R380 for 2hr.)* Hazyview's main attraction is the southern section of **Kruger National Park.** Big Five Backpackers and Kruger Park Backpackers (see **Accommodations and Camping,** p. 260) offer **safaris** into the park. Longer trips include accommodation in the park and/or at the respective backpacking establishments. *(Daytrips around R275; nighttime trips around R120.)*

KRUGER NATIONAL PARK   ☎ 013

A vast stretch of wilderness comparable in size to Israel or Taiwan, Kruger National Park is one of the largest and most successful conservation areas in the world. Supporting a staggering variety of plants and animals within 12 different

MPUMALANGA

ecosystems, the park also documents the history of human diversity through a number of cultural heritage sites. Balancing flat *bushveld* and rolling savanna with a meticulously planned network of campsites and roads, Kruger is an accessible and deservedly popular attraction drawing over one million visitors each year.

AT A GLANCE

AREA: 20,000 sq. km.

CLIMATE: Hot summers with frequent midday rains; drier winters with frigid evening temperatures.

FEATURES: Olifants River; Limpopo River; gorges and rock formations.

GATEWAYS: Nelspruit (p. 354); Phalaborwa (p. 351); Hazyview (p. 364); Thohoyandou (p. 342).

CAMPING: Permitted only in designated bush camps; 2-person sites R40-70 with advance reservations.

FEES & RESERVATIONS: R30 per person (see **Practical Information**, p. 368), plus R24 per vehicle. Reservations essential; call National Parks main line (☎ 012 343 1991). See **Practical Information** to book guided tours.

The oldest and largest national park in South Africa grew from a collection of smaller conservation projects. In 1898, President Paul Kruger launched the first of these by establishing the Sabie Game Reserve, a protected area between the Sabie and Crocodile Rivers. His efforts were threatened by the Anglo-Boer War, which destroyed much of the area's wildlife. Afterward, the British government renewed conservation efforts and officially founded the Shingwedzi Game Reserve (north of the Olifants River) in 1903. In 1926, the National Parks Act joined these reserves to form Kruger National Park.

Today, Kruger protects 2000 plant species (50 of which are endangered), and 507 bird, 114 reptile, 34 amphibian, 49 freshwater fish, and 147 mammal species, including the endangered wild dog and roan antelope. Successful relocation projects and an aggressive anti-poaching program have stabilized the park's rhino population, contributing to South Africa's status as one of the only remaining countries with a significant population of both black and white rhinos. There are roughly 1300 white and 200 black rhinos in the park today.

The Parks Board has recently adopted new policies concerning wildlife management and human resources. With an eye toward minimizing disturbance by humans, park authorities have embraced a minimal interference management plan, which includes the controversial ban against culling animals (the "scientific" shooting of animals to keep their numbers in check). Meanwhile, authorities are trying to maximize human benefits from the park by negotiating land restitution claims with citizens evicted by the colonizers long ago. They are also maintaining affordable access to the park, and encouraging neighboring communities to participate in conservation efforts. An ambitious plan is currently underway to link the northern section of Kruger to protected areas in Mozambique, Zimbabwe, and Botswana, which would create an enormous trans-national park and allow for the reopening of traditional elephant migration routes

Kruger is dry and mild in the winter months (Apr.-Aug.), with warm days and cool nights. In the summer (Sept.-Apr.), the park is rainy, hot, and humid, especially in the southern region. But the land is rich and green, alive with the movement of newborn mammals and migratory birds.

✳ ORIENTATION

Kruger National Park is a finger-shaped strip of land in the northeastern corner of the country. The park stretches 350km from the Crocodile River in the south to the

WHEN TO GO. The dry winter months (about Apr.-Oct.) are the most ideal for animal sightings in Kruger. The reduced water supply means that the game congregate at watering holes and rivers, which become the best places for animal watching. By December, the grass has grown high enough to hide most game. Kruger has enjoyed a generous supply of rainfall in the last few years. As a result, the vegetation is exceptionally green during the summer months, and the water holes are unusually active in the winter.

Limpopo River in the north and measures 60km from its western limits to the border of Mozambique in the east.

There are eight entrance gates (from south to north): **Crocodile Bridge** (close to Komatipoort and Maputo); **Malelane** (near the N4, the most convenient gate from Johannesburg and Pretoria); **Numbi** (convenient from Nelspruit and Hazyview); **Paul Kruger** (close to Hazyview, Sabie, and Graskop); **Orpen** (near Blyde River Canyon and Hoedspruit); **Phalaborwa** (convenient from Pietersburg and Tzaneen); **Punda Maria** (near Thohoyandou); and **Pafuri** (accessible from Messina and Beitbridge). The absolutely essential *Kruger National Park Map* is sold at all gates and rest camp shops (R22); the *Find It* guide (R35) is an excellent companion to this map, providing information on the park's geology, plants, and animals.

Visitors congregate in the bottom third of the park, south of the Timbavati and Nwanetsi rivers. This is partly because the majority of visitors approach Kruger Park from the south, and partly because wildlife is more plentiful in the central and southern sections of the park. However, the area north of the Letaba River offers a more authentic wilderness experience; here, visitors can camp in privacy and drift through the bush on deserted roads.

☐ TRANSPORTATION

The only way to see Kruger is by car. Travelers without wheels have three options: take public transportation to Skukuza camp and hire a car there; take public transportation to a rest camp that offers bush drives and night drives (Berg-en-Dal, Skukuza, and Letaba); or join one of the many organized tours into the park (see **Practical Information,** p. 368). **Don't even think about hitching around Kruger Park.**

Flights: South African Airways Express (☎011 978 6927) has daily flights between **Johannesburg** and **Skukuza** (1hr., 3 per day, round-trip R1939).

Trains: The **Spoornet** Komati train (☎011 773 2944 or 011 773 2992) runs from **Johannesburg/Pretoria** to **Malelane** (10hr.; daily; 2nd-class R106, 1st-class R75). **Minibus taxis** run from Malelane to Skukuza.

Buses: Greyhound (☎753 2100) and **Translux** (☎011 774 3333) run buses to **Nelspruit.** From there, Nelspruit Backpackers organizes tours into Kruger, or travelers can hop a minibus taxi to Hazyview, Skukuza, or a rest camp with bush drives. **North Link** (☎011 773 5857) has buses to **Hoedspruit** and **Phalaborwa.** In Phalaborwa, travelers can take a Kruger tour with Elephant Walk Backpackers. There are no tours from Hoedspruit, but there are minibus taxis.

Minibus Taxis: Minibuses will take travelers from Hazyview to **Skukuza** via **Belfast.** In Skukuza, both walks and drives are available into the park.

Car Rental: Cars can be hired from **Avis** (☎741 1087 or 0800 021 111) in Nelspruit, Hazyview or at the Phalaborwa airport. Avis also rents within Kruger at Skukuza camp (☎735 5651; M-F 8am-5pm, Sa-Su 9am-1pm). **Budget** (☎0800 016 622) or **Imperial** (☎0800 131 000) also rent.

MPUMALANGA

⚡ PRACTICAL INFORMATION

Medical Assistance: There is a medical practitioner at Skukuza (☎ 735 5638), with consulting hours M-F 8am-noon, Sa 8-11am. Malaria medication is available from the shop at Skukuza.

Reservations: Reservations are necessary for all camps and for any tours booked through the camps. Though the summer months and school holidays (June and July) are especially busy, the park is busy year-round. Make reservations as far in advance as possible, especially for tours. Contact the **National Parks Board,** Pretoria office (☎ 012 343 1991; fax 343 0905; reservations@parks-sa.co.za; www.parks-sa.co.za) or Cape Town office (☎ 021 422 2810; fax 424 6211). Accommodations can be booked through the web site.

Gate Hours: Nov.-Feb. daily 5:30am-6:30pm, Mar. and Oct. 5:30am-6pm, Apr. 6am-6pm, May-July 6am-5:30pm, Aug.-Sept. 6am-6pm.

Entrance Fees: R30; ages 2-15 R15. Vehicles R24; caravans R18; trailers R9. Visitors must keep their entrance permit with them at all times.

Tours: In Hazyview, backpacker hostels offering trips into Kruger include **Nelspruit Backpackers** (☎ 741 2237), **Big 5 Backpackers** (☎ 737 7378), and **Kruger Park Backpackers** (☎ 737 7224). **Elephant Walk Backpackers** (☎ 015 781 2758) offers trips from Phalaborwa. **Bundu Bus** (☎ 011 675 0767) runs a variety of tours from Johannesburg to the Panorama Route and Kruger Park (see **Game Viewing,** p. 370).

Petrol Stations and Auto Repair: Petrol stations are at all main rest camps and near most entry gates. They only accept cash. AA stations are at Skukuza (☎ 735 4037; after hours 082 990 5374), Satara (☎ 082 990 5375), and Letaba (☎ 082 990 5376).

Telephone: At all main rest camps; phone cards available at reception offices. International calling cards can be used at any phone. **Phone codes** vary by region.

Banks: First National Bank, with an **ATM.** Open M-F 8:30am-3:30pm, Sa 8:30-11am.

Credit Cards: MasterCard and Visa accepted at all camps, shops and restaurants.

Post Office: At Skukuza, with fax and *Poste Restante.* Open M-Tu and Th-F 8:30am-1pm and 2-4:30pm, W 9am-1pm and 2-4:30pm, Sa 8am-noon.

Postal Code: 1350.

⚡⚡ SAFARI CAMPS

There are three types of wilderness lodging in Kruger Park: rest camps, *bushveld* camps, and bush lodges. **Rest camps** have the most facilities and a variety of accommodations, ranging from campsites to family cottages. Each rest camp has its own restaurant and shop, unless otherwise indicated. Restaurants are open daily 7-9am, noon-2pm, and 6-9pm. Shops are open from 8am to half an hour after gate closing time. Some rest camps have laundromats and most have wheelchair-accessible accommodations and facilities. All rest camps offer day and night game drives (R75), and guided walks into the park (R100-140). Bush drives can be booked at the reception area of all camps. Many also offer a bush breakfast, a morning drive including outdoor breakfast (R150), and a nightly *braai* (R175). Call camp receptions to inquire about activities. *Bushveld* camps are smaller, more remote, and more expensive. **Bush lodges** are luxurious private camps, each with a single cottage that sleeps 12-19 people.

The following recommended rest camps are listed by location, from south to north. Northern rest camps tend to be cheaper because of lower demand.

Berg-en-Dal (☎ 735 6106 or 735 6107). "Mountain and dale" is the park's newest camps, situated amidst lush *bushveld* on the banks of the Matjulu River. Its location means excellent views of the nearby Matjulu Dam, where klipspringer, white rhino, and waterbuck congregate. It's the only camp that is fully wheelchair-accessible. Other amenities include a swimming pool and "braille trails," nature trails accessible to the blind. The nearest gate is **Malelane** (12km). Double bungalows with kitchen and bathroom R315; four-person cottages R600; 2-person campsites R70, R20 per extra person. ❶

Pretoriuskop (☎ 735 5128 or 735 5132). The oldest camp in Kruger sits amidst granite hills with sprouting rock figs and shrubbed, grassy valleys. There is a relatively high concentration of white rhino in the area. Situated at a high altitude, the camp is slightly cooler than others in the summer. Pretoriuskop has a sociable atmosphere, with *rondavels* arranged in a circle around a green, as well as a natural rock swimming pool and nature trails. The nearest gate is **Numbi** (9km). Double huts with communal baths R100; four-person cottages R600; 2-person campsites R70, R20 per extra person. ❶

Lower Sabie (☎ 735 6506 or 735 6057). Surrounded by rolling savanna and shady marula trees, Lower Sabie is on the edge of a dam where many animals come to drink. Expect to see waterbucks, kudus, zebras, and giraffes. The nearest gate is **Crocodile Bridge** (34km). 1-person huts with A/C and fridge R80, 2-person R160; 4-person cottages R600; 2-person campsites R70, R20 per extra person. ❶

Skukuza (☎ 735 4152). This is the largest camp, housing up to 3000 people. With a post office, bank, library, museum, airfield, and amphitheater, Skukuza feels more like a small town than a wilderness rest camp. Nevertheless, the camp's services and lively atmosphere, as well as the hippo pool below the camp, make it an appealing destination. The nearest gate is **Paul Kruger** (12km). Double safari tents R160; double bungalows R350; 4-person cottages R600; 2-person campsites R70, R20 per extra person. ❷

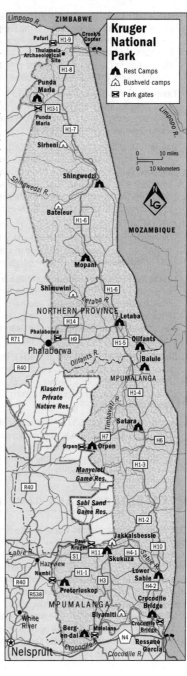

Kruger
National
Park

▲ Rest Camps
△ Bushveld camps
☒ Park gates

Satara (☎735 6306 or 735 6307). The second-largest camp after Skukuza is on flat marula savanna near the center of the park. Although it is probably the park's least aesthetically pleasing camp, it is in an area known to have a high concentration of lions. Also look out for cheetah, waterbuck, buffalo, and hyena. There is an AA emergency service station in the camp. The nearest gate is **Orpen** (48km). Double bungalows R350; four-person cottages R600; 2-person campsites R70, R20 per extra person. ❷

Tamboti (call Orpen camp at 735 6355). A small tented camp surrounded by wide grassy plains. There are no facilities, so bring everything you need. Near the Timbavati River and perfect for those who want convenience and privacy. The nearest gate is **Orpen** (5km). 2-person safari tents R160. ❷

Balule (call Olifants camp at 735 6606). A small camp in rugged *veld*, punctuated by black boulders and thorny bush. Remote and rustic, Balule is the favorite camp of many regulars. Only 11km from the beautiful Olifants camp, it is quieter and cheaper than anywhere else in the park. Campers are likely to see wildebeest, elephant, and especially hyena. The nearest gate is **Phalaborwa** (83km). Double huts with communal bath R100; 2-person campsites R70, R20 per extra person. ❶

Olifants (☎735 6606). A large camp positioned on a 100m cliff overlooking the rushing Olifants River. Shaded terrace overlooking the valley provides an ideal place to spot elephants, hippo, and antelope drawn to the river during the hot afternoons. The nearest gate is **Phalaborwa** (83km). Double bungalows R315; four-person cottages R600. ❹

Letaba (☎735 6636). One of the most beautiful rest camps in the park, Letaba is in dense *mopane bushveld* on a bend in the Letaba River. Safari tents, huts, and campsites are pleasantly shaded by apple-leaf trees and skirted by green lawns. Many animals roam the area, including eland, roan, sable, leopard, and jackal. Letaba has an AA emergency service station. The nearest gate is **Phalaborwa** (51km). Double huts or safari tents R160; 4-person cottages R600; 2-person campsites R70, R20 per extra person. ❶

Shingwedzi (☎735 6806 or 735 6807). The largest camp in the northern *mopane bushveld* section of Kruger. Visitors are likely to see an abundance of elephant, steenbok, zebra, and possibly lion. Swimming pool. The nearest gate is **Punda Maria** (71km). Double huts R150; double bungalows with kitchen R315; four-person cottage R400; 2-person campsites R70, R20 per extra person. ❶

Punda Maria (☎735 6873). The northernmost camp in the park. The terrain here is completely different from the rest of the park, with richly vegetated flatland occasionally pushing up into sandstone hills. Animals frequenting the area include wild dog, buffalo, nyala, and Sharpe's grysbok. The nearest gate is **Punda Maria** (9km). Double bungalows R315; four-person cottages R600; 2-person campsites R70, R20 per extra person. ❷

⚠ 🐾 OUTDOORS AND GAME VIEWING

THE GAME. Most visitors come to the Kruger Park to see the Big Five—elephant, lion, leopard, buffalo, and rhino—but the search for these stars shouldn't blind visitors to the park's spectacular array of birds and smaller mammals. Oft-sighted birds include the marabou stork, bee-eater, grey loerie, ground hornbill, bateleur, fish eagle, and hooded vulture. Vervet monkeys and baboons line the roads, herds of impala often hold up cars, and giraffe and zebra commonly stroll in close view. Visitors are also likely to see kudu, waterbuck, and warthog. Hippo and crocodiles are often seen near water. The patient and observant will probably glimpse a lion or two; the truly blessed may spot a leopard. The best times to see animals are between sunrise and 10am and from 4pm to sunset; during the day, most vanish into the shade of the bushes. Predators are most likely to be seen around sunset.

MPUMALANGA

WHEN LIONS ATTACK... Visiting Kruger Park is not like visiting a zoo, and tourists who underestimate the dangers of the Park have often paid with their lives. Every guide knows the story of the tourists who came upon a pride of sleeping lions. They decided the lions were too "lifeless" to make a good picture. One of the tourists got out and pulled a lion's tail, and the lion turned around and ate him, so the story goes, while his friends took pictures. Other stories revolve around a lion who has been nicknamed "Breakdancer" because of the way he moves when approaching a car. One carload of tourists who encountered Breakdancer on the road stopped their car, rolled down the windows, and turned off the ignition in hopes that the lion would come closer. Come closer he did. Because the car windows were electric, the tourists could not roll them up when Breakdancer attacked, and the only thing that saved them was the fact that the lion's head was too big to fit through the windows.

More tragic than the stories of misguided tourists are the statistics of animal attacks on illegal immigrants who cross the park from Mozambique and Zimbabwe into South Africa. Moving in the middle of the night, the immigrants walk in single-file through the park, oldest and weakest people first, stepping in each others' footsteps so that park rangers will think their trail was made by only one person. Prides of lions tend to specialize in hunting a particular kind of prey, and there are now prides in Kruger Park that specialize in hunting people.

FINDING THE LIONS. Visitors who come to Kruger with a big game checklist can become frustrated when the Big Five fail to appear on cue. Leopards and lions are the most sought-after and can be particularly elusive. Some tips: first, most of the rest camps have maps of the park marked with daily sightings of the Big Five. By mid-afternoon, the map should be filled with pushpins from morning sightings—use this information to plan a late afternoon drive, when many of the animals awake from afternoon naps. Second, plan on at least one night drive—lions are attracted to the relative warmth of the tar roads after dark. Third, watch and listen for cues from the animals. Antelope and giraffe will often stare in the direction of approaching predators and hold their ground, while baboons and monkeys will shriek and climb into the trees.

VESTIGES OF THE ANCIENTS. With 78 cultural heritage sites signposted throughout the park, Kruger has a strong reputation for preserving a rich human heritage in addition to nature. Signs mark art shelters with San paintings, old trade routes from the eastern harbors, and the **Makahane** and **Thulamela heritage sites** in the northernmost section of the park (near Punda Maria and Pafuri), where evidence of prehistoric habitation has been unearthed. Remains suggest a Late Iron Age settlement, with artifacts including gold beads, charcoal, ivory rings, and ornamental cowrie shells. The Punda Maria organization organizes twice-daily trips to Thulmela (R50). The **Masorini hill** heritage site, near the Phalaborwa gate, has provided archaeologists with rich details about its Iron Age inhabitants.

BUNDU SAFARIS. This tour company offers a unique (if expensive) way to get a well-rounded feel for the Kruger area. Their famous four-day **Ultimate Bundu Adventure** starts by traversing Blyde River Canyon and then continues to a home-stay experience in the Shangan village of Nyani. The group enters the national park for the next three days, experiencing a range of day drives, night drives, game walks, and open *bushveld* camping. Professional guides are great, and camp cooking is surprisingly good. (☎ *011 675 0767 or 082 567 7041; www.bundusafari.co.za. Departs every Tu from Johannesburg and Pretoria; other tours of varying lengths also available. R2800 per person, including pick-up/drop-off from Gauteng.)*

MPUMALANGA

▣ WILDERNESS WALKING TRAILS

Those seeking the ultimate Kruger experience should book a hiking trip on one of its seven amazing trails. Though far from cheap, the trails are well worth the price, since they offer a rare opportunity to explore the bush without the obstruction of a vehicle. Groups are limited to eight people and are led by a knowledgeable ranger and tracker who offers explanations of the plants, animals, and tracks found along the way. Often walking in silent single-file, hikers will feel the fullness of the sights, sounds, and smells of the wilderness: birds gliding overhead, antelope snorting, elephants blowing water over their bodies, and the strong scent of potato bushes and stagnant hippo pools. The ranger and tracker are armed to protect hikers in the unlikely case an animal charges. Hikers will not get as close to the game while walking as they would in their cars, since the animals are, oddly enough, more accustomed to vehicles. *(Trails last 3 days and 2 nights, with 2 days of 10-15km early morning hikes and 4-6km late afternoon hikes. Overnight accommodation and meals provided. Bring binoculars and a flashlight. Don't pack obsessively light, as all your things will remain in the camp while you hike with light rucksacks provided by rangers. Book up to a year ahead of time through the National Parks Board. R1500 per person.)*

Bushman Trail. Near Berg-en-Dal camp, this path winds through the southwest corner of the park. Hikers romp through *bushveld* to the tops of granite hills, which have lookout points providing likely glimpses of white rhino, elephant, and buffalo. Unique to this trail are the San paintings visible on the walls of many rock shelters.

Wolhunter Trail. Just north of the Bushman Trail, this covers mountainous and woodland terrain. Hikers are likely to observe lion, leopard, zebra, and buffalo drinking at the Miambane Stream, as well as abundant birdlife at the Stolsnek and Newu dams.

Napi Trail. Situated in the bushwillow woodlands between Skukuza and Pretoriuskop camps, this trail offers ample white rhino, elephant, lion, and buffalo sightings.

Metsimetsi (Water-Water) Trail. Aptly named for the riverine *bushveld* through which it winds, this trail traverses savanna and rocky gorges, and traces the Nwaswitsontso River, where hippos, crocodiles, and a bounty of birdlife congregate. The camp overlooks a water hole frequented by herds of elephant, warthog, impala, and other wildlife.

Olifants Trail. This trail, in the park's center, takes hikers through the rolling terrain of the Lebombo foothills and along the banks of the beautiful Olifants River. Lion, buffalo, and elephant often appear, as do the African fish eagle and the rare Pel's fishing owl.

Sweni Trail. Located in terrain most commonly associated with the African bush: harsh marula and knobthorn savanna, dry and brown in the winter, greener but still sparse in the summer. A chance few will encounter the Sweni lion pride, so hope for luck.

Nyayaland Trail. At the northern end of the park, this trail passes among fever tree and baobab forests. Hikers walk along the Lanner Gorge to elevated points with spectacular three-country *bushveld* views. This trail features nyala as well as fishing owls, buffalo, elephants, hippos, and crocodiles.

THE PANORAMA ROUTE

The Panorama Route is the name given to a particularly scenic part of northeastern Mpumalanga, roughly defined as the area around and between Graskop, Pilgrim's Rest, Lydenburg, and Sabie. The "Route" can be literally that, a scenic drive along the escarpment that includes historic towns, the dramatic Blyde River Canyon, some notable waterfalls, and rugged mountain passes that afford tremendous views of the area's towering hills and rocky gorges. But travelers who see the Panorama Route only from a car window are missing out on good hiking, swimming, and a range of outdoor adventure activities. While the towns can seem overly touristy at times, the countryside offers ample room to escape, and the Route makes for a laid-back meander of anything from a few days to a few weeks.

GRASKOP ☎ 013

Graskop is a small town surrounded by forests, smack in the middle of the Panorama Route. Another town born from the glint of gold in the mountains, Graskop got its name from the vast tracts of tree-less grassland in the area. Within a half hour's drive of Sabie, Pilgrim's Rest, God's Window, and the Bourke's Luck Potholes, Graskop is a convenient home base for touring the *lowveld* escarpment. Tour buses have discovered the convenience of Graskop as well—at peak times, the town's main street, with its collection of restaurants and curio shops, resembles the Johannesburg airport duty-free shopping area.

■ ▉ **ORIENTATION AND PRACTICAL INFORMATION.** Graskop lies 90km north of Nelspruit, at the intersection of the R532, R533, R534, and R535. There are few public transportation options, as there is no rail line in the area and coach buses have difficulty negotiating the winding mountain roads. Nonetheless, **minibus taxis** run to **Lydenburg** (R16) and **Sabie** (R10) from the rank across from the Total station on Hoof St. The two main streets in town, **Louis Trichardt St.** and **Main St.** (also called **Hoof St.**), form an "L": Louis Trichardt St. leads east to the R534/R532 (toward God's Window), and Main St. heads south to Hazyview. One block south of this main intersection, **Pilgrim's Way** intersects Main St. and leads west to Pilgrim's Rest and Sabie. The verbosely-titled **tourist office, Wild Adventures Graskop Information and Central Reservations** is inside Spar at the corner of Richardson Ave. and Kerk St. (☎767 1833. Open M-Sa 8am-5pm.) Services include: **First National Bank** and **ATM** on Kerk St. (open M-F 9am-12:45pm and 2-3:30pm, Sa 8:30-11am); **camping equipment** at the Forest Shop, on Main St. (☎767 1020; open M-F 8:30am-5pm, Sa 8:30am-1pm); the **police station** (☎767 1122); and **Internet** at Blyde Chalets, on Louis Trichardt St. at Oorwinning St. (☎767 1377; open daily 8am-6pm; R1 per min.). The **post office,** at Hoof St. and Louis Trichardt St., has public phones. (Open M-Tu and Th-F 8:30am-4pm, W 9am-4:30pm, Sa 8:30-11am.) **Postal code:** 1270.

▉ **ACCOMMODATIONS AND CAMPING.** On the corner of Voortrekker St. and Market St., **Summit Lodge ❶** offers two-bed or four-bed compartments in an old train car, pleasant thatched two-person *rondavels* with en suite bathrooms and TVs, self-catering units that sleep up to 6, and an adjoining campground with *braai* and self-catering facilities. Take Pilgrim's Way about 1km west from the center of town; the lodge will be on your left. Its restaurant and the bar next door are two of Graskop's hot spots. (☎767 1058 or 072 149 6181; www.wheretostay.co.za/summitlodge. Swimming pool. Dorms R60 or R90 with breakfast; *rondavels* R180 per person with breakfast; self-catering units R320 for 2-4 people, R420 for 5-6 people; camping R30.) A bit farther away is the **Mac Mac Forest Retreat ❶**, 15km south of Graskop on the Sabie Rd. Their large rustic houses deep in the woods are within easy hiking distance of the Mac Mac Pools and Forest Falls (see **Waterfalls,** p. 378) and command a pleasant view of the surrounding forests. (☎764 2376 or 083 228 6176. Self-catering forestry houses sleep up to 8 and cost R200-300 per house during the week, R260-450 during weekends and school holidays.) At the mouth of the Graskop Gorge, 2km southeast of town on the road to Hazyview, is the **Panorama Rest Camp ❶**, which boasts a great bird's-eye view of the *lowveld* expanse. (☎767 1091. Fully equipped double chalets R160 or R190 with a view; quads R260; campsites R50 plus R10 per person.) Good, simple value for your money is available at **Blyde Lodge ❷,** on Oorwinning St. one block from Louis Tri-

MPUMALANGA

chardt St. behind the pricier Blyde Chalets. Eight basic doubles with bath and TV and one luxurious honeymoon suite are all R170 per person, including dinner and breakfast. The lodge also features a swimming pool.

◪◪ FOOD AND NIGHTLIFE. ◪Thistles Country Kitchen ❶ (☎082 467 5276), a local legend for its innovative menus and home-cooked food, has moved from its old location on Pilgrim's Way to a new house on Louis Trichardt St. Dinners are by prior arrangement only, so call the proprietress, Bevvie Myburg, in advance. **Harrie's Pancake House ❶,** on the corner of Louis Trichardt St. and Kerk St., serves delicious sweet and savory crepes. The bright atmosphere entices diners to linger over coffee and another pancake or two. Sadly, the convenient parking entices tour buses to disgorge hordes of hungry tourists at lunchtime. Pancake offerings include one with apricots, cream, and liqueur (R17.50) and one with chicken and mushroom for the same price. (☎767 1273. Open daily 7am-6pm; last orders 5:20pm.) **Leonardo's Trattoria ❷,** on Louis Trichardt St. between Kerk St. and Oorwinning St., serves a good selection of pasta (R30-50), grills (R40-60), and pizzas (R20-40). Spaghetti marinara comes with a tomato cream and seafood sauce. (☎767 1078. Open daily 11am-3pm, 5:30pm-9pm.) The **House of Beers ❶,** at Hoof and Richardson, has 31 kinds of beer, darts, big-screen TV, and occasional live entertainment. (☎767 1403. Open daily 10am-late.)

◪ OUTDOORS. About 2km north of Graskop, the R534 loops off the R532 and leads to the town's several worthy sights. **The Pinnacle** is a column of quartzite peeking out 30m from the bottom of a rocky cleft. Farther north is **God's Window,** the star tourist attraction in the area. One look down from the 750m high drop and you'll see why. For the best lookout point, hike away from the crowds and up into the forest, where clearings afford heavenly views of the subtropical expanse far below. (Gate open daily 7am-5pm. Free.) A few kilometers north of God's Window, **Wonder View** is the highest car-accessible point on the escarpment (1730m). On a clear day, this perch offers a 360-degree panorama of the peaks, plateaus, smooth hills, and curling towns that make up the *lowveld* area.

Returning to the R532, the **Berlin Falls** lie about 2km north of the T junction with the R534. These small falls are worth seeing for the huge ravine that gulps down their cascade. About 2km back toward Graskop are the 92m **Lisbon Falls,** the highest in the area. After the Lone Creek Falls (see p. 378), they are the most beautiful on the Panorama Route. It's possible to climb down the first slope of rocks to reach a few small pools set back from the sheer cliff edge. During summer, the falls are especially powerful and the rocks perpetually slick, so descend with care.

◪◪ HIKING AND ADVENTURES. Aside from the self-made hikes around the falls, there are a few marked trails of varying intensity around the *veld*. The most serious of these is the **Jock of the Bushveld** trail, which commemorates every place the beloved Jock raised his leg (See **Who the *&*% is Jock,** p. 361). The trail begins at the Graskop Holiday Resort and winds its way for about 8km along the escarpment east of Graskop, heading south at Paradise Camp and returning to the Resort. The route takes around 3hr., and trail markings depict Jock's doggy outline in a circle. Hikers with less time on their hands can opt for the **Fairyland Trail,** a shorter version of the Jock of the Bushveld trail that comprises only the trail's southern portion. Another short trail, the **Swartbooi Trail,** also begins at the Graskop Holiday Resort. (☎767 1377, or contact the tourism office. Open M-Sa 8am-5pm. R15.) Hiking enthusiasts should consider the two- to three-day **Blyde River Canyon (Blyderivierspoort) Trail,** which begins at Paradise Camp near Wonder View and descends 30km to Bourke's Luck Potholes, with strategically placed huts along the way. (☎013 759 5432, or contact the Blyde River Nature Reserve Visitors

Center at 015 795 5643; www.linx.co.za/trails/grading/gradtral.html. Trail markings are yellow. R35.) For those not satisfied with viewing the Graskop Gorge from its edge, there is the **Graskop Big Swing,** a 65m free fall on the cliff's edge at Mogodi Lodge, just out of town on the R535 to Hazyview. (☎ 072 223 8155. R235.)

PILGRIM'S REST   ☎ 013

Once a precious little mining village, Pilgrim's Rest is now more of a tour bus rest stop than a real town. Its history dates back to 1873, when pioneering Scottish miner Alex "Wheelbarrow" Patterson discovered gold at Pilgrim's Creek. Fortune seekers came rushing by the hundreds, and by the end of that year South Africa's first mining town was born. The gold lasted until 1972, after which Pilgrim's Rest was declared a national monument and its corrugated iron buildings aggressively restored. Unfortunately, the restoration went a bit too far (as facelifts sometimes do), and the nipped-and-tucked, brightly painted buildings filled with overpriced, scented candles hold few reminders of gold rush days.

7 PRACTICAL INFORMATION. Pilgrim's Rest is 16km from Graskop off the R533. From the R533 there are **uptown** and **downtown** entrances 1km apart. The tourist office, museums, and practical services are uptown; restaurants, shops, and budget lodgings tend to be downtown. **Pilgrim's Rest Information Center,** on the main road near the uptown exit, is a good one-stop place to plan your tour and buy your museum tickets. (☎ 768 1060. Open daily 9am-12:45pm and 1:15-4:30pm.) Just down the main road is a **First National Bank** with no ATM (open M and Th 9-11:30am) and a **post office** with **phones** (open M-F 9am-4pm, Sa 9am-1pm).

7 ☐ ACCOMMODATIONS AND FOOD. Your best bet for budget accommodations in Pilgrim's Rest is the **Environmental Education Center ❶.** Driving along the main road from uptown to downtown, turn left after Jubilee Potters Restaurant onto the road to the Old Cemetery and continue up the hill; the Center will be on your left. Perched on a hilltop overlooking the surrounding fields, the Center has pleasant self-catering cottages that sleep between two and 12 people. (☎ 768 1201 or 082 872 9469. 12-person guest house R250; 6-person or 10-person guest house R220; other cottages R50 per person. Book in advance.) At the bottom of the single road leading through town, **Pilgrim's Rest Caravan Park ❶** stretches along the banks of the Blyde River, across the street from an active mine. Campsites are available, as are tents with toilet, shower, and cooking facilities. (☎ 768 1427. Double rooms R100; double tents R85. 2-person campsites R50, each additional person R10, electricity R10. Prices are higher during December, Easter, and school holidays.)

For such a tiny town, Pilgrim's Rest has a surplus of places to feed hungry busloads of tourists. Downtown, **The Vine ❷** serves good sandwiches (R20-25) and main dishes (R20-45), including a great chicken curry, in an informal, tavern-style setting. (☎ 768 1080. Open daily 8am-7pm.) Uptown, the **Royal Hotel ❷** offers marinated ostrich fillet (R38) and brandy in an elegant Victorian atmosphere. (☎ 768 1100. Open daily noon-3pm and 6-9pm.)

☐ ☒ SIGHTS AND OUTDOORS. The town's museums offer an interesting look into the way things used to be. The **News Printing Museum** displays antique printing presses and old photographs; the **House Museum,** a typical wood and corrugated iron structure, recreates a middle-class, turn-of-the-century house; and the **Dredzen Shop Museum** exhibits the goods of a general store from the town's golden years in the mid-1940s. (All open daily 9am-1pm and 1:30-4pm. A single R10 ticket, available at the Visitors Center, is good for all three museums.) Outside of town on Graskop Rd. is the **Diggings Site Museum,** which has exhibits on the lives of the

MPUMALANGA

early diggers and offers a gold panning demonstration. Watch the hordes re-emerge in search of gold, especially on weekends. (Guided tours at 10, 11am, noon, 2, and 3pm. R10.) The **Alanglade House Museum,** west of downtown, is the opulent former residence of the Pilgrim's Rest mine manager and is decorated in early 20th-century furnishings. (Tours M-Sa 11am and 2pm. All tours begin from the Visitors Center and should ideally be booked 30min. in advance. R10.)

The **Prospector's Hiking Trail Network** is an extensive series of trails that traverse the forests northwest of Pilgrim's Rest. The first section of the trail, known as Peach Tree Creek, leads from Pilgrim's Rest to the Morgenzon Forest Camp (16.3km). From there, the Clewer Section continues 14km to Blackhill Lookout. From Blackhill Lookout, the Morgenzon Trail leads to Excelsior Camp (10.5km). Robbers Pass trail continues 15.7km from Excelsior back to Morgenzon Forest Station, and the Columbia Race trail leads from Morgenzon Hut (not to be confused with Morgenzon Forest Camp or Morgenzon Forest Station) 8.3km back to Pilgrim's Rest. Call SAFCOL (info ☎012 804 1230; reservations ☎012 764 1058).

Pilgrim's Rest briefly reconnects with its mining roots during the **South African Gold Panning Championships,** held annually in late November and early December, and the town will host the **World Gold Panning Championships** in 2004. Amateurs can join the swishy-swishy fun. Or, decompress on the way up from the depths of touristy tackiness at the **Mt. Sheba Nature Reserve.** Located about 20km from Pilgrim's Rest, down a long dirt road off the R533 to Lydenburg, this small reserve is a peaceful place to stroll while watching monkeys scamper among the indigenous trees. A number of hiking trails wind their way through the reserve, ranging 1-5km in length. Maps are available at reception. (☎768 1241. Reception 6am-10pm.)

SABIE ☎013

Sabie, the largest town on the Panorama Route, owes its existence to a trigger-happy hunting party whose intoxicated ailment accidently sparked the area's fourth gold rush. In 1871, Henry Glynn and his posse were out tracking game near Sabie Falls when some of the more inebriated men began shooting bottles on a rock ledge. When a few fateful bullets flew past the bottles and struck the cliff wall, they exposed glints of gold beneath the rock. Over the next 55 years, one million ounces of gold were extracted from the reef. Today, the town's "green gold" timber industry has replaced the old gold mainstay, and the more than one million acres of pine and blue-gum trees surrounding the town constitute the largest human-made forest in the world. Beautiful indigenous forests also boast excellent hiking and biking possibilities near the area's famous waterfalls.

✦ ❷ ORIENTATION AND PRACTICAL INFORMATION

Sabie lies 60km north of Nelspruit on the R37 and R537. Though Sabie is the largest development in the area, it is still no more than a single street, **Main Rd. (Hoof St.),** which runs north-south and connects to the R532 north of town and the R37 south of town. In the center of town, Main Rd. splits in two; one road continues south toward the R37 and Nelspruit, while another road heads east toward the R536, R537, and Hazyview. At the intersection where Main Rd. splits is a shopping center called Market Square, which contains many useful shops and services. The **Panorama Information and Central Reservation** center in Market Sq. offers trip planning services and a wealth of information. (☎764 1125; fax 764 1134. Open M-F 9am-5pm, Sa 9am-2pm, Su 9am-noon.) Taxis depart from the **minibus taxi** rank behind the Kwik Spar at the southern end of town for: **Lydenburg** (R15); **Nelspruit** (R16); **Graskop** (R10); **Hazyview** (R12). Services include: **Standard Bank,** Main Rd., with foreign exchange. (☎764 1261; open M-F 8:30am-3:30pm, Sa 8:30-11am); **Big**

Sky Outdoors—for camping, hiking, and fishing permits/equipment—in the center of town off Main Rd. (☎764 2214; open M-Sa 8am-5pm); **bike rental** at Bike Doc, corner of Main Rd. and Louis Trichardt St. (☎082 878 5527; open M-F 9am-6pm, Sa 8am-1pm; mountain bikes R70 per day); **Panorama Link Pharmacy,** next to the Standard Bank on Main Rd. (☎764 2213 or 631 8572; after hours 764 3060; open M-F 8am-7pm; alternates open Sa 8am-1pm and 5pm-6pm); **Long Tom Pharmacy,** two doors down (☎764 1268; open on alternating Sa, same times as Panorama); **Sabie Hospital,** on Simmons St., on the northeastern side of town (☎764 1222; open 24hr.); **Internet** at Soft Net, Market Sq., below Spar (☎764 3485; R10 for 30min.; open M-Sa 9am-5pm, Su 2-5pm); **Spar** Supermarket, Market Sq. (open M-Sa 8am-6pm, Su 8am-1pm, 4-6pm); **A to Z Laundromat,** Market Sq. (☎764 3333; open M-F 7:30am-5pm, Sa 8am-1pm); the **post office,** on Main Rd. near Market Sq., with *Poste Restante* and telephones (☎764 2211 or 764 2212; open M-Tu and Th-F 8:30am-4:30pm, W 9am-4:30pm, Sa 8am-noon). **Postal code:** 1260.

ACCOMMODATIONS

Sabie Backpackers Lodge (☎764 2118 or 082 507 9108; www.satic.co.za), on Main Rd. north of the center between Simmons and Lydenburg Rd. This lively hostel also offers a popular extreme adventure package. Wood stove-heated pool allow guests to swim under the stars year-round. Basic kitchen and common areas. *Braai* facilities available. Dorms R50; doubles, including a two-person treehouse, R60 per person. Shuttle pick-up from Nelspruit R60 for 1 person, R10 per person thereafter. ❶

SerINNdipity Guest House, 7 Power St. (☎764 2685; fax 764 2687; www.east-cape.co.za/serinndipity). Just off Main Rd. at the northern end of town. Heading toward Graskop, turn right just before the bridge. Massive breakfasts and comfy accommodations for the most reasonable prices in town. Extensive collection of nature books prep you for the trip to Kruger. Pool on the premises. Breakfast R15. Smaller rooms with twin beds R100 per person; larger rooms with double beds, TVs, and bath R120-130 per person. Self-catering flats R160-180 for 2, R50 per extra person. ❷

Jock-Sabie Lodge (☎764 2178; jocksabi@netactive.co.za), at Main Rd. and Glynn St. north of the center. Sprawling family resort complex offering a variety of accommodations along with a pub, restaurant, and pool. Very basic cabins with 2 bunks R100 for one person, R140 for two people, R30 per extra person; double lodge rooms R160 or R120 per person sharing; self-catering double flatlets R300; camping R60 for one person, R100 for two people, R25 per person thereafter; under 2 free. ❷

FOOD

Woodyglen Coffee Shop, 102 Main Rd. (☎764 2209). At Ford St., across from CNA. Terrific little coffee shop with filling breakfasts and tasty pita sandwiches. Hearty "health breakfast" with yogurt and muesli, stewed fruit, home-baked bread, juice, and coffee is a bargain (R16). Open M-F 7:30am-5pm, Sa-Su 8am-2pm. ❶

The Woodsman Pub and Restaurant, 94 Main Rd. (☎764 2204). In Woodsman Center on the branch of Main Rd. that heads east toward the R536 and R537. Bustles with people lunching on outdoor deck during the day; at night, bar and restaurant brim with mellow diners warmed by firelight. Serves delicious, mainly Greek food. Woodsman platter (R37) is a great combination of *saganaki* (fried cheese), *dolmades* (grape leaves stuffed with rice and beef), and chicken livers. *Moussaka* R33, "Hercules" breakfast R33. Open daily 7:30am-late, kitchen closes at 8:30pm. ❷

Country Kitchen (☎764 1901), on Main Rd. in the center of town. An upscale restaurant serving local specialties. Gazpacho R13, trout fillets with herb cream R47. Open M-Sa 6-9pm, call ahead to confirm. ❷

◉ ⬛ SIGHTS AND ADVENTURES ON THE WILD SIDE

FORESTRY MUSEUM. Sabie is the heart of Mpumalanga's forestry industry, and visitors learn all about the "green gold" biz at this museum, at the intersection of Ford and 10th St., off Main Rd. just north of the center. Visitors can plan a hike on SAFCOL lands and get permits here. (☎ *764 1058. Open M-F 9am-4pm, Sa 9am-noon.*)

WATERFALLS. Aquaphiles rejoice. There are no less than seven (touristed) waterfalls in the Sabie area. Drive north on Main Rd. and turn left onto Old Lydenburg Rd. to reach **Bridal Veil Falls, Horseshoe Falls,** and **Lone Creek Falls.** The most beautiful of these—and the only one to be declared a national monument—is Lone Creek Falls. Unlike other cascades in the area, Lone Creek can be seen up close at the bottom, where the single chute of water thunders into a wide pool. The surrounding indigenous forest has picnic spots shaded by moss-covered trees. With a flat paved pathway, the Lone Creek Falls are also the most accessible to the elderly and those in wheelchairs. (*All waterfalls open daily 8am-5pm. Each waterfall R5 per person.*)

  Sabie Falls, Forest Falls, Mac Mac Falls, and **Maria Shire Falls** are along the R532 to Graskop. Sabie Falls are 2km north of town; turn at the sign for Castle Rock and Mac Mac Family Resort. Mac Mac Falls are about 10km north of town, and Forest Falls and Maria Shire Falls are about 5km beyond Mac Mac. The most appealing of these waterfalls, and by far the least touristed because hiking is required to reach it, is Forest Falls. To get there, park your car at the Green Heritage Picnic Site, on the R532, and hike 3km through pine forests to the falls, which, for a change, are wider than they are tall. In the same area, also off the R532, are the **Mac Mac Pools.** These stone-dammed pools and the surrounding wilderness are well worth an extended visit for swimming and a picnic lunch. Starting from the pools, the 3km Secretary Bird Walk winds over rocky terrain with scattered patches of indigenous trees. (*Waterfalls and pools all open daily 8am-5pm. Each site R5 per person.*)

TRAILS. Numerous trails, ranging from easy to hard-core, originate at the Ceylon Forest Station; contact SAFCOL at ☎ 764 1058 or 012 481 3615 for more information. Maps are sometimes available at Panorama Information, Market Sq. ☎ 764 1125. Several **mountain biking** trails begin in Sabie, leading riders through indigenous forests, past waterfalls, and even through the Long Tom Pass. Cabins are available. **Bike Doc,** on the corner of Main Rd. and Louis Trichardt St., has permits and maps. (☎ 082 878 5527. Open M-F 9am-6pm, Sa 8am-1pm. Mountain bikes R70 per day; permits R20 per day, R45 for 3 days, or R75 for 5 days.) Biking permits are also available at the **Merry Pebbles Resort** (☎ 764 2266), signposted off Old Lydenburg Rd.

OTHER ADVENTURES. Sabie Horse Trails offers rides and tours through pine forest along the Sabie River. (☎ 082 938 2060. 1hr. R50; 2hr. R80; 3hr. R100, 5hr. R200.) **Trout fishing permits** on the Sabie River are available at **Big Sky Outdoors,** in the center of town off Main Rd. (☎ 764 2214 or 083 966 5089; open M-Sa 8am-5pm.)

BLYDE RIVER CANYON ☎ 015

Carved by the flow of the Blyde River, the canyon is a spectacle of precipitous cliffs dropping into a bush-covered valley. A ribbon of water snakes calmly along the canyon floor, branching off into a second stream south of the reserve. Voortrekkers etched their names into the rock and christened the two streams *Blyde* ("Joy") and *Treur* ("Sorrow"). In winter, the canyon's quartzite mountains take on an intriguing pinkish-red hue, and tracks of flowing water appear as tiers and ridges in the bare mountain walls. In summer, the canyon is a vibrant green, with trees and shrubs covering all traces of the rock beneath the canopy.

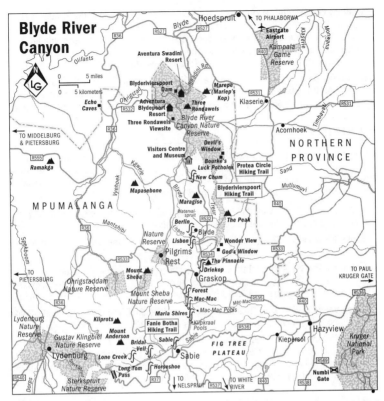

Blyde River Canyon

TO PHALABORWA
Hoedspruit
Eastgate Airport
Kampala Game Reserve
R527
R36
Blyde
R527
Olifants
Aventura Swadini Resort
R40
Swadini Rd.
Blyderiviespoort Dam
Marepe (Mariep's Kop)
Klaserie
R531
Echo Caves
R532
Adventura Blydepoort Resort
Three Rondawels
Ohrigstad
Blyde River Canyon Nature Reserve
R531
Three Rondawels Viewsite
R36
Acornhoek
TO MIDDELBURG & PIETERSBURG
Visitors Centre and Museum
Devil's Window
NORTHERN PROVINCE
Kgwele
Bourke's Luck Potholes
Protea Circle Hiking Trail
Sand
R555
Ramakga
New Chum
Blyderiviespoort Hiking Trail
Wehoek
Mapasebone
Blyde
Mutlumuvi
MPUMALANGA
Maragise
Waterval-spruit
R40
Mantshibi
Berlin
R532
The Peak
R36
Nature Reserve
Lisbon
Lisbon
Blyde
Wonder View
R533
Pilgrims Rest
R534
God's Window
TO PIETERSBURG
Mount Sheba
Driekop
The Pinnacle
TO PAUL KRUGER GATE
R533
Graskop
R536
Ohrigstaddam Nature Reserve
Mount Sheba Nature Reserve
Forest
Mac-Mac
Mac-Mac Pools
R535
R40
R36
Maria Shires
Lydenburg Nature Reserve
Kliprots
Fanie Botha Hiking Trail
Klipkraal Pools
R536
Hazyview
Gustav Klingbiel Nature Reserve
Mount Anderson
Sable
Sable
FIG TREE PLATEAU
Kiepersol
Kruger National Park
Lydenburg
Lone Creek
Bridal Veil
Sabie
R569
Long-Tom Pass
Horseshoe
Numbi Gate
R538
Sterkspruit Nature Reserve
R540
Doring
R37
TO NELSPRUIT
R537
TO WHITE RIVER
R40

TRANSPORTATION AND ORIENTATION

Blyde River Canyon runs roughly north-south and is bordered on the west by the R532, on the north by the R36 and R527, on the east by the R531 and R40, and on the south by the R533. Using these roads, it is possible to make a complete loop around the Canyon, beginning and ending in Graskop. To reach the canyon floor, take the R40 north from Hazyview or south from Hoedspruit, turn west onto the R531, and then turn onto the tar road marked "Swadini."

ACCOMMODATIONS AND FOOD

Staying around beautiful Blyde River Canyon may be nice, but it is often significantly cheaper to make the canyon a day trip, spending the night in Hazyview or Graskop.

■ **Moholoholo Mountain View** (☎ 795 5684), 1km from the R531 on the Swadini road. Pleasant accommodations attached to wildlife rehab center. Spacious, fully equipped chalets near the canyon. Each chalet has a porch affording spectacular views of the escarpment, punctuated by Marepe Mountain (the highest point in the range). Booking essential. Tours available of the wildlife rehab center. Tours R40. 2- and 4-bed chalets with communal kitchens R130 per person. ❷

Aventura Eco Swadini (☎ 795 5141; fax 795 5178), near the end of the Swadini road off the R531. In the spectacular heart of the canyon. Provides clean youth hostel accommodations to those who call in advance. Used mostly by school groups, the hostel is often booked, but will attempt to accommodate travelers in need. Dorm beds R115 weekdays, R125 weekends and holidays; campsites R50-100 plus R20 per person. ❷

Mad Dogz Cafe (☎ 795 5425), on the R527 a few kilometers from the R36 junction. Pleasant little place to stop for a good lunch. Open-walled deck overlooks a trickling pond. Quiche R18.80. Tomato and mozzarella salad R18. Open daily 7:30am-5pm. ❶

🎒 HIKING

Follow the Swadini Road past the Aventura Resort, turn right at the end of the road, and continue over the bridge a few kilometers farther to reach the Blyde River Nature Reserve. At the end of the road is a visitors center (☎ 015 795 5643; open M-F 9am-4pm) and the head of the 2.3k **Peninsula Trail.**

Waterfall Trail (2km). Waterfall Trail is an easy walk along the Blyde stream to the waterfall. Starts opposite the nature conservatory's office by the bridge.

Eagle/Mariepskop Hike (4-5km). This trailhead is toward the reserve's entrance gate and loops through the foothills of the Mariepskop Peak.

Belvedere Day Walk (5hr.). This is a difficult, steep day trail which allows only 10 people at a time. Trail markings are blue. Belvedere permits available at visitors' center. Maps (R5) are available at Bourke's Luck Potholes information office. (☎ 013 769 6019 or 759 5432.)

Hippo Valley Trail (10km). This route stretches along the Blyde Dam and Rodille Peaks to Hippo Valley. Permits available at visitors center. R15.

Blyde River Canyon (Blyderivierspoort) Hiking Trail (30km, 5 day). The mother of all hikes, this trail starts at God's Window and traverses the canyon, nature reserve, and Treur River Valley before ending near Bourke's Luck Potholes. Trail markings are yellow. (☎ 013 759 5432) or contact the visitors' center. R35.

👁 SIGHTS

THREE *RONDAVELS*. The R532 marks the northernmost section of the Panorama Route. The Three *Rondavels* is the most famous postcard shot around here, with good reason. The lookout point offers a stunning view of the canyon and an eye-level perspective of the peaks. It doesn't take much imagination to see why the *rondavels* were originally named after three women (the wives of a local chief).

ECHO CAVES. This vast network of dolomite caves was formed by an underground river and was used long ago as a Sotho hiding place from Swazi warriors. Many of the stalactites are broken off, as their sharp points were used to make spears. You can test the echoes by tapping a stalactite with a piece of metal. *(On the R36 3km south of the R532 junction. Open daily 8am-6pm. R30, not including guide tip.)*

BOURKE'S LUCK POTHOLES. No, we're not talking about chunks missing from a concrete highway. These potholes are enormous circular wells in the mountainside formed by grinding sand and swirling water at the confluence of the Blyde and Treur rivers. Climb into the nearby waterfall gorge, or take the hike over colorful calcium-rich rocks to the small **Kadish Waterfall,** 500m away from the potholes. *(On the R532 a few kilometers south of the Three Rondavels. A few kilometers down the main road. Gate open daily 7am-5pm.)*

LYDENBURG ☎013

Lydenburg was named "the town of suffering" by its Voortrekker founders, who established the town in 1849 after a malaria epidemic forced them to abandon their original swampy settlement and rebuild in the mosquito-free Drakensberg Valley. Today, Lydenburg offers good trout fishing, beautiful waterfalls, and a few examples of historic Voortrekker architecture. If nothing else, the small town is a public transport connection between Gauteng and the Mpumalanga escarpment.

⬛ TRANSPORTATION. Translux/Intercape (☎011 774 3333) buses go to **Johannesburg** (5hr.; M, W, F, Su 10:25am; R90) and **Phalaborwa** (3hr.; Tu, Th-F, Su 1:25pm; R65). Buy tickets at Anne Louise Florist, at Voortrekker St. and Kantoor St. (open M-F 8am-5pm, Sa 8am-noon). You can also catch a **minibus taxi** at the corner of Voortrekker and De Clerq St. Taxis run to **Sabie** (R16) and **Nelspruit** (R28). To reach **Johannesburg** and **Pretoria,** take a taxi to **Witbank** (R45); from there, minibuses to Gauteng cost about R25.

⬛ ⏹ ORIENTATION AND PRACTICAL INFORMATION. Lydenburg is about 50km west of Sabie on the R37. The main road through town is **Voortrekker St.,** which runs east-west and leads to Sabie over the Long Tom Pass. Coming south from Ohrigstad, the R36 becomes **De Clerq St.;** take a left onto Voortrekker to reach the center of town. East of the center, **Viljoen St.** intersects with Voortrekker St. and leads south to Dullstroom. There is no tourist office in town, but local businesspeople are generally happy to answer your questions. A particularly good bet is a fishing supply shop called **Starlings,** in a shopping plaza called Jock's Country Stalls, about 2km south of town on Viljoen St. (☎235 4037. Open M-Th 9am-5pm, F 9am-6pm, Sa 9am-2pm.) Services in town include: **ABSA Bank** with **ATM,** in the Spar center at the corner of Voortrekker and Kantoor St. (open M-F 8:30am-3:30pm, Sa 8-11am); **Link Pharmacy,** on Voortrekker St. between Kantoor and Burger St. (☎235 3200 or 083 377 3791; open M-F 8am-5:30pm, Sa 8am-1pm and 5-6pm, Su 10am-noon and 5-6pm); **Medical Clinic** at the corner of Viljoen and Kerk St. (☎235 2205; open M-F 8am-1pm and 2-5pm, Sa 8am-noon); **police** on Rensburg St. (☎253 2222); **Internet** at Comrite, down Kantoor St. from the ABSA bank (☎235 1486; open M-F 8am-5pm, Sa 8am-1pm; R15 per 30min.). The **post office** with *Poste Restante* is at the corner of Voortrekker and Burger St. (Open M-Tu and Th-F 8:30am-4:30pm, W 9am-4:30pm, Sa 8am-noon.) **Postal code:** 1120.

⬛ ⬛ ACCOMMODATIONS AND FOOD. Perched atop the highest point of Long Tom Pass, **Hops Hollow Country House and Brewery ❸,** 22km from Lydenburg on the R37, is a lovely country house with spacious, comfortable rooms, excellent food, and views of the hills and valleys below. The welcoming hosts also brew three kinds of delicious beer. One room is partially handicapped accessible. (☎235 2275 or 083 281 7113. No children under 14. Breakfast included, dinner available upon prior request. Doubles R250 for 1 person, R230 per person sharing.) The **Manor Guest House ❸** is on the corner of Potgieter St. and Viljoen St., one block south of Voortrekker St.; look for the mustard-colored wall. Touches of comfort and class ornament this pleasant guest house. Each bedroom has a different nature theme and overlooks the garden. All rooms have TV, electric blanket, and bath, as well as access to a swimming pool and secure parking. (☎235 2099; fax 235 2251; manorgh@intekom.co.za; lydenburgmanorhouse.com. Breakfast included. Singles R210; doubles R430.)

The **Trout Inn Restaurant & Pub ❷,** at Lange and Potgieter St., sports a lovely candlelit dining room stuffed to the gills with locals enjoying freshly caught fish. The boneless trout with vegetables runs R45. (☎235 1828. Open M-Sa 10am-11pm, Su noon-11pm.) **Froukje's Coffee Shop ❷,** at Voortrekker St. and Rensburg St., offers a welcome reprieve from the busy thoroughfare in town. Their light lunch platters include Quiche Lorraine (R21.50), lasagna (R24.50), and seafood dishes. (☎ 235 3016. Open M-F 8:30am-4:30pm, Sa 8:30am-2pm.)

◙ ⚞ **SIGHTS AND OUTDOORS.** Lydenburg has a few Voortrekker buildings of the Cape Dutch style: the **Voortrekker School** (1851) and the **Voortrekker Church** (1852), both near the corner of Kantoor and Kerk St., one block north of Voortrekker, and the **Dutch Reformed Church** (1894), near the corner of Kerk and Lange.

The well-hidden cascades of **Lydenburg Falls** are the town's best attraction and arguably the most spectacular waterfalls in Mpumalanga. A short forest walk from the power station leads to a roped ledge overlooking the three main falls, which have a combined height of 244m. Steep paths also lead down to the bottom of the ravine, but be aware that it takes an hour to re-ascend. (Contact Kudu Ranch at 234 6251 for information on visiting the falls.) Those craving a more interactive (and less active) experience with nature should consider **trout fishing** in one of Lydenburg's rivers. (Required license R20 per year.) The R37 route from Lydenburg to Sabie via the **Long Tom Pass** is one of the most beautiful mountain drives in South Africa. The pass is named for the Long Tom artillery guns used to defend the pass in the Boer War; bullet marks are still visible along the walls of the pass.

FREE STATE

The Free State (*Vrystaat*) isn't the milk-and-honey paradise that the first *Voortrekkers* once envisioned. Originally named the Orange Free State, most of the province consists of jutting, flat-top sandstone mesas and scrubland possessing its own understated beauty. The terrain houses the memories of the Anglo-Boer War and British concentration camps, and you may still encounter the occasional Boer who longs for a separate Afrikaner *volkstaat* within the province. Despite having once-sacred status among Afrikaners, the Free State is no longer the openly prejudiced place it once was. You may find the province to be the most authentic mixture of traditional Boer and native African culture of any province in South Africa.

HIGHLIGHTS OF THE FREE STATE

An outpost of alternative lifestyles and unconventional thinking, **Rustler's Valley** (see p. 389) is home to music festivals, permaculture, and traditional medicines.

All the rugged hikes and dizzying views of the Lesotho Highlands can be found in **Golden Gate Highlands** and **Qwaqwa National Park** (see p. 394), without actually crossing the border.

Tours of the **Intabazwe township** near Harrismith (see **P. 394**) offer an opportunity to see the way of life of many South Africans.

BLOEMFONTEIN   ☎051

A seemingly ordinary city, Bloemfontein (Afrikaans for "flower fountain," though the Tswana call it *Maugaung*, meaning "place of cheetahs") has it all. Not only is Bloemfontein the capital of the Free State, but it is also South Africa's judicial capital. First, the Voortrekkers lugged their weary bones across the Orange River and set up parliament in a one-room, thatched-roof house. Then the British invaded during the Anglo-Boer War, razing Boer farms and deporting their women and children to concentration camps. Finally, in 1854, the city was restored to its current role as capital of the (Orange) Free State.

▐▀ TRANSPORTATION

Flights: Bloemfontein Airport (☎433 2901), on the N8 10km east of town, with **South African Airways/Airlink** (☎433 3225 or 408 4822) offices. Daily flights to: **Cape Town** (1hr. 40min.; M-F 8:05am, 1:10pm, 7pm; R2340); **Durban** (1hr. 15min.; M-F 8:25am, Su 5:45pm; R2060); **Johannesburg** (1hr. 10min., 2-8 flights daily 6:20am-8pm, R1560); **Port Elizabeth** (1hr. 35min., M-F 10:50am, R2260).

Trains: Bloemfontein Station (☎408 4861 or 086 000 888), at the intersection of Maitland and Harvey St. One-way to: **Cape Town** (daily, 2nd/1st class R235/R330); **Durban** (Tu, R135/R195); **East London** (daily, R100); **Johannesburg** (3 per day; R80/R130); **Kimberley** (3hr., Su-F, R45/65); **Pretoria** (daily, R105/R150). Student discount 25% on 2nd class round-trip tickets. Ticket office open M-F 7:30am-4pm.

Buses: Buses depart from and are ticketed at the **Transit Center,** a part of the Bloemfontein Tourist Center on Park Rd. Open 24hr.

    Intercape (☎447 1575) runs to: **Cape Town** (12hr., daily 11:30pm and M, Tu, Th, Sa 2:45am; R300); **Durban** (8hr.; M, Tu, Th, Sa 6:30am; R150) via **Harrismith** (3hr. 45min., R130) and **Pietermaritzburg** (6hr. 45min., R140); **Plettenberg Bay** (11½hr., M-Sa 11:30pm, R235) via **George** (10hr., R215) and **Graaff-Reinet** (5hr. 15min., R145); **Port Elizabeth** (7hr.; M, Tu, Th, Sa 11:30pm; R195); **Pretoria** (7hr., daily 6:30am, R160) via **Johannesburg** (5½hr., R160).

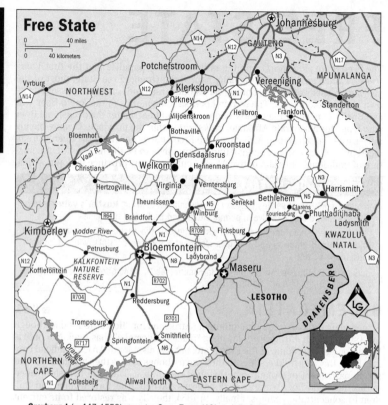

Free State

0 ——— 40 miles
0 ——— 40 kilometers

Johannesburg

GAUTENG

Potchefstroom

Vyrburg

NORTHWEST

Klerksdorp

Orkney

Vereeniging

MPUMALANGA

Standerton

Viljoenskroon

Heilbron

Frankfort

Bloemhof

Bothaville

Kroonstad

Vaal R.

Christiana

Odensdaalsrus

Welkom

Hennenman

Hertzogville

Virginia

Verntersburg

Theunissen

Senekal

Bethlehem

Harrismith

Clarens

Phuthaditjhaba

Ladysmith

Brandfort

Winburg

Fouriesburg

Modder River

Ficksburg

KWAZULU-NATAL

Kimberley

Petrusburg

Bloemfontein

Ladybrand

Maseru

KALKFONTEIN NATURE RESERVE

Koffiefontein

LESOTHO

DRAKENSBERG

Reddersburg

Trompsburg

Smithfield

Springfontein

Orange River

NORTHERN CAPE

Colesberg

Aliwal North

EASTERN CAPE

Greyhound (☎447 1558) goes to: **Cape Town** (12hr., daily 8:45pm, R300); **Durban** (8hr., daily 11:45pm, R160) via **Harrismith** (5hr. 15min., R145) and **Pietermaritzburg** (6hr. 30min., R160); **East London** (6hr. 45min., daily midnight, R190); **Port Elizabeth** (9hr., daily 11:15pm, R200) via **Grahamstown** (9½hr., R200); **Pretoria** (6½hr., daily 5:05am, R150) via **Johannesburg** (5hr. 45min., R150).

Minibus Taxis: Majakathata Taxi (☎448 5082), at Harvey and Douglas St., runs to: **Ficksburg** (R50); **Johannesburg** (R80); **Kimberley** (R45); **Maseru, Lesotho** (R30); and **Wepener** (R35). Taxis leave daily as early as 6am; just show up with lots of patience. Alternatively, look for the fleet of minibus taxis at Central Park, along Peet between Hanger and Harvey.

Taxis: Silver Leaf Taxi (☎430 2005 or 080 043 0200) and **Pro-Taxi** (☎523 3779 or 080 044 4333) are 24hr. radio taxi companies. You should be able to get anywhere in Bloemfontein for under R40. **Gerardo Odendaal** (☎526 2745) makes trips to **Lesotho** on demand. One-way from Bloemfontein to **Malealea** or **Maseru** (R180 per person, min. 2 people); or to **Semonkong** (R200 per person, min. 2 people).

Car Rental: Avis, 123 Nelson Mandela St. and in the airport (☎433 2331 or 086 102 1111). Open in town M-F 8am-5pm, Sa 8am-1pm; at the airport M-F 6:30am-8pm, Sa 9am-5pm, Su 8am-8pm. **Tempest** (☎433 2146 or 082 463 0392) in the airport. Open M-F 6:30am-8pm, Sa 9am-5pm, Su 8am-8pm. **Budget** (☎433 1178 or 083 903 3846) in the airport. Open M-F 6:30am-8pm, Sa 8am-4pm, Su 9am-8pm.

FREE STATE

▟ ORIENTATION

The N1, which runs between Cape Town and Johannesburg, passes through Bloemfontein. The R64 runs west to Kimberley, the N6 south to East London, and the N8 east to Maseru and the N3, which stretches between Johannesburg and Durban. Coming from the north on the N1, exit the highway at Zastron/Nelson Mandela St. From the south, exit at Haldon Rd. Downtown Bloemfontein is defined by **Zastron St.** to the north, **St. Georges St.** to the south, **Markgraff/Pres. Boshoff St.** to the west, and **Harvey St.** to the east. The northwest corner of town is known as the **Westdene**, marked by **Nelson Mandela St.** to the south and **First (Eerste) Ave.** to the east. Westdene is the hub of Bloem nightlife and the hangout of local college students. South of Westdene is **Loch Logan**, where Bloemfontein has focused its gentrification . The constellation of restaurants, shops, and night spots that surrounds the lake forms a commercial district known as the **Waterfront**, a diminutive sterile version of the Victoria & Alfred Waterfront in Cape Town.

▟ PRACTICAL INFORMATION

Tourist Offices: Bloemfontein Tourist Information Office, 60 Park Rd. (☎405 8489/90; blminfo@iafrica.com), in Tourism Center, on south side of the Waterfront and sporting grounds. Open M-F 8am-4:15pm, Sa 8am-noon. **Transgariep** (☎447 1362; transgariep@intekom.co.za), next to Bloemfontein Tourist Center, covers activities in all of Free State. Open M-F 8am-4pm.

Tours: Anglo-Boer War Battlefield Tour (☎447 3447). A 2-day play-by-play program complete with reveille at dawn. **Astra Tours** (☎430 2184 or 082 696 4309; astratours@intekom.co.za), next to the tourist office on Park Rd., arranges tours throughout the country as well as local excursions (open M-F 8:30am-5pm). More adventurous folk may want to try a trip with **Adventure Exposed** (☎448 6452 or 082 907 1122; adventureexpo@worldonline.co.za), in Showgate Center on Curie Ave. south of downtown. They offer outdoor opportunities from abseiling to paragliding at some of the finest locations in South Africa (open M-F 8:30am-5:30pm, Sa 8am-4pm).

Travel Agencies: STA Travel (☎444 6062, fax 444 6065; bloemfontein@statravel.co.za; www.statravel.co.za), in Mimosa Mall (the intersection of Nelson Mandela St. and Parfitt/Gen. Dan Pienaar St.). Open M-F 9am-6pm, Sa 9am-1pm. **Usit Adventures** (☎447 7629; www.usit-adventures.co.za), in Waterfront Mall. Open M-Th 9:30am-6pm, F 9:30am-6pm, Sa 9:30am-2pm.

Weather: ☎012 310 3611.

Banks: First National Bank, 88 Maitland St. (☎505 3111; fax 505 3297). No commission on American Express or Visa traveler's checks. Open M-F 9am-3:30pm, Sa 8:30-11am. **24hr. ATM** on the premises.

Currency Exchange: American Express Foreign Exchange (☎444 6938; fax 444 6928), in Mimosa M-F 9am-4:30pm, Sa 9-noon.

Laundromat: Johnny's Laundromat & Fun Center, 30 1st Ave. (☎447 1080). Corner of Zastron St. Wash R7 per load; Dry R2 for 10min. Not as "fun" as you might desire. Open Su-Th 7:45am-11pm, F-Sa 7:45am-midnight.

Camping Supplies: OFS Canvas, 66 West Burger St. (☎447 8018). At the corner of Cricket St. A wide array of tents, stoves, and a bit of everything else. Open M-F 8am-5pm, Sa 8am-1pm. Also try **Outdoor Warehouse** (☎448 6882), in Showgate Center on Curie Ave., has an extensive range of outdoor gear. Open M-F 8:30am-5:30pm, Sa 8am-1pm. In the same shopping mall, **Adventure Exposed** (see **Tours,** above) has a selection of more technical gear. Open M-F 8:30am-5:30pm, Sa 8am-4pm.

Public Swimming Pool: Stadium Swimming Bath, on Park Rd. next to the Tourist Center. R6 per person. Open M-Sa 6am-7:30pm, Su 10am-5pm.

Emergency: Police (☎10 111); **ambulance** (☎10 177 or 447 3111).

Police: At Park Rd. and President Boshof St.

Pharmacy: Checmed (☎444 3871) in College Sq. shopping center. On Zastrom St. near the intersection with Parfitt/Gen. Dan Pienaar. Open 24hr.

Hospital: Medi-Clinic (☎404 6666) on Kellner St. **Universitas Hospital** (☎405 3911), on Logeman St.

Internet Access: Connix Internet (☎448 5648), in the Waterfront Mall. R40 per hr. Open M-F 8am-9pm, Sa 9am-9pm, Su 10am-4pm.

Books: M&M Booksellers (☎448 8575), in the Tourist Center on Park Rd. A good selection of J.R.R. Tolkien. Open M-F 8:30am-5pm, Sa 8:30am-1pm. **Bloemfontein Library** (☎405 8250), on the corner of West Burger St. and Charles St. Open M-F 9am-6pm, Sa 8:30am-noon.

Post Office: Groenendal St. (☎403 0600). On Hoffman Sq., between St. Andrews and Maitland St. Fax and *Poste Restante*. Open M-F 8am-4:30pm, Sa 8am-12:30pm.

Postal Code: 9300.

■ ACCOMMODATIONS AND CAMPING

The legion of hotels, guest houses, and Bed & Breakfasts in town drives prices down, making reasonable, if not budget, lodging easy to find. For extra peace and quiet, try the "guest rooms" available through the Tourist Center; though little more than a bed in someone's home, singles are only R50-60 and doubles are R100-120.

■ **Naval Hill Backpackers,** 7 Delville Street (☎430 7266 or 082 579 6509; info@naval-hillbackpackers.co.za; www.navalhillbackpackers.co.za). Follow the signs for Naval Hill Game Reserve. Take West Burger Street north until it ends. Turn left onto Union St., and then turn right onto Delville. This is the best Bloem has to offer. A restored water pump station from the Anglo-Boer War divided into funky sleeping quarters and common area. Stellar view of the city and nature reserve next door; your neighbors are giraffes. Customized tours (shuttle to Lesotho R180 per person, minimum 4), Internet (R10 for 30min.), self-catering kitchen and wood-burning pizza oven, TV lounge. Linen R5; laundry R15. Free pick-up from bus/train station and airport. Dorms R55; doubles R130. Camping R35. ❶

Arete Inn, 28 Kellner St. (☎430 7667). Near the corner of Kellner St. and Markgraaf (Market). Great location close to the Waterfront and the heart of Westdene with simple and clean rooms and a great deal on doubles. 24hr. reception. Check-out 10am. Rooms with shared bath R130, with private bath R150. ❷

City Lodge (☎447 9888), at the corner of Nelson Mandela and Parfitt. A sparkling new establishment that sets the standard for motel accommodation in Bloemfontein. 24hr. reception. Check-out 11am. Rooms R370 (single or double). ❹

Dagbreek Accommodation (☎/fax 433 2490; www.satic.co.za/accommodation/dag-breek/index.html). Take Andries Pretorius St. 8km north from city center, and follow signs. Though a bit far from town, it's is a good option for travelers seeking quiet. Offers camping/caravan sites, chalets, guest house, and beds in train sleeper coaches. Hot shower, self-catering kitchen, and pool. Camping R40 for 2; self-catering caravan R50; train beds R50; 4-person guest house R145; 6-person chalets R200. ❶

FREE STATE

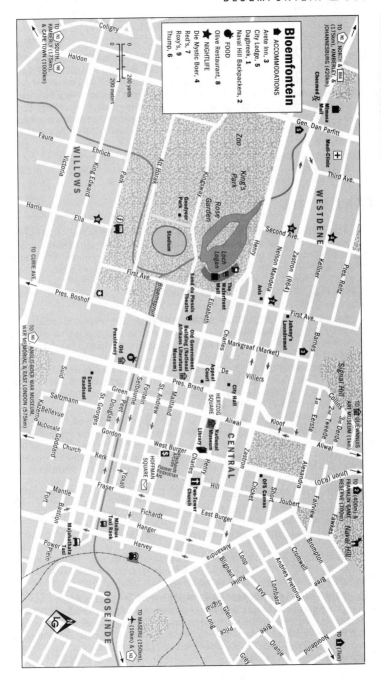

Bloemfontein

➤ ACCOMMODATIONS
Arete Inn, 3
City Lodge, 5
Dagbreek, 1
Naval Hill Backpackers, 2

🍴 FOOD
Olive Restaurant, 8

★ NIGHTLIFE
Die Mystic Boer, 4
Reds, 7
Roxy's, 9
Thump, 6

◘ FOOD

▓ **Fishpaste,** 31 Pres. Steyn Ave. (☎ 430 2662 or 430 7240). Near the corner of 2nd Ave. and Pres. Steyn Ave. Serves up Bloemfontein's most creative dishes (R35-55) for meat-eaters and vegetarians alike in a relaxed, funky setting. Open M-Sa 7am-late. ❷

Olive Restaurant (☎ 430 8121), on the grounds of the Old Presidency near the corner of Pres. Brand and St. Georges St. The training ground for students at Bloem's Cordon Bleu Chef School. Thankfully, they seem to have been hitting the books; the restaurant is home to some of the best food in town. Lunch and snacks R20-35. Dinner R35-60. Open daily 9am-5pm; W, F-Sa 6-9pm. ❷

Jazz Time Cafe (☎ 430 5727), on the Waterfront. Might feel a bit pre-packaged, but with a huge deck, it's the best place in town to see and be seen. Good dinners (R25-60) make it ideal for a nice evening. Open daily 8am-midnight. ❸

◉ 🄻 SIGHTS

OLIEWENHUIS ART MUSEUM. Set in a manor house originally built to house governors and state presidents, the museum features a cross-section of South African artists. Themes include idyllic, oil landscapes from the 19th century, 20th-century bronze and wood sculptures, and postmodern works constructed of anything and everything. A superb wood-sculpture exhibit is designed specifically for the visually impaired. *(Take Aliwal St. north and turn left onto Harry Smith St.; entrance is up the hill on the right. ☎ 447 9609. Open M-F 8am-5pm, Sa 10am-5pm, Su 1-5pm. Free.)*

NATIONAL WOMEN'S MEMORIAL & WAR MUSEUM. The museum commemorates the 26,000 Afrikaner women and children who died in concentration camps; a chilling reminder of the horrors of war. The building contains a treasury of war artifacts, including heartwrenching photographs from the camps and a just acknowledgement of the black regiments that fought for both sides. *(On Monument Rd. From downtown Bloemfontein, take Kerk St. south and bear right at the fork onto Monument Rd. ☎ 447 3447; www.anglo-boer.co.za. Museum open M-F 8am-4:30pm, Sa 10am-5pm, Su 2-5pm. Memorial open daily 7am-7pm. Museum admission R5.)*

NATIONAL MUSEUM. This museum was established in 1877 and now houses a collection that includes exhibits on natural history, cultural history, sciences, and art. Once interesting display focuses on a collection of clay pots originating from traditional black population groups of the country and their differing character and function. *(At the corner of Charles St. and Aliwal St. ☎ 447 9609. Open M-F 8am-5pm, Sa 10am-5pm, Su noon-5:30pm. Admission R5.)*

FRANKLIN GAME RESERVE. Hiking trails criss-cross Naval Hill with only slightly less frequency than artillery fire did when it was home to British guns during the Anglo-Boer War. There are a number of good view points for panoramas of Bloemfontein, and you're likely to see the springbok and wildebeest which call the reserve home. Three roaming giraffes are named for their relative sizes: Small, Medium, and Large. If you're not up for a walk, a number of trails are negotiable by car. *(On Deville Rd., up the street from the Naval Hill Backpackers. Gates open dawn to dusk. There is no central information office, but trails are marked.)*

OLD PRESIDENCY (OU PRESIDENSIE) MUSEUM. Designed with turrets and arches, this European manor was home to three Free State presidents between 1886 and 1899. It's seen better days, but the luxurious lifestyle enjoyed by the leaders of the Orange Free State is easy to imagine. *(Corner of St. George's and President Brand St. ☎ 448 0949. Open Tu-F 10am-noon and 1-4pm, Su 2-4pm. Free. Chamber music concerts Su afternoons in the ballroom.)*

FIRST COUNCIL CHAMBER (EERSTE RAADSAAL). This one-room thatched roof building was built as a schoolhouse 150 years ago and has since been repeatedly face-lifted into a Dutch Reformed Church, a meeting house, a council chamber, an Anglican church, and finally a quiet museum featuring a brief history of Bloemfontein. *(On St. George's near the intersection with Pres. Brand St. ☎447 9609. Open M-F 10am-1pm, Sa-Su and holidays 2-5pm. R2.50, children R1.50.)*

🔊 🎵 NIGHTLIFE AND ENTERTAINMENT

Die Mystic Boer, 84 Kellner St. (☎430 2206). Near 2nd Ave. "The Mystic," as it's known, is the most happening spot in Bloem on pretty much any night. A smoky hangout for college kids and local twentysomethings of all races, with thumping music, a dance floor, pool tables, and a chill vibe. Live local bands. Open daily noon-late.

Red's (☎083 370 8181), 2nd floor at the corner of Nelson Mandela and First Ave. Loud and packed, this is the place to head when "all you want is to dance." Th and Sa are "pig-out" nights (cover R15) where drinks are very cheap. Open Th-Sa 8pm-6am.

Thump (☎447 7907), on 2nd Ave. between Nelson Mandela and Zastron St., on 2nd fl. A new club swamped with a relatively diverse student crowd. House music, techno grooves, and psychedelic rave. Head to the *lapa* balcony for a cool breather. Cover R10. Open Tu-Sa 8pm-late.

Roxy's Rhythm Bar (☎082 979 1761), on Ella St. Off of Park Rd. neat the Bloemfontein Tourist Center; look for the flashing red squiggle. Comfortable place for gay travelers in the midst of conservative Bloem. Live music on Su. No cover. Open daily 6pm-late, but things get pumping on W, F, and Sa nights.

DJ's, on the Waterfront, features a state-of-the-art pool hall (R2 per game, R10 deposit) as well as a full-on dance club. It serves as the focal point for Waterfront nightlife. Pool hall open daily noon-late. Dance club open W-Sa 8pm-late.

Nu Metro Loch Logan (☎448 7485), on the Waterfront. 6 cinemas. Showtimes from noon-9pm. R20-22, Tu R15.

Sand du Plessis Theatre (☎447 7771), on Markgraaf St., between Elizabeth and St. Andrew St. Ballet, opera, jazz, symphony orchestra (R15-50), and children's theater (R10). Booking office open M-F 9am-5pm, Sa 9am-noon. Tours W 2:30pm (R2, children R1). Student discounts available for some performances.

Free State Stadium (☎407 1701; www.fscheetahs.co.za), on Att Horak St., between the Tourist Center and the Waterfront. Home of the Free State's rugby team. Season runs Mar.-Aug. R20, under 16 R10. Call for schedule.

Goodyear Park (☎430 6365), on Att Horak St. R10 for domestic test matches, R50 for international test matches. Season Oct.-Mar. Call for schedule.

RUSTLER'S VALLEY

In a secluded grassland valley surrounded by sandstone, Rustler's Valley faces the heart of the eastern Free State. Life here centers on **Rustlers Valley Mountain Lodge ❶**, which serves as a backpackers, restaurant, workshop center, and festival venue, among other things. The individuals who live in the valley and the thousands of Rustlers devotees who journey here on a regular basis are united by a common goal: creating a model for sustainable multiculturalism and arts. The vision is imparted through music festivals traditionally held each year at Easter, the spring equinox, and the New Year. Although they differ in ethos and attendance (from 500 to 5000), each is a testament to the eclectic, culturally diverse vibe of the place, with music and musicians from around the world. The festivals are in a bit of flux now, so check the web site (www.rustlers.co.za) for more info. Gate fees for the two- to four-day events run R150-300 per person. Workshops on such subjects as permaculture, traditional medicines, and drumming bring experts to the valley. The workshops are held on weekends throughout the year and cost between R500 and R100. Alternatively, a sweat lodge ceremony—a cathartic experience involving alternating deep sweats and plunges into the reservoir—occurs every full moon, and poetic sound journeys are organized whenever there's enough interest. There's also plenty of hiking and climbing around, including forays into the Thabo Thabo game reserve next door.

The town has had some recent bad luck: most of Rustlers burnt to the ground several years ago. Since then, many new buildings featuring funky architecture and unique interiors have gone up, including a beautiful restaurant and bar with a stunning view of the surrounding hills (meals R20-50). Despite its ecofriendliness, Rustlers is not wanting for technology; the Mountain Lodge features a TV lounge, Internet access, and a surround-sound system. Of course, to experience Rustlers fully, you have to stay a night or two, and there are myriad accommodation options from which to choose. (Large, lavish dorms R60 per person, R50 each additional night; more upscale doubles with attached bath R180-500; all include use of communal kitchen. Camping R25.) From Fouriesburg travel 23km south on the R26 before turning right onto a dirt road at the Rustlers sign. Follow the road 13km over a mountain pass and make another right at the Rustlers sign. The main gate is about 1km along that road. From Ficksburg, travel 9km north on the R26 and make a left turn onto a dirt road at the Rustlers sign. Follow that road 15km through two crossroads, and the main gate will be on the right. They'll do pick-ups from Ficksburg during the day, but make sure to call ahead. (☎ 933 3939; fax 933 3286; wemad@rustlers.co.za; www.rustlers.co.za)

FOURIESBURG (MASHAENG)   ☎ 058

When the British took over Bloemfontein in 1906, the Boers named Fouriesburg the temporary capital of Free State. Ever since then, it's been on the downswing. The crumbling roads, dearth of amenities and lack of real infrastructure make it feel as though Fouriesburg is trying to commemorate its past by remaining in it. As a jumping-off point for outdoor adventurers, however, the town is hard to beat. Surrounded by a few heavenly multi-day hikes and just down the road from a border post that plunges you into the heart of Lesotho's Maluti Mountains, Fouriesburg caters to those travelers trying their best to escape civilization.

■ ◪ **ORIENTATION AND PRACTICAL INFORMATION.** Fouriesburg is between Bethlehem (49km) and Ficksburg (53km) just off the R26. The town is laid out in a grid and is small enough that, despite the almost complete lack of street signs, travelers are never really "lost;" they're just a block or two from where they should be. **Minibus taxis** run to Bethlehem (R22) and Clarens (R18-25). The minibus taxi depot is across from the post office in the middle of town. The **tourist office** (☎ 223 0207) doubles as the reception for Fouriesburg Country Inn (see **Accommodations,** below) and has information on the town and guided tours, including tours of Bushman painting sites. (Open daily 6am-11pm.)

Services include: **First National Bank,** with a 24hr. **ATM,** on Brand St. (☎ 223 0255; open M-F 9am-12:45pm and 2-3:30pm, Sa 8:30-11am); **emergency ambulance** services (☎ 223 0255); **emergency police** (☎ 10 111); **police station,** on Martin St. (☎ 223 0260); the **post office** (☎ 223 0215), with *Poste Restante,* on the corner of Robertson and Martin. (Open M-Tu, Th-F 8:30am-1pm and 2-4:30pm; W 9am-1pm and 2-4:30pm; Sa 8am-noon.) **Postal code:** 9725.

ACCOMMODATIONS AND FOOD. Accommodations in Fouriesburg proper are limited. The ancient **Fouriesburg Country Inn ❷**, on Reitz St., a few blocks from the town center, is a relic out of the late 1800s that's still going strong. The interior decor is reminiscent of Boer homes in larger cities' museums, but rooms are clean and comfortable. The exterior is still the original sandstone and Oregon pine. (☎223 0207; fax 223 0257. Follow the Inn signposts from the main road. Singles R150; doubles R300. Rates included breakfast.) Attached to the Inn is the only proper **restaurant** in Fouriesburg. Steaks (R40) are delicious, and other entrees range between R25 and R50. (Open daily 6am-9:30pm.) Take Robertson east out of town, make a left on Commissaris St. and follow signs to reach **Meiringskloof Nature Park ❶**, the only campground in the vicinity. Idyllic in its placid setting, the park rests in a kloof surrounded by caves, cliffs, Bushman paintings, and a few of the Free State's best hikes. Sites include toilets, hot showers, and *braai*. The *swaelnes* (swallow's nest) hut is only R10, but it provides little more than a roof against the rain and wind, 400m from the facilities. For a more decadent option, stay in a chalet with full kitchen, bed linen, heaters, and fireplaces. There's also a pool, rope swing, and an exciting African *foefie* slide. (☎223 0067. R40 plus R10 per person per night. Singles R70-100; doubles R140-200; each additional adult R65-70; children under 18 R30-35.)

HIKING. Hiking trails abound in the Fouriesburg area. The **Brandwater Hike** is a spectacular, strenuous five-day hike through the Witteberger, which is dotted with a number of enormous sandstone caves used as places of refuge for the Bushmen, Basotho, and Boers. One of these, Saltpeterkrans, is the largest overhang in the Southern Hemisphere and is still used by the Basotho for ancestral worship and fertility rituals. Since the path runs through private property, permits are necessary; they can be purchased for R70 from **Father Mostard** (☎223 0050 or 496 5503), chairman of the local Heritage Fund. The overnight **Venterberg Hike** is slightly tamer; the good Father sells permits (R60). The tourist office can arrange for the **Tepelkop, Lesoba,** and **Queen Victoria** hikes, all daytrips into the surrounding area and the Lesotho border regions.

ADVENTURES. Didibeng Mountain Park claims to be the first caravan park exclusively for 4x4 enthusiasts and offers 30km of challenging 4x4 trails through the Rooiberg Mountain Range. (☎223 0067. Day entry R30 per vehicle plus R5 per person. Camping R20 per person.) **Abseiling** (R75) and **horseback riding** (R35 per hr.) can also be arranged through the tourist office or the Meiringskloof Park. For those with an aerial fetish, you can get an hour's worth of breathtaking view by chartering a five-passenger Cessna plane (pilot included, don't worry) for R1000. Terrain includes the Eastern Free State, Northern 'Berg, and Lesotho Highlands. Contact Crause Steyl (☎223 0429) to set it up.

CLARENS (KGUBETSOANA)   ☎058

Sitting on a hilltop several kilometers west of Golden Gate and surrounded by superb mountain vistas, Clarens is atypical among small South African towns. Founded in 1912 and named after the Swiss Village where President Paul Kruger spent his last days, the town is young even by South African standards. Paradoxically, it contains none of the strip malls, fast food restaurants, or chain stores that typify the recent growth of most of South Africa. Clarens is far the major highways that link the country's urban centers, but it is filled with art galleries, luxurious guest houses, and inventive restaurants. It is much more cosmopolitan than many of South Africa's other hamlets. As a result, white, upper-middle class Johannesburg and Pretoria residents have increasingly chosen Clarens as a retirement destination. Still, life is not entirely harmonious in this little town. The stark contrast between the posh homes of many whites and the township-like suburbs that house the poor black population working in the area manifests the socio-economic divide that continues to persist in South Africa.

☏ PRACTICAL INFORMATION. Minibus taxis run to Fouriesburg (R18), Bethlehem (R20), and Phuthaditjaba (R25). The **tourist office,** in the mall on Market St. by President Sq., has information on restaurants, accommodations, and activities in Clarens. (☎256 1542; clarens@bhm.dorea.co.za; www.clarenstourism.co.za. Open daily 9am-1pm and 2-5pm.) The **Clarens Adventure Tourism** office, in the Clarens Meander, is an excellent resource for local exploration as well as journeys into Lesotho. (☎256 1903. Open M, W-Sa 9:30am-1pm and 2-4pm; Su 10:30am-1pm.) While there's **no bank** in town, there is a 24hr. **ATM** by the **Maluti Superette** in the Clarens Meander on Main St. **Bibliophile,** 313 Church St., is a great little bookstore with a surprisingly wide selection. (☎256 1692. Open M-F 9am-4:30pm, Sa-Su 9am-1pm.) In case of **emergency,** call ☎10 177. The **police station** is at the corner of Market and Church St. The **post office** is at the corner of Church and Van Zyl St., with **public phones** out front. (☎256 1300. Open M-Tu, Th-F 8:30am-1pm and 2-4:30pm, W 9am-1pm and 2-4:30pm, Sa 8am-noon. Closed 2nd and 3rd Sa of each month.) **Postal code:** 9707.

☏☐ ACCOMMODATIONS AND FOOD. B&Bs are generally the best way to go in Clarens, as the prices are usually below R100. For reservations and info on all lodging options, contact the tourist office. The **Village Square Guest House ❷** (☎256 1064) is right on President Sq., down the street from the tourist office and kitty corner to the affiliated street cafe (see below). The rooms are beautifully decorated, have a luxurious feel, and some even boast spectacular views. The cheapest rooms go for R100 per person. Spacious doubles with TVs, among other amenities, are R250. Prices for families and backpackers may be negotiable. **Clarens Inn and Backpackers ❶,** 93 Van Reenen St., offers austere dorms situated at the base of one of the nearby mountains. Entering on the R712, take Main St. past the President Sq. and turn right on Van Reenen. The Inn is at the road's end. There are no official hikes to the top of the ridge, but the climb is an easy 20min. scramble from the lodge. (☎256 1119 or 082 377 3621; schwin@netactive.co.za. Linen R10. Dorms R60; doubles R140.)

Clarens boasts good restaurants, and one of the best is the **Street Cafe ❶,** on Main St., adjacent to President Sq., where the locals come for flavorful pastas and juicy burgers. The spot has an air of unaffected romance with warm colors, wood furniture, and candlelit dinners. (☎256 1060. Breakfasts around R20; sandwiches R7-15; lunches from R20; dinner served from 5:30pm starts at R25. Open daily 8:30am-10pm.) The **Grouse and Claret ❷,** on the corner of Main St. and Van Zyl St., is the place to catch a rugby match with the locals while enjoying some good grub. (Open daily noon-3pm and 6-9pm. Entrees R25-40.) For breakfast, afternoon tea, or anything in between try **Post House ❷,** 276 Main St. Inquire about the quiche of the day and tantalizing cakes. (☎256 1534. Breakfast around R25; lunch and dinner a bit more. Open M and W-F 7:30am-4pm and W, F, Sa 7:30-10:30pm.) For a dollop of comfort a short walk from downtown head to **Thistle Stop Bed and Breakfast ❸,** 53 Le Roux St. Take Main St. to Van Teenen and turn right, then turn left on Le Roux; it's on your right. This lovely home offers a sumptuous B&B as well as a separate self-catering bunkhouse. (☎256 1003. B&B R150-R175 per person. Bunkhouse R85 per person, 3 or more R75 per person.)

☏OUTDOORS. With sandstone scenery like this, you would hope that the Clarens area had some outdoorsy stuff going on. If desired, you can stay out of the art galleries and explore marvelous terrain instead. The St. Fort Country House lies

4km along the road to Fouriesburg (R711) and is the trail head for three excellent hikes: Mushroom Trail (1hr.), Kloof Trail (1½-2hr.) and St. Fort Trail (15km). A couple of good walks start from downtown as well, including Kloof Hike (2½-3hr) and Scillia Walk (1-2hr). More information about all hikes is available at the information center (see above). There is also some excellent rock art at the Schaapplaats farm southeast of Clarens, which provides insight into the religious practices of the Bushmen as well as a look at their remarkable skill. Ask for directions at the information Center. **Bokpoort Horseback Adventures** is as close as you could get to a South African dude ranch, 5km out of Clarens off the Golden Gate road (R172) and about 3km up the hillside. The owners proudly claim that their farm is not a hotel, but a way of life. Indeed, roaming horses, pigs, cats, and dogs might get in your way as you stroll around the grounds. The farm's speciality, as the name implies, is horses and **horseback riding.** The farm organizes two-hour saunters (R400 per day per person), two-day "Snowyhill" trips (R800 per person), and three-day-or-more trips (R900) into the surrounding countryside. If you're not camping out on the trail, Bokpoort's dorm-cum-barn, rustic mountain huts, and chalets give you a comfortable, reasonably priced bed for the night. (Dorms R50, no linen; 3-person mountain huts R220; chalets R150 per person, breakfast included.) **4x4, mountain bike** and **hiking trails** also abound (R100 per vehicle; R15 per bike).

GOLDEN GATE HIGHLANDS NATIONAL PARK   ☎ 058

Full of towering sandstone faces that glow in deep yellows, oranges, and reds, and enclosed by the brooding Maluti Mountains which soar into the stratosphere, Golden Gate feels as though it was hewn in an age of fire and brimstone. The park's landmark feature, Brandwag Buttress, serves as the gate to a heaven on earth for black wildebeest, eland, blesbok, lammergeier, bald ibis, and human beings. In the summer, the Little Caledon River and its tributaries spring from green slopes, and in the winter, the rock is mirrored by the rich colors of the surrounding grasslands. The entire region is relatively undeveloped.

⚷ ACCOMMODATIONS AND CAMPING. The **Glen Reenen Rest Camp ❷** is in the middle of the park on the R172, 23km from Clarens and 70km from Harrismith. Bungalows with bathrooms and kitchens available, as well as lavish *rondavels*, and camping/caravan sites with showers and *braai*. Make reservations a month in advance during high season. (☎ 012 343 1991; fax 012 343 0905. Two-person bungalows R205, each additional adult R45, child R25; two-person *rondavels* R190, each additional adult R45, child R25. Two-person camping and caravan sites R60, each extra person R20, maximum 6 people.) One kilometer down the road, **Brandwag Camp ❸** lies in the shadow of the Buttress and offers the sort of extravagant lodging that perplexes those budget travelers simply looking for a place to rest their heads before hitting the trail. (☎ 012 343 1991; fax 012 343 0905. R195-520.)

◨◪ HIKING AND OUTDOORS. The park **information center** (☎ 255 0012) is at the Glen Reenen Camp. Pick up a free map of the park. (Open Oct.-Apr. daily 7am-5:30pm; May-Sept. Su-Th 7:30am-5pm and F-Sa 7:30am-5:30pm. Ribbok Hiking Maps R2.50.) In case of **emergency,** call ☎ 255 0021. If you come directly from the higher Drakensberg to Golden Gate, you'll find the terrain more forgiving and easier to navigate. The distinctive crags and dense foliage that characterize most of the Drakensberg Range do not exist here; instead, Golden Gate is marked by rolling *veld* and sandstone domes laced with trails of all difficulty levels. The best way to experience the park is on the **Ribbok Trail,** a two-day, 27km hike limited to 18 people at a time. The climax of the trail is an ascent of Mount Generaalskop, with its 360-degree view of Lesotho, the Caledon River, and the park's own sandstone wonders. The R50 permit available at the park reception includes a night at the

Ribbok hut. For those without the time for the Ribbok Trail, the park offers a number of hikes, including **Echo Ravine** (45min.), with climbs into a remarkable stream cut, and Wodehouse Peak (4hr.), which tops out for great views at 2438m. A **game-viewing self-drive** features zebra, oribi, springbok, and baboons. A permit (R12) is necessary for the hikes and the drives.

QWAQWA NATIONAL PARK   ☎ 058

Ecologically and geologically indistinguishable from its famous neighbor, Golden Gate, Qwaqwa (pronounced "!wa-!wa," with a sharp click at the beginning of each syllable) National Park offers scenery and wildlife without the crowds. The park, with its brilliant rock formations and expansive *veld*, recently came under the jurisdiction of the Free State Environmental Affairs and Tourism Office after a long period of private ownership. It has since undergone minimal development. Eventually Qwaqwa will most likely be incorporated into Golden Gate and garner the attention associated with federally protected land, but until then this pristine wilderness is out there for the exploring. The park offices are at the Alma turn-off on the R712, just east of the road to Kestell. (☎713 530; fax 713 5302; ecotour@dorea.co.za. Open M-F 8am-5pm; someone may be around on the weekends.)

Accommodation in Qwaqwa Park consists of rustic farmhouses renovated to be dorms. Options including **Welgedacht** (sleeps 9), **Avondrus, Spelonken,** and **Klipriver** (sleep 15 each); reservations are available from the park offices (☎721 0300; ecotour@dorea.co.za). Each is equipped with running water, toilets, showers, and *braai*. The centerpiece of the park is the two-day, 27km **Spelonken Hiking Trail** which weaves through the mountains and provides the chance to view white rhino, eland and zebra up close. The Spelonken overnight huts sit at the half-way point (permit required). Guides may be arranged through the park offices. There are several good spots on the R712 to get out for a day hike, but no real trails apart from the 4x4 roads, that criss-cross the terrain. Qwaqwa also hosts the picturesque and insightful **Basotho Cultural Village.** (☎721 0300; fax 721 0304; basotho@dorea.co.za; www.dorea.co.za/ecotourism). Though sanitized and tourist-friendly, the village provides rare opportunities to learn about the hierarchical structures of traditional Basotho culture. The tour takes visitors through time—from the 16th century to the present day—via a numbering system on beautifully constructed homes, and includes a drink of sorghum beer (one percent alcohol, so indulge) with the "chief." The spiritually inclined can roll the bones with the *sangoma*—a traditional doctor. (One-on-one sessions R15, children R10. R60 package includes tour, lunch, and a traditional Basotho dance.) Also available are the **Museum Tour** (R15, children R10) and **Herbal Trail** (R20, children R10). Unlike many other "cultural villages" in South Africa, this one is run by the Basotho themselves, and does not reek of cultural kitsch.

HARRISMITH (INTABAZWE)   ☎ 058

Harrismith's wide thoroughfares lined with Victorian, sandstone buildings and its quiet, relaxed feel, aptly named in honor of British Governor Sir Harry Smith (Ladysmith in KwaZulu-Natal was named after his wife), belie the fact that this town has some dark splotches on its history. In the midst of the Anglo-Boer War, Harrismith was occupied by British troops who liked the town so much that they stuck around 11 years after the conflict's conclusion. During much of this time, Boer women and children were confined to concentration camps. The spectacular views of the 2377m Platberg from downtown are a treat and will inspire you to head into the surrounding hills. Harrismith is among the best places in the eastern state to stock up on provision for outdoor adventures, including steaks; the town is the capital of the country's top red-meat producing region. Contact the Harrismith Taxi Association (☎623 1188) for more information.

TRANSPORTATION. The **minibus taxi** depot is behind (and downhill from) the city hall, between Southey and Bester St. **Minibuses** run to Qwaqwa (R15), Bergville (R20), and Johannesburg (R50). **Buses** can be booked through **Hirundo Travel** (☎ 622 2579, open M-F 8am-12:30pm and 1:30-4:30pm), in Spur Village. **Greyhound** goes to Cape Town (18hr., daily, R355) via Bloemfontein (5½hr, R145), Durban (4¼hr., daily, R140) via Pietermaritzburg (3¼hr., R130). **Intercape** goes to Cape Town (17¼hr.; Su, M, W, F, Sa 9:45pm; R355) via Bloemfontein (4¼hr., R130), Durban (4¼hr., daily, R125) via Pietermaritzburg (3hr., R110), and Pretoria (4½hr., daily, R125) via Johannesburg (3hr., R125). **Translux** goes to Cape Town (17¾hr., daily, R365) via Bloemfontein (5hr., R140), Durban (5¼hr., daily, R125) via Pietermaritzburg (3hr., R75), and Pretoria (6¼hr., daily, R125) via Johannesburg (3¾hr., R125). R20 booking fee.

ORIENTATION AND PRACTICAL INFORMATION. Harrismith is just off the N3 between Johannesburg (314 km) and Durban (315); the N5 from Bethlehem points west and terminates in Harrismith. Coming from Johannesburg, the N3 exit to town (after the Intabazwe township) joins **Warden St.,** which runs into the city square. From Durban the exit (near the Spar Village) joins **McKechnie St.;** turn right onto **Piet Retief St.** to get to the city square. Downtown Harrismith is a mini-grid of just a few streets; most stores are in the few blocks around the square. The **Tourist Office** (☎ 622 3525; fax 623 0923) is on Pretorius St., at the back of the city hall. (☎ 622 3525; fax 623 0923. Open M-F 8am-5pm, Sa 9:30am-12:30pm.)

Services include: **First National Bank,** 25 Southey St., on the corner of Southey and Warden St. (☎/fax 622 1044; open M-F 9am-3:30pm, Sa 8:30-11am); **ABSA Bank,** 31a Southey St., near the corner of Southey and Stuart, with a 24hr. **ATM; laundromat,** 76 McKechnie St. (☎ 612 1292; open M-F 7:30am-4:45pm); **weather,** ☎ 082 162; **emergency services,** ☎ 10 177; the **police station,** on Piet Retief St. next the post office (☎ 622 1050; open 24hr.); **Harris Pharmacy,** 26a Piet Retief St. (☎ 622 2612; open M-F 8am-5pm, Sa 8am-1pm); the **Harrismith Provincial Hospital,** on Mauritz St., east of town (☎ 622 1111; open 24hr.); **Internet** at Cyber Cafe in the **Yes Print and Copy Shop,** 49 Stuart St., opposite the post office (open M-F 8am-1pm; R10 per 30min., R20 per hr.); the **post office,** on the corner of Piet Retief and Stuart St. (☎ 622 1200. Open M-Tu, Th-F 8:30am-4:30pm, W 9am-4:30pm, Sa 8am-noon.) **Postal code:** 9880.

ACCOMMODATIONS AND FOOD. Down the road, **Harrismith Backpackers** ❶, 44 Piet Retief St., is a pleasant home downtown converted into a backpackers. More a spot just to hit the hay than a destination in its own right, it's the perfect place for budget travelers in transit. (☎ 623 0007 or 083 412 6728; jmentz@oldmutualpfa.com. Dorms R50; doubles R130. Camping R25.) The **Grand National Hotel** ❷, on the corner of Warden and Boshoff St., is more than a century old and full of character. It may be a little dingy, but the atmosphere grows on you. (☎/fax 622 1060. Breakfast R20. Dinner R40. Singles R100; doubles R180; singles and doubles with bath and TV R150/R220. Weekend prices negotiable.) The pricier **Harrismith Inn** ❸, behind the Spur Village in the southern end of town, has atypically large rooms that include a bath, phone, double beds, TV, and, in some cases, couches. The fairly luxurious establishment also sports a pool, restaurant, and **"Sir Harry's Bar,"** a good post-dinner meeting spot. (☎ 622 1011; fax 622 2770. Reception 24hr. Check-out 10am. Restaurant open 6:30am-9:30pm, later on F and Sa. Breakfast R20-R30. Lunch and dinner R30-50. Bar open 3-10:30pm. Singles R199; doubles R279 including breakfast.)

About 23km from Harrismith on the R712 to Qwaqwa, off the N5 to Bethlehem, is the **Sterkfontein Dam Nature Reserve** ❶, which has self-catering chalets with sweeping panoramic views of the dam and Drakensberg, as well as camping. All the chalets are equipped with kitchen and fireplace, and some have TVs. They also offer bird-watching, vulture feeding, and game drives. (☎622 3520 fax 622 1772. Chalets may have to be booked in advance. 4-bed chalets R170; 5-bed chalets R210; 8-bed chalets R320. Campsites R30, with power R40. R20 entrance fee.) At **President Brand Park ❶,** you can pitch your tent within walking distance of downtown and still be lulled to sleep by the gurgling of the Wilge River. From the center of town, take Murrat St. west. Pass under the railroad bridge, and the park will be on your left. (☎622 1818. Reception 24hr. Camping R30 per site for two, each additional person R10; with electricity R35; caravans R50.) With a spacious garden and a bar full of outlandish odds and ends, **The Princess and the Frog ❷,** 17 Voew St., serves some of the best grub around (R25-60) in what is almost a fairy-tale setting. (☎622 2476. Open Tu-Sa 10am-late.) For refreshingly light and creative breakfasts and lunches, as well as terrific milkshakes, try **Odell's Street Cafe ❶,** on Stuart St. across from the post office. (Open M-Sa 8am-4pm.) The sparkling Harrismith Spar, east of downtown on Hamilton St., is the place to stock up on rations for the back country. (☎622 3045. Open daily 7:30am-8pm.)

🔲 **SIGHTS.** The **Intabazwe Township Tour** demonstrates how the effects of apartheid survived its demise. With a population of 60,000 black South Africans, Intabazwe is smaller than the townships surrounding the larger cities. Tours include revealing snippets of day-to-day life at the township's schools, *shebeens* (taverns), and *spaza* shops (improvised general stores). Local children put on traditional dances or drum performances. You can book 3hr. or overnight tours through the tourist office, a day in advance. Overnight tours include a stay with a host family. (Day tours R25; overnight tours R130 including dinner, bed, and breakfast.)

NORTHWEST PROVINCE

Nicknamed the "platinum province," the Northwest Province has historically been of more interest to geologists nosing out the big mineral cache than to tourists seeking game. The area's booming mining industry, as well as its cultivation of citrus fruits, corn, tobacco, and sunflowers, have pushed tourism down on the list of income-generating ventures. Things are changing, however, as small-scale operators begin to offer trips to some of the region's previously overlooked sights.

During the Apartheid Era, most of the region's black population resided in Bophuthatswana, one of the less impoverished South African homelands (see p. 58). Because of the relatively higher standard of living of blacks here, racial turmoil and anti-apartheid activism were not as pronounced, and in the post-apartheid era, the province has remained a conservative corner of the country.

The Northwest's climate is generally hot and dry year-round. *Bushveld*, interrupted only by thicket and woodland on the rocky slopes of the Magaliesberg Mountains, dominates the landscape. These weathered peaks and the massive Pilanesberg crater are two of the oldest geological formations on earth. Rustenburg, with its numerous B&Bs and small-town feel, is a great base for Pretoria and Johannesburg daytrips. However, the absence of reliable inter-city transport networks makes a car necessary for getting around efficiently.

HIGHLIGHTS OF THE NORTHWEST PROVINCE

Pilanesberg National Park (see p. 402) showcases the Big Five in an immense reserve.

The forested slopes of the Magaliesberg lie within the **Rustenberg Nature Reserve** (see p. 400), where hikers might spot an elusive leopard on one of the excellent hiking trails.

RUSTENBURG   ☎ 014

Seated at the base of the obsidian cliffs and rolling slopes of the Magaliesberg, this booming town is enjoying a vibrant economy thanks to mining, agriculture, and tourism. With its beautiful scenery and proximity to Sun City and Pilanesberg National Park, the number of visitors is gradually increasing. All this, along with over half of the world's platinum production, make Rustenburg one of the fastest growing urban centers in South Africa. One of the area's early Afrikaner settlers was Paul Kruger, whose homestead still stands just outside the town. Rustenburg held political and religious importance for the first Boer republic, and even served briefly as the seat of the *Zuid Afrikaansche Republiek* (South African Republic) before Pretoria was named its capital.

▐ TRANSPORTATION

To get in and out of Rustenburg, **minibus taxis** are often the only option other than driving yourself. The minibus station, at the corner of Van Staden and Malan St., has continuous service to destinations throughout the country (R15 to Sun City, R35 to Johannesburg). Caution should be exercised in this area during the day, especially if traveling with bags. Avoid the station after dark. The **bus terminal** is at

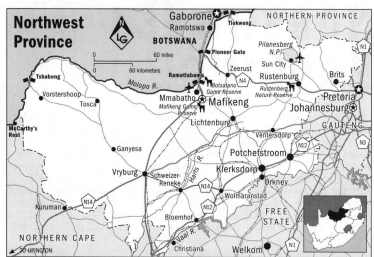

the junction of Smit and Van Staden St. **Intercape** buses (☎592 0251) go to **Gaborone** (4¾hr., 5:30pm, R85) and **Johannesburg** (1½hr., 9:30am, R70). **John's Taxi** (☎082 771 2146), driven by John himself, provides service in and about Rustenburg. About R25 should get you anywhere in the area, although he does not drive late at night.

✈ 🛈 ORIENTATION AND PRACTICAL INFORMATION

Rustenburg is just over 100km west of Pretoria on the **N4** and about 120km northwest of Johannesburg along the **R24,** which runs into the N4 on the outskirts of town. The N4 runs through the city center as **Van Staden St.,** and intersects **Smit St.** at the town center.

The **Rustenburg Tourism Information and Development Center** is at the corner of Kloof and Van Staden St., just off the N4/R24 when entering from Johannesburg or Pretoria. (☎597 0904. Open M-F 7:30am-4pm, Sa 8am-noon.) Services include: **Standard Bank,** on Van Staden St. in the MKTV Plaza (☎597 0760; open M-Tu and Th-F 8:30am-3:30pm, W 9am-3:30pm, Sa 8:30-11am); **ABSA Bank** (☎590 1000), at the corner of Van Staden and Burger St., which handles AmEx Travelers Checks (open M-F 8:30am-3:30pm and Sa 8-11am); **emergency services** (☎10 111); **ambulance** (☎594 3444); **Kloof Pharmacy,** at the corner of Van Straden and Postma St. (☎592 6251; open M-F 8am-9pm, Sa 8am-1pm and 5-9pm, Su 9am-1pm and 5-9pm); **police** (☎594 4115), on Kruis St. near Burger St.; **Paul Kruger Memorial Hospital** (☎592 2112), along Van Staden St. on the east side of town; and the **post office** (☎597 1931), at the corner of Pretorius and Loop St, behind MKTV Plaza (open M-Tu and Th-F 8:30am-4:30pm, W 9am-4:30pm, Sa 8am-noon). **Postal code:** 0300.

▮ ACCOMMODATIONS

The city's increasing popularity as a base for excursions has caused a number of quality B&Bs to sprout up.

■ **Travellers Inn,** 99 Leyds St. (☎592 7658). Near the corner of Van Zyl and Leyds St. Close to minibus station. In a lush garden setting, the Travellers Inn has a hint of the tropics with banana trees, swimming pool, and cabin pub with grass shutters. Large

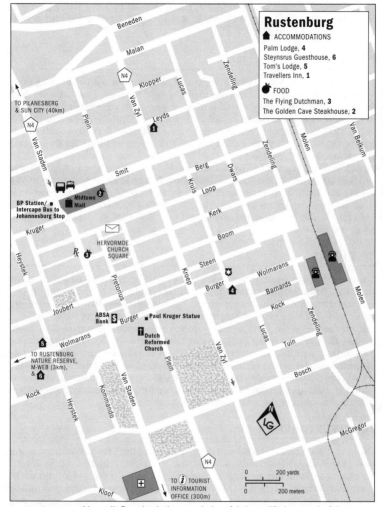

Rustenburg

ACCOMMODATIONS
Palm Lodge, **4**
Steynsrus Guesthouse, **6**
Tom's Lodge, **5**
Travellers Inn, **1**

FOOD
The Flying Dutchman, **3**
The Golden Cave Steakhouse, **2**

guest rooms with sunlit French windows and cheerful decor lift the mood of the weary. Carport parking and security. Rooms R145 per person. AmEx/D/MC/V. ❷

Tom's Lodge, 51 Heystek St. (☎592 0435/6). From Van Straden St. turn left into Wolmarens St. and continue until the lodge's sign. Conveniently located with comfortable, well-equipped rooms in an apartment-like complex. Carport parking and security. Breakfast R15 per person. Singles R125; doubles R180. ❷

Palm Lodge, 99 Wolmarens St. (☎597 2520). Near the corner of Burger and Kruis St. Huge palms decorate the entrance of this polished establishment. Rooms have phone, coffee machine, and TV. Meals on request (R25). Singles R130; doubles R200. ❷

Steynsrus Guesthouse, 158 Kock St. (☎597 3071). West of downtown. Steynsrus boasts numerous honors from the national tourism industry, and deserves them: the suburban lodge offers privacy and class. Comfortable setting with a homey feel. Small pool, private parking, and well-furnished rooms. English Breakfast included. Singles R155; doubles R270. ❷

☕ FOOD

Grocery stores line Van Staden and Smit St., and various coffee shops and fast food chains populate the numerous malls. Locally acclaimed **Karl's Bauernstube** ❷, 5km east of town along the R24, offers a world-class menu combining local game with German and Austrian flavors. Dishes are surprisingly cheap at R20-50. (☎ 537 2128. Reservations recommended. Open Tu-F noon-2:30pm and 6-10pm, Sa 6:30-10pm, Su noon-2:30pm; closed for first three weeks of Jan.) **The Golden Cave Steakhouse** ❷, 56 V. Staden St., in the Midtown Mall, has a broad range of offerings (R25-50), many with a Greek flair. (☎ 592 3469. Open M-Sa 10:30am-2:30pm and 6:30-10pm, Su 10:30am-2:30pm.) **The Flying Dutchman** ❷, on the corner of Van Staden and Kerk St, is a restaurant-pub that has a reasonably priced menu for steak and seafood. Lunch from the bar menu costs R20-30; dinners go up to R60. (☎ 592 4021. Evening reservations vital. Open M-F 10:30am-11pm, Sa 6-11pm. AmEx/DC/MC/V.)

◎ SIGHTS

Rustenburg retains reminders of its key role in 19th-century Afrikaner history. The city's first **Dutch Reformed Church** is a grand, if not elaborate, building in the city center. Its imposing form stands directly opposite the **Town Hall,** on whose front lawn stands the statue of **Paul Kruger,** the founder of the Afrikaner state.

Rustenburg is often used as a base for excursions to the surrounding areas. (Some skittish Johannesburg visitors stay here to avoid the big city at night). Day trips to the exclusive, pocket-draining resort of **Sun City** are easy to make, while the nearby small German village of **Kroondal,** a few kilometers southeast along the N4, will provide a welcome getaway for those seeking simpler distractions. Kroondal's population has retained its distinct culture for over a century, as is evident from the hundreds of German handicrafts available here.

⚔ ADVENTURES

The slopes and cliffs of the **Magaliesberg,** also called the **Cashan Mountains,** tower over Rustenburg. Named after Kgwashwane, the powerful leader of the Kwena Mmatau, the mountains are largely uninhabited and are protected as part of the **Rustenburg Nature Reserve,** west of downtown. The visitors center provides info on trails in the 4247ha park, which is one of the few protected habitats of the rare sable antelope. (☎ 533 2050; www.parksnorthwest.co.za. Open Sept.-Mar. daily 5:30am-7pm; Apr.-Aug. 6am-6:30pm. Entrance fee R10 per adult, R5 per child, R10 per vehicle. Hiking R90 per person. Camping R40 per site.)

PILANESBERG NATIONAL PARK

Set within the breathtaking backdrop of a gigantic extinct volcanic crater, Pilanesberg provides a game-viewing experience that ranks among the best in South Africa. The history of the park, South Africa's fourth largest game reserve, can be traced back 1.3 billion years to a volcanic eruption. The national park opened in 1979 and occupies 550 sq. km, of which 140 are open for viewing the estimated 12,000 animals of 364 different species.

⬛🔢 ORIENTATION AND PRACTICAL INFO.

Pilanesberg is about 40km north of Rustenburg at the end of the R565. From Rustenburg, take the N4 west to the R565 turn-off and head north for 35km. There are three entrances to the park: Bakubung Gate (south side), Manyane Gate (east side), and Bakgatla Gate (north side). The Bakubung Gate gets the most use because it is the closest to the R565 and Sun City, but all the gates are connected by roads within the park. Although minibus taxis do run from Rustenburg to Sun City, a car is essential (and required) to explore the park. The park entrance fee is R20 for adults and R15 for children, plus R15 per vehicle. Each of the entrance stations provides maps and visitor information. (☎ 555 5351; www.parks-northwest.co.za.ark. Park gates open Nov.-Feb. 5:30am-7pm; Mar.-Apr. 6am-6:30pm; May-Aug. 6:30am-6pm; Sept.-Oct. 6am-6:30pm.)

🔢 CAMPING.

The National Park offers campsites at two locations: **Bakgatla Resort ❺** (campsites ❷), in the northeast off the road to Saulspoort, and **Manyane Resort ❺** (campsites ❷), in the east section off the Rustenburg-Thabazimbi road. Both resorts have campsites (R120, R140 with electricity) and chalets (singles start at R550 and sharing at R210 per person; Bakgatla Resort chalets host up to 5, Manyane up to 6). Two-bed safari tents start at R295. Both resorts contain restaurants, bars, pools, convenience stores, and *braais*. All overnight visitors must register and pay park entrance fees. **Golden Leopard Resorts** (☎ 014 555 6135; goldres@iafrica.com; www.goldenleopard.co.za) handles bookings for both camps.

🔢 ADVENTURES.

The park is divided into five areas defined by the flora and fauna indigenous to each specific habitat. Lion and cheetah prey on herds of wildebeest and antelope in the grasslands but rarely disturb the larger white rhinos or the more aggressive buffalo. Thickets and woodlands support black rhino, giraffe, and elephant. Nimble leopards and their main food source, baboons, camouflage themselves in the high, stony cliffs. Fierce Nile crocodile and hippos lounge about in the park's watering holes. In addition to the game, the park is filled with 6000-year-old **rock paintings** created by the Bushmen, who made Pilanesberg their home back in 40,000 BC. Pilanesberg is reputed to be one of the longest continually inhabited sites by humans. Expeditions have unearthed artifacts dating back to the early Stone Age, while the most recent inhabitants left only 30 years ago. Visitors interested in viewing archaeological sites should speak directly with Resort or park staff at the gates.

THE BIG SPLURGE

FUN IN THE SUN

Pilanesberg National Park shares a border with the resort town of Sun City, one of the most popular (and expensive) tourist destinations in Southern Africa. While it's out of reach for most budget travelers, it's worth considering as a weekend splurge. The Sun City complex features four hotels: the Cabanas, Sun City Hotel, Cascades, and the Palace (part of the recently built Lost City). With golf courses, gorgeous pools, mouth-watering buffets, endless casinos, and one of the best outdoor waterparks in South Africa, it's tough to match the luxury of Sun City. The complex also organizes game-viewing trips to Pilanesburg National Park, and they have a variety of children's programs to keep the kids busy while parents relax.

Room prices range from R1125 per night at the Cabanas to almost R4000 per night at the Palace. If you're on a budget, don't even think about trying to stay anywhere but the Cabanas. The Cabanas's rooms are clean and comfortable, overlooking a beautiful lake teeming with swimmers and watersports.

For more information on staying at Sun City, visit the remarkably handy web site: www.suncity.co.za.

Gametrackers Wildlife Adventures is the official park tour operator. It offers 2½hr. game drives that depart from the Manyane and Bakgatla Resorts (R130) in open-air vehicles. Bring warm clothing; temperatures in the crater fall rapidly after dusk. (☎555 6135 or 556 2710; gametrac@netactive.co.za. Book in advance.) To see Pilanesburg as its 300 bird species do, Gametrackers also books **balloon safaris.** (R1850 per person, includes 2½hr. driving tour, breakfast, and 1hr. in the sky.)

MAFIKENG AND MMABATHO   ☎018

Mafikeng's relatively recent history is a tale of conflict among the Barolongs, the Setswana-speaking indigenous inhabitants, the early Afrikaners, and the British. The town traces its modern roots back to the 1880s, when the British set about establishing Mafikeng as the administrative center of Bechuanaland (now Botswana), even though this makeshift capital lay well outside the borders of the territory it was supposed to administer. In October of 1899, the outbreak of the Anglo-Boer War precipitated the famous Siege of Mafikeng. For the following six months, 2000 British and Barolong troops under Commando Colonel Robert Baden-Powell defended the town against an 8000-man Boer force.

With the conclusion of the siege and the war, Mafikeng resumed its role as a regional administrative center. In 1977 the decision was made to create a capital for the new "independent" homeland of Bophuthatswana, and the town of Mmabatho ("mother of the people" in Setswana) was built largely from scratch right next to Mafikeng. Today, both the old (Mafikeng) and the new (Mmabatho) are combined under a single Mafikeng municipality that is the capital of the Northwest Province. It is one of the few towns where a middle-class family is just as likely to be black as white. The result is a more tolerant society than that found in much of the rest of the Northwest Province. The city has taken steps to preserve its history, which, along with excellent game reserves nearby, is its primary draw.

▐ TRANSPORTATION

Buses: Intra-city buses depart from Megacity and Mafikeng railway station (R2). Bus service to **Johannesburg** (☎381 2680 or ☎011 333 4412) leaves from Megacity (7am) and the corner of Carrington and Main St. in Mafikeng (7:15am). Tickets are available from the driver (R70, children R30).

Minibus Taxis: Local minibus taxis are based near the rail station on Station Rd. at Martin St. and at a rank outside Megacity. Minibuses to **Rustenburg** (R35), **Johannesburg** (R40), and **Pretoria** (R60) run from the corner of Tillard and Station St.

▟ ▍ ORIENTATION AND PRACTICAL INFORMATION

Mafikeng is about 40km from Zeerust along the **R49/R27** and just under 275km west of Pretoria and Johannesburg. Coming from Zeerust, the R49 enters Mafikeng and turns into **Shippard St.** before continuing southwest to Vryburg (150km). Shippard St. intersects **Nelson Mandela Dr.** (Mafikeng's closest thing to a main drag) and marks the eastern limit of the downtown business district. The **train station** is on the western edge of town on **Station St. Moroka Dr.** runs parallel to Nelson Mandela Dr. along the eastern edge of downtown Mmabatho, which is northwest of downtown Mafikeng. Separating the two centers is an industrial area and a large stadium. The **Megacity** shopping mall is on Moroka Dr. in Mmabatho.

Tourist Office: Tourism Information and Development Center (☎381 3155; fax 381 6058; tidcmf@yebo.co.za). Follow Mandela Dr. south over the bridge and look for the

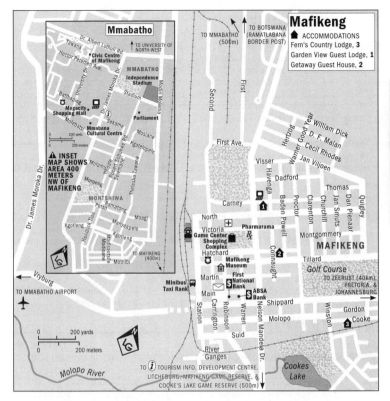

hutted roofs on the left. The center offers a wealth of information on the area and the Northwest Province in general. Open M-F 8am-6pm, Sa 8:30am-noon.

Bank: ABSA (☎381 0610), on Main St. near Warren St. Open M-F 8:30am-3:30pm, Sa 8-11am. It has a 24hr. **ATM,** as does **First National Bank** (☎381 6342) on Robinson St., between Shippard and Main St. Open M-F 9am-3:30pm, Sa 8:30am-11am.

Supermarket: Spar (☎381 7774) at the Game Center complex. Open M-Su 8am-8pm.

Emergency: Police (☎10 111); **ambulance** (☎392 3333).

Pharmacy: Pharmarama (☎381 6270 or 381 3584), at Mandela Dr. and Victoria Rd. in the Game Center shopping complex. Open M-F 8:30am-8pm, Sa 8:30am-2pm, 5-8pm, Su 10am-1pm and 5-8pm. MC/V.

Hospital: Victoria Hospital (☎381 2043), on Victoria Rd. off Mandela Dr.

Internet Access: The Internet Cafe in the Megacity Complex. R10 per 30min., R20 per hr. Rates double if staff help required.

Post Office: (☎381 4628), along Carrington St., between Martin and Main St. in Mafikeng. Open M-Tu and Th-F 8:30am-4:30pm, W 9am-4:30pm, Sa 8am-noon. In Mmabatho (☎381 0489), adjacent to Megacity.

Postal code: Mafikeng 2745, Mmabatho 2735.

ACCOMMODATIONS

■ **Garden View Guest Lodge** (☎381 3110 or 381 4076), centrally located on corner of North St. and Havenga St., off Mandela Dr. Large rooms with kitchenettes and private bath make this the best bang for your buck. Pool, tennis courts, sauna, and TV provide resort feel. Filling meals served out of country kitchen. Book in advance. Reception 7am-9pm. Singles R120, with bath R180; doubles R180, with bath R260; 4-person flats with bath R440. Rooms with private bath include breakfast. AmEx/DC/MC/V. **Getaway Guest Lodge** (☎381 1150), closer to the town center at the corner of Tillard and Baden-Powell St, has the same management as Garden View. ❷

Fern's Country Lodge, 12 Cooke St. (☎381 5971). South of Shippard St. Tucked away from the hustle and bustle of downtown Mafikeng but still close to the center of things. The elegant rooms have access to a pool and a lovely garden. Singles R300; doubles R350. ❹

FOOD

■ **Garden View Country Kitchen and Pub** (☎381 3110). At the Garden View Guest Lodge. Burgers so fat and juicy they fall out of the bun, sweet ribs that slide off the bone, sandwiches, and salads (all R10-35). An intimate dining room, and a small attached pub to wash it all down. Open noon-2pm and 6:30pm-9pm. AmEx/DC/MC/V. ❷

Fern's Country Lodge, 12 Cooke St. (☎381 5971). Affordable gourmet dining. Comfortable atmosphere and mouth-watering meals. The owners are proud to boast Nelson Mandela as a customer. Light lunches from R26. Steak R40-66. Seafood specials R39-66. Reservations recommended. Open daily 1:30-3pm and 7-9pm. ❷

ENTERTAINMENT

Mafikeng is somewhat short on kicks. However, casino games can be found at the **Tusk Mmabatho Casino Resort** (☎389 1111), along Nelson Mandela Dr. 4km north of Mafikeng. For non-gamblers, Tusk offers miniature and full-size golf courses and a dance club, **Tuskers,** that rocks on Friday nights. One Wednesday a month is Ladies' Night and special acts entertain guests. (Cover varies. Open 8pm-late.)

SIGHTS AND ADVENTURES

Mafikeng Museum (☎381 6102), on Martin St., between Carrington and Robinson St., is a valuable learning center for those who wish to know more about the city's fascinating history. Exhibits on the 1899-1900 Siege dominate, with details of the Anglo-Boer War. Other displays include a piece on Sol Plaatje, a prominent African leader and admired political activist who helped found the ANC. (Open M-F 8am-4pm, Sa 10am-1pm. Admission is free, but remember to sign the guest book.)

The **Mafikeng Game Reserve,** on the outskirts of town along Lichtenburg Rd., is home to giraffes, antelope, white rhinos, ostriches, and a wealth of bird life. (☎381 5611. Open daily 7am-6pm. R10 per person plus R5 per vehicle.) The park is next to **Cooke's Lake Reserve ❶,** just behind the Tourist Information and Development Center on Nelson Mandela Dr., where camping is available for R15 per person (tent) and R60 per person (caravan). There is also a R5 per person entrance fee. Campers have access to ablutions and electricity. Reception 7am-6pm daily.

Botsalano Game Reserve (☎386 2433), 30km north of town off the Ramatlabana Rd., has one of the most successful white rhino breeding centers on the continent. The park is laced with trails, and despite its proximity to town, you get the feeling you are in the heart of the *veld.* Giraffes, ostriches, buffalo, warthogs, and zebras are common sightings. (Open daily 6:30am-6:30pm. Admission R10, under 12 and seniors R5; cars R5 extra. Camping R40 per person.)

NORTHERN CAPE

South Africa's least populous province accounts for close to a third of the country's area. It is a wild, untamed region where nature still rules; the geographic remoteness and harsh, dry climate have hindered (thankfully) human settlement of the land. The result is vast tracks of pristine wilderness where hardy flora and fauna have enjoyed a little peace and quiet, apart from the occasional intrepid soul. People might have stayed away altogether were it not for the large quantities of diamond-bearing rock discovered first in the fields of Kimberley (on the eastern side of the province, now known as the Diamantveld) and later in alluvial deposits at the mouth of the Orange River on the Atlantic seaboard.

The province's sparse population and wild terrain, not to mention the characters attracted to its mines, once gave it a reputation for lawlessness reminiscent of the American Wild West. Bandits like Scotty Smith often led the lawmen of the Northern Cape on merry chases. From these humble origins, Kimberley, with its diamond wealth, transformed its reputation to become one of South Africa's more innovative and genteel cities. Today, the Northern Cape offers a rare opportunity for visitors to commune with nature on its own terms—in the overwhelmingly colorful fields of Namaqualand or in the expanse of Kalahari Gemsbok National Park. If hiking is your forte, don't miss the sensational trails of Augrabies National Park.

HIGHLIGHTS OF THE NORTHERN CAPE

The diamond mines in **Kimberley** (see p. 405) made Cecil Rhodes a millionaire. Stare down Kimberley's Big Hole and imagine how profits soared (and miners struggled) as the hole grew ever deeper.

The sixth largest waterfall in the world plummets down the Ararat Canyon in **Augrabies National Park** (see p. 414). Landlubbers may view the falls from the safety of the banks, while the nautically inclined can paddle to within 300m of the top of the falls.

In the **Kalahari Gemsbok National Park** (see p. 416), the largest continuous protected ecosystem in Southern Africa, gemsbok antelope graze over the dunes as birds of prey circle above, but the black-maned Kalahari lion is the real king of the desert.

KIMBERLEY   ☎ 053

Kimberley began with a monumental bargain. In 1871, a chap named De Beers sold his farm for £6000, certain he had the good end of the deal. But the company of buyers had secured a pot-bellied empire for a pittance. Slavering speculators scrambled to mine and milked the hell out of what became known as "the Big Hole," the everflowing diamond fountain of the De Beers Company (yes, it was named after that unfortunate man). The Big Hole has a significance beyond its sparkly finds: It represents the lifelong toil of thousands of miners digging towards the center of the earth to enrich an empire from which they received little gain. Nevertheless, some of the De Beers fortune was put back into the city, and the surprisingly high quality of Kimberley's museums as well as the preservation of many historical and beautiful buildings owes this to this "recycling."

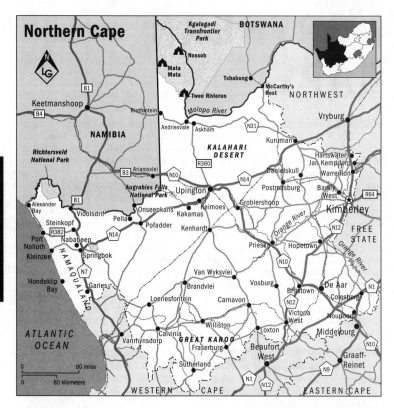

Kimberley still yields diamonds for De Beers, but shafts and tunnels have replaced the spades and buckets on pulleys that once worked the open mine. One thing that hasn't changed, however, is the hold this most successful of international monopolies has over this town.

These days, the most coveted commodity in town isn't measured in carats; its the few shade trees that block the scorching *veld* sun. If you're headed west enjoy them. They might be the last you see for a long while.

■ TRANSPORTATION

Flights: South African Airlink (☎838 3337), 8km south of town on Oliver Rd. toward Bloemfontein. Flies to **Cape Town** (1½hr.; M-F 8:15am and 6pm, Su 6pm; R1620) and **Johannesburg** (1¼hr., 1-4 flights daily 7:45am-7:35pm, R1140).

Trains: Spoornet (☎080 052 4804 or 838 2731/2060) runs to: **Bloemfontein** (3hr., Su-F, 2nd class R45, 1st class R65); **Cape Town** (17hr., daily, R200/R295); **Durban** (20hr., Tu, R150/R205); **Johannesburg** (10hr., Su-F, R100/R150); **Pretoria** (12hr., daily, R125/R170). Ticket office open M-F 8am-1pm and 2-4pm, Sa 8-11am.

Buses: Tickets 4 Africa, 121 Bultfontein Rd. (☎832 6040 or 832 6045). The very useful local booking office and departure point for all buses. In the same building as the

Visitors Center. Open M-F 8am-5pm, Sa 8am-noon. **Greyhound** runs to **Cape Town** (12hr., 8pm and 10:40pm, R280) and **Pretoria** (8hr., 1:30am and 7am, R175) via **Johannesburg** (8hr., R175). **Big Sky** runs between **Upington** (R110) and **Bloemfontein** (R60) via **Kimberley** on the weekends. Check the Visitors Center.

Minibus Taxis: Kimberley Long-Distance Taxi Association (☎831 8977), on Bultfontein/Pniel Rd. in the Indian Center, just north of downtown. To **Bloemfontein** (R45). **Vrystaat Toere** (☎051 523 3620) runs shuttles to **Bloemfontein,** departing from the Kimberley Holiday Inn on du Toitspan Rd. (2hr.; M, W, F, and Su 4pm).

Taxis: A&A Taxis (☎861 4015 or 083 283 0558) or **Rikki's Taxis** (☎842 1764 or 083 342 2533) are pretty much your only options. Both charge R2.50 per km and operate 24hr. Shuttle to or from the airport is R25.

Car Rental: Avis (☎851 1082), **Budget** (☎851 1182), **Hertz** (☎851 1547), **Imperial** (☎851 1131), and **Tempest** (☎851 1516) have offices at the airport. Open M-F 6:30am-8pm, Sa-Su with arriving flights.

ORIENTATION

Kimberley's winding streets are a confusing jumble; most of the major roads change names at least once. The **N12** runs north-south and the **R64/N8** runs east-west through town. The city center is defined roughly by the Big Hole to the west, the train station to the east, and the Anglo-Boer War Memorial to the south. **Old Main Rd.** is just that: the former main drag of the boom years. It remains a commercial center, but one more notable for fast-food and street vendors than the stately shops of Rhodes's days. Most businesses have relocated to the south side of town, and the major commercial center is the Sanlam Center on **Lennox St.** between Sidney and Chapel. Most of the nightlife can be found in the bars of **du Toitspan Rd.**

PRACTICAL INFORMATION

Tourist Office: Diamantveld Tourist Information Center, 121 Bultfontein Rd. (☎832 7298; fax 832 7211; tourism@kbymun.org.za; www.kimberley-africa.com), as it becomes Dalham Rd. between Lyndhurst Rd. and Eureka St. Open M-F 8am-5pm, Sa 8am-noon.

Banks: Standard Bank, 10 Old Main Rd. (☎838 4861). Cashes traveler's checks and exchanges currency. Open M-F 9am-3:30pm, Sa 8:30-11am. For best rates on traveler's checks, try **ABSA Bank** (☎839 5200), on the corner of Long and Bultfontein. Open M-F 8:30am-3:30pm, Sa 8-11am. Both banks have 24hr. **ATMs.**

Bookstore: Words Unlimited, 157 du Toitspan Rd. (☎832 5232). Open M-F 10am-6pm, Sa 8am-6pm, Su 2-6pm. **Kimberley Library** (☎830 6244), between Sidney and Chapel, next to the Sanlam Center. Open M-F 8:30am-7:30pm, Sa 8am-1pm.

Supermarkets: Pick 'n Pay (☎832 9481), on Sidney St. Open M-F 8am-7pm, Sa 8am-3pm, Su 9am-1pm. **Checkers,** 470 Eden (☎831 2348), near Bultfontein Rd. Open M, W-F 8am-6pm; Tu 9am-6pm; Sa 8am-3pm. **ShopRite** (☎831 2130), on Chapel St. Open daily 8am-8pm. **Spar** (☎831 2966), on Bultfontein Rd. Open M-Th 8am-6:15pm, F 8am-5pm, Sa 9am-1pm.

Laundromat: Cut-a-Cost Laundromat, D'Arcy St. (☎833 2467). R24 per load. Open M-F 8am-9pm, Sa 8am-6pm, Su 9am-6pm.

Pharmacies: Center Pharmacy (☎831 1941), Sanlam Center. Open M-F 8am-5:30pm, Sa 8am-1pm.

NORTHERN CAPE

Public Toilets/Showers/Swimming Pool: Big Hole Caravan Park (☎830 6322), on W. Circular Rd., across from the Big Hole. R10 per person for toilets, showers, and pool.

Weather: ☎851 1021.

Emergency: ☎10 177 (ambulance); ☎10 111 (police).

Police: 31 Transvaal Rd. (☎838 4331 or 838 4341).

Hospital: Kimberley Hospital (☎802 9111), on the corner of Lyndhurst and du Toitspan Rd. Open 24hr.

Internet Access: Small World Net Cafe, 42 Sidney St. (☎831 3484). South of the Pick 'n Pay. R15 for 30min. Open M-Sa 9am-5pm.

Post Office: (☎839 5900), in Market Sq., on the corner of Old Main and Stead Rd., next to City Hall. *Poste Restante.* Open M-Tu and Th-F 8am-4:30pm, W 8:30am-4:30pm, Sa 8am-noon.

Postal Code: 8300.

▌ ACCOMMODATIONS

▨ **Savoy Hotel,** 19 De Beers Rd. (☎832 6211; fax 832 7021; savoy@icon.co.za). This charming hotel is one of the few relics from Kimberley's glory days that has been able to preserve its stature. An unassuming exterior in the heart of downtown belies sophisticated rooms that serve as a welcome oasis from the desert of fast food restaurants and strip malls that dominate much of the city. Meals at the upscale Tiffany's (R35-65) or the relaxed Teemane Pub (R25-50). Reception 24hr. Check-out 10am. Singles R249, weekends R199; doubles R279/R229. ❸

Gum Tree Lodge (☎832 8577; lawrie@global.co.za), on the R64 to Bloemfontein, 5km from town. Converted old jail delivers the essentials with pool, playground, and kitchen. The wooded grounds offer a pleasant respite from the uniformity of the surrounding *veld* and shade to boot. Meals available at the Old Digger Restaurant (R25-35). Reception 7am-10pm. Dorms R40; singles, doubles, and quads R70 per person. ❶

Stay A Day, 72 Lawson St. (☎832 7239). Headed south on Bultfontein from the center of town, make an immediate right onto Lawson St. (after the Game Shopping Center). Continue for 800m. A 10min. walk from downtown. More dorm beds than you could imagine in a safe, suburban neighborhood. Kitchen. Breakfast R15-25. Dorms R40; singles R70, with bath R100; doubles R140/R160. ❶

Big Hole Caravan Park (☎830 6322), on W. Circular Rd., across from the Big Hole. Quiet, out-of-the-way setting with shady trees, pool, and easy access to Kimberley's pride and joy. Hot showers, baths, and *braai*. Laundry R4. Reception 6am-8pm, but they'll "stay up" if you call ahead. Campsites R20 per tent plus R10 per person; Caravan sites R35 plus R10 per person; seniors R20 plus R9 per person. Day visitors R10 per car plus R10 per person. ❶

◖▩ FOOD AND NIGHTLIFE

▨ **Star of the West** (☎832 6463), corner of N. Circular and Barkley Rd. One of the Northern Cape's most famous attractions and the oldest pub in South Africa, established in 1870. It once was a buy-a-room-number brothel—women weren't allowed downstairs until 1987. There are rumors of roaming ghosts and lost fortunes in gold coins beneath the floorboards. Bar and liquor cabinet are the original hardwood, salvaged 130 years ago from the "Star of the West," a ship that foundered off the Cape Coast. Limited but delicious pub menu. The steaks are an astounding deal at R35. Open M-Sa 8:30am-1am, Su 11:30am-4:30pm. DC/MC/V. ❷

NORTHERN CAPE

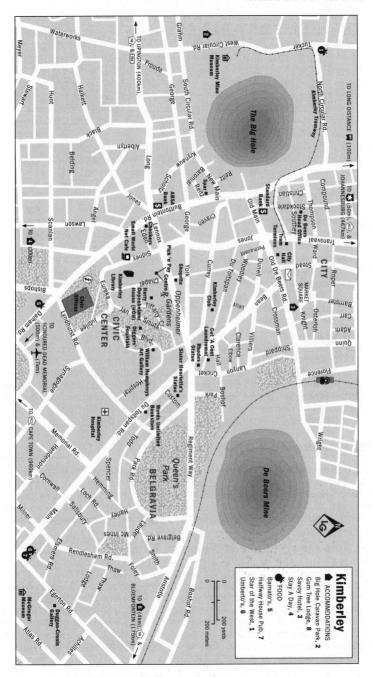

Kimberley

ACCOMMODATIONS
Big Hole Caravan Park, **2**
Gum Tree Lodge, **8**
Savoy Hotel, **3**
Stay A Day, **4**

FOOD
Barnato's, **5**
Halfway House Pub, **7**
Star of the West, **1**
Umberto's, **6**

THE GUMBOOT DANCE The syncopated, synchronized steps of the Gumboot dance got their start in the mining camps of Kimberley and the Witwatersrand, where workers from all over Southern Africa eked out a subterranean living. It is perhaps best known outside the region for lending its name to the title of a Paul Simon song on the *Graceland* album. The name of the dance comes from the long, sturdy rubber boots that the miners wear, which are stomped and slapped to generate the dance's distinctive rhythms. The lighthearted vigor of the line dancers is punctuated by periodic calls and whistles from the leader, a form of expression that brought humor to the daily drudgery of the shafts. Stingy employers and stone-faced supervisors are the objects of relentless parody in the slang of the satirical calls, which in days past were also laced with political resistance against the exploitation of black miners. The Gumboot dance is more than clever movements and tricky steps—it's a humorous and often poignant dramatization of one of the toughest occupations imaginable.

Barnato's, 6 Dalham Rd. (☎833 4110). Between Memorial Rd. and Bishops Ave. Simple single-story house in which Barney Barnato (of diamond lore) was born. Specialties such as Karoo Lamb Chops and Northern Cape steaks. Entrees R40-60. Open M-F 11:30am-2:30pm and 6:30-10:30pm, Sa 6:30-10:30pm. AmEx/DC/MC/V. ❷

Umberto's (☎832 5741), corner of du Toitspan and Egerton/Carrington Rd. A convincing facsimile of a pseudo-Italian restaurant in the heart of Kimberley, with red-checkered tablecloths and lots of garlic. Whatever it may be lacking in ambiance, it makes up in food with wood-oven pizzas (R26-50), salads (R20-30), pasta dishes (R20-30), and a number of South African takes on Italian cuisine (R45-60). Open M-F noon-2:30pm and 6-10:30pm, Sa 6-11pm. AmEx/DC/MC/V. ❷

Halfway House (☎831 6324), on corner of du Toitspan and Egerton/Carrington Rd., in same building as Umberto's. Cecil Rhodes himself used to drop into the "Half" (est. 1875) when commuting between mines. Being quite a diminutive man, it was only on horseback that his stature matched his ambition. Rather than make the diamond emperor self-conscious, the staff brought him his brew while he remained mounted. Tradition became law: the bar now has the distinction of being one of only two licensed drive-in pubs in the world. Enter on foot for lunch or dinner. Steak roll R24. T-bone R30. Fish 'n chips R21. Castle draft R6. Open M-Sa 10am-2am. ❷

🅖 SIGHTS

The **Diamond Route** (8km), marked by the yellow diamonds painted down the middle of the road, connects the city's many museums and sights. One way to see a cross-section of Kimberley is to catch the historic tram from the center of town to the Big Hole. The tram stops on request at the Star of the West pub; have a quick peek or a brew. *(Departs daily from City Hall on the quarter hour 9:15am-4:15pm and from Big Hole and Mine Museum on the hour 9am-4pm. R5 one-way.)*

BIG HOLE AND KIMBERLEY MINE MUSEUM. Kimberley's most famous attraction has impressive numbers—240m deep, 14.5 million carats of diamonds mined—but nothing compares to the raw feeling of staring down the maw of this beast. This is, in no uncertain terms, a big hole. On the rim, a number of buildings have been abandoned by De Beers, like some latter-day Pompeii. Shops and houses full of boom-era artifacts sit in deserted silence as though their inhabitants vanished into thin air the day the last diamond was uncovered. *(Corner of N. Circular and W. Circular Rd. From Tourist Center, take Bultfontein Rd. north to N. Circular and make a left. Take your next left onto Tucker, which becomes W. Circular. The Big Hole will be on your left. ☎833 1557. Open daily 8am-6pm. R17, children R10.)*

CECIL JOHN RHODES Often described as the most important

South African politician of the 19th century, Rhodes (1853-1902) was not simply a diamond magnate; he was also a raging imperialist with a vision of a white-dominated Africa. Born in England, he was sent to work on a cotton farm in South Africa in 1870 due to his poor health. In 1871, attracted to the diamond mines of Kimberley, he established himself as an entrepreneur by buying claims in De Beers, the biggest mining corporation in the country, over which he eventually gained full control. As he moved back and forth between Oxford, England, and South Africa, he fascinated his colleagues not only with his business skills, but also with his grandiose musings: "Why should we not form a secret society with but one object—the bringing of the whole uncivilized world under British rule—for making the Anglo-Saxon race one Empire. What a dream, but yet it is probable, it is possible." Rhodes was prime minister of the Cape Colony from 1890-1896. During this time he formed the Diamond Syndicate, the harbinger of the Central Selling Organization, which controls nearly 80% of the world diamond trade today. Rhodes made sure his name and legacy would continue after his death by establishing a scholarship to some little-known university in England.

MCGREGOR MUSEUM. Previously a sanatorium, convent, and refuge, the museum now houses an impressive range of insightful and polished exhibits on a span of African history ranging from the origins of man to the Boer siege of Kimberley. *(Between Atlas St. and Egerton Rd. in Belgravia, next to the Duggan-Cronin Gallery. ☎842 0099. Open M-Sa 9am-5pm, Su 2-5pm. R8, children and students R4.)*

DUGGAN-CRONIN GALLERY. A small sampling of the over 8000 photographs taken by Alfred Matrin Duggan-Cronin in the 1920s and 30s are on display in this gallery. They depict indigenous cultures from all over Southern Africa at a time when many peoples were besieged by western modernization. Most compelling are the black and white portraits of mothers and children. *(On Egerton Rd. in Belgravia. ☎842 0099. Open M-F 9am-5pm, Su 2-5pm. Donations appreciated.)*

WILLIAM HUMPHREYS ART GALLERY. This private collection of a wealthy diamond magnate includes 16th- and 17th-century Dutch and Flemish oil paintings alongside traditional Zulu and Xhosa pottery and beadwork. Contemporary South African art is a recent addition and the most engaging portion of the gallery. *(Inside the Civic Center on Cullinan Crescent near the corner of Lennox St. and Jan Smuts Blvd. ☎831 1724. Open M-Sa 10am–5pm, Su 2-5pm. R2, children R1; W free.)*

UPINGTON   ☎054

Upington (pop. 75,000) rests on the quiet and desolate edge of the Kalahari Desert. It's little more than a large base camp en route to the Kalahari Gemsbok (300km north) and Augrabies National Park (120km west). Upington tenders its wares to adventurers stocking up for a wilderness safari. Hulking 4x4s saddled with camping gear, a supermarket spanning one city block, banks swapping currency, and a street market filled with vendors hawking al kinds of supplies can meet almost any adventurer's needs. In October, the annual Raisin Festival brings a carnival atmosphere to the town, with flea markets and amusement rides. During the rest of the year, the town slows to the lethargic pace of the neighboring Orange River.

▣ TRANSPORTATION

Upington lies roughly 900km west of Johannesburg and Pretoria along the N14, entering town from the northeast as Schroder St. From Cape Town, take the N7

NORTHERN CAPE

north to Clanwilliam, the R364 to Soetwater, and then the R27 to Keimoes, on the N14 southwest of Upington. The whole trip is about 820km.

Flights: Upington Airport on Diedericks Rd. north of town. **South African Airlink** (☎332 2161) flies to **Cape Town** (1¼hr., daily 8:05am, R1528) and **Johannesburg** (1½hr., 5:20pm, R1540).

Buses: Intercape (☎331 2102) buses depart from Lutz St., between Scott and Schroder St. to: **Cape Town** (10hr.; M, W, F-Sa 6:30pm; R200) via **Citrusdal** (7hr., R180); **Pretoria** (11hr., M-Tu and Su 7:15am, R250) via **Johannesburg** (10hr, R250); **Windhoek** (13hr.; Tu, Th-F, Su 5:45pm; R275) via **Keetmanshoop** (7hr., R210). **Big Sky** (☎072 290 4849 or 053 832 2006) buses depart from Lutz St. between Scott and Schroder St. on Sundays to **Kimberley** (5hr., R110) and **Bloemfontein** (7½hr., R170). Call for departure times.

Minibus Taxis: Douglas Taxi (☎339 1017 or 021 904 5352) offers door-to-door service between Upington and **Cape Town** (M, W R120; F, Su R140). Other long-distance minibuses depart from the Upington railway station off Keimoes Rd. They leave very early in the morning, so show up at 6am and be patient. To: **Johannesburg** (R100); **Kimberley** (R60); and **Springbok** (R60).

Car Rentals: 4x4 vehicles permit the most adventurous touring, but sedans work fine for the main roads of the parks and getting around in towns. ■**Kalahari 4x4 Hire,** 57 Scott St. (☎332 3098 or 082 490 1937; www.kalahari4x4hire.co.za). Very helpful and friendly staff. Rents sturdy 4WDs which are available with CD players and A/C. R650 per day plus R100 for camping equipment and insurance. Book in advance via the web site. **Venture 4x4 Hire** (☎337 8400), in the Oasis Protea Lodge on Schroder St. R650 per day plus R150 for camping equipment. Insurance included. **Kgalagadi 4x4 Hire** (☎337 8560 or 083 456 4702), at the corner of Market and Park St. Offers a range of vehicles from R627-695 per day. Open M-F 7:30am-5:30pm. **Avis** (☎332 4746 or 082 459 7119), and **Tempest** (☎337 8560), at the airport.

■ ⚡ ORIENTATION AND PRACTICAL INFORMATION

Downtown Upington is quite compact, with all major stores and consumer services along four streets running parallel to the river. Closest to the river, **Schroder St.** is home to the town's best restaurant. West of Schroder St., Upington's large supermarkets and outfitters are found on **Scott St.** and **Mark St. Le Roux St.,** stretching between the **N14** west to Augrabies National Park and the **R360** north to Kgalagadi Transfrontier Park, is the downtown area's westernmost street, running past the stadium, schools, and the Pick 'n Pay Center.

Tourist Office: (☎/fax 332 6064; greenkal@mweb.co.za), inside the Kalahari Oranje Museum at the southern end of Schroder St., between Basson and Kort St. Open M-F 8am-5:30pm, Sa 9am-noon.

Banks: ABSA Bank, 40 Schroder St. (☎337 3300). On the corner of Schroder and Hill St. Offers currency exchange and **ATM.** Open M-F 8:30am-3:30pm, Sa 8-11am. **First National Bank** (☎332 1186), on the other corner of Schroder and Hill St. Open M-F 9am-3:30pm, Sa 8:30-11am.

Library: ☎332 5911, on Le Roux St. between Lutz and Hill St. Open M-F 8:30am-5:30pm, Sa 9am-noon.

Laundry: Coin-O-Wash (☎331 3115), on Scott St. R6 per kg for wash, dry, and iron. Open M-F 7am-7pm, Sa 8am-3pm.

Municipal Swimming Pool, on Borcherd St. north of downtown. R4, students R2.50. Open Oct.-Apr. M-Sa 11am-8pm, Su 2-6pm.

Camping Equipment: Midas, 53 Market St. (☎337 5200). At Hill St. Rents and sells camping equipment. Open M-F 7:30am-5:30pm, Sa 8am-1pm. **Walker's Guns and Sports,** 18 Scott St. (☎332 1555). Sells arms, ammunition, and knives, as well as camping gear. Open M-F 8am-5pm, Sa 8am-1pm.

Weather: ☎331 1171.

Emergency: ☎10 177 (ambulance); ☎10 111 (police).

Police: ☎337 3400, on Schroder St. towards Jo'burg.

Pharmacy: Upington Apteek, 33 Schroder St. (☎332 3071, after hours 332 2785). Next to First National Bank. Open M-F 8am-5:30pm, Sa 8am-1pm, Su 11:30am-12:30pm.

Hospital: Upington Medi-Clinic (☎338 8900), corner of Du Toit and 4th Ave.

Internet Access: Internet Cafe, in the Kalahari Pick 'n Pay Center, at the corner of Le Roux and River St. R10 for 30 min. Open M-Sa 9am-9pm, Su 1-9pm.

Post Office: (☎332 3021), corner of Market and Park St. Offers *Poste Restante.* Open M-Tu, Th-F 8:30am-4:30pm; W 9am-4:30pm; Sa 8am-noon.

Postal code: 8800.

⬛ ACCOMMODATIONS AND CAMPING

Yebo Guest House, 21 Morant St. (☎331 2496; teuns@intekom.co.za). Follow Le Roux St. north. After crossing the bridge over the train tracks, bear left onto Swartmodder, and then make an immediate left onto Morant. It's at the corner of Hertzog and Morant. Airy bungalow and spacious backpackers dorm with kitchen, *braai,* and pool. Call for free pick-up. Meals and laundry available. Dorms R50; doubles R85 per person, with bath R100. Camping R35. ❶

Die Eiland Resort (☎/fax 334 0286), along Palm Ave., on one of the Orange River islands. Off the N10 southeast of town; follow *Die Eiland* signs. Easily the best municipal accommodation in South Africa. Self-catering lodgings, tennis courts, bowling, and pool. Monkeys hang about the lush grounds. Reception 24hr. Reservations recommended. 4-person huts R172-215; 3-person bungalows R215; 4-person chalets R293; 4-person cottages R446; 5-person chalets 319; caravans and campsites R44 for 2, extra person R9. DC/MC/V. ❶

The Islandview House (☎331 1328 or 082 717 2340), alongside the river on Murray St., behind ABSA bank. A tranquil B&B offering spectacular views of the Orange River and the *veld* beyond. Pool and pleasant garden. Ideal lodging for families. Breakfast included. Singles R190; doubles R280. ❷

Kalahari Junction Backpackers, 3 Oranje St. (☎332 7874 or 082 435 0007; www.upington.co.za/kalahari-junction.html). Take Le Roux St. north. After crossing the bridge over the tracks bear left onto Swartmodder and make an immediate left onto Morant. You'll see the sign. Owner and manager Dieter welcomes you into his home at this cozy backpackers, and you'll benefit from his wealth of Kalahari knowledge. Free pick-ups. Dorms R50; doubles R85 per person, en suite R105 per person. ❶

🍴 FOOD

To stock up on provisions, head to **Pick 'n Pay** (☎331 2719), in the Kalahari Center, at the corner of Le Roux and River St. (open daily 8am-8pm) or the massive **Shop-Rite** (☎331 1587), on Scott St. (open M-F 8am-6pm, Sa 8am-3pm, Su 9am-1pm).

◾ **Le Must,** 11 Schroder St. (☎332 3971). Between Basson St. and Park St. Upington's undisputed culinary champ; not to be missed whatever your budget. Traditional Malay,

African, and Provençal cuisines served with local wines in an intimate interior. Starters R20-R30. Salads R25. Vegetarian entrees R35. Grills R45-55. Open Su-F noon-2pm and 6-10:30pm, Sa 6-10:30pm. Reservations recommended. AmEx/DC/MC/V. ❷

Lyndi's Book and Coffee Shop, 34 Schroder St. (☎332 4793). Run by an international cordon bleu chef, this friendly little spot dishes out divine breakfasts (R12-30) as well as other light dishes (R7-21). Internet R15 for 30min. Open daily 7:30am-6pm. ❶

🎵 🎭 ENTERTAINMENT AND NIGHTLIFE

We won't lie: this town ain't got much. Don't expect any of the spots listed below to ever get really full; the crowds can be pretty sparse. That said, Upington livens up on Wednesday, Friday, and Saturday nights. Locals flit into the shadows on all other evenings, leaving streets eerily desolate by 7pm, and even the most popular pubs empty out by 10pm. **CF's Action Cafe,** 65 Market St. (☎332 1414), plays a high-decibel selection of techno, alternative, rock, and traditional *boeremusiek*. Local Afrikaner youth come out for the occasional raves and live bands. (Open W and F-Sa 7pm-4am. 18+. R10, W R5.) **Club Fantasy,** on Sendeling St. off Le Roux St., is popular with Upington's black youth and welcoming to all. It rocks nightly with *kwaito,* hip-hop, and the occasional live band. Expect to pay a nominal cover charge (R10 at most) when it's busy. (☎339 1580. 18+. Open W and F 9pm-late, Sa 2pm-late.) Perhaps your best bet for entertainment is **Nu Metro Cinemas** in the Kala-hari Pick 'n Pay Center at the corner of River and Le Roux St. (R18).

👁 🏔 SIGHTS AND OUTDOORS

Upington is home to the **Oranjerivier Wine Cellars,** South Africa's (and the southern hemisphere's) largest cooperative, located northwest of town along Industrial Rd. Wine connoisseurs rejoice; the wine cellar offers over 30 varieties to choose from and free **tasting sessions,** which allow you to make an "educated" choice. (☎337 8800. Open M-F 8am-5pm, Sa 8:30am-noon.)

If you arrive in Upington and are thirsting for wide open desert and a sampling of local wildlife, stop by **Spitskop Nature Reserve** (☎332 1336), 13km north of town on the R360. The 5641ha reserve is home to several species of antelope, zebra, camel, and bird. From the telescope observation post at the top of *kopje,* one can only begin to appreciate the infinite size and majesty of the flat, harsh wilderness of the Green Kalahari. The reserve's 37km of **hiking** and **4WD trails** are good warm-ups for the more challenging routes of the Augrabies and Kalahari Gemsbok National Parks. Spitskop Reserve organizes **safaris** and camping trips to the Gems-bok, Augrabies, and the natural springs of the Molopo River Canyon, and also provides overnight huts (R50 per person; with electricity R70, R50 per child) and serviced campsites (R20, R10 per child).

AUGRABIES FALLS NATIONAL PARK

Established in 1966, the 50,000ha Augrabies Falls National Park stretches from the banks of the Orange River into the heart of the Green Kalahari. Often overlooked by visitors en route to the more well-known parks to the north and west, Augra-bies' surreal moonscapes and thundering falls remain some of South Africa's best-hidden treasures. The Orange River carves an 18km gorge through granite bedrock as it roars west toward the Atlantic. The park owes its name to the Nama people, who made their home on the river's bank and called the spot *!oukurubes,* or "the place of the Great Noise." The river was the lifeblood of their existence, and they considered it to be a place of great spiritual energy. The mighty Orange plunging

56m into the gorge below is one of the more awesome displays of the force of nature to be found in Southern Africa.

⌷▮ TRANSPORTATION AND PRACTICAL INFORMATION

The park is 120km west of Upington and 360km northeast of Springbok. From Upington, take the N14 toward Springbok to the petrol/supply station of Kakamas (80km). From Springbok, take the N14 towards Upington to Kakamas (320km). From Kakamas, follow the well marked tar access road (R359) 40km to the park gates. (Open Apr.-Sept. daily 6:30am-8pm; Oct.-Mar. 6am-8pm.) Park reception and the visitor Center, with some interesting displays on history, flora, and fauna, are on the main road just beyond the entrance. (☎054 452 9200; fax 451 5003. Open daily 7am-7pm. Entrance fee R12, under 16 R6.) A store that stocks a basic selection of supplies is located next to the reception. (Open daily Apr.-Sept. 8am-6:30pm, Oct.-Mar. 7:30am-7pm.) A filling station is also on the premises. (Open daily 7am-10am and 12:30-5pm.) The gravel roads within the park are well maintained and navigable by sedan vehicles.

▮ ACCOMMODATIONS AND CAMPING

The **Parks Board** in Pretoria (☎012 343 1991; fax 343 0905) arranges reservations for the several housing options at the **main camp ❸** in Augrabies. Spacious two-bedroom cottages come complete with air-conditioning and self-catering kitchen (R520 per cottage; up to 4 people). Two- and three-person bungalows are also available (R270-R345 per bungalow). Fully serviced **camp and caravan sites ❶** equipped with communal baths are the best way to experience the desert in its essence. Camping in the park is restricted to the campground. (R50 for 1-2 people, R20 per additional person. Nov.-Jan. 20% seasonal discount on all accommodations; does not apply on school holidays or long weekends.) Self-service (open daily 7:30am-6pm) and a la carte **restaurants** (open daily noon-2pm and 6-10pm) are next to the park office. About 14km south of the park off the R359, the **Kalahari Adventure Center ❶** offers camping (R20), dorms (R60), and private self-catering doubles (R120). Guests can also take advantage of a number of amenities including a rustic outdoor shower, TV lounge, Internet access (R15 for 30min.), *braai*, dining room (meals R25-50), and a variety of outdoors activities, such as rafting, canoeing, and hiking. From Kakamas take the R359 for about 20km towards Augrabies Falls and look for the Adventure Center sign. (☎054 451 0177; info@kalahari.co.za; www.kalahari.co.za. Reservations recommended. MC/V.)

▚ ADVENTURES

AUGRABIES FALLS. Plunging 56m to the floor of Ararat Canyon and enveloped in veils of mist, the falls are the centerpiece and namesake of the national park. Many believe that an untold fortune in alluvial diamonds lies at the foot of these falls. Visitors can appreciate the thundering spectacle from a variety of vantage points easily accessible via a well marked trail from the reception. A guardrail traces the cliff edge so you don't get too close. Hopping from point to point is also a great way to see the park's flora and fauna. Notable resident species include *dassies* (rock hyrax), the fleet-footed klipspringer antelope, and the psychedelically colored Augrabies flat rock lizard. To see the quieter, more pristine side of the Orange and the stark solitude of its surroundings, take the well-maintained road from the main camps to the outlying overlooks, including Moonrock, Ararat, Oranjekom, and Echo Corner. (Open Apr.-Sept. 6:30am-8pm, Oct.-Mar. 6am-8pm.)

HIKING AND BIKING. Augrabies also offers several **hiking** and **mountain biking trails,** among them the self-guided three-day, 40km **Klipspringer Hiking Trail.** This classic South African trek threads through breathtaking but harsh desert landscapes, affording spectacular views of the river, its gorges, and the great variety of plants, reptiles, rodents, and mammals who have adapted to life in this arid region. Access to this popular trail has been limited to only 12 hikers per day, so visitors are encouraged to book at least one year in advance. Still, if you're interested, contact the park office in Pretoria (☎012 343 1991) for any openings or cancellations. (Open Apr.-Oct. 15th. Trail suitable for fit and experienced hikers only. Overnight huts are equipped with bunks, drinking water, fire pits, and toilets. Hikers must be self-sufficient and carry their own provisions and equipment. Trail starts and ends at the rest camp. R70 per person.) For those without a year's foresight, the self-guided **Gariep Three-in-One Route** combines mountain biking, hiking, and a brief canoeing stint on the Orange River. (3km canoeing, 4km hiking, and 11km biking. Departure at 7am from park reception. Route map, canoes, bikes, and vehicle provided. Book at reception by 4pm the previous day. Groups of 2-6 R120 per person, under 16 R60.) The more docile 3km **Dassie Trail** makes for a couple of hours of easy hiking, providing opportunities to view the ravine and its resident monkeys and klipspringers. (Starts from the campground; no prior reservation necessary.)

NIGHT DRIVES. Group night drives enable sightings of the park's elusive nocturnal game, including jackals, owls, and leopards. (Departs in winter at 7:30pm, in summer at 8pm from the park office. Bookings must be made before 4pm on the day before the drive at park reception. R50, under 16 R25.)

KALAHARI ADVENTURE CENTER. The Adventure Center offers a variety of heart-pounding activities. Most popular is the **Augrabies Rush,** an 8km guided rafting adventure covering Class II-III rapids above the waterfall and ending only 300 perilous meters from the final precipice. The excursion begins and ends at the Augrabies Park main reception. (4hr. R225 per person, 4 person min. Reasonable fitness required.) The Center also offers **Augrabies Canoe Trail** trips (4 day, 5 nights; R1450) and **Orange River Gorge Rafting.** (Experienced rafters only. 2-day trips from R995 per adult.) For desert adventures, the **Kalahari Backroads Safari** traverses Kgalagadi Transfrontier Park, Riemvasmaak Hot Springs, and Augrabies Falls, and rafts the Orange River (5 days, 4 nights; from R2450).

KGALAGADI TRANSFRONTIER PARK (SOUTH AFRICA)

The Kgalagadi Transfrontier Park (37,991 sq. km) is far and away the largest continuously protected ecosystem in Southern Africa; the Netherlands could fit within its borders. For most of the last century, the area now protected by the park was composed of two separately managed pieces: South Africa's Kalahari Gemsbok National Park and Botswana's Gemsbok National Park. In 1992, a joint management committee was established, and the region was formally designated Kgalagadi Transfrontier Park, the first of its kind in Africa. The portion of South Africa-Botswana frontier within the park has no physical barrier, enabling the natural movement of the animals across the border. In the heart of the Kalahari, hundreds of kilometers from most of the features of modern society, this park is one of the most remote places in Southern Africa—a distinction which is both its greatest asset and the biggest barrier to visitors. To most, "The Kalahari" conjures up a vista of sandy sameness, dunes like jaundiced monoliths, and the odd bush holding on for dear life. Indeed, Kgalagadi affords much in the way of dusty landscape, but a closer look reveals a myriad of flora plugging away successfully, punctuated by such striking sights as the furious greens of the Jurassic camelthorn trees.

The true treasures of this vast wilderness are its animal inhabitants, roaming with impunity through the dry river beds of the Nossob and Auob. Blue wildebeest, more concerned with the nearest leopard than the curious human, hardly notice the occasional car. Adorned with black and brown racing stripes, gemsbok stare at motorists with indifference. Though cheetahs are as elusive as water in this land, occasionally lucky travelers witness the incomparable sight of a cheetah in full sprint. The park is known above all for its lions, just as much kings of the desert as they are of the jungle. Adult males have a thick black mane around their neck, endowing them with a particularly majestic appearance.

▐ TRANSPORTATION

If you're entering the park from South Africa, Upington is the best if not the only good spot to stock up on provisions and take one last look at civilization. From Upington, you'll drive 260km north along the **R360** to Twee Rivieren, the administrative center and South African entry point to the park, in its southeast corner. While there's gas available along the way in Andriesvale, as well as in the park, it makes sense to fill your gas tank and jerry cans in Upington. The last 50km are well-graded gravel roads through somewhat treacherous sandy terrain. Because of the distances involved, it is advisable to leave Upington before noon in order to reach the park before nightfall.

The main roads within the park are well-maintained sand (within the river beds) or gravel (dune-roads). Though it is possible to pass in sedan vehicles, the higher your ground clearance (or rental car insurance) the better. It never hurts to have a 4WD, especially on the rare occasion when the weather takes a turn for the worse.

For those with more extreme aspirations, such as entering the park in South Africa and leaving from Botswana, a 4WD convoy along with off-road expertise and desert wherewithal are required. The Nossob-Mabuasehube access track is passable by 4WD vehicles. The Wilderness Train to the Kaa Entrance Gate in Botswana should be attempted only if you're willing to meet your maker in the middle of the desert. Permits are required for all 4WD excursions. Be sure to speak with a ranger before even considering setting out. An entrance fee of R25 per adult per day, under 16 R12, and R5 per car per day is levied at Twee Rivieren over and above any accommodation costs of your stay. (Park office ☎ 054 561 2000; fax 561 2005. Park gates and the roads between camps open Jan.-Feb. daily 6am-7:30pm, Mar. 6:30am-7pm, Apr. 7am-6:30pm, May 7am-6pm, June-July 7:30am-6pm, Aug. 7am-6:30pm, Sept. 6:30am-6:30pm, Oct. 6am-7pm, Nov.-Dec. 5:30am-7:30pm.)

▐ PRACTICAL INFORMATION

Two dry rivers diverge in a yellow desert, but luckily you can travel both. Deep and narrow **Auob Riverbed** veers northwest toward the Namibian border, while wider and shallower **Nossob Riverbed** at first follows a northeasterly course before bending northwest to **Union's End,** the point where South Africa, Botswana, and Namibia converge. The park's principal roads run along these dry washes through harsh scrub, thorny bush, grassland, and the occasional shade of lone trees—a contrast to the waterless landscape beyond the rivers' banks. Both roads access rest camps complete with accommodations, shops, and refueling stations. Either way, it's the road less taken, and that makes all the difference. 130km from Twee Rivieren at the Namibian border, **Mata Mata** sits on the banks of the Auob. The **Nossob rest camp** is 160km from Twee Rivieren, a little over halfway to the road's end.

The sole entrance to the park for cars without a 4WD is at Twee Rivieren. From here, many visitors spend a day traveling to one of the interior rest camps, where they spend the night. Two dune-roads connect the riverbeds, so visitors need not return to Twee Rivieren to travel from one camp to the other. While Mata Mata lies at the end of the Auob road, the Nossob road continues beyond the Nossob rest camp for 125km to Union's End. Above the camp, the riverbed opens up, and one gets a true sense of the Kalahari's great expanses. Though 50km per hour is the speed limit on all park roads, most cars drive more slowly. It will take no less than 3½ hours to reach Nossob from either of the other camps and 2½ hours to travel between Twee Rivieren and Mata Mata. You cannot cross the border into Namibia within the park. Plan your movements accordingly, and remember that leaving your vehicle (except in designated locations) and driving after dark are prohibited.

▶ ACCOMMODATIONS AND CAMPING

The park's sheer size and remote location make a real visit impossible without an overnight stay, preferably within the park grounds. The **National Parks Board ②** (☎ 012 343 1991; fax 343 0905) offers cottages, bungalows, huts, and campsites at the three rest camps. Due to the park's growing popularity, it is advisable to book accommodations through the Parks Board in advance. Expect to pay R460 for a four-person self-catering cottage with private bath, R610 for a six-person, and R275-R425 for two- to four-person bungalows and cottages with shared or private bath. For spur-of-the-moment visitors, **camping ①** on the park's fully serviced site may be the only option, so come prepared (R65 per night). During the blazing hot summer months, camping offers a cost-effective alternative for all visitors. In winter, precautions against the icy desert nights are necessary. Visitors searching for a truly *Out of Africa* experience should ask park headquarters about the free backcountry campsites in Botswana accessible from the Nossob road. There is a 20% discount on both accommodations and camping from Nov. 1 to the end of Feb. The **Lapa Restaurant ②** (open daily 7:30-9am and 6:30-9pm; take-away 7:30am-6pm) and **Lion's Den Pub ②** (open Su-Th 10am-9pm, F-Sa 10am-10pm) offer a welcome change of scenery after one too many burnt meals in the bush.

An increasing number of neighboring landowners are starting to cash in on their location by offering **guest house accommodation** within easy driving distance of the park. A comprehensive catalogue of these establishments can be obtained from the Upington tourist office (see p. 411). A number of affordable accommodations can be found in or around the town of Askham, 60km south of the park. For restless travelers who want to stretch their legs after days of watching game from behind the windshield, these are two more adventurous options:

Kalahari Trails Nature Reserve (☎ 054 902 916 341; fax 082 786 7615; kalahari.trails@intekom.co.za), 35km south of park on the Askham (R360). Dune hiking trails, game drives (3hr., R40), and guided walks (2hr. morning R35, 1½hr. night R30) on a 3500ha reserve. Self-catering facilities include: doubles and triples (R170-190); triples and quads with bath (R250); 4-person luxury chalets (R300). Camping on attractively sheltered sand with hot shower, kitchen, *braai*, and lapa (R60 per tent, 4-person maximum, R10 per extra person). Alternatively, try a tented bushcamp overlooking a waterhole (R100 per person). Discounted prices Nov.-Mar. ①

Molopo Kalahari Lodge (☎/fax 054 511 0008; reservations@molopo.com; www.molopo.com), 58km south of park on the R360 to Askham (15km southeast). Posh establishment offers camping with pool, hot showers, and lounge area. Arranges 4x4 trips, game drives, and *spoorsny* (tracking) with Bushman guides. Restaurant/bar serves breakfast, lunch, and dinner. Reservations recommended. R120 per person per night, breakfast included. Camping R25 per person, ages 6-12 R12.50, under 6 free. ②

◣ GAME VIEWING

The park's dunes may appear barren and lifeless, but they are actually home to several hardy species of **plant life,** including the shepherd and camelthorn trees, which bind the sand together with their extensive root systems and provide much needed fodder for grazers. Just as vital are the *tsamma* melons, whose fruit is often the only source of water for the animals of the Kalahari and the Bushmen. These plants and tough grasses grow in greater profusion along the river valleys, which become invaluable feasts for grazers after rains.

The park counts five species of **antelope** among its inhabitants, ranging from the 20kg duiker to the elusive 900kg eland. Both springbok and gemsbok are plentiful. With the exception of the eland, which prefers life among the dunes, you are likely to see the most antelope in the river valleys, especially after rains. To see the park's flora and fauna up close and personal, take a day walk with a ranger from one of the rest camps. These informative jaunts into the bush provide a rare opportunity to experience the Kalahari in a pristine state. (Book at the rest camp reception. R60 per adult, R30 per child.)

Africa's three great **feline predators**—the lion, the leopard, and the cheetah—all thrive in the park. Sparse vegetation makes for ideal viewing conditions. In this land where water is so scarce, animals congregate near the watering holes beside the park's roads. Only the cheetah hunts primarily by day, relying on keen eyesight and high speed to run down its prey. If you're lucky enough to see one, the Nossob and Auob riverbeds offer excellent confined spaces from which to watch these speed demons do their deadly work. The Auob riverbed, in particular, is regarded as one of the best places in the world to catch sight of cheetahs as they hunt. The Kalahari lion is a nocturnal hunter, lazing in the shade for most of the day. Keep a sharp eye out for these kings lounging beneath the park's occasional tree. The camps at Twee Rivieren and Nossob organize night game tours; otherwise, the ban on nighttime driving makes it difficult to watch a lion hunt its prey. Leopards are almost exclusively nocturnal and are very rarely seen because of their camouflage.

During the day, the best way to spot predators in the park is to keep an eye on their potential prey; look in the direction of their nervous glances. At night, you might catch a glimpse at the watering-hole hides near each of the three camps. The best chance to see a hunt is on a **night drive,** a three-hour guided trip on an open bus that leaves daily from Twee Rivieren and Nossob rest camps. (Book in advance at the rest camps. R60, under 16 R30; 6-18 people.)

Should you tire of earthbound hunters, the skies above the park are filled with a wide variety of **raptors,** ranging from the huge martial eagle, the largest flying predator in the world at 1m in height, to the tiny, 20cm-tall pygmy falcon, the smallest bird of prey in Africa. Birds of prey share the skies above the Kalahari with the kori bustard, the world's heaviest flying bird, weighing just under 20kg. The park is also home to a myriad of smaller creatures, ranging from the tiny sociable meerkat to a wide range of snakes, lizards, and, of course, scorpions.

For those visitors who truly want to immerse themselves in the Kalahari the park offers guided **4x4 drives.** These excursions provide an amazing opportunity to plunge into the heart of the desert with someone intimately knowledgeable about the land. (You must provide your own vehicle and supplies. 3 days, R1200 per vehicle, minimum 2 vehicle.)

If you've always wanted to try **dune surfing,** be sure to check out **Rooiduin Experience** (☎ 082 589 6659), 30km south of the park on the R360. Surf the red sands to your heart's content for R20.

NORTHERN CAPE

KGALAGADI TRANSFRONTIER PARK (BOTSWANA)

The section of the Kgalagadi Transfrontier Park within Botswana is like a big brother to the South African portion of the park. In addition to being three times larger (28,400 sq. km), it is more desolate, more inaccessible, and more spacious. The park features no signs of human presence apart from the scattered roads and shelters. The nearest town of any size is 80km away, 60km of which is like driving through a giant sandbox. Lions, cheetah, blue wildebeest, and a multitude of antelope all call this desolate landscape home. Due to its remote, difficult-to-access location, game viewing here takes place in a pristine, unfettered environment. A trip here truly feels like a journey into the wild.

▟ ⬚ ORIENTATION AND PRACTICAL INFORMATION. The main entrance to Kgalagadi in Botswana is in the Mabuasehube section of the park off the road between Tsabong and Tshane. The road from Tsabong is navigable only by 4x4 and presents quite a challenge even then. The first 55km out of town are on a newly graded gravel road that requires no special care. The remaining 55km or so to the entrance station are along an incredibly treacherous single-lane of sand. Only the ruts from other intrepid explorers allow any sort of progress in a straight line. This stretch of road should be approached with extreme caution. Extra fuel, water, repair/emergency supplies, and a detailed map are all musts.

Tsabong is the nearest town to the McCarthy's Rest border post (open daily 8am-4pm), about 20km south. To reach McCarthy's Rest from the South African portion of the park, take the R31 from Andriesvale east to Van Zylsnus before heading northeast and joining the R380 to the border. The whole drive covers about 260km. From Kuruman to McCarthy's Rest along the R31 and R380 is about 190km. To reach Tsabong from the McCarthy's Rest border post, turn right before making a left at the turnoff for Tshane. Continue straight for 50m, and then make the first right onto a gravel road, which arrives at the park 110km later.

The really adventurous with a couple of 4WD vehicles might consider traveling between the parks along the Nossob-Mabuasehube access track, which not surprisingly runs between Nossob camp in South Africa and the Mabuasehube entrance gate in Botswana. The route is usually tackled in two days, and there are a couple of nice campgrounds along the way.

The visitors center (at the entrance station) for the Mabuashebe section along the Tsabong-Tshane Rd. provides a good deal of information about exploring the park, including invaluable **maps.** There is also water and a small campground here. (P20 per adult, P10 per child, P4 per vehicle.) There's a Barclays Bank in Tsabong, where you can exchange currency if you're coming from South Africa. (Open M-F 8:30am-3:30pm, Sa 8:15pm-10:45am.)

▛ ACCOMMODATIONS AND CAMPING. One of the most appealing features of Mabuasehube is the proximity of the campsites to the wildlife. There are six campgrounds, each overlooking a pan, some with ablution facilities and *braai* areas. One of the sites is right next to the main entrance, but the sites closest to the wildlife are 12km to 30km west of the park entrance. (Camping P30 per adult, P15 per child.) If you're looking for a bit more comfort, the **Berry Bush Camp ❶** provides a pleasant indoor alternative. This family camp/farm organizes tours into the Gemsbok (P600 per day) and serves as the local tourist information center. If you run into trouble or an emergency situation out in the bush, make a beeline here for a safe haven. (From downtown Tsabong, head east for 8km before turning north at the Berry Bush signs. The camp is 3km in. ☎267 540 540; berrybush@mega.bw. Modest singles P125; camping P25 per person.)

LESOTHO

> **PRICE RANGES.** Price ranges, marked by the numbered icons below, are now included in food and accommodation descriptions. They are based on the lowest cost for one person, excluding special deals or prices. In the case of campgrounds, we include the cost of a car. The table below is a guide to how prices and icons match up.

SYMBOL	❶	❷	❸	❹	❺
ACCOMM.	M1-100	M101-200	M201-300	M301-400	M401+
FOOD	M1-25	M26-50	M51-100	M101-200	M201+

There are many disreputable jokes about what Lesotho (*le-SOO-too*) looks like, most of which have something to do with "hole in South Africa." Lesotho, of course, is not a part of South Africa, but it is entirely surrounded by it. This mountain kingdom may be no more than a tiny pocket of land on the map, but it feels anything but claustrophobic. Windswept landscapes seem to stretch out into eternity from the capital city of Maseru. One glimpse at the breathtaking Drakensberg mountains in the east is enough to understand why J.R.R. Tolkien used them as a model for the Misty Mountains. Of course, Lesotho more than satisfies the standard Southern African pants-wettingly-cool wildlife requirement. However, throughout its history, Lesotho has been faced with the struggle to remain whole in the shadow of a huge neighbor. Today, the country continues to search for a way out of its seemingly permanent state of poverty. In the meantime, however, visitors will be inspired by the flawless sense of hospitality and generosity that permeates the Basotho culture in both good times and bad.

FACTS AND FIGURES

Official Name: Kingdom of Lesotho

Government: Constitutional monarchy

Capital: Maseru

Land Area: 30,355 sq. km

Geography: Lowlands in the west; Drakensberg mountains in the east.

Climate: Temperate, with hot, wet summers and cool, dry winters—greater extremes are reached in the Highlands

Head of State: King Letsie III

Major Cities: Maseru

Population: 2,143,141

Languages: English, Sesotho

Religions: Christian 80%, indigenous 20%

GDP Per Capita: US$2240

Major Exports: Clothing, footwear, vehicles, wool, mohair, livestock

LIFE AND TIMES

HISTORY

ALL YOU EVER WANTED TO KNOW ABOUT PRE-1990 LESOTHO. Basotho farmers became the first permanent residents of Lesotho in about 1500. Their destiny changed forever in 1820, when refugees of all nationalities began to seek protection from Shaka Zulu's troops (see p. 268) atop the fortress-like cliffs of the Drakensberg. The powerful leader of the Basotho, **Moshoeshoe** (*moh-SHWAY-shway*), offered asylum; from these grateful new subjects, the kingdom of **Basutoland** (now Lesotho) was formed. Thus began a long monarchical tradition in Lesotho, one that has seen enough ups and downs and conspiracies to fill a Shakespeare play.

Amidst the politics, the discovery of diamonds in nearby Kimberley, South Africa in 1870 proved a watershed moment. Young Basotho men migrated to the mines, bringing back wages and infusing the country with more hard currency than it had ever known. Britain, Lesotho's nominal "protector," held a low opinion of the country, seeing it as a labor reserve for South Africa destined for eventual absorption. Lesotho thus remained underdeveloped. Despite failed stabs at political independence in 1910, the first democratic elections took place in 1960. Ntsu Mokhekle's **Basutoland Congress Party (BCP)** won a majority and crafted a constitution that splits power between the king, prime minister, and National Council.

Thing got a little crazy after independence: the Lesotho military took over in the 1970s and ruled the country for the next two decades. It was not until the early 1990s that Lesotho democratized once more, paving the way for Ntsu Mokhekle's re-election as prime minister and for the return of the monarchy from exile.

TODAY

DISBANDMENT, ABDICATION, DEATH, CONTROVERSY. Ever since democracy returned to Lesotho in 1993, the relationship between King Letsie III and the elected government has been on edge. In 1994, things came to a head when the king single-handedly disbanded the BCP government. When the move was greeted with deafening international criticism and the threat of sanctions, Letsie was forced to back down and reverse his order. Publicly humiliated, the king then abdicated the throne back to his father, Moshoeshoe II. Following Moshoeshoe's death in a car accident two years later, however, the controversial Letsie III returned to the throne.

MASSIVE ELECTION FRAUD AND COUP (WELCOME TO AFRICA). In March 1997, BCD founder and prime minister Ntsu Mokhekle was discharged from his own heavily divided party over allegations of misrule. He remained prime minister, however, and formed the absurdly named **Lesotho Congress for Democracy (LCD).** In the May 1998 elections, the new LCD, amid charges of widespread fraud, won every national assembly seat except one. Anti-LCD protests began, grew, and then erupted into violence; the government was forced to ask South African troops to occupy the country in order to avoid a military coup. Breakaway members of Lesotho's army put up armed resistance to the South Africans, but were soon subdued. Meanwhile, in central Maseru, the chaos sparked widespread looting and burning, directed in large part at businesses owned by people of Chinese descent, who are often the target of Basotho resentment. The South African troops left within two months, and a compromise **Interim Political Assembly (IPA)** has been established as a shaky power-sharing agreement between the factions. Reminders of the turmoil can still be seen in central Maseru, where most lots are either empty, under construction, or occupied by brand-new buildings.

PEOPLE

Lesotho has approximately 2.3 million citizens. It is one of Africa's only nations almost entirely composed of a single ethnic group, the **Basotho** (singular: Mosotho). There are also small groups of Xhosas, Europeans, and Asians. The official **languages** are Sesotho and English. The largest (and official) **religion** is

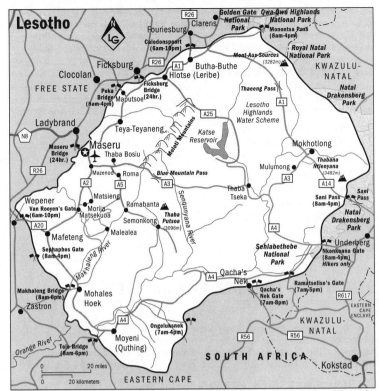

Lesotho

Christianity—predominantly Roman Catholic, but also Protestant and Lesotho Evangelical. Islam and indigenous religions are also present to lesser degrees.

Nearly a fifth of Lesotho's citizens live in urban areas, primarily in Maseru. Despite the pressures of migrancy and modernization, the Basotho are generally attached to their traditional ways of life. In rural areas, Basotho culture is centered in villages, presided over by **chiefs** who derive their authority from (and are often related to) the king. As many as five or six families live together in villages made up of *rondavels,* round or rectangular huts built of brick, mud, stone and sometimes cow dung, and often painted with intricate designs. The chief's *rondavel* is usually in the center of the village, as is the fenced-in *kraal* of livestock.

CULTURE

Culturally, you won't find much difference between the Lesotho and its Southern African neighbors. For additional information, please refer to p. 64.

THE ARTS

Reenforcing the country's relatively high literacy rates (around 70%), the newspaper *Leselinyana Le Lesotho* has been published for over 100 years. **Thomas Mokopu Mofolo's** classic novel *Chaka* (1925) portrayed the tragedy of Shaka Zulu's life, and **Mpho 'M'atsepo Nthunya** wrote her stirring autobiography *Singing Away* *the Hunger* (1996) in English. Many of the country's crafts derive from traditional objects of everyday use, such as the **Basotho Hat** (see p. 431). This woven head-dress is worn by both men and women, and is supposedly modeled after **Qiloane,** a hill situated next to the sacred Thaba Bosiu national monument (see p. 432).

HOLIDAYS & FESTIVALS (2003)

Note that Lesotho celebrates Boxing Day on December 26. All dates listed below are fixed from year to year except for **Ascension**, which changes dates each year. When these dates fall on Sunday, they are usually observed the following Monday.

11 March: Moshoeshoe's Day

Second Monday in March: Commonwealth Day (non-holiday observance)

21 March: National Tree-Planting Day (non-holiday observance)

4 April: Heroes' Day

1 May: Workers' Day

17 July: King Letsie III's Birthday

4 Oct.: National Independence Day

ESSENTIALS

DOCUMENTS AND FORMALITIES

VISAS

Visas are not required of citizens of Australia, Canada, New Zealand, South Africa, the United States, or the European Union for stays up to 90 days. Citizens of other nations and those requiring longer stays should contact the **Director of Immigration and Passport Services,** P.O. Box 363, Maseru 100, Lesotho (☎323 771; fax 310 438).

LESOTHO EMBASSIES ABROAD

South Africa: 391 Anderson St., Menlow Park, Pretoria. P.O. Box 55877 (☎012 467 648; fax 467 649).

United Kingdom: 7 Chesham Pl., Belgravia, London, SW1 8HN (☎0171 235 5686).

United States: 2511 Massachusetts Ave. NW, Washington, DC 20008 (☎202 797-5533; fax 202 234 6815).

EMBASSIES AND CONSULATES IN MASERU

South Africa: (☎315 758; fax 310 127), 10th fl. of Lesotho Bank Center, on Kingsway. Open M-F 8am-12:30pm and 2-4:30pm.

United Kingdom: (☎313 961; fax 310 120; hcmaseru@lesoff.co.za), on Linare Rd. behind the Treasury. Open M-Th 8am-4:30pm, F 8-10am.

United States: 254 Kingsway (☎312 666; fax 310 116), between Maseru Bridge and the beginning of downtown. Consular hours M,W 9am-noon and 2-4pm, but open to enquiries anytime.

CURRENCY AND EXCHANGE

Lesotho's unit of currency is the **loti** (plural **maloti**), and is fixed one-to-one to the South African rand. One loti is divided into 100 lisente (singular: "sente"). Maseru is the only city in Lesotho in which you can exchange money (M-Sa, banking hours). South African rand are accepted anywhere in Lesotho—travelers entering from South Africa should not need to convert currency. Change for cash purchases, however, will likely be issued in maloti. Try to use up any spare maloti before you leave Lesotho; they may be very difficult to change back to rand within South Africa. Credit cards (DC/MC/V) and traveler's checks (including AmEx/MC/ Thomas Cook/V) are accepted on a limited basis in Maseru, but very rarely elsewhere. **ATM machines** in Maseru do not accept foreign bank cards. Left with few other options, travelers should consider carrying a well-hidden cash reserve. For more on money matters, see **Essentials** p. 13.

TRANSPORTATION

BY AIR. Maseru Airport is 21km from town, on the Main South Rd. Commercial flights service only Johannesburg (see p. 428).

BY CAR. If you plan to rent a car in South Africa to travel overland to Lesotho, be sure that the rental company's insurance will cover you in Lesotho. Cars may enter Lesotho through any of the twelve border posts listed below. Those with the steadiest traffic include Maseru Bridge, Ficksburg/Maputose Bridge, Caledonspoort and Van Rooney's Gate. Sani Pass, Qacha's Nek, and all other Highland posts are generally accessible only by 4WD vehicles, at least on the way up. Lesotho charges a M5 tax for compact cars and a M10 tax for larger vehicles. Since the recent paving of some of Lesotho's roads, the most convenient way to see the country is by car; many of the drives outside Maseru are quite beautiful. A 4WD vehicle is helpful for navigating the more remote roads of the Highlands. Be sure to stock up on gas before heading into the mountains; rural fueling stations can be rare. Compact cars and 4WDs are available from agencies at the airport, but renting in South Africa is a much more reliable option and offers more choices.

BORDER POST	HOURS	NEAREST S.A. TOWN	NEAREST LESOTHO TOWN
Maseru Bridge	24hr.	Ladybrand, FS	Maseru
Peka Bridge	8am-4pm	Gumtree, FS	Peka
Ficksburg Bridge	24hr.	Ficksburg, FS	Maputsoe
Caledonspoort	6am-10pm	Fouriesburg, FS	Butha Buthe
Mononts'a Pass	8am-4pm	Wetsieshoek, FS	Oxbow
Van Rooyen's Gate	6am-10pm	Wepener, FS	Mafeteng
Sephaphos Gate	8am-4pm	Zastron, FS	Mafeteng
Makhaleng Bridge	Sa-Su 8am-4pm	Zastron, FS	Mohale's Hoek
Tele Bridge	8am-6pm	Sterkspruit, EC	Moyeni
Qacha's Nek Gate	7am-8pm	Matatiele, KZN	Qacha's Nek
Ramatseliso's Gate	7am-5pm	Matatiele, KZN	Sehlabathebe
Bushman's Nek/Nkonko-ana (Hikers only)	8am-4pm	Underberg, KZN	Sehlabathebe
Sani Pass	8am-4pm	Himeville, KZN	Mokhotlong
Ongeluksnek	7am-4pm	Mapheelle, EC	Mphaki
Ongeluksnek	7am-4pm	Mapheelle, EC	Mphaki

BY BUS OR MINIBUS TAXI. Travelers without wheels often hop into minibus taxis from Bloemfontein (see p. 383), Ladybrand, or Fouriesburg (p. 390). Sani Pass Carriers (☎033 701 1017) has buses from Pietermaritzburg to Underberg (M-F; one-way R65). Travelers can also catch a minibus taxi from Pietermaritzburg to Underberg (early morning until 1-2pm, R20). From Underberg, guests can catch a

4WD taxi on to Mokhotlong (R40). Based in Underburg, **Thaba Tours,** arranges day-trips to Mokhotlong (R175) and overnight trips to Mokhotlong or Katse Dam. Within Lesotho, buses and minibus taxis en route to destinations throughout the country are cheap and relatively convenient; most major towns in both the Lowlands and Highlands are accessible by minibus taxi from Maseru.

BY BASOTHO PONY. In some areas, especially the Highlands, the best way to travel is by **Basotho pony.** Pony trekking is a great way to access the beautiful hikes of the Highlands and, in some cases, is the only way to reach remote mountain villages. Bosotho ponies are amazingly sure-footed and can negotiate hairpin turns in mountain passes. Lesotho's major pony trekking centers are the **Basotho Pony Trekking Center** (p. 432) and at **Malealea Lodge** (p. 433).

BY THUMB. *Let's Go* strongly urges you to consider seriously the risks of hitching. However, many drivers will happily let passengers swing up into the back, for free or a small contribution toward petrol. (For important safety information regarding hitching, see **Essentials** p. 29).

KEEPING IN TOUCH

TELEPHONES. Country code: 266. Directory assistance: ☎ 151. **Collect calls:** ☎ 100. International operator ☎ 109; to call directly, dial ☎ 00 and the country code. For major calls, it may be cheapest to cross over to South Africa.

MAIL. The postal code for Maseru is **100.** Postal codes generally aren't used outside of Maseru. There is no reliable *Poste Restante* service at post offices in Lesotho. To **send mail** from Lesotho, take your chances with the local post offices or use one of the express mail services in Maseru, like **FedEx** (see p. 429).

TIME DIFFERENCE. Greenwich Mean Time plus two hours (the same as South Africa). Lesotho does not observe daylight savings time.

HIGHLIGHTS OF LESOTHO

Malealea Lodge (see p. 433) will introduce visitors to Basotho culture and arrange pony trekking or hiking into some spectacular countryside.

Semongkong (Sesotho for "Place of Smoke") is in the heart of the Highlands and is worth visiting just for the drive. However, once you arrive be prepared to be blown away by **Maletsunyane Falls,** the second-highest straight drop waterfall in Southern Africa.

MASERU

This scraggly city unfortunately provides many visitors with their first glimpse of Lesotho. Thankfully, most are not so put off that they don't venture any farther. In a country filled with beautiful mountains, unspoiled valleys, and smiling people, you would expect its capital to share at least some of these attributes. In almost complete contrast, however, Maseru is something of an urban wasteland, half-finished, dirty, and packed with bustling masses. The realities of a country that was long little more than a labor reserve for South Africa's mines are brought to bare in this metropolis. As bleak as the image of Maseru may seem now, though, it has been worse. In 1998, political discontent and violent riots shook this city almost to pieces. Bombed-out buildings, broken windows, burned cars, and extensive looting turned Maseru into a smoldering husk of its former self (see **Recent News,** p. 422). A profound sense of pessimism hung with the dust from the wreckage in the

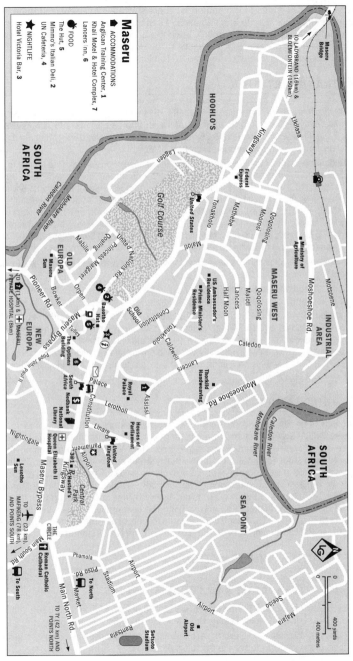

Maseru

♦ ACCOMMODATIONS
Anglican Training Center, **1**
Khali Motel & Hotel Complex, **7**
Lancers 'inn, **6**

🍴 FOOD
The Hut, **5**
Mimmo's Italian Deli, **2**
UN Cafeteria, **4**

★ NIGHTLIFE
Hotel Victoria Bar, **3**

LESOTHO

streets. Imposing signs for commercial centers loomed over charred buildings, announcing stores that no longer existed. Even the Basotho Hat—Maseru's signature building—was burned down. Since then, investment projects are slowly bringing some economic improvements, technological advances are making their way to this growing city, and the Basotho Hat has been rebuilt.

⌐ TRANSPORTATION

Flights: The **airport** is off the Main South Rd., 21km from downtown. **South African Airlink** (in Maseru ☎314 536; in South Africa ☎0800 211 11) flies to **Johannesburg** (1¼hr.; M-Sa 8:25, 10:55am, 5:25pm; Su 10:55am, 5:25pm; M890). Outbound travelers are charged an **airport departure tax** of M20.

Regional Transportation: Minibus taxis, 4WDs, and larger buses make the rounds to the vast majority of Lesotho's towns and villages with an impressive frequency. Buses headed into southern and central Lesotho leave from Main South Rd. and its environs and can be found around the market district north of the Main North Rd. If you can't find a bus headed to your exact destination, catch one to a nearby town. Other minibus taxis will almost certainly cover the remaining distance. To: **Mafeteng** (M15), **Maputsoe** (M17), **Mohale's Hoek** (M24), **Morija** (M8), **Quthing** (M35), **Semonkong** (M26), **Teya-Teyaneng** (M8), and **Thaba Bosiu** (M6).

Minibus Taxis: Local minibus taxis run up and down Kingsway, honking away. M2 for any destination within the city.

Taxis: Moonlight Taxi Service (☎312 695 or 852 695). Prices depend on destination, but fare shouldn't exceed M20 within Maseru.

Car Rental: Avis (☎314 325 or 350 328; ☎0800 021 111 in South Africa) at Lesotho Sun and **Budget** (☎316 344) at Maseru Sun have a very limited selection of 4WD and regular cars. Both have offices at the airport that are only open when South African Airways flights arrive. Renting in South Africa and driving into Lesotho is a much more reliable option. If you're hankering for a 4x4 to do some real exploring try **Thipane Transport** (☎332 067).

◪ ORIENTATION

Kingsway is the main road through town. At the western end of Kingsway is the **Maseru Bridge Border Post** and at the eastern end is the roundabout called **The Circle**; most of Maseru lies in between the two. **Main North Rd.** (to places north of Maseru) and **Main South Rd.** (to places south) shoot out from The Circle. The new Maseru Bypass runs from the start of downtown to The Circle and allows you to skip the congestion of Kingsway, or Maseru, all together. The industrial **Moshoeshoe Rd.** branches off Kingsway after the Maseru Bridge and meets up with it again at the roundabout. **Pioneer Rd.**, across from the **post office**, drops south from the middle of Kingsway. The **Basotho Hat** is jauntily perched at the corner of Kingsway and **Orpen Rd. Ladybrand, SA** is on the R26 just off the N8, 16km north of Maseru.

⚏ PRACTICAL INFORMATION

TOURIST, FINANCIAL, AND LOCAL SERVICES

Tourist Office: Lesotho Tourist Board (☎318 968 or 312 896; fax 323 638), on Kingsway just under the Hotel Victoria. Open M-F 8am-5pm, Sa 8:30am-1pm.

Tours: Since Lesotho lacks extensive infrastructure for the independent traveler, guided tours are a good way to see the country in depth.

Lesotho Tours (☎322 782 or 857 805; africacanman@hotmail.com). Packages ranging from day-trips to 5-day tours. Can also arrange airline flights. Full-day trips start at around R200.

Lesotho-Durban Link (☎325 166; fax 312 614). Outdoor activities, including mountain climbing, abseiling, canoeing, and rafting.

Thaba Tours (☎340 678 or 864 296, fax 310 275; tours@thabatours.de; www.thabatours.de). Extensive pony-trekking and sightseeing tours of the countryside. From R1790 for 5 days, all-inclusive.

Banks: Major banks are in central Maseru on Kingsway. Currency exchange commission rates are generally 1% on cash with a variable minimum charge, around 0.75% for traveler's checks issued by AmEx/MC/Thomas Cook/V. **Standard Bank** (☎312 423), on Kingsway between the post office and the Senate building. Open M-F 8:30am-3:30pm, Sa 8:30-11am. **NedBank** (☎312 696), on Kingsway. Open M-F 9am-3:30pm, Sa 8:30-11am.

Laundry: **Qwik Clean Laundromat** (☎323 697), on Pioneer Rd. in Options Building. M36 for 10kg wash/dry/press. Open M-F 8:30am-5pm, Sa 8:30am-1pm.

EMERGENCY AND COMMUNICATIONS

In case if a serious medical emergency, Bloemfontein (150km east of the N8) is the best option. For major phone calls and mail services, it's cheaper and probably more reliable to cross the border to Ladybrand.

Emergency: police ☎123; **ambulance** ☎121.

Police: (☎317 262 or 317 263), on Parliament Rd.

Pharmacy: Husted's Pharmacy (☎324 917; 24hr. emergency ☎312 464). In Tradorette Mall on Kingsway. Open M-F 7am-5pm, Sa 7am-1pm, Su 8am-12:30pm.

Hospital: Maseru Private Hospital (☎313 260), on Pioneer Rd. about 8km south of downtown. Open 24hr.

Telephones: You can call within Lesotho from telephones on most street corners in Maseru. There are no local phone codes. International calling is significantly more difficult and expensive. 3@1 (see below) is a relatively reasonable option, but the cheapest option for long distance phone calls is to take a minibus taxi (M6) across the border to Ladybrand, South Africa.

Internet Access: Leo Internet (☎322 772), on Orpen Rd. next to the Basotho Hat, M0.60 per min. Open M-F 8am-5pm, Sa 9am-1pm.

Shipping Services: Fed Ex (☎311 277), in the shopping center at the corner of Moshoeshoe Rd. and Kingsway. Open M-F 7:30am-6pm. **DHL** (☎311 082), in the Options Building on Pioneer Rd. **3@1** (☎313 982), in the Carlton Center on Kingsway. Also a good place to make international phone calls. Internet M10 for 30min. Open M-F 8am-6pm, Sa 8am-3pm, Su 10am-3pm.

Post Office: Post Office/Posong (☎325 668), on Kingsway. Mail takes an awfully long time (up to 3 weeks) to get overseas; it is cheaper and faster to cross the border and post from Ladybrand. Open M-F 8am-4:30pm, Sa 8am-noon.

Postal Code: 100.

▛ ACCOMMODATIONS

Budget accommodations are scarce in the budding metropolis of Maseru, so plan accordingly. One option is to spend little time in the city and head for more pleasant destinations in the country, planning Maseru as a day stop if possible. Another possibility is to stay at one of the multitude of B&Bs or guesthouses in Ladybrand (6km from the border post) which are generally clean and reasonably priced. One of the best is **Don's Inn** (☎051 924 1316 or 082 445 9540) on Joubert St. It has spa-

FROM THE ROAD

HACKING IN LESOTHO

When I saw her running with an outstretched arm alongside the road, I thought what harm could there be in giving her a lift. I slowed to a stop and threw all of my books and notes in the passenger seat into the back to make room for her. She got in next to me with her blue and yellow school sweater tied around her head, and when I stepped on the accelerator to go, she said, "Wait!" and pointed to a friend. The friend soon clamored into the back seat behind me, tossing water bottles, bag sand, and my laptop to the other side of the truck.

As we rattled along the dirt road, they fingered everything I had in the truck—CDs, cell phone, sunglasses—with interest, making me embarrassed as well as uneasy. We tried our best at pleasantries and introductions as we climbed up to their village, and I had much more difficulty with their names than they did with mine. When one of them asked if I had anything to drink, I produced a bottle of Coca-Cola. I think we all enjoyed the silence that followed as they gulped down tremendous mouthfuls. I pulled over to the side of the road on the outskirts of a large group of rondavels, and they hopped out amid a crowd of young boys who swarmed around the truck. Waving goodbye, I headed on my way toward Sani Pass. When I stopped the truck 20km up the road to make a few notes, I looked into the back seat and realized my laptop was gone.

(Continued on next page)

cious self-catering apartments that sleep up to six (R100 per person), as well as singles (R175) and doubles (R250; both include breakfast).

Anglican Training Center (☎322 046), near Royal Palace. From Kingsway, walking away from the Circle, turn right on Palace, and right again onto Constitution Blvd. Then make a left on Lerotholi and eventually make a left on Assisi. It's at the top of the hill. This conference center/training facility for future pastors is the best option for budget beds in Maseru. Ablution facilities. Breakfast M15. Lunch M25. Linen provided. Reception M-F 8:30am-4:30pm; on weekends and after hours ask in kitchen. Curfew 7pm. Rooms M40 per person. ❶

Khali Motel & Hotel Complex (☎878 0271 or 878 9679), in New Europa district. From Kingsway, head south on Pioneer Rd. Turn left on Matlaka Rd. and again on Manong Rd. 15min. walk from town. Modest rooms available in a large complex. Pick-up from Maseru Bridge and airport (daily 6am-6pm, approx. every 30min.). Meals M14-40. Reception 24hr. Check out 11am. Singles and doubles M220. ❸

Lancers Inn (☎312 114), at the corner of Kingsway and Pioneer Rd. Inviting rooms, two happening bars, and a restaurant popular with the international crowd. Central location. Reception 6:30am-11:30pm. Check out 10am. B&B single R330, double R425. ❹

🍴🎵 FOOD AND ENTERTAINMENT

Kingsway is lined with **stalls** hawking a wide array of snacks from roasted corn (M1) to heaping helpings of meat (M3) to all sorts of fruits (50 lisente), as well as simple crafts and supplies. For sit-down meals try **Mimmo's Italian Deli ❷** in the Maseru Club on UN (United Nations) Rd., which serves brick oven pizzas and calzones (R20-35) as well as other Italian specialities. (☎860 552. Open M-Sa noon-10pm, Su noon-9pm.) **The Hut ❷**, on Orpen Rd. next to the Basotho Hat, provides uncharacteristically hip dining in the heart of downtown Maseru. (☎325 102. Open daily noon-10:30pm. Lunch and dinner R30-50.) **The United Nations Cafeteria ❶**, in the United Nations House on UN Rd., is a good place to catch up with Maseru's large ex-patriot population. (Open M-F noon-2:30pm. Chinese lunches for under M20.)

Two of the more happening night spots are the **Lancer's Inn Bar** and **Hotel Victoria Bar and VIP Lounge.** They attract much the same crowd, although the Victoria has pool tables (R1 per game) and less glamorous atmosphere. (Both open Su-Th 9am-11pm, F and S 9am-midnight.) For more upscale diversions head to one of the hotel casinos—either the **Maseru Sun,** on Orpen Rd. just east of downtown, or the **Lesotho**

Sun, on a hill above QEII hospital—which feature blackjack and roulette from 7pm on and slot machines anytime.

CRAFTS

The big sellers in Lesotho are the conical Basotho hats. The **Basotho Hat Building** (see p. 429), downtown at the Maseru Bridge end of Kingsway, sells such hats, as well as crafts, beads, books, and clothing for the entire extended family. (☎ 311 011. Open daily 8am-4:30pm; holidays 9am-3pm.) The blankets that the Basotho wrap themselves in for most of the year are more a local necessity than a cultural novelty; you can join the masses and pick one up for M150-400 at any of the "blanket and shoe" stores around town. Unlike their ubiquituous counterparts, the blankets from the **Thorkild Handweaving Shop** on the roundabout side of Moshoeshoe Rd., are dyed and woven in Lesotho. Wool blankets are M250; ponchos are M275. (☎ 322 378. Open M-F 7:45am-4:30pm and Sa 7:45am-1pm.)

BEYOND MASERU

Lesotho's tourist industry is definitely in its infancy, which makes it an exciting, if challenging, place for independent travelers to explore. The destinations below are listed roughly north to south.

TEYA-TEYANENG (BEREA)

Teya-Teyaneng (or TY, as everyone calls it) is home to workshops that create Lesotho's finest mohair tapestries and other handwoven goods. More of a pit stop while traversing the country or a day trip from Maseru than a bona fide tourist destination, this town, nonetheless, should not be missed by those interested in quality craftsmanship. The **Hellang Basali,** on the Maseru side of town (follow the signs from the highway), is the best choice for tapestries, both in terms of quality and variety. Tapestries range from M50 to M1300. (☎ 501 546. Open M-Sa 8am-5pm, Su 10am-5pm.) Right along the main highway (the A1), on the Maseru side of town, are two other workshops, **Elelloang Basali** (☎ 501 520; open M-Sa 8am-5pm and Su 9am-5pm) and **Hatooa-Mose-Mosali** (☎ 500 772; open daily 7am-7pm). They offer tapestries as well as a range of other woolen products. In downtown TY, **Sesotho Design** (☎ 500 353), left off Main St. past the post office coming from the main road, is the most professional of the workshops and features a wide selection of hand crafts in addition to weavings.

(Continued from previous page)

I turned around and, attempting not to let my anger overwhelm my driving, made my way to the police station in Mokhotlong. After waiting what seemed an interminable amount of time, I finally went through the drawn out process of filing a report and making a statement. Judging from the reaction of the officer handling my case, I resigned myself to the fact that I had seen my laptop for the last time. Maybe they would get more use out of it anyway. It started to drizzle as I retraced my tracks on what was now a road too often traveled when, just up the hill from where I had dropped them off, there stood the girls and an older man, laptop in hand. He said with a smirk that they had found it by the side of the road and wanted to return it to me. I thanked them profusely and thanked my lucky stars that it wasn't one of the new Apple iBooks.

—Bryden Sweeney-Taylor

Minibus taxis run here from **Maseru** (M8) and **Leribe** (M10). The town consists of a central street (the **Main Road,** as it's called) perpendicular to the main highway and two cross streets. Services include: the **police station,** on the main road west of downtown (☎500 200; open 24hr.); the **hospital,** north of town (☎500 272; open 24hr.); **S&T Pharmacy,** on Mafolo Rd. (☎869 804); and the **post office,** on the main road in the center of town, with **public phones** in front. (☎500 290. Open M-F 8am-1pm and 2-4:30pm, Sa 8am-noon.) Overnight visitors can stay at the unspectacular **Blue Mountain Inn ❷,** which has house rooms with TV, carpeting, and attached bath, as well as a restaurant and two bars. (☎/fax 500 362. Reception and restaurant open daily 7am-11pm. Meals M25-49. Singles M190; doubles M220; triples M270. Camping M60.)

THABA BOSIU

If Lesotho is the "Kingdom in the Sky," then **Thaba Bosiu** ("Mountain at Night") is the kingdom's fortress. From here, King Moshoeshoe the Great defended his steadily increasing domain against Zulu, British, and Boer forays over the course of nearly a half-century (see **History,** p. 421). The plateau can only be reached via six easily defendable passes and boasts bountiful grasslands as well as several springs, making it ideal for enduring sieges. Thaba Bosiu itself is now a national monument and is extremely significant to the Basotho for both the role it played in the rise of their kingdom and as a final resting place of the line of kings that began with Mashoeshoe. The present monarch, King Letsie III, as well as many members of the cabinet, visit Thaba Bosiu several times a year to pay tribute to the country's past rulers and this important geographic feature.

Minibus taxis run from **Maseru** (M6). By car, follow Main South Rd. out of Maseru, take the turn-off toward Roma (18km), and follow the signs to Thaba Bosiu. There is a M5 entrance fee payable at the **tourist information office** at the base of the monument; excellent **guides** (free, but a tip is appreciated) can also be arranged there. (☎850 166. Open M-F 8am-4:30pm, Sa and Su 8am-1pm.) **Mmelesi Lodge ❷,** nearby, has excellent *rondavels* with hot shower and TV, and a restaurant on the premises. (☎885 2116. Breakfast M25. Lunch M35. Dinner M45. Singles M150; doubles M200.)

BASOTHO PONY TREKKING CENTER

This government-run center, approximately 60km from Maseru on the road to Thaba Tseka in the heart of the highland, offers a number of pony treks into the mountains. This region is a world away from the hustle and bustle of the lowlands. Livestock rather than people are your primary company as you traverse sweeping mountains and isolated river valleys. Trips include all the essentials: something to ride, something to eat, and someone to show you where you're going. There are one-hour saunters (M25) and day treks to **Leboela Falls** (2hr., M35) or the majestic **Qiloane Falls** (4hr., M50), as well as overnight excursions for one to six nights (1 night M125; 2 nights M175, 2 person min.; 4 nights M250, 4 person min.; 6 nights to Semonkong M405, 4 person min., summer only). Treks leave every day at 9:30am in the summer and 10:30am in the winter, but it's a good idea to call ahead so they know you're coming. Try to arrive before 9am to prepare for overnight trips. Room and board isn't included in the price for the overnight treks so bring your own food and cooking supplies. Villages along the way offer *rondavels* (M20) or you can ask permission to pitch a tent (M10), either way, remember to bring appropriate camping gear. (Basotho Pony: ☎314 165 or 327 284; fax 311 500. Open daily 8am-4:30pm.)

Buses run past to the Center from **Maseru** on the way to Thaba-Tseka (1½hr., daily, M8), as do **minibus taxis** (M9). Driving from Maseru, head down Main South Rd. and take the Roma turnoff. In the town of St. Michael's, take the road towards Thaba Tseka; the Center is 32km in along this amazing engineering feat of a road after several winding mountain passes, all of which are well-paved. Simple, comfortable rooms with bath can be found at **Mabotlenyane Lodge ❶,** about 10km from St. Michael's on the Thaba Tseka road, 22km from the Center. (☎181 209 or 347 766; mobile 854 319. Bar and restaurant open 24hr. Meals M22-38. Singles and doubles M90, M50 per extra person. Accommodation also available at the Center guest house.)

MORIJA

Founded in 1833 by pioneer French Protestant missionaries, Morija is the oldest mission station in Lesotho, and was a prominent educational and religious center in the 19th century. This historical legacy is embodied in the old buildings scattered throughout the village, a number of schools, and the country's only museum. Morija is one of the most pleasant towns in Lesotho, a lovely place to stop either for a daytrip or overnight stay. The **Morija Museum and Archives** is a wonder of artifacts that somehow successfully manages to compress into two rooms remnants of the land and its inhabitants from many millions of years. Musical instruments, fertility dolls, and the first books published in Sesotho sit beside relics from a more ancient era, including casts of dinosaur footprints from the area and fossilized ferns. (☎360 308; after hours 360 309. Open M-Sa 8am-5pm, Su 12-5pm. M5, students and children M2.) The museum also plays middleman for the local **pony trekking** association, which offers guided rides around Morija and up to the Makhoarane Plateau. (☎360 309. M40 per hr., half day M50, full day M100, overnight M100. Book in advance.) **Maeder House Crafts Center,** down the hill from the Museum, is home to **Morija Iponeleng Handicrafts,** which offers some fine wares produced by Morija locals. (☎360 487. Open M-Sa 9am-5pm, Su 2-5pm.)

  Minibus taxis run here from **Maseru** (M8). Driving from Maseru, head down Main South Rd. for 42km and turn left at the signs for Morija. The museum is about 1.5km from the turn-off, up the hill from the center of town. Services include: the **police station** (☎360 211), on the turn off to the Scott Hospital Sign; **Scott Hospital** (☎360 237), a marked right turn off the main street that runs between the Main South Rd. and downtown; and the **post office,** in the center of downtown. (☎360 220. Open M-F 8am-4:30pm, Sa 8am-noon.) Museum staff can book overnight visitors at the **HaMatela Guest House ❷,** three historic cottages in different parts of town. (☎360 309. M100 per person.) The museum is also home to a tea room that serves fine lunches (M15) and tasty snacks. (Open M-Sa 8am-5pm, Su noon-5pm.)

MALEALEA

Malealea Lodge, the focal point of the small town from which it takes its name, is one of Lesotho's gems. It's a great base for hiking, pony trekking, and relaxing, but the lodge alone is a reason to visit this country's mountainous interior. Di and Mick Jones, both born and raised in Lesotho, have created a Shangri-La nestled amongst the Highland's most picturesque scenery. It's an unparalleled springboard to the heart of Lesotho, whether by foot or pony.

🖪 TRANSPORTATION. By car, take Main South Rd. out of Maseru for 52km until you reach the village of Motsekuoa. At the Taxi Rank Restaurant, make a left onto a tarred road, and follow it for 10km. At the fork, make a right and continue for another 15km. Make a left turn at the Malealea sign, head over a mountain pass and you'll arrive at the lodge after 7km. Minibus taxis run from Maseru to Motsekuoa (M10) several times a day. If you have trouble finding one, ask a driver heading farther south (to Mafeteng, Mahale's Hoek, or Moyeni) if he can drop you off in Motsekuoa, which will be on his way. From Motsekuoa, you should be able to get a ride to Malealea (M6) as long as you don't arrive too late in the day.

⌐┌ ACCOMMODATIONS AND FOOD. Accommodations at the lodge ❶ include camping and caravaning with a sunrise view over the valley (M40); back-packer dorm beds with bedside tables (fashioned from beer cans), shared kitchen, toilets, hot showers, and lounge (M60 per person); *rondavels* with communal kitchen and facilities (M80 per person); and doubles with private bath (M120-165). There is also a **dining room and bar** ❷, serving scrumptious breakfast (M25), lunch (M35), and dinner (M50), as well as necessary libations. (☎27 51 447 3200 or 082 552 4215 in South Africa; malealea@mweb.co.za; www.malealea.co.ls.) A **general store**, next door in "downtown" Malealea, offers basic provisions. (Open M-F 8:30am-5pm, Sa 8:30am-1pm.)

▓ ADVENTURES. The lodge is home to the Basotho-run **Malealea Pony Trekking Association,** which runs day trips as well as overnights of up to six days. The four-day journey swings toward Ketane Falls and back, and the six-day hike stretches to Semonkong and the towering Maletsunyane Falls. Trips into the mountainous region around Malealea provide a glimpse of the precarious Arcadia that exists in Lesotho beyond the Lowlands squalor. Small villages, composed of just a few *rondavels*, are perched precipitously above sparkling waterfalls. The struggling inhabitants and their ubiquitous sheep and goats cling on to the sheer slopes of the towering peaks in search for an economic foothold.

Pony trekking includes the pony, panniers, a guide, and, for the overnight trips, nights in remote Basotho *rondavels*. The *rondavels* contain only the basics: a foam mattress for sleeping, utensils for eating, a pail of drinking water, and some spartan furniture for relaxing. Your typical well-packed pannier—the only resource you'll have access to on the voyage—should contain the bare minimum: food (catering available), a sleeping bag, rain gear, warm clothing, a towel, sun-screen, a flashlight, sun hat, first-aid kit, water bottles, and water purification tablets. (Day rides M90-135; overnights M160-185 per person, plus M30 per person per night.) If you are short on time, try the quicker **hikes** to waterfalls, Bushman art sites, gorges, and caves. It is well worth the small expense to hire a guide (M10 per hr.). Abseiling between the twin streams of Botsoela Waterfall and exploring the countryside via 4WD, either on your own or with a guide in a Land Rover, are also possibilities. For the more culturally inclined, trips to the school or around the village (M7-10 per hr.) can be arranged. In the afternoon, two *sangomas* from the village accept visits (M20 per person), and the local band and choir perform.

SEMONKONG

As you drive to Semonkong, the rise and fall of the mountains will take even the most jaded traveler's breath away. Undoubtedly the highlight of the area is the awesome 192m Maletsunyane Waterfall, the second highest single drop waterfall in Southern Africa and third highest in the world. In the summer, the water level reaches it peak. In winter the falls are at their most beautiful and most surreal: the base freezes over, and water and ice crash down thunderously from above. The two major **pony trekking** groups in Lesotho—**Malealea** (see p. 433) and the **Basotho Pony Trekking Center** (see p. 432)—both run six-day treks with Semonkong as the turning point. To reach the falls, take the dirt road that leaves the main road to Semonkong and crosses the Maletsunyane River a few kilometers before town. This track, which is worse than the road up to this point, winds through *rondavel* villages and is good spot for a game of dodge-the-cow. You'll drive about 7km before you see the falls, but the land starts to drop away into the river gorge beforehand. Park wherever you wish and look for a good vantage point on foot.

The other way to reach the falls is to walk from the only traveler-oriented accommodation in town, ▓**Semonkong Lodge** ❷, which is tucked into a valley next to the bubbling Maletsunyane River. The hike only takes an hour. The lodge itself is worth a stop for an excellent meal or even a cozy room. The backpackers' thatched-roof bunkhouse has a kitchenette, outhouse, and hot showers in separate buildings. More upscale rooms include a beautifully renovated *rondavel* dating back from the lodge's founding years in the early part of the last century. Delicious breakfasts (M10-26) and other meals (M25-35) can be enjoyed in the rustic dining room. (Reception 24hr. Dorms M50; singles M167; doubles M264. Camping M28. Major credit cards accepted. Contact the Lodge in South Africa at ☎ 27 51 933 3106; bookings@placeofsmoke.co.ls; www.placeofsmoke.co.ls.)

Semonkong Lodge organizes **pony treks** and **hikes** for guests. Overnight trips involve accommodation in villages along the route and last two to seven days. (Day pony treks M72-138; overnight trips M155-190; additional pack horse M70 per day. Overnight hikes including guide M86; with packhorse M151. All prices per person. Prices decrease with larger groups.)

Buses and **minibus taxis** run to and from Maseru throughout the day (5hr., M26). Driving from Maseru, take the Main South Rd. to the Roma turn-off, and keep driving past Roma. Continue to Moitsupeli; here the road becomes dirt. The entire trip is about 115km, 50km of which is on a dirt road.

LESOTHO

SWAZILAND

PRICE RANGES. Price ranges, marked by the numbered icons below, are now included in food and accommodation descriptions. They are based on the lowest cost for one person, excluding special deals or prices. In the case of campgrounds, we include the cost of a car. The table below is a guide to how prices and icons match up.

SYMBOL	❶	❷	❸	❹	❺
ACCOMM.	E1-100	E101-200	E201-300	E301-400	E401+
FOOD	E1-25	E26-50	E51-100	E101-200	E201+

Swaziland is roughly the size of Wales or New Jersey. The land outside of Mbabane and Manzini is sparsely settled, consisting of protected nature reserves, quilted farmland, and sprawling timber plantations. Nevertheless people are friendly. Because Swaziland is relatively homogenous—most Swazis belong to the same tribe—there is little racial and ethnic strife. Royalty is still an active and powerful presence: King Mswati III holds court in his several palaces, and the king's many half-brothers, half-sisters, and cousins (most with the Dlamini surname) walk with red feathers affixed to the backs of their heads to indicate royal status.

Swaziland's monarchy has both detractors and defenders. On the positive side, the royal family has used its influence to preserve the country's rich cultural heritage. One can witness the homage ceremonies and reed dances that take place annually. Many modern Swazis proudly wear colorful traditional dress to their urban jobs. On the negative side, however, "traditionalism" has often corresponded, in practice, to an entrenched patriarchy. Polygamy is common (the king himself has an ever-growing number of wives), women's rights independent of their husbands are limited, and gender roles are strictly defined. Many Swazis (of both genders) complain that the king has too much power, and want the government to take steps toward becoming a full democracy.

FACTS AND FIGURES

Official Name: Swaziland

Government: Monarchy

Capital: Mbabane and Lobamba

Land Area: 17,363 sq. km

Geography: Higher in the west, flattening to low hills in the east

Climate: Temperate, with a wet season in October-April. Rare cases of snowfall in June-August

Head of State: King Mswati III

Major Cities: Mbabane, Manzini

Population: 1,010,000

Languages: English, siSwati

Religions: Christianity (60%), Indigenous Beliefs (40%)

GDP Per Capita: US$4200

Major Exports: Pineapples, sugar, wood pulp, soft drink concentrate

HISTORY

THEY CAME, THEY SAW, THEY CONQUERED (PRE-1875). Originally, the Swazis were a loose confederation of Nguni-speaking ethnic groups whose ancestors migrated from east-central Africa around 1400. First settling in southern Tsonga-

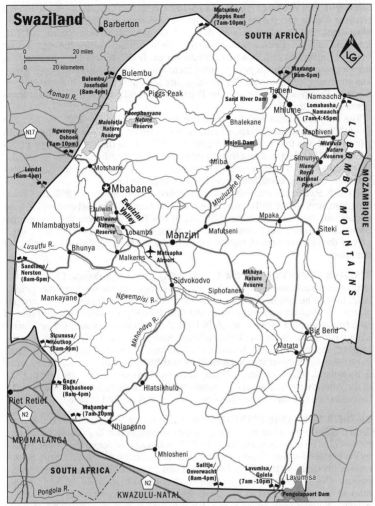

Swaziland

land (now in Mozambique), these ancestors eventually moved southwest, reaching what is now modern Swaziland in 1770, during **King Ngwane III's** reign. There they displaced the area's Sotho inhabitants and built a permanent capital, Lobamba, on the northern bank of the Pongola River. Ngwane's grandson, **Sobhuza** (known to his people as Somhlolo, "the wonder") pushed north due to Zulu threats. His son **King Mswati II** continued to expand the Swazi kingdom until it was almost twice the size of modern Swaziland.

King Mswati II (from whom the present nation derives its name) successfully unified and stabilized the nation after becoming king in 1839. The type of nationalistic kingdom that he fashioned still exists, in a modified form, today. In his fiercely patriarchal kingdom, Mswati II had a monopoly on all wealth, land, and war spoils, and he could marry any and all women he choose (not a bad deal).

SOLD OUT FROM UNDER THEM (1875-1922). Mswati's death in 1865 sparked a ten-year war of succession that was only settled when a compromise candidate, **Mbandzeni,** was crowned in 1875. Although the new king's non-confrontational, innocent character made him an ideal "middle ground" choice, he was a poor leader. Unlike Mswati, who established a professional civil service and an uncompromising foreign policy, Mbandzeni was easily manipulated by Europeans streaming into the area. The Swazi granted so many land and mineral concessions to Europeans, especially the British, that foreigners soon owned a large percentage of their land.

The Boers and Brits both had their eye Swaziland in the late 19th century. The Boers' plans to make Swaziland part of South Africa were dashed when South Africa itself was taken over by the British in 1877. Even though the Pretoria Convention of 1881 declared that Swaziland would be independent, both Brits and the Boers continued to watch over their stakes in the country. After the Anglo-Boer war ended in 1902, Swaziland became a British protectorate.

Though Swaziland was officially controlled by Britain until 1968, the Swazi kingdom was never fully conquered. Queen Labotsibeni, Mbandzeni's wise widow, successfully encouraged Swazis to buy back land from the Europeans. Swaziland's traditional political system remained strong, and during the greater part of the colonial period, traditional authorities retained political leadership of the nation.

STRIDING TOWARDS FREEDOM (1922-1968). In 1922, **Sobhuza II** became the king of Swaziland and immediately set about completing the recovery the nation's land. In 1924 he initiated court proceedings in London, beginning a legal struggle that would drag on until 1940, when the British finally allowed a meager piece of land to come under Swazi control. In 1960, the European Advisory Council, sensing a trend towards African independence, launched an initiative aimed at maintaining white control in Swaziland. Sobhuza II created his own political movement, the **Imbovokodzo National Movement (INM)** to oppose Britain's presence in Swaziland. When the British finally allowed elections in 1964, the INM got 85% of the vote, giving Sobhuza the political confidence to cut ties with his white allies. He continued to press for independence until it was granted in 1968.

ON THEIR OWN (1968-PRESENT). Swaziland was able to avoid the violent conflicts that besieged other newly independent nations in part because its ruling clan represented most of its inhabitants. In 1973, Sobhuza II replaced the British constitution created for Swaziland with one more in keeping with Swazi culture. By the time of his death in 1982, King Sobhuza II had guaranteed that his country would endure. His successor, King Mswati III, has ruled since 1986. In 1995, a year marked by a general strike and student riots, the king's autocratic power began to weaken. Some Swazis today argue that it is time to end royal rule and embrace democracy.

TODAY

CONSTITUTIONAL REFORM. As other countries have democratized, Swaziland has been pressured, both internally and externally, to make similar reforms. Although King Mswati appointed a "Constitutional Review Commission" in 1998 to propose changes, most reformist Swazis consider the royalist-headed commission a farce and refuse to participate. The commission's report, now several years overdue, is expected to argue for the maintenance royal power.

JAILED OPPOSITION. Mario Masuku was jailed in October 2001 for saying that the monarchy should be abolished. Though political parties are illegal in Swaziland, Masuku leads the underground **People's United Democratic Movement (Pudemo)**. He faces up to 20 years in prison if convicted.

FACING STARVATION. In 2002, Swaziland desperately asked for food aid as nearly 40% of its population was at risk of starving to death due to poor crops, the depletion of maize reserves, problems importing maize, the departure of the United Nations World Food Program and food thefts. Ben Nsibandze, the chairman of the National Disaster task force, said the country needed 60,000 metric tons of maize in order to prevent wide-spread starvation.

A UNIQUE WAY TO FIGHT AIDS. King Mswati III has come up with a new way to fight the AIDS virus devastating Africa. In the fall of 2001, he ordered Swaziland's young women to not have sex for five years. Women are supposed to wear a collection of brightly colored tassels, called an *umcwasho*, to discourage potential suitors. If a man is caught sleeping with a young woman, he might have to give her family a cow (which is not cheap). If a girl is caught, she can be fined $160 or put in jail for three months. Girls are also no longer allowed to wear pants. The new orders met with extensive opposition. Swazis have been especially indignant because the king himself has been violating the decree—he recently took a 17-year-old girl as his eighth wife. The United Nations estimates that 20% of Swazi adults are HIV-positive, and that 20,000 Swazis have died of AIDS.

PEOPLE

POPULATION, LANGUAGE, AND RELIGION. Ethnic Swazis comprise approximately 97% of the population of Swaziland; many of the remaining 3% emigrated from South Africa to escape persecution during the apartheid years. The Swazi nation is historically made up of more than 70 African groups. The *ngwenyama* (king) and *ndlovukazi* (queen mother), as well as many modern business leaders and politicians, come from the largest clan, the **Dlamini.** The contemporary Swazi language, **siSwati,** shares the title of "official language" with **English.** English is the accepted official language of written communication. Slightly over half of Swazis belong to **Christian** churches, both Roman Catholic and Protestant, with the remainder adhering to **indigenous beliefs.**

TRADITIONS. Swazi traditions are still a very important component of Swazi life. Two key rituals are still observed. The *Umhlanga* (Reed Dance) takes place in July or August as young, unmarried girls and women travel to the royal *kraal* where they perform dances in honor of the queen mother (*ndlovukazi*), and in recognition of female beauty and virtue. On the journey to the *kraal*, they gather long reeds which they use to repair the queen mother's home. However, with more educational opportunities becoming available, many young women are now refusing to participate in the *Umhlanga* because they feel it reinforces the nation's patriarchal structures. Many women today also object to polygamous marriage, to the customs of *levirate* (in which a widow is given to her late husband's brother) and to *sororate* (in which a younger sister replaces a deceased older sister as wife).

CUSTOMS & ETIQUETTE

In Swaziland, as in the rest of Southern Africa, ask locals about specific traditions you should follow. There are numerous guidelines regarding tourist photography. Always ask before you take a picture of someone. You might be asked to give a tip,

S W A Z I L A N D

THE INCWALA CEREMONY
The *incwala*, a three-week celebration of the king's importance and virility, is the most sacred Swazi tradition. The ceremony begins in early January with the journey of the Bemanti, or "water people," to the ocean off the coast of Mozambique, where they collect foam from the waves. The return of the Bemanti to the royal *kraal* commences the celebration of the first part of the *incwala*, which occurs before the full moon. The king tosses natural medicines in all directions to symbolize the regeneration of the earth, men and women sing songs of praise, and youths venture into every corner of the country to search out the sacred branches of the *lusekwane* shrub. Swazi myth declares that the shrub's leaves will wilt in the hands of any youth who has been intimate with a married woman or who has impregnated a young maiden. The *lusekwane* is then carried to the royal *kraal*, where it is used to build a small enclosure. The *denouement* of the ceremony is the "Day of the Bull," when the blackest of bulls is pummeled to death to celebrate the king's potency. The celebrations' climax is without doubt the "Great Day": the king, garbed in lavish traditional dress, his body glistening with scented ointment, partakes of the first fruits of the season. After the king eats, the people can finally enjoy the fruits of their harvest and the bedding and household items of the royal *kraal* are burnt. Thus the king purges the nation and hails the new year.

especially if your photography subject has put on traditional clothing or taken other measures to help you get a good photo. You are not allowed to photograph the royal family, the royal palace, police in uniform, army personnel and equipment or banks. If you want to take photos at a traditional ceremony, write to the government at PO Box 451, Mbabane. People usually tip 10% in restaurants and hotels.

HOLIDAYS & FESTIVALS

Swaziland's main festivals are the *Umhlanga* and the *Incwala* festivals, both of which celebrate the monarchy. Tourists are allowed to observe at least part of these festivals and should do so if they want to see truly traditional pageantry. The dates of National Flag Day and Somholo Day, as well as Christian Easter Holidays and Ascension Day, vary each year.

2 April: Easter Sunday

5 April: Easter Monday

19 April: King's Birthday

25 April: National Flag Day

1 May: Independence Day

21 May: Ascension Day

22 July: King Sobhuza II's Birthday

End of August/Early September: Umhlanga Reed Dance

6 Sept.: Somholo (Independence) Day

25 Dec.: Christmas Day

26 Dec.: Boxing Day

Sometime in December or January: Incwala Day

ESSENTIALS

DOCUMENTS AND FORMALITIES

VISAS

Citizens of the USA and all commonwealth countries (with the exception of Nigeria) don't need visas; everyone else must have one. Visas may be obtained free of charge from the **Swaziland Consulate** (☎ 011 403 2050) in Johannesburg, or at the Lavumisa, Mahamba, Matsamo, and Ngwenya border posts. Visitors entering from South Africa with South African visas or work permits must get multiple entry or re-entry visas from a South African Department of Home Affairs (branches are in most larger towns). Swaziland has no vaccination requirements.

EMBASSIES ABROAD

Canada: 130 Albert St., # 1204, Ottawa, ON, KIP 5G4 (☎ 613 567 1480; fax 567 1058).

South Africa: 165 Jeppe St., 9th fl., P.O. Box 8030, Johannesburg 2000 (☎ 012 344 1917; fax 299 763).

United Kingdom: 20 Buckingham Gate, London SW1E 6LB (☎ 207 630 6611; fax 630 6564).

United States: 3400 International Dr. NW, Suite 3M, Washington D.C. 20008 (☎ 202 362 6683 or 6685; fax 244 8059).

EMBASSIES AND CONSULATES IN

Mozambique: Highlands View, Princess Dr. (☎ 43 700; fax 43 692).

South Africa: Mall St., 2nd fl. (☎ 40 44 651; fax 46 944).

United Kingdom: 2nd fl. Lilunga House Building, Gifillan St. (☎ 40 42 581; fax 42 585).

United States: Central Bank Building, 7th fl., Warner St. (☎ 40 46 441; fax 45 959).

CURRENCY AND EXCHANGE

The Swazi **lilangeni** (plural: **emalangeni**) is pegged 1:1 to the South African rand. Although rand is not legal tender in Swaziland, rand and emalangeni are often used interchangeably. It is very easy to change rand into emalangeni, and it is fairly easy to change emalangeni back into rand (many hostels will do so). Cashing travelers' checks can be problematic; a passport is required, and presenting the travelers' checks' receipts may expedite the process. Although there are many ATMs in Swaziland, only two accept bank cards from outside of Swaziland: One is the right hand ATM outside the Standard Bank in Swazi Plaza, and the other is inside the Royal Swazi Sun Hotel in the Ezulwini Valley.

HEALTH AND SAFETY

In an **emergency** dial ☎ 999. For **police**, dial ☎ 40 42 051 in Mbabane and ☎ 50 52 221 in Manzini. Swaziland is a relatively safe and peaceful country. Muggings, burglaries, car thefts, and other economic crimes, however, do occur from time to time. Petty street crime is quite frequent in Mbabane and Manzini; avoid walking alone in the downtown areas of these cities at night.

SWAZILAND

TRANSPORTATION

BY AIR. The **Matsapha International Airport** (often called the Manzini Airport) is 8km from Manzini off the main Ezulwini Valley road. There is an airport departure tax of E20. **South African Airways** (in Swaziland ☎ 518 6155) flies to and from Johannesburg (45min., 3-4 per day, US$120 round-trip), where transfers can be made to intercontinental destinations. There are taxis from the airport to Ezulwini Valley (E60), to Mbabane (E80), and to Manzini (E60).

BY CAR. The most scenic drive into Swaziland is over the Saddleback Pass to the **Bulembu Gate.** The unpaved road, however, is in bad shape, and those without 4WD vehicles will have a slow trip. The tarred route through KwaZulu-Natal to **Mahamba** is also beautiful. **Oshoek,** the central access point for most visitors from South Africa, is the busiest post. Most hired cars may be brought into Swaziland from South Africa (ask your company), but an E15 vehicle tax must be paid at the border. Non-hire cars will be taxed E5. **Rental cars** are available at Matsapha airport in Manzini and at Mbabane; drivers must have a valid license and be at least 24.

BY BUS AND MINIBUS TAXI. The **Baz Bus** (☎ 021 439 2323 in South Africa; info@bazbus.com; www.bazbus.com) travels from **Capetown** to **Johannesburg,** stopping at many places along the way, including **Manzini** (departs M, W, F 6:30pm; Tu, Th, Sa 7:30am) and **Mbabane** (departs Tu, Th, Sa at 8:30am). **Minibus taxis** travel to **Manzini** from: **Durban** (E60); **Johannesburg** (via **Mbabane,** E55); and **Maputo** (E25). Taxis from **Nelspruit** go to **Mbabane** (E45). It is possible to get around Swaziland using **buses** and **minibus taxis.** As buses do not come very frequently, minibus taxis are often a cheaper and more regular way to get around. Although *Let's Go* does not recommend **hitchhiking,** some travelers in Swaziland use it as their primary form of transportation.

DRIVING. Swaziland has a good network of national and secondary roads, and driving is a good way to get around. Most of the major gravel roads are in fairly good condition, although some become impassable in the rainy season. In addition, Swazi drivers, much like their South African neighbors, have a reputation for being speed demons. Large, often unmarked speed bumps abound; watch out for them or risk hurting your car. Car rental rates are similar to those in South Africa. Some rental agencies in South Africa allow cars to be taken into Swaziland; check with your agency ahead of time.

KEEPING IN TOUCH

TELEPHONES. Country code: 268. **International dialing prefix:** 00. From outside the country, dial international dialing prefix (see inside back cover) + 268 + 7-digit local number.

MAIL. The postal code for Mbabane is M100, and for Manzini is M200. *Poste Restante* services are available in Mbabane and Manzini.

INTERNET. Internet access is available at several cafes in Mbabane and Manzini. Rates average E20/hr.

TIME DIFFERENCE. Greenwich Mean Time plus two hours (the same as South Africa). Swaziland does not observe daylight savings time.

SWAZILAND

HIGHLIGHTS OF SWAZILAND

The traditional capital of **Lobamba** (see p. 447) contains the country's tiny Parliament, museum, and the monumental tomb of King Sobhuza II.

Malolotja Nature Preserve (see p. 452) features Swaziland's highest waterfall (a 100m plummet), enough trails to keep serious backpackers busy for days, and sweeping views across the whole of Swaziland and neighboring Mozambique.

North of Mbabane, the **Mthunzi Village** (see p. 446) allows visitors to participate in the daily life of a living Swazi community, from soccer matches to church services to chores.

MBABANE

Perched amidst some of the mountains that define Swaziland's terrain, Mbabane is a particularly calm capital city. Tourists mix with locals at restaurants and bars, at the inevitable craft markets, or on the streets of the central business district. However, all this tranquility has its downside, as travelers are unlikely to find things to do in Mbabane for more than a day or two. Ultimately, the city is best used as a convenient place to stock up on food and supplies before heading off into the rural villages and nature reserves that constitute Swaziland's real attractions.

◨ TRANSPORTATION

Buses: Rank behind Swazi Plaza. To **Johannesburg** (5hr., E90) and **Manzini** (1hr., E5).

Minibus Taxis: Also behind Swazi Plaza. To **Nelspruit** (E55) via **Barberton.**

Car Rental: Affordable Car Hire (☎404 9136 or 606 0268, after hours 404 1345 or 404 1722), in Swazi Plaza. Excellent service. Volkswagen Golf E109 per day without insurance, plus E1.10 per km. MC/V/DC.

◪ ORIENTATION

The main road coming east from the Oshoek border becomes **Bypass Rd.** in town. The first intersection coming from Oshoek is with **Commercial Rd.** A left turn at this intersection leads to the two big shopping plazas in town, **The Mall** and **Swazi Plaza.** Past these shopping plazas, Commercial Rd. intersects **Western Distributor** and then becomes Walker St. Walker continues east and intersects **Allister Miller St.** Allister Miller, which runs north-south, is the main road through town, where restaurants, hotels, and supermarkets can be found.

⁊ PRACTICAL INFORMATION

TOURIST, FINANCIAL, AND LOCAL SERVICES

Tourist office: There is a government-run tourist information office in Swazi Plaza. (☎416 1136; fax 416 1040.)

Mozambican Consulate (☎404 3700), 3km from town near the Mountain Inn, off the Manzini Rd. 2 photos and a passport needed to obtain a visa for entry into Mozambique. Allow 1 week for processing. 1-month single entry E45, 3-month multiple entry E140. For same-day service (drop-off before 11am, pick up after 2pm): single-entry E85, 3-month E265. For 24hr. service, single-entry E75. A local man with a camera stands outside the consulate and snaps ID photos for a small fee.

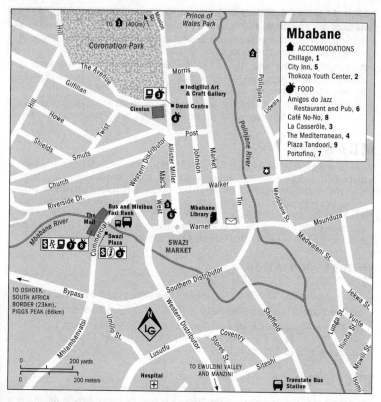

Banks: Standard Bank (☎404 6930), with **ATM,** in Swazi Plaza. Open M-F 8:30am-2:30pm, Sa 8:30-11am. **First National Bank** (☎404 1218), in the mall. Open M-F 8:30am-2:30pm, Sa 8:30-11am. **ATMs** are at the First National Bank on the corner of West and Warner. Many ATMs in Swaziland will not accept international ATM cards. If you run into problems, try the right-hand ATM at Standard Bank in Swazi Plaza.

Bookstores: Webster's Books (☎404 6619), in the mall. Has **maps** of town (R10). Open M-Sa 8am-5pm.

Library: Mbabane Library (☎404 2633), on Walker St. Open M and W 9am-5pm, Tu and Th 9am-7pm, F 9am-4:45pm, Sa 9am-1pm.

Laundry: Kayalami Laundromat, in the mall. Open M-F 7:30am-5:15pm, Sa 7:30am-2pm.

Supermarket: Spar (☎404 1722), in the mall. Open M-F 8am-6:30pm, Sa 8am-5pm, Su 8:30am-1pm.

EMERGENCY AND COMMUNICATIONS

Emergency: ☎999.

Police (☎404 2221), on the corner of Walker St. and Polinjane Rd.

Pharmacy: Green Cross Pharmacy (☎404 3450), in the mall. Open M-F 8:30am-5:30pm, Sa 9am-1:30pm, Su 10am-1pm.

Hospital: Mbabane Clinic Service (☎404 2423). **Mbabane Government Hospital** (☎404 2111). Both open 24hr.

Internet access: Internet Cafe (☎404 1676), in the Omni Center on Allister Miller Rd. north of Gilifillan St. E5 per 15min. Open M-F 8am-8pm, Sa 8am-5pm, Su 9am-noon. **Real Image** (☎404 8545), in the mall. E10 per 30min. Open M-F 8am-6:30pm, Sa-Su 9am-1pm.

Post office: (☎404 2341), in a bright coral building on the corner of Warner St. and Market St. *Poste Restante* available for E4. Open M-F 8am-4pm, Sa 8am-noon.

Postal code: M100.

ACCOMMODATIONS AND CAMPING

Accommodation options in Mbabane are somewhat limited. Travelers with cars might want to crash in nearby Ezulwini Valley (see p. 446).

The Chillage, 18 Mission St. (☎404 8854 or 605 9297; thechillage@mailfly.com). From Allister Miller St. going north, pass Morris St. and turn left onto Mission St.; Chillage is on the right, near the end of road. A relaxed hostel with kitchen, TV lounge, and Internet access. The owners can arrange a variety of trips into Swaziland. Breakfast and dinner available on request. Internet E15 per 30min. Dorms E50; private rooms with twin beds E120; cottage with bath and lounge E200. Camping E40. ❶

Thokoza Youth Center (☎404 6681), on Walker Street going east, turn left at the police station onto Polinjane Rd.; it's a few hundred meters down the road on the left. Part of an Evangelical Church, the basic, lockable rooms with two beds each ensure a bit more privacy and security than most hostel dorms. Breakfast included. Book in advance. Singles with communal bath E85; doubles E110, E130 with private bath. ❶

City Inn (☎404 2406), on Allister Miller St. Convenient central location. Rooms have TVs, heaters and phones. Breakfast included. Singles E190; doubles E270. ❷

FOOD AND NIGHTLIFE

Restaurants in Mbabane are surprisingly good. Excellent lunches and dinners can be had at a number of restaurants around the city.

La Casseröle (☎404 6426), in the Omni Center on Allister Miller St. Possibly the best restaurant in Swaziland. Prompt, courteous service complements the sumptuous, well-presented food. Although the dining room is immaculate, you many want to sit outside on the attached veranda, surrounded by mountainous terrain. Special of the day E30-35. *Zuricher Geschnetzeltes* (sliced veal in mushrooms and cream with butter rosti and salad) E45. *Three Musketeers* (beef, lamb, and pork served with a variety of sauces) E59. Several dishes for vegetarians, all under E25. Open daily 9:30am-11pm. ❷

Plaza Tandoori, in Swazi Plaza. Good, inexpensive Indian food to eat in or take out. Vegetable curry with salad and rice or roti E21. Open M-Sa 10am-10pm. ❶

Portofino and **Cafe No-No,** in the mall. These popular cafes are under the same management but in different parts of the mall. Portofino serves breakfast and lunch; a baguette with brie cheese is E11.50. Cafe No-No serves lunch and early dinner; spaghetti bolognese is E27.50. Portofino open M-F 8am-6pm, Sa 8am-5pm, Su 8:30am-2pm. Cafe No-No open M-Th 11am-7pm, F-Sa 11am-8:30pm. ❶

The Mediterranean (☎404 3212), on Allister Miller St. near the Omni Center. South Asian and Portuguese food in a very mellow atmosphere with Moorish arches, green tablecloths, and flickering candles. Good selection of seafood and vegetarian dishes. Vegetable curry E37. Spanish omelette E31. Chicken tandoori E45. Open daily 10:30am-midnight. ❷

Amigos do Jazz (Jazz Friends) Restaurant and Pub, on Allister Miller St. Popular night-spot with occasional live music. Open daily 8am-late. Happy hour Th 6-7pm.

CRAFTS

Mbabane Market, on Warner St., has crafts varying from the ubiquitous hippo statues to beautiful wax-print tapestries. The market is less hectic than the one in Manzini, but also has a smaller selection. Prepare for very assertive sales pitches. More upscale crafts are found at the **Indigilizi Art and Craft Gallery** on Johnson St. near Morris St., a great place for people who like to look at local art more than they like to pay for it. The Gallery carries wooden and stone figurines typical of other craft shops in the country, but also exhibits pricier framed prints for serious art-collecting tourists. Check out the rows of stone masks for sale hanging on the walls, imported mostly from Zambia and the DRC. A pleasant tea garden out back serves sandwiches and dessert. (☎404 6213. Open M-F 8am-5pm, Sa-Su 8:30am-4pm.) The **Siyavuka Swaziland National Arts Festival** (☎404 7454; siyavuka@real-net.co.sz) takes place at the end of August in venues throughout town.

NEAR MBABANE: MTHUNZI VILLAGE

Mthunzi's tours take you into a *highveld* village where you can experience Swazi cooking, dancing and singing, hikes with breathtaking views, football matches with locals (Saturday and Sunday only), and church ceremonies (Sundays only). Stay overnight in beehive huts or traditional mud hut homesteads and see the night sky and Milky Way like you never have before. *(Take a Pigg's Peak-bound bus from Mbabane and ask to be let off at Nkomanzi Station. ☎608 0469; swazivillage@hotmail.com; www.swaziplace.com/mthunzi/index.html. One-day tours E120; overnight E160.)*

EZULWINI VALLEY

The Ezulwini Valley is a long corridor of mountains, farms, and elevated highway stretching between Mbabane and Manzini. The most touristed area of Swaziland, this valley is the traditional seat of royal power: King Mswati's lavish palaces are interspersed with resorts, shops, and tourist amenities. While the valley is definitely worth a visit, the roadhouse atmosphere quickly gets tiresome. After a few days, travelers will be thankful for the swift highway passage to the countryside.

ORIENTATION AND PRACTICAL INFORMATION

The main road through the Ezulwini Valley is the **MR103,** which diverges from the M3 just south of Mbabane and is signposted as the road to Ezulwini and Malkerns. Following the MR103 south from Mbabane, drivers will pass through the town of Ezulwini and will pass Timbali Lodge on the right. Continuing south, drivers will pass the Swaziland Spa and several hotel casinos, including the Royal Swazi Sun and Lugogo Sun. Farther south is the turn-off, on the right, for Mantenga Lodge and the Mantenga Craft Center. Even farther south on the left is Happy Valley Hotel and its attached disco and go-go bar. Continuing south, Mlilwane Nature Reserve will be on the right, followed by the royal village of Lobamba on the left, followed by the turn-off, on the right, for Malkerns. Farther along the MR103 is the town of Matsapha and Swaziland Backpackers, followed soon after by Manzini. **Tourist Information** is available at **Swazi Trails,** inside Mantenga Craft Center. (☎416 2180. Open daily 8am-5pm.) The only internationally networked **ATM** in the valley is at the Royal Swazi Sun Casino. Drivers should be wary of **speed bumps** on the MR103, which are large and frequently unmarked.

ACCOMMODATIONS AND CAMPING

Sondzela Backpackers (☎528 3117 or 528 3944; reservations@biggame.co.sz), in the Mlilwane Wildlife Sanctuary. If the stunning sunsets, hippo feedings, and beautiful hikes don't suck you in, the peaceful lifestyle and comfortable lounge will. Looks and feels more like an upmarket lodge than a hostel. Swimming pool, bar with pool table and ping-pong, and clean kitchen and bath facilities. Run by park staff. Hiking, biking, horse riding, and game drives can be arranged. On the Baz Bus route. One-time E20 entrance fee to the reserve. Dinner E20. Dorms E50; singles E100; doubles E150; camping E35. Book ahead. ❶

Swaziland Backpackers (☎/fax 518 7225; info@swazilandbackpackers.com), in Matsapha, 12km from Manzini on the MR103, next door to the Salt and Pepper Club. A relaxed hostel with decent dorms, a large outdoor lounge area, and a restaurant and bar next door. A Baz Bus overnight stop. Laundry facilities. Internet. Tours arranged, including river rafting, paragliding, and trips to local markets and the "cuddle puddle" (see **Sights and Crafts**, p. 447). Phones answered 24hr. Breakfast E15. Dinner E25. Laundry E1 per item. Dorms E50; doubles E140. Camping E35. ❶

Mantenga Lodge (☎416 1049 or 416 2168; fax 416 2516; mantenga@africaonline.co.za; www.iafrica.sz/biz/mantenga.), 16km south of Mbabane. Follow signs from the MR103 onto the road to Mantenga Falls. Pricey, but you're paying for the most peaceful view in the Ezulwini Valley: the lodge sits on a densely vegetated hill overlooking a valley lined with rock formations. The attached Mantenga Restaurant is superb. Breakfast included. Singles E300; doubles E400; single chalets E360; double chalets E470. ❸

FOOD

Malandela's (☎528 3115 or 418 3115), on the Malkerns road, next to Tishweshwe Crafts. This restaurant delights diners with its delicious and original menu. The decor is earthy, with sepia-toned walls and tables and inviting benches cushioned with sunny throw-pillows. Lovely outdoor seating area in summer. Avocado salad E18.50. Chicken and mushroom pancake E18. Spinach and feta quiche E29. Pecan pie E13.50. Open M-Sa noon-3pm and 6-9pm, Su noon-3pm. M curry night. Bar open daily 9pm-late. ❶

Mantenga Lodge Restaurant (☎416 1049), next to Mantenga Lodge, 16km from Mbabane. Wide patio and pleasant mountain view. Greek salad E14.50. Pasta alfredo E29. Kingklip curry E38. Splurge on Sunday morning, when E60 gets you an amazing buffet brunch with huge mussels and smoked salmon. Open daily 6am-10pm. ❷

The Great Taipei (☎416 2300), in the Gables Shopping Complex (centered around a Pick 'n Pay Supermarket) on the MR103. Come here for cheap, tasty Chinese food. Veggie chow-mein E22. Spring rolls E3.75. Set menus E27.50. Open daily noon-11pm. ❷

SIGHTS AND CRAFTS

The Ezulwini Valley has the highest concentration of craft markets in Swaziland. Along the main road, about 14km south of Mbabane, is the **Long Market**, a long line of curio stalls with a broader selection of woodcarvings, *batiks*, and soapstone animals than you'll find in any other spot in the country. So much competition makes haggling easier, but avoid playing the "ugly tourist" by taking financial advantage of talented, hard-working artisans.

LOBAMBA. As the spiritual and administrative heart of Swaziland, Lobamba is the center of Swazi culture and politics. It is here that the annual *Incwala* and *Umhlanga* festivals (see p. 440) take place, outside King Mswati II's royal *kraal*. Any other time of the year the place may be deserted, but even when quiet it provides a perfect entry point to Swazi culture. The royal complex houses the **Embo State Palace,** the **King Sobhuza II Monument and National Park, the House of Parliament,** and the **Sonhlolo National Stadium,** a venue for political events and international soccer matches. The National Museum takes you on a journey from prehistoric sites through the Iron Age, the Bantu people, the formation of Swaziland, the struggle against invaders, and Independence. *(23km from Mbabane down an unmarked paved road off the MR103. Coming from Mbabane, turn left off the MR103 near the metal pedestrian bridge over the highway, after the casinos but before the turn-off for Malkerns. Museum open M-F 8am-4pm, Sa-Su 10am-3pm. Admission R10, students R5. Guided tours of the House of Parliament daily 8:30am-12:30pm and 2-3pm. Women must wear knee-length skirts and cover their hair to enter Parliament. Call the National Museum at ☎ 416 1489 for more information.)*

MANTENGA CULTURAL VILLAGE. A traditional village of beehive huts and an open-air museum where visitors can experience Swazi craftwork, song, dance, and everyday life. *(Past Mantenga Lodge on the road to Mantenga Falls. ☎ 416 1151 or 416 1178. E25. Guided tours available all day; special events including dancing and walks to Mantenga falls daily at 11:15am and 3:15pm. Double tents E250.)*

MANTENGA CRAFT CENTER. This village of specialty shops may be a bit more expensive than some of the city market craft stalls, but it offers more interesting crafts: soaps, candles, intricate carvings (not just of animals), and hand-made sandals, as well as pottery, cotton clothing, and jewelry. *(On the way to Mantenga Lodge. ☎ 416 1136. Open daily 8am-5pm.)*

SWAZILAND SPA HEALTH AND BEAUTY STUDIO. Nicknamed the "Cuddle Puddle," the spa is an excellent place to pamper your palpitating nerves. Here the weary traveler can rejuvenate himself for refreshingly affordable prices. Outside is a large pool filled with natural spring water. Inside are separate sections for men and women containing a sauna, hot spa bath, showers, gym, aerobics area, and massage and aromatherapy rooms. The best time to visit is during the week, as the place is often crowded on weekends. The best deal is a sauna, spa, and 45-minute massage package for E100. *(11km from Mbabane on the MR103. ☎ /fax 416 1164. Pool open daily 10am-11pm. Massage section open daily 10am-6pm. Gym and aerobics area open daily 10am-8pm. Entrance E10, children E4.)*

GONE RURAL. This atypical women's cooperative, 700 artisans strong, has some of the most beautiful crafts around. The center serves as a symbol for emerging Swazi female liberation and as a showcase for some of the country's emerging female talent. The shop sells a wide selection of woven mats and baskets, pots, candles, a variety of decorations for the home, as well as mohair rugs and scarves. *(Next to Malandela's on the Malkerns Road; see **Food,** p. 447. ☎ /fax 528 3078 or 528 3439. Open daily 8am-4:45pm.)*

SWAZI CANDLES. This combination workshop/craft store sells unique, handmade wax creations in a rainbow of colors. Watch the artisans at work on psychedelic spheres and zebra-striped hippos. *(On the Malkerns Road; follow signs. ☎ 528 3219; swazi-candles@realnet.co.sz; www.swazicandles.com. Open daily 9am-5pm.)*

▨ NIGHTLIFE

Anyone traveling from South Africa to Swaziland may be unsettled by the journey back to the 1970s club atmosphere. The **Mlilwane Nature Reserve** hosts live Sibhaca dancing several times a week starting at 8pm in the main camp. Wednesday is "pub night" at the **Lugogo Sun.** Gamblers, meanwhile, may want to visit the **casino** at the **Royal Swazi Sun** hotel. Both are on the MR103 at the northern end of the valley.

Attached to Malandela's Restaurant is the **House On Fire,** an open-air theater that offers plays, concerts, and dancing. (Check the local papers or call ☎528 2110 for more information.) The most popular nighttime hangout is the kitsch **Why Not? Disco,** with its **If Not Go-Go Bar,** on the MR103 across from the Gables Shopping Complex. When the place is packed, you'll find yourself lost in the bad music and Swazi smiles. (☎416 1061 or 416 1898. Cover E20-E25 for bar and disco. Bar open daily 8pm-3 or 4am; disco open daily 10pm-3 or 4am, with occasional live bands and special shows at 11:45pm and 1:30am.)

MANZINI

All roads converge in Manzini, the hub of Swaziland and the industrial heart of the nation. Although Manzini offers fewer attractions for the average traveler than Mbabane, its quiet streets have a charm of their own, which is enhanced by the absence of tourist hordes. Manzini can feel more genuine than Mbabane, as shops and restaurants are not done up for tourists and generally just go about their day-to-day business. If you happen to be in the area on a Thursday or Friday at the end of the month, make time to browse through the craft market, where artisans from all over will have their wares on display.

▐ TRANSPORTATION

Minibus taxis: The rank is on Louw St. north of Ngwane St. To: **Big Bend** (E10); **Durban** (E100); **Johannesburg** (E100); **Lobamba** (E3.50); **Maputo** (E35); **Mbabane** (E5).

Taxis: Taxis can be found on Louw St. near the minibus rank. Useful for transport to **Hlane** (E150) and **Mlilwane** (E80) nature reserves.

Car Rental: Avis (☎508 4928 or 508 6226) and **Hertz/Imperial** (☎508 4393 or 508 4862) at Matsapha Airport. **Inter-Tour Travel** (☎505 2983), in the Hub Mall, is also an authorized Avis and Imperial branch.

✈ ❼ ORIENTATION AND PRACTICAL INFORMATION

The MR3 from Mbabane splits into two one-way streets, which become the main roads in town. **Ngwane St.** runs eastward toward Siteki, and **Nkoseluhlaza St.** runs westward back toward Mbabane. The big **shopping centers** in town are the Bhunu Mall, on Nkoseluhlaza St. between Sandlane and Louw St., and the Hub Mall, at Mhlakuvane and Tenbergen St.

Tourist Office: Inter-Tour Travel (☎505 2983), on the corner of the Hub Mall. Open M-F 8:30am-1pm and 2-5pm, Sa 8:30-11am.

Banks: Standard Bank (☎505 195), on Nkoseluhlaza at Louw St. Open M-F 8:30am-2:30pm, Sa 8:30-11am. **First National Bank** (☎505 3181 or 505 3185), on Ngwane St. in the Bhunu Mall. Open M-F 8:30am-2:30pm, Sa 8:30-11am.

Police: ☎505 2221, on Mancishane St. near Louw St.

Supermarket: ShopRite, in the Bhunu Mall. Open daily 8:30am-6pm.

Internet: Real Image, in the Bhunu Mall. E20 per hr. Open M-F 9am-6pm, Sa 9am-1pm.

Pharmacy: The **Mall Pharmacy** (☎505 5010), in the Bhunu Mall. Open M-Sa 8am-5pm, Su 9am-1pm.

Hospital: R.F.M. Hospital (☎505 2211).

Post Office: On the corner of Nkoseluhlaza and Martin St. *Poste Restante.* Open M-F 8am-4pm, Sa 8am-noon.

Postal Code: M200.

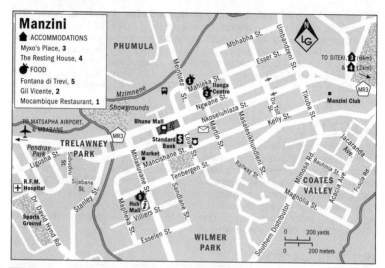

Manzini

🏠 ACCOMMODATIONS
Myxo's Place, **3**
The Resting House, **4**
🍴 FOOD
Fontana di Trevi, **5**
Gil Vicente, **2**
Mocambique Restaurant, **1**

PHUMULA

TO SITEKI, **3** (6km)
& **4** (2km)

Manzini Club

TO MATSAPHA AIRPORT,
& MBABANE

Bhunu Mall

TRELAWNEY
PARK

Pendray
Park

Standard
Bank

Market

R.F.M.
Hospital

Sports
Ground

Hub
Mall

WILMER
PARK

COATES
VALLEY

0   200 yards
0   200 meters

🏕 ACCOMMODATIONS AND CAMPING

Myxo's Place/Woza Nawe Hostel (☎ 505 8363 or 604 4102; mzn136@postcafe.co.sz), 6km from Manzini. Take the Siteki/Big Bend Rd. past Impilo Clinic, turn left at the Big Surprise Bottle Store, and follow signs down a bumpy dirt "road." The only Swazi-owned and operated backpackers in Swaziland, in the countryside far from the dirt and noise of Manzini. Myxo and Daniel love to teach about Swazi culture, and if you're lucky you may even learn how to make the SiSwati click sound. The house is relaxed and friendly, with comfortable lounges and dorms that have the feel of a meditation center. Myxo arranges overnight trips to a traditional Swazi village (E340). Free rides to and from town three times daily; call ahead. Dorms E60; doubles E160. Camping E35. ❶

The Resting House, 540 Logwaja St. (☎ 505 2037; harrys@iafrica.sz), 2km from Manzini; follow the MR3 about 1.5km out of Manzini toward Siteki, turn left at Inyati St., then left at the first intersection, and finally right onto Logwaja St. Located in an affluent suburb, it seems a world away from the gritty center of Manzini. Bedrooms have attached baths and are showered with afternoon sunshine. Internet. English breakfast included. Singles E170; doubles E265. ❷

🍴 FOOD

🍽 **Fontana di Trevi** (☎ 505 3608), in the Hub Mall, a 10min. walk from the center of town. This cafe has a book-length menu of Italian and Portuguese food, with an entire page devoted to hot drinks. Outdoor seating as well as a spacious indoor dining room that's pleasant for a quick lunch or a leisurely dinner. Omelettes E15. Vegetarian pizza with zucchini and eggplant E26. Open M-Sa 9am-9pm. ❶

Gil Vicente (☎ 505 3874), in the Ilanga shopping center on Martin St. near Mahleka St., close to the center of town. Famous for its seafood, but also serves pizza (E30-40), meat dishes (E40-45), and salads (E15-18). Toasted sandwiches (E10-12) make a cheap and tasty lunch. Open Tu-Su 8am-midnight. ❷

Moçambique Restaurant (☎ 505 2489 or 505 2586), on Mahleka St. near the bus rank at the Moçambique Hotel. The fine food and lively clientele will help you forget about the city life bustling outside the dining room. A dozen prawns E46-100. Portuguese-style meat, chicken, and fish E30-50. Open daily 8am-midnight. ❸

SWAZILAND

SWAZI NATURE RESERVES AND PARKS

Between 1930 and 1960, Swaziland's wildlife was nearly wiped out by a scourge of hunting, poaching, and commercial development. Today, though, the country has a strong conservation policy and boasts some of the best-managed wildlife reserves in the southern hemisphere. Conservation was first promoted in earnest by King Sobhuza II, who patronized efforts to preserve what little wildlife remained in the country. In 1959, Ted Reilly turned Sobhuza's promotion into practice by converting his family farm into the Mlilwane Wildlife Sanctuary. Reilly's efforts launched a movement which created three big game parks and five nature reserves, an impressive quantity of protected zones in such a small country. These reserves give travelers great incentive to get out of the cities and the valley, and into the Swazi wilderness.

MLILWANE WILDLIFE SANCTUARY. Mlilwane Wildlife Sanctuary is Swaziland's pioneer conservation area. Located in the Ezulwini Valley, Mlilwane ("little fire" in SiSwati) is a well-developed *middleveld* reserve with a high population of blue wildebeest, impala, kudu, and bushbuck. Warthogs, hippos, zebras, crocodiles, and buffalo may also be seen. There are 30km of **hiking trails** of varying intensity in the park, traversing various ecosystems. The Hippo Trail is a mild 2hr. hike along the hippo pond, through the blue-gum forests and rocky terrain. The 5hr. round-trip **Mhambanyatsi River Trail** takes you to Nyonyane Peak (Execution Rock). Though the hike is intense at times, the view at the end is worth the sweat and toil.

The reserve is very close to Mbabane and Manzini and has its own backpackers lodge, **Sondzela Backpackers** (see p. 447), which helps make it the most touristed park in Swaziland. It doesn't feel like much of a nature retreat, and those seeking a so-called "escape" should make a run for one of the other reserves. The **main rest camp ❷** is much closer to the park gate than Sondzela Backpackers, but book in advance or arrive early in the day, as accommodations fill up by late afternoon. There is a rustic timberlog dormitory with solid wooden bunkbeds (E120 for one person or E75 per person sharing), comfortable beehive huts (E150 for one or E100 per person sharing), nicer huts with attached bath (E240 or E140 per person sharing), and a campground with kitchen and laundry (camping E35). For any of the accommodations, it's wise to bring your own food, as the nearest market is a 15min. drive away on the road to Manzini. Alternatively, you may wish to eat at the rest camp's **Hippo Haunt Restaurant ❷**, which serves buffet breakfast (E28.50), a la carte lunch, and *braai* dinner (E58), all near the hippo pool, where rangers feed the resident beasts daily at 3pm. *(On the MR103 in the Ezulwini Valley. Minibus taxis from Manzini to Lobamba E2. ☎528 3943 or 404 4541; reservations@biggame.co.sz; www.biggame.co.sz. E20 entrance fee. Game drives E100, min. 2 people. Horseback riding E75 per hr. Mountain-biking E45 per hr. Swazi dance display E10 per person, free for large groups.)*

▧ PHOPHONYANE NATURE RESERVE. This private nature reserve near Piggs Peak is arguably the loveliest place in all of Swaziland. Failing to appear on most maps, Phophonyane (pronounced *PO-po-NYA-ne*) is also the nation's best-kept secret: a lush, green reserve, perfectly suited to the independent hiker who wants to explore without a guide. This 500ha Garden of Eden is centered around the Phophonyane Falls, a cascade said to be formed from the tears of a Swazi maiden grieving for her lost suitor. The falls tumble over the world's oldest sedimentary rock (estimated to be 3.6 billion years old), chunks of which lie exposed along the river, making great sunbathing slabs and picnic spots. A few easy trails wind through the dense forest toward views of the falls and surrounding mountain peaks. Overnight stays here are a real treat; the cottages and safari tents are private and so well placed that they seem to grow out of the trees. Safari tents are more affordable than the cottages and still very comfortable, with one twin bed and one double bed, carpeting, electricity, and heaters. A sundowner bar perches on stilts near the falls, and the **Dining Hut restaurant ❷** serves excellent food in the intimate fire-warmed atmosphere of the Phophonyane bar. The restaurant is open to the public for lunch and includes a good selection of vegetarian dishes; breakfast runs E35, while lunch and dinner are a la carte. Lentil curry is E35.50. (☎437 *1319 or 437 1429; lungile@iafrica.sz. Gates open daily 6am-7:30 pm. E15, E10 if staying overnight; children E7.50. Open daily noon-3pm. Bookings should be made at least 1 month in advance; 50% due at booking. Safari tent singles E268; doubles E356. Prices exclude VAT and are higher over holidays and long weekends. Cottage singles E407; doubles E542.)*

MALOLOTJA NATURE RESERVE. This 18,000ha hiker's paradise in northern Swaziland has over 280 bird species, a fair population of wildebeest, zebra, and buck, and 200km of trails winding through the Ngwenya and Silotwane mountains. Malolotja (pronounced *MA-lo-LO-cha*) is mostly untouched, offering a true wilderness experience in Swaziland's *highveld* and *middleveld* grasslands. In summer, the mountains glow with wildflowers. In winter, the blooms are sparse and often burned by fire, offering ideal terrain for game. There are several day hikes with views of the 100m **Malolotja Falls** (the highest in the country), as well as overnight and multiple-day hikes to the northern part of the reserve, where stunning views stretch across Swaziland to the Lubombo mountains on the Mozambique border.

Camping areas have common baths and *braai* facilities. Backpacking trails with 20 different campsites are close to water, but have no facilities. Bookings and permits for overnight trails must be arranged through the office at the reserve's entrance. Bring a compass and gas stove—fires are not permitted on the trails. Spacious six-person log cabins are also available for a moderate price; there are a limited number, so book ahead. The **Malolotja Trail,** which travels from View Point to Malolotja Falls, is a 3.5km hike and travels through indigenous forest. The **Mapahadakazi Trail** (7km, 5hr.) leads to the waterfall of the same name, and is a much more intense hike. Permits can be obtained at the office and are free. *(35km from Mbabane, before Piggs Peak. Minibus taxis go from Mbabane toward Piggs Peak, with a stop outside the gate; E7. ☎442 4241 or 442 1179; fax 442 4241; mnr@iafrica.sz. Gates open daily 6am-6pm. E15; E6 per car. Morning drives 7am; E60. Night drives 6pm; E40. Book a day in advance. Log cabins E250, F-Sa and public holidays E350. Camping E18; backpacking E15.)*

NAMIBIA

 PRICE RANGES. Price ranges, marked by the numbered icons below, are now included in food and accommodation descriptions. They are based on the lowest cost for one person, excluding special deals or prices. In the case of campgrounds, we include the cost of a car. The table below is a guide to how prices and icons match up.

SYMBOL	❶	❷	❸	❹	❺
ACCOMM.	N$0-75	N$76-170	N$171-250	N$251-400	N$401+
FOOD	N$0-10	N$11-25	N$26-55	N$56-100	N$101+

An enchanted land of shifting desert sand, rolling dunes, *bushveld*, and mountain peaks, Namibia stretches across the southern Atlantic seaboard. Home to one of Africa's most diverse populations, Namibia has a cultural history that is as impressive as its natural wonders. After being punted from one colonial power to the next, in 1989 it became the last African country to gain independence. Today, Namibia's first president is still in office, and this nation of hard-working, friendly people is shaping its future.

Countless sites and artifacts document Namibia's cultural history: 6000-year-old San rock art, Portuguese shipwrecks, a German mining ghost town, and recent memorials to Namibia's fight for independence. Today, Namibia is a rich tapestry of traditions and customs from nearly a dozen different ethnic groups, including the San, whose roots can be traced back to the beginning of humanity. The influence of European colonization can still be felt: the west coast ports of Swakopmund and Lüderitz are in many ways museums preserving 1920s German architecture and culture. Although half the population inhabits the central plateau on which Windhoek sits, urbanization in Namibia has occurred at a relatively slow pace. Namibians of all ethnicities are extremely proud of their young country and eagerly welcome travelers to explore the large rural areas and blossoming urban centers that hold its treasures.

Outdoor adventures, from the harmless to the hair-raising, abound here, and the landscapes have something for everyone. You can simply enjoy the enigmatic features of the Etosha Pan, Hoba Meteorite, or the bizarre Giant's Playground, or you can get physical and hike the Fish River Hiking Trail, one of the most challenging trails in Africa. Etosha National Park offers game watching opportunities that rival those of Kruger or the Serengeti. Namibia's impressive big game includes huge elephants (some of the world's largest), lions, giraffes, rhinos, and hartebeests. Namibia's biggest draw, however, is its haunting landscapes: the desiccated lakes of Etosha National Park, the eerie dunes of the Skeleton Coast and Namib Desert, the deep crevices of the Sesriem and Fish River Canyons, and the great interior sand dunes will amaze travelers with their beautiful solitude.

LIFE AND TIMES
HISTORY

IN THE BEGINNING. The hunter-gatherer **San** are generally believed to be Namibia's first inhabitants. An estimated 37,000 prehistoric rock paintings, many still undiscovered, have preserved a picture (so to speak) of the San's existence in

NAMIBIA

FACTS AND FIGURES

Official Name: Republic of Namibia

Government: Parliamentary Democracy

Capital: Windhoek

Land Area: 825,418 sq. km

Geography: Central high plateau; the Namib desert and coastal plains in the West, Kalahari desert and mountains in the East; wooded *bushveld* in the North

Climate: Hot and dry desert and semi-desert, with sporadic rain

Head of State: Pres. Samuel Nujoma

Major Cities: Windhoek, Walvis Bay

Population: approx. 1,800,000

Languages: English, Oshivambo, Otjiherero, Nama, Damara, Afrikaans, Rukavango

Religions: Christian (90%); Indigenous

GDP Per Capita: US$4300

Major Exports: Diamonds, copper, gold, cattle, fish

the area northeast of Swakopmund and the Namib Desert, around the Tsisab Ravine. Nomadic **Khoi-Khoi** herders arrived after the San and competed with them for the area's resources. The Bantu-speaking **Herero** migrated from the Great Lakes region of Central Africa in the 16th and 17th centuries. They fought with and eventually defeated the Khoikhoi. The South African Oorlam Khoikhoi group, the ancestors of the modern day Nama, resisted the Herero from the 1840s to the 1880s. By the late 1800s, the Ovambo, Namibia's only agriculturalists at the time, had settled along Kunene River in northern Namibia and southern Angola.

AN INHOSPITABLE LANDSCAPE. Although the Portuguese **Diego Cao** and **Bartolomeu Dias** came to Namibia in the late 1480s, treacherous fog, desolate beaches and rough waters made it hard for anyone to get very far. Many attempts to sail down the coast resulted in shipwrecks. Dutch and British explorers were a little more successful. During the late 18th century, these explorers managed to stake claim to some parts of coastal Namibia, but their governments were not interested in conquering what they thought was desert wasteland. British missionaries from the **London Missionary Society** became Namibia's first permanent European residents in 1802 and opened new ivory trade routes. German missionaries followed in the 1840s, introducing firearms to the various indigenous communities.

HERE COME THE OORLAMS. Around the same time the missionaries arrived, the **Oorlams,** herders of mixed Khoi-Khoi, slave, and "coloured" descent, migrated into Namibia from the Cape Colony in South Africa. Though at first peaceful, they soon became embroiled in land rivalries between the Nama and the Herero. The opening of ivory and cattle trade routes, combined with the introduction of South African firearms, soon led to increasing violence. In 1830, Oorlam leader **Jonker Afrikaner** moved to Windhoek with a huge group of well-armed followers, gaining control of the trading routes between Walvis Bay and the Cape Colony, and establishing a quasi-Oorlam nation which favored the Nama over the Herero. This nation lasted until Afrikaner's death in 1861, at which point relations between the Nama and Herero became even more violent. Over the next 29 years, between 1863 and 1892, the bloody Nama-Herero wars raged incessantly.

A BLOODY TAKEOVER. The Nama-Herero wars provided Germany with the opportunity to annex Namibian land by using divide-and-rule strategies, falsified treaty documents and sometimes direct theft. In 1884, German Chancellor **Otto von Bismarck** proclaimed the strip of land running from the Orange River to just north of present-day Lüderitz a protectorate.

The German acquisition of Namibia was not peaceful. The Herero launched the first resisted German subjugation in 1885. Though the **Herero Revolt** was initially successful in pushing back the Germans back, it only strengthened Germany's

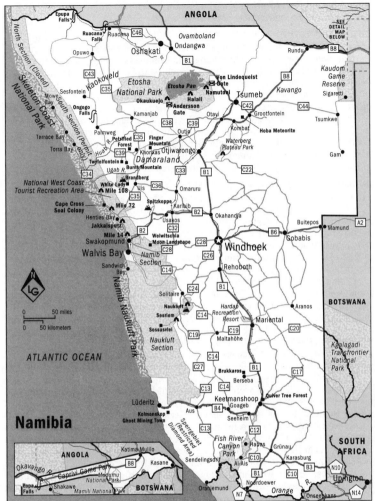

Namibia

resolve. The discovery of diamonds in Lüderitz and Oranjemund, and the start of profitable copper mining in Tsumeb and Swakopmund made Germany determined to capture the land. The **German-Namibia War** raged from 1904-1907. During the war, the Germans launched a genocide against the Herero, slaughtering almost half of them by using such tactics as hanging, extermination, and detention in concentration camps. At least another 24,000 Herero died of starvation and thirst when the Germans pushed them into the Kalahari Desert after winning the **Battle of Waterberg**. By 1910, the Herero population was almost entirely wiped out; the remaining 5-10% went into exile in neighboring Bechuanaland (now Botswana). The Nama's attempt to fend off German colonization was crushed by 1907. The Germans killed half to two thirds of the Nama population. Following the subjugation of the Herero and Nama, the newly conquered land was brought under direct German rule and named **German South West Africa.** The territory stretched from Tsumeb-Grootfontein in the north to the Orange River in the south.

OUT OF THE FRYING PAN, INTO THE FIRE. With the outbreak of WWI in 1914, white South Africa seized the opportunity to kick out the Germans by invading German South West Africa. The subjugated Namibians willingly helped the South Africans fight. In 1915, the Germans surrendered to South African military leader **General Louis Botha,** effectively ending 30 years of German rule. Namibians hoped that they would now be able to reacquire their land. South Africa, however, had other plans: In 1920 it convinced the **League of Nations** to establish South West Africa as a South African protectorate. Confronted by another era of colonial rule, the Nama revolted in 1921-22 but were crushed by South African forces. In 1946, South Africa asked the United Nations for permission to incorporate South West Africa into South Africa. Though the UN denied their request, South Africa refused to hand the territory over to the UN Trusteeship Council.

AN INTERNATIONAL FIGHT FOR FREEDOM. Once the Apartheid Era began in earnest, the new, isolationist South African regime became determined to control Namibia. The government created homelands for blacks (dividing different ethnic groups), introduced a slightly diluted version of the apartheid system to Namibia, and appropriated huge tracts of fertile land and rich mineral resources. In addition, South Africa used Namibia as a buffer zone between it and the rest of Africa and as a launching point for military excursions against ANC sympathetic governments (see Apartheid in Crisis, p. 60).

Beginning in 1947, South West Africans began to petition the UN for liberation from South African rule. In 1958, the **Ovamboland People's Organization** was established and quickly mobilized strikes against the contract labor system that forced blacks to work for South African-owned enterprises for subsistence wages. By 1960, the Ovamboland People's Organization became the **South West Africa People's Organization (SWAPO).** SWAPO initially resisted peacefully, but after a 1959 demonstration in **Old Location, Windhoek** (see p. 469) degenerated into a massacre, they started fighting back. In 1960, SWAPO declared a guerrilla war to expel South Africa, beginning a conflict that dragged on until 1989.

The **Windhoek Shootings** were a turning point in the struggle for independence because the international community became aware of South Africa's ruthlessness in Namibia. In 1966, the UN General Assembly passed Resolution 2145, terminating Namibia's status as a mandate of South Africa. South Africa, however, refused to yield to UN pressure and proceeded with plans to further institutionalize apartheid in Namibia by creating 10 *Bantustans* (African homelands).

Angola's imminent independence from Portugal further complicated matters for South Africa, who viewed Angola as a necessary buffer zone between itself and the rest of Africa. On the eve of Angolan independence in 1975, South Africa marched troops into Angola to protect its interests and to crush the Popular Movement for the Liberation of Angola (MPLA), a rebel movement supported by the Soviet Union. South Africa supported the MPLA's rival, the National Union for Total Independence (UNITA), because it thought UNITA would support South Africa's Angolan interests.

Cold War politics brought the Angolan and Namibian civil wars to a head. Some 18,000 Soviet-allied **Cuban troops** joined forces with the MPLA and SWAPO guerrillas in Angola. Soon, South Africa and the white Namibian population grew weary of the wars' economic burden. By December 1988, South Africa agreed to participate in a UN-brokered peace deal. It was agreed that Cuba would withdraw its support from the Angolan rebels and South Africa would withdraw from Namibia, though South Africa was allowed to hold onto profitable Walvis Bay until 1994. The peace deal also called for elections in Namibia in 1989 with universal suffrage.

TODAY

PUSHING FOR FASTER LAND REFORM. Black communal farmers in Namibia are encouraging the government to quicken the pace of land reform. The government's policy of "willing-seller, willing-buyer" has failed to rectify the inequity in land ownership because many white farmers refuse to sell their land. The Namibia National Farmers' Union has warned that if land reform does not happen faster, a situation similar to one in Zimbabwe, in which blacks seized white farms, might develop. In Namibia, whites own 75 million acres of farm land and blacks own 5.5 million. President Nujoma has upheld the "willing seller, willing buyer" policy, calling on commercial farmers to aid the government in helping those hurt by colonial rule. The government estimates it will need $109 million dollars for future land reform.

HERERO'S SEEK THEIR DAY IN COURT. In 2001, the Herero tribe filed German government and two German companies. The Herero, who were almost completely exterminated while Namibia was a German colony, seek $2 billion in reparations from each institution it is suing. Namibia's ruling party, the South West African People's Organization (SWAPO) does not endorse the Herero's suit. Germany, who is Namibia's largest bi-lateral donor, has repeatedly refused to give reparations to the Herero because they argue that their aid to all Namibians has benefitted the Herero.

PEOPLE

DEMOGRAPHICS

POPULATION AND DEMOGRAPHY. With only two people per sq. km and a total population of just under two million, Namibia is one of the least densely populated countries in sub-Saharan Africa. Approximately 87.5% of Namibians are black, 6% are white, and 6.5% are of mixed racial heritage. The Bantu-speaking **Ovambo,** who live mainly on the Namibian-Angolan border east of the Kaokoveld, comprise about 50% of the total black population. The **Kavango** (9%) inhabit the northeastern territory between the Caprivi Strip, southeastern Angola, and Ovamboland. Other major ethnic groups include **Herero** (7%), **Damara** (7%), **Nama** (5%), **Tswana** (0.5%), **Caprivian** (4%), **San** (3%), and **Baster** (2%). Most of the overall population occupies the Central Plateau upon which Windhoek is situated, the outlying regions of the nation—particularly the Kaokoveld—tend to be the least populated.

LANGUAGE AND RELIGION

English is Namibia's official language. Other national languages include Oshivambo, Nama, and Herero. Most Namibians are multi-lingual, speaking indigenous, national and colonial languages. Namibian languages generally fall into two groups—Bantu languages and Khoikhoi languages. Clicks are an important component of Khoisan languages. Namibia's colonial history ensures that both **German** and **Afrikaans** are widely used, particularly in the German post-colonial towns of Lüderitz and Swakopmund. **Portuguese** can also be heard in the northern regions of the country, particularly along the border with Angola.

As in the rest of Southern Africa, the predominant religion in Namibia is **Christianity.** Approximately 80-90% of Namibians are Christian, at least 75% of them being Lutheran. Other major denominations include Roman Catholicism, Anglicanism, and Methodism. The remaining 10-20% of the Namibian population practices indigenous religions, including **animism.**

CULTURE

FOOD AND DRINK

Namibian cuisine mixes local and German recipes. *Mahango*, a millet, is a staple of the Ovambo, while the **!nara melon,** a tangy desert cucumber, is a chief food of the Nama. *Tsamma* melon, while not widely served in restaurants, is popular among the San, who eat it by cutting off the top and using a stick to mash the inner contents to an edible pulp. The melon provides a hydrating fluid, and the oil in its seeds can be used for cooking. **Game meat,** including antelope, crocodile, and ostrich, is also hugely popular in Namibia. Snails are a common appetizer and *braai* is ubiquitous. Usually smothered in garlic sauce and fried, this dish is served alongside main meals of kudu, ostrich steaks, or *Wienerschnitzel*.

THE ARTS

Namibian art usually serves both decorative and practical purposes. The Ovambo mold enormous clay pots to store beer, and huge, intricate handwoven baskets to store grain and protect it from insects and pests. Himba women craft leather belts studded with shells and ivory beads. Their jewelry is even more remarkable; heavy brass bracelets adorn their arms, and whelk shells hang from metal coils around their necks. The Damara are known for intricate jewelry fashioned from nuts and ebony seeds. The San and the Nama decorate themselves with ostrich egg beads, and the San use the larger ostrich eggs to store water. The Ovambo, Himba, and Herero also craft exquisitely detailed wood carvings.

CUSTOMS AND ETIQUETTE

In Namibia, as in most Southern African countries, following European and American standards of politeness will generally keep you in everyone's good graces. There are, however, some Namibian courtesies that you should be aware of. Namibians typically shake hands when saying hello or goodbye—people do not kiss or hug when greeting each other. If you see another car while driving on a road in a national park or in a rural area, it is polite to wave to the driver. Finally, if you are invited to visit a native village, bring a small gift for the chief's wife—doing so will make the villagers more likely to accept you and show you their traditions.

HOLIDAYS & FESTIVALS

Mar 21: Independence Day

May 1: Workers' Day

May 4: Cassinga Day

May 9: Ascension Day

May 25: Africa Day (Anniversary of the OAU's founding)

Aug 26: Heroes' Day

Dec 26: Family Day

ADDITIONAL RESOURCES

Chronology of Namibian History: From Prehistorical Times to Independent Namibia (1999), by Kalus Dierks.

Namibia–The Struggle for Liberation (1983), by Alfred T. Moleah.

Katatura: A Place Where We Stay: Life in a Post-Apartheid Township in Namibia (1996), by Wade C. Pendelton.

Coming On Strong: Writing by Namibian Women (1996), edited by Margie Orford and Nepeti Nicanor.

ESSENTIALS

DOCUMENTS AND FORMALITIES

VISAS
Visitors from most European Union and North American countries will only need their **passport** to visit Namibia. Those arriving from **yellow fever** zones need proof of vaccination.

EMBASSIES AND CONSULATES ABROAD

South Africa: 197 Blackwood St., Arcadia Pretoria (☎012 481 9100; fax 012 343 7294).

UK: Namibian High Commission, 6 Chandos St, London WIG 9LU (☎020 7636 6244; fax 020 7637 5694).

US: 1605 New Hampshire Ave NW, Washington DC 20009 (☎202-986-0540; fax 202-986-0443).

EMBASSIES AND CONSULATES IN WINDHOEK
Malawi: 56 Bismarck St. (☎22 1391).

South Africa: Corner of Jan Jonker Ave. and Nelson Mandela Ave. PO Box 23100 (☎205 7111).

UK: 116 Robert Mugabe Ave. (☎27 4800; fax 22 8895).

US: 14 Lossen St., Ausspannplatz (☎22 1601; fax 22 9792; www.usembassy.namib.com).

Zambia: Corner of Sam Nujoma and Madume N. Ave. (☎23 7610).

Zimbabwe: Corner of Independence Ave. and Grimm St. (☎22 8134).

NAMIBIA

CURRENCY AND EXCHANGE

The **Namibian dollar** (N$) is tagged directly to the South African rand, so it remains rather stable. Although prices are listed in N$, rand are also accepted. Almost all banks, even in small towns, offer currency exchange. Expect a commission of between N$16 and N$33. Visa, MasterCard, and Diner's Club are widely accepted; AmEx acceptance is rarer. ATMs are increasingly common, though not universally compatible. If your card is not accepted at one ATM, try ATMs at a different bank or go inside the bank during business hours for cash withdrawals.

WHEN TO GO. Summer (Dec.-Mar.) in Namibia's interior is miserably hot. On the west coast, summers are blissful and packed, as all of Namibia flocks to the water for relief from the heat. The dry winters (May-Sept.) are prime angling season, and the best time to visit national parks; the temperature is comfortable and thirsty game must come to strategically placed waterholes to drink. Plus, travelers during these months avoid dangers and delays from flooded rural roads, particularly risky if one does not have a 4WD.

TRANSPORTATION

BY AIR. Virtually all international flights to Namibia fly to Windhoek's **Eros Airport** (☎ 061 239 850). Most local airports only offer charter flights and flights to and from Windhoek. **Air Namibia** (☎ 061 299 6140 or 061 299 6141; www.air-namibia.com.na), the national airline, flies regularly to Victoria Falls, Johannesburg, Cape Town and other cities within the region. **South Africa Airways** (in Namibia ☎ 061 237 670; fax 061 235 200; in the US 800-722-9675; in London 44 20 8897 3645; fax 44 20 8564 9245; www.flysaa.com) also flies to Johannesburg and Cape Town, with connecting flights to the rest of the world. Other airlines that fly to and from Windhoek include **British Airways/Comair** (☎ 061 248 528; fax 061 24 8529) and **Lufthansa** (☎ 061 22 6662).

BY TRAIN. Trains are very slow, but very cheap. **TransNamib Starline** has rails between most major cities, and buses to those off the railroad grid. Be sure to pick up a TransNamib schedule, including both train and bus routes, at a train station to find out dates, times and locations. Unfortunately, Namibia's major attractions are often far from the nearest major city, making both train and bus transportation impractical.

BY BUS AND MINIBUS TAXI. Intercape (in Namibia ☎ 061 227 847; in SA ☎ 021 386 4491; info@intercape.co.za; www.intercape.co.za) offers service to Windhoek and other cities within Namibia from Cape Town, Upington, Pretoria, and Victoria Falls. **Ekonolux** (in Namibia ☎ 064 205 935) also runs from Cape Town; it's cheaper, but runs less regularly. **Minibus taxis** travel regularly to Windhoek from Cape Town, via Upington. To get around by **bus** or **minibus taxi** within Namibia, it is usually necessary to start in Windhoek, as most routes radiate outward from the capital to the small towns.

BY CAR. The distances between places and the remoteness of many sights often makes a car is the independent traveler's only option. Citizens of most western countries entering Namibia by car need their passport and, if the car is a rental, a permission letter from the company. Other paperwork may be necessary. Be sure to ask the rental company before you attempt the border crossing.

Foreign visitors planning to drive in Namibia need an international drivers license, which can only be obtained in your home country prior to arrival. Those planning to use a **rental car** should consider renting one in South Africa as rates at all major agencies in Namibia are more expensive. If you do rent a car in Namibia, go with one of the smaller, domestic agencies; international firms charge exorbitant rates. International rental agencies include **Budget** (☎ 061 22 8720; fax 22 7665; www.budgetrentacar.com) and **Imperial** (☎ 062 54 0278; fax 54 0046; www.imperialcarrental.co.za). Local rental agencies are listed in the **Transportation** section of cities and towns. Another option for getting around Namibia is **buying a car;** see p. 40 for more advice. All cars driven in Namibia are charged a **road tax** of N$80.

KEEPING IN TOUCH

TELEPHONES. Country code: 264. **Domestic/international directory assistance and collect calls:** 1188/1199. Drop the zero from in front of city codes when calling from abroad. **Grab-A-Phone** terminals are a reliable, but expensive, way to call overseas.

PHONE. To call Namibia from overseas, dial the appropriate international access code followed by **264** (Namibia's country code), and then the local phone code and the six-digit local phone number. When calling from overseas, do not use the zero in the local phone code; use the zero when calling internally in Namibia. **International calls** and **collect calls** are difficult, as external calling cards rarely work.

MAIL. There are no postal codes in Namibia; simply address mail with the town or city name. *Poste Restante* is available only in medium to large towns. Mail to Windhoek from North America or the EU generally takes 1-2 weeks; mail to elsewhere within Namibia can take considerably longer.

TIME DIFFERENCE. Namibia, like South Africa, is two hours ahead of GMT between October and April, but is the only country in Southern Africa that observes daylight savings time. It is one hour ahead of GMT (and one hour behind South Africa) between April and October.

HIGHLIGHTS OF NAMIBIA

Swakopmund (see p. 494) is one of the adrenaline capitals of Africa. Jump out of a plane, snowboard down a dune, drive off-road, sea kayak...and then do it all over again.

Sossusvlei (see p. 510), in **Namib-Naukluft National Park,** is home to Namibia's most famous sand dunes—giants as tall as skyscrapers that come to life in the morning sun.

Etosha National Park (see p. 484) is the classic safari experience. Hundreds of species of animals, from tiny birds to some of the world's largest elephants, gather here to drink at the springs that well up through the desert clay.

WINDHOEK ☎061

Windhoek (pop. 300,000), Namibia's commercial hub and national capital, is a sprawling metropolis located in the center of the country. The area was once referred to as fire-water by the Nama because of its hot springs. Oorlam leader Jonker Afrikaner bestowed its current name in 1840, naming the town after the South Africa farm where his father was born. Today, Windhoek is largely segregated by neighborhood, from the rich, white Klein Windhoek in the northeast to the poor, black Katatura township in the northwest. However, the city centers around a vibrant core where locals of all colors mix.

For all its capital-city pomp, from its impressive Supreme Court building to Sam Nujoma's presidential mansion, Windhoek seems at times to be a small farm town. Due to its sprawl and the hills upon which it sits, visitors cannot see more than one neighborhood at a time; thus the town feels smaller than it is. Nevertheless, Windhoek has a vibrant nightlife and an overflowing roster of restaurants. Most travelers mistakenly cut their stay in Windhoek short, not knowing that there really is something here for everyone—you can take hiking day trips to Daan Viljoen National Park, barter at street markets, visit museums and government buildings, or simply sit and watch the world go by in this colorful metropolis.

▐▛ INTERCITY TRANSPORTATION

Flights: Eros Airport (information ☎ 70 2102), near the Southern Industrial Area, offers domestic and charter flights, as well as some flights to South Africa. **Hosea Kutako International Airport** (☎ 062 702 401) is off the B6, 40km east of Windhoek. Transportation to the International Airport is best provided by **VIP Shuttle** (☎ 081 256 3657; N$70 per person) or **Crown Shuttle** (☎ 081 129 9116; N$150 for up to 2 people). **Local taxis** run to Eros Airport for around N$10 per person.

Air Namibia (☎ 299 6140; Eros ☎ 061 299 6058; Kutako Int. ☎ 061 299 6600), in Gustav Voigts Ctr. on Independence Ave. To: **Cape Town** and **Johannesburg** (both N$1680); **Lüderitz** (2½hr., Su-F 9am, N$950); **Ondangwa** (2hr., twice daily, N$710); **Swakopmund** (50min., Su-F 9am, N$380); **Walvis Bay** (50min., Su-F 9am, N$380); **Victoria Falls** (W, F, Su 8:45am; N$2310).

South African Airways (☎ 231 118), corner of Independence St. and Bulow St., flies to **Cape Town** and **Johannesburg** (both daily N$1830).

Trains: The train station lies north of Bahnhof St., which runs parallel to John Meinert St. **TransNamib's Starline** (☎ 298 2175; after hours 122 6062), at the station. Ticket office open M, W, and F 6am-8pm; Tu and Th 6am-7:30pm; Su 6-10am and 3:30-7:30pm. Buying tickets on the train costs N$5 more. Trains run to: **Keetmanshoop** (11½hr.; Su-F 7:10pm; 2nd class N$54, 1st class N$71), via **Mariental** (6¼hr.); **Tsumeb** (16hr.; Tu, Th, Su 5:45pm; N$44/N$54); **Walvis Bay** (11hr., Su-F 7:55pm, N$49/N$65); **Swakopmund** (9½hr., N$49/N$65). For **South Africa,** trains connect **Keetmanshoop** and **Upington** (13hr., W and Sa 8:50am, N$54/N$71). 33% senior discount; students always pay off-peak fare.

Buses: Four bus lines connect Windhoek to the rest of the Namibia and its neighbors.

Trans-Namib's Starline (☎ 298 2175) runs buses from the train station to **Otjiwarongo** (4½hr., F and Su 8am, N$50).

Intercape, 2 Galilei St. (☎ 227 847), stops at the Grab-a-Phone bus terminal on Independence Ave. and runs to: **Walvis Bay** (5½hr.; M, W, and F-Sa 6am; N$110) via **Swakopmund** (5hr., N$110); **Cape Town** (20hr.; M, W, F, and Su 5pm; N$430) via **Keetmanshoop** (5½hr., N$240); **Upington** (13hr.; M, W, F, and Su 5pm; N$295); **Victoria Falls** (21hr.; M and F 7pm, N$440) via **Tsumeb** (5hr.; N$215). Intercape offers 15% discounts for students, seniors, and HI members.

Audi Camp (☎ 256 580) runs a door-to-door shuttle to **Maun, Botswana** (16hr.; departs W 7:30am, returns M 7:30am; US$55).

Namibia Contract Haulage, 68 Bismarck St. (☎ 234 164), runs from Soweto market in Katatura to: **Ondangwa** (N$60); **Oshakati** (N$65); **Oshikango** (N$70); **Ombalantu** (N$80). Buses leave for all destinations on M at 6am and F at 6am and 5pm.

Minibuses: To **Gobabis, Swakopmund, Walvis Bay, Keetmanshoop, Tsumeb, Ondangwa** leave from Rhino Park; to **Rehoboth** from Wernhil Park Mall. Inquire with drivers for fares (usually similar to those of train).

✦ ORIENTATION

Windhoek is situated in the valley between the Auas and Eros Mountains to the east and the Khomas Hochland in the west. The former township of **Katatura** (see p. 469) borders the north, and the suburbs **Olympia** and **Pioneers Park** lie to the south. The suburbs **Windhoek West** and **Hochland** are on the west side of the city, while **Klein Windhoek** sits to the east. The main downtown area, however, is quite compact and walkable, split in half by **Independence Ave.,** the main north-south thoroughfare where most shops and civil services are located. The **B6,** as **Sam Nujoma Dr.,** splits downtown into quarters by running east-west through the city, leading to Botswana in the east. North of Sam Nujoma Dr., in the heart of downtown on **Independence Ave.,** is **Post St. Mall,** an open-air pedestrian-only shopping area with boutiques, major banks, and a lively street market. Its western end con-

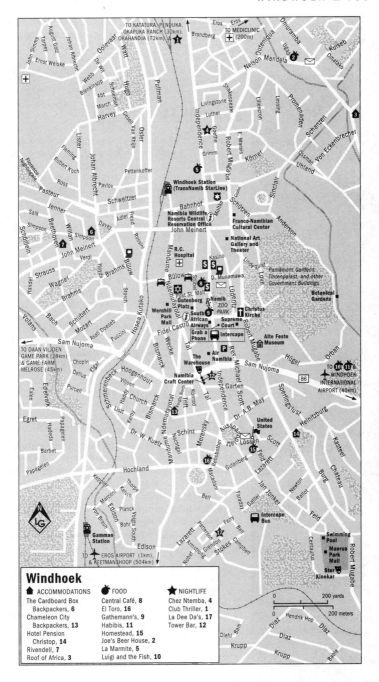

NAMIBIA

Windhoek

🏠 **ACCOMMODATIONS**

The Cardboard Box
  Backpackers, **6**
Chameleon City
  Backpackers, **13**
Hotel Pension
  Christop, **14**
Rivendell, **7**
Roof of Africa, **3**

🍎 **FOOD**

Central Café, **8**
El Toro, **16**
Gathemann's, **9**
Habibis, **11**
Homestead, **15**
Joe's Beer House, **2**
La Marmite, **5**
Luigi and the Fish, **10**

⭐ **NIGHTLIFE**

Chez Ntemba, **4**
Club Thriller, **1**
La Dee Da's, **17**
Tower Bar, **12**

FROM THE ROAD

I AM WOMAN, HEAR ME ROAR

Trekking the globe alone is a big step for anyone. Even though I had extensively explored Europe and North America, Namibia was more of a leap, the size of which I was to be reminded of at every turn. At every tourist sight, with every inquiry at a hostel, after the initial introductions came a quick, questioning glance and the inevitable, "Are you alone?" How people responded when I said "yes," depended upon their sex. Women, in a hushed voice, asked if I was afraid to be alone, especially when registering for a campground. Men tended to look upon it as an opportunity to sometimes make inappropriate comments, ranging from offering their company to offering their bed. A few daring Romeos even proposed, something not uncommon in African countries. After politely declining their request, the only extra baggage I carried home were a few pieces of jewelry given as tokens. As I travelled, I learned that women travelling alone is Namibia is unusual, if not extremely rare. Otherwise, there might eventually be a shortage of eligible African bachelors.

There are reasons why women historically haven't travelled alone in Namibia. The country is rightfully known for its challenging hiking trails, lonely drives, and harsh landscapes.

(Continued on next page)

nects to **Wernhil Park Mall.** Many of Windhoek's historic buildings, including the president's house and all the museums, are on **Robert Mugabe Ave.,** which runs parallel to and one block east of Independence Ave. The **B1** skirts the city at the **Western Bypass,** continuing on to South Africa.

⌐ LOCAL TRANSPORTATION

Taxis: Most taxis run pre-set routes that start downtown and end in Katatura. Taking a taxi anywhere on this route is N$5 per person; destinations anywhere off this route cost more. Taxis with or without routes can be waved down on most streets but rack at Wernhil Park Mall, Zoo Park, and on Bülow, west of Stübel. Taxis are scarcer on weekends, but there are 24hr. radio taxis: **Kalahari** (☎263 333) and **Crown** (☎081 129 9116) charge N$10-20 per car for trips anywhere in town. Prices rise somewhat after 10pm.

Car Rentals: Car rental agencies in Windhoek tend to be pricier than their counterparts in South Africa. Rental agencies for 2WD include **Andes Car Rental,** 25 Voigts St. (☎25 6334; andescar@iafrica.com.net), and **Kalahari Car Hire,** 109 Daan Bekker St. (☎25 2690), in Olympia. Both charge N$300-400 per day with limited mileage. For 4WD, contact **African Tracks,** 3 Sandpiper St. (☎24 5072), which has a single cab 4WD with unlimited mileage for N$605 per day.

⚡ PRACTICAL INFORMATION

TOURIST AND FINANCIAL SERVICES

Tourist Offices: Windhoek is the best place to make reliable advance arrangements for the rest of a Namibia itinerary. Tourism offices in the rest of the country will be helpful for local arrangements but will be less useful in booking ahead for other towns.

Tourist Information Office (☎/fax 290 2092), inside Post St. Mall. Open M-F 7:30am-1pm, 2-4:30pm.

Tourist Junction, 40 Peter Muller St. (☎23 1246; fax 23 1703; info.tjunction@galileosa.co.za), is a private info center that provides advice, bookings (beware of commissions), day trips, phones, and Internet (N$15 for 30min.). Luggage storage N$50 per day. Open M-F 7:30am-4:30pm, Sat 9am-noon.

Namibia Wildlife Resorts (NWR) Central Reservation Office (☎23 6975/6/7/8; fax 22 4900; reservations@mweb.com.na; www.namibiawildliferesorts.com), at Moltke and John Meinert St., is an essential stop for those going to Namibia's parks and reserves. Bookings open M-F 8am-5pm.

Tours: Windhoek is the starting point for most safaris, especially those to Etosha National Park. Tour companies offer 3-day and 6- to 15-day tours, generally N$300-500 per day, depending on duration, distances traveled, and type of accommodations. Carless travelers may find this their best option. All companies offer regular tours, trips further afield to neighboring countries, and tailor-made safaris.

Crazy Kudu Safaris (☎22 2636; fax 25 5074; namibia.safaris@crazykudu.com; www.crazykudu.com), runs the cheapest 3-, 6-, and 10-day tours (US$120 per person, US$260, US$360). The 10-day tour covers Etosha and the Sossusvlei. The 5-day Kaokoland tour is the only regular tour to Opuwo and surrounding Himba villages (US$300; min. 4 people). All trips leave on Sa.

Wild Dog Safaris, 19 Johann Albrecht St. (☎25 7642; fax 24 0802; wilddog@iafrica.com.na), has 3-day trips to the Sossusvlei (US$160), 7-day trips north or south (US $340), and 6-day Etosha and Sossusvlei trips (US$350).

Chameleon Safaris, 22 Wagner St. (☎/fax 24 7668; info@chameleon.com.na), offers 18-day Namibian Extravaganzas (N$7500 per person) and shorter trips with custom routes.

Cardboard Box Travel Shop, 15 Johann Albrecht St. (☎/fax 25 6580; namibia@bigfoot.com; www.namibian.org), books car rentals (inquire about Tempest Sedan car rates), adventure tours, and Intercape buses, as well as organizing self-drive tours. A one-stop shop for all of Namibia.

Banks: Bank of Windhoek, 262 Independence Ave. (☎299 1122), opposite Bülow St. **First National Bank** (☎299 2222), at Post St. Mall and Independence Ave. **Standard Bank,** 261 Independence Ave. All have *bureau de change,* **24hr. ATM,** and are open M-F 9am-3:30pm, Sa 8:30-11am. The **American Express Office,** in the Kaiser Krone building on Post St. Mall, cashes and exchanges traveler's checks on commission. Open M-F 9am-3:30pm. **Namibia Bureau de Change** (☎/fax 229 667), in the Levinson Arcade off Independence Ave. just north of the Post St. Mall, is the local Thomas Cook agent and handles traveler's checks and international money transfers in addition to foreign exchange. Open M-F 8am-5pm, Sa 8:30am-1pm.

LOCAL SERVICES

Bookstores: Book Den (☎23 9976), on Stübel St. in the Gutenberg Platz, one of the best bookstores in Namibia. Open M-F 9am-5pm, Sa 9am-1pm. To buy and sell used books, go to **Uncle Spikes,** at Tal and Garten St., one block from Namibian Craft Center. Open M-F 9am-5:30pm, Sa 8:30am-1pm.

Cultural Centers: The **Franco-Namibian Cultural Center,** 118 Robert Mugabe St. (☎22 2122), is accessible to French and English speakers, offering a library, French classes, art exhibits and subtitled films W at 7:30pm. Open M-Th 9am-7pm, F 9am-12:30pm.

(Continued from previous page)

Still, for a prepared woman, these potential obstacles should not be a deterrent. I contacted people in Southern Africa, who aptly warned me that vehicles post the biggest safety concern, as they break down, roll over, and generally strand you in the middle of nowhere quite frequently.

To combat this I only travelled on well-marked roads and trails, where help, if needed, would be arriving sooner rather than later. I never travelled roads, even tarred ones, after dark, and I always kept speeds at a controllable level (at most 120km. per hr. on tar and 80km per hr. elsewhere). Protection at night, especially with the high percentage of HIV/AIDS, was a personal concern, and so I set certain rules for myself. I never camped by the side of the road and I stayed in a private room instead of a dorm if I could. From past experience, I knew that long pants were the best clothes to wear, since my goal was to see the country, not be a Marilyn Monroe look alike. Eventually I learned to trust my instincts: a place that made feel unsafe probably was. Despite taking precautions, my number one rule remained "Have a good time." Namibia is a wonderful and rewarding country to travel in, whether you're alone or with twenty people, so be aware and have fun.
—Kelzie Beebe

Supermarkets: Model Pick 'n Pay, in Wernhill Park Shopping Ctr. Open M 9am-7pm, Tu-F 8:30am-7pm, Sa 8am-7pm, Su 9am-7pm. **ShopRite,** corner of Independence Ave. and John Meinert St. Open M-Th 8am-6pm, F 8am-6:30pm, Sa 7am-4pm, Su 9am-1pm.

Laundromat: Laundraland (☎224 912), in Elsa building on Sam Nujoma Dr., in Klein Windhoek. Self-service wash N$15; dry N$7. Open M-Th 7am-8pm, F 7am-5pm, Sa closed, Su 8am-5pm.

Camping Equipment: Adventure Camping Hire (☎/fax 24 2478; adventure@nation.net) rents and delivers camping supplies. **Cymot,** 60 Mandume Ndemufayo (☎234 131), and **Le Trip** (☎233 499), inside Wernhill Park Shopping Ctr., sell camping equipment.

EMERGENCY AND COMMUNICATIONS

Emergency: ☎10 111.

Police: ☎10 111. On Bahnhof St. at Independence Ave.

Pharmacies: Several on Independence Ave. including **Namib Pharmacy,** 195 Independence Ave. (☎237 103).

Hospitals: Medi-Clinic (☎222 687), on Heliodoor St. in Eros Park. **Roman Catholic Hospital,** 92 Stubel St. (☎237 237), is another good private hospital. Open 24hr. The **public hospital,** at the intersection of the B1 and Independence Ave., is best avoided.

Internet Access: Internet Cafe (☎255 570), on Daniel Munamava St. across from post office. N$10 per 30 min. Open M-F 8am-late, Sa 9am-late, Su 10am-late. **Club Internet,** 78 Bulow St. (☎230 997), has the same rates. Open M-F 8am-8pm, Sa 9am-2pm.

Post Office: Windhoek Post Office (☎201 3025), on Independence Ave. across from Post St. Mall. *Poste Restante* (around back), fax, photocopying, money transfer, phones, and international calls available. Open M-Tu, Th-F 8am-4:30pm; W 8:30am-4pm; Sa 8am-noon.

⌂ ACCOMMODATIONS AND CAMPING

Windhoek hosts nearly a dozen hostels, with the best options clustered in the city's northwest quarter. Most accommodations listed below offer a pool, TV lounge, *braai*, self-catering kitchen, and secure off-street parking. Reservations are recommended, especially for private rooms.

▨ **The Cardboard Box Backpackers,** 15 Johann Albrecht St. (☎22 8994; namibia@bigfoot.com; www.namibian.org). At John Meinert St. and Simpson St. With a brand new restaurant and bar, the Box continues to be the epicenter of the independent-traveler scene. Its lively atmosphere, large self-catering kitchen, and in-house travel center draw guests and staff from far and wide, all with stories to tell over beer or soda. Internet (N$0.50 per min.), free shuttle from Intercape bus, pool table, and resident pets. Key deposit N$25. Dorm N$65; private room (single or double) N$150. Camping N$40 per person. MC/V. ❷

▨ **Rivendell,** 40 Beethoven St. (☎25 0006; fax 25 0020; rivendell@touthfairy.com; www.rivendell-namibia.com). Its tastefully decorated rooms with huge windows are a great value. The best place for a quiet stay, it has all the amenities of a backpackers without the hectic feel. Breakfast N$20. Self-catering kitchen, TV lounge, laundry, and free pick-up from Intercape bus (book ahead). Doubles N$135, with bath N$150; triples without bath N$165. MC/V. ❷

Chameleon City Backpackers, 5 Voigts North (☎24 4347; fax 24 7668; chamnam@namib.com; www.chameleonbackpackers.com). Follow Church St. (parallel to Sam Nujoma) west from Tal St., turn left on Triff St., and at its end take the hairpin left turn; Chameleon is at the end of the street. This great, low-key place for travelers is dominated by its TV and movie collection. Though it has a pool and a new bar, it can be less personable than other places. Breakfast included. Internet, free shuttle to town, and laundry. Dorms N$40; 4-bed dorms N$50; doubles N$120. ❶

Hotel Pension Christop, 33 Heinitzburg St. (☎24 0777; fax 24 8560; christoph@mweb.com.za). At Robert Mugabe Ave. For a more comfortable alternative away from other accommodations that is still centrally located, try this cheery pension surrounding a lush courtyard. Rooms have bath, TV, fridge, and telephone. Breakfast included. Single N$250; double N$350. MC/V. ❸

Roof of Africa, 124 Nelson Mandela Ave. (☎25 4708 or 081 124 4930; fax 24 8048; info@rooofafrica.com; www.rooofafrica.com). Located in slightly remote Klein Windhoek in a gated community, this is a well-equipped backpackers where most people keep to themselves. Its redeeming characteristic is its proximity to Joe's Beerhouse. Restaurant, bar, pool, and TV lounge. Travel advice and bookings, free shuttle from Interscape, laundry, Internet and kitchen. Dorms N$50. Private rooms with breakfast: Singles N$245; doubles N$295. Camping N$45 per person. ❶

Penduka (☎25 7210; penduka@namibnet.com), a 15min. drive from downtown on the far side of Katatura township, on the lakefront next to Goreangab Dam. Take Independence Ave. north from city center, through Katatura, until it intersects Otjomuise Rd. Continue on Eveline St., turn left onto Green Mountain Dam Rd. Look for the sign on the left. Backpackers dorms and camping as well as individually decorated thatched-roof bungalows make for a good, quiet retreat with amazing views of Windhoek and nature. Convenient for hiking along the dam and Katatura tours (book in advance). Free pick-up from Grab-a-phone (☎081 129 4116; not open on Su; N$25 per person, min. 3 people). Restaurant and *braai*. Dorms N$30; bungalow singles with bath N$115; doubles N$155. MC/V. ❸

◖ FOOD

Windhoek has a lineup of excellent restaurants. Carnivores, particularly, will find fulfillment, and there are a surprising number of restaurants offering traditional African fare. No matter how much you skimp elsewhere, restaurants in Windhoek are worth the splurge—your stomach will thank you.

▨ **Luigi and the Fish,** 320 Sam Nujoma Ave., Klein Windhoek (☎25 6399; luigi@iafrica.com.na). A lively place with great food, the atmosphere suits groups for either dinner, drinks, or late nights in the cigar lounge. Unlike many other Namibian restaurants, vegetables abound in game, seafood, and vegetarian dishes, with the Game Wrap (N$40.95) and Espantada topping the list. Tapas N$22. Fish N$28-79. Beef N$33-80. Open daily noon-3pm and 6pm-late. AmEx/DC/MC/V. ❸

▨ **Joe's Beer House** (☎232 457), 700m from Independence Ave. on Nelson Mandela. Colossal new location still packed with diners feasting their eyes on the quirky decor and filling their gullets with meat. Bushman *sosatie* (a kebab of chicken, ostrich, kudu, crocodile, and zebra; N$70) stands out above the rest. Sunday lunch buffet noon-5pm N$70. Open M-Th 5pm-late, F-Su 11am-late. Reservations strongly recommended. AmEx/DC/MC/V.

Habibis, in Klein Windhoek on Sam Nujoma Ave. opposite Luigi and the Fish. A Middle Eastern restaurant whose name means "friend," Habibis is a great place to lounge on the floor, feast on Lamb Meat Schwarma (N$44), and share a hookah (N$40) with friends. Table seating also available. Fabulous Lebanese Pastry (N$10-26) with taboule and hummus highly recommended. The only drawback is that some of the more well-known dishes and tobacco flavors are routinely out of stock. Open M 6-11pm, Tu-Sa 11:30am-3pm and 6-11pm, Su 11:30am-3pm and 6-10pm. DC/MC/V. ❸

La Marmite, 383 Independence Ave. (☎24 0306; fax 24 8026). Offers excellent Came-roonian food created by the owner/head chef/host Martial. The menu may be short, but ask Martial for his nightly improvisation or try the Cameroonian curry with couscous (N$39.50). Also try the chicken with peanut butter stew (N$34.50). Open daily 6-10pm. ❸

Homestead, 53 Feld St. (☎22 1958; fax 22 1846). Just off Lossen St. and the Ausspann-nplantz. Located in one of Windhoek's oldest homes, Homestead is excellent for an upscale night out. The owner can help you pick one of the 300 wines or 40 whiskeys to best suit your meal. The fireplace will warm you as you enjoy ostrich medallions (N$68.50) or Roman Oxtail ragout (N$59.50). Large vegetarian menu. Great granadilla parfait (N$24.50). Reservations for 4 or more reccommended. Open M-Sa 6-10pm. AmEx/DC/MC/V. ❹

Gathemann's, 179 Independence Ave., upstairs (☎22 3853). Very classy joint with a large price range. Namibian Beef Fillet N$74. Filled Chicken Breast N$52. For lighter fare, try the green salad with caramelized apples and goat cheese (N$32) or the cheese platter (N$40) and a bottle of port. Reservations recommended for open-air balcony. Open daily for lunch noon-2pm, cake and coffee 2-6pm, and dinner 6-11pm. AmEx/DC/MC/V. ❹

Central Cafe (☎22 2659), in the Levinson Arcade across Independence Ave. from the post office. The cheapest option for lunch or cake and coffee, this lively open-air cafe is decorated in early 20th-century pictures of Namibia. Excels at pizza (N$24-37), but also has salads (N$25) and *sosaties* with rice (N$24.50). Apple cake N$8.50. Open M-F 6:30am-10pm, Sa 7am-10pm. ❷

El Toro Steakhouse, 4 Rehobother Rd. (☎22 2797). South of Ausspannplatz. Local and visiting carnivores flock to the best steakhouse in town for legendary 1kg steaks (N$90-120), seafood (N$55-245), and burgers (N$27). Vegetarians are satisfied as well with a well-stocked salad bar (N$10-20). Open daily noon-2pm and 6-11pm. AmEx/DC/MC/V. ❹

◉ SIGHTS

ALTE FESTE. The Alte Feste (Old Fort), built in 1880, is one of the oldest buildings in Windhoek. Originally occupied by German and then South African Union Forces, it housed POWs during the National Liberation Struggle of 1904-1908. Today the National Museum of Namibia, opened in 1957, is inside and showcases Namibian culture and history, including extensive displays on the first open elec-tion after independence and Bushman rock art. The museum helps visitors piece together the country's political and social history, something which is sometimes left incomplete in other museums. *(On Robert Mugabe Ave., between Fidel Castro St. and Sam Nujoma Ave. ☎293 4362. Open M-F 9am-5pm, Sa-Su 10am-noon and 3-5pm. Free, but donations encouraged.)*

NATIONAL ART GALLERY. This small yet excellent gallery is even more notable for its exhibitions of famous Namibian and African artists. It also has prints, sculp-ture, silk screening, water colors, and oil paintings. An artsy craft shop sits next to the colorful courtyard. *(Corner of Robert Mugabe Ave. and John Meinert St. ☎23 1160. Open Tu-F 9am-5pm, Sa 9am-2pm. Free.)*

PENDUKA PROJECT. Located about a 15min. drive from downtown Windhoek next to Goreangab Dam in Katatura township, this non-profit development project trains and works with women, most of whom are physically handicapped, in rural and underdeveloped areas in Namibia. Penduka, which means "wake up" in Ovambo and Herero languages, teaches women to make traditional crafts and become self-sufficient by earning more income. The crafts produced include household goods, pottery, jewelry, and natural beauty products. Accommodations and a restaurant are available; hiking trips and cultural tours require advanced booking. (☎25 7210; penduka@namibnet.com. Take Independence Ave. north from city center, through Katatura, until it intersects Otjomuise Rd. Continue on Eveline St., turn left onto Green Mountain Dam Rd. Look for the sign on the left. Restaurant and craft shop open M-Sa 8am-5pm. Cultural tour of Katatura N\$35 per person.)

KATATURA All South African and Namibian towns had "townships" during the Apartheid Era, and, in December 1959, the township of Katatura ("the place we don't want to stay") became famous when 13 blacks resisting relocation were shot and killed by police. The massacre encouraged the liberation movement to fight harder, but thousands were still "relocated" into shoebox houses in Katatura, where they were not even allowed to own their own property until the late 1970s. Although much has changed since then, the vast majority of blacks in Windhoek still live in Katatura today. Though new neighborhoods are quickly developing to try to close the divides created by colonialism and apartheid, hardship, poverty, and distrust still exist. It is still not advisable to enter Katatura alone; a day trip with a well-known resident is quite safe and offers a rare opportunity to glimpse township life. Katatura has a growing gentry of intellectuals, former SWAPO revolutionaries, and schoolteachers who welcome foreigners into their mix with generosity and curiosity.

🎵 ENTERTAINMENT

The Warehouse, 48 Tal St. (☎23 7966). Windhoek's most popular performing arts space offers close-up contact with hip performers. Grab a seat at the bar or a candlelit table for stand-up comedy, bands, dance revues, and plays. Tickets available through the National Theater box office; inquire for times and prices.

National Theatre (☎23 4633 or 23 7966), on Robert Mugabe Ave. next to National Art Gallery. Mainstream and traditional African performances including orchestras, operas, and ballets.

Ster Kinekor (☎24 8980 or 24 9267), in Maerua Park Mall, at Robert Mugabe Ave. and Jan Jonker Rd. Recent Hollywood flicks. Buy tickets early. Before 8pm N\$22; F-Sa 8pm shows N\$22. W shows N\$11.

🛍 SHOPPING

The **Namibia Crafts Center,** 40 Tal St., next to The Warehouse (see **Entertainment,** p. 469), offers three floors of quality crafts at excellent prices (from N\$5). Stalls, representing projects and cooperatives established to bolster both women's roles and the income of traditional families, sell everything from hand-embroidered textiles, ostrich eggshells, and baskets to wood carvings, pottery, and jewelry. Killer health shakes (N\$15.50) and salads (N\$29.50) are served in the cafe on the second floor. (☎24 2222. Open M-F 9am-5pm, Sa 9am-1:30pm.) You can find a remarkable collection of art and kitsch from all over Africa at admittedly inflated boutique prices in **Bushman Art,** 187 Independence Ave., just south of Post St. Mall. (☎22 8828. Open M-F 8:30am-5:30pm, Sa 8:30am-1pm, Su 10am-1pm.) For quality crafts and souvenirs in a less touristy—and cheaper—atmosphere, peak into **Omatako Curios,** in Levinson Arcade, past Central Café on the left. (Open M-F 8:30am-5pm, Sa 8:30am-1pm. AmEx/DC/MC/V.) Great prices, especially for those willing to bargain or trade, can be found at vendor displays of curios along the **Post St. Mall** and at the

NAMIBIA

Grab-a-phone, on the corner of Independence Ave. and Fidel Castro St. The best place in Namibia to buy quality **wood cravings** are the markets in Okahandja. (1hr. north on the B1 from Windhoek, the markets are at both the North and South exits from the B1. Open daily.) Finding traditional Namibian art is the most difficult part of souvenir shopping, as much wooden merchandise actually originates in Zimbabwe. Namibian carvings tend to have a rougher finish, whether they be animals, masks, or bowls. Also, Namibian elephants have their trunks up in the air. Some of the more imaginative bugs and scorpions, most with detachable legs, are Namibian. For insurance of authenticity, purchase signed art or buy from craft projects where you can meet the artisan.

◙ NIGHTLIFE

In Windhoek's clubs, the latent racism still evident in most of Namibian society melts away. The best nightclubs are all enthusiastically integrated. However, Windhoek's current hot spots can be hard to find as clubs can have a short lifespan: it's smart to ask around to find places that are trendy and still open. Bars have a longer life, but few offer the occasion to shake your booty. If you do get jiggy with it, however, be sure to watch your wallet, as pickpockets are common.

Chez Ntemba, on Uhland St. at Independence Ave., has a healthy mix of more traditional African artists and European house music. Upbeat and almost always near capacity, this is the club of the moment. Open Th-Su 8pm-late. Cover varies, but is usually only a few Namibian dollars.

Club Thriller, in Katatura. This is the longest lasting and most famous club in Windhoek. It is also one of the safest nightclubs in the city; there is a weapons search at the door. A bar and fantastical lights compliment the house and rap music. While it may not be in the safest of neighborhoods, its staying power means that it will most likely continue to welcome clubbers for a long time to come. A taxi is the only reliable way to get there.

La Dee Da's, 4-6 Ferry St. (☎081 240 6880). Behind Hyundai south of Lazarett St. This huge warehouse has the biggest dance floor in Namibia. Soul, jazz, hip-hop, electronica, and occasionally live music. 18+. Cover N$20 after 10pm. Open Th-Sa 9pm-4am, Su 6pm-midnight.

Tower Bar (☎081 249 8455), on Tal St. between The Warehouse and Namibian Crafts Center. Occasional live music. Call for performers and prices. Open daily 6pm-2am.

⚄ OUTDOORS

DAAN VILJOEN GAME PARK. Perched atop the rolling hills of Khomas Hochland, west of Windhoek, the **Daan Viljoen Game Park** and its animals are in a world removed from the nearby metropolis. Located 2000m above sea level, Daan Viljoen is a beautiful and spacious home for 301 plant species and 260 bird species, as well as mountain zebra, eland, blue wildebeest, and black backed jackal. The hiking trails and hour-long self-drive game drives make this an excellent day trip from Windhoek (taxis will make the trip for N$30-40 per person). It is also a great way to see Namibia's flora and fauna if you can't visit other game parks. The signposted, self-guided hiking trails are relatively easy, but be sure to carry enough water. The two-day **Soet-Doring Trail** (32km) starts at the park swimming pool. Hikers may see kudu, gemsbok, zebra, and many birds. (N$75 per person. Book well in advance at the NWR office in Windhoek. Hikers must be self-sufficient and carry a backpacker's stove. There is an overnight shelter.) The 3km, 2hr. **Wag'n Bietjio Trail** is a roundtrip trail to Stengel's Dam, following a riverbed and going right through prime game territory. It starts across the road from the park reception office. The

9km, 6hr. **Rooibos Trail** passes the highest point in the park which offers a superb view of Windhoek. It starts at the swimming pool and ends at the restaurant. Neither of these hikes needs to be reserved in advance, and both are free for day visitors. *(24km west of Windhoek on the tarred C28, then left on the D1526 for 6km. ☎22 6806; fax 23 2393. Reception open sunrise to sunset. Gates open for day visitors from sunrise-1pm and 2-5pm; open for night visitors from sunrise-1pm and 2pm-midnight. Day visitors must leave by 6pm. N$20, ages 6-16 N$2; vehicles N$20. Picnic sits N$110 for up to 4 people. Restaurant open 7-8:45am, noon-1:45pm, and 6:30-8:30pm. Bungalow rooms with breakfast: singles N$210; doubles N$280. Camping N$125 for up to 4 people.)*

NATIONAL BOTANICAL GARDENS. Along with the National Botanical Research Institute, the Gardens span the hill and valley between downtown Windhoek and Klein Windhoek. Laced with self-guided walking paths, the area comes to lush life during the wetter seasons but can be fairly unspectacular, apart from small animals, during the drier months. However, year round it provides excellent views of the Eros and Auas mountains to the east of Windhoek. *(Just east of Robert Mugabe St. on Independence Ave. Turn left onto Hügel St.; follow it up the hill for 700m, and the Gardens are on the right. Open M-F 8am-5pm. Free.)*

GUEST FARMS AND RANCHES. Numerous private guest farms and ranches within 50km from Windhoek offer day visitors a laundry list of outdoor activities, including hiking, cheetah feeding, horse riding, game drives, helicopter flips, and bow-and-arrow target shooting. For a comprehensive list, inquire at the tourist information offices in Windhoek. Advance booking is necessary for most of the activities described below, and all prices are per person.

Okapuka Ranch (☎23 4607), 30km north of Windhoek on the B1, is a private farm offering game drives (N$90), mountain drives (3hr.; N$190; min. 4 people), horse riding, lion feeding (N$60), and helicopter flip (N$520). **Game Farm Melrose** (☎23 4298), 43km southwest of Windhoek off the C26 in Khomas Hochland, offers cheetah-feeding (N$20), game drives (N$80), and horse riding (N$60 per hr.). The game here includes impala, hartmann zebra, cheetah, and leopard. Camping costs N$40.

NORTH-CENTRAL NAMIBIA

N
A
M
I
B
I
A

Receiving a higher-than-average amount of rainfall, North-Central Namibia has a lush plant life that supports large commercial cattle farms. Windhoek's relatively close proximity, however, can be felt in the faster pace of town life. The B1 Junction here makes the region important to shipping and industry, since roads split from here to all the other northern regions. The area's commercial importance, however, has not stopped culture from flourishing both in urban and rural settings. Natural attractions abound here. Etosha National Park is renowned for its plentiful game, Waterberg National Park for its colorful geology, and the placid garden town of Tsumeb for its 200 unique minerals. This varied land provides excellent outdoor opportunities, including hiking, game-viewing, bird watching, horseback riding, and camping next to the largest single chunk of meteorite in the world, the Hoba Meteorite near Grootfontein.

OTJIWARONGO ☎067

Otjiwarongo (pop. 28,000) was founded in 1892 in the wake of an agreement between the Herero Chief Kambazembi and the Rhenish Mission Society. A growth spurt came fourteen years later with the construction of railway connection to Swakopmund in 1906. Now the commercial and transportation hub of northern Namibia, the city derives its name from the Herero word for "beautiful

BACKPACKER'S RULES TO SOUTHERN AFRICA

1. Never, under any circumstances, assume *anything*.
2. To determine how long anything will take, add three hours to your best estimate. Double it.
3a. "24hr. service" does not mean all in a row.
3b. "*Just* now" does not mean "*now* now."
4. National holidays may be randomly declared.
5. What you need or want is always "finished," "coming just now," or "not possible."
6. There is no such thing as a full bus.
7. Always avoid physiological excess whenever the chance arises.
8. You can always unload *something*.
9. If you're eating and unexpectedly crunch on something, just swallow and...
10. Accept it.

place." Although travelers primarily use Otjiwarongo as a stopover for trips into nearby Etosha and Waterberg National Parks, the town has its own attractions, including a cheetah conservation center and Namibia's sole crocodile ranch. Farms and guest lodges teem with the wildlife of the *bushveld* plains, and the town environs offer relief for those fleeing the bustle of big cities.

⌐ TRANSPORTATION

Otjiwarongo lies at the junction connecting Windhoek to Etosha, Waterberg, Damaraland, and the Caprivi region in the northeast. It is 245km north of Windhoek and 400km east of Walvis Bay. Waterberg National Park is an hour southeast.

Trains: The **station** is on Dr. Libertina Amathila Dr., on the west edge of town. The ticket office inside is open M, W, F 7am-4pm; buying tickets on the train costs N$5 more than the normal price. **TransNamib's Starline** (☎305 202) runs trains to: **Tsumeb** (6½hr.; Tu, Th, Su 3:15am; N$20); **Walvis Bay** (13hr.; M, W, F 3pm; N$35) via **Swakopmund** (11hr., N$35); **Windhoek** (14¼hr.; M, W, F 3pm; economy N$35, business N$45).

Buses: Intercape buses depart from the BP Service Station on Hage Geingob St. to: **Swakopmund** (10hr., F 10:55am, N$160); **Victoria Falls** (17hr.; M and F 11:15pm; N$370) via **Tsumeb** (2hr., N$110); **Windhoek** (3hr., M 12:45am, N$140). **Welwitschia Travel** (see **Orientation and Practical Information,** below) is the local ticket agent. **TransNamib Starline** buses run from the train station to: **Walvis Bay** (11hr., Su 8am, N$129) via **Outjo** (1½hr, N$20); **Khorixas** (4½hr., N$54); **Swakopmund** (10½hr., N$121).

Car Rental: Out of Africa Car Hire, 94 Tuin St. (☎30 3397 or 081 124 7185). 2WD from N$330 per day; 4WD from N$795 per day, both with unlimited km. **C'est Si Bon Car Hire** (☎30 1240; fax 30 3208), at the west end of Hospital St., has 2WD cars for N$390 per day.

■✚ 🛈 ORIENTATION AND PRACTICAL INFORMATION

The B1 is **Hage Geingob Street** as it runs north-south through town, and has most of the town's shops and services. The corner of **Dr. Libertina Amathila Drive** and **Market Square** is the center of town. **St. George's Street,** one block north, is another commercial center.

Tourist office: 5 St. George's St. (☎/fax 303 830). Inside the Omaue Namibia Gem shop. Open M-F 8am-1pm and 2-5pm, Sa 8am-noon.

Travel Agency: Welwitschia Travel (☎/fax 30 3437), on Hage Geingob St. Handles bookings for Intercape buses. Open M-F 8:30am-12:30pm and 2-4:30pm.

Bank: Bank of Windhoek, 14 Hage Geingob St. (☎30 2541); and **First National Bank,** 7 St. George's St. (☎30 3176), provide **24hr. ATMs** and currency exchange. Both open M-F 9am-3:30pm, Sa 8:30-11am.

Camping Gear: Otjiwarongo Arms and Ammunition (☎30 2947), on Hage Geingob St.

Supermarket: Spar, 9 Hage Geingob St. Open M-Sa 7am-8:30pm, Su 8am-8pm. **Model Pick 'n Pay,** on Tuin St. Open M-Sa 8am-7:30pm, Su 9am-1pm and 4-7pm.

Police: (☎10 111), at St. George's and Van Riebeeck St.

Pharmacy: F.H. Badenhorst Pharmacy, 24 Hage Geingob St. (☎30 2501 or 30 2942). Open M-F 8am-1pm and 2-5:30pm, Sa 8am-1pm.

Hospital: Medi-clinic (☎303 734), on Sonn St.; or the **State Hospital** (☎30 2491) on Dr. Libertina Amathila Dr.

Emergency: Ambulance ☎303 734/5; **fire** ☎304 444. **State hospital** (☎30 2491) on Dr. Libertina Amathila Dr.

Public Telephones: At the post office.

Internet access: Communication Center (☎30 3852), on Market Sq., charges N$15 per 30min. **ITS,** 5 Dr. Libertina Amathila Dr. (☎30 1177), charges the same.

Post office: (☎302 000), on Hage Geingob St. near Market Sq. *Poste Restante,* phonecards, fax, international calls, and photocopies. Open M-Tu and Th-F 8am-4:30pm, W 8:30am-4:30pm, Sa 8am-noon.

ACCOMMODATIONS

▨ Wesrand Farm (☎30 4108 or 081 124 5606). Take Dr. Libertina Amathila Dr. west from town and turn left onto the C33 south. After 10km, turn right onto the gravel road at the small Wesrand sign, and continue 6km to the farm. A classic Afrikaner farm with beautiful camp sites and excellent views right smack in the middle of *bushveld* plain. The open-air communal ablution facilities are some of the best in Namibia, including an open-air bath tub that overlooks a nearby mountain range. Guests are welcome to take part in the farm's cattle business, interact with the free-roaming goats, and hike. Pick-up from nearby cities can be arranged. One spacious bungalow with nearby bath. Bungalow N$75 per person. Camping N$40 per person, with firewood and electricity. ❶

Out of Africa, 94 Tuin St. (☎30 3397; fax 30 3504). Slightly out of the city center with sunny, well-decorated rooms surrounded by lush plant life. A great value for the money. Breakfast, secure parking, a pool, private bath, and TV all included. Singles N$175; doubles N$255; triples N$325. ❸

Falkennest Guesthouse, 21 Industrial Rd. (☎30 2616; otjbb@iafrica.com.na). Follow Dr. Libertina Amathila Dr. three blocks west from Market Sq. and turn left onto Industrial Rd. A centrally located, family-owned B&B with TV lounge/breakfast room, pool, and aviary. *Braai,* self-catering kitchen, and secure parking also available. Reception 24hr. Check-out 10am. Singles N$130; doubles N$220; triples N$300. ❷

FOOD AND ENTERTAINMENT

O. Carstensen Bäckerei (☎30 2326), on St. George's St. A bustling place offering the authentic taste of a *Dampfbäckerei* (German chimney bakery) in a diner-like setting. Fresh bread, cakes (N$3.50-8), and sandwiches (N$6-11) grace the menu along with full meals (N$14-34) including meat, pasta, and vegetarian options. ❷

IN RECENT NEWS

LOVING NATURE TO DEATH

Even though Namibia is not extremely populated for its size, its growing population density and tourist industry are beginning to tax the land and animals. Key problem areas include the Kaokoveld and Fish River Canyon. Certain animal populations, especially the cheetah, as 20% of the worldwide cheetah population lives within Namibia's boundaries, are also being negatively affected.

The Himba people of the Kaokoveld, are becoming increasingly affected by tourism as better roads enable more tourist traffic. Fish River Canyon is suffering from refuse left by hikers and campers. Among animals, cheetahs and Cape Fur seals are two the most hurt populations: Farmers shoot cheetahs, blaming them for livestock deaths, and seals suffocate or become unable to swim due to ocean garbage.

Efforts, ranging from government programs to private companies, are underway to preserve Namibia's resources. One of the most established programs in the Cheetah Conservation Fund (CCF), started in 1990 to educate Namibian farmers and perform research in an attempt to curb the population decline that may make cheetahs extinct by the 21st century. Based near the Waterberg Plateau, the CCF also started an Anatolian Shepard dog program, raising and training them from birth to aggressively protect livestock from predators, thereby decreasing the number of cheetahs killed due to livestock deaths. The decrease in the

(Continued on next page)

Kameldon Bistro, 17 Hindenburg St. (☎081 244 5967). Follow Hage Geingob two blocks south from Market Sq. and turn right onto Hindenburg St. Set in an extremely relaxed atmosphere, tables are surrounded by lush plants and filled with locals who come to recoup after a long day. The menu is filled with breakfasts (up to N$32), light meals (N$15-35), and inexpensive dinner specials that abound with fresh vegetables. Open M-F 7:30am-7pm, Sa 7:30am-1pm. ❷

Prime Rib Restaurant, 12 River St. (☎30 3165). Just off Hage Geingob. The best meat place in town has steaks (N$28-46), create-your-own pizza (from N$10), burgers (N$12-20), and salads for the non-carnivore (N$10-12). Open M-Sa noon-2pm and 6-9pm. Cash only. ❷

Ojtibamba Lodge Restaurant (☎30 3133). Take Hage Geingob St. 3km south of town; Ojtibamba is on the right. This more upscale, *a la carte* restaurant offers seafood (N$35-52), pork (N$35-42), and beef (N$40-60). Both the ostrich (N$61) and the Ruben fillet stuffed with mushrooms (N$66) are recommended. ❸

Kipple's Dance Bar, next to the Prime Rib Restaurant. Otjiwarongo's liveliest bar, featuring dancing, DJs, pool tables, and the occasional live band. 18+. Open M-Sa 5pm-midnight (often later). ❷

🔍 SIGHTS

CHEETAH CONSERVATION CENTER. Started in 1990 for both research and educational purposes, the center has informative and interactive displays that take visitors through the history of the area's burgeoning cheetah population. Both wild and tame cheetahs live at the center, and you can see them feed daily at 3-3:30pm; call to make sure a feeding is scheduled for your arrival. Lure coursing (to see the cheetahs run at nearly 110kph) and demonstrations with the center's cheetah ambassador, Chewbacca, are also available if booked in advance. The center also breeds and trains Anatolian Shepard dogs to be flock herders, protecting livestock from predators. This arrangement in turn protects the cheetahs from local farmers who shoot them for killing precious livestock. Shepard dog demonstrations are also available. *(44km east of Otjiwarongo on the D2440, which is on the right heading north out of town. ☎067 30 6225; fax 067 30 6225; www.cheetah.org. Open daily 9am-5:30pm. Suggested donation N$35; inquire for demo prices.)*

CROCODILE FARM. This farm, which breeds crocodiles primarily for their skin, can house between 50 to 3000 Nile crocs at a time. Visits are especially interesting around Christmas, when the eggs begin to hatch, and in July, when crocodile love is in the air. *(At the corner of Zingel St. and Hospital St. Guided tour lasts 15-20min. Open M-F 9am-4pm, Sa-Su 10am-1pm. N\$20, ages 4-10 N\$10.)*

WATERBERG PLATEAU ☎ 067

Waterberg Plateau National Park, established in 1970 as a sanctuary for rare and endangered species, stands in stark contrast to its surrounding *bushveld*; its presence on the horizon can be seen over a hundred kilometers away. The beautiful rusty-pink sandstone cliffs stretch 50km northeast to southwest and 20km northwest to southeast, providing a home for 25 mammal and over 200 bird species, including the endangered white and black rhino, sable and roan antelope, buffalo, kudu, gemsbok, giraffe, and leopard. Waterberg is also the only breeding colony of the Cape Vulture. Close to the Bernabé de la Bat Rest Camp, at the foot of the plateau, lies the site of the historic Battle of Waterberg, fought between the Herero and German colonial forces in 1904. A commemorative graveyard was established for the few dozen Germans killed in the battle, though no such memorial exists for the few *thousand* Herero mowed down by the German colonists' superior weaponry.

🛂 **PRACTICAL INFORMATION.** The gate is open daily from 6am to 10pm. After signing in at the gate, check in with the reception (☎ 067 30 5001) to obtain permits and accommodations. Reception is open daily 6am-6pm. Day visitors must exit the park by 6pm. (Entry permits N\$20 per day, ages 6-16 N\$2, N\$20 per vehicle.) Services at Bernabé de la Bat Rest Camp include a **gas station** (open daily 8am-1pm and 2-5pm), a **kiosk,** and **provision shop** (open 7-9:30am, 11am-2pm and 3:30-6pm). There is **no public transportation** to the park. From Windhoek, drive 220km north on the B1 and turn right on the C22. After 41km turn left onto the D2512. From December through March, the graveled D2512 can get dangerously wet and slippery and is usually only accessible by 4WD. Call ahead to reception to check road conditions.

📷📷 **ACCOMMODATIONS AND FOOD. Bernabé de la Bat Rest Camp ❷,** 17km after the D2512 turn-off on the left, offers campsites and bungalows of various sizes. Though finding an open campsite is rarely a problem, bungalows are in higher demand; reserve in advance, especially during high season (Jul.-Oct.). Campsites are sandy and large with hot showers, *braai*, wash/iron rooms, field kitchens with hot plates, and immaculate ablution facilities. All bunga-

(Continued from previous page)

cheetah's free range hunting ground due to increased farming has created the problem between man and beast that CCF is trying to remedy.

Garbage left by travelers has also caused problems in recent years. Tens of thousands of people hike in Namibia each year, and garbage is piling up. Total oil and service stations have begun a campaign to clean up Fish River Canyon and make hikers more aware of their behavior. To help conservation efforts, don't litter and don't leave marked trails or destroy sensitive areas.

In some cases, even the most well-meaning tourists can do harm. Contact between tourists and some Namibians is slowly destroying the traditional cultures. As tourists introduce modern objects and capitalist ideas into societies where share and share alike used to be the mentality, tradition communities loose their beliefs, sometimes to such a degree that they degenerate into mere tourist attractions. While Namibia's native cultures is one is its main tourist draws, visitors need to be aware of their actions, especially when they are in villages and around younger community members. When camping visitors should be sure not to cross village and sacred boundaries. If in doubt about where to camp, opt for established campsites and leave the rest of the land intact for the next Namibian generation.

—Kelzie Beebe

lows feature hot plate, fridge, bath, *braai*, and bedding. Wheelchair-accessible bungalows are available. The rest camp also features a beautiful sandstone pool, a bar and a decent restaurant. (Sites N$100 for 4 people, N$10 per extra adult up to 8. Bungalow doubles N$330; triples N$360; quads N$400. Pool open 24hr. Bar open daily noon-1:30pm, 7-9:30pm. Restaurant open daily 7am-8:30am, noon-1:30pm, and 7-8:30pm. Breakfast N$40, children N$20; lunch and dinner N$27-55. MC/ V.

◼ **HIKING.** Several unguided hiking trails, most of which explore the flat area at the foot of the mountain, leave from the Bernabé de la Bat Rest Camp. Trail maps and information can be found at the camp's reception desk.

Forest Walk (15min.). Offers a brief introduction to the thick bush.

Francolin Walk (20min.). Originating at the restaurant, this short trail presents the opportunity to view mongoose and francolin birds in the wild.

Kambazempi Trail (3km, 2½hr.). The best hike to see wildlife, it follows the base of the plateau. The path, while flatter than most, is populated with baboons, antelopes, and enough birds and butterflies to darken the sky. Bring plenty of water, and watch where you step—the trail is covered in leopard scat.

Mountain View Trail (2km, 1½hr.). The only day hike that reaches the top of the plateau and accessible to those who are in moderately good health. Although it is quite steep and involves some scrambling over rocks, those who reach the top are rewarded with amazing views of the plateau and *bushveld* beyond.

Waterberg Trail (50km, 3-4 days; unguided). The only trail that explores the top of the plateau in any depth. Aside from the initial climb up the plateau, the trail is very flat. Stick to the trail and stay alert for frequent rhino encounters. Basic campsites at Huilboom and Antephora offer shelter and water; hikers must carry everything else. N$100 per person; Apr.-Nov. hikers must depart on W. Call the park office to book ahead.

Okarakuvisa Trail (3-4 days; guided). Though this trail lacks much of the big game found on the Waterberg Trail, it explores the beautiful wildernesses surrounding Okarakuvisa Mountain. Hikers generally cover about 15km per day, carry their own supplies, and sleep in rustic farmhouses en route. Hikes depart from Onjoka Gate Apr.-Nov. every 2nd, 3rd, and 4th weekend. N$220 per person. Book ahead.

◼ **GAME VIEWING.** Departing daily from the rest camp, 4WD game drives offer a quick and convenient initiation to the park's wildlife. For those who have already spent time at Etosha, the drives can be unexciting. Giraffe and various antelope are often spotted, but some game drives return with binoculars unused. Bundle up for the extremely chilly morning drives. (3hr. Apr.-Sept. depart 6am and 3pm; Oct.-Mar. depart 7am and 4pm. N$90 per person, under 12 N$40. Book ahead.)

TSUMEB
☎ **067**

The difference between Tsumeb and other Namibian towns can be seen and felt almost immediately. Streets are lined with well-kept trees, and kids play soccer in the parks and ride their bikes around town. Despite being one of the centers of Namibia's mining industry, the dust prevalent in other northern towns is absent. Whether stopping in Tsumeb to stock up on provisions—it is the best gateway to Etosha—or to get a relaxed taste of culture, no visitor will leave disappointed.

◼ **TRANSPORTATION.** Tsumeb is 426km north of Windhoek via the B1, 181km north of Otjiwarongo, and 60km west of Grootfontein via the C42. The airport serves charter flights only, so train, bus, or driving are your best transportation options. The **train station** is north of town on the B1. From Main Rd., turn right onto the B1 and take the left fork towards Ondangwa; the station is 500m ahead on the left. **TransNamib Starline** (☎ 067 29 8203) goes to Windhoek (7hr.; M, W, F 10:25am;

N$40) and Walvis Bay (5½hr.; M, W, F 10:25am; N$40). Buses stop at Travel North Namibia, 1551 OMEG Allee. **Intercape Mainliner** has buses to Windhoek (5hr.; W, Su 9:45pm; N$215) and Victoria Falls (15hr.; Tu, Sa; N$310). **Imperial Car Rental** (☎22 0728; fax 22 0916), in Travel North Namibia, offers 2WD and 4WD, including Etosha specials with limited and unlimited mileage. Cars can be delivered and collected anywhere in Southern Africa. **Avis** (☎22 0520), on Jordann Rd., has 4WD with unlimited kilometers for N$698 per day.

■ ▌▌ **ORIENTATION AND PRACTICAL INFORMATION.** The B1, called **Hage Geingob** around here, borders the west and south of the square that is the downtown area. **Main Rd.** runs perpendicular to it as the northern side of the square where most shops and services are located. **OMEG Allee** completes the square in the east, running in the south back into the B1. **Travel North Tourism Services,** 1551 OMEG Allee (☎22 0728; fax 22 0916; travelnn@tsunamib.com) is the one-stop-shop for all travel needs north of Windhoek. The services offered here include information, **car rental, Internet** (N$25 for 30min., N$40 for 1hr.), airline reservations, and tailor-made safaris. (Open M-F 7:30am-6pm, Sa 8am-noon.)

Standard Bank (☎22 0956), **First National Bank** (☎22 1794), and **Bank of Windhoek** (☎22 0823), are all on Main Rd. and have **24hr.** ATMs and bureaux de change (open M-F 9am-12:45pm and 2-3:30pm, Sa 8:30-11am). **Model Supermarket** (☎22 1171) is on Post St. opposite the post office. Other services include: **Tsumeb Dry Cleaners & Laundry,** on Main Rd. (☎22 0139; laundry N$18 per kg); **emergency/police** (☎10 111), on the corner of 6th St. and 8th Rd.; **Tsumeb Apteek,** on Main Rd. (☎22 2455; open M-F 8am-1pm and 2-5pm); the **State Hospital** (☎22 1082), on Hage Geingob, next to the Caltex Service Station; **T.C.L. Hospital** (☎22 1001), on Hospital St., north of the park; **Internet** at the Dot Com Café, on OMEG Allee (☎22 1628; N$10 per 30min.; open M-Th 9am-6pm, F-Sa 9am-10pm, Su 11am-6pm). The **post office,** on Post St. at 5th Rd., offers phones, fax, phonecards, photocopies, and *Poste Restante.* (☎20 0211. Open M-Tu and Th-F 8am-4:30pm, W 8:30am-4:30pm, Sa 8am-noon.)

▌ **ACCOMMODATIONS. Pension Kreuz des Südens** ❷, on 3rd St., is a quiet and inexpensive alternative to a bigger hotel. All three large rooms have bath, safe facilities, and access to a communal TV lounge and secure parking. (☎22 1005. Reception 6am-9pm. Check-out 10am. Breakfast N$20. Singles N$110; doubles N$170.) **Pension OMEG Allee** ❸, on OMEG Allee, one block south of Travel North Tourism, is a comfortable option, slightly out of the town center, with good-sized rooms that have air-conditioning, bath, fridge, and TV. It is also on a tree-lined street in a residential neighborhood with secure parking and self-catering kitchen. (☎22 0631 or 22 0520; fax 22 0821. Breakfast included. Singles N$195; doubles N$285. Credit cards accepted with surcharge.) **Tsumeb Municipality Caravan Park** ❶, on Hage Geingob 1km south of town, is situated around a small pond, completely lined with lush grass. Although it is small with no privacy, it is clean and offers a playground, *braai,* communal ablution facilities, and security. (☎22 1056; fax 22 1464. Showers N$15.31. Tent sites with *braai* N$61.23; N$15.31 per adult and per vehicle; N$7.66 per child under 16.) **Makalani Hotel** ❹, at the corner of 3rd St. and 4th Rd., has a central location and is quietly situated around an inner pool courtyard. Tsumeb's upscale accommodations are tastefully decorated, with rooms including breakfast, TV, telephone, shower and A/C. For relaxation and a meal there is a restaurant and *lapa* with a big-screen TV, bar, and the country's only L-shaped pool table. (☎22 1051; fax 22 1575. Secure parking. Singles N$320; doubles N$450. Credit cards accepted.) **Etosha Café and Biergarden** ❷, on Main St., is a well-kept local favorite. The accommodations are inexpensive and a little drab, decorated in '70s-style decor. Bathrooms are down the hall. (☎22 1207. Secure parking. Reception M-F 7am-5pm, Sa 8am-1pm. N$90 per person.)

NAMIBIA

🗗 **FOOD. Minen Hotel ❸,** at Post and Hospital St., has garden and indoor seating where guests can get inexpensive yet delicious German food. (☎22 1071 or 22 1021. Breakfast buffet N$30 per person. Open 7-9am, 12:30-2pm, and 7-9:30pm. Credit cards accepted.) **Bäckerei Steinbach & Café ❶,** on Main St., serves both traditional German and Italian food and is run by a friendly couple who love travelers. Fresh bread is baked daily. You can enjoy pizza (N$3) made to order or pasta (N$13.50) as you sit at this sidewalk cafe, watching the world go by. (☎22 0135. Open M-F 7am-5:30pm, Sa 8am-2pm.) **Etosha Café & Biergarden ❷,** on Main St., is a local favorite that offers breakfast and light meals in a lush courtyard. (☎22 1207. Cake N$3-8. Toasted sandwiches N$6-15. Open M-F 7am-5pm, Sa 8am-1pm.)

◪ **SIGHTS AND SHOPPING. Tsumeb Museum,** on Main St., one block east of Hospital St., has an extensive collection focused on local mining and culture, in addition to the historical *Schutztruppe* POW camps built in Tsumeb in the early 20th century. Highlights include the Khorab Chamber, which holds artillery found in Otjikoto Lake after the Germans dumped it there to keep it out of British hands; and the colorful rock collection showing local geology. (☎/fax 22 0447. N$9, students N$4, children N$2. Open M-F 9am-noon and 2-5pm, Su 9am-noon.) Tours of the OMEG open cast mine and the surrounding area are available. Tours use 4x4 vehicles and leave the museum every Tuesday and Thursday at 10am. (N$30 per person. Book ahead.) **Tsumeb Arts and Crafts Center,** 18 Main St., was started to help local people become self-sufficient by earning an income from making and selling traditional crafts. A showroom displays wares for sale. (☎/fax 22 0257. Open M-F 8:30am-1pm and 2:30-5:30pm, Sa 8:30am-1pm. Call to arrange other hours.)

GROOTFONTEIN ☎067

Grootfontein (pop. 18,000) is one of the centers of the farming industry in northern Namibia. The open expanses of *bushveld* bordering the town are home to large commercial farms, which keeps the area from becoming too built up. Gateway to Kavango, Bushmanland, Caprivi, and Botswana, this sleepy town received its name from the San and Bergdamara who called it "Gei-ous," meaning big fountain. In the late 19th century, Grootfontein was settled by Dorstland Trekkers and Germans who bestowed the Afrikaans moniker that refers to the same waters. A German fort originally built in 1896 now serves as a museum that chronicles local history. Nearby is the Hoba Meteorite, the largest meteorite in the world.

🚍 **TRANSPORTATION.** Grootfontein is 60km east of Tsumeb and 207km north of Otjiwarongo via the B8. **TransNamib Starline** runs buses from the Spar parking lot on Okavango Rd. to Gam, Bushmanland (7½hr., Th 11:30am, N$73) via Tsumkwe (6½hr., N$65). **Intercape Mainliner** goes from the Shell service station on Okavango Rd. to Windhoek (5½hr., W and Su 9:30pm, N$240) and Victoria Falls (15½hr., Tu and Sa 1:15am, N$600). **Minibuses** to Rundu (N$100) stop at the Total service station on the eastern end of Okavango Rd. Those headed to Windhoek and Tsumeb (N$15) stop at the Caltex service station on the western end of Okavango Rd.

▣🔳 **ORIENTATION AND PRACTICAL INFORMATION.** The B8 runs east-west through town as Okavango Rd., with Sam Nujoma Dr. and Hage Geingob Ave. being the major roads that intersect it. Most shops and services line these three streets. The **Tourist Information Center** and **Meteor Safaris** is on Okavango St., next to the Meteor Hotel. It has fax, telephone, and **Internet** (N$30 per hr.) while booking for Intercape, lodges, national parks, and tailor-made safaris. (☎24 0086; cell 081 124 8208. Open M-Sa 8am-5pm.)

First National Bank, 18 Hage Geingob Ave., has an **ATM** and offers currency exchange. (☎24 2112. Open M-F 9am-12:45pm and 2-3:30pm, Sa 8:30-11am.) **Spar Supermarket** is on Okavango St. (Open M-Sa 7:30am-7pm, Su 9am-1pm and 4-7pm.) Other services include: **Makalani Apteek,** on Dr. Toivo ya Toivo St. (☎24 2728, after hours 24 2289; open M-F 8am-1pm and 2-5pm, Sa 8:30am-1:30pm; MC/V); **Northern Arms and Ammunition** (☎24 3469), on Dr. Toivo ya Toivo St., for camping equipment; **police** (☎10 111), on the corner of Hage Geingob Ave. and Gauss St.; **ambulance** (☎24 2141); **fire** (☎24 3101 or 24 2321); **State Hospital** (☎24 2041) on Moltke St.; **private hospital** (☎24 0064), at the west end of Nickey Iyambo St. The **post office,** on West St., has phones, photocopies, fax, telecards, and *Post Restante.* (☎24 2200. Open M-Tu and Th-F 8am-4:30pm, W 8:30am-4:30pm.)

▮▯ ACCOMMODATIONS AND FOOD. Courtyard Guesthouse ❹, 2 Gauss St., has extremely comfortable doubles with bath, breakfast, cable TV, A/C, and a mini-bar, pool and secure parking. (☎/fax 24 0027; platinum@iway.na. Internet N$35 per hr. Singles N$350; doubles N$500. DC/MC/V.) **Simply the Best ❷,** 6 Weigel St. (☎24 3315), is an excellent option, with self-catering kitchen, secure parking, common TV, and pool. Light and airy rooms are N$150 per person. **Olea Municipal Caravan Park ❶,** at Okavango and Museum Rd., is a shaded, quiet, but also slightly worn-out campsite. Pool, playground, *braai,* and power outlet available. (☎24 3100. 2-week maximum stay for chalets. Check-out 10am. Shower N$6.70, included if staying at Olea. Chalet quads with bath, fridge, hot plate, and kettle N$131.40, not including bedding. Camping site N$27.10; adults N$6.70, ages 6-16 N$5.40; vehicles N$9.80.) For meals, you can go to **Le Club ❷,** on Hidipo Hamutenya St., for pizza (from N$15), meat (N$30-60), pasta, and a game of pool. (Open M-F 6:45am-2:30pm and 5-11pm, Sa 8:30am-2pm and 5:30-11pm, Su noon-2pm and 6-9pm. **Meteor Restaurant ❷,** 33 Okavango Rd., is a good choice for seafood (N$30-70), create-your-own pizza (F 6-10pm; N$45), and a N$45 Sunday buffet. (☎24 2078. Open M-Sa noon-2pm and 6-11pm, Su noon-2pm and 6-10pm. DC/MC/V.)

NORTHEASTERN NAMIBIA With as much as 1m of summer rainfall, Namibia's water-rich northeast is made up of a unique landscape of flood *veld*, swamps, and lush riverine forests. Taller trees and grass grow in the *veld*, and waters attract more abundant game. This region is thickly populated compared to the rest of Namibia, with subsistence farmers growing *mahangu* and other crops, raising cattle, and fishing in the rivers. The far northeast island of Impalila—where the borders of Namibia, Zambia, Zimbabwe, and Botswana meet—is known for its papyrus-lined channels, serene backwaters covered with water lilies, and fertile flood plains inhabited by herds of red lechwe. The lodges, like Impalila Island Lodge, Ichingo Chobe River Lodge, King's Den, and the Zambezi Queen, offer excellent game-viewing opportunities. Unfortunately, the recent political and military situation in Zimbabwe and the Caprivi Strip have brought regular tourist traffic visiting this fascinating area to a halt.

◧ ▨ SIGHTS AND OUTDOORS. The German Fort and Museum (Das Alte Fort), on Eriksson St., has exhibits on local history (including German *Schutztruppe* paraphernalia), and a great photo collection of the Himba of Kaokoveld region. (Call ☎24 2351 for additional hours. Open Tu 4-6pm, W 9-11am, F 4-6pm.)

The largest single meteorite known in the world, **Hoba Meteorite,** was discovered by Johannes Hermanus Brits in 1920. Weighing in at 50 tons and measuring 3m by 1m, it is believed to have fallen to earth up to 80,000 years ago. The site was declared a national monument in 1955 after people started taking pieces home as souvenirs. You can camp around it (N$10 per person, children free), but cold showers and thoughts about when the next meteorite might fall convince most people to stay in town. From Grootfontein, follow the C42 towards Tsumeb for about 4km. Turn left onto the D2859 and continue for 18km. Follow the signs from there. (N$10, children N$1. Open daily 7am-7pm.)

ETOSHA NATIONAL PARK ☎ 067

With an area of 22,912 sq. km, Etosha National Park is one of Africa's premier game reserves. The word "etosha," meaning "Great White Place" in the Ovambo language, describes the pan around which the park is centered. Covering 4590 sq. km, Etosha Pan is actually the bottom of an immense, shallow lake that dried up millions of years ago. Now there is only a desiccated sandy clay expanse that fills very slightly during the wet season, when floodwaters flow south from the Ekumu and Oshigambo Rivers. The greenish hue of the soil in its northern parts is attributed to minerals deposited during floods and to the algae growing in the shallow water. In the southern parts of the pan, water reserves formed during the rainy season filter into its impermeable clay floor, creating permanent springs where thirsty game flock during the dry season. Of course, where there's game, there are tourists. As they circle the cobweb of roads and search for elusive predators, tourists take in some of the best game-viewing in Africa; Etosha's marvels rival even those of the Serengeti and Kruger. The big game, including four of the Big Five, inhabit Etosha's southern edges, where vegetation is comparatively lush. Be aware, however, that during the dry season (Dec.-Feb.), the pan still holds enough water for game, and waterholes often go unvisited.

> Even the most seasoned outdoorsmen may encounter some surprises while camping in Namibia. Due to the lack of light pollution, Namibian nights are very, very dark. Most campsites do not have light markers or, in some cases, lights in the bathroom to navigate you through the night. To avoid stumbling into the toilet, bring flashlights or lanterns and a larger supply of batteries or kerosene than you think you'll need. Namibian nights are also cold due to the country's arid environment. As soon as the sun goes down, the temperature drops. Even if the temperature isn't that low, the change between day and night is enough to make anyone shiver. Long pants, long-sleeved outer layers, and closed-toed shoes are a must. Bring lots of layers, including a hat and gloves, to sleep in.

TRANSPORTATION

To get to **Okaukuejo** on the southwestern side of the park, take the B1 to Otjiwarongo (245km north of Windhoek), and then the C38 190km to Okaukuejo past Andersson Gate. For **Namutoni,** on the park's eastern side, continue on the B1 for 78km past Tsumeb, then turn left onto the C38; it is 32km to Namutoni past Von Lindequist Gate. There is no public transportation in the park, and hitching is prohibited, so it is best to hire a rental car in Tsumeb or Otjiwarongo (see p. 471), or arrange a safari with a budget tour operator in Windhoek (see p. 461).

ORIENTATION AND PRACTICAL INFORMATION

Though the western half of the park is only open to registered tour operators, visitors to Etosha's public eastern half are not missing much; both regions feature the same wildlife. Two gates allow entrance to Etosha: **Andersson Gate** from the southwest and **Von Lindequist Gate** from the east. The three public rest camps within the

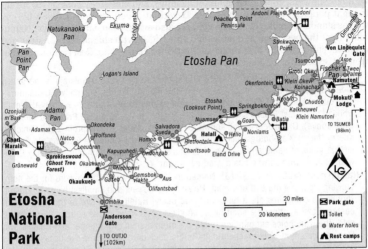

Etosha National Park

(Map labels: Natukanaoka Pan, Ekuma, Qshigambo, Andoni Plain, Andoni, Poacher's Point Peninsula, Stinkwater Point, Von Lindequist Gate, Pan Point Pan, Etosha Pan, Logan's Island, Tsumcor, Aroe, Groot Okev, Fischer's Pan, Tweep, Palms, Namutoni, Okerfontein, Klein Okev, Koinachas, Ngobib, Chudob, Mokuti Lodge, Ozonjuitj m'Bari, Adamx Pan, Etosha (Lookout Point), Springbokfontein, Kalkheuwel, Klein Namutoni, TO TSUMEB (98km), Adamax, Okondeka, Salvadora, Nuamses, Goas, Batia, Chari Marais Dam, Natco, Wolfsnes, Sueda, Halali, Helio, Noniams, Grünewald, Sprokieswoud (Ghost Tree Forest), Leeubran, Kapupuhedi Pan, Homob, Rietfontein, Charitsaub, Eland Drive, Okaukuejo, Ondongab, Nebrowni, Okaukuejo, Gaseb, Gemsbok Vlakte, Aus, Olifantsbad, Ombika, Andersson Gate, TO OUTJO (102km))

Legend: 0 — 20 miles; 0 — 20 kilometers; ⊠ Park gate; 🚻 Toilet; ● Water holes; ▲ Rest camps

park are **Okaukuejo,** 15km north of Andersson Gate; **Namutoni,** 12km west of Von Lindequist Gate; and **Halali,** halfway (75km from each) between Okaukuejo and Namutoni. Etosha's gravel roads (speed limit 60km per hour due to dust) are in surprisingly good condition and accessible by 2WD. Gates open on a celestial schedule with the sunrise. Gates close at sunset, before which day visitors must exit the park and overnight visitors must return to their campsites. Allow yourself plenty of return time before dark, or else you'll incur fines and other penalties.

Visitors must pay a daily **entrance fee** (N$30, ages 6-16 N$2) and a one-time vehicle fee (N$10). Day visitors may use all facilities except rooms, bungalows, and campsites. **Maps** of Etosha (N$8.85) are sold at bookstores in major towns and at the rest camps.

No game drives are offered by the NWR, so if you would rather photograph than read a map or drive, contact one of the upscale lodges just outside Von Lindequist or Andersson Gate. Rest camp receptions can provide a short list of options. Remember to keep *all* accommodations receipts and entrance permits, as you need them to exit the park. If you lose them, you may have to pay again. Nights without receipts and unaccounted for in the park's computer system are sometimes assumed to have been spent outside a rest camp and can lead to penalties and/or fines. The **Etosha Park Post Office,** at Okaukuejo, offers *Poste Restante* services. (Open M-F 8am-noon and 1-4:30pm, Sa 8:30am-noon; stamps also available at the Namutoni reception.)

🏠🍴 ACCOMMODATIONS AND FOOD

Each of Etosha's rest camps has its own character and waterhole. Those who have several days can spend time at each camp and its waterhole. Only the three public camps provide nighttime viewing. Navigate the 75km between camps at a leisurely pace, stopping to visit the groups of animals gathered about each waterhole. Each camp is equipped with a petrol station, pool, *braai*, ablution blocks, a restaurant/bar, and a provision store. Campsites at Okaukuejo and Halali also have field kitchens. The reception and petrol station at each camp is open from sunrise to sunset, and all restaurants serve enormous all-you-can-eat buffets. (Breakfast N$45, 7-8:30am. Lunch N$60, noon-1:30pm. Dinner N$80, 6-8:30pm.) **Campsites ❷** with hot showers, communal ablution facilities, and electricity cost N$160 for up to eight people. Two-bedroom **chalets** ❹ with attached kitchens (N$380-420) as well as standard **doubles** ❹ (N$255-295) are also available at each campsite. Namutoni offers the best deal on doubles ❸ (only N$220 with shared bath). Ask at rest camp reception for the best rooms and rates for your group. Reservations recommended, especially for June-August.

Okaukuejo (☎22 9800; fax 22 9852). First opened in 1955, Okaukuejo is the park's oldest camp and its administrative center. The main buildings, originally a German military outpost built in 1901, house the **Ecological Institute**, a non-governmental agency working to protect Etosha's game, and the Etosha **post office** (see **Practical Information**, above). Okaukuejo is well known for its tower, added to the fort in 1963, which is one of the park's photographic icons. Okaukuejo and its flood-lit waterhole draw the largest influx of game and visitors of Etosha's three camps. Its name, originally Okakwiju, means "woman who has a child every year" or "prolific woman."

Halali (☎22 9400; fax 22 9413). Named in 1967 after the German word for the horn-blowing signaling the end of a hunt, Halali is the newest and smallest camp in Etosha. Though its campsites are a bit barren and dusty, Halali is the site of the only hills in eastern Etosha, offering a short hike that gives good views of the surrounding *mopane veld*. The waterholes surrounding Halali are often teeming with game, and Halali's own Moringa waterhole gets excellent night traffic, including rhinos and the occasional lion or leopard. However, Halali draws fewer tourists than do Okaukuejo or Namutoni. Halali is also the best place to swim, as its crystal clear natural swimming pool lacks the hazardous chemicals found in the other two camps' pools.

Namutoni (☎22 9300; fax 22 9306). Originally called *Omutjamatinda* in Herero to describe "the strong water coming from a raised place," Namutoni features a natural spring. Originally built in 1902-03 as a German military outpost, the white-washed **fort** was destroyed by Ovambo the day after 7 Germans defended the fort by day before retreating under the cover of night. Rebuilt in 1906, it was declared a national monument in 1950 and today houses a **museum** featuring *Schutztruppe* paraphenalia. It was opened to tourists in 1957. The view from the top of the **watchtower** (open sunrise-sunset) is superb. If you book well in advance, you may be able to stay in a room inside the fort (small double N$140), adding a pioneer charm to your visit. The waterholes around Namutoni are frequented by eland, giraffe, and blue wildebeest, but Namutoni's own waterhole draws little game. The camp's provision shop is the best of the three.

🦏 GAME VIEWING

Etosha is home to an amazing animal kingdom; 114 mammal, 50 snake, and 340 bird species live within the park's boundaries. Several of these species qualify as "endangered" or "threatened," so try not to run over anything. In fact, the **black-faced impala** is unique to Etosha. Four of the big five—lion, elephant, leopard, and rhino—roam within the park. Among the kaleidoscope of other creatures that will grab your attention are **giraffe, springbok, gemsbok, zebra, blue wildebeest, red hartebeest, eland, kudu, black rhino, roan antelope, ostrich,** and **cheetah.** Of course, catching a glimpse of the great predators isn't always a walk in the park. The general scarcity and nocturnal hunting patterns of the elusive **leopards** make sightings rare. Halali and Okaukuejo are the most promising waterholes for spotting that feline. **Lions** are most visible in the morning, stalking large groups of more common mammals. You may spot them in the long grass at the edge of a field, across the road from the group, or lazing by the waterholes in the afternoon. While their kills are rarely seen, **cheetahs** can sometimes be spotted crossing roads or lying low in long grass near larger groups of animals. Though the idle grazing of **gemsbok, zebra,** and **springbok** may seem slow and unspectacular, these herbivores actually put on quite a show, usually visible on the Pan.

Learning when, where, and how to spot game is difficult, but *Let's Go* will now provide you with the 30-second summary on how to become an expert. Animals are most active in the morning and early evening, making the four to five hours after dawn and two to three hours before sunset the best times for game drives. Nights are key viewing periods for leopard, elephant, and rhino. Since rest camp waterholes are the only ones to allow night viewing, tourists often gather at them around sunset and don't disperse until after sunrise. If you want to pull a game-watching all-nighter, bring a blanket; Pan nights can be freezing.

Waterholes differ in spring type and amount of water, and the game therefore varies. Rest camps abound with stories of the day's sightings. Start some conversations to get the best tips on where to go the next day. Each reception office has a register book of recent sightings, notable or otherwise, which can be useful in route-planning. Ask the receptionist for tips, as most of them have spent long nights by the waterholes. Oftentimes, simply driving the roads and checking the bushes along them can produce many sightings; most animals spend the day moving from waterhole to waterhole. Just remember to *always stay in the vehicle*, unless you want to be eaten.

One of the best places to look for game is in the divisions between trees, bushes, and grass. Animals congregate here because of shade and food, and predators are drawn to such areas for cover as they stalk large groups in the fields. Anthropology enthusiasts should be sure to spend some time at waterholes watching how opposite sexes and different species interact for some great insight into group dynamics and individual signalling.

Besides the predators, giraffes and elephants can be the most elusive attractions. Thanks to their height, **giraffes** notice vehicles very early and have plenty of time to disappear among the trees. To spot a giraffe, look above the short trees and bushes; quietly drive closer once you spot one. **Elephants** frequent the rest camp waterholes by night but blend into the brush during the day. Pay attention to areas beside the road for, literally, a wall of grey.

Finally, if you're not into endless driving, hang out at the **Kalkheuwel waterhole.** It may be the best spot for waterhole photography.

NEAR ETOSHA

OUTJO

For those who miss making it to Okaukuejo before sunset, staying overnight in Outjo (about 120km to the south on C38) is an inexpensive alternate plan. ◙**Outjo Backpackers ❶,** 74 Hage G. Geingob St., is an excellent option. (☎31 3470. Dorms N$60. Camping N$25.) Both come with bath and a self-catering kitchen including dish ware, cookery, and hot plates. About 2km north toward Etosha is **Buschfeld Park ❶,** which provides nicer accommodations for those looking to live it up before entering Etosha. Bungalows include 2 or 4 beds, fridge, *braai*, pool, and restaurant/bar. Camping, on small but quiet and shady sites, includes pool, *braai*, and communal ablution blocks. (☎31 3665; fax 31 3072. Check-in 24hr.; not open in Jan. Bungalows N$195 per person. Camping N$35.) For a meal, try the **Aloe Steakhouse ❷,** at Hage Geingob and Herold St., opposite the Total station. Self-caterers will be pleased with the **OK Grocer,** on Sam Nujoma Dr. (Open M-F 7:30am-6:30pm, Sa 7:30am-1:30pm, Su 8:30am-1pm and 4-7pm.) The **tourist office** is at 8 Hage Geingob Ave. (☎/fax 313 072). **Standard Bank,** one block down from Outjo Backpackers on Geingob St., has a 24hr. **ATM** and *bureau de change.* **Internet access,** inside the excellent **Outjo Backerei,** is N$20 for 30min., N$35 for 1hr. Be sure to try the vanilla-creme-filled elephant ears. (Open daily 6am-5pm.)

THE NORTH

Northern Namibia is prime farmland where thick trees, instead of *bushveld*, create a lush, green environment. Receiving more rain than any other region and almost completely bordered by rivers, the North is primarily comprised of Ovamboland's four regions: Omusati, Oshana, Oshikoto, and Okavango. Since many Ovambo are subsistence cattle farmers, this region boasts Namibia's highest population density. There are few large cities or towns, as most Ovambo live in small villages along the rivers and still follow traditional ways.

Due to its proximity to Angola, the north's two largest cities were used as bases for the SADF (South African Defence Force) and their buildings still bear the scars of numerous bombings. A trip to the now non-existent Ruacana Falls (a hydroelectric dam has stopped the water flow) and to smaller villages off the B1/C46 is one way to see the beauty behind the industry.

ONDANGWA   ☎ 065

Like its larger neighbor city Oshakati, Ondangwa revolves around commerce. Even the open market where Ovambo women sell their baskets is geared toward large-scale buyers rather than individuals. Although Oshakati is the region's capital, Ondangwa is a much nicer and safer place to visit for a respite from rural Ovamboland. One highlight is Olukonda National Monument and Nakambale Museum, an excellent place to see traditional Ovambo culture and spend the night in a traditional Ndonga homestead.

⬛ TRANSPORTATION. Ondangwa is 271km north-west of Tsumeb on the B1, and 33km east of Oshakati on the C46. The B1 turns north just west of Ondangwa, leading 60km to the Oshikango Angolan border crossing. The **Air Namibia** office is in the game shopping center on Okatana St. in Oshakati, but flights leave from the Ondangwa airport 5.5km west of the Main Rd. and Post Office St. intersection. Air Namibia flies to Windhoek Eros (2½hr; M-Tu 8:20am, W-Su 9:20am; 1½hr., Su-F 5pm, N$803). **Minibuses** leave when full for Oshakati, Otjiwarongo, and Windhoek from the open market on the southwest corner of the Main Rd. and Ya Tovo St. intersections. Inquire with drivers for prices. Car rental is available through **Santorini Car Hire**, in Oshakati. (☎ 22 1803; info@santorini-inn.com.)

⬛⬛ ORIENTATION AND PRACTICAL INFORMATION. Although most services and shops line Main Rd. (the B1 as it runs east-west through Ondangwa), the center of Ondangwa is the intersection of Main Rd. and Post Office St., where the **First City Center shopping mall** is located. East of this intersection are small neighborhoods (the biggest of which is Oniipa), which have own names. **First National Bank** and **Bank of Windhoek** (☎ 24 2800), both in the First City Center shopping mall, and **Standard Bank,** on Post Office St. in the Old Mutual building, all have 24hr. **ATMs** and *bureaux de change.* (Open M-F 9am-3:30pm, Sa 8:30-11am.) Self-caterers can choose between the **Bela Vista Supermarket,** in the First City Center shopping mall, and **OK Grocer,** on Main Rd. (Open daily 7am-7pm.)

Services include: **Emergency/Police** (☎ 10 111); **Oshana Pharmacy and Optics,** on Post Office St., one block north of Main Rd. (☎ 24 0144 or 081 129 6928; open M-F 8am-5pm, Sa 8:30am-1pm); **Onandjokwe Lutheran Hospital** (emergency and ambulance ☎ 24 0111), 5km north of Main Rd. on the D3622 in Oniipa; **telephones,** at the intersection of Main Rd. and Post Office St.; **Internet access** at Cresta Lodge, at the intersection of Main Rd. and C46 (N$1 per min.; open 24hr.); the **post office,** Nampost (☎ 24 0015), at the northern end of Post Office St., offering fax, photocopies, and public **phones.**

⌐⌐ ACCOMMODATIONS AND FOOD. Nakambal Museum Rest Camp ❶ can be reached by taking Main Rd. east from Post Office St. and turning right at the D3629 to Olukonda; the museum is 5km ahead on the left. Combined with the Finnish mission museum and the Ndonga Homestead, the restcamp offers accommodations (including camping) in a traditional Ndonga hut or the missionary cottage. This is the best chance to experience a traditional feel without needing a 4WD. (☎24 5668; fax 24 0472; olukonda.museum@elein.org.na. *Braai* and communal ablution facilities on site. Book in advance. Traditional Owambo lunch/ dinner N$40 per person. Camping N$35 per site plus N$12 per person over 14; traditional hut N$70 per person with bedding and breakfast, N$40 per person without; 4-person Missionary cottage N$80 per person with breakfast, N$65 without.)

Ondangwa Rest Camp ❶, on Post Office St., is one block north of Main Rd. Situated in what must have once been a beautiful pond area, Ondangwa is now less attractive but the only camping option that offers a central location, restaurant, and bar. Day visitors are welcome. (☎24 0354. Day visitors N$10, under 12 N$5. Restaurant open M-F 7:30am-5:45pm and 7-9:45pm, Sa 8am-1:45pm and 7-9:45pm; breakfast N$20.50. Camping N$35 per person. Pre-constructed tents with beds single/double N$90/N$120.) **Elcin Guest House ❶**, on the D3622, 5km north of Main Rd. in Oniipa, is set inside a Lutheran church, offering excellent chances to get an up-close glimpse of Ovambo culture. Dorms are sparse and a bit dark, but mosquito nets are provided. (☎24 8189. Restaurant and reception open M-F 8am-6pm, Sa 7am-6pm, Su noon-6pm. Dorms N$60-90.)

Cresta Lodge Pandu Ondangwa ❺, at the intersection of the B1 and the C6, is the twinkle in Ondangwa's eye, featuring tasteful and traditional art and architecture and rooms with shower, telephone, and cable TV. (☎/fax 24 1900. Breakfast included. Fax, Internet, and laundry. Reservations recommended. Check-out 10am. Singles N$430; doubles N$580; family N$1000. Inquire for great weekend specials. AmEx/DC/MC/V.) **Chatters Restaurant ❸**, the lodge's restaurant, has a chef who should be commended for his unusual and delightful creations. Try the Fillet à la Greque (filet filled with feta; N$56), the Minted Yogurt Chicken (N$43), and Cappucino Mousse (N$16) for dessert. (Open 12:30-2:30pm and 6:30-10:30pm.)

◪ SIGHTS. Olukonda National Monument and Nakambale Museum is a monument and museum on the site of the first Finnish Mission Station in Ovamboland, home of Rev. Martti Rautenen (Nakambale) from 1880 until his death in 1924. The museum, along with the original mission house, shows visitors the cultures of northern Namibia and the history of Ovamboland. Perhaps most interesting is the traditional Ndonga homestead, where you can try traditional Ovambo food and accommodations. Take Main Rd. east from Post Office St., and turn right onto the D3629 to Olukonda. The museum is 5km ahead on the left. (☎24 5668; fax 24 0472; olukona.museum@elcin.org.na. Open M-F 8am-1pm and 2-5pm, Sa 8am-1pm, Su noon-5pm. N$5, guided tours N$10; book in advance. Ndonga tour N$10 per person.)

THE NORTH-WEST

Consisting of Damaraland and the Kaokoveld, North-West Namibia is a vast and beautifully desolate land which is home of some of Namibia's most distinct ethnic groups. Damara, Herero, Himba, Dhimba, and Nama have adapted to the extremely harsh and arid conditions that minimize tourism. Here traditional villages are interspersed among the few emerging towns. Moving east from the coast or west from the B1, roads to the cities are well-maintained but not tarred, becoming 4WD tracks into the bush. The scenery and culture are well-preserved, once-in-a-lifetime sights.

N A M I B I A

The most obvious differences between Damaraland and the Kaokoveld are manifested in their culture and language. Traditional languages abound throughout the North-West; both Bantu and Khoisan dialects are prominent. The Damara's language, along with the languages of the Nama and San, make up the Khoisan dialects, informally referred to as "click languages." In the Kaokoveld, the traditional Herero and Himba language is a Bantu dialect called Oshiherero, and the Dhimba dialect is Orudhimba. Almost all inhabitants speak both. English is now the school language, but Afrikaans is known, though spoken infrequently. Oshiwambo, the bantu dialect of the Ovambo people from Ovamboland, is also prevalent due to social and industrial movement between the two regions.

 CRIME. With an unemployment rate between 30 and 40%, some Namibians have turned to crime to survive, whether it be mugging or breaking into houses or vehicles. Crime rates have risen partly due to the lack of educational opportunities; Many educational programs are open by selection only and are expensive. To remedy the crime problem, larger towns and cities have brought in security services who install alarm systems and provide 24hr. emergency response. Both people and statistics report success, showing that such prevention has caused crime to drop drastically. There are still some personal precautions, however, that you can take to stay safe while you travel. Be aware of people's hands and of any unnecessarily close approaches. One criminal technique is shoving newspapers for sale into your face as they reach for your wallet. Leave backpacks, large cameras, and large amounts of money somewhere safe (i.e. not on you). Backpacks send up the "I am a tourist" flare, which can be spotted by anyone looking for mugging prey. If you must where a backpack, carry it on your front, rather than on your back. Put small amounts of money into several pockets and invest in a camera that's small enough to fit in a front pocket. Save your large camera for shots that are worth the possibility of theft.

OPUWO   ☎ 065

Opuwo, the capital of the Kaokoveld, is commercial and dusty, but nevertheless offers a fascinating lesson in Namibian ethnicity. Himbas and Hereros, from both the bush and Opuwo, go about their daily business in traditional dress. An eclectic mix results when Himba women, painted in rusty ochre and butter and wearing only elaborate head-dresses and game-skin skirts, walk among Hereros, who wear huge, full-length dresses and accompanying headwear made from vibrant fabrics in every pattern imaginable. Many walk in from neighboring villages, while others have transplanted themselves here from the bush, drawn by the lore of the "big city" and tourists' money. Tourism is nowhere near the level it is elsewhere in the country, but problems are developing as people abandon their village and traditional community for Opuwo, where tourists pay to take photos of them. If you do decide to take a photo, you should pay as a way of showing respect and should be very clear about explaining that the money is for a photo and not just a donation.

■ ⊓ **ORIENTATION AND PRACTICAL INFORMATION.** While there is no public transportation to Opuwo, the best towns to rent cars to get here are Otjiwarongo and Oshakati. The main road, **Mbumbuazo Muharuku Ave.,** runs perpendicular to the C41, the main road into town from the south, as it follows the bottom of the hill on which Opuwo sits. The intersection of **Marthi Athisari St.** and Muharuku Ave., one block east of the C41, is the commercial center. **Kaoko Info Center,** at the intersection of Muharuku Ave. and the C41, next to the Oreness Restaurant, offers guided tours of Himba and Herero villages. They also have information about the Kaokoveld. (☎27 3420. Tours N$80 per person for one village, N$90 for 2. Open M-Su 8am-5pm.) There are no banks or ATMs in Opuwo. Supermarkets include **Power Save,** on Marthi Athisari St., one block from Muharuku Ave. (open M-Sa 8am-8pm, Su noon-8pm); and **Agra,** at the BP service station on the C41 (open M-F 8am-5pm, Sa 8am-noon). Services include: **police** (☎27 3041); an **ambulance** at the clinic (☎27 3026); **post office** (☎27 3013). For **public phones,** turn left on Athisari St., take the first right, and they are one block ahead on the left. (Open M-Tu, Th-F 8am-4:30pm, W 8:30am-4:30pm, Sa 8am-noon.)

⌂ ACCOMMODATIONS. At the center of town, **Okahane Lodge ❹,** on Marthi Athisari St., is a large, comfortable hotel, although its gates separate guests from the tradition-filled streets. Amenities include swimming pool, restaurant (dinner N$75), and bar/coffee shop. (☎27 3031. Breakfast included. Singles N$350; doubles N$500. Credit cards accepted.) To get to **Oreness Campsite ❶,** the only campsite in town, turn right opposite the Shell Service and drive 300m. It is small but extremely clean and protected from the wind featuring grassy sites, communal ablution blocks with only cold showers, and *braai.* Ask Bernard, the security guard, for advice on what to do in town. (N$35 per person.) Set a little out of the city, the **Uniting Guest House ❷** is a good option for inexpensive accommodations. With large but sparse rooms, this converted house brings you out of the commercial area. Take the second left after Marthi Athisari St., at the Uniting Guest House sign, and follow the road around the slight bend for 600m; the house has a small sign in front on the left. (☎27 3400. N$100 per person, with private bath N$120.) For a traditional feel, **Ovahimba Village and Camping of Kaokoveld ❶** is a good option. Located in a valley outside town, the camping is small but protected from the wind, with *braai,* communal ablution blocks, and a bar. Guided tours to a nearby Himba village are also available. From C41 take Muharuku Ave. left, past the road to Sesfontein, for 3km; the camp is on the left at the sign. (Sites N$30 per person.)

⚏ FOOD. For breakfast or an excellent traditional lunch go to the **Kunene Craft Café ❷,** nestled within the Kunene Craft Center. While you watch Herero women make traditional crafts, you can have toasted sandwiches (N$10), pasta (N$25), or Mahangu pancakes made with local Magangu flour (N$15). The Ondundukaze tea (a Himba herbal speciality, N$4) is recommended. For a traditional Herero meal of porridge and meat goulash (N$25), order in advance. From the C41, cross Muharuku Ave., and go up a small hill; the Craft Center is at the top on the hill on the right. (☎27 3209. Open M-F 8am-5pm, Sa 9am-1pm.) Heartier meals and dinner are served at the **Oreness Restaurant ❸,** on the corner of the C41 and Muharuku Ave. Decorated in over 400 pieces of Himba creation, the restaurant offers seafood (N$50), omelettes (N$15-40), and rice and meat meals (N$50-70). The traditional Himba tea is a must. (Open daily 8:30am-10pm. Cash only.) Fresh bread, cold drinks, and baked goods can be found at the **Bakery,** on the corner of Vita Thom St. and Muharuku Ave.

◨⌂ SIGHTS AND SHOPPING. Kunene Craft Center and Café, across Muharuku Ave. from the C41, up the hill and to the right, hires Himba and Herero women in the community to make traditional crafts in the workshop and then sells them on consignment. Opened in January 2002, the center holds workshops for local artists and puts the resulting work on display. It also has a showroom for art on sale. The cafe provides excellent tea and light meals (see **Food,** above) in a pleasant setting. (☎27 3209. Open M-F 8am-5pm, Sa 9am-1pm.) Several groups in the area offer tours of Himba and Herero villages: **Kaoko Info Center** (see **Practical Information,** above); **Okahane Lodge** (N$200 per person, 3hr., min. 4 people; book in

N A M I B I A

advance); and **Ovahimba Village and Camping of Kaokoveld** (see **Accommodations, above**). The **Curio Shop**, on Muharuku Ave., half a block from Okahane Lodge, buys traditional Himba and Herero crafts on consignment and provides a showroom. (Open M-F 8am-4pm.)

DAMARALAND

Traditionally home to the Damara, an ancient cultural group of Bantu origin that speaks a Khoisan dialect, Damaraland is famous for its hauntingly desolate and mysteriously beautiful desert wilderness. Some of Namibia's tallest mountains cast their imposing shadows here over greenish-yellow flatlands dotted with small villages and farmsteads. Dry riverbeds, lush with vegetation and greenery, streak through desolate deserts, while lone black and white rhino and great herds of desert elephants roam the barren expanse.

Despite Damaraland's emptiness, it contains a number of the country's most interesting attractions. Easily within a day's drive from the coast and even closer to Usakos is Spitzkoppe. Rising suddenly form the terrain, this peak is a climber's and hiker's delight. Central Damaraland is home to the Brandberg massif and the Konigstein, Namibia's highest peak at 2573m. Shorter hikes at Brandberg take you to the White Lady, one of Africa's most famous rock paintings. At Twyfelfontein, a 2hr. drive north of Khorixas, are numerous preserved Bushman rock engravings and paintings. You'll also find mineralogical marvels, such as Burnt Mountain and the Organ Pipes, formed by volcanic actions thousands of years ago.

KHORIXAS ☎ 067

The fact that this tiny town is Damaraland's administrative capital shows how truly deserted this area is. With only a few thousand residents, a couple of restaurants, and one petrol station, most view Khorixas as a place to a stop for petrol and provisions. It fits this role well, providing a good base for Damaraland trips. There is, however, more to Khorixas than gas and groceries: with frequent traditional music and dances, discos packed with locals on the weekends, and surrounding hills offering pleasant afternoon hiking opportunities, Khorixas is also a good place to relax and experience the culture of rural Namibia.

◪◪ **TRANSPORTATION AND PRACTICAL INFORMATION.** The C39 is the main road through town. Simson Tjongarero St. runs parallel to the C39 and is connected to it by Gottfried A. Uiseb St. **Trans-Namib's Starline** runs buses to: **Otjiwarongo** (3½hr., F 9pm, N$30) and **Walvis Bay** (6½hr., Th 12:30pm, N$50). **Minibuses** run to: **Otjiwarongo** (N$30); **Outjo** (N$20); **Petrified Forest** (N$20). Both Starline and minibuses stop at the Total station on the C39. Most shops and services line these three streets. **Standard Bank** (☎33 1184), with 24hr. **ATM**, is on Tjongarero St. (open M-F 9am-12:45pm). The grocery store is **Mini Market General Dealer,** on the corner of C39 and Simson I. Gobs St. (open daily 8:15am-7:15pm). The **post office** (☎33 1011), which has *Poste Restante* and **pay phones,** is on Tjongarero St., a block from the bank. In case of emergency, call the **police** (☎10 111), on Tjongarero St., past the post office, or the **state health clinic** and **ambulance** (☎33 1064), on the C39.

◪◪ **ACCOMMODATIONS AND FOOD.** 3km west of town off the C39, **Khorixas Lodge Restcamp and Restaurant** ❶ offers a tranquil base from which to explore nearby sights. Campsites come with ablution blocks and *braai*; bungalows have a private bath and phones. Both have access to a pool, TV lounge, and laundry facilities. (☎33 1111; fax 33 1388. Bungalow singles N$295; doubles N$500. Camping

SAFARI SURVIVAL SKILLS. When traveling in Damaraland and the Kaokoveld, it is important to remember that only a few towns have gas stations and adequately stocked provision shops. Besides strategically planning one's itinerary so that necessary stops are made at the towns for refueling and provisioning, it is imperative that you carry extra fuel tanks, spare tires, plenty of water, and the necessary repair equipment for a vehicle breakdown. Tourists and Namibians alike get killed on these treacherous roads, and vehicles flip with remarkable ease. Drive slowly (50km per hr. at most), try not to travel alone, and never travel at night except in emergencies. When Namibians part by saying "Drive safely," they're not just being polite. In most of the Kaokoveld, it is advisable to travel in convoys of two or more 4WD vehicles in case of breakdown. Most of the gravel roads in Damaraland are accessible by 2WD in the dry season, but become treacherous to navigate even with 4WD in the rainy season (Jan.-Apr.).

N$35 per person. Day visitors N$5. Restaurant open daily 7-9am, noon-2pm, and 6-9pm. Steaks N$38-45. AmEx/DC/MC/V and traveler's checks accepted.) The **church** ❶ (☎ 33 1051 or 081 256 2720) in the center of Khorixas has 32 dorm beds that are technically intended for church affiliates. However, they usually will let backpackers stay for N$50 a night. To get there, follow the C39 west out of town to the high school, turn left onto Amathila St., drive for 500m, and take the third left. The dorm is in the middle of the church and school complex, so expect lots of interaction with the locals, especially children. Very cold showers and secure parking are available. For meals on the run, try the take-out counter at the **Total** petrol station (open daily 7am-9pm) or **Mirabelle's Bar & Restaurant** on the C39, one block from the Total station (open when the front doors are open).

🔁 DAYTRIPS FROM KHORIXAS

All of the following sights are within a 1½hr. drive from Khorixas and can be easily covered in a daytrip. Use Khorixas as your base or spend the night at the Aba-Huab Camp in Twyfelfontein (see p. 489).

VINGERKLIP. Precariously perched 35m above a red sandstone hill, Vingerklip (finger rock) is a stark contrast to the surrounding tabletop mountains and low-lying plains. This popular and peculiar rock formation was formed by the erosion of the Ugab River plateau more than 15 million years ago. Though the rock itself only takes a few minutes to admire, you could spend all day hiking the nearby plateaus. Rock climbers with their own gear can climb to the top of Vingerklip and other nearby natural monuments. The upscale Vingerklip Lodge, which has a wonderful view of the rock itself, can arrange hiking tours (4hr., N$345 per group) and has self-guided hiking trails. Those looking for a bite to eat will have to pay N$80.50 for lunch and N$108.10 for dinner, though the lodge offers complimentary tea and coffee to all visitors. *(From Khorixas, take the C39 east for 55km, turn right onto the D2743, and continue for 18km. From Outjo, take the C39 west for 78km, and turn left onto the D2743. ☎067 29 0318; fax 29 0319. No camping allowed. Restaurant open daily 8am-9pm.)*

TWYFELFONTEIN. One of the richest collections of prehistoric rock engravings in Africa (dating back to 4000-2000 B.C.), Twyfelfontein ("doubtful spring") is a vast open-air museum where ancient Bushmen released their creative energies by producing lively depictions of animals, footprints, and ceremonial scenes on rusty sandstone slabs. The over 2000 individual engravings decorating the surfaces of this rocky mountain slope were first seen by Europeans in 1947. According to one theory, these engravings were used to help children learn about wildlife by match-

NAMIBIA

THE BIG SPLURGE

VINGERKLIP LODGE

Nestled deep within the Ugab River valley, the Vingerklip Lodge is noticeably different from other Namibian Lodges. From a distance the lodge practically disappears into the neighboring table mountain and the surrounding *bushveld*. The Lodge plays off the best features of the valley, nicknamed the "Arizona of Namibia." Its bungalows span the saddle between two table mountains. This gives them privacy and stunning views of nearby Finger Mountain. The sounds of nature—animals at the lodge's personal waterhole and water tinkling in the two swimming pools—relax those who have spent the day hiking the mountains and river valley floor.

For a late afternoon treat, have a seat in the 360° open-air lookout, enjoy a drink from the fully-stocked bar, and watch shadows chase each other along the canyon walls as the sun sets, bringing out the stunning colors of the local geology. After dark, dine in an open-air restaurant which specializes in game and is replete with animal prints. There are also fireplaces where you can warm you feet during a nightcap.

Bungalows, doubles, and family suites, with bath, await weary travelers looking for all the luxurious comforts of home. (☎067 29 0318; fax 067 29 0319; www.vingerklip.com.na. Breakfast and dinner included. Single N$747.50; double N$626.75 per person. Children 4-14 yrs. N$290.95; children under 4 free.)

ing footprints to the appropriate animal. Etosha Stone, the largest slab at the site, portrays all the hoofed animals which can be spotted today in Etosha National Park. The area is named after a nearby spring, which has an inconsistent water supply. For local camping, contact the **Aba-Huab Camp ❶**, 2km towards Twyfelfontein from the D2612-D3254 intersections. Aba means "to carry a baby on one's back" in Damara, and this endearing term was used to name the Aba-Huab, the nearby tributary of the Huab. The camp boasts a great hot outdoor shower sheltered by a large mopane tree and enclosed by a thatched wall where water taps grow out of the tree's trunk. Campsites come with restaurant, bar, self-catering kitchen, braai, laundry, and toilets. (*To get to Twyfelfontein from Khorixas, follow the C39 west for 69km, then turn left/south onto the D2612. Continue on the D2612 for 16km and turn right onto the D3254. After 8km, bear right at the fork in the road; the site is 5km further on. The road can be treacherous in the winter months; call Aba-Huab for updates. Aba-Huab camp: ☎33 1104; fax 33 1749. Reception 24hr. Camping or outdoor thatched A-frame shelters N$35 per person, with tent and blanket N$60 for two; vehicles N$10. Free picnic facilities for day visitors. Twyfelfontein entrance: N$5 per person, N$5 per vehicle. Hikes to rock paintings and engravings must be accompanied by a guide: N$30 per hr., N$20 for 30min. Twyfelfontein open daily Sept.-Apr. 8am-6pm, May-Aug. 7am-5pm.*)

BURNT MOUNTAIN AND ORGAN PIPES. These two natural fascinations, just 1km apart, showcase Namibia's geological diversity. A charred, cinderlike mass of dark maroon, black, and charcoal rock created over the course of 100 million years, Burnt Mountain stands in stark contrast to the low-lying mountains surrounding it. The Organ Pipes are dolomite slabs, standing 2m high on average. They split along fault lines to create long, thin pipes of rock nestled tightly together. Eventually, the pipes begin to break away from each other, forming a sort of rock-flower, and then crumble completely. (*From Khorixas: west on the C39 for 69km, then left onto the D2612; after 16km turn right onto the D3254. 8km later bear right at the fork; the site is 5km farther on. The Organ Pipes are 1km before Burnt Mountain off the D3254 on the left; look for small "Orralpype" signs. The Pipes are in a small gorge as you look down from the turnoff.*)

PETRIFIED FOREST. Declared a national monument in the 1950s, the Petrified Forest is home to the remnants of at least 50 trees that turned to stone after being buried by high-pressure sediment 250 to 300 million years ago. The trees, the longest of which measures 35m, are so well preserved that it would be hard to believe they are actually fossilized if it weren't for the salt and quartz crystals found in some tree trunks. You can't visit the forest without a guide. Beware of prices, however, as the guides often demand outrageous sums. Try to agree on a fee before leaving. *(From Khorixas, follow the C39 west for 45km; turn right at the sign reading "Versteende Woud." Open 8am-dusk. Guided tours: N$20 for the Ministry of Tourism, then another N$20 for the guides plus tips.)*

UIS
☎ 064

A tiny former mining village 120km south of Khorixas, Uis is a welcome relief from the Damaraland's rigorous sojourns. Most people stock up here before heading to Henties Bay (128km southwest on the C35) or the Brandberg massif. Uis is also a great place to spend the night before a long day of hiking or driving in southern Damaraland.

⁊ PRACTICAL INFORMATION. There is no scheduled **public transportation** to this lonely outpost. Minibuses may stop en route between Henties Bay and Khorixas, but don't count on it. All shops and services are on or just off Uis St., the road that leads into town from the C36. **Brandberg Supermarket** (open M-F 7:30am-5pm, Sa 7am-5pm, Su 8am-5pm; MC/V) and **1 Stop Super Shop** (open daily 7:30am-5:30pm) are opposite each other on Uis St. and serve as the commercial center. A **health clinic** (☎50 4011) and **police station** (☎10 111) are also on Uis St. There is only one petrol station, next to the Brandberg Supermarket. **Brandberg Rest Camp** and 1 Stop Super Shop offer **Internet access.** The **post office,** next to the petrol station, has pay phones and *Poste Restante* services. (Open M-F 9-11:30am and 1:30-3:30pm.) For a local guide to Brandberg massif or mineral deposits, contact Monti Van Der Smit (☎50 4096; monty@iway.na; www.montina.com.na).

⁊ ACCOMMODATIONS AND CAMPING. ◙Ugab Wilderness Camp ❶, forty miles away from Uis, lies at the at the foot of the Brandberg. To get there, drive fifteen kilometers north of Uis on the C35 and make a left onto D2359. After 18km, follow signs to the right; the camp is 10km farther. Ugab gives new meaning to those midnight rustling sounds; here they are as likely to be caused by elephants as by the wind. Nestled on the lush bank of the Ugab river and hidden beneath the shelter of willowy acacia trees, the camp is an excellent spot from which to explore the mountain range, either by hiking or by sitting and admiring its fiery red glow at sunset. Campsites are private and spacious, with *braai* and communal open-air flush toilets and hot showers. Herds of elephants commonly walk by the camp, but in case you miss them, Ugab offers a game drive. (☎50 4110. Reservations not necessary, but can be made with the Tsiseb Conservancy Office; see **Outdoors,** below. Day visit N$10. Guided hikes N$25 per hr. Game drive N$60 per person. Meals N$55. Firewood N$10. Traditional songs and dances. Campsites N$35 per person, N$20 per vehicle. "B&B tent" single N$160; doubles N$240.)

In Uis proper you'll find the **White Lady Bed and Breakfast ❶,** an oasis-like complex on the edge of town, offering camping and rooms. Both come with a swimming pool, *braai*, secure parking, and laundry; rooms also come with mosquito gauze, breakfast, a fridge, phone, and bath or shower. Campers can use the communal ablution block. Visitors can find meals at the White Lady Restaurant on Uis St. Reservations are recommended. (☎50 4102; nicovdyk@iway.na. Reception 7am-10pm. Single N$220; double N$350. Camping N$30 per person.)

⁊ OUTDOORS. The **Brandberg massif,** topped by Konigstein (meaning King's Rock) at 2573m, is Namibia's highest mountain range. Formed 115 million years ago when a single mass of granite pushed itself through the earth's crust during the break-up of the African and American continents, the massif is much younger and larger than its neighbors, Spitzkoppe and Erongo. Its fiery red hue, seen best at sunrise and sunset, makes it look as if the mountain is permanently on fire. Appropriately, "Brandberg" roughly means "burning mountain" in Afrikaans. The Tsiseb Conservancy Office in Uis, along with the Daureb Mountain Guides in the Brandberg Mountain parking lot, arranges hikes in the area with negotiable lengths and prices. While shorter hikes in the valley are good exercise, a two- to three-day hike to the summit offers breathtaking views.

The Brandberg is also famous for the **White Lady** rock painting, first discovered in 1917 by German surveyor Dr. Reinhard Maack. The oft-misinterpreted painting actually depicts a young boy's ceremonial initiation into manhood. The Brandberg massif is home to at least 43,000 other rock paintings in over 1000 locations. (From Uis, drive 14km north towards Khorixas on the C35 and turn left onto the D2359; after 28km the road ends at the Daureb Mountain Guides office. Open June-Aug. daily 7am-4:50pm, later during peak periods; Sept.-May 8am-4:50pm. Tsiseb Conservancy Office ☎50 4162. Open M-F 8am-1pm and 2-5pm. 2hr. hikes to White Lady N$10; to White Lady and other paintings N$15. Other hikes have negotiable prices. Hiking requires physical agility, plenty of water, and food for both the hikers and their guides.)

DUDE LOOKS LIKE A LADY The "White Lady" rock painting of Brandberg was first seen by Europeans in 1917, but it wasn't until Abbé Henri Breuil came across it in 1955 that the painting gained international fame. Due to the figure's white pigment and long hair, Breuil supposed that the image must be that of a white European woman, and he announced that Westerners had mysteriously inhabited the area thousands of years ago, causing an international stir. In spite of Breuil's assumptions, the painting was in fact the work of local Bushmen some 7,000-20,000 years ago, and the painting depicts a young teenage boy, not a white western woman. The large genitalia clearly visible in the painting should have been Breuil's first clue.

USAKOS ☎064

In 1906, Usakos' star was on the rise: it boasted the biggest railway station in the colony, and plans were in the works to fashion the outpost into a major city. Plans changed, however, and Windhoek became the major city. Nevertheless, Usakos is an excellent base for those interested in exploring the Spitzkoppe mountain range (40km northwest), hiking, or spending the night on the way to the coast. Visitors need only walk out the front door to find hiking opportunities in this tiny town nestled in a little mountain range. Its small-town atmosphere makes Usakos a welcome relief from the hustle and bustle of the larger towns and cities around it.

The **Bahnhof Hotel ❸**, 72 Theo Ben Gurirab St. (☎53 0044; fax 53 0765), is a comfortable new hotel with a beer garden that provides most of the town's nightlife. Rooms have A/C, TV, telephone, bath, and secure parking. The hotel also has a bar, restaurant, swimming pool, Internet service, gym, and regional guided tours. (Restaurant open daily 7am-3pm and 6-10pm. Breakfast included. Check-in 24hr. Call 53 0044 if the bar is closed. Singles N$185; doubles N$280. Cash and traveler's checks only.) The **Namib Wüste Farmstall ❶**, 1km west of town on the B2, is a family-run B&B, campground, restaurant, and bar. Beds lie in a converted first-class sleeper train. The campsite includes a treehouse, *braai*, bath, power outlets, peacocks, goats, and springbok. (☎53 0283. Restaurant open daily 7am-8pm. Dorms N$85 per person. Breakfast included. Campsites N$60 per person.) **Padstal Beergarden** has a full-menu restaurant and drinks in a relaxed outdoor setting where the walls and roof consist of creeper plants. (☎53 0407. Open daily 8am-9pm.)

TransNamib Starline (☎061 298 2032) and **Intercape Mainliner** both occasionally stop here; call the companies for specific schedules and fares. From the east, the B2 turns into Bahnhof St., which makes a sharp turn halfway through town and becomes Theo Ben Gurirab St. Eventually it becomes the B2 to Swakopmund. All shops and services line the B2. On the B2, heading east to Windhoek, is the 24hr. **Shell petrol station,** which sells petrol, groceries, and hot food. Next to Shell is the **Chameleon Traveler's Shop** offering tourist information, 24hr. **ATM,** public restrooms, and a quiet cafe. (Open M-Sa 7am-5:30pm, Su 7am-4pm.) Services Include: **First National Bank,** on the corner of Bahnhof and Theo Ben Gurirab St. (☎53 0002; open M-F 9am-12:45pm and 2-3:30pm, Sa 8:30-11am); **emergency** ☎10 111 or 53 0003; **ambulance** ☎53 0023.; and a **doctor,** ☎53 0013. **Usakos Self-Help,** a pharmacy and grocery store, is a block from First National Bank, on Theo Ben Gurirab St. (☎53 0058. Open M-F 8:30am-12:30pm and 2:30-6:30pm, Sa 8am-1pm, Su 11am-noon.) **Internet access** can be found at the Bahnhof Hotel, 72 Theo Ben Gurirab St., for N$18 per 30min. The **post office** is on Theo Ben Gurirab St., two blocks down from the bank (open M-Tu, Th-F 8am-4:30pm; W 8:30am-4:30pm; Sa 8am-noon).

SPITZKOPPE

Spitzkoppe and the Pondoks peaks (1728m and 1692m, respectively) rise like island mountain mirages out of the arid plain between Swakopmund and Usakos. Nicknamed the Matterhorn of Namibia and having a volcanic origin, Spitzkoppe offers steep challenges to rock climbers, while the Pondocks has mostly hiking trails up its loose rock faces. All hiking trails and rock climbs can be done without a guide by experienced hikers, but must be completed in a single day. Camping is allowed only at the **Spitzkoppe Community Tourism Restcamp** at the base of the mountains. All guided hikes are the responsibility of the rest camp and can be booked on-site. A guided hike to the top of **Groot Spitzkoppe** (4-5hr.) costs N$150 per group with a maximum of five people. While the first 45min. of the hike are misleadingly gentle, the remainder of the trail is both slippery and steep. Though the climb up is barren, monotonous, and very challenging, the spectacular view from above makes it all worthwhile. A similar but less time-consuming challenge leads to the top of the adjacent **Pondoks** (1½-2hr.; N$100 per group). Guides can also take hikers on tours of magnificent San **rock paintings,** including the famous **Bushman's Paradise** (N$50 and up). The best time for hiking or rock climbing in the Spitzkoppe is winter (June-Aug.), as Namibian summers are stiflingly hot. Because there are no readily available printed maps to take with you, be sure to ask at reception to see the map of the park before setting out.

The **Spitzkoppe Community Tourism Restcamp** (☎53 0879) offers both private and scenic campsites situated around the base of the mountains, each with a slightly different feel and flavor. Campsite #26, at the bottom of the hike to Bushman's Paradise, is most probably best for hiking, whereas #10 is perfect for bird-watchers, and Swakop Camp and Campsite #11 are great for sunsets. Campsites are minimalist; many are only a sandy clearing, but some have primitive shelter and field toilets. Ablutions are near the reception office. Traditional dance is available on request at the on-site restaurant/pub. While the roads to Spitzkoppe are bumpy but 2WD accessible, roads in the park are best done with 4WD, even in dry season. From the B2, turn north 25km west of Usakos onto the D1918, then turn right onto the D3716 after 19km; the rest camp is 15km farther on. (Day visitors N$10, ages 6-16 N$5. 4WD vehicle N$10, cars N$5, motorbikes N$3. Showers (N$5). Firewood (N$10). Bungalow N$70 for one night, N$120 for three; no bath. Camping N$20 per person, 6-16 N$10. Entrance fees included with accommodations.)

NAMIBIA

THE COAST

Extending 1600km from the Orange River in the south to the Kunene River in the north, Namibia's coastline is an eerie, desolate, and exceptionally beautiful area. The icy cold Benguela current sweeps up from Antarctica, bestowing a life-giving fog on the fragile ecosystem found in the narrow strip of coastal desert called the Namib. Due to an almost total absence of rain, the flora and fauna of this desert area—from small herds of gemsbok and springbok to lizards and snakes to that botanical oddity, *Welwitschia mirabilis*—are sustained only by the fog pushed inland during the night. This same current supports seals, penguins, and dolphins, as well as some of the best angling in Southern Africa.

Though now home to inviting towns and awesome adventures, the coast has not always been welcoming to visitors. Many an unfortunate ship has run aground here, giving Skeleton Coast its name. The few towns that dot this otherwise uninhabited coastline, however, are all worth a visit. Their harbors offer amazing aquatic adventures as well as serene scenic beauty. The 30km drive on the coastal B2 between Swakopmund and Walvis Bay is one of the most scenic drives in Namibia, with gigantic wind-swept sand dunes on one side and the raging waves of the mighty Atlantic on the other. Outdoor activities available in this desert coastal region include sand-boarding, quad-biking, sky-diving, scenic desert flights, sea-kayaking, dolphin tours, angling, and bird-watching.

SWAKOPMUND ☎ 064

A favorite among Namibians and foreigners alike, Swakopmund (pop. 30,000) is an oasis of German culture sandwiched between the Atlantic Ocean and the world's most ancient sea of sand, the Namib Desert. Officially founded by Hauptmann Curt von Francois in 1892 at the *Mund* ("mouth") of Swakop River, this area has been inhabited by Nama people since time immemorial. Though an unsuitable place for building a port, Swakopmund nevertheless grew into the principal gateway to German Southwest Africa. It was stripped of its function as a trading center during WWI, when the Union of South Africa took over and transferred all harbor activities to neighboring Walvis Bay, a real port with a perfect natural harbor. Swakopmund subsequently became a vacation spot. With its palm-lined promenades and beach, it is now a tourist mecca with a first-rate infrastructure.

Swakopmund enjoys a temperate climate that ranges between 15-25° C, perfect for all the overland adventures that take place in the area. The town receives virtually no rain (less than 15mm per year) and is packed with vacationers during the Namibian school holiday season of December and January, when it becomes a cool haven for those fleeing from the heat in the interior. While Swakopmund is an excellent stop for any visitor to Namibia, those who like to avoid the crowds and delve deeper into the culture should try to visit during the winter.

▐ TRANSPORTATION

Swakopmund lies 360km west of Windhoek on the tarred **B2,** which turns into the main east-west thoroughfare, **Sam Nujoma Ave. (Kaiser Wilhelm St.),** before continuing via the perpendicular **Nathaniel Maxuilili St.** to Walvis Bay 34km south.

> **Trains: TransNamib's Starline** (☎ 061 298 2175) runs from the train station on Schlosser St. to: **Tsumeb** (15¾ hr.; Tu, Th, and Su 6:05pm; off-peak N\$40, peak N\$50) via **Otjiwarongo** (9hr.; off-peak N\$35, peak N\$45); **Windhoek** (10¼hr.; Su-F 8:45pm; 2nd class off-peak N\$35, 1st class off-peak N\$50; peak N\$45/N\$60; high peak N\$55/

N$70). Students with letter of proof from school always pay off-peak prices. Senior citizens get 33% discount on all tickets.

Buses: TransNamib's Starline (☎061 298 2175) stops at the train station on Schlosser St. and runs to: **Otjiwarongo** (10¼hr., F 2pm, N$121) via **Henties Bay** (1½hr., N$20); **Khorixas** (7hr., N$69); **Walvis Bay** (30min., Th 6:30pm, N$17). **Intercape** (☎061 227 847) runs to **Walvis Bay** (30min.; M, W, F-Sa 10:45am; N$70) and **Windhoek** (5¼hr.; M, W, F, and Su 12:15pm; N$110). **Intercape** picks up people at the bus terminal at the corner of Roon and Brücken St.

Car Rental: Avis (☎40 2527) at the Swakopmund Hotel; **Budget** (☎46 3380) in the Woermann Brock Mall on Moltke. St.

CELEBRATING PAY DAY For Namibians, the end of the month usually means one thing in particular: pay day. Many Namibians, especially contractual workers, are paid at midnight on the last day of the month. Once the sun comes up, people take the day off work to stand in line at the bank and deposit their checks. Bankers and retailers hold extra hours to handle the influx of money into the community. After depositing their money, some people hit the bars to do some rowdy celebrating. Be careful as you roam about: bar fights and drunk patrons looking for trouble sometimes spill out into the streets. Hostels are often filled to the point of overflowing as rural workers come to town to buy supplies and have fun, so make reservations early if you plan to be in an area with limited accommodations.

■★■ ORIENTATION AND PRACTICAL INFORMATION

The **B2** runs into Swakopmund's east side, where it turns into **Sam Nujoma Ave.,** the linchpin of downtown's simple grid. Sam Nujoma Ave. ends at **Schad Promenade,** which borders the Atlantic Ocean and beach.

TOURIST, FINANCIAL, AND LOCAL SERVICES

Tourist Offices: Namibi, 28 Sam Nujoma Ave. (☎/fax 40 4827; swainfo@iafrica.com.na). At Roon St. Open M-F 8am-1pm and 2-5pm, Sa 9am-noon; July-Sept. also open Sa 3-5pm, Su 10am-noon. **Namibia Wildlife Resorts** (☎40 2172, reservations ☎40 5513; fax 40 2796), on 23-26 Bismarck St., south of Sam Nujoma Ave., arranges permits and accommodations for **Namib-Naukluft Park** and the **Skeleton Coast.** Office open M-F 8am-1pm and 2-5pm; reservations open M-F 8am-1pm and 2-3:30pm. Park permits available on weekends at **Hans Kries Service Station.**

Banks: Commercial Bank of Namibia (☎40 4925), **Standard Bank** (☎40 5011), and **Bank of Windhoek** (☎40 5068), all on Sam Nujoma Ave., near Moltke St., have **ATMs** and *bureaux de change.* Open M-F 9am-3:30pm, Sa 8:30-11am.

Bookstores: CNA, on Roon St., near the tourist office. Open M and W-F 8:30am-5:30pm, Th 9am-5:30pm, Sa 8am-1pm, and Su 9am-1pm.

Supermarkets: Woermann Brock Supermarket and Bottle Store, in the Woermann Brock Mall (entrance on Moltke St.). Open M-F 8am-8pm, Sa 8am-7pm, Su 8am-1pm and 4-7pm. **Model Pick 'n Pay,** at Sam Nujoma Ave. and Roon St. Open M 8:30am-6pm, Tu-Sa 8am-6pm, Su 9am-1pm and 4-6pm.

Camping Equipment: Cymot (☎40 0319), on Sam Nujoma Ave., east of Mazuilili St. Sells camping gear. Open M-F 8am-1pm and 2-5pm, Sa 8am-noon.

EMERGENCY AND COMMUNICATIONS

Police: ☎10 111, on Post and Garnison St., next to the post office.

Ambulance: ☎40 5731.

Pharmacy: Swakopmunder Apotheke (☎40 2825, after hours 46 3610), on Sam Nujoma Ave. Open M-F 8am-1pm and 2:30-6pm, Sa 8am-1pm and 5-6pm, Su 11am-noon and 5-6pm.

Hospitals: Cottage Private Hospital (☎41 2201). **Bismarck Medical Center and Private Hospital** (☎40 5000/1), on Sam Nujoma Ave., at Bismarck St.

Internet Access: Swakopmund Internet Cafe and Coffee Shop, inside Woermann Brock mall on Moltke St. N$10 per 30min. Open M-Sa 7am-10pm, Su 10am-10pm. **Desert Explorers,** on Woermann St., next to Rafter's. N$20 per 30min., N$40 for 1hr. and above. Open M-Su 8am-8pm.

Post Office (☎40 2222), at Daniel Tjongarero and Garnison St. From Kaiser Wilhelm St. facing the water, turn right onto Moltke St. Offers email, fax, pay phones, photocopies, and *Poste Restante.* Open M-T, Th-F 8am-4:30pm; W 8:30am-4:30pm; Sa 8am-noon.

⌐ ACCOMMODATIONS AND CAMPING

◪ **Alternative Space Backpackers,** 167 Lazarett St.(☎/fax 40 2713; nam00352@mweb.com.na). Head 1.5km out of town to the eastern end of Brucken St., take a left at the dead end, and look for the flat-roofed gray building ahead on the right. A traveler's dream, this backpackers is proof that a house can be a work of art. Silbylle and Frenus equip their guests with open-air bathrooms, a well-stocked self-catering kitchen, and a TV lounge with libraries of books and vinyl, all decorated with local artists' work and scrap metal scavenged from the desert. The dunes, where you can see fantastic sunsets, are only a 10min. walk away. Secure parking. Free transport to and from town (daily 7am-9pm). Laundry N$20. Free traditional fish *braai* on Fridays. Breakfast included. Dorms N$50; doubles N$150; triples N$200. ●

Desert Sky Backpackers, 35 Lazarett St. (☎40 2339; cell 081 257 5606; dsbackpackers@swakop.com). A central location near the beach and a full range of facilities make this a good backpackers. The atmosphere is lively in this converted house, where the guests have the run of the place and swap travel stories. Offers TV lounge, self-catering kitchen, secure parking, pool room, tourist info, and Internet (N$30 per hr.). Dorms N$50; doubles N$140; private singles N$110. Camping N$40. ●

Hotel Grüner Kranz (☎40 2039; fax 40 5016; swakoplodge@yahoo.com), on the corner of Leutwein and Maxuilili St. This hotel has a touristy feel, and its upstairs bar hosts the majority of the city's nightlife. Central location, full bar/restaurant, and TV facilities. When the overlander trucks come into town, the influx of tourists can be a bit much. Laundry (N$15), *braai*, self-catering kitchen, secure parking, and 24hr. check-in. Reservations recommended. Dorms N$40; singles N$200; doubles N$240. Cash and traveler's checks only. ●

Hotel Dig by See, 4 Brücken St. (☎/fax 40 4130/70; stelgodl@iafrica.com.na). An older hotel with large rooms, some with ocean views. Its location, sightly out of the town center toward the beach, gives it a quiet atmosphere, nice for those not wanting a backpackers feel. Secure parking, restaurant, and laundry. Breakfast included. Reservations recommended Dec.-Feb. Call ahead if arriving late. Singles N$180; doubles N$250. Cash only. ❸

Alte Brücke Caravan and Camping Site (☎40 4918; fax 40 0153; accomod@imlnet.com.na), on the southern end of Strand St. An extremely clean campground featuring the roar of the Atlantic, power outlets, and bathrooms for each campsite. *Braai*, public phone, and security. Reservations recommended. 3-person suite N$150; N$50 per person extra. ●

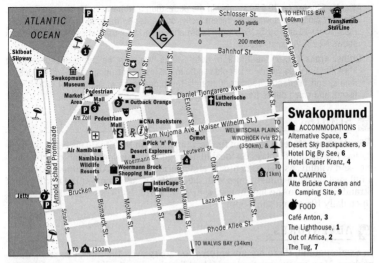

ATLANTIC OCEAN

Schlosser St.
TO HENTIES BAY (60km)
TransNamib StarLine
Bahnhof St.
Skiboat Shipway
Swakopmund Museum
Market Area
Pedestrian Mall
Am Zoll Pedestrian Mall
Outback Orange
Daniel Tjongarero Ave.
Lutherische Kirche
CNA Bookstore
Sam Nujoma Ave. (Kaiser Wilhelm St.)
Cymot
Pick 'n' Pay
Desert Explorers
Woermann St.
Woermann Brock Shopping Mall
Air Namibia
Namibia Wildlife Resorts
Brucken St.
InterCape Mainliner
Lazarett St.
Rhode Allee St.
TO WALVIS BAY (34km)
TO 9 (300m)
Leutwein St.
Otavi St.
Nathaniel Maxuilili St.
Lüderitz St.
Moltke St.
Roon St.
Bismarck St.
Strand St.
Molen Way
Arnold Schad Promenade
Jetty
Koch St.
Gamison St.
Schul St.
N. Maxuilili St.
Esstorff St.
Windhoek St.
Moses Garoeb St.
TO WELWITSCHIA PLAINS, WINDHOEK (via B2) (350km), &
TO 5 (1km)

Swakopmund

▲ ACCOMMODATIONS
Alternative Space, **5**
Desert Sky Backpackers, **8**
Hotel Dig By See, **6**
Hotel Gruner Kranz, **4**

▲ CAMPING
Alte Brücke Caravan and Camping Site, **9**

🍴 FOOD
Café Anton, **3**
The Lighthouse, **1**
Out of Africa, **2**
The Tug, **7**

FOOD AND ENTERTAINMENT

Out of Africa, 13 Tjongarero St. (☎ 40 4752). Near Moltke St. With its motto of "Life's too short to drink bad coffee," this is the only place in town that brews its coffee (N$4.50) with and sells fresh-ground beans, making it an early-morning favorite among locals. *Crêpe*-like pancakes (N$8.50-25), fruit shakes (N$13.50), and the Ploughman's Platter (N$30) for the truly hungry give this café the perfect feel for any time of day. Open M-F 7am-8pm, Sa-Su 7am-10pm. ❷

The Tug (☎ 40 2356), next to the jetty on Arnold Schad Promenade. Arguably the best seafood restaurant in town is in a tugboat's pilot house overlooking the ocean. An excellent choice for a romantic dinner or an expensive night out. The menu includes seafood (from N$50), meat, and vegetarian options. Reservations essential, even for drinks. Open M-F 6-10pm, Sa-Su noon-3pm and 6pm-late. AmEx/DC/MC/V. ❸

The Lighthouse (☎ 40 0894), on Koch St., opposite the Museum. Known for its fish and pizza, this restaurant has the best ocean view around, whether you sit on the patio or inside. Beside serving drinks all day, the menu has seafood (from N$32), pizza (N$20), and pasta (N$35-45). One of the better-known restaurants in town, the nightlife can be lively. Open for lunch M-Sa 11:30am-2:30pm, Su 11:30am-3pm. Open for dinner M-Sa 6:30-10:30pm, Su 6:30-10pm. Credit cards accepted. ❸

Cafe Anton, 1 Bismarck St. (☎ 40 0331). In the lobby of Hotel Schweizerhaus. Elegant cafe with outdoor seating, a nice ocean view, and enticing German confections. The menu, featuring sandwiches (N$10-20), cakes (N$5-10), and Costa Rican coffee (N$5.50), pulls in small groups of locals and hotel guests. End a meal with a piece of amazing Apple Cake (N$8). Full meals include vegetarian (N$20-38), meat (N$31-40), and seafood (N$32-210). Open daily 7am-9pm. MC/V. ❸

Swakopmund Brauhaus (☎ 40 2214), in the pedestrian mall between Moltke and Roon St., north of Nujoma Ave., is the best place in town for German eats and drinks. A large restaurant with seasonal outdoor seating, it has a full dinner menu including fish (N$40-125) and game (N$30-63). The Filled Chicken Breast (N$39.50) and Pork Roast with Dumplings (N$40) are both excellent choices. Lunch features lighter dishes (N$20-36). Don't skip dessert, especially the vanilla ice cream with hot raspberries (N$19). Open daily for lunch 11:30am-2:30pm and for dinner 6-10pm. ❸

Atlantic Cinema (☎ 40 2743), also in the pedestrian mall between Moltke and Roon St. The only cinema in town plays recent Hollywood notables daily. M-Th 10am-10:30pm, F-Sa 10am-11pm, Su 5:15-10pm. 11am shows N$18; 2-6pm shows N$20; 8-10pm shows N$23; VIP seats N$30.

Grüner Kranz Bar, on the 2nd fl. of Hotel Grüner Kranz, on the corner of Leutwein and Mazuilil St. A wide variety of people can be found inside, including skydiving instructors, locals, and overlander tourists. Certainly the place to be at night. Pool tables, shot menu, and small dance floor. Open 8pm-late.

⊙ SIGHTS

▧**Swakopmund Museum** is one of the best museums in Namibia. This catch-all facility has fascinating displays on local history, geology, ecology, ethnology, technology, and wildlife, as well as dentistry and pharmaceuticals. Allow at least 1½hr. for a full visit. Arrange guided tours with the curator in advance. (At the north end of Strand St., next to the lighthouse. ☎ 40 2046. N$14, students N$9, children N$5. Open daily 10am-1pm and 2-5pm.)

⚒ ADVENTURES

In Swakopmund, there are adventures to satisfy even the most daredevil thrill-seekers. Most unique are those which utilize the gigantic 30km coastal dunebelt: sandboarding and quad-biking are local specialties. The close proximity of the Atlantic Ocean, with its Benguela current and Walvis Bay Lagoon, enables deep sea and beach fishing, kayaking, and dolphin/seal cruises. ("We use what we've got," says one Namibian tour operator.) The sky above Swakopmund and the Skeleton Coast is filled with hot air balloons, sky divers, parasailors, and scenic flights. Half and full-day trips and safaris can provide a wide range of activities in one tour. Bookings for all activities listed below can be made through ▧**Outback Orange** (☎ 40 0968; cell 081 129 2877), next to the Out of Africa café (see p. 497) on Tjongarero. They also offer township tours (3hr., N$400 per person including dinner and drinks) and book massages to soothe you after a harrowing day of adventure. **Desert Explorers Adventure Center** (☎ 40 6096; fax 40 5038; swkadven@iafrica.com.na) is on Woermann St., next to Rafter's (open daily 8am-8pm). Operators based in Windhoek also offer tours to the Swakopmund/Walvis Bay region.

OVERLAND ADVENTURES

With an impressive variety of landscapes close at hand, it's no wonder Swakopmund is a center of overland adventure. The sand dunes south of Swakopmund are among the world's tallest, the Kuiseb and Swakop River deltas start just east of town, and the Skeleton Coast to the north has its own barren charm.

▧ **Alter-Action** (☎ 40 2737 or 081 128 2737; www.alter-action.com). Sandboarding, comparable to snowboarding and sledding, offers the adrenaline rush for those in need of speed. After "Little Nellie," the first training run, get bolder on progressively bigger dunes until you take on the Terrible Twins, "Dizzie" and "Lizzie," at 80km per hr. Snowboard-style stand-up boarding lets you off skill, but face-first lie-down boarding is where the speed is. Open 9:30am-1:30pm. Lie-down US$20, stand-up and lie-down US$30. Safety gear, lunch, and transport to and from the dunes included.

Namib Tours (☎ 40 4072, 40 4054, or 081 128 6111; fax 40 4072), in Namib Center next to Hansa Hotel on Roon St. Only company in town offering historical tours of Swakopmund (1hr., N$95). They also have a Rössing Mountain gem tour (N$230) and a tour of the Cape Cross Seal Colony (including salt mines, Bird Paradise, Henties Bay, and Lichenfields; N$250). Full-day tours (N$250) departing at 9am as well as shorter tours (N$200) explore the Namib Desert. There are also 1- or 2-day Spitzkoppe tours. All prices per person, and tours are by booking only.

Charly's Desert Tours, 11 Sam Nujoma Ave. (☎40 4341; fax 40 4821; charlydt@mweb.com.na). Specializes in tailor-made tours anywhere in Namibia. Stay in lodges or camp. Full-day (9am-4pm) tours include the environmental Namib Desert tour (N$330 per person) and the Kuiseb Delta tour, which features Walvis Bay Lagoon and a traditional Topnaar community. Inquire for rates. All tours by booking only.

AQUA ADVENTURES

The Atlantic coast, extending from Walvis Bay to 200km north of Swakopmund, is one of Africa's best fishing grounds, drawing thousands of anglers in December and January. From November to March there's superb angling for west-coast steenbras, kob (kabeljou), galjoen, blacktail (dassie), geelbek, and white stumpnose. Predator sharks can be caught throughout the year. The Swakopmund coastline and Walvis Bay Lagoon offer chances to view aquatic birds and other marine animals, including dolphins and seals. While Swakopmund companies offer excellent tours, see Walvis Bay for more options.

Blue Marlin Adventures (☎/fax 40 5070; cell 081 127 5070). Offers daily fishing tours, from shore or boat, including special shark fishing trips (9am-2:30pm, N$450 per person). Dolphin tours (including Walvis Bay and eco-sightseeing) run from 8am-1pm (N$300 per person) and include snacks and drinks. Trips by booking only.

AERIAL ADVENTURES

🖎 **Ground Rush** (☎081 124 5167; fax 40 2064; freefall@iafrica.com.na), at the Swakopmund Airport. You can pre-book through Outback Orange or just drop-in to jump. You get a 25min. scenic flight over Swakopmund, the Atlantic Coast, sand dunes, and the Namib Desert. Your flight is interrupted by the "tandem master" strapping himself to your back. At 9500 ft., you shuffle to the door, and out you go. Key statistics: 30 seconds of free-fall; 220km per hr.; 5min. of parachuting descent. All this, of course, while enjoying the best view in Namibia. A cameraman along for the ride to record your reaction is optional. (US$150 for flight and jump, US$30 for still photos or video, US$40 for both). Also offers a Static-Line certification course that includes 6hr. ground instruction. Be sure to stick around the Clubhouse after jumping for the day to find out why it's easy to become a drop-zone groupie after your first time.

African Adventure Balloons (☎/fax 40 3455; cell 081 242 9481; flylo@swk.namib.com). Desert balloon safaris from Swakopmund include 30min. jaunts (US$125) and 1hr. sunrise champagne flights (US$175 per person). Pricey, but worth it if your purse can take it. They collect you at 5:15am and return you by 10am. Dress warmly and bring a hat. Advance booking essential.

Scenic Air (☎/fax 40 3575/71; flying@iway.na). Offers scenic and photographic flights over all of Skeleton Coast and the Namib Desert from Swakopmund (from N$50 per person, including refreshments). Specialities are Sossusvlei (2½hr.); Damaraland, Brandberg, and Skeleton Coast Shipwrecks (2½hr.); and Kaokoveld, including a Himba tour and lunch (5hr.). Inquire for specific rates.

THE SKELETON COAST

North of Swakopmund, the Namib Desert stretches along the coast all the way to the Angolan border. The northernmost 500km of this 30-40km wide swath of gravel plains, from the Ugab River north to the Kunene River, make up the Skeleton Coast Park. Dense coastal fog once blinded sea captains to the rocky coast, causing violent wrecks. The survivors who made it to shore found a bleak land-

FROM THE ROAD

SKYDIVING: THE NEXT DIMENSION

In the beginning, there was the flight. For twenty-five glorious minutes, I was part of the sky, peering down on the world below from a small plane. Then my "tandem-master," Simon, strapped himself onto my back, a feeling which must be familiar only to Siamese twins. He gave me the rundown of technique one last time. Seconds later, my camera-man took one last interview and I found myself hanging out the door, looking down through the clouds at the earth below. And away we went.

I had expected to experience that stomach-in-throat feeling I get going off the high dive. However, because there was no immediate danger of impact, my body didn't go through its normal alerts. Instead it became completely attuned to the feeling of falling with nothing holding it back. Then came the intense realization that the ground was hurtling up at me: falling through the clouds showed me just how fast I was dropping. Although I was reluctant at first, now jumping seemed easy, and definitely worth it.

The parachute opening was not as abrupt as I expected it to be. There was a momentary painless jolt and then a gradual decrease in speed. For five minutes, I had an amazing view of the desert, as I safely spiraled toward the landing target. My feet touched the ground within mere meters of the airstrip, another perfect landing to add to a cumulative 100% safety record. And with that, as promised, another dimension was added to my previously two-dimensional world.

—Kelzie Beebe

scape with no surface water, scarce game, and windswept plains covered with sand, pebbles, and scattered desert plants. For desert enthusiasts, this is enchanting country; for anglers, it's paradise. For most other visitors, the skull-bedecked main gate is far more exciting than anything inside the park, which is marked by a lack of skeletons, shipwrecks, and just about everything else.

◼⃝ 🗹 ORIENTATION AND PRACTICAL INFORMATION. Between Swakopmund and the Ugab River is the **National West Coast Recreation Area,** open to everyone, no permit required. Everything north of this, from the Ugab River to the Kunene River, is **Skeleton Coast Park,** open only to visitors with a permit. The tarred **C34** runs directly from Swakopmund up the coast and through the Park. The road is in good condition and is 2WD-friendly. Skeleton Coast Park is divided into two sections: north of Terrace Bay, where no one is allowed; and south of Terrace Bay, open to both day and overnight visitors. Day visitors to the south of Terrace Bay can obtain permits (N$20 per person, N$20 per vehicle) at both Ugabmund and Springbokwasser gates, while campers and anglers must reserve sites at Terrace Bay or Torra Bay in advance at the NWR offices in Windhoek or Swakopmund.

There are two entrances to the Skeleton Coast Park. **Ugabmund** lies right on the coast and marks the northernmost point of the West Coast Recreation Area. **Springbokwasser** is 150km west of Khorixas on the **C39.** Day visitors who only want to drive through the park between Ugabmund and Springbokwasser can obtain the necessary transit permit at either of the two entry points but must enter the park by 3pm and exit by 5pm. Visitors must enter and exit at different gates. Overnight visitors must reach Ugabmund by 3pm or Springbokwasser by 5pm to ensure punctual arrival at their accommodations. Permits for angling are granted automatically with accommodations reservations. Provision shops are only open December and January, but there is a year-round petrol station at Mile 108. The nearest **banking** facilities are in Henties Bay.

🖬 ACCOMMODATIONS AND CAMPING. There are four windy, minimalist **campsites ❷** spread through the West Coast Recreation Area: **Mile 14, Jakkalsputz** (12km south of Henties Bay), **Mile 72** (35km north of Henties Bay), and **Mile 108** (140km north of Henties Bay). Toilets are available, but visitors must bring their own camping equipment, food, and firewood. Camping is N$110 at all four sites and can be booked through the NWR Central Reservations Office in Windhoek or Swakopmund. Reception and showers at all campsites are open M-Sa 8am-noon and 3-7pm. ("Mile 14" indicates the campsite is 14 mi. north of Swakopmund. Signs along C34 for other sites marked "Mile number X" only have toilets and fish washing facilities and are not for camping.)

For accommodations in the West Coast Recreation Area, look to **Cape Cross Lodge** (see **Big Splurge** p. 504) or **Fisherman's Inn ❷** (☎/fax 064 20 2309 or 081 262 8499). The inn, at mile 62, offers large but sparse rooms, without bathrooms, that open onto a central restaurant, bar, and pool table area. The Inn is a welcome respite from the never-ending wind outside, with a nightlife that is sure to be lively during the peak angling season. (Reservations recommended between September and February. Rooms N$100, with breakfast N$125.)

Inside Skeleton Coast Park, accommodations are only available at **Torra Bay ❷**, 130km north of the Ugabmund entrance, or **Terrace Bay ❺**, 50km north of Torra. Torra Bay, open December and January, provides only basic camping facilities. Communal ablution facilities, water, firewood, and a provision shop are on the premises. (N$100 per site.) Terrace Bay has year-round bungalows, but no camping is allowed. There is also a shop and a restaurant. Rates include breakfast and dinner, bath, bedding, and towels. (Singles N$500; doubles N$350 per person.) Both areas have petrol station, but no bank. Make all bookings through NWR.

🌄🏊 **OUTDOORS AND HIKING. Cape Cross Seal Reserve,** 50km south of the Ugabmund entrance on the C34, is the second largest colony of Cape fur seals in the southern hemisphere. Some 80,000 to 100,000 of these flapping, whinnying creatures produce a terrific stench, but the sight is awesome and definitely worth the detour. The free-for-all that is the November/December mating season is especially fun. A replica of the cross planted by Portuguese explorer Diego Cao in 1485 stands at the original site with picnic facilities and toilet nearby. (Open daily 10am-5pm. N$20, ages 6-16 N$2. Vehicles N$20.)

The three-day, 50km **Ugab River Hiking Trail** winds along the Ugab River, departing with a group of three to eight people on the 2nd and 4th Tuesday of every month between April and October. This guided hike kicks off at Ugabmund at 9am and also ends there. Hikers should spend the night before the hike at Mile 108 and provide and carry their own equipment and food. Medical certification of physical fitness, issued within the preceding 40 days, is required. (Medical certification obtained by collecting the appropriate forms at the NWR or MET offices in Windhoek or Swakopmund and seeing a local doctor for a brief consultation, usually about N$50. Trail permit N$220. Book well in advance at NWR offices in Windhoek (see p. 464) or in Swakopmund.)

HENTIES BAY ☎064

A small, coastal village 70km north of Swakopmund off the C34, Henties Bay has only 3500 residents but welcomes 20,000 anglers during December and January, who flock to the great fishing spots found on the 200km crystal stretch north of Swakopmund. The turnoff from C34 becomes **Jakkalsputweg,** which bears most shops and services. Benguela Rd., the other commercial center, is the next street over towards the ocean from Jakkalsputweg. There is no public transport to or from Henties Bay. The **tourist information office** is inside the **Total Service Station,** opposite the Eagle Shopping Center on Jakkalsputweg. (☎/fax 50 1143; info@hentiesbay.com; open M-F 8am-1pm and 2-5pm.) **West and Skeleton Coast Angling Tours and Safaris** (☎/fax 50 0171), next to Spar on Benguela Rd., specializes in angling, Damaraland tours, Kaokoland safaris, and boat tours. **Maxi Adventures** (☎50 0574; fax 50 0708; eaglesc@iafrica.com.na) also rents camping equipment and offers camping trips to Damaraland, the Kaokoveld, and coastal destinations. The **Bank**

NAMIBIA

of Windhoek (☎50 0298), on Jakkalsputweg, has a *bureau de change* and 24hr. **ATM**. For grocery stores, try **Spar,** 17 Benguela Rd., or **Your Family Store** in the Eagle Shopping Center. Other services include: **laundromat** (☎50 1311), inside Video Cave, which is next to Spar on Bengwela Rd.; **police** (☎10 111, open 24hr.); **Henties Bay Pharmacy** (☎50 0599; after hours 081 127 0599), on Jakkalsputweg; the state **clinic** (☎50 0020); **Internet access,** N$15 for 30min., inside Video Cave on Bengwela Rd.; the **post office** (☎50 0006) on Jakkalsputweg. Except for the police, all keep regular business hours (M-F 8am-1pm and 2-5pm).

If you plan to stay in Henties Bay overnight, **Eagle Holiday Flats ❶,** 172 Jakkalsputweg (☎50 0032), offers the best value in town for budget travelers, featuring colossal two-bedroom chalets (with bath, shower, self-catering kitchen, TV, secure garage, and *braai*) or backpackers doubles (with bath, fish freezer, secure parking, self-catering communal kitchen and *braai*). Reservations require a 15% deposit. (4-person chalets N$80 per person; 2-person backpackers rooms N$50 per person. AmEx/DC/MC/V.) **Henties Bay Guest House ❹** (☎/fax 50 1111/77; jfoost@mweb.com.na), on Auas St. has the comfort of a hotel but a B&B atmosphere and a view overlooking the ocean. Double rooms with bath, breakfast, secure parking and TV are N$265 as singles or N$170 per person as doubles. Bar and lounge, *braai*, lunch and dinner available with advanced booking. There are lunch boxes for fisherman. Follow the posted road signs or ask at the information office. **Buck's Camping Lodge ❷** (☎/fax 50 1039) offers small, sandy campsites, each with its own bathroom and power outlet. (From Jakkalsputweg, turn right onto Nicky Iyambo St., and then left at Buck's sign. N$100 per site.) For a *bona fide* restaurant, try **Eagle Steak Ranch ❹,** on Jakkalsputweg in Eagle Shopping Center. The meat (N$32-70), seafood (N$80-120), and salads (N$15) are extremely filling. (☎50 0574. Open M-Sa 9am-2am, Su 9am-3pm. AmEx/DC/MC/V.)

WALVIS BAY ☎064

Walvis Bay (pop. 40,000) is Namibia's premier port and industrial center. The quality of the port's deepwater harbor and the quantity of its industrial resources have drawn so many companies that the port may soon rival the town in size. Bartolomeu Dias was the first European to rest his sails here in 1487, on his way around the Cape. Britain annexed the bay and the surrounding 1124 square kilometers in 1840, passing it on to the newly formed Union of South Africa in 1910. Namibia only gained control of Walvis Bay in 1994. Due to its focus on other industries, the tourist industry sputtered to a start, but is now quickly growing. The **lagoon,** one of the best bird-watching sites in the world, and the towering **sand dunes** northeast of town keep adrenaline-seekers busy with top-notch quad biking and duneboarding.

▐ TRANSPORTATION

Flights: Walvis Bay Airport (☎20 0403 or 20 7428) has domestic and international flights. **Triple Three Rentals** (see **Car Rental**) runs airport shuttles from/to: Walvis Bay Airport/Walvis Bay (N$65), Walvis Bay Airport/Swakopmund (N$110), Swakopmund Airport/Swakopmund (N$55). Call ahead for reservations. **Air Namibia** flies to **Windhoek Eros** (1hr.; daily 1:20pm; N$380, seniors and children N$350) and **Lüderitz** (1hr.; N$640/N$580). **South African Express** flies to **Cape Town** (2hr.; M-F 12:05pm, Su 9:10am; N$1650/N$1250) and **Johannesburg** (2½hr.; M-F 12:35pm, Su 3:50pm; N$1890/N$1410).

Trains: TransNamib's Starline (☎061 298 2175) travels to **Tsumeb** (17½hr.; Tu, Th, Su 4:15pm; N$40) via **Swakopmund, Otjiwarongo,** and **Otavi;** and **Windhoek** (12hr.; Su-F 7pm; economy class N$45, business class N$60) via **Swakopmund.** Tickets sold at the train station M-F 8am-1pm and 2-4pm, Su 2-4pm.

Bus: Intercape (book through SAA City Center Ultra Travel at 20 7997) runs to **Windhoek** (5hr.; M, W, F, Su 11:30am; N$115) via **Swakopmund** (45min., N$70). Picks up in Spur Restaurant's parking lot on Mbumba Ave. **TransNamib's Starline** (☎061 298 2175) goes to **Otjiwarongo** (11¼hr., F 1pm, N$129), via **Swakopmund, Henties Bay, Khorixas,** and **Outjo.** Picks up at the train station.

Car Rental: Triple Three Rentals, 42 12th Rd. (☎20 0333 or 081 127 3331; fax 20 6686), in the same building as the tourist info bureau. **Budget** (☎20 4128 or 081 128 6900; fax 202 931), inside Protea Lodge at 10th Rd. and Sam Nujoma Ave. **Avis** (☎20 7527 or 081 128 1206; fax 20 9150) is in the airport.

⚒ 🔋 ORIENTATION AND PRACTICAL INFORMATION

All roads into town lead through Diaz Circle on the northeast side of town. The town is laid out on a grid, with "streets" running from southwest to northeast and "roads" running from northwest to southeast. Streets and roads are numbered, and numbers get lower as you move closer to the water (i.e., **1st St.** is on the bayfront, while **18th St.** and **18th Rd.** are both well inland). This orderly system would be easily navigable, except for the fact that the streets in the center of town recently changed their names in honor of famous Africans. For example, 7th St. became **Sam Nujoma Ave.,** 8th St. became **Hage G. Geingob St.,** 9th St. became **Theo-Ben Gurirab St.,** and 10th St. became **Nangolo Mbumba Dr.** To add to the confusion, locals use the new and old names interchangeably, although the street signs have all been changed. Mbumba Dr. is the main street for civic buildings and services, while Hage G. Geingob and Sam Nujoma Ave. are the commercial center.

Tourist Office: Tourist Information Bureau, 42 12th Rd. (☎20 9170; fax 20 9171; walvisinfo@iml.com.na), between Theo-Ben Gurirab St. and Nangolo Mbumba Dr. Sells permits for Namib-Naukluft Park. Open M-F 8am-1pm and 2-5pm, Sa 9am-noon.

Travel Agencies: SAA City Center Ultra Travel Services, 161 Nangola Mbumba Dr. (☎20 7997; fax 20 3167), is the local agent for Intercape and handles a range of services, from airplane flight reservations and travel packages to bookings for incoming tours. **Harvey World Travel,** 151 Sam Nujoma Ave. (☎20 6925; fax 20 3778). Books flights, leisure packages, and the majority of tour operators in the area.

Banks: Commercial Bank (☎20 6006), on the corner of Sam Nujoma Ave. and 11th Rd. **First National Bank** (☎20 1811), on Sam Nujoma Ave., next to Commercial Bank. **Bank of Windhoek** (☎21 9600), on 13th Rd. All three open M-F 9am-3:30pm, Sa 8:30-11am, with 24hr. **ATMs** and *bureau de change.*

Bookstore: CNA (☎20 7643), on Hage G. Geingob St. between 11th and 12th Rd., inside Seagulls Shopping Mall. Open M, W, and F 8:30am-5:30pm; Tu and Th 9am-5:30pm; Sa 8am-1pm and Su 9am-1pm.

Supermarkets: Model Pick 'n Pay (☎20 5912), on Hage G. Geingob St. between 11th and 12th Rd., inside Seagulls Shopping Mall. Open M and W-F 8:30am-6pm, Tu 9am-6pm, Sa 8am-2pm, Su 9am-1pm. **Spar,** 102 Sam Nujoma Ave. (☎20 4916). Open M-Sa 8am-9pm, Su 9am-1pm and 4-8pm.

Camping Equipment: Cymot, 136 8th St. (☎20 2241). Open M-F 8am-1pm and 2-5pm, Su 8am-noon. Credit cards accepted.

Police: ☎10 111, at Nangolo Mbumba Dr. and 13th Rd. Also try **The Security School** (☎20 4412).

Ambulance: ☎20 5443. Also try **Aeromed** (☎20 7207 or 081 129 4444).

Hospitals: State Hospital (☎20 3441), on 14th St. between 7th Rd. and 9th Rd., and **Weltwitschia Hospital** (☎20 9000), on 13th Rd. Both are open 24hr.

THE BIG SPLURGE

CAPE CROSS LODGE

If you are going to travel this far to get away from it all, why not stay in the lap of luxury? The Cape Cross Lodge sits on the edge of the desert and overlooks the ocean. After you walk through the sliding glass doors into a lobby with plush couches and crackling fireplaces, the Atlantic Surf is only 30ft. away.

The lodge's eight rooms each have individual balconies overlooking the ocean, a full bath, and beds for two with the facilities for a family suite. These rooms coddle the weary traveler returning from a day of fishing in the South Atlantic, surfing one of the best point breaks in Africa, or quad biking the Skeleton Coast (the lodge organizes all of these activities).

After a day of exploring the Skeleton Coast's vast beauty, you can relax in the bar and full-menu restaurant, which has open Atlantic-air seating. In the cellar below, there is a wine tasting and cigar lounge for those who like to end the day with some of the finer comforts in life.

The only thing the Cape Cross Lodge lacks is a crowded feeling. It is 60km away from the nearest town. The Cape Cross Seal Reserve and the Diaz Cross are right next door, but otherwise it is just you, the Atlantic, and the Skeleton Coast. (Lodge: ☎/fax 064 69 4012/3; capecross@africaonline.com.na. Windhoek reservation office: ☎061 25 5488; fax 061 25 5400. Reservations highly recommended. Lunch N$65./ Dinner N$110. Singles (Mar.-Oct./ Nov.-Feb.) N$800/N$675; doubles N$1000/N$850.

Internet Access: Internet Cafe, 144 Sam Nujoma Ave. (☎20 5667), in Computerland. N$10 for 30min. Open M-F 8am-1pm and 2-8pm, Sa 9am-1pm and 4-8pm, Su 10am-1pm.

Post Office: ☎20 1451, at Sam Nujoma Ave. and 14th Rd. Offers *Poste Restante*, faxes, international calls, and photocopies. Open M-Tu, Th-F 8am-4:30pm; W 8:30am-4:30pm; Sa 8am-noon.

🏠 ACCOMMODATIONS AND CAMPING

The Spawning Ground, 84 Hage G. Geingob St. (☎/fax 20 4400; spawning@iafrica.com.na). On the corner of Hage G. Geingob St. and 8th Rd. A new location, great interior decorating, and the cozy and homey atmosphere make this *the* place to stay in Walvis Bay. Guests have full use of house and backpacker's lodge. The owner and manager are happy to organize sandboarding, quad biking, and other activities. 2 self-catering kitchens, TV lounge, *braai*, secure parking, fireplace, laundry, and hot showers. Dorms N$60; doubles N$160. Camping available. ❶

Lagoon Chalets (☎20 7151), towards the lagoon, then left on 8th Rd. Best deal in town for groups. 29 spacious, well-equipped chalets. Each chalet has a loft area, 6 beds, full self-catering kitchen, bathroom, cable TV, secure parking, *braai*, and patio. Reservations recommended. N$260 for chalet, up to 6 people. ❹

Esplanade Park Bungalows (☎20 6145; cell 081 129 4970; fax 20 9416), bordering the lagoon on Nangolo Mbumba Drive. Fairly comfortable two-bedroom bungalows have 5 beds and a double couch bed in addition to a garage, spacious living room, and self-catering kitchen. Single room bungalows are similar, but contain only 3 beds and a double couch bed. *Braai*, laundry, and garage. Key deposit N$200. Reception open M-F 8am-1pm and 2-9pm, Sa-Su 8am-1pm and 3-6pm. Reservations recommended. 1-bedroom N$270; 2-bedroom N$30. MC/V. ❹

The Caravan Park at Long Beach (Langstrand) Resort (☎20 3134; fax 20 9714), on the coast off the B2, 17km north of Walvis Bay. Semi-private and sometimes windy camping in a beach resort. Breathtaking ocean views, *braai*, communal ablution blocks, and power outlets. Offers some of the best camping in town. Facilities include a full bar, restaurant, oyster bar, laundry, public phones, and ice/firewood/charcoal for sale. Reception open M-F 8am-1pm and 2-5pm; Sa, Su 8am-1pm and 3-6pm; see security guard for off-hour check-in. Sites N$57.50 plus N$6.90 per person. MC/V. ❶

📷 📑 FOOD AND ENTERTAINMENT

🍴 **Crazy Mama's,** 133 11th Rd. (☎20 7364). At Sam Nujoma Ave. Two thumbs up for mouth-watering pizzas and pastas, courteous service, reasonable prices, and a kitchen area that opens into the seating area. Offers salads (N$18-26), seafood (N$50-90), pasta (N$26-50), and pizza (small/medium N$18-40); try the Filetto with vegetables and strips of beef fillet. Bar and take-away available. Reservations are highly recommended for dinner. Open M-F 12:30-5pm and 6:30-10:30pm, Sa 6:30-10:30pm. DC/MC/V. ❸

Willi Probst Cafe & Restaurant, 148 9th St. (☎20 2744). At 12th Rd., opposite the tourist office. Willi's German pastries and desserts are not to be missed, especially the custard slice with creme (N$4.50). Indoor/outdoor seating. Offers pork (N$28-40), vegetarian (N$25-35), and other German fare. For lunch, try sandwiches made to order in the cafe (N$4.30-8). Open M-F, Su 6:15am-5:30pm; Sa 6:15am-2:15pm. Reservation for restaurant recommended. AmEx/DC/MC/V. ❷

The Raft (☎20 4877), located on the Esplanade. Very popular among the tourists, this upscale restaurant has one of the best locations in Namibia: it is 80 meters out in the lagoon on stilts. Beautiful views of flamingo, jellyfish, pelicans, and sometimes even dolphins. Vegetarian fare (N$27-40), meat (N$35-60), and seafood (N$50 and up) all have a traditional South African flavor. Try the South African Sweet and Sour Chicken (N$39). Open M-Sa noon-3pm and 5-10pm. Reservations recommended. AmEx/DC/MC/V. ❸

👁 🏔 SIGHTS AND OUTDOORS

There is no public transport to any of Walvis Bay's outlying sights; drive yourself or contact a tour company listed below. **Dune 7** is the highest dune in the area and gets lots of local and tourist traffic. You can climb up it, sand-board down it, or picnic under the palm trees at its base. (About 10km southeast of town, off the C14 on the way to Namib-Naukluft Park.) **Walvis Bay Lagoon,** a Ramsar Site since 1964, is one of the most important habitats for coastal birds in Africa. In August, it is home to 70% of the flamingos in Southern Africa. The permanent population of 70,000 to 120,000 birds includes flamingos, pelicans, and the rare Damara tern. Add in 200,000 additional migratory visitors, which join in March and August-October, and the lagoon starts to look like it is covered in a pink blanket. The Esplanade, a paved, 5km walkway bordering the lagoon, brings you close enough that binoculars are practically unnecessary. The lagoon is currently having a salination crisis brought on by the local salt works. The problem needs to be solved in five years before the damage becomes irreversible. The **Salt Works** are huge heaps of white salt tower over the gates to one of the largest solar evaporation facilities in Africa (5000ha). The salt pans, each 40ha, have directly contributed to the lagoon's circulation and salination problems. Oyster farms lie in some of the outer pans, and, with flamingos, they filter plankton from the water. Tours of the Works, pans, and oyster farms are only available through Inshore Safaris. Tours include oysters, flamingo watching, and a glass of champagne. (At the southwestern end of Nangolo Mbumba Dr., on the lagoon past Esplanade Park.) **Bird Island,** at the inland end of 13th Rd., is a bird sanctuary that allows for great bird-watching from observation towers. Shallow ponds shaded with reeds and tall grass draw birds from both the lagoon and the desert. On days when the nearby sewage treatment facility becomes unbearable, opt for the short trails along the ponds.

ADVENTURES

For all of the listings below, book your adventure way in advance before you arrive in Namibia, especially if you plan to visit in December or January. Most of these companies will negotiate prices, so call for the latest rates and terms. Solo travelers may get better rates with freelance guides. **Tas von Solms** (☎ 20 3056 or 081 128 6182), a desert survival specialist, is an excellent choice.

LAND ADVENTURES

Inshore Safaris (☎ 20 2609; cell 081 129 2619; fax 20 2198; info@inshore.com.na; www.inshore.com.na), on 12th Rd., between 9th St. and Nangolo Mbumba Dr., opposite the tourist bureau. The only operator allowed to tour the salt works and oyster farms, this office also books a wide range of desert activities from quad biking to catered meals in the desert. Their Namib Desert Highlights tours are excellent for those who like to keep their feet on the ground and learn about the ecosystem. Check the web for an extensive list of tour and package options.

African Heritage Tours (☎/fax 20 7401; afrherit@iafrica.com.na; www.african-heritage-tours.com), on Nangolo Mbumba Dr. at Scheppman St. Specializes in anything 4WD, including self-drive environmental tours and Sandwich Harbor. Their Mini Dune Jeep vehicles are one-of-a-kind in the area. Self-driving trips available. Tours always include tasty snacks and a glass of champagne.

AQUA ADVENTURES

Eco Marine Kayak Tours, 63 Theo-Ben Gurirab St. (☎/fax 20 3144; jeannem@iafrica.com.na). Kayaks are the best way to get right down in it with lagoon birds or go hand-to-flipper with rambunctious seal pups on the Pelican Point and Dolphin Experience, which begins with a 4WD trip past the lagoon to Pelican Point and features quality open-water kayaking. Morning tours only. Inquire for rates.

Mola Mola Marine & Desert Adventure (☎ 20 5511; fax 20 7593; cell 081 127 2522; mola-mola@iafrica.com.na; www.mola-mola.com.na), corner of the Esplanade and Atlantic St. Specializes in dolphin and seal cruises that depart from Walvis Bay Yacht Club. The boats are big, but not nearly as exciting as kayaks. Morning cruises (9am-12:30pm) N$350. Also organizes angling adventures and open-sea bird watching.

EXTREME ADVENTURES

Dare Devil Adventures (☎ 20 9532 or 081 127 5701; fax 20 9584; daredadv@iafrica.com.na), opposite the Long Beach (Langstrand) Holiday Resort on the B2, 15km north of Walvis Bay. Specializes in sand dune adventures (dune boarding and quad-biking) on the dune fields between Swakopmund and Walvis Bay.

Albatross Paragliding (☎ 20 0250 or 081 241 5483; abstauch@iway.na), next to Dare Devil Adventures. Offers paragliding lessons and a full pilot licensing course. Tandem flights over Long Beach (Langstrand) sand dunes 18km north of Walvis Bay.

NAMIB-NAUKLUFT NATIONAL PARK

Shifting dunes, wind-swept gravel plains, rugged canyons of volcanic rock, and looming mountain ranges all lie within the boundaries of Namib-Naukluft National Park, one of the largest national parks in the world. Established in 1979, when the Namib Desert Park and Naukluft Mountain Zebra Park were combined with state lands and Diamond Area 2, Namib-Naukluft is an impressive 23,000 sq. km., making it Namibia's largest conservation area. In summer, this desert and semi-desert area gets scorchingly hot during the day. However, the icy Benguela Current sweeps up the Namibian coast from Antarctica, bestowing a life-giving fog that pushes inland at night to cool the earth and enable the survival of the many animal and plant species that have adapted to this unforgiving environment. Regarded as the oldest desert in the world, the Namib enjoys the distinction of being the only desert that is home to elephants, lions, rhinos, and giraffes, as well as *Welwitschia mirabilis*, Namibia's national plant. Within Namib-Naukluft are some of Namibia's top tourist destinations, including the Weltwitschia Plains, the Naukluft mountains and the dunes around the Sossusvlei. These dunes, among the world's largest, dazzle many a visitor as they rise in peachy gold mounds that sparkle purple when hit by the late-day sun.

NAMIB-NAUKLUFT AT A GLANCE

AREA: 23,000 sq. km	**GATEWAYS:** Swakopmund (p. 494), Solitaire, Lüderitz (p. 514), Walvis Bay (p. 502)
CLIMATE: Semi-arid to arid	
FEATURES: Namib Desert, Naukluft Mountains, Sossusvlei Dunes, Kuiseb River	**CAMPING:** Campsites throughout the park; make reservations at 061 23 6975; fax 22 4900
HIGHLIGHTS: Hiking trails, dune boarding and climbing, quad biking, camping, 4WD trails, game viewing	**FEES:** Vary by gate. Day permits N$20-30 per person plus $20 per vehicle; camping N$80-160 per campsite

■ ⌐ ORIENTATION AND TRANSPORTATION

Namib-Naukluft Park stretches from east of Swakopmund in the north to the Lüderitz-Keetmanshoop road in the south, extending from the coast approximately 100km inland and jutting further east in the middle to include the Naukluft mountains. Most of the park has no roads and is completely inaccessible. The exceptions, however, are among Namibia's top tourist attractions. They are: the **Namib Region** southeast of Swakopmund, with its **Welwitschia Plains; the Naukluft Mountains** 100km south; the **dunes** at **Sesriem** and **Sossusvlei;** and **Sandwich Harbor,** directly south of and accessible from Walvis Bay.

A network of well-maintained, 2WD-friendly, and often scenic gravel roads provide what access there is to the park. **C28** and **C14** run west to east through the Namib area, making it the most readily accessible of the park's sections. At the picturesque Gaub Pass, C14 bends to the southeast, and later passes through the Naukluft mountains. **C19** strikes off to the west at Solitaire and goes to Sesriem, then approaches scenic perfection further southeast in the **Zarishoogte Pass.** There is no road to Sandwich Harbor, though 4WDs can make it from the north. Several roads provide views of the southern end of the park, particularly **D707** north of Aus and **D826** south of Sesriem.

Forget about public transportation around the park, and don't count on hitching; traffic is just too light and weather conditions too extreme to make thumbing a safe or reliable option. The car-less should opt for a guided tour from Windhoek (see p. 461) or Swakopmund (p. 494), or Walvis Bay.

⌐ ACCOMMODATIONS

Indoor accommodations options are along a 50km stretch of road just northwest of the Naukluft range, in an area outside of the park's boundaries. They are within an easy day's drive of both Windhoek and Swakopmund and an ideal launching point if you want to approach the park from the north. Accommodations can also be found, closer to Windhoek, near Maltahöhe.

Solitaire (rest camp ☎/fax 063 29 3387; lodge reservation 061 24 0375), 200 km southeast of Walvis Bay on the C14 and 80km north of Sesriem on the C19, is an oasis of hospitality make world-famous by commercials, documentaries, an original 1937 shop, and Moose's apple strudel (N$8). After recent additions, the rest camp will include a restaurant, open daily for lunch and sandwiches (N$10), a provision shop (with Moose's homemade bread; N$7), 24hr. petrol station, camping and lodge accommodations. 24 hr. check in. Lodge (with breakfast) single N$150, double N$215. Camping with hot shower and *braai* N$20 per person; N$30 per car. Reservations recommended. Credit Cards accepted. ❶

Weltevrede Farm (☎063 29 3374; fax 29 3375; aswarts@mweb.com.na). On C19 47km north of Sesriem and 37km south of Solitaire. The 12,000ha farm borders the park's dunes and mountains and has hiking and 4WD trails near recently-discovered ancient San paintings. Reputably excellent food. Swimming pool and bar. Laundry. Sunset drives to the tops of nearby dunes (2hr.; N$80 per person with drinks). Reservations necessary for bungalows. Bungalows with 2 beds and private bath, and family suites with 2 bedrooms and private bath, N$350 per person with full board. Campsites with hot shower and *braai* N$90 for 3 people, then N$30 per person. MC/V. ❷

Namib Restcamp (☎/ fax 063 69 3376/7). North of Weltervrede Farm on C19 (27km south of Solitaire, 57km north of Sesriem). Centered around pastures full of animals, bungalows and campsites have astonishingly close views of the Petrified Dunes. Sunset dune drives (2hr.; N$100 per person including drinks). Swimming pool, bar/restaurant, *braai*, horseback riding. Reservations recommended. Bungalows with bath, lounge, and kitchen N$360 per person, with breakfast and dinner; N$400 per person with full board. Camping with hot shower N$40 per person. Cash only. ❶

CAMPING

IN THE PARK

Namib Section. Minimalist camping sites are available at Kuiseb Bridge, Mirabib, Homeb, Vogelfederberg, Tinkas, Ganab, Weltwitschia, Aruvlei, Kries Rus, Blutkopje and Rock Arch. Campers must provide their own camping equipment, food, water, and firewood. No shower or kitchen, and only field toilets. N$80 per campsite per night for up to 4 people, N$10 each additional person. ❷

Naukluft Section. To get to the Naukluft/Koedoesrus Campground, about 50km northeast of Sesriem, head southeast on the C14 from Walvis Bay, turn right onto the D854, 50 km past Solitaire. After 15km, turn right at the Naukluft gates; follow this road another 11km to the campground office. These seven sites are nestled deep within the Naukluft mountains, shielded from the morning sun by valley walls. Though mornings are chilly, there are frequent animal sightings, including baboons. Firewood (N$12 per bag) and hot showers are available, but there are no other facilities or electricity. Reservations recommended—contact NWR in Windhoek. Reception open dawn to dusk. Campsites N$90 per site up to 4 people, N$10 per additional person, not including park permits. Cash only. ❷

Sesriem. The park office has 27 large, well-kept campsites that look out on Elim Dune from beneath spacious camel-thorn trees. Clean ablution block with hot shower, *braai* facilities, bar, fuel, public phone, and firewood (N$15 per bag). N$160 per campsite with up to 4 people, N$10 per additional person, not including park permits. ❷

NEAR THE PARK

Sossusvlei 4WD Rental (☎/fax 063 69 3223/7; adventure@sossusvleilodge.com). One kilometer outside the gates of Sesriem Camp. A recent change in ownership means that

Namib-Naukluft National Park

LODGES (PRIVATE)
Namib Restcamp, 14
Solitaire, 13
Weltevrede Farm, 15

MAJOR CAMPSITES (PRIVATE)
Sossusvlei 4WD Rental, 18
Sossusvlei River Campsite, 19

MAJOR CAMPSITES (PARK-OPERATED)
Naukluft, 16
Sesriem, 17

MINOR CAMPSITES
Aruvlei, 10
Blutkopje, 5
Ganab, 7
Groot Tinkas, 3
Homeb, 12
Kriess Rus, 8
Kuiseb Bridge, 9
Middel Tinkas, 2
Mirabib, 11
Rock Arch, 4
Swakop River, 1
Vogelvederberg, 6

paved roads
gravel roads
park roads
4WD roads

the nearby Sossusvlei Lodge Adventure Center, which campers can use to organize tours and adventures, now runs the site. Offers hot shower and *braai*, but no electricity or, surprisingly, car rental. This campground is an excellent alternative to the pricier Sesriem Campground, which is practically next door. Reception closes at 8pm. N$40 per person. ❶

Sossusvlei River Campsite (☎063 29 3236). 28km south of Sesriem on the D826. Geared towards larger groups, you need a 4WD to get to this peaceful spot in a meadow. It's near a mountain, but there's no river. Reservation required. N$40 per person. ❶

Solitaire, **Weltevrede Farm**, and **Daweb Guest Farm** (see **Accommodations**) also have camping facilities.

◎ ⚠ SIGHTS AND OUTDOORS

NAMIB DRIVE AND THE WELWITSCHIA PLAIN. The thirteen stations of this **scenic drive** on the **Welwitschia Plains** can be completed in four hours on a daytrip from Swakopmund, where the NWR office distributes the permits and the glossy, informative guide to the drive. The road first traverses a barren plain which supports only blackish crusty lichens—sprinkle a few drops of water onto some of these and watch how they blossom and change color within a few minutes. The road continues to several lookouts over the vast expanse of undulating desolation and the sweeping vistas of **Swakop Valley Moon Landscape.** It finally reaches the **Welwitschia Plains**, the only habitat of Namibia's national plant, *Welwitschia mirabilis*, a bizarre desert denizen with no close relatives. A corral at site number twelve protects a colossal specimen estimated to be more than 1500 years old. Though less glamorous, the road to Welwitschia campsite, which splits off to the left of the scenic route at site number 11, provides a better, less touristed encounter with this living fossil—a tree related to the pine tree that seems to have many intertwining leaves, but really has only two leathery ones that have been ripped into shreds by wind over time. *(From Swakopmund, follow the B2 towards Windhoek. Turn right onto the C28 just after the Martin Luther steam engine; continue on this road for 17km. Shortly after the Namib-Naukluft park sign, turn left at the Welwitschia Drive sign; soon you will see the first of the 13 stone beacons indicating sites of interest. Day Permits for N$20 per person plus N$20 per vehicle from the NWR office and most service stations in Walvis Bay/ Swakopmund.)*

SOSSUSVLEI. Sossusvlei, meaning "the vlei" (or flooded hollow people never return from," actually has two separate attractions: the 60km of paved road runs west from Sesriem campsite through some of the world's highest dunes and the vlei itself. At day break, the dunes are a warm apricot color with shadows that playfully chase each other across the dunes' faces. Throughout the day, the colors change, until sunset when they have a purple glow, the by-product of their high iron content. The vleis document the history of plant and Bushman life with its petrified trees and ancient rock tools.

Dune 45, 45km from Sesriem on the way to Sossusvlei, is the most accessible and thus most-walked dune in the area. A parade of caravans leaves the Sesriem gates an hour before dawn to claim dunetop seats for sunrise. While there are few better places to greet the sun, many dune connoisseurs prefer to wait and leave Sesriem as the sun rises, when the dunes along the road are at their most beautiful and game is the most active and visible. If you don't fancy an early morning dune

 DUNE BUGGING. A walk up one of Sossusvlei's dunes is no walk in the park. Dune 45 is almost 50 stories tall, and the popular sunrise walk up it will give your legs a serious workout. Keep these tips in mind will make great trek a little easier. Walk *along* dune crests, not across them. Avoid the slip face--the side of the dune away from the wind, characterized by the softest sand and the steepest slope. Always wear closed shoes: midday heat is dangerously hot. And, finally, always bring water, a hat, and sunscreen.

climb, Sossusvlei is also a delight place to watch the sunrise. If you head out soon after daybreak, you can beat the rush of 4WD traffic to the vleis.

The 2WD parking lot for Sossusvlei is 60km west of Sesriem. Sossusvlei is 5km farther; those without 4WD must walk the sandy road or take a 4WD shuttle (N$60 per person; runs 7am-4pm). The *vlei's* appearance varies with the water level: when there little rain its hardly more than a barren lime flat, but with heavy rain it becomes a vibrant and active oasis of trees, plants, and animals. **Hiddenvlei,** just

NAMIBIA

2km from the 2WD parking lot, is just as beautiful as its more famous sibling. **Deadvlei**, 1.1km off the 4WD track, is named for the dead camel-thorn trees, some of which are almost a thousand years old, that make it a photographer's favorite.

SESRIEM CANYON. This canyon, 4.5km from Sesriem Campground down a road behind BP petrol station, makes a great afternoon stopoff after a morning at Sossusvlei. Carved by the Tsauchab River, the canyon is 25-30m deep. Its nearly vertical walls make for a cool and calm canyon floor, the nesting ground for numerous birds that fly about constantly. Steps lead down onto the canyon's short and easy hiking trail from the parking lot (look on the right as you enter the canyon).

SANDWICH HARBOR. A favorite with birders and nature lovers, this body of water is a sanctuary for thousands of coastal and fresh water birds. Once an open bay freshened by water filtering from inland aquifers, silt has more recently created a long, brackish strip of water separated from the ocean by a sand bar. Continuing siltation will likely fill the lagoon completely within five years, but for now, flamingos, pelicans, terns, and other birds frolic here. It is strongly advised that explorers go with a guide and more than one 4WD, as roadless dune driving along treacherous shores is involved. The last 1.7 km before the lagoon must be walked. *(48 km south of Walvis Bay along the coast. Day permits are available at the Walvis Bay Tourist Bureau or through any Sandwich Harbor guided tour operator.)*

NAUKLUFT 4-WHEEL-DRIVE TRAIL. This self-guided, 73km trail is marked with points of interest along the way and can be completed in two days; a shorter, one-day version is also available. The track is for the die-hard 4WD enthusiast, and includes some very steep and narrow passes. On any of these trails, one may spot baboons, kudu, zebra, springbok, oryx, and dassies, as well as numerous bird species. When parking, lock up your car and roll up the windows to prevent baboons from invading. Those wishing to form caravans should ask around in Windhoek or Swakopmund. *(Overnight camp consisting of partially open shelters includes toilets, shower, and water. Equipment, food, and firewood must be provided. N$220 per vehicle. Check in at the Koedoesrus Campsite office no later than 2pm to begin and again when finished. Day trip permits N$20 per person, plus N$20 per vehicle.)*

⬛ HIKING TRAILS

NAUKLUFT TRAIL. For experienced and fit hikers, this eight-day, 120km trail offers the most thorough exposure to the Naukluft range. Scenic challenges include chain-assisted waterfall scaling and several steep ascents. A stay in Koedoesrus Campground's simple Hikers Haven, with self-catering kitchen, hot shower, and *braai*, the first and last nights of the hike, is included in the price. There are overnight shelters with pit toilets and drinking water on the self-guided, signposted trail. Hikers should begin each day carrying at least two liters of water, have sturdy hiking boots, and take a sleeping bag and gas stove for cooking. A four-day version covering the first half of the full trail can also be walked. *(Trail open Mar.-Oct. Hike permit N$100. Medical certificate of physical fitness required. Contact the NWR or MET office in Windhoek for details.)*

OLIVE TRAIL. This 10km, five-hour trail begins by ascending slowly to the top of a plateau affording breathtaking vistas from over 1800m of the surrounding canyons. It then descends into the largest of these, a (mostly) dry riverbed, before passing between banks blessed with quiver trees and the nests of sociable weaverbirds. *(Check in at the Koedesrus Campground office, then drive back 4km toward the main entrance. Follow the white footprints. Check in with the office when done.)*

N A M I B I A

WATERKLOOF TRAIL. Waterkloof (17km, 6-7hr.) explores the heart of the Nauk-luft mountains. It features pools, caves, quiver trees and a view from a 1900m elevation. Hikers should be physically fit, as there are some steep climbs. *(Check in at the Koedoesrus Campground office. The trail starts at the campground itself, 1 km past the office. Follow the yellow footprints.)*

THE SOUTH

Namibia's arid southern region spans two of Africa's most interesting deserts, the Namib in the west and the Kalahari in the east. Vast tracts of sunbaked savannah and rugged mountains fall in between. Along the Atlantic coast lie areas chronicling Namibia's past and present. **Sperrgebiet,** a forbidden diamond area open only to diamond barons, holds one of the keys to Namibia's economy. **Lüderitz,** resembling a morsel of Bavaria left in between the Namib's dunes and the Atlantic's waves, is a testament to the Germans' impact on Namibia and a history buff's delight. Further inland, **Fish River Canyon** surrounds an area where over the course of hundreds of thousands of years the forces of nature have created a natural spectacle unrivaled in most of Africa. From the basins to the peaks, the South offers a variety of challenging activities, including one of the most challenging trails in all of Africa, the Fish River Hiking Trail, and the world's longest 4WD trail.

KEETMANSHOOP ☎ 063

Located at the intersection of the two biggest roads in southern Namibia, Keetmanshoop (pop. 22,000) is certainly the "Capital of the South." Prior to 1866, when Rhenish missionaries arrived from Germany, the area was known as Nu-gouses ("Black Marsh"). It was renamed Keetmanshoop to honor Johan Keetman, a wealthy German businessman who donated the money to build the first church here. Although many people use Keetmanshoop as a launching pad for expeditions to surrounding sites, including such natural wonders as the Quiver Tree Forest and Giant's Playground, the town itself is worth a look.

TRANSPORTATION. Keetmanshoop is 500km south of Windhoek on the B1, 334km east of Lüderitz on the B4, and about 280km from the Hobas gate in Fish River Canyon Park via the B1. From the station on Daan Viljoen St. in the northern part of the town, **TransNamib Starline** (☎ 22 9202) runs train service to Windhoek (12hr., daily, N$40-60) via Mariental (5hr., daily, N$35-40); and Upington, South Africa (12hr., W and Sa 8:50am). For reservations, visit or call the train station daily 8am-4pm. **Intercape** tickets (☎ 22 3063) can be bought at the **Engen Service Station** (☎ 22 2690), on 5th Ave., three blocks south of Kaiser St. Buses stop at the BP service station across 5th Ave from Engen Service Station and run to: Windhoek (7hr.; T, Th-F, Su 11:45pm; N$240); Cape Town (M, W, F, and Su 10:45pm; N$320); Upington (M, W, F, and Su 10:45pm). TransNamib Starline also offers bus services to Lüderitz (5hr.; M, W, F 7:30am; N$67) from the train station.

ORIENTATION AND PRACTICAL INFORMATION. The roads to Keetmanshoop from the east and south both lead to Kaiser St., with the center of town two blocks north. Accommodations, food and services are located primarily in a rectangle formed by Mittel St. to the north, Fenschel St. to the south, 8th Ave. to the west, and 4th Ave. to the east. Most municipal services, shops and banks are concentrated on Fenschel St. and Mittel St. around 5th Ave. The **Southern Tourist Forum,** 33 5th Ave., is half a block south of Fenschel St. (☎ 22 1166; fax 22 3818. Open M-Th 7:30am-12:30pm and 1:30-4:30pm, F 7:30am-12:30pm and 1:30-4pm.)

Keetmanshoop

🏠 ACCOMMODATIONS
Burgervereniging van
Keetmanshoop, 1
Municipal Caravan Park, 5

🍎 FOOD
Andre's Restaurant, 4
Balathon Hungarian Food Shop, 3
Lara's Restaurant, 2

Services Include: **Standard Bank,** at Fenschel St. and 5th Ave., with *bureau de change* and **ATM** (☎22 3274; open M-F 9am-3:30pm, Sa 8:30-11am); **Commercial Bank,** at Mittel St. and 5th Ave., with *bureau de change* (☎22 3354; open M-F 9am-4:30pm, Sa 9-11am); **Spar Supermarket,** at Mittel St. and 4th Ave. (☎22 3590; open M-F 8am-1pm and 2:30-6:30pm, Sa 7:30am-1pm); **Sentra supermarket,** on 5th Ave., half a block south of Kaiser St. (open M-F 7:30am-5pm, Sa 8am-1pm); **police** (☎11 011), at the corner of 5th Ave. and Kaiser St.; **Khabuser Pharmacy,** on Mittel St. between 6th and 8th Ave. (☎22 3309; open M-F 8am-1pm and 2:30-5:30pm, Sa 8am-12:30pm); **state hospital** and **ambulance service** (☎22 3388), off the B1 north of town; **Internet access** at the **iway Internet Cafe,** on 6th Ave. between Mittel and Fenschel St. (☎22 5902; open daily 8am-10pm; N$15 per 30min.). The **post office** is on the corner of Fenschel St. and 5th Ave., opposite the tourist office. A private **pay phone** is inside. (☎22 3211. Open M-Tu, Th-F 8am-4:30pm; W 8:30am-4:30pm; Sa 8am-noon.)

🏠📷 ACCOMMODATIONS AND FOOD. Burgervereniging van Keetmanshoop ❶, 12 Schmeide St., between 3rd and 4th Ave., has the bare necessities: a bed, a roof and hot water. (☎22 3454. Self-catering kitchen. No check-in 10pm-8am; those are "quiet hours." Reservations recommended. N$70 per person, payable on arrival. Cash only.) The **Municipal Caravan Park ❶,** at 8th Ave. and Kaiser St., offers characterless but safe camping with hot showers (N$8), electricity hookup and *braai.* (☎22 1211. 24hr. check-in. N$35 per person, under 14 N$14; N$17 per vehicle per day. Traveler's checks accepted.) **Andre's Restaurant ❶**, on Fenschel St. between 7th and 8th Ave., offers food including pizza (N$11-46), sandwiches (N$5.50-7.50), and burgers (N$10-13) at good prices. (☎22 2572. Open M-F 8am-8pm, Sa 8:30am-2pm and 5:30-8pm, Su 6:30-8pm.) One of the few full-fledged restaurants in town is **Lara's Restaurant**, at 5th Ave. and Schmiede St. Lara's serves German grub for breakfast (N$18-35), lunch, and dinner (N$15-50). (☎22 2233. Open M-Sa 8am-10pm, Su 11:30am-2pm. Cash only.) **Balathon Hungarian Food Shop ❷**, on Mittel St. between 5th and 6th Ave., also serves breakfast (N$15-25), lunch and dinner. (☎22 2539. Open daily 8am-5pm.)

◨◩ SIGHTS AND ADVENTURES. The **Rhenish Mission Church**, at Kaiser St. and 7th Ave., houses the **Keetmanshoop Museum**, which details the history and culture of both the town and region. The beautifully simple church was rebuilt in 1895 after the original building was washed away in 1890 by the Aub River. In addition to the museum, the church houses art and geological displays. (☎22 1256. Open M-Th 7:30am-12:30pm and 1:30-4:30pm, F 7:30am-12:30pm and 1:30-4pm. Free.)

Shrubs and hills dotted with strange-looking aloe trees combine to form an otherworldly atmosphere in the **Quiver Tree Forest National Monument,** 17km northeast of Keetmanshoop off the C17. Although their exact age is unknown, the trees are between 200 and 300 years old and stand 9m tall. They are called "Quiver Trees" because the bushmen used to make arrow quivers from their bark.

About 3km past the forest on the C17 lies **Giant's Playground**, a bizarre geological wonder of massive boulders piled one on top of another as if a giant had playfully heaped them together. Both of these wonders belong to a private farm, **Quiver Tree Forest Rest Camp** on Gariganus Farm, which charges day visitors N$10 entry fee and N$20 per vehicle for both sites and the cheetah feeding daily at 4pm. Overnight visitors can choose to camp at large impersonal campsites or stay in bungalows. (☎/fax 22 2835; quiver@iafrica.com.na. 24hr. check-in. Reservations recommended for bungalows. Bungalow singles N$165; doubles N$250. Camping N$50 per person. MC/V and traveler's checks.)

BRUKKAROS CRATER

One of the only geological formations which rises vertically from the flat plains between Asab and Keetmanshoop, this once-active volcano-*cum*-crater is 80,000 years old. To get there, take the B1 78km north from Keetmanshoop, turn left onto the C98 at Tses, and make a right after 40km onto the D3940. Brukkaros comes from the Nama word, *Kaitsi !Gudeb*, which refers to the large features around a Khoi-Khoi woman's waist. In the 1930s the Smithsonian had a sunspot observation center on the crater's rim, but now all that remains is the **Brukkaros Community Campsite ❶** at the crater's base. (Campsites N$25 per person, N$10 per vehicle. *Braai* sites N$15 per person; N$10 per vehicle.) The number of stars you can see here, in the midst of clean air free of light pollution, is unimaginable. Water and firewood is for sale and only small shelters, *braai* pits, and long drop toilets mark the campsites. There are two camping areas, one outside the crater and one on the floor of the crater, at the end of a very bumpy 4WD track. Otherwise, the **hike** into the crater is 6hr. roundtrip and features crystal rock formations, quiver trees, and the now-deserted Smithsonian station. Inquire at the gates for guides.

LÜDERITZ ☎063

Lüderitz (pop. 22,000) is a bizarre yet colorful windy Bavarian town which is besieged by black rock formations embracing the icy blue waters of Lüderitz Bay. The bay is a collection of caves, reefs, lagoons, and unspoiled beaches where the mighty waves of the wild Atlantic crash against the rocky coastline and produce

CAR GUARDS Namibians have an anti-theft device for their cars that is a little more comprehensive then the club. In many parking lots, there are car guards to watch your car. Working only for tips from car owners, car guards cannot have a criminal record and stand losing their lucrative and respected position if any complaints are brought against them. At first car guards can be startling, since they approach drivers as they exit their vehicles, but their presence is both worthwhile and assuring. Registered car guards, who pay the city a small sum to have the right to watch vehicles, are distinguished by their brightly colored bibs. Tipping, while not necessary, is advisable.

furiously white, foamy splashes. Nearby are beaches with seal and jackass penguin colonies. Desert winds often whirl about, sometimes blanketing the well-preserved German colonial buildings with sandy dust. Founded by the Bremen tobacco merchant Adolf Lüderitz in 1884, this was the first German settlement in what was then *Sudwestafrika*. Most of the historical German buildings owe their existence to the discovery of diamonds at nearby Kolmanskop in 1908. Now the center of Namibia's rock lobster industry, Lüderitz is also famous for its fresh oysters, bred in the icy Benguela current.

TRANSPORTATION

Flights: Air Namibia (☎ 20 2850), at the train station opposite the post office, has flights to **Cape Town**, Eros Airport in **Windhoek, Walvis Bay**, and **Oranjemund**. Open M-F 8-10am and 2-5pm.

Buses: TransNamib's Starline (☎ 20 1220) has buses to **Keetmanshoop** (5hr.; M, W, and F 12:30pm; N$76) from Bahnhof St. across from the post office. Buy tickets in the office or on the bus.

Car Rental: Avis (☎ 20 3965; fax 20 3967) on Bahnhof St. at Moltke.

ORIENTATION AND PRACTICAL INFORMATION

Situated at the northwestern corner of the diamond area known as *Sperrgebiet* ("forbidden territory"), Lüderitz is connected to Keetmanshoop, 334km away, by the tarred B4, which turns into Bay Rd. as you enter town. Most shops and services are on **Bismarck St.**

TOURIST AND FINANCIAL SERVICES

Tourist Office: Lüderitz Safaris & Tours (☎ 202 719/622 or 081 129 7236; ludsaf@africaonline.com.na), on Bismarck St. Extremely helpful office issues permits for Kolmanskop and Sperrgebiet, organizes custom safaris, books tickets for other tour companies, and sells cultural souvenirs. Open M-F 8am-1pm, 2-5pm, Sa 8-noon, Su 8:30-10:30am.

Tours: Visits *anywhere* in the diamond area are possible only with a valid permit issued by the Namibian police through NAMDEB. Permits can be obtained by applying one month in advance to **Lüderitz Safaris and Tours** (see Tourist Office) or another tour company depending on trip destination. Kolmanskop permits can be acquired the day of the trip. For additional tours, see **Sights and Adventures** p. 517.

Banks: Commercial Bank of Namibia, (☎ 20 2577) on Bismarck St., has *bureau de change*, **ATM,** and cash advances. (Open M-F 9am-12:45pm and 2-3:30pm, Sa 8:30-11am).

LOCAL, EMERGENCY, AND COMMUNICATIONS SERVICES

Supermarket: Spar (☎20 2667), on Bahnhof St. at Moltke. (Open M-F 7:30am-5:30pm, Sa 8am-1pm).

Camping Equipment: Augra Electric (☎20 2625; cash only) and **M&Z Hardware** (☎20 2036), both on Bismarck St.

Pharmacies: Reichs Pharmacy (☎202 806), on Bismarck St. Open M-F 7:30am-1pm and 2-5pm, Sa 8am-1pm.

Police (☎202 255), at Lessing Brucken St. and Bay Rd.

State hospital (☎202 466) and **ambulance service** (☎202 466); at end of Hafen St.

Internet Access: Club Internet Lüderitz, 16 Bismarck St. (☎206 061), opposite Lüderitz Safaris and Tours. N$20 per 30min. Open M-F 8am-1pm and 2-5pm, Sa 9am-noon; cash only).

Post Office: Corner of Bismarck St. and Nachtigal St. Fax, photocopying, public phones, and *Poste Restante*. Open M, T, Th, F 8am-4:30pm. W 8am-4pm, Sa 8am-noon.

▐ ACCOMMODATIONS

Backpackers Lodge, 7 Schinz St. (☎/fax 20 2000 or 20 2742; toya@ldz.namib.com). A central location, wealth of tourist information, and cool fellow backpackers make this converted house a comfortable and extremely well-kept home away from home. Everything from the TV lounge to the self-catering kitchen is alive with color. Laundry service. Checkout 10am. Dorms N$60; doubles N$140; passage beds N$50. Cash only. ❶

Shark Island Camp Ground and Bungalows (☎20 2752), on Shark Island in the harbor, reached by Kreplin Insel. A nice campground with a scenic view of Lüderitz Bay and the ocean, set on rocky and sandy soil and often very exposed to gusty winds. Decently well-kept, Shark Island has *braai*, 24hr. check-in, and communal ablution facilities. The bungalows have 6 beds with kitchen, bath, and bedding. Reservations recommended; contact the NWR office in Windhoek (☎25 6447) or Swakopmund (☎402 172). Sites N$95, vehicle N$10; bungalows N$300. Cash at gate; traveler's checks and credit cards can be used at office in town. ❷

Kratz Platz, 5 Nachtigal St. (☎/fax 20 2458), between Diaz and Berg St. Extremely nice, remodelled rooms. All have a TV, most have a bath, and some have a kitchen. Its central location and clean facilities make these rooms an excellent deal for the weary traveler. Reservations (not required) need a 25% deposit. Arrivals after 6pm should call ahead. Check-out 10am. Singles N$150; doubles N$220. Traveler's checks and credit cards accepted. ❷

Roman Catholic Guest House (☎20 3071, ask for Maria), corner of Bay Rd. and Lessing Brucken St. Coming into town from Keetmanshoop, the B4 turns into Bay Rd.; turn left onto Lessing Brucken St., and then, immediately before the bridge over the railway tracks, turn left onto the gravel road. Look for the little wooden gate in a red brick wall in rear of Roman Catholic Church. Away from the town center, these rooms are quiet and clean, with full bath and kitchen. Reservations recommended. Singles and doubles N$90 per person. ❷

▶ ♫ FOOD AND ENTERTAINMENT

▓ **Badger's Bistro/Ritzi's Seafood Restaurant** (☎202 818 or 081 124 335), on Diaz St., right off the rondo. If you're craving a burger (N$12) or want to drink beer at a hoppin' bar, go to Badger's. If you're in the mood for a beautifully decorated, quiet seafood restaurant with a great grilled tuna steak (N$60), head to Ritzi's. At both, the food is terrific and the waiters are friendly. Various menu options include breakfast (N$15-30), salads

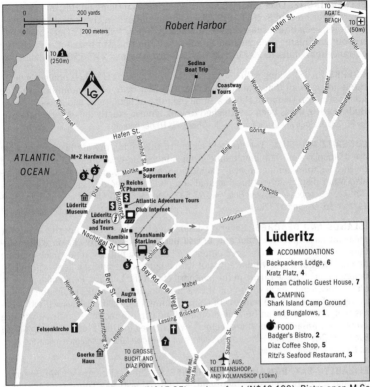

Lüderitz

🏠 ACCOMMODATIONS
Backpackers Lodge, 6
Kratz Platz, 4
Roman Catholic Guest House, 7

⛺ CAMPING
Shark Island Camp Ground
and Bungalows, 1

🍎 FOOD
Badger's Bistro, 2
Diaz Coffee Shop, 5
Ritzi's Seafood Restaurant, 3

(from N$15), light meat meals (N$15-35), and seafood (N$40-100). Bistro open M-Sa 9am-2am. Ritzi's open M-Sa 6-11pm, reservations recommended. ❶

Diaz Coffee Shop (☎ 203 147), corner of Bismarck and Nachtigal St. The light and airy seating area, complete with magazines, is a nice spot for a good breakfast (N$20-40), lunch (N$7-20) or random milkshake (N$13). Cakes (N$10) and the menu, changed monthly, are sure to spice up your life. Open M-F 7:30am-5pm, Sa 8am-1pm and 3-5pm, Su 8am-1pm. Credit cards accepted. ❶

👁 🗾 SIGHTS AND ADVENTURES

For information on organized tours, see **Adventure Outfitters,** below.

KOLMANSKOP. The best-known among the ghost mining villages in Sperrgebiet, this once-thriving town is an eerie testimony to mankind's obsession with glittering objects. The once opulent buildings have been invaded by the desert, with some almost completely engulfed in a sea of sand. Kolmanskop is a must see, whether you choose to climb in and among the buildings or just see the museum, which displays the history of the diamond industry, accompanied by photos and mining instruments. (Located 10km east of Lüderitz, off the B4 to Keetmanshoop. Visitors must obtain permit from Lüderitz Safaris & Tours (see **Practical Information,** p.457). 1hr. tours M-Sa 9:30 and 10:45am, Su 10am. Tour and ½ day permits adults N$30, age 6-14 N$15; tour and all day photo permits N$100 per person.)

NAMIBIA

FELSENKIRCHE. Overlooking Lüderitz Bay from atop Diamond Hill, this Lutheran Church was erected in 1911-1912. The colorful and extremely intricate stain-glass windows, seen best a sunset, were donated by Kaiser Wilhelm II. Once a month a traveling minister preaches on Sunday, see the bulletin board at the church entrance for details. *(☎ 20 2381. Open M-Sa 6-7pm in summer, 4:45-5:30pm in winter.)*

GOERKE HAUS. Along with the church, Lieutenant Hans Goerke's opulently decorated house is all that remains of Lüderitz's first taste of diamond dollars. The house sits atop Diamond Hill in a small paradise of palm trees and grass terraces. Built in 1910, it has been refurbished to look almost exactly like its original style. *(☎ 20 2312. Open M-F 2-4pm and Sa-Su 4-5pm. N$10 per person.)*

LÜDERITZ MUSEUM. The greatest assets of this small, private history museum are its displays on Namibian ethnic groups, including weaponry and clothing, and on the diamond mining process, including *Schutztruppe* memorabilia. There are also other displays about local animal and plant life, geology, and marine fossils. *(On Diaz St., opposite Bayview Hotel. ☎ 202 532. Open M-F 8:30-11am and 3:30-5pm, Sa 9-11am. N$5, children N$3.50.)*

ISLANDS AND BEACHES. Several islands and beaches near Lüderitz make for pleasant daytrips. **Diaz Point** and **Grosse Bucht,** accessible by car on well-maintained gravel roads, can be seen either in a ½ day or a full day, if you pack a picnic lunch. Diaz Point is a windswept spot with a light house and sea lions within binocular range. Grosse Bucht, at the southern end of the Lüderitz Peninsula, is a desolate. Dark sand beach where the waves crash against the rocks as flamingos play in the surf amongst the remains of a small shipwreck. **Halifax Island,** with its jackass penguin colony, can be visited on a sailing trip offered by Atlantic Adventure Tours (see **Adventure Outfitters,** below), which goes to Diaz Point. *(To reach Grosse Bucht and Diaz Point, take Bismarck St. south from downtown Lüderitz and then follow the signs on the gravel roads. Dress warmly.)*

ELIZABETH BAY, POMONA, AND BOGENFELS. These sites are within Sperrgebiet and are only accessible by organized tours. Coastways Tours' (see **Adventure Outfitters** below) goes to Pomona and Bogenfels, while the Ghost Town Tours organizes trips to Elizabeth Bay. Both Pomona and Elizabeth Bay are Consolidated Diamond Mines' ghost towns south of Lüderitz. Elizabeth Bay is known for its weathered, honeycombed walls, while Pomona, further away and less well-known, holds more historic interest with a cemetery and mining equipment. Even further south is Bogenfels, a 55m high sea arch.

ADVENTURE OUTFITTERS

Apart from **Lüderitz Safaris & Tours** (see **Practical Information,** above), the following also offer organized trips and tours (many including the sights listed above).

Atlantic Adventure Tours (☎/fax 204 030; 081 127 9565; sedina@iafrica.com.na) runs sailing trips to seal and penguin colonies on Diaz Point and Halifax Island. About 2½hr.; depart from Lüderitz Harbor daily at 8am, also occasionally at 2pm during peak season. All trips weather permitting. Dress warmly. N$150, ages 2-12 N$75.

Coastways Tours Lüderitz (☎ 202 002, fax 202 003; lewiscwt@iway.na) organizes 4WD trips to Pomona, Bogenfels, and into the Namib Desert to Saddle Hill and Spencer Bay. Namib Desert trips are three-day, self-drive guided tours with overnight stays at a shelter with ablution facilities and kitchen. Highlights are beautiful desert scenery, untouched beaches, isolated shipwrecks, and desert wildlife. Off-road driving experience essential; min. 8 persons and 2 vehicles per trip. Inquire for rates.

Ghost Town Tours (☎204 031; kolmans@iafrica.com.na) operates informative 1hr. guided tours of Kolmanskop (see **Sights and Adventures**). Trips to Elizabeth Bay require a minimum of 4 people. Children under 14 prohibited. Inquire for rates.

FISH RIVER CANYON NATIONAL PARK   ☎063

Located in the lower reaches of Namibia's longest river, the mighty Fish River Canyon is one of the continent's most awesome geological phenomena. This spectacular wonder is second in size only to the Blue Nile Gorge in Ethiopia, measuring 160km in length and up to 27km across. Since this is one of the few rivers in Namibia regularly supplied with water, the change in seasons here is obvious and is directly connected to the rivers' flow. In winter, the Fish River is little more than a muddy trickle, and its plants lose their bright green. In summer, however, the canyon flourishes with the renewed strength of the river's flow, bringing life back to plants and animals alike. The **Fish River Canyon Hiking Trail**, 85km in length and one of Africa's most challenging trails, is only open to hikers April to September because there are high temperatures and floods during the summer.

⊏⊏ TRANSPORTATION AND ORIENTATION. There is no public transportation to the canyon, but some lodges (see **Accommodations,** below) do offer lifts for a fee. The Canyon is in the south-central part of Namibia, 150km from the South African border. There are two entrances to the park: **Hobas** and **Ai-Ais**. To get to Hobas from Keetmanshoop, take the B4 west 43km to Seeheim, turn left onto the C12, and then turn right onto the D601 after 75km, following the signs to the Fish River Canyon. After Seeheim, all roads are gravel. To get to Ai-Ais from Keetmanshoop, take the B1 south 186km to the C10, turn right, and follow the C10 west 73km. Both entrances are 2WD accessible.

⊓ PRACTICAL INFORMATION. Hobas, at the canyon's northern tip, is only 10km from the canyon's main viewpoint, and is a logical starting point for exploring the park. It suffers from (or is blessed by) a lack of infrastructure and accommodations, so arrive stocked with food, camping gear, and petrol. **Ai-Ais,** at the southern end of the park, is the main resort area, with a shop, restaurant, pools and saunas, and lodging. The nearest vistas, however, are quite a drive. The gates at **Hobas** (☎26 6028) are open daily 6am-10pm (reception 7am-5pm). The gates at **Ai-Ais** (☎26 2045; fax 26 2047 or 26 2048) are open 24hr. (reception sunrise-sunset). Daily fees N$20, ages 6-16 N$2, and vehicles N$20.

⊓⊓ ACCOMMODATIONS AND FOOD. Campsites ❷ at **Hobas** and **Ai-Ais** include communal ablution blocks, power outlets, *braai*, and use of the pools. Ai-Ais also has field kitchens with stoves and ovens. Bookings for accommodations can be made through the **Central Reservations Office** in Windhoek (☎061 236 975; 223 903; fax 224 900). Hobas' campgrounds are a bit smaller than Ai-Ais', but they have more shade and privacy, and are closer to the viewpoints. (Sites N$125 up to 4 people, N$10 each additional person up to 8; provision shop open 7am-5pm.) The posher lodgings at **Ai-Ais** are geared to exhausted canyon hikers and to relaxing vacationers. Guests can use the hot springs (N$15, children N$10), as well as the restaurant (open daily 7-8am, noon-1:30pm and 6-8:30; breakfast and dinner buffet N$60, lunch *a la carte*). There is also a provision store (open daily 8am-6pm) and a gas station. (Sites N$125; self-catering chalet quads N$220, with bath N$300-360.)

Several other accommodations lie near the park. **Cañon Roadhouse ❶**, 14km east of Hobas on the D601, offers large and semi-private campsites, peacefully set in the shade, with well-kept ablution blocks, *braai*, pool, and an *a la carte* restaurant. A 2hr. hiking trail skirts the mesa ridge that abuts the property. (☎26 6031; nature.i@mweb.com.na. Cash only.)

About 60km north of the Hobas Gate is **Fish River Canyon Lodge** ❹ (camping ❶), which offers private rooms, self-catering dorm beds, and camping. To get there, follow the C12 60km south from Seeheim and turn right at the sign marked Springfontein; it's 22km farther by gravel road which is 2WD accessible if cautious. The dorm, housed in "The Stable," has communal ablution blocks and a kitchen, but does not include bedding. Private rooms in the main building include bath and breakfast (single N$260; double N$420). Alternatively, you can camp at a spot beside the Fish River as it flows through this private property. These campsites and 6 huts are a 12km 4WD trip from the lodge, and have communal ablution facilities and a field kitchen with a fridge and a hot plate. (☎/fax 22 3762; frlodge@iafrica.com.na. Backpackers "trips" are also available, including transport to and from Keetmanshoop, accommodations, and activities for 2 days. Bush camping without/with facilities N$50/N$180 per vehicle plus N$10 per person. Huts in canyon N$180 per vehicle plus N$10 per person. 4WD transport to canyon N$70 per person each way. Dorm backpacker trip with self-catering N$580 per person. Private room backpacker trip with full board N$950 per person.)

⚠️🏕 OUTDOORS AND ADVENTURES. The Fish River Canyon's main attraction is the 85km **hiking trail,** one of the most challenging in Africa, that furrows through the canyon from Hobas to Ai-Ais, taking 4-5 days. Due to the heat, the trail is normally only open from April 15 to September 15 (in some heavy rainfall years, however, the trail has not opened until June). It's best to spend the night at Hobas before starting the strenuous hike. (N$100 per person, 3 person min. Call the **Central Reservations Office** in Windhoek at 061 23 6995, 061 23 6996, or 22 3903; fax 22 4900 for information and bookings.) Hikers must find their own transport from Hobas to the trail and from Ai-Ais back to Hobas. One option is to contact Cañon Lodge (☎23 0066; fax 25 1863).

Hobas is the best place for views of the canyon, with the **Main Viewpoint** only 10km away. **Hiker's Point,** where canyon hikes begin, and **Sulphur Springs,** 3km and 10km from the Main Viewpoint respectively, also offer jaw-dropping vistas from different angles. Both are accessible by gravel roads that, while passable by a 2WD, can become treacherous during the rainy seasons. Hikers point is also accessible along a trail, starting at the Main Viewpoint, that skirts the canyon's edge. This is the only trail left to satisfy hikers who don't want to walk a full 85km.

Both **Fish River Lodge** and Cañon Lodge, which owns the Cañon Roadhouse, offer a wide variety of activities. **Hiking, 4WD trails,** and **scenic drives** are available on the 15,000ha private canyon property owned by Fish River Lodge and on the 100,000ha Gondwana Cañon Park owned by the Cañon Lodge. At Fish River Lodge, all trails are marked and self-guided, and fires are allowed. The landscape includes fascinating rock formations, crystal-clear waterpools, and a variety of small game. (Contact lodge for reservations. 1½-day trail N$250; 30km, 2-day trail N$275; 40km, 3-day trail N$300; 85km, 5-day trail N$350.) All trails can be completed by anyone physically fit; prices are per person, and 5-day trips include first and last nights spent in the dorm. The 4WD trails are of medium difficulty and take about 4hr. Ask in particular about those along the Löwen River. (Contact lodge for reservations and prices.) Activities offered by Cañon Lodge (☎26 6029; nature.i@mweb.com.na) include **sunrise walk** (N$90), **sunrise drive** (N$185), **horse riding** (N$130 per hour), and **scenic flights.** All prices are per person; book ahead.

BOTSWANA

PRICE RANGES. Price ranges, marked by the numbered icons below, are now included in food and accommodation descriptions. They are based on the lowest cost for one person, excluding special deals or prices. In the case of campgrounds, we include the cost of a car. The table below is a guide to how prices and icons match up.

SYMBOL	❶	❷	❸	❹	❺
ACCOMM.	P0-80	P81-165	P166-270	P271-350	P350+
FOOD	P0-30	P30-45	P45-60	P61-80	P80+

Botswana, sometimes called "Africa's Cinderella," has been blessed with a sparkling sense of timing. One of the 20 poorest places in the world when Britain walked away from it in 1966, Botswana discovered its diamond fields the very next year and never looked back. It soon catapulted itself from the bottom of Africa's economic ladder to the top. Botswana now boasts a fast-growing economy, strong currency, successful democracy, and professional civil service. The country's largest concern today is the enormous income gap between rich and poor.

Botswana's natural areas, meanwhile, are nothing short of spectacular—so spectacular, in fact, that the country can afford to be choosy about who gets to see them. The official tourism policy is "low-density, high-cost;" thus revenue is generated by attracting a relatively small number of tourists willing to pay dearly for the privilege of having the place nearly to themselves. This is excellent for Botswana's environment, but spells disaster for the budget traveler. Still, there are few who would dispute that Botswana's magnificent game viewing is worth every penny. Even if it means eating macaroni for the next month, budgeteers should let themselves splurge in this unparalleled destination.

HISTORY

ONCE UPON A TIME. Khoisan-speaking groups of hunters and gatherers, or **"Bushmen,"** have occupied the land for thousands of years. At the Depression Shelter site in the Tsodilo Hills (p. 557), experts have found evidence of continuous occupation from about 17,000 BC until only about 350 years ago. In the last few centu-

FACTS AND FIGURES

Official Name: Republic of Botswana
Government: Parliamentary Republic
Capital: Gaborone
Land Area: 600,370 sq. km.
Geography: Predominantly flat; savanna with gently rolling hills; Kalahari Desert in the southwest
Climate: Semiarid, with warm winters (May-Aug.) and hot summers (Nov.-Mar.)

Head of State: Pres. Festus Mogae
Major Cities: Gaborone, Francistown, Lobatse, Selebi-Phikwe
Population: 1,576,000
Languages: English, Setswana
Religions: Christianity (50%), Indigenous Beliefs (50%)
GDP Per Capita: US$3900
Major Exports: Diamonds, copper

ries BC, **Bantu**-speaking peoples moved in from the north, bringing with them iron tools. Over time, a number of other groups also moved into what is now Botswana, including **Shona**-speakers, who probably arrived around AD 1000.

DON'T ANSWER IT; IT'S THE MISSIONARIES. British interest in modern-day Botswana began in the early 1800s with exploratory expeditions originating in the South African Cape colonies. In 1813, John Campbell of the **London Missionary Society (LMS)** crossed the Orange River into **Tlhaping** in South Africa's Transvaal, where the locals warmly invited him to send instructors. In 1821, the LMS sent **Robert Moffat,** the man who completed a translation of the entire Bible into Tswana (1857) and, more importantly, encouraged the Scottish missionary **David Livingstone** (see **Dr. Livingstone, I Presume?,** p. 523) to come to the region north of the Kalahari. Livingstone established himself as a trusted ally of the Kwena tribe and even baptized Kwena **King Sechele**, a highly influential Tswana ruler.

THE REDCOATS ARE COMING! The discovery of gold in 1867 brought the first major wave of white prospectors to the region. That influx was followed by the so-called **Scramble for Africa** of the 1880s. The Germans colonized **South West Africa** (present day Namibia), which threatened to join forces with the Boer Transvaal by way of the Kalahari. In 1883, the British reacted by proclaiming a protectorate over the country "outside the Transvaal," a region whose boundaries they clarified and expanded in 1885. What is now most of Botswana was designated as the Bechuanaland Protectorate.

Over the next several decades, investment and economic development were largely overlooked; in fact, in 1895 the administrative capital of Bechuanaland was established at **Mafikeng,** in South Africa's Transvaal, rather than within the boundaries of the protectorate. Controversy arose in 1948 when **Seretse Khama,** heir to the Ngwato chieftainship, married an English woman. The British government, supposedly acting in accordance with Ngwato tradition, claimed that by marrying a white woman Seretse had invalidated his right to royal succession. They exiled Seretse from the protectorate in a hotly debated political move that made many people question the extent to which the British government was acting on behalf of South Africa rather than the Bechuanaland Protectorate.

INDEPENDENCE DAY. By the late 1950s, the British finally began taking steps to ensure the nation's self-sufficiency, and a nationalist spirit rose within the protectorate. In 1960, a temporary constitution was drafted, and 1962 saw the birth of the **Bechuanaland Democratic Party,** led by Seretse Khama, who had returned from exile in 1958. A new administrative capital was constructed in Gaborone. The first general election, held in March 1965, resulted in the newly knighted Sir Seretse Khama taking office as the premier of Bechuanaland. In 1966, the country became the **independent Republic of Botswana**, with Seretse Khama as its first president.

Following the diamond discoveries of the 1970s and 80s, Botswana became increasingly involved in international politics and took a strong stance against South Africa's apartheid regime. During the Civil War prior to Zimbabwe's independence in 1980, Botswana became known as a haven for refugees from Rhodesia. In 1985, Botswana again found itself accepting refugees from a liberation struggle, this time from South Africa. On this occasion, however, a commando raid and bomb blasts killed 11 suspected ANC members in Gaborone. Recognizing serious vulnerability, Botswana's government asked the ANC to withdraw from the country and tightened security against illegal immigrants. Once South Africa's apartheid government crumbled in the 1990s, relations between Botswana and its neighbors improved dramatically.

DR. LIVINGSTONE, I PRESUME?

Sure, many have heard the phrase, but relatively few know about its origins. Born into a poor Scottish family in 1813, **David Livingstone** was already working in a cotton mill by the time he was 10. While still working part-time at the mill, he began to study Greek, theology, and medicine in hopes of becoming a missionary. Accepted in 1833 by the **London Missionary Society,** Livingstone was China-bound before the Opium War put a damper on his plans. After meeting **Robert Moffat** in 1840, he decided to head to Africa instead. Several months later he was on his way to Cape Town, and by the summer of 1842 he had already ventured further north than any European before him. By learning the local languages and becoming involved in Tswana political struggles, Livingstone succeeded not only in his Christian missions, but also in gaining the respect of indigenous peoples. A trusted ally of the Kwena, Livingstone lashed out against Boer attempts to invade the region; he also strongly opposed slavery and sought to end the slave trade throughout the African continent. After surviving a lion attack in 1844 and assisting in a royal expedition in 1849, the missionary quickly made a name for himself as an explorer. He is perhaps best known today as the first white person to lay eyes on **Victoria Falls**. After returning to England several times, Livingstone set off in 1866 to locate the source of the Nile. Despite poor health and having been deserted by his followers, he continued to push farther into the interior of the continent. British and American supporters grew concerned, and in 1869, *New York Herald* special correspondent **Henry Morton Stanley** was sent to find him. Leading a well-equipped caravan and mischievously refusing to explain his purpose to the British, Stanley eventually did find Livingstone—whom he supposedly greeted with the oft-quipped line. Livingstone was sick and in desperate need of medicine and supplies. Reinvigorated (though not fully recovered) by the replenished supplies, Livingstone insisted on resuming his quest, but succumbed to illness in 1873.

TODAY

ELECTORAL POLITICS. Despite the growth of several opposition parties (most notably the **Botswana National Front,** or **BNF,** and the **Botswana Congress Party, BCP**), Seretse Khama's original **Botswana Democratic Party** (**BDP**) continues to be favored by the Botswana electorate. Following Quett Masire's retirement in 1998, his vice-president, **Festus Mogae,** was sworn in as his successor. He was officially voted into office in October 1999 in landslide elections that left the BDP with a powerful 33 out of 40 parliamentary seats. Since then, the government has become increasingly unsettled. While the BNF has recently been torn in half by a leadership dispute, factional fighting within the ruling party has threatened to break up the BDP as well. In January 2000, Mogae's vice-president, **Lt.-Gen. Ian Seretse Khama** (son of

BOTSWANA

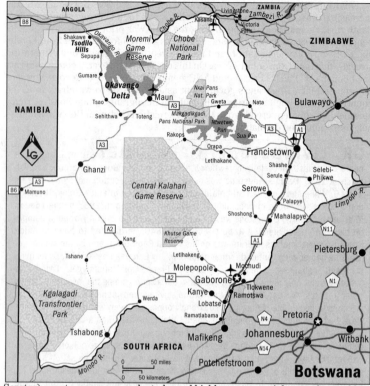

Seretse), went on an unprecedented—and highly controversial—year-long sabbatical. Mogae recalled him from the sabbatical in August 2000 to boost the government's national development plan, giving Khama more powers. Now, many observers compare Khama's new role to that of a prime minister.

OTHER ISSUES. Current hot issues on Botswana's plate include **environmental concerns** (such as how to deal with the overwhelming number of plastic shopping bags littering the country) and complications from increased **infrastructure development** (such as the fate of those currently living in squatters' camps).

PEOPLE

Botswana has over 1.6 million citizens (called **Batswana,** singular **Motswana**), only about half of whom live in urban areas. The largest city, Gaborone, only has a population of 250,000. The dominant ethnic identity is indisputably **Tswana.** Most citizens of Botswana can still probably identify themselves with one of the eight early Tswana states that developed out of the precolonial kingdoms: Tswana, Ngwato, Kwena, Ngwaketse, Kgatla, Tlokwa, Malete, and Rolong.

At least 34 different languages are spoken by Batswana around the country. The official language is **English,** which is spoken to some degree by a majority of the population, although **Setswana** (or just Tswana) is the national language, spoken by almost all adults. Most of the home languages fall into one of four different language groups, reflecting the group's origins before settling permanently in Botswana: Indo-European/Germanic languages (including Afrikaans); Khoi-Khoi languages, descending from the pastoral groups (including Nama); Khoisan/San languages, descending from the hunter-gatherer groups; and Niger-Congo/Bantu languages (including Herero and Yeyi).

The missionaries were successful in establishing **Christianity** as the official religion in all five major Tswana states by the late 19th century. Today, the two most popular churches are the Zion Christian Church and the Roman Catholic Church. **Traditional beliefs** and religious practices have largely been discarded.

HOLIDAYS & FESTIVALS (2003)

When these dates fall on Sunday, they are usually observed the following Monday.

2 Jan.: Second Day of New Year

Second Monday in March: Commonwealth Day (non-holiday observance)

1 May: Labour Day

29 May: Ascension

1 July: Sir Seretse Khama Day

15-16 July: President's Day

30 Sept.: Botswana Day (Independence Day)

ADDITIONAL RESOURCES

GENERAL HISTORY AND LITERATURE

Historical Dictionary of Botswana (1996) by Jeff Ramsay. Useful for travelers looking to fill in some knowledge gaps about the nation beforehand.

Serowe: Village of the Rain-Wind (1981) by Bessie Head. Head is one of the greatest literary minds in Botswanan history.

FILM

The Gods Must be Crazy (1980) and its sequel, *The Gods Must Be Crazy II* (1989); both dir. Jamie Uys. It might not be saying much to call these two flicks the best movies ever made about Botswana, but they're both funny and worth watching.

Animals Are Beautiful People (1974), dir. Jamie Uys. A great primer for the safari-bound. By the same director as *The Gods Must Be Crazy*, it's perhaps the funniest documentary you will ever see. Don't miss the part about monkeys with hangovers.

ESSENTIALS

DOCUMENTS AND FORMALITIES

VISAS. Visas are not required for citizens of the United States, the British Commonwealth (except Ghana, India, Sri Lanka, Pakistan, and Nigeria), or the EU (except Portugal and Spain), for stays under ninety days. For citizens of all other nations, **visa applications** may be obtained from Botswanan Embassies, or, in countries where Botswana is not represented, from the **British High Commission.** Visas are initially issued for a maximum of thirty days, but may be extended to ninety days by the Department of Immigration and Citizenship (P.O. Box 942, Gaborone, Botswana (☎361 1300; fax ☎267 395 2996). Travelers at border crossings are often required to present proof of onward travel or adequate means of subsistence.

BOTSWANA EMBASSIES AND CONSULATES ABROAD

South Africa: Infotech Building, 1090 Arcadia St., Suite 404, 4th Floor, Pretoria. **Consulate:** Botswana Trade Mission. 122 De Korte St., Braamfontein, Johannesburg (☎27 11 403 3748).

United Kingdom: Botswana High Commission. 6 Stratford Place, London, W1C 1AY (☎44 20 7499 0031) or, for visa-specific info, (☎44 20 08 9160 0335; fax 44 20 7495 8595).

United States: Embassy of the Republic of Botswana. 3400 International Drive, NW, Suite 7M, Intelsat Building, Washington, DC, 20008. (☎202-244-4990).

Zambia: Botswanan Embassy. Plot no. 5201 Pandit Nehru Road, Diplomatic Triangle, Lusaka, Zambia. PO Box 31910 (☎260 1 253 9032).

Zimbabwe: 22 Phillips Avenue, PO Box 563, Harare (☎263 4 721 360).

EMBASSIES AND CONSULATES IN GABORONE

Ireland: Irish Consulate, Mutual & Federal Insurance Company of Botswana, First Floor, Standard House, The Main Hall, Gaborone, P.O. Box 715 (☎390 5807; fax 303 400).

South Africa: Private Bag 00402, Gaborone (☎390 4800 or 390 4801; fax 305 502).

United Kingdom: British High Commission. Queens Road, The Mall. Private Bag 0023, Gaborone (☎395 2841; bhc@botsnet.bw).

United States: American Embassy. P.O. Box 90, Gaborone (☎395 3982; http://usembassy.state/botswana).

Zambia: Zambia High Commission, Zambia House. PO Box 362, Gaborone (☎395 1951; fax 353 952).

Zimbabwe: Zimbabwe High Commission, The Mall, Plot 8850. PO Box 1232, Gaborone (☎391 4495; fax 305 863).

CURRENCY AND EXCHANGE

The **Botswanan Pula** (P) is divided into 100 thebe (t). Bills come in the denominations of 5, 10, 20, 50, and 100P, and coins in 1P, 2P, as well as 1, 5, 10, 25, and 50t. **Foreign Currency** may be brought into and out of the country without restriction, as long as it is declared upon entry. **Traveler's cheques** may enter and exit the country in unlimited amounts. Outside of major cities, **Credit** and **Debit Cards** should be used with caution. Banks or bureaus of exchange are generally not to be found in rural areas. Inquire at branches in larger cities and towns about the **mobile banks** that make occasional payday visits to outlying areas. National banking hours *usually* run M-F 9:30am-2:30pm, and Sa 8:30am-noon.

HEALTH AND SAFETY

EMERGENCY. General Emergency: ☎999 (Gaborone), ☎212 222 (Francistown). **Police** ☎999; **ambulance** ☎997; **fire** ☎998.

TRANSPORTATION

BY AIR. Most international budget flights to Gaborone, Botswana, fly via Johannesburg, South Africa. **South African Airways** (Johannesburg ☎ 0861 359 722 or 0861 722 2480; US office ☎ (800) 722 9675; www.flysaa.com) flies to **Johannesburg** (M-F 8:05, 11:20am, 2:35, 5:55pm; Sa 11:20am, 5:55pm; round-trip approx. US$110) $25 airport departure tax from Johannesburg. **Air Botswana** (☎ 267 390 5500) also flies to Johannesburg for similar fares.

BY TRAIN. There is no passenger rail service running between Botswana and other countries. Botswana Rail (☎ 267 395 1401) offers domestic service.

BY CAR. At border crossings, visitors are required to pay a vehicle tax (P5) and must have their passport, rental registration, and proof of onward travel (see **Visa and Permit Info**, p. 525). 4WD is essential for most roadways, especially those in game reserves. As in South Africa, cars in Botswana drive on the left side of the road. Recommended maps include the Shell Tourist Map of Botswana and the red and green Freytag & Berndt Series road map, available at www.mapsworldwide.com. Exercise extreme caution on the road; poor lighting, high speed limits (120km/hour), frequent sand patches, and game crossings make driving extremely dangerous, especially past dusk.

BY BUS OR MINIBUS TAXI. Intercape (☎ 012 660 0070) runs buses to **Gaborone** from: **Pretoria** (6½hr., daily 3pm, R150); **Johannesburg** (5½hr., daily 4pm, R150); **Rustenburg** (3¾hr., daily 5:45pm, R90). **Minibus taxis** travel to Gaborone from **Johannesburg** (P90) and **Mafikeng** (P80).

KEEPING IN TOUCH

MAIL. Botswana's mail system operates at the swift speed of cold molasses. Allow two to three weeks for mail to reach Botswana from Europe and the US. Most post offices are open from 8am-4pm (with hour-plus lunch breaks).

TELEPHONES. State-owned **Botswana Telecommunications Company (BTC)** recently altered the nation's telephone numbers by changing all 6-digit numbers to 7-digit numbers. At press time, information about how some rural phone numbers were changing was not available. Look at www.btc.bw for the latest updates concerning these areas. Cellular service is available only in major city centers and along connecting routes; the two private providers are **Mascom** and **Simply Cell.**

 TELEPHONES. Country code: 267. **International dir. assistance and collect calls:** ☎ 101.

TIME DIFFERENCE. Greenwich Mean Time plus two hours (the same as South Africa). Botswana does not observe daylight savings time.

GABORONE

A dusty agricultural center for much of the 20th century, Gaborone morphed into a major African capital virtually overnight. The result is a place reminiscent of an overgrown village putting on airs. New cars now cruise past highrises downtown, and top-level bureaucrats go home to opulent gated suburbs at night. One of the world's fastest-growing cities, Gaborone's chaotic sprawl may be difficult to love, but the city provides a good introduction to Botswana's national culture.

HIGHLIGHTS OF BOTSWANA

Tsodilo Hills (see p. 557), tucked into the northwest corner of the country, are covered with some of the finest examples of indigenous rock art in the entire world.

Chobe National Park (see p. 558) is the metropolis of the elephant world—more than 55,000 pachyderms wander the place. In many parks, visitors are lucky to spot two or three elephants in a day—here, it's a slow day if they see less than 100.

Central Kalahari Game Reserve (see p. 541) is the epitome of remote. Traveling through this surreal landscape in a convoy of Land Rovers, visitors get the sense of being on another planet. Only the now-familiar giraffes and rhinos break the spell.

⊑ TRANSPORTATION

INTERCITY TRANSPORTATION

Flights: Air Botswana (☎390 5500; in South Africa ☎011 447 6078), in the BIC Building on the east end of the Main Mall. Open M-F 7:30am-12:30pm and 1:45-4:30pm; Sa 8:30-11:30am. They fly from **Sir Seretse Khama Airport** to **Francistown** (1hr.; M, W, F 6:40am and 5:15pm, Tu 10:40am, Th 6:40am; US $82); **Harare** (2hr.; M, W, Sa 9:40am; US$224); **Johannesburg** (1hr.; daily 7, 10am, 1:30, 5, 7pm; US$141); **Kasane** (2hr.; M, W, and Su 12:20pm, F 9am; US$144); and **Maun** (1½hr.; M, W-Th, Su 12:20pm, Tu 6:30am and 3pm, Th 9am and 3pm; US$144). **South African Airways** (☎397 2397) flies to Jo'burg (3-4 times per day between 8am and 5:30pm; US$145).

Trains: Botswana Railways (☎395 1401), across Nelson Mandela Dr. from downtown, along the Mogoditshane Hwy. Trains run to **Francistown** (depart daily 10am and 7pm, arrive 5pm and 6am; first-class prices range from P15 for towns near Gaborone to P116 for Francistown; stops frequently).

Intercity Buses: Intercape (☎012 660 0070) runs buses to **Johannesburg** (5½hr., daily 6:30am, R110) via **Rustenburg** (3¾hr., R85).

Long distance minibus taxis: Travel to **Johannesburg** (P90) and **Mafikeng** (P80). They leave most frequently from 6-10am.

LOCAL TRANSPORTATION

Local buses: Local buses rank next to the train station and are cheap, but not always quick or available. Don't hesitate to ask drivers and conductors for help sorting out routes. Prices start at P1.25 and are rarely more than P5.

Taxis: Taxis are everywhere, with the main rank at the bus station, and cost P10-25 for most destinations. If your taxi doesn't have a meter (most don't), agree on a fare before hopping in. **Delta** (☎391 9237) and **Gaborone Cab** (☎597 0001) have meters and good reputations.

Car Rental: Budget (☎390 2030) tends to be cheapest; rates start at P95 per day for a sub-compact. **Avis** (☎391 3093; avisbots@botsnet.bw) and **Imperial** (☎390 7233) are in the same range. All are in the airport. No one rents to drivers under 21.

Hitchhiking: Although *Let's Go* does not recommend hitching, some travelers and locals find rides by holding their hand out and waving it up and down slightly (using a thumb can be offensive). Riders typically pay the prevailing minibus rate for the lift. If hitching, be clear on the price before embarking.

BOTSWANA

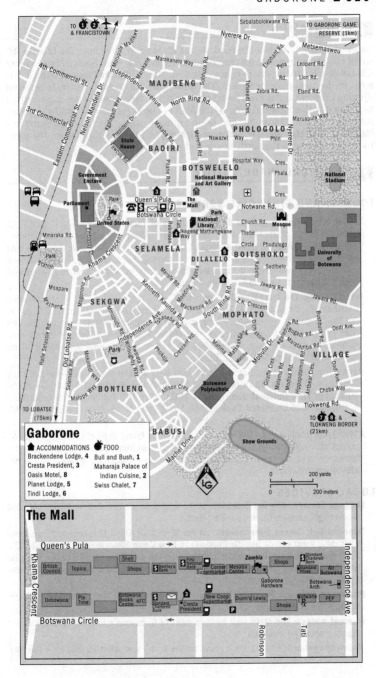

Gaborone

♠ ACCOMMODATIONS
Brackendene Lodge, 4
Cresta President, 3
Oasis Motel, 8
Planet Lodge, 5
Tindi Lodge, 6

● FOOD
Bull and Bush, 1
Maharaja Palace of
  Indian Cuisine, 2
Swiss Chalet, 7

BOTSWANA

 ORIENTATION

Gaborone's main north-south road, **Nelson Mandela Dr.**, becomes **Old Lobatse Rd.** south of Karma Crescent. A series of roads radiate out from Nelson Mandela Dr./ Old Lobatse Rd. to the east in concentric semi-circles. **Kharma Crescent** is the inner-most of the semi-circular streets. The **Main Mall**, Gaborone's center, is between Kharma Crescent and the next semi-circular street, **Independence Ave.** A pedestrian zone lined with shops and offices, the Mall is bracketed on one end by the Pula Arch and National Museum, and on the other by the complex of Government buildings. **Motsetse Highway, Tlokweng Highway,** and **Lobatse Highway** are the main roads out of town to the north, south, and west.

⁊ PRACTICAL INFORMATION

TOURIST AND FINANCIAL SERVICES

Tourist office: Government of Botswana Office of Tourism (☎395 3024), 2nd fl. of Standard House at the Mall. Walk into the 2nd fl. lobby and ask for the "Information Office"; it's sequestered down a maze of hallways. While resources at the office may seem sparse and information is less than forthcoming, maps, tourist guides and general info are readily available to the traveler who comes armed with a planned itinerary and specific questions. Open M-F 7:30am-4:30pm.

Travel agency: The Travelling Co., Inc. (☎395 2021; fax 390 5552; travelco@it.bw), Debonairs Building/Mesaba Center, first fl. (Americans would consider it the 2nd fl.), at the Mall. Excellent clearinghouse for many tour operators and safari companies. Ser-vices include domestic, regional, and international flight bookings, vehicle reservations, safaris, and package tours. Commission charged on all bookings. Open M-F 8:30am-12:45pm and 2-5pm, Sa 8:30-11:30am.

Banks: Most banks have offices along the Mall strip; all offer foreign exchange and cash advances. **Barclays Bank** (☎395 2041; open M-F 8:30am-3:30pm, Sa 8:15-10:45am); **First National Bank** (☎391 1669; open M-F 8:30am-3:30pm, Sa 9am-noon); **Standard Chartered Bank** (☎360 1500; open M-F 8:30am-3:30pm, Sa 8:30-11am).

ATMs: Teller machines line the Main Mall and can be found at most shopping malls. All accept Visa; *none* accept MasterCard. If you need cash from your MasterCard, go to the forex counter on the upper floor of Barclay's (see above), and it will be advanced to you with no commission.

LOCAL SERVICES

Luggage Storage: City Dry Cleaners, at the long-distance bus station. P3 for 3hr., but no overnight storage. Open daily 7am-6pm.

Supermarket: Corner Supermarket, on the Main Mall. Open M-F 7am-6pm, Sa 7am-1pm. MC, V accepted. Directly opposite is **New Coop Supermarket** (☎395 2632). Open daily 8am-8pm. For a wider selection, try the new **Spar** (☎395 6860) in Kgale Hills Center on the Lobatse Hwy. Open M-F 8:30am-8pm, Sa 8:30am-5pm, Su 9am-1pm.

Pharmacy: Notwane Pharmacy (☎395 1853), at the Main Mall. Open M-F 8:15am-5:30pm, Sa 8:15am-1pm.

Internet access: The Main Mall houses most of Gaborone's Internet services. Don't expect a speedy connection.

Letloa Internet (☎318 1442), Rm. 1 above the New Coop Supermarket. P5 per 30min. Open M-F 8am-8pm, Sa 8am-4pm, Su 10am-2pm.

Postnet Business and Communications Services, near Standard House. P5 per 30min. Open M-F 8am-7pm, Sa-Su 8am-3pm.

AIM Internet Access, next to the Cresta President Hotel. P6 for 30min.

Sakeng Internet Access (☎397 2109), basement of Debonairs Bldg. P6 per 30min, P10 per hr. Open M-F 8am-8pm.

Camping Supplies: Cape Union Mart (☎397 4780), in the RiverWalk complex on Tlokweng Hwy., sells a variety of high-end backpacking equipment. Open M-F 9am-8pm, Sa 9am-5pm, Su 9am-1pm. Visa accepted. Gaborone Hardware (☎391 4474), on the Main Mall, sells camping and car supplies. Open M-F 8:30am-12:45pm and 2-5pm, Sa 8:30-11:30am.

Souvenirs: BotswanaCraft (☎395 3577), in the Cresta President building on the Main Mall, sells high-quality crafts and books. Open M-F 8am-5pm, Sa 8am-1pm. AmEx/MC/V. The **street vendors** on the Main Mall also sell curios of highly variable quality.

EMERGENCY AND COMMUNICATIONS

Emergency: Ambulance, ☎997; **Medical Rescue,** ☎911.

Police: ☎999.

Hospital: Gaborone Private Hospital (☎390 1999), on Segoditshane Way opposite Broadhurst North Mall, has the best medical care in the city. For non-emergency procedures at a lower price tag, try the government-run **Princess Marina Hospital** (☎395 3221), along Churchill Way near the Main Mall.

Telephones: Public telephones and phone shops are widespread throughout Gaborone. Phone cards (available from pharmacies, supermarkets, and street vendors) are more convenient than coin slot phones which sometimes accept only certain denominations. Scratch-and-dial cards offer even more flexibility. International collect calls cannot be made from public telephones.

Post Office: (☎390 0278), on Main Mall. Visitors who stay in Gaborone longer than one month can avail themselves of the *Poste Restante* service. Open M-Tu and Th-F 8:15am-4pm, W 8:45am-4pm, Sa 8:30-11am.

▌ ACCOMMODATIONS AND CAMPING

Although "Gabs" has nothing that is quite cheap enough to fit neatly in the "hostel" category, its cozy lodges and upscale hotels provide the weary wanderer with a variety of homes away from home.

Planet Lodge Bed and Breakfast (☎390 3295; fax 390 3229), on South Ring Rd., a 10min. walk from downtown. A new Gaborone institution, Planet offers top-notch rooms at a great value: each room has a satellite TV, fridge, alarm, writing desk, A/C, and other goodies. Continental breakfast included; kitchen available for self-catering. Singles P95; doubles P160. ❷

Tindi Lodge (☎317 0897), on South Ring Rd., 50m from Planet Lodge. Tindi offers sparse but clean rooms with shared kitchen facilities, a TV room, and a public telephone. A well-kept but no-frills option for those on a tight budget. Singles P90-P100; doubles P120-P180, depending on room size and quality. ❷

Brackendene Lodge (☎391 2886; fax 390 6246), on Ikageng Way. From the east end of the Main Mall, facing away from The Mall, turn right and walk along Independence Ave.; Ikageng Way is the 1st right after the traffic light. A quick hop from the Main Mall, Brackendene is more convenient but pricier than most. The few extra pula, however, buys superb service, classy rooms, and access to a common kitchen and TV room. Breakfast included. Key deposit P50. Reception daily 6:30am-10pm. Singles P133.50, with bath P146.20; doubles P167.50, with bath P186. V. ❷

Oasis Motel (☎ 392 8396), on Tlokweng Rd., 4km outside of town. Somewhere between a motel and a luxury resort, Oasis offers swanky public areas, several pools, and a lush garden. Rooms include all the amenities one would expect from a major hotel. Chalets take it a step further, offering a sitting room, bedroom, private kitchen, and a yard with a picnic table. Supermarket next door for self-caterers. Go for the weekend special: Rooms are P179 on F and Sa. Normally, singles P220-240; chalets P250-280. V. ❸

Cresta President (☎ 395 3631; bwpresident@info.bw). The centerpiece of the Main Mall, this modern high-rise caters to an international business clientele with room service, soft beds, in-room coffee makers, and sweeping views of Gaborone. Normally beyond the reach of budget travelers, but students with valid ID get an impressive break: 50% off all room prices. Regular rates are singles P367; doubles P402. ❺

▟ FOOD

For a range of standard burger, chicken and pie options, try the Main Mall area and the Africa Mall, just off Kenneth Kaunda Rd.

▧ **Maharaja Palace of Indian Cuisine** (☎ 391 1060), next to Bull and Bush. Operated by an established Indian-Botswanan family, the Maharaja offers Punjabi specialties such as *shahi korma* (P30) and *hanadis* (meals served from special copper pots, P20-42). Popular lunch buffets (P50) feature a blend of Indian and Continental cuisine M-F and regional Indian dishes on Su. Elegant wood-carved decorations complete the authentic experience. Open daily 12:30-2:30pm and 6:30-10:30pm. ❷

Swiss Chalet Restaurant (☎ 392 5172), 2km out of town along Tlokweng Hwy. (Tlokweng 1 or 3 minibus passes Swiss Chalet on the left). Botswana's spot for Swiss and Continental cuisine. Meals served outside on shaded terrace. Features **Crash Site Bar,** where the remains of a wrecked airplane cheekily display Visa and Mastercard logos. The younger crowd (or young at heart) can enjoy the swimming pool (summer only) or swings. Steak and chicken dishes P34-65. Vegetarian pastas P21-50. Flambe specialties P50-68. Fine wines and full bar. Open daily 10am-2pm and 6pm-late. ❸

Bull and Bush (☎ 397 5070), just north of the city (passed by the Broadhurst 4 minibus); heading out of town, look for the green "Bull and Bush" sign on the left side of Nelson Mandela Dr., just past the Independence intersection. Gaborone's hot spot, attracting everyone from suit-clad executives to the off-duty police officers who live across the road. Extensive menu offers everything from pizza (P25-31) to grill items (P30-49). Crowds *really* start pouring in after dinner, when it becomes a vibrant nightclub. Choose between outdoor pub atmosphere or a lively dance club with Tswana "house" music and the occasional rave or R&B. Open M-F 12:30-2:30pm and 6:30pm-2am; Sa-Su 12:30-3pm and 6:30pm-2am. AmEx/DC/MC/V. ❷

Mike's Kitchen (☎ 390 2087), several kilometers out of town in the Kgale Hill Shopping Ctr. at last circle en route to Lobatse next to the Engen station. An American-style bar and grill, Mike's dishes up a wide variety of steaks (P28-42), burgers (P17-22), and seafood (P23-49). **Bourbon Street,** next door but under the same management, is a popular sports bar that's packed to capacity whenever big games are on TV. Both open M-F 10:30am-11:30pm, Sa 9:30am-11:30pm, Su 9am-10:30pm. MC/V. ❶

◉ SIGHTS

NATIONAL MUSEUM. Botswana's most important museum is a historical record of the country, with displays spanning from the Big Bang to the colonial and post-colonial eras. Thoughtful attention is given to the evolution of human society in the country, as well as to the ever-changing savannah plains and diverse animal life. The never-ending passageways enthrall visitors and the startlingly life-like models of cave and rural life are delightful. The museum highlights modern Botswanan artists with an art gallery in an octagonal room, and rotating craft and art displays from local artists. The museum shop is a good spot for high-end curios and crafts. *(☎ 397 4616. Open Tu-F 9am-6pm, weekends and holidays 9am-5pm. Free.)*

GOVERNMENT ENCLAVE. Built in the late 1960s after Botswana became a democracy, the modest Parliament building is surrounded by gardens with palm trees, and its courtyards feature majestic marble fountains, all of which can be leisurely wandered around. Members of the Botswanan government are happy to give free, private tours of the working Parliament to visitors, provided advance notice is given. *(Across from the Main Mall. To set up a guided visit, write to the Clerk of the National Assembly, PO Box 240, Gaborone, attn: Public Relations Officer. Include the desired date and time of your visit, number of visitors, and contact info in Gaborone. You will get a call the day before to confirm your visit. Grounds open dawn-dusk.)*

GABORONE GAME RESERVE. In Gaborone proper, this small reserve has picnic and *braai* spots for those seeking a quick escape from the city. Bird- and animal-watchers won't be disappointed—there is an abundance of antelope, monkeys, warthogs, and kingfisher, among other creatures. A separate "rhino area" is home to a breeding pair of white rhino, introduced several years ago. The reserve is also used by scientists to experiment with new wildlife management techniques before using them in national parks. Animals are best viewed in the early morning and late afternoon. *(To get there by minibus, take Broadhurst Rte. 2 and ask to be let off at the turn-off for the reserve; it's a quick walk to the end of the road. ☎ 397 1405. Open daily 6:30am-6:30pm. P1 per person, P2 per vehicle; braai/picnic 50 thebe.)*

◪ DAYTRIPS FROM GABORONE

KGALE HILL. Gaborone's only hiking opportunity, this modest mountain dominates the city's skyline and offers panoramic views well into South Africa from its summit. Though the top is a bit of a letdown—a fenced-in radio tower surrounded by graffiti-covered rocks—the trail itself is frequented by families of dassies and baboons, and requires some vigorous rock scrambling. Most hikers ascend via the gentler "Transveldt Trail," on the left, and come back down the more direct "Rusty's Route." A map at the trailhead outlines the options. The return trip can be made in 1½hr. *(8km out of Gaborone, look for an unmarked parking area on the right side of the Lobatse highway, just before a cluster of satellite dishes on the left; this is the trailhead.)*

OODI WEAVERS. Although it's a long haul from central Gaborone, the weavers are unforgettable. The Lentswe-la-Oodi Weavers, in a rural village to the northeast of Gaborone, is one of the most successful community self-help projects in Southern Africa. To get there, drive 18km north of Gaborone on the Francistown road and turn right at the turn-off to Oodi. It is then 7km to the village, where a sign marks a left turn onto a dirt road, and from here small white and blue signs mark the last 1.5km to the weavers' site. Minibus taxis also go direct to Oodi from downtown Gaborone.

Founded in 1967 by Swedish volunteers to empower local women outside the home, the women of Oodi have personalized weaving and turned it into a world-renowned art form. The imported wool is dyed over an open fire, spun, and used by each weaver to create fascinating designs and scenes of rural life. Each stitch is deliberate and unique; every square meter of tapestry takes over one month of work to complete. Even a seemingly simple placemat can take up to three days. The weavers are proud to show their craft and don't mind if you sit in the workshop and watch a tapestry progress.

Financially healthy and currently expanding, the weavers' shop is filled with place mats (P25-45), bedspreads (P350), jackets (P260), and of course the famous tapestries, priced around P700 per sq. m. *(☎310 2268. Open M-F 8am-4:30pm, Sa-Su 10am-4:30pm. Visa, US dollars, and traveler's checks accepted.)*

MOCHUDI VILLAGE. The **Phuthadikobo Museum** is the focal point of the village of Mochudi (pop. 21,000), the historical and cultural center of the Bakgatla people. Housed in a 1923 community school, the museum was established by the District Tribal Council to actively preserve the community's heritage. The schoolhouse displays a craft history of the Bagkatla. Outbuildings and side rooms bring Bakgatla culture to life with a printing workshop that produces colorful Bagkatla cloth hangings, a series of special exhibits, and numerous community outreach programs with local schoolchildren. *(Drive 35km north of Gaborone on the Francistown road and turn right at village of Pilane. Turn left at the T junction 8km down the road, in center of Mochudi village, and follow signs for museum. Minibus taxis cost P3-5 and leave from the long-distance bus station in Gaborone when full; ask a kombi driver for "Mochudi." ☎397 7238. Open M-F 8am-5pm, Sa-Su 2-5pm.)*

NATIONAL PARK BASICS The fees for all national parks in Botswana are standard: **non-citizens** P120 per person per day; **camping** P30 per person per day, ages 8-15 P15, under 8 free; **vehicles** with foreign registration P50, with Botswana registration P10. Always apply for overnight accommodation permits well in advance of your trip (in some cases, up to a year). To obtain the permits, you must make reservations with the Botswana Department of Wildlife National Parks and Reserves Reservations Office (in Maun ☎686 0368, fax 686 1264; or in Gaborone ☎397 1405, fax 391 2354; dwbots@global.bw). Permits for day visitors are generally available at the gates of the national park, but overnight permits MUST be arranged prior to arrival. The best map of the National Parks, including campsites, is the **Shell Tourist Map,** available at most lodges and service stations for P40-60.

EASTERN BOTSWANA

The A1 shoots north from Gaborone, all the way to Francistown and beyond into Zimbabwe. For a long time, this was Botswana's only true highway, a division between the relatively barren western part of the country and the populous and inhabitable east. Most of Botswana's population lived in the southeast; the arid Kalahari in the west and the salt-heavy north were too harsh for most humans. The majority of people settled by the lush banks of the Limpopo, tilling the fertile soil for crops and, later, rich minerals. Don't expect greenery though; the dominant flora are grasses and bush adapted to arid climates.

The locals in Eastern Botswana are mainly of Tswana background, although the area surrounding Francistown is rich with Shona influence from Zimbabwe. The relaxed atmosphere, striking landscape, and game of the Tuli Block make the eastern corridor a worthwhile route to adventures farther north.

FRANCISTOWN

Conveniently located at the crossroads of several of Botswana's main roads, Francistown, the second largest city in Botswana, is a hub of activity, none of which is geared towards tourists. Historically, the region is Shona, and the predominant language is Kalanga rather than Setswana. In 1867, gold was discovered, drawing prospectors from all over the world, including Daniel Francis, the Englishman for whom the city is named. Francistown remained a mere dot on the map with a couple of mine shafts until Rhodesian firms seeking stability migrated here shortly before Zimbabwe's independence. Though there's not much to see here, Francistown is an excellent place to take care of finances, shopping, communication, and other logistics before shipping out to wilder locales.

▐ TRANSPORTATION

Flights: Air Botswana (☎241 2394) flies only to **Gaborone** (1hr.; M, W, F 8:20am and 6:50pm, Tu 12:10pm, Th 8:20am; one-way US$82). Office in the **airport,** 4km west of town on the road to Nata.

Trains: From the station (☎241 3444) at Haskins and Baines St., trains leave to **Gaborone.** (Day train: 6hr.; 10am; economy P15, 1st class P27. Night train: 9hr.; 9pm; economy P22, 2nd-class sleeper P96, 1st-class sleeper P114.)

Buses: Depart from parking lot south of Haskins St. Buy tickets on bus to: **Bulawayo** (2½hr.-5hr., depending on border delay; hourly 6am-6pm; P12); **Gaborone** (5hr., every 30min. 5am-6pm, P33); **Kasane** (5hr., hourly 6:30-11:30am, P57) and **Maun** (6hr., hourly 6:30am-6:30pm, P42), both via **Nata** (2hr., P17); **Selebi-Phikwe** (1½hr., 2pm, P11).

Car Rental: Avis (☎241 3901), at airport. Start around P95 per day plus P0.93 per km.

ORIENTATION

The A1 from Gaborone circles through three roundabouts around Francistown. It becomes **Blue Jacket St.** after the middle roundabout, outside the Thapama Lodge, and houses the city's main shops and services. One block west of Blue Jacket lies **Haskins St.,** which runs one-way from south to north. A left turn (west) off the A1 at the Thapama roundabout leads to the **airport,** Maun, and Kasane. Following the A1 north for 80km will take you to the **Ramokgwebana border crossing** into Zimbabwe (open daily 7am-8pm).

▐ PRACTICAL INFORMATION

Banks: Barclays Bank (☎241 3439), on Blue Jacket St. at Lobengula Ave., has **ATMs** and currency exchange. Open M-F 8:30am-3:30pm, Sa 8:15-10:45am.

Supermarkets: Spar, in Francistown Mall at the south end of Blue Jacket St. Open M-F 8:30am-8pm, Sa 8am-3pm, Su 9am-2pm. **Score Supermarket,** next to Francistown Mall. Open M-F 8am-7pm, Sa 8am-5pm, Su 9am-1pm.

Safari/Outdoor Equipment: Metsef Trade Center (☎241 3008), 3km east of the Thapama roundabout, past the hospital. One of the biggest stores in Africa, this mammoth complex occupies several city blocks and sells *everything,* from food to automotive supplies to camping equipment. Open M-F 9am-6pm, Sa 9am-2pm, Su 9am-1pm.

Police (☎241 2221 or 241 2222), at north end of town on A1, after Caltex but before the roundabout. Open 24hr.

Pharmacy: Phodisong (☎241 3943), shop 3 in Francistown Mall, on Blue Jacket St. Open M-F 8:30am-7pm, Sa 8:30am-2pm, Su 9am-1pm.

Hospital (☎241 2333). From Gaborone, turn right at the Thapama roundabout; the hospital is on the left.

Internet Access: Postnet (☎241 3872), on Blue Jacket St. between Baines and Lobengula Ave.; another branch inside Cresta Thapama Hotel. P10 for 30min. Open M-F 8am-8pm, Sa 8am-1pm. **Jemm Computer** (☎241 7073), on Blue Jacket St., around the corner from Barclays. P7 for 30min., P12 for 1 hr. Open M-F 8am-7pm, Sa 8am-1pm.

Post Office (☎ 241 2371), on Blue Jacket St. between Baines and Lobengula Ave. *Poste Restante* and public phones. Open M-Tu and Th-F 8:15am-4pm, W 8:45am-4pm, Sa 8:30-11:30am.

◪ ◪ ACCOMMODATIONS AND FOOD

Because Francistown is geared more toward business travelers than tourists, budgeteers don't have many options. It's possible to get a high-quality room at a decent price, but don't expect much in the way of social atmosphere. For food, there is little beyond the hotel restaurants, fast-food joints, and supermarkets.

Marang Hotel (☎ 241 3991; fax 241 2130; marang@info.bw). Coming from Gaborone, turn right at the Thapama roundabout and look for the large sign 5km down on the right. This luxury hotel, Francistown's best, offers unadvertised "budget" rooms for backpackers— hotel rooms with private bath almost as plush as regular rooms, for a fraction of the price. Campers, meanwhile, enjoy an idyllic site along the river and have access to the pool, restaurant, and casino. Budget rooms P175 each; regular rooms P455. Camping P27.50 per person. Breakfast buffet P39.50; lunch buffet P55. MC/V. ❸

YWCA (☎ 241 3046; fax 241 8404). From Gaborone, turn right off the Thapama roundabout and go past the hospital. Turn right at Botsalano Bar; it's 200m on the left. Simple, affordable accommodations with absolutely no frills. Clean and tidy 4- and 6-bed dorms. Check-out 11:30am. Breakfast P16, lunch P21.50, dinner P21.50. Call ahead to arrange check-in. Dorms P85. ❷

Grand Lodge (☎ 241 2300; fax 241 2309), in town center, on Haskins at Selous St. Tidy en suite rooms with TV, A/C, and kitchens; pots and plates available at reception. Check-out 10am. Singles P160, doubles P185; slightly nicer rooms with carpets and microwaves P195. Long-term discounts available. MC/V. ❷

Town Lodge (☎ 241 8802 or 241 8803, fax 241 5610), 1450 Leeba St. Headed north on Blue Jacket St., turn right on Guy St., right on Tlhangwe Dr., right at the T junction onto Morubisi, and an immediate left onto Leeba. Set in a pleasant suburban neighborhood, this new hotel is clean, if a bit sterile. Rooms have coffee makers, cable TV, phones, and A/C. Breakfast P25. Singles P180; doubles P235. MC/V. ❸

Oriental Restaurant (☎ 241 7324), on Lobengula Ave., next to Barclays Bank. Curries P5-7. Open M-F 7am-7pm, Sa 7am-5pm, and occasionally Su. ❶

Tina's Coffee Shop (☎ 241 0472), corner of Tainton Ave. and Blue Jacket St. Classy take-away with good coffee and curios. Huge full English breakfast P19.50. Food and coffee all under P20. Open M-F 8:30am-5:30pm, Sa 8:30am-1pm. ❶

♫ ENTERTAINMENT

If you came to Francistown looking for historical sites, roaring parties, or pretty much anything else, you'll be disappointed. There are few bars and clubs in the city center, and the scene is quiet. There's a young crowd and mostly house music at the **Nite Moves** club, at the north end of the town center on Blue Jacket St. (☎ 241 4103. Cover P5 weeknights, P10 weekends. Open Su-Th 3pm-4am, F-Sa 6pm until the wee hours.) Check the postings at the intersection of Blue Jacket and Guy St. for info on touring bands and organized parties that hit Francistown almost every weekend. Admission is usually around P20; the events take place at the Civic Center and other community centers around town. Fairly recent movies rotate every three to four days at the **Cine 2000,** on Blue Jacket St. near Francis Ave. (☎ 241 7175. Showings nightly at 8pm. W-Sa P10, Su-Tu P7.)

SEROWE

Serowe (pop. 48,000) is known as one of the "largest villages in Southern Africa." Donkeys and goats graze just beyond the Main Mall, and winding cattle trails lead past miles of mud huts and concrete dwellings. Besides being a good base for the Khama Rhino Sanctuary, Serowe offers a number of sights for history buffs. Sir Seretse Khama was born here, and the leader is now buried along with his ancestor, the beloved Chief Khama III (1875-1923), in Serowe's Royal Cemetery. In the 1960s, Serowe was the birthplace of the Brigade Movement, founded by a South African political refugee to solve rural unemployment by teaching practical skills.

⚑⚐ ORIENTATION AND PRACTICAL INFORMATION. Taking the A1 north from Gaborone, Serowe is 50km northwest of Palapye on the highway to Orapa. The main highway branches right toward the rhino sanctuary before reaching Serowe; another road continues straight and becomes Serowe's main street 5km later. The town center is a large pedestrian mall on the left. Just after the hill with the TV tower, a turn-off to the right links back with the main road to Orapa. **Buses** depart from next to the PEP on the southern side of the mall, and run to **Francistown** (P14) and **Gaborone** (2-4hr., daily 8 and 9am, P26). **Minibus taxis** make the run to **Palapye** (30min., whenever full, P10). Buy tickets on the bus.

Services include: **Barclays Bank** (☎463 0264) and **Standard Chartered Bank** (☎463 0249), both behind the Spar complex in the mall, with **ATMs** and **currency exchange** (both open M-F 8:30am-3:30pm, Sa 8:15am-10:45pm); **Spar Supermarket,** in the mall (open M-F 8:30am-7pm, Sa 8:30am-3pm, Su 8:30am-2pm); **police station** (☎463 0512), past the mall and left on Tshekedi Rd.; **Serowe Pharmacy,** in the Spar complex (☎463 2078; open M-F 8:30am-5:30pm, Sa and last Su of the month 8:30am-1:30pm); the public **hospital** (☎463 0333), all the way along the main road and past the center, where the road turns left; the private **Dr. Paul's Clinic** (☎463 1074), behind the main mall; **Internet** and **public phones** at **Serowe Comm.** on the Orapa road (☎463 7357; P6 per 30min.; open M-F 8am-8pm, Sa-Su 9am-6pm); and the **post office,** to the left of the Spar complex, with your back to the main road. (Open M-Tu and Th-F 8:15am-4pm, W 8:45am-4pm, Sa 8:30am-11:30pm.)

⚐⚐ ACCOMMODATIONS AND FOOD. Lentswe Lodge ❸, 3km from town, dominates its own mountaintop. To get here, follow the large signs that lead north from the main road. Though it appears a bit ramshackle in places, its setting, relaxing chalets, and warm management more than compensate. Chalet #5 is worth requesting: though it costs P20 more per person, its front porch has a commanding private view of the entire Serowe valley. The Lodge also has an outdoor and indoor bar, pool, and restaurant serving delicious pizza (P6-16) and a fixed menu (around P40). Trips to the Khama Rhino Sanctuary and other local sites are available; prices negotiable. Free pick-up from Palapye and Serowe. (☎463 4333; lentswe@mopane.bw; www.lentswe-lodge.bw. Breakfast included. Check-out 10am. Singles P180; doubles P200; triples P300; quads P360. MC/V.) **Tshwaragano Hotel ❷** offers chalets overlooking the town center. From town, turn up the road to Orapa, and make a right at the sign. The chalets are tidy with old and slightly grimy bathrooms; the hotel is geared more toward salesmen than tourists. A restaurant and popular bar are also on site. (☎463 0377. Restaurant open daily 6:30am-2:30pm and 5-8pm. Traditional food P7-35. Check-out 10am. Singles P145; doubles P165.)

◼ SIGHTS. The **Khama III Memorial Museum,** Botswana's best historical museum, commemorates the Khama family, widely regarded as Botswana's founding dynasty. The collection houses the artifacts of the Khama chiefs as well as some of the personal belongings of Sir Seretse Khama. The museum also covers the local

B O T S W A N A

history of the Serowe and Palapye area. (Off the central turn-off to Orapa, 300m from the T junction with Serowe's main road. ☎463 0519. Open Tu-F 8am-4:30pm, Sa 11am-4pm. Free; donations appreciated.) The **royal graves** of the Khama family sit on the hill in the center of town near the TV tower. A sculpture of a duiker guards the grave of King Khama III; the king chose the animal as his totem after an incident in which he claimed a duiker saved his life. The graves are highly treasured by locals; those who wish to ascend to them must sign in at the *Kgotla* (village council). Depending on availability, they may ask a guide to accompany you to the site, in which case a small tip is in order. (Take the small road on the right just before the Caltex station when coming from the A1. The road ends at the *Kgotla*.)

NEAR SEROWE

KHAMA RHINO SANCTUARY

Follow the road to Orapa for 23km from Serowe; the sanctuary is on the left. Gates open daily 8am-6:30pm; small provisions store open at gate during business hours. ☎463 0713. P10 per person per day and P15 per vehicle. Chalets P200-350; campsites with hot showers and toilets P25 per person. Those with 4x4 and high-clearance 2x2 can drive themselves. Guided game drives (P200 for up to 4 people, P50 each extra person) and nature walks (P40 per person) available at 4pm. Night drives leave at 7pm (P300 for up to 4, P60 per extra person).

In 1993, when the Botswanan rhino population was plummeting due to extensive poaching, the Ngwato Land Board allocated an area of land around the Serowe Pan, then used as a cattle post, to the Khama Rhino Sanctuary Trust. The area is ideal not only because it is a suitable habitat for rhinos, but also because it is adjacent to a military base whose troops protect the rhinos from poachers around the clock. Since the initial introduction of four rhinos, more have been transferred from all over Southern Africa, and others have been born within the sanctuary, bringing the total number to 14. Today, the sanctuary is a community trust governed by trustees elected from the surrounding community, and it relies on tourist revenue for survival. Eland, zebra, wildebeest, hartebeest, kudu, duiker, gemsbok, leopard, and ostrich thrive, and the reintroduction of black rhino is planned.

A highlight of the sanctuary is the **Serowe Pan,** a grassy expanse in the northern section of the park that is popular with zebra and kudu. **Malema's Pan,** just north of the entrance gate, is perhaps the best place to see the often elusive rhinos; park here and sit patiently, and many of the park's species are likely to parade past. In the park's southwest corner, a **bird hide** offers visitors the opportunity to see the 140-plus species that frequent the area. Visitors may camp at the edge of the sanctuary at the **Mokongwa Camp,** which features 12 campsites and five chalets that accommodate four people each. The camp can be reached by 2WD vehicles.

SELEBI-PHIKWE

A mining center east of the A1 highway, Selebi-Phikwe doesn't have anything of interest to tourists, but it makes a decent overnight stop on the way into or out of the Tuli Block. **Traveller's Rest House ❷,** on Kopano Rd., is a cheery converted home with a family atmosphere. To get there, turn right on Borakanelo Rd. when coming from the highway, and right again at the T junction onto Kopano Rd.; the lodge is on the left. (☎261 0044. Breakfast P15. Check-out noon. Rooms P80-P170, some with private bath and TV.) **Score Supermarket,** on Tshekedi Rd. opposite the mall, is open M-F 8am-7pm, Sa 8am-3pm, Su 8am-2pm. Although Selebi-Phikwe has all the basic services (banks, post office, etc.), it's better to take care of business elsewhere; the town's population has expanded much faster than its infrastructure, and as a result, long queues are typical here.

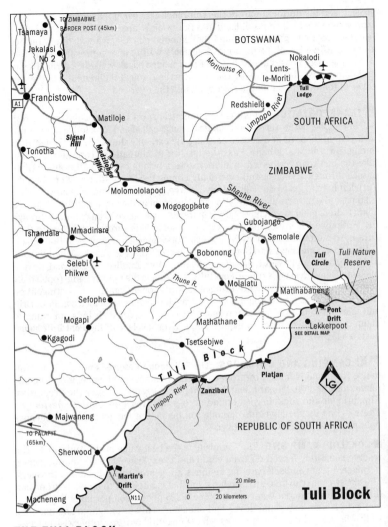

Tuli Block

THE TULI BLOCK

The Tuli Block, set apart from Gaborone and the adventures of the north, is not often visited by travelers. However, striking landscape, abundant wildlife, and more inexpensive game-viewing and accommodations than the national parks make the Tuli Block a worthwhile detour for the budget traveler. The area is a 350km long, 10-20km wide strip of land along the Botswana side of the Limpopo River (which, notwithstanding Kipling's characterization, is rarely great or grey-green but is somewhat greasy), ceded to the British by the Ngwato people as the Boers were advancing northward. The Ngwato believed the British strip would protect them from the Boers, while the British were set on building a railway from the Cape to Cairo. Uneven land, however, forced the British to abandon the project, and the northern part of the Tuli Block was eventually bought by private farmers and gradually consolidated into Botswana's largest privately owned game reserve. Trees and greenery around the Limpopo quickly give way to dry bushes and magnificent rock formations; **Solomon's Wall** is one impressive example. Where the road crosses the Motloutse River, a huge basalt wall once formed a natural dam across the river. Now the river carves through the middle, but the two edges of the wall jut out of the river bank into the river bed.

⊑ TRANSPORTATION. There is no public transport into the Tuli Block. From Selebi-Phikwe, **buses** run as far as **Matlhabaneng;** call ahead for a lodge operator to pick you up there or at a border crossing. By **car,** take the tar road through Bobonong towards Mathathane. Pass the turn-off to Mathathane (on the right) and take the dirt road to the left, which crosses a bridge over the Motloutse River, passes through a village, and eventually comes to a large four-way crossroads. Turn left here to get to the Tuli Nature Reserve. Alternately, continue down the tar road past Mathathane all the way to the T junction at the border, turn left, and go 15km to Redshield. If you have a 4WD in the dry season, you can continue through the Motloutse River into the Tuli Nature Reserve 5km further, and then to Pont Drift border crossing 17km away. The last Botswanan gas station is in Bobonong.

Four **border crossings** into South Africa puncture the Tuli Block's lengthy flank. They are, from southwest to northeast: **Martin's Drift, Zanzibar, Platjan,** and, next to Mashatu Game Reserve's office, **Pont Drift.** The first is the most reliable (open daily 8am-6pm). The other three are bridgeless fords (open 8am-4pm), contingent on the Limpopo's height. During the deluge, travelers can leave vehicles at Pont Drift and take Mashatu's cable car across (P20), arranging for their lodge or camp to claim them at the border. To inquire about river levels, call the **Pont Drift border post** (☎ 845 260).

⚍ ⚑ CAMPING AND OUTDOORS. The **Tuli Nature Reserve** is north of the Motloutse River and is fenced off from cattle. Large numbers of game, including elephant, giraffe, lion, leopard, eland, antelope, and zebra, wander the properties. Klipspringer and rock dassies bound across the area's distinctive *inselbergs.* There is one inexpensive accommodation inside the fenced area, and cheaper options south of the Motloutse River.

▨ NOKALODI CAMP SITE. This campsite is the best value in the Tuli Block. The reserve is entirely fenced off from cattle and is exclusively game (*lots* of game). Permanent tents and self-catering facilities are geared towards budget travelers. The classy camp can take up to eight people but is hired out to only one group at a time with no minimum number of people. P225 per person per night buys either two 1- to 2-hour-long game drives and one short walk or one drive and one long walk. The camp lies in the Tuli Block's most beautiful territory, otherwise inaccessible to those not staying in the Tuli or Mashatu Reserves. (Call for directions or ask at Pont Drift border post 5km away. ☎ 082 532 3308; ask for Hugh. Book ahead.) ❸

REDSHIELD. Across the Motloutse River from the Tuli Nature Reserve, Redshield is the second of the string of private farms that make up the Tuli Block. Once the kind of farm that actually grew things, Redshield is now an unfenced expanse for nomadic elephant antelope herds. Fewer carnivores compared to the fenced reserve across the river, but the scenery is just as stunning. (For directions, see **Transportation,** p. 540. ☎ 195 643; hartls@global.co.za. Simple rooms with hot shower P250, including 3 meals and 2 game drives. Camping at new site 30min. into the bush P100 per person, P750 for entire site.) ❷

CENTRAL KALAHARI DESERT

Stretching from northern South Africa to Gabon, the Kalahari Desert is the largest swath of sand in the world. Unlike stereotypical dunefield deserts, though, this sandscape is overlaid with acacia scrub, woodland, and *veld*. About 85% of Botswana is part of the Kalahari. These dry plains support the profuse wildlife that makes Botswana a tourist destination. Even for those who aren't born Kalahari-philes, it's easy to learn to love this desert.

THE CENTRAL KALAHARI GAME RESERVE

Closed to the public until 1990, the Central Kalahari Game Reserve (CKGR), slightly smaller than Ireland at 52,800 sq. km, is almost untouched by tourists. The reserve's campsites are isolated islands of greenery, surrounded for miles by raw desert. The CKGR is one of only a few areas in the world where you can be sure you're the only human being for a hundred miles in any direction. Here, your companions are wandering game, searching for the precious pools of standing rainwater and patches of green grass. During the rainy season (Nov.-Mar.) big game are especially common. Once the pans dry out, however, many of the animals leave for greener pastures and return the following season.

T A GLANCE

AREA: 52,800 sq. km.

CLIMATE: Dry season normally lasts from May-Dec.; Oct. and Nov. tend to be uncomfortably hot

FEATURES: Deception Valley, Piper's Pan, Sunday Pan, Passarge Valley

RANGERS/EMERGENCY ASSISTANCE: Game scouts are posted at Matswere Gate and Xade village.

GATEWAYS: Rakops, Maun (p. 552), Letlhakane (p. 547).

CAMPING: 20 minimalist sites; no wild camping permitted.

FEES & RESERVATIONS: The same as in all Botswanan parks; see **p. 534**. Sites are rarely full. Reservations required; no day-trippers permitted.

■ **TRANSPORTATION.** A self-guided trip into the Central Kalahari is not for novices. **Matswere Gate,** the main entrance to the park, is on the reserve's northeastern boundary. The best way to approach the gate is via the town of **Rakops,** 40km to the northeast on the Maun-Orapa highway. A Shell station in town (open daily 7am-10pm) usually has petrol (call 420 304 to make sure), and several grocery stores stock the basics. The well-maintained dirt turnoff to the park leaves the main road 2km west of Rakops and is clearly marked. Although it's possible to reach the gate directly from Maun, it's smart to make the Rakops detour in order to get fuel. The rare traveler who chooses to approach CKGR from the south should follow directions through Khutse Game Reserve (p. 543). The Shell Tourist Map of Botswana has an excellent detailed map of the CKGR on the back.

 WHEN TO GO. The dry season (especially June-Sept.) is an ideal time to visit CKGR; the grass is low, animals congregate around water holes, and the temperatures are bearable. Rainy season (Jan.-Mar.) is known for the dramatic and spectacular afternoon thunderstorms that race across the flat desert. Late in the wet season, however, grass grows extremely high between the wheel ruts in the road; drivers must stop every few minutes to scrape the grass seeds out of the vehicle's radiator and undercarriage, nearly doubling travel time.

ORIENTATION. A dirt track crossing the reserve from northeast to south serves as the park's main drag. In the north, a second track makes a loop that passes most of the park's pans, water holes, and prime camp sites. As the main road proceeds south, the road deteriorates, wildlife dwindles, and the landscape becomes less unique. This section of the park is typically visited only by those making the trans-Kalahari journey to Gaborone, although it may also appeal to those with a cultural interest in the area's indigenous communities (p. 542).

> **ROAD CONDITIONS.** Always inquire at a company that runs Kalahari safaris about up-to-date road conditions before setting off. A trip into the CKGR is not to be taken lightly. A 4WD is absolutely necessary, and familiarity with your vehicle is paramount. The chance of not seeing another person is quite high, so try to travel in a convey of more than one car. If you can only take one car, be sure you have plenty of spares and several people. All water, food, and fuel must be taken into the reserve with you. Be very generous calculating fuel consumption, and allow about 5L of water per person per day. If you don't have a 4WD, off-road experience, or enough people to do a trip into the CKGR safely, your best bet is to head to Maun (see p. 552) and organize a tour through one of the tour operators.

PRACTICAL INFORMATION. CKGR travel takes the term "self-sufficient" to a new level: if anything happens, it may be the better part of a *year* before another vehicle rolls past. There is **no petrol** anywhere in the park; the nearest is (unreliably) Rakops. **Game scouts** are posted at Matswere Gate and at Xade, on the park's western edge. **Water** is available reliably at Xade and sporadically at Matswere. In an emergency, pumped water is available at man-made wildlife water holes in the north of the park. **Airstrips** are at Xade, Xaxa, and just beyond the park's northern boundary at Deception Valley Lodge.

> **DECLINE OF A CULTURE** When the Central Kalahari Game Reserve was originally designated in 1961, it was established in part to protect the way of life of the indigenous San people, otherwise known as Bushmen. The San had managed to maintain their nomadic hunter-gatherer lifestyles for tens of thousands of years, until the latter half of the 20th century. By closing the area to the general public and protecting the wildlife, the CKGR's creators hoped to preserve the San's cultural isolation and food supply. Government priorities soon changed, however. A prohibition against herding cattle inside the park was followed by a decree requiring all game-hunters to obtain official government licenses. Both of these new rules make the San's life difficult. Finally, in the 1990s, the CKGR's San population was "encouraged" to resettle in permanent towns outside of the park's boundaries. These new towns were (and are) afflicted by contemporary problems such as alcoholism, unemployment, and venereal disease. A few dozen defiant San, mostly older individuals, have refused to make the move and continue to live in places like the enclosure of Molopo and the "ghost town" of Xade. If you travel around the central and western parts of the reserve, you may meet some of these people; be aware that they have had little contact with outsiders. Stand outside the boundaries of an enclosure until invited in, and ask before taking pictures. The San usually don't mind posing for photographs, but a token gift of food or other supplies (money is almost meaningless) is in order.

CAMPING AND SIGHTS. The undisputed highlight of CKGR is **Deception Valley**, 38km southwest of Matswere Gate. Hardly a "valley" at all (its sides are perhaps 3m high), this elongated pan earned celebrity status after naturalists Mark and Delia Owens wrote *Cry of the Kalahari,* chronicling their 10 years here studying the brown hyena. The Owenses' abandoned camp and airstrip are on the valley's northwestern edge; with a little luck, you might spot their beloved hyenas. Several **campsites** (CKK 1-4 and CKD 1-6) line the valley's western edge. About 40km southwest of Deception Valley on a good track, **Letiahau Waterhole** is a reliable place to see dozens of large game when the pump is active (inquire at the gate). Camp at the small, shaded site just across the road (called CKL 3) to watch the herds migrate to and from the water. Continuing 50km west, the spectacular **Piper's Pan** is a haven for wildlife of all kinds. Two camp sites (CKP 1-2) make an excellent place to pause for several days in order to take in the Kalahari in all its glory. North of Piper's Pan, a side road winds for 36km through **Passarge Valley,** a "fossil riverbed" that still shows signs of the river that coursed through it almost 10,000 years ago. Three camp sites (CKA 1-3) overlook the dozens of small pans that occupy the valley. Finally, **Sunday Pan,** 17km northwest of Deception, is a beautiful spot with three campsites (CKS 1-3). All campsites must be reserved in advance through the National Parks Office, and rangers won't let anyone past the gate without reservation in hand. It is extremely rare to find a site booked, however, even at the last minute. All campsites lack water and facilities of any kind. ❶

KHUTSE GAME RESERVE

*To get to Khutse from Gaborone, drive 111km through Molepolole to Letlhakeng, the last place where you can refuel. Here, the road turns to dirt and sometimes can become deep sand. It continues 104km to the reserve gate through the villages of Khudumelapye and Salajwe. In Salajwe, look carefully for green "Khutse" signs, as dirt tracks wind in every direction. The roads in Khutse are solid, but if you go north into the CKGR, the sand can get deep and loose. Entry fees are the same as other parks in Botswana. See **National Park Basics**, p. 534.*

This small reserve, situated along the southern border of the Central Kalahari Game Reserve, offers some of the same experiences as its northern neighbor without all of the logistical nightmares. Travelers come here from Gaborone in order to get the "feel" of the central Kalahari—the vast flat expanses, millions of stars on a moonless night, and famous "Kalahari silence." A series of pans, including **Moreswe Pan,** are beautiful in every season. Game in the park is extremely varied—this small area supports an ecosystem with many hundreds of plant and animal species—but the animals are often difficult to see, and one shouldn't expect the same kinds of numbers that are visible farther north. One 170km road in decent condition loops all the way around the park and crosses briefly into the CKGR. Most visitors spend three to four days exploring this road in its entirety in order to see all of Khutse's highlights. There are six areas where you can camp in the reserve, but only the **Khutse Campground** ❶, about 11km from the gate, has facilities. Bring your own water, allowing 5L per person per day.

KALAHARI SALT PANS

About 10,000 years ago, there was a lake called Lake Makgadikgadi. Then plate tectonics shook things up, rivers shifted their courses, and the lake evaporated. What was left behind—the Okavango Delta and the Makgadikgadi and Nxai Pans—is a sight that must be seen to be believed.

North of the vast Central Kalahari and south of the lush Chobe Valley, the pans are a landscape reminiscent of another planet. Trees float and shimmer in the distance beyond a sea of white, blasts of hot air race across the perfectly flat salt, and baobabs the size of houses stand as lone sentinels. In the rainy season, the desert becomes an ocean, and hundreds of thousands of flamingoes descend from the skies creating a horizon of bright pink.

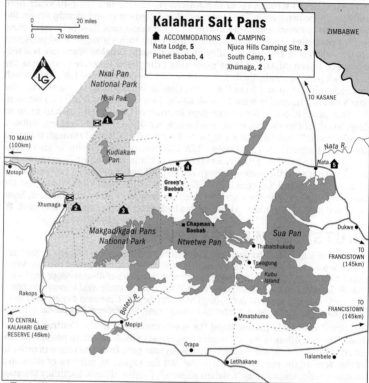

Kalahari Salt Pans

♠ ACCOMMODATIONS   ▲ CAMPING
Nata Lodge, **5**   Njuca Hills Camping Site, **3**
Planet Baobab, **4**   South Camp, **1**
                          Xhumaga, **2**

Two adjacent national parks, described below, give protected status to a relatively tiny corner of pan country. Botswana's two largest pans, Ntwetwe and Sua, stretch for hundreds of kilometers south and east of the parks. For those who prefer to bypass the expensive national parks, there are a number of less pricey ways to experience the pans and their surroundings, starting from bases in the tiny towns of Nata, Gweta, or Lethlakane.

MAKGADIKGADI AND NXAI PAN NATIONAL PARKS

In **Nxai Pan National Park** (the "x" is a click), animals congregate around the relatively small pan to lick the salt or drink the water, depending on the season. Nxai is especially well-known for its sizeable lion population and **Baines' Baobabs.** This landmark, accessible from a right-hand turn-off 20km down the main entrance road to Nxai (just follow the most pronounced jeep trail thereafter), is a cluster of baobab trees overlooking a salt pan that was immortalized by the British painter Thomas Baines and many a photograph. For those who wish to stay in the park, **South Camp,** on the south end of Nxai Pan just past the game scout station, has unheated ablution blocks surrounded by excellent game drives. A hide overlooking a pan is within walking distance.

Makgadikgadi National Park (the "kg" sounds are pronounced like a harsh "h") is Nxai's larger and less-visited sibling on the other side of the highway. One of Makgadikgadi's most striking features is the broad **savannah** that cuts a swath down the center of the park. Roamed by ostrich, antelope, and the occasional elephant, this mini-Serengeti seems to stretch on forever, its flat horizon punctuated only by the slender palm trees in the distance.

On the west side of the park, 9km north of the Xhumaga entrance gate along the Boteti River, a side road overlooks a small **hippo pool** where about a half-dozen of the creatures typically lounge. The main campsite, **Xhumaga** , sits on a bluff above the Boteti and has a very basic ablution block with running water. An undeveloped campsite called **Njuca Hills** is on two hillocks surrounded on all sides by endless savannah that makes for some incredible sunsets. The site has basic outhouses but no water. Gather firewood before driving out of the acacia forest, because you won't find any nearby.

> **DRIVING IN THE PANS.** Exercise extreme caution when driving through the salt pans. Roads are manageable by 4x4 only and are mere tracks that change after each rainy season. It is extremely dangerous to drive off the wheel ruts. Entire cars have been known to sink, as the pans are only a crust lying over endless mud. Always be aware of the depth and consistency of the wheel tracks in front of you, and don't go where others have clearly had difficulty before you. The vegetated pans are no less dangerous. In Makgadikgadi National Park, you may not see anyone for days, so take vehicle necessities and enough supplies for a few days. A good map is extremely important; the Shell Tourist Map, available at service stations and accommodations nationwide, is excellent.

ORIENTATION & PRACTICAL INFORMATION

The **Nata-Maun road** runs through Makgadikgadi and Nxai Pan National Parks. The parks are managed as one unit—the 2000 sq. km north of the road are called Nxai Pan National Park, while the 5000 sq. km south of it is Makgadikgadi Pan National Park. You only have to pay one entrance fee to go into both parks. **Park gates** to Makgadikgadi are in Xhumaga village off of the road to Orapa and on the Nata-Maun road; the entrance to Nxai is on the Nata-Maun road, but you pay at the gate further north at South Camp. All gates are open from 6am-6pm.

> **WHEN TO GO.** The rainy season (Jan.-Apr.) offers the most bird life in the pans. The trade-off, however, is that visitors can only reach the edge of the pans, and not go out on them. The shoulders of the rainy season (normally Dec. and May) see the migration of elephants and other large game through pan country. The dry season presents the pans at their most austere, with mirages and blinding white salt; October and November, however, can be ungodly hot.

Camping and entrance fees are the same as for all national parks (see p. 534). Makgadikgadi's sites can often be reserved on a few days' notice, though Nxai's are more likely to be full. **Game scouts** and **emergency assistance** are posted at Makgadikgadi's Xhumaga gate, just south of the highway in Makgadikgadi, and at the south end of the pan in Nxai. The nearest **fuel** and **supplies** can be found in Gweta, 12km east of Makgadikgadi's border on the Nata-Maun highway.

BOTSWANA

KUBU ISLAND

Far down a sandy track on the western side of Sua Pan, this hauntingly beautiful spot makes visitors feel like the only people on earth. The island's official name is *Lekhubu*, meaning "rocky outcropping," but locals and tourists alike always have called it *Kubu*. When the pans were all part of one inland sea, waves lapped against the shores of this island. Evidence of Kubu's past life still exists in the form of wave prints and fossilized bird droppings. Later, the descendants of the Great Zimbabwe civilization used the island for sacred rites, creating stone walls and ceremonial beads that remain today. Kubu's giant baobabs, rock formations, and meandering footpaths make for great hiking, with the vastness of the salt pans never more than a few feet away. For those who spend the night camping here, seeing the sun rise over the shimmering salt is an unforgettable experience.

■ 🛈 ORIENTATION AND PRACTICAL INFORMATION

You will get lost at least once trying to reach Kubu; just accept it now. The best way to tackle it is from the south. Heading west on the **Francistown-Orapa road,** make a right onto a gravel track 215km from Francistown, where a white sign displays a map of the pans and the title "Lekhubu Island." The village of Mmatshumo is 25km down this road; take a gentle left at the very beginning of the village at a green sign saying "Lekhubu." Stay to the right as this track bends around the side of a yellow building. After passing through town, you should find yourself on an wide sandy track. This track will fork many times—stay on the wider, more heavily-traveled track at each junction. Just over 14.5km after leaving town, you will drive out onto a salt pan—a veterinary gate is at the other end. Pass through this gate and proceed across 7.5km of grassland to a fork in the road with two rusty, twisted poles. Make a right here, and you will soon see Kubu advancing across the pan. Allow 1½hr. from the highway. Kubu is completely inaccessible during the wet season (roughly Jan.-Apr.). On the wet season's fringes, when the pan is still damp, you will need to approach the island via Tswagong; ask the gatekeeper at the veterinary gate for directions.

A community trust maintains the island and charges P5 per person plus P25 per vehicle for entrance and P10 per person for camping. The ranger will amble out and find you, "mobile office" in hand, as you wander the island.

CHAPMAN'S BAOBAB

In the northern edge of Ntwetwe Pan, six giant baobabs twist around a common trunk to form **Chapman's Baobab,** claimed to be the largest and one of the oldest baobabs in the world; experts believe it began growing about 5500 years ago. With a circumference of 80 feet at the base, this tree dwarfs everything else on the horizon. The road leading here is a straight shot south from the village of Gweta. Take the jeep track for 40km. When you emerge from the acacia brush onto a savannah, look for the first track that crosses, make a left, and drive 3km.

On the way to Chapman's, 23km from Gweta, the road passes **Green's Baobab** on the right. Though tiny compared to its cousin to the south, the tree is historically important as a frequent stopover point for a motley crew of early European traders, many of whom carved their names into the trunk.

NATA

The tiny town of Nata consists of little more than the main road and a few service stations useful to those on their way to Maun and Kasane. Nata is a good choice for those wishing to explore the pans or to break up the exhausting, 1000km trip between Gaborone and Kasane or Maun. Detailed information about road conditions and directions can be obtained from the Nata Lodge (see below).

⊞⁊ ORIENTATION AND PRACTICAL INFORMATION. Driving west from Francistown, the road crosses Nata River before passing the Shell and Northgate Caltex service stations to the left and right, respectively. The turn-off to Maun is immediately after, on the left; the main road continues straight to Kasane. Coming from the west, the **police station** (☎621 1222) is on the left, just over the bridge. A tiny **clinic** (☎621 1244) is on the right, just over the bridge in the same direction. Public **phones** are outside Northgate. There is a **post office** behind the Sua Pan Lodge by the Shell service station. (☎621 1211. Open M-F 8am-4pm, Sa 8am-noon.) **Buses** stop at Northgate Caltex station and run twice daily to **Kasane** (3hr., P40), and hourly to **Francistown** (2hr., P17) and **Maun** (4hr., P25) via **Gweta** (1hr., P12). Maun-bound buses can be asked to stop at the turnoff for Planet Baobab (p. 546).

⌐◻ ACCOMMODATIONS AND FOOD. Nata Lodge ❶, 10km toward Francistown, is the town's best accommodation option, enveloped by palm-fringed and thatched scenery. Chalets (P340) are luxurious and well-decorated; one "family chalet" (P380) with bunkbeds sleeps 6 and is a good option for groups. Huge tents (P280), meanwhile, are also electrified, furnished, and have full bathrooms. Campers (P27 per person) have their pick of woodsy sites and can fully use the lodge's facilities, including a pool with a cascading waterfall. Their restaurant, with bar, features buffets (P50) on Saturday, and a la carte the rest of the week (entrees P15-45). The lodge offers three-hour game viewing trips to Makgadikgadi National Park in the morning and evening; the trips are a bargain (P77 per person), but actual game-viewing time is quite short. (☎621 1260; fax 621 1265; natalodge@info.bw; www.natalodge.com. MC/V.) In Nata proper, the **Sua Pan Lodge ❷** has budget *rondavels* with stone floors and tiny bathrooms, as well as camping facilities. The lodge makes an adequate night stop, but its location—attached to the Shell gas station—is less than picturesque, and the noise of highway traffic and bar patrons filters into the rooms. Their restaurant, with attached bar, serves standard fast-food fare for around P20. (Restaurant open M-Th 6am-11pm, F-Sa 6am-midnight, Su 6am-10pm. Check-out 10am. *Rondavel* singles P133; doubles P154; triples P176. Camping P25 per person. MC/V.) **Nata Sanctuary ❶** (see below) offers campsites set in a stand of *mopane* trees for P15 per person plus entrance fees.

◨ SIGHTS. Nata Sanctuary, reached by a turnoff 18km south of the Nata junction on the A1, occupies a small "bay" in the northeastern corner of Sua Pan. Although this reserve is not a must see for those who plan on venturing out into pan country, it's an essential stop for anyone who wouldn't otherwise get a glimpse of the pans. Visitors can experience the feeling of standing on the edge of the pans' vastness, and the sanctuary's bird life makes it famous among birding enthusiasts. The forested section of the sanctuary, crossed by a web of sandy jeep tracks, is home to game such as antelope and gemsbok. (Open daily 7am-7pm. Admission P20.)

LETLHAKANE

Just south of Botswana's two largest salt pans, the mining town of Letlhakane owes its existence to a huge diamond deposit that lies just underfoot. The town isn't a destination in itself, but it makes a good launching pad for those approaching the pans from southern Botswana or for those intending to enter the Central Kalahari through Rakops. Everything you'd want, including a **Standard Bank** and **Shell filling station,** is on the one main road, which branches northwest off of the highway. For a place to sleep, **Granny's Guesthouse ❷** (☎297 8246), just behind the Shell station, has simple rooms with desks and shared bathrooms for P110. **Granny's Kitchen ❶** (☎297 8246), also attached to the Shell complex, serves up English breakfasts (P19), curries (P20), and steaks (P30) on tables with checkered tablecloths, candles, and flowers. The Kitchen also serves as the guest house's reception. (Open daily 7:30am-10pm.)

BOTSWANA

GWETA

The tiny town of Gweta, 100km west of Nata on the Nata-Maun highway, is worth visiting if only for a stay at ▧**Planet Baobab ❷**. Planet Baobab combines superb indigenous architecture with a playfully creative touch of the absurd (beer-bottle chandeliers are just the beginning). Set among fifteen colossal baobabs, guests here can camp, stay in an authentically recreated San grass hut, or enjoy one of the Bakalanga huts, which are nothing short of masterpieces. The operators also run three-day, all-inclusive tours to the pans, as well as shorter trips to other locales. (☎ 6 21 2277; fax 621 3458; unchart@info.bw. San grass hut singles P82.50; doubles P150. Bakalanga hut singles P220; doubles P275. Camping P20 per person. Three-day tours P565 per person.)

OKAVANGO REGION

The Okavango Delta is unspoiled African wilderness at its most magnificent. The Okavango River snakes southeast from Angola into the north of Botswana, where it meets the Kalahari Desert. The sands split the waters into radiating rivulets, forming an inland delta of over 15,000 sq. km. of twisting canals, islands, and reed-choked marsh land. Come June, the outer fingers of the Delta swell as rains from the wet season filter down to northern Botswana. When the water recedes, wild-life gathers close around disappearing pools. Throughout the year, an astounding number and variety of birds, game, and plants thrive in and around this watery wonderland. Hippos and crocs abound, and other game find their way onto the many fingers of dry land that extend out into the lily-bedecked waterways.

There are several ways, outlined below, to experience the Okavango. The most popular option is to arrange a *mokoro* (traditional dugout canoe) trip from **Maun** (p. 552); these pre-arranged trips are the easiest and most hassle-free, but prices start at US$50 per person, per day for the most minimalist trips and go up from there. Those with wheels (or enough determination) can make their way to the remote village of **Seronga** (p. 549), where a community *mokoro* polers' trust offers an experience that is richer than that of the Maun operators in many ways, for a fraction of the price. **Moremi National Park** (p. 551) has a network of roads and camp sites in the southeastern part of the Delta, allowing visitors to experience the Delta by vehicle rather than canoe. Finally, lodges in the **Okavango Panhandle** (p. 558) offer motorized boat trips that explore the panhandle section of the river; the experience is different from that of the Delta but worthwhile nonetheless.

Most visitors prefer to explore the Okavango between July and October, when the waters are brimming and the rain has stopped. A wet safari can be miserable. It may prove difficult to find either poler or accommodation in the rainy season (Jan.-Mar.), as some lodges close altogether. Those that do stay open during the summer rains may offer discounts and will certainly be less crowded.

A typical day of *mokoro* exploration is spent only partly in the boat. After break-ing camp in the morning, the poler will spend two or three hours cruising through the Okavango's seemingly endless waterways. The boat is ill-suited for game-view-ing—you can expect to see mostly reeds and sky—but birders will be blown away by the abundance of bird life around them.

At least once or twice a day, the poler pulls up onto solid ground and leads sev-eral-hour game walks through the grasses and brush. The polers are experts in tracking animals by their prints and droppings; over the course of the trip, they will teach you the basics of game tracking. Elephants, giraffes, and cats are often sighted on these walks, but after a few grisly misadventures in the 1990s, guides are now extremely cautious and most animals are viewed from afar. After a day divided between boating and walking, camp is pitched somewhere along the shore, dinner is made, and everyone goes to bed not long after sunset.

As you may have guessed by now, you will be spending a *lot* of time in close company with your poler. One of the biggest factors influencing the happiness of your trip, therefore, will be how well the two of you get along. In many cases, guests have some degree of control over whom they choose to guide them; take this decision seriously and have a chat with your prospective guide before you commit. On self-catering trips, it's a nice gesture to share one's own dinner with the guide, even though it's not required.

THE BASICS OF MAUN-BASED MOKORO TRIPS. Maun is the *mokoro* capital of the world; the town is full of booking companies (the best of which are listed on p. 555) that put together *mokoro* trips ranging from basic to luxurious. Make the following considerations while choosing your trip:

—Number of days. One of the beauties of *mokoro* travel is the ability to enter a wilderness untouched by roads or people. This is only true, however, if the poler has enough time to penetrate the heart of the delta, instead of lingering by the launch points. A minimum of three days in the water is recommended. Although one-day jaunts are available, they are a pale shadow of the full experience.

—Drive-in or fly-in. Fly-in trips drop guests at airstrips deep in the central delta and have the advantage of a scenic over-flight of the Okavango's watery mazes. Round-trip airplane transfer fees are usually US$80-150 per person.

—All-inclusive or self-managing. Budget trips usually include only transportation, the boat, and the guide. Everything else (food, stove, tent, etc.) is the responsibility of the visitor; full equipment can be hired in Maun for about US$30. On more upmarket trips, the company takes care of the gear, cooking, tents, and other chores, allowing visitors to sit back and relax.

—Delta camps. The wilderness camps inside the Okavango are all out of a budget traveler's reach (Oddball's and Gunn's Camp, see p. 556, are the only ones that come close). For some, however, the experience is worth the splurge. It's hard to match a gourmet, candlelight dinner after a long day exploring the Delta.

OKAVANGO DELTA

SERONGA MOKORO OPTION

All of the Maun *mokoro* trips have one thing in common—their high cost. This is due in part to the fact that the government of Botswana has granted a license to one concessioner, and all *mokoro* polers and tour companies must operate through this highly profitable monopoly. This is a sore point for a number of people in the Maun area, since the government's licensing scheme was originally intended to nourish community self-help programs, not a large company.

Residents in the village of Seronga, 500km north of Maun by road, are not constrained by this license; the town is one of the only places in the delta where travelers can (legally) hire a *mokoro* and poler directly, without going through a middleman. The village has established the **Okavango Polers' Trust** (☎676 861; fax 676 939; mbiroba@okavango.co.bw; www.mokoro.org) to handle the increasing flow of tourists alienated from the Maun scene. Unlike in Maun, 100% of the proceeds are reinvested in the community. Moreover, the Northern Delta, near Seronga, is thought to be superior in beauty and wildlife activity to the regions in the south. For those travelers with the time, resources, and will to transport themselves to the northern side of the Delta, the trip is certainly worthwhile.

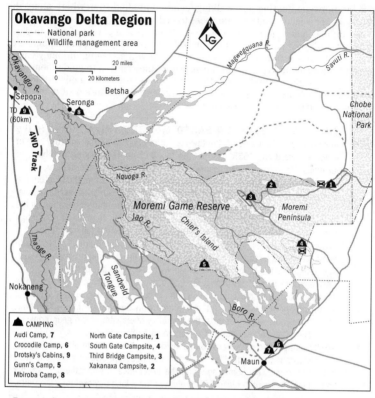

Okavango Delta Region
-·-·-·- National park
·········· Wildlife management area

CAMPING
Audi Camp, **7**
Crocodile Camp, **6**
Drotsky's Cabins, **9**
Gunn's Camp, **5**
Mbiroba Camp, **8**

North Gate Campsite, **1**
South Gate Campsite, **4**
Third Bridge Campsite, **3**
Xakanaxa Campsite, **2**

By road: Seronga is 500km from Maun; allow 7hr. for the trip. Proceed west on the main highway to Sehithwa (101km) and turn north. At Etsha 6 (288km), to the right off of the main highway, fill up at the gas station; there is no other gas anywhere in the region. Continue to Shakawe (404km), near the Namibian border; the blacktop passes straight through town and leads to the edge of the Okavango, where a free vehicle ferry crosses continuously from dawn to dusk. Once on the other side, follow the sand and gravel track (4WD highly recommended) southeast along the bank of the Okavango River for 100km to Seronga village. The camp is 2km south of the village; signs mark the way.

By boat: a motorized launch, filled with supplies and local residents, makes the 1½hr. trip to Seronga from the village of Sepupa, 350km northwest of Maun (departs daily at 2pm, returns daily at noon; P20). Drivers can get to Sepupa from Maun in 3-4 hours; those without wheels are confined to minibus taxis, which leave Maun primarily in the early morning, take 4 hours, and cost P25.

By air, chartered 5-passenger aircraft fly directly to Seronga from Maun, take 40 min., and cost about US$250 each way for the entire plane. Charter companies in Maun, all with offices at the airport, include **Delta Air** (☎686 0044), **Mack Air** (☎686 0675), **Sefofane Air** (☎686 0778), and **Swamp Air** (☎686 0569). Call ahead to the polers' trust to be met at the airstrip. If you're lucky, you may be able to coordinate with a group that's returning from Seronga when you're flying up or vice-versa; in this case, the cost of the plane can be split in half.

BOTSWANA

Two-passenger *mokoros*, with guides, cost P150 per boat per day. A one-time fee of P70 per person is also levied for booking and transportation to the launch site. Equipment is hired for those who need it (tents P25-40 per night, cook kit P20 per night, sleeping bag P5 per night).

The small village of Seronga makes an excellent base for the first and last night of the trip; some visitors opt to stay longer and enjoy the riverside location. The Polers' Trust operates **Mbiroba Camp ❶**, which offers a variety of accommodations. (*Rondavels* with shared bath P50 per person. Luxurious two-level chalet singles P200 single; doubles P250; triples P330; quads P400. Camping P25 per person.)

MOREMI GAME RESERVE

Since its creation, the Moremi Game Reserve has thrived as one of the premier nature reserves in the world, serving as a role model for conservation efforts and as proof that limiting tourism can make a big difference. The government's tight restrictions on lodges and tourist numbers in the reserve have kept the area very close to its natural state; this place is as wild as they come.

Today, after several enlargements, the game reserve includes the secluded **Chief's Island** at its heart and the magnificent **Moremi Peninsula** on its eastern edge. Chief's Island is accessible only by air or water; most *mokoro* trips from the interior will explore this area. The entire region is superb for bird watching, and the abundant eagles, owls, and egrets will astonish even those who aren't avid birders. The spectacular flora is rich with *mopane* trees, and swamps of reeds and lilies tease the solid land. It's possible to sight lion, leopard, wild dog, and cheetah, and where there's enough water, crocs and hippos are in it.

⛭ ⛬ ORIENTATION AND PRACTICAL INFORMATION. There are two automobile entrances to Moremi, and only 4WDs are allowed into the park. The government has left the roads sandy—*very* sandy. The roads around Third Bridge are especially notorious for their deep sand, and the northern part of Moremi Peninsula (particularly the road between Khwai and Xakanaxa) becomes submerged in several feet of water during the rainy season. The road to Moremi from Maun is paved until the village of Shorobe (47km), where it becomes good gravel, forking shortly thereafter; take the left fork. 15km after the fork, the road passes through a veterinary gate and abruptly turns into a deep, rutted sand track. After a total of 99km, the **South Gate,** with camp sites and ablutions, is reached. When returning from Moremi, plan on reaching Maun before sunset; it isn't wise to make the drive after dark. The Shell Map to Moremi (P20), superimposed on satellite images and available anywhere in Maun, is indispensable. No fuel or automobile assistance is available anywhere beyond Maun, but basic staples and cold drinks can be picked up in Khwai village, just past the north gate.

A standard self-drive tour of the park might start at **South Gate** in the morning, pass by the several roadside waterholes and cross the four beautiful *mopane* **pole bridges** in the afternoon, and then camp at **Third Bridge** at night. Day two could be spent exploring the wildlife-rich **Mboma Island** and its sibling, **Dead Tree Island,** and then camping at **Xakanaxa.** On day three, proceed east to visit several small **pans** and the **hippo pools** before arriving at **North Gate Camp.** On day four, you could either return to Maun via South Gate or continue north to Chobe National Park.

⛭ ⛬ ACCOMMODATIONS AND FOOD. There are four campsites within the reserve: **South Gate, Third Bridge, Xakanaxa** (*KA-ka-na-cka*), and **North Gate ❶.** You must attain a permit to camp in the park, and reservations are often filled one year in advance. The campsites within Moremi have been recently remodeled to include water taps and ablution facilities with hot showers and toilets (although these are seldom cleaned). Campers are responsible for all other necessities and are expected to leave campsites immaculate. The sites are not fenced, and wildlife are free to roam. If you didn't plan your trip a year in advance and therefore missed out on reservations, your only choices are to go through one of the safari operators in Maun or make daily visits to the national parks reservations office in Maun and hope for last-minute cancellation (which are frequent).

MAUN

When, just a few decades back, the Botswanan government realized the tourism potential of the country's unspoiled north, Maun's fate was forever changed. What was but a wee hamlet has since been pumped up into a bustling way station of over 30,000 and is now the undisputed tourist capital of Botswana. In the rush from Tswana cattle post to international tourist base, the town has come to resemble one long, long strip mall. All accommodations are sensibly located well north of the soulless town center; if you're here, you're bound for somewhere else. Turn that frown upside-down and get out of Maun.

▐ TRANSPORTATION

Flights: Air Botswana (☎686 0391 for the booking office in Gaborone) flies to **Gaborone** (1½hr.; daily 5pm, Tu at 8:30am, F 3:20pm; US$82), **Johannesburg** (2hr., 3pm, US$220); **Kasane** (55min.; M, W, and Su 2:20pm, F 12:30pm; US$76); **Victoria Falls** (50min.; Th, Sa 2:20pm; US$90). The office is off the main road on the way to the airport. Open M-F 7:30am-12:30pm and 1:45-4:30pm, Sa 8:30-11:30am.

Buses: Leave from the Maun Old Mall, across the street from Spar. Buses run daily to **Nata** (4hr., P25), where you can transfer to **Kasane** and then to **Francistown** (6hr., P42), where you can transfer to **Gaborone.** Buses run approximately every hr. on the ½hr., 6:30am-4:30pm. **Audi Camp** (☎686 0599) runs a shuttle to **Windhoek, Namibia** (11hr., M 7:00am, US$50).

Minibus Taxis: Leave from the Maun Old Mall. Fares are P3-10 for most nearby destinations. Good for travel to **Ghanzi** (P25), **Sepupa** (P30), **Etsha** (P30), and **Shakawe** (P50). Local minibuses make the run from the town center to the end of Sir Seretse Khama Rd. every 10min. or so (P1.25).

Car Rental: Avis (☎686 0039), 200m up the road from the airport, rents **4WD** double cabs for P349 per day, plus P3.19 per km.

Taxis: Cabs cruise along Maun's main street and make the run to Matlapaneng (where most accommodations are located) for P20-25. Drivers generally expect some haggling.

▐ ▐ ORIENTATION AND PRACTICAL INFORMATION

The town of Maun is on the northwest bank of the Thamalakane River. The one major road parallels the river and is split by a central roundabout. On the south side of the roundabout, the road is called **Tsheko-Tsheko.** Just behind the Barclay's bank on this road, obscured from street view, is the pedestrian-only **Old Mall,** the commercial heart of the city, which contains banks, supermarkets, and the post office. North of the roundabout, the road changes to **Sir Seretse Khama** and passes the police station, the New Mall, and the airport on the way to the village of Matlapaneng, 9km away, where all budget accommodations are located.

Department of Wildlife and National Parks (☎686 1265; fax 661 264; dwnp@gov.bw), off the main road close to the central roundabout. A required stop for individual national park reservations. Open M-F 8:30am-5pm, Sa 8:30am-1:30pm.

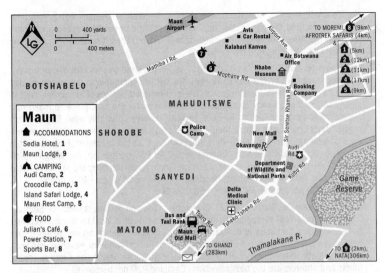

Bank: Standard Bank (☎ 686 2209) and **Barclay's Bank** (☎ 686 0210), both in front of the Maun Old Mall. Both offer currency exchange, Visa **ATMs,** and credit card advances. Open M-F 8:30am-3:30pm, Sa 8:30-11am.

Camping gear: Kalahari Kanvas (☎ 686 0568; fax 686 0035; kal.kanvas@info.bw), next to Avis. Rents tents (from P22 per night), as well as all other equipment needed for a *mokoro* trip. Open M-F 8am-1pm and 2-5pm, Sa 8:30am-12:30pm.

Police: (☎ 686 0223), off the main road near the central roundabout.

Pharmacy: Okavango Pharmacy (☎ 686 2049), in the Maun New Mall. Open M-F 8am-1pm and 2-5:30pm, Sa 8:30am-1pm.

Hospital: Delta Medical Center (☎ 686 2999), opposite Rileys Garage. Open 24hr.

Internet Access: Postnet (☎ 686 5606), just behind the Engen station off of Seretse Khama, is the fastest, largest, and most reliable in town. Also handles all mail, phone, and fax needs. P15 per 30min. Open daily 8am-6pm. **Sedia Hotel** (☎ 686 0177), 5km north of town. P2.50 per 5min. Open M-F 8am-8pm, Sa-Su 10am-5pm. **Ensign Agencies** (☎ 686 0351), opposite the Power Station complex, has one Internet-enabled computer (P14.50 for 30min.). Open M-F 8am-1pm and 2-5pm, Sa 9-11am.

Book Exchange: At **Ensign Agencies** (see above). Books are P2 to exchange, P5 to buy.

Post Office: (☎ 686 0245), on the main highway 200m south of the Old Mall. *Poste Restante* and **phones.** Open M-Tu and Th-F 8:15am-4pm, W 8:45am-4pm, Sa 8:30-11am.

ACCOMMODATIONS AND CAMPING

Audi Camp is the best place to find other travelers going to the delta; all of the following also organize trips into the surrounding national parks (see **Adventures,** p. 555). The **Power Station** (see **Food,** p. 555) has a hard-to-beat deal for campers.

■ **Island Safari Lodge** (☎ 686 0300; fax 686 2932; island@info.bw), 10km north of Maun on Sir Seretse Khama, and 7km down the signposted dirt road. Thanks to its long access road, the lodge has its side of the river all to itself; the verdant shoreline feels like it's a million miles from the bustle of Maun. Recently renovated chalets with bath are top-notch, and the bar, restaurant, and pool make it possible to spend a day here just relaxing. Also coordinates excellent drive-in *mokoro* trips. Chalets P250 including full breakfast. Camping P20 per person. ❶

 Audi Camp (☎ 686 0599; fax 686 0581; audicamp@info.bw; www.audi-delta.com), 12km north of town on the way to Moremi. The heftiest contender in the budget market and popular with the overlander crowd. The ever-crowded bar, great restaurant, crystal-clear pool, and big, sandy campground make this by far the best place to make new friends in Maun. Those looking for quiet serenity, however, probably won't find it at this regular party spot. Open-roofed reed showers are unforgettable; some love the experience of bathing under the stars, while others find it a bit too...exposed. Free rides from the Power Station daily at 5pm. Canoes rented for P50 per person, including drop-off upriver. Self-catering kitchen. Laundry service. Dome tents with cots: single P66; double P88. Canvas tents with furnishing, bedding, and electricity: single P110; double P143. Camping P20 per person. MC/V with P50 min. ❶

Maun Rest Camp (☎/fax 686 3472), 9km north of town on Sir Seretse Khama. Emphatically not a municipal campground, this lush riverfront oasis is ideal for those who prefer bougainvillea to breakfast and dryads to drunken locals: there's no restaurant or bar here, just a quiet campground with friendly owners. Hungry campers, however, can walk down the path to the Sports Bar (p. 555). Campsites overlooking the river are idyllic; toilets and showers are the best anywhere. Camping P20 per person. ❶

Crocodile Camp (☎ 686 0796; fax 686 0793; croccamp@yahoo.com), next to Audi, has the best-located bar in town, perched over a particularly beautiful stretch of river. The campsite, however, is sandy and rather characterless, and the chalets don't live up to their price tag. Chalets US$60; singles and double US$70. Camping P20 per person. ❶

Sedia Hotel (☎/fax 686 0177), 5km north of town on Sir Seretse Khama. Campers here get the best river view, as well as use of the facilities (including a resort-style pool) and the cheapest rate of any developed, electrified complex in town. The hotel's rooms and restaurant, however, don't meet the mid-range standard. Free transport to and from town center. Internet. Tent singles with beds US$10; tent doubles US$15; unremarkable chalets and rooms US$55 and up. Camping US$1 per person. MC/V. ❶

Maun Lodge (☎ 686 3939; fax 686 3969; maun.lodge@info.bw; www.sausage.bw/maunlodge/), 2km from town. Take the western most turnoff to Francistown and follow it across the river; Maun Lodge is on the left. The newest player on Maun's tiny upmarket scene, the lodge offers quality hotel rooms with A/C, room service, and satellite TV. Restaurant and pool; free airport pick-up. Singles P330; doubles P390. MC/V. ❹

NAVIGATING YOUR WAY TO NAMIBIA

If you're planning on heading to Windhoek (see p. 461) from Maun, the town of **Ghanzi** is your godsend. Overnight here to split your time on the road. Though there isn't much of interest to see, the town gained infamy from a merciless past inhabitant, **Hendrik Matthys van Zyl,** who supposedly discouraged Boer Dorsland Trekkers from settling around Ghanzi because of his ruthlessness. Van Zyl wandered the Botswana wilderness in the late 1800s, slaughtering San and elephant with the same disregard. From the ivory ripped from over 400 elephants, he built a massive mansion in Ghanzi and lived the high life until his mysterious death, after which his wife and four children left the area and were never heard from again. Besides the gory story, Ghanzi also offers accommodation at the **Kalahari Arms Hotel** (☎ 659 6311). Singles and doubles are about US$40 and *rondavels* are US$40-50. Camping is US$4 per person.

FOOD

Island Safari Lodge and **Audi Camp** (see above) both have popular restaurants. Self-caterers can visit the **Spar supermarket** in the Ngami Center off of Seretse Khama just north of the roundabout (☎ 686 0094; open M-Sa 8am-8pm, Su 8am-1:30pm).

Sports Bar and Restaurant (☎ 686 2676), 5km out of town off of Sir Seretse Khama; when coming from town, look for a black sign on your right, and drive through the gate. Don't let the name fool you: with a broad selection of pastas (P18-35), seafood (P25-50), and steaks (P32-50), the Sports Bar's refined dining room is the closest thing Maun has to a fine culinary experience. The actual bar, meanwhile, has several TV screens with the latest games, free-flowing beer, and pool tables to bring you back to earth after an other-worldly delta adventure. Open M-Th 5-11pm, F-Sa 5pm-midnight, Su 5-10pm. Bar closed M. ❷

Power Station (☎ 686 2037), south of the airport on Mophane Rd. Unfinished electricity complex turned Art Nouveau restaurant. The food, from burgers (P15) to Indian (P15-20), isn't fabulous, but the surroundings are. Even better, there's free camping around back, with hot shower and toilet. Open M-Sa 8am-10:30pm; bar closes at midnight. ❶

Julian's Cafe (☎ 686 2905; fax 686 2842), facing the airstrip on Mathiba I Ave., near the intersection with Mophane Rd. Quality menu of fusion cuisine (P15-35) changes weekly. Fully-loaded burgers with chips P20. Open M-F 8am-5pm, Sa 9am-1pm. ❶

◎ SIGHTS

Housed in a historic complex of colonial-era buildings, the **Nhabe Museum,** on Seretse Khama just past the New Mall, displays the Ngamiland region in all its vibrance. Rotating exhibitions spotlight some of the area's most talented artists. The museum also stages festivals and dramatic performances. Nhabe is also one of the best places in the area to acquire museum-quality crafts and artwork. Objects are more expensive than the standard roadside curios but worth it. *(☎ 686 1346. Open M-F 9am-5:00pm, Sa 9:30am-4:30pm. Free, but donations appreciated.)*

ADVENTURES

Maun is the epicenter of northern Botswana's nature tourism boom. From here, tours depart to Moremi, Chobe, the Makgadikgadi and Nxai Pans, the Central Kalahari Game Reserve, and Tsodilo Hills. While all these tours are offered by Maun operators, it is the Okavango Delta *mokoro* trip that is the typical house specialty.

GENERAL TOURS

Audi Camp (☎ 686 0599 or 686 3005; fax 686 0581; audicamp@info.bw; www.audi-delta.com). Offices next to Power Station and at their lodge (see **Accommodations,** p. 554). All *mokoro* trips are self-catering, but gear can be hired from Audi. The operators shy away from running single-person trips; all rates are per person for 2 or more, and Audi's staff can help coordinate solo travelers into groups. Drive-in *mokoro* trips: 1-day US$60; 2-day US$100; 3-day US$130. Fly-in *mokoro* trips start at US$220 per person for a 2-day/2-night excursion. 3-day fully catered Moremi safari US$360 per person with 4 people; 5-day Moremi/Chobe or Central Kalahari safari US$600 per person with 4 people. 3-day Kalahari/Bushman experience US$295 per person with 4 people.

Afro Trek (☎ 686 0047), at the Sedia Hotel, is run by the personable Richard Randall, who was chosen to be U.S. President Bill Clinton's personal safari guide during his African state visit. 1-day *mokoro* trips US$55; 2-day trips US$85 (US$130 single); 3-day trips US$110 (US$170 single). Guests provide food and equipment. 4-hour *mokoro* ride and game walk P100. Scenic delta flights US$230 per 5-passenger plane. All-inclusive, custom-designed safaris to Central Kalahari, Moremi, and/or Chobe US$150 per person, per day. Open daily 8am-5pm.

Okavango Tours and Safaris (☎686 0220; OkavangoTours@okavango.bw; www.okavango.bw), inside the Power Station (see **Food,** above). Handles bookings for the popular Oddballs' Camp, a former backpacker mecca that has recently decided to go upscale. In "low season" (usually April-June), however, it's still possible to buy an all-inclusive 4-night fly-in mokoro outing for a bargain price of P2300 per person, including air. Otherwise, the rack rate is US$180 per person per night sharing (all-inclusive), plus a US$130 return air transfer fee.

Maun Rest Camp (☎/fax 686 3472 or 071 655 475; simonjoyce@info.bw). Specializes in safaris to Moremi, Central Kalahari, Chobe, and combinations of the above. All-inclusive prices work out to about US$100 per person, per day for 6 people—the cheapest anywhere for trips of this quality. Prices rise for smaller groups. All safaris are custom-built and personally led by the amiable Simon and Joyce. Day safaris to Moremi or Nxai Pan US$80 per person for 6 people. (See **Accommodations,** p. 554).

Gunn's Camp (☎686 0023; fax 686 0040; gunnscamp@info.bw) has a booking office in Julian's Cafe (see **Food,** above). One of the cheapest real delta camps, Gunn's is a short distance from Chief's Island in Moremi, allowing for some of the best game-viewing exploration in the area. 3-day safari US$294 per person, US$56 per additional day, more if travelling alone. Prices include meals and round-trip flight from Maun. Hot showers and store on site.

SPECIALIZED TOURS

Grey Matters (☎/fax 686 0198; grey.matters@info.bw) offers 1-day elephant trips where you can learn all you ever wanted to know about pachyderms. Includes transport to site, 4hr. with the ellies, and a nature walk. The trips can also be booked through Okavango Tours and Safaris (see above). US$100, children US$50.

Maun Birdwatching Center (☎686 2257) is a one-man show run by Roger Hawker, one of Botswana's most knowledgeable and experienced birding experts. For P25 per person, Roger leads 2-3 hour walks (preferably in early morning or late afternoon) and introduces visitors to some of of species that inhabit the Okavango. Bring binoculars if you have them. Roger is also available to accompany safaris and game drives, turning any outing into a specialized birding expedition. Call for all arrangements.

OKAVANGO PANHANDLE

In Botswana's northwestern corner, the same geological system that created the Delta squeezes the Okavango River into a channel just a few kilometers wide. The panhandle, as this area is called, is a nature-lover's dream. Dozens of bird species take refuge in the Okavango's reeds, and the river's strong channel is an angler's paradise. The panhandle's clear champion is ◙**Drotsky's Cabins ❶** (☎675 035; fax 675 043), down a long drive 5km south of Shakawe (look for the signs). Chalets (P200) are decent but basic; campsites (P30 per person), however, are among the best in Southern Africa, surrounded by lush forest and looking onto the beautiful Okavango River. The owners' warm, genuine hospitality is also legendary. There are home-cooked meals for P50/60/70 for breakfast/lunch/dinner and an honesty bar. Fishing excursions and boat tours are arranged. Further south, the **Sepupa Swamp Stop ❶** (in Maun ☎686 0300) is, despite the name, a beautiful campsite on the Okavango River. Camping is P30 per person. A private ferry to the Seronga *mokoro* launch is P140, and a 3-night *mokoro* trip is US$130. Flights can be charted from Maun to the airstrips in Sepupa and on the property of Drotsky's; expect to pay about US$250 each way for an entire 5-passenger plane.

TSODILO HILLS

40km west of the Okavango River and 150km northeast of the other nearest out-croppings, the Tsodilo Hills gleam amid acres of Kalahari sand. Despite their modest size, the hills seem to tower over the immense flatness that surrounds them, prompting a hushed reverence from even the most jaded traveler. The hills play important roles in the creation legends of both the Mbukushu and !Kung peoples; !Kung elders, especially, have been bitterly disappointed to see an increasing trickle of tourists hike through the sacred spot. Covered in over 4500 rock paintings dating back to AD 700-1100, with a few faded drawings dating to 3000 BC, the hills have recently been inducted as a United Nations World Heritage Site under the remarkable name "Tsodilo: Mountain of the Gods." The slick publicity campaign that has followed the new UN money hasn't damaged the area's magic yet: a trip here is still a spiritual journey to the very marrow of the land.

TRANSPORTATION. A good 4WD is needed to get to Tsodilo; even under excellent conditions, your vehicle and body will sustain considerable abuse before you arrive. Three awful roads approach the hills from the Sehithwa-Shakawe highway; the middle of the three routes is the least treacherous and is in the process of being upgraded. It should be 2WD-friendly by mid-2004. Look for a western turnoff 2.3km south of Nxamasera village; a corrugated metal building and an enclosure of huts sit near the intersection. The road soon degenerates into a 38km ordeal that will take at least 90 minutes. When the road comes abreast of Male Hill, there is a small cluster of houses and a yellow arrow pointing right; follow it through Tsodilo's entrance gate, and continue following the arrows straight to the museum. There is no food, petrol, or services of any kind after you leave the black-top. Flights can be chartered from Maun, though the 2km from Tsodilo's airstrip to the Visitors Center must be walked. For those without 4WD, Drotsky's Cabins and Sepupa Swamp Stop (see below) both offer pricey one-day trips (US$200-300) with advance notice. Prices will plummet once the hills become 2WD-accessible.

ORIENTATION AND PRACTICAL INFORMATION. Four hills make up the Mountain of the Gods, in a rough north-south line. The southernmost and tallest, at 320m, is the **Male Hill.** Next to it is the **Female Hill,** which is the most richly decorated of the four. Further north is **Child Hill,** then a few kilometers of flat brush, and finally a hummock known officially as **North Hill** (though sometimes called "Grand-child Hill," and occasionally said to be a previous wife of Male Hill, now jilted for a more shapely hill). All four hills are in fact gorgeous, streaked in red, orange, gold, and white, with shocking neon green lichens dramatically offsetting the other colors. A sandy 4WD track leads along the west side of the three major hills, skirting the cliffs in places. Another track leads through the saddle between Male and Female Hill; this track has two offshoots, one which leads to the Male Hill trail-head and the other which leads up near "Dancing Penises" (see below).

A new **museum** and **visitors' center** is at the foot of Female Hill and makes a good starting point for a visit. The museum contains few artifacts, but the care-fully-designed interpretive displays give some background to the hills. The Visitors Center is the park's sign-in point, and also contains a wall map of the trails. **!Kung guides** (P50-70 per day) can be arranged here, and their use is encouraged by the rangers to stimulate the local economy and prevent lost tourists. Though the !Kung are extremely knowledgeable and visit paintings that an independent hiker would undoubtedly miss, language barriers often prove limiting. The museum and visitors' center both have informal hours; they'll unlock it when you get there.

BOTSWANA

◪ TRAILS. Tsodilo has four official trails, as well as numerous side tracks. On all of the trails, look for the brown **Tsodilo rock gecko,** which is unique to this area. The most popular route is the circular **Rhino Trail,** which explores Female Hill and passes much of the most famous rock art. Ascending from the museum (the ranger can point you to the trailhead), the trail climbs up to a seemingly unremarkable swampy pit next to the **Tree of Knowledge;** the pool is said by the Mbukushu to be the origin of all life on earth. Curving up to the crest of the hill, the trail descends into a small valley that houses the **Dancing Penises,** a group of sexually aroused dancers with exaggerated members, and the **Large Rhinos,** one of the most exquisitely executed paintings at the site. Reaching the foot of the hill, the trail passes the **penguin and whale,** crude drawings which have been controversially cited as proof that the San had contact with cultures in coastal Namibia. A branch of the trail then squeezes hikers through a natural rock tunnel before emerging at the foot of the **van der Post Panel.** Rock scramblers can climb to the actual panel at the top of the cliff; the group of paintings found here is more remarkable for its sweeping vista than for the artistry itself. The trail then returns to the museum; a full loop, with stops at each painting, can take two to four hours.

The **Male Hill Trail** leads up from a small parking area on the north side of the hill, and climbs steadily over boulder fields to the summit of Male Hill, yielding a view of all of northwestern Botswana. The trail is devoid of rock art except for one unusual lion painting, but it is a rewarding challenge from a pure hiking standpoint. The round-trip takes three to four hours; bring plenty of water.

The **Cliff Trail** encircles Child Hill, visiting several important paintings along the way. The **stylized zebra** on the hill's northeast face is different in technique from most of the other rock art and has been adopted as the official logo for Botswana's national museums. The **Origin of Sex** is one of the few paintings that depicts a creation story. Finally, the **Lion Trail** meanders through the saddle between Male and Female Hills; it explores a beautiful section of the hills.

⚑ CAMPING. Tsodilo has four camping areas that can be nabbed on a first-come, first-served basis; at least half of them are typically vacant even in high season. **Rhino Camp ❶,** next to the museum, is the "main" camp site; it has ablution blocks with hot and cold running water, although the water source has been unreliable lately. **Overland Camp ❶** is tucked into the cliffs just above the museum and feels more remote, despite the 2-minute walk to the ablutions. **Makoba Woods ❶,** off the entrance road, is the closest camping spot to the saddle and its spectacular paintings. Finally, the little-used ▩**Malatso Camp ❶** is possibly one of the most beautiful sites in this part of Africa; embraced on three sides by the cliffs of Child Hill, campers truly feel like they are part of the magic. All of the camps are positioned to catch the fiery sunset against the cliffs. No camping fees are currently collected, but this may change as administration becomes more formalized.

CHOBE NATIONAL PARK

Occupying over 10,000 square kilometers in the northeastern corner of the country, Chobe is the place to go for virtually guaranteed sightings of more animals than you've ever imagined. A typical game drive yields animal counts well into the thousands, and the sweeping beauty of the Chobe River flood plain provides a breathtaking backdrop. Roughly 45,000 of Botswana's 75,000 elephants reside within the boundaries of the park, and they often blacken the riverbank with their sheer numbers. Although Chobe is jam-packed with tourists any time of year, the park is still large enough to offer plenty of places for tranquil silence.

AT A GLANCE

AREA: 10,566 sq. km.

CLIMATE: Dry season normally lasts from May-Dec.; Oct. and Nov. tend to be uncomfortably hot.

FEATURES: Chobe flood plain; Linyanti River; Savuti Marsh.

GATEWAYS: Kasane (p. 561); Maun (p. 552).

CAMPING: Ihaha, Savuti, and Linyanti sites. No wild camping is permitted.

ORIENTATION

Chobe can be divided into three regions of primary interest to tourists: the Chobe River flood plain, Savuti Marsh, and Linyati Swamps.

CHOBE FLOOD PLAIN. The Chobe flood plain is by far the most visited area of the park because of both its easy proximity to Kasane and the number and variety of animals that drink at its river banks. Most visitors enter via Sedudu Gate, 5km west of Kasane—a series of roads follows the river westward. Look for lions beneath the shade of the bushes by the river; leopards tend to stay farther inland. **Nanyanga peninsula,** about 25km west of the gate, offers excellent views of the winding Chobe River in three directions. The game-viewing drive continues along the river west of Ihaha all the way to Ngoma Bridge, but animals are rather scarce compared to other segments, and the scenery becomes mundane.

SAVUTI MARSH. This region, in the park's more remote western side, is worth the effort required to reach it. Although the name Savuti "Marsh" is misleading—the Savuti River is undergoing an extended dry spell and last flowed in 1982—it is still a haven for animals of all shapes and sizes, which occupy the area so densely that it could be their capital city. Safari experts consider this one of the best wildlife-viewing locations in Africa today. Though Savuti can be accessed from Maun via the Mababe Gate, the rutted track is a disaster and should only be attempted under ideal conditions. Ask for advice about road conditions.

LINYANTI. Located in the park's extreme northwest corner, Linyanti has been described as a "forgotten paradise." It is extremely difficult to reach, and drivers must be well prepared and completely self-sufficient. Once here, however, they will find themselves in complete and peaceful solitude with only the elephants, buffalo, and waving grass for companions.

PRACTICAL INFORMATION

WHEN TO GO. During the rainy season (Jan.-Apr.), it is an ordeal to visit Chobe; the sandy roads turn to thick muck, mosquitoes invade, and the thick underbrush makes it difficult to see animals. June to September is the prime tourist season; the roads are dry, but the weather is still relatively cool. October to December still offers plenty of game-viewing opportunities, but daytime temperatures can be boiling.

Before exploring Chobe, try to get some experience driving in deep sand; some parts of the tracks are a mess. Travelers visiting Linyanti are especially advised to go in a convoy in case of breakdown.

Rangers/Emergency Assistance: Game scouts are posted at Sedudu, Ihaha, Ngoma, Savuti, Linyanti, Mababe, and Nogatsaa.

BOTSWANA

Fees and Reservations: The same as in all Botswanan parks; see p. 534. Ihaha and Savuti are extremely popular and usually fill up months in advance. Day permits are not issued at the gate and must be reserved in advance through Central Reservations.

Gear: There are no fuel or supplies between Maun and Kasane, so stock up before going. To navigate Chobe, the Chobe Shell Map is crucial. Ihaha camp is not plotted, but the map is otherwise accurate. The map can be purchased just about anywhere in Kasane.

Tours: The **Chobe Safari Lodge** offers game drives in Chobe. Otherwise, all Chobe safari tour operators are based in Maun.

DO IT YOURSELF SAFARI BASICS For the independent traveler, the idea of striking out into the African bush alone is very appealing. Every year, thousands of people plan their own African safaris and conduct them safely. Before going on safari alone, however, ask yourself some honest questions.

Do you have the 4x4 experience? Areas in Southern Africa require that you take your vehicle through heavy sand, mud, rivers, pans, and other hazards. Without the proper training, it's easy to swamp your vehicle or—worse yet—roll it.

Are you comfortable in the wild? You must know wilderness first-aid, as well as other skills (fire building, camp basics, etc.). Wilderness common sense and the ability to improvise are also essential.

How important is wildlife to your experience? Guided safaris have one huge advantage: the guide. Good leaders can track animals and can provide lots of information about their characteristics and behavior. If you travel alone, your wildlife experience will likely be less in-depth.

If you still want to go one your own safari, think about logistics. When you pick a location, take into account seasonal driving conditions and animal migrations. Vehicle wise, its best to rent from a 4x4 company that offers vehicles containing all necessary supplies (including cookery, jerry cans, tents, etc.). Be generous when calculating fuel, water and food consumption. Make a detailed outline of where you want to go and always have backup plans. Travel with least two vehicles, in case one breaks down. If you're venturing far into the bush, consider renting a small GPS system. Finally, before you leave, obtain as much information and advice from as possible locals and professional safari operators.

Once you're out there, remember to lock all food in your vehicle's cab (as opposed to its canopy) to seal in its smell. Always sleep in a tent with all doors zipped up tight—you might become animal food if you try to sleep "under the stars." Never try to touch an animal: even the cuddly-looking herbivores deliver one hell of a kick. Most importantly, on the rare occasion when you're walking outside your vehicle never let an animal get between you and your car.

CAMPING

Ihaha Camp. Located just west of the Nanyanga Peninsula in the Chobe flood plain region of the park, Ihaha is a relatively new site featuring top-notch ablutions with hot running water. Campsites hug the shore and offer views of Namibia. Vervet monkeys like to cavort through the sites during the day, and the caretakers allow day visitors to use the sites' *braai* facilities for picnic lunches. ❶

Savuti Camp. This amazing campsite is in Chobe's Savuti Marsh region. After the sun goes down, you can hear the growling of lions, crunching of elephants, and sneezing of God-knows-what just feet from the tent. With the adequate precautions, however (just ask the ranger), all of these critters will (probably) give you space. The recently renovated site has hot showers and a game scout office. ❶

Linyanti Camp. The last of the park's camps yet to be renovated, this campsite in the Linyanti region has rustic facilities, although hot showers are often available. This camp can usually be booked with less advance notice than Savuti or Ihaha. ❶

KASANE

This village is the gateway to Chobe National Park and to Zimbabwe's Victoria Falls via the Kazungula border post 10km away (open daily 6am-8pm). Beyond that, it doesn't have a whole lot to offer. Most eating options and planned activities are provided by the pricey safari lodges; those on a tighter budget should consider Kasane to be little more than a supply stop. A walk down the friendly main road reveals a few new craft shops and a limited but pleasant open-air market that sells the ever-popular dried fish, fresh fruits, and vegetables.

TRANSPORTATION. Air Botswana (☎267 390 5500) flies to **Johannesburg** (3¼hr.; Tu, Th, Su 3pm; one-way US$211, round-trip US$249) via the **Tuli Block** (1½hr.; US$136/US$152) and **Gaborone** (2¾hr.; M, W, Su 3:40pm and F 2pm; US$144) via **Maun** (55min., US$76). **Buses** run at 6am and 10am to **Nata** (3hr., P45) and on to **Francistown** (5hr., P80) from "The Cool Joint" in town. Transfer in Nata for **Maun** (4hr., P25). Transfers by **Chobe Safari Lodge** to **Victoria Falls** (1½hr.; US$35/US$45), **Victoria Falls Airport** (1½hr., US$40/50), and the **Kazungula border** (15min., US$5).

ORIENTATION AND PRACTICAL INFORMATION. Every service and government office in Kasane lies on the highway that runs right through the center of town. Coming from Kazungula 12km to the east, the road first passes a few lodges, then the Shell service station, bank, post office, police, and hospital. At this point there is a fork: the left branch heads up a hill to the airport and Chobe's Sedudu gate, while the right fork passes Chobe Safari Lodge and the supermarket.

Services include: **Barclays Bank,** in the middle of town, offering an exchange and cash advances (☎625 0221; open M-F 8:30am-3:30pm, Sa 8:30-10:45am); the **police** (☎625 0335 or 217), in the center of town past the Audi Center Plaza; **Pharma Africa,** next to the Audi Center Plaza (☎625 1492; open M-F 8am-6pm, Sa 8am-1pm); the **Kasane Primary Hospital,** along the main road (☎625 0333; open 24hr.); a **private clinic,** 200m before the Shell station, coming from the east (☎625 1555; open 24hr.); **Internet** at The Cool Khaya in the Audi Center Plaza (☎625 1609; P10 for 30min.; open M-F 8am-12:45pm and 2-5pm, Sa 8am-1pm); and the **post office** (☎625 0355; open M-F 8:30am-4pm), on the main road on the western edge of town.

ACCOMMODATIONS AND FOOD. Chobe Safari Lodge ❶, 8km from the Chobe gate, is a picturesque complex of rooms for all budgets, making it the only lodge in Kasane to acknowledge the existence of the backpacker. To persuade you to spend your entire holiday within the camp, they offer every activity imaginable, including boat cruises, game drives, fishing, and boat hire. All activities are booked through an office beyond the gift shop. (Office open daily from 8am-6pm). There's also a lavish buffet open to walk-ins, and an outdoor bar that overlooks the Chobe River. After your full day of activities, you can camp, rest in a *rondavel*, stay in a conventional hotel room, or try their boat-shaped dorm. (☎625 0336. Check-in 2pm. Check-out 10:30am. Park fee P70 per day. Dorm P50; *rondavels* and standard hotel rooms, with bath, TV, and coffeemakers, P385; max. 2 people. Camping P40. Permanent tent with 4 beds P150. Boat cruises P65. Game drives P85. Fishing P90 per hr., including equipment. Boat hire P90 per hr. for up to six

BOTSWANA

people. Buffet P55-75. MC/V.) **Liya Guest Lodge ❷** is clean, new, friendly, and a good choice for those just passing through on their way to Chobe or the Falls. To get there, follow the signs from Plateau Rd., which leaves the highway 1km west of town. (☎625 1450; liyaglo@botsnet.bw. Free pick-ups from town. Singles P175, with bath P185; doubles P260/P280. Camping P90 per person.) **Sedudu Guesthouse ❸**, 300m east of the Shell service station, has very small caravan rooms with bathrooms and larger, nicer rooms in the main house, with shared bathrooms. A lack of social spaces for guests, however, makes for a rather cheerless stay. (☎/fax 625 1748. Wheelchair access in main house. Check-out noon. Caravan singles P166; doubles P222. Main house singles P199; doubles 277. Family room P554. MC/V.)

There are few food choices outside the lodges. **The Hotbread Shop ❶**, in the complex next to Shell service station, is a locally popular take-away place selling good pies (P3) and sandwiches. (Open M-F 8am-7pm, Sa 7am-2pm.) The **Tea Garden ❶**, in the Audi Center, makes hot breakfasts (P16-22) and offers a selection of sandwiches and burgers (P18-20) for lunch. (Open M-F 8am-5pm, Sa 8am-1:30pm.) The **Savas Stores Supermarket** is on the left just past the entrance to Chobe Safari Lodge when coming from town. It stocks basic safari supplies and accepts payment in foreign currency at fair rates. (Open M-F 7am-1pm and 2-5:30pm, Sa 7am-1:30pm.)

NEAR KASANE: BORDER CROSSINGS

 VISITING ZIMBABWE AND THE FALLS. If you want to visit Victoria Falls without driving through Zimbabwe, a trip through Kasane may be your best option. From Kasane, take the Kaungula Ferry (see below) into Zambia. You can then take a bus or drive to Livingstone, Zambia. You can see some of the Falls from Livingstone. If you're willing to travel into Zimbabwe, see p. 586.

KAZUNGULA ROAD. The major portal for those transiting between Chobe and Victoria Falls, the border is reached by a clearly marked right turn off of the Nata highway. Botswana will ask to see the vehicle's registration papers when leaving; Zimbabwe issues single- and double-entry visas, and temporary import permits for vehicles. Zimbabwe also charges a carbon tax for vehicles (rates vary from US$2-10 depending on engine size). Shacks across the road sell mandatory third-party vehicle insurance (about US$2, foreign currency accepted at parallel rates). Travelers report that staff on the Zimbabwean side sometimes ask for "gifts;" a polite refusal usually ends the matter, however. The border is open daily from 6am-8pm.

KAZUNGULA FERRY. The ferry makes sense for those planning to visit Vic Falls primarily from Zambia, where you can trade a longer road for escape from immigration hassles. Go straight north on the highway from Nata until you hit water. Cars with Botswanan and Zambian registration, as well as foot passengers, cross for free; others must pay US$10 per car or US$20 per pickup truck at a small window next to the immigration office on either side. The ferry runs from 6am until 6pm, but has a very small capacity, so be prepared to wait for the boat to make several trips. Zambian immigration does not issue on-the-spot visas to those who require them; send away for the visa beforehand.

NGOMA BRIDGE. The most hassle-free of the Chobe border posts is about an hour from both Kasane and Katima Mulilo. Although the actual crossing is usually painless, those entering Namibia with non-Namibian vehicles will need to stop in Katima Mulilo to buy a CBC import permit (N$80 for a car or pickup). The permits are sold daily from 8am to 5pm at an office on the left side of the highway when entering town; the white signs mark where to turn. Only the South African Rand is accepted at the CBC office. The border itself is open daily from 6am-6pm.

THE FREEDOM FERRY The rusty ferry that chugs across the Zambezi between Botswana and Zambia may seem unremarkable, but its predecessor was once one of the most symbolic boats in Africa. For over a decade, between Botswana's independence in 1967 and Zimbabwe's in 1980, a tiny sliver of water in the Zambezi was Botswana's only geographical connection to the rest of independent Africa. Surrounded on four sides by white-controlled Southern Rhodesia, Southwest Africa, and South Africa, black intellectuals and political leaders who had made it safely into Botswana took the ferry to Zambia, where they boarded a train and traveled to places like Dar-es-Salaam and Addis Ababa to further their education and play important roles in the pan-African liberation movement. When Zimbabwe gained its independence, the crossing lost its strategic importance and went back to being a simple transportation link. However, it will always occupy a warm place in the hearts of those who remember the "freedom ferry."

ZIMBABWE

 PRICE RANGES. Price ranges, marked by the numbered icons below, are now included in food and accommodation descriptions. They are based on the lowest cost for one person, excluding special deals or prices. In the case of campgrounds, we include the cost of a car. The table below is a guide to how prices and icons match up.

SYMBOL	❶	❷	❸	❹	❺
ACCOMM.	US$0-2	US$2-5	US$5-10	US$10-15	US$15+
FOOD	US$0-2	US$2-5	US$5-9	US$9-15	US$15+

From the thundering Victoria Falls in the West to the dramatic mountain peaks in the East, Zimbabwe is a land of striking beauty on a grand scale. Zimbabwe has it all: big game, thatch-roofed villages, scenery that varies from desert to savannah to rain forest, a thriving and unique artisanal community, and modern, Westernized cities and tourism amenities. In a sense, Zimbabwe takes the "highlights" of many other African countries, and combines them within one set of borders.

In the past few years, however, Zimbabwe has also experienced the difficulties of many of its African neighbors. The country has become familiar to nightly news viewers who hear of rural violence, street riots, and the desperate actions of an increasingly autocratic President and ruling party. Images of occupied farms and clouds of tear gas have prompted most outsiders to cancel travel plans to the country, dealing severe blows to the country's once-thriving tourism and hotel industries. Slowly, Zimbabwe has attempted to rehabilitate its reputation, but the country's many treasures continue to go largely unseen by international travelers.

Although average Zimbabweans are doing their best to overcome difficult times, the country still remains as warm and inviting to travelers as it has always been. Elephants and zebra still graze at Hwange's water holes; clouds still congregate around the highest peaks of Chimanimani; the sun still sets in a fiery blaze over Lake Kariba. And, most importantly, the people of Zimbabwe continue to extend their hospitality to travelers of all nations—despite the headlines (and admittedly serious problems), the country is an ideal destination for any traveler to Africa.

FACTS AND FIGURES

Official Name: Zimbabwe
Government: Parliamentary Democracy
Capital: Harare
Land Area: 390,580 sq. km.
Geography: Mostly high plateau; arid in the West, mountainous in the East. Lowest elevations are in the Zambezi Valley
Climate: Tropical, with a rainy season from November to March

Head of State: Pres. Robert Mugabe
Major Cities: Harare, Bulawayo, Mutare
Population: approx. 11,000,000
Languages: English, Ndebele, Shona
Religions: Christian/Syncretic 75%; Indigenous 24%; Jewish, Muslim 1%
GDP Per Capita: US$2400
Major Exports: Tobacco, gold, cotton, iron, sugar

LIFE AND TIMES

HISTORY

PRE-COLONIAL HISTORY (PRE-1888). The high plateau of Zimbabwe is believed to have been inhabited as early as 2000 years ago, but the **Shona civilization** did not take firm root in the area until about 1050 A.D., with the construction of the first stone settlements. By about 1500, this stone construction had advanced to an art form, culminating in the city and religious site of **Great Zimbabwe.** From Great Zimbabwe and other cities, Shona leaders controlled a gold-trading empire that extended to the Indian Ocean, and had links with India and China. By the late 1600s, the relative influence of the Shona had faded, and most of present-day Zimbabwe had come under the control of another leader, **Changamire.** His **Rozwi Empire** fell in turn and was replaced by that of the **Ndebele,** a people who had recently fled the Transvaal. The Ndebele leader, **Mzilikazi,** established political control over the Shona people, exacting occasional tribute.

THE SCHOLARLY RHODES (1888-1965). By the mid-19th century, British and Dutch settlers in South Africa began to eye territory further north. It was British politician and financier **Cecil Rhodes** who soon gained the upper hand. Negotiating a mineral rights contract with Mzilikazi's Ndebele successor, **Lobengula,** in 1888, Rhodes gained the right to occupy a vast territory stretching for thousands of square miles north of the Limpopo River. The British Government responded by granting Rhodes a charter to form the **British South Africa Company,** with the responsibility to administer the new territory. Two years later, Rhodes led a well-armed "settler column" into Zimbabwe to gain physical control over the inhabitants. Rhodes poured a small fortune into "settling" the territory, building forts, roads, and infrastructure, because of his confident expectation of a major gold strike in Zimbabwe. As it turned out, they discovered very little gold in Zimbabwe,

ZIMBABWE

and the British South Africa Company found itself on the brink of collapse. Ever resourceful, Rhodes solved this quandary by attacking his Ndebele hosts, driving them off of their ancestral lands and redistributing their land and cattle to white farmers. The Shona people of central Zimbabwe soon met the same fate, and by the turn of the century, Rhodes had established a full-fledged British colony, named (modestly) Southern Rhodesia. For the next 60 years, Southern Rhodesia developed under colonial rule, with railroads and cities. Whites settled the best land along the railroads while blacks were forced to congregate in rocky "communal areas" or seek wage labor on the white farms in order to meet tax burdens.

WAR OF LIBERATION (1965-1980). By the 1950s and 60s, British colonies around the world were entering negotiated periods of decolonization, and joining the Commonwealth as independent states. Nyasaland (Malawi) and Northern Rhodesia (Zambia) gained independence in 1963; by 1965, the **Rhodesian Front Party,** a white political party led by **Ian Smith,** demanded Southern Rhodesian independence with a continued white-dominated government. This was unacceptable to Britain and to the colony's black African population, both of whom wanted to see Southern Rhodesia move down the road toward black rule. Unable to find common ground, Ian Smith and the RFP issued a **Unilateral Declaration of Independence (UDI),** establishing a white government in Southern Rhodesia free from British control. Over the next few years, this move earned Smith condemnation and sanctions from the rest of the world, except (predictably) from apartheid South Africa. Meanwhile, the country's black population began to mobilize into guerrilla movements against the UDI government. In Ndebele areas, they were organized by **Joshua Nkomo,** leader of the **Zimbabwe African People's Union (ZAPU);** in Shona areas, they were led by **Robert Mugabe,** head of **Zimbabwe African National Union (ZANU).** By the mid-1970s, the aim of both groups was the overthrow of the white government by military force; surprise attacks became more frequent and effective as the decade wore on. By 1980, after a series of failed peace talks, Britain finally helped to mediate the **Lancaster House agreements,** which were signed in London by the Smith regime, ZANU, and ZAPU. The document guaranteed black rule for the new nation (although with a number of concessions to the white minority), and arranged for the country's first democratic elections. The elections ushered Robert Mugabe into power by a decisive margin, marking the beginning of a brutal political reign that continues to this day.

RECENT EVENTS

LAND REFORM. In 1997, President Mugabe announced a plan to redistribute a large portion of white-owned farmland to black subsistence farmers over the succeeding years. After a series of largely unproductive negotiations with the white farmers, Mugabe introduced legislation in 1998 that gave the government the power to designate farms for redistribution, with or without the consent of the farmers. Although this legislation passed, it was struck down later that year by the country's Supreme Court as unconstitutional. In response, Mugabe introduced a new Constitution that solved this problem by eliminating the troublesome section. The proposed Constitution was put to a national referendum, where it was defeated by Zimbabwean voters. This was widely seen as a "slap in the face" to the Mugabe regime, and marked one of Mugabe's first losses at the polls in twenty years of power. Following this defeat, veterans from the country's liberation war began a strategy of **"farm invasions,"** in which a number of well-armed veterans would move onto a white-owned farm, set up makeshift huts, and often prevent the farm from operating. Farm workers and owners who resisted were beaten, tortured, and, in some cases, murdered. The link between the war veterans and the

Zimbabwe

ZAMBIA

Lusaka
Zambezi R.

Lago de
Cahora Bassa

MOZAMBIQUE

Chirundu

Mucumbura

Lake
Kariba

Kariba

Karoi

Mvurwi

Mount
Darwin

Nyamapenda

A1

Chinhoyi

Zambezi/
Victoria Falls
National Park

T1

Binga

Mutoko

A2

Harare

Livingstone

Mlibizi

Chegutu

A5

Chitungwiza

Rhodes
Inyangani NP

Victoria Falls

Victoria Falls

Deka

Hwange

Gwayi
River

Shangani R.

Kadoma

A4

Marondera

A3

Rusape

Sinamatella

Robins

Dete

Main

Kwekwe

Chivhu

Mutare

Hwange
National Park

Lupane

Gwayi R.

A9

Libuti

A8

Gweru

Mvuma

Save R.

Chimanimani

Masvingo

Birchenough Bridge

A5

A18

A9

Chimanimani
NP

Bulawayo

A6

Zvishavane

A9

Runde

Mount Selinda

A7

Matobo
NP

Espungabera

BOTSWANA

A3

Plumtree

A1

Gwanda

R.

Triangle

Chiredzi

Francistown

Rutenga

Gonarezhou
National
Park

N
LG

A6

A4

MOZAMBIQUE

0   50 miles

A1

Selebi
Phikwe

Thuli
R.

Limpopo R.

Beitbridge

Messina

Beitbridge

0   50 kilometers

SOUTH AFRICA

Mugabe regime became extremely suspicious when the government failed to investigate or prosecute any of these incidents; further, Mugabe refuses to denounce the actions of the war veterans despite mounting worldwide protest.

POLITICAL OPPOSITION. In 1999, a coalition of trade unionists, white business leaders, and disenchanted ZANU-PF officials joined together to form the **Movement for Democratic Change (MDC),** led by union leader **Morgan Tsvangirai** (CHAN-gee-RAH-yee is close). In the parliamentary elections of June 2000, MDC stunned the ruling party by picking up nearly every seat in both Matabeleland and Harare, breaking ZANU's veto power in Parliament. The elections were preceded by political violence, including the torture and/or murder of a number of opposition supporters. The balloting itself was said to be highly irregular, and some election results have been overturned in the courts. Since then, although MDC has not officially been banned, it has suffered intimidation on a number of fronts, including the repeated jailing of its key leaders and the bombing of its Harare headquarters. Tsvangirai is expected to run against President Mugabe in the 2002 elections.

MEDIA REPRESSION. In 1999, Zimbabwe's first independent daily newspaper, **The Daily News,** started printing in Harare. Adopting a tone often critical of the government, the newspaper has been singled out for attack, lawsuits, and attempts at closure by Zimbabwe's Minister of Information, **Dr. Jonathan Moyo.** The paper's offices were mysteriously bombed in mid-2000, and the printing press was destroyed by another bomb in early 2001. No suspects have ever been indicted in

ZIMBABWE

either case. The publisher of the paper, **Mr. Geoff Nyarota,** has been charged several times with criminal defamation of the President and risks jailing. Meanwhile, the country's only independent radio station, **Capital Radio,** was shut down several weeks after starting because it lacked government permission to operate.

AIDS CRISIS. Zimbabwe, with a growing HIV-positive population of at least 25%, has one of the highest AIDS rates in the world. It has been estimated that one out of every two Zimbabweans who is now 15 years of age or younger will die of the virus. Although the government has initiated an aggressive campaign to educate Zimbabweans about AIDS, it struggles to keep pace with rapid infection rates.

PEOPLE

POPULATION AND DEMOGRAPHY. Zimbabwe's two primary ethnic groups are the **Shona,** who make up about 75% of the country's population, and the **Ndebele,** who make up most of the remainder. Traditionally, the Shona have inhabited the areas in Central and Eastern Zimbabwe now encompassed by the Mashonaland and Manicaland provinces, while the Ndebele have inhabited Matabeleland, in the western part of the country near Botswana. The last few decades, however, have seen an increasing urban migration, and Harare and Bulawayo are now somewhat ethnically mixed. In addition, a number of minority ethnic groups inhabit the areas near the Zambian border. Finally, small but economically powerful groups of **European and Asian descendants** make up about 1% of the population.

LANGUAGE. English is the official language, and is used in most business settings. Virtually all urban Zimbabweans speak English well, as do many rural Zimbabweans, especially those of a younger generation. Some rural Zimbabweans, however, especially those living in the so-called "communal areas," have little or no knowledge of English. At home, most Zimbabweans speak their primary language, either **Ndebele** or **Shona** depending on their ethnic background. All three languages are taught in schools.

ESSENTIALS

DOCUMENTS AND FORMALITIES

VISAS

Visas are not required for citizens of the British Commonwealth, the European Union, Norway, Switzerland, the USA, or Japan. Visas for citizens of all other countries must be acquired in advance, except for South Africans, who can pick one up at the border.

EMBASSIES ABROAD

Canada: 332 Somerset St. West, Ottawa, ON K2P 0J9. ☎(613) 237 4388.

South Africa: 798 Mertons, Arcadia, Pretoria. ☎012 342 5125.

United Kingdom: Zimbabwe House, 429 The Strand, London WC2R 0SA. ☎0171 836 7755.

United States: 1608 New Hampshire Ave. NW, Washington, DC 20009. ☎202-332-7100.

Zambia: Memaco House, Cairo Rd., Lusaka. ☎01 229 382.

ZIMBABWE

EMBASSIES AND CONSULATES IN HARARE

Australia: 29 Mazowe St. ☎ 757 774.

Canada: 45 Baines Ave., PO Box 1430. ☎ 733 881.

Mozambique: 152 Herbert Chitepo Ave. ☎ 790 837.

New Zealand: Eastgate Center, 8th Floor. PO Box 5448. ☎ 759 221.

South Africa: Temple Bar House, Nelson Mandela Ave. and Angwa St. ☎ 753 147.

United Kingdom: Stanley House, Jason Moyo Ave. ☎ 793 781.

United States: 172 Herbert Chitepo Ave. ☎ 703 169.

Zambia: 1266 Kenneth Kaunda. ☎ 492 452.

CURRENCY AND EXCHANGE

The Zimbabwe dollar (Z$) has been inflating rapidly on the world market, and is almost impossible to re-exchange into foreign currency. Zimbabwe's currency foibles necessitate careful money management, and a thorough understanding of the difference between the bank rate and the parallel rate. The **bank rate,** used by all credit card companies, ATMs, and all other financial institutions, is set by the government. The government maintains this rate at an artificially low level, making credit cards, cash cards, and bank exchanges nearly worthless. A **parallel rate,** which reflects what the Zimdollar is actually worth on the open market, is used by virtually everyone else. *Bureaux de change* offer the standard parallel rate, and are by far the best bet. Illicit money hawkers offer rates that range from good to phenomenal, but this method carries large risks: what looks like a roll of Z$100 bills is often stuffed with Z$5 bills, newspaper, or (most entertainingly) Zambian *kwacha*, at 3700 to the US dollar. In addition, plainclothes police sometimes set up stings to nab less scrupulous tourists.

HEALTH AND SAFETY

Zimbabwe has quite good medical facilities, with excellent private hospitals in Bulawayo and Harare, although availability of prescription medicines may be limited due to the currency shortage. Some smaller rural hospitals may present an increased risk for tuberculosis infection; get to a city if possible for any extended stay. Most hospitals take credit or insurance cards as payment. For more information on staying healthy, see **Health,** p. 19.

EMERGENCY. Harare: ☎ 99. Bulawayo: ☎ 999. Victoria Falls: ☎ (13) 4646 (Medical Air Rescue Service).

TRANSPORTATION

BY AIR. Harare (see p. 571) is the country's hub for air transport. **Victoria Falls** (see p. 586) also has an international airport with service to South Africa and the United Kingdom, but direct intercontinental flights to the Falls have dwindled with the drop in tourist visits. **Air Zimbabwe** is one of the more comprehensive regional carriers, serving eleven other countries and twenty destinations; their long-distance jet, however, is sometimes removed from service on short notice to carry President Mugabe on official visits. Small towns and bush camps, especially in the north, are served by private bush pilots on a charter basis.

ZIMBABWE

BY TRAIN. Zimbabwean National Railways (☎ 04 733 901) travels between **Harare, Bulawayo, Mutare,** and **Victoria Falls.** First-class cabins consist of modernized four-person sleeper compartments with sinks. Many second-class cabins are modernized, with polyester, high-backed seats and televisions; some, however, are the antiquated wooden variety. Third-class cabins tend to be extremely crowded, with padded benches. The year 2000 saw two fatal derailments on the Bulawayo/Victoria Falls line; check for the latest updates and use your judgment.

BY CAR. To cross the Zimbabwean border, you must pay a US$8 **vehicle tax** both when coming and going. You also need your passport and, if the car's a rental, a permission letter from the company. **Beitbridge** is the main border crossing from South Africa (open 6:30am-10pm). Most of the other crossings are open 6am-6pm. Watch out for pickpockets in the chaotic jostle of the immigration queues.

BY BUS. Greyhound (in South Africa ☎ 011 830 1301; in Harare ☎ 04 253 227; in Bulawayo ☎ 09 65 548) runs from **Johannesburg** to **Bulawayo** (13 hrs.; Sa-Th 8am, F 10pm; returning daily 4pm; R230 one-way) and **Harare** (16hrs.; Su-Fr 10:30pm, Sa 1:30pm; returning Mo-Sa 10pm, Su 1pm; R285 one-way). College students get 5% off return tickets. **Translux** (in South Africa ☎ 011 774 3333; in Harare ☎ 04 792 778; in Lusaka ☎ 01 228 682) runs from **Johannesburg** to **Harare** (17 hrs.; daily 10pm; returning daily 9pm; R270 one-way) and **Bulawayo** (13 hrs.; daily 9pm; returning daily 5pm; R220 one-way). They also travel weekly from **Lusaka** to **Harare** (9 hrs.; leave Su 1pm; return W 2am; US$14). The old **Baz Bus** route to Victoria Falls has been discontinued because of the political situation. Within Zimbabwe, travelers may choose between **express coaches,** which generally leave from city centers, and **township buses,** which leave from sprawling terminals several miles away. Express coaches have the advantage of being faster, more comfortable, and having convenient drop-off/pick-up points in the center of town; township buses have the advantage of being cheaper, much more frequent, traveling to many places that express coaches don't go, and connecting easily to other buses and minibuses at the terminals. Pickpockets, however, are a concern at these terminals, and township buses do tend to break down on the road with greater frequency. See city listings for details.

BY MINIBUS TAXI. Minibus taxis operate over a wide range of distances: some go from Harare to the suburbs, while others run from Harare to Johannesburg. They are much more frequent and comprehensive in their routes than regular buses; on the other hand, they can be extremely confusing to navigate without a local to help show you the ropes. Taxis travel from Park St. Station in **Johannesburg** to and from **Bulawayo** (US$27) and **Harare** (US$30), leaving, as always, when they fill up. Most minibuses tend to leave before 8am.

KEEPING IN TOUCH

TELEPHONES. Country code: 263. **International operator:** ☎ 966. Most public phones in Zimbabwe use **prepaid cards,** available at local post offices.

MAIL. There are no postal codes in Zimbabwe; the town or city name is all that is required. *Poste Restante* is generally available in the larger cities. First class mail to and from the United States, Canada, and Europe generally takes 15 to 25 days.

TIME DIFFERENCE. Greenwich Mean Time plus two hours (the same as South Africa). Zimbabwe does not observe daylight savings time.

GAY AND LESBIAN TRAVELERS

Zimbabwe is notorious for its official anti-gay attitude. President Mugabe has called homosexuality a "sickness;" the practice of homosexuality is against the law; and the nation's first President, **Rev. Canaan Banana,** is currently serving a prison sentence for charges stemming from homosexual conduct. Although most Zimbabwean citizens are tolerant of homosexual lifestyles, and homophobic violence is not common, discretion is recommended.

NATIONAL HOLIDAYS AND FESTIVALS

April 18: Independence Day
May 1: Workers' Day
May 25-26: Africa Days
August 11-12: Heroes' Days

NORTHERN ZIMBABWE

The northern region of Zimbabwe highlights the country at its most cosmopolitan, but also at its most rugged. Standing on a high sandstone mound at sunset, one can look off and see the twinkling lights and skyscrapers of Harare in the distance; in the other direction, the sun sets over rock outcroppings and tobacco farms. Not far over the horizon, the land begins to slope steadily downward, meeting the mighty Zambezi River and submerging itself beneath the artificial coasts of Lake Kariba. Northern Zimbabwe showcases all the things for which Zimbabwe deserves to be proud. The country's intellectual community converges at Zimbabwe's largest university; world-class Shona sculpture and art is displayed at prestigious galleries and humble markets alike; the national soccer team energizes tens of thousands of cheering fans at international matches; big game drink along the shores of the Zambezi, amid scenery worthy of any postcard; and middle-class Zimbabwean families spend holidays together above the waters of one of the great engineering projects in Southern Africa. Traveling through this part of Zimbabwe, one gets the sense of a country that is alive, indomitable, and always on the road to self-improvement, no matter what obstacles it faces.

HARARE ☎ 04

The "Sunshine City" is Zimbabwe's thoroughly modern capital, pulsating with the alternate sounds of the traditional and the Western worlds. Though five-star hotels, Internet access, and high-rises have become a part of the city's personality, Harare is also Zimbabwe's center for traditional art, music, and craftsmanship.

Recent political misfortunes have depressed Harare's heartbeat. Astronomical inflation, fuel shortages, and a currency crisis (see p. 569) have made life very difficult for Zimbabweans everywhere, but the crunch is perhaps most evident here in the capital city, where modern towers go dark from lack of electricity, and petrol queues filled with smartly-dressed businessmen often snake around city blocks. Despite the difficulties, however, most Harareans remain good-humored, optimistic, and ever-proud of their hometown.

Although there are many sights and places of interest in and around Harare during daylight hours, the city's main claim to fame for passing tourists is its nightlife; late-night revelers have learned to deal with hangovers as efficiently as they have with fuel shortages. As Zimbabwe's travel hub and the logical first stage of any trip to the country, Harare offers a welcome touch of the metropolitan, with the country's traditions and culture never far away.

ZIMBABWE

▛ TRANSPORTATION

Flights: Harare Airport (☎575 188). Several km south of town off the Seke Rd. Airport **departure tax** US$20. **Taxis** from the airport to the town center cost around US$5.

Air Malawi (☎04 753 346) flies to **Lilongwe/Blantyre** (US$125/US$145).

Air Mauritius (☎04 735 738) flies to **Port Louis** (US$320).

Air Tanzania (☎04 752 537) flies to **Dar-es-Salaam** (US$380).

Air Zimbabwe (☎04 575 111) flies to **London** (US$800+) and **Nairobi** (US$366).

British Airways (☎737 200) flies to **Johannesburg** (R1710) and **London** (US$800+)

South African Airways (in S.A. ☎0861 FLY SAA; in Bulawayo ☎09 713 37; in Harare ☎04 738 922) runs frequent flights to: **Bulawayo** (Su-F, US$139); **Johannesburg** (daily, US$170); **Victoria Falls** (daily, US$186).

Trains: The **train station** (☎786 000/1, reservations 786 033/06) is along Kenneth Kaunda Ave. between Angwa and Sam Nujoma St. Reservations office open M-F 8am-1pm and 2-4pm, Sa 8-11:30am; ticket office open 6am-9pm. Trains to: **Bulawayo** (9hr.; daily 8pm; M-Th and Sa 2nd class/1st class US$4/US$8, F and Su US$5/US$10) and **Mutare** (9hr.; daily 9:30pm; M-Th and Sa US$2/US$4, F and Su US$2.50/US$5). The overnight train has become increasingly unreliable, as theft of copper wires along the tracks has caused severe delays (as much as 9 hr.).

Buses: For an explanation of the bus service levels, see **By Bus and Minibus Taxi,** p. 37.

Express Buses: Blue Arrow (☎726 725 or 729 514/8), at Chester House, on Speke Ave. near 3rd St. Buses to **Bulawayo** (6hr.; M-Th and Sa 8am, F 8am and 5pm, Su 2pm; US$18) and **Mutare** (5hr.; W and F 7:30am, Su noon; US$11). Blue Arrow's international carrier, **Greyhound** (☎720 801) goes to **Johannesburg** (17hr.; M-Sa 10pm, Su 1pm; US$21) as do **Translux** (☎725 132; M, W, F 9pm, Su 1pm; US$14) and **Intercape** (☎701 821/3; Th 11:30am, US$21). Three final bus lines depart from the **Roadport station** at the corner of Robert Mugabe Ave. and 5th St.

Semi-Luxury Coaches: While not as plush, some bus companies offer comfortable coaches that operate from Roadport and Mbare to national and regional destinations. The following buses depart from Roadport. Munenzwa to: **Bulawayo** (6hr.; daily 7am and 1pm; US$8); **Johannesburg** (17hr.; M, Tu, Th, F noon; US$10) via **Beitbridge**; **Mutare** (4hr.; daily 8am and 3pm; US$5). Express Motorways to **Johannesburg** (17hr.; M-F and Su noon; US$12) via **Masvingo** (4hr.; US$6). Chigubu to **Johannesburg** (17hr.; daily noon; US$10) via **Masvingo** (4hr.; US$4), and **Lusaka** (10hr.; daily 7am and 9pm). Tenda Buses to **Mutare** (5hr.; daily 8, 10am, noon; US$5). Kariba Power Coach (☎702 798) to **Kariba** (5½hr.; daily, every 2hr 5am-5pm; US$6) via **Chinhoyi** (2hr.; US$2). Munorurama (☎721 581) to **Johannesburg** (17hr.; daily noon and 9pm; US$10), and **Lilongwe** (up to 18hr.; daily 7am; US$15) via **Blantyre** (12hr.; US$13).

Township Buses: Most township buses operate from the bus rank at Mbare Musika (see p. 577). Destinations and fares at Mbare do not differ significantly from the semi-luxury coaches at Roadport, though efficiency, comfort and cleanliness are vastly inferior in comparison to the above coaches. The one major advantage is that buses here leave more frequently, and tend not to sell out in advance. The risk of theft or loss at Mbare Musika is significantly greater than at Roadport. **Chitanda Bus Services** go to **Gaborone** (22hr.; daily 6am; US$12). Other destinations served with regularity include **Beitbridge, Bulawayo, Chirundu, Masvingo, Mutare,** and **Nyamapanda.**

Minibus Taxis: Swerving, honking white minibuses are the lifeblood of Harare's city transportation system. Departing from multiple ranks, their ordered chaos can be understandably confusing. Minibuses to **Avondale, Greencroft, Mbare,** and **Westgate Shopping Center** depart from the **Speke Ave. rank,** on the corner of Leopold Takawira. Minibuses to **Borrowdale** and **Domboshawa** run from the **Rezende St. rank,** at the corner of Nelson Mandela. The **Park Lane Rank,** next to the Crowne Plaza hotel, runs minibuses to **Johannesburg** daily before 9am (US$15). Seats to South Africa are competitive; you have to be assertive to get your name on the master list as soon as you arrive. Fares to most local destinations are less than US$0.40.

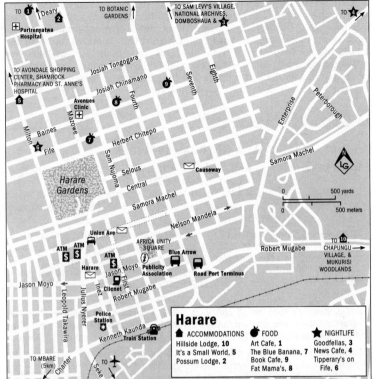

Harare

▲ ACCOMMODATIONS	🍴 FOOD	★ NIGHTLIFE
Hillside Lodge, **10**	Art Cafe, **1**	Goodfellas, **3**
It's a Small World, **5**	The Blue Banana, **7**	News Cafe, **4**
Possum Lodge, **2**	Book Cafe, **9**	Tipperary's on
	Fat Mama's, **8**	Fife, **6**

Taxis: Harare's main taxi rank is at Union Ave. between Julius Nyerere and Angwa St. Major metered taxi companies include **Yellow Cab** (☎ 758 746), **A1** (☎ 703 334 or 700 158), and **Rixi Taxi** (☎ 753 080 or 720 460). **Avondale Taxi** (☎ 335 883 or 336 616) has ranks at both the Avondale and Westgate shopping centers. A number of non-metered (or optional meter) taxis also congregate at the Union Ave. rank and fares should be negotiated in advance. Expect to pay around US$1 in the city center, or US$2 to Avondale.

Car Rental: Transit, 80 George Silundika Ave. (☎ 706 919; fax 734 121), at 6th St.; **Budget,** 145 Samora Machel Ave. (☎ 701 858; fax 701 860 or 724 645), near 6th St., and at the airport (☎ 575 421; fax 575 422). **Avis** (☎ 732 789 or 732 795), on 3rd St. near Jason Moyo Ave., by Meikles Hotel, and at the airport (☎ 575 144).

■ ORIENTATION

Like most Zimbabwean cities, Harare's colonial influence is reflected in its classic rectangular grid plan, where numbered vertical streets crisscross named horizontal avenues. The main road through town is **Sam Nujoma St.,** which runs south past **Africa Unity Square** and terminates at the railway station on **Kenneth Kaunda Ave.** Harare's center lies at the intersection of Sam Nujoma St. and **Samora Machel Ave.,** a busy thoroughfare which leads toward Bulawayo as it runs west out of town. The city's other main east-west artery, **Robert Mugabe Rd.,** forms the shopping district's

ZIMBABWE

southern border and passes the Fourth St. bus terminus as it runs east to Mutare. Most worthwhile shops lie between **Fourth** and **First St.**, the latter being a pedestrian mall on the western edge of town. Downtown's upper-left quadrant is dominated by the **Harare Gardens,** bordered by **Herbert Chitepo Ave.** to the north and **Leopold Takawira St.** to the west. At the southeast corner of the Gardens, **Julius Nyerere Way** runs south to become **Seke Rd.,** which then turns off to the airport after crossing **Charter Road.** Charter Rd. itself is the extension of Kenneth Kaunda Ave. and leads to the incredible **Mbare *musika*** (market).

ᵇ PRACTICAL INFORMATION

TOURIST, FINANCIAL, AND LOCAL SERVICES

Tourist Office: Zimbabwe Tourist Authority, 1 Union Ave., stocks various publications and event listings for shows and festivals. (☎758 730/4 or 758 712/4. Open M-F 8am-4:30pm.) Less helpful is the **Harare Publicity Association,** in Africa Unity Square at the corner of Sam Nujoma St. and Jason Moyo Ave. (☎705 085/6. Open M-F 8am-noon and 1pm-4pm, Sa 8am-noon.)

Tours: Canvas Safari Tours, 7 Deary Ave. (☎722 803 or 726 851), behind Possum Lodge (see **Accommodations** p. 575). Their trips, which lack a commercial, pre-packaged feel, stand out from the crowd. Tours in and around Harare, as well as major tourist destinations in Zimbabwe, can be arranged. A number of tour companies geared toward foreign visitors operate from the **Travel Center,** along Jason Moyo Ave. between 3rd and 4th St.

Banks: Barclay's Bank (☎758 280/9), in 1st St. Mall, at the corner of Jason Moyo Ave. **Standard Chartered,** on Sam Nujoma St. and Nelson Mandela Ave. Both have **ATMs** that accept foreign cards. Open M, Tu, Th, F 8am-3pm; W 8am-1pm; Sa 8-11:30am.

Currency Exchange: Rennie's/Thomas Cook, along Jason Moyo near the corner of 4th St. Charges slightly lower commissions and fees than do banks. For all intents and purposes, buying foreign currency with Z$ is impossible in Zimbabwe—don't buy more Zimdollars than you know you can spend.

Camping Equipment Rental: Rooney's Hire Service, 144 Seke Rd. (☎771 557/9, 748 621/9), in Graniteside. MC/V.

Laundromat: Fife Avenue Launderette (☎794 867 or 091 600 274), at the Fife Ave. Shopping Center. Wash and dry US$0.70 each per 5kg load; iron US$0.80; detergent/fabric softener US$0.30 each. Drop-off service US$2.50 per 5kg load. Open M, Tu, Th, F 7:30am-6pm; W 7:30am-2pm; Sa 8am-5pm. Phone ahead on Su.

EMERGENCY AND COMMUNICATIONS

Emergency: ☎99 or 112.

Police Station: (☎772 033, 733 033/733), at the corner of Kenneth Kaunda Ave. and Inez Terrace, near the railway station at the southern end of town.

Pharmacy: Shamrock Pharmacy (☎336 730 or 339 339), along King George Rd., opposite Avondale Shopping Center. Open daily 8am-8pm.

Hospitals: Parirenyatwa Hospital (☎701 555/7) is the general hospital, with entrances on Mazowe St. (vehicles) and Leopold Takawira Ave. (pedestrians). **St. Anne's Hospital** (☎339 933), on King George Rd. near Lomagundi Rd. **Avenues Clinic** (☎241 180/99) is a more expensive, but higher quality, private facility at the corner of Mazowe St. and Baines Ave. All open 24hr.

Internet Access: Clicnet (☎/fax 759 624), in Batanai Mall, at the corner of 1st St. and Jason Moyo Ave. Up to 10min. US$0.20, 10-15min. US$0.25, 15-30min. US$0.50. 22% student discount. 22% Su discount for all customers.

Telephones: Functioning public telephones are a rarity in Harare. A few booths can be found on the 1st St. pedestrian mall and at the Avondale Shopping Center. Phone cards in Z$100 and Z$200 denominations are available at the post offices. Calls and faxes to the US, UK, and Australia available at **Clicnet** (see Internet, above). Calls US$0.25 per min. Faxes US$0.50 per page. Rates to other countries available upon request. Open M-F 8am-8pm, Sa 8am-6pm, Su 9am-5pm.

Post Office: Main Post Office (☎ 794 491), on the corner of Inez Terrace and George Silundika Ave. Less hectic alternatives: **Union Ave.** branch, between 1st and Sam Nujoma St. (☎ 725 613), or **Causeway** (☎ 704 135/8), at the corner of Central Ave. and 3rd St.

▌ ACCOMMODATIONS AND CAMPING

Possum Lodge, 7 Deary Ave. (☎ 726 851; fax 722 803; possum@zol.co.zw). Turn onto Mazowe St. (parallel to Sam Nujoma St.), heading away from town with the hospital on your left; Deary Ave. is on the right. By minibus, take "Avondale/Greencroft" to Parirenyatwa. A thriving hostel in a huge 2-story colonial, with a busy bar and travel/tour service. Convenient 20min. walk from downtown. Typically grubby ablution facilities. Cosy TV lounge. Internet access US$0.40 per 15 min. Transfers to: train station (US$1.50); bus station (US$2.30); airport (US$5.40). Dorms US$5; doubles US$14-16; camping US$2. ❶

Hillside Lodge, 71 Hillside Rd. (☎ 747 961 or 091 325 202; jacas@samara.co.zw or hillside2001@yahoo.co.uk). By minibus, take "Msasa," "Mavbuku," or "Tafara" routes to the children's home on Robert Mugabe Rd. From Robert Mugabe Rd. heading away from town, turn right onto Chiremba Rd., then left onto Hillside Rd. A laid-back suburban place, Hillside is perhaps Harare's most homey hostel. Oft-used graffiti wall for guests' musings. Easy access to city center and Mukuvisi Game Reserve. TV lounge, bar, swimming pool, laundry, and cooking facilities. Bike hire US$1 per hr. or US$5 per day. Dorms US$2.30; cabins and cool treehouses US$5.40; camping US$1.40. ❶

It's a Small World, 25 Ridge Rd. (☎ 335 341 or 335 176), at the corner of Argyle Rd. Take Leopold Takawira Ave. north from town, continue just past the Avondale Shopping Center, then turn left onto Argyle. Cross the traffic lights at Prince Edward Rd. and continue to Ridge Rd., turning left at the top of the hill; the hostel in on the left corner. By minibus, take "Mabelreign via Quendon" to the corner of Ridge Rd. and Argyle. Lovely accommodations in an enormous suburban bungalow. Carpeted dorms, plush bathrooms, new furniture and amenities. Snacks available. Full bar. Laundry US$1.60 per load. Dorms US$6; doubles US$15; en suite rooms US$20; camping US$4. MC/V. ❷

◖ FOOD

▩ **Art Café,** 30 Bath Rd. (☎ 333 413), behind the Avondale Shopping Center. Take Leopold Takawira north to the Shopping Center, cutting through the parking lot past Bon Marché supermarket and then across the field. Avondale minibuses run from downtown to the shopping center. Peach walls and lilac chairs surround a sculpture garden with pond and water lilies. Inspired diners are invited to purchase and complete unfinished paintings and pottery items. Lunch specials from US$0.75. Sandwiches from US$1. Home-made cakes from US$0.60. Open M-Sa 9am-10pm, Su 9am-4pm. ❶

🖼 **Fat Mama's** (☎ 702 026), in the Russell Hotel at the corner of 3rd St. and Baines Ave. Mama isn't the only person likely to get fat at this fantastic Italian restaurant. Nearly always full, Fat Mama's offers perhaps Harare's best deal for filling meals, from pasta (US$1.60-2.10) to chicken, pork, and beef (US$2.30-3.50). *Involtini* made with beef so tender a baby could chew it, and rolled with ham and mozzarella (US$3). Family atmosphere. Reservations recommended, especially for large groups. Open M-F 12:30-2pm and 6pm-late, Sa 6pm-late. MC/V. ❷

Blue Banana (☎ 702 613 or 705 320), on Fife Ave., between Sam Nujoma and 3rd St. Splendid decor and equally splendid food. A taste of exotic Thai food amid South African cuisine. Entrées US$2.50-5. Open M-F 12:30-3pm and 7pm-late, Sa 7pm-late.

Book Café (☎ 728 191 or 792 551; fax 726 243; bookshop@bookcafe.icon.co.zw), at the corner of Fife Ave. and 6th St., above OK Supermarket. The favorite haunt of Zimbabwe's literary and performing arts circle. Bookshop stocks works by celebrated African authors and aspiring Zimbabweans. Weekly events range from Africa night, with African food and music (W), Literary and Open Mic (Th), Starlight Music and Comedy (F), and Jazz (Sa lunch and evening). Vegetarian Tuesdays. Internet access during bookshop hours. Café open M-Sa 10am-late. Bookshop open M-F 8am-5pm, Sa 8:30am-1pm. ❶

🗂 SIGHTS

CHAPUNGU SCULPTURE PARK. "The home of Zimbabwean Stone Sculpture," Chapungu is a community of established and aspiring artists who celebrate traditional values in contemporary artwork. Works for sale and display are set in the grounds and indoor galleries. Visitors can experience tours with the artists as they explain their works. Do not expect oft-imitated souvenir curios at Chapungu—there is an element of the spiritual in the art here. *(On Harrow Rd. in Msasa, 8km from Central Harare. From the Samora Machel East, turn right at the Caltex Garage traffic lights. Msasa, Tafara, and Mabvuku-bound minibuses stop at the Garage. The village is at the end of the short road. ☎ 486 648 or 486 656. Open M-F 8am-6pm, Sa-Su 9am-6pm. US$0.10.)*

MUSEUM OF HUMAN SCIENCES. Called the Queen Victoria Museum until only recently, the MHS records the natural history of the man and mammals of Mashonaland in captivating style, exhibiting life-sized models of animals and displays of traditional Shona life. *(In the Civic Center on Rotten Row, behind the Sheraton Hotel. ☎ 774 208 or 752 876. Open daily 9am-5pm. US$2.)*

NATIONAL ARCHIVES. The storehouse of the nation's history, the Archives have been keeping the public records of the Zimbabwean people since 1935. Galleries emphasize the events and heroes of the two wars leading to independence, and explain important landmarks in Zimbabwean history. The library and research center are typically off-limits to non-Zimbabweans, though guests may visit the gallery while supervised by an Archives official. Well-kept gardens of cactus and aloe surround statues of educational benefactor Alfred Beit, as well as a controversial statue of Cecil John Rhodes. *(Along Borrowdale Rd., with vehicle entrance on Ruth Taylor Rd., parallel to Borrowdale Rd. Minibuses to Borrowdale, Hatcliffe, and Domboshawa drive past the Archives. ☎ 792 741. Open M-F 8:30am-4pm, Sa 8am-noon. Free.)*

NATIONAL GALLERY OF ZIMBABWE. The gallery has a permanent collection of European and African pieces, as well as rotating special exhibits and an indoor and outdoor sculpture gallery. *(Along Julius Nyerere Way, near Sam Nujoma St. ☎ 704 666/8. Open Tu-Su 9am-5pm. US$0.15, free Su.)*

SHOPPING AND MARKETS

SHOPPING CENTERS. The **Avondale Shopping Center** is conveniently located and easily accessible, filled with supermarkets, restaurants, clothing stores, movie theaters, and pharmacies. The Center is along King George Rd., the extension of Leopold Takawira Ave., heading northwest out of town. Far and away Zimbabwe's largest shopping center, **Westgate Shopping Center,** on the western edge of Harare, is an attractive and modern outdoor mall. It has all the offerings of Avondale and much more, though all at slightly higher prices. **Sam Levy's Village,** along Borrowdale Rd. in the wealthy and predominantly white suburb of Borrowdale, is modeled on Tudor-style English cottages. It features several bars, clubs, and shops, as well as Harare's only bowling alley. *(Minibuses run from downtown to all three centers. See* **Minibus Taxis,** p. 572.)

MARKETS. Mbare Musika, Harare's biggest market, is a mini-economy in its own right. Crowded under an expansive metal roof, Mbare is a thriving trading ground for carvings, sculptures, second-hand clothing, traditional medicines, fruits, and vegetables. Bargaining skills go a long way here—a few strategically-chosen Western items can be traded for pieces of remarkable craftsmanship. As Mbare is one of Harare's poorest areas, pickpocketing and petty thievery are very common here. Take a minimum of cash, keep minibus taxi fare tucked away in a separate spot, and leave watches and jewelry elsewhere. (5km south of the city center along Charter Rd., off Leopold Takawira. Minibuses from downtown depart for the market regularly. See **Minibus Taxis,** p. 572. Open daily 6am-6pm.) Other market sites include: **Africa Unity Square,** along Jason Moyo Ave., between Sam Nujoma and 3rd St.; **Robert Mugabe Ave.,** a few blocks east of downtown; **Enterprise Rd.,** near the Newlands shopping center; **Avondale Plaza,** behind the Avondale shopping center; and near **Sam Levy's Village,** along Borrowdale Rd. A dozen smaller craft markets lie throughout the city.

NIGHTLIFE

Harare boasts enough bars, clubs, and combinations of the two to cater to nearly every taste (only metalheads might struggle to find a midnight niche). **The Book Café** (see p. 576) is an excellent venue for performances of traditional and contemporary African music.

Tipperary's on Fife (☎ 708 041 or 722 210), at the corner of Leopold Takawira and Fife Ave., not to be confused with Tipperary's in Greendale. An Irish-style tavern that is Harare's favorite central watering hole, "Tipper's" also has a fine restaurant, *braai* facilities, karaoke, and live music. Cover F-Sa US$0.75. Open daily 6pm-late.

Stars Studio, in the Sheraton on Herbert Chitepo St. Thoroughly popular with Zimbabwe's young black professionals who come to hear their favorite hip-hop, R&B, and South African *kwaito* until the wee hours. Leave your thirst at the door; with bartenders often overwhelmed, it takes a while to get a drink. Cover US$3-4. Open F-Sa 10pm-late.

Goodfellas, at Sam Levy's Village in Borrowdale. Stars' counterpart for Harare's young white revellers, Goodfellas pounds out Top 40 tunes for the young and chic of Harare's more affluent suburbs. Cover US$4. Open M-Sa 9pm-late.

News Café, at Newlands Shopping Center along Enterprise Rd. Popular with trendy and diverse twentysomethings, the News Café serves sophisticated cocktails, imported and local brews, snacks, and meals. Glitzy, yet relaxed and convivial. Open M-Sa noon-late.

⚠ OUTDOORS

Harare is known throughout Zimbabwe for its gardens, parks, and public spaces, all reminders of the days of colonial pomp. In October and November, the blooming Jacaranda trees paint the city spectacular pink and violet hues. Visitors to these parks should watch their belongings, and steer clear after sunset.

HARARE GARDENS. The most centrally located park, in the shadows of Harare's tallest skyscrapers, Harare Gardens feature an open-air theater, bandstand (free live music Su afternoons and occasional weekdays), *al fresco* restaurant, and municipal swimming pool. The shady gardens are the site of many popular national festivals, including the Zimbabwe International Book Fair and the Harare International Festival of Arts. *(Main entrance on Nyerere Way, near the Crowne Plaza.)*

NATIONAL BOTANIC GARDENS. A popular picnic site, with 58ha of indigenous and exotic vegetation, the Gardens offer myriad pleasant walks. Its hideaways make this the ideal spot for the leisurely passing of a sunny afternoon. *(On Downie Ave., off Josiah Tongogara in Alexandra Park. Open daily 7:45am-6:30pm. Nominal fee.)*

AFRICA UNITY SQUARE. The focal point of downtown Harare, this small park has a large fountain, a thriving curio, and an open flower market. Originally dubbed Cecil Square, this park was laid to commemorate Britain's founding of Fort Salisbury on this spot a century ago. After independence, Zimbabwe's leaders renamed the square to symbolize a strong and independent nation and continent. The colonial-era plaque honoring the British ironically remains. *(Off of Jason Moyo Ave.)*

MUKUVISI WOODLANDS. Crocodiles, elephant, duiker, ostrich, and zebra populate this nature reserve on the southeastern outskirts of Harare. A walk-through aviary features several species of birds. Guided foot safaris and horse safaris traverse the entirety of this small wilderness. *(8km east of town off of Robert Mugabe Ave., at the corner of Glenara Avenue and Hillside Rd. Msasa, Mabvuku, and Tafara minibuses run past the corner of Mugabe and Glenara. ☎ 747 111 or 747 123. Foot safaris daily 2:30pm, US$1.50; horse safaris daily 8:30am and 3pm, US$2.30. Admission without safari US$60. Book horse safaris in advance.)*

🗓 DAYTRIPS FROM HARARE

DOMBOSHAWA ROCK PAINTINGS

25km from Harare on the Domboshawa (Borrowdale) Road. Domboshawa-bound minibuses (30min., US$0.40) leave from the rank opposite the OK Supermarket at the intersection of Cameron St. and Charter Rd. in Harare. ☎ 790 044 or 752 876. Open M-F 9am-6pm, Sa-Su 6am-6pm. Admission US$2.

A massive granite hill of great cultural importance to the Shona people, Domboshawa (translated either as "red rock" or "hill of the eland people") is a serene but commanding presence over the surrounding countryside. **Gudu's Cave,** thought to be the site of an ancient rain-making ceremony, is decorated with San paintings and surrounded by a starkly beautiful rock landscape. At nearby **Chawaroyi** ("witches'") **Hill,** suspected sorceresses were once made to run laps around the base to rid themselves of evil spirits. **Rambakurimwa** ("land that cannot be tilled") is a grove of *muzhanje* trees which produce a delicious wild fruit. The grove's name derives from local legend that claims that fresh trees would re-emerge whenever the Shona would attempt clear the land. The *muzhanje* still stand.

CHINHOYI CAVES

8km beyond the city of Chinhoyi on the Kariba highway. The Kariba Power Coach departs from Harare. (90 min., every 2hr. 5am-5pm, US$2). Confirm that the bus will go past the caves. Alternately, township buses run frequently from Mbare to Chinhoyi city; from there, Alaska Mine minibus taxis (US$0.30) can take travelers to the Alaska turn-off, a several-minute walk from the caves along the main road. Returning to Harare, Power Coach buses may be difficult to flag down; in this case, Alaska Mine minibuses run back into town, and frequent Harare-bound buses go from there. Caves ☎ (167) 223 40. US$5.

In the countryside of Mashonaland West, the pools, rocks, underground tunnels, and geological formations of these caves make for a fascinating afternoon of exploring. A self-guided tour of the caves might begin at the Sleeping Pool (315 ft. deep), a still lagoon of green, blue, turquoise, and aquamarine that has inspired many myths and tales of mermaids. Backtracking a little, another path leads to a view of the Sleeping Pool 50m above water level. From this vantage point, the rock faces appear suspended in the air above the pool, an awesome sight. A series of winding paths and tunnels above and under the ground eventually lead to another awe-inspiring view of the pool from the Dark Cave, which features calcium-formed stalactites hanging from the roof of the tunnels. Unfortunately, no guided tours of the site are available. Overnighters can camp at the attached park (tents and caravans US$0.30 per person), while the on-site Caves Motel is a passable venue for basic meals and snacks.

KARIBA

For thousands of years, the northern fringes of Zimbabwe were a parched, scrubby landscape, interrupted only by the muddy flow of the Zambezi. In the 1950s, a group of enterprising Rhodesians and Europeans changed all that by sticking a giant concrete plug in the river, turning the area into Zimbabwe's brand-new seaside (and drowning lots of unsuspecting critters in the process). Nowadays, the glimmering waters of Lake Kariba, stretching to the horizon, help Zimbabweans pretend that their country isn't landlocked—those who can afford it come here in droves to pilot houseboats, zip around on jet-skis, and watch elephants and hippos immerse themselves in this unlikely inland sea. Elephants and tourists alike can be glad there's water here: temperatures are routinely the hottest in the region, baking the ground and making visitors long for air-conditioned refuge.

▛ TRANSPORTATION

Buses and Minibus Taxis: Direct buses leave from in front of Spar to **Harare** (6hr., every 90min. 6am-3pm, US$6). For all other destinations, minibus taxis run to the highway junction **Makuti** (75min., every 30min. 6am-6pm, US$0.75), where buses can be flagged down for **Harare, Chirundu,** and **Lusaka, Zambia** until mid-afternoon.

Ferries: Every week or two, a large ferry transports visitors down the lake to **Mlibizi,** near **Victoria Falls.** The spectacular 22hr. journey beats the land route, but tickets are so comically overpriced for foreigners that few travelers will want to take it. Those willing to cough up the US$90 can contact **UTC Safaris** (☎ (27) 11 888 4037 in South Africa; reservation@adventures.co.za; http://africanadrenalin.co.za).

▚ ▛ ORIENTATION AND PRACTICAL INFORMATION

Kariba is a sweltering mess of roads, hills, trees, and water. To get around it, you'll need a vehicle of your own, enough money for a series of taxis, or good hiking shoes and a knack for not getting eaten or stomped on by the large animals that wander through town. It's not easy to get lost, in part because not many travelers venture away from the few campsites, hotels, and restaurants in operation. **Kariba Heights,** the city's upscale center, overlooks the lake from a perch 7km from the budget-traveler haunts on the lakefront below (the "Lows"). Kariba's **post office** (open M-F 8:30am-3pm) is in the center of Kariba Heights, as are several shops that double as safari companies and the **Church of Saint Barbara,** whose uninspired modern Christian architecture can only be described as televangelical. At the low end of the road between the Heights and the Lows is a **Shell station.** The low-lying areas of Kariba don't have much going for them, except proximity to wild beasts and the **bus stand.** At the bus stand is a **Spar supermarket** (open daily 7am-5:30pm) and a *bureau de change* that buys US dollars at reasonable rates and traveler's checks at unreasonable ones.

ACCOMMODATIONS AND FOOD

Kushinga Lodge (☎613 041; buffalo@internet.co.zw). One of Zimbabwe's friendliest and most welcoming campsites. The one drawback is its remote location—you'll have to walk 30 hilly minutes to get anywhere. For the backpack-laden, the walk may prove too strenuous. Once there, the friendly staff and idyllic site will charm you into staying for days. Food is available, but bring things from town to avoid having to trek out unnecessarily. Chalet doubles US$12.50; camping US$1.40. ❶

M.O.T.H. Campsite, 20min. walk southwest of bus stand. Conveniently located, cheap, and relatively secure, but no prizes for luxury or service. The owner arranges safaris and boat trips. Campers must coexist with several other species of lakeside visitor: don't camp between the hippos and the shore, or they may kill you. Doubles US$3.25; pre-erected tents US$1.50; camping US$0.75. ❶

Kariba Yacht Club, ten minutes west of M.O.T.H. Breakfast every day and set dinners most days (after 6:30pm). Popular piri-piri chicken night (US$1.80, usually Th). ❶

SIGHTS AND ADVENTURES

OPERATION NOAH MONUMENT. The impressive man-made Lake Kariba extends nearly to the horizon from most viewing points in Kariba town. Environmental damage notwithstanding, the lake is a remarkable blue and well worth a few minutes' appreciative gazing. Operation Noah monument, in Kariba Heights, is one of the best places to do so. The phenomenal panorama also offers a cool breeze, which during the summer, is a rare and precious Kariba commodity. The monument itself is a small plaque to "Operation Noah," which took place in the early 1960s. When the waters of the reservoir started to rise, countless animals were stranded on fast-disappearing islands of land in the middle of the Kariba. This project sought to transfer as many animals as possible to the shore before they drowned. Although they succeeded in saving thousands, many more perished.

KARIBA DAM. One of the greatest engineering feats in Africa, this 128-meter high concrete dam straddles the Zimbabwe-Zambia border and powers much of Zimbabwe. Visitors can get a close-up view by walking along the top of the dam, gazing down at the flowing water and crocodiles far below. The dam is in the "no-man's-land" between Zimbabwe and Zambia, so you'll need to get the Zimbabwean border officials to hang onto your passport while you take your stroll. Another viewpoint, up the steep hill above the border post, offers the classic panoramic view of the dam, and is complemented by a gift shop and some basic historical information. *(Dam access open with border post, daily 6am-6pm.)*

ZIMBABWE

HOUSEBOATING. Kariba's most popular vacation pastime isn't especially cheap, but it does provide the opportunity to cruise the lake while admiring the thirsty elephants, giraffes, and buffalo that congregate along the shoreline by the hundreds to drink. Expect to pay US$40-100 per person per night, including a 2-3 person crew, petrol, all meals, and drinks. Some reputable booking agents for Kariba houseboats include **African Safari Consultants** (in US ☎ (805) 968 7394; info@classic-safaris.com; www.classicsafaris.com) and **What a Pleasure** (in South Africa ☎ (27) 31 766 3638; wap@afrizim.com; www.afrizim.com/whata).

 BORDER CROSSING: KARIBA If you enjoy getting your passport stamped amid dramatic scenery, enter Zambia at Kariba. The sleepy border post on the Zimbabwe side is along a cliff ten minutes' walk from Kariba Dam; you'll have to walk or drive across the dam, then up a twenty-minute scenic road on the Zambian side, where a slightly more active border patrol welcomes visitors to Zambia. No regular public transport leaves from either of these points, but some travelers do hitch lifts. Better still, take a slow walk from border to border and savor the view. Lifts to Lusaka (2-3hr.) are few, though some travelers manage to get one after a wait. Open daily 6am-6pm.

MATABELELAND

As its name indicates, Matabeleland is home to most of Zimbabwe's ethnic Ndebele population. Unlike the Shona, the Ndebele speak a "click" language quite close to Zulu, and have much closer ancestral ties to the ethnic groups of South Africa than to the ethnic groups of Zambia, Congo, and East Africa. The land they inhabit is at the brink of the Kalahari Sands; the relatively green terrain of central Zimbabwe fades into tans and oranges as one moves closer to Botswana, and the large commercial farms of the Midlands dissipate into smaller and drier patches of crops and pastures, before giving way entirely to the arid, untilled *bushveld* that borders the true desert. On the northern edge of Matabeleland, of course, is Southern Africa's crown jewel: the world-famous Victoria Falls, a world wonder that no traveler can afford to miss.

The inhabitants of Matabeleland have always existed in an uneasy marriage with the rest of the country. From the first days of the war of independence, there were two separate guerrilla armies, one for each ethnic group; in 1980, when Robert Mugabe (a Shona) assumed power in an independent Zimbabwe, many Ndebele were dissatisfied by their lack of political influence, and a number spoke of secession. As these plans matured and became known to Mugabe, his government declared a "state of emergency," and from 1983 to 1987, special government troops (the so-called "fifth brigade") swept through Matabeleland, arresting and interrogating anyone thought to be pro-secessionist. During these dark years, euphemistically referred to as the "Disturbances," an estimated 20,000 Ndebele were killed. Some of the bad blood between the government and the Ndebele has since been vetted; Matabeleland's lingering resentment was more than apparent in the 2000 election, however, when every single parliamentary seat in the region went decisively to the opposition party.

BULAWAYO ☎ 19

Bulawayo, known as the "City of Kings," considers itself Zimbabwe's royal citadel, although its name means "place of killing." The Ndebele first came to Bulawayo in the 1830s when Mzilikazi, a Zulu Kumalo general, fled his ruthless king, Shaka,

ZIMBABWE

with a band of warriors and their families. The break-away Zulus tore their way north from Natal, battling and incorporating everyone they encountered; by the time they arrived here, they had gained a reputation far and wide as a bellicose people. Today, Bulawayo is a serene city, a far cry from its historic days of plunder. An unhurried ambience characterizes this modern city. It is the southern gateway to the spectacular Victoria Falls, Great Zimbabwe, and the Eastern Highlands, as well as an important transport link to Botswana and South Africa. Bulawayo also boasts its own captivating attractions in the Matobo and Khami monuments, museums, and cultural places of interest.

▐ TRANSPORTATION

Flights: The **Bulawayo Airport** (☎26 423) is north of town off Robert Mugabe Way.

Air Zimbabwe (☎72 051), in Treger House on Jason Moyo between 11th and 12th Ave. flies to **Harare** (1 hr.; 2 per day; US$49) and **Johannesburg** (1hr.; M, F; US$202 incl 15% sales tax).

South African Airways (☎71 667), in Africa House on the corner of Fife St. and 10th Ave. flies to **Johannesburg** (T, Th, Su 12:55pm).

Trains: The **train station** is just off the southern end of Lobengula St., near the city center. To **Harare** (9hr., daily 8pm, weekday economy/2nd/1st class US$3/US$4/US$8, weekends US$4/US$5/US$10) and **Victoria Falls** (12hr., daily 7pm, weekdays US$2.50/US$4.50/US$6, weekends US$3/US$5/US$7) via **Dete** (the nearest town to Hwange National Park). The train arrives in Dete around 1am. Ticket office open M-F 7am-8:45pm, Sa-Su 7am-2pm and 6-8:45pm.

Buses: Township buses leave when full from the **Renkini bus terminal** at the 6th Ave. extension to the west of town, and run to most major towns. Other buses include:

Blue Arrow (☎65 548) stops in front of its office at the Unifreight House, 73a Fife St. near the corner of Leopold Takawira, and books tickets on Translux and Greyhound. To **Harare** (6hr.; M-Th 8am, F 8am and 5pm, Su 2pm; US$18) and **Victoria Falls** (6hr.; Tu, Th, F 9am; US$19) via **Hwange Safari Lodge** and **Dete.**

Translux (☎66 528) leaves from the corner of 12th Ave. and Mugabe to **Johannesburg** (13hr., daily 5pm, US$12).

Minibus taxis: From the rank at City Hall, behind the tourist office, minibuses leave when full to **Harare** (US$5), **Johannesburg** (US$8), and **Victoria Falls** (US$5). Minibuses to **Masvingo** (US$5) depart from the BP service station.

Taxis: Rixi Taxi (☎61 933, 61 934, or 60 666), on the corner of 4th Ave. and George Silundika St. Taxis also rank in the City Hall car park on Leopold Takawira Ave., and outside the Bulawayo Rainbow Hotel on the corner of Josiah Tongogara and 10th Ave.

Car Rental: Budget, 106 Josiah Tongogara Ave. (☎72 543 or 65 566) near the corner of 10th Ave. **Europcar** operates with **Imperial,** 9a Africa House (☎67 925 or 226 445). **Transit,** 86 Robert Mugabe Way (☎76 495 or 76 496) near 8th Ave.

Bike Rental: Packers Rest Lodge (see p. 584) has bicycle rental facilities. US$1 per hr. Daily rates also available.

▐ ORIENTATION

Central Bulawayo is an extremely navigable grid of numbered horizontal avenues intersected by named vertical streets. The road from Beitbridge border becomes **Leopold Takawira Ave.** (7th Ave.), the main road through town, which hits **Josiah Tongogara St.** and **Robert Mugabe Way** on the eastern edge of downtown. Most of the best restaurants line Robert Mugabe, which also runs north to the airport and south to become the **Matopos Rd.** leading to the Matobo National Park. Small shops and businesses lie on **George Silundika, Fife,** and **Jason Moyo Sts.,** while banks, and

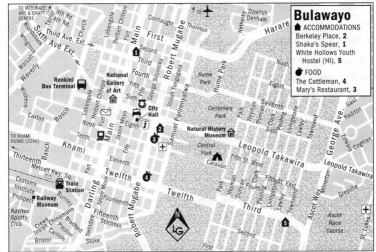

Bulawayo

♦ ACCOMMODATIONS
Berkeley Place, 2
Shaka's Spear, 1
White Hollows Youth
Hostel (HI), 5

● FOOD
The Cattleman, 4
Mary's Restaurant, 3

the post office are on **Main St. First Ave.** becomes the Harare road as it runs east from town, and the road to Hwange National Park and Victoria Falls is accessible by turning left onto **Masotsha Ndlovu Ave.** at the northern end of the city. Unless traveling to the railway station or the Renkini bus terminal (on the 6th Ave. extension), do not linger west of **Fort St.** due to crime concerns.

🔲 PRACTICAL INFORMATION

TOURIST, FINANCIAL, AND LOCAL SERVICES

Tourist Office: The **Bulawayo Publicity Association** (☎ 60 867 or 72 969; fax 60 868; bulawayo@telconet.co.zw; www.arachnid.co.zw/bulawayo), in City Hall car park on Leopold Takawira St., offers maps and comprehensive lists of accommodations, tour operators, and campsites in and around Bulawayo, including Matobo Hills. Open M-F 8:30am-4:45pm, Sa 8:30am-noon.

Tours: Gemsbok Safaris (☎ 63 906 or 66 002; fax 70 009), in the Old Mutual Center on the corner of Jason Moyo St. and 8th Ave., is among the largest of the local tour companies. On average, a full day tour of Matobo Hills costs about US$60, half day about US$45. Of the many local companies offering trips to Matobo Hills and other local attractions, the most reputable are: **Black Rhino Safaris** (☎/fax 241 662; black-rhino@telconet.co.zw or blackrhino@hotmail.com), **Adventure Travel** (☎ 66 775), and **Circle Court Tours** (☎ 76 838 or 61 857). For a taste of contemporary rural Zimbabwean life, **Mzingeli Cultural Tours** (☎ 76 986; fax 78 264), operating from the Municipal Caravan Park, offers trips to rural villages (full day US$40, half day US$30 including refreshments).

Bank: Barclays (☎ 540 061), on the corner of Main St. and 8th Ave., has an **ATM** friendly to foreign cards. **Standard Chartered** (☎ 63 861), on Fife St. at 10th Ave. Banking hours are M, Tu, Th, F 8am-3pm, W 8am-1pm, Sa 8-11:30am.

Currency exchange: CFX Foreign Exchange, 97 Robert Mugabe Way (☎ 75 834 or 71 121), between 9th and 10th Ave., charges no commission. Open M-F 9am-5pm. Many hostels will exchange foreign currency for their guests at competitive rates.

Laundromat: **Bulawayo Laundry Services,** 56a Josiah Tongogara St. between 4th and 5th Ave.

EMERGENCY AND COMMUNICATIONS

Emergency: ☎999 or 71 717

Police: (☎72 515), on the corner of Leopold Takawira and Fife St. Open 24hr.

Pharmacy: Plus 2 Pharmacy, 91 George Silundika St. (☎64 441 or 64 582) at 9th Ave., and **Plus 2 Emergency,** 94b Robert Mugabe Way (☎68 667 or 68 668). Both open daily 8am-9pm.

Hospital: Bulawayo Central Hospital (☎72 111) is on St. Luke's Way off Leopold Takawira Ave. east of town. **Galen House Emergency Unit** (☎540 051), Josiah Tongogara St. at 9th Ave. Open 24 hr.

Telephones: Few, far between, and often out of order. There are phones inside the post office, behind City Hall, and outside the video arcade on the corner of 9th Ave. and Robert Mugabe Way. Phone cards are available at the post office.

Internet Access: Afrinet, 5a Bulawayo Center, on Main St. between 9th and 10th Ave. Open M-F 8am-5pm, Sa 8am-1pm.

Post Office: (☎62 535), a large white colonial building on the corner of Main St. and 8th Ave. *Poste Restante* available. Open M-F 8:30am-4:30pm, Sa 8-11am.

▓ ACCOMMODATIONS AND CAMPING

▓ **Shaka's Spear** (☎/fax 79 788 or 091 227 018; after hours 246 376; shakass-pear@hotmail.com), at the corner of Sam Nujoma Ave. and Jason Moyo St. Heading west on Leopold Takawira, turn right on Jason Moyo and continue 5 blocks to the corner of 2nd Ave. Conveniently located, Shaka's Spear is a buzzing backpackers' stop with a convivial atmosphere and accommodating staff. Hospitality, currency exchange, and friendly advice doled out in good measure. Self-catering or meals available on request with traditional dinners (US$2) the specialty. Internet US$0.50 for 15min. Laundry available for a fee. Tours arranged. Dorms US$3; doubles US$7. ❷

Packers Rest, 1 Oak Ave. (☎71 111; fax 74 058; packers@mweb.co.zw). Along 12th Ave. going east from town, 500m from downtown. Despite the busy main road at its threshold, the hostel manages to capture a suburban feel in its neat, well-kept quarters. A comprehensive range of services includes tour bookings, Internet (US$2 for 30min.), and luggage storage. Dorms US$3; singles US$8; doubles US$10. Camping US$2. Day guests US$1. ❶

Berkeley Place, 77 Josiah Tongogara St. (☎/fax 67 701) near the corner of Leopold Takawira Ave. Like a hotel for backpackers: small rooms with twin beds, shower, and tea and coffee facilities in a pink apartment-style complex. Not luxurious, but clean and private. Extras include laundry services, curio shop selling African art, and currency exchange facilities. Late arrivals call ahead. Breakfast included. Reception open until 8pm. US$6 per person. ❸

White Hollows Youth Hostel (HI), 52 Townsend Rd. (☎76 488). On the corner of 3rd St. (12th Ave.). For clean, reputable, and economic budget accommodations, this cannot be beat. If the whitewashed narrow hallways, high ceilings, and stale furniture make this place feel like a nursing home, it's no coincidence—it used to be one. Only 2km from town, but in a quiet residential area. Curfew 10:30pm. Dorms and private rooms US$0.50 per person. ❶

FOOD

Let's not mince words: Bulawayo is the place to eat a sumptuous meal, as the city holds firm to traditional standards of fine dining and good service. Be it a slice of cake, a light pasta lunch, or a thick *lowveld* steak, Bulawayo's restaurants spoil a visitor for choice. Among the most highly recommended are:

Ester's Coffee Shop (☎ 70 126), in the courtyard of the National Gallery of Art on the corner of Takawira Ave. and Main St. Faintly evocative of a Parisian café, Ester's enriches guests with delightful meals (pastas and salads US$0.75-1.25) in the art-intellectual shade of the gallery. Tempting vegetarian choices stray from the usual cheese and tomato variety. Teatime treats US$0.30-0.50. Open Tu-Sa 9am-5pm. MC/V. ❶

Mary's Restaurant, 88 Josiah Tongogara St. (☎ 76 721 or 64 790) near the corner of 8th Ave. A Greek family restaurant with tables patriotically decked in blue and white gingham, Mary's is always packed at lunchtime—and for good reason. Massive and hearty entrees (US$2-2.70) with daily specials (US$1.50) will fill a growling stomach. Afterwards, heavenly desserts will rapidly make you forget that your stomach was ever full: rich chocolate mousse cake or spongy carrot cake US$0.70. Open M-Th 7:30am-4pm, F 7:30am-4pm and 6:30pm-late, Sa 8am-noon and 6:30pm-late. DC/MC/V. ❷

The Cattleman (☎ 76 086 or 60 873), at the corner of Josiah Tongogara and 12th Ave. A Texan-style steak house in the middle of the *lowveld*, complete with stars and stripes banner and lasso-man logo. Waiters in cowboy denim deliver fine juicy steaks (US$2.75-4). Beef regionally renowned. Open Tu-Su noon-2pm and 6-10pm. MC/V. ❷

☉ SIGHTS

MUSEUM OF NATURAL HISTORY. Housed in a large rotunda in the attractive Centenary Park, this museum records the cultural, colonial, and natural history of Zimbabwe with eye-opening, life-size models, including the world's 2nd-largest mounted elephant. Exhibits will leave visitors wide-eyed as they move from kings and rulers to stuffed animal displays. *(East of Bulawayo along Leopold Takawira Ave. Admission US$2. Open daily 9am-5pm.)*

AMAKHOSI THEATRE. The Amakhosi troupe is Bulawayo's nationally-acclaimed performing arts group, and their repertoire includes plays and drama, modern dance, poetry, and traditional dance and music. Visitors are welcome to watch rehearsals; a calendar of performances is available at the office. *(Extension of Masotsha Ndlovu Ave., just after the traffic lights. Open 9am-5pm.)*

MZILIKAZI ART AND CRAFT CENTER. Visitors can witness the creation of beautiful works of pottery, as well as sculpture, drawing, and painting. Nearby is the **Bulawayo Home Industries Center,** where batiks and tapestries are made and sold. *(Off the Old Victoria Falls Rd. along Taylor Ave. north of town. Open M-F 8am-12:30pm, 2-4pm.)*

NATIONAL GALLERY OF ART. This modest gallery, housed in an old colonial building, displays batiks and abstract/contemporary art exhibits by talented high school students. *(Corner of Main St. and Leopold Takawira Ave. ☎ 70 721. Open Tu-Su 9am-5pm. Admission US$0.15, free on Su.)*

WILDLIFE SANCTUARIES. The **Chipangali Wildlife Orphanage** is a fascinating animal rehabilitation project with penned black rhino, lion, cheetah, and leopards. *(23km from Bulawayo along the Gwanda road to Beitbridge. Open Tu-Su 10am-5pm. Nominal entrance fee.)* On the road to Matobo National Park is the **Tshabalala Sanctuary,** home to giraffe, zebra, kudu, and wildebeest. Driving, walking, and cycle safaris are permitted. *(10km from Bulawayo along the Matobo Rd. Open daily 6am-6pm.)*

ZIMBABWE

⚡ DAYTRIP

KHAMI RUINS

22km from Bulawayo on the extension of 13th Ave. No consistent public transport serves Khami, but a determined visitor can cycle to the ruins, take a taxi, or find a ride in a hostel. Museum collects admission to the ruins. Admission US$2.

With a history inextricably tied to that of Great Zimbabwe, the less-renowned Khami nonetheless displays even more sophisticated architecture than its predecessor. Constructed circa 1500AD, this site is all that remains of the capital of the Torwa people. The ruins consist of circular platforms filled with soil. These platforms, connected by paths and passages, supported huts of the Shona nobility. As at Great Zimbabwe, excavation of the Khami Ruins uncovered Chinese porcelain and Portuguese trading goods. One of the site's highlights is a Portuguese cross cut into the rock at one of the ruins. There is also a tiny on-site museum.

VICTORIA FALLS ☎ 113

One of the largest and most spectacular waterfalls in the world, the Victoria Falls have a width of over 1700m, plunging more than 100m into the gorge below at an estimated rate of 500 million liters per minute. The water's force of impact sends spray up to five times the height of the Falls themselves, giving rise to the local name of *Mosi oa Tunya* ("the smoke that thunders"). When the moon is full, a lunar rainbow is almost always visible. The Falls have earned their place among the world's Seven Natural Wonders.

The Falls have also become the adventure capital of Southern Africa. Only ten years ago, the first rafting company began capitalizing on the Zambezi River's churning turbulence; now, many rafting companies, safari guides, microlight pilots, booze cruisers, and bungee operators compete fiercely for clients. They charge foreign-level prices, as does the Victoria Falls National Park itself. This has caused a domino effect, leading to expensive hotels, bureaux de change, and street hawkers pawning soapstone hippos and black market currency. Though the Falls themselves are definitely a must-see in Zimbabwe, the over-touristed atmosphere of the Vic Falls town makes it a pleasure to hit the road again, or at least defect to the more pleasant Zambian side.

The Falls are weakest in November, when everything east of the bridge is bone-dry, and fullest (but hardest to see due to spray) in March. All Zambezi River activities depend upon the water's height; if your trip involves rafting or other activities, call your company in advance to inquire which rapids (if any) are open.

▮ TRANSPORTATION

Flights: Victoria Falls International Airport is 20km west of town. **Air Zimbabwe** (☎ 43 16) has an office between the post office and banks on Livingstone Way. Flights to: **Harare** (1hr.; M-Tu and Th-F 3:30pm, W 12:30pm, Sa-Su 5:15pm; US$108); **Johannesburg** (3-4 flights per day, US$246); **Kariba** (M, W, F, and Su 3pm; US$78); **Maun** (Tu-W and F 12:10pm, US$228); **Windhoek** (W, F, and Su 3:30pm; US$385). **South African Airways** flies to **Johannesburg** (1½hr; daily 11:45am, Th-Su 4:35pm; US$225). **British Airways** (☎ 13 20 53) has a special one-way fare to **Johannesburg** (1½hr.; daily 1:45pm; US$104) that can only be bought within Zimbabwe (your travel agent can't do it); call the Vic Falls office for reservations. There is a US$20 airport tax, payable in foreign currency, for international departures. A taxi into town costs US$15. Cheaper flights can sometimes be found from Livingstone, Zambia (see p. 595).

ZIMBABWE

Trains: The **train station** (☎ 43 91) is next to the Victoria Falls Hotel off Livingstone Way across from the Kingdom Hotel. Reservations office open M-F 7am-noon and 2-4pm, Sa-Su 7-10am. Ticket office open M-F 7am-noon and 2-6:15pm, Sa-Su 7-10am and 4:30-6:15pm. To **Bulawayo** (12hr.; daily 6:30pm; 2nd class US$8, 1st class US$10) via **Dete** (US$3/US$5).

Buses: Blue Arrow (☎ 09 655 48 or 22 90 35) stops outside the Shearwater office in Soper's Arcade on Park Way, headed to **Bulawayo** via Express (6hr.; Su, W, and F 9am; US$32) or Local (8hr., daily 8am, US$10); and to **Harare** via Express (14 hr., Su, US$37). **Trans Zambezi Express** (☎ 091 31 28 55) stops outside the post office, headed to **Johannesburg** (M and Sa noon, US$45).

Taxis: Mosi Taxis (☎ 20 87 or 59 54). A taxi from town to the waterfall costs US$1.25.

Car Rental: Transit, 18 Soper's Arcade (☎ 21 09, 47 29, or 58 02), is usually the cheapest. **Europcar** (☎ 45 98; airport ☎ 43 44), in the Sprayview Hotel 1km west of town on Livingstone Way, and at the airport. **Budget** (☎ 22 43), Zambezi Center, 1st fl., on Clark Rd. by Jay's Spar; and at the airport.

◼ ORIENTATION

The town of Victoria Falls, 2km from the waterfall of **Victoria Falls,** wheels and deals along the **A8** from Bulawayo, which becomes **Livingstone Way** in town. Entering town, **Reynard Rd.** heads left at the Sprayview Hotel and leads to dozens of small lodges in a quiet suburb. Continuing straight to the **Wimpy** corner (sadly, the center of town), **Park Way** shoots off to the left just before the railroad tracks. Most of the shops and tour companies are on Park near the corner, housed in the **Phumula Center** and **Soper's Arcade.** Banks, the **train station,** and the **post office** line Livingstone Way, which passes a couple of obscenely lavish hotels before continuing on to the Falls and Zambia.

A FLOOD OF UNWANTED SOLICITATIONS

Before you set foot in central Victoria Falls (particularly the area around Shearwater and Soper's Arcade), be prepared to be harassed by an onslaught of aggressive money-changers, car-watchers, "tour operators," and others looking for ways to separate you from your money. These harassers, mostly young men, are usually persistent and always bad news. *Never* do business with them, no matter how cheap their tour or attractive their rate of exchange; stick to established businesses with physical offices. To shake them, maintain a confident air and pretend like you know exactly what you're doing and where you're headed, even if you haven't got a clue. Pretending not to speak English may also help at times. If the touts really get to be too much, you can relocate to the Zambian side of the Falls, where such nuisances are mercifully absent.

◼ PRACTICAL INFORMATION

Tourist office: The **Backpackers Bazaar** (☎ 46 11 or 58 28; backpack@africaon-line.co.zw), behind Wimpy on Park Way. Disarmingly helpful, they will book tour and travel reservations, and keep tabs on all the specials around town. Open M-Sa 7:30am-5:30pm, Su 7:30am-4pm.

Currency exchange: Bureaux de change line Park Way; shop all of them for the best rates, and remember to get a receipt. Most are open M-F 8:30am-5:30pm, Sa 8:30am-1:30pm. If you need an **ATM, Standard Chartered** (☎ 42 49), on Livingstone by the post office, has one that accepts Visa and Mastercard. Banks are open M-Tu and Th-F 8am-3pm, W 8am-1pm, Sa 8-11:30am.

Pharmacy: Vine Pharmacy (☎33 80 or 011 212 014), in the Kingdom Hotel on Livingstone Way. Open M-F 8am-8pm, Sa 9am-3pm and 6:30-8:30pm, Su 10am-4pm.

Hospital: Dr. Nyoni's Victoria Falls Surgery, 13 West Dr. (☎33 56), off Park Way. Open M-F 9am-5pm, Sa 9am-1pm. In an emergency, call the **Medical Air Rescue Service** (☎46 46).

Internet access and telephones: The **e-World Cyber Cafe,** in the Kingdom Hotel, has reliable connections and a quiet, comfortable atmosphere for US$2 per hr. Open daily 8am-10pm. The **Victoria Falls Cyber Café** (☎46 84) and the **DMZ Internet Village** (☎21 09) are upstairs in Soper's Arcade. The former has a quicker, more reliable connection and higher prices (US$2 for 30min., compared to US$1.15 for 30 glacial minutes at DMZ). The DMZ Internet Village, though, has the best phone rates in town (US$1 per min. to the US). Both open daily 8am-6pm.

Post Office: On Livingstone Way, just past the railroad tracks. *Poste Restante* and **EMS** available. Open M-F 8am-4pm, Sa 8-11:30am.

ACCOMMODATIONS AND CAMPING

With the sharp drop in tourist visits to Victoria Falls, a number of guest lodges are open but empty, leading to a rather lonely and spooky stay. The places listed here have all managed to maintain a loyal following through lean times, preserving their friendly, social atmosphere. All places prefer payment in foreign currency, but accept Zim at the prevailing parallel rate.

Club Shoestrings, 12 West Dr. (☎01 67 or 011 80 07 31; backpack@africaonline.co.zw). Turn left off Park Way just past the Codfather sign and look for the multi-colored wall with the big number "12." A colorful backpackers with a tranquility that is the perfect antidote to tourism overdoses. Huge gated shady yard, self-catering kitchen, social bar, book exchange, and swimming pool by which beer is often tranquilly (or not) consumed until very late. Dorms US$7; doubles with bath US$20. Camping US$3. ❷

Victoria Falls Backpackers, 357 Gibson Rd. (☎22 09). 1km from town. From Park Way, turn left onto West Dr., right onto Soper's Crescent, and then right onto Gibson Rd. Nightly campfires create a familial feel at this pleasant backpackers, where owners Dennis and Marina take care to learn every guest's name. A thoughtful renovation has added a tree-level viewing platform, TV lounge with video library, and hut doubles. Dorm rooms are more like bedrooms, with six beds or fewer. Well kept yard, self-catering kitchen, swimming pool. Dorms US$8; doubles US$10 per person. Camping US$4. ❷

Villa Victoria, 165 Courteney Selous Crescent (☎/fax 43 86; villavic@telcovic.co.zw). From Park Way, turn left onto West St. and right onto Courteney Selous; Villa Victoria is on the right. Owners Tony and Sue make this little guest house the best of the bunch; impeccable rooms with bath US$40 single, US$50 double. Inquire about discounts. Check-in from 8:30am-4:30pm only, unless prior arrangements are made. ❻

Penny Wise Cottages (☎45 55; pwc@mweb.co.zw), is on King's Way. Driving away from Livingstone Way on Reynard Rd., make a right on King's Way and go 100m. Although Penny Wise lacks the welcoming, social feel of the other places, it offers hotel rooms with cable TV, en suite baths, and large closets (but somewhat lumpy beds) for an unreal Z$1500/US$3 per person. Self-catering kitchen, laundry service. ❷

FOOD & NIGHTLIFE

Vic Falls isn't restaurant country; the lack of locals here means most eateries are touristy and expensive. The hungry will do well by eating at lodge buffets, particularly for breakfast, when a big meal can hold you until dinner. **Panarotti's,** in the Kingdom Hotel, has periodic bottomless pizza or pasta nights.

ZIMBABWE

▧ **The Boma** (☎ 32 38), at the Victoria Falls Safari Lodge, off Park Way, 3km from town. Out of town, but worth the trouble at least once. Although every lodge offers a huge buffet, few go to such lengths to offer exotic, traditional, and other non-Continental choices. The amazing African buffet (US$12) includes game starters, campfire soup, a vast salad bar, a spectacular *braai* (including game, beef, pork, and chicken), *potjies*, and desserts. Vegetarian options. Enthusiastic mix of traditional (dance troupe and music) and touristy (do you really deserve a certificate for eating a *mopane* worm?). Open daily 9am-4:30pm and 7-10pm. ❹

The Codfather (☎ 011 214 750), a mere window in an alley off of Park Way next to Phumula Center. Marlon Brando has had men for less than this take-away's great fish'n'chips (US$2) or pizza (US$2.75). Open daily 10am-midnight. Free delivery. ❷

Ilala Lodge Restaurants (☎ 47 38), on Livingstone Way on the Falls side of the railroad. The **Palm Grill** ❷ serves good buffets in lodge fashion, while **Kubika** ❷, next door, serves a Mongolian grill buffet in an open-air patio. Pick beef, lamb, pork, chicken, ostrich, kudu, crocodile, and hake, as well as sauces and veggies, and give it to the chef to fry up for you. Breakfast is less exotic, with an omelette station and fresh pastries. Breakfast buffet US$2.75, dinner buffet US$7. Open daily 7-9:30am, 10:30am-6pm, and 7-9:30pm.

◪ THE FALLS

The entrance to Victoria Falls National Park is 2km from town along either Livingstone Way or a number of footpaths. A path passes by a tiny museum with basic displays on the Falls, before continuing to the statue of a determined David Livingstone. It then runs parallel to the five major Falls that make up Victoria Falls: **Devil's Cataract, Main Falls, Horseshoe Falls, Rainbow Falls,** and the **Eastern Cataract.** At their highest, the Falls are 111m high, and depending on the season, between 500,000 and 9 million liters of water hurtle over their 1.7km wide lip every second. The path ends at slippery spray-soaked **Danger Point,** an unfenced promontory overlooking **The Boiling Pot,** the bottleneck at the cascade's base where all of the Falls' water converges to create the Zambezi's famous rapids. Near Danger Point, a path branches off to the right, ending at a lookout high above the **Victoria Falls bridge** and its bungee activity. The **Cataract View** viewpoint, down a slippery flight of stairs from the Livingstone Statue, is worth visiting for its bewildering view lengthwise down the ravine (especially at sunrise) and for the chance to gaze *up* at the Devil's Cataract. Single-entry admission to the Falls

THE BIG SPLURGE

VICTORIA FALLS HOTEL

On a bluff overlooking the Zambezi gorge and the spray of the Falls beyond stands one of the world's most elegant lodgings: the storied Victoria Falls Hotel. A long-preferred locale for kings, queens, presidents, and sultans, the hotel's guests pay US$348 and up for rooms here. Budget-minded travelers, however, can wash up, don some dressy casual attire, and sample some of the hotel's many luxuries.

Most popular is the **afternoon tea** (Z$1500) served daily on the terrace from 3:30-5pm. After choosing from a selection of fine imported teas, a three-tiered tray is placed on your table with a wide variety of cakes, scones, jams, and finger sandwiches. For lunch and dinner, visitors can enjoy the **Terrace Restaurant** (open daily 12-3pm and 5:30-10pm), which serves artistically prepared ostrich steaks (Z$2000), as well as lighter fare such as *monte cristo* sandwiches (Z$1750). The **Jungle Junction** restaurant (open daily 12-3pm and 7-10pm) offers a buffet for Z$4000 that features starters, grills, curries, exotic specialties such as crocodile tail, and a crepe station for dessert. A third restaurant, the **Livingstone Room,** offers culinary masterpieces and a live orchestra, but requires semi-formal attire (coat and tie for the men).

Still not satisfied? Retire to the sofas in the **Bulawayo Room** (open nightly 5:30-10pm) to sip champagne and smoke a Havana cigar (prices vary).

ADVENTURE COMPANIES IN VICTORIA FALLS AND LIVINGSTONE

Unless noted, all phone numbers are in Victoria Falls, Zimbabwe.

1. **Abseil Zambia,** 215 Mosi-ua-Tunya Rd., Livingstone (in Livingstone ☎321 292; theswing@zamnet.zm). Full-day ropes challenges include unlimited abseiling, high-wire, gorge swings, and rap jumping; half-day tours include a choice of three. Full-day US$95, half-day US$80. Videos US$30.

2. **Adrift Zimbabwe** and **Kandahar Safaris** (☎35 89; fax 013 20 14; adrift@africa-online.co.zw; www.adrift.co.nz), in the old train across Park Way from Soper's Arcade. The only truly international white water rafting operator on the Zambezi, Adrift rafts five other rivers worldwide, but keeps its operation here small and personal. Half-day and full-day US$85; full-day and overnight US$145; 2 days, 2 nights US$290; 6 days, 5 nights US$1000. All-inclusive canoe safaris US$75-415.

3. **Baobab Safaris** (☎/fax 42 83; safaris@telconet.co.zw), on West Dr. Walking safaris US$98-202 per day, canoeing trips US$46-70, village tours US$36-44.

4. **Bundu** (in Livingstone ☎324 407; fax 324 406; zambezi@zamnet.zm; www.africa-insites.com/zambia/bundu.htm), on the Zambian side. Rafting (US$65 half day, US$70 full day), riverboard/raft combo (full day US$95), canoeing (US$65 half day, US$70 full day, US$140 overnight), game drives (3hr., US$30).

5. **Bush Birds Flying Safaris** (☎/fax 22 10; ulazim@samara.co.zw, www.samara.co.zw/ulazim), Soper's Arcade, 2nd fl. Ultralight trips over Victoria Falls (35min., US$100) and game flights (50min., US$170).

6. **Del-Air** (in Livingstone ☎/fax 232 095; delair@zamnet.zm), on gorge on Zambian side. Zambian helicopter company. Call for prices.

7. **Frontiers Adventures** (☎35 87, fax 58 09), in the Phumula Center on Park Way. White water rafting (full-day US$85), riverboarding (half-day US$85, full-day US$115), and flat-water canoeing (half-day US$75, full-day US$95).

8. **Good Memories Cultural Tours and Safaris** (☎33 05; goodmemo@tel-covic.co.zw; http://goodmemo.hypermart.net), Soper's Arcade, 3rd fl. Rural village tour (US$40), Chobe tour (full day, US$140), Zambia tour (full day, US$120), cruises (US$30-35), canoe trips (½ day US$65, full day US$85).

9. **Jet Extreme,** 12 Tanzania Rd. (in Livingstone ☎321 375; fax 321 365). Jetboating. Half-day trips US$60.

10. **Kalambeza Safaris and Lodge** (☎42 93; fax 46 44; kalambez@pci.co.zw). On Park, 75m from Livingstone Way. Cruises (US$25-30), guided village tours (US$40). Also does transfers on request (US$8-50).

11. **Kiwi Extreme** (in Livingstone ☎324 231; fax 324 238; bridge@zamnet.zm). Bungee jumping (US$90 per jump).

12. **Makora Quest** (in Livingstone ☎324 253; fax 320 732; quest@zamnet.zm), in the Adventure Center, Livingstone. Canoe safaris (half-day US$70, full-day US$85).

13. **Raft Extreme** (in Livingstone ☎324 156; fax 324 157; grotto@zamnet.zm; www.zambiatourism.com/raftextreme/), in Zigzag Coffee House (see p. 566) in Livingstone. Zambian rafting company with renowned guides and excellent personalized trips. Full-day rafting trip including three meals (US$95).

14. **Sabonani Safaris** (in Livingstone ☎208 120; rnsinganu@yahoo.com), in Livingstone near Park Way. Elephant safaris. Call for prices.

15. **Safari Par Excellence** (in Livingstone ☎700 707; speres@mweb.co.zw; www.sri-parx.com). Rafting, canoeing, riverboarding. Call for prices. (US$18). Lots of combo packages available.

16. Shearwater (☎ 44 71; fax 43 41; shearadv@shearwater.co.zw; www.shearwateradventures.com), Soper's Arcade, First fl. Huge, impersonal activity company. Really. Rafting (full-day US$85), riverboarding (US$115), helicopters (US$75), microlights (US$75), fixed-wing flights (US$55), ultralights (US$100), tethered balloons (US$25), elephant safaris (half-day US$90), bungee jumps (US$90), horseback riding (US$40), abseiling (half-day US$80, full-day US$95), Zambezi cruises.

17. Southern Africa Touring Services (☎ 58 23; sats@samara.co.zw, www.sats.co.zw), Soper's Arcade, 2nd fl. Chobe day trip US$160, bungi jumping US$90, fixed-wing flight US$65, helicopter flight US$75, half-day game drive US$55, cruises US$25, white-water rafting US$95.

18. Spirit of Africa Adventures (☎ 091 770 077; butternutsafaris@yahoo.co.uk), Soper's Arcade, 2nd fl. Cruises (US$20-35), village tours (US$40).

19. Taita Falcon Lodge and Safaris, (☎/fax 332 1850 or 011 208 387; taita-falcon@zamnet.zm, www.africa-insites.com/zambia/taita). Game drive US$45, sunset cruise US$45, both US$80.

20. Trumpet Safaris and Tours (☎/fax 20 65; trumpsaf@yahoo.com, http://trumpetsafaris.bizland.com), Soper's Arcade, 2nd fl. Rafting (full-day US$85), jet boating (US$135), Chobe day tour (US$115), helicopter flights (US$75-150), microlight flights (US$75), ultralight flights (US$100), fixed-wing flights (US$50-100), cruises (US$20-35), bungi jumps (US$90), elephant rides (US$90), canoeing (half-day US$70, full-day US$85).

21. Ulinda Safari Trails (☎/fax 20 78; ulinda@samara.co.zw). Contact through Backpackers Bazaar. Game drives, safaris. Call for prices.

22. United Air Safaris (☎ 33 83; agricair@samara.co.zw). Fixed-wing and float-planes. Call for prices.

23. Victoria Falls Safari Express (☎ 46 82; fallsexp@mail.pci.co.zw, www.samara.co.zw/victoriaexp). Luxurious adventures aboard a restored steam train across Vic Falls Bridge. Call for prices.

24. Viva Rafting (☎ 42 10; fax 22 64), Soper's Arcade, First fl. Small locally-run rafting company with just 3 boats. Call for prices.

25. Wild Horizons (☎ 20 04, fax 43 49; wildhori@samara.co.zw), next to Backpackers Bazaar. Elephant safaris. Call for prices.

26. Wild Side Tours and Safaris, 131 Mosi-oa-Tunya, Livingstone (☎ 323 726; fax 322 895; wild@zamnet.zm, www.zambiatourism.com/wildside). Sundowner cruises US$35, half-day Zambezi cruise US$50, full-day Zambezi/Chobe cruise US$150.

27. Zambezi Helicopter Safaris (☎ 45 13; fax 58 06; heli@id.co.zw). 13min. flights US$75, 30min. flights US$150.

28. Zambezi Horse Trails (☎ 011 209 115; alison@horsesafari.co.zw), 3km out of Victoria Falls on Park Way. Horse safaris. Call for prices.

is US$20. (Open 6am-6pm. Open late for full moon viewing US$30. Note that the rangers now require entry payment in foreign currency, unless visitors can produce an exchange receipt from a bank (not a *bureau de change*).

There is often quite a crowd at the Falls, but the wealth of lookout points eases the tourist crush. Midday spray often makes viewing problematic, especially during the high water season (Mar.-Sept.), so shoot for the morning and late afternoon. Bring a poncho or raincoat if you don't want to get drenched. Ponchos are for rent inside the gate for US$1. It's worth the missed sleep to arrive at the gate for its 6am opening; this is the one time each day when the Falls, nearly deserted, still feel wild and undiscovered. Zimbabwe is the place to be for the best perspec-

ZIMBABWE

FROM THE ROAD

THE MIGHTY ZAMBEZI

On the day I stepped into a raft to shoot the Zambezi, I found myself sitting opposite a professional rafting guide visiting from West Virginia. Her eyes brimmed with excitement: "Every rapid I've run has always been compared to this. I can't believe I'm finally doing the real thing."

The Zambezi is the celebrity of rivers among those who know, and I soon found out why. Dropping into a rapid known by the guides as "Milky White Buttocks," our boat pitched steeply down into a trough, and then flew through the air as the waves boiled and crashed around us. As we reached a calm section and gasped for breath, our guide nonchalantly remarked, "ah, it's not so exciting this time of the year." Every few minutes, the river boiled into a fury once again and sent our hearts racing.

After surviving ten or so of these gauntlets unscathed, we were all feeling pretty good about ourselves: perhaps this whitewater thing wasn't so hard after all. Then came "Oblivion," a roaring, seething mess that seemed to drop straight down. We smashed head-first into a wave, and before I even felt the sensation of flipping I was deep inside the rapid, my body tossed about like laundry and my eyes frantically seeking the surface of the water. After an eternity (maybe six seconds), my head bobbed above water long enough for a gasp, and then the Zambezi shot me flailing through the tumult and, eventually, into a pool. I flopped back into the raft shaking and newly humbled, like so many before me.

—*Owen Robinson*

tive of the Falls' immensity. For a closer view with less spray (usually), head to Zambia. Your single-entry Zimbabwe visa will still be valid if you don't spend the night in Zambia. For true cheapskates, or those without forex, there is a free view of a small section of the Falls from the Victoria Falls bridge; bring your passport, and tell the Zimbabwean border guards you're only going out onto the bridge.

🏃 ADVENTURES

Victoria Falls is the adventure capital of Southern Africa. The market is extremely competitive, so check around for the latest specials. A US$10 river fee is added to water-based activities in Zimbabwe. There is a 15% sales tax on all activities purchased with cash in Victoria Falls, Zimbabwe, but none on those paid with traveler's checks; bring plenty of the latter. **The numbers appearing after each activity refer to the operator listings on p. 590.**

IN THE ZAMBEZI

WHITE WATER RAFTING. Victoria Falls' first adventure option is white water rafting on the Zambezi below the Falls. It is the wildest raftable river in the world. If your timetable is flexible, try to be here in October. You won't regret it. On the white-water scale of I to VI, with VI being commercially unraftable, the October Zambezi has nine class V rapids. Rapid 5, **Stairway to Heaven,** has the biggest vertical drop of any commercially rafted rapid in the world. Whereas most rafted rivers get their rapids from rocks, the Zambezi is virtually rockless; the channel is too deep nearly everywhere for rocks to enter the rafting experience. This, along with precautions like helmets and safety kayaks, allows lucky novices to raft the Zambezi relatively safely. Even the moderately fit will do all right, at least until day's end, when the walk out of the gorge is 220 vertical meters of pain. In low-water season (Aug.-Jan.), the Zambian companies put in at Rapid 1 and their Zimbabwean counterparts at Rapid 4, but Rapids 1-3 are warm-ups. All companies portage around Rapid 9, "Commercial Suicide," and usually around a series of whirlpools later in the river. During high water (Jan.-Mar., June-July), everyone rafts Rapids 11-23. The river is closed in April and May, when the water is too high. All trips include breakfast and lunch, and the Zambian companies throw in a barbecue dinner. Rafters must be 14 years old or older. You can choose to paddle or let a guide with oars do all the work. **2, 4, 7, 13, 15, 16, 17, 20, 24.**

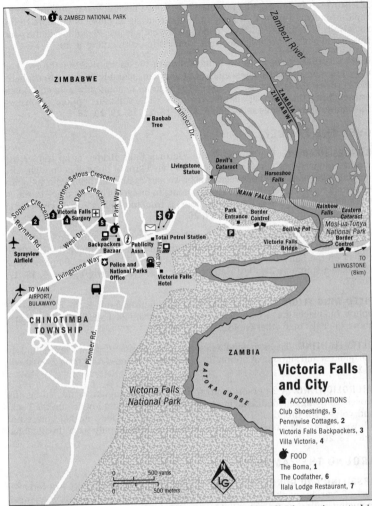

Victoria Falls and City

🏠 ACCOMMODATIONS
Club Shoestrings, **5**
Pennywise Cottages, **2**
Victoria Falls Backpackers, **3**
Villa Victoria, **4**

🍎 FOOD
The Boma, **1**
The Codfather, **6**
Ilala Lodge Restaurant, **7**

RIVERBOARDING. Riverboarding (basically boogie-boarding) was invented in New Zealand in 1989 and is perfect for waves of the Zambezi's rocking rockless rapids. Boarders are outfitted with wet-suits, flippers, and boards. They raft the pools between the rapids and board the rapids themselves. Compared to rafting, riverboarding is more intimidating and more of a rush. It also requires more fitness and is more expensive. Rafting-riverboarding combos are available. **4, 7, 15, 16.**

CANOEING. Canoe safaris run above the Falls, and are the best for spectacular game-viewing opportunities. Participants are able to see and hear animals and birds that might be frightened away by an outboard motor. Most canoe safaris actually use touring kayaks with double-bladed paddles. Some of the safaris shoot some relatively tame white-water above the Falls, as well. **3, 4, 7, 8, 12, 15, 20.**

ZIMBABWE

JET BOATS. Big 9-person jet-powered boats have been uniquely modified to be rapid-friendly. These yellow monsters buzz tourists as close as possible to the rock walls of Rapids 23-25. Since half-day trips include just 40 minutes in the boat, this option might make more sense in combination with rafting. **9, 20.**

BOAT CRUISES. Cruises in the calm waters of the Zambezi above the Falls all offer more or less the same scenery, but vary considerably in their atmosphere. Meal cruises and sunset cruises appeal to the more romantically inclined. "Booze cruises" bring the party set out onto the river, while still other options emphasize the natural surroundings and wildlife. **8, 10, 16, 17, 18, 19, 20, 26.**

OVER THE ZAMBEZI

BUNGEE JUMPING. The jump off the Victoria Falls Bridge is no longer the world's highest, but many would contend that 111m of bungee is enough. The jump is in no-man's-land between Zimbabwe and Zambia, so bring your passport to immigration and tell them you're just going to bungee. The best place to watch the jumpers (who go in groups on the hour) is from the Boiling Pot, down a trail in the Zambian national park. **11, 16, 17, 20.**

HELICOPTER FLIGHTS. Chopper pilots hover over the Falls for the best photo ops, but the noise of the rotors and turbulence of the ride make it difficult to reflect on the Falls' beauty. Typical trips last about 13 minutes; 20-minute trips also take a spin over Zambezi National Park to see (and terrify) game. **6, 16, 17, 20, 27.**

FIXED-WING FLIGHTS. Standard, Cessna-type light aircraft is the cheapest air option, but places the most structure between you and the Falls. It also flies higher above the Falls than other choices. **16, 17, 20, 22.**

ULTRALIGHTING. These specially-designed two-person airplanes are definitely the quietest and smoothest option for photo buffs. Offered only from Zimbabwe. **5, 16, 20.**

MICROLIGHTING. A 2-person contraption with a triangular wing, this is the closest to flying unaided. Imagine a hang-glider with a window fan on the back, and you've got the idea. There's so little structure under you that you're not allowed to bring a camera for balance reasons. Offered only from the Zambian side. **16, 20.**

AROUND THE ZAMBEZI

ABSEILING AND GORGE SWINGING. Ropes activities are usually offered as a sort of "variety pack," taking participants through a multitude of challenges including zipline, gorge swing (swinging off a bridge—far more frightening than bungee), and abseiling: descend the face of the gorge on a rope, then get inched back up. This last activity is widely considered the scariest thing around. **1.**

HORSE SAFARIS. Guided rides wander through nearby game parks, offering many of the standard game-viewing opportunities from a truly different perspective. Some trips are designed for novice riders, while others require some more experience. **16, 28.**

ELEPHANT RIDES. View game parks and surrounding areas from the back of one of these mammoth and elegant beasts. Tours range from 2hr. spins to overnight extravaganzas, and combine traditional game-viewing with plenty of pachyderm interaction and opportunities to learn about the creatures. **14, 16, 20, 25.**

ZIMBABWE

BORDER CROSSING: VICTORIA FALLS-LIVINGSTONE
The Vic Falls-Livingstone border is open from 6am-8pm. **Taxis** from Livingstone to the Zambian border post cost K3000, from Vic Falls to the Zimbabwean border post US$1.25, and between the two posts K2000, though the 1km **walk** is across beautiful Victoria Falls Bridge. The 7km from the border to Livingstone are dangerous, and should not be walked or biked. **Zambian Visas** are US$10 for a day visa, US$25 for a double-entry 30-day visa, and US$40 for a multiple-entry 6-month visa. Australians, New Zealanders, and South Africans are exempt. Both countries require pricey 3rd-party **insurance** for drivers (US$36 in Zimbabwe and US$30 in Zambia), and Zimbabwe further soaks drivers with a carbon tax, based on engine size (about US$10). Those pre-booking an **organized tour** with a Zambian operator get a free 2-week visa. **Jollyboys** offers great "organized tours" including 2 nights accommodation, multiple meals, and transfer to the border for around US$20. Book in Vic Falls 24 hours in advance.

LIVINGSTONE, ZAMBIA   ☎ 03

Initially called Old Drift and situated right on the river, Livingstone was forced to relocate 7km north to its present site because of malaria and blackwater fever. From 1907 to 1935, Livingstone was the capital of various bits of Rhodesia. Notwithstanding Lusaka's present prominence, Livingstone continues to be a friendly gateway to stunning Victoria Falls. The difference between Livingstone and its Zimbabwean sister city is dramatic: it's easy to see why the Vic Falls bridge is often said to be the gateway between Southern and Central Africa. In contrast to the fast-paced, touristy, over-hyped atmosphere across the river, African charm positively oozes from Livingstone's colonial facades and local market. Indian proprietors run many local businesses and curry dishes and *pakoras* are readily available among the city's main road. Tourism seems to be a side presence here, not the city's reason for being. As a result, tourists can stroll the main street without the catcalls of "my friend...change dollars...cheap tours..." With the Zambezi's countless activities nearby, many travelers have found a planned short stay stretching out into "Africa time's" vague eternity.

▛ TRANSPORTATION

Flights: From Livingstone International Airport, **South African Airways** (in Lusaka ☎ 01 254 372) flies to **Johannesburg** (M, W, F, and Su 1:45pm; US$316). **Nationwide Air** (in Jo'burg 011 327 3000; www.flynationwide.co.za) also flies to **Johannesburg** (1½hr.; M, W, F, and Su 1:45pm; US$106 each way). The international departure tax is US$20; the domestic departure tax is US$5.

Trains: The **train station** (☎ 321 001) is on Mosi-oa-Tunya Rd. on the side of town closest to the Falls. TAZARA trains leave to: **Kitwe** (31hr.; M, W, and F 9am; economy US$7.50; standard US$9.25; sleeper US$11.50); **Lusaka** (13½hr.; Su, Tu, Th 4:30pm; US$5.25/US$6.25/US$9.75). To go to **Dar-es-Salaam, Tanzania,** take the Kitwe train to Kapiri Moshi; a train with narrower gauge departs when that train arrives, and continues on (48hr., US$45).

Buses: From the bus terminal across from ShopRite, **Sierra Couriers** (☎ 288 425) sends A/C coaches to **Lusaka** (5hr.; daily 6, 7, 10am, 1pm; US$12), while **EuroAfrica** sends one there for the same price (5hr., daily 9am). African buses also leave frequently for Lusaka (6hr., US$7).

EMBASSIES IN ZAMBIA

United States: PO Box 31617, Independence Avenue, Lusaka. ☎01 228 595.
United Kingdom: PO Box 50050, Independence Avenue, Lusaka. ☎01 251 133.
Canada: 5199 United Nations Avenue, Lusaka. ☎01 250 833.
Mozambique: 46 Mulungushi Village, Kundalile Road, Lusaka. ☎01 290 451.
Malawi: Woodgate House, Cairo Road, Lusaka. ☎01 228 296.
Zimbabwe: Memaco House, Cairo Road, Lusaka. ☎01 229 382.
Botswana: 2647 Haile Selassie Ave., Lusaka. ☎01 250 555.
Namibia: 6968 Kabanga Rd., Rhodes Park, Lusaka. ☎01 252 250.

ZAMBIAN EMBASSIES ABROAD

United States: 2419 Massachusetts Ave. NW, Washington DC 20008. ☎202 265-9717.
United Kingdom: 2 Palace Gate, London, W8 5NG. ☎44 0 20 7589 6655.
Malawi: Convention Drive, Capital City, Lilongwe. ☎782 100.
South Africa: 1159 Ziervogel St., Arcadia, Pretoria. ☎012 326 1847.
Zimbabwe: 6th Floor, Zambia House, Union Ave, PO Box 4698. ☎04 773 777.

 ZAMBIAN TELEPHONES. Country code: 260. International calls are most reliably made from the public telephone offices in cities and towns.

Minibuses: Minibuses leave the bus terminal for the **Zimbabwean border** (10min., frequently all day, US$0.50) and **Kazungula** (1hr., most often in morning, US$1.75).

Taxis: Sky-blue taxis head to the border with Zimbabwe for US$0.85 if someone else is along; they're easiest to find in front of Barclay's. Flagging an empty taxi constitutes a booking and raises the price to US$3.25.

Car Rentals: Livingstone 4x4 Hire (☎320 888; 4x4hire@zamnet.zm) is on Mosi-oa-Tunya near the tourist office.

Bike Rentals: Bikes can be hired at **Jollyboys** and **Fawlty Towers** (see **Accommodations,** p. 597).

⊁🛈 ORIENTATION AND PRACTICAL INFORMATION

Livingstone is 7km north of the border with Zimbabwe. The highway from Victoria Falls turns into **Mosi-oa-Tunya Rd.,** the main street. Coming from Vic Falls, Mosi-oa-Tunya passes the **railroad station** on the right, **tourist office** and **Livingstone Museum** on the left, **post office** and **banks,** also on the left, and **ShopRite,** on the right.

Tourist office (☎321 404; fax 321 487; zntblive@zamnet.zm). Helpful and eager to please. On Mosi-oa-Tunya next to the Livingstone Museum. Open M-F 8am-1pm and 2-5pm, Sa 8am-noon.

Currency exchange: Banks surround the post office, closing early and charging exorbitant commissions. **Barclays Bank** (☎321 114), with Visa **ATM.** Open M-F 8:30am-2:15pm. **Mo Money Bureau de Change** (☎323 43), across the street, is a better option. Cash advances on Visa and Mastercard. Open M-F 8am-5pm, Sa-Su 9am-1pm.

Market: Lively African market with local crafts behind ShopRite. Open daily 7am-4pm.

Police (☎320 888), on Akapelwa St. across the railroad tracks from Mosi-oa-Tunya.

Pharmacy: LM Pharmacy (☎324 486), next to the post office. Open M-F 8am-5:30pm, Sa 8am-1pm, Su 8:30-11:30am.

Hospital: Livingstone General Hospital (☎320 221), on Akapelwa St. uphill from Mosi-oa-Tunya.

Internet access: Cyberpost, next door to Fawlty Towers on Mosi-oa-tunya, charges US$1 per 10min., 50% off after 30min. Open M-F 9am-5pm, Sa-Su 9am-noon.

Post office: Next to the banks on Mosi-oa-Tunya Rd. in the center of town. Open M-F 8am-5pm, Sa 8am-1pm.

▐ ACCOMMODATIONS AND CAMPING

With Zimbabwe's recent trouble, Livingstone's backpacker scene is on the rise. Staying here is a great way to avoid the tourist zoo of Victoria Falls, but has the disadvantage of being beyond walking distance from the Falls.

▨ Jollyboys Backpackers, 559 Mokambe Rd. (☎324 229; jollybs@zamnet.zm). Coming from Victoria Falls on Mosi-oa-Tunya, turn right just after the Total petrol station; Jolly-boys is on the right. The heart of Livingstone's budget travel scene, boys and girls alike get their jollies here. Wonderful staff, self-catering kitchen, swimming pool, ping-pong table, and happening bar. Great package deal (see "Border Crossing," above). Dorms US$6; doubles US$10. Camping US$2. ❷

Papagayo, 56 Mwela St. (☎320 237; papagayo@zamnet.zm). Coming from Zimbabwe, pass the banks and curio-filled park. Turn left on Mwela; Papagayo is at the very top, on a traffic circle. Somewhere between backpacker hostel and upmarket guest lodge, Papagayo's pride and joy are the air-conditioned and tasteful private rooms with desks and en suite baths. Camping facilities are the best in town. The squash court, not surprisingly, is the only one in Livingstone. Swimming pool, bar. Meals available. Kayaks for hire (US$20). Free pick-up from Zimbabwe border. Doubles and 4-bed family room US$15 per person; dorms US$8. Camping US$3. ❷

Fawlty Towers, 215 Mosi-oa-Tunya Rd. (☎323 432). Near the train station. Popular with huge overlander tour groups, who often dominate the place. Swimming pool, bar, restaurant, TV lounge. Doubles with A/C and shared bathroom US$20, with bath US$30; dorms US$10, with A/C US$12. Camping US$5. ❷

▐ FOOD

Zigzag Coffee House (☎324 081), on Mosi-oa-Tunya amidst the banks. A backpacker favorite, with big, overstuffed couches, magazines, sidewalk tables, and heaps of atmosphere. Enormous mugs of coffee US$1. Scrumptious muffins US$0.85, stack of pancakes US$1. Stuffed pitas US$2.50, creative desserts US$1-3. Also doubles as a booking agency. Open M-Sa 8am-5pm. ❶

48 Hrs. Pub and Restaurant, between post office and Barclays on Mosi-oa-Tunya. A popular place preparing hefty servings of pub chow (burgers and mash US$2.25) and Zambian staples like *nshima* (mashed corn US$1.50). Really gets hopping during sporting events. Open daily 8am-11:30pm. ❶

Funky Munky (☎320 120), on Mosi-oa-Tunya near Fawlty Towers. Hip little eatery, if a bit shadowy, specializing in excellent pizza (Zambezi pizza: tuna, onions, and corn US$4). Good shawerma, too (US$2). Open daily 7:30am-9pm. ❷

Utsav Indian Restaurant (☎322 259), on Mosi-oa-Tunya around the corner from Shop-Rite. Utsav's dishes are favorites among the city's large Indian community. Backpackers Special (2 curries, rice, *naan*, drink) US$4.25. Tandoori dishes US$3-5. Open M-Sa 8:30-10:30am, 11:30am-3pm, and 6-9:15pm. ❷

SIGHTS

LIVINGSTONE MUSEUM. This museum, styled after a Spanish mission, has one of the world's best collections of David Livingstone's relics (see p. 523), including the famous explorer's bedside table, next to which he was found dead on his knees. An anthropological room, featuring prehistoric tools and human remains unearthed across Zambia, is fascinating. The museum also houses Kenneth Kaunda's old motorcycle (which the ex-president stops by occasionally to visit) and a large room filled with the wildlife of Zambia in all their stuffed, glass-eyed glory. Try to politely decline the offer of a guide if possible; most guides, though well intentioned, simply read the exhibit labels out loud, one after another. (☎321 204. Next to the tourist office on Mosi-oa-Tunya. US$3, children US$1. Open 9am-4:30pm.)

RAILWAY MUSEUM. This museum is worth a quick visit, particularly if you're a train buff. Zambezi Sawmills at one point had the longest private rail line in the world; the wood used to build the London Stock Exchange rode these rails. In the wake of independence, the process of "Zambianization" led the government to take 52% of all private businesses. This inspired Zambezi Sawmills to close up shop. Since its 1973 abandonment, this stretch of track has been home to old engines and various railroad knicknackery. Most are in various states of disrepair, but the relics give a good sense of the importance of the rails to Livingstone's prosperity. (☎321 820. Follow the tracks 1km left off Mosi-oa-Tunya, from south of the train station. Open daily 8:30am-4:30pm. US$2.75.)

THE FALLS. Zambia's share of one of the natural wonders of the world is 7km from Livingstone. As compared to the more heavily touristed Zimbabwean side of Victoria Falls, the Zambian side of the Falls offers a much closer approach to the colossal cascade. From this side in particular, the Falls will boggle your mind just as surely as they did Dr. Livingstone's (I presume). The precarious **Knife Edge Footbridge** crosses directly in front of the Eastern Cataract on its way to a viewpoint across from Zimbabwe's **Danger Point.** Trails also lead upstream and down into the gorge, to the **Boiling Pot.** In the shadow of Vic Falls bridge, this is the best place to watch bungee jumpers plummet in terror toward the Zambezi. When the water is low enough, hardy (or foolish) visitors rock-scramble along the lip of the Eastern Cataract to **Livingstone Island** and beyond, generating panic and astonishment among the camera-snapping tourists peering across at them from Zimbabwean lookout points. A small exit gate allows visitors to leave the park after closing, and rangers usually don't mind if guests linger to witness the sunset and see the Falls by moonlight; just be sure to ask first. The curio market just opposite the entrance is a good place to acquire certain items not widely available in Zimbabwe: high-quality carvings made of mahogany and other hard woods, common here, are especially difficult to find across the river. (Open daily 6am-6pm. US$10, children US$5.)

UPSTREAM FROM LIVINGSTONE

MOSI-OA-TUNYA NATIONAL PARK

The only ways to see the park are with your own vehicle or through a Livingstone game drive; pedestrians are strictly forbidden. Open daily 6am-6pm. US$3.

Just 1600 fenced hectares along the Zambezi above the Falls, miniscule Mosi-oa-Tunya National Park is nevertheless full of game. The highlight here is the white rhino. There are only five, but one rhino is enough to make your day. Most forays into the park successfully find the rhinos, as well as elephants, giraffes, zebra, and antelope galore—basically everything but cats, which the park is too small to support. Six rhinos were introduced in 1993, and other than one de-horning-related death in 1996, the park's record is impressively unscathed.

JUNGLE JUNCTION

Advance booking required. Book through office at 21 Obote Ave., Livingstone (☎/fax 332 4127; jungle@zamnet.zm; www.junglejunction.net), on the eastern end of town at the corner with Mosi-oa-Tunya.

This private island in the middle of the Zambezi 50km upstream of Victoria Falls is a self-styled paradise. Designed as a "chill zone," this is the perfect place to unwind for a few days, surrounded by the sights and sounds of nature. Hammocks, rope swings, and sand beaches have a do-nothing appeal, while more active visitors can go on canoe trips, game walks, fishing excursions, and visits to nearby villages. Campers, unfortunately, have been booted 11km downstream to a new development on less attractive Bovu Island, leaving the original island to a higher-budget crowd. Still, the slightly hefty price is more than fair, considering the all-inclusive benefits it brings. Reed huts come in three sizes: small (US$75 for first night, US$25 each subsequent night), medium (US$85, US$35), and large (US$95, US$45). All prices include canoe transfers from Livingstone, a range of activities, and meals. Bovu Island, for campers, with a shop and bar, is US$6 per night. Transfers to Bovu cost US$20, and discounts accrue for longer stays. For both islands, pick-ups can be arranged from the Victoria Falls and Kazungula borders.

EASTERN HIGHLANDS

Forming a natural border with neighboring Mozambique, the Eastern Highlands range from the gentle, understated hillocks of northern Nyanga to the sheer faces and cloud-covered peaks of Chimanimani. The mountains provide welcome relief from the flatter terrain that stretches west for thousands of miles to the Atlantic, and feel oddly un-Zimbabwean with their pine forests, Swiss-style chalets, alpine meadows, and mountain goats. At times, only the occasional wandering baboon preserves the sensation of being in Africa.

The mountains have long played a role in the heritage and history of the region. A number of the sites considered to be most sacred by many Shona are located among the heights here, and spiritual significance is accorded to every rock, stream, and wisp of mist. More recently, the highlands have played a crucial role in the Mozambican civil war: guerrilla soldiers from both sides used the caves and forests as staging areas, venturing across the border for quick strikes and quickly returning to Zimbabwe. Up until the recent crash of Zimbabwe's economy, illegal Mozambican migrant workers often trekked across the passes in search of work in Zimbabwe; if Zimbabwe's unemployment rate continues to skyrocket, however, perhaps the flow of job-seekers will begin in the opposite direction.

MUTARE ☎020

Zimbabwe's third largest city has—so far—been spared the worst of the violence and trauma of recent years. Residents brag that their city has comparative peace, balmy weather, and the country's best access to parks and natural beauty. A trip to Chimanimani or Nyanga will almost certainly include a stop in Mutare to stock up on provisions at the supermarket or to change buses or trains. Travelers to or from south and central Mozambique will pass through as well; the crossing to Machipanda is only 9km away.

ZIMBABWE

◖ TRANSPORTATION

Trains: Nightly from the railway station (just south of the bend in Herbert Chitepo St.) to **Harare** (9hr., 9pm, US$5). Tickets generally available at the station at departure, or call **National Railways** (☎ 62801) to book in advance.

Buses and minibuses: The Blue Arrow express bus is managed through Rennie's Travel, on Aerodrome Rd. one block north of Herbert Chitepo St. (☎ 64112. Open M-F 8am-5:30pm.) The bus to Harare leaves from the Holiday Inn, two blocks south of Rennie's (4 hr.; W, F, Su; US$9). Buses to Chimanimani leave from the Sakubva terminal 3km west of the city center (3-4hr., 4-5 per day 7am-noon, US$2). The same buses pass Wengezi Junction, the turnoff point for Bulawayo and areas farther south. The 7am bus to Chimanimani also meets the incoming train from Harare at the central station before departing. Buses and minibuses bound for Juliasdale and Nyanga leave from near the intersection of Avenue D and First St. (3hr., 6-7 per day 7am-4pm, US$2). Minibuses to the Mozambican border leave every half hour from a depot south of Herbert Chitepo St. near Avenue C (20min., US$0.50).

Taxis: Rosewise Taxis covers the rest (☎ 66195; Sakubva from city center US$1).

▓ ORIENTATION

Mutare's main drag, **Herbert Chitepo St.**, runs fairly straight through town, except for a major bend near the **railway station**. Its main cross street is **Robert Mugabe Rd.** Numbered avenues lead northeast and lettered avenues lead southwest parallel to Robert Mugabe. Streets are parallel to Herbert Chitepo with higher numbers further south. The road to Harare crosses **Christmas Pass** 12km from the city center. The **border crossing** to Mozambique (see **Machipanda,** p. 600) is 9km east.

 BORDER CROSSING: MACHIPANDA Until Zimbabwe's export market collapsed, the Machipanda crossing was a major trade route—the beginning of the Beira Corridor, the country's path to the sea. Commercial traffic still trickles through, but queues remain short enough to guarantee passage through both checkpoints in 30 minutes tops. Money changers hover on both sides of the border; the Mozambican side seems to have better rates. Both checkpoints were selling visas as of June 2001, but this may not be permanent. Get your visa before you reach Machipanda if you can. The checkpoints are a few hundred meters apart and, though *Let's Go* does not recommend hitching, travelers frequently find lifts to Mutare or Chimoio.

▐ PRACTICAL INFORMATION

Stores and offices in other Eastern Highlands towns sell all the basics, but only Mutare stocks a full range of international goods and services. Take care of business here if you have special needs.

TOURIST AND FINANCIAL SERVICES

Tourist Office: (☎ 64711; publicity@mutare.icon.co.zw.) On Robert Mugabe. 40m south of Herbert Chitepo St. Shirley can provide any information about Mutare and the Eastern Highlands that this book doesn't provide. Open M-F 8:30am-12:45pm and 2-4pm.

Currency Exchange: Clustered near the tourist office, and inside the lobby of the Holiday Inn. Excellent rates. Exchange money here as it will be more difficult to do so in Chimanimani or Nyanga.

ZIMBABWE

Banks: Standard Chartered at the corner of Herbert Chitepo St. and Aerodrome Rd. **24-hour ATM** on the Cirrus/MC/Plus network, but it exchanges at a highly unfavorable rate.

EMERGENCY AND COMMUNICATIONS

Emergency: Police (☎ 425031/5); **ambulance** (☎ 422002/8708).

Internet: Africa Online cybercafé, at 63/67 Fourth St. Connects clients for US$2 per hour. Open M-F 8am-8pm, Sa 8am-1pm. Another cybercafé is set to open soon on Herbert Chitepo St. just east of Robert Mugabe Rd. US$1 per hr.

DHL: Accepts packages at its office on Herbert Chitepo St., one block west of Aerodrome Rd. 500g of documents to North America for US$16. Open M-F 8am-5pm.

Post Office (☎ 64621). On Robert Mugabe Rd. 600m north of Herbert Chitepo St. *Poste Restante* service available. Open M-F 8am-5pm, Sa 8-11:30am.

■ ACCOMMODATIONS AND CAMPING

⊠ Mrs. Ann Bruce, 99 Fourth St. (☎ 63569). Mrs. Bruce runs a guest house out of her home—or a home out of her guest house; it's hard to tell which. A longtime Mutare resident and incomparable resource on local history and sights, she cooks excellent, cheap homestyle meals and (along with her menagerie of affectionate pets) warmly welcomes backpackers. Beds US$1.25-5, with varying degrees of privacy. ❶

Border Home, 3A Jason Moyo Dr. (☎ 63346). On a side-street off Upper Third St. Campsites are quiet and well-protected by gruff security guards, but lacking in character. Self-catering US$0.40 per person. Camping US$1; dorms US$1.40. ❶

Tracy's Bed and Breakfast, 10 Aerodrome Rd. (☎ 65972). 300m N. of Mutare Museum. Tracy's seems relatively deserted and is good for seeking privacy. Singles US$4.25; doubles US$5.50. ❷

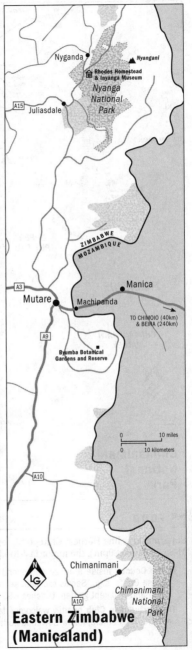

Eastern Zimbabwe (Manicaland)

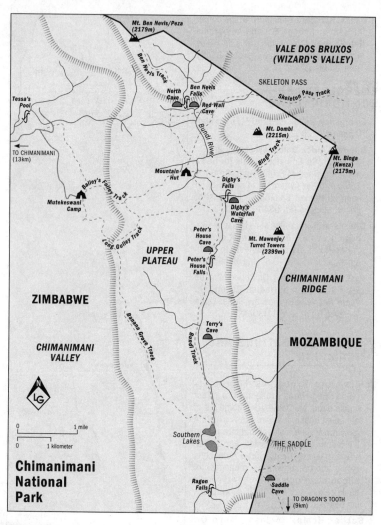

🍽 FOOD

Supermarkets line Herbert Chitepo St., especially near Robert Mugabe Rd. (Open M-Sa 7:30am-6:30pm); the major fast-food chains are also along this stretch.

Green Coucal. Inside a house on Second St. between Eighth and Ninth Ave.; look for "Nyasa Crafts" sign. Serves excellent set-menu lunch. Doubles as a craft shop, cheese store, and well-kept garden. Lunches US$1.50-2.30. Open M-Sa 10am-4:30pm. ❶

The Portuguese Club heartily welcomes Mutare's expats (and others), but it's slightly remote. To get there, follow C Avenue north to the Police Camp, then turn left and follow

Hosgood St. 50m to the Club. Ignore the sign that says "Members Only"; it refers to the now-broken mechanical bull. Steak sandwich US$1. Open 11am-11pm. ❶

Stax. In the First Mutual arcade near First Ave., has good service and prices. Cheese pizza US$1.40. Open daily 7:30am-9pm. ❶

🔆 🎵 SIGHTS AND ENTERTAINMENT

Though natural beauty is easier found outside Mutare than in, the **public gardens** south of the city center offer prime picnicking real estate. Three kilometers east of Mutare, the **Cecil Kop Nature Reserve** hosts forest and animals, but is inaccessible by public transport. **Tiger's Kloof Dam** does draw some pedestrians to witness the evening feedings in the park. (US$1.50.)

The vehicularly-challenged are better off joining a tour of the nearby **Bvumba** and **Nyanga** areas. Contact **UTC,** at the corner of Herbert Chitepo St. and Second Ave., to see if any tours are leaving soon or stop by Mrs. Ann Bruce's (see p. 601) to gather enough people to organize one. (☎ 64784. US$20-40 per person per day.)

The **Mutare Museum,** on Aerodrome Rd. 500m north of Herbert Chitepo St., houses an impressive collection of tractors and Chevys, as well as an informative weapons exhibit, an ethnological and biological display on Manicaland, an aviary (to learn about the birds...), and an apiary (and the bees). Guides may not let you leave if they feel you haven't sufficiently reflected on all the exhibits. (Open M-F 9am-5pm. US$2.) Mutare's other museum receives few visitors. **Utopia House,** on a hill above Jason Moyo Dr., preserves **Kingsley Fairbridge's** turn-of-the-century colonial shack. Fairbridge, famous for building European and Canadian farm schools, lived in Zimbabwe as a child at his father's Gold Belt property. Surveying equipment, household items, and an out-of-tune upright piano are highlights of this unguided, unlabeled museum. (Open daily 6am-6pm.)

Meanwhile, back in the 21st century, you can always catch the latest Schwarzenegger flick at the **cinema** across from the post office. The **Courtauld Theatre,** opposite the cinema, hosts drama and dance on weekends. (Tickets US$0.60-1.15.) Art in the **National Gallery,** at the corner of Third St. and Eleventh Ave., varies widely in quality. For those in the market for Manica stonework or craving more art than Schwarzenegger provides, the National Gallery is a must. (☎ 61000. Open daily 8am-4:30pm. Sculptures from US$0.25. Admission US$0.10.)

MOZAMBIQUE

USD $1 = Mt23,360	Mt100,000 = USD $4.28
AUD $1 = Mt12,848	Mt100,000 = AUD $7.93
CAD $1 = Mt14,974	Mt100,000 = CAD $6.68
EUR €1 = Mt22,892	Mt100,000 = EUR €4.37
GBP £1 = Mt35,974	Mt100,000 = GBP £2.78
BWP P1 = Mt3,737	Mt100,000 = BWP P27
MK10 = Mt3,145	Mt100,000 = MK318
NAD $1 = Mt2,214	Mt100,000 = NAD $45
ZAR R1 = Mt2,214	Mt100,000 = ZAR R45
ZWD Z$1 = Mt427	Mt100,000 = ZWD Z$234

PRICE RANGES. Price ranges, marked by the numbered icons below, are now included in food and accommodation descriptions. They are based on the lowest cost for one person, excluding special deals or prices. In the case of campgrounds, we include the cost of a car. The table below is a guide to how prices and icons match up. **Mozambique has three price ranges.**

SYMBOL	❶	❷	❸
ACCOMM.	US$3-10	US$10-25	US$25 plus
FOOD	US$1-4	US$4-7	US$7 plus

Mozambique is a country in transition—uncertain of its future and recovering from a painful and traumatic past. Since the end of the civil war in 1992, cyclones, droughts, devastating floods, and outbreaks of famine have dealt one setback after another to this unfortunate nation and combined to keep it one of the poorest and least developed corners of the world. For the first time in decades, however, Mozambique is peaceful, optimistic, and planning for development and growth. Budget travelers will need to make do with only the basic trappings of comfort, but those who are willing to make this sacrifice will discover beautiful Indian Ocean beaches, diverse cultures, grand colonial architecture, and immense markets where the entire economy seems to converge in a chaos of colors, noises, and aromas. Although visitors can be daunted by the country's poverty and lack of infrastructure, this underdevelopment can also be thought-provoking and eye-opening, providing sensitive travelers with extraordinary and diverse experiences.

HISTORY

FROM THE IRON AGE TO GREAT ZIMBABWE. Humans have inhabited Mozambique for over 100,000 years. In the third century, pastoral **Bantu** people moved to Mozambique from central Africa. A basic command of agriculture resulted in population expansion and permanent settlements. At the end of the first millennium, settlements composed of stone enclosures, called **zimbabwe**, emerged. As the Bantu and **Afro-Arab (Swahili)** visitors from the North began to uncover gold in the

MOZAMBIQUE

FACTS AND FIGURES

Official Name: Republic of Mozambique

Government: Multiparty Republican Democracy

Capital: Maputo

Land Area: 799,380 sq. km.

Geography: Coastal plain in the South and East; mountains and plateaus in the North and West

Climate: Tropical, with a rainy season Oct.-Mar.

Head of State: Pres. Joachim Chissano

Major Cities: Maputo, Beira, Nampula

Population: approx. 17,000,000

Languages: Portuguese (official), Emakhuwa, Tsonga, Yao, Sena, Shona, Echuwabo, Nyanja, Ronga, Shimaconde, Nyungue, Bitonga, Swahili, Shangana

Religions: Indigenous beliefs 50%; Christian 30%; Muslim 20%

GDP Per Capita: US$220

Major Exports: Prawns, cashews, cotton, citrus, coconuts, timber, electricity

region, these *zimbabwe* civilizations were integrated into the Indian Ocean trade network. Ports sprouted up along the Mozambican coast and rivals contended for trading positions. Bantu groups traded initially within Africa, and later with the Middle East, India, and China. The Iron Age city, **Great Zimbabwe,** controlled the political and economic activities of the region until the 15th century, supporting a population of over 10,000 Bantu-speaking people of the **Shona** culture.

EUROPEAN CONTACT AND COLONIZATION (1498-1960). After Portuguese explorer **Vasco da Gama** rounded the Cape of Good Hope and stopped in Mozambique en route to India in 1498, Europeans intersected the centuries-old Arab-African trade. Da Gama and other Europeans saw the importance of the Mozambican coast in establishing a trade route between Europe and India, and created coastal settlements to restock ships making the long journey. As these ports developed, they were used as bases for extracting gold, ivory, and slaves from the African interior and as launching points for Jesuit missionary expeditions. The Portuguese then established a *prazo* (land grant) system that brutally controlled the people and reduced the political power of their kingdoms. In effect, this system granted virtual ownership of land and labor to European colonists.

The slave trade, merciless droughts, and increasing Portuguese influence combined to weaken the authority of African kingdoms. After slavery was abolished, Portuguese settlers shifted their sights to agriculture and resource extraction, and outright slavery was replaced by wage labor, only a marginal improvement. The nature of Portuguese rule in Mozambique changed dramatically with Portugal's 1926 coup and the subsequent dictatorial rule of **António de Oliveira Salazar.** While Portugal had previously taken a relatively "hands-off" approach to its colonies, the new government now planned the Mozambican economy from Lisbon, and actively recruited Portuguese citizens to settle in Mozambique.

WAR OF INDEPENDENCE (1960-1975). The brutal colonial administration under Salazar combined with the formation of independence movements elsewhere in Africa to fuel the growth of revolutionary groups in Mozambique. In 1960, violence began when Portuguese soldiers killed 600 unarmed Africans who were peacefully demonstrating against burdensome taxes. Two years later, the **Front for the Liberation of Mozambique (*Frente de Libertação de Moçambique,* or Frelimo)** was formed by exiled Mozambicans in Tanzania, and its leaders soon mobilized a guerrilla insurrection. The Portuguese tried unsuccessfully to counter the guerrilla war with a mixture of military force and development programs designed to pacify the discontented population. Fighting dragged on until a 1974 revolution in Portugal, sparked in part by unpopular wars in Mozambique and Angola, toppled Salazar. A peace was negotiated, and Mozambique declared its independence a year later.

CIVIL WAR (1975-1992). The end of Portuguese rule was not the end of Mozambique's crises. The euphoria of victory was short-lived: a shattered country, weak economy, and uneducated population greeted Frelimo's new government. The government instituted significant and radical reforms, including the collectivization of agriculture, the extension of women's rights, and the support for neighboring independence movements in South Africa and Southern Rhodesia (now Zimbabwe), but many of the reforms spurred dissent both from those that claimed they went too far and those who claimed that they didn't go far enough.

During the era of Cold War politics, Frelimo's openly Marxist-Leninist orientation startled the Western Bloc of countries who were concerned with the spread of communism. In addition, white governments in South Africa and Southern Rhodesia, fearful of Frelimo's support for revolution in their own countries, also sought ways to undermine it. As a result, money and weapons flowed into the hands of an anti-Frelimo guerrilla group called *Resistência Nacional Moçambicana,* or **Renamo.** Born in 1980, Renamo waged an all-out war against the Mozambican government. A 1983 drought and famine further weakened the faltering postcolonial regime.

As the war continued and the government's strength dissipated, Frelimo sought to regain support and legitimacy by cutting ties with neighboring revolutionary movements and distancing itself from Marxism-Leninism. The 1984 **Nkomati Accord** ended Frelimo support for the revolutionary African National Congress (ANC) of South Africa, and a **1990 constitution** repudiated Marxism-Leninism and established a **multiparty democracy.** With these developments, as well as the crumbling of the Soviet Empire, foreign interests lost the motivation to finance the Renamo. Starved of arms and money, Renamo quickly lost its ability to continue fighting. A 1992 **peace treaty** solidified the war's end, and led to 1994 **democratic elections**. Frelimo president, **Joachim Chissano,** was narrowly reelected.

TODAY

In the 1990s, a ravaged Mozambique began to rebuild with the help of foreign aid. One of the world's poorest nations, Mozambique struggled to stabilize a shaky government while simultaneously rebuilding infrastructure, removing land mines, and coping with natural disasters. Mozambique's largest barrier to stability is beyond its control: destructive and extreme weather patterns devastate the country with tragic regularity. Most recently, in 2000 and again in 2001, nationwide floods destroyed harvests and roads, and made thousands of Mozambicans homeless.

In addition to the challenges presented by Mother Nature, Mozambique struggles with the challenges of upholding a fledgling democracy. In the December 1999 elections, President Joachim Chissano garnered 52% of the vote. Chissano's closest competitor, **Afonso Dhlakamo** of Renamo, won 48% of the vote in a close race that drew 80% of eligible voters. Challenged as fraudulent by Dhlakamo and Renamo, the election was nevertheless unanimously certified by the Supreme Court.

GOVERNMENT

Only a decade ago, Mozambique's constitution provided for a one-party socialist state under Frelimo leadership, with a *Politburo* and a People's Assembly. Now, Mozambique's popularly elected president is the head of state, and a 250-seat **National Assembly** is elected with a five-year mandate. In the years since Mozambique's governmental transition, initial feelings of optimism about the country's potential have shifted to more guarded hopes that Mozambique's government will go the way of Mandela and Mbeki's South Africa rather than Mugabe's Zimbabwe.

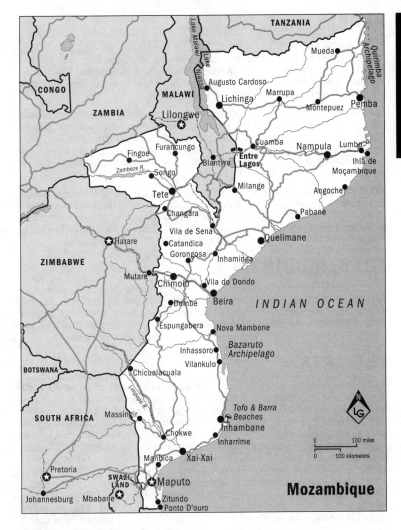

MOZAMBIQUE

Mozambique

ECONOMY

In the 1970s, Mozambique's predominantly agricultural population worked on collective farms under an economic structure that was highly controlled and Marxist. In the late 1980s, under international and domestic pressure, the government began steadily liberalizing its economy. The government has cut subsidies, encouraged investment, privatized over 900 state enterprises, and disbanded collective farms. A promising start (a 10% annual growth rate from 1997 to 1999, one of the highest in the world) preceded a painful fall when the floods of 2000 ravished the infrastructure and destroyed the year's crops. As the country attempts to stand on its feet, it depends heavily on foreign aid and remains one of the world's poorest countries.

MOZAMBIQUE

PEOPLE

POPULATION AND DEMOGRAPHICS. Like its neighbors, Mozambique's arbitrarily created borders encompass many ethnic groups. The largest of Mozambique's 16 major groups are the **Makua, Makonde, Sena, Shanagaan, Chokwe,** and **Manyika.** There are very few non-black Mozambicans, and most of these are native Portuguese (less than 0.5%) or Indian (less than 0.1%).

LANGUAGE. Mozambique's official language is Portuguese, but there are 13 main national languages, many of them Bantu, spoken by the country's diverse population: Emakhuwa, Tsonga, Yao, Sena, Shona, Echuwabo, Nyanja, Ronga, Shimaconde, Nyungue, Bitonga, Swahili, Shangana. Portuguese is spoken by a quarter of the population, usually as a second language. Within the tourist industry, most people speak either Portuguese or English.

RELIGION. Indigenous religions are still practiced by a majority of the population, though early Portuguese missionaries successfully spread **Catholicism** to roughly a quarter of the population. More recently, **Protestant** missions have become active in the northern interior, Maputo, and Inhambane. **Islam** was introduced by Swahili traders in the 14th century and is now practiced by 20% of the population.

FOOD & DRINK

Cornmeal, millet, rice and hot stews are common dishes in Mozambique. Much of the cuisine is influenced by Portuguese traditions, a trend that is particularly evident in cities. Portuguese wine is used both in cooking and as a beverage. Mozambican specialities include fresh seafood (especially prawns), *piri-piri* (chicken with hot pepper relish) and *matapa* (cooked cassava leaves with fixings).

THE ARTS

Mozambique's ethnic and cultural diversity make for rich and varied artistic traditions. The Makonde people in northern Mozambique are famous for their carved wooden masks and sculptures. In the south, Chopi musicians are renowned for their marimba orchestra performances (called *midogo*). While oral poetry, song and story-telling have survived within the indigenous cultures of Mozambique, the written word also become important in the 20th century. Luís Bernardo Honwana, José Craveirinha, and Orlando Mendes are well-known Portuguese-language authors, while Bento Sitoe writes short stories in Tsonga.

Mozambique's most influential visual artist is Malangatana Ngwenya, whose work is internationally celebrated. Born in 1936, Malagatana creates colorful murals and drawings that reflect his indigenous heritage and Mozambique's turbulent history. Instrumental in establishing the Mozambican National Museum of Art and the country's Center for Cultural Studies, he was named an UNESCO goodwill ambassador in 1997.

ESSENTIALS

DOCUMENTS AND FORMALITIES

VISAS

All visitors to Mozambique need a visa. Visas are obtained at embassies in nearby African countries or in various international cities. A visa costs US$20 for one month, single entry, US$30 for three months, $40 for multiple-entry, and US$5 for 7-day transit. You can extend a visa at immigration offices in provincial capitals. The process takes several days.

EMBASSIES AND CONSULATES ABROAD

Malawi: Commercial Bank Building, African Unity Ave., Lilongwe (☎265 784 100 or 784 696; fax 781 342; mozambique@malawi.net). The Blantyre consulate (☎265 643 189), Masauko Chipembere Highway, Nunes Building, next to Maselema Post Office, is open for visas.

South Africa: 252 Jeppe St., Cape York Building, 7th fl., Johannesburg (☎27 01 336 1819; fax 336 9921); Mozambican Consulate, 45 Castle St., 7th fl., Cape Town (☎27 21 26 29 45; fax 26 29 46).

Swaziland: Highlands View, Princess Drive Rd., Mbabane (☎ 268 437 00, fax 436 92).

United Kingdom: 21 Fitzroy Sq., London (☎44 171 383 3800; fax 383 3801).

United States: 1990 M St. NW, Suite 570, Washington, DC 20036 (☎202-293-7146; fax 202-835-0245; embamoc@aol.com; www.embamoc-usa.org).

Zambia: 9592 Kacha Rd., Northhead, Lusaka (☎260 1 220 333 or 239 135; fax 220 345; mozhclsk@zamnet.zm).

Zimbabwe: 152 Herbert Chitepo Ave., Harare (☎ 263 4 790 837; fax 732 898).

EMBASSIES AND CONSULATES IN MAPUTO

Australia: 95 Ave. Zedequias Manganhela, 2nd fl. (☎422 780; fax 307 369; stephens@mail.tropical.co.za).

Canada: 1128 Ave. Julius Nyerere. (☎492 623; fax 492 667).

Malawi: 75 Ave. Kenneth Kaunda (☎491 468, fax 490 224).

South Africa: 41 Ave. Eduardo Mondlane (☎491 614; fax 493 029).

Swaziland: 608 Ave. de Zimbabwe 608 (☎492 451; fax 492 117).

UK: 310 Ave. Vladimir Lenine (☎ 420 111; fax 421 666).

US: 193 Ave. Kenneth Kaunda (☎492 797 or 491 916; fax 490 448; consularmaputo@state.gov).

Zambia: 1286 Ave. Kenneth Kaunda (☎492 452 or 491 893).

Zimbabwe: 1623 Ave. Martires da Machava (☎490 404; fax 490 492).

CURRENCY AND EXCHANGE

The currency unit is the metical (Mt, plural meticais). Get used to carrying around bills in large quantities; Mt100,000 in your pocket makes you feel richer than you are. Keep US dollars or South African rand handy when outside of Maputo. (In southern Mozambique, you can often use South African rand for purchases.) Banks charge high commissions (sometimes as much as 10%) for changing money, especially traveler's checks, which are difficult to exchange outside of Maputo anyway. You can save money by changing currency at private bureaus or in supermarkets. You can rarely use credit cards outside Maputo. All prices in *Let's Go* are listed in US dollars. Visitors are expected to pay with Mozambican meticais.

HEALTH AND SAFETY

MALARIA. Malaria is worse in Mozambique than in other countries in the region. Bring a mosquito net, insect repellent, and malaria medicine if you are planning on traveling in Mozambique. (See **Health,** p. 19.)

MOZAMBIQUE

 LAND MINES. Mozambique's civil war has many lasting effects; one of these is the presence of over million landmines still scattered throughout the countryside. Although most mines are far away from tourist destinations, and some minefields are marked, travelers should exercise common sense. **Never walk or drive on unmarked paths, and avoid wandering through open fields.**

EMERGENCY. Maputo: ☎425 031 or 425 035 (police), ☎422 002 (ambulance). **Beira:** ☎213 094 (police), ☎325 055 (hospital). **Nampula:** ☎425 031 or 425 035 (police), ☎213 001 (hospital).

TRANSPORTATION

BY AIR. Most international flights go to Maputo or Beira and travel through South Africa. The national airline is **Linhas Aereas de Moçambique (LAM)** (☎465 810; fax 421 091; reservas@lam.co.mz; www.lam.co.mz). Other regional airlines that service Mozambique include **South African Airways** (☎420 740 or 420 742; fax 422 481; www.flysaa.com), **Air Zimbabwe** (☎423 302; fax 303 696; www.airzimbabwe.com), **Metavia Airlines** (☎465 487). Major international airlines that fly from Europe and the US include **TAP Air Portugal** (☎303 927, US: (800) 221 7370, UK: 0207 630 0746; reservas@tap.pt; www.tap-airportugal.pt). Expect to pay US$1400 to fly from New York to Maputo or US$800 to fly from London to Maputo. To save money, fly to Johannesburg and continue by air or land from Johannesburg to Maputo. Remember to save US$20 for international flights and US$10 for continental flights (in US dollars or South African rand) to pay the airport departure tax. See **Maputo: Transportation** (p. 613) for locations, prices, and destinations for regional flights.

BY TRAIN. Trains in Mozambique are sporadic and slow, with tracks ravaged by weather and war. **Portos e Caminhos de Ferro de Moçambique EP (CFM)** does, however, have domestic and regional train routes (☎431 269). A May 2002 train crash killed two hundred passengers, the worst train accident in the country's history.

BY BUS AND MINIBUS TAXI. Buses servicing Mozambique include **Intercape/ Tropical Air** (☎27 21 380 4400 in Cape Town; www.intercape.co.za), and the amenity-packed **Panthera Azul** (☎494 238; South Africa: ☎27 11 333 4249). **Minibus taxis** or *chapa-cems* **(transport trucks)** are the most common means of transport.

BY CAR. Foreigners must pay a visitors' tax of US$5 or R12 entering Mozambique. Drivers pay more (as much as US$35 or R70)—and prices vary at border crossings. Drivers are also charged US$35 or R85 for insurance. (Make sure you get a receipt, passport stamps, and forms for all payments made at border crossings.) Driving can be hazardous because of robbery and erratic drivers. If traveling by car outside of Maputo, get updates on the safety of your route. Rental companies in Mozambique include: **Avis** (☎465 497 or 465 498; fax 494 498; www.avis.com), **Emauto** (☎422 506; fax 426 045), **Europcar** (☎497 338; fax 465 634; www.europcar.com), **Hertz** (☎465 534; fax 426 077; www.hertz.com), **Iberica** (☎422 341 or 300 531), and **Imperial** (☎493 545; www.imperial.ih.co.za).

BY THUMB. *Let's Go* does not recommend hitchhiking. Hitchiking is, however, common in Mozambique, and there is an etiquette: travelers form a line, wait their turn, and pay the driver approximately the bus fare to their destination. Locals wait on the side of the highway near town or at petrol stations and border posts.

KEEPING IN TOUCH

TELEPHONES. Country code: 258. **Pre-paid telephone cards,** available at kiosks and post offices, are used to make international calls. Many travelers find it cheaper and much more reliable to arrange in advance for others to call them at a predetermined number in Mozambique (a hostel, for example).

MAIL. Most letters to the US or Europe take a couple of weeks, but as with most countries in Southern Africa, the success rate for letters is inconsistent. Your letter stands a good chance of reaching its designated recipient if you mail it from Maputo, but chances are slimmer from smaller cities or towns.

INTERNET. Most cities have Internet access, usually for US$3-12 per hr.

TIME DIFFERENCE. Mozambique is on Greenwich Mean Time plus two hours (the same as South Africa). Mozambique does not observe daylight savings.

HIGHLIGHTS OF MOZAMBIQUE

Ilha de Moçambique (Mozambique Island, see p. 631) is an outpost of living history, with 500-year-old homes and forts once inhabited by Portuguese spice traders.

Bazaruto Archipelago (see p. 623), though pricey, combines coral reefs, unspoiled beaches, and palm tree-covered islands in the middle of the turquoise Indian Ocean.

Pemba (see p. 635) offers diving, snorkeling and cultural riches off the beaten track.

HOLIDAYS & FESTIVALS

DATE	NATIONAL HOLIDAY
January 1	New Year's Day
February 3	Heroes' Day
April 7	Women's Day
May 1	International Workers' Day
June 25	Independence Day
September 7	Victory Day
September 25	Revolution and Armed Forces Day
December 25	Christmas (Family Day)

ADDITIONAL RESOURCES

Mozambique: A Country Study, ed. Harold D. Nelson. Foreign Area Studies, American University, 1985.

A History of Mozambique, Mayln Newitt. Indiana University Press, 1993 (US$30).

Complicated War: The Harrowing of Mozambique, William Finnegan. University of California Press, 1993.

The Economist, www.viewswire.com. Up-to-date information on Mozambique's economy. By subscribing online, you can gain access to the Mozambique home page. The annual **Mozambique: Country Profile** can also be purchased for a steep US$215.

SOUTHERN MOZAMBIQUE

Though much of Southern Mozambique is within 150km of South Africa, life here is a world apart. By crossing a border, travelers move from the ordered, European-ized world of a regional superpower to the dirt roads, thatched huts, and street markets of a nation struggling to get by. Though Mozambique is squarely within Southern Africa, travelers may feel transported to West or Central Africa. The south's cities and towns provide opportunities to explore this experience in depth, absorbing the sights, sounds, and realities while reflecting on the palatial, white-washed buildings that stand as eerie monuments to a would-be empire that has long since vanished. For water-lovers, Mozambique is also the only place in South-ern Africa with true tropical beaches. Those in search of warm sun, palm trees, and white sand won't be disappointed here.

MAPUTO ☎01

Mozambique's capital and largest city has a fairy-tale history. Just a decade ago, civil war and African socialism had ravaged Maputo, leaving it crime-ridden and bereft of infrastructure. Peace and privatization have been the city's Prince Charming: today's Maputo boasts modern supermarkets, an energetic cultural scene, and safe, palm-lined boulevards. The markets have been restocked with crafts, vegetables, and traditional remedies; streetside *pastelarias* (small pastry cafes) and restaurants provide meals with ingredients not available ten years ago. From the seaside Avenida Marginal, one can look over Maputo Bay, where the Portuguese explorer Lourenço Marques landed in 1548. After independence, Samora Machel, Mozambique's first president, changed the city's name from "Lourenço Marques" to "Maputo," the name of an early chieftain who fought the Portuguese. Though Maputo was spared the worst of the fighting in the civil war, its economy and people suffered acutely, and its subsequent recovery has been a small miracle.

Security in Maputo is relatively good, although muggers lurk near the beach. If you walk around the city at night, your greatest worry should be the holes in the rotting sidewalks. Nevertheless, take basic precautions to ward off robbers: stay alert, dress down, and for God's sake, hide that camera.

PROVE YOUR IDENTITY. Mozambican law requires you to carry identifi-cation at all times. In practice, this means Maputo cops will pull you aside to demand your *documentos* or *identificação* once every few days. Corrupt police have exploited their power to snatch passports from tourists' hands, then insist on payment for their return. Never pay—instead, offer to accompany the cops to their station so you can call your embassy. Notify the embassy duty officer of their badge numbers, and be civil but confident. To avoid the shakedown alto-gether, you can go to your embassy immediately on arrival in Maputo to request a notarized copy of your passport; police must accept the copy in lieu of the orig-inal, which you should leave somewhere safe. Police have also been known to pull aside motorists and demand exorbitant on-the-spot fines for traffic violations that may or may not have actually occurred. Drive carefully and have your docu-ments in order; if you do get pulled over, calmly negotiate and don't lose your cool. If you do show your passport, maintain a firm grip so any attempt to snatch it will result in a brief tug-of-war, which you will win.

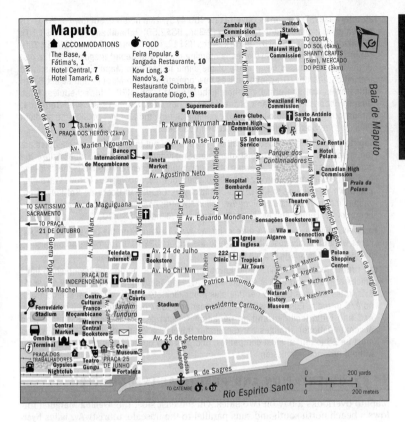

Maputo

🏠 ACCOMMODATIONS

The Base, **4**
Fátima's, **1**
Hotel Central, **7**
Hotel Tamariz, **6**

🍴 FOOD

Feira Popular, **8**
Jangada Restaurante, **10**
Kow Long, **3**
Nando's, **2**
Restaurante Coimbra, **5**
Restaurante Diogo, **9**

Baia de Maputo

Zambia High Commission
Kenneth Kaunda
United States
Malawi High Commission
TO COSTA DO SOL (6km), SHANTY CRAFTS (5km), MERCADO DO PEIXE (3km)

Av. de Accodos de Lusaka

Av. Kim II Sung

Swaziland High Commission

Supermercado O Vosso
Aero Clube
Santo António da Polana
TO (3.5km) & PRAÇA DOS HERÓIS (2km)
R. Kwame Nkrumah
Zimbabwe High Commission

Av. Marien Ngouambi
Av. Mao Tse-Tung
US Information Service
Parque dos Continuadores
Car Rental
Hotel Polana

Banco Internacional de Moçambicano
Janeta Market
Canadian High Commission

Av. Agostinho Neto
Hospital Bombarda
Praia da Polana

Av. Salvador Allende
Av. Tomas Nduda
Av. Julius Nyerere

TO SANTISSIMO SACRAMENTO
Av. da Maguiguana
Xenon Theatre

TO PRAÇA 21 DE OUTUBRO
Av. Eduardo Mondlane
Sensações Bookstore

Av. Vladimir Lenine
Av. Amilcar Cabral
Vila Algarve
Connection Time

Av. Karl Marx
Igreja Inglesa
Polana Shopping Center

Teledata Internet
Av. 24 de Julho
Bookstore
222 Clinic
Tropical Air Tours

Av. da Marginal
R. Jose Mateus
R. de Argelia

PRAÇA DE INDEPENDÊNCIA
Cathedral
Av. Ho Chi Min
Patrice Lumumba
R. M.S. Muthemba

Josina Machel
Tennis Courts
Natural History Museum
R. de Nachinwea

Centro Cultural Franco-Moçambicano
Jardim Tunduro
Stadium
Presidente Carmona

Ferroviário Stadium

Central Market
Minerva Central Bookstore

Omnibus Terminal
Av. 25 de Setembro

PRAÇA DOS TRABALHADORES
Coin Museum
R. de Obadias Muianga

Gypsies Nightclub
Teatro Gungu
PRAÇA 25 DE JUNHO
Fortaleza
R. de Sagres

TO CATEMBE
Rio Espírito Santo

0   200 yards
0   200 meters

▮ TRANSPORTATION

Flights: Maputo International Airport (☎465 828, ext. 216), 3km northwest of the city. **South African Airways** (☎27 11 722 2480; www.flysaa.com) flies to **Johannesburg** (1hr., 1-2 per day, US$120) and **Durban** (1hr., M-F 1 per day, US$130). Mozambique's airline, **LAM** (☎465 810; www.lam.co.mz), flies to: **Beira** (1hr., 2-4 per day, US$150); **Lichinga** (4hr.; Tu, Th; US$240); **Nampula** (3hr., 1-2 per day, US$235); **Pemba** (4hr., 1 per day, US$260); **Quelimane** (2hr., 1 per day, US$260); **Tete** (1½hr.; M, W, F; US$195). International departures include: **Dar-es-Salaam** (6hr.; Tu, Th, Sa; US$365); **Harare** (3hr.; Th, Su; US$230); **Johannesburg** (1hr., 1-2 per day except Sa, US$140); **Lisbon** (10hr., M-Sa, US$1200). 40% discount for passengers under 25. 50% discount for those over 60. Regional departure tax US$10. International departure tax US$10.

Trains: Maputo's railway station (☎431 269), next to the Praça dos Trabalhadores, serves trains headed daily to the South African border at **Komatipoort** (7hr.; 7:55am, 11am, 6:10pm; US$3), the Swazi border at **Goba** (4hr., 8:15am and 6pm, US$0.40), and the Zimbabwean border south of **Chimanimani** (22hr.; W only, 8am; US$2.50). Connection to **Johannesburg** at Komatipoort costs R125, although at the time of writing, a June 2002 train accident had suspended service.

MOZAMBIQUE

Intercity buses: Transportes Oliveiras (☎400 475), 2km northwest of town at Praça 16 de Junho, runs buses north to: **Xai-Xai** (2-3hr., US$2.50); **Inhambane** (6hr., US$3.10); **Vilankulo** (12hr., US$5.10); **Beira** (24hr., US$12.75); **Chimoio** (30hr., US$16); **Tete** (48hr., US$18). Buses leave in early morning hours, and depart irregularly for the rest of the day. **Minibuses** cover many of the same routes from Maputo's Benfica suburb throughout the day. **Greyhound** buses now operate between Maputo and select South Africa cities; call the office in Johannesburg (☎011 249 8900) for schedules. **Minibuses** *(chapas)* cover many of the same routes from Maputo's suburb, **Benfica,** throughout the day. You can also take minibuses from the terminal outside the stadium (see map) to **South Africa** and **Swaziland** (US$9-12).

Maputo buses: Regular buses ply all the main roads, but their routes and schedules are too chaotic for a passing tourist to master. Small minibuses called *chapas* follow the same paths and provide somewhat of an adventure; passengers often include chickens and women returning from market with bushels of fruits and veggies in tow. Wave *chapas* down by pointing to the road in front of you. *Chapas* to **Costa do Sol** leave from various major intersections along Av. Julius Nyerere; *chapas* to **Benfica** leave from the corner of Av. Lenine and Av. Eduardo Mondlane. All rides US$0.20.

Taxis: Av. Julius Nyerere, Av. 24 de Julho, Av. Mao Tse-tung, and the *baixa* all have taxis. Fares within the city cost US$2.50-4; to the airport US$5-10. There are no meters, so make sure to negotiate a price beforehand.

Car rental: Avis (☎494 473) and **Europcar** (☎497 338; europcar@virconn.com) have offices at the airport and at the corner of Av. Mao Tse-Tung and Av. Julius Nyerere. At Avis, rates begin at US$46 per day plus a per-kilometer fee for a compact vehicle with no A/C or radio. Europcar is slightly cheaper at US$57 per day for a small car with the A/C and radio included and no per-kilometer charge. The owner of **Fatima's** (see Accommodations) arranges car rentals for travelers a discounted rate (US$45). You must be 25 to rent at most companies, and cars may not be taken out of Mozambique without advance permission.

■ 🛈 ORIENTATION AND PRACTICAL INFORMATION

Maputo overlooks a bay on two sides. On the east side, the **Avenida Marginal** follows a beach north-south and runs parallel to the upscale, touristy **Av. Julius Nyerere.** Maputo's port is on the south coast; the downtown area, or *baixa,* is here as well. Av. Kenneth Kaunda, lined with embassies, cuts through the north part of town, and **Catembe,** the village south across the water, is a short ferry ride away.

TOURIST, FINANCIAL, AND LOCAL SERVICES

The **Public Information Bureau,** at the corner of Av. Eduardo Mondlane and Av. Francisco Magumbwe, has postcards and academic monographs on Mozambique. Mainly for scholars. Open M-F 7am-3:30pm, Sa 8am-2pm. For maps and guides, you're better off at Sensações (see below).

Tours and Travel Agent: Tropical Air Tours, 909 Av. 24 de Julho (☎425 078; tropical@teledata.mz). Books tours to all points north. English-speaking staff. Open M-Sa 9am-5pm. Backpackers' hostels (see **The Base** and **Fatima's,** below) can also arrange day trips from Maputo and are the best places to go for budget options.

Currency Exchange and ATM: The private exchange bureaux, on Av. Mao Tse-Tung near the Av. Julius Nyerere intersection, offer good rates and charge 5% commission for traveler's checks. On of these, **Mundo de Câmbios** (☎449 995), allows you to draw money off of a Visa for a 5% commission. The **ATM** opposite the Polana Shopping Complex at the corner of Av. 24 de Julho and Av. Julius Nyerere and any of the banks in the *baixa* area will also allow you to do this. Most will charge US$5-10 commission.

Western Union: Banco Comercial de Moçambique, Av. 24 de Julho #1016 (☎420 465). Open M-F 7:45am-3:30pm.

Bookstores and Music: Sensações (☎497 465), next door to Mundo's on Av. Eduardo Mondlane at Av. Julius Nyerere, carries books, maps and guidebooks of the city, and current periodicals. Open M, W, F 3pm-9pm, T and Th 9am-3pm. **Livraria Escolar Editora** (☎302 469; livescolar@pcimoz.com), on Av. 24 de Julho, 100m east of Av. Lenine, has a better selection of English literature and helpful, English-speaking staff. Open daily 9am-7pm. For books in Portuguese, try **Minerva Central** (☎422 092) in the *baixa* area, 1 block east of the main police station on Rua Consiglieri Pedroso. Open M-F 8am-12:30pm and 2pm-7:30pm, S 8am-1pm. MC, V.

Hash House Harriers: Everyone's favorite "drinking club with a running problem" meets twice per week: once for running and beer, and once for, well, beer. Formed by British soldier Albert Stephen Ignatius Gispert in the 1930s, the global hash movement has since grown to 1500 clubs. Maputo's is *the* place to mingle with expats. Meetings at the Aero Clube de Moçambique on Av. Kwame Nkrumah. Sa 3pm for running, W 8pm for drinking only. US$3.10. For more info on hashers worldwide: www.gthhh.com.

EMERGENCY AND COMMUNICATIONS

Emergency: Dial ☎119 or 112 from any pay phone.

Police: The head station in the *baixa* is on Rua do Bagamoyo just west of Praça 25 de Junho. If you are robbed and need to file a report, your best bet is to talk first to your hotel manager, then your embassy. For emergencies, dial ☎119 or 112 from any pay phone, or call the main police line (☎422 001 or 422 002).

Pharmacy: Farmácia Calendula (☎497 606), Av. Mao Tse-Tung, next to Nando's (see Food). Modern facility with medications as well as a full selection of European fragrances and beauty products. Open daily 9am-8pm.

Hospital: 222 Clinic (☎082 319 207 for emergencies, or 431 736), Av. 24 de Julho, at Rua do Com. Augusto Cardoso. Arranges malaria tests and provides 24hr. emergency care. The **Swedish doctor** (☎082 300 261) speaks English, makes house calls and handles 24hr. emergency cases.

Telephones: For local calls, look for yellow **"Telefone Pública"** signs. US$0.10 per call. Buy a **telephone card** *(cartão telefónica)* to make international calls from any pay phone in Maputo. To Europe and North America, expect to pay at least US$4 for the first 3min. and far more in frustration with the Portuguese-speaking operators. For cheaper rates and less of a headache, try **Telecomunicações de Moçambique** (☎425 394), on 24 de Junho one block east of Rua Francisco Malange, where 3min. to Europe or North America costs US$3. The friendly manager allows incoming calls for free.

Internet: Teledata Mozambique (☎302 580), Av. 24 de Julho at Av. Lenine. US$3.10 per hour. Open M-F 7:30am-8pm, Sa 9am-6pm. **Connection Time Cyber Cafe,** upstairs from Mundo's at the corner of Av. Mau Tse-Tung and Av. Julius Nyerere (☎499 147), is cheaper at US$2.75 per hr. Open M-F 8am-9pm, Sa 8am-7pm, Su 11am-7pm.

Post Office: Av. 25 de Setembro 1/2 block east of Av. Samora Machel. *Poste Restante.* Expect 1-2 weeks delivery to Europe and North America. Letters US$0.90. Open M-Sa 8am-noon and 2-7pm.

Couriers: DHL, 1622 Av. 25 de Setembro (☎307 290).

ACCOMMODATIONS

Maputo's once dry market for budget accommodation, parched even more after the civil war and recent flooding, has recently started to flourish. While still more expensive than other African capitals, the quality and quantity of budget accommodations has risen.

MOZAMBIQUE

Fátima's, 1317 Av. Mao Tse-Tung (☎302 994; fatima@virconn.com). Just west of Av. Lenine and Janeta Market. Maputo's long-standing backpacker haunt and the place to come to meet travelers heading to or coming from the north. Rooms are basic, but lively owner Fátima and her Mozambican lieutenants provide incomparable service and traveling advice. Dorms US$3.30; doubles US$13. ❶

The Base (☎302 723; thebasebp@yahoo.co.uk), Av. Patrice Lumumba, at Av. Salvador Allende. Warm staff and sterile white rooms give this place the atmosphere of a friendly dentist's office. Quiet location on a street lined with fading colonial villas. Stunning view of Maputo's harbor. Kitchen. Free pick-up within city. Dorms US$5; doubles US$16. ❶

Costa do Sol (☎450 115; rcs@teledata.mz), on Av. Marginal, 5km north of the city. To get there, take any *chapa* headed north on Av. Julius Nyerere. Spacious rooms with TV, phone, and private bathroom adjacent to the popular restaurant of the same name. The friendly Greek owners speak English and offer the best accommodation in town for the price. Continental Breakfast included. Singles US$25; doubles US$46. MC/V. ❸

Hotel Ibis (☎352 200; www.ibishotel.com), near the intersection of Av. 25 de Setembro and Av. Karl Marx. An international chain with a brand-spanking new Maputo location. A bit of a splurge for the budgeteer, but modern, sparkling-clean rooms with all the amenities are a steal at US$48 for singles/doubles (US$38 on weekends). Continental breakfast included. Breakfast buffet on weekends US$4. MC/V. ❸

Hotel Tamariz (☎422 596), on Rua Consizleri Pedroso, just east of Av. Karl Marx. It's worth tolerating the kitschy, mirror-lined interior for a clean room (most with private bath) in the center of the *baixa* area. Singles US$20; doubles US$25 with continental breakfast included. MC/V. ❷

Hotel Central (☎309 254), south of the Old Mosque on Rua da Mesquita. Murals line the walls and drumming from the nearby national dance academy wafts through the breezy corridors. Though tranquil by day, the area blooms to rowdiness at night, especially on weekends. Rooms with unattached bath are tidy and pleasant. Singles US$7.75; doubles US$15.50. ❶

Parque de Campismo, on Av. Marginal, 1km out of town. Remote site and ratty grounds make camping in Maputo a lousy deal. US$10 per person. ❷

🍴 FOOD

Maputo's restaurants are the highlight of the city and offer a melange of Portuguese, Indian and local flavors. The country's staples include *xima* (a corn flour paste, usually mixed with vegetables and spices) and *matapa* (a mix of cassava, coconut milk, peanuts, and fixings), though you won't find these dishes in most restaurants. Egg sandwiches sold at markets will tide you over for breakfast and between meals (US$0.25), or stop at a *pastelaria* for small pastries (US$0.15-0.50). **Supermercado Novo** on Av. 24 de Julho and **Supermercado O Vosso** on Av. Amilcar Cabrad, north of Av. Mao Tse-Tung, sell Western brands at Western prices.

Costa do Sol, on Av. Marginal 5km northeast of the city center. Prawns leap from the sea into fishing boats for the honor of being grilled on the Costa's coals. During the civil war, the Costa was the only restaurant in Maputo that stayed in operation and has since gained legendary status. Lovely beachfront location and Art Deco building. Grilled shrimp US$9, cocktails US$2.50; the cafe next door has pastries and ice cream from US$2. Open daily 11am-11pm. Cafe open daily from 7am-11pm. V/MC. ❸

Feira Popular, on Av. 25 de Setembro near the waterfront. The fairgrounds draw a combination of local, expat, and tourist clientele eager for Maputo's choicest cuisine, which is served up in restaurants and bars alongside a dusty ferris wheel and bumper cars. **Escorpião** ❶ (☎302 180), the most expensive spot, does seafood and Portuguese

MOZAMBIQUE

dishes. Grilled calamari US$4. **O Coqueiro** serves cheap, delicious Mozambican fare; **Lua** is the ranking Chinese spot. For the best cheap meal, head to **Farhan's ❶** (☎302 600), where half a chicken and fries costs a mere US$1.25. Some restaurants are open from 10am, but the place won't get properly thumping with activity until 8 or 9pm.

Restaurante Diogo (☎082 390 840), on the Catembe beachfront. From the ferry, turn left and walk 1km. Prawns (US$3) and calamari (US$2.80), grilled and fried, are the specialties of this low-key establishment where modest surroundings meet spectacular city views. Open daily 7am-9pm. ❶

Jangada (☎082 317 673), 2 steps east of the boat landing at Catembe. High ceilings and high prices greet visitors to the newest of the town's restaurants, known for live jazz on Saturday afternoons and prawn curry (US$7). Grilled cod US$6. The owner arranges daily boat tours of the harbor for US$45 including lunch, leaving from the Maputo ferry at 10am. Call for reservations. Open daily 9am-midnight, closed M. MC/V. ❷

Kow Long (☎495 216), on Av. Julius Nyerere north of Av. 24 de Julho. Maputo's best Chinese joint does take-away. Beef chow mein US$3.10. Open daily 11am-11pm. ❶

Restaurante Coimbra (☎430 719), opposite the stadium on Av. Romão Farinha. Built in the 1950s, this popular luncheonette serves lobster with garlic butter (US$8) and various dishes from northern Portugal. The shady patio overlooks the street, which is safest by day. Open daily 11am-10pm. ❸

Nando's and Pizza Inn (☎490 099), on Av. Mao Tse-Tung, 700m west of Av. Julius Nyerere. Bad American rock music accompanies cheap fast food and take-away: hamburgers, pizza, fries, ice cream, gizzards. US$3-7. Open daily 6am-midnight. MC/V. ❷

🖸 SIGHTS

BAIXA (DOWNTOWN). Near the port and adjacent to the Praça 25 de Junho stands a small red stone **fortaleza** (fort), Maputo's oldest and best-kept landmark. The Dutch built the original fort in 1720, but subsequent occupations and invasions by the English and Portuguese have left it in smouldering ashes several times since. Today its ramparts are 10m tall at their highest point; the structure houses a tiny historical museum and art exhibition, as well as bronze statues of various commanders. *(Open Tu-Su 9am-noon, 2-5pm; closed Friday afternoons.)* A short walk west on Rua da Consiglieri Pedroso leads to Maputo's oldest **mesquita** (mosque) near the corner of Rua da Mesquita and Av. 25 de Setembro, a crumbling white structure built around 1800. *(Open daily noon-sunset.)* Farther west is the large **Praça dos Trabalhadores** (Workers' Square) featuring a large statue built in memory of soldiers in World War I. The figure is of a warrior-woman draped with a snake she killed after it terrorized her village. Gustave Eiffel designed the mint-green **train station,** built in 1910, on the west side of the square, not long after designing a little-known tower somewhere in Europe. The station houses models of the first four- and ten-wheeled cars to leave Maputo for surrounding towns.

PRAÇA DA INDEPENDÊNCIA. Independence Square, north of the *baixa*, is surrounded by sights of political, religious, and architectural import. Overlooking the wiry metal statue in the center of the square is the **Câmara Municipal (City Hall),** a neoclassical structure erected by architecturally homesick Portuguese colonists in 1945. Next door is the blocky white **Cathedral de Nossa Senhor da Conceição,** which appears to have been built during a cube sale at the Poured Concrete Wholesale Shop. Its huge barrel vault is deteriorating, but the bas relief on the inside is worth a look. **Jardim Tunduru,** the botanical gardens southeast of the cathedral, attracts wedding parties on weekends; you'll hear celebratory singing if you stick around long enough. The **Café da Radio Moçambique,** at the corner of Av.

Lenine and Av. Patrice Lumumba, overlooks public **tennis courts** in the center of the gardens. (☎427 027. *US$3 per hour. Open daily 6am-8pm.*) One block west is the **Centro Cultural Mocambicano,** a colorful complex where one can enjoy live music and French films. The **Tribunal** is at the gardens' east edge and is Maputo's sole example of Dutch architecture. On the opposite side, at Av. Lenine, is **Casa de Ferro (Iron House),** a notorious architectural folly perpetrated by Eiffel in 1892. At great expense, builders brought steel from the Belgian Congo to construct a governor's residence. Only after completion did they notice that steel would rust in the salty, wet air of Maputo. In 1910 the home became an orphanage; now it houses museum offices. Next door is a statue of Samora Machel, first president of Mozambique.

OTHER SIGHTS. Vila Algarve has some of the best colonial architecture in Maputo. The Portuguese tortured and executed political prisoners there. The structure is now decrepit and rotten. *(At the corner of Av. Ahmed Sekou Touré and Av. Mártires de Machava. Interior closed for renovations.)* Maputo's second major church, the **Igreja de Santo António Polana,** built in 1962, looks like an enormous concrete orange-juicer. Blame Portuguese architect António Geddes for this monstrosity. *(On Av. Zimbabwe.)* Mozambique's most famous mural is at the **Praça dos Heróis Moçambicanos (Heroes' Square).** The 100m long collaborative effort may not be photographed. *(2km northwest of the city on Av. Acordos de Lusaka.)* **Catembe,** across the bay from Maputo, is a quiet dusty town. It's worth a look if you want to see rural Mozambique but haven't got the time to head farther north. *(Ferries take 10 minutes and leave every half-hour from Maputo port, 6am-midnight. US$0.20)*

🏛 MUSEUMS

Museums aren't fastidious about providing English translations of exhibits, but you can probably figure out what's going on.

Museu Nacional da Arte, 1233 Av. Ho Chi Minh. Paintings and wood sculptures by Mozambican artists. Small selection of books and postcards. Open Tu-Su 3-7pm. Free.

Museu da Moeda (☎420 290), at Praça 25 de Junho. This building, shaped and painted like a gold ingot, houses an exhaustive collection of Mozambican coins and bills. Enjoy. Open M-Sa 9am-noon and 2-5pm, Su 2-5pm, closed F 2-5. US$0.10.

Museu da Revoluçao, 3003 Av. 24 de Julho. Four floors packed with memorabilia from Mozambique's war for independence. Highlights include original correspondence between revolutionaries, jungle-rusted artillery, and Psych 101 textbooks from Liberation Front President Edouardo Mondlane's frat-boy days at Oberlin College, USA. Open Su-F 9am-noon and 2-6pm. US$0.75.

Museu da História Natural, on the Praça da Travessia do Zambezi. The city's location for stuffed mammals and beasts floating in jars. A fine introduction to Mozambique's fauna. The gorgeous gothic structure was renovated in 2000. Open Tu-Su 9-11:30am and 2-4pm. US$2.60; Su US$0.50.

Museu da Geologia, at the corner of Av. 24 de Julho and Av. Mártires de Machava. Strictly for rock hounds. Excellent displays of Mozambican rocks and minerals, including a relief map and pitchblende. Open Tu-F 3-6pm. Free.

🛍 MARKETS AND SHOPPING

Maputo has many markets, some quaint, some sprawling. Crafts markets focus on Mozambican woodwork. Most markets are open 7am to 6pm, Monday to Saturday; some open Sunday morning.

Mercado Xipamanine, 1km northwest of the city. Take *chapas* from Av. Mao Tse-Tung or from the Catembe ferry landing. A gargantuan spread of exotica. Ask around to find the witch-doctors' area (*secção dos curandeiros*), where magi sell all sorts of mysterious curative potions and powders: hen's beaks, hippo feet, spices, Ortho-Novum, and much more. Watch for pickpockets.

Mercado do Artesanato, on Praça 25 de Junho. Artists and their dealers hawk statuary, batik, and wire figurines. Increasingly touristy, but still a good venue. Bargain hard, as vendors quote high prices initially. Sa mornings only. Other places to buy crafts include **Av. Julius Nyerere** outside Hotel Polana and at its intersection with Av. 24 de Julho.

Shantycrafts (☎450 305; fion@tropical.co.mz), on Av. Marginal near the Costa do Sol. An excellent shop selling jewelry, clothing, and Mozambican handicrafts run by a Canadian expat and his pet heron. Open daily 10am-6pm. MC/V.

Mercado do Peixe (Fish Market), on Av. Marginal, 2km past the camping park. Take *chapas* from Av. Julius Nyerere to get there. Fishermen show up throughout the day to drop off buckets of still-slithering fish and prawns. Don't wear clothes you care about. Restaurants nearby.

🎵 🎭 ENTERTAINMENT AND NIGHTLIFE

Most travelers to Maputo come with visions of a city in perpetual *festa* mode, expecting to hear music on every street. While Mozambicans like to party, the town is quiet on most weeknights. When they do go out, however, the locals dance until sunrise. For more mellow evenings, look out for *bares* scattered around town; they provide the best venue for drinking locally brewed 2M and Laurentina beers and meeting Mozambicans. It's a good idea to check *Notícias* (the local newspaper) for listings and concert info.

Centro Cultural Franco-Moçambicano (☎420 786), opposite the Cathedral on Av. Patrice Lumumba. The French sponsor the best local cultural center, offering Internet access and a library, cafe, and concert area. Call ahead for schedules of African dance, music, and international cinema shows. Entry is free.

Charlot, on Av. Eduardo Mondlane, west of Av. Romão Farinha towards the Alto Maé part of town. Shows Bollywood films from India.

Xenon, on Av. Julius Nyerere just north of Av. Eduardo Mondlane. Maputo's best movie theatre. Entry US$3.

Gungu, on Av. Mástures de Inhaminga, near the Praça 25 de Junho. A theater committed to socially aware drama. Shows are in Portuguese, but English speakers can usually follow along without much difficulty. US$0.50-5. Open F-Su.

Gaivota, 2km north on Av. Marginal at the Maritime Club. Beachside dining and live Brazilian *bossa nova* music in the summertime. US$1 to enter, or included with dinner. Head to **Minigolf,** a nearby discotheque, afterwards for dancing. US$4.

Gypsies, in the *baixa* area on Av. Mártires de Inhaminga, is a popular bar with South Africans in the late evenings. Be prepared to pay Western prices. Gets crowded around midnight on F and Sa. Open 10pm-2am. Most head to **Luzo's,** the strip club next door, after getting sufficiently drunk.

Africa Bar, on Av. 24 de Julho between Av. Karl Marx and Av. Olof Palme, is the place to go for live jazz and African music and serves a mostly expatriate clientele. Best on Th nights. Entry US$2.50 for concerts.

Discoteca Tara, on Av. Marginal, 4km from the city center. An outdoor club with African, pop, and rave music. Great place to meet Mozambicans. US$2.75. Women get in free after 11:30pm. Open 10pm-6am.

Sanzala, near the Feira, plays African and salsa dance music and packs in locals on weekends. US$2.50. Open Th-Su 10pm-sunrise.

XAI-XAI ☎22

Xai-Xai's beaches have little to recommend them and are tough to get to without a car. Still, the town's proximity to Maputo and relaxed atmosphere make it a convenient stop for travelers heading north to Inhambane or Vilankulo. The town's tourist infrastructure was devastated by the 2000 floods, as evidenced by the countless crumbling and abandoned hotels lining the streets. Accommodations and food are generally overpriced and are likely to stay that way for the next few years.

▉▊ ORIENTATION AND PRACTICAL INFORMATION. Along the EN1 heading north from Maputo, the Banco Internacional de Moçambique (BIM) office on the right side of the street charges a 1% commission on Visa card advances and is usually packed in the mornings. (☎22966. Open M-F 8am-3pm.) Banco Austral, 1.5km north along the same road in a dusty old building, does Visa and Mastercard advances for the same price. (☎26334. Open M-F 8am-3pm.) The red and white post office, one block west from the BIM building, is currently under renovation but operates from a temporary location behind the construction. (Fax 22314. Open M-F 7:30am-5pm, Sa 7:30am-noon.) The Transportes Oliveiras bus station is 2km north of the BIM on the left side of the road. Oliveiras express buses leave twice every day for Maputo (2-3hr., US$2.85) and Inhambane (4hr., US$3.25). Buses depart around 5:30am and 1pm. Braver souls can head to the minibus stand 2km south of the Oliveiras stand on the main road, where minibuses depart when full for Maputo, Inhambane, and in-between destinations throughout the day. The beach, Praia de Xai-Xai, is 10 km east of town. *Chapas* (US$0.20) run regularly along this route, which ends 0.5km uphill from the beach at a small traffic circle.

▐▐ ACCOMMODATIONS AND FOOD. Budget options for lodging at Xai-Xai beach are few and far between. The **Xai-Xai Camping and Caravan Park ❶,** known locally as Campismo de Xai-Xai, is at the north end of the main strip of beach and has spartan accommodation with unattached bath in a pleasant campground (ZAR130). The **restaurant ❷** does grilled seafood, by far the best value on the beach. You can have spicy prawns or fish dishes with chips and salad (US$5; open daily 10am-10pm). During South African holidays in December, the place gets packed with trailers heading north. (☎35022; fax 35016. Diving and fishing can be arranged; call in advance for rates and schedules. 2- or 4-bed bungalows ZAR260. Camping ZAR40 per person; ZAR20 per caravan plus SAR40 per person.) **Complexo Halley ❷** is the mid-range two-storey hotel next door. The hotel's **restaurant ❷** is on a breezy veranda and serves calamari and fish dishes for US$5. (☎35003. Singles US$20; doubles with TV and attached bath with hot water US$25; suites US$30. V.) **Restaurante Golfinho Azul ❶,** 800m south of the camping park, specializes in mediocre chicken and seafood but has recently branched out to provide mediocre accommodation as well. Inquire at the restaurant and you will be provided a guide to bring you on foot 3km north of the camping ground to the wooden buildings of the Golfinho Azul. (Spartan rooms in nonelectrified shacks US$5.25 per person.) The **Miau Miau Discoteca,** off the main road 3km east of the bus station, is the town's weekend hangout spot and plays a mix of local and international music. The party starts around 11pm and goes strong until dawn (US$1).

INHAMBANE   ☎023

The declining global demand for elephant tusks and slaves has transformed Inhambane from a thriving port city to a quiet and relaxed seaside town. The second-oldest municipality in Mozambique (after Ilha de Moçambique), it figured prominently in Portuguese colonists' commercial schemes from Vasco da Gama's landing in 1498 until the 1950s, when overland travel to Maputo became feasible. Vestiges of its former prominence remain in the city's wide avenues, its 18th-century church, fading colonial-era architecture (especially near the jetty), and a small slavery monument. Inhambane's political prominence has waned, although it is still the capital of the province bearing the same name. For travelers, its main attractions are easy-to-navigate streets lined with murals and old buildings, a good selection of restaurants, and the town's relaxed atmosphere. Nearby **Tofo and Barra beaches,** renowned for crystal-clear water and abundant marine life, are the first decent budget-oriented strips of sand on the Mozambican coast north of Maputo.

■ ⚠ ORIENTATION AND PRACTICAL INFORMATION. The city borders a shallow bay on its north and east edges. The main **pier** and waterfront are on the east edge. A central **market,** 800m southwest of the pier on **Avenida da Revolução,** doubles as a **bus stand** and town center. Avenida da Revolução meets **Avenida da Independência** at a rotary, which stands in front of the old, disused railway station. **Transportes Oliveiras** and **TSL buses** leave from the central market to Maputo (6hr., daily 5:30am, US$3.75). For other long-distance destinations, head first by **dhow** to Maxixe (every 15min., 6am-sunset, US$0.20). More buses depart from the bus stand there. Be careful at low tide: dhows can get beached on sandbars, turning a 20min. trip into an afternoon at sea. Dhows leave from the pier on the eastern waterfront; from here, one can also arrange dhow transport to **Linga Linga** (US$4), a remote peninsula north of Maxixe. Allow 2-3hr. each way. **Banco Austral** (☎20256), on Av. da Independência, has an **ATM** machine for Visa withdrawals. (Visa advances US$5. Open M-F 7:45am-3pm.) **Banco International de Moçambique** (☎20251), on Av. Acordos de Lusaka opposite Maçaroca restaurant, provides the same services, **Western Union** money transfers, and currency exchange. (Open M-F 8am-3pm.) About 500m south of the pier on the waterfront and next door to the main secondary school is the town's **library,** housing a number of old Portuguese texts. (Open M-F 8am-5pm.) The **pharmacy** on Av. da Independência has basics; for anything serious, head for Maputo. (Open daily 8am-5pm.) The **Telecomunicações de Moçambique** is opposite the pier in a grandiose yellow-and-white building. (Open M-F 7:30am-5pm.) The **EPCI Internet café,** next to the library, allows clients to send and receive international faxes (US$0.30 per minute) and has scanner and photocopier access. (☎21138; cpepci@teledata.mz. US$3 per hr. Open M-F 8am-8pm, Sa-Su 9am-1pm.) The **post office,** south of the rotary, offers EMS express mail service. (☎20494; fax 20956. Open M-F 7:30am-noon, 2-6pm.)

▐ ▐ ACCOMMODATIONS AND FOOD. Pensão Pachiça ❶, on Rua 3 de Fevereiro along the waterfront, is the only backpackers' in Inhambane. Camping is more affordable than the dorm, although you'll have to pitch your tent on a tiny patch of lawn opposite the popular bar and pizza joint. (☎20565; inhambane@africanmail.com. Dorm beds US$4.50; private rooms US$10 per person. Camping US$4.) The other budget option, the **Escola Ferroviária de Moçambique ❶** at the train station, has clean and comfortable rooms open to the public, but its sterile rooms and manicured lawns give it an institutional feel. (☎20712. US$5.25 per person.) Food options abound. **A Maçaroca ❷,** on Av. Acordos de Lusaka one block south of Av. da Independência, is owned by a friendly Swiss-Mozambican couple and serves the best cuisine in town. (☎20489. Prawn curry US$5, omelettes US$2.

Open M-Sa 8am-11pm.) **Tijamu ❶,** at the base of the pier, is the place to party on Friday and Saturday nights and is an equally popular restaurant by day, particularly for those on a budget. The menu includes hamburgers (US$1) and half-chicken and salad (US$3). (☎20408. US$0.80 cover after 10pm. Open M-Sa 7am-11pm; Su 10am-10pm.) **Bar Prancha,** next door to Pensão Pachiça, plays hip-hop and is a good place to meet locals. (Open Tu-Su 3pm-midnight.)

◪ TOFO AND BARRA BEACHES.

The beaches near Inhambane win top honors in Mozambique for their friendliness to budget travelers and idyllic setting in a white-sand, palm-fringed paradise. **Tofo,** the more accessible of the two, has a number of accommodation options for backpackers and a good dive shop. For luxurious rooms at a price, **Hotel Marinhos ❸,** just opposite the *chapa* drop-off and central market, has clean rooms with private bath and TV and can arrange special rates for groups of 12 or more. (☎29015. Breakfast included. Singles US$30; doubles US$55.) Less expensive options are numerous. An expat couple have built a well-known campsite and hut complex called **Bamboozi Backpackers' ❶,** by far the most popular lodge in Tofo. To get there, you'll have to walk about 25min. north along the beach. Leave your luggage at the dive shop near the Tofo drop-off point; Bamboozi staff will drive to collect it later. The bar/restaurant sits prettily on a veranda atop a sand dune and is worth a visit. (www.moztravel.co.za; bamboozi@teledata.mz. Dorms US$4. Camping US$3. Sixth night free.) **Campismo de Tofo ❶,** 200m west along the beach and run by Fatima's in Maputo, is the cheapest option. Individual huts with spectacular ocean views are a steal, but you'll have to endure cold bucket showers in communal bathrooms. The buffet-style dinner is the cheapest in town; all-you-can-eat seafood and salad is only US$4. (Huts US$3. Camping US$1, $2 to borrow a tent.) **Nordin's ❶,** a 5min. walk north of the drop-off, has a different atmosphere, but it has clean, comfortable dorms and doubles. Its location lacks Bamboozi's seclusion but shares its gorgeous view. (Dorms US$4.50; doubles US$12.00.) Aside from in-house options at all the lodges, there are only a handful of restaurants. The best by far is **Restaurante Albatroz ❶** (☎29005), a few steps up a hill from Dino's Bar. Friendly staff serve up heaping portions of chicken, beef, calamari, and even *boerewors* (Afrikaner sausage) for US$3.50-6. The view of Tofo and neighboring Tofinho is not to be missed. **Dino's Bar ❶,** at the east end of the beachfront, is home to nightly beach bonfires and a range of creative cocktails (including the "White African" with Amarula, Kahlua, and vodka). It also serves grilled sandwiches (US$1.50) and fish dishes (US$3). (Open daily from 10am until the last man leaves; closed W.) **Diversity,** in the bright yellow building next to the Restaurante Ferriário, is a PADI scuba center offering a full range of services. Packages of four dives cost US$105 (equipment included) for licensed divers; wannabes can take the open water course (US$160), including four nights accommodation at a nearby lodge. (☎29002; info@diversityscuba.com. Open daily 9am-6pm. Group discounts available.)

Barra beach has recently become much more developed for tourism. To get to either beach from Inhambane, some travelers catch a truck from the central market (every hr., 6am-6pm, US$0.25). At the Cruzamento de Josina Machel, the road forks in front of Zimbabwean-owned **Bar Barbalaza ❶,** specializing in crab curry (US$3) and cold beers. (☎083 897442. Open daily 6am-1am.) At the fork, the trucks will head to Tofo. It's harder to find vehicles heading along the branch toward Barra. A more reliable way to go to Barra is to spend a night at one of the lodges in Tofo or Inhamnae, all of which can arrange transport for guests. Prices vary; call in advance for pick-ups. In any case, the trek is worth the effort: Barra boasts the most spectacular beaches in the region and its lodges cheaply offer many amenities. The **Barra Lodge Beach Resort ❶** is touristy but offers the best deal for backpackers; tidy dorms with hot showers cost a mere US$5.50 in the low season (Jan.-

Nov.) and US$7.50 in the high season (Dec.). Camping is US$4-6 per person. Diving, fishing, horseback riding, and quad bike riding are just a few of the activities one can indulge in at Barra. Prices are lower than at any of the northern resorts. (☎20561; barralodge@teledata.mz.) Two hundred meters further down the main road is **Barra Reef ❶**, smaller and quieter than its more commercialized cousin. Still, amenities are excellent. The campground has hot showers and power outlets, and the bar/restaurant overlooking the sea is recommended even by Barra Lodge staff. Inquire about trips to Linga Linga nature reserve and diving/snorkeling. (☎20864; mozbarrareef@hotmail.com. Camping US$3.)

MAXIXE ☎023

Inhambane's twin across the bay functions mostly as a transit hub for travelers heading up the coast. It draws no one with its drab and concrete-themed waterfront, and its streets hold zero historical interest.

⬛🄙 ORIENTATION AND PRACTICAL INFORMATION. Dhows bound for **Inhambane** leave from Maxixe's only pier (every 20min., 6am-sunset, US$0.20). Ascend the hill from the pier and in 300m you'll be at the **bus stand;** 300m farther is the central market. A **Banco Comercial de Moçambique** is between the pier and the bus stand. (Open M-Sa 7:30am-5pm.) Express buses leave Maxixe for Maputo (6hr., 5:30am and 1pm, US$1), Vilankulo (5hr., 5am and 1pm, US$3.60), and Beira (15hr., 6am, US$10.20). Slow buses heading in both directions depart every 30min. throughout the day. Opposite the Don Carlos restaurant and behind the bus stand is the town's small **post office.** (open M-F 8am-5pm).

🄵🄲 ACCOMMODATIONS AND FOOD. Tight security and clean grounds make **Maxixe Camping ❶**, next to the pier, the most welcoming of the city's few accommodation options. (☎30351. Doubles US$30; caravans US$2.50-8, depending on size. Camping US$3 per person.) The tentless should consider **Pousada de Maxixe** (☎30780; singles US$5.25; doubles US$8.25; triples US$9.25), opposite the pier, or the nearly identical **Hotel Golfinho Azul ❶** next door (☎30071; doubles US$7.75-10.25). Food options are also limited. Cheap Mozambican-style *piri-piri* chicken (US$3) and an oceanfront location make **Stop Snack Bar ❶** the town favorite. (Located at the end of the pier on the right. ☎30025. 10am-11pm daily.)

VILANKULO AND THE BAZARUTO ARCHIPELAGO ☎023

For snorkeling, sailing, and sun-drenched laziness, no destination in Mozambique matches Vilankulo and the Bazaruto Archipelago. The blue waters and diverse marine life put the archipelago in a league with the Maldives and Andaman Islands, the most beautiful and best-known resorts of the Indian Ocean. Several top-end hotels and lodges have developed the five main islands of the archipelago, but they have succeeded in keeping their structures discreet. Quiet, untarnished beaches are not hard to find, and if you're looking for hot Mozambican sand, you're unlikely to come across a better location. Vilankulo, the mainland town across the bay from the islands, serves as a transportation hub and center for tourist services, and as an accommodation spot for those unwilling to empty their pockets at the overpriced Bazaruto lodges.

The best time to visit the archipelago, if you wish to have the best budget travel experience possible, is 1997. In the last few years, territorial luxury resorts have slowly bought up land, edged out campers and backpackers, and gentrified the islands beyond the last notch on a shoestring traveler's money belt. The right to pitch a tent at Benguerra Island's one basic campsite will cost about as much as a double room on the mainland; a single room at the island's resort costs a minimum SAR400. Unless more budget options appear—and this is very unlikely—travelers on the cheap will be confined mostly to the main land (or to the comparably beautiful beaches of Tofo and Barra farther south).

■♦ ⑦ **ORIENTATION AND PRACTICAL INFORMATION.** Oliveiras and TSL buses drop passengers at the **station** a few hundred metres north of the roundabout in the center of town. *Chapas* run often along this main road, which meets the **Central Market** at its south end and stretches 2km north to the beach road. The **airport,** 3km west of the town center, serves the jet-setting crowd of the expensive hotels and lodges. **LAM** flies to Maputo (W, F, Su; US$100) and Beira (W, F; US$60). Call the central reservations office in Maputo to book flights (☎01 465810; www.lam.co.mz). A more reliable option is TTA, a new service run by South African Airways, with regular flights to Johannesburg. (☎011 973 3649 in South Africa; tta@icon.co.za. US$170 one-way; T and Th flights depart from Vilankulo at 2pm.) **Transportes Oliveiras** runs buses to Maputo (US$5.25) and Beira (US$6.25) every morning at 5am. Expect a 12hr. journey in either direction. Slower buses leave from the bus stand near the central market. There are no express buses, except to Maputo, so count on significant travel time. From the market, a perpendicular path leads west to the beach and to **Baobab Beach;** the **SEA Supermarket** is on the right side of this road and carries a good selection of food and toiletries—stock up here before visiting the islands. (Open M-F 9am-7pm, Sa 9am-2pm.) Just north of Baobab along the beach, a friendly South African named Margie Toens offers a range of tourist services and information on Vilankulo from her home on weekday afternoons. To get there, ask any local child for the **casa de Margarita.** (☎82228; margie@teledata.mz.) Another path 200m down the main road from the market leads to the yellow **Telecomunicações de Mocambique (TDM)** office. (☎82701. International calls US$1-5 for first 3min.) Everything else is along the main road. The **police station** (☎82011), **post office** (open M-F 7:30am-4:30pm, Sa 7:30am-12:30pm), and **hospital** (☎82062), where malaria tests are available, are all near or after the roundabout, as is a small **Banco Austral** branch. (☎82289. Open M-F 8am-3pm. Visa advances.) **Banco Internacional de Moçambique,** past Na Sombra at the north end of town, cashes traveler's checks for a US$20 fee. (☎82081. Open M-F 8am-3pm.) Parallel to the main road, a dirt vehicle path runs along the waterfront and curves east at Vilankulo's small **pier** and the abandoned **Hotel Dona Ana,** a tribute to the unfortunate architecture of the 1960s. A few kilometers further east is a cluster of upscale accommodation, including the **Águia Negra** (Black Eagle) **Lodge.**

▐╷▐╷ **ACCOMMODATIONS AND FOOD.** The Belgian-run **Na Sombra ❶** hotel and restaurant cooks an impossibly luscious peanut chicken-curry, some of the finest cuisine in Mozambique. Local food is less than US$6 per person and should not be missed. The seven rooms have shared bath and no view, but they are clean and secure. To get there, walk to the north end of the main road. (☎82090; nasombra@go.to. Singles and doubles US$9.50-20.) For a beach experience, the cheapest and most popular option is the new **Baobab Beach ❶** backpackers, 1km west of the Central Market on a dirt road. There are grand plans, but for now Baobab is just a very friendly, laid-back campground with a bar, shower, and hammocks. Stop by here to meet other budget travelers and organize shared transport to the archipelago. Dhows can be arranged for US$10 per person return, including snorkeling at Two Mile Reef. (☎82202; 2baker@bushmail.net. Dorms US$5.25; camping US$3.) A less lively coast is available out the front gate of the tiny **Casa Josef e Tina,** on the waterfront road 600m north of the market. All rooms are hut doubles (US$12). The

camping park ❶, 500m farther north, lacks a functional fence and should be avoided unless you bring your own security guard and pit bull (camping US$3.75). Other than Na Sombra, dining in Vilankulo distinguishes itself in no way whatever. **Bar Ti-Zé ❶,** near the central market, serves decent fish and is the best place to meet locals. (Fish US$2.50-3.10. Open daily 9am-11pm.) The **Tropical ❶,** between Casa Josef e Tina and the campground, has some of the better seafood and chicken in Vilankulo. The location is fantastic, but service is painfully slow and the attached *discoteca* is usually deserted, possibly because of excessive playtime devoted to Bart Simpson CDs. (Half-chicken US$3.10. Open daily 9am-midnight.) Expats converge nightly at **Smugglers ❷** sports bar, which also has two guest rooms away from the noise. (Doubles US$10.25-15.50. Open daily 11:30am-2am.)

◪ THE BAZARUTO ARCHIPELAGO. The islands lie two to three hours off the coast by dhow across blue waters so shallow you can almost walk to the archipelago during low tide. Most of the islands have some permanent luxury lodge; only **Benguerra** has a functional campsite. Authorities declared much of the archipelago a national park in 1971 and have since monitored tourism carefully by banning most camping and licensing just a few high-end resorts. The vastly overpriced **Gabriel's ❷,** on Benguerra, is the cheapest of the lot and has a monopoly on its price range. The campsite is poorly equipped, the dorms plain, and the staff's disinterest in their clients has irked some travelers. The food is palatable, though dishes are pricey (chicken US$6) and there are few options. (Snorkeling trips to the other side of the island US$15. Dorms US$15.00; camping US$7.50.) If you insist on the beach for days on end, you'll have to pay Gabriel's fees, plus a one-time US$4 parks fee, collected by roving rangers.

For day trips, dhow operators in Vilankulo will take you to any of the islands. **Bazaruto Island,** 30km away and 30km long, is the farthest and not really feasible as a day-trip destination. Nor is tiny-but-picturesque **Santa Carolina,** a rock with an abandoned 100-room hotel. The small, idyllic island of **Magaruque** lies just 12km from Vilankulo, but it has no budget accommodation. **Benguerra,** 14km from Vilankulo, has three lodges, sand dunes in the east, and freshwater crocodile lakes. Dhow operators seem to be quite diligent about approaching any foreigner within a minute's walk of the ocean to see if he or she wants a lift to the islands. Be wary of going with an independent operator; several tourists have reported being forced into paying double or triple the agreed-upon price once the dhow reaches the middle of the ocean. Trust us: it's much better to go with an established professional. Rodrigues of **Amor do Sol,** near the Tropical, has standard rates. (US$10-15 per person return; inquire at Baobab Beach.)

Two Mile Reef, the coral formation between Bazaruto and Benguerra, teems with fish. Spear-fishing is not permitted, but the snorkeling and diving are some of the world's finest. **Vilankulo Dive Charters,** at the Águia Negra lodge 2km north of the town center, offers two-dive excursions, equipment provided, for US$75. Open water courses are offered when there is demand. Snorkeling day-trips cost about US$175 for four snorkelers, depending on fuel cost, and pick-up can be arranged from the center of town. (☎82387; an01@bushmail.net. Open daily 9am-3:30pm.) Those hoping not just to *see* fish but to eat them should contact Roger at **Mozambican Game Fishing Safaris,** also at the Águia Negra. Four to eight fishermen can have a day on the water for US$390-420, again depending on fuel cost and consumption.

The operation that wraps all these services into one is **Sail Away** (kerry@ecoweb.co.zw), on a minor road parallel to the beach 500m south of the jetty. For US$35-45 per person per day, Sail Away ferries clients to Benguerra Island, feeds and houses them at Gabriel's, and brings them to snorkeling and fishing sites. Trips leave periodically, though advance booking is recommended. Sail Away arranges dive trips as well.

BEIRA ☎ 03

When the Portuguese left Beira, they clogged the sewer system with cement and threw away the drainage maps. This accounts for the city's peculiar odor, or so local lore would have us believe. The city does present an urban image different from what one sees in Maputo, which looks as if it has been dolled up for international eyes. Beira is filled with moldy buildings that haven't been renovated since they were built, including picturesque Art Deco theatres and the once accurately named Hotel Grande, now occupied by hundreds of squatters. Although it is the commercial capital of Mozambique, Beira sees few tourists; most visitors head straight to the Bazaruto Archipelago. As a result, the city has an air of authenticity sadly absent from some towns to the south. Locals are surprised to meet travelers and are often genuinely welcoming. The city has virtually no tourist sights and precious few budget hotels, but visitors can be sure that they are seeing Mozambican city life in all its commercialism and natural charm.

▐ TRANSPORTATION

Flights: The **airport** is 7km from the city center and is best reached by taxi. The **LAM** office (☎323 711), north of Praça da Metical on Rua Costa Serrão has English-speakers on staff. Open M-F 7:30am-3pm. Flights to: **Maputo** (daily, US$97); **Johannesburg** (Tu, Th, Sa; US$237); **Harare** (Tu and Th; US$137); **Nampula** (M, Tu, Th-Sa; US$156); **Vilankulo** (W, F; US$56); **Quelimane** (M-Th, Su; US$103). **South African Airlink** (☎011 978 1111 in SA; www.saairlink.co.za) now offers direct flights to **Johannesburg** (Tu, Th, Su; US$250).

Rail: Beira's train station is an immense, modern building on the eastern side of town near the docks. Trains depart daily for **Chimoio** (3hr., US$5) and less frequently to other cities in central Mozambique. Reservations ☎321 051.

Intercity buses and *chapas:* Depart from Praça do Maquinino, in the center of the *baixa*. Oliveiras express buses depart from here to **Maputo** (24hr., US$18) every morning at about 5am. For all other destinations, show up as early as possible and search for a bus with a sign indicating your destination. Most leave when full. Show up before 3pm for a bus bound for **Chimoio** (2½hr., US$3), where there are numerous connecting buses bound for **Tete** and **Mutare, Zimbabwe.** For all other destinations, including **Vilankulo** (12hr., US$9.50), show up by 5am at the latest. *Chapas* traverse most of the city (US$0.20). *Chapas* to **Makuti Beach** run from the *baixa,* starting from near the Mobil station on Rua Major Serpa Pinta, and near ShopRite Supermarket.

⚒ ▐ ORIENTATION AND PRACTICAL INFORMATION

Most of Beira's useful and pleasant shops and restaurants are within a 15min. walk of the city center (*baixa*). Two small squares—Praça do Metical, which has a big bronze one-metical coin in the center, and Praça do Município, which has a park—are the business hubs. The former is adjacent to Rua Luis Inácio, Beira's bank-lined Wall Street. The Púngoè River abuts the city's west side and is to blame for the dingy, silt-filled shores of the Indian Ocean to the south. Avenida das FPLM traces the ocean shore east from the city center about 4km to a historic lighthouse, at which point it joins Estrada Carlos Pereira, the north-bound route to the airport.

Currency exchange: Most banks are open M-F 8am-3pm; the sole exception is the BIM branch at ShopRite (open Sa 8am-5pm). The newest and most professional is the **Banco de Fomento** (☎323 975; bfe.moc@teledata.mz), on Rua Major Serpenta across from the Mobil Station. Any of the banks around Praça do Metical will change cash and traveler's checks, and **Banco Internacional de Moçambique** (☎329 459), just northwest of the square, gives Visa advances. Private *casas de cambios* offer better rates and more convenient hours; **786 Cambios** (☎328 527), 31 Rua Machado dos Santos, in Maquinino, is recommended by locals. Open M-F 8am-5pm, Sa 8am-noon.

Markets: The vast **Tchungamoyo Market** east of the *baixa* is a crowded set of stalls with a vast array of improbable merchandise. Watch for pickpockets and be aware of Mozambican instant justice: if you are robbed and yell *"ladrão"* (robber) while pointing at your thief, prepare for the local mob to apprehend and punish the thief on the spot. For the thief's sake, avoid doing this in the hardware section. If you get robbed at the **ShopRite** (☎327 500), on the opposite corner, report the incident to the security guard near the frozen foods aisle. Open M-F 9am-8pm, Sa 9am-7pm, Su 9am-3pm. V.

Medical assistance: The **Avicena Clinic** (☎327 990; avicena.clinic@teledata.mz), on Av. Poder Popular north of Praça do Metical, has 24hr. service and an on-site pharmacy. The central **Hospital** (☎312 075), on Av. Mártires Revolução off Macuti Beach, has been renovated and has similar services at lower cost.

Police: On Rua de Albuquerque, opposite the Escola Bons Sonhos, near Pensão Moderna. (☎321 153; emergency ☎119). Open M-F 9am-5pm.

Telephone and Internet: Telecomunicações de Moçambique (TDM), is in the *baixa,* southwest of Praça do Metical. Buy phone cards (*cartões telefônicas*) and make international calls here. The attached **Internet cafe** charges US$3 per hr. Both close late for Beira, though women travelers should brace themselves for after-dark catcalls from the hordes of men peering out of the **prison** next door. Open M-Sa 7am-9pm.

Post office: (☎322 800), near the municipal library, on Rua Correia de Brito near the cathedral. *Poste Restante.* Open M-Sa 7am-7pm. **DHL** (☎328 829) has an office near the northwest corner of Praça do Município on Rua Castilho. Delivery time to North America or Europe is 4 business days. Open M-Sa 8am-5pm.

▐ ACCOMMODATIONS AND CAMPING

Backpackers will have to pay a little more in Beira than they may be used to paying elsewhere. No accommodation offers dormitory beds, and low-range hotels generally double as brothels.

Pensão Moderna (☎324 537), 2 blocks southwest of the cathedral. Pensão Moderna has a nice outdoor restaurant, and the children's park across the street lends it a relatively wholesome feel. Doubles US$12. ❷

Hotel Miramar (☎322 283), at the end of Av. Edouardo Mondlane, 1.5km southwest of the *baixa.* The only option if you want a room near the waterfront. Doubles US$9. ❶

Biques (☎313 051), a campsite on Makuti Beach 5km from the city center. Biques also has an excellent cheap restaurant and sports bar. Huge rusted cargo ships beached nearby make the campsite scenic; a hot water ablutions block makes it worth the hike from town. Club sandwich US$2. Camping US$3 per person, kids under 6 free. ❶

Hotel Infante (☎326 603), on Rua Jaime Ferreira west of Praça do Município. Though it stretches the means of budget travelers, the central location, elevator, and private bathrooms make it a good deal for the price. Doubles with hot water, TV, and A/C US$24. ❷

Hotel Tivoli (☎320 300; www.hoteltivoli.co.mz), on Av. Bagamoyo at R. Madeira outside the *baixa,* is Beira's newest and best-equipped luxury hotel. For those willing to shell out some cash, the satellite TV, impeccable rooms, and professional staff are sure to impress. Reservations recommended. Doubles US$65. V. ❸

MOZAMBIQUE

FOOD

Biques and **Hotel Miramar** both have good restaurants; the bar at **Hotel Embaixador** next to the Banco de Fomento has live music on weekends and is popular with Beira's monied set. The *baixa* has several other noteworthy options.

Cabinete do Capitão (☎322 781), 50m northwest of the Praça do Metical. One of the few seafood restaurants in Beira that is reliably stocked with all the items promised on the menu, provided the overdone nautical theme doesn't kill your appetite for all things oceanic. Waiters sport sailor costumes. The blue light interior warms up on Sa with a live band at 9pm. *Peixe grelhado* (fried fish) US$4. Open daily 8am-midnight. ❶

Pic-Nic, north of the Praça do Metical next to the LAM office. Despite its name, this is a rather posh indoor restaurant with attentive waitstaff. The *cozida* (bean and meat stew; US$2.50) prepared every Sa is a cheap and filling option. Open daily 7am-11pm. ❷

Johnny's Place (☎322 266), on Av. Poder Popular, north of the Praça do Metical. Lures locals with low prices and a nice outdoor cafe. Oysters US$2.50. Prawn curry US$3.75. *Lagosta* (lobster) US$12 per kg. Open daily 9:30am-11pm. ❶

Café Capri (☎329 305), on the east side of Praça do Município. A European feel and nerve-tingling, Italian-strength espressos. **Café Riviera,** its rival across the square, offers concentrated Nescafé wannabes for the same price. Fresh pastries, including the local favorite, *bolo de arroz* (rice cake), US$1. Open 7am-9pm. ❷

Clube Palmeiras (☎312 947), near Nautico on the way to Macuti Beach. Classy decor and several excellent dishes, including *bife na pedra* (beef on a rock), a mouth-watering hunk of meat served raw on a hot grill for you to cook to your liking with provided seasonings (US$5). Most entrees US$4-9. Open daily 10am-11pm. ❷

Clube Nautico (☎312 615). A theoretically private but practically public sporting club on Av. FPLM near Macuti. Boasts beachside dining with a pool table and fills up with families on weekends. Chicken curry US$4. Use of the swimming pool US$2. ❷

ENTERTAINMENT AND NIGHTLIFE

Complexo Oceana, on Av. FPLM on the waterfront, has a sports bar, restaurant, and disco, but doesn't run any of them particularly well. The disco's zebra-striped wall is the closest you'll get to wildlife in Beira's urban expanse. Entry US$1.50, free for women (hence its popularity with prostitutes). **Monte Verde,** on Estrada Carlos Pereira 3km north of Macuti beach, is where international DJs meet Beira's clubbing crowd, yielding a surprisingly pleasant mix of Mozambican *marrabenta* music and J. Lo. (Cover US$2. Cocktails US$2-5. Open M-Sa 8pm-4am.)

NORTHERN MOZAMBIQUE

The two fingers that make up northern Mozambique hold little of conventional interest to visitors: they are extremely poor and underdeveloped, and their residents get by almost exclusively on subsistence and small-scale agriculture. The huge exceptions to this generalization, however, are the hauntingly fascinating **Ilha de Moçambique (Mozambique Island),** an aging remnant of the Indian Ocean spice and slave trade, and **Nampula,** the northern commercial capital that Mozambicans affectionately dub "Dubai." For tourists, shop-filled Nampula merely serves as a convenient rest stop en route to the Ilha, Malawi, or Tanzania. In contrast, Mozambique Island is a traveler's gem. Due to its remoteness, little has changed since the days when Portuguese sailors and Arab sheiks walked the streets, their ships anchored nearby laden with spices and ivory. Those willing to make the uncomfortable two-day journey across the rest of northern Mozambique (or shell out the cash to fly into Nampula) can explore this historical treasure.

CUAMBA ☎71

Mozambicans from all over say the residents of Cuamba are among the warmest people in the country. This is fortunate, since Cuamba has little else to draw tourists besides its role as a stopover for travelers en route to Nampula, Malawi, or Ilha de Moçambique. Cuamba is over 300km west of Nampula; an early-morning **train** connects the two cities (☎62 634; 6am, US$5.25). Practically speaking, one could rent a bicycle in Cuamba for the same price and get to Nampula before the train, which has been known to take as long as 40 hours to arrive at its destination. The service between Cuamba and Entre Lagos has been temporarily suspended; to get to the border, walk to the transport stand across the train tracks on the main *estrada* (highway) and catch an early-morning truck. (4-5am daily, US$2.) You can also obtain Malawian kwacha here at decent rates from any of the eager changers. If you'd prefer to get to Blantyre unaccompanied by chickens, maize sacks, and 18 other people crammed into the back of a pick-up, try the new Cuamba-Nampula-Blantyre flight operated by SAR. (W, Su. US$150. Book through Vision 2000 Hotel, below). **Banco Internacional de Moçambique** in the center of town, changes money and has a 24hr. **ATM.** (Open M-F 8am-3pm. Visa.) Next door is the **post office** (open M-F 7:30am-noon and 2-5:30pm) and **Telecomunicações de Moçambique** cabin where you can make international calls (open daily 7am-10pm). If stranded overnight, **Namaacha Hotel ❶** has excellent doubles for US$7. **Pensão São Miguel ❶**, just west of the bank, has good doubles (US$9) and allows camping at a mutually agreeable price. For luxury seekers, **Vision 2000 Hotel ❸** (annex ❶) has carpeted rooms with satellite TV, hot water, and breakfast included for US$30-45. The hotel also has a decent **restaurant** and an annex behind the main complex with simpler rooms for US$7-10. (☎62 632/714; h-vision2000@teledata.mz. V.) The owner is an enterprising former-pilot who runs a **garnet mine** 5km from town that is open to visitors; he also maintains a surprisingly chic rooftop jazz and blues on Sundays and a monthly outdoor weekend disco. (US$2 cover. Entry to jazz bar free with drinks.)

BORDER CROSSING: NAYUCHI/ENTRE LAGOS The desolate and desperately remote frontier post at Entre Lagos is, believe it or not, the most active crossing between Malawi and northern Mozambique. 99% of the time, the border is utterly deserted, with more chickens than people and a snoozing guard on either side of the line. Three times per week, however, a **passenger train** from **Liwonde, Malawi** (see p. 647) leaves at 6:45am and arrives at Nayuchi sometime before noon (third-class only; M, W, F; MK80). The border jumps to life as passports are stamped, forms are filled, and the Mozambicans collect a 30,000Mt entry tax. Money-changers give mediocre rates, but better than you'll get anywhere else in northern Mozambique. *Chapas* and pick-up trucks greet Cuamba-bound passengers from the Liwonde train at Entre Lagos (4hr., US$2). The Malawian train chugs back to Liwonde from Nayuchi, and the border dozes off again until the next train comes.

NAMPULA ☎06

Nampula is a relatively large city, but few visitors do more than change money and bask in "urban life" and its amenities before hopping on a plane, train, or *chapa* to Ilha de Moçambique, Malawi, or Tanzania. Still, it's a pleasant city with a diverse ethnic heritage (Muslims, Hindus, and Christians have inhabited the area for centuries), and an increasing commercial importance as a trading center for Northern Mozambique. For tourists, the two main attractions are the city's large cathedral and the National Ethnological Museum.

⌐ TRANSPORTATION

The **LAM office**, on Av. Manyanga near the train station, provides the only efficient transport to the rest of Mozambique. (Open M-F 8:30am-5pm. ☎212 801 or 213 011. Visa.) **Flights** leave for **Beira** (M-Tu and F-Sa, US$170), **Pemba** (M, W, Su; US$100) and **Tete** (W, US$170). The land-lover's alternative is to take a series of buses and *chapas* over wretched roads to Quelimane and on to Caia and Beira; count on at least 72hr. of bumpy travel. Daily **trains** run to **Cuamba** (10hr.; 6am; 3rd-class US$1, 2nd-class US$6, first-classUS$30). *Chapas* and **buses** leave from in front of the train station on Ave. de Trabalho for **Ilha de Moçambique** (4hr., 5am-1pm, US$4), **Pemba** (4hr., 4am-1pm, US$4) and **Monapo** (3hr., US$2.10). Chapas to Ilha stop in **Lumbo**, on the mainland, where you'll have to board a connecting bus to the island itself. Within the city, a small fleet of yellow taxis provides efficient transport; a trip to or from the airport costs US$2. (☎082 598 459. Available 24hr.)

■ ⚐ ORIENTATION AND PRACTICAL INFORMATION

Nampula is conveniently tiny for tourists; the entire downtown area can easily be traversed in a few hours. The southern end of the city is bordered by **Rua dos Continuadores,** which meets **Av. Kankhomba,** the town's bank- and business-filled central artery, at a major traffic circle. The **train** and **transport station** is on Av. do Trabalho, which runs along Nampula's northern edge.

Currency exchange: The main **BIM** branch, across from the bright yellow MCell building on Av. da Independência, has a 24hr. Visa **ATM** and changes cash and traveler's checks (2% commission). Western Union service. Open M-F 8am-5pm, Sa 9am-noon.

Markets: Shops carrying everything from henna powder to frozen hamburgers can be found on all main streets. For more adventurous consumers, the open-air **Mercado Central,** across from the post office on Av. Kanhomba, offers a patchwork of stalls and better bargains. Open daily from 8am-dusk.

Camera and Film: Photo Expresso Boutique (☎212 772), on Av. Kankhomba north of the traffic circle. Develop and purchase film and photographic equipment. Open M-F 8am-6pm, Sa 8am-1pm.

Medical Assistance: The **Avenida Clinic** (☎218 090l; emergencies ☎082 457 720), on Rua Monomatapa opposite the TDM office, has reliable malaria tests and a variety of specialists. Open 24hr.

Pharmacy: Farmácia Calendula (☎217 966) has a branch on Av. Mondlane, west of the museum. Open M-Sa 8am-8pm, Su 9am-1pm.

Police: ☎213 131. On Av. Mondlane east of Av. Kankhomba. Open M-F 9am-5pm.

Telephone: Telecomunicações de Moçambique (☎213 200), for local and international calls, is on Rua Monomatapa next to the cathedral. Open M-F 7:30am-5:30pm; phone cabins open daily 7am-10pm.

Internet Access: Teledata de Moçambique (☎218 372; teledata.nampula@teledata.mz), the cybercafe across the street, has 10 new computers and a friendly staff. US$2 per hour. Open M-F 7:30am-12:30pm and 2-7pm, Sa 9am-1pm and 3-7pm.

Post Office: The unmistakable red-and-white *Correios de Moçambique* (☎212 114) is on Av. Cidade de Moçambique. Open M-F 7:30am-5pm, Sa 7:30am-noon.

♖ ACCOMMODATIONS

Nampula's market for accommodations has blossomed in recent years, though budgeteers should expect to shell out a lot more than they're used to in the coastal regions. Cheapest are the numerous *pensões* (boarding houses), along Av. Kanhomba, most of which have undergone renovations to meet the increasing influx of tourists.

Pensão Parque (☎212 307), near the traffic circle. 7 airy rooms with shared bath and veranda off a freshly painted, garishly colored hall. US$7-10. ❶

Residênciel Estrela (☎214 902), half a block north of Pensão Parque. A step up that boasts new interior tiling. Rooms with a small fridge and TV. US$12-25. ❷

Pensão Marques (☎212 527), on Av. Independência. Old-world charm and doilies on the furniture. Rooms are equipped with a rarity for Nampula's budget travelers: hot water. Clean singles and doubles US$20-30. ❷

Residênciel Brasília (☎217 531), on Rua dos Continuadores in the southern end of town. With a sterile atmosphere, its only real attribute is proximity to several tasty restaurants. Overpriced rooms. Singles and doubles US$30-40. ❸

◪ FOOD

Trendy eateries are Nampula's latest addition; every evening streetside patios are beehives of activity and provide great opportunities for people-watching (or BMW-ogling, as the town's gentrification continues).

Pastelaria Aurora, on Rua dos Continuadores west of Residênciel Brasília. The best selection of Indian and Chinese food in town. Chicken makani US$3. Manchurian vegetables US$2. Open daily 7am-midnight. ❶

Oceanus, near the Pastelaria Aurora. A bit more upscale, featuring European dishes. Pizza US$5. Open daily 7:30am-11:30pm. ❷

Restaurante Sporte's, near the museum. This bougainvillea-covered patio is particularly popular with expats. While a splurge for the budgeteer (olive steak costs US$7), a visit to the swankiest of Nampula's restaurants is worth the extra cash. ❸

◪ SIGHTS

Other than shops and urban conveniences, Nampula has only two sights of interest. The gargantuan **Cathedral de Nossa Senhora de Fátima**, near the governor's residence on Av. Mondlane, is notable mainly for its size. Inside there is nothing to see but bare walls and unremarkable stained glass.

Across Av. Kanhomba on the same street lies the equally huge and far more interesting **Museu Nacional de Etnologia** (National Ethnological Museum), home to iron tools from the 14th and 15th centuries, striking Mapiko masks made by the Makonde, and pipes for smoking *suruma*, an indigenous plant similar to marijuana. (Open Tu-Th 2-4:30pm, F 2-6pm, Sa 10am-noon and 2-4pm. The sympathetic receptionist occasionally opens the museum on Mondays for those unable to master the museum's perplexing schedule. US$1.50 suggested donation.)

ILHA DE MOÇAMBIQUE

Named a UNESCO World Heritage site in 1991, Ilha de Moçambique (Mozambique Island) is a colorful former colonial capital. Once the headquarters of Arab trade and Portuguese eastward expansion, the country's most intriguing tourist attraction now seems frozen in history. The 3km stroll from end to end is an eerie glimpse of 500 years of colonial domination, cultural mongrelization, and architectural good taste. The Makua people first inhabited the island in the third century after the Bantu migration into Mozambique, and Makua remains the most widely spoken language on the island. Vasco da Gama first arrived in 1498 and ejected a local sheik, Mussa-al-Bique, from whom the present-day country derived its name. Within a decade, Ilha had become a necessary haven for any Portuguese vessel heading east, and it was declared the colonial capital in 1763 following the removal of the Jesuits (whose convent later became the Governor's Palace). It remained strategically important until 1898, when the colonial capital was moved to Lourenço Marques (now Maputo). In 1930, the Portuguese laid the terminus of the railway track from Lake Malawi at nearby Lambo; twenty years later, a branch was laid to Nacala. These two cities siphoned away Ilha's commercial importance, leaving it the historical artifact and cultural curiosity that it is today. Ilha's dominant Muslim Swahili culture shares the stage with a significant Christian minority, which arrived from Goa in the 1500s. Hindus once made up a small religious community, though none are left on the island, and the lone temple caters solely to worshippers from Nampula and surrounding areas. The compactness of the island ensures that all these fragments of the past are inescapable even on a casual walk.

▐ TRANSPORTATION

To get to Ilha from Malawi (perhaps the most logical starting point for a trek here), take the train from Liwonde, Malawi to Cuamba, Mozambique (see p. 629). In Cuamba, stay overnight and continue by train the next morning to Nampula (p. 629), then hustle onto a *chapa* headed to Ilha. The entire journey, barring mishaps, should take two full days.

▐ ▐ ORIENTATION AND PRACTICAL INFORMATION

Just 3km long and 500m wide, Ilha is perfect for walking. Indeed, you will have missed much of its charm if you don't explore some of the backstreets and neighborhood alleys. Off the extreme south end of the island is tiny **São Lourenço (St. Lawrence) Island,** almost every square meter of which is covered by a small stone fort. At low tide you can walk there. A causeway on the west side of Ilha's south tip leads 3km to the mainland; vehicles wider than 81 in. (204cm) cannot pass. All transportation to and from the island stops at the causeway. For a vehicle to **Nampula** (4hr., US$4), it would be wise to leave no later than 9am. The north end of the island is dominated by the fort. Just south of the fort, on the west shore, are a large park, a **Telecomunicações de Moçambique** office, and the tourist information center.

Tourist Information: The **tourist office** (☎610 081; ilha@teledata.mz), also next door to the Palácio, is the most helpful one in Mozambique. They list and book budget accommodations, provide excellent guide service and historical literature, and rent bikes (US$4 per day). They also operate a beauty parlor that will apply *msiro* (a traditional white vegetable-meal mask used to beautify the skin) to your face for US$0.50. Open daily 9am-noon and 2-5pm. For an astounding array of old books in Hindi, Portuguese, French, and English, as well as the must-read 1985 Dutch-Mozambican historical report *Ilha de Moçambique*, visit the library at the **Conselho Municipal** (☎610 132), on Av. dos Herois, in the center of town. Open M-F 7:30am-3:30pm.

Banks: Banco Internacional de Moçambique (☎610 135), near the center of the island, changes cash. Open M-F 8am-3pm.

Markets: The **Mercado Central,** on the east side of the island off Av. dos Herois, offers little for tourists. For handmade jewelry and traditional khamau blouses, try **Missanga,** in the shopping arcade on Rua Alvares Cabral. The shop's Makua name refers to strands of old Portuguese trading beads, now sold by young children all over the island for about US$1 each. Open M-Sa 9am-5pm. The **tourist office** (see above) carries locally-produced silver jewelry based on the Goan collections of the early Portuguese aristocracy (US$3-30).

Medical Care: A crumbling **hospital** on Rua da Saude still operates, though it's best to visit as a tourist rather than a patient; go to Nampula for any serious medical problem.

Pharmacy: Farmácia de Ilha de Moçambique (☎610 088), next to Missanga in the shopping arcade. Open M-F 7:30am-noon and 2:30-6pm, Sa 7:30am-1pm.

Internet Access: Ilha's new Internet Café is located next to the Palácio de São Paulo. (US$3 per hr.) Open M-Th 7am-8pm and F-Sa 7am-9pm. In the same building is the trusty **Telecomunicações de Moçambique** (☎610 000; same hours).

Post Office: Across from Relíquias on Rua Cabral. A great place to stock up on old Mozambican **stamps.** Open M-F 7:30am-noon and 2-5pm, Sa 7:30am-noon.

ACCOMMODATIONS AND CAMPING

Backpackers head to the **Casa de Luís ❶**, on the north edge of Makuti town. Despite the friendly owners and lovely backyard garden, a lack of space makes this option less than ideal, particularly if you intend to camp. (Doubles US$8. Camping US$4.) Numerous B&Bs dot the island and provide a glimpse into family life. **Residênciel Amy ❶**, just south of the central market, has spacious quarters and pristine bathrooms. (☎082 455 142. US$9.) If Amy's is full, try the equally charming **Alojamento Chiamo ❶** next door (☎610 044, US$7), or the smaller **Hospedagem Kerro ❶** across from Complexo Indico and covered in passion fruit vines. (☎610 084. US$9.) One step up is **Casa Branca ❷**, up a set of small steps on the east side of the island opposite the statue of poet Luís Camões. (☎610 076. US$18.) Far less charming and far more expensive is the four-star **Hotel Omuhipiti ❸** (☎610 101), easy to find with its obtrusive fluorescent signs. Luxurious rooms cost US$65; the restaurant is a better value and has decent dishes for US$6. The sandy grounds at **Causalina Camping ❶**, on the Lumbo mainland 50m north of the bridge, are run by former model Helena and her cats. (☎082 446 990. Single huts US$7; double huts US$10. Camping US$3.)

FOOD

Ilha's classiest eatery is **Relíquias (Relics) ❷**, in an arcade just south of the museum. The atmosphere is remarkably trendy and the food is outstanding. (Entrees US$4.75-10.25. Open Tu-Su 11am-11pm.) The **Complexo Indico ❶**, on the east side of the center of the island, boasts an ocean breeze and a beautiful view. Here is your chance to sample *matapa*, the delicious cassava mush that is a Mozambican staple but curiously rare on menus. (*Matapa* with *xima* US$3.75. Open M-W and F-Su 9am-10pm.)

SIGHTS

FORTALEZA DE SÃO SEBASTIÃO. Weedy, deserted, and immense, the fort over-looks the entrance to the bay and, from its construction between 1558 and 1620 to the end of Ilha's glory days, was the center of the region's military operations. It looks as if the 2000 or so inhabitants of the fort left in a hurry and hired no house-sitters: the whole complex is overgrown with weeds and, on a typical day, devoid of human activity. Cannonballs lie rusting in gutters. Cannons line the edges of the four main ramparts and, in some cases, still point feebly out to sea. At the fort's center stands an enormous cistern, built to sustain the 2000 or so former inhabitants during the six-month dry season. Ilha's current residents still use the tank as an emergency water supply. You can walk around the fort freely, but nothing is labeled, so you'll have to use your imagination (or hire a guide from the tourist office) to envision the place as it once was—teeming with soldiers, families, priests, and prisoners. Immediately south of the fort is a park with an **obelisk** commemorating the World War I dead. *(Located on the extreme north point of the Ilha.)*

CAPELA DE NOSSA SENHORA DE BALUARTE (CHAPEL OF OUR LADY OF THE BULWARK). Built in 1522 by Don Pedro de Castro, the chapel is reportedly the oldest European building in the Southern Hemisphere. Seasick new arrivals from Portugal sank to their knees in this modest late-medieval worship house; the stone bosses at the intersection of the chapel's vaults are imported from Portugal. The tombstones are too faded to read, but one of them marks the final resting place of the first bishop of Japan (1588). The bones in a box in the cramped north transept are those of a Portuguese commandant. Just outside the chapel is a firing range where countless political prisoners were murdered during the most macabre moments of Portuguese domination. *(Located east of the fort. Fort open daily 6am-6pm. Guided tours available from the tourist office.)*

STONE TOWN. **Stone Town** was Ilha's commercial and administrative district. The flat-roofed structures, built over 400-odd years, are strictly planned and in various stages of decay. All follow a distinctive model of limestone and wood construction. This uniformity was one of the factors behind the island's classification as a UNESCO World Heritage Site in the early 1990s. The organization has since pledged to renovate over 50 buildings in the stone town. Unfortunately, the only project to date is the handsome but permanently-locked public bathroom, built to encourage cleaner beaches. Stone Town's other notable buildings are the **colonial capital offices** in the white buildings in the center of the island. *(South of the fort.)*

PALÁCIO DE SÃO PAOLO. Stone Town's historical crown jewel is the **Palácio de São Paulo.** The governor stayed here from its construction in 1610. Docents at the entrance are responsible for maintaining the palace grounds and happily offer tours (in Portuguese only). Doff your shoes in the reception; a walk through the posh residence takes about 30min. and plays like a Robin Leach-style exploration into 17th-century elite life. The bedrooms, kitchens, and halls are packed with exotic furniture and art from the colonial era, in a collection that rivals those of many European museums. The ornate rosewood tables and cabinets from Goa and Ming-dynasty vases from China are authentic, although scholars generally agree that the Cuisinart in the kitchen is a contemporary addition. *(Located on the west side of the island, near the fort. Open M-F 8am-noon and 2-5pm. US$2 suggested donation.)*

MUSEU DE ARTE SACRA (MUSEUM OF SACRED ART). The museum consists of a single room of Christian woodwork and metalwork, removed from the chapels of the island and nearby Mussoril in the 1960s. Artifacts include 17th-century Goan paintings and the religious objects of Mozambique's first bishop. To enter, seek out the old caretaker and ask him for a tour (again, in Portuguese only); he'll be happy to oblige for a small tip. *(Next to the palace. Open W-Su 9am-5pm.)*

MAKUTI TOWN. Makuti Town is a crowded residential area much newer than Stone Town. Its name is derived from the Makua word for palm fronds, from which the houses are constructed. The houses and winding lanes are unzoned, leaving a vibrant chaos for pedestrian exploration. Ask around if you want to see **traditional dance** in Tufo or Ntsope styles; women traditionally dance while men drum. Informal performances common at night, but you might have to put some effort into your search to get invited. The tourist office may be able to assist in arranging something. *(Located on the southern region of the Ilha.)*

MOZAMBIQUE

◢ BEACHES

In terms of beaches, the island has little to offer due to the unfortunate fact that most residents use the sea as a giant public toilet. Still, the beach just south of the Fort remains fairly clean for swimming, and the guards at Hotel Omuhipiti's oceanfront have also managed to deter bathroom-seekers.

A better option is to arrange a trip to nearby Chocas or Cabaceira Pequena beaches or the islands of Goa or Sena; this is best done through the **Dugong Dive Center,** south of Reliquias, as local *dhow* owners have been known to double their prices in the middle of the ocean. The center also arranges snorkeling and scuba driving excursions. (☎610 156, ask for Caku; torquip@iafrica.com; diving US$30, boat trips US$20-40). The waters surrounding the island contain centuries' worth of sunken ships, galleons, and untold riches in the form of Chinese porcelain, art, and gold. A few intrepid foreigners have set up an archaeological exploration company, **Arqueonautas,** to investigate these tales.

PEMBA

Still unknown to most tourists due to its remote location on a peninsula along Mozambique's northern coast, Pemba is a beach-lover's paradise with intriguing links to Tanzania's Swahili Coast. Coconut palms and white sands are standard fare at popular Wimbe Beach, and the 30-odd islands of the Quirimbas Archipelago provide unparalleled diving and snorkeling with sea turtles and corals. Though situated above the third largest bay in the world, Pemba has yet to take on the urban edge of its sister ports, Beira and Maputo. Ten thousand people still inhabit Pemba's first settlement, Paquitequete, a maze-like cluster of *makuti* (palm-frond) houses which becomes an island at high tide. The *Estaleiro Naval* is the only place left in the country where lateen-rigged *dhows* are made using a centuries-old method handed down from Arab traders. For travelers who don't mind the 2500km journey from Maputo, Pemba's unbeatable combination of cultural riches and coastal bliss is sure to please.

THAT WHICH WE CALL A ROSE... As local lore has it, a group of Swahili sailors from Zanzibar were stationed in Pemba Bay centuries ago when a a swarm of flies descended on their boat. Their desperate cries of **"pembe!"** (the Swahili word for "fly") gave the city its present name. When Pemba became the capital of Cabo Delgado province in 1900, it was renamed Porto Amélia de Orleans e Bragança, after the former queen of Portugal. Seventy-five years later, when the newly independent Republic of Mozambique broke its ties with Portugal, mapmakers cringed as Porto Amélia endured yet another name change and became Pemba once again.

▣ TRANSPORTATION

Pemba's international **airport** is 5km from the city center. **LAM** (☎204 34 or 202 51; www.lam.co.mz), on Av. 25 de Setembro at Av. Eduardo Mondlane, operates flights to Dar es Salaam (Tu, Th and Sa; $150), Nampula, and Maputo, with connecting service to Tete and Beira. **STA** has good rates to most Mozambican cities but is like an airborne version of a *chapa*—plan on stopping three or four times in out-of-the-way towns before you reach your destination. (Nampula Tu, Th; US$70.) **SAR** flies directly to Nampula, Lichinga, and Nacala from Pemba, with connecting flights to Blantyre and Lilongwe, Malawi. Contact the booking office in Nampula for rates and schedules. (☎06 212 401; electro@teledata.mz.) **Minibuses** travel to Nampula (6hr.; US$5) and Nacala (4hr.; US$4) every morning and depart from the bus stand opposite the post office on Av. 25 de Setembro. To head north to Tanzania, catch the **Mekula Group** bus to Moçimboa da Praia (7hr., daily 6am, US$4) from in front of the Telecomunicações de Moçambique cabin on Av. 25 de Setembro at Av. Mondlane. From there, transport leaves to Palma between 4 and 5am, and then on to Namiranga, the Mozambican border post. A new 10-ton passenger ferry traverses the **Rovuma River** to the Tanzanian border. At the same intersection, **MC Taxi's** (☎20 187) bright yellow, metered cabs wait to pick up passengers; this is the only way to get to Wimbe Beach (US$0.50 per km). **Boats** can be arranged for transport to the islands; inquire at **Pemba Dive** (see **Sights**, p. 638) for schedules and information.

◼🛈 ORIENTATION AND PRACTICAL INFORMATION

Pemba's tiny *baixa* (downtown) is along **Av. Eduardo Mondlane** and **Av. 25 de Setembro**, which meets the neighborhood of **Paquitequete** at its east end and the **airport** at its southwest end. Another *estrada* (highway) runs along the beach 6km east of the *baixa* to the center of all tourist activity: **Praia do Wimbe** (Wimbe Beach), a lively strip of sand dotted with bars and restaurants. The immense Pemba Beach Hotel marks the start of Wimbe, which continues east for another 5km.

Travel Agent: Viatur (☎214 31 or 204 94; viatur@teledata.mz), in the Banco Austral plaza at 10 Av. Mondlane, 1 block south of Av. Setembro. English-speaking staff arranges charter flights and boat trips to the Quirimbas, as well as **car rental.**

Banks and Currency Exchange: BIM Expresso (☎214 39), on Av. Mondlane opposite Flor d'Avenida. **Western Union**, a 24hr. **ATM** that accepts Visa cards, and **currency exchange** (3% commission). Open M-F 8am-3pm. **Banco Austral** (☎20837), in the complex across the street, charges $5 commission for V/MC advances and doesn't have an ATM. Open M-F 8am-3pm.

Craft Markets: For curios, try **CeeBee Pemba** (ceebee@teledata.mz), on Av. 25 de Setembro 2km east of the city center; the shop also offers pricey Internet access. **Cooperativa Karibu**, behind the Internet café adjacent to Complexo Caracol, has a smaller selection of wood carvings and jewelry.

Pharmacies: Farmácia Novo (☎202 27), at 393 Av. Mondlane opposite the Banco Austral Complex. The brand-new interior is stocked with instant malaria tests and designer lenses. Open daily 7:30am-8:30pm.

Telephone and Internet: On Wimbe Beach, the small **Internet/telephone cabin** has one computer with a fast (though expensive) connection; bringing fruit or bread for the staff's pet monkey might win you extra surfing time. You can also send or receive international calls and faxes. Internet US$4 per hr. Open M-Th 7am-11pm; F-Su 7am-midnight. In town, **Telecomunicações de Moçambique** has several *cabines telefónicos*; try the one opposite the LAM office on Av. 25 de Setembro. Open daily 7:30am-9pm.

Post Office: On Rua 25 de Setembro, ½ block west of Av. Mondlane. One computer with Internet access; US$5 per hr. Open M-F 7am-noon and 2-5pm.

Courier: DHL (☎206 25) has an office behind Viatur on Av. Mondlane. Open M-F 7am-noon and 2-5pm.

🛈 ACCOMMODATIONS AND CAMPING

Wimbe Beach is not (yet) equipped to handle masses of backpackers; most of the accommodation caters to middle- and upper-range budgets. Still, compared to other parts of Mozambique, travelers to Pemba will be happily surprised at the quality they'll get for the price. Should you prefer to stay in town (for reasons unknown to man), this does not hold.

THE BIG SPLURGE

▨ **Quilalea.** (see Big Splurge sidebar.)

Russel's Place (also known as Blackfoot or Cashew Camp), is the only spot with dorm beds and camping. Luckily, a monopoly on the budget market hasn't jacked up Russel's prices nor ruined his spacious, secluded locale. Getting there is tough—you'll have to take a taxi or walk 4km east from Wimbe Beach on the sand road—but worth the hassle. Bucket showers (with hot water). Giant wall map of Africa behind the bar tempts your wanderlust into even more remote corners of the continent. Basic kitchen for self-caterers. Dinner US$2.50. Dorms US$5; A-frame chalet (sleeps 2) US$16. Camping US$3. Book through Ceebee Pemba, ceebee@teledata.mz. ❶

Centro Turístico Caracol (☎201 47, fax 201 08; sulemane@teledata.mz), opposite Pemba Dive, is a gated blue-and-white apartment complex overlooking Wimbe Beach. Clean, furnished rooms start at US$15 (single with fan, private bath) and go up to US$55 for a triple with fridge, air-con, and ocean view veranda. Popular with expats and NGO workers. Discounts available for longer-term stays. Laundry service. ❷

Complexo Nautilus (☎215 20; nautilushtl@teledata.mz), at the west end of the beach, is Wimbe's fanciest lodging, complete with a palm-fringed pool, bar and wooden esplanade connecting the self-contained chalets. Bright, airy 3-room chalets sleep 4 and are equipped with A/C, fridge, and hot-water kettle. Chalets US$88. Use of pool US$2; under 12 US$1. On-site **CI Divers** (☎201 02; cidivers@teledata.mz) runs a full range of scuba courses. PADI Open Water Course US$265; Advanced Open Water US$250; guided dive including equipment US$35. ❸

Hotel Cabo Delgado (☎215 52), on Av Mondlane opposite the Banco Standard Totta, has friendly staff and spacious rooms with hardwood furniture and verandas overlooking Pemba's sad cityscape (and, if you squint, the sea). Singles US$33; doubles US$40; suites (with two rooms) US$53-56. Bathrooms have hot water, a rare luxury. MC/V. ❸

ISLAND FOR RENT: QUILALEA

Quilalea, a minuscule dot along the Quirimbas Archipelago, has been uninhabited and well-hidden for centuries; even major nautical surveys left it out. That is, until 2002, when an enterprising South African couple bought the island and established an exclusive hideaway for a very moneyed minority. Now, privacy-seekers can have the place to themselves (not counting complimentary on-site waitstaff) for the tidy sum of US$450 per day—a steal when compared to steep rental rates on similar islands in the Seychelles.

A further plus: Quilalea lies within the Ibo Marine Reserve, and, thanks to the prohibition of commercial fishing, its waters are teeming with tropical fish, sea turtles, sharks, dolphins, and even the occasional whale in transit. To book (or simply drool), check out the web site: www.quilalea.com.

▶ FOOD

The beachside restaurants at Wimbe Beach are favored by weekend merry-makers and serve succulent seafood; head into town for more variation or to splurge on a sumptuous evening buffet at the Pemba Beach Hotel.

Restaurante Mar e Sol (☎201 34), a spot for basic grilled prawns and fish fillets (US$3). On Sunday afternoons, try the Portuguese *fejoada* (bean stew) or local *matapa* with *xima*, a cassava and maize dish (both US$3). Open daily 8am-10pm. ❶

Restaurante do Wimbe (☎201 00). Giant fish and prawn painted on the walls oversee the delicious smells emanating from the kitchen. Steaming *lagosta* (lobster, US$8). Fried *rissões* (prawn-filled dumplings, US$2), This is the place to be after 11 on Fr and Sa nights to boogie to Angolan rap and Mozambican *marrabenta* music; Sunday's party caters to the 16+ set and starts at 7:30pm. Cover US$1. ❷

Aguila Romana (☎219 72), Pemba's best Italian restaurant. A soothing Mozambican guitarist sets the mood on Su nights. Pastas US$5. Oven-hot pizzas (Th, Sa-Su only) US$4-8. Open 11am-11pm, closed Tu. ❶

Restaurante/Bar 556 (☎214 87), on Rua de Commerçio at Rua III, is a South African meat joint with sparse decor and a fine selection of beer; vegetarians beware. Tender rump steak US$5. Be sure to specify *mal passado* unless you like your meat thoroughly cooked. Open M-Sa 11:30am-2pm and 5:30pm until the last man stumbles home. ❷

Pemba Beach Hotel, with a restaurant that serves lunch and dinner buffets fit for a king, and, for the five-star quality, priced for a pauper. Full buffet US$16. Cold entrees US$6; hot entrees US$10. Happy hour 5-7pm nightly. (☎217 70; www.pembabeach.com. Open daily 11am-10:30pm). ❸

⊙ SIGHTS

Pemba offers few museums or historical relics, but has a thriving cultural scene. The Casa de Cultura, near the Pemba Beach Hotel, hosts *tufo* dancing and other movement arts. Several local groups perform upon request for a flat fee (usually between US$20-40); contact the tourist office at the Pemba Beach Hotel for a list and rates (see Food, p. 637).

For a glimpse of traditional life, head to the Paquitequete *bairro*, on the western tip of the peninsula; the bridge from the mainland seems useless until the tide comes in and the place becomes an island. A walk through the densely packed huts yields markets, mosques, and women with their faces covered in white paste, a beauty treatment made from pieces of the *nsiro* plant pounded with water. Stay away from the beaches, as many are used as public toilets—only a handful of the houses have private bathrooms.

Ibo Island, about 170km north in the Quirimbas Archipelago, was used by the Portuguese in the mid-18th century as a gateway to the northern reaches of Mozambique and for the export of slaves and ivory. The Fortaleza de São João Baptista, which currently houses three expert silversmiths, is one of the only remaining European buildings. To get to Ibo, take a *chapa* heading north to Quissanga (2hr; US$3) and then on to Tanganyanga; *dhows* depart infrequently from there to the island for a negotiable price. Viatur (see Practical Information, p. 636) also arranges flights to Ibo for US$75 per person and up, depending on the size of your group.

The reefs around Pemba are some of the best in the world for diving and snorkeling. CI Divers (see **Accommodations,** p. 636) offers PADI courses and certification; Pemba Dive's friendly and knowledgeable owners don't certify divers but offer snorkeling and beach buggy tours (US$5) and dive packages (5 dives plus equipment US$135). They can also arrange transport to the islands and yacht rental. (Opposite the Caracol Complex. ☎208 20. Open daily 9am-4pm.)

MALAWI

CURRENCY		
USD $1 = MK74		MK100 = USD $1.35
AUD $1 = MK40		MK100 = AUD $2.49
CAD $1 = MK48		MK100 = CAD $2.10
EUR €1 = MK73		MK100 = EUR €1.37
GBP £1 = MK114		MK100 = GBP £ 0.87
BWP P1 = MK12		MK100 = BWP P8.42
MZM Mt10,000 = MK32		MK100 = MZM Mt28,953
NAD $1 = MK7.04		MK100 = NAD $14.27
ZAR R1 = MK7.04		MK100 = ZAR R$14.27
ZWD Z$1 = MK1.36		MK100 = ZWD Z$73.62

 PRICE RANGES. Price ranges, marked by the numbered icons below, are now included in food and accommodation descriptions. They are based on the lowest cost for one person, excluding special deals or prices. In the case of campgrounds, we include the cost of a car. The table below is a guide to how prices and icons match up. **Malawi has three price ranges.**

SYMBOL	❶	❷	❸
ACCOMM.	MK100-500	MK500-1000	MK1000 plus
FOOD	MK100-200	MK200-300	MK300 plus

Wedged into the southern end of the Great Rift Valley, Malawi is a land of astonishing beauty. With plateaus rearing up from the shores of the lake and craggy mountains peering over lush valleys in The exotic fish in Lake Malawi make it a diver's and snorkeler's paradise, while houseboats, sailboats, and dugout canoes ply the surface of this inland sea. For landlubbers, Malawi's mountain trekking opportunities are equally enticing. This chapter presents the highlights of Malawi, including the majestic Lake Malawi and Liwonde National Park.

ESSENTIALS

DOCUMENTS AND FORMALITIES

VISAS
Citizens of Commonwealth countries, EU countries, South Africa, and the United States do not need visas. All others must pay US$25 for a tourist visa, which is usually issued in about three days. As requirements tend to change frequently, it's a good idea to check beforehand.

EMBASSIES ABROAD
Canada: 7 Clemow Ave., Ottawa, K1S2A9 (☎613-236-8932).

MALAWI

FACTS AND FIGURES	
Official Name: Malawi	**Head of State:** Pres. Bakili Muluzi
Government: Multiparty Democracy	**Major Cities:** Lilongwe, Blantyre
Capital: Lilongwe	**Population:** 10,385,000
Land Area: 94,080 sq. km	**Languages:** English, Chichewa
Geography: High plateaus rising west and south of the Lake	**Religions:** Protestant 55%; Roman Catholic 20%; Muslim 20%
Climate: Tropical in Shire Valley; temperate in highlands. Wet season Nov.-Apr.	**GDP Per Capita:** US$940
	Major Exports: Tobacco, tea, sugar

South Africa: P.O. Box 11172, Brookhlyn, Pretoria (☎012 477 853).

United Kingdom: 33 Grosvenor St., London (☎0171 491 4172).

United States: 2408 Massachusetts Ave., Washington, DC 20008 (☎202-797-1007).

Zambia: Woodgate House, Cairo Rd., Lusaka (☎228 296).

Zimbabwe: 42/44 Harare St., PO Box 321, Harare (☎04 752 137).

EMBASSIES AND CONSULATES IN LILONGWE

Canada: P.O. Box 51902, Blantyre-Limbe (☎645 441).

Mozambique: Commercial Bank Bldg., African Unity Ave., Lilongwe (☎784 100).

South Africa: Impco Bldg., Capital City, Lilongwe (☎730 888).

United Kingdom: P.O. Box 30042, Kenyatta Rd., Capital City, Lilongwe (☎782 400).

United States: P.O. Box 30016, Area 40, City Center, Lilongwe (☎773 166).

CURRENCY AND EXCHANGE

Malawian kwacha (MK), though relatively stable, are not easily exchanged back into foreign currency. Most businesses will accept US dollars or South African rand at fair rates. **Traveler's checks** are exchanged for cash in Lilongwe and Blantyre.

KEEPING IN TOUCH

TELEPHONES. Country code: 265. International calls can generally only be made at public phone offices. Prices for calls outside Africa can range from US$10 to US$25 for three *minutes!*

MAIL. There are no postal codes; just use the town name. *Poste Restante* is available in most larger towns. Air mail to and from Europe/USA takes about 3 weeks.

TIME DIFFERENCE. Malawi is two hours ahead of Greenwich Mean Time and does not observe daylight savings.

BLANTYRE

A city of little aesthetic or cultural interest, Blantyre nevertheless attracts travelers in need of cash, email, transportation, and other urban amenities. The bland but walkable city center stocks most of the services and luxuries travelers crave. The handful of colonial-era historical sights can be seen in a morning, leaving ample time to catch an onward bus before nightfall.

╔ TRANSPORTATION

Malawi

Blantyre (and its smaller twin city, **Limbe**) will be the first destination of size for travelers arriving overland from Mozambique or across the Tete Corridor from Zimbabwe. Within the city itself, most distances are short enough to walk, except for the stretch from Blantyre to Limbe, which is serviced by a stream of **minibus taxis** (20min., MK10-15). At night, it's worth taking a taxi if you must go between the bus stand and the city center; cabs congregate outside the bus stand and the **Meridien Hotel** (MK200). A few travelers have been mugged outside the tiny stretch of road that leads from Doogles Backpackers to the main bus station, so make sure to have cabs drop you off *inside* the hostel gates rather than at the station.

Flights: The airport is a 20-30min. taxi trip north of the city (MK800, negotiate in advance). A **$20 departure tax** must be paid in dollars for international flights; many airlines include the fee in the ticket price. **Air Malawi** (☎ 620 811) flies to: **Lilongwe** (50min., 4-5 per day, MK4634); **Johannesburg** (1-2 per day, US$348); **Harare** (3 per week, US$179); **Lusaka** (3 per week, US$238); **Nairobi** (2 per week, US$452); **Dar-es-Salaam** (2 per week, US$315). **Serviço Aéreo Regional (SAR),** a charter company, now operates direct flights to northern Mozambique: **Nampula** (W, Su; US$100); for **Pemba, Nacala, Cuamba, and Lumbo,** flight tables vary. Book through **Inter-Ocean Travel** (see **Practical Information** p. 642) or in Mozambique at the **SAR office** in Nampula (☎258 06 212 401; electro@teledata.mz).

Buses: Blantyre's intercity bus depot is opposite the train station, near Doogles Backpackers. **Monorurama/Vee's Venture** (☎ 624 735), next to Safari restaurant at the bus depot, goes daily to **Harare** (11hr., 7am, MK1200), with connecting service to **Johannesburg** (17hr., 9pm, R250). The driver will drop you off in **Tete** (5hr.) if you ask, provided you pay the full fare for a ticket to Harare. Minibuses to **Liwonde** and **Monkey Bay** are numerous and depart from early morning to late afternoon every day (2-5hr., MK100-200). To get to **Mulanje,** first take a minibus to the station in Limbe (MK15), then board a bus to the border town (MK80). The most reliable and comfortable transport out of Blantyre, operated by **Translux** and **City to City,** is not found at the bus depot. Their office is behind the Petroda station near the main traffic circle. Schedules posted. Purchase tickets one day in advance. (☎ 621 346; open daily 8am-4:30pm)

Taxi: Cabs sit outside the bus stand and at Le Meridien Hotel. To **Limbe** (MK120). For transit to **Cape Maclear,** you might be able to find enough travelers at Doogles to hire a minibus for a fast, direct journey. Expect to pay at least MK500-600 per person.

Car Rental: Avis (☎622 748), on Victoria Avenue south of the Mount Soche Hotel. Basic rental runs MK3-4000 per day, plus MK520 for insurance, MK20 per km, and a 20% tax. Open M-F 7:30am-5pm, Sa 7:30am-noon.

✦ ORIENTATION

The city center is bound on its north edge by **Glyn Jones Rd.** and on its south edge by **Haile Selassie Rd.** The posh **Meridien Mount Soche Hotel** is a major landmark in the northwest corner of the city center. At the **traffic circle** 100m east of the intersection of Glyn Jones Rd. and Haile Selassie Rd., two new roads branch off. **Kamuzu Highway** goes southeast to **Limbe** (6km away) and **Chileka Rd.** goes northeast to the Blantyre **bus station** (500m) and **Chileka airport** (20km).

❼ PRACTICAL INFORMATION

Lilongwe is Malawi's capital, so for international flights and bureaucracy, head there. For travel information and supplies, however, Blantyre is the spot to be.

TOURIST, FINANCIAL, AND LOCAL SERVICES

Tourist Info: The one-room **tourist office** (☎620 300), on Victoria Ave. and Chilembwe Rd., sells maps of Blantyre (MK40) and stocks brochures from the lakeside luxury resorts. Open M-F 7:30am-5pm. The walls at **Doogles** (see **Accommodations,** p. 643) are plastered with information; staff members are helpful but less readily available.

Travel Agency: Lloyd's Travel Center (☎623 910 or 624 128), on Haile Selassie Rd., across from Ali Baba restaurant. Books international flights and has a *bureau de change*. (Open M-F 8am-noon and 1:30-5pm, Sa 9am-noon.) For charter flights to Mozambique, contact **Inter-Ocean Travel**, in Limbe (☎642 944; open M-F 9am-5pm).

Mozambican Consulate: On the road to Limbe, 1km past the soccer stadium and ShopRite Center. The **visa section** (☎643 189) is open 9am-noon and charges MK1000 for tourist visas, issued in 4 days (2 passport photos, available at ShopRite down the road, are also needed). Same-day service costs MK600 extra. Transit visas are normally issued the same day at no additional cost. Visas are now available at all Mozambican border posts, although these are 25% more expensive. **Doogles** also offers visa service.

Immigration: Visa extensions are easy and free. The office is a block south of the Mount Soche Hotel on Victoria Avenue and usually doesn't accept requests after 1pm M-F.

Maps: If you plan to hike around Mulanje or Zomba, stop by the **map sales office** on Victoria Ave., south of Haile Selassie Rd. Excellent topographical maps cost MK600 and are unavailable in Mulanje and Zomba. Open M-F 7:30am-5pm.

Currency Exchange: Banks will change money for you in Blantyre, but the **Victoria Foreign Exchange Bureau** (☎621 026), opposite the Meridien Hotel, has faster service, better rates, and more convenient hours. MC/Visa advances incur a MK200 surcharge. Open M-F 8am-4pm, Sa 8am-noon. If you plan to travel in rural Malawi, change as much money in Blantyre as you think you'll need; exchange is difficult elsewhere.

Bookstore: Central Bookshop, near the intersection of Henderson St. and Haile Selassie Rd. in the city center, sells a respectable range of titles, including several shelves devoted to Malawiana. Open M-F 8am-5pm, Sa 8am-12:30pm. MC/V.

Markets: For **crafts,** head to the intersection of Victoria Ave. and Chilembwe Rd., where you can bargain for ebony woodcarvings and malachite. The **street vendors** along Haile Selassie Rd. sell toiletries and shoes at a fraction of their in-store prices.

Supermarket: ShopRite, the South African megastore, has recently opened its doors in Blantyre, at Chichiri Mall on the main road to Limbe. The attached food court with generic European, Chinese, Indian, and Middle Eastern cuisine caters to Western tastes at Western prices. Other shops in the complex include a bookstore, photo studio, communication center, and bank (open M-F 8am-7pm, Sa 8am-5pm, Su 9am-1pm). Closer to the city center on Glyn Jones Rd. at Haile Selassie, **Metro** sells everything from camping gear to baby food in bulk. Open M-Sa 8am-7pm, Su 8am-2pm.

EMERGENCY AND COMMUNICATIONS

Pharmacy: Mudi Pharmacy (☎ 633 074), on Haile Selassie Rd. 300m east of the main fork. Stocks malaria medication and Biltricide, a new treatment for bilharzia (MK200-400, depending on body size). Open M-F 8am-6pm, Sa 8am-2pm.

Hospital: Mwaiwathu Private Clinic, next to the bus stand, will test you for malaria for MK200 and have your results (usually) that afternoon. **Queen Elizabeth Central Hospital,** on Kamuzu Highway 500m west of ShopRite, is immense and crowded. For anything more serious, consider investing in a flight to South Africa.

Internet: Post dot Net (☎075 288), in the ShopRite Complex on the road to Limbe, offers telephone, Internet, copy, and DHL services at good rates. Internet MK 250 per hr. Open M-F 8am-7pm, Sa 8am-5pm, Su 9am-1pm.

Post office: The chaotic **general post office** (☎ 621 711) is on Glyn Jones Rd., 300m west of the traffic circle. DHL service. Open M-F 7:30am-4:30pm, Sa 8-10am.

ACCOMMODATIONS AND CAMPING

Blantyre doesn't have much for budget travelers. If you want to save money, go up-country as fast as possible.

Doogles Backpackers (☎ 621 128; doogles@africa-online.net), 50m north of the central bus station. Accommodates nearly every budget traveler who comes through Blantyre and is accordingly far too institutional to be cozy. Its expensive but atmospheric bar attracts legions of expats and affluent locals, filling the dorms with noise until the wee hours; the decibel level rises again when the bus announcers get going at 4:30am. Still, it's the only central meeting place for backpackers and operates one of the few vegetarian-friendly restaurants in Malawi. Internet access MK400 per hr. Dorms MK420; doubles MK840-1680. Camping MK220. ❶

Kabula Lodge (☎ 621 216), on Michiru Rd., 1kilometer west of Sharpe Rd. A quiet hilltop escape from the city that's worth the 3km hike out of town. To get there, walk north on Sharpe Road past Glyn Jones Rd.; turn left on Michiru Rd. and follow the signs. A string of simple rooms, shared bathrooms with hot water, and a well-equipped kitchen for self-catering are set aside from the main lodge. Singles MK500; doubles MK780. ❶

Aunty Vee's B&B, 19 Henderson St. (☎623 474). Near the New Reserve Bank in the city center. An intimate, familial atmosphere and convenient location make Aunty Vee's the polar opposite of Doogles. The doubles are big and well furnished, and security for campers is good. Satellite TV in the main lounge. For people in dorms (MK1000) and campers (MK500), breakfast is not included. ❷

Alendo Hotel (☎ 621 866), at the intersection of Chilembwe Rd. and Sharpe Rd. Operated by the Malawi Dept. of Tourism as a hotel management school. Nearly all of the staff are students, eager to please the passing tourist. Clean rooms with fridge, fan, and satellite TV are pricey at US$55-60, but the peaceful grounds and professionalism of the staff probably will convince you that your money is well spent. ❸

⬤ FOOD

What Blantyre lacks in accommodation options, it makes up for in a diverse selection of restaurants, from cheap and hearty local joints to four-star dining. Malawi's staple food is *nsima*, the same maize filler available as *sadza* in Zimbabwe and *xima branca* in Mozambique. *Nyemba* (spicy bean stew) is the usual complement, sometimes prepared with beef or trout-like *chambo* from the lake.

Safari Restaurant, at the main bus station opposite Doogles. Perhaps the best deal in Malawi. The place lacks decor and the staff doesn't speak English, but you get heaping plates of beef curry with rice or *nsima* for a mere MK80. ❶

Fat Angela's (☎835 960), on Independence Dr. at Hanover Av., also prepares inexpensive local dishes and solid, home-cooked meals, but with considerably more charm and a pleasant veranda. *Nsima* with beef stew MK115. Too bad Angela doesn't stick around for dinner. Open M-F 7:30am-5pm, Sa 7:30am-3pm. ❶

Café Chez Maky (☎622 124), set back from the street in a tiny building on Sharpe Rd. at Chilembwe Rd. Has a secluded, vine-covered patio where you can enjoy delicious iced coffee (MK60) and crepes (MK85). Blantyre's closest thing to a French bistro gets packed around noon with families and expats craving toasted sandwiches (MK100-300); come later if you'd rather mingle with the intellectuals. Open M-Sa 8am-5pm. ❷

Kip's Take-away (☎635 247 or 624 221), opposite the Reserve Bank on Hanover Ave. American-style hot-fudge sundaes (MK150) and cream sodas, plus standard fast-food fare. Steak burgers MK175. Open Su-Th 7:30am-10pm, F-Sa 7:30am-midnight. ❶

Ali Baba (☎621 560), on Haile Selassie Rd., 200m west of the junction. The Middle-Eastern version of take-away, specializing in *shawerma* and cross-cultural pizzas; try "The Indiana." Open daily 10:30am-8pm. ❶

Gypsy's, at Le Meridian Mt. Soche Hotel. May be out of daily range but is a good value for the posh surroundings. Dinner buffet US$12. If stuck in Blantyre, you can also float in Le Meridien's pool for MK200. Open daily 11am-2pm and 7-10:30pm. MC/V. ❸

◉ ♫ SIGHTS AND ENTERTAINMENT

Blantyre looks and feels like a young city, but a few antique edifices remain and may entertain colonial history buffs. Most others can safely skip sightseeing here, save for a brief trip to the **National Museum,** on the main road to Limbe east of Mankata Rd., to see the exposition on slavery or view traditional arts and weapons. (Open M-Th 9am-5pm. Free.)

A few minutes' walk east of the bus stand, 100m set in from the road, is the **Church of Central Africa Presbyterian (CCAP)** house of worship. The modest brick church was southern Malawi's Church of Scotland headquarters after its construction between 1889 and 1891. Few tourists visit here, and there isn't any museum or historical exhibit, so you'll have to find one of the friendly (but not always English-speaking) church staff to show you around. The **Cathedral of St. Paul,** on Glyn Jones Rd., 200m west of the Mount Soche Hotel, is architecturally less elegant but has a better collection of memorial plaques commemorating holy men who have died during service to the church in Malawi/Nyasaland.

Another colonial relic, the **Mandala House,** almost totally unmarked and rarely visited, has served as headquarters for the African Lakes Corporation since its founding in the 1870s. It was from this two-story house that British entrepreneurs planned the development of a trade infrastructure in Southern and Eastern Africa. (To get there, walk toward Limbe on Chilembwe Rd., then turn right on the first uphill residential road. Mandala House is by the car dealership at the road's end.)

For those who don't hanker for the good ol' days of pith helmets and dead missionaries, there's always beer. The **Carlsberg** brewery, 1km south of the CCAP Church, gives occasional tours of its facility and (strictly for connoisseurs) tasting sessions of its lagers. You'll need to join a group prior to arriving at the brewery; stop by Doogles (see **Accommodations,** p. 643) to see if a group is scheduled, or call the facility (☎670 022) for more information.

Doogles is where the backpackers and expats congregate nightly; if you want to meet more locals or play pool, head to the lively bar at **Legend's** on Hanover Ave., north of Independence Dr. On Friday and Saturday nights, the downstairs **disco** draws major crowds; Saturday afternoon outdoor *braais* are for the 12- to 18-year-old set. MK100 cover on weekend nights. Movies are shown daily at the complex's new **Web Bar** for MK100.

MONKEY BAY

It's a testament to the beauty of Lake Malawi that travelers still flock to Monkey Bay, even though its reputation has been sullied by travelers' stories of fending off persistent street kids and getting scammed by seemingly helpful tourist "guides." These irritations peaked a few years ago. Now, most travelers head directly to Senga Bay and the northern beaches, taking the hagglers with them. Evening strolls along the beaches of **Cape Maclear**—Monkey Bay's nearby lakeside paradise—are warmed by the sunset glow over the lake, but visitors still occasionally find the romance killed by five or six local teenagers who may tag along in case you decide to buy something on impulse. Those who can deal with the annoyances get to experience one of Southern Africa's best coastal destinations, a cheap and picturesque heaven for beach bums, kayakers, and beginning scuba divers.

■⃰ ⁊ **ORIENTATION AND PRACTICAL INFORMATION.** Monkey Bay is a tiny little lint-trap of a town, hardly 1km along the highway. Towards the center of town, a couple of market stalls are rigged as **telephone centers.** Don't fall for their tempting signs advertising email access, as none of them actually have computers. At **Ermac Communication Bureau** (☎587 407), accurately self-described as "the best in town," where one can send and receive faxes and international calls. It's best not to wait until you get to the Cape to make calls, as phone infrastructure is in its infancy and may not be functioning. (Open Sa-Th 6am-9pm, F 6am-6pm.) The tiny **post office** (☎587 702) is further north along the highway, across from the turn-off to Venice Beach Backpackers. (Open M-F 7:30am-noon and 1-4:30pm.) Adjacent to the postal window in the same room is the **Malawi Savings Bank** (☎587 216), which can change money and, in the unlikely event that you find a way to spend all your money on the Cape, arrange Western Union Transfers. Aside from these basic services, a couple of restaurants, some general stores, and a **superette** (open daily 8am-6pm), there is little else in Monkey Bay. For credit card advances, hop on one of many minibuses during daylight hours and head to **Mangochi** (2-3hr., MK90), where you'll find a larger **bank.** For anything more, count on a 6hr. trip to **Blantyre** (MK140) for which you will most likely have to change buses in **Mangochi, Liwonde** (40min., MK80), or **Zomba** (2hr., MK120), all along the same route.

⁊⃰ ⁊ **ACCOMMODATIONS AND FOOD. Venice Beach Backpackers ❶,** a 1km trudge east of the highway, is the pick of most travelers. Their prices can't compete with Cape Maclear, but the scenery and convenience can. The lively bar and huts are right on the lake and are ideal if you are forced to spend a night in Monkey Bay. (Snorkel and mask rental MK200 per day. Singles MK300. Camping MK150.) **Zawadi Lodge ❶** (☎587 232), further south along the highway opposite the bus stand, is a better option if you arrive at night and can't make your way along the pitch-black highway. Clean doubles with private bath and concrete floors are MK350.

MALAWI

LAKE MALAWI NATIONAL PARK AND CAPE MACLEAR

To drive here from Monkey Bay, head south (toward Mangochi) on the main road, and make a right turn onto the gravel road at One-Stop Junction, 5km away. From here, the winding road crosses the peninsula, arriving in Cape Maclear 14km later. Public transport from Monkey Bay to Cape Maclear is tricky, mostly due to persistent efforts by locals to waylay you in Monkey Bay—perhaps long enough to spend some money—or overcharge you for transport. Some travelers loiter around the petrol station and ask drivers if they are making the journey to Cape Maclear. A few times each day, a pickup truck carrying more passengers than you might expect, even in Malawi, runs to Cape Maclear from the petrol station; get there by 7am to avoid waiting indefinitely for more passengers. The standard charge is MK70. Other than the pickup, traffic is sparse along the road to the Cape.

⚄ PRACTICAL INFORMATION. As blue and beautiful as the ocean a few hundred kilometers away, Lake Malawi is the country's surrogate sea and main tourist draw. Some 600km long and 87km wide, it would be indistinguishable from an ocean to the naked eye were it not for its low salinity and lack of coral and cargo ships. Numerous colorful species of cichlid fish, unique to the ancient lake, make the area one of the world's best diving spots. On a typical afternoon, you'll see a few fishing boats, a couple of water-skiers, and even a small number of locals commuting to work in traditional dugout canoes. The islands closest to the Cape are Thumbi, Domwe, and Mumbo, and make picturesque getaways from the mainland.

⚄⚄ ACCOMMODATIONS AND FOOD. At the north end of the Cape, **Fat Monkeys Backpackers Lodge ❶** boasts a fantastic location and the best bar in town. Transfers from Monkey Bay are free for guests if arranged far enough in advance. The restaurant serves excellent pizzas and calzones, and though it's pricey, there's no better place to enjoy a beer and watch the sun hit the lake. (boris@fat-monkeys.com. Hot water ablution block available. Cheese pizza MK300. Doubles MK400. Camping MK100.) **Chembe Lodge ❸,** about 1km north of Fat Monkey's on the main road, offers discounted luxury. Full-day catamaran charters are US$40 per person, including snorkeling equipment and food. Accommodations are in luxury chalets in a grassy, gated area; campers have access to the shared and impeccable bathrooms. (☎950 575; info@chembelodge.com. Sunset catamaran cruise US$15. Breakfast and dinner included. Chalets US$55. Camping US$5. MC/V.) **Chirwa Lodge,** half-way between Scuba Shack and Fat Monkey's on the sand road, has basic doubles for MK250, plus a kitchen for self-caterers. The bar has cheap cocktails (MK100), but is not reliably stocked.

Across from the Scuba Shack, **Steven's Rest House ❶** is cheap and central, and it was the first accommodation built on the Cape. The pizzas are best avoided for lack of any discernible signs of cheese, but otherwise the food is tasty. Order well in advance. The concrete-block beachfront bar used to compete with the bar at Fat Monkeys for the title of top evening meeting place, but now the generator is turned off at 8pm, and the stereo only plays warped Bob Marley tapes. (Giant doubles with private bath MK250.) **Thomas's Restaurant ❶** is 150m south of Steven's and makes delicious French toast and banana pancakes (MK60) for breakfast, plus a variety of lunch and dinner options. (Open daily 6am-9pm. Chapati, beans, and salad, MK120.) Local boys also arrange home-cooked dishes and will bring them to your lodge; make sure to bargain the price down before hand. Traditional *nsima* with *nyemba* (maize dough with spicy bean stew) should cost around MK100. Rounding out the food options is a smiling Malawian with a McDonald's t-shirt who cooks **chips,** served hot and fresh for MK30, on the sandy strip outside Steven's. Self-caterers must buy food in Monkey Bay, as even basic ingredients are unavailable in Cape Maclear.

◪ **WATER ADVENTURES. Scuba Shack,** on the beach at the center of Cape Maclear's 2km strip, is the best dive shop in the area. Courses are offered on demand by a well-trained and professional staff. (☎ 09 934 220; scubashack@africa-online.net. Open water US$195, advanced open water US$150, refresher US$50, dives US$20-30, specialty and technical courses available. Open daily 7am-5pm. MC/V.)

A great way to get away from the commercial atmosphere of the beachfront is to rent a **kayak** and paddle out to one of the two islands just off the Cape. Most kayakers can reach the near island in 30min.; keep an eye on the weather. **Kayak Africa,** 50m south of Scuba Shack, rents out boats and arranges guides. They also arrange all-inclusive boat-supported **safaris** to the islands, with accommodation in luxury tented camps for US$120, and an Open Water scuba certification course for US$165. (Cape Town booking office ☎ 27 21 689 8123; www.kayakafrica.co.za; letsgo@kayakafrica.co.za. Double kayaks US$10 per half-day. Two-dive trip to one of the islands with lunch included US$60. MC/V.) A cheaper alternative and better way to benefit the local economy is to ask a local canoe operator to take you around to the islands for snorkeling. Half a day should cost no more than US$10-15 and include a hot lunch cooked on the spot. A reliable operator, according to many travelers, is **Greevn** (☎ 08 861 827), who can be located by asking around at the craft stalls.

Another splurge option is **Danforth Yachting,** at the southern tip of the main road, which organizes sunset cruises (US$20) and day trips to the islands (US$60, includes lunch and all equipment) on its impressive yacht. Overnight stays in the well-furnished, airy guest house or on the yacht include meals and unlimited use of all scuba and water sports equipment for US$120. (☎ 09 960 077 or 09 960 770; danforth@malawi.net; www.danforthyachting.com. Min. 4 people.)

LIWONDE

Liwonde town doesn't see too many foreign visitors, since most are clever enough to head straight to its nearby world-class game park or to a Mozambique-bound train.

■⁊ **ORIENTATION AND PRACTICAL INFORMATION.** The town's pride is the Shire ("shee-ray") River, which cuts it into a tiny western section and a more substantial commercial and residential district on the east. A 10min. walk north of the Shire is a railway station. Buses and bicycle taxis leave from the depot 500m to the west. They run throughout the day to all the standard destinations on the Blantyre-Monkey Bay route, including Blantyre (2hr., MK120), Mangochi (90min., MK90), and Zomba (1hr., MK90). The telephone bureau, on the east side of the market, allows free call-backs. (☎ 592 813. Open daily 8am-5pm.) Minibuses to Blantyre also stop at the west side of the Shire bridge, across the river from the boat depot run by Mvuu Camp (see Liwonde National Park, p. 648).

◪◪ **ACCOMMODATIONS AND FOOD.** The best—perhaps the only—reason to spend a night in Liwonde is because you missed a train to Mozambique. In this sad scenario, the cheery **Liwonde Holiday Hotel ❶,** on the south side of the market, has the best reasonably-priced accommodations in town. The neighborhood has a few noisy beer halls, but those quiet down by a tolerable hour. (☎ 542 338. Doubles MK500-600.) The quiet atmosphere and low prices of **Liwonde Holiday Resort ❶,** on the west side of the river, are its only virtues. (MK100 per person.) The adjoining **restaurant ❶** serves good *nsima*, though (as usual) you have to order in advance if you want to make sure your menu selection is available.

MALAWI

◪ LIWONDE NATIONAL PARK

Getting to Liwonde National Park can be done the easy way or the cheap way. The easy way is to take a boat on the Shire; Mvuu sends one at least once per day. The boat is fast, but will pause if you see any good game. The average rides lasts around 1¼hr. The boats leave Liwonde town from near the Shire bridge. (Booking ☎771 393; wildsaf@eomw.net. US$20 per person each way.) The cheap (and considerably more adventurous) way is to catch any northbound minibus or chapa from Liwonde and get off at Ulongwe (30min., MK40). From there, locals on bicycles can take travelers 14km to the park entrance for a negotiable fee (about MK200). This is by far the best way to get a sense of the surrounding villages and park vegetation. Make sure that the guide takes you all the way to the river, which is several kilometers past the park entrance. A ferry from Mvuu camp fetches people from there. Park entrance fees are US$5 per person, payable whenever you enter the park.

Malawi's splendid wildlife flocks to Liwonde like college students to an open bar. The combination of dry African bush and the mighty Shire River ensures a diverse and crowded population of animals ready to pose for tourists. Hippos lounge in abundance on the riverside—listen for their cacophonous honks during the night and early morning—and elephants chew up flora everywhere. On the banks of the Shire, crocodiles lurk in anticipation of their next meal—local fishermen get pounced upon a few times a year, especially October, when waters are highest. A few rhinos are fenced in for their own protection in the center of the park, but it's not guaranteed that they'll show their faces for you. Over the last year, a couple of lions wandered into the park from Northern Mozambique, though these are the most elusive of the resident wildlife and you probably won't see them.

Mvuu Camp ❶ has a virtual monopoly on budget accommodations within the park; in practice, this is limited to a good campsite near the camp's ritzier chalets. At night you will hear wild beasts scrounging around the campsites, but you won't be physically disturbed unless you do something foolish, like slathering the outside of your tent with raw meat (inadvisable under any circumstances). For the hippo-weary, guards are around to escort you to and from the restaurant and ablution block. Mvuu also has excellent boat safaris and game drives (US$18 per person), as well as early morning foot safaris (US$10). The guides are all bush-savvy and good-natured. The only prepared food consists of meals at Mvuu; the nearest supply shop for self-caterers is in Liwonde town. (Meals US$8-15. Camping US$8. Chalet rental US$35 per person per night. Full safari package US$120, including game drives and boat safaris, 3 meals, and chalet.)

Another option is to stay at the **Njobu Village Cultural Lodge ❶**—set up by Peace Corps volunteers, local villages, and Mvuu Camp—4km outside the park gate and accessible only by bike taxi. Here, guests forsake luxury in exchange for a glimpse of local life. The accommodation are mud huts with drop toilets, and the food includes traditional dishes like field mice kebabs and *nsima*. In addition to the Mvuu park safaris, you can spend your days learning about traditional medicine from a village healer or watching dances or local bands. All profits go towards development projects in the area. Contact Mvuu for booking and rates.

APPENDIX

TEMPERATURES

Avg Low/High Temp (C/F)	January		April		July		October	
Blantyre	20/28	68/82	18/28	64/82	13/24	55/75	19/32	66/90
Cape Town	16/26	60/79	12/23	53/73	7/18	45/64	11/21	51/70
Durban	21/28	70/82	17/26	63/79	11/23	51/73	17/24	62/75
Gaborone	22/30	72/86	16/26	61/79	7/20	45/68	18/28	64/82
Harare	17/25	63/77	15/25	59/77	9/20	48/68	15/26	59/79
Johannesburg	15/26	58/78	10/21	51/70	4/17	39/62	11/24	52/75
Maputo	22/30	72/86	19/27	66/81	13/24	55/75	18/28	64/82
Windhoek	17/29	63/84	13/25	55/77	7/20	45/68	15/29	59/84

MEASUREMENTS

MEASUREMENT CONVERSIONS

1 inch (in.) = 25.4 millimeters (mm)	1 millimeter (mm) = 0.039 in.
1 foot (ft.) = 0.30 m	1 meter (m) = 3.28 ft.
1 yard (yd.) = 0.914m	1 meter (m) = 1.09 yd.
1 mile = 1.61km	1 kilometer (km) = 0.62 mi.
1 ounce (oz.) = 28.35g	1 gram (g) = 0.035 oz.
1 pound (lb.) = 0.454kg	1 kilogram (kg) = 2.202 lb.
1 fluid ounce (fl. oz.) = 29.57ml	1 milliliter (ml) = 0.034 fl. oz.
1 gallon (gal.) = 3.785L	1 liter (L) = 0.264 gal.
1 acre (ac.) = 0.405ha	1 hectare (ha) = 2.47 ac.

APPENDIX

PHRASEBOOK

AFRIKAANS

ENGLISH	AFRIKAANS	ENGLISH	AFRIKAANS
PHRASES			
Hello.	Hallo.	**How are you?**	Hoe gaan dit?
Pardon.	Ekskuus.	**Yes/no**	Ja./Nee.
Thank you.	Dankie.	**No thanks.**	Nee dankie.
Good-bye.	Tot siens.	**It's a pleasure.**	Dis 'n plesier.
When?	Wanneer?	**What?**	Wat?
Who?	Wie?	**Where?**	Waarheen?
How much?	Hoeveel?	**Why?**	Waarom?
Stop/enough.	Disgenoeg.	**What is your name?**	Wat is jou naam?
Please speak slowly.	Praat stadig asseblief.	**My name is...**	My naam is...
I can't speak Afrikaans.	Ek kan nie Afrikaans praat nie.	**Please repeat.**	Herhaal asseblief.
NUMBERS			
one	een	**eleven**	elf
two	twee	**twelve**	twaalf
three	drie	**fifteen**	vyftien
four	vier	**twenty**	twintig
five	vyf	**thirty**	dertig
six	ses	**forty**	veertig
seven	sewe	**fifty**	vyftig
eight	agt	**sixty**	sestig
nine	nege	**one hundred**	honderd
ten	tien	**one thousand**	duisend
FOOD			
bread	brood	**main dish**	hoofgereg
salad	slaai	**meat**	vleis
water	water	**fruit**	vrugte
TIMES AND HOURS			
open	oop	**closed**	toe
What time is it?	Hoe laat is dit?	**morning**	môre
afternoon	middag	**night**	nag

Afrikaans pronunciation, with its numerous gutterals, is an adventure for many English-speaking foreigners. The letters *g* and *ch* represent the gutteral sound. The vowel combinations *ui* and *ei* both make a long *a* sound, as in *day.* For instance, the capital of Mpumalanga, Nelspruit, sounds like *NEL-sprait.* The correct pronunciation of *apartheid* rhymes with "a start date." In general, Afrikaans vowels represent different sounds than they do in English. For more information, check out any Afrikaans grammar book from your local library, or pick one up in a South African airport.

XHOSA

ENGLISH	XHOSA	PRONUNCIATIONS
PHRASES		
Good morning/afternoon.	Molo.	moh-loh
Good night.	Ulale kakuhle.	oo-LAH-leh kah-KOO-Hleh
Good-bye.	Uhambe/Usale kakuhle.	oo-HAH-mbeh/oo-SAH-leh kah-KOO-Hleh
What is your name?	Ngubani igama lakho?	ngoo-BAH-nee ee-GAH-mah- LAH-kaw?
My name is...	Igama lami wu...	ee-GAH-mah lah-MEE woo
Pleased to meet you.	Ndiyavuya ukukwazi.	ndee-yah-VOO-yah oo-koo-KWaH-zee
How are you?	Kunjani kuwe?	oon-JAH-nee
Fine thanks. And you?	Ndikhona enkosi. Kunjani kuwe?	ndee-KOH-nah eNKAW-see. koo-NJAH-nee KOO-weh.
How much?	Kangakanani?	kah-ngah-kah-NAH-nee
Where is/are...?	Iphi?Ziphi i...?	EE-pee/ZEE-pee ee
Please.	Nceda.	N!C!EH-dah
Yes./No.	Ewe./Haya.	EH-weh/HAH-yi
Thank you (very much).	Enkosi (kakhulu).	eh-NKAW-see kah-KOO-Hlooh
Help!	Ndicela!	ndee-CHEH-dah

ZULU

ENGLISH	ZULU	PRONUNCIATIONS
PHRASES		
Good morning/afternoon.	Sawubona.	sah-woo-BOH-nah
Good night.	Ulale kahle.	oo-LAH-leh kah-Hleh
Good-bye.	Uhambe kahle/Usale kahle.	oo-HAH-mbeh kah-Hleh/oo-SAH-leh-KAH-leh
What is your name?	Ngubani igama lakho?	ngoo-BAH-nee ee-GAH-mah LAH-kaw?
My name is...	Igama lami ngu...	ee-GAH-mah lah-MEE ngoo
Pleased to meet you.	Ngiyajabula ukukwazi.	ngee-yah-jah-BOO-ah oo-koo-KWAH-zee
How are you?	Unjani?	oon-JAH-nee
Fine thanks. And you?	Ngiyaphila. Wena unjani?	ngee-YAH-PEE-lah.weh-nah-oo-NJAH-nee.
Where do you come from?	Uyaphi?	oo-YAH-pea
I'm from...	Ngibuya...	ngee-BOO-yah
I don't understand.	Angizwa.	ah-NGEE-zwah
What does this mean?	Isho ukuthini lento?	ee-SHOH-oo-koo-TEEn-ee LEH-ntaw
Please speak slowly.	Ngicela ukhulume ngokun-gasheshi.	ngee-!C!Elah oo-koo-KOO-lew-meh ngaw-koo-ngah-SHEH-shee
How much?	Kangakanani?	kah-ngah-kah-NAH-nee
Where is?	Iphi i...?	EE-pee ee
How far?	Kude kangakanani?	koo-deh kah-ngah-kah-NAH-nee
How long?	Isikhathi esingakanani?	ee-see-KAH-tee eh-see-ngah-kah-NAH-nee
Please.	Ngiyacela.	nghee-yah-!c!ehla
Yes./No.	Yebo./Cha.	YEH-baw/!C!AH
Thank you.	Ngiyabonga.	ngee-yah-BOH-ngah
Help!	Siza!	SEE-zah
Stop.	Yima.	YI-mah
bread	isinkwa	eeh-sink--wah
meat	inyama	eeh-NYAH-mah

ENGLISH	ZULU	PRONUNCIATIONS
in the morning	ekuseni	eh-koo-SEH-nee
during the day	emini	eh-MEE-nee
in the evening	entambana	eh-ntah-MBAH-nah
at night	ebusuku	eh-boo-SOO-koo
yesterday	izolo	ee-ZOH-loh
today	namhlanje	nah-MHLAH-njay

SESOTHO

ENGLISH	SESOTHO	PRONUNCIATIONS
PHRASES		
Good morning/afternoon.	Dumela!	doo-MEH-lah
Good night.	Robala hantle.	ro-BAH-lah HANT-lay
Good-bye.	Kgotso.	HOH-tsoh
What is your name?	Le bitso la hau u mang?	leh-BEE-tsoh lah how oh mang
My name is...	Ke...	kai
How are you?	U kae?	oh kai
Fine thanks. And you?	Ke teng. Wena?	keh-tehng WAY-nah
Where do you come from?.	O tsoa kae?	oh tswah kai
I'm from...	Ke tsoa...	keh tswah
I don't understand.	Ha ke utloisise.	hah keh oot-loh-SEE-see
What does this mean?	Ke eng hoo?	ke heng hoh
Please speak slowly.	Bua butle.	BOO-ah BOOT-lay
How much?	Ke bokae?	keh-BOH-kai
Where is/are...?	E kae?	eh kai
How far?	Hole-hole?	HOH-lay-HOH-lay
How long?	Dihora bokae?	dee-OH-rah boh-KAI
Yes./No.	E./e-e.	ay/eh-eh
Thank you.	Kea leboha.	ke-hya leh-BOH-ha
Help!	Nthuse!	in-TOOs-ee
Stop.	Ema!	AY-mah
FOOD		
bread	bohobe	boh-HOH-beh
meat	nama	NAH-mah
TIMES AND HOURS		
in the morning	hoseng	HOH-seng
during the day	motsheare	moh-tse-HAH-reh
in the evening	ka phirimana	kah-pee-ree-MAH-nah
at night	bosiu	boh-SYOO
yesterday	maobane	ma-hoh-BAH
today	kajeno	kah-JEH-noh

SHONA

ENGLISH	SHONA	PRONUNCIATIONS
PHRASES		
Hello	Mhoroi	MOH-roh-ee
Goodbye	Chisarai	CHEE-sah-rah-yee
Good Morning	Mangwanani	mah-NGWAH-nah-nee

APPENDIX

ENGLISH	SHONA	PRONUNCIATIONS
Good Afternoon	Masikati	mah-SKAH-tee
Good Evening	Manheru	mah-NAY-roo
Father/Mother	Baba/Amai	BAH-bah/ah-MAH-yee
What is your name?	Zita rako ndiani?	ZEE-tah RAH-kow NJEE-ah-nee
My name is...	Zita rangu...	ZEE-tah RAH-ngoo
How is your day?	Maswera sei?	mah-SKWAY-rah SAY-ee
How did you sleep?	Marara sei?	mah-RAH-rah SAY-ee
My day is/I slept well.	Ndaswera/Ndarara	n-dah-SKWAY-rah/n-dah-RAH-rah
Where are you from?	Unobva kupi?	oo-KNOW-bvah KOO-pee
I'm from...	Ndinobva ku...	n-DEE-know-bvah koo
I don't understand.	Handinzwisisi	ha-NDEE-nzwi-see-see
How much is this?	I marii ichi?	EE mah-REE EE-chee
That's good.	Zvakanaka	SHA-kah-NAH-kah
Yes/No	Ehe/Aiwa	eh-HEH/EYE-wah
Yes/No (deeper Shona)	Hongu/Kwete	OHN-goo/KWAY-tay
Please	Ndapota	n-dah-POH-tah
Thank you	Ndatenda	n-dah-TAYN-dah
Excuse me.	Pamusoroi	pah-moo-SOW-row-ee
I'm sorry.	Ndine urombo	n-DEE-nay oo-ROHM-bow
Yesterday	Nezuro	nay-ZOO-row
Today	Nhasi	NAH-see
Tomorrow	Mangwana	mahn-GWAH-nah
Stop here.	Mirai pano	mi-RAH-yee PAH-no
I don't have any money.	Handina mari	an-DEE-nah MAH-ree
Leave me alone.	Ndisiye	n-dee-SEE-yay

The following list is comprised of general, widely used terms in Southern Africa.

abseiling: rapelling
ablutions/ablutions block: toilet and shower facilities
apteek: chemist, pharmacy
baas: deferential term ("boss"), sometimes used by blacks when speaking to whites
backpackers: hostel/lodge
bakkie: open pickup truck
berg: mountain
biltong: dried, spiced meat
Blair toilet: type of rural outhouse
boerewors: spiced sausage
bottle store: business selling soda and beer
braai: barbecue
Bushman: Khoisan (offensive to some)
CBD: central business district
Cde.: comrade
chapa: pickup truck used as public transport
chinja: change (Zimbabwean opposition slogan)
college: secondary boarding school
coloured: in South Africa, any person of mixed race
combi: minibus taxi
creeking: abseiling, sliding, and/or swimming in a creek
dagga: marijuana
E.T.: minibus taxi (literally "emergency taxi")
foofie (or fufi) slide: zip line
F.T.: f-ing tourist
hire: rent
hold your thumbs: cross your fingers
hostel: university dormitory
"is it?"/"isn't it?": commonly said to express interest or emphasize a point
jol: to party
kaffir: derogatory term referring to black Africans (extremely offensive)
kak: shit
kloofing: cliff-jumping
knopknerrie: walking stick
kombi: minibus taxi
kopje (or koppie): small hill
kraal: African homestead
kwaito: a type of South African pop music

lapa: open air hut with cooking facilities
lekker: nice, pleasant, sweet
lobola: dowry paid by a potential husband to his wife's family
location: township
mampoer: moonshine brandy
Madiba: Nelson Mandela
mbanje: marijuana
mbira: hand-held instrument played with the thumbs
mealie meal: dry ground maize
mealie pap: maize meal
motor: car
mozzie: mosquito
my china: my friend
muti: medicine
pan: a basin or depression in the land
pap: maize meal
paraffin: kerosene
pensioner: senior citizen
petrol: gasoline
pronk: show off
pronking: jumping (antelopes only)
rank: bus/taxi stand
Rhodey: term used by blacks to refer to white Zimbabweans and Zambians (mildly offensive)
robot: traffic light
rock up: show up
rondavel: small round hut
rooibos: herbal tea
sadza: maize meal
sangoma: traditional healer
shandy: alcoholic drink made with bitters and citrus
"shame"/"for shame": expression of sympathy or disapproval
shebeen: township pub
sis: expression of disgust
slip-slops: flip-flops
strand: beach
sundowner: sunset drinks
supertube: waterslide
take-away: takeout
takkies: tennis shoes or sneakers
veld: ("felt") grassland

INDEX

A

B

O

MAP INDEX

MAP LEGEND

Hospital	Airport	Hotel/Hostel	Mountain
Police	Bus Station	Camping	Internet Access
Post Office	Minibus Taxi Rank	Food & Drink	Pedestrian Zone
Tourist Office	Taxi Stand	Shopping	Park
Bank	Train Station	Nightlife	
Embassy/Consulate	Ferry Landing	Museum	Beach
Site or Point of Interest	Church	Park Gate/Entrance	Water
Telephone	Synagogue	Border Crossing	
Theater/Cinema	Mosque	Battlefield	The Let's Go compass always points NORTH.
Library	Hindu Temple	Wildlife Reserve	

MAP INDEX (CONT.)